International Directory of
COMPANY
HISTORIES

International Directory of

COMPANY HISTORIES

VOLUME 63

Editor

Jay P. Pederson

ST. JAMES PRESS

An imprint of Thomson Gale, a part of The Thomson Corporation

Detroit • New York • San Francisco • San Diego • New Haven, Conn. • Waterville, Maine • London • Munich

International Directory of Company Histories, Volume 63

Jay P. Pederson, Editor

Project Editor
Miranda H. Ferrara

Editorial
Virgil Burton, Donna Craft, Louise Gagné, Peggy Geeseman, Julie Gough, Linda Hall, Keith Jones, Lynn Pearce, Maureen Puhl, Holly Selden, Justine Ventimiglia

Imaging and Multimedia
Randy Bassett, Lezlie Light

Manufacturing
Rhonda Williams

LIBRARY OF CONGRESS CATALOG NUMBER 89-190943

ISBN: 1-55862-508-9

BRITISH LIBRARY CATALOGUING IN PUBLICATION DATA

International directory of company histories. Vol. 63
I. Jay P. Pederson
33.87409

Printed in the United States of America
10 9 8 7 6 5 4 3 2 1

CONTENTS _____

Preface . . . . page vii
List of Abbreviations ix

Company Histories

PREFACE

The St. James Press series *The International Directory of Company Histories (IDCH)* is intended for reference use by students, business people, librarians, historians, economists, investors, job candidates, and others who seek to learn more about the historical development of the world's most important companies. To date, *IDCH* has covered over 6,700 companies in 63 volumes.

Inclusion Criteria

Most companies chosen for inclusion in *IDCH* have achieved a minimum of US$25 million in annual sales and are leading influences in their industries or geographical locations. Companies may be publicly held, private, or nonprofit. State-owned companies that are important in their industries and that may operate much like public or private companies also are included. Wholly owned subsidiaries and divisions are profiled if they meet the requirements for inclusion. Entries on companies that have had major changes since they were last profiled may be selected for updating.

The *IDCH* series highlights 10% private and nonprofit companies, and features updated entries on approximately 50 companies per volume.

Entry Format

Each entry begins with the company's legal name, the address of its headquarters, its telephone, toll-free, and fax numbers, and its web site. A statement of public, private, state, or parent ownership follows. A company with a legal name in both English and the language of its headquarters country is listed by the English name, with the native-language name in parentheses.

The company's founding or earliest incorporation date, the number of employees, and the most recent available sales figures follow. Sales figures are given in local currencies with equivalents in U.S. dollars. For some private companies, sales figures are estimates and indicated by the abbreviation *est.* The entry lists the exchanges on which a company's stock is traded and its ticker symbol, as well as the company's NAIC codes.

Entries generally contain a *Company Perspectives* box which provides a short summary of the company's mission, goals, and ideals, a *Key Dates* box highlighting milestones in the company's history, lists of *Principal Subsidiaries, Principal Divisions, Principal Operating Units, Principal Competitors,* and articles for *Further Reading.*

American spelling is used throughout *IDCH*, and the word "billion" is used in its U.S. sense of one thousand million.

Sources

Entries have been compiled from publicly accessible sources both in print and on the Internet such as general and academic periodicals, books, annual reports, and material supplied by the companies themselves.

Cumulative Indexes

IDCH contains three indexes: the **Index to Companies**, which provides an alphabetical index to companies discussed in the text as well as to companies profiled, the **Index to Industries**, which allows researchers to locate companies by their principal industry, and the **Geographic Index**, which lists companies alphabetically by the country of their headquarters. The indexes are cumulative and specific instructions for using them are found immediately preceding each index.

Suggestions Welcome

Comments and suggestions from users of *IDCH* on any aspect of the product as well as suggestions for companies to be included or updated are cordially invited. Please write:

The Editor
International Directory of Company Histories
St. James Press
27500 Drake Rd.
Farmington Hills, Michigan 48331-3535

AB	Aktiebolag (Finland, Sweden)
AB Oy	Aktiebolag Osakeyhtiot (Finland)
A.E.	Anonimos Eteria (Greece)
AG	Aktiengesellschaft (Austria, Germany, Switzerland, Liechtenstein)
A.O.	Anonim Ortaklari/Ortakligi (Turkey)
ApS	Amparteselskab (Denmark)
A.Š.	Anonim Širketi (Turkey)
A/S	Aksjeselskap (Norway); Aktieselskab (Denmark, Sweden)
Ay	Avoinyhtio (Finland)
B.A.	Buttengewone Aansprakeiijkheid (The Netherlands)
Bhd.	Berhad (Malaysia, Brunei)
B.V.	Besloten Vennootschap (Belgium, The Netherlands)
C.A.	Compania Anonima (Ecuador, Venezuela)
C. de R.L.	Compania de Responsabilidad Limitada (Spain)
Co.	Company
Corp.	Corporation
CRL	Companhia a Responsabilidao Limitida (Portugal, Spain)
C.V.	Commanditaire Vennootschap (The Netherlands, Belgium)
G.I.E.	Groupement d'Interet Economique (France)
GmbH	Gesellschaft mit beschraenkter Haftung (Austria, Germany, Switzerland)
Inc.	Incorporated (United States, Canada)
I/S	Interessentselskab (Denmark); Interesentselskap (Norway)
KG/KGaA	Kommanditgesellschaft/Kommanditgesellschaft auf Aktien (Austria, Germany, Switzerland)
KK	Kabushiki Kaisha (Japan)
K/S	Kommanditselskab (Denmark); Kommandittselskap (Norway)
Lda.	Limitada (Spain)
L.L.C.	Limited Liability Company (United States)
Ltd.	Limited (Various)
Ltda.	Limitada (Brazil, Portugal)
Ltee.	Limitee (Canada, France)
mbH	mit beschraenkter Haftung (Austria, Germany)
N.V.	Naamloze Vennootschap (Belgium, The Netherlands)
OAO	Otkrytoe Aktsionernoe Obshchestve (Russia)
OOO	Obschestvo s Ogranichennoi Otvetstvennostiu (Russia)
Oy	Osakeyhtiö (Finland)
PLC	Public Limited Co. (United Kingdom, Ireland)
Pty.	Proprietary (Australia, South Africa, United Kingdom)
S.A.	Société Anonyme (Belgium, France, Greece, Luxembourg, Switzerland, Arab speaking countries); Sociedad Anónima (Latin America [except Brazil], Spain, Mexico); Sociedades Anônimas (Brazil, Portugal)
SAA	Societe Anonyme Arabienne
S.A.R.L.	Sociedade Anonima de Responsabilidade Limitada (Brazil, Portugal); Société à Responsabilité Limitée (France, Belgium, Luxembourg)
S.A.S.	Societá in Accomandita Semplice (Italy); Societe Anonyme Syrienne (Arab speaking countries)
Sdn. Bhd.	Sendirian Berhad (Malaysia)
S.p.A.	Società per Azioni (Italy)
Sp. z.o.o.	Spólka z ograniczona odpowiedzialnoscia (Poland)
S.R.L.	Società a Responsabilità Limitata (Italy); Sociedad de Responsabilidad Limitada (Spain, Mexico, Latin America [except Brazil])
S.R.O.	Spolecnost s Rucenim Omezenym (Czechoslovakia
Ste.	Societe (France, Belgium, Luxembourg, Switzerland)
VAG	Verein der Arbeitgeber (Austria, Germany)
YK	Yugen Kaisha (Japan)
ZAO	Zakrytoe Aktsionernoe Obshchestve (Russia)

$	United States dollar		ITL	Italian lira
£	United Kingdom pound		JMD	Jamaican dollar
¥	Japanese yen		KPW	North Korean won
AED	Emirati dirham		KRW	South Korean won
ARS	Argentine peso		KWD	Kuwaiti dinar
ATS	Austrian shilling		LUF	Luxembourg franc
AUD	Australian dollar		MUR	Mauritian rupee
BEF	Belgian franc		MXN	Mexican peso
BHD	Bahraini dinar		MYR	Malaysian ringgit
BRL	Brazilian real		NGN	Nigerian naira
CAD	Canadian dollar		NLG	Netherlands guilder
CHF	Swiss franc		NOK	Norwegian krone
CNY	Chinese yuan		NZD	New Zealand dollar
COP	Colombian peso		OMR	Omani rial
CZK	Czech koruna		PHP	Philippine peso
DEM	German deutsche mark		PKR	Pakistani rupee
DKK	Danish krone		PLN	Polish zloty
DZD	Algerian dinar		PTE	Portuguese escudo
EGP	Egyptian pound		RUB	Russian ruble
ESP	Spanish peseta		SAR	Saudi riyal
EUR	euro		SEK	Swedish krona
FIM	Finnish markka		SGD	Singapore dollar
FRF	French franc		THB	Thai baht
GRD	Greek drachma		TND	Tunisian dinar
HKD	Hong Kong dollar		TRL	Turkish lira
HUF	Hungarian forint		TWD	new Taiwan dollar
IDR	Indonesian rupiah		VEB	Venezuelan bolivar
IEP	Irish pound		VND	Vietnamese dong
ILS	new Israeli shekel		ZAR	South African rand
INR	Indian rupee		ZMK	Zambian kwacha
ISK	Icelandic krona			

International Directory of

COMPANY
HISTORIES

Advanced Fibre Communications, Inc.

1465 North McDowell Boulevard
Petaluma, California 94954
U.S.A.
Telephone: (707) 794-7700
Fax: (707) 794-7777
Web site: http://www.fibre.com

Public Company
Incorporated: 1992
Employees: 773
Sales: $333.5 million (2003)
Stock Exchanges: NASDAQ
Ticker Symbol: AFCI
NAIC: 334210 Telephone Apparatus Manufacturing

Operating out of Petaluma, California, publicly traded Advanced Fibre Communications, Inc. (AFC) offers multi-service broadband solutions to more than 800 telecommunication companies. AFC's products provide a connection between a telecom's central office and end users, with the ability to deliver not only voice but also video and high-speed internet services over a single network infrastructure. Moreover, AFC technology allows customers to enter the broadband era using an existing network. In this way, telecoms can maximize their previous investment in copper wire technology without the immediate need to engage in the costly conversion to a fiber-optic network. AFC's customers range from regional Bells to small Third World telephone companies. The company maintains sales offices in California, Florida, Kansas, Texas, and Mexico, and research and development and technical assistance offices in California, Florida, and Texas.

Founding the Company in 1992

AFC was founded in May 1992 by Donald Green, James Hoeck, John Webley, and Henri Sulzer. Hoeck and Webley were engineers with DSC Communications, who struck out on their own to design a product ultimately named the Universal Modular Carrier, or UMC 1000. The UMC 1000 was a variation on digital loop carrier technology (DLC) developed in the early 1980s, which used fiber to connect highly concentrated groups of customers, such as those found in a housing development or a rural community, to a telephone company's central office. Because fiber was not used in many locations, Hoeck and Webley developed the UMC 1000, which could use traditional copper wire to connect as few as six and as many as 672 subscribers.

Hoeck and Webley enlisted Donald Green, because of his reputation, management skills, and proven ability to attract venture capital. Green was regarded as the founding father of "Telecom Valley"—Sonoma County, California, which became the home of a number of telecom services companies, many of which had ties to the British-born Green. After receiving an engineering degree from the British Institute of Electrical Engineers, he worked as a design engineer, first with British Telecom, and later with U.K.-based RCA Standard Tele Cables and Lynch Communication Inc. He began his career as an entrepreneur in 1969 with the launch of Digital Telephone Systems, a Novato, California-based company that developed digital loop carriers for long distance signals. He later sold the business to Harris Digital Telephone Systems, where he served as vice-president until his first attempt at retirement in 1986. A year later he founded another start-up company, Optilink Corporation, a Petaluma company that developed a fiber digital loop carrier system called Litespan, supplemented later by an expanded version called Starspan. (Hoeck and Webley were both Litespan engineers who left in 1990 to cofound a design consulting company, Quadrium, before starting AFC.) In 1990 Green sold the business to DSC Communications, a Plano, Texas-based company, for $54 million. After staying on as a vice-president of DSC and president of DSC Optilink, in 1991 he retired a second time, only to change his mind a year later when he agreed to become involved in the creation of AFC.

One of the first moves that AFC made in 1992 was to enter into an agreement with the government of Taiwan and its Industrial Technology Research Institute (ITRI) to jointly develop telecommunications technology. It appeared to be a good deal at the time, bringing the young company much needed funding, engineering resources, and credibility. In exchange, ITRI and its member companies received the right to sell a European version of the UMC 1000 to markets outside North

Company Perspectives:

Through its market proven solutions, AFC enables carriers to deliver the most advanced broadband services to their customers, providing newer, richer experiences and more exciting ways for people to communicate.

America on a royalty basis until 2002, after which ITRI members would be allowed to sell the technology anywhere in the world without paying a royalty. Because the two partners were competing against one another in a number of international markets, tensions developed, and eventually led to litigation. Before matters reached that point, however, AFC was already embroiled in legal problems.

In April 1993, Green sued DSC, claiming that the company still owed him millions of dollars for the stock he sold three years earlier. Several months later, in July 1993, DSC sued AFC for $20 million, claiming that it owned the UMC 1000 because the system relied on proprietary information used in the Litespan and Starspan products. Green responded by having AFC sue DSC, charging the Texas firm with violating antitrust provisions and engaging in sham litigation and industrial espionage. Green told *Fibre Optics News* that DSC was "attempting to put a competing company out of business by inappropriately using the legal system." He also suggested that DSC did not even care if it won the case: "All they have to do is spend enough of our money that we can't continue in business."

Installing the First UMC System in 1993

While the DSC litigation moved slowly through the court system, AFC began to ship its product. The first UMC 1000 system was installed in Mexico in 1993. Within a year a dozen countries adopted the technology. In the United States the first customer was the Sioux Valley Telephone Company, located in South Dakota. By mid-1994, some 40 systems were installed in the United States. Also in 1994 AFC entered into a joint venture with Tellabs Operations to develop a system that could transmit telephone and cable television service into a home over a single line. AFC would sell the product to telephone companies and Tellabs would market to cable companies. Revenues during these early years grew at a rapid pace for AFC, totaling just $620,000 in 1993, then increasing to $18.8 million in 1994 and $54.3 million in 1995. The company also turned profitable in 1995, posting net income of $2.3 million.

In June 1996, after three years in court, AFC reached a settlement with DSC. Although the terms were not publicly disclosed at the time, both sides acknowledged that neither company would be denied the use of its own technology, and it was later reported by *Communications Week* that AFC agreed to pay $10.1 million in cash and 719,424 shares of stock to settle the matter. Because Tellabs owned an interest in AFC, it was included in the settlement, but the relationship between the partners would soon come to a close when their joint venture was dissolved in 1996.

AFC was only free of litigation for a brief period. In July 1996 it filed suit against ITRI and its member companies for breach of

contract, trade secret misappropriation, and other claims. A month later ITRI member companies sued AFC, alleging breach of contract. This litigation would be settled two years later when the two sides reached an agreement that awarded three Taiwanese telecom companies a license to produce and sell the European version of what was now older AFC technology. In return, AFC received an undisclosed payment plus royalties.

On a far more positive note, in 1996 AFC completed a highly successful initial public offering of stock. Underwritten by Morgan Stanley & Co., Merrill Lynch & Co., Cowen & Company, and Hambrecht & Quist, the offering netted AFC approximately $118.1 million. Initially priced at $25, the stock quickly soared to $47 by the next day. A major cause for investor confidence was the adaptability of the UMC 1000, able to help telecoms in the switch from copper wire to fiber optics, and also a highly desirable product for the global marketplace, especially in Third World countries where the UMC 1000 was an inexpensive way to create a telephone system. For the year, AFC saw its revenues grow to $130.2 million in 1996, with net income improving to $7.2 million.

Several months later, in May 1997, AFC began shipping the next generation of its digital loop carrier product, the UMC 1000 DLC. It was a far more robust system, able to provide standard telephone service and high-speed broadband service to as many as 2,000 users, and offer speeds of 155 megabits per second for a single subscriber, as opposed to 1.5 megabits per second for the UMC 1000. Moreover, standard telephone lines were capable of carrying only 64 kilobits of data per second, roughly 2,500 times less than the capacity of the UMC 1000 DLC. Management hoped that the new product would triple its market potential, since it could now sell to larger telecom companies, which represented the lion's share of the market. In fact, business in 1997 improved dramatically, especially due to new contracts in Asia, Latin America, and South Africa. Revenues for 1997 more than doubled the previous year's total, reaching $267.9 million, while net income grew fivefold to $36.8 million.

Green took steps to groom a successor to the CEO post. In July 1995, Carl J. Grivner, the former president of the Enhanced Business Services unit of Ameritech Corp., was named a vice-president with the understanding that he would eventually replace Green at the top. He became president and chief operating officer in January 1996, and in July 1997 he replaced Green as CEO. Green, who was now 66 years old, stayed on as chairman of the board and planned to remain involved in charting the company's course. His tenure as CEO, however, would last only one year.

Difficulties Arising in 1998

In mid-1998 AFC was stunned by a series of adverse developments. First, selling to the larger regional Baby Bells proved to be more challenging than anticipated, requiring costly levels of custom design and operational support. As a result, the company was forced to lower earnings estimates for the second quarter of 1998. Next, AFC had to admit that it was having problems at its China operations and that it had lost its largest customer, GTE. To make matters even worse, Grivner quit in order to become CEO for the Western hemisphere operations of Cable & Wireless plc, a London-based international telecommunications company. Investors punished the company, quickly bidding down its stock. In just two months, the stock lost almost three-quarters of its value, and AFC was rumored to be a takeover target, despite a poison pill provision the board of directors had installed only months earlier. The company also was beset with lawsuits initiated by disgruntled shareholders. Green was forced to take over as CEO on an interim basis, faced with the challenge of putting out fires while attempting to recruit Grivner's replacement. He asserted that the company continued to have excellent prospects because "the fundamentals of the company have not changed." By early October he had a verbal commitment from AFC's top candidate for the CEO post, allowing the unnamed executive six weeks to complete an employment contract. At the end of that period, however, the candidate informed Green that he was now considering a counteroffer from his current employer. Green immediately withdrew AFC's offer, explaining to the press, "You should live by your word. The guy wasted two months of our time, which is the most annoying thing."

Back to square one in the search for a new CEO, Green continued to head AFC. Finally, in April 1999 the company settled on a new president and CEO, hiring 50-year-old John A. Schofield, a senior executive at Minnesota-based ADC Telecommunications. Born in Australia, Schofield had lived in the United States for nearly 20 years and boasted 30 years of experience in selling telecommunications equipment around the world. He took over a company that was clearly in turmoil, its reputation with investors in tatters. According to Schofield, AFC "was drifting, in terms of customer focus. It was drifting in terms of product focus. And the internal processes associated with development were not in the shape that they needed to be."

Schofield's first step in turning around the company was to lower investors' expectations, a move that gave him some breathing room to effect some changes. He shut down engineering projects that he did not think could help the balance sheet in the near term. More important, with the help of an outside consultant, the Massachusetts firm of PRTM, he revamped the company's two-headed engineering organization, which previously had prevented AFC from pursuing a focused, long-term strategic plan. Now there was a single manager overseeing a unified engineering unit. Schofield withdrew from marginal foreign markets, in the process cutting about 9 percent of the company's global workforce, instead electing to target large European telecoms and distributors. He also beefed up the company's domestic sales operations to improve sales in the United States.

These steps soon paid off, as within 18 months AFC was posting record results. In 2000 AFC recorded sales of $416.9

million and net income in excess of $77.5 million. Also of note during 2000 was the acquisition of GVN Technologies, a Largo, Florida company that developed integrated access device equipment, the addition of which expanded AFC's product portfolio.

In 2001 Green retired as AFC's chairman at the age of 70, adhering to an age requirement that he had instituted. Schofield assumed the added responsibility. Overall, it was a difficult year for the telecommunications industry and AFC in particular, due to the effects of a slowing economy and the September 11 terrorist attacks. AFC experienced a major drop in sales, mostly occurring in the fourth quarter. As a result, management was forced to cut its workforce by 9 percent. For the year, sales fell to $327.6 million. Nevertheless, AFC remained a cash-rich company and was well positioned to wait until economic conditions improved. In 2002 it was able to invest in the future by acquiring AccessLan Communications, a San Jose, California, company that strengthened AFC's bid to be a technology leader in the development of next generation networks.

To adapt to changing conditions, in 2002 AFC restructured its supply chain to accommodate customers' preference for "just-in-time" purchasing. With the telecom industry still in the doldrums in 2003, AFC laid off another 11 percent of its workforce. The company essentially treaded water and remained profitable while waiting for customers to once again invest heavily in infrastructure. It also remained receptive to investing in the future through acquisitions if the right deal appeared. In February 2004, AFC paid approximately $240 million in cash to acquire Marconi's North American Access Group, part of London-based Marconi Corporation plc. The deal added a successfully deployed "Fiber-to-the-Curb" solution, greatly enhancing AFC's product offerings.

Principal Subsidiaries

GVN Technologies Inc.

Principal Competitors

Alcatel S.A.; Lucent Technologies Inc.; Nortel Networks Corporation.

Further Reading

Appel, Ted, "Advanced Fibre Lays Off 84," *Press Democrat,* October 19, 2001.

——, "Telecom Turnaround," *Press Democrat,* November 12, 2000, p. E1.

Bernier, Paula, "AFC Has Big Appeal for Small Telcoms," *Telephony,* May 16, 1994, p. 10.

Bollinger, Brad, "AFC's Stunning Reversal," *Press Democrat,* August 23, 1998, p. E1.

——, "A Slip by AFC Brings a Rout," *Press Democrat,* July 5, 1998, p. E1.

Chaffee, C. David, Charley Hartley, and Ellen Mullally, "DSC, Advanced FibreCom Battle Over Fibre Product Rights," *Fiber Optics News,* February 20, 1995, p. 1.

Karpinski, Richard, "Will AFC's Green Be Three Times Lucky," *Telephony,* July 5, 1993, p. 11.

—Ed Dinger

Aerojet-General Corp.

Highway 50 & Aerojet Road
Rancho Cordova, California 95670
U.S.A.
Telephone: (916) 355-4000
Fax: (916) 351-8667
Web site: http://www.aerojet.com

Wholly Owned Subsidiary of GenCorp Inc.
Incorporated: 1942 as Aerojet Engineering Corp.
Employees: 1,400
Sales: $321.0 million (2003)
NAIC: 336414 Guided Missile and Space Vehicle
   Manufacturing; 336415 Guided Missile and Space
   Vehicle Propulsion Unit and Propulsion Unit Parts;
   336419 Other Guided Missile and Space Vehicle Parts
   and Auxiliary Equipment

Aerojet-General Corp. is a leading U.S. rocket propulsion company. Founded during World War II, Aerojet has supplied most of the space programs in the United States, including the Apollo rockets and Space Shuttle, and has produced thousands of munitions for the military. The company is a subcontractor for body panels on advanced aircraft programs. Aerojet's satellite sensing technology detects missile launches as well as changes in the environment. Its high-tech research has spawned spinoffs in medical and other fields.

World War II Origins

Aerojet-General Corp. began by making jet-assisted takeoff (JATO) rockets in World War II. They were first demonstrated on August 16, 1941, by a group of enthusiasts from the California Institute of Technology led by professor Theodore von Karman. These provided an extra boost for aircraft taking off from short runways and aircraft carriers.

The company was incorporated March 19, 1942, as Aerojet Engineering Corp., and received its first production contract three months later. The first plant was located in Pasadena, California.

General Tire and Rubber Company, forerunner to GenCorp, was an early investor, acquiring the company in 1948. Aerojet produced thousands of JATO units during World War II.

In the spring of 1945, a number of scientists from Germany's V-2 rocket program surrendered to U.S. forces. Some of them, like Rudi Beichel, began working for Aerojet. Beichel is credited with leading the team that designed the Redstone rocket that Alan Shepard, Jr., rode into space in 1961.

Demand, production, and employment were cut back sharply following the war's end. However, some of the propeller-driven civilian airliners of the day could be fitted with JATO units to allow them to take off in the thin air of high elevation airports.

According to company literature, Aerojet became the first major U.S. company to develop expertise in both liquid and solid propellant rockets. The company was also responsible for the first U.S. rocket to probe the edge of space. The Aerobee class (eventually designated the X-8 series by the Air Force), launched in 1947, was used for decades.

Closing the Missile Gap

Aerojet employed nearly 2,800 people in 1952, when sales were $21 million. In 1953, the company established a weapons plant in Rancho Cordova, near Sacramento, California. Two years earlier, as the community of Pasadena grew around its original facility, the company had begun buying enough land for the new plant to isolate it from future development. The plant would be considered the free world's largest rocket engine facility.

Aerojet was called the "General Motors of U.S. Rocketry" by *Time* magazine in 1958; five years later, the company employed 34,000 people working on missiles such as the Polaris, Minuteman, Trident, and Titan. Revenues were $605 million in 1962.

In 1959, the company created two new divisions: Ordnance and Electronic Systems. The Electronic Systems Division created infrared technology allowing satellites to observe missile launches around the world—a vital component of U.S. defense during the Cold War. In May 1959, Aerojet bought a Downey,

California defense business from the Rheem Corporation. This was combined with a small defense operation acquired three years earlier to form the Ordnance Division.

Space Race and Vietnam

In the 1960s, Aerojet built a plant near the Everglades to supply NASA with solid fuel rockets. It was closed after NASA chose liquid fuel for the Saturn V program.

Aerojet powered many of the rockets used in the Apollo program, culminating in the first moon landing on July 20, 1969. The company was also developing its microwave and infrared sensing systems, used to monitor weather and the environment from satellites. At the same time, Aerojet was mass producing rockets and other ordnance for the Vietnam Conflict.

Employment fell to 8,000 by the early 1970s. Aerojet worked with Textron Inc. unit Bell Aerospace Co. to develop a pair of experimental surface-effect ships for the U.S. Navy in the early 1970s, but dropped out of the program.

More enduring were contracts for the Combined Effects Munitions program and 30mm ammunition. Aerojet began producing depleted uranium rounds after the 1976 acquisition of a factory in Jonesborough, Tennessee.

Aerojet-General Corp. earned $25.5 million on revenues of $670 million in 1975. Aerojet had 14 operating companies, according to *Business Week*, including Aerojet Electrosystems, Barnard & Burk Inc. (energy-related construction and engineering), Chemical Construction Corp., CESSCO (oil tanks), Cordova Chemical Co., Howe Richardson Scale Co., and Liquid Rocket Co. Aerojet acquired Chemical Construction Corp., a builder of natural gas plants, in a bid to diversify from government defense contracts. Other subsidiaries produced chemicals, pumps, and valves. A food flavorings unit, H.A. Johnson Co., was sold to Sands, Taylor & Wood of Cambridge, Massachusetts, in February 1975.

Company President Jack H. Vollbrecht embraced an ''80-20'' system, reported *Business Week*, urging managers to spend most of their time on the most important matters. Jack L. Heckel replaced Vollbrecht as president in 1981, and was named chairman and CEO in 1984.

Booming in the Reagan Era

Sales were $349.4 million in 1980, with earnings of $26.6 million. The Reagan era defense buildup was just beginning. Aerojet was a supplier of solid fuel propulsion systems for the new MX missile system, among other projects. While rival Morton Thiokol Inc. won the initial contract to build solid fuel booster rockets for the Space Shuttle, Aerojet would supply the liquid fuel maneuvering engines. Aerojet also designed and produced elements of the Strategic Defense Initiative, a system designed to intercept incoming ballistic missiles.

In the early 1980s, Aerojet's corporate parent, General Tire, was, according to *Business Week*, considering spinning off its many holdings into three separate companies in order to raise its share price. Aerojet itself was divesting some of its subsidiaries as it refocused on its lucrative aerospace business. The General Tire and Rubber Company became GenCorp. in the mid-1980s.

Aerojet's 13,500-acre complex near Rancho Cordova, California, was designated a Superfund site by the Environmental Protection Agency in 1983, and the company was forced to spend millions treating the groundwater underneath it. Since the 1960s, it had been poisoned by 30 different types of contaminants, alleged one lawsuit by a local water supplier. Aerojet would commit to a $100 million cleanup program of its Rancho Cordova site even before the discovery of perchlorate contamination prompted the closure of 18 wells in California in 1997. (A 1992 report by the General Accounting Office estimated the potential total cleanup cost to be up to $1 billion.)

Aerojet had begun applying some of its technology to medical applications, such as a cryogenic brain probe. The company also had an artificial heart research program, which was spun off in the mid-1980s as Nimbus Inc. Aerojet employees formed a number of other enterprises, such as Clean Energy Systems, launched in 1993 to apply Rudi Beichel's ideas for developing steam power using rocket technology.

Aerojet reached sales of $1 billion in 1988, when it had 8,000 employees. A slowdown in defense spending soon resulted in layoffs and factory closings. During the year, the company traded 5,100 acres in the Everglades to the federal government for 53,000 acres near its testing site in Nevada.

In 1989, NASA chose Aerojet and Lockheed Corporation to produce solid fuel rocket motors for the Space Shuttle program, replacing Morton Thiokol Inc., which had been dropped after the *Challenger* disaster. However, the booster rocket replacement program was canceled by Congress in October 1993. Aerojet was researching a cleaner, nitrate-based oxidizer for solid rocket motors, which until then left a noxious trail of hydrogen chloride exhaust.

1990s Cutbacks

Aerojet announced a reorganization in May 1990. Its two Sacramento propulsion units were combined into the Aerojet Propulsion Division. Three other divisions were renamed: Aerojet Space Boosters, which was producing advanced solid rocket motors (ASRM) for the Space Shuttle, was renamed the Aerojet ASRM Division; Aerojet ElectroSystems, based in Azusa, California, became the Aerojet Electronics Division; and Downey, California-based Aerojet Ordnance became the Aerojet Ordnance Division.

Aerojet's satellite technology was used to detect Iraq's Scud missile launches during the Persian Gulf War. Aerojet also supplied cluster bombs for the war effort; in 1994 it and the only other supplier, Alliant Techsystems Inc., were fined for price fixing related to these armaments.

In 1993, Aerojet unveiled a refueling system for natural gas vehicles. It used mobile fuel tanks constructed of high-tech composite materials. In the 1993 fiscal year, sales were $872 million, down from $1.1 billion, but they still accounted for nearly half of the parent company's total revenues. Aerojet employed 5,000 people in the early 1990s. The company trimmed 1,250 jobs in 1993; cutbacks at NASA resulted in the layoffs of another 650 workers in 1994.

Portions of the munitions business were sold to Olin Corporation of Stamford, Connecticut. In December 1994, GenCorp announced it would sell the rest of Aerojet as well. At the time, Aerojet had 1,350 employees at its electronics plant in Azusa, California, and 1,650 at its propulsion plant near Sacramento. The sale of Aerojet was not completed, however.

New Ventures in the Late 1990s and Beyond

Aerojet was developing new lines of business in the late 1990s. The company had won contracts to supply fuselage panels for the new F-22 Raptor fighter, but the long-running Peacekeeper missile program was canceled.

Aerojet Fine Chemicals was one of Aerojet's fastest growing new ventures. The unit manufactured chemicals for pharmaceutical companies. By 1999 sales were $45 million a year. In 2000, Aerojet Fine Chemicals was partially merged with Pharbil Technologies, an investor group associated with Donaldson, Lufkin & Jenrette Inc. GenCorp bought back ownership of Aerojet Fine Chemicals one year later.

A space propulsion joint venture with United Technologies Corp.'s Pratt & Whitney unit was discussed in 2000 but not consummated (Aerojet's environmental cleanup costs were one factor cited in the press). The rocket-propulsion industry, which then had a half-dozen competitors, was consolidating due to shrinking demand and excess capacity.

In 2001, Northrop Grumman Corporation bought Aerojet's Electronic and Information Systems (EIS) business for $315 million. EIS had 2000 revenues of $323 million, but was considered too small to compete with prime contractors such as

Boeing, Lockheed-Martin, and TRW. It employed about 1,350 people, most of them near Los Angeles. EIS was merged into Northrop's Space Systems Division.

In August 2001, Aerojet successfully test fired the world's largest one-piece rocket motor to date. It was built for Lockheed Martin's Atlas V rocket.

A 2,600-acre section of the Rancho Cordova property was removed from Superfund status in 2002 and was slated to be commercially developed. Aerojet sold the Lake Natoma Office Park located on this property in August 2003.

Major Acquisitions in 2002 and 2003

Aerojet made a couple of acquisitions that together doubled its size. In late 2002, it paid $93 million for General Dynamics' Ordnance and Tactical Systems Space Propulsion and Fire Suppression unit, based in Redmond, Washington, which employed 300 people and had sales of about $60 million a year. Renamed Aerojet Redmond after the acquisition, this company had been founded in 1968 as Rocket Research. It specialized in small thrusters used to guide satellites in space.

The space propulsion business of Atlantic Research Corp. (ARC) was acquired in the summer of 2003 for $133 million. ARC's propulsion unit had sales of $150 million a year and 900 employees. The addition of the two programs expanded Aerojet's range of offerings, including more rockets for the Space Shuttle program. Aerojet was also involved in the propulsion systems behind the Mars rovers Spirit and Opportunity. Aerojet's profits slipped 2.3 percent to $43 million in 2003 as revenues rose 18 percent to $321 million.

Principal Divisions

Propulsion Systems; Specialty Metals; Munitions Loading & Packing.

Principal Competitors

ATK Thiokol Inc.; Boeing Integrated Defense Systems; Northrop Grumman Corporation.

Further Reading

"Aerojet 80-20s Itself Toward Profits," *Business Week,* June 21, 1976, p. 88B.
"Bomb Makers Paying Fine in Antitrust Suit," *Austin American Statesman* (Texas), January 20, 1994, p. C28.
Bowman, Chris, "California Approves Aerojet Pollution Pact," *Sacramento Bee,* March 22, 2003.
——, "Rancho Cordova, Calif., Water Utility Targets Rocket Builder's Move," *Sacramento Bee,* October 21, 2001.
Calvan, Bobby Caina, "Chemical in Rocket Fuel Spurs Public Health Debate," *Boston Globe,* May 25, 2003, p. A20.
Clifford, Frank, "Toxic Chemical Shuts 18 Water Wells in State," *Los Angeles Times,* August 1, 1997, p. 1A.
"Connecticut-Based Firm Ends Talks with California-Based Aerospace Company," *Waterbury Republican-American,* November 11, 2000.
Cuff, Daniel F., "Executive Has Faith in Hearts of Tomorrow," *New York Times,* September 1, 1982, p. D2.

Downey, Dave, "Chino Hills Ammunition Plant Cited for Violations," *Press-Enterprise* (Riverside, California), Bus. Sec., December 24, 1991.

Draper, Heather, "Atlas V Launch in California a Thunderous Hit; Rocket Motor Built for Lockheed Martin Rattles Windows, Scares Schoolkids in Test Firing," *Rocky Mountain News* (Denver), September 4, 2001, p. 2B.

"GenCorp. Inc.: Deal Will Return Ownership of Aerojet Fine Chemicals," *Wall Street Journal,* November 26, 2001, p. B8.

"General Tire: Pondering Spinoffs to Make the Most of Its Assets," *Business Week,* September 7, 1981, p. 98.

Glover, Mark, "Sacramento, Calif.-Based Rocket Science Firm Advances with Times, Technology," *Sacramento Bee,* May 1, 2000.

Hynes, Mary, "Industrial Zoning for Aerojet Complex Creates Stir," *Las Vegas Review-Journal,* November 9, 1993, p. 1B.

LePage, Andrew, "GenCorp Says Aerospace Future Bright Despite Drop in 2003 Earnings," *Sacramento Bee,* January 29, 2004.

Leusner, Jim, and Christopher Quinn, "Some Weapons Makers Keep Development at Bay," *Orlando Sentinel,* March 20, 1990, p. A6.

Little, Robert, "Northrop Now Running New Linthicum Division; Satellite-Borne Defense-Tech Unit Bought from Aerojet," *Sun* (Baltimore), October 23, 2001, p. 1C.

Lusk, Steven, "Dwindling Defense Projects Spur Job Shop, Subcontractor Competition," *Orange County Business Journal,* June 19, 1989, p. 1.

Middleton, Richard H., Jr., "Asbestos Cartel Insulates Truth," *Washington Times,* December 15, 2002, p. B5.

"Northrop to Buy Aerojet-General Electronics Unit," *New York Times,* April 21, 2001, p. C3.

Payne, Melanie, "Hot Economy to Soften Blow of Aerospace Firm's Move Out of Sacramento, Calif.," *Sacramento Bee,* July 18, 2000.

Pollack, Andrew, "Coup for Pioneer Leader in Rocketry," *New York Times,* Sec. 1, April 22, 1989, p. 37.

Pounds, Marcia Heroux, "Pratt Out of Aerojet Merger; Palm Beach Figures into Growth Plans," *South Florida Sun-Sentinel* (Fort Lauderdale), November 15, 2000, p. 1D.

Richards, Bill, "Big Cleanup Costs to U.S. from Aerojet, Boeing, Lockheed Called 'Tip of Iceberg'," *Wall Street Journal,* October 26, 1992, p. B6.

"Rocket Company Sells Land," *Orlando Sentinel,* July 23, 1988, p. B1.

Sandoval, Ricardo, "Aerojet Unveils Fueling System for Natural Gas," *Journal Record* (Oklahoma City), May 5, 1993.

Skeen, Jim, "Aerojet Considers Relocating Test Site," *Daily News* (Los Angeles), Antelope Valley ed., October 16, 2001, p. AV.1.

Smith, Emily, "Rocket Fuel That Leaves a Cleaner Trail," *Business Week,* November 13, 1989, p. 136.

Swett, Clint, "GenCorp to Build Office Space in Rancho Cordova, Calif.," *Sacramento Bee,* March 27, 2003.

——, "Rocket Maker to Sell Southern California Unit to Northrop Grumman," *Sacramento Bee,* April 21, 2001.

Walter, Bob, "Rancho Cordova, Calif., Rocket Maker to Buy Virginia Firm's Propulsion Assets," *Sacramento Bee,* May 6, 2003.

Yerak, Becky, "Gencorp's Aerojet Unit Is Up for Sale," *Plain Dealer* (Cleveland, Ohio), December 22, 1994, p. 1C.

—Frederick C. Ingram

Aetna Inc.

151 Farmington Avenue
Hartford, Connecticut 06156-0001
U.S.A.
Telephone: (860) 273-0123
Toll Free: (800) 872-3862
Fax: (860) 273-3971
Web site: http://www.aetna.com

Public Company
Incorporated: 1982 as United States Health Care
    Systems, Inc.
Employees: 27,548
Total Assets: $40.95 billion (2003)
Stock Exchanges: New York
Ticker Symbol: AET
NAIC: 524114 Direct Health and Medical Insurance
    Carriers; 524113 Direct Life Insurance Carriers

Specializing in managed healthcare, Aetna Inc. is one of the largest providers of health insurance and related benefits in the United States. In addition to health insurance, the company offers dental, pharmacy, group life, disability, and long-term-care products. Aetna offers plans to businesses large and small, in all 50 states. Nationwide, the company's networks include more than 362,000 primary care and specialty physicians, 3,626 hospitals, more than 62,000 dental practices, and more than 62,000 participating pharmacies. Aetna health plans cover about 13 million individuals, and its dental plans have nearly 11 million members. Of the members in Aetna's health plans, 36 percent are enrolled in health maintenance organizations (HMOs), 34 percent in preferred provider organizations (PPOs), 17 percent in point-of-service (POS) plans, and 11 percent in traditional indemnity plans. The company started out in the mid-19th century as a life insurer and then slowly evolved into a multiline insurer. Between 1995 and 2000, however, Aetna shed the bulk of its operations that fell outside of health insurance and related group benefits. It also completed several acquisitions during this period to build its health business into a national player.

Establishment by Prominent New England Lawyer: 1850s–60s

Aetna was founded in Connecticut in 1853 as the Aetna Life Insurance Company. Aetna Life was originally formed as an affiliate of the older Aetna Insurance Company, which specialized in fire insurance (and was named after Mt. Etna, the Sicilian volcano), and it profited from its association with Aetna's reputation for reliability and speed in paying claims. However, a new state insurance regulation passed in nearby New York state in 1849, and strengthened in 1853, prohibited the same company from providing both fire and life insurance. In 1853 the Connecticut legislature granted a petition for the separate incorporation of the Aetna Life Insurance Company.

Aetna Life's founding president, Eliphalet Bulkeley, originally divided his time between practicing law and developing the fledgling life insurance firm. He was also active in the formation of the Republican Party in Connecticut, starting a long tradition of political activism by Aetna leaders. Bulkeley guided Aetna through its difficult first years, when new insurance laws in some states required capital deposits beyond the stockholders' resources, hindering Aetna from doing business in those states. The depression of 1857 further threatened the firm's financial stability, but Aetna survived in the face of multiple bank closings. During this period the company regained its financial footing in part by hiring its first midwestern agent, a Connecticut man, who opened an office in Wisconsin to serve the burgeoning market in those states.

The year 1861 was important for Aetna for two reasons: the Civil War began and Aetna modified its form of ownership. Both events profitably affected the company's growth. Seeking security during the uncertain war years, many people bought life insurance policies for the first time. In addition, Aetna modified its form of investor ownership to permit policyholders to control their own funds in a separate mutual department that operated within the overall management structure. Originally, Bulkeley had resisted the mutual plan that placed ownership in the hands of policyholders. He disliked the speculative nature of dividend payment and could not countenance an approach to management that divided responsibility among all policyholders.

Pressure from the public and from competing insurance companies helped change Bulkeley's mind. The result was the creation of a mutual department whose accounting system was separate from that of management. Within this department, policyholders controlled their own funds and received dividends, but did not vote for the management of the company. The firm as a whole continued as an investor-owned company with all the efficiency of management Bulkeley believed was inherent in that arrangement. Partly because of this revision of the ownership structure, in just five years, from 1861 to 1866, Aetna jumped from 15th among 40 life insurance companies nationwide to fifth among 80.

Policyholder Resistance to Changes in the Insurance Industry in the Late 19th Century

Bulkeley died in 1872 and was succeeded by Thomas O. Enders, who had served as both a clerk and secretary for the firm. Bulkeley had presided over Aetna during the speculative postwar years, and had maintained careful control of the risks the company assumed. The 1870s was a period of nationwide economic crisis, and Enders was hard-pressed to keep the firm alive, despite its earlier successes. Not only did he have to contend with a nationwide depression that began in 1873, but he also was burdened with the disastrous results of a major change in the method of premium payment made toward the end of Bulkeley's presidency. Until then, Aetna and most other insurance companies had accepted interest-bearing notes as half payment for premiums. In the wake of questions from the state insurance commissioner about the booking of these notes as assets, and the negative press elicited by the commissioner's report, Aetna management decided to start requiring full cash payment for premiums. Although Aetna was innovative in this change and most other insurance companies soon began to follow the new practice, the firm's policyholders were outraged. Many canceled their policies, and new policyholders were not forthcoming. In desperate straits following the policy change and weakened by the financial crisis of the 1870s, Aetna steadily declined. Enders resigned in 1879.

Aetna passed back into family hands when Morgan G. Bulkeley, Eliphalet Bulkeley's son, took over leadership of the firm, a position he was to retain for the next 43 years. Although Morgan Bulkeley had been a director on the Aetna board since his father's death, he had chosen to apprentice as a dry goods merchant rather than rise through his father's firm. His primary interest was in politics. He was active in the state Republican Party his father had helped to form. By 1879 he had been a

councilman and alderman and was successfully running for mayor of Hartford. He subsequently became governor of Connecticut and then a U.S. senator. Bulkeley maintained firm control over both his government office and his corporate office. While governor, Bulkeley loaned the state of Connecticut $300,000 from Aetna's funds during a period of financial need. In 1911 Bulkeley lost his senate seat and returned full-time to his position with Aetna.

Moving into the 20th Century: Advancing Through Diversification and Innovation

Aetna did very well under Morgan Bulkeley. Its total assets increased from $25.6 million in 1879 to $207 million in 1922, while premium income increased more than 20-fold during the same period. The number of employees grew from 29 to 2,000. Aetna's success was in large part due to innovations in forms of insurance. The first years of Bulkeley's presidency were spent getting the ailing company back on its feet, but in the 1890s Aetna made its first move to diversify, initiating a period of rapid expansion. In 1891, under its existing charter, Aetna began to write accident insurance, and in 1899 added health insurance. In 1893 its charter was expanded, allowing the company to become a pioneer in the development of liability insurance. In 1902 Aetna opened a separate accident and liability department to handle employers' liability and workmen's collective insurance. Eager to profit from the rapidly growing market for automobile insurance, in 1907 Aetna management transformed the liability department into Aetna Life's first affiliate, the Aetna Accident and Liability Company.

For a few years, this new company issued all the new forms of insurance Aetna offered, but soon further diversification was necessary. In 1912 Aetna offered the first comprehensive auto policy, providing all kinds of auto insurance in one contract, and in 1913 a second Aetna affiliate was formed, the Automobile Insurance Company. The charter of this second affiliate also allowed it to handle other insurance lines including loss of use, explosion, tornado and windstorm, leasehold, and rent. In 1916 Aetna Auto began to offer marine insurance, a line that was greatly broadened during World War I. Meanwhile, the Aetna Accident and Liability Company was expanding its business in fidelity and surety bonds, and in 1917 changed its name to the Aetna Casualty and Surety Company. In 1913 Aetna formed a group department to sell group life insurance. Group disability policies were offered for the first time in 1919.

Streamlining Procedures Under a New President in the 1920s

When Morgan Bulkeley died in 1922, Morgan Bulkeley Brainard, grandson of Eliphalet Bulkeley, succeeded his uncle as president. Unlike his uncle, Brainard was a company man. Following college, law school, and two years in a law firm, he joined Aetna as assistant treasurer, later becoming treasurer and then vice-president. According to Richard Hooker's *Aetna Life Insurance Company: Its First Hundred Years, A History*, Brainard described his uncle as having ''built up an unusually strong organization by the sheer force of his personality.'' Brainard, by contrast, intended to initiate a new style of leadership. ''Where Governor Bulkeley could bring men around him and have them work for him by the inspiration of his presence, I cannot. I have

Key Dates:

1853: Aetna Life Insurance Company is incorporated in Connecticut, with Eliphalet Bulkeley serving as founding president.
1891: The company diversifies into accident insurance.
1899: Aetna enters the field of health insurance.
1913: A group department is formed to sell group life insurance.
1936: The first group hospitalization policy is offered.
1960: Aetna enters the international market by purchasing Toronto-based Excelsior Life Insurance Company.
1967: Aetna Life & Casualty Company is created as a holding company, with these subsidiaries: Aetna Life Insurance Company, Aetna Casualty and Surety, Standard Fire Insurance, and the Automobile Insurance Company.
1968: The company's stock is listed on the New York Stock Exchange.
1973: A health maintenance organization (HMO) subsidiary is created.
1981: Aetna reorganizes into five insurance divisions: employees benefits division, personal/financial/security division, commercial insurance division, American Re-Insurance Company, and international insurance division.
1992: American Re-Insurance is divested for $1.31 billion.
1996: Aetna sells its property-casualty operations to Travelers Group for $4.1 billion; company pays $8.9 billion for HMO provider U.S. Healthcare, Inc., which is renamed Aetna U.S. Healthcare Inc.; parent company Aetna Life & Casualty is renamed Aetna Inc.
1998: The U.S. individual life insurance business is sold to Lincoln National Corporation.
1999: Aetna acquires the healthcare business of the Prudential Insurance Company of America.
2000: Aetna Inc. spins Aetna U.S. Healthcare off to its shareholders; the remnants of Aetna—the company's international and financial services units—are acquired by ING Groep N.V. for about $7.75 billion; Aetna U.S. Healthcare is renamed Aetna Inc.

got to surround myself with as able a group of men as I possibly can.'' Accordingly, Brainard focused on efficiency of administration, concentrating particularly on relations and communications with agents in the field. He streamlined procedures, regularized paperwork, and reduced the costs of doing business. The new approach worked. In 1922 life insurance in force was $1.3 billion. By 1929 assets amounted to $411 million and life insurance in force to $3.79 billion. In 1924, Aetna also had acquired a third affiliate, the Standard Fire Insurance Company, which further strengthened its position.

Such expansion, however, did not come without costs. The Automobile Insurance Company, one of Aetna Life's affiliated companies, had contributed to the spectacular increases of the 1920s. In 1922 the affiliate's premium income reached $11 million; in 1923, $19 million; and in 1924, premium income reached $30 million. The affiliate's success, however, was not

grounded in a solid financial base. In March 1926, Brainard discovered that the Automobile Insurance Company had understated its liabilities and taken on more business than it could handle. The marine division of the affiliate had expanded swiftly during the war years, but had exercised poor judgment in the selection of risks, especially following World War I, when solicitation of marine business should have been curtailed. The Automobile Insurance Company also had gained new business by assuming risks from other companies. Brainard rapidly retrenched. He cut business drastically, resulting in premium income of just $7.9 million in 1927 for the auto affiliate. Reserves were increased to cover liabilities and future underwriting losses.

This crisis during the mid-1920s helped prepare Aetna for the economic shock of the Great Depression. Brainard had, in effect, stemmed the tide of financial speculation within Aetna while the rest of the business community continued to speculate until the stock market crash of 1929. As a result, during the worst years of the Depression, Aetna's income dropped by only a little more than 10 percent. Cautious management kept the company solvent. Dividends were not paid between 1932 and 1934, but no Aetna employees were dismissed. In 1929 only 11.7 percent of Aetna's assets were in common stock, and almost half of that in the stock of Aetna affiliates, another condition that helped Aetna survive during the 1930s. Although the company did suffer because it had assumed growing numbers of farm mortgages that defaulted during the Depression, Brainard's careful business practices kept the losses to a minimum. Aetna also opened up two new lines of business during these difficult years: pensions in 1930 and group hospitalization policies in 1936.

Renewed Expansion During the War Years

World War II finally helped pull Aetna and the nation out of the Depression. The war gave Aetna several opportunities to develop new types of insurance coverage. In cooperation with other insurers, Aetna issued a bonding contract for $312 million that insured the construction of seven aircraft carriers. Aetna also was involved in insuring the production of the atom bomb under the Manhattan Project, a uniquely challenging actuarial task because much of the information was classified. In addition, Aetna was centrally occupied with developing its lines of employee group insurance during these years. Ordinary life insurance premiums remained almost steady during World War II, but group insurance rose dramatically, increasing overall premium income by almost 65 percent. Group insurance premiums declined quickly after the war with the switch to a peacetime economy, but Aetna's prewar experience with group insurance helped the company rally with relative ease.

In the postwar years, Aetna continued to diversify cautiously. The company explored the possibilities of insurance coverage for air travel, became involved in several large bonding issues, and became a pioneer in the area of driver's education. In 1955, two years after Aetna's centennial, Brainard resigned the position of president to become Aetna's first chairman. Vice-President Henry Beers succeeded him as Aetna's fifth president.

With Beers's inauguration, the long history of family control ended and a new era of shorter presidencies began. In 1962

Beers became chairman and J.A. Hill took over as president. One year later Olcott D. Smith succeeded Beers as chairman. In 1972 John H. Filer succeeded Smith as chairman, and Donald M. Johnson was named president in 1970. In 1976 William O. Bailey succeeded Johnson. Through these years of fairly rapid changes in management, the position of chairman and chief executive officer gained ascendancy over that of president and chief operating officer.

Going International in the 1960s

In 1960 Aetna entered the international market with the purchase of Excelsior Life Insurance Company of Toronto. Six years later Aetna entered into an international cooperation agreement with Italy's Assicurazioni Generali S.p.A. through which each company provided reciprocal services to the other's clients while abroad. To facilitate flexible management of these expanding operations and allow diversification into non-insurance fields, Aetna Life & Casualty Company, a holding company, was created in 1967 with subsidiaries Aetna Life Insurance Company, Aetna Casualty and Surety, Standard Fire Insurance, and the Automobile Insurance Company. Later that same year Aetna purchased the Participating Annuity Life Insurance Company, becoming the first major insurance firm to enter the variable annuity market. In 1968 Aetna was first listed on the New York Stock Exchange.

In the late 1960s Aetna experienced a sharp drop in earnings, a trend that reflected an industrywide increase in claims. The decline was reversed in the early 1970s, in part because of nationwide decreases in losses and increases in premiums and in part because of Aetna's move to control costs and concentrate on the most profitable lines of insurance. Nevertheless, rapid diversification into non-insurance fields later in the same decade undermined earlier gains. Particularly ill-fated acquisitions were Geosource Inc., an oilfield services concern, and Satellite Business Systems, a communications firm.

Diversification Followed by Reorganization in the 1970s

In 1972 Chairman Smith initiated a management change that resembled Brainard's initiation of his new leadership style 50 years before. In place of administration by one man, Smith introduced the "corporate office" approach, a consensual relationship of the four top managers—chairman, president, and two vice-presidents—with the chairman still slightly dominant. Corporate structure also was reorganized. In addition, in a move that would become much more important in subsequent decades, Aetna created a health maintenance organization (HMO) subsidiary in 1973.

In 1981 the company reorganized its operations into five insurance divisions. The employees benefits division offered group insurance, healthcare services, and pension and related financial products to business, government units, associations, and welfare trusts. The personal/financial/security division provided automobile and homeowner insurance, life and health insurance, and retirement funding and annuity products to individuals, small businesses, and employer-sponsored groups. The commercial insurance division marketed property-casualty insurance and bonds for businesses, government units, and associ-

ations, including workers' compensation. The American Re-Insurance Company reinsured commercial property and liability risks in domestic and international markets. The international insurance division handled insurance and investment products in non-U.S. markets. The activities of these five insurance sectors were supported by the operations of a financial division that managed all of the firm's investment portfolios.

Back to the Insurance Basics in the 1980s

Income declined in the early 1980s. In 1981, hoping to lead industrywide price increases, Aetna raised commercial insurance prices, a mistimed move that cost the company as much as 10 percent of its business. In addition, Aetna was forced to lower its 1982 statement of earnings by 39 percent, in response to a ruling by the Securities and Exchange Commission that disallowed Aetna's practice of booking future tax credits as current earnings.

In 1984 James T. Lynn became chairman and CEO. Like his predecessors in the Bulkeley family, Lynn was active in Republican politics when he accepted the post with Aetna. Trained as a lawyer, he served as secretary of Housing and Urban Development from 1973 to 1975, and as director of the Office of Management and Budget from 1975 to 1977. Lynn implemented a policy of prudent retrenchment, selling subsidiaries that were not performing well and emphasizing Aetna's longstanding priority on insurance. This policy once again proved profitable for Aetna: earnings more than doubled from 1984 to 1985, with record increases in 1986 and 1987.

Ronald E. Compton became president of Aetna in 1988. Earnings declined by 23 percent from the previous year, a downturn reflecting increased competition in the commercial property-casualty business, rising loss costs in auto and homeowners insurance lines, and losses in its highly competitive multinational corporations operations. In 1989 the decline continued at the rate of 5 percent from the previous year, with commercial property-casualty insurance lines affected by two natural disasters, Hurricane Hugo and the San Francisco Bay area earthquake.

New Challenges from Changing Economy in the Early 1990s

In the fluctuating economic climate of the 1990s, Aetna began to redraw its traditional market sector, as well as to reorganize its three domestic insurance divisions into 15 strategic business units. In response to several state legislatures' efforts to roll back or otherwise restrict the rise in auto insurance rates, the company attempted to pull out of both Pennsylvania's and Massachusetts' auto insurance markets, although such efforts drew resistance from both state regulators and consumers. The company would withdraw from the auto insurance business in 13 other states over the next few years. The company also began to curtail its expansion of personal property and casualty insurance markets in several states, and cut back personal mortgage insurance early in the decade.

While pulling out of the auto insurance market, the company was investing heavily in the growing field of managed healthcare insurance. By 1990 Aetna Life & Casualty had spent more than $400 million to establish its own HMO, a profitable venture that helped buoy net income for that year to $614 million, against a slight drop in overall earnings. Losses taken against plummeting real estate prices in the northeast further eroded earnings in 1991 because of the company's extensive property holdings. Net income for 1991 was reported at only $505 million, the downturn aggravated by property claims resulting from Hurricane Bob.

A further sign that Aetna was serious in its efforts to reposition itself by narrowing its focus to health and life insurance and financial services came in November 1991, when the company announced that Aetna President Ronald E. Compton would be appointed chairman upon the retirement of James T. Lynn in early 1992. The company also divested itself of its American Re-Insurance subsidiary in September 1992, selling it to American Re Corporation for $1.31 billion and raising much needed cash. In an effort to retain customers lured away from insurance by mutual fund offerings, Aetna Life & Casualty began offering five mutual funds on the retail marketplace in September 1992.

Despite a slowly improving national economy, the continuing deterioration of the company's mortgage loan portfolio would force Aetna to engage in further streamlining efforts, and in June 1992 the company laid off 10 percent of its workforce. Plagued by natural disasters and bad weather for the remainder of the year—the winter storms during the fourth quarter alone generated almost 18,000 claims totaling $118 million—as well as a $55 million charge for withdrawing its automobile insurance services from Massachusetts, the company saw its 1992 net income eroded to $56 million.

Retrenchment and Cutbacks in the Mid-1990s

Continuing its slide, Aetna posted a net loss of $365 million in 1993, although much of that loss was attributable to charges related to downsizing. By April 1994 the company announced further layoffs, cutting staff by 4,000 jobs. Despite the layoffs, the efforts to shrink the company's unprofitable pension business, and the implementation of other cost-containment measures, industry analysts were skeptical that the sprawling insurance giant could stem continued losses.

In mid-1994 Aetna took another hit: $1.75 billion charged toward loss reserves for the purpose of paying out pollution- and asbestos-related claims against policies written for large industrial businesses as long ago as the 1950s. This action, which shadowed a similar charge against reserves made in 1992, made it the first among the nation's insurance giants to recognize corporate environmental liability.

Efforts to enter the Mexican market after the passage of NAFTA were among the company's attempts to forestall further decreases in net earnings in 1994 and 1995. Aetna also moved into the Philippines, where it was granted a license in 1995, to Latin America, where it invested $390 million in Brazil's Sul America Seguros in 1997, and to China, where it established two offices with the expectation that the country would soon be open to foreign insurance offices. Year-end 1994 saw net income rise to $467.5 million.

Against this long awaited rise in net income, the company announced that it intended to sell its property-casualty subsid-

iary, which had contributed mounting losses to the corporate balance sheet over the past several decades through its policies for individuals and businesses. Travelers Group agreed to a merger with the Aetna division in November, paying Aetna $4.1 billion for a 72 percent interest in the company and making the newly formed Travelers/Aetna Property Casualty Corp. one of the fifth largest carriers of such insurance in the nation. The deal closed in April 1996.

Series of Health Insurance Acquisitions in the Late 1990s

In 1996, under Compton and newly appointed Chairman of Strategy and Finance Richard L. Huber, Aetna began to shed both its corporate malaise and its tradition-bound methods of operation. Continuing to divest itself of losing real estate investments after the sale of its property and casualty division, Aetna now focused on aggressively growing its interests in managed healthcare and retirement services, a potentially risky mix according to some industry analysts, and about which Huber himself would acknowledge in the *Hartford Courant* that "demographics are destiny." In April 1996 the company paid $8.9 billion for HMO provider U.S. Healthcare, Inc., transforming Aetna into the nation's largest managed healthcare provider. The parent company Aetna Life & Casualty was renamed Aetna Inc., with the company realigning itself around the new name and new identity. Aetna's existing health insurance operations were merged into U.S. Healthcare, which became an Aetna subsidiary and was renamed Aetna U.S. Healthcare Inc.

A change of leadership in mid-1997 saw former banking executive Richard L. Huber named president and CEO, continuing the efforts to streamline Aetna and focus the company's manpower on what it had proven it does best. "We take care," Huber stated, "of what matters most to the vast majority of the population, their health and their wealth." In February 1998 Huber was named chairman as well, succeeding the retiring Compton.

Huber oversaw several deals in the late 1990s that further bolstered Aetna's position as a major health insurer. In July 1998 the company spent more than $1 billion to acquire New York Life Insurance Company's health insurance operations, which were known as NYLCare Health Plans. The deal added 2.5 million members to the 13.7 million people already enrolled in Aetna plans. NYLCare HMOs operated in several large metropolitan areas, including Washington, D.C., Houston, and Dallas, as well as a number of cities in the states of Illinois, Maine, New Jersey, New York, and Washington.

Continuing to shed noncore operations, Aetna sold its U.S. individual life insurance business to Lincoln National Corporation for $1 billion in cash in October 1998. Then in August 1999 Aetna completed its third major acquisition in as many years, spending about $1 billion for the money-losing healthcare business of the Prudential Insurance Company of America. The deal increased the number of Americans covered by Aetna health plans from 16 million to 22 million, and it also more than doubled Aetna's dental insurance business to 15 million members. To gain antitrust approval from the U.S. Department of Justice, Aetna had to divest its NYLCare HMO businesses in Dallas and Houston. The Texas Medical Association had opposed the deal, concerned that it would give Aetna too large a share of the market in those two cities. The American Medical Association was also against the deal, arguing that it would give Aetna too much power over physicians and be bad for consumers as well.

In fact, by this time many doctors and healthcare consumers were in open rebellion against the policies that had prevailed at Aetna since its purchase of U.S. Healthcare. It turned out that Aetna had made this acquisition at a peak point and, therefore, had paid a premium price. The company began squeezing both doctors and patients to improve profits. Physicians did not like the restrictions that Aetna contracts placed upon them, and the company began facing a rash of class-action lawsuits not only from doctors but also from patients claiming they had been denied care. Aetna's travails were compounded by the difficulty it had integrating its operations with those of U.S. Healthcare and also by the discovery that the newly acquired Prudential health unit was losing more money than anticipated. Despite steadily increasing revenues, profits were falling, dropping from $901 million in 1997 to $848.1 million in 1998 to $716.9 million in 1999.

Divesting Global Health and Global Financial Services in 2000

By February 2000 Aetna's stock had fallen to $39, having lost two-thirds of its value since August 1997. Mounting pressure from shareholders led to Huber's sudden resignation that month. William H. Donaldson, cofounder of the investment banking firm Donaldson, Lufkin & Jenrette, Inc., was named chairman and CEO. In late February managed-care firm WellPoint Health Networks Inc. and the U.S. arm of the Dutch financial services giant ING Groep N.V. jointly approached Aetna about a $10.5 billion takeover. But the company's board rebuffed this unsolicited bid and instead announced in March that the company would split, creating two separate businesses focusing on healthcare and financial services.

ING remained interested in a deal, however, and in July the two parties reached an agreement. The complicated transaction was completed in December 2000. Aetna Inc. spun off to its shareholders the Aetna U.S. Healthcare Inc. subsidiary. What remained of Aetna—the company's international and financial services units—was acquired by ING for about $7.75 billion. Aetna U.S. Healthcare was then renamed Aetna Inc. (meaning that the "new" Aetna would trace its incorporation back to that of United States Health Care Systems, Inc. in 1982). As a result, the new Aetna was focused almost solely on U.S. medical and dental insurance and related products; it did retain much smaller operations in group life, disability, and long-term-care insurance and in large-care pensions.

To turn around the troubled company, Donaldson brought John W. Rowe onboard as president and CEO in September 2000. A noted gerontologist, Rowe had most recently served as head of Mount Sinai NYU Health, a group of nonprofit New York City hospitals. Rowe was appointed chairman of Aetna as well in April 2001. Another key appointment was that of Ronald A. Williams, who was named executive vice-president and chief of health operations in March 2001. Hired away from Aetna rival WellPoint Health Networks, Williams was promoted to president of Aetna in May 2002.

One of the key steps taken by the new leadership team was to mend fences with both doctors and patients. Aetna changed many of the restrictive policies that it had implemented in an attempt to contain costs. It began providing clearer information on coverage to both doctors and patients, speeded up payments, and reduced red tape. In May 2003 the company broke ranks with its industry rivals and agreed to settle a massive class-action lawsuit that had been brought against the nation's major managed-care insurers. The suit, whose class included nearly all U.S. physicians, had listed a number of complaints, including unfair billing practices and interference with treatment recommendations. The value of the settlement was estimated at about $470 million. Aetna also introduced new health plans, such as Aetna HealthFund (launched in 2001), that gave plan members more direct control over their healthcare decisions.

To repair the company's finances, Rowe cut about 15,000 jobs and raised insurance premiums by about 16 percent per year to keep ahead of medical inflation. He also shrunk Aetna's customer base from 19 million members to 13 million by abandoning unprofitable markets, including almost half of the counties nationwide in which it offered Medicare products. Because of the drop in membership, Aetna was no longer the nation's largest managed-care insurer, but it appeared to be a stronger company. After reporting a net loss of $279.6 million in 2001, the firm was profitable the following year before the effects of a charge taken because of a change in accounting principles. The $2.97 billion charge translated into a net loss of $2.65 billion. For 2003, although revenues fell to $17.98 billion from $19.88 billion, Aetna netted $933.8 million. Wall Street responded to this turn of events by pushing the company's stock up to $75 per share by early 2004, signaling that Aetna was well on its way to recovery.

Principal Subsidiaries

Aetna Health Inc.; Aetna Health of California Inc.; Aetna Health of the Carolinas Inc.; Aetna Health of Illinois Inc.; Aetna Dental Inc.; Aetna Dental of California Inc.; Aetna Life Insurance Company; Aetna Health Insurance Company of Connecticut; Aetna Health Insurance Company of New York; Corporate Health Insurance Company; Aetna Health Administrators, LLC.

Principal Competitors

Anthem, Inc.; UnitedHealth Group Incorporated; Blue Cross and Blue Shield Association; Kaiser Foundation Health Plan, Inc.; CIGNA Corporation; Humana Inc.; PacifiCare Health Systems, Inc.; Health Net, Inc.

Further Reading

"Aetna: A Long Way to the Recovery Room," *Business Week,* July 16, 2001, p. 56.

"Aetna Chairman Details New Direction," *Wall Street Journal,* April 3, 1996.

"Aetna Explodes," *Economist,* March 18, 2000, p. 79.

"Aetna: Where Group Management Didn't Work," *Business Week,* February 16, 1976, p. 77.

Anders, George, "Aetna Will Sell Unit to KKR for $1.4 Billion," *Wall Street Journal,* June 9, 1992, p. A2.

Benko, Laura B., ''Makeover at Aetna Lags,'' *Modern Healthcare,* March 18, 2002, p. 38.

Brady, Diane, ''Aetna's Painful Recovery,'' *Business Week,* December 8, 2003, pp. 86–88.

——, ''The Volcano Behind Aetna: Under Jack Rowe, It's a Force for Health-Care Reform,'' *Business Week,* June 9, 2003, pp. 98, 102.

David, Gregory E., ''Opportunity Knocks,'' *Financial World,* April 12, 1994, pp. 42 + .

Gentry, Carol, ''Aetna's Shares Catch Cold from Its New Health Unit,'' *Wall Street Journal,* September 29, 1999, p. B4.

——, ''As Aetna's Woes Pile Up, Its Chairman Is Under Fire,'' *Wall Street Journal,* February 16, 2000, p. B1.

Gentry, Carol, and Nikhil Deogun, ''Aetna to Split into Two Separate Businesses,'' *Wall Street Journal,* March 13, 2000, p. A4.

Gorham, John, ''Train Wreck in Hartford,'' *Forbes,* March 6, 2000, pp. 70–71.

Hardman, Adrienne, ''Reinventing Aetna,'' *Financial World,* November 24, 1992, pp. 22 + .

Hooker, Richard, *Aetna Life Insurance Company: Its First Hundred Years, A History,* Hartford, Conn.: Aetna Life Insurance Company, 1956.

Jackson, Susan, ''Aetna's Brave Old World,'' *Business Week,* March 30, 1998, p. 180.

King, Resa W., and Marc Frons, ''How Government Groomed Jim Lynn for Aetna,'' *Business Week,* June 2, 1986, pp. 54 + .

Lagnado, Lucette, ''Personality Change: Old-Line Aetna Adopts Managed-Care Tactics and Stirs a Backlash,'' *Wall Street Journal,* July 29, 1998, p. A1.

Lagnado, Lucette, and Joann Lublin, ''Hospital Chief Picked to Revive Distressed Aetna,'' *Wall Street Journal,* September 6, 2000, p. B1.

Levick, Diane, ''Another Adventure Beckons,'' *Hartford Courant,* August 11, 1997.

''Listening to Its Own Drummer,'' *Forbes,* August 17, 1981, pp. 34 + .

Lohse, Deborah, ''Aetna to Sell Some Assets to Lincoln,'' *Wall Street Journal,* May 22, 1998, p. A3.

Loomis, Carol J., ''Behind the Profits Grow at Aetna,'' *Fortune,* November 15, 1982, pp. 54 + .

Martinez, Barbara, ''Aetna to Announce Settlement with Physicians,'' *Wall Street Journal,* May 22, 2003, p. A3.

——, ''Aetna to Expand Its Catalog of Health-Plan Products,'' *Wall Street Journal,* July 30, 2001, p. B8.

——, ''Making Amends: Aetna Tries to Improve Bedside Manner in Bid to Help Bottom Line,'' *Wall Street Journal,* February 23, 2001, p. A1.

''Profit Pains at the New Aetna,'' *Business Week,* August 1, 1983, pp. 50 + .

Rifkin, Glenn, ''Reengineering Aetna,'' *Forbes,* June 7, 1993, pp. 78 + .

Roush, Chris, ''Aetna's Heavy Ax,'' *Business Week,* February 14, 1994, p. 32.

Rublin, Lauren R., ''Temperature Rising,'' *Barron's,* March 27, 2000, pp. 21–22.

Scism, Leslie, ''Aetna to Buy New York Health Unit,'' *Wall Street Journal,* March 16, 1998, p. A3.

——, ''Travelers Stock Jumps on Plan to Buy Aetna Unit,'' *Wall Street Journal,* November 30, 1995, p. A3.

Smart, Tim, ''Moving Mount Aetna: What It Will Take to Make the U.S. Healthcare Merger Pay,'' *Business Week,* February 10, 1997, p. 100.

Smart, Tim, and Keith H. Hammonds, ''Aetna's Booster Shot: An $8.9 Billion Merger Makes It No. 1 in Managed Care,'' *Business Week,* April 15, 1996, pp. 41 + .

Smart, Tim, and Richard A. Melcher, ''The Floodwaters Rise Around Aetna,'' *Business Week,* June 5, 1995, p. 110.

Steinmetz, Greg, ''Aetna Revamps, Taking a Charge of $1.28 Billion,'' *Wall Street Journal,* January 31, 1994, p. A3.

Treaster, Joseph B., ''Aetna Agreement with Doctors Envisions Altered Managed Care,'' *New York Times,* May 23, 2003, p. A1.

Winslow, Ron, ''Aetna to Acquire Prudential Health Unit,'' *Wall Street Journal,* December 11, 1998, p. A3.

Winslow, Ron, and Leslie Scism, ''Aetna Agrees to Acquire U.S. Healthcare,'' *Wall Street Journal,* April 2, 1996, p. A2.

Winslow, Ron, Leslie Scism, and Elyse Tanouye, ''Aetna Hopes for Breath of New Life from Acquisition,'' *Wall Street Journal,* April 3, 1996, p. B4.

Wojcik, Joanne, ''Aetna's Shift to Health Focus Brings Struggles,'' *Business Insurance,* August 13, 2001, p. 1.

—Lynn M. Voskuil
—updates: Pamela L. Shelton, David E. Salamie

Air Mauritius Ltd.

Air Mauritius Centre
5 President John Kennedy Street
Port Louis
Mauritius
Telephone: (230) 207-7070
Fax: (230) 208-8331
Web site: http://www.airmauritius.com

Public Company
Incorporated: 1967
Employees: 2,500
Sales: EUR 360.44 million (2003)
Stock Exchanges: Mauritius
Ticker Symbol: AIRM
NAIC: 481111 Scheduled Passenger Air Transportation;
481112 Scheduled Freight Air Transportation; 481212
Nonscheduled Chartered Freight Air Transportation;
481211 Nonscheduled Chartered Passenger Air
Transportation; 488190 Other Support Activities for
Air Transportation; 721110 Hotels (Except Casino
Hotels) and Motels

Air Mauritius Ltd. (AM) is the official airline of its namesake island, located to the east of Madagascar. AM has been called the Indian Ocean's leading airline. It flies to 30 destinations, as far as Europe, Asia, and Australia. According to Mark Twain, "God created Heaven based on Mauritius"; with only 1.5 million or so residents of its own, the country relies on upscale tourism, and attracts 650,000 visitors a year (60 percent from Europe).

Every year about one million passengers fly Air Mauritius, and the cargo operation carries 42,000 tons of freight (cargo operations accounted for one-fifth of revenues). The diverse fleet includes five Airbus A340 aircraft, two A319s, one ATR 72 turboprop, two ATR 42s, and three Bell Ranger helicopters. The Republic of Mauritius has a 51 percent controlling interest in the airline, which *African Business* dubbed "African Airline of the Year" in 2003.

Origins

Air Mauritius Ltd. (AM) was formed on June 14, 1967, as a ground handling agent for other airlines. Mauritius was then a colony of the United Kingdom; it became an independent state within the Commonwealth in March 1968. The island's economy was dependent upon sugar. The government owned 42.5 percent of the company when it was formed; other shareholders were shipping company Rogers & Co. (17.5 percent), British Airways and Air France (15 percent each), and Air-India (10 percent).

In 1972, AM began its own flight operations with a single, six-seat Piper Navajo leased from Air Madagascar. The first island-hopping flights were to neighboring Reunion and Rodrigues. The next year, AM launched a Mauritius-Nairobi-London flight with a Vickers Super VC 10 aircraft leased from British Airways. The airline took the *phaeton rubicola* or Paille-en-Queue, a fish-eating tropical bird, for its symbol. Communications minister Harry Tirvengadum joined the airline in 1972 and became managing director in 1978, a position he held for nearly two decades.

Nonstop Growth in the 1980s

In 1984, AM began operating nonstop service flying Boeing 747 jumbo jets to major European cities including London, Paris, and Rome. In April 1987, Air Mauritius began leasing two Boeing 747s for use on long routes, including one to Munich. It also ordered two Boeing 767 airliners worth $130 million.

As the network expanded to the east, AM began serving Singapore in 1985, using the stop as a regional hub. Three years later, the airline started flying to Kuala Lumpur in cooperation with Malaysian Airlines System (MAS).

Air Mauritius ordered five Airbus A340s, two of them leased, in 1993. The next year, the carrier began operating joint flights to neighboring territories with Air Madagascar and Air Austral of Reunion Island. The Air Austral link included connections to Nairobi.

Company Perspectives:

Air Mauritius maintains its commitment to high quality service because the Mauritian carrier acts as an ambassador for the country and reveals the image of its people. Those who fly Air Mauritius realise that multiple elements in its offices and on board celebrate "L'Esprit de l'Ile Maurice," the Soul of Mauritius. This concept tries to express the blend of an innate sense of human encounter with the urge to improve constantly.

Public in 1994

The airline offered 20 percent of its shares on the Stock Exchange of Mauritius in November 1994. British Airways, which competed with Air Mauritius on an Indian Ocean route, owned about 13 percent of the company. At the time, Air Mauritius had a 60 percent share of the local air travel market.

Revenues of FRF 1.5 billion in the 1995–96 fiscal year produced a profit of FRF 200 million (MUR 610 million). The airline connected 25 destinations at the time. In 1995, AM moved its headquarters to the 18-story Air Mauritius Centre in downtown Port Louis.

In February 1997, Nash Mallam Hassam, an 18-year veteran of British Aerospace, succeeded Tirvengadum, who had left to lead Air Afrique. He would remain AM's head for another four years.

It was a difficult time to take the reins, reported *Airline Business*. Profits and cash reserves were down drastically, thanks to skyrocketing fuel costs, aircraft lease prices that doubled, and unfavorable exchange rates. In addition, one of the company's A340 aircraft had caught fire on the ground in October 1996 and was out of service for ten months.

In July 1997, AM joined several other carriers (Air Comores, Air France, Air Madagascar, and Air Seychelles) in establishing a regional feeder airline called Air Ocean Indien (AOI). Coordination difficulties between the founding airlines, however, prevented AOI from taking off.

AM was developing Singapore as a hub for the Asian region, although the carrier did not yet fly there nonstop. Plans for expanding in the region were arrested by the Asian financial crisis.

Maintaining an Edge in the Late 1990s

In 1998, the French Direction Générale de l'Aviation Civile certified Air Mauritius as a JAR (Joint Aviation Requirements) 145 Maintenance Organization, a valuable endorsement. Within a few years, the company would be setting up a third party maintenance operation. Air Mauritius had been in talks with Irish airline Aer Lingus in the early 1990s about setting up a maintenance center in Africa. Most of the region's 220 airliners were flown to Europe for upkeep.

Mauritius was growing in importance as a destination for business travelers from India, and Air-India owned an 8.82 percent equity stake in AM's holding company, and 2.56 percent in

the airline itself. In 1999, the airline contracted Cambridge Technology Partners of India to develop its e-business strategy.

AM got a new managing director, Vijay Poonoosamy, in October 2000, but he resigned six months later, returning to his former post as AM's legal director. Sir Harry Tirvengadum (he had been knighted in 1987) remained CEO throughout. Vinod Chidambaram replaced Poonoosamy; he had held this role during Nash Mallam Hasham's administration. Unfavorable exchange rates and rising fuel costs pushed AM into a MUR 214.4 million loss for the 2000–01 fiscal year.

Following the ouster of Poonoosamy, who was the brother of a high-ranking official in the Mouvement Militant Mauricien (MMM) party, allegations of embezzlement surfaced regarding the previous administrations' dealings with Rogers & Co., its general sales agent for certain destinations. The resulting scandal in turn forced the resignation of Harry Tirvengadum; he was replaced as chairman by Arjoon Suddhoo, an aeronautical engineer by training with experience at Rolls-Royce plc and the Massachusetts Institute of Technology. Vinod Chidambaram was the company's managing director. Nash Mallam Hasham, managing director from 1997 to 2000, was convicted of embezzlement. He died of a heart attack in November 2001.

Restructuring in 2002

AM launched a major corporate restructuring program in March 2002. The airline also moved its Asian hub from Singapore to Malaysia during the year, attracted by modern facilities and breaks on fees at Kuala Lumpur International Airport (KLIA). The airline added a second weekly flight to KLIA and opened a new office in Kuala Lumpur.

AM launched a scheduled cargo service to Johannesburg, South Africa, in October 2002. A McDonnell Douglas DC-8 was leased from African International Airways for the purpose, reported *Air Transport Intelligence*. Cargo accounted for 20 percent of revenues.

Service to India was expanded in the spring of 2003 with a new weekly flight to the country's "Silicon Valley," Bangalore. AM lured Indian tourists to Mauritius with the offer of a free visit to the island's new water park.

The airline's thriving business in Asia was deeply affected by the SARS epidemic in the spring of 2003. AM suspended flights to Hong Kong, Kuala Lumpur, and Singapore. The war in Iraq had a smaller impact on AM's traffic.

In May 2003, AM canceled services to the neighboring Seychelles Islands, where the government there prevented airlines from withdrawing profits from local banks. Other international airlines also were withdrawing from that market.

Yet another new managing director arrived at AM in September 2003. Megh Pillay had formerly led Mauritius Telecom. In late December 2003, AM launched a new turboprop service between Reunion and Rodrigues Island, a newly autonomous country that was eager to develop its tourist trade.

About 850,000 passengers flew Air Mauritius in 2002–03, and the cargo operation carried 42,000 tons of freight. The

Key Dates:

1967: Air Mauritius is established as a handling agent.
1972: AM launches island-hopping flight operations.
1973: The route to London via Nairobi is opened.
1984: Nonstop flights to Europe are launched.
1985: The Singapore hub is established.
1994: AM begins trading shares on the Mauritius Stock Exchange.
2002: A major restructuring program is launched.
2004: The annual passenger count tops one million.

diverse fleet included five Airbus A340 aircraft, two A319s, one ATR 72 turboprop, two ATR 42s, and three Bell Ranger helicopters. Passenger count exceeded one million for the first time in 2003–04.

Principal Subsidiaries

Mauritius Estate Development Corporation Ltd. (MEDCOR) (93.7%); Pointe Coton Resort Hotel Company Ltd. (54.2%); The Mauritius Shopping Paradise Company Ltd. (41.7%).

Principal Operating Units

Cargo; MK Consulting; Helicopter Services; Business Extensions.

Principal Competitors

Air Austral; Air Seychelles.

Further Reading

"Air-India, Air Mauritius to Relook at Fares," *Business Line* (India), February 12, 1999.

"Air Mauritius—A Tricky Customer; Skillful Management Secures Attractive Aircraft Purchasing Deals," *Airline Business,* September 1, 1990, p. 96.

"Air Mauritius: Managing Director Replaced at Air Company," *Indian Ocean Newsletter,* March 31, 2001.

"Air Mauritius May Extend South Links," *Business Line* (India), February 18, 1999.

"Air Mauritius on Its Way Out," *Indian Ocean Newsletter,* May 17, 2003.

"Air Mauritius to Take Off from Silicon Valley in Q1 (It Will Have a Flight with a Weekly Frequency)," *India Business Insight,* February 15, 2003.

"Air Mauritius's New Organizational Chart," *Indian Ocean Newsletter,* April 6, 2002.

"Arjoon Suddhoo (Mauritius)," *Indian Ocean Newsletter,* September 29, 2001.

"BA Increases Share in Air Mauritius," *Times,* November 28, 1994.

Bani, Eirmalasare, "Air Mauritius to Increase Frequency to KLIA," *Business Times* (Malaysia), June 22, 2002, p. 5.

Bowman, Louise, "Making Waves," *Airline Business,* July 1, 1998, p. 56.

"Cambridge India's Partnership with Air Mauritius," *Hindu* (Madras, India), July 26, 2000, p. 1.

"Cargo Helps National Airline Buck the Global Downward Trend," *Lloyd's List,* March 9, 2004.

Chan, Felix, "Air Mauritius to Expand South Asia Hub in S'pore," *Business Times* (Singapore), October 8, 1997, p. 18.

Chidambaram, Vinod, "Air Mauritius: African Airline of the Year," *African Business,* January 1, 2003, p. 37.

"God Created Heaven Based on Mauritius," *New Straits Times* (Malaysia), March 12, 2004, p. 31.

"Harry Tirvengadum (Mauritius)," *Indian Ocean Newsletter,* November 16, 1996.

Ionides, Nicholas, "Air Mauritius Adds Scheduled Freighter Services," *Air Transport Intelligence,* October 22, 2002.

Jeziorski, Andrzej, "Tropical Life—Air Mauritius," *Flight International,* August 17, 1994, p. 40.

"Lower Air Mauritius Profits," *Indian Ocean Newsletter,* September 27, 1997.

"Mauritius-Boeing Deal," *New York Times,* Sec. 1., April 18, 1987, p. 30.

"Mauritius/Madagascar: Airline Agreements," *Indian Ocean Newsletter,* April 2, 1994.

"Mauritius: Tandem Project with Aer Lingus," *Indian Ocean Newsletter,* February 6, 1993.

"Mauritius: Vengeance Reveals Scandals Galore," *Indian Ocean Newsletter,* September 22, 2001.

"Nailed to the Tarmac," *Indian Ocean Newsletter,* July 18, 1998.

Toh, Eddie, "Air Mauritius to Move Regional Hub to KLIA from S'pore," *Business Times Singapore,* June 6, 2002.

Versi, Anver, "The Focus Is on Smart," *African Business,* April 1, 2003, p. 38.

—Frederick C. Ingram

Alabama Farmers Cooperative, Inc.

121 Somerville Road, Southeast
Decatur, Alabama 35601-2446
U.S.A.
Telephone (256) 353-6843
Fax: (256) 350-1770
Web site: http://www.alafarm.com

Cooperative
Incorporated: 1936 as Tennessee Valley Fertilizer
   Cooperative
Employees: 2,000
Sales: $324.12 million (2003)
NAIC: 115110 Support Activities for Crop Production

Based in Decatur, Alabama, Alabama Farmers Cooperative, Inc. (AFC) is a federated cooperative, made up of 52 local, farmer-owned cooperatives, serving Alabama and the Florida panhandle. AFC is one of the largest farmer-owned agribusinesses in the Southeast. It operates some 80 stores, which are each governed by a local cooperative. All members share in the profits of the stores and other ventures, as well as benefit from AFC research and systemwide marketing efforts. Local co-op stores, which sell to the general public as well as farmers, offer a full range of agricultural supplies and services. The feed department not only offers horse, cattle, hog, and poultry feed, but also fish feed, sheep and goat feed, rabbit feed, deer and wild animal feed, and dog and cat food. Co-op stores supply a wide variety of medications, vitamins, and supplements. In addition, AFC offers many products that cater to non-farming customers: home and garden accessories, such as gifts and home decorating, outdoor furniture, and lawn and garden ornaments; landscape supplies, including greenhouse and nursery supplies; bird and wildlife feeders and accessories; pond and water gardening products, including pond fertilizer; fertilizers, repellants, and plant foods; pet supplies; sporting goods; and even toys. Other store product lines include farm equipment, lawn and garden equipment, fencing supplies, tool boxes and fuel tanks; and tires. AFC operates a gin division, peanut division, and plant division. The gin division, Currie Gin, operates two cotton gins in Alabama,

one of which is among the largest in the state. Peanuts are handled through Opp, Alabama-based Anderson's Peanuts, a leading marketer of seeds and peanuts, which it also sells internationally. The plant division is comprised of Bonnie Plant Farms, a Union Springs, Alabama, business that is one of the nation's largest sellers of annual flowers and vegetable plants. In addition, AFC and partner Southfresh Farms own SouthFresh Aquaculture, providing feed, fingerlings, and two processing plants to Alabama and Mississippi catfish farmers. More recently, AFC and the Midwestern Land O'Lakes cooperative have joined forces to create Agriliance-AFC, LLC, an effort to increase buying power in the purchase of seed, crop protectants, and crop nutrients. To keep members informed, AFC produces a monthly publication, *Cooperative Farming News.* AFC is governed by a board of directors comprised of working farmers and is a member of the National Council of Farmers.

Farmers Cooperatives Grow Out of 19th-Century Conditions

As long as farming was done for subsistence there was no great need for cooperatives, but with the rise of commercial farming the need for farmers to band together for their mutual benefit began to mount. During the 1800s the railroads, as well as grain elevators, spread across the United States, making commercial farming more viable but also putting farmers in the difficult position of dealing with a local monopoly that was interested in charging the highest possible price. The Granger movement, which started in 1866, attracted a number of farmers who wanted to band together to combat the exorbitant rates charged by the railroads and grain elevators. Farmers formed cooperatives to pool their buying power for needed supplies and to cut out the middleman when selling their products, as a way to negotiate the best price. It was not until 1922, when the United States Congress passed the Copper-Volstead Act, that farmers and ranchers were able to legally form cooperative associations for their mutual benefit.

In 1936 representatives of several local county cooperatives met in Decatur, Alabama, and agreed to pool their money in order to receive a price break on a large order of nitrogen fertilizer. To achieve this purpose they formed a new cooperative, the Tennessee Valley Fertilizer Cooperative, AFC's predecessor. In 1937 Edmond P. Garrett, Sr., was named general manager and chief executive officer of the co-op, a position he would hold for the next 31 years. Garrett, born in 1898, was college educated, a graduate of Alabama Polytechnic Institute in Auburn, Alabama.

Over the years, Tennessee Valley Fertilizer gradually added to its purpose. By World War II it was making food for cattle and hogs, and in the final years of the decade beginning to clean and process seeds. During the 1950s the co-op expanded its fertilizer facilities, eventually possessing storage facilities for both liquid and dry fertilizer. In addition, the co-op expanded well beyond fertilizer, feed, and seeds, and during the 1950s used its buying power to offer member farmers tires, lubricants, and farm tools. In 1957, a grain marketing service was added to sell the grain produced by north Alabama farmers. Eventually the co-op would own ten granaries.

Adoption of AFC Name: 1961

In 1961 Tennessee Valley Fertilizer acquired the Farmers Marketing and Exchange Stores and changed its name to Alabama Farmers Cooperative. In addition to serving the needs of member farmers, these co-op stores were also open to the general public, to gardeners and homeowners, thereby further increasing AFC's buying power. The network of co-op stores, operating under a variety of names, would eventually number 80. The 1960s also marked the end of Edmond Garrett's term as AFC's general manager. He retired in 1968 and died ten years later at the age of 70.

In 1969 AFC completed another major acquisition, adding Anderson's Peanuts. The man behind the Anderson name was Robert B. Anderson, who became interested in peanuts while working one summer in a Greenwood, Florida, peanut shelling operation. In 1933 Anderson left his family's farm and along with a man named Bryant Pender started the Anderson-Pender Peanut Company, a small buying and shelling operation. Two years later Anderson bought a shelling plant in Andalusia, Alabama. He and Pender split in 1938, and now Anderson took in his brothers, Edward and Alban, as partners. Together they formed another buying and shelling operation, the Hartford Peanut Company. Anderson continued to grow his peanut holdings in the 1940s. He launched a harvest season buying office in Jay, Florida, in 1945, gaining a good supply of high-quality seed stock. In that same year, he also established the Luverne Peanut Company. Anderson's connection to the company's present-day location of Opp, Alabama, came in 1955 when he bought a local shelling plant, which he renamed the Opp Peanut Company and brought in his son, James B. Anderson, to manage it. The Anderson family now owned four shelling operations and a network of buying locations in Alabama and Florida. After the family sold its peanut business to AFC in 1969, the

Andersons remained very much involved. James headed the division until he retired in 1982. John W. Anderson succeeded him and ran the peanut division until 1989, at which point he took over as president and CEO of AFC. In the 35 years of AFC ownership, Anderson's Peanuts significantly upgraded its facilities, replacing two outdated shelling facilities with a state-of-the-art plant in Goshen, Alabama, in 1977. Then, in 1986, AFC added a 12-million-pound cold storage facility to the Goshen grounds. In addition, AFC added more buying locations and warehouses.

Acquisition of Bonnie Plant Farm: 1975

AFC's next major acquisition came in 1975 when the co-op acquired Union Springs, Alabama-based Bonnie Plant Farm. The business was started in 1918 by Livingston and Bonnie Paulk in Bullock County, Alabama. The couple started out with a small truck farm in Boynton, Florida, but were ruined by a freeze that killed all of the area's vegetables and fruits. They moved back to his hometown of Union Springs, Alabama, in June 1917, living on his uncle's farm, and started some small-scale planting of cotton, corn, and peanuts, as well as hogs, but were only able to scrape by. To make ends meet during the winter months, they decided to raise cabbage plants in their garden to sell to area merchants. The following winter they planted a much larger crop and began to advertise the plants in the local newspaper, which drew out-of-town orders. As the business grew, so did the accounting and paperwork. Now in need of letterhead, Livingston went to a printer to have some made. When asked the name of the business, he decided on the spot to name it after his wife, calling it the Bonnie Plant Farm.

The Bonnie Plant Farm began to advertise in farm newspapers throughout the south, which led to a much greater cabbage crop and the addition of onions, strawberries, and potato plants. After seven years of growing the plant business on their uncle's farm, the Paulks were able to buy their own 200-acre farm. To keep up with competition they began to deliver their plants, a move that not only retained old customers but brought in new ones. In 1936 they built a greenhouse where they could plant seed in boxes, transfer the small plants to pots, and later transplant to the fields. In this way the Paulks were able to get their produce to the market early and receive a better price. Next, they built a packinghouse with one room sealed off to serve as a seed room.

By 1940 the Paulks had established a steady business in their winter crops, but it provided little more than a good living. In the postwar years, however, that would begin to change as the Bonnie Plant Farm evolved into a true business. Bonnie reached the $1 million mark in annual sales in 1967. At this stage the farm mostly offered field-grown vegetable plants, but within a few years, in answer to customer demand, Bonnie began to focus on greenhouse potted plants. As a result, the farm began to build more greenhouses. After AFC bought Bonnie in 1975, Paulk family members, like the Andersons, stayed on to run the business. With AFC's support, Bonnie began to expand rapidly, adding trucks and building new greenhouses to serve an ever-growing market. By 1983 Bonnie marketed to 13 states and annual sales reached $9 million. Expansion was fueled even further by the rising popularity of garden centers by mass market retailers. Bonnie built up its sales staff, constructed

Key Dates:

1936: Co-op is formed as Tennessee Valley Fertilizer Co-operative.
1957: Grain marketing service is added.
1961: Company changes name to Alabama Farmers Cooperative.
1969: Anderson's Peanuts is acquired.
1975: Bonnie Plant Farms is acquired.
1997: Currie Gin is acquired.

more greenhouses, and as a result was well positioned to enjoy great success in the 1990s. In 2000 Bonnie would take in more than $42 million in revenues. As was the case with the Anderson family, one of the Paulks would eventually rise to the top at AFC. In 1996, Tommy Paulk, grandson of Bonnie's founders, became AFC's CEO, the fourth in the co-op's history.

AFC also enjoyed a period of strong expansion in the 1990s. In 1993 it formed a financing subsidiary to serve the seasonal and long-term needs of local cooperative members. A year later, AFC formed Dixieland Express, a transportation division with some 200 tractor trailers that served the eastern United States. (This business would be sold off in 2001.) McCullough, Alabama-based Currie Gin was acquired in 1997. The business was founded by the Currie family in Atmore, Alabama, in 1913 and moved to McCullough in 1950. AFC created SouthFresh Aquaculture, LLC, in 1999, a joint venture with Indianolia, Mississippi-based Southfresh Farms, and became involved in supplying the needs of Alabama and Mississippi catfish farmers.

AFC continued to launch new initiatives in the new century. It established the Co-op Calf Marketing Program to provide added value and better markets for cattle breeders through state-of-the-art preconditioning. In 2000 SouthFresh opened the first fish processing plant in Alabama's history, providing the state's catfish farmers with another marketing option. In 2003 AFC and regional cooperative Land O'Lakes formed a partnership, Agriliance-AFC, LLC, to pool their buying power to help members achieve better prices in the purchase of seed, crop protectants, and crop nutrients. By now, AFC was generating over $300 million in annual revenues. In 2003 the co-op recorded a net margin of $7.5 million before taxes.

Principal Divisions

Anderson's Peanuts; Bonnie Plant Farms; Currie Gin.

Principal Competitors

Farmland Industries, Inc.; Gold Kist Inc.; Southern States Cooperative, Incorporated.

Further Reading

Martin, James D., ''Alabama Fish Processing Plant to Start Up,'' *FeedStuffs,* September 25, 2000, p. 18.
''Paulk New CEO at Alabama Farmers Co-op,'' *Rural Cooperatives,* May/June 1996, p. 34.

—Ed Dinger

Alico, Inc.

640 S. Main Street
LaBelle, Florida 33935
U.S.A.
Telephone: (863) 675-2966
Fax: (863) 675-6928
Web site: http://www.alico.com

Public Company
Incorporated: 1960 as Alico Land Development
   Company
Employees: 143
Sales: $48.3 million (2003)
Stock Exchanges: NASDAQ
Ticker Symbol: ALCO
NAIC: 111998 All Other Miscellaneous Crop Farming

Alico, Inc., based in LaBelle, Florida, is primarily an agribusiness company involved in the production of citrus fruit, sugarcane, cattle, sod, and forest products, as well as crop insurance through wholly owned subsidiary Agri-Insurance Company, Ltd. In addition, the company rents land for farming, cattle grazing, oil exploration, the mining of materials for the construction industry, and recreational and other uses. Through subsidiary Saddlebag Lake Resorts, Inc., Alico also is involved in retail land sales and development. All told, Alico owns approximately 140,000 acres of Florida land. With more than 11,000 acres in production, it ranks among the top 15 citrus producers in Florida.

Tracing Roots to 1800s Railroad

Alico grew out of the land holdings of The Atlantic Coastline Railroad, which was originally known as the Wilmington & Weldon Railroad. The line was chartered in 1933 to connect the towns of Wilmington and Weldon, North Carolina. When completed in 1840, its length of 161.5 miles made it the longest continuous railroad in the world. During the Civil War, 20 years later, the line was critically important to the Confederacy as the major carrier of supplies from the deep South to the capital in

Richmond, Virginia. After the war, the line became The Atlantic Coastline Railroad. Because the company accumulated a great deal of land in connection to its road building, in 1898 it incorporated a subsidiary to manage the holdings, named The Atlantic Land and Improvement Company (the initials of which led to the Alico acronym). It was not until 1948 that the subsidiary opened its LaBelle, Florida, office, located 40 miles east of Fort Meyers. The company, owning more than 250,000 acres, became heavily involved in agribusiness during the 1950s. It began developing citrus groves as well as a cattle ranch, and also began managing its forest holdings. Later in the decade, the company started to lease some of its land for mining and oil exploration. While more and more acres were devoted to citrus growing and the raising of cattle, Atlantic Land sold several thousands of acres to real estate developers to take advantage of the rising demand for new housing following World War II, when the Baby Boom generation and their parents fled the cities in favor of the new suburbs.

In February 1960, The Atlantic Coast Railroad spun off some of the Florida real estate holdings of Atlantic Land and Improvement Company, forming Alico Land Development Company, based in LaBelle, Florida. According to its first annual report, Alico had assets of $2.8 million. Of its $247,000 in revenues, most resulted from the sale of forest products, followed by cattle sales. Citrus was third. Over the course of the 1960s, the business mix would undergo a complete reversal. The company took a number of steps to build up its citrus and cattle operations, investing in infrastructure—building roads and irrigation systems and improving pastures—so that by the close of the decade Alico's fruit sales was the biggest contributor to the balance sheet. Cattle sales came next, followed by oil leases, land rentals, and forest products. According to the 1970 annual report, Alico posted revenues of $2.5 million and net income of $157,000.

Ben Hill Griffin, Jr.—Gaining Control, Fostering Growth: 1960s–80s

It was also early in the 1960s that the man most responsible for the growth of Alico in the 1970s and 1980s would become associated with the company: Ben Hill Griffin, Jr. In 1961 he

Company Perspectives:

Alico, Inc., is an agribusiness company, primarily engaged in the production of citrus, sugarcane, cattle, sod and forest products. The Company's operations are located in central and southwest Florida.

was named to Alico's board, and over the next dozen years quietly accumulated a controlling interest in the company. According to *Florida Trend* magazine, Atlantic Coast Line Railroad officials "asked Griffin Jr. to serve on the board of the new company to help it break into citrus, cattle and timber. In 1972, [he] traveled to New York City and bought concentrated control of Alico for $15.9 million in a private, hidden bid."

Griffin was already a successful citrus grower and wealthy man. Born in 1910, he grew up on a farm and then attended the University of Florida, studying economics and agriculture before going to work for his father. As a wedding gift from his father in 1933, Griffin received a ten-acre orange grove. Throughout the Depression of the 1930s, while others were selling, he was buying up their land at bargain prices, just $2 to $3 an acre. In 1938 he picked up 16,000 at once when he acquired his first ranch, the Peace River Ranch. He later added a 55,000-acre spread. During the 1940s he took several key steps that would make his fortune. In 1945 Florida Department of Citrus researchers made a breakthrough in the development of orange juice using the "cutback" process. As a result, an increasing number of citrus growers began to focus on frozen concentrate rather than fresh fruit. Griffin anticipated, as a consequence of this switch, the price of fresh fruit would rise. This was a major assumption in 1948, given that the price of oranges had fallen from $1.50 per box to just 35 cents. Nevertheless, he bought a packing plant in 1948, launching Bill Hill Griffin Inc. Griffin also proved lucky because, that same winter, the California orange crop was devastated by a major freeze, which drove up the price of Florida oranges even higher. These events laid the foundation for Griffin's personal fortune. Moreover, while other growers began selling out to corporate farming interests, he remained independent, and by working hard and keeping his operations lean, he prospered.

As Alico entered the 1970s, it began to sell off noncore acreage and also achieved some diversity by becoming involved in the development of residential real estate. At this point the chairman of the board was W. Thomas Rice, but in 1972 Griffin made his play, gaining a controlling share of Alico through Ben Hill Griffin Inc. His son, Ben Hill Griffin III, was named to the board, and then in 1973 the elder Griffin took over as chairman of the board of directors. That year was also significant because it was the first time that the company declared a dividend. A year later, in 1974, it officially adopted the Alico name. With the autocratic Griffin in charge, Alico entered a new phase in its history.

Alico's total assets topped the $20 million mark by 1980, when the company recorded $15.2 million in sales and net income of $4.2 million. By now, Alico owned 187,000 acres of land, more than 4,300 of which was devoted to citrus fruit,

which accounted for more than half of the company's revenues. Under Griffin's leadership, Alico added even more acreage for citrus, buying neighboring land to supplement current holdings. The company reached a significant milestone in the 1987–88 season when it surpassed the two million box mark in citrus production.

During the decade of the 1980s Alico first became involved in sugarcane production, an area in which Florida was fast becoming a major player. In 1989, Alico devoted 845 acres to the planting of its first sugarcane crop. Although very much devoted to agriculture, Alico also was finding even more lucrative uses for its land because of Florida's rapidly increasing population. Some 300,000 people were moving into the state each year, and Alico owned a good deal of land close to such boom areas as Fort Myers and Tampa. Citrus acreage could be sold from $10,000 to $15,000 per acre, but land that could be developed close to a population center could command a price in the $60,000 per acre range. As it entered the 1990s, Alico controlled assets of nearly $70 million, with net sales steadily eclipsing $20 million and net income ranging from $4 million to $10 million.

In March 1990 Griffin died at the age of 79, leaving his estate (*Forbes* estimated his personal wealth at $300 million) to his five children but appointing his only son as the sole trustee to his business empire. As for Alico, the younger Griffin had taken over the daily running of the business in January 1988 when he succeeded his father as president (although the elder Griffin continued to hold the CEO title and chairmanship). The four sisters had been actively involved in the family's business affairs. They included Sarah Jane Alexander, Lucy Anne Griffin Collier, Francie G. Milligan, and Harriet G. Harris, the mother of Katherine Harris (who as Florida's Secretary of State would gain national prominence for her involvement in the Florida recount controversy in the 2000 Presidential election). The sisters soon became disenchanted with the way their brother ran the businesses, claiming that he acted as if he were sole owner. But Griffin, who had been groomed since childhood to take over, acted in very much the same manner as his father, exerting strong control. He insisted that their father never intended the family businesses to be run by committee. Ultimately the sisters would sue him, maintaining, according to *Florida Trend*, that he steered "their mother's shares of BHG Inc. into his own hands" and "systematically fired or forced out every member of the plaintiffs' families whom Griffin Jr. had hired." Moreover, he promoted his son, Ben Hill Griffin IV, to a position of prominence.

Family Dispute in the 1990s Affecting the Company's Future

The tensions within the Griffin family increased throughout the 1990s until finally erupting into a very public lawsuit. In the meantime, Alico continued to buy desirable land for its agricultural operations, while unloading surplus acreage and devoting some land for highly profitable real estate development. Even when the company made charitable contributions, it found a way to turn a profit. In 1992 Alico donated land in Lee County to the State of Florida for the founding of a new state university, Florida Gulf Coast University. Alico was not alone in its willingness to provide land. Another two dozen companies were interested, but after a process of elimination conducted by

Key Dates:	
1898:	Atlantic Land and Improvement Company is formed as a subsidiary of the Atlantic Coastline Railroad.
1948:	The LaBelle, Florida, office is opened.
1960:	Atlantic Coast Railroad spins off Alico Land Development Company.
1972:	Ben Hill Griffin, Jr., acquires a controlling interest.
1990:	Griffin dies and is succeeded by his son, Ben Hill Griffin III.
2004:	Griffin III resigns, as part of litigation settlement.

Florida's 14 university system regents was completed, only Alico and corporate giant Westinghouse remained in the running. On the surface, it appeared that Westinghouse had the inside track. The 560-acre site it offered was located close to Florida International Airport and already had connecting roads to I-75 in place. Alico's site was large, encompassing 760 acres, but it was isolated and consisted of forested wetlands. In the words of *Florida Trend,* "More than Alico's health was at stake for Griffin. He was still trying to fill the huge boots of his father. . . . Sensing that the regents were leaning toward Westinghouse, Griffin decided, on the spot, to sweeten Alico's bid by offering an additional $3 million to fund endowed professorships for the new university. Westinghouse executives cried foul as the regents accepted Griffin's offer." Griffin, who had received all the authority he needed in the negotiations from the Alico board, claimed that he "got caught up in the magnanimity," but the donation was in reality a reasonable investment in Alico's future. *Florida Trend* reported in October 2001, "As Florida Gulf Coast University grows and adjacent cattle lands are bulldozed for development, Alico's 10,000 acres around the university are skyrocketing in value, in some cases, from $5,000 an acre to upward of $90,000."

As Alico closed the 1990s its assets totaled more than $175 million. But now the future of the company would be caught up in the litigation that would consume the Griffin family. The lawsuit went to trial in March 2001, but it never came to a judgment because after three days of testimony the two parties agreed to a settlement, which called for Griffin to receive a 40 percent share of the family's total assets and the four sisters to share the remaining 60 percent. But the Harris family refused to sign on and two months later sued the three other sisters and Griffin to prevent the settlement from being implemented. The matter would linger for another two years. Then, in June 2003, all parties reached final agreement on the matter. It was believed that the split of the estate remained the same, but under the terms of the agreement the controlling interest in Alico was turned over to the sisters through a company named the Four Sisters Family Corporation.

The transfer of Alico stock was completed in February 2004, at which point Griffin resigned as chief executive officer and chairman of the board along with four directors. Five new board members were then named. John R. Alexander became the new chief executive officer and chairman of the board. Providing continuity was President and Chief Operating Officer Bernie Lester, who had been employed by Alico for 17 years. Upon his election, Alexander commented, "We share the philosophy with the past management for the love of the land and our commitment to Florida agriculture. We look forward to working with Bernie Lester and the Alico staff to enhance shareholder value and commit to working diligently for the benefit of the shareholders. We plan to continue the company's involvement in the Central and Southwest Florida regions and its close association with Florida Gulf Coast University." For his part, Griffin wished the new board great success, as Alico took the first steps into a new era in the company's history.

Principal Subsidiaries

Agri-Insurance Company, Ltd.; Saddlebag Lake Resorts, Inc.

Principal Competitors

Cactus Feeders, Inc.; Imperial Sugar Company; Sunkist Growers, Inc.

Further Reading

Barnett, Cynthia, "His Father's Will," *Florida Trend,* October 1, 2001, p. 68.

Bouffard, Kevin, "Florida Citrus Magnate's Heirs Agree to Resolve Long-Standing Issues," *Ledger,* August 6, 203, p. 1.

Hackney, Holt, "Frozen," *Financial World,* February 6, 1990, p. 24.

Trussell, Tuit, "The Last of the Citrus Barons," *Nation's Business,* February 1989, p. 46.

—Ed Dinger

Alliance Capital Management Holding L.P.

1345 Avenue of the Americas
New York, New York 10105
U.S.A.
Telephone: (212) 969-1000
Fax: (212) 969-2229
Web site: http://www.alliancecapital.com

Public Company
Founded: 1971
Employees: 4,100
Total Assets: $1.16 billion (2003)
Stock Exchanges: New York
Ticker Symbol: AC
NAIC: 551112 Offices of Other Holding Companies

Alliance Capital Management Holding L.P., a publicly traded limited partnership, holds about 30 percent ownership of Alliance Capital Management L.P. Alliance Capital is a leading global investment management firm with about $489 billion in assets under management. AXA Financial, Inc., a subsidiary of the global French insurer AXA, holds about 55 percent. The company serves both the retail and institutional markets. The Bernstein unit focuses on high-net-worth individuals.

Establishing a Presence: 1960s–80s

William H. Donaldson, Dan W. Lufkin, and Richard H. Jenrette established a partnership in 1959, buying a seat on the New York Stock Exchange and opening up a small office. In 1962 Donaldson took over the investment banking area, marking the beginning of the firm's asset management department. Donaldson, Lufkin & Jenrette's (DLJ) pension fund business flourished, and Alliance Capital Management L.P. began operating as a subsidiary in 1971.

During the first half of the decade, two of DLJ's principals left the company. Jenrette, now at the helm, faced a challenging economic environment. During a period of restructuring, DLJ announced that it would sell off Alliance Capital for $7 million. The sale did not materialize and the subsidiary remained in the fold.

Alliance Capital continued to grow its offerings and geographic reach. In 1978, its first money market fund was introduced. That same year a London office opened—its first overseas. Beginning in 1983, a load mutual fund was offered to the public. The company also expanded through the purchases of other companies.

In 1984, the company had $18 billion under management, according *to American Banker.* The bulk of the assets were for corporate employee benefits plans, endowment funds, foundations, and public employee retirement systems. As a DLJ subsidiary, Alliance Capital had grown into one of the largest pension fund managers on Wall Street. Moreover, it provided its parent company with its chief source of income.

Jenrette agreed, in late 1984, to sell majority control of DLJ to The Equitable Life Assurance Society of the United States, the third largest insurer in the country. The next year, Alliance Capital was split off from DLJ and began operating as an independent subsidiary of The Equitable. In 1987, Alliance opened an office in Tokyo. The company was taken public on the New York Stock Exchange, in 1988, as a master limited partnership, a structure that yielded tax and liquidity advantages.

Building Worth: 1990–2000

In the spring of 1993, Alliance acquired the business of Equitable Capital Management Corporation, a wholly owned subsidiary of The Equitable. The deal put Alliance Capital among the top three money management companies in the country, with assets under management approaching $100 billion. Prior to the deal, Alliance had about $62 billion in assets under management.

Alliance planned on keeping half of Equitable Capital's ten mutual funds—those that added diversity to the company's offerings. The remaining five would be rolled into other Alliance funds. Alliance, ranked 20th in mutual fund assets, had been positioning itself to expand mutual fund sales made through banks. Alliance had been an early player in bank sales, beginning them in 1987.

Company Perspectives:

Diverse products, consistent investment style, solid perform-ance. Alliance Capital's mission is to be the premier global research and investment management organization through superior performance across a broad range of investment disciplines for a diverse group of clients.

Alliance also pitched mutual funds in developing markets. A joint venture in Hong Kong was entered into in 1997 to offer funds owning both local and U.S. stock. During the year, similar operations were established in Brazil, Russia, South Africa, and South Korea. Meanwhile, the Alliance Japanese operation had begun to flourish, thanks to a combination of economic condi-tions and regulatory changes. Investors held $1.6 billion in Alliance funds, up from just $100 million the prior year. Con-versely, a four-year-old joint venture in Bombay had only $40 million in assets under management. "That's less than Alliance collects in a single day from U.S. investors," observed Jon Birger in *Crain's New York Business.*

Emerging markets looked good to Alliance in light of a number of factors, according to *Crain's.* The U.S. mutual fund market was maturing and was unlikely to sustain its decade-long 18 to 25 percent growth rate. Capital investment to start a new business in these markets was relatively low. The demographics in countries such as India and Brazil held positive indications, such as high rates of savings. In addition, early entry in emerging markets gave Alliance first crack at developing local financial management partners. On the down side, evaluation of local stock was more difficult due to accounting practices. But Alliance felt that its solid research capabilities were up to the task.

In 1998, according to the *Bond Buyer,* Alliance had nearly $7 billion in assets in 27 tax-free bond portfolios and institu-tional accounts. The company had begun building up this area of the business beginning in 1984, when it had just $90 million in money market funds. The addition of five municipal portfo-lios pushed the class of assets above the $1 billion mark in 1990. When the bond market collapsed in 1994, Alliance saw it as a time of opportunity instead of panic.

The company bought up fixed-income investments others had abandoned. Denver International Airport bonds, suffering from lengthy construction delays and baggage system woes, looked like a poor deal, but Alliance took a chance and invested heavily. "The deal is a tale of almost mythical proportions within the fund complex. It has all the elements of Alliance's approach at its best—the undervalued credit, the cash-rich fund ready to pounce, and finally, the market vindication," Ilana Polyak, wrote for the *Bond Buyer.*

Alliance moved to strengthen its position in Europe with the purchase of Whittingdale Holdings, Limited, London-based fixed income manager. According to an October 1998 *Financial Times* article, Alliance was making the move "ahead of mone-tary union and anticipated growth in funded pension schemes."

In 1999, The Equitable changed its name to AXA Financial, Inc., when it became a part of AXA Group, a global French

insurer. Alliance, in turn, reorganized into a two-tier partner-ship. Alliance Capital Management Holding L.P. traded on the New York Stock Exchange and owned an interest in Alliance Capital Management L.P.

Alliance and Sanford C. Bernstein Inc. would merge in 2000 in a $3.5 billion deal, according to a June *Investment News* report. The cost to Alliance was slightly more than 4 percent of the assets under management for Bernstein, on the upper end of the industry range for such an acquisition. The companies held disparate philosophies: Alliance was growth driven and Bern-stein was value driven. Together the pair held $475 billion under management. Institutional clients numbered 2,600 and private clients totaled 15,000.

Turning Point: 2001–04

Alliance entered 2001 facing changing market conditions. In late 2000, technology and growth stocks fell off, hurting the company's fourth quarter earnings. Circumstances continued to deteriorate. Alliance lost millions on Enron stock. Three share-holder lawsuits and the loss of a pair of institutional investors and their $343 million in assets compounded the problem.

The situation evolved from the purchase of Enron stock by large-cap growth fund Premier Growth. The fund bought heav-ily in October and November 2001, in the wake of a slide in Enron stock. An expected purchase of the Houston-based Enron fell apart; bankruptcy soon followed. The stock Premier accu-mulated was sold off at a large loss.

Longtime client and major investor the Florida Retirement Fund took a huge hit and dumped Alliance. According to *Invest-ment News,* Alliance, like many others caught in the fiasco, maintained that Enron had been misleading investors by pro-viding inaccurate information.

Alliance stock took a tumble during the fray. A decline in assets under management translated to lower revenue from related fees. Moreover, the company had fallen behind its peers in fund performance, weakening its competitive position.

Bad news continued to surface. In late 2003, Alliance was faced with investigation for improper trading. The company had suspended two employees at the end of September. In one case, a portfolio manager was "allowing investors in Alliance hedge funds to make money trading in and out of Alliance mutual funds," according to *Crain's.* Because the company allowed a single manager to oversee both hedge and mutual funds, there was concern that the practice was widespread. In November, Alliance asked for the resignation of two top execu-tives over the matter.

New York State Attorney General Eliot Spitzer had begun investigating market-timing practices in the fall of 2003. The Securities and Exchange Commission (SEC) set up its own probe of the matter. U.S. lawmakers began pushing greater oversight of the $7 trillion mutual fund industry, in which about 95 million Americans had put their savings. Alliance was not the only company under the spotlight. Bank of America, Put-nam Investments, Strong Capital Management, and Bank One already had been examined and more would follow.

Key Dates:

1962: The firm is established originally as the investment management department of Donaldson, Lufkin & Jenrette (DLJ).

1971: Alliance Capital Management Corporation begins operating as a DLJ subsidiary.

1978: The first overseas office is opened, in London.

1985: Alliance Capital is acquired by The Equitable Life Assurance Society of the United States.

1987: The Tokyo office is opened.

1988: A minority interest is offered to the public.

1993: Equitable Capital Management Corporation business is acquired.

1997: A joint venture is formed in Hong Kong.

1999: The firm is reorganized into a two-tier partnership.

2000: Sanford C. Bernstein Inc. is acquired.

2003: An investigation hits the mutual fund business.

In December 2003, Alliance agreed to cut management fees by an average of 20 percent over the next five years as part of a settlement with Spitzer involving improper trading. In an agreement made jointly with Spitzer and the SEC, Alliance would pay $250 million to reimburse investors hurt by its activities.

Critics of the agreement, according to the *New York Times,* said fee adjustment should not be a part of the deal. Market forces, not government agencies, should set fee levels. The action dropped Alliance fees below the industry average; prior to the agreement, fees were on the high side of average.

In March 2004, Alliance reported an increase in assets under management. Companies responding less quickly to the mutual fund scandal had not fared as well.

Principal Subsidiaries

Alliance Capital Management L.P.

Principal Competitors

FMR Corp.; ING, B.V.; Merrill Lynch & Co., Inc.

Further Reading

''Alliance Capital Earnings Fall Short of Expectations,'' *Futures World News,* February 2, 2001, p. 1.

Atlas, Riva D., ''In Settlement, Alliance Agrees to Cut Fees,'' *New York Times,* December 17, 2003, p. C1.

Barreto, Susan, and Fred Williams, ''Alliance-Bernstein Deal: Blessings and Questions,'' *Investment News,* June 26, 2000, p. 8.

Birger, Jon, ''Fund Company Has Money, Will Travel,'' *Crain's New York Business,* October 27, 1997, p. 47.

Elstein, Aaron, ''Mutual Funds in NY Holding on to Assets,'' *Crain's New York Business,* November 17, 2003, p. 1.

''Equitable Life Assurance Society of the U.S.,'' *Best's Review—Life-Health Insurance Edition,* April 1993, p. 114.

Gold, Jacqueline S., ''Stock Watch: Bottom Fishers Cautioned on Misalliance,'' *Crain's New York Business,* November 10, 2003, p. 4.

Guthrie, Jonathan, ''Companies & Finance: UK,'' *Financial Times USA Edition,* October 13, 1998.

''In Brief: Alliance Reports Feb. Managed Assets Up,'' *American Banker,* March 29, 2004.

Moore, Michael D., ''Alliance Capital Puts Wholesalers on Banks' Front Lines,'' *American Banker,* March 31, 1993, p. 9.

Plasencia, William, ''Chief of First Chicago's Brokerage Arm to Run Bank Effort at Top Firm,'' *American Banker,* September 28, 1995, pp. 1+.

Polyak, Ilana, ''With the Bets It Placed Paying Off, Alliance Says 'Call Us Contrarian,' '' *Bond Buyer,* July 13, 1998, p. 1.

Wipperfurth, Heike, ''Alliance Battered by Enron Losses and Lawsuits,'' *Investment News,* February 11, 2002, p. 20.

Yacoe, Donald, ''Donaldson Lufkin Subsidiary to Buy Marsh & McLennan Investment Unit,'' *American Banker,* November 1, 1984, p. 8.

—Kathleen Peippo

Allmerica Financial Corporation

440 Lincoln Street
Worcester, Massachusetts 01653
U.S.A.
Telephone: (508) 855-1000
Toll Free: (800) 533-7881
Fax: (508) 853-6332
Web site: http://www.allmerica.com

Public Company
Incorporated: 1995
Employees: 5,300
Total Assets: $26.57 billion (2002)
Stock Exchanges: New York
Ticker Symbol: AFC
NAIC: 524126 Direct Property and Casualty Insurance
    Carriers; 511120 Offices of Other Holding Companies

Allmerica Financial Corporation is a holding company for a group of financial services companies. After more than a century and a half of selling life insurance, tough times forced the company to exit the sector in order to survive. The core focus is now on its property and casualty end of the insurance business, offering products through The Hanover Insurance Company and Citizens Insurance Company of America. In its other business area, Allmerica vends insurance retirement savings, and investment management products and services.

Mutual Insurer's Deep Roots: 1800s–1995

The history of Allmerica Financial began with the chartering of State Mutual Life Assurance Company in 1844. John Davis, a former Massachusetts governor, founded the Worcester-based entity to sell individual life insurance. From those New England roots, the company grew and diversified. In 1989, a top executive from Fidelity Investments took the helm and set out to turn a regional operation into a national concern.

During the 1990s, State Mutual Life Assurance Company earned recognition as the linchpin of a group of insurance and financial services companies. State Mutual was the fifth oldest life insurer in the United States and ranked among the top 20 mutual life insurance companies in terms of assets. The Hanover Insurance Company and Citizens Insurance Company of America provided property and casualty coverage.

The State Mutual group of businesses began operating under the Allmerica name in 1992. The founding life insurer retained its name but some subsidiary companies and divisions were renamed. In addition to the life and the property/casualty companies, the Allmerica Financial umbrella covered several investment management companies, a registered mutual fund broker-dealer, and a registered investment advisor, according to a 1992 *PR Newswire* article.

Allmerica Financial posted a fifth straight year of record financial results in 1992. Net income from operations climbed 21 percent to $104 million. The company's financial position enabled development of new products and services.

The company's record-setting ways continued into 1993. Its steadily growing contingency reserve level was indicative of the company's strength relative to its industry. In addition, assets topped the $10 billion mark.

Contributing to the positive results were increased revenues from variable products, growth of the institutional services division, the strength of managed care and claims management services, and solid property/casualty performances.

The policyholder-owned State Mutual had financed its growth and improvements by means of income generated by operations. But as it entered its 150th year of operation in 1994, the company was planning a demutualization. By converting to a stock insurance company, State Mutual gained access to new sources of capital and entry into new financial services markets. Eligible policyholders would receive stock, cash, or policy credits in exchange for their illiquid membership interest. Policies would remain unchanged. The demutualization process required a public hearing, approval by the Massachusetts Commissioner of Insurance, and acceptance by two-thirds of policyholders.

State Mutual's majority ownership of publicly held Allmerica Property and Casualty Companies, Inc. would not

---

Company Perspectives:

Managing Risk, Managing Assets, Managing to Make a Difference: By maintaining an evenhanded approach to the two crucial elements of financial well-being—risk management and financial security—we offer a richer source of financial solutions to the individuals, families and organizations we serve. The Allmerica Financial companies operate in two primary businesses, asset accumulation and risk management, which are comprised of smaller more specialized enterprises.

---

change. But State Mutual would become the subsidiary of a new holding company and operate under the name First Allmerica Financial Life Insurance Company.

The initial public offering (IPO) of the holding company Allmerica Financial Corporation took place concurrently with the conversion of State Mutual to a stock company. The IPO offered 11 million shares of common stock at $21 per share, in October 1995.

Selling, Selling, and More Selling: 1996–99

Allmerica's products included personal and commercial lines of property and casualty insurance, plus health insurance and life and retirement savings products to individuals and institutional clients nationwide.

In 1996, First Allmerica began offering a product targeting wealthy couples. The variable universal life policy combined insurance protection and investments in one program. Private banks and trusts would sell the product and well-known money managers would handle investments for people wanted to protect assets destined for their heirs. Sales via banks accounted for about 15 percent of annuity sales, according to *American Banker*.

Beginning in 1997, O'Brien led the company on an all out selling spree of variable products. Allmerica also moved to settle a class-action lawsuit in 1998. The company had been accused of making erroneous statements concerning life insurance premiums payments, churning, and misrepresenting policy benefits. Allmerica denied the charges, according to *Bestwire*, but wanted to avoid the time and expense of a lengthy litigation process.

Final approval of the $31 million settlement came in 1999, on 400,000 policies issued from 1978 to May 31, 1998. Injured policyholders could buy discounted life insurance or annuities or have an independent referee determine compensation and benefits, according to the *Boston Globe*.

Allmerica was not the only insurer to be hit by deceptive practices claims. The country's largest insurer, Prudential Insurance Co. of America, was expected to pay up to $2 billion to eight million policyholders. John Hancock Life Insurance Co. of Boston had also settled on a suit.

Allmerica was hit hard by another kind of claim during 1998. Severe weather in the Midwest, Northeast, and South added up to total catastrophic losses of $90.3 million, compared

with $26.5 million in 1997. It was a record loss. During the year, the company embarked on some cost-cutting measures. As it moved into 1999 it also began repurchasing shares of its common stock.

The property and casualty insurance business generated a significant portion of Allmerica's earnings. Property/casualty contributed pretax operating profits of $199.6 million in 1999, up from $149.6 million in 1998. Company-wide cost-cutting efforts had aided efforts, but slim margins and hefty competitors created a difficult environment.

Meanwhile, the company continued to push its variable products, which were linked to underlying investment portfolios. Allmerica's fee income generated in this business line had climbed from $87 million in 1995 to $291 million in 1999.

Eve of Destruction: 2000–04

In 2000, the red hot stock market began to cool. By October 2001, Allmerica was looking at a dark horizon. World Trade Center-related claims alone cost the company $17 million. Investments eroded as the market nose-dived in the wake of the September 11 attacks. Allmerica's profits and stock price plummeted.

Twelve months later, Allmerica was looking for a way out of its life and annuity business. The bear market prevented Allmerica from earning the level of investment it needed to meet the promised level of payoff to holders of variable annuities.

"The firm tripled yearly sales of its annuities between 1997 and 1999 by offering a guaranteed death benefit on annuities, with a minimum annual return of as much as 5 percent," reported Scott Bernard Nelson for the *Boston Globe*, in October 2002.

When insurers, such as Allmerica, began selling the products, they had a different future in mind than the one that manifested itself. For the first time in history, the market experienced three consecutive years of declining numbers. Plus, the guaranteed death benefit proved to be a hot product. The situation produced a scenario in which Allmerica experienced greater than expected costs and less than expected income. Capital reserves on future claims had to be boosted.

Allmerica President and CEO John F. O'Brien, who put variable annuity sales in the forefront, resigned in October 2002. A new office of the chairman was created to oversee the company until a new leader was found.

Some larger companies had the financial capacity to withstand the pressures on variable annuities. Reinsurance coverage helped, as did product diversity. Also, not all the products on the market had guaranteed the 5 percent return Allmerica had offered.

Rick Miller observed, in an *Investment News* article in October 2002, Allmerica "just might be worth more dead than alive." Stock traded around the $7–$8 mark, less than 20 percent of its book value.

Colin Devine, an insurance industry analyst for Salomon Smith Barney Inc., told *Investment News*, "You can chop up this company and sell it and generate a healthy return from where you can buy the stock today."

<table>
<tr><td colspan="2">Key Dates:</td></tr>
<tr><td>1844:</td><td>Business is formed as a life insurance company in Worcester, Massachusetts.</td></tr>
<tr><td>1989:</td><td>John F. O'Brien comes on board with plans to transform company.</td></tr>
<tr><td>1992:</td><td>Company records its fifth straight year of record results.</td></tr>
<tr><td>1995:</td><td>Company converts from mutual to stock company.</td></tr>
<tr><td>1997:</td><td>Sales of variable annuities ramp up.</td></tr>
<tr><td>2002:</td><td>O'Brien resigns after company falters under his watch.</td></tr>
<tr><td>2003:</td><td>Allmerica returns to profitability as it undergoes major reorganization and an exit from life insurance products.</td></tr>
</table>

Allmerica's credit rating was downgraded. Some analysts speculated the development would hurt the property casualty business, which had been holding its own. Allmerica reported a net operating loss of $275.4 million for 2002 and worked diligently to turn things around. Fixed life insurance products were sold to John Hancock Financial Services in 2003. Allmerica retained a large block of variable products on their books but no longer sold them. A reinsurance deal was struck. The reorganization, which followed in the wake of O'Brien's departure, allowed capital to move to hard-pressed areas of the company. In addition, the resurgence of the stock market was a godsend.

Frederick Eppinger was named CEO in August 2003. The CPA-trained turnaround specialist was an executive vice-president overseeing The Hartford's property and casualty divisions. His 100-day plan for the company included an effort to improve the company's financial ratings. The policies being sold and the productivity of the agents selling them would be reviewed. Organizational streamlining, including employment losses, was in the offing. The property/casualty operation would be the core business.

Allmerica returned to profitability in 2003. Net income was $306.1 million. Stock had recovered, climbing to around the $35 mark. Allmerica's financial strength ratings saw upgrades.

Principal Subsidiaries

The Hanover Insurance Company; Citizens Insurance Company of America.

Principal Competitors

American International Group, Inc.; State Farm Insurance Companies.

Further Reading

"Allmerica Financial Corporation Announces Initial Public Offering of 11 Million Common Shares," *PR Newswire*, October 11, 1995.

"Allmerica Financial Posts 29% Drop in 4th-Quarter Net," *A.M. Best Newswire*, February 9, 1999.

"Allmerica Financial Reports Record Income for 1992," *PR Newswire*, March 16, 1993.

"Allmerica Financial Reports Sixth Consecutive Record Year: Celebrates 150th Anniversary of Founding," *PR Newswire*, March 15, 1994.

"Allmerica Financial Settles Shareholder Lawsuit," *Bestwire*, December 7, 1998.

Fraser, Katherine, "Allmerica Policy Targets Estate Planning for Rich," *American Banker*, June 25, 1996, p. 10.

Gjertsen, Lee Ann, "Entangled in Death Benefit Guarantee Woes," *American Banker*, October 3, 2002.

Hillman, John, "Allmerica Turns Profit As Exit from Broker-Dealer Business Proceeds," *A.M. Best Newswire*, October 28, 2003.

Lehmann, Raymond J., "Allmerica Posts Lower Profits, Cites Investments, Restructuring," *A.M. Best Newswire*, April 29, 2003.

——, "Restructuring Helps Allmerica Return to Profitability," *A.M. Best Newswire*, February 3, 2004.

Mason, Edward, "Allmerica Suffers from Insurance-Sector Slump," *Boston Business Journal*, October 12, 2001, p.4.

McDonald, Lee, "Allmerica President: There's Still a Role for Diversified Insurers," *Bestwire*, May 24, 2000.

Miller, Rick, "A Poster Child for What Ails Variable Annuities: Allmerica CEO Pays Price for Bungles," *Investment News*, October 28, 2002, p. 3.

Nelson, Scott Bernard, "CEO to Leave Allmerica Financial Corp.," *Boston Globe*, October 26, 2002.

——, "John Hancock Financial to Buy Policies from Struggling Allmerica," *Boston Globe*, January 9, 2003.

——, "New Chief Executive for Life Insurer Allmerica Has Plan to Start Turnaround," *Boston Globe*, August 22, 2003.

——, "Worcester, Mass.-Based Insurance Firm Taps Turnaround Specialist for Revival," *The Boston Globe*, August 19, 2003.

Roush, Matt, "Citizens Insurance Owner Reverts It to Private Status," *Crain's Detroit Business*, December 14, 1998, p. 7.

"State Mutual Adopts Plan to Convert to Stock Company," *PR Newswire*, February 28, 1995.

"State Mutual Introduces New Identity: Allmerica Financial," *PR Newswire*, September 21, 1992.

Suszynski, Marie, "Allmerica's Net Income Falls on Accounting Change," *A.M. Best Newswire*, April 27, 2004.

Syre, Steven, "The Boston Globe Capital Column," *Boston Globe*, July 31, 2003.

"Worcester, Mass.-Based Insurer May Settle Deceptive Sales Complaints," *Boston Globe*, May 26, 1999.

—Kathleen Peippo

Ansoft Corporation

4 Station Square, Suite 200
Pittsburgh, Pennsylvania 15219-1119
U.S.A.
Telephone: (412) 261-3200
Fax: (412) 471-9427
Web site: http://www.ansoft.com

Public Company
Incorporated: 1984
Employees: 285
Sales: $47.3 million (2003)
Stock Exchanges: NASDAQ
Ticker Symbol: ANST
NAIC: 511210 Software Publishers

Ansoft Corporation is a Pittsburgh, Pennsylvania-based developer of electronic design automation (EDA) software, used by electrical engineers in the design of such products as cellular phones, internet networking, satellite communications systems, computer chips and circuit boards, and electronic sensors and motors. EDA software is a modeling tool that can be used throughout the design process—logic design and synthesis, design and analysis, and physical design and verification. As a result, physical prototypes are not needed, product performance is maximized, and the time to market is greatly reduced. Ansoft's products fall into three market categories: high-frequency software, a three-dimensional electromagnetic field simulator for high frequency, radio, frequency, and wireless product design; signal integrity software, used to analyze printed circuit boards, components, and combinations of these structures; and electromechanical software to produce an accurate representation of electric or magnetic field behavior. Ansoft also offers add-on modules that link the company's products to popular design software programs. Ansoft sells its products on a global scale to the communications, semiconductor, automotive/industrial, computer, consumer electronics, and defense/aerospace industries. Major customers include Boeing, Cisco, Ericsson, Ford Motor, General Motors, IBM, Intel, Motorola, NASA, Sony, and Sun Microsystems. Ansoft maintains North American sales and support offices in Arizona, California, Florida, Illinois, Massachusetts, Michigan, New Jersey, Ohio, Pennsylvania, Texas, and Wisconsin. To serve the Asia-Pacific market, Ansoft maintains sales and support offices in China, Japan, Korea, Singapore, and Taiwan. In Europe, Ansoft operations are found in Denmark, England, France, Germany, and Italy. Ansoft is a public company, trading on the NASDAQ.

Founding the Company in 1984

Ansoft grew out of research conducted at Pittsburgh's Carnegie Mellon University by Ansoft's chairman and chief technology officer, Zoltan J. Cendes, and his colleagues. After earning an M.S. and Ph.D. in electrical engineering from McGill University in Montreal, Canada, he went on to work for General Electric Corporation (GE), initially involved in the large steam turbine generator division and later responsible for the development of finite element computer codes in GE's corporate research and development center. He returned to McGill University in 1980, taking a position as Associate Professor of Electrical Engineering, and two years later joined the faculty at Carnegie Mellon. Cendes and his colleagues conducted important research that would make finite element modeling practical for electrical engineering. Soon their research partners, who provided the funding, requested that they develop commercial software tools to put their research to practical use. Thus, with no product, no organization, and just a vision, Ansoft was born in 1984. Its founders were Cendes, his brother Nick Csendes (who retained the original spelling of their last name), Thomas A.N. Miller, and David Shenton. Nick Csendes, a nonscientist, was instrumental in helping to arrange the funding to launch the business. He had 15 years of investment experience and had helped to establish start-ups in Boston and Houston. Finding seed money in Pittsburgh, however, proved to be a difficult task. Recalling those early days, Csendes told the *Pittsburgh Post-Gazette* in 2002, ''I talked to every banker in town . . . I know that if I had a steel plant, they would have lent me money. But because I was in software, I couldn't get a penny.''

Introducing the First Product in 1986

Ansoft was able to scrape by until 1986 when it introduced its first product, a 2-D Field Simulator, which was called Eddy because it computed Eddy currents in AC conductors. Compared with later developments made by the company, it was a crude program. Nevertheless, it was a much appreciated new tool for electrical engineers, allowing them to conduct "what-if" analysis on product designs. Factors such as size, material properties, and excitation levels could be factored together to determine electromagnetic field simulation. Eddy was followed by two-dimensional microwave simulation programs. Ansoft's cutting edge work was so respected in its field that in 1989 Hewlett-Packard (HP) asked the company to help in developing a three-dimensional finite-element simulator. HP's customers had been clamoring for an alternative to traditional test-and-measure instrumentation in the hope of cutting down product development time. According to Csendes, "We [looked] upon that as a very important milestone for the company. It reinforced the value of our product and made us aware of the real market potential. That is when the company took off." The HP alliance also moved Ansoft into higher-frequency design, which was a difficult area in which to work. As Zoltan Cendes explained to *Microwaves & RF* in a 2001 interview, "At that time, solving high-frequency electromagnetic problems using finite elements often resulted in unphysical spurious modes. This was a severe limitation, and presented us with a great challenge, We invented procedures to avoid these problems, which made it possible to solve three-dimensional electromagnetic field problems using finite elements for the first time. . . . The culmination of our work was the software program HFSS, which was the first commercial program that could simulate complete three-dimensional geometries. After we finished the initial software development, HP marketed the product exclusively for us. We began shipping the product in 1990." A key to Ansoft's breakthrough in the development of the software program—called HFSS, or High-Frequency Structure Simulator—was a dramatic improvement in computer hardware performance with no increase in cost at this time. As a result, the company was able to solve three-dimensional problems without imposing unrealistic costs.

In 1990 Ansoft reported sales in the $2 million range. By mid-1991, Ansoft employed 38 people and maintained sales offices in Pittsburgh, Boston, and Los Angeles, with the capability of distributing its products to Europe as well as the Pacific Rim. The company began to expand in a number of ways. It acquired Parametric Integrated Circuits Inc., a Tempe, Arizona-based company that had developed electronic circuitry-packaging design software. The deal combined Ansoft's work on electrical systems analysis with Parametric's electronic package design technology, which led to software that could help in computer circuit board design. Because circuit boards were becoming ever more powerful, relying on smaller computer chip packages, designers were faced with a problem of "cross talk," as electronic impulses from one chip spilled over to interfere with a neighboring chip. The Parametric acquisition

then led to an agreement with Motorola Inc. to aid in the design of new software to help in the development of semiconductor products by speeding up the design of complex integrated circuits.

In 1992 Ansoft launched a new software product, Maxwell Spicelink, which represented a departure for the company. Instead of marketing to a broad range of design engineers in a variety of industries, Ansoft now looked to target a specific market, in this case, electronic design engineers. Spicelink essentially combined Ansoft's electro-magnetic-field-simulation technology, marketed under the Maxwell name, with SPICE, an established software program used to design and simulate electronic circuits. Spicelink allowed designers to simulate performance of a product without having to actually build a prototype. Because electronics were changing so rapidly, the ability to simulate performance before going to market was becoming of paramount importance. Not only would time be saved, but functionality could be maximized, which could very well be the key to the product's success with consumers.

Completing an Initial Public Offering in April 1996

During the early 1990s, Ansoft grew steadily, as management prepared to take the company public. Revenues totaled $3.47 million in 1993, $5.1 million in 1994, and $6.15 million in 1995. The company was still losing money but was on the verge of becoming profitable. In 1996 Ansoft, which by now had established sales offices in Japan and England, was ready to make an initial offering of stock to the public. It was completed in April 1996, netting some $12 million for the company. A few months later, Ansoft used some of those proceeds to make an acquisition, paying $5.6 million in cash to buy MacNeal Schwendler Corporation's electronic business unit, thereby adding products to complement Ansoft's line of electromechanical analysis software programs. For the fiscal year, the company recorded revenues of nearly $8.7 million and a net profit of $1.3 million. It was also during this period that Ansoft's relationship with HP soured, as the two companies differed on how to develop HFSS. They became competitors, as HP, and later an HP spinoff named Agilent Technologies, vied for supremacy in the 3D electromagnetic modeling market.

Ansoft continued to grow its customer base through acquisitions in the second half of the 1990s. In April 1997 it completed the purchase of Compact Software Inc., a move that added a full line of RF and microwave circuit-design tools and filled out Ansoft's wireless solution suite. Next, in August 1997, Ansoft acquired Boulder Microwave Technologies Inc. at a cost of $1.5 million in cash and stock, as a result adding a simulator for printed microwave circuits. In June 1998, Ansoft grew internationally, acquiring the South Korean assets of Jason Tech Inc., which led to the creation of Ansoft Korea. Jason Tech had served as the distributor of Ansoft products in South Korea since 1991. Also in 1998, Ansoft expanded its European presence by opening a sales office in Paris to serve France, Belgium, Portugal, and Spain. The final acquisition in the decade came in April 1999, when Ansoft completed the $3.2 million purchase of Pacific Numerix, Inc., a Scottsdale, Arizona, company that developed a suite of integrated tools for signal integrity simulation. With this addition in technology, Ansoft now offered designers much greater expertise in electrical design validation.

As a result of these acquisitions, Ansoft was able to improve revenues to $24.5 million in 1999.

In 2000 Ansoft elected to change its business model, forming a pair of ventures to pursue niche opportunities while it focused the core business on higher growth markets. First, it spun off Altra Broadband Inc. to focus on the development of new hardware technology to increase the speed of broadband wireless and optical communications products. By making Altra a separate business, Ansoft hoped that the new company could attract its own outside financing. Ansoft planned to remain in the wireless and optical market, but only as an engineering software company. Later in 2000, Ansoft created Automotive Product & Technology Solutions to concentrate on the automotive industry and the electronic and electromechanical systems it employed in its vehicles.

Ansoft completed a pair of significant transactions in 2001. Early in the year it bought SIMEC GmbH & Co. KG, a German company that made software to assist automobile designers in modeling. In July 2001 Ansoft announced that it would purchase Agilent's HFSS product line. In effect, Agilent and HP agreed that Ansoft's approach to HFSS was better and the former strategic partners were once again working together. Agilent customers would now be transitioned to Ansoft solutions by way of translators that would automatically convert Agilent 2-D and 3-D models to the Ansoft format.

With the restructuring of its business model complete by early 2001, Ansoft hoped to improve its standing on Wall Street. Despite a general crash in the tech sector, Ansoft continued to show steady growth in revenues, which totaled $33.5 million in 2000, $43.6 million in 2001, and $53.4 million in 2002. For the most part, however, the company was operating at a loss. Only in 2002 did Ansoft record a net profit ($1.2 million). Moreover, Ansoft's efforts to sell telecommunications hardware through Altra Broadband were discontinued. With telecoms mired in a prolonged slump, there was simply not enough investment in this area to sustain the business. As a result, in September 2002, Ansoft announced that it would close Altra's Irvine, California, office and lay off some 20 people. Another 20 Ansoft employees also were laid off. Altra's Boston office and its ten people would not be affected, because that group was working on technology that could contribute to Ansoft's core software business.

Ansoft's revenues fell to $47.3 million in 2003 while the company posted a $3.1 million loss. On the positive side, Ansoft finished the year strong and was positioned to enjoy growth in the 10 to 15 percent range in 2004. With the economy improving, there was good reason to believe that Ansoft, a leader in its field, would resume its long-term pattern of growth.

Principal Subsidiaries

Ansoft California, Inc.; Compact Software Inc.; Ansoft Korea KK; Boulder Microwave Technologies, Inc.; Pacific Numerix Corporation.

Principal Competitors

ANSYS, Inc.; Mentor Graphics Corporation; Synopsys, Inc.

Further Reading

Allen, Anna, ''Software Built on Vision,'' *Design News,* March 23, 1998, p. 86.

''An Interview with Dr. Zoltan Cendes,'' *Microwaves & RF,* September 1, 2001, p. 47.

''Pittsburgh-Based Software Company Sees Rapid Growth,'' *Pittsburgh Post-Gazette,* May 16, 2001.

Sabatini, Patricia, ''Pittsburgh-Based Software Developer to Close Irvine, Calif., Technology Center,'' *Pittsburgh Post-Gazette,* September 17, 2002.

Shinkle, Kirk, ''Don't Be Paranoid—It's Just High Frequency,'' *Investor's Business Daily,* July 17, 2001, p. A10.

—Ed Dinger

Apex Digital, Inc.

2919 East Philadelphia Street
Ontario, California 91761
U.S.A.
Telephone: (909) 930-0132
Web site: http://www.apexdigitalinc.com

Private Company
Incorporated: 1997
Employees: 101
Sales: $1.5 billion (2004 est.)
NAIC: 334310 Audio and Video Equipment Manufacturing

Apex Digital, Inc. is a leading importer of DVD players and other consumer electronics to the United States. It is believed to sell more DVD players than anyone else in the country, and is the fourth leading producer of televisions. The scourge of more established rivals, Apex competes at the low end of the price spectrum. It is able to keep prices low by working closely with its Chinese suppliers. The company also has been innovative, however, in making new technologies accessible to the mass consumer. As company cofounder David Ji told *Forbes* in 2002, "We are the only real American brand. That should give the Japanese the willies." According to an NPD Group study cited in *Fortune* magazine, the average price of DVD players fell 90 percent between 1997 and 2004; Apex Digital was a huge factor in that price drop.

Not many companies achieve annual sales of $1 billion with only 100 employees and without having to pay for advertising. Apex made this happen by outsourcing production to China and using a low-price strategy to rapidly gain market share. Apex products are found in more than 20,000 stores.

Origins

Digital video disks (DVDs) first entered the U.S. market in 1997. DVD players cost $600 at the time. While the price of VHS videocassette technology had fallen relatively slowly in the previous 20 years, that of DVD players would tumble drastically in a few short years, in large part thanks to Apex Digital, Inc.

Apex Digital, Inc. was founded in August 1997 by David Ji and Ancle Hsu. According to *Time,* the two met while working for a Los Angeles scrap metal dealer. Ji, from Shanghai, China, arrived in the United States in 1987 to work on his M.B.A. Hsu arrived from Taiwan in 1984.

In May 1992, the duo formed their own business exporting scrap metal to China, called United Delta, Inc. Ji also started a car stereo speaker business in City of Industry, California. Other ventures included herbal supplements and rubber gloves, reported *Forbes.*

The pair then began producing DVD players with a Chinese manufacturer, Visual Disc and Digital Video Corporation (VDDV). According to CNN.com, the first microchips were sourced in California. According to *Fortune,* the availability of standard, digital components found in DVD players would allow their price to fall much faster than that of videocassette players, which used more specialized parts.

Ji was Apex Digital's CEO, while Hsu served as chief operating officer. Stephen Brothers, who originally led sales and marketing efforts, was named president in September 2003.

First Big Sale in 2000

Apex first broke into the U.S. market in a big way with its AD-600A DVD player. These players were an instant sensation due to their unique ability to play MP3 files; the format was used mostly to download music files off the Internet during the height of the Napster controversy. The player also had a karaoke feature. Adding to the popularity was a retail price of $179—about $100 less than others. Apex kept prices down by working closely with its low-cost suppliers in China and by eschewing advertising.

Circuit City bought 5,000 of these in February 2000, reported *Electronic Business,* and sold out of them quickly. Best Buy and Wal-Mart soon followed. Sales were $120 million in 2000.

A programming quirk in the company's first DVD players enabled users to disable the Macrovision copyright protection. The ability to play DVDs from any region in the world and to

Key Dates:

1997: The company is founded in Ontario, California, by David Ji and Ancle Hsu.
2000: The first Apex DVD players are introduced in the United States via Circuit City.
2001: Apex enters a TV set partnership with Changhong Electric Co. of China.
2002: Apex becomes the fourth leading TV brand in just ten months.
2003: Plasma screen HDTVs and the ApeXtreme game console are launched.

Fourth in TVs in 2002

Eager to stay on top of consumer electronics trends, Apex introduced a couple of new products in 2002, including a DVD player with a built-in hard drive for downloading TV programs, and a line of 18 television sets. The TVs were developed in partnership with Sichuan Changhong Electric Co. Ltd., China's largest manufacturer of color televisions and a supplier of some of Apex's DVD players. According to *Consumer Electronics*, Sichuan had 13,000 employees, $2.5 billion worth of annual production, and had been making television sets since the 1980s. It was founded in 1958 as a defense electronics contractor. At the time of its partnership launch with Apex, oversupply in the domestic TV market had been cutting into its profits.

After a copyright infringement suit in January 2002, Apex agreed to pay Philips, Sony, and Pioneer a $7 patent royalty fee for each DVD player it made, becoming the first Chinese manufacturer to do so. Apex had already been paying a licensing fee to these companies; most Chinese manufacturers balked at paying additional royalties since the makers of the components they used had already done so.

Apex had sales of nearly $1 billion and only 100 employees of its own, most of them in California. The company also did not advertise. In one effective and unique marketing ploy, however, it sold 142,000 20-inch television sets through the Albertson's grocery store chain in the run-up to Christmas 2002. By the end of 2002, Apex was in more than 15,000 stores across the United States. In ten months, Apex had become the fourth leading TV brand.

A Proliferating Product Line in 2003

In 2003, Apex commanded a 10 percent share of the U.S. DVD player market by unit volume—still second place to Sony—according to one estimate. Its somewhat stripped-down AD-2600 model retailed for just $60, and was sometimes marked down to half that price. At $399, Apex's DRX-9000 DVD+RW recorder was priced about $100 lower than competitors' models. According to *EE Times*, a single-chip DVD encode/decode processor from California's LSI Logic made this low price possible. Apex was getting microchips for its DVD players from Zoran Corp., Media Tek, and Cirrus Logic, reported *EE Times*.

record them onto videocassettes did not seem to bother buyers, but it offended copyright owners, and this loophole was closed in subsequent models.

By the end of 2001, Apex was the second leading marketer of DVD players in the United States, with a market share of 13 percent to Sony's 22 percent, by one count. Another estimate placed Apex just ahead of Sony, with a little more than 15 percent market share.

At $100 to $350, Apex DVD players were priced below the major brand names. Apex sales for 2001 were about $600 million and growing furiously. It then had just 50 employees at its Ontario, California headquarters.

Apex paid $9 million for a 60 percent interest in Zhenjiang Jiangkui Electronic Group, a state-owned DVD player manufacturer near Shanghai, China, in November 2001. This business was soon renamed Apex Zhenjiang Ltd.

Apex was typically one of the first to bring new innovations to the mass consumer market. The DVD line was expanding to include higher-end models priced up to $350. In 2001, Apex became the first company certified to produce DVD players compatible with Eastman Kodak's Picture CDs. Its AD-7701 was the first to play Super Audio CD and DVD-Audio music formats. The AD-7701 was plagued by quality control problems, however, and its production was stopped. Apex's ViDVD player featured a modem for connecting to the Internet, allowing users to browse web pages, e-mail, and purchase licenses to view special high-capacity "locked," encrypted DVDs developed by Vialta of Fremont, California.

Apex began shipping 42-inch high definition plasma screen TVs in March 2003. LCD monitors followed the next month. Apex expected to sell 60,000 of the plasma TVs, which retailed for $4,000 each, during the year.

The company continued to roll out a large variety of new products, from portable DVD players with LCD screens to 65-inch projection TVs. In January 2004, Apex introduced its ''ApeXtreme'' console for playing PC video games on a television screen. The expanding DRX line of DVD recorders added software geared to converting VHS home movies into DVDs. They also included a chip for filtering out offensive content from movies. Revenues were expected to reach $1.5 billion in 2004.

Principal Subsidiaries

Apex Zhenjiang Ltd. (China; 60%).

Principal Competitors

Matsushita Electric Industrial Co., Ltd.; Pioneer Corporation; Royal Philips Electronics N.V.; Samsung Corporation; Sony Corporation; Toshiba Corporation.

Further Reading

''Apex Brand to Expand Through Exclusive with Chinese TV Maker,'' *Consumer Electronics,* November 19, 2001.

''Apex Derides Sony DVD Suit, Wants 'Level Playing Field' on Royalties,'' *Audio Week,* April 8, 2002.

''Apex to Have $299 DVD/SACD Combo, Web DVD for Locked Content,'' *Consumer Electronics,* February 5, 2001.

Arensman, Russ, ''Watch Out Sony; Apex, Already No. 1 in U.S. DVD Players, Is Taking Aim at TVs,'' *Electronic Business,* May 1, 2002, p. 38.

Ascenzi, Joseph, ''Digital Technology Unveiled This Week Will Replace Outmoded Videotape,'' *Business Press* (Ontario, Calif.), January 7, 2002, p. 13.

——, ''Ontario, Calif., Digital Video Disk Player Company Settles Licensing Dispute,'' *Business Press* (Ontario, Calif.), April 29, 2002.

Baig, Edward C., ''Low-Cost Apex Shoots High, But Falls Short,'' *USA Today,* March 20, 2002, p. D4.

Berestein, Leslie, ''David Ji and Ancle Hsu: Founders of Apex Digital,'' *Time,* December 2, 2002, p. 70.

Botelho, Greg, ''At Its Apex: California Firm Rallying to Become Home Electronics Stalwart,'' *CNN.com/TECHNOLOGY,* November 27, 2002.

Clark, Don, ''Apex to Unveil Console to Play PC Games on TV,'' *Wall Street Journal,* January 6, 2004, p. B5.

Einhorn, Bruce, ''Learning to Play Fair in China,'' *Business Week Online,* May 7, 2002.

——, ''Twilight of the DVD Pirates,'' *Business Week,* May 13, 2002, p. 22.

Frasher, Steven, ''Ontario, Calif.-Based Tech Company Concentrates on Plasma-Screen Televisions,'' *Business Press* (Ontario, Calif.), March 17, 2003.

Gautschi, Heidi, ''Apex Closes the Loop on Code-Cracked DVD,'' *EMedia Magazine,* June 2000, p. 19.

Katzanek, Jack, ''Ontario-Based Company Rises in DVD Market,'' *Press Enterprise* (Riverside, Calif.), December 15, 2001, p. E1.

Lashinsky, Adam, ''Shootout in Gadget Land,'' *Fortune,* October 26, 2003.

Lyons, Daniel, ''Smart and Smarter,'' *Forbes,* March 18, 2002, p. 40.

Takahashi, Dean, ''Ontario, Calif.-Based DVD Maker to Roll Out PC Game Console,'' *San Jose Mercury News,* January 6, 2004.

Walker, Rob, ''The Payoff from a $29 DVD Player Is the Cultural Capital of Savvy That Goes with Finding a Bargain,'' *New York Times Magazine,* March 7, 2004, p. 28.

Yoshida, Junko, ''New Processor Drives DVD Recorder Price Tag Below $400,'' *EE Times,* June 2, 2003.

—Frederick C. Ingram

Aquarius Platinum Ltd.

Level 4 Ste. 5, S Shore Centre/8
Perth
WA 6151
Australia
Telephone: +61 8 9367 5211
Fax: +61 8 9367 5233
Web site: http://www.aquariusplatinum.com

Public Company
Incorporated: 1996
Employees: 23
Sales: $96.9 million (2003)
Stock Exchanges: Australian London
Ticker Symbol: AQP
NAIC: 212299 Other Metal Ore Mining; 551112 Offices of Other Holding Companies

A minnow compared with the big fish in the PGM (platinum group metals) mining market, Aquarius Platinum Ltd. is also the industry's only publicly listed, independent pure-play platinum producer. Aquarius is an Australia-based, Bermuda-registered company operating mines in South Africa and Zimbabwe. The company owns and mines property on South Africa's Merensky Reef, in the so-called Bushveld Complex, one of the world's major PGM deposits. Aquarius operates two mines at Bushveld, including Kroondal, which is expected to ramp up to more than 500,000 ounces per year by the end of the 2000s, and Marikana, which will reach 155,000 ounces per year. The company also is developing a third site at Bushveld, the Everest South, with deposits forecasted at more than 225,000 ounces per year. Aquarius also owns a 50 percent stake in the Mimosa mine at Zimbabwe's Great Dyke, which produces 135,000 ounces per year. The company expects production to top 600,000 PGM ounces by 2005. Aquarius bills itself as the industry's lowest-cost producer, in part because it operates using a highly mechanized mining model. The company has also avoided the costs associated with constructing and operating smelting plants, instead turning to primary partner Impala Platinum Holdings (Implats), the world's second largest plati-

num producer, which processes Aquarius's ore, and is also the group's largest shareholder, with stakes in the Aquarius South African subsidiary and the Mimosa mine as well. Aquarius is listed on the Australian and London stock exchanges, with shares available in the United States through ADR sales. The group reports sales in dollars, the world standard currency for the platinum market. It is led by CEO Stuart A. Murray.

Exploring the Platinum Market in the 1990s

Aquarius Platinum represented the evolution of a mining group rooted in the Australian gold rush of the 1920s. The company's earliest incarnation was as Mount Monger Gold Mining Company, set up in 1920 as one of many small-scale mining groups exploiting the Kalgoorlie goldfield. The Mount Monger group later developed a successful mine site, at the Penny West deposit, but faded away again when that deposit was exhausted. In 1984, the company listed on the Australian stock exchange as part of a real estate divestment effort. Joining the company's board at that time were Peter Briggs, an entrepreneur based in Perth, and Jim Del Piano, who became instrumental in steering the company into its next phase as Aquarius Platinum.

The idea behind the company's entry into the South African platinum market came from Ed Nealon and Mike Tuite. Both were geologists working for CRA—later known as Rio Tinto—one of the world's largest mining groups. Nealon and Tuite had recognized an important trend in the metals market, that of a coming rise in demand for platinum group metals, or PGMs, a group including platinum, rhodium, and palladium, as well as osmium, iridium, and ruthenium. These metals were becoming increasingly vital components in a variety of industries, ranging from the high-technology and electronics industry, to the automotive industry, where both platinum and palladium were necessary materials used in catalytic converter systems, and to the jewelry and related industries, such as eyewear, where platinum increasingly replaced gold as the metal of choice.

Although PGM deposits—the various metals composing the group were generally found in the same seams, often alongside base metals such as copper—had been found in Russian Siberia, in Montana, and in Ontario, the overwhelming majority of known PGM deposits were located in South Africa and Zimbabwe. The Merensky Reef, site of the massive Bushveld Complex itself, represented more than one-third of all South African PGM deposits. Yet this real estate lay almost entirely in the hands of a small number of major mining groups. Several small-scale ''junior'' mining companies attempted to enter the region, without success.

Led primarily by Nealon, Aquarius began acquiring property in the Bushveld Complex. As part of this effort, Aquarius acquired three companies, Gemex Exploration & Mining Company and Randex Platinum Holdings in 1995, and Pacific Platinum Limited in 1996. These purchases gave Aquarius two sites near the village of Kroondal. The company then commissioned a feasibility study to determine whether the sites offered enough ore to support the full-scale implementation of a mining complex. That study was completed in September 1997, and the Kroondal project, with deposits estimated at 25 million tons, classified as ''robust.''

Yet the simple presence of strong reserves was not enough to ensure the company's viability. Because platinum tended to be present only in narrow seams, mining platinum was traditionally labor-intensive and costly. Extraction costs ran as high as nearly $400 per ounce (platinum prices on a global scale remained expressed in U.S. dollars), a fact that raised an extremely high entry barrier for junior companies such as Aquarius.

Aquarius, however, had developed a unique mining model based on a ''wide reef'' concept. Instead of sending a large number of miners down into narrow tunnels, Aquarius proposed to open tunnels that were large enough to allow the use of mechanical mining equipment. The use of machinery meant that the company was able to drastically reduce its manpower needs—cutting the cost of extraction in half.

Another feature of Aquarius was its willingness to avoid investing in costly smelting and processing equipment. Instead, the company went looking for a larger partner for processing the ore it produced. In the meantime, Aquarius moved ahead with construction of the mining site, raising AUD 5 million in a private placement.

The company found its partner in January 1998, signing a life of mine sales agreement with platinum mining giant Impala Platinum Holdings (Implats), then the world's second largest platinum concern. As part of the agreement, Implats agreed to buy Aquarius's production according to the daily spot rates, rather than according to a fixed discount rate, which was then an industry standard. This meant that Aquarius remained in posi-

tion to profit from the coming boom in global PGM prices. Another important part of the agreement held that Aquarius received first rights to acquire properties that did not meet Implats' own development criteria.

The next step in the Kroondal project came in July 1998, when Aquarius successfully brought the Kroondal project, through a subsidiary Kroondal Platinum Mines (later Aquarius Platinum South Africa), to the Johannesburg stock exchange. Aquarius itself retained a 45 percent stake in Kroondal, and Implats acquired stakes in both Aquarius and Kroondal.

Flushed with the proceeds of the public offering, and armed with the backing of a major platinum producer, Aquarius launched construction of the Kroondal site. At the same time, the company also began preparing for the future, acquiring a second site at Marikana, also located in the Bushveld complex.

Production began at the Kroondal site in 1999. The company quickly began the ramp-up to full production, which was expected to top 100,000 ounces of platinum, 50,000 ounces of palladium, and 15,000 ounces of rhodium per year. The total of more than 165,000 ounces represented some 100,000 more per year than the company had originally planned.

With its share price languishing in Australia—which, with no platinum resources, was said to remain indifferent to platinum stocks—Aquarius decided to make its stock more easily available to the European market. In 1999, the company obtained a dual listing on both the London and Australian stock exchanges through a share-swap Bermuda-registered entity, Strategic Platinum Mines Ltd. Aquarius's stock was then placed on the London Stock Exchange's AIM index, where it quickly became one of the listing's hottest stocks.

Platinum Success Story in the 2000s

Aquarius and Implats deepened their relationship in 2000, when the companies agreed to exchange Implats' holdings in the Everest North, Everest South, and Chieftains Plains mining projects for a 24.5 percent stake in Aquarius Platinum South Africa, under which Aquarius had been developing the Marikana project. Aquarius, which by then had favorably completed its feasibility study, projected bringing the Everest South site online by the end of 2002, a move that, together with the launch of production at the Marikana site in 2001, would boost the company's total production past 500,000 ounces per year.

The Kroondal site, meanwhile, was boosted in the middle of 2000 with the announcement of an agreement between Aquarius and Anglo American Platinum Corp. that called for a tripling of Kroondal's production over a 16-year period. Aquarius now moved to regain complete control of the Kroondal project, in a restructuring move that placed it as a subsidiary under the Aquarius Platinum South Africa operation. By 2001, the company had retaken control of the subsidiary, which was then delisted from the Johannesburg exchange.

Demand for platinum and other PGMs increased markedly by the dawn of the 21st century. Platinum jewelry had become extremely popular and represented a major portion of worldwide platinum sales. At the same time, the use of platinum and palladium for catalytic converters also had stepped up demand for the metals. Meanwhile, new platinum-based fuel cell technologies were expected to provide a new boost to demand in the early part of the new decade.

As a result, platinum prices soared, prompting Aquarius to step up its efforts to expand its production. In 2002, the company acquired a direct 50 percent stake in ZCE Platinum, which owned the Mimosa Platinum Mine in Zimbabwe's Great Dyke. Joined by partner Implats, Aquarius now controlled a prime site in the world's second largest known platinum deposit. Soon after, the company transferred its London listing to the London Stock Exchange main board, where it soon joined the FTSE 250 index.

By the end of 2002, Aquarius had boosted its total production past 220,000 ounces per year. As the company ramped up the Marikana site in 2003, production forecasts were raised to 600,000 ounces per year by 2005. Yet Aquarius seemed only at the beginning of a new growth phase, with plans to begin construction on its Everest South site slated for that year as well. Into 2004, the company was hampered somewhat by the strength of the South African rand—the currency used for paying its costs—against the U.S. dollar, in which Aquarius received its revenues. Nonetheless, the company remained highly profitable and encouraged by the expected continued demand in PGM metals. Aquarius had successfully developed into the world's only independent "pure-play" platinum company.

Principal Subsidiaries

Aquarius Platinum (Australia) Limited; Aquarius Platinum (South Africa) (Pty) Ltd.; Kroondal Platinum Mines Limited; Malfeb (Pty) Ltd.; Rossal No. 9 (Pty) Ltd.; Magaliesburg Properties (Pty) Limited; TKO Investment Holdings Ltd.

Principal Competitors

Lonmin Platinum Div.; Impala Platinum Holdings Ltd.; Anglo American PLC; Western Platinum Ltd.; Metallgesellschaft AG.

Further Reading

"Aquarius Re-structure Boosts the South African Image," *Australasian Business Intelligence,* June 13, 2002.

Chung, Joanna, "Aquarius Rises Despite Strength of SA Rand," *Financial Times,* February 11, 2004, p. 26.

Foley, Stephen, "Aquarius Platinum Worth a Gamble," *Independent,* August 28, 2002, p. 18.

Gooding, Kenneth, "Aquarius Takes Fresh Look at Platinum," *Financial Times,* March 10, 1998, p. 37.

"Implats Helps Aquarius Platinum Restructure Debt," *African Mining Monitor,* January 11, 2002.

Innocenti, Nicol Degli, "Platinum Groups to Merge," *Financial Times,* July 25, 2000, p. 33.

Moodie, David, "Aquarius Star Poised to Rise," *Advertiser,* October 6, 1997, p. 17.

O'Connor, Gillian, "Aquarius Platinum Wins Kroondal," *Financial Times,* May 7, 2001, p. 22.

"Palladium Price Could Provide Added Boost to Strong Performance Expected from Aquarius Platinum This Year," *Minews,* February 3, 2004.

Phaceas, John, "Junior Platinum Miner Plans the Age of Aquarius," *Australian,* April 24, 2000, p. 43.

—M.L. Cohen

COMIC PUBLICATIONS, INC.

Archie Comics Publications, Inc.

325 Fayette Avenue
Mamaroneck, New York 10543-2306
U.S.A.
Telephone: (914) 381-5155
Fax: (914) 381-2335
Web site: http://www.archiecomics.com

Private Company
Founded: 1939 as MLJ Magazines
Employees: 23
Sales: $15 million (2002 est.)
NAIC: 511120 Periodicals Publishers; 511199 All Other
     Publishers

Everyone knows Archie, the flagship creation of Archie Comics Publications, Inc., even though they might not know his last name (Andrews). Add Betty, Veronica, and Jughead to the mix and millions of fans will respond in more than a dozen languages. Archie and his Riverdale sidekicks have long been a favorite among comic book and newspaper readers, but the Archie gang has appeared in animated and live-action television productions, topped the music charts, educated the public to the dangers of alcoholism and AIDS, and raised awareness of cerebral palsy, missing children, and environmental issues. Archie Comics, the company behind the lovable icon, also brought Sabrina the Teenage Witch, Josie and the Pussycats, and Sonic the Hedgehog to comic book and television prominence. Archie, however, still reigns supreme with an average monthly circulation of 850,000 or 16 million comic books annually.

Three Guys and an Idea: 1939–43

In November 1939 three gentlemen with loads of creativity and big dreams formed MLJ Magazines. The M came from Maurice Coyne, the L from Louis Silberkleit and the J from John Goldwater. The new company's goal was to produce comic books, the first series of which was Blue Ribbon Comics. A second series was called Top-Notch Comics, and a third, Pep Comics, appeared in 1940. The first volume of Pep Comics featured a superhero called ''The Shield.'' The Shield was an American patriot, battled international foes, and appealed to a predominantly male audience.

In order to attract more female comic book readers, the founders of MLJ decided to create an average, wholesome type of character experiencing the ups and downs of daily life. Goldwater (the J of the firm's name) came up with a character loosely based on Mickey Rooney's Andy Hardy roles beginning in the late 1930s, with some real life inspiration from Goldwater's own friends growing up in New York. Goldwater's creation was Archie Andrews, a redhead with freckles. Archie's best friend, Jughead, was based on Goldwater himself and his relationship to a high school pal who also happened to be named Archie.

The first likeness of Archie Andrews came courtesy of Bob Montana who became the principal artist for the Archie series. The first Archie comic, written by Vic Bloom, debuted in December 1941 (a rather infamous month in U.S. history) in Pep Comics volume 22. Archie was the standout in this issue, not because his story was outstanding but because he was an average kid and not a superhero like other characters in the issue. Goldwater and his partners had little idea they had just launched what would become an international phenomenon.

The first Archie story revolved around a new girl who came to town (Riverdale), Betty Cooper. Also introduced was Jughead Jones, Archie's best friend, who had no interest in females whatsoever. Archie and a growing number of Riverdale folks were featured in both Pep Comics and another line called Jackpot Comics. By the time Pep Comics volume 26 arrived in April 1942, Archie and his antics were gaining an audience. This particular comics issue was pivotal, as it introduced a character who would shape stories for decades to come. Wealthy, attractive Veronica Lodge arrived in Riverdale and Archie found he was attracted to two gals—flashy Veronica and wholesome Betty. Hence one of the most famous love triangles was born, as Veronica and Betty became rivals for Archie's affection.

Despite the era's love of larger-than-life heroes, especially as the United States fought in World War II, Archie brought a fresh and welcome perspective to comic books. He was ordinary, silly, and willing to go to outrageous lengths to impress the girls of his dreams. Veronica was feisty and added a spark of mischief to the

---

Company Perspectives:

Archie Comics is the only family-owned and independent publisher in the industry. Goldwater's and Silberkleit's fathers formed the comic book publishing company, MLJ Magazines, in November 1939. MLJ Magazines was named after its three founders, Maurice Coyne, Louis Silberkleit and John Goldwater. Archie was first introduced in comics in December 1941, and the company adopted the name of its flagship character in 1946. Today, Michael Silberkleit and Richard Goldwater provide millions of loyal fans across the country with more than 25 Archie Comics titles published each month.

---

stories, while Betty was America's sweetheart. Jughead was comic relief but also demonstrated loyalty to pal Archie.

As MLJ Magazines realized Archie's potential, the young everyman was given an increased presence in its comic books. The first *Archie Comics* volume came out in 1942, while Archie received his first Pep cover in 1943 (volume 36); became Pep's lead story by volume 49; and filled an entire Pep comic by volume 51 (while also filling the pages of his own line, *Archie Comics*).

Laughter Takes Center Stage: 1944–59

Archie had taken center stage at MLJ by 1944 and soon his teen and merry band had their own comic book line. Archie was not, however, MLJ's only product. The firm had several different comic book lines and was continually trying out new characters. One of these was Katy Keene, a beauty queen introduced in 1945. Katy became a popular pinup girl with GIs fighting overseas and was soon featured in several comic book series. The following year, 1946, MLJ Magazines changed its name to Archie Comics Publications (ACP), reflecting the growing popularity of Archie and his gang.

By the early 1950s ACP had several popular comic book lines, and had segued into a radio show featuring the Archie characters. While there were still a few action heroes in the company's comics, comedy had become the firm's primary credo. In addition to Archie and Pep comics, other lines such as *Laugh Comics, Archie's Pal Jughead, Archie's JokeBook, Life With Archie*, and a spinoff title featuring Betty and Veronica were added. ACP had also begun making yearly "jumbo" editions of its titles, and added new characters to the Archie saga including bad guy Reggie Mantle, shop owner Pop Tate, Jughead foil Big Ethel, and personnel from Riverdale High School.

Changing Times: 1960s

As America experienced the 1960s, so did Archie and the gang. Clothing, attitudes, and language changed in the comic books to reflect the times. Katy Keene was no longer the belle of the ball and her comic line was discontinued in 1961 (though she would return in the future). *Batman* and *The Man from U.N.C.L.E.* were popular television programs and Archie mirrored the renewed interest in superheroes and spies. Archie became a Batman-like action hero called Pureheart the Power-

ful in 1965, while a *Man from U.N.C.L.E.* spoof, *The Man from R.I.V.E.R.D.A.L.E.* hit store shelves.

Archie mania swept the nation but the teen really hit the big time when the company inked a deal with Filmation to produce a Saturday morning television show featuring the Riverdale kids. Debuting in 1968, the animated series was wildly successful and even spawned a musical group called the Archies who produced an album of catchy tunes. One of the album's singles, "Sugar Sugar," went all the way to the number one slot on the *Billboard* music charts in 1969.

Archie Comics did not rest on its Riverdale laurels but continued to come up with new storylines in the 1960s. One of these was Sabrina, a teenaged witch who was given her own TV show and shared space with Archie in a new series called *Archie's TV Laugh Out* (though Sabrina was given her own comic series later). Another female, Josie, who had been introduced back in the 1940s, received little attention until she donned a cat suit and started a girl band called "Josie and the Pussycats" in 1969. Both Sabrina and Josie had their own TV shows (the former produced by Filmation and the latter by cartoon giant Hanna-Barbera) and graced the pages of comic books, but each would make a bigger splash in the decades to come.

Turbulent Times: 1970s–80s

The dawn of a new decade, the 1970s, brought toy licensing agreements and numerous spinoff titles for Archie characters including Betty's first solo outing and editions in varying sizes and slants. One brilliant marketing endeavor was the release of "digests," reprinting original stories from ACP's earliest years and offering them to readers who had not been born at the time of their publication. Archie's appeal was soon crossing generational boundaries, as the grandparents and parents of Riverdale's current audience were brought back into the fold. In 1975, however, everyone at ACP was saddened by the death of Bob Montana who had drawn Archie for three decades. Don DeCarlo, who had created the likenesses of Josie (of Pussycat fame), took the reins and became the principal artist for Archie and his Riverdale pals.

In a nod to one of the more important issues of the decade, several ethnically diverse characters were introduced to Riverdale High School. African Americans Chuck Clayton and Nancy Harris, and Hispanic Americans Frankie Valdez and Nancy Rodriguez became regular features in the comic books. Despite racial diversity and reprinting early Archie stories, the Archie television show was canceled in 1976 as comic book sales slumped in the last years of the decade. Many titles were cut and the ACP's corporate belt tightened. One bright spot, however, was the unexpected return of World War II pinup Katy Keene who was revived by a Saks Fifth Avenue window designer who featured blowups of Katy in her displays.

The 1980s found ACP making bold moves to revive its audience. A racy new character, Cheryl Blossom, stirred up controversy in 1982 when she was introduced in *Betty and Veronica* volume 320. Cheryl had no shame and liked to show off her well-endowed body, much to the dismay of Betty and Veronica. Cheryl also had a twin brother named Jason, and the two immediately caused trouble for Riverdale's wholesome

Key Dates:

1939: MLJ Magazines is founded by three partners.

1941: Archie Andrews makes his first appearance in a comic strip.

1942: The infamous Archie-Betty-Veronica love triangle is born and Archie gets his own comic book.

1943: Archie is featured for the first time on the cover of a comic book.

1946: MLJ Magazines is renamed Archie Comics Publications.

1968: Filmation's animated Archie television series debuts on Saturday mornings.

1969: "Sugar Sugar" by the musical group Archies tops the pop charts.

1987: An updated Archie animated series returns to television.

1990: Adult versions of Archie and his pals star in a live-action television movie.

1993: Archie Comics produces a *Sonic the Hedgehog* comic book insert for Sega.

1994: The "Love Showdown" between Betty and Veronica hits the comic books.

1997: *Archie Comics Online* debuts on the Internet.

2000: Archie's 500th issue is published.

2001: Archie Comics Entertainment LLC is established.

2002: The 60th anniversary of *Archie Comics* is celebrated.

2004: IDT Entertainment buys an equity stake in Archie Comics Entertainment.

high schoolers. After two years, Cheryl Blossom and her brother disappeared; like their predecessors who vanished, however, they would turn up again.

Despite fluctuating sales in the comic book industry, ACP continued to find new niches for its characters. *Betty's Diaries* began publication as a standalone title in 1986 after years as a feature in *Archie's JokeBook* while the Riverdale pals went back in time to middle school in another animated television series called *The New Archies* in 1987. Neither of these ventures, however, did exceedingly well and they were consequently discontinued.

An Archie Renaissance: 1990s

Early Archie experiments in the 1990s proved outlandish as the United States was in the thrall of George Lucas and his *Star Wars* saga. ACP responded with space adventures such as *Archie 3000* and Jughead's *Time Police*. While the new titles were imaginative, they did not last. One change that did last was ACP's switch to soy-based inks and recycled paper after readers wrote in about environmental concerns. A risky move was a 1990 live-action television movie called *Archie: To Riverdale and Back,* featuring grown up versions of the Riverdale gang. Aired on NBC against popular shows of the time, the movie did not fare well—in part because most of the adult characters were portrayed as embattled and unhappy, but also because most longtime fans never equated their favorite comic book heroes as dealing with such heavy issues as divorce.

While Archie faltered, however, something else took hold in the minds of kids around the world. Sega mascot Sonic the Hedgehog, created in 1991, was given its first comic book treatment by the artists at ACP in 1993. Designed as a promotional leaflet for Sega products and based on the character's cartoon show likeness, the comic proved so successful Archie and Sega inked a deal to produce a comic book series. Sonic went on to star in two different animated series and was featured in numerous product tie-ins throughout the decade and into the next.

While Sonic rocketed to fame, the Archie-Betty-Veronica love triangle got a major boost in 1994. Still torn by his feelings for both Betty and Veronica, Archie receives a blast from the past in the form of a letter. Though the letter-writer is kept a secret, Betty and Veronica learn the author is female and has feelings for Archie. This, of course, stirs up a whirlwind of feminine competition by Betty and Veronica to secure Archie's heart. Carried over several titles and weeks, readers find the mystery woman is none other than Cheryl Blossom, last seen in 1985. Cheryl's return was met with so much enthusiasm that she was featured in several titles over the next few years, until she was given her own comic book series in 1997. Her twin Jason had been resurrected as well.

Sabrina, the teen witch who had been starring in her own comic series since the 1960s, was given the star treatment when Showtime produced a full length movie featuring her character in 1996. The movie scored high with young viewers because of its star, Nickelodeon actress Melissa Joan Hart, and led to a new television series on ABC. As Sabrina won over audiences on Friday nights during prime time, ACP launched *Archie Comics Online* in 1997. ACP had also become active in fundraising and cultural awareness by the middle and late 1990s; Archie was an official ambassador for United Cerebral Palsy in 1995 and ACP characters endorsed such healthy life choices as staying away from drugs and alcohol.

ACP lost one of its original founders, John Goldwater, the creator of redheaded Archie Andrews, at age 83 in 1999. At the time of Goldwater's death, Archie comic books were sold in three dozen countries worldwide.

A New Era: 2000s

Archie in the 21st century was not too different from Archie in the 20th, just that he had millions of virtual fans in addition to his diehard comic book readers. In 2000 Archie and his Riverdale pals joined select company when the 500th Archie comic book was published. This put Archie in league with such comic book legends as Superman, Batman, and Mickey Mouse. The millennium also brought a new business caveat: that everything old was new again.

Favorite heroes of bygone decades including Scooby Doo, Spider-Man, the Hulk, and the Teenage Mutant Ninja Turtles were back on television and even on the big screen and the folks at ACP, which included the sons of two founders (Michael Silberkleit, chairman and publisher, and Richard Goldwater, president and publisher) were poised to take advantage of the renaissance. In 2001 Archie Comics Entertainment LLC (ACE) was formed to license and market ACP characters. A big screen live-action version of Josie and her Pussycat pals debuted in

April 2001 starring hipsters Rachel Lee Cook, Tara Reid, and Rosario Dawson. A music CD and video version were also produced and released later in the year.

In 2003 ACE announced that Betty Cooper and Veronica Lodge were headed to the big screen; Miramax had signed on to produce a live-action motion picture starring the Riverdale duo. While Archie, Jughead, and others would be part of the *Betty & Veronica* film, the ladies were the headliners.

In 2004 ACE sold a 5 percent stake in its operations to IDT Entertainment, a subsidiary of the telephone and network giant IDT Corporation. The equity stake partnered IDT and ACE to develop and market animated projects based on ACP's popular characters. Testament to the enduring appeal of Riverdale's high schoolers was the publication of well over two dozen issues a month featuring Archie and his gang. For six decades Archie comic books had enthralled American youth without resorting to sex, violence, or profanity. Other comic book heroes had come and gone, but Archie remained a consistent voice for generations of kids.

Principal Subsidiaries

Archie Comics Entertainment LLC.

Principal Competitors

Marvel Publishing; DC Comics Inc.; Image Comics, Inc.

Further Reading

Ames, Lynne, "Archie: A Teenager in His 60th Year," *New York Times,* January 6, 2002, p. 11.

"Archie Comics Names New President," *Home Accents Today,* April 2003, p. SS31.

"Archie Comics Pitches in to Help Save Environment," *Playthings,* October 1991, p. 10.

Cohen, Jeffrey, "Publications: Comic Books Take Off," *Progressive Grocer,* December 1995, p. 83.

Duke, David, "Licensors to Seek to Broaden Exposure," *Playthings,* October 1987, p. 66.

"DVD Insider: IDT Entertainment Acquires an Equity Stake in Archie Comics Entertainment LLC," *Playthings,* January 28, 2004.

Fuchs, Marek, "Archie, Model of Sobriety, Fights Teenage Drinking," *New York Times,* October 9, 2003, p. B1.

Hennemeyer, Doug, "Comic Relief for the Toy Industry," *Playthings,* October 1985, p. 62.

Henry, Gordon, M., "Bang! Pow! Zap! Heroes Are Back!," *Time,* October 6, 1986, p. 62.

McCormick, Moira, "Warner Vid Gets Head Start on *Josie and the Pussycats*," *Billboard,* March 3, 2001, p. 57.

Napoli, Lisa, "Why a Big Player in Telecom Bigwig Added Archie and Jughead to His Holdings," *New York Times,* February 2, 2004, p. 8.

Reysen, Frank, Jr., "Comic Books Turn the Page," *Playthings,* July 1995, p. 28.

Schulman, Milt, "Action Figures Gear Up for Comeback," *Playthings,* April 1992, p. 28.

—Nelson Rhodes

Assurances Générales de France

87, rue de Richelieu
75113 Paris Cedex 02
France
Telephone: +33 1-44-86-20-00
Fax: +33 1-44-86-29-60
Web site: http://www.agf.fr

Public Company
Incorporated: 1818 as Société Anonyme des Assurances
  Générales
Employees: 34,000
Operating Revenues: EUR 18.28 billion ($22 billion)
  (2003)
Stock Exchanges: Euronext Paris
Ticker Symbol: AGF
NAIC: 524113 Direct Life Insurance Carriers

Assurances Générales de France, or AGF, is one of France's oldest and largest insurance companies, offering a full range of insurance products and financial services to the private, commercial, and government sectors. Present in more than 20 countries worldwide, with a workforce of more than 34,000 people, AGF is particularly strong in Belgium, the Netherlands, and Spain, and also has a significant Middle East and South American presence. AGF's primary operations are in the life and health insurance sector, which accounts for 41 percent of the group's EUR 18 billion in annual revenues, and in the property and liability sector, which adds 38 percent to AGF's revenues. Other areas of operation include financial services (10 percent) and credit insurance and assistance (11 percent). France remains the company's largest single market, at 65 percent of revenues. Despite the company's worldwide presence, Europe remains its major market, combining to reach 92 percent of sales. Hit hard by the economic slump beginning in 2000, AGF has moved to streamline parts of its business, such as selling off its subsidiaries in Brazil and Chile, as well as its banking operation in Belgium, and divesting its majority stake in property lending wing Entenial in 2003. AGF itself is majority controlled by Allianz, the leading insurance group in Eu-

rope. Yet AGF, listed on the Euronext Paris exchange, has retained much of its autonomy under Chairman and CEO Jean-Philippe Thierry.

Founding the French Insurance Industry in the 19th Century

Emerging from the chaos of the French revolution, France found itself lagging behind as the insurance industry developed into a potent financial force in the neighboring European economies. Yet the relative calm of the Restoration period, starting in 1815, enabled the emergence of an insurance industry within France that would ultimately develop into the world's fourth largest domestic insurance market.

An important factor in the creation of the French insurance industry came from the return of many of the country's nobles and their families, who had fled the country during the revolution. Educated in the other European capitals, and especially in London, the émigrés brought with them a background in British-styled insurance methods. Among them was Auguste de Gourcuff, who had began lobbying the French government for permission to launch the first modern French insurance company.

Gourcuff found support from a number of prominent bankers of the time, and particularly Martin d'André, who had built up one of the country's largest trade and banking empires. With backing from d'André and others, Gourcuff led the formation of a new company, Société Anonyme des Assurances Générales in 1918. The company quickly developed into an umbrella for three primary components: Compagnie d'Assurances Générales Maritimes, la Compagnie d'Assurances Générales contre l'Incendie, and la Compagnie d'Assurances Générales sur la Vie, which received authorization to begin business in 1819. This marked the first time the three most prominent branches of the insurance industry—marine, fire, and life—were combined into a single organization in France.

Les AGF, as the company came to be known, received official support from the French government under King Louis XVIII and quickly gained a leading position among the country's growing number of insurance companies. Among these was another major insurance group, founded in 1820, la

Compagnie Française du Phénix. That company remained les AGF's main rival for the leadership of the French insurance sector until the middle of the 20th century—at which time the two companies merged into a single entity.

Gourcuff, a native of the Brittany region, brought in fellow Breton and protégé Alfred de Courcy to take over direction of the company toward the middle of the 19th century. Together Courcy and Gourcuff developed a number of innovations in the French insurance sector, such as the launch of employee pension and protection plans, starting in 1844, that later became a key component of the French social security system.

Les AGF continued to develop new insurance products as well. Responding to the changing economic and social landscape brought on by the Industrial Revolution, les AGF launched a range of new policies, covering such events as railroad accidents and gaslight explosions. Originally confined to the trading sector, les AGF led the extension of insurance coverage into a broader market, adding agricultural insurance policies—a popular policy offered protection against damage brought on by hailstorms—and policies spanning the wide range of newly developing industries and machinery.

The new insurance markets and products attracted a steadily increasing number of new players into the industry. Les AGF found itself facing rising competition, not only from the new entries but from such major rivals as La Phénix and other prominent companies founded during that period, including GAN and UAP. In response, the company became one of the first in the insurance sector to invest in newly developing advertising techniques. As a result, the company quickly became one of France's most well-known brands.

Surviving Nationalization in the 21st Century

The turn of the 20th century brought new changes to the French insurance industry as it moved to its modern form. Laws promulgated at the end of the 19th century required employers to insure workers against industrial accidents as well as provide other social protections. The insurance industry responded by developing a whole range of products, policies, and services to the country's industrial and corporate sectors. Yet the administration of these policies by private companies led to a great deal of complaints and worker unrest. In 1910, the French government took over the workers' indemnity sector.

Instead, les AGF and other insurance groups, including La Phénix, began developing a whole new category of insurance products. Whereas les AGF, like other insurance companies,

had previously targeted the nation's industries and wealthy for its clientele, in the early decades of the 20th century, it now began to create a new class of consumer-oriented policies and services. This trend picked up especially with the beginnings of the development of the French social security system in the 1920s and under the Front Populaire government of the 1930s. During this period, les AGF introduced policies offering health insurance and accident and theft insurance. The company's clientele extended to include customers from a variety of social backgrounds.

If France's insurance companies thrived during the interwar period, the sector was threatened with complete collapse as the country emerged from World War II. In 1946, therefore, the government under General Charles de Gaulle passed new legislation nationalizing nearly all of the French insurance sector, including its 25 largest players. Les AGF now became owned and operated by the French government. The government then reformed much of the insurance sector, creating the new social security system covering health, accident, and retirement benefits.

The next major step in AGF's evolution came in 1968, when the French government decided to merge its nationalized insurance companies into just four large-scale companies. The move marked the emergence of national heavyweight UAP, GAN, and MGF-Mutelles du Mans. It also created a "new" AGF, composed of the former Assurances Générales and rival La Phénix.

In the 25 years that followed, les AGF developed a distinct identity among its sister insurance companies. Starting in the 1970s, les AGF became the spearhead for the French government's drive to create a global insurance giant. As such, les AGF launched a drive into a number of foreign markets, capturing strong positions in Belgium, Germany, the Netherlands, Switzerland, and Spain in Europe, and building up positions in a number of Middle East and North African markets, including Egypt, Lebanon, and Tunisia. The company also entered the South American market, with holdings in Chile, Argentina, Brazil, Colombia, and Venezuela.

In the 1980s and early 1990s, les AGF went on a buying spree, building up a leading position in the industrial insurance sector, and acquiring such entities as Coface, which provided insurance and financial services to the government, and the insurance group SCOR. Part of the stimulus behind the company's growth drive was the promise of its coming privatization. The company had originally hoped to be released from government control during the Socialist-led government's privatization efforts in the mid-1980s. Les AGF appeared slated for privatization in 1987, but was passed up in favor of other government holdings.

The French government nonetheless reduced its stake in Les AGF, down to just 51 percent in the mid-1990s. In the meantime, les AGF had joined in the jockeying for position among Europe's insurance industry, as it prepared for the lowering of trade barriers slated for 1992. As part of its effort, les AGF began wooing Germany's AMB Aachen Munchen, the country's third largest insurance company, ultimately acquiring nearly 35 percent of its stock.

Les AGF's turn to be privatized finally came in 1996, when the French government agreed to spin off its share in the company

Key Dates:

1818: Société Anonyme des Assurances Générales (AGF) is founded by Auguste de Gourcuff, Martin d'André, and others.

1846: AGF launches first social security policies.

1946: Nationalization of French insurance industry by French government under Charles de Gaulle.

1968: AGF is merged with another nationalized insurance company, La Phénix, creating Les AGF.

1996: French government privatizes Les AGF.

1997: After hostile takeover attempt by Generali of Italy, AGF acquires Athena Assurance then agrees to be acquired by Germany's Allianz.

2001: AGF acquires Zwolsche Algemeene Europe from Hartford Group.

2002: AGF acquires Euler Hermes credit insurance company.

2003: AGF restructures, selling off Chile and Brazil holdings.

2004: AGF sells off property lending business, Entenial.

to the public market. Flush from its successful listing, AGF began making plans to boost its position in the French market. In 1996, for example, the company acquired majority control of SFAC, originally founded in 1927. That company was renamed EULER under AGF. Yet in 1997, AGF shortly became the target of a hostile takeover attempt by Italy's Generali.

AGF at first sought a partner in France to help it fight off Generali's advances. In November 1997, the company agreed to acquire Worms et Cie in order to gain control of its insurance group, Athena, then the 12th largest French insurance company. Athena had been formed in 1989 through the merger of PFA, owned by Worms, and the GPA. By the end of that year, AGF had completed its acquisition of Athena. Yet AGF required a still larger partner in order to defeat the Generali bid. The company then began looking beyond France, and fell into the arm of Germany's Allianz.

Allianz itself had been seeking growth, particularly after it lost its position as European insurance leader following the merger of two French companies, AXA and UAP. Allianz's offer proved more attractive—in large part because Allianz agreed to take only a minority stake in Les AGF as well as a minority position on its board of directors. At the same time, les AGF was to operate autonomously within the Allianz empire, with its own chairman and CEO and exclusive responsibility for key geographic areas, including France, Belgium, the Netherlands, Spain, and other countries corresponding to les AGF's international profile.

The appearance of Allianz as white knight led to intense negotiations among the various players, including the French government, which was unwilling to allow certain parts of les AGF, and especially its holding in Coface, fall into the hands of foreign owners. The talks ultimately resulted in what some considered a splitting in two of Les AGF. The company agreed to cede Coface to the French government, and its stake in AMB

Aachen Munchen to Generali. At the same time, the recently acquired Athena insurance group was divided into its component parts, with AGF retaining PFA and other parts, and Generali taking the GPA operations. Generali then agreed to relinquish its own stake in AGF.

The "new" AGF now found itself one of the primary subsidiaries of Europe's leading insurance group. With the addition of the former Athena operations and the French operations of parent company Allianz, les AGF claimed the position as the number three French insurance company.

At the turn of the millennium, les AGF began exploring new frontiers. As part of that effort, the company began repositioning itself for the growing e-commerce and Internet markets, developing a new series of insurance products—focusing especially on providing credit transaction insurance and assistance policies and services. Les AGF also targeted entry into the financial services market, launching its own assets management services through subsidiary Banque AGF. In 2002, the company changed its name, to AGF, in order to highlight its new, more unified status.

AGF continued to eye international expansion within the larger Allianz group. In 2001, for example, the company acquired the Netherland's Zwolsche Algemeene Europe, as well as its subsidiary The Hartford Luxembourg (THL), sold by U.S.-based Hartford Group. The following year, AGF acquired the recently formed Euler Hermes, combining AGF's and Allianz's credit insurance operations into a single entity.

The difficult economic situation at the beginning of the 2000s led AGF into losses by the end of 2002. In 2003, the company began a restructuring, which included shedding a number of its operations, including its holdings in Brazil and Chile. The company's restructuring continued into 2004, when it received permission from the French government to sell off its majority stake in its property lending operation, Entenial. These moves helped AGF restore its profitability. After nearly 200 years, AGF remained a powerful force in the French—and world's—insurance industry.

Principal Subsidiaries

Adriatica de Seguros (Venezuela; 96.97%); AGF Afrique; AGF Allianz Argentina Generales (Argentina); AGF Asset Management; AGF Assurances Financières; AGF Belgium Insurance (94.19%); AGF Immobilier; AGF International; AGF La Lilloise; AGF Life Luxembourg (94.19%); AGF Vie; Alliance Nederland Groep; Allianz Seguros y Reaseguros (Spain; 48.31%); Arcalis; Astrée (Tunisia; 42.08%); Banque AGF; Calypso; Colombiana de Inversion (92.82%); Compagnie de Gestion et de Prévoyance; Coparc; Elmonda (Mondial Assistance) (Spain; 50%); Euler Hermes (70.46%); Génération Vie; La Rurale; Les Assurances Fédérales; Mathis Assurances; Phénix Vie (Switzerland); Protexia France (65.99%); Qualis; Société Nationale d'Assurances (SNA SAL) (Lebanon; 56.15%); Spain; W Finance.

Principal Competitors

American International Group Inc.; AXA Insurance PLC; China Insurance Company Ltd.; Fortis; AEGON N.V; Aetna Life Insurance Company of America; Prudential Financial Inc.

Further Reading

''Assurance Generales de France May Sell Off Its Stake in Frank Bank Entenial to Credit Foncier de France,'' *Euroweek*, July 25, 2003, p. 10.

''French Insurer Posts 63% Fall in 2002 Profits,'' *Euroweek*, January 5, 2001, p. 33.

Kielmas, Maria, ''AGF Making Bid for Worms et Cie,'' *Business Insurance*, October 13, 1997, p. 25.

——-, ''France Putting AGF up for Sale,'' *Business Insurance*, May 13, 1996, p. 17.

Fabre, Thierry, ''L'impossible privatisation des AGF,'' *L'Expansion*, September 4, 1995.

Schmid, John, ''Allianz Makes $10 Billion Bid for AGF,'' *International Herald Tribune*, November 19, 1997, p. 15.

—M.L. Cohen

Avecia Group PLC

PO Box 42, Hexagon House, Blackl
Manchester
M9 8ZS
United Kingdom
Telephone: +44 161 740 1460
Fax: +44 161 795 6005
Web site: http://www.avecia.com

Private Company
Incorporated: 1999
Employees: 2,700
Sales: £485 million ($776 million) (2003)
NAIC: 325412 Pharmaceutical Preparation
Manufacturing; 325320 Pesticide and Other
Agricultural Chemical Manufacturing; 325510 Paint
and Coating Manufacturing; 325998 All Other
Miscellaneous Chemical Product Manufacturing

Avecia Group PLC is in the process of redefining itself as a focused specialty and fine chemicals group. Originally part of Zeneca (and before that, part of Imperial Chemical Industries), Avecia has shed a number of its former operations in order to concentrate itself around a new core of biotechnology products and fine chemicals, specifically niche pharmaceutical intermediates, as well as genetically engineered chemicals and products, including a vaccine for anthrax, on the one hand, and ''neoresins'' on the other. Under neoresins the company includes its fast-growing light-emitting polymers (LEP) segment, the world's leading manufacturer of LEP-based screens for portable telephones and other applications. As part of its paring down, Avecia sold off or shut down a number of its subsidiaries, including its largest revenue-generator, the Stahl leather chemicals group in 2002, as well as its color additives business, sold to Lubrizol, and its biocides (primarily water treatment and pool cleaning products), sold to Arch in 2004. Motivation for Avecia's streamlining comes in part from the group's owners, investment groups Cinven and Investcorp, which have indicated an interest in cashing in on their investment through a public offering or sale of parts or all of Avecia by the middle of the 2000s. The company in

the meantime is making strategic acquisitions to boost its core operations, such as its 2003 purchase of the chirals operations of Synthon Chiragenics. Avecia is led by CEO Jeremy P. Scudamore. In 2003 the company's sales stood at £485 million.

Born from a Breakup in the 1990s

Imperial Chemical Industries (ICI) long held the title of the United Kingdom's largest company. Formed from a merger of the country's three largest chemical companies—Nobel Industries, British Dyestuffs, and Brunner, Mond & Co—in 1926, ICI grew into an internationally operating conglomerate with more than 500 widely diversified subsidiaries operating throughout the world. ICI's focus tended toward the production of dynamite, chlorine, dyes, metals, and a variety of general chemicals, as well as agricultural chemicals and leather treatment chemicals. In general, the company concentrated on bulk chemicals, such as fertilizers, leaving the specialty chemicals realm to competitors.

By the 1970s, ICI had become a massive—and massively bloated—organization, generating little profit in proportion to its revenues. Part of the group's difficulties came from its over-dependence on low-margin bulk chemicals, as well as its production of its own invention, polyethylene, which by then was already under pressure from rising competition from Asian producers. Fertilizer also remained a core company product. Yet ICI's range of hundreds of products left it unfocused, even while it depended on a single area, bulk chemicals, for some 40 percent of its total products.

This situation started to change in the early 1980s, with the arrival of Sir John Harvey-Jones as the head of the company in 1982. Harvey-Jones began a ruthless cost-cutting program, closing several dozen of ICI's outdated manufacturing sites and slashing thousands of jobs from its payroll. Harvey Jones began the long process of reshaping ICI, reducing its reliance on bulk chemicals, shifting its focus from polyethylene and instead stepping up the group's investments in pharmaceuticals and fine chemicals, while also building up its specialty chemicals offering.

By the end of the 1980s, pharmaceuticals and fine chemicals—now grouped under a new division, ICI Bioscience—had grown into the group's largest revenue and profit centers. Meanwhile, ICI had been developing its specialty chemicals division, which was to form the core of the later Avecia. That business took off in the early 1980s, with the launch of a new type of polyester, produced by using genetically altered bacteria. The resulting thread found use as surgical stitching materials. It also pointed the way toward the group's entry into the biotech market in the 1990s. Other important Specialty Chemicals division products included biocides, used as chlorine alternatives for water treatment, and the development of a biodegradable plastic, Biopol. In the late 1980s and early 1990s, ICI's Specialties division also refined a myco-protein-based meat substitute, Quorn.

In the meantime, ICI had gone on a new buying spree, making a number of large-scale acquisitions. Among these were the chemicals division of Beatrice Corporation, in 1984, and Glidden Paint in 1986. The following year, after Harvey-Jones had retired, replaced by Sir Denys Henderson, the company bought Stauffer Chemical, a move that made ICI one of the world's largest agro-chemical companies, with sales of more than $20 billion. That acquisition, too, was to play a major part in the development toward the formation of Avecia.

Corporate Mitosis in the 1990s

Nonetheless, Specialties remained ICI's smallest division, accounting for less than 10 percent of its revenues. In the meantime, ICI once again appeared to be plagued by its inability to achieve focus. Although ICI had rebuilt itself around a dual core of chemicals and pharmaceuticals, including specialty chemicals, the two sides were in fact unrelated businesses and failed to achieve synergies between them. At the same time, each division's profits were too heavily reliant on a single product line. With prices falling rapidly in the bulk chemicals and pharmaceuticals market, accompanied by a global economic slump at the beginning of the 1990s, ICI's lagging stock price left it the target of a potential takeover by Hanson Plc, which began acquiring ICI shares in 1990.

ICI defeated that effort, and restructured in order to block any future takeover attempts. Nonetheless, ICI's share price stagnated, as the company slipped into losses. By 1992, ICI's losses mounted to nearly £600 million. The company at last gave in to shareholder pressure, announcing its plan to accomplish what it called a "hive-down" of its operations, splitting off its ICI Bioscience division as an autonomous company. The process, which required a team of several hundred over most of the year to come, involved separating ICI's nearly 500 subsidiaries into two separate operations. At the end of 1992, ICI announced a new name for its Bioscience division: Zeneca.

With more than 16,000 products and sales of more than £4 billion ($6.5 billion), Zeneca operated in three primary divisions: Pharmaceuticals, its largest operation; Agrochemicals; and Specialties, which included the group's work with Biopol and Quorn, as well as strong business providing pharmaceutical intermediates and other fine chemicals, grouped as the Life Science Molecules division. The Specialties division also grouped ICI's former leather chemicals business, operating under the Stahl name.

Zeneca's major focus, however, remained on its pharmaceutical development, with specialty chemicals receiving only a small share of the company's research and development funding into the late 1990s. In the meantime, the wave of mergers consolidating the global pharmaceutical industry began creating a new class of drug giants. A similar process was occurring in the specialty chemicals field, as a number of major players emerged to claim dominance in their targeted niche sectors. At the same time, the investment community began favoring "pure play" pharmaceutical and specialty chemicals companies.

These factors convinced Zeneca to undergo a new round of corporate "mitosis" and in 1998, the company announced its intention to sell off its specialty chemicals operations. The company began looking for buyers in early 1999. Yet Zeneca itself made the first move, announcing its intention to merge its pharmaceuticals side with Sweden's Astra, forming AstraZeneca in April of that year.

In the meantime, Zeneca Specialties began preparing itself for its de-merger by adding to its range of business. The company took a step in what was to become a major corporate direction in April 1999, when it acquired Covion Organic Semiconductors, a maker of light-emitting polymers (LEPs) owned by Hoescht, through its Aventis Research & Technologies wing. The purchase complemented Zeneca Specialties' existing businesses in Neoresins and other high-technology chemicals, which included an array of chemicals for inkjet technologies. LEPs, brighter, less expensive, and more energy efficient than LEDs, promised to become a dominant display technology at the dawn of the 21st century.

Finding an industrial buyer willing to purchase Zeneca Specialties as a single entity proved difficult. For a short period, AstraZeneca considered splitting the division up into its component parts, a move that might have generated a higher value for the company. Instead, AstraZeneca decided to open up the bidding to institutional investors, and in May 1999 reached an agreement to sell Zeneca Specialties to a management buyout sponsored by investment groups Cinven and Investcorp.

Under terms of the £1.3 billion ($2.1 billion) buyout agreement, Cinven and Investcorp, and CEO Jeremy Scudamore, agreed to maintain the company as a single entity for at least a year following the sale. The newly independent company then adopted a new name, Avecia Group PLC. (In December of that

Key Dates:

1992: Imperial Chemical Industries (ICI) announces its intention to split off its Biochemicals division.

1993: The Biochemicals division is spun off as Zeneca, and includes ICI specialty chemicals operations, renamed as Zeneca Specialties.

1998: Zeneca announces plans to split up into three separate companies, including the creation of a new company for its specialties operations.

1999: Zeneca Specialties acquires Covion LEP manufacturing group in Frankfurt, Germany; Zeneca merges with Astra, forming AstraZeneca, which then sells off Zeneca Specialties in a management buyout backed by Cinven and Investcorp; the company is renamed as Avecia, and acquires Boston BioSystems in a move to boost its Life Science Molecules (LSM) operations.

2001: Avecia begins selling off noncore operations to focus on LSMs and NeoResins, selling Novacote packaging, adhesives, and coatings business to Chimica Organica Industriale Milanese, in Italy.

2002: The company sells off the Stahl leather chemicals operation to Investcorp for EUR 375 million.

2003: The company acquires chiral technologies from Synthon Chiragenics; the company sells its mining chemicals division.

2004: The company sells its color additives and biocides operations.

year, Zeneca sold off its agrochemicals business as well, into a merger with Novartis creating Syngenta.)

Avecia began business with operations in five primary sectors: the fast-growing Life Science Molecules (LSM) and Specialist Colors and Display; and the more stable, if not mature, Biocides, color additives, and Stahl leather chemicals groups. Avecia quickly turned its expansion focus on its fastest-growing businesses, and in September 1999 made its first acquisition, of Boston BioSystems, for $6 million. The U.S.-based company, founded in 1996, had already gained a leading place as developer of oligonucleotides—also known as DNA molecules—complementing Avecia's own newly established DNA medicine plant, opened in Scotland in 1998 and expanded in mid-1999.

Narrowing Focus in the 2000s

LSM remained Avecia's key growth area in 2000, with an agreement to acquire the ribozyme manufacturing process and technology from Colorado-based Ribozyme Pharmaceuticals. In June of that year, the company acquired Torcan Chemical Ltd., based in Ontario, Canada. The company also boosted its Neoresins operations, forming Image Polymers, a 50–50 joint venture partnership with Mitsui Chemicals to develop biomodal toner resins.

Avecia now began the process of narrowing its focus to its high-growth businesses. In 2001, for example, it sold off its Novacote packaging, adhesives, and coatings business to Chimica Organica Industriale Milanese, in Italy. Then in 2002, the company sold the Stahl leather chemicals business—which represented more than one-third of Avecia's total revenues—to Investcorp for EUR 375 million ($335 million). Sales of noncore operations continued, including the group's mining chemicals business, bought by Cytec Industries in 2003; its color additives operation, acquired by Lubrizol in January 2004; followed by the sale of its biocides division to the United States' Arch Chemicals, for $210 million, in March of that year.

The pared-down Avecia nonetheless continued to boost its LSM and electronics materials operations. The group's fine chemicals division expanded its scope in 2003 with the purchase of the proprietary chiral technologies and other operations from Synthon Chiragenics in the United States. Yet a number of investment analysts criticized Avecia's drive toward focus, in part because much of the group's cash flow depended on the businesses sold off by the beginning of the century. Nonetheless, with Cinven and Investcorp said to be looking to cash in on their investment, the stripped down company appeared a strong candidate for a public offering—or even an acquisition by a larger partner. In the meantime, Avecia remained a leading player in the global specialty chemicals market.

Principal Subsidiaries

Avecia Inc. (U.S.A.).

Principal Competitors

Merck and Company Inc.; GlaxoSmithKline PLC; Pfizer Inc.; Bayer AG; Roche Holding AG; Celesio AG; Bristol-Myers Squibb Co.; Abbott Laboratories.

Further Reading

Alperowicz, Natasha, "Avecia Seeks Higher Growth," *Chemical Week,* January 9, 2002, p. 17.

"Avecia Expands North American Portfolio," *Speciality Chemicals,* June 2000, p. 168.

D'Amico, Esther, "Arch to Buy Avecia's Biocides Business," *Chemical Week,* March 10, 2004, p. 6.

Kennedy, Carol, *ICI: The Company That Changed Our Lives,* London: P. Chapman, 1993.

Scott, Alex, "Avecia Buys Synthon Chiragenics' Chirals Business," *Chemical Week,* February 19, 2003, p. 51.

——, "Avecia to Produce Anthrax Vaccine," *Chemical Week,* October 8, 2003, p. 22.

Van Arnum, Patricia, "Avecia Stakes Role in Specialties," *Chemical Market Reporter,* March 27, 2000, p. 30.

Walsh, Kerri, "Lubrizol to Buy Avecia's Color Additives Unit," *Chemical Week,* January 7, 2004, p. 9.

—M.L. Cohen

Banca Fideuram SpA

Piazzale Giulio Douhet 31
Roma
I-00143
Italy
Telephone: +39 06 59021
Fax: +39 06 59022634
Web site: http://www.fideuram.it

Public Company
Incorporated: 1968 as Fideuram
Employees: 1,995
Total Assets: $5.48 billion (2001)
Stock Exchanges: Borsa Italiana
Ticker Symbol: FIBK.MI
NAIC: 522110 Commercial Banking

Banca Fideuram SpA is Italy's leading assets management and investment banking group, with more than EUR 58 billion in assets under its control. Italian financial powerhouse San Paolo IMI, the country's largest commercial bank, controls nearly 74 percent of Banca Fideuram. Nonetheless, Banca Fideuram has long maintained operations independent of its parent company. Most of Banca Fideuram's business is focused on its core assets management services, which account for more than 80 percent of the group's total net revenues. The remainder is generated, in large part, through a range of retail banking services. Although Italy continues to account for the large majority of Fideuram's business, at 85 percent of its revenues, the company has been making a push into the broader European market since the late 1990s. The company has set up subsidiaries in Switzerland and Luxembourg. In 2000, Fideuram moved into France through the acquisition of that country's Wargny Associes, since renamed Fideuram Wargny, giving the company a strong brokerage arm. In Italy, Fideuram also acquired Sanpaolo Invest Network from San Paolo IMI in 2002. Fideuram has been active in the insurance business as well, particularly through its 76 percent holding of Fideuram Vita. In 2004, however, Banca Fideuram agreed to de-merge Fideuram

Vita as a separate company directly under San Paolo's control. Banca Fideuram is listed on the Borsa Italiana and is part of the exchange's MIB30 index of top Italian companies.

Mutual Fund Provider in the 1970s

Banca Fideuram developed as an offshoot of Italy's Instituto Mobiliare Italiano, or IMI, created in 1931 out of the chaos of Italy's post-World War I economy. Founded in large part to aid in the reconstruction of Italy's ruined business sector, IMI operations became more focused in the middle of the decade with the Banking Law of 1936. Under this legislation, which remained in place into the 1990s, IMI targeted the medium- and long-term loan market, providing funding for businesses as well as for public works projects. Over the next several decades, the bank developed a range of commercial banking services.

In the years following World War II and with the rising economy of the postwar reconstruction period, IMI developed a strong business in investment banking, asset management, and other private banking services. The decision of International Overseas Services in the late 1960s to withdraw from the operation of mutual fund investments opened a new opportunity for IMI. In 1968, IMI created a new subsidiary, Fideuram, which began offering the Luxembourg-based Fonditalia and Interfund mutual fund products to the Italian market.

The new company was backed by a team of more than 300 private bankers, who began promoting its products throughout the country. Into the next decade, Fideuram remained limited to promoting foreign fund investments. With the passage of new legislation in 1983, however, the bank gained access to the first mutual funds offered within Italy itself. In 1984, Fideuram began marketing Italy's first domestic funds, Imirend and Imicapital, backed by parent IMI.

Fideuram represented just one part of IMI's mutual funds and assets management operations, which by the late 1980s had grown into one of Italy's largest. Another important part of IMI's assets management business was Banca Manusardi, which functioned as IMI's inhouse bank, providing back-office processing for its mutual funds business.

Company Perspectives:

Mission: Banca Fideuram brings private investors highly-sophisticated portfolio management services that were previously available to institutional investors only.

At the beginning of the 1990s, IMI began making moves to streamline these operations ahead of the coming European economic unification, which, accompanied by new legislation and deregulation of the banking industry, promised a new era of banking competition in Italy. In 1987, the bank took Banca Manusardi public, with a listing on the Borsa Italiana. Next, IMI began preparing to merge its assets management businesses into the newly public company, a process that resulted, in 1992, in the merger between Banca Manusardi and Fideuram. The new company was then named Banca Fideuram with its shares listed on the Borsa Italiana.

International Assets Management Giant in the 21st Century

Banca Fideuram started out as a giant in Italy's investment banking sector, with 22 Fideuram bank branches and a nationally operating army of more than 2,200 sales agents working from 220 sales offices. The new Banca Fideuram also included insurance products, notably through subsidiaries Fideuram Vita (held at more than 76 percent by Fideuram) and Fideuram Assicurazioni, which was 99 percent owned by the bank. Mutual funds remained the company's primary focus, however, and, with control of such mutual fund products as Fideuram Gestioni and part-ownership of Imigest, another top Italian mutual fund, Fideuram was the clear market leader. By the early 1990s, Banca Fideuram controlled more than 21 percent of the total mutual fund market.

Fideuram grew strongly into the middle of the 1990s. By 1996, the company was valued among the top Italian public companies, and its listing was added to the prestigious MIB 30 index. By then, Fideuram had begun to diversify its product offering. Among the company's new products was a new "Umbrella Fund" launched in 1995 and modeled after the British-styled multilevel funds. In 1997, the company branched out into personalized financial planning and other private banking services through a partnership with the United States' Frank Russell group.

The late 1990s and early 2000s marked a new phase in Fideuram's growth as the company turned toward developing an international base of operations. In 1998, the bank established its first foreign subsidiary, in Luxembourg. This was followed in 2001 by the creation of a Swiss subsidiary, in the town of Lugano. By then, Fideuram had moved into the French market as well, when it acquired Groupe Wargny in 2000.

Wargny had been established in 1806 as the company Charge d'Argent de Change Warngy. Specialized in asset management and with a particular focus on brokerage services, Wargny had developed a strong business in providing back-office services to institutional investors by the 1970s. After

Key Dates:

1931: IMI, which specializes in medium- and long-term loans, as well as assets management services, is created in Italy.
1968: IMI creates a new subsidiary, Fideuram, to market Luxembourg-based mutual fund products.
1984: Fideuram launches the first Italy-based mutual fund.
1987: IMI lists the back-office subsidiary Banca Manusardi on the Borsa Italiana.
1992: IMI merges Manusardi and Fideuram and creates Banca Fideuram, which is listed on the Borsa Italiana.
1995: The "Umbrella Fund" is launched, in a first attempt at diversification.
1996: Fideuram is listed on the Borsa Italiana's MIB 30 index.
1997: Fideuram diversifies into private banking operations.
1998: The first foreign subsidiary is established in Luxembourg.
2000: Groupe Wargny, in France, is acquired, adding its brokerage services.
2001: A subsidiary is launched in Switzerland.
2002: Banca Sanpaolo Invest is acquired from parent San Paolo IMI.
2004: Fideuram agrees to de-merge the Fideuram Vita life insurance subsidiary to parent San Paolo IMI.

going public in 1982, Wargny had pioneered telephone-based financial transactions in France, with the launch of Telebourse in 1985.

The 1990s had marked a period of expansion for Wargny, which created a new subsidiary, Financiere Wargny, devoted to providing assets management and consulting services to the corporate sector. Wargny also began a period of acquisitions in the early 1990s, starting with its purchase of Societe de Bourse FIP in 1994. The company completed several more acquisitions through the 1990s, including Societe de Bourse Fauchier-Magnan in 1995, and Temps Reel Intermediation in 1996.

Wargny's expansion also included the opening of new offices in Lyon in 1994 and in Monaco in 1995. The company moved into new virtual quarters with the launch of its Internet-based e-broker site, Wargny.com, in 1999. That year, the company developed a new assets management operation, Wargny Gestion, backed by the purchase of Cap Finance.

Under Banca Fideuram, however, Wargny found a strong financial partner for its continued growth. In 2001, Fideuram consolidated its French presence, regrouping its operations in that country under a new subsidiary, Banque Privee Fideuram Wargny. Fideuram, in the meantime, had seen its own parent company grow strongly at the beginning of the century, through the merger of IMI with another leading Italian bank, San Paolo, creating San Paolo IMI. The subsequent merger of that bank with Banco di Napoli created one of Italy's largest publicly listed commercial banking empires.

The growth of Fideuram's international operations—which, by 2003, represented 15 percent of the bank's total net revenues—enabled Fideuram to sharpen its focus around a core of assets management and private banking services. In 2002, the group's operations were boosted through an agreement to acquire San Paolo IMI's own financial services and investment consulting arm, Banca Sanpaolo Invest. The addition of the new operation, with its own strong brand and more than 1,500 financial consultants, boosted the total assets under Fideuram's control from slightly less than EUR 50 million to more than EUR 59.6 million, placing Fideuram among the top assets management groups not only in Italy but throughout Europe.

With its newly fortified focus as a provider of financial services, assets management, and private banking, Fideuram moved to simplify its own structure at the beginning of 2004. In February of that year, Fideuram and San Paolo IMI announced their intention to de-merge Fideuram Vita from Fideuram, transferring ownership of the insurance operation to San Paolo IMI. That transaction awaited approval by Italian banking authorities.

In the meantime, Fideuram became embroiled in the controversy surrounding a law voted in by the Berlusconi-led govern-ment, which granted a tax amnesty on savings invested outside of Italy. In March 2004, a number of Fideuram sales agents in Italy and in Switzerland were accused of laundering clients' money, making it appear as if assets originated outside of Italy, in order to claim the tax amnesty. Fideuram agreed to cooperate with authorities, while asserting the company acted within the letter of the contested legislation.

Principal Subsidiaries

Banca Fideuram Luxembourg; Banca Fideuram Suisse; Banque Privee Fideuram Wargny (France).

Principal Competitors

Banca d'Italia; Banca Monte Parma S.p.A.; Banca Monte Dei Paschi di Siena S.p.A.; Banca Nazionale del Lavoro S.p.A.

Further Reading

"Banca Fideuram in Money Laundering Investigation," *Private Banker International,* March 26, 2004.
"Banca Fideuram Takes Full Control of Wargny," *European Report,* October 11, 2000, p. 600.

—M.L. Cohen

Bank of China

1 Fuxingmen Nei Dajie, Xicheng D
Beijing
100818
China
Telephone: 86 10 6659 6688
Fax: 86 10 6601 4024
Web site: http://www.bank-of-china.com

Government-Owned Company
Incorporated: 1912
Employees: 192,000
Total Assets: $433.78 billion (2003)
NAIC: 522110 Commercial Banking

Bank of China (BOC) is that country's oldest bank, and also one of its four largest banks, with assets of more than $433 billion—which also places it in the top 20 banks worldwide. BOC's function as the country's foreign exchange specialist for more than 40 years has made it the country's most international bank, with 580 branches and subsidiaries in 26 countries. At home, Bank of China is backed up by a network of more than 12,000 branch offices. Altogether, the bank employs nearly 193,000 people. Although BOC remains under Chinese government control, its subsidiary Bank of China (Hong Kong) Limited is the first Chinese-held bank to list on a foreign stock exchange. BOC offers a full range of traditional banking services, including commercial, private, and investment banking, foreign currency deposit and exchange services, as well as assets management and insurance services. BOC also holds note-issuing privileges in Hong Kong and Macau. Since the start of the 2000s, BOC has been undergoing a steady restructuring of its operations in order to shrug off the poor reputation of the Chinese banking industry in general as it prepares its own initial public offering (IPO). The bank's listing is slated for 2005 if it meets its restructuring targets—and the arrival of foreign banking competition after China's entry into the World Trade Organization.

Domestic Bank in the 1910s

Although China was the first civilization to introduce paper currency—in the 12th century—the country remained without a modern banking system until after the First Opium War in 1842. With China brought under colonial influence, the country opened up to foreign banks. In part by providing loans to the ruling Qing dynasty, the foreign banks quickly dominated China's economy.

Growing nationalist sentiment against the Qing government at the end of the century led to the first attempts to establish Chinese banks, beginning with the formation of the Imperial Bank of China in Shanghai in 1897. The Qing government responded by authorizing the creation of a new Chinese-owned bank in Beijing. The Bank of the Board of Revenue, as it was called, was created in 1905 and was jointly held by private citizens and the government. In 1908, the bank changed its name, to Da Qing Bank. At that time, the Qing government authorized the bank to issue money and oversee the treasury. Da Qing also coordinated the government's debts.

The Qing dynasty was overthrown during the republican revolution of 1911. The new provisional government, led by Sun Yatsen, authorized Da Qing Bank to change its name, to Bank of China. Now the Sun government's central bank, BOC became headquartered in Shanghai. In the meantime, the overthrow of the Qing dynasty and the Chinese monarchy led to the emergence of a large number of new domestic banks. These remained rather small, dwarfed by the more established foreign competitors.

BOC remained a central component of the Sun government through the troubled decades ahead. In 1928, BOC took on a new facet as the government's international exchange bank. This position was solidified with the opening of a branch office in London in 1929, marking the first time a Chinese bank had opened an office outside of China. BOC quickly extended its foreign network, and by the end of the 1940s had opened 34 branches outside of China, including a number of branches in Britain-dominated Hong Kong.

The arrival to power of the Communist government under Mao marked a new era for BOC as well. Foreign banks were forced to exit the country. At the same time, the domestic banking sector was brought entirely under government control and reformed into four primary bodies. BOC, which remained one of the country's four prominent banking operations, was then specialized as the government's foreign exchange bank, responsible for foreign trade and international banking operations.

BOC remained China's most public banking face as the country plunged into some three decades of political and economic isolation from the rest of the world. At the end of the 1970s, however, the Chinese government became determined to end its attempt at self-sufficiency, and instead initiated a thaw in its international relations—and a gradual relaxation of its economic policies.

Full-Service Banker in the 1990s

BOC played a primary role in reintroducing China to the global market. As such, BOC acted as an intermediary in negotiating a number of important trade agreements, such as the country's first energy loan agreement with the Export and Import Bank of Japan in 1979. The following year, BOC itself entered Japan, opening its first branch office in Tokyo. That year, too, BOC acted as the first Chinese bank to offer export sales credits. In 1984, BOC achieved another first, becoming the first Chinese bank to issue bonds on the foreign market. These came in the form of ''Samurai'' bonds worth ¥20 billion.

The thawing of relationships with China and the West enabled BOC to entered the U.S. market in the early 1980s as well, starting with the opening of its first branch office in New York in 1982. Meanwhile, the decentralization of China's banking system enabled BOC to come home, as it were. Throughout the 1980s and into the 1990s BOC established a powerful domestic banking network. At the same time, BOC developed a full range of both consumer and corporate banking services. Among these was the issuing of China's first credit card, the Great Wall Credit Card, in 1986.

Into the 1990s, BOC played a prominent role in adding new technologies, as the Chinese banking system rushed to catch up to its foreign counterparts. In 1991, BOC became the first Chinese bank to offer telephone-based banking services. In 1994, the bank also became the first to install an automated teller network and to begin issuing debit cards to its customers.

By then, BOC had become one of the pillars of China's foreign exchange reform, an important component to China's emergence as one of the world's most powerful economies at the beginning of the 21st century. BOC itself had begun to gain increasing stature on the world market. In 1994, the bank became the first in China to issue bonds to the U.S. market. In that year, also, BOC's Hong Kong subsidiary was granted the au-

thority to issue notes in colony, a privilege extended the following year to Macau as well.

In 1998, BOC extended its range of services again, founding BOC International Holdings Ltd. in Hong Kong as an investment banking specialist. That operation, backed by BOC's fast-growing international network of more than 500 foreign branch offices by the end of the decade, established itself as China's leading investment banker. By the end of the decade, BOC had entered the insurance market as well, founding Bank of China Group Insurance Co., which, together with BOC International, began building its own retail network on the Chinese mainland. This development enabled BOC to reposition itself along a three-pronged strategy of commercial banking, insurance, and investment banking.

Reforming for Competition in the 2000s

China's decision to join the World Trade Organization by 2006 promised to open the country's banking market to a new era of competition. The deregulation of the industry offered the prospect of free market-based growth within the sector, both the country's domestic banks and for their foreign competitors, eager to share in what promised to become the world's most vigorous economy. As part of the run-up to deregulation, BOC, like its state-controlled counterparts, was forced to institute a massive restructuring.

Indeed, decades of serving as the government's bank had led to years of corruption, bad loans, and spending to prop up the many inefficiently run government-owned companies in China. Particularly troubling for BOC, as for the other three main state-controlled banks, was its extremely high level of nonperforming loans. In some sectors, such as the entertainment sector, nonperforming loans ran as high as 60 percent of the bank's portfolio. Working with outside consultants, BOC began developing new loan criteria designed to push its nonperforming loan portfolio down to acceptable international standards. At the same time, BOC was able to look to the Chinese government for help in writing off parts of its nonperforming loan portfolio.

Into the 2000s, BOC had operated in Hong Kong through some 12 different banks and a credit card operation, with little to no coordination among them. In 2001, however, BOC merged these companies together to form a single, unified entity, Bank of China (Hong Kong) Ltd. The new bank now became Hong Kong's second largest bank, behind only HSBC. After more than a year spent integrating its operations, BOC Hong Kong was ready for the next stage in BOC's development: its public offering. Worth more than $2.8 billion, and oversubscribed by some 7.5 times, BOC Hong Kong's IPO marked a new milestone for the Chinese banking system, becoming the first Chinese-owned bank to go public.

The listing of BOC Hong Kong was widely recognized as the precursor for the public listing of parent BOC in the near future. By 2004, BOC had acknowledged its plans to go public, suggesting that its IPO might take place as early as 2005 if it met its own restructuring schedule. As part of the move toward listing publicly, BOC continued to push down its nonperforming loan levels—selling an additional 10 percent stake in BOC Hong Kong in December 2003 in a cash-raising effort. That sale

Key Dates:

1905: The Qing government gives authorization for the founding of Chinese-owned Bank of the Board of Revenue in Beijing.

1908: The bank changes its name to Da Qing Bank and begins issuing notes.

1912: After the overthrow of the Qing government, the bank changes its name to Bank of China (BOC), and becomes the central bank.

1929: BOC becomes the government's international exchange bank and opens its first foreign office, in London.

1949: After the Communist revolution, BOC specializes in foreign exchange operations for the government.

1979: BOC signs the first energy loan agreement between China and Japan as China launches its "Open Door Policy"; the bank establishes its first branch office in Japan.

1982: The bank opens its first branch office in the United States, in New York City.

1984: BOC becomes the first Chinese bank to issue bonds to the Japanese market.

1986: BOC introduces the first Chinese credit card.

1991: Telephone-based banking services are launched.

1994: BOC begins issuing notes in Hong Kong; the bank issues the first Chinese bonds in the U.S. market.

1995: BOC begins issuing notes in Macau.

1998: BOC International Holdings, the group's assets management business, is launched.

2001: BOC merges 12 Hong Kong banks and a credit card subsidiary to form Bank of China Hong Kong.

2002: BOC becomes the first Chinese bank to launch a public offering, listing Bank of China Hong Kong on the Hong Kong stock exchange.

2004: BOC begins preparations for its own public offering in 2005; the bank opens its first branch office in the Middle East, in Bahrain.

reduced BOC's stake in its Hong Kong subsidiary to just 66 percent.

BOC appeared to be coming closer to its IPO in 2004, especially after receiving a massive cash injection—taken from the country's huge foreign exchange reserves—in order to reduce still further its nonperforming loan levels. The bank also announced that it was actively seeking strategic investors as part of the process of going public. As it braced itself for the coming international competition, BOC also continued to expand its own foreign banking network. In April 2004, for example, BOC announced its intention to open a branch office in Bahrain, marking its entry into the Middle East market. With assets approaching $500 billion, BOC promised to remain a major player on the international banking stage.

Principal Subsidiaries

Bank of China (Hong Kong) Limited; Nanyang Commercial Bank, Ltd.; Chiyu Banking Corporation Ltd.; BOC Credit Card (International) Ltd.; BOC International Holdings Ltd.; BOCI Asia Ltd.; BOCI Asset Management Ltd.; BOCI Capital Ltd.; BOC Group Trustee Co., Ltd.; BOCI-Prudential Asset Management Ltd.; BOCI-Prudential Trustee Ltd.; Bank of China Group Insurance Company Ltd.; BOC Group Life Assurance Company Ltd.; Bank of China Group Investment Ltd.

Principal Competitors

Westpac Banking Corporation; Industrial and Commercial Bank of China; China Construction Bank; Agricultural Bank of China; First Pacific Bank.

Further Reading

"Bank of China Establishes First Middle East Branch," *Asia Pulse,* April 20, 2004.

"Bank of China Has Yet to Choose Where to List," *Asia Pulse,* April 15, 2004.

"Bank of China Prepares 2004 IPO by Selling 10% of BOC Hong Kong in Red Hot Markets," *Euroweek,* December 19, 2003, p. 14.

"Banking in China: The Future Is Clear," *Banker Magazine,* January 29, 2003.

"BOC Still Looking for Key Investors," *Standard,* April 9, 2004.

"Botox Shot," *Economist,* January 10, 2004, p. 65.

"Chinese Bank Breaks the Barriers," *Project Finance,* July 1999, p. 9.

Clifford, Mark, "The Bank of China's Real Scandal," *Business Week Online,* June 20, 2003.

——, "The Long March Begins," *Business Week,* August 5, 2002, p. 44.

—M.L. Cohen

Bank of East Asia Ltd.

10 Des Voeux Road Central
Hong Kong
Telephone: +852 2842 3200
Fax: +852 2845 9333
Web site: http://www.hkbea.com

Public Company
Incorporated: 1918
Employees: 5,400
Total Assets: HKD 189 billion ($24.3 billion) (2003)
Stock Exchanges: Hong Kong
Ticker Symbol: BKEAY
NAIC: 522110 Commercial Banking

One of Hong Kong's oldest Chinese-owned banks, Bank of East Asia Ltd. (BEA) is also one of its largest, ranking in the top five among the city's banks in terms of deposits, and among the top ten in terms of its loan portfolio. BEA offers a full range of commercial banking services to the corporate and personal banking markets, as well as investment banking and a range of services geared specifically for the mainland China banking sector. BEA offers a variety of services, including foreign currency savings, mortgage and consumer lending, credit cards, online banking, syndication loans, as well as insurance products through subsidiary Blue Cross (Asia-Pacific) Insurance Ltd. The company also provides business, corporate, and investor services through another subsidiary, Tricor Group. Hong Kong remains BEA's center of operations, with more than 130 branches. Nonetheless, BEA has built up a strong international component, with operations in the United States and Canada and branch offices in much of southeast Asia. BEA is also highly active in China—the bank has maintained a presence on the mainland for some 75 years—with plans to play a primary role in the offshore renminbi market. Publicly listed BEA remains controlled by the founding Li family, represented by David Li as chairman and CEO.

Founding a Hong Kong Banking Institution in the 1920s

British banking institutions dominated colonial Hong Kong's banking sector into the 20th century. In the years following World War I, however, the colony saw the rise of a growing number of local, Chinese-owned banks founded specifically to provide banking services to the island's Chinese population. The Chinese banks were typically small, family-owned businesses. Yet they also provided the start for many of the city's wealthiest business empires.

One of the earliest and longest-lasting of the local banks was The Bank of East Asia (BEA). Four families, the Lis, Wongs, Kans, and Fungs, joined together to found their own bank in 1918 and began providing financial services to the local Chinese community. By 1919, the group's operation had grown enough to open its first headquarters, on 2 Queen's Road. While the other families retained their shares in the bank, the Li family proved the most active in its direction, and ultimately became BEA's chief shareholders—and one of the island's wealthiest families.

From the start, BEA had international ambitions and by 1920 had already established two branches outside of Hong Kong, opening offices in Shanghai, and another in the former Saigon, in Vietnam. That country remained a key foreign market for BEA, which opened a second Vietnamese branch in 1930 in Haiphong. By then, BEA had already grown into one of Hong Kong's most prominent locally owned banks, underscored by the construction of its distinctive new headquarters building in 1935.

The years of World War II, and China's communist-led Cultural Revolution, transformed Hong Kong's banking community. The Mao-led government now forced foreign banks to exit the mainland market. Only BEA was allowed to remain on the mainland, where its Shanghai branch maintained its operations, albeit on a limited scale. Nonetheless, BEA's presence enabled the bank, and the Li family, to establish strong ties with many of China's leaders. Ties with China's large expatriate community also led BEA to develop its international network, and particularly in the Southeast Asian region, where the Chi-

<table>
<tr><td colspan="2">

Company Perspectives:

Mission Statement: We at BEA strive to provide best in class financial services, always demanding the highest standard of professionalism and integrity of ourselves. With a commitment to quality of service, we focus on satisfying customer needs. We aim to grow, together with our customers, our shareholders and our colleagues.

</td></tr>
</table>

Key Dates:

1918: The Bank of East Asia is founded as a family-owned bank for the Chinese community in Hong Kong.
1920: Offices are opened in Shanghai and in Saigon, Vietnam.
1930: A second office is opened in Vietnam.
1952: A branch office is opened in Singapore.
1969: The bank becomes the first Chinese bank in Hong Kong to introduce computer technology.
1975: The bank becomes the first Chinese bank in Hong Kong to launch a credit card.
1979: The first foreign credit card is accepted in mainland China.
1982: The bank introduces automated teller machines to Hong Kong.
1984: The bank opens its first branch office in the United States.
1985: The bank opens an office in Shenzhen, China.
1990: The bank opens a branch in London.
1991: The bank acquires Blue Cross (Asia Pacific) Insurance Ltd.
1992: A subsidiary is established in Canada.
1995: United Chinese Bank in Hong Kong is acquired.
2000: First Pacific Bank in Hong Kong is acquired.
2001: The Grand National Bank in the United States is acquired, expanding corporate banking services to the West Coast.
2003: The bank upgrades its Beijing office to a full branch.

nese community quickly established itself as a driving commercial and industrial force. In 1952, BEA opened a new foreign branch, this time in Singapore.

In the late 1960s and through the 1970s, BEA played the role of an innovator among Hong Kong's Chinese banks. In 1969, the bank became the first Chinese-owned bank on the island to computerize its operations. The bank was also the first Chinese bank on the island to list its stock on the Hong Kong Stock Exchange, becoming one of the mainstays of the exchange's Hang Seng index. In another innovation, BEA joined with Bank of America to launch the first credit card based on the Hong Kong dollar in 1975.

By then, however, the bank was forced to withdraw from the Vietnamese market, as that country came under control of the communist government. Instead, BEA turned its attention to mainland China, where the first signs of a thaw had begun to show. The company's continuous presence in the mainland made it an important foreign partner for the Chinese government as it prepared to institute the economic reforms that were to transform China into the world's most vibrant market in the next century.

BEA became the first foreign bank to form a joint venture in China, joining in the creation of China-Beijing Air Catering Ltd. in 1979. In a move more closely related to its banking operations, BEA's credit card became the first foreign card to be accepted for use on the Chinese mainland.

International Bank in the 1980s

BEA continued to seek opportunities to expand its mainland presence, particularly with the creation of the Shenzen and Guangzhou free trade zones, across the channel from Hong Kong. BEA also partnered in the founding of Joint Electronic Teller Services Ltd., or Jetco, which became the first company to launch automated teller machines in Hong Kong, as well as in Shenzen and Zhuhai, and also on Macau.

David Li joined the bank in the early 1980s and became chairman at the middle of the century. The new generation of the Li family now stepped up the bank's expansion efforts, in preparation for the handover of Hong Kong to China slated for the middle of the 1990s.

BEA's growth followed two primary paths over the next two decades. The bank began a diversification effort, such as the launch of a life insurance joint venture with the United States' Aetna in 1983. The bank expanded its insurance operation again in 1991 when it acquired Blue Cross (Asia-Pacific) Insurance

Ltd. In 1984, the bank joined with Bank of China (Hong Kong) Ltd. to form the leasing joint venture Trilease International. The following year, BEA established a securities trading arm, originally called Tung Shing Securities Company, but which later changed its name to East Asia Securities Company in 1998. The company also became the cofounder of the first foreign financing company launched by a Chinese company, China International Finance Company Ltd., in 1986.

The second part of BEA's development came through a more aggressive international expansion. The bank especially began targeting markets with large Chinese populations, such as the United States, where it opened its first branch in New York in 1984. In 1986, the bank opened a new subsidiary on Grand Cayman Island. The following year, the bank established a branch in Guangzhou, then upgraded its office in Shenzhen to a full branch.

Further abroad, BEA opened a second office in the United States, in New York's Chinatown, in 1989, then opened its first office in Europe, in London, the following year. The company's Western development continued into the 1990s, with the opening of a new office in Los Angeles in 1991, and the formation of a subsidiary in Canada, as well as an office in Toronto, in 1992.

Mainland Ambitions in the New Century

Yet the Chinese mainland remained the company's primary expansion market. Through the 1990s, the company began opening new offices in most of the mainland's major urban markets, such as Xiamen in 1991, Dalian in 1992, Fuzhou, Taipei, and Beijing in 1993, Qingdao in 1994, Wuhan in 1995, and Tianjin in 1996. Although the company was restricted to opening representative offices in most of its new markets, during the 1990s it began receiving permission from the Chinese government-run Bank of China to upgrade its offices to full branch status. Such was the case in Dalian, in 1993, and Taipei in 1997.

While it continued to build up its international network in the late 1990s and early 2000s, BEA launched a still more aggressive expansion campaign in the late 1990s, now targeting growth through acquisition. In 1995, the bank reached an agreement to acquire United Chinese Bank Ltd., boosting its Hong Kong banking network by 19 branches. That bank was fully merged into BEA in 2001. BEA added another prominent Hong Kong bank, First Pacific, in December 2000, helping to boost the group into the top five among Chinese banks on the island. At the same time, the company considerably boosted its presence in the United States with the acquisition of California's Grand National Bank. That purchase enabled BEA to introduce its corporate banking services to the U.S. West Coast market.

In the new century, BEA once again acted as an innovator, becoming one of the first Chinese banks in Hong Kong to launch Corporate Cyberbanking services in 2000. In 2002, the company also became the first foreign bank to win approval to launch online banking services on the Chinese mainland as well.

The dawn of the 21st century represented new growth prospects for BEA. On the one hand, the bank continued to build up its mainland China business, becoming the first foreign bank to enter the northwestern province of Xian in 2001. In 2003, the bank upgraded its Beijing office to full branch status. The bank also began a new expansion drive into the southeast Asian region, entering Malaysia, Vietnam, the Philippines, Indonesia, and Taiwan. From a small family-owned concern, BEA had grown into a regional financial institution. The company's strong position in booming mainland China made it likely that BEA would remain a banking powerhouse into the new century.

Principal Subsidiaries

The Bank of East Asia (BVI) Limited; The Bank of East Asia (Canada); The Bank of East Asia (Nominees) Limited; The Bank of East Asia (Nominees) Private Limited; The Bank of East Asia (U.S.A.) N.A.; Abacus Share Registrars Limited; Bank of East Asia (Trustees) Limited; Blue Cross (Asia-Pacific) Insurance Limited; East Asia Asset Management Company Limited; East Asia Corporate Services (BVI) Limited; East Asia Facility Management Limited; East Asia Futures Limited; East Asia Property Agency (China) Company Limited; East Asia Property Agency Company Limited; East Asia Property Management (China) Limited; East Asia Secretaries Limited; East Asia Securities Company Limited; Friendly Registrars Limited; Progressive Registration Limited; Secretaries Limited; Standard Registrars Limited; Strath Corporate Services Limited; Tengis Limited; Tricor Investor Services Limited; Tricor Services Limited.

Principal Competitors

Westpac Banking Corporation; Sumitomo Mitsui Financial Group Inc.; HSBC Holdings PLC; Bank of Tokyo-Mitsubishi Ltd.; Bank of China Beijing; China Construction Bank; Agricultural Bank of China.

Further Reading

Cheung, Clare, and Michele Batchelor, ''Bank of East Asia Net Rises As Loan Provisions Shrink,'' *Bloomberg News,* February 10, 2004.

Hamlin, Kevin, ''Asia's Most Influential Bankers,'' *Institutional Investor International Edition,* August 1999, p. 41.

Lau, Justine, ''BEA's Jump in Profits Hints at Recovery,'' *Financial Times,* February 11, 2004, p. 28.

Loong, Pauline, ''The Challenge for David Li,'' *Asiamoney,* December 2002, p. 22.

Racine, John, ''Bank of East Asia Plays for Position in the High-Stakes Contest for China,'' *American Banker,* August 16, 1995, p. 5.

Ridding, Jan, ''Bank of East Asia Sees Better Conditions This Year,'' *Financial Times,* January 27, 1998, p. 27.

Robinson, Karina, ''An Iron Fist in a Velvet Glove,'' *Banker,* December 2001, p. 20.

—M.L. Cohen

BEST BUY™

Best Buy Co., Inc.

7601 Penn Avenue South
Richfield, Minnesota 55423-3645
U.S.A.
Telephone: (612) 291-1000
Fax: (612) 292-4001
Web site: http://www.bestbuy.com

Public Company
Incorporated: 1966 as Sound of Music, Inc.
Employees: 80,000
Sales: $24.54 billion (2004)
Stock Exchanges: New York
Ticker Symbol: BBY
NAIC: 443112 Radio, Television, and Other Electronics
    Stores; 443111 Household Appliance Stores; 443120
    Computer and Software Stores; 443130 Camera and
    Photographic Supplies Stores; 451140 Musical
    Instrument and Supplies Stores; 451220 Prerecorded
    Tape, Compact Disc, and Record Stores; 454110
    Electronic Shopping and Mail-Order Houses

Minnesota-based Best Buy Co., Inc. is the leading consumer electronics retailer in the United States, far outpacing archrival Circuit City Stores, Inc. in revenues if not in store count. In early 2004, the company's flagship Best Buy chain included more than 600 stores in 48 states (the exceptions being Hawaii and Wyoming) as well as 19 more in Canada. In addition to personal computers, computer peripheral equipment, and consumer video and audio products, Best Buy outlets, which are on average about 44,000 square feet in size, offer large and small appliances, ranging from refrigerators to coffeemakers, and entertainment software, including compact discs, video games, DVD and VHS movies, and computer software. In the early 2000s, Best Buy acquired two other chains: Seattle-based Magnolia Audio Video and Burnaby, British Columbia–based Future Shop. By early 2004, Magnolia Audio Video, formerly called Magnolia Hi-Fi, operated 19 stores in Washington, Oregon, and California offering high-end consumer electronics and providing expert design and installation services. These stores

are about 10,000 square feet on average. Future Shop, operating more than 100 stores throughout Canada, is that nation's largest electronics retailer, offering a wide selection of digital products, televisions, computers, music, and appliances. The average Future Shop outlet occupies approximately 21,000 square feet of retail space. Each of the company's business units also runs an electronic shopping web site on the Internet. Overall, Best Buy's revenue mix has consumer electronics generating 37 percent of the total revenues; home office products, 35 percent; entertainment software, 22 percent; and appliances, 6 percent.

Early History

Best Buy is the brainchild of the company's founder and chairman, Richard M. Schulze. In 1966 Schulze and a partner established Sound of Music, Inc. and opened their first store in St. Paul, Minnesota, in an attempt to capture a share of the Twin Cities' home and car stereo retail market. First-year sales reached $173,000. Four years later Schulze bought out his partner and proceeded to expand his retail chain; his product line, however, was limited to audio components until the early 1980s. Then, according to an Executive of the Year cover story for *Corporate Report Minnesota,* Schulze said, "The lights began to turn on." Writer S.C. Biemesderfer explained: "Schulze had come to realize that there wasn't much of a future in a market glutted with vendors, serving a shrinking audience of 15- to 18-year-olds with limited resources." His ability to alter the course of his company was enhanced by a weeklong management seminar he attended in 1981. Departing the seminar as a "reformed controller," Schulze saw the dynamic possibilities that lay ahead and turned them into reality.

His first step was to expand Sound of Music's offerings to include appliances and VCRs. Schulze saw sales quickly climb. In 1982 revenues reached $9.3 million; the following year the company renamed itself Best Buy Co., Inc. and firmly oriented itself toward an older, broader, and more affluent customer base. Then, in 1984, Schulze took another major step by introducing the superstore format and quickly capturing 42 percent of the local market. At the time the company operated just eight stores in the Midwest, but by 1987 this number had tripled, while sales and earnings had spiraled upward to $239 million and $7.7 million, respectively. In addition to greatly expanded warehouse size and product offerings, the superstore format meant significantly smaller margins to maintain its good service, low prices image. Meantime, Best Buy was taken public in 1985, raising $8 million through an IPO, and two years later gained a listing on the New York Stock Exchange (NYSE).

Price Wars in the Late 1980s

Of course Best Buy was not alone among upstart chains during the 1980s in capitalizing on the superstore format and such hot-ticket consumer items as VCRs. "But after a raft of these chains went public," wrote Mary J. Pitzer in 1987, "they expanded rapidly and began colliding head-on. As a result, many companies took a beating on profit margins and are now gravely wounded." It was, in a very real sense, the best of times and the worst of times for Best Buy. Although sales had practically doubled to $439 million in 1988, net earnings had declined by 64 percent. Price wars were the chief culprit, and they were still escalating to a frenzied pitch in Best Buy's core Twin Cities market, which Highland Superstores had boldly entered in early 1987.

For a while, both companies benefited from market share increases, if not profit gains, by the battle. Then, finally, a saturation point was reached, with too many stores in the same area competing for the same dollars. According to Biemesderfer, "Rumor had it that, as Best Buy limped into the fall of 1988 Schulze tried to sell his company to Sears and failed because of his demands for certain perks." Biemesderfer went on to write, "Schulze denies the allegation, but to this day, even his backers question his version of the story." Schulze's own explanation was as follows: "At no point in time were there ever any concerns or fears about the future of the company. . . . Our discussion with Sears Roebuck was simply an attempt to understand the interest they would have in supplying capital necessary to grow the company independently."

Despite the earnings downturn in 1989 (net profits for the year ending March 31 slumped 26 percent, to just $2 million) and the looming presence of Highland, revenues were still climbing, albeit more slowly. In Schulze's mind, the key to regaining the momentum of the mid-1980s was to stand out from the competition, for the average customer recognized little difference among superstores, with their discount prices, multiple-step purchase processes, commissioned salespeople, and

ubiquitous service plan and extended warranty packages. Schulze's answer? Concept II stores.

The unveiling of Best Buy's first Concept II stores in 1989 was the culmination of a daring new advance by Schulze. The idea behind Concept II was that the traditional superstore format was out of sync, in large part, with the needs or preferences of most shoppers. Shoppers were entering electronics discount stores with only a limited need for sales help and a desire for hassle-free buying (no service plan contracts, no waiting for merchandise from the back room, no switching from counter to counter). Thus the revamped Best Buy stores would feature well-stocked showrooms averaging around 36,000 square feet, fewer salespeople, more self-help product information, Answer Centers for those requiring personal assistance, and one-stop purchasing. As a veteran Best Buy analyst, quoted by Biemesderfer, proclaimed: "Concept II is the most innovative thing to happen in this industry—ever." The revenue Best Buy sacrificed in de-emphasizing service plans was compensated for by lowered employee costs. Stores without commissioned sales help now were able to operate at two-thirds of the workforce required in the past.

Continued Expansion in the Early 1990s

In April 1991, even before Best Buy had gotten around to converting its ten Twin Cities stores, loss-ravaged Highland exited the metropolitan area, conceding defeat and closing all six of its stores there. Best Buy itself reported a loss of $9.4 million for 1991, but this was due to a $14 million change in its method of accounting for extended service plans. From 1992 to 1993, Best Buy reported "the best financial performance in the company's 27-year history." In addition to its stunning increases in revenues and earnings, the fast-growing retailer opened 38 new stores and saw comparable store sales (sales from stores open at least 14 months) increase by 19.4 percent.

During the calendar year 1993, Best Buy opened nine more stores in Chicago, for a total of 23, to solidify its leadership position in the Midwest, and entered the key Circuit City markets of Atlanta and Phoenix with an additional 13 stores. Numerous other openings, including a small number of megastores (40,000- to 50,000-square-foot self-service warehouses emphasizing the emerging growth lines of prerecorded music and computers), brought Best Buy's tally to 151 stores by year-end 1993. At that point the only internal factor seriously saddling the company was a hefty 43 percent debt-to-capital ratio. Best Buy's "push" distribution system, however, in which products are automatically shipped to outlets based on computer analysis of past sales trends, along with its rapid turnover time and its expectation of rising sales per store, indicated that the company could hold its costs while continuing to expand.

Its greatest concern for the future was the bottom line impact of Circuit City's latest moves. Just as Best Buy had looked to the outer corridors of the country, Circuit City had looked inward. It, too, had embraced Chicago, where price wars began anew. The Virginia company also had plans to enter Kansas City, Missouri, and the Twin Cities in 1994.

By 1993 both superstore titans had virtually vanquished the remaining competition, which included such former number two retailers as Highland Superstores (forced to liquidate) and Dixons Group's Silo Holdings (forced to downsize and sell to Fretter Inc.). Best Buy's growth had been nothing short of spectacular. From 1989 to 1992 corporate sales rose annually by 23 percent, while the industry as a whole expanded by a yearly average of just 3 percent. From 1992 to 1993 revenues catapulted for the first time beyond the $1 billion mark, from $929 million to $1.6 billion, for an increase of 74 percent. During this same period net earnings soared 107 percent to just less than $20 million. Although Circuit City was a significantly larger and more stable company in the eyes of investors, with a history of wider profit margins and negligible debt, it was Best Buy that generated the most excitement on Wall Street. For the first half of 1991, Best Buy outshone all other NYSE stocks in percentage appreciation. With excitement, however, came volatility: in 1993 the stock nearly doubled within a three-month period but then dropped by 10 percent in a single day in mid-November.

Part of this roller-coaster pattern stemmed from Best Buy's increasingly heated battle with Circuit City, which had many analysts wary.

The roller-coaster ride continued into 1994, with Best Buy's stock hitting a high of $37 a share in April, then falling almost 40 percent in the next five months to $22. It rose again to $45 only to drop by December to $34. Competition with Circuit City remained fierce, with Best Buy challenging its archrival by entering its traditional strongholds in California, Washington, D.C., and Ohio. The head-on clash prompted renewed price wars, which Best Buy was positioned to withstand because of its low cost structure. Lowered prices, however, meant lower earnings for Best Buy. In the meantime, Best Buy moved forward with the introduction of its larger Concept III stores, which were 45,000 to 58,000 square feet in size and offered customers a greater selection of products and more information, particularly through hands-on displays.

The company's strategy of cutting service to help offer lower prices continued to cost the company suppliers. By 1995 the electronics manufacturer Hitachi had stopped supplying Best Buy, as had the appliance maker Kenwood. In addition, Whirlpool pulled its top-line Whirlpool brand from the store, although it continued to supply its lower-priced Roper brand. President of Mitsubishi Consumer Electronics America Jack Osborn explained to *Forbes* in 1995 that his company chose to sell through smaller retailers because they offer better service and cannot use their size to pressure Mitsubishi into offering lower wholesale prices. Osborn said at the time, "We will not be in a national chain."

In an effort to reverse this trend, Best Buy announced in 1995 that it would revamp its merchandising format for high-quality audio products. Brad Anderson, the president of Best Buy, told *Forbes* that the move was needed because, "We could not land some of the products we wanted."

Expanding Territory and Market Share in the Late 1990s

Despite these problems, Best Buy continued to broaden its territory and bolster market share. In 1995 the company added 47 new stores and moved into new areas, including Miami and Cincinnati. By late 1995 Best Buy was breathing down the neck of Circuit City in terms of market share. With 8.7 percent of the consumer electronics market, Best Buy stood only a tenth of a percent behind Circuit City.

The company added almost 50 new stores in 1996 and moved into additional new territories, including Philadelphia. Revenues rose to more than $7 billion in fiscal 1996 from 1995 revenues of $3 billion. Earnings, however, actually dropped, from about $58 million in 1995 to $48 million in 1996. This decline forced Best Buy to rethink its product offerings. For instance, the company began offering cut-rate compact discs in 1988 as a loss leader and pushed the idea in the mid-1990s. Although people bought the low-priced discs, they did not stay to purchase the big-ticket, high-margin items. In 1997 the company cut back its CD selection and raised the remaining titles' prices slightly. It also added an assortment of books and magazines to its entertainment section. In addition, it decided to concentrate on higher margin items, such as computer peripherals, high-end appliances, and service plans.

By 1997 Best Buy had achieved its goal of becoming the industry leader, but it paid the price in profits, which had fallen to a dismal $1.7 million on revenues of $7.77 billion, translating into a minuscule profit margin of 0.02 percent. The company was particularly hurt that year by an ill-timed decision to borrow heavily to add $300 million of merchandise, mainly computers, for the 1996 holiday season. Soon after the products began arriving at the stores, chipmaker Intel Corporation announced plans to introduce its latest chip, a Pentium featuring MMX technology designed to improve the multimedia performance of personal computers. Demand for existing computers running earlier generation processors fell almost immediately. In early 1997, saddled with mountains of unsold PCs, Best Buy had to ask its creditors and vendors for an extra 60 days to pay its bills. Its stock tanked, dropping as low as $1.31 per share during the year, and finishing at $1.54, and it appeared that Best Buy might be destined for the dustbin, joining the legion of electronics retailers already there.

Schulze, however, brought in outside consultants from Andersen Consulting LLC for advice on a range of areas. Significant changes were made to the product mix, particularly by eliminating slower selling product lines and models; a greater emphasis was placed on selling service plans to customers; and ''high touch'' areas were added to the stores to help sell the burgeoning array of digital consumer products, such as cameras, cellular phones, satellite systems, and the fast-selling DVD player (first introduced in 1996) for which customers often needed more assistance. The management team was also overhauled; 40 new vice-presidents were hired, most coming from the outside and replacing much of the company's old guard. While this restructuring proceeded, the chain's expansion was slowed considerably, and only 12 new stores opened during the fiscal year ending in February 1998. The changes that were implemented succeeded in turning the company around. Inventory began turning over at a quicker pace, a key criterion for retail success, and net profits for 1998 jumped to a record $94.5 million on record revenues of $8.36 billion. By June 1998, following a two-for-one stock split, Best Buy's stock had soared 900 percent since February 1997, to a split-adjusted $36 per share.

In March 1998 Best Buy officially entered the e-commerce realm by launching an online music store at its bestbuy.com web site. Later in the year the company unveiled its Concept IV format. Typically sized between 43,000 and 45,000 square feet—actually slightly smaller than the previous model—these stores featured more high-tech products, had a more open layout with products grouped in such departments as home theater and digital imaging, and added cash registers throughout the store. The recently introduced ''high touch'' areas were retained, and additional hands-on features were added to the car audio section, where customers could now listen to different audio components in a ''Boom Room'' and a ''virtual car.'' As Schulze described it in the company's annual report: ''The new format reinforces our brand position as the destination for new technology in a fun, informative and no-pressure shopping environment.'' Also during 1999, Best Buy began selling digital televisions, and the company returned to more robust store growth, opening up 28 new stores and entering the New England market

for the first time. Revenues increased 21 percent for the year, hitting the $10 billion mark, while profits surged 138 percent, to $224.4 million. Best Buy's stock leaped 233 percent, prompting another two-for-one stock split in March 1999. Shortly thereafter, the stock was added to the prestigious Standard & Poor's 500 index.

Early 2000s: Reaching New Heights, Turning Acquisitive

During the next fiscal year, 47 more stores were opened, bringing the total to 357, as the chain moved into the major California markets of Sacramento, San Diego, and San Francisco, and also into Richmond, Virginia. Best Buy also introduced a new and smaller, 30,000-square-foot format designed specifically for markets with populations under 200,000. Nine of these stores were opened during fiscal 2000, and it was hoped that the new format would enable the company to continue its expansion even as its penetration of larger metropolitan areas neared saturation. The smaller stores were also expected to serve as models for a planned move into high-density urban markets, such as New York City, where it would be impossible to build massive superstores. Fiscal 2000 profits jumped 60 percent, to $347.1 million, and revenues grew smartly again, reaching $12.49 billion. This translated into a profit margin of 2.8 percent, significantly better than the 1.1 percent figure from two year's previous.

In June 2000 Best Buy relaunched an expanded bestbuy.com web site, which now offered not only music and DVDs but also consumer electronics, computers and peripherals, software, and games. In addition to choosing delivery to the home, customers could also elect to pick up the merchandise they ordered through the web site at a Best Buy store, and they could return items there as well. Customers at the stores, meanwhile, now had the option of logging onto an in-store computer to order products not available at that outlet. Best Buy entered into a number of partnerships to help with the content of the site and the technology behind it. The most prominent deal was with Microsoft Corporation, which invested $200 million for a 2 percent stake in Best Buy. In return, Best Buy began promoting the Microsoft Network as its preferred Internet service to buyers of new computers. Microsoft also agreed to give bestbuy.com ''prominent and preferred placement'' on several Microsoft web sites. Bestbuy.com quickly became one of the most visited e-commerce sites on the Internet.

Among the 62 new Best Buy stores opened during 2001 were 15 located in the greater New York City area. The first store on Manhattan opened the following year. In August 2000, through an agreement with Whirlpool Corporation, Best Buy stores began selling KitchenAid brand appliances. Next, Best Buy turned acquisitive. In December 2000 the company completed its first ever acquisition, that of Magnolia Hi-Fi, Inc. Bought for $88 million, the privately held Magnolia was based in Seattle and operated 13 high-end consumer electronics stores in Washington, Oregon, and California. (It had gotten its name from the Magnolia district of Seattle, in which its first store was sited.) The company generated more than $100 million in annual revenues from the sale of audio, video, and home theater products. Magnolia was founded in 1954 by Len Tweten, who built the firm into one of the most respected audio-video retailers in the nation based on the high quality of its merchandise, its dedication to exceptional customer service, and its renowned in-house repair/installation department. At the time of its acquisition, Magnolia had won *Audio/Video International* magazine's prestigious Retailer of the Year award for 22 straight years. Magnolia was headed by Jim Tweten, son of the founder, who continued to run the company as an autonomous Best Buy subsidiary. Best Buy hoped to leverage Magnolia's experience as a retailer catering particularly to early adopters of new gadgets, gaining strategies for maximizing sales early in the product life cycle, when profits were at their peak.

Having conquered most of its electronics retailing rivals, and gaining the upper hand over archrival Circuit City, Best Buy set off after new challenges with its next acquisition. In January 2001 Best Buy acquired Musicland Stores Corporation, based in nearby Minnetonka, Minnesota. The purchase price was $425.1 million in cash plus the assumption of $271.2 million in debt. Musicland, whose 1999 revenues totaled $1.89 billion, operated more than 1,300 stores in 49 states and Puerto Rico: approximately 650 Sam Goody stores (4,500 square feet on average), selling prerecorded home entertainment products, primarily in suburban shopping malls; 400 Suncoast Motion Picture Company stores (2,400 square feet), selling video, DVD, and movie-related products, primarily in metropolitan shopping malls; around 75 Media Play superstores (46,000 square feet), selling books, music, videos, software, and other products in select large to midsize markets; and some 200 On Cue stores (6,000 square feet), selling a variety of entertainment products in small town markets. Each of these stores also had a sister e-commerce site. Best Buy planned to retool some of Musicland's store formats and was particularly interested in gaining a presence within shopping malls by revamping the Sam Goody format through the addition of such consumer electronics goods as MP3 players, cellular products, and gaming items. In addition, shopping malls, a retail environment frequented by women and preteens, provided Best Buy with an opportunity to expand its core customer demographic, which had remained dominated by young to middle-aged males. Having largely conquered the nation's major markets, Best Buy also coveted the access to the smaller markets that would be gained through ownership of the On Cue chain, which served communities of 30,000 people or fewer.

Heightened competition and a slowdown in consumer spending cut into fiscal 2001 profits, which increased only 14 percent over the previous year. Revenues climbed 23 percent, reaching $15.33 billion. Despite the onset of a recession, Best Buy bounced back the following year, reporting record profits of $570 million on revenues of $19.6 billion, also a record. Sales of digital products reached 17 percent of total sales, compared to the 4 percent figure for fiscal 1999. This rapid growth in digital product sales also inspired a shift in the overall product mix: sales of consumer electronics products (33 percent of the total) surpassed the sales of home office products (31 percent) for the first time (in 1999 these figures were 27 percent and 36 percent, respectively). Among the 62 Best Buy stores opened in 2002 were the first ones in Seattle, which had been the only major U.S. market the chain had not penetrated.

That year Best Buy also set its sights north of the border in its quest for further expansion opportunities. In November 2001 the company spent $368 million for Future Shop Ltd., the largest consumer electronics retailer in Canada. Based in Burnaby, British Columbia, Future Shop operated 88 stores throughout Canada and had annual sales of $1.32 billion. Future Shop outlets had a product mix similar to that of a Best Buy store, although the specific brands and products carried differed. At an average of 21,000 square feet, the typical Future Shop was also considerably smaller than a Best Buy, but the key difference was that the Canadian chain used commissioned sales associates, a practice that Best Buy had so famously—and successfully—done away with years earlier. Future Shop had been founded by Hassan Khosrowshahi, who opened the chain's first outlet in Vancouver, British Columbia, in 1982. He later expanded the chain throughout the remaining Canadian provinces and even made an abortive move into the U.S. market in 1992, opening 28 stores in five states and losing millions before beating a hasty retreat. Khosrowshahi relinquished his position as chairman and CEO following the takeover, but Future Shop's president and chief operating officer, Kevin Layden, a former Circuit City executive, stayed on to head up the new Best Buy subsidiary.

Returning to the Core: 2003 and Beyond

Despite the completion of this acquisition, Best Buy pushed ahead with a previously planned expansion of the Best Buy chain into Canada, opening eight stores in the Toronto area in the fall of 2002. The company appeared confident that it could successfully operate the dual Canadian brands given their distinguishing characteristics. Meanwhile, in July 2002 Schulze turned over his CEO duties to Vice-Chairman Brad Anderson, who had also served as president and chief operating officer since 1991 and had been with the company since 1973. Schulze remained involved in the company he founded as chairman and continued to be the largest shareholder in the company, owning a stake of nearly 17 percent.

As the Best Buy chain pushed past the 500-store mark in 2003 with the opening of 67 new stores in the United States, including the first stores in Alaska, Idaho, Utah, and West Virginia, the situation at the Musicland chains was deteriorating. Sales at music retailers were ratcheting down not only because of the downloading of music over the Internet that had been made steadily more popular by Napster and other online music services but also because consumers were increasingly buying the cheaper CDs that were now being offered by such mass merchants as Wal-Mart Stores, Inc. and Target Corporation. Musicland's mall-based chains suffered a further blow with the dwindling of mall traffic post-9/11. Best Buy announced in April 2002 that it would rebrand the On Cue stores under the more nationally known Sam Goody name. Then in January 2003, 90 Sam Goody stores were closed, along with 20 Suncoast outlets. Musicland continued to lose money, however, and in March 2003 Best Buy announced it would sell the entire division. During 2003 Best Buy took $410 million in charges to write down the value of its Musicland acquisition, and coupled with additional charges of $90 million, net profits for the year totaled just $99 million. In another early 2003 development, Best Buy shifted its corporate headquarters from Eden Prairie, Minnesota, where it had operated out of eight scattered buildings, to a more compact 37-acre campus in nearby Richfield.

In June 2003 Best Buy offloaded Musicland, essentially giving the unit away to Sun Capital Partners Inc., a private investment firm based in Boca Raton, Florida. Paying no cash in the transaction, Sun Capital simply assumed Musicland's debt and lease obligations. In what was perhaps an understatement, Anderson told the *Minneapolis Star Tribune* that "this was a very expensive, but a powerful learning experience for Best Buy." Investors reacted positively to Best Buy's return to its roots. The stock had performed poorly ever since the Musicland acquisition, but during the 2003 calendar year, shares of Best Buy ascended 124 percent. In December, Best Buy rewarded those shareholders who had stuck with the company by issuing its first dividend ever of 30 cents per share. In November 2003 the Best Buy chain opened its 600th U.S. store, during a fiscal year in which 78 new Best Buys made their debut. In September, meantime, Magnolia Hi-Fi adopted the more contemporary name of Magnolia Audio Video, a move that accompanied that chain's entrance into the Los Angeles market. Magnolia, now 22 outlets strong, was just beginning to recover from a severe post-9/11 downturn in sales of high-end electronics.

Fueled by a 7.1 percent increase in comparable store sales, the newly refocused Best Buy rebounded with its best year ever in fiscal 2004. Overall revenues rose 17 percent, reaching nearly $25 billion, while net income totaled $705 million. During the next year, Best Buy planned to open 60 more U.S. stores, including the first store in Hawaii, as well as ten Best Buys and three Future Shops in Canada. Faced with the ongoing challenges of shorter product cycles, severe downward pricing pressure, and heightened competition from mass merchants, Best Buy was also in the process of rolling out a new store concept, one the company described as "customer-centric." In addition to featuring more high-tech digital gadgets, particularly products promoting the integration of multiple technologies, the new stores were customized to meet the needs of local markets. They also placed a greater emphasis on high-end electronics coupled with service and installation—taking a page from the Magnolia playbook. Toward this same end, Best Buy had bought Minneapolis-based Geek Squad, Inc. in October 2002 for about $3 million. Founded in 1994, Geek Squad was a computer-maintenance company providing at-home/in-office technology support services. Through these initiatives, Best Buy hoped to stay ahead of its many rivals in what was perhaps the most ruthlessly competitive segment of the retail market.

Principal Subsidiaries

Geek Squad, Inc.; Magnolia Hi-Fi, Inc.; Best Buy Canada Ltd.; Future Shop Ltd. (Canada).

Principal Competitors

Circuit City Stores, Inc.; CompUSA Inc.; Wal-Mart Stores, Inc.; CDW Corporation; RadioShack Corporation; Staples, Inc.; Office Depot, Inc.; Amazon.com, Inc.; Boise Office Solutions; Sears, Roebuck and Co.

Further Reading

Bernstein, Elizabeth, "Best Buy Breaks into Book Market," *Publishers Weekly,* September 1, 1997, p. 9.

Berss, Marcia, "High Noon," *Forbes,* December 20, 1993, pp. 44–45.

——, "We Will Not Be in a National Chain," *Forbes,* March 27, 1995, p. 50.

"Best Buy Files for New Stock Offering," *Minneapolis Star Tribune,* April 21, 1993, p. 1D.

"Best Buy Inc.," *Chain Store Age Executive with Shopping Center Age,* December 1992, pp. 64, 66.

Biemesderfer, S.C., "Laughing Last (Executive of the Year: Richard M. Schulze)," *Corporate Report Minnesota,* January 1992, pp. 33–42.

Brown, Ken, "Best Buy Faces a Continuously Rising Bar," *Wall Street Journal,* December 8, 2003, p. C1.

Carvell, Tim, "The Crazy Record Business: These Prices Really Are Insane," *Fortune,* August 4, 1997, pp. 108–15.

Haran, Leah, "Best Buy, Circuit City Raising the Stakes in Electronics Warfare," *Advertising Age,* September 27, 1995, p. 4.

"Hi-Fi Store to Superstore: Growing with Best Buy," *Chain Store Age,* December 1987, pp. 17+.

Hisey, Pete, "Facing a Rapidly Changing Competitive Landscape," *Retail Merchandiser,* February 2002, pp. 24+.

Kurschner, Dale, "Best Buy Harder," *Corporate Report Minnesota,* August 1997, pp. 66–71.

Levy, Melissa, "Best Buy Cuts Musicland Loose," *Minneapolis Star Tribune,* June 17, 2003, p. 1D.

Marcotty, Josephine, "Best Buy Co. Stock Takes a Beating As Possible Price War with Circuit City Looms," *Minneapolis Star Tribune,* November 12, 1993, pp. 1D-2D.

Masters, Greg, "Best Buy: On Top. Now What?," *Retail Merchandiser,* March 2003, pp. 15+.

Moore, Janet, "A Global Growth Strategy," *Minneapolis Star Tribune,* December 8, 2000, p. 1D.

——, "Best Buy's Global Ambitions," *Minneapolis Star Tribune,* August 15, 2001, p. 1D.

Palmer, Jay, "Stop the Music!," *Barron's,* January 27, 2003, p. 27.

Pitzer, Mary J., "Electronics 'Superstores' May Have Blown a Fuse," *Business Week,* June 8, 1987, pp. 90, 94.

Ramstad, Evan, "Best Buy Makes Two Acquisition Pacts," *Wall Street Journal,* December 8, 2000, p. B8.

"Sales at Best Buy Coincide with Rally of Its Stock," *Minneapolis Star Tribune,* July 9, 1993, pp. 1D, 7D.

Schafer, Lee, "Richard Schulze's Manifest Destiny," *Corporate Report Minnesota,* March 1995, pp. 26–31, 33.

Spagat, Elliot, "Best Buy Inc. Slims Down to Continue Expansion," *Wall Street Journal,* March 12, 2002, p. B4.

Sullivan, R. Lee, "Appealing to the Technophiles," *Forbes,* April 27, 1992, pp. 52, 54.

Tatge, Mark, "Fun and Games," *Forbes,* January 12, 2004, p. 138.

Voskoboynik, Henry, "Best Buy: A Best Buy Indeed," *Financial World,* September 1, 1994, p. 12.

Weimer, De'Ann, "The Houdini of Consumer Electronics: Dick Schulze Has Pulled Off an Astonishing Turnaround at His Best Buy Chain," *Business Week,* June 22, 1998, pp. 88, 92.

Wieffering, Eric, "Best Buy Clicks Online," *Minneapolis Star Tribune,* November 5, 2000, p. 1D.

——, "Has Wal-Mart Met Its Match?," *Minneapolis Star Tribune,* December 21, 2003, p. 1D.

—Jay P. Pederson
—updates: Susan Windisch Brown, David E. Salamie

Bob Evans Farms, Inc.

3776 South High Street
Columbus, Ohio 43207-4000
U.S.A.
Telephone: (614) 491-2225
Toll Free: (800) 272-7675
Fax: (614) 492-4949
Web site: http://www.bobevans.com

Public Company
Incorporated: 1957 as Bob Evans Farm Sales, Inc.
Employees: 40,446
Sales: $1.09 billion (2003)
Stock Exchanges: NASDAQ
Ticker Symbol: BOBE
NAIC: 722110 Full-Service Restaurants; 311612 Meat
   Processed from Carcasses

Bob Evans Farms, Inc. owns and operates more than 520 full-service, family restaurants in 22 states, mainly in the east north central, mid-Atlantic, and southern regions of the United States. Most of these operate under the Bob Evans Restaurant banner, but there are a handful of Bob Evans Restaurant and General Store outlets, which are combined restaurants and gift shops, as well as nine Owens Restaurants located in Texas. About 83 percent of the company's revenues are generated by its restaurant operations. The remaining sales come from Bob Evans's food products operations, which include seven production facilities in Hillsdale, Michigan; Galva, Illinois; Bidwell, Springfield, and Xenia, Ohio; and Richardson and Sulfur Springs, Texas. These operations also are supported by a distribution center in Springfield, Ohio. The company produces and distributes fresh, smoked, and fully cooked pork sausage and ham products under the Bob Evans, Owens Country Sausage, and Country Creek Farm brands, as well as a variety of other complementary food items sold in the refrigerated and frozen sections of grocery stores. The company's food products are distributed through more than 15,000 grocery stores in 30 states.

Early Years

Bob Evans Farms got its start when founder Bob Evans began preparing farm fresh sausages for the 12-seat, 24-hour restaurant—the Bob Evans Steak House—he opened in 1946 in Gallipolis, Ohio. Although the restaurant was a success, the difficulty Evans experienced in obtaining high-quality sausage prompted him in 1948 to start making his own from hogs raised on the farm. Favorable reports from his customers, many of whom were truck drivers who bought ten-pound tubs of the sausage to take home to their families and friends, prompted Evans to take some time away from his restaurant and concentrate on building a business to distribute the sausage products. He delivered the product himself and operated his sausage business only during the cool months of the year when storage was possible. Eventually distribution was expanded to grocery stores and, as the popularity of his sausage grew, Evans invited grocery store managers to come to the family farm, known as the Homestead, in Rio Grande, Ohio (Gallia County), to witness the sausage-making process.

The Homestead, where Evans and his wife Jewell raised their six children, was once an inn and stagecoach stop and is now on the National Register of Historic Places. Visitors may hike or ride horses on the farm's 1,100 acres of rolling hills or visit the farm's museum and authentic log cabin village. Craft fairs and other special events are held at the farm on many weekends during the tourist season, which runs from Memorial Day weekend through Labor Day weekend.

In 1953 a group of friends and family recognized the growing demand for Bob Evans Farms Sausage and became business partners. When a packing plant in Xenia, Ohio, came up for sale, the partners, led by founding Chairperson Emerson E. Evans, bought it and went into the sausage business on a larger scale. Sausage distribution was expanded into southwestern Ohio. The Xenia plant not only allowed for increased production of Bob Evans Farms Sausage but also gave many of the company's current top management their start in the business.

By 1957, the year that the company was incorporated as Bob Evans Farms Sales, Inc., 14 delivery trucks delivered fresh Bob Evans Farms Sausage overnight to central and southern Ohio outlets. By 1963, when the company changed its name to Bob Evans Farms, Inc., the sales territory covered most of Ohio. That same year, the firm went public, offering 160,000 shares of stock on the NASDAQ exchange at $9 per share. The first move out of Ohio was into Michigan in 1964. In conjunction with that year's introduction of sausage into Detroit, the company opened a third sausage plant in nearby Hillsdale, Michigan. The company also expanded west, beginning sausage distribution in Indiana in 1966 and in Illinois in 1968, and in 1974 Galva, Illinois—a concentrated hog producing area—became the site of Bob Evans Farms' fourth sausage production plant. The corporate headquarters were shifted from Gallipolis to 3776 South High Street, Columbus, Ohio, in 1968. There was also expansion of sausage distribution to the east, to West Virginia in 1969, to Pennsylvania in 1971, and to New Jersey in 1973. Bob Evans's cousin, Daniel E. Evans, became company chairman and CEO in 1971; Bob Evans continued serving as president.

First Bob Evans Restaurant: 1968

As the reputation of Bob Evans Farms Sausage grew, and more people began coming to his farm, Evans built another restaurant at the family farm in Rio Grande in 1962. The success of the Sausage Shop encouraged the company to open the first of what would become the Bob Evans restaurant chain in 1968. A further incentive to opening a restaurant was to maintain consistent returns for shareholders amid the ups and downs of the sausage business. Located in Chillicothe, Ohio, the pilot restaurant featured a design reminiscent of the farm, including a red exterior with white trim, which would eventually serve as the model colors for the entire Bob Evans chain. The restaurant's first menu, however, was not quite as successful as the building design. The Chillicothe restaurant was initially intended as a fast-food outlet featuring sausage sandwiches, hamburgers, french fries, and milk shakes. When business started to decline, a team of employees, including top management, closed the restaurant for one weekend, redesigned the interior as a sit-down, full-service facility, hired waitresses, put in a new menu, and reopened with great success.

Bob Evans Restaurants were initially known for their hearty breakfasts, available at the restaurants at all hours of the day. The company's reputation for high-quality breakfasts, however, began to overshadow the lunch and dinner hours, and some restaurants were so slow after 2 p.m. that they had trouble keeping staff. In response to this problem, management sought to develop and refine its menu to meet changing consumer tastes and lifestyles. To build the dinner business, platters of charbroiled ribs, chicken, and catfish were added, nightly dinner specials were offered, and advertising targeted both adults and families with children. Moreover, a greater variety was eventually introduced

into the Bob Evans dinner menu, including such dishes as veal parmigiana, spaghetti with meat sauce, and the Mexican-inspired Skillet Breakfasts and taco salad. Bob Evans was also active in promoting healthier menus by introducing a new summer menu with lighter, health-oriented foods such as grilled chicken salad, egg substitutes, and a new skillet breakfast line.

The Bob Evans Restaurant chain was built gradually over the years, financed completely through the company's own earnings and without any franchising or independent operators in order to ensure chainwide consistency. After expanding to Columbus in 1969, the company opened its first restaurant outside of Ohio in Florence, Kentucky, in June 1974. During the remaining years of the 1970s, the chain expanded to Indiana, West Virginia, Michigan, and Pennsylvania. It then moved into Illinois (1980), Tennessee (1984), Florida (1985), Missouri (1986), Maryland (1988), and Virginia (1989). The 100th restaurant opened in Schaumburg, Illinois, in November 1983, while the 200th began operations in Port Charlotte, Florida, in February 1988.

In the meantime, Bob Evans Farms reached an agreement in September 1980 to be acquired by nationwide food conglomerate Beatrice Foods Inc. The deal fell apart, however, three months later. At the end of 1986, Bob Evans retired as president of the company, which continued to be run by his cousin Dan. By the fiscal year ending in April 1988, the company was reporting net profits of $29 million on revenues of $395 million.

Establishment of Foodservice Division: 1991

In June 1991 the company established Bob Evans foodservice division, which sold food products directly to distributors and institutions. Items such as gravies, burritos, sausage and biscuit sandwiches, soups, ham, and specialty sausages were sold to convenience stores, restaurants, and noncommercial foodservice segments. In 1993, the food products segment made up 30 percent of sales for Bob Evans Farms. Bob Evans had established a position of market leadership in sausage products and a major competitive advantage based on the direct-store delivery system. The company distributed many types of sausage produced at its manufacturing plants, and its products gained a reputation for premium quality based on whole-hog ingredients, proprietary recipes, and unparalleled freshness. With a fleet of trucks making deliveries to more than 14,000 grocery stores each week, Bob Evans had a unique ability to place refrigerated products on grocery store shelves within 24 hours of making the products, circumventing the distributors and chain warehouses.

In order to maintain its market share and market success, the food products segment introduced many new items. For customers looking for products lower in fat, Country Lite Sausage was test-marketed in Chicago, St. Louis, Buffalo, Houston, and Dallas in the early 1990s, and was soon available in much of the company's marketing territory. Plans were also underway to enter the gourmet food market as several new items were in development and were slated for testing in the mid-1990s.

Several other new products included bratwurst, Italian dinner links, and smoked sausage. Moreover, Bob Evans Harvest Salads were targeted to consumers looking for a high-quality prepared item. The Harvest Salad line included tuna salad,

Key Dates:

1946: Bob Evans opens a 12-stool, 24-hour restaurant—the Bob Evans Steak House—in Gallipolis, Ohio.

1948: Evans starts making his own sausage for his restaurant and soon expands into distributing the product to grocery stores.

1953: Evans and a group of friends and family members join as partners in the sausage production operation; they buy a packing plant in Xenia, Ohio.

1957: The company is incorporated as Bob Evans Farms Sales, Inc.

1962: Evans opens a new restaurant—the Sausage Shop—on the family farm.

1963: The company changes its name to Bob Evans Farms, Inc. and goes public.

1964: The first expansion outside Ohio occurs, with the opening of a new plant in Hillsdale, Michigan.

1968: The first Bob Evans Restaurant opens in Chillicothe, Ohio.

1971: Bob Evans's cousin Daniel E. Evans becomes company chairman and CEO.

1974: The fourth sausage production plant opens in Galva, Illinois.

1983: The 100th Bob Evans Restaurant opens in Schaumburg, Illinois.

1987: Bob Evans Farms acquires Owens Country Sausage, Inc. of Richardson, Texas.

1988: The first Owens Restaurant opens in Irving, Texas.

1991: Mrs. Giles Country Kitchens, a producer of refrigerated deli salads, is acquired.

1992: The company opens its first Cantina del Rio, a Mexican-style restaurant and bar.

1996: The Cantina del Rio chain is shuttered.

1999: Mrs. Giles is divested.

2000: Stewart K. Owens becomes the first non–Evans family member to serve as CEO.

2001: Revenues top $1 billion for first time.

2002: The company opens a distribution center in Springfield, Ohio; its 500th restaurant opens in Canton, Michigan.

2003: A food production plant in Sulphur Springs, Texas, is purchased.

macaroni salad, Italian pasta salad, and others. This salad line complemented the sausage business, because sausage volumes were highest in the fall, whereas the salad business was at its best in the spring and summer.

Late 1980s–Early 1990s Acquisitions

The Bob Evans Farms food products division grew not only through new products but also through acquisitions. Owens Country Sausage, Inc., based in Richardson, Texas, was purchased by Bob Evans Farms on January 16, 1987, in a stock transaction worth nearly $16 million. Bob Evans Farms acquired all Owens's outstanding common stock in exchange for shares of Bob Evans Farms stock. Until the Bob Evans Farms acquisition, Owens was a privately held company.

Owens Country Sausage was founded in 1928 by Clifford Boyce Owens and was chaired by his son, Jerry Owens, in the early 1990s. Selling a variety of food products in the Southwest, Owens offered a new market for Bob Evans Farms and provided the company with a wealth of opportunities for restaurant expansion. The first Owens Family Restaurant, opened in Irving, Texas, in March 1988, retained the Owens name, but resembled the Bob Evans design and menu concept. By 1993 there were 13 Owens Family Restaurants in the Dallas/Fort Worth area.

Bob Evans Farms acquired Mrs. Giles Country Kitchens—a food production company operating in Lynchburg, Virginia—on September 13, 1991, from an affiliate of the Campbell Soup Company, for $2.9 million. Mrs. Giles, founded by Zena Giles in 1933, produced refrigerated deli salads and distributed most of its products in bulk, unbranded, to delicatessens around the United States. In May 1992, Bob Evans Farms upgraded several of the Mrs. Giles recipes and marketed them under the Bob Evans brand in Columbus and Cincinnati, Ohio.

Another acquisition occurred in March 1992, when Bob Evans Farms bought Hickory Specialties, Inc. for $3 million. Hickory specialized in charcoal products, grills, liquid smoke seasonings, and application systems. The company had two major divisions, Nature-Glo Charcoal and Zesti Smoke Flavor. Nature-Glo produced several lines of grills (under the Champion brand) as well as charcoal, hickory, and mesquite wood smoking chips. The charcoal and smoking chips were sold under the Mr. Quick, Old Hickory, and Mountain Hardwood names. The company also manufactured the Jack Daniel's line of charcoal and smoking chips. The company patented technology to produce a new line of gas grill briquets that provided a hickory or mesquite flavor. The Zesti Smoke Flavor division produced liquid smoke flavorings to the meatpacking and the processed food industries. Major customers included Nabisco, Kraft, Carnation, and Heinz. The commercial flavor products were used in the manufacture of such items as potato chips, pet foods, nuts, pharmaceuticals, smoked hams, and barbecue sauces.

Bob Evans continued its growth in foodservice sales as it increased its product line and marketed its products to more schools, hotels, convenience stores, and other foodservice customers. The food production operation expanded as well, opening another production facility in Springfield, Ohio, in August 1992, and the Bob Evans Restaurant chain moved into New York and South Carolina in 1990, Iowa in 1992, and New Jersey and Delaware in 1993.

New Restaurant Concepts and Strategies for Improvement in the Early 1990s

In the early 1990s, Bob Evans Farms management realized that in order to enhance future growth while retaining the commitment to quality, the company had to diversify. Although it developed a strong network of restaurant and sausage operations through a coordinated marketing and expansion strategy, the company needed to minimize dependence on the breakfast business and sausage products. The sausage business remained subject to volatile hog costs and, because of health concerns, continual declines in U.S. pork consumption. For this reason the company increasingly emphasized new developments in its restaurant business. Consequently, the restaurant segment generated approximately 70 percent of total revenues in 1993, up from approximately 52 percent in 1982.

In April 1992, Bob Evans opened its first Cantina del Rio, a Mexican-style restaurant and bar, in Columbus, Ohio. Bob Evans's entry into the Mexican food market was well planned. The Mexican food business was the fastest growing segment in the restaurant industry in 1991 at 18.3 percent. In order to create a quality restaurant and menu, Bob Evans chose Phillip Torres, the owner of the successful Guadalajaran Mexican Grille and Bar (located in Houston, Texas) to head the operations. Management was pleased with the initial results and anticipated further success because of the restaurant's atmosphere and recipes. Six more Cantina del Rios were scheduled to open in the Midwest in 1994.

Further expansion of the restaurant business included the development of Bob Evans General Store and Restaurants. Designed to recall the country stores of the mid-1800s, the stores were constructed of red oak and wooden pegs and featured ceiling-high shelves displaying country crafts and homemade goods. The adjacent restaurants featured gift shops that sold pottery and other craft goods, a restaurant with a new country-style menu, and an in-house bakery. The first General Store and Restaurant opened in April 1991 near Kings Island Amusement Park in Mason, Ohio, and over the next three years seven more went into operation. Intended for high-traffic sites near tourist attractions, resorts, and junctions of interstate highways, the Restaurants and General Stores were in direct competition with Cracker Barrel Old Country Stores, another restaurant and gift shop chain whose territory Bob Evans attempted to penetrate.

Another development in the restaurant segment was the launching of the Bob Evans "small town" restaurants. "Small town" outlets were smaller versions of the traditional Bob Evans family restaurants, featuring 90 percent of the chain's traditional menu and targeting locals in cities of fewer than 50,000 residents, many of whom used to travel up to 50 miles to enjoy a Bob Evans meal. The first unit was opened in Bellefontaine, Ohio, in the spring of 1993. It was hoped that this 3,200-square-foot, 96-seat version of the traditional restaurant would provide a boost to the company as it was less expensive to build and operate than traditional Bob Evans Restaurants and that it would allow the company to expand to smaller towns where building a traditional restaurant would not have been feasible. Several dozen of these smaller restaurants were subsequently opened, but these were all later converted to full-size Bob Evans Restaurants.

Even though the new restaurant concepts were certainly in the spotlight during the early 1990s, Bob Evans realized that the traditional Bob Evans and Owens Family Restaurants were the strength of the company. These restaurants generated average unit sales of $1.6 million annually, and all were company owned, with no plans to franchise. Bob Evans owned the buildings and equipment at every location and owned the land for nearly all sites. For these reasons the company focused on several strategies to improve these restaurants.

First, as part of its long-term strategy, Bob Evans was involved in a continual remodeling, renovating, and redesigning plan. All existing units, on a three-year basis, were given new coats of paint and were furnished with new carpeting and drapes. About every eight years the company purchased new furniture as well as new kitchen equipment. Renovation or remodeling costs per unit ran approximately $50,000 to $75,000.

Beginning March 4, 1991, a new Bob Evans prototype restaurant was unveiled, from a design featured in an Indianapolis restaurant. The new design was larger, consisting of 5,500 square feet, compared with 5,000 square feet in the original building. The dining room had more than half of the 150 seats designed for nonsmoking customers, a large foyer was added, and the restrooms were moved to the front of the building for the customers' convenience. While the new prototype featured an interior decorated in oak wood and light country colors, the Bob Evans style of food and logo remained the same.

Another pivotal change at Bob Evans was the enhancement of the restaurant manager position. As a result of the 1990 management restructuring, managers received higher compensation, stock options, and better training. Unit managers were given greater autonomy and increased accountability for the performance of their individual units. Managers were encouraged to localize their operations—from menu items to service strategies and in-store decorative accents—reflecting the taste of the community served, and were asked to send new product ideas and management approaches on to headquarters.

These company innovations resulted in a sharp decline in management turnover and an improvement in customer satisfaction. Bob Evans continually strove to enhance its benefit packages, providing medical coverage and paid holidays and vacations. Consequently, hourly employee turnover in 1993 was about half of the 300 percent industry average. In return, the company expected a commitment from its employees. Each new management employee underwent comprehensive training, including a 14-week program for new Bob Evans Restaurant managers, which helped to ensure that Bob Evans's standards of quality were upheld.

Another strategy aimed at enhancing the profitability of the restaurant segment and heightening customer satisfaction was the development of a point-of-sale (POS) computer system, which increased accuracy and efficiency in the restaurants. This highly specialized computer program handled customer orders and inventory, tracked sales trends, monitored buying patterns by region and unit, and kept a tally of store costs.

Refocusing on Core Restaurant Operation: Late 1990s and Beyond

In January 1994 Stewart K. Owens, grandson of the founder of Owens Country Sausage, was named chief operating officer and executive vice-president of Bob Evans Farms, having previously served as group vice-president of food products and president of Owens Sausage. In August 1995 he was named Bob Evans Farms' president and chief operating officer. Bob Evans Farms continued to expand on all fronts during this period. In February 1994 the company's 300th restaurant opened in Kent, Ohio. The food product line grew with the additions of maple sausage links and frozen biscuits and rolls in 1995, and bacon, ham steaks, and frozen entrees the following year. Distribution of Bob Evans Farms Sausage in Wisconsin began in early 1995.

Fierce competition in the restaurant sector hit the company's dining operations hard in the mid- to late 1990s. Same-store stores (sales at stores open more than one year) declined for much of 1995 and 1996, leading to depressed earnings of $29.2 million and $36.1 million for fiscal years 1996 and 1997, respectively. Seeking to turn around the core family-style restaurants, the company in 1996 closed down its 14-unit Cantina del Rio chain, which never quite met expectations. Late that same year, Bob Evans Farms reached an agreement to sell off Mrs. Giles Country Kitchens to an investment banking company, but the deal soon fell apart. In September 1996 the menu at Bob Evans Restaurants was revamped to replace some pasta dishes and contemporary American cuisine with more traditional and heartier items such as chicken pot pie, charbroiled catfish, and pork chops. The company also worked hard to improve service and cleanliness at the restaurants and to slow down turnover in staff. Backing this effort was an advertising campaign with a ''We're family'' theme. In the fall of 1997 Bob Evans began adding Carry Home Kitchens and Corner Cupboards to some of its restaurants; the former offered carryout customers home-meal replacement menu options, and the latter were small areas featuring a variety of gifts and novelties for sale. Early results from these changes were encouraging as same-store sales for the fiscal year ending in April 1998 were up 4.6 percent. Profits that year increased to $45.7 million on revenues of $886.8 million. Meantime, an accelerated pace of new restaurant openings—though slowed down in 1997—meant that the company's 400th restaurant, located in Columbia, Missouri, opened in August 1997, less than three and a half years after the 300th. The first restaurants in North Carolina and Massachusetts debuted in 1997, and Kansas got its first Bob Evans Restaurant in 1998.

To heighten its focus on its core restaurants, Bob Evans Farms divested two more peripheral businesses in April 1999: Mrs. Giles and the charcoal manufacturing business of Hickory Specialties (the liquid smoke portion of the latter company was retained), which sold for a combined $29.2 million; the two businesses generated less than $50 million in annual revenues. The restaurants now accounted for nearly 80 percent of total revenues for Bob Evans Farms, compared with the 75 percent figure that had prevailed for some time. During 2000, the company opened another two dozen restaurants and spent about $85 million as part of a remodeling effort that aimed to revamp about 60 percent of the existing restaurants. At the end of that year, Dan Evans, who was suffering from a heart ailment, retired from the CEO position, remaining chairman, with Stewart Owens replacing him and becoming the first non–Evans family member to hold that office.

Owens's tenure got off to a somewhat rocky start when he had to organize opposition to three shareholder resolutions that were voted on, and ultimately defeated, at the September 2000 annual meeting. Bob Evans Farms shareholders were an increasingly disgruntled lot. At the time of the annual meeting, the stock traded for about $17 per share, only a little better than what it sold for in 1987, and $6 less than the peak that was hit in early 1994. One of the defeated proposals, which called on the company to sell itself to the highest bidder, was initiated by Deborrah Donskov, daughter of founder Bob Evans. Evans supported his daughter's proposal and also offered to return to his previous role as advertising spokesperson for the company, a proposal quickly spurned by Bob Evans Farms. There was much discussion in the press about a reported rift between Bob and Dan Evans that had developed over the years. The cousins apparently did not always agree on the way the company should be run.

Dan Evans retired as chairman in April 2001, having served 30 years in that position. He remained on the board of directors, however, while Owens added the chairmanship to his duties. That same month the company opened a restaurant in its 22nd state, Mississippi. For the fiscal year ending that month, Bob Evans Farms reported that its revenues surpassed the $1 billion mark for the first time.

Although the company maintained a much slower growth rate over the next two years, profits jumped from $50.8 million to $75.1 million in 2003, while net profit margins increased from 5 percent to 6.9 percent. Bob Evans Farms opened 27 restaurants in 2002 and 29 the following year. In October 2002 the company's 500th restaurant opened in Canton, Michigan. Also during 2003, a new restaurant prototype was tested in Zanesville, Ohio, that cost about $150,000 less to build than the previous version because of a smaller footprint, fewer decorative elements, and a smaller porch. The new design also sported a separate entrance for carryout orders, a design element that was increasingly common among casual-dining restaurants.

On the food products side, the firm successfully rolled out a new refrigerated potato product line, which included home fries, hash browns, and regular and garlic-flavored mashed potatoes. In May 2002 a new line of frozen, microwavable products called Brunch Bowls debuted. This line included such selections as country gravy and sausage with potatoes, and grilled chicken and potatoes. The Bob Evans Express line was introduced into grocery stores in February 2003. This product line featured three varieties (original, maple, and lite) of fully-cooked, microwavable sausage links. Another significant development on the food products side was the September 2002 opening of a $6 million, 55,000-square-foot distribution center in Springfield, Ohio—the company's first such facility. Also during 2002 Hickory Specialties, the smoke flavorings subsidiary, was sold to Kerry Group plc, an Irish food product manufacturer, for $16.3 million.

In June 2003 the company purchased a 56,000-square-foot food production plant in Sulphur Springs, Texas. In November of that year the company reopened the plant, where it began producing its SnackWiches line of convenience sandwich items for the retail, foodservice, and convenience store markets. Also during the fall of 2003, the Bob Evans Restaurant chain rolled out its Dinner Sensations line of entrees in an effort to boost dinner business. The line included four protein-rich choices: T-bone steak, grilled chicken, pork chops, and salmon fillet. Another effort to increase dinner business came via the testing of a curbside carryout service in which customers parked in designated spaces where they could pick up and pay for their orders from their cars. Such efforts made it clear that Bob Evans Farms was determined to remain one of the key players in the U.S. family-dining sector, while keeping its commitment to quality and ''down on the farm'' hospitality.

Principal Subsidiaries

Owens Country Sausage, Inc.; Owens Foods, Inc.; Owens Country Foods, Inc.; BEF Aviation Co., Inc.; Bob Evans Restaurants, Inc.; Bob Evans Restaurants of Michigan, Inc.; Bob Evans Restaurants of Indiana, L.P.; Bob Evans Transportation Company, LLC.

Principal Competitors

CBRL Group, Inc.; Shoney's, Inc.; Applebee's International, Inc.; Denny's Corporation; Brinker International, Inc.; Waffle House, Inc.; IHOP Corporation; The Restaurant Company; American Hospitality Concepts, Inc.

Further Reading

Amatos, Christopher A., ''Texan Leads Drive to Update Image at Bob Evans Farms,'' *Columbus Dispatch,* February 28, 1994.

''Bob Evans Farms Chairman Says Company to Remain Independent,'' *Wall Street Journal,* January 2, 1981.

''Bob Evans Farms' Founder Cuts Links to Sausage Firm,'' *Wall Street Journal,* November 21, 1986.

Brammer, Rhonda, ''Hog Heaven Soon?,'' *Barron's,* February 17, 1997, p. 19.

Carlino, Bill, ''Bob Evans Goes Casual with Cantina del Rio,'' *Nation's Restaurant News,* May 13, 1991, pp. 3 + .

——, ''Bob Evans Shutters Cantina del Rio Chain,'' *Nation's Restaurant News,* August 19, 1996, pp. 3, 118.

——, ''Daniel E. Evans: From the Slaughterhouse to the Boardroom, Bob Evans Chief Drives Chain with Down-Home Smarts,'' *Nation's Restaurant News,* October 14, 1996, pp. 156, 158.

''Conservatism, Feud Slow Growth at Bob Evans Farms,'' *Wall Street Journal,* April 19, 1982.

Elder, Martin, ''Bob Evans Wins the Heartland,'' *Restaurant Business,* February 10, 1988, pp. 128–32.

Evans, Daniel E., *Bob Evans Farms, Inc.: Fine Family Restaurants and Farm Fresh Sausage,* New York: Newcomen Society of the United States, 1988.

''From Oink to Ah,'' *Forbes,* June 21, 1982, pp. 79 + .

Gebolys, Debbie, ''Bob Evans, 82, Offers Seasoned Pitch to Aid Company,'' *Columbus Dispatch,* September 8, 2000, p. 1B.

——, ''Bob Evans Sides with Dissidents But Namesake Company Defeats Shareholders' Shake-Up Proposals,'' *Columbus Dispatch,* September 12, 2000, p. 1E.

Gorman, John, ''At Bob Evans, Breakfast War Can't Hurt 'em,'' *Chicago Tribune,* April 28, 1986.

Lohmeyer, Lori, ''Bob Evans Plans Expansion, Push for Lunch, Dinner Crowds,'' *Nation's Restaurant News,* June 16, 2003, pp. 8, 89.

McKenna, Peter, ''Cheaper Goods Haven't Hurt,'' *Restaurant Business,* July 20, 1992, pp. 110–14.

Murray, Matt, ''In the Grinder: Lean Business Times Add to Family Friction at Bob Evans Farms,'' *Wall Street Journal,* October 22, 1996, pp. A1 + .

Newpoff, Laura, ''Cultivating the Farm: CEO-to-Be Owens Sees Plenty of Prospects to Expand Bob Evans' Restaurant Business,'' *Business First—Columbus,* October 8, 1999, pp. 1, 82.

Papiernik, Richard, ''Bob Evans: Up on Restaurants But Not So High on the Hog,'' *Nation's Restaurant News,* September 20, 1999, p. 11.

Peters, James, ''Bob Evans Growth Plan Falls Flat As Unit Expansion Falters,'' *Nation's Restaurant News,* December 3, 2001, pp. 4, 6.

Phillips, Jeff, ''Bob Evans Changes Style from Laid-Back to Flat Out,'' *Business First—Columbus,* May 13, 1991, pp. 1 + .

Scarpa, James, ''Branding,'' *Restaurant Business,* October 10, 1991, pp. 145–61.

Schlossberg, Howard, ''Bob Evans Farms Personifies Success,'' *Restaurants and Institutions,* March 4, 1987, pp. 118 + .

''Through the Years with Bob Evans Farms, 1953–2003,'' Columbus, Ohio: Bob Evans Farms, Inc.

Walters, Rebecca, ''Chairman Rides Herd on Leaner Bob Evans,'' *Business First—Columbus,* May 4, 1992, pp. 1 +

——, ''Smaller Is Better in Growth Strategy at Bob Evans Farms,'' *Business First—Columbus,* January 10, 1994, pp. 1, 31.

Wolf, Barnet D., ''Scrambled Earnings, Sales at Bob Evans Eating at Bottom Line,'' *Columbus Dispatch,* August 18, 1996, p. 1G.

Yanez, Luisa, ''Food Fight on the Interstate,'' *Restaurant Business,* September 20, 1992, p. 50.

—Carol Kieltyka
—update: David E. Salamie

Bob's Red Mill Natural Foods, Inc.

5209 SE International Way
Milwaukie, Oregon 97222
U.S.A.
Telephone: (503) 654-3215
Toll Free: (800) 349-2173
Fax: (503) 653-1339
Web site: http://www.bobsredmill.com

Private Company
Incorporated: 1978 as Moore's Natural Foods, Inc.
Employees: 1,121
Sales: $25 million (2003 est.)
NAIC: 311812 Commercial Bakeries; 445291 Baked
    Goods Stores

Bob's Red Mill Natural Foods, Inc. mills all common grains and many unique grains into healthful flours and meals, cereals, bread mixes, pancake and waffle mixes, and muffin and quick bread mixes. Its 400-plus products sell through 70 different distributors in both the natural food class of trade and the specialty grocer class of trade throughout the United States and Canada as well as through the company's onsite retail store. The company only purchases organically grown and Identity Preserved seed grown commodities (in accordance with the California Organic Food Act of 1990).

1978–88: The First Ten Years

The initial idea for Bob's Red Mill started in the 1950s when Bob and Charlee Moore lived on a five-acre dairy goat farm in northern California. Bob worked as a Firestone tire store manager, while Charlee stayed at home to raise the couple's three boys. Charlee valued whole grain foods, and her interest in grinding her own flour, coupled with Bob's lifelong love of machinery, started the Moores thinking about setting up a mill of their own. "Coupled with an interesting history, I wanted to eat right, live right, be independent, do something fruitful and healthy, work with my family and not contaminate the world," Moore said in *Horizon Air Magazine*.

Around the year 1800, high-speed steel roller mills ended the need for the old, slow-turning stone mills that had supplied the world with flour for centuries. However, modern grinding processes often pulverized the grains. Stone grinding, to the contrary, used flint-hard, quartz millstones that blended the germ, its oil, the bran, and the endosperm. The lower temperatures at which stone grinding took place preserved the "good fats," vitamins, and minerals of the grain. Moore learned what he needed to know about mill operations from old milling journals and books. After a chance reading in 1968 about old stone grinding flour mills, Bob visited more than 50 old flour mills around North America and the British Isles searching for usable millstones from the 1880s. With the help of an old miller who was inventorying old American gristmills, he was able to acquire several sets of stones from an old, water-powered flour mill in North Carolina in 1969, and, in 1972, he and his sons set up Moore's first operation in Redding, California.

In 1977, Bob and Charlee moved to Portland, Oregon, with the idea of going to seminary, but within six months, they had discovered and purchased a 19th-century flour mill near Milwaukie, Oregon. They painted the building red and began stone grinding grains into flours and cereals using two sets of stones from the former Boyd mill near Dufur in north central Oregon and other sets from old mills in Tennessee and Indiana. Their stone grinding process involved suspending grain above the mill in 2,000-pound sacks and pouring it across the chiseled surface of the slowly turning stones to turn it into a soft, warm flour that poured onto a narrow conveyor belt at the rate of 1,200 pounds an hour. The buhrstones weighed approximately 2,000 pounds— a bit larger and thicker than two manhole covers.

Moore's Natural Foods sold its products almost exclusively in the Portland area, and business grew steadily, helped along by the growing commitment on the part of consumers to natural foods. Among the mill's steady customers were both local health food stores (which Moore's supplied with its small, cellophane-wrapped bags of flours and larger bags for sale in bulk) and Safeway and Fred Meyer supermarkets. Then, in 1988, with annual sales approaching $3 million, an arsonist burned down the company's historic grist mill, destroying everything except the stone buhrs. Almost indestructible to begin

---

Company Perspectives:

Bob's Red Mill is dedicated to the production of natural foods in the natural way. With all the sophisticated knowledge of recent times, no machinery has yet been developed that grinds grain into flours quite as well as the flint-hard quartz millstones used by millers since Roman times. Bob's Red Mill products are still ground this way. Automated packaging equipment efficiently places our premium stone ground flours into colorful ''down home'' style bags that are recognized throughout the U.S. and Canada. Milling expertise gleaned from old milling journals, coupled with over 30 years of innovative, hands-on milling experience has given Bob Moore the hard-won ''secrets'' to milling success.

Key Dates:

1978: Bob and Charlee Moore found Moore's Natural Foods, Inc.
1988: The company mill is burned by an arsonist.
2002: Bob's Red Mill begins construction on a new multipurpose building.
2004: The company doubles its warehouse and distribution.

---

with, the stones were saved when hundreds of pounds of stored grain fell on them from the second floor during the fire and snuffed out the flames, keeping them from shattering in the heat, as well as preserving the gears that turned them.

1988–94: Bob's Red Mill Begins Broader Distribution

''After the fire,'' according to Moore, ''it took incredible effort to sustain business with Fred Meyer. I had a responsibility to stay in business for both my customers and employees.'' Friends flew Moore over the state of Oregon to search for another old mill, but Moore decided to reestablish his business in a Milwaukie, Oregon industrial park. The Moores borrowed $2.5 million to build a 60,000-square-foot warehouse that had plenty of storage, power, and space for expansion—and a sprinkler system—for the new Bob's Red Mill, Inc.

In 1996, the Moores brought on two new partners, Dennis Gilliam, who became vice-president of sales and marketing, and John Wagner, who became vice-president of administration in an effort to increase revenues rapidly and pay off the new company's debt. Gilliam had experience in the printing business and led the company to expand into wholesaling its products. He persuaded the Moores to attend a national trade show in California where the company hooked up with Quality Brokerage of California, a food brokerage that had just lost a national supplier. This connection led to another important one with Nature's Best, the company's first regional distributor.

Gilliam sought out other trade show opportunities for Bob's Red Mill. To distinguish itself at these shows, the company built an elaborate exhibit with large pictures of old grist mills and a miniature working mill that actually ground grains at the booth. ''We went all out for the first five years or so,'' Moore admitted in a 1999 *Oregonian* article. The strategy worked. In 1992, the company succeeded in persuading Chicago-based Kehe Food Distributors, Inc. to showcase the company's entire product line. Kehe opened doors to the company to accounts in new regions. By 1999, Bob's generated more than 90 percent of its sales by supplying wholesalers throughout the United States and Canada and had grown 310 percent since 1990. It had further broadened its distribution network in 1994 when Tree of Life in Florida became its first nationwide distributor.

1995–2004: Rapid Growth Culminates in New Construction

The rapid growth that followed brought new challenges for Bob's Red Mill, including debt. The company saved money by repairing its own equipment, creating its own production machinery, and buying used machinery from Seattle-based Fisher Mills, Inc. It also bought used equipment at auctions and used packaging equipment from Boyd's Coffee of Portland, which it was able to implement because coffee is the same granulation as ground cereals. However, despite cost, the company continued its practice of employing a three-stage screening and grain cleaning system, testing every load of its product for moisture, proteins, and purity, and conducting random tests for fiber and fat content at local laboratories.

By the mid-1990s, the company's sales were approaching $6 million. During the second half of the decade, revenues grew 25 percent annually. By 1999, business boomed as consumers stocked up on supplies in anticipation of Y2K. Mail-order profits leapt by 133 percent, while sales at the company's small store jumped 80 percent. The company, which by then had 40 distributors, 20 brokers, and web-based sales, added a 10,000-square-foot warehouse and bought three new milling machines.

Sales continued to increase at an average of 25 percent a year into the next century as consumers maintained their interest in eating whole-grain foods. With Safeway and Fred Meyer taking the company's products beyond North America, and General Nutrition Stores selling them in Saudi Arabia, Bob's Red Mills employed 80 workers on round-the-clock shifts. ''When times are tough, people move away from the more esoteric, more frou-frou foods and move back to the basics where they perceive a full value and good nutrition,'' Gilliam explained in a 2004 *Portland Daily Journal of Commerce* article. Bob's Red Mill responded to the greater interest in its products by launching five new wheat-free, gluten-free products and adding a gluten-free milling area and lab testing in 2001.

In 2002, it began construction on a new multipurpose building, its Whole Grain Store and Visitors Center. The two-story building, which housed the company's corporate offices, and mail-order warehouse and 50,000-square-foot manufacturing plant, also contained an 18-foot-tall operational water wheel, a working stone mill that used French buhrstones from the 1800s, a breakfast and lunch café, outlet store, bakery, deli, bookstore, historical milling equipment displays, and cooking classroom. Designed to resemble a 19th-century mill building, the building's interior featured heavy timbers and wrought iron connections.

Still needing more space, the company doubled its warehouse and distribution capacity to 65,000 square feet by moving its distribution facility half a mile down the road from its new building two years later in 2004.

"This is a proud moment for Bob's Red Mill," Moore had announced in a 2003 *Portland Daily Journal of Commerce* article. "We started this company with a dream to support the health and well-being of the community, and 25 years later, we have built a strong foundation in whole grain nutrition across the nation. Now we are able to share the history of stone milling and provide a first-hand look at how our hundreds of products can be used. Business is good, and we keep growing and growing." Business promised to keep on growing in 2004 as Gilliam represented the company at an Oregon Department of Agriculture trade mission to Seoul, South Korea, and Osaka, Japan.

Principal Competitors

General Mills, Inc.; Goya Foods, Inc.; Pepperidge Farm, Inc.

Further Reading

"Back to the Grindstone; Grist Miller Abandons Old-World Romance for Practical Solution," *Horizon Air Magazine* (XXXX), n.d.

Perry Sara, "A Couple in Love with the Daily Grind," *Oregonian*, August 17, 1997, p. L14.

Riege, Rick, "Bob's Red Mill Natural Foods Opens Store, Visitors Center," *Portland Daily Journal of Commerce*, October 27, 2003, pp. 1, 16.

Rumler, John, "Trade Shows Build Bob's Red Mill," *Oregonian*, January 29, 1999, p. B1.

—Carrie Rothburd

Bodycote International PLC

Hulley Road
Macclesfield
SK10 2SG
United Kingdom
Telephone: +44 1625 505300
Fax: +44 1625 505313
Web site: http://www.bodycote.com

Public Company
Incorporated: 1923 as G.R. Bodycote Ltd.
Employees: 7,400
Sales: £448.4 million ($716 million) (2003)
Stock Exchanges: London
Ticker Symbol: BOY
NAIC: 332813 Electroplating, Plating, Polishing,
    Anodizing, and Coloring; 332811 Metal Heat
    Treating; 332812 Metal Coating, Engraving, and
    Allied Services (Except Jewelry and Silverware) to
    Manufacturing; 531210 Offices of Real Estate Agents
    and Brokers; 541380 Testing Laboratories; 551112
    Offices of Other Holding Companies

The United Kingdom's Bodycote International PLC is the world's leading provider of metallurgical services to the steel, engineering, aerospace, defense, automotive, and other industries. The company has developed four core specialties: Heat Treatments, including metal joining processes using electron beam and laser welding, and vacuum and exothermic brazing; Metallurgical Coatings, using electroplating, mechanical plating, nickel and zinc alloy plating and other coatings technologies to provide anti-corrosion, anti-wear, decorative, and other surfaces; Hot Isostatic Pressing (HIPping), a method for hardening metals and other materials using high-temperature and high-pressure treatment techniques; and Materials Testing of a large range of materials, from metals to textiles to organic materials, using a variety of testing methods. Bodycote operates nearly 250 plants in 21 countries—primarily in North America and Europe, but with a limited presence in the Middle and Far East. The United Kingdom accounts for just 14 percent of overall group sales, which topped £448 million ($716 million) in 2003; North America represents 40 percent of sales, while the rest of Europe generates more than 45 percent of group sales. Traded on the London Stock Exchange, Bodycote is led by CEO John Hubbard.

Knitting Beginnings in the 1920s

The Bodycote International entering the 21st century bore little resemblance to the company founded in Hinckley, Leicester, in the heart of the English textile industry in the early 1920s. The original G.R. Bodycote Ltd. began as a textile manufacturer in 1923, and remained under the control of the Bodycote family into the 1950s. Bodycote, which went public in 1951, originally specialized in manufacturing underwear under the Guardian brand name, then added its own line of Aero brand outerwear, including raincoats.

By the late 1960s, Bodycote had come under the control of rapidly expanding British conglomerate Slater, Walker. Founded in 1964, with a market capitalization of just £3 million, Slater, Walker had expanded rapidly into a variety of industrial and financial areas. By the end of the 1960s, Slater, Walker's value had leapt to more than £280 million. The conglomerate by then counted more than 500 companies under its control, including Bodycote. As part of its acquisition by Slater, Walker, Bodycote then took over a number of textiles operations from its new parent.

Under Slater, Walker, Bodycote launched its own expansion and diversification effort. In 1969, Bodycote paid some £140,000 to acquire fellow Leicester knitwear manufacturer Arthur Gee, adding that company's line of women's outerwear. The following year, Bodycote acquired another textile group, Simla Textiles, a merchant converter, for £150,000, while targeting new acquisitions. By mid-1971, Bodycote had completed several more acquisitions, adding Smith Blankets, D. Spiro and Sons, Heathgate, Joyce Fabrics, Henshaw Knitwear, and Selwyn Textiles. In that year, the company reorganized its divisional structure around its three primary business areas of knitwear and outerwear manufacturing, blankets and household utensils, and textile merchanting and converting.

The company, initially focused on the U.K. markets, began exporting more of its products, and in 1971 set up a new export sales subsidiary. The company also took on a new name, Bodycote Holdings, with the original company, G.R. Bodycote, remaining as a subsidiary.

By then, however, Slater, Walker had already begun dismantling its industrial conglomerate ahead of its mid-1970s repositioning as an investment and financial services provider. In 1971, Slater, Walker began preparing to spin off Bodycote as an independent company. As a first part of this process, Slater, Walker backed Bodycote's acquisition of Valdown Jersey Fabrics, owned by the Dwek family. Under terms of the cash and shares agreement, Valdown's owners acquired 44 percent of the enlarged group—in which Valdown's operations accounted for 59 percent of revenues—and the right to increase their stake in Bodycote to up to 50 percent. At the same time, Arthur Bodycote, who had remained with the company after its acquisition by Slater, Walker, agreed to step down, and buy out G.R. Bodycote at the same time.

Changing Markets in the 1980s

Joe Dwek now became the driving force behind Bodycote's growth through the 1970s. Bodycote's first move was to turn to the international markets, and in 1972 the company paid £1.4 million to acquire Dutch textile group Ehco. The purchase marked the group's diversification into industrial work clothing and safety garments, and also brought it onto the European continent for the first time. Another purchase that year, of Taylor and Hartley Group, had added to the group's industrial clothing operation, as well as adding women's dress production. By the end of that year, Bodycote, now with sales of more than £15 million, was ready to regain its independence.

Renamed Bodycote International, the newly independent company included the former Bodycote and Valdown operations, as well as other Slater, Walker textile interests, including Brocklehurst Fabrics and Ormerod Brothers. Dwek continued the group's move into industrial textiles and household textiles, and in 1972 led the sale of the company's knitwear division to Stirling Group. Instead, the company made a new series of acquisitions, including Supercraft Garments and head- and eye-safety products and garments maker Wm Stephens in 1974. The company continued its exit from consumer textiles markets as it repositioned itself as a focused industrial textiles group. Bodycote also pursued its international expansion through the

decade, building a manufacturing presence in Germany and Sweden, and becoming one of Europe's largest integrated industrial textiles producers.

Yet the oil crisis of the 1970s, the resulting British recession, and especially the flood of cheap textiles from Asian markets at the end of the decade forced Bodycote to make an unusual decision. At the end of the decade, the company decided to abandon its traditional operating sector and instead move into a new industrial market altogether. That process got underway with the acquisition of Blandburgh Ltd., based in Macclesfield, in Cheshire. Dwek remained Bodycote's chairman, but now was seconded by Blandburgh's John Chesworth, who had founded the company in 1972.

Blandburgh had grown quickly into a major provider of heat treatment services in the United Kingdom, and formed the basis of Bodycote's transformation into a metallurgical services company. Bodycote quickly began making new acquisitions, picking up Zinc Alloy Rust Proofing from Astra Industrial Group for £700,000. Another company acquired at this time was the dyeing and finishing group William Denby and Sons, which primarily added its textile coating and laminating capacity to Bodycote. By the end of 1980, Bodycote had already reduced its reliance on textiles from 90 percent to just 10 percent of sales, and continued selling off the majority of its textile holdings into the early 1980s.

Bodycote continued to build its metal treatment capacity through the decade. A notable acquisition for the group came in 1983, with the purchase of Nemo Heat Treatments, based in Stockport, adding its specialty in vacuum hardening techniques. Not all of Bodycote's expansion involved metallurgical services. In the mid-1980s the company made a foray into the packaging sector. Yet those operations remained marginal for the group and were abandoned in the late 1990s.

Metallurgical Services Leader in the 21st Century

Instead, Bodycote began refocusing itself as a metallurgical services specialist. A major step toward that goal came in 1990 with the acquisition of Metallurgical Testing Services Ltd., based in Edinburgh, Scotland, allowing the company to add a new prong to its range of metal treatment services. The next step came with the formation of Bodycote HIP—and the group's entry into the emerging Hot Isostatic Pressure market (HIP).

Having established its core competencies, Bodycote now began constructing its international presence. The company moved into North America, acquiring Industry Metal Technology Inc. in 1992. The company also opened operations in Belgium that year. At the same time, Bodycote established a number of new plants. While Heat Treatment remained its largest operational division into the next decade, the company successfully built its HIP division into the world's leading hot isostatic pressure specialist.

By the mid-1990s, Bodycote's industrial empire stretched over 50 plants worldwide. The North American market remained a primary target for the group. In 1996 the company bought Hinterliter Heat Treating, adding six new plants in the United States and Canada. That purchase was followed by the acquisitions of Texas-based Metallon in 1996, and Ohio's

Key Dates:

1923: The company is founded as G.R. Bodycote, a maker of underwear, in Leicester, England.

1951: G.R. Bodycote goes public on the London Stock Exchange.

1969: The company is acquired by fast-growing industrial and financial conglomerate Slater, Walker.

1972: The company acquires Valdown Jersey Fabrics, in a cash-share deal giving Joe Dwek the right to acquire up to 50 percent in the company; renamed Bodycote International, the company is spun off from Slater, Walker as an independent company; Bodycote then begins to specialize in the industrial textiles sector.

1979: Bodycote acquires Brandburgh Ltd., a heat treatment specialist, launching its transformation into a metallurgical services group.

1983: Bodycote acquires Nemo Heat Treatments, based in Stockport, adding its specialty in vacuum hardening techniques.

1990: Bodycote acquires Metallurgical Testing Services, in Scotland.

1991: The company forms Bodycote HIP, entering the hot isostatic pressing market.

1992: International expansion begins with Industry Metal Technology Inc. in the United States.

1996: The company acquires Hinterliter Heat Treating in the United States.

1997: The company sells off the last of its former industrial textiles operations; the company acquires Brukens Thermotreat in Denmark and HIT, based in France.

2001: The company acquires Lindberg, based in the United States, for $102 million.

2003: The company begins cost-cutting measures in response to a slump in the metals market.

Alpha Heat Treating Co. in 1998. Elsewhere, the group continued its expansion as well, such as its 1996 acquisition of Poole, England's Lymington Plating. The following year the group strengthened its Scandinavian presence with the purchase of Brukens Thermotreat in Denmark. In 1997, also, Bodycote became the leading heat treatment specialist in France with its acquisition of that country's HIT, which also gave the company operations in Spain, Portugal, and Italy.

By then, the company had sold off the last of its textiles operation—a maker of bulletproof vests—as well as its remaining packaging operations. Now fully focused on metallurgical services, Bodycote continued its global expansion. In 1999, the company acquired Metal Treating and Progressing Heat Treatment, in the United States, then Sweden's Dala Plating Gruppen. Back at home, Bodycote boosted its U.K. position with the purchase of Thermal Processing Group in 1998.

Bodycote continued its acquisition spree into the new century, buying up a number of companies in Sweden, Canada, and France. In 2001 the company stepped up its presence in Germany with the purchase of that country's Nussbaum Metal Technology. The company also gained market leadership in the United States that year through its acquisition of finishing specialist Lindberg, paying more than $102 million.

The company next prepared to continue its expansion into the Far East. Yet the economic slowdown at the beginning of the 21st century, coupled with a drastic drop in the aerospace and other key industries, put Bodycote under pressure. With revenues slipping, and profits falling, the company was forced to abandon its expansion drive, and instead institute cost-cutting measures, including the shedding of a number of employees. By 2003, the company had managed to stabilize itself, but forecasted a return to market growth only in 2006. Nonetheless, Bodycote clearly had positioned itself as a global leader in the metallurgical services sector.

Principal Subsidiaries

Bodycote de Mexico SA de CV; Bodycote H.I.P. Limited; Bodycote Heat Treatments Limited; Bodycote IMT Inc. (U.S.A.); Bodycote IMT NV (Belgium); Bodycote Industrial Materials Technology GmbH (Germany); Bodycote Materials Testing A/S (Norway); Bodycote Materials Testing BV (The Netherlands); Bodycote Materials Testing Limited; Bodycote Materials Testing Srl (Italy); Bodycote Metallurgical Coatings Limited; Bodycote Omnitest Inc. (U.S.A.); Bodycote Powdermet AB (Sweden); Bodycote Technitrol Inc. (Canada); Bodycote Warmebehandlung GmbH (Germany); Bodycote Ytbehandling AB (Sweden); Coutherm (France); Hauzer Coating Centrum BV (The Netherlands); HIT Industries (France); Staalharderij NEVE NV (Belgium); Traitement Thermique Belge (Belgium).

Principal Competitors

Arcelor S.A.; LNM Holdings N.V.; W.C. Heraeus GmbH und Company KG; Outokumpu Oyj; Engelhard Corporation; Rautaruukki Oyj; Wagon PLC; ODS B.V.

Further Reading

Aldrick, Philip, "Bodycote Needs Time to Knock Itself in Shape," *Daily Telegraph,* August 30, 2003.

"Bodycote Says No Full Recovery Until 2006," *Birmingham Post,* August 28, 2003, p. 19.

Dick, Philip K., "Bodycote Raises the Temperature," *Independent,* October 19, 1997, p. 5.

Jones, Sheila, "Bodycote Expands in US with $103M Lindberg Buy," *Financial Times,* March 24, 2000, p. 30.

Lumsden, Quentin, "Born-Again Chain Shows Its Mettle," *Independent,* October 27, 1996, p. 8.

Withers, Malcolm, "British Metal-Testing Firm Bodycote Plans Cost-Cutting Measures," *Evening Standard,* August 28, 2002.

—M.L. Cohen

Bruegger's Corporation

159 Bank Street
Burlington, Vermont 05402
U.S.A.
Telephone: (802) 660-4020
Toll Free: (888) 822-5379
Fax: (802) 652-9293
Web site: http://www.brueggers.com

Private Company
Incorporated: 1983
Employees: 1,600
Sales: $85 million (2002 est.)
NAIC: 311822 Flour Mixes and Dough Manufacturing
from Purchased Flour; 722211 Limited-Service
Restaurants

Bruegger's Corporation, the first major bagel chain in the United States, operates a chain of approximately 250 stores in 18 states. Bruegger's offers a selection of more than a dozen varieties of bagels and cream cheeses, as well as sandwiches, coffee products, salads, muffins, and scones. The company is owned by Sun Capital Partners Inc., an investment firm with a diverse portfolio of holdings.

Origins

Bruegger's played a leading role in what industry observers termed the "bagel wars," a reference to the heated competition among national chains who attempted to exploit the enormous popularity of bagels during the mid-1990s. Bruegger's founders, Nordahl Brue and Michael Dressell, were the first operators to field a national chain of bagel shops, and their early success touched off a wave of excitement. "Bagel fever" led to the bagel wars, as a host of national bagel chains staked their future on rapid expansion, endeavoring to achieve national dominance of what became a more than $2-billion-in-sales market. Bruegger's was the first company that could claim national dominance, but before it developed into an industry giant, the company's founders followed a measured and methodical approach to growth.

Brue and Dressell first met each other in 1980. Both men lived in Burlington, Vermont, where Brue worked as a lawyer and Dressell worked as a commercial builder, operating his own construction company. The pair met when Dressell's construction company employed Brue's law firm. Their introduction led to talks about starting a business together, with each expressing a desire to enter the fast-food segment of the restaurant industry with a low-cost item tailored for customers with busy lifestyles that would be largely resistant to the capriciousness of the economy. As the vehicle to drive their entrepreneurial careers, the partners selected the bagel, which was largely unavailable outside ethnic metropolitan enclaves until the 1970s. It was a propitious decision, one that positioned Brue and Dressell to capitalize on the burgeoning demand for bagels. According to a research firm that charted food trends, per capita consumption of bagels increased 169 percent between 1984 and 1993, the formative years of Bruegger's history.

Brue and Dressell used their own money to start Bruegger's, convinced that their focus on a single item would prove to be successful. With the help of a baking expert in New York City, Brue and Dressell developed an authentic production process, boiling their bagels and hearth-backing them on site, adopting a preparation method used by Eastern European immigrants who first brought bagels to the United States in the early 20th century. By 1983, the partners were ready to open their first store, selecting Troy, New York, as the first market to be introduced to their concept. A bigger market than Burlington, and only a short drive away from Burlington, Troy struck Brue and Dressell as an ideal starting point for their enterprise. Stephan Finn, Bruegger's chief executive officer for much of the 1990s, offered his own explanation for the reasoning behind Brue's and Dressell's decision to select Troy rather than their hometown of Burlington for the company's debut. "They didn't want to embarrass themselves," Finn remarked, in a May 22, 1995 interview with *Nation's Restaurant News*.

Brue and Dressell did not rush headlong into expansion. After the February 5, 1983, opening of the first Bruegger's, the partners wanted to make sure they had sufficiently honed the operational and design complexities of their concept before unveiling it to their neighbors in Burlington, much less before they took the bold step toward national expansion. Brue and Dressell risked failure to arrive at success, developing a plan to open six units in six markets over the course of six years—the pair's six-plus-six-plus-six business plan—to see what worked and what did not work. They experimented with different layouts of stores, and they selected some challenging markets. In the years following the opening of the Troy location, Brue and Dressell opened stores in markets such as Boston, but they also selected markets that tested the Bruegger's concept more fully, exposing it to the same sort of challenges that would be presented once they moved forward with national expansion. During the 1980s, they opened Bruegger's units in eastern Iowa, Minneapolis-St. Paul, Minnesota, and Raleigh-Durham, North Carolina, testing the acceptance of their bagel concept in markets not readily associated with an "ethnic" delicacy found almost exclusively in pockets of metropolitan areas.

After thoroughly testing the strengths and weaknesses of the Bruegger's format, Brue and Dressell became convinced of the viability of their business model. In the early 1990s, they began opening stores at an accelerated pace. Between 1990 and 1993, Brue and Dressell built Bruegger's into an 84-unit chain, enjoying enough confidence to bring the concept to their hometown, the site of the 38th Bruegger's opened. They also realized their own limitations and hired a veteran of the food industry, Stephan Finn, to help expand the company. Finn had spent years working for Burger King. By the end of this initial expansion spree, the partners were ready for the chain's next big leap. In late 1993, they began to franchise Bruegger's, a decision that was made only after the company-owned stores began to attract educated and affluent clientele. Through franchising, the Bruegger's chain achieved its greatest growth, quickly turning into the national behemoth that convinced other entrepreneurs to jump into the bagel business.

Franchising Beginning in the Early 1990s

With the help of Finn, Brue and Dressell developed a franchising program whose design promised growth and stability. They only recruited individuals with experience in foodservice and they required franchisees to become owners in Bruegger's by purchasing $350,000 worth of the company's preferred stock. Further, prospective franchisees were required to commit to developing a minimum of ten stores in each of the markets they operated.

As the Bruegger's franchising program made its debut, the retail bagel segment began to exhibit tremendous growth. Between 1994 and 1996, bagel sales increased 240 percent in the United States, developing into a $2.3 billion market. For Bruegger's, the surge in growth attracted a crowd of entrepreneurs more than willing to sign on to the company's franchising program. Within 18 months of franchising its concept, Bruegger's grew into a 155-unit chain with stores in 16 states. Systemwide, the company generated $81 million in sales in 1994, ranking as the largest bagel chain in the nation. The market's second largest competitor, New Jersey-based Manhattan Bagel Inc., trailed far behind, collecting $15 million in sales in 1994. Bruegger's widened its lead in 1995, recording an explosive rise in sales that lifted its annual revenue volume above the $220 million mark. The company expected to reach nearly 300 units by the beginning of 1996 and 1,000 stores by the end of 1998. By the following year, Bruegger's executives expected to reach $1 billion in sales. Clearly, the mood was optimistic at the company's Burlington headquarters. "We intend to dominate every market we enter," Finn remarked in a July 17, 1995 interview with *Nation's Restaurant News*.

The prognostications made in mid-1995 reflected the confidence of Bruegger's executives. The company had swept across the country and secured a commanding position in one of the fastest growing segments of the foodservice industry. Its lead over the second largest chain suggested that the company may have already won the race for national supremacy by achieving great strides at the start, but no one could have predicted how frenetic the chase would become from 1995 afterwards. As it turned out, Bruegger's main rival in the race ahead would not be Manhattan Bagel but a company that was gearing up for expansion in 1995. At a presentation given by Finn in mid-1995, a group of foodservice operators, investment analysts, and bankers gathered to listen to the wisdom of the bagel industry's leading operator. In attendance was Scott Beck, chairman and CEO of Boston Chicken Inc., who was preparing to enter the fast-growing retail bagel market with a new chain of stores that were expected to debut under the Einstein Bros. banner. Beck's entry into the market, along with the competition presented by a host of other nationally oriented chains, greatly intensified the race for national dominance, creating what pundits referred to as the bagel wars. "It's not there yet, but the bagel wars will come," the operator of Big Apple Bagels said in a July 17, 1995 interview with *Nation's Restaurant News*. "It will be like the yogurt wars of the late 1980s and early 1990s," he added.

1996 Acquisition by Quality Dining

As the need to expand at a rapidly accelerated pace gripped every competitor with national ambitions, initial public offerings (IPOs) served as the quickest way to obtain the resources to pay for expansion. Within an 11-month period beginning in November 1995, four bagel chains completed IPOs, giving investors a chance to place their bets on the bagel wars. As its competitors turned to the public marketplace for their capital, Bruegger's took an alternative route to filling its expansion coffers. In the spring of 1996, Bruegger's announced it was being acquired by Quality Dining Inc. in a stock deal valued at $145 million. Based in Indiana, Quality Dining was formed in 1982, beginning as a franchisee of Burger King restaurants.

Quality Dining began operating Bruegger's stores as a franchiser in 1994 and acquired rights to Chili's Bar and Grill, Grady's American Grill, and Spageddies Italian Kitchen restaurants in the years immediately preceding its deal with Brue and Dressell. The acquisition was completed in June 1996, when Quality Dining gained control over the Bruegger's chain, which operated 332 units at the time the transaction was completed. Finn stayed on as president and chief executive officer, stewarding Bruegger's fortunes as an independent subsidiary of Quality Dining. Brue and Dressell became substantial minority shareholders in Quality Dining, holding a 26 percent interest in the company.

The corporate marriage between Quality Dining and Bruegger's was an unmitigated disaster. Quality Dining expanded the chain rapidly, often paying too much for poorly located sites. Bruegger's franchisees began to revolt. Less than a year after the acquisition was completed, Brue and Dressell had had enough, announcing in March 1997 that they planned to pursue an auction of Quality Dining's various restaurant holdings. Quality Dining's stock, which traded at $34.35 per share when it acquired Bruegger's, plummeted following the acquisition, dropping to $7.25 per share by the spring of 1997, which meant Brue and Dressell's 26 percent stake in Quality Dining was worth far less than when they sold Bruegger's to the company.

As the Bruegger's chain's vitality wilted under the stewardship of Quality Dining, the other competitors in the bagel segment advanced across the country, expanding at a rapid pace. By mid-1997, Boston Chicken's bagel chain, which earlier had acquired Noah's Bagels to become Einstein/Noah Bagel Corp., had passed Bruegger's to become the largest operator in the country. In the fall of 1997, the situation with Quality Dining was resolved, with Brue and Dressell emerging as the successful high bidders for the bagel business they had created. The founders acquired Bruegger's in a deal valued at $45 million. Finn resigned shortly before Quality Dining announced the divestiture, leaving to join a Minnesota-based, quick-service Chinese food chain named Leeann Chin.

In the wake of the Quality Dining debacle, Brue and Dressell attempted to salvage what they could of the chain's former success and begin anew. The late 1990s were years of retrenchment for the founders, as they exited unprofitable markets and shuttered ailing stores. When Bruegger's was acquired from Quality Dining in the fall of 1997, there were more than 475 stores scattered throughout nearly 30 states. Before Brue and Dressell could entertain the idea of embarking on any expansion drive of significance, they needed to give Bruegger's a strong foundation again.

Recovery in the 21st Century

As Bruegger's entered the 21st century, its escape from the wild excitement of the 1990s was cause for some celebration. The company had suffered from the fast-paced expansion that pervaded the retail bagel segment, to be sure, but it had escaped. Some of its competitors had not escaped, such as Einstein/Noah Bagel Corp., which filed for bankruptcy in April 2000. By the beginning of the 21st century, Bruegger's was ready to grow again, having trimmed its store count to 275 units, primarily by shuttering franchised units. Geographically, the company narrowed its scope as well, pulling out of many unprofitable markets across the country and abandoning cities in Texas, Colorado, and the Pacific Northwest.

Despite hopes for expansion, the Bruegger's chain contracted during the early years of its third decade in operation. The company's store count dropped to 250 units as it contested with recessive economic conditions and its hangover from the bagel wars. Renewed hope for growth arrived in early 2004, however, when the company gained a benefactor. In January 2004, Boca Raton, Florida-based Sun Capital Partners Inc. bought Bruegger's from Brue and Dressell for an undisclosed price. Sun Capital specialized in leveraged buyouts of leading, yet struggling companies of all types. Under Sun Capital's management team, led by Jim Greco, the promise of expansion returned. ''We think it was a business that needed some attention,'' Greco said in an April 1, 2004 interview with the *Burlington Free Press.* ''For a number of years,'' he added, ''it was constrained because of its access to capital.''

As Bruegger's prepared for its future, the intervention of Sun Capital appeared to be a positive development for the chain. Greco and his team planned to open 100 units by 2006. New menu items were added to the chain's offering, including salads, muffins, and scones—additions meant to position Bruegger's in the fast-casual segment of the dining industry. Typically, once Sun Capital was able to restore luster to an acquired business, it sold the company or spun it off in an IPO within three to five years. Accordingly, there was a good chance Bruegger's would be on its own again by the end of the decade. In the interim, company executives were looking forward to reaping the rewards of the chain's affiliation with Sun Capital. ''We're very excited about the prospect of the months and years ahead,'' Bruegger's vice-president of marketing said in an April 1, 2004 interview with *Burlington Free Press.* ''What happened [with the changes enacted by Sun Capital] is really the starting point of the rebirth of Bruegger's in many ways.''

Principal Subsidiaries

Bruegger's Enterprises.

Principal Competitors

Brinker International, Inc.; New World Restaurant Group, Inc.; Panera Bread Company.

Further Reading

Allen, Robin Lee, ''Bruegger's Bagel Bakery,'' *Nation's Restaurant News,* May 22, 1995, p. 88.

Ambrose, Eileen, ''Minnesota's Quality Dining to Sell Bruegger's Bagel Business,'' *Knight Ridder/Tribune Business News,* September 5, 1997.

Forster, Julie, ''Long Lines, a Simple Menu, Fast Food,'' *Corporate Report-Minnesota,* December 1997, p. 44.

''Founders of Bruegger's Corp. Steer Bagel Shop Chain Back Toward Success,'' *Knight Ridder/Tribune Business News,* June 4, 2001.

Fryer, Alex P., ''Bruegger's Ready to Roll Out Seattle-Area Expansion,'' *Puget Sound Business Journal,* June 16, 1995, p. 4.

Hamstra, Mark, ''Quality Bags Bagel Race: Bruegger's for Sale,'' *Nation's Restaurant News,* May 26, 1997, p. 1.

Harrison, Kimberly P., ''Holey Bagel: Shops Popping Up All Over,'' *Crain's Cleveland Business,* October 31, 1994, p. 1.

Key, Peter, ''Founders of Bruegger's Bagels Want to Reclaim Mismanaged Creation,'' *Knight Ridder/Tribune Business News,* May 13, 1997.

Kim, Nancy J., ''Bagel Vendors Quickly Filling Up Holes,'' *Puget Sound Business Journal,* July 19, 1996, p. 7.

Kukolla, Steve, ''Bagel Chain Founders Seek Split from Indiana's Quality Dining,'' *Knight Ridder/Tribune Business News,* March 22, 1997.

Papiernik, Richard L., ''Quality Dining Battles for Control of Bruegger's Rollout,'' *Nation's Restaurant News,* March 31, 1997, p. 2.

——, ''Quality Dining Bids for Top Bagel Spot; Bruegger's Acquisition Heats Up Battle for Segment Dominance,'' *Nation's Restaurant News,* March 4, 1996, p. 1.

——, ''Rolling in Dough: Bagel Chains Bake Up Big Bucks,'' *Nation's Restaurant News,* July 17, 1995, p. 47.

''Quality Dining Inc. Completes Bruegger's Buy,'' *Nation's Restaurant News,* June 17, 1996, p. 58.

Upbin, Bruce, ''Burned by Bagels,'' *Forbes,* September 8, 1997, p. 134.

Walkup, Carolyn, ''Jacobs Bros. Bagels Acquires 14 Bruegger's Units,'' *Nation's Restaurant News,* March 16, 1998, p. 8.

Wieneke, Heidi Prescott, ''The Bagel Debacle,'' *Indiana Business Magazine,* January 1, 1999, p. 8.

Wright, Leslie, ''Bagel Chain's New Owners Have Big Plans,'' *Burlington Free Press,* April 1, 2004, p. 6.

—Jeffrey L. Covell

Burns, Philp & Company Ltd.

Level 23, 56 Pitt Street
Sydney
NSW 2000
Australia
Telephone: 292591111
Fax: 292473272
Web site: http://www.burnsphilp.com

Public Company
Incorporated: 1882
Employees: 14,000
Sales: AUD 1.88 billion ($1.41 billion) (2003)
Stock Exchanges: Australian
Ticker Symbol: BPC
NAIC: 311423 Dried and Dehydrated Food
Manufacturing; 325411 Medicinal and Botanical
Manufacturing; 424490 Other Grocery and Related
Product Merchant Wholesalers

Long a part of Australia's corporate establishment, Burns, Philp & Company Ltd. has reinvented itself at the beginning of the 21st century as a leading supplier of yeast, yeast extracts, and other baking and food ingredients, including the Fleishmann yeast brand, and also as one of Australia's top branded food products groups—the latter in large part through the company's 2003 acquisition of Goodman Fielder Ltd. and its Meadow Lea and Uncle Tobys. In 2003, also, the company acquired the South American Fleischmann operations from Kraft Foods. Altogether, Burns, Philp maintains a manufacturing presence of 114 facilities in 28 countries, with sales in more than 60 countries. After an extended financial crisis during the late 1990s, the result of an ill-fated attempt to enter the spices and seasonings market, Burns, Philp has refocused and returned to profitability by shedding a number of its holdings, including much of its longstanding shipping terminals operation, its North American industrial vinegar division, and even its historic headquarters. At the same time, the group has been selling off its spices and seasonings operations, a process that neared completion at the beginning of 2004 with the announcement of its impending sale of Tone's, the group's North American herbs and spices division. The company's turnaround, and especially its purchase of Goodman Fielder, has boosted its revenues to nearly AUD 1.9 billion ($1.4 billion) in 2003.

Founding an Australian Business Empire in the 19th Century

Scottish-born James Burns was just 16 years old when he joined his older brother and immigrated to Australia in 1862. While John Burns founded a retail business in Brisbane, James Burns went to work as a jackaroo in the Australian outback—it was there that Burns recognized a number of retailing and wholesaling principles that enabled his later success. In 1867, Burns returned to Brisbane and became a partner in his older brother's business. The discovery of gold in Gympie led Burns to set up a branch store supplying miners. That store was followed by several others; yet Burns shrewdly sold off these stores in 1869, before the end of the first gold rush.

With the money earned from the sale, together with a family loan, Burns moved to Townsville to establish his own retail and wholesale business in 1872. Two years later, Burns hired another Scottish immigrant, Robert Philp. The pair hit it off, and before long established a partnership together. Philp took over operation of the Townsville store, while Burns moved to Sydney in order to build on a growing interest in shipping. From then on, Burns and Philp rarely saw each other, yet remained loyal and dedicated business partners.

Townsville quickly developed into Queensland's major port city, connected by rail to such primary industries as the mining, ranching, and sugar industries. Burns and Philp expanded their investments and operations to include a wide range of business interests, and expanded their retailing and shipping operations to new ports, including Normanton, and to the outlying islands. In 1882, Burns and Philp decided to convert their partnership to a full-fledged corporation, creating Burns, Philp & Company Ltd. with a capital of £150,000.

Burns, Philp grew into a major force in the eastern Australian trade regions, with shipping interests extending throughout much of the South Pacific. Through Robert Philp, the company

Company Perspectives:

Our products have been well accepted in markets where we operate and are often exported to other neighboring markets.

Our global operations are supported by an extensive and diverse team of approximately 14,000 employees at 114 production facilities in 28 countries. The company has developed a strong reputation for reliable sales and technical support services.

then became involved in the so-called "blackbirding" trade, that is, the illegal transport of forced labor from the Pacific Islands into Australia. Yet the company ended its involvement in "labor trading" in 1886. Instead, the company began opening branch stores on the islands. As a complement to its shipments to the islands, the company began exporting goods as well, such as oil-rich copra.

By the end of the century, this shipping business had become the company's largest, supported by a fleet of some 60 ships. The company's more or less organic growth led it into a variety of new business areas. A major example of the group's ability to pursue offshoots of its core operations came in 1886 when the company backed the founding of the North Queensland Insurance Company in Sydney, which later grew into QBE Insurance. Burns, Philp was to retain its stake in QBE into the early 1990s.

Failed Diversification in the 1970s

Through the first half of the 20th century, Burns, Philp grew into one of Australia's leading corporations, listing on the Australian Stock Exchange where it became a blue-chip mainstay. Through the 1960s, the company's strategy was characterized as conservative. The company continued to seek out new business opportunities, however, such as the ownership of copra plantations, even though the company exited that activity, for the most part, following World War II. Nonetheless, the company's growth centered mostly on its three core operations of retailing, shipping, and insurance and other financial services. Through this period, the Burns family remained in control of the company, providing it leadership.

The late 1960s and early 1970s, however, saw the emergence of a new breed of corporate conglomerates—giant companies investing in wide-ranging and extremely diversified businesses. Burns, Philp's management caught conglomerate fever in the early 1970s, launching a buying spree that lasted for nearly a decade. By the early 1980s, Burns, Philp had been transformed into a sprawling, internationally operating empire of more than 200 companies involved in some 100 separate industries, including toy manufacture, perfumes, automobile sales and rentals, production of penicillin and other antibiotics, and an extension of retail operations into the hardware segment through the Australia-based BBE Hardware store chain.

The attempt at diversification severely strained the company, all the more so because nearly all of the group's diversified operations were losing money. Attempts to rein in costs, in large part by emphasizing a centralization of management con-

trol, only tended to make matters worse. Despite its huge array of businesses and expanding revenues, Burns, Philp barely managed to scrape out more than AUD 5 million in profits at the beginning of the 1980s.

In response, Burns, Philp brought in a new CEO, Andrew Turnbull, in 1984. Turnbull, the first from outside the Burns family to head the company, quickly began to restructure the group, selling off most of its smaller operations. Turnbull then rebuilt the company around a new core composed of its retail hardware stores and one of its most recent activities—food ingredients.

In 1982, Burns, Philp had made its first food products purchase, acquiring Australia's Mauri Bros., a leader in the production of yeast, with operations in the United Kingdom, Malaysia, and Indonesia as well as in Australia. The company backed up that acquisition with another, Thompson Limited, which brought it into the European yeast market as well. Burns, Philp quickly added a number of other yeast- and fermentation-related purchases, and by the mid-1980s had already become one of the world's leading providers of yeast and fermentation technologies.

In 1986, the company claimed leadership in its new core area when it bought up RJR Nabisco's North American yeast business, trading under the Fleischmann's name, the leading North American producer of consumer yeast, and a top producer of baker's yeast. The Fleischmann acquisition also gave the company its market-leading branded and industrial vinegar production.

The Fleischmann purchase not only boosted the weight of yeast production in Burns, Philp's overall operations, it made the group the world's dominant yeast and vinegar company. Yet this position left the company with little room for further significant growth.

Into the late 1980s, Burns, Philp once again turned toward diversification for its expansion. Yet, eager to avoid repeating its mistakes of the previous decade, the company now sought to diversify into an area more closely related to its now core yeast and vinegar businesses. Turnbull and the other members of Burns, Philp's management soon identified the herbs and spices market, which they considered a natural extension of their existing food products business.

In 1988, Burns, Philp, through Fleischmann, agreed to acquire Specialty Brands Inc. from then parent United Biscuit Holdings Plc. That acquisition gave Burns, Philp control of the Spice Islands brand of herbs and spices, then touted as the leading gourmet brand of herbs and spices in North America. Yet that purchase was to lead the company into head-to-head competition with McCormick and Company, which in fact dominated the U.S. herbs and spices consumer market with a more than 40 percent market share.

Burns, Philp moved to build up its international herbs and spices wing, investing massively to acquire a number of regional players around the world, with an emphasis on European markets, such as Germany, The Netherlands, France, and the United Kingdom. In its push to build up scale, the company paid handsomely for its acquisitions, driving up its debt.

Key Dates:

Key Dates:

1862: James Burns arrives in Australia from Scotland at the age of 16.

1872: Burns opens store in Townsville and begins retail and wholesale business.

1874: Burns hires Robert Philp, also from Scotland, who later becomes Burns's partner, taking over the store as Burns moves to Sydney to pursue shipping interests.

1882: The company incorporates as Burns, Philp & Company Ltd.

1973: Burns, Philp begins diversification program, acquiring some 200 companies in 100 separate businesses.

1982: The company acquires Mauri Bros., a leading producer of yeast, in Australia, and Thompson Limited, which produces yeast in the United Kingdom.

1984: Andrew Turnbull is appointed CEO, leading the company on a restructuring that refocuses it around a core of foods and retail hardware operations.

1986: The company acquires Fleishmann yeast and vinegar from RJR Nabisco.

1992: The company acquires Durkee-French from Reckitt Colman.

1994: The company acquires Ostmann of Germany and Euroma of The Netherlands.

1995: The company acquires Tone Brothers, Inc., based in Iowa, sparking an intense price war with McCormick and Company.

1997: After Turnbull's death, the company announces its intention of selling off the herbs and spices business.

1998: The company launches a restructuring, shedding a number of holdings, including the last of its shipping line, and corporate headquarters.

2000: The company returns to profitability, posting AUD 86 million in net profits.

2003: The company acquires Goodman Fielder Limited for AUD 2 billion; Fleishmann in South America is acquired from Kraft Foods.

2004: Plans to sell off the remaining Tone's herbs and spices unit are announced.

In 1992, the company returned to the United States, paying Reckitt-Colman nearly $90 million to acquire the Durkee-French spices and seasonings group. While that acquisition added a wide range of products, it firmly established Burns, Philp as the number two producer of spices and seasonings in the North American market. Nonetheless, Burns, Philp had only just begun this new leg of its herbs and spices expansion, purchasing Germany's Ostmann in 1994, then The Netherlands' Euroma, and, finally, Iowa-based Tone's in 1995.

This last acquisition brought Burns, Philp into full head-to-head competition with McCormick and exposed the company's lack of understanding of the international spices market, and especially in its differences with the yeast market. Tone's had long been McCormick's chief rival on the important wholesale spices market, fighting for essential supermarket slotting contracts.

Burns, Philp was unprepared for the response from McCormick, which rushed to protect its lead, inaugurating a price war and effectively knocking Burns, Philp off many of the market's leading supermarket shelves. Meanwhile, the company was forced to sell off a number of assets in an effort to pay for the debt incurred by its expansion effort. In 1993, the company sold off its 45 percent stake in QBE Insurance as well as its BBC Hardware chain at what were described as "fire sale" prices.

Turnaround for the New Century

By the mid-1990s, Burns, Philp's failed foray into herbs and spices was draining the company, which saw its profits drop drastically. Turnbull retired in 1995, taking up the company chairmanship, but was replaced by longtime protégé and friend Ian Clack, who, like others on the company's board, refused to call into question Turnbull's decision to enter the herbs and spices market. As the price war with McCormick intensified, Turnbull became ill with cancer, reducing the company to a degree of inaction.

Turnbull's death in 1997, followed by Clack's resignation, signaled a new start for the company, which announced its intention to sell off its herbs and spices operation. Now with Thomas Degnan in place as company CEO, Burns, Philp began seeking buyers for its herbs and spices business. Yet, when the company proved unable to find a buyer, it was forced to slash the value of its assets. As a result, the group's share price plummeted in 1998—from a market capitalization of more than AUD 1.5 billion, the group's value fell to just AUD 150 million. Burns, Philp appeared on the verge of collapse and unlikely to make it to the next century.

Yet along the way, Burns, Philp had picked up a new major shareholder, New Zealand's Graeme Hart, who had acquired nearly 20 percent of the company just months before its share collapse. With his own investment gone awry, Hart stepped in to help the company pick up the pieces. As Degnan led a new divestment drive, shedding much of the group's herbs and spices division, while also exiting a number of other businesses, including the last of the group's shipping holdings and even its former Sydney headquarters, Hart convinced the group's bankers to renegotiate its debt.

These efforts gave Burns, Philp the breathing room to rebuild itself around its core yeast operation, which accounted for more than half of the group's revenues. As it returned to profitability, posting more than AUD 82 million in 2000, the company began scouting for new growth prospects. By 2003, the company had found its new direction with the acquisition of bakery products and branded consumer foods group Goodman Fielder Ltd.

That acquisition, which cost the company AUD 2 billion, boosted the group's sales by more than AUD 600 million, and extended the company's operations to include 114 manufacturing facilities in nearly 30 countries. It also gave the company a new range of branded products, chiefly under the Uncle Toby's and Meadow Lea brand names. Following the integration of Goodman Fielder, Burns, Philp prepared to complete its exit from the herbs and spices market. In March 2004 the company announced its intention to sell off its North American holdings, by then grouped under the Tone's name. In the meantime, the company had achieved new growth for its yeast business, buying up the Fleischmann business in South America that had been owned by Kraft Foods. The transformed Burns, Philp now looked forward to smoother sailing in the new century.

Principal Subsidiaries

Burns-Philp Food Inc. (U.S.A.); Burns Philp UK PLC; Fleischmann's Yeast (U.S.A.); Goodman Fielder Ltd.; Provesta Flavor Ingredients (U.S.A.).

Principal Competitors

Altria Group Inc.; Nestlé S.A.; Unilever PLC; Kraft Foods Inc.; Astor Products Inc.; Edison S.p.A.; Associated British Foods PLC; CSM N.V.

Further Reading

Buckley, K., and K. Klugman, *The History of Burns, Philp: The Australian Company in the South Pacific,* Sydney: Allen and Unwin, 1981.

''Burns, Philp Fire Sale Follows Company Collapse,'' *Chemical & Market Reporter,* May 4, 1998, p. 3.

Dann, Liam, ''Burns, Philp Pleased with Goodman Takeover,'' *New Zealand Herald,* November 6, 2003.

Lipari, Kathy, and Aap Burns, ''Burns, Philp Fights Back into Black,'' *Courier-Mail,* October 31, 1996, p. 27.

McGuire, Michael, ''Building a Future,'' *Australian,* February 2, 1999, p. 32.

Talbot, Jillian, ''Burns, Philp Cuts the Fat and Makes Profit,'' *The Press,* November 6, 2003, p. 7.

Westfield, Mark, ''Dreams of Empire Die with Turnbull,'' *Australian,* May 20, 1997, p. 23.

—M.L. Cohen

Caffè Nero Group PLC

3 Neal Street, 2nd Floor
London, England WC2H 9PU
United Kingdom
Telephone: (44) 20 7520 5150
Fax: (44) 20 7240 5332
Web site: http://www.caffenero.com

Public Company
Incorporated: 1997
Employees: 1,100
Sales: £39.39 million (2003)
Stock Exchanges: London
Ticker Symbol: CFN
NAIC: 722110 Full-Service Restaurants

Caffè Nero Group PLC ranks as one of the three largest operators of espresso shops in the United Kingdom, trailing Starbucks Corporation and Costa Coffee. Caffè Nero operates more than 150 shops in more than 50 cities and towns in the United Kingdom, with sites stretching from Brighton, England, to Glasgow, Scotland. Although the company strives to convey a single, branded identity to the chain, it also endeavors to tailor each store to the peculiarities of its location. Caffè Nero intends to greatly increase its store count by opening units in both large metropolitan markets and in smaller regional markets. The company also intends to expand into mainland Europe.

Origins

The first Caffè Nero opened in 1990, debuting in the South Kensington section of London. The coffee shop drew its inspiration from a small espresso bar in Milan, a city where thousands of shops catered to millions of people accustomed to having their coffee while standing. In London, where the first Caffè Nero offered no seating for its patrons, the custom of drinking coffee while standing was foreign. Moreover, Londoners, as a whole, did not demonstrate a particular taste for the espressos, lattés, and mochas that were ingrained in the daily lives of those in Milan and throughout Italy. The first Caffè

Nero, not surprisingly, drew its clientele largely from London's Italian community, who enjoyed their traditional coffee drinks and samplings of their native cuisine, prepared in a kitchen located downstairs from the espresso bar.

The debut of the first Caffè Nero occurred well before the sight of Italian-style espresso shops would become commonplace in London. Despite the lack of general appeal for its format, Caffè Nero thrived on Old Brompton Road in South Kensington, its success sufficient to justify the establishment of other, similarly designed espresso bars. Within the next six years, four more Caffè Neros were opened in London, with each opening signaling an increasing acceptance and demand for espresso and all its derivative variations.

By the beginning of the late 1990s, espresso shops had begun to become big business in London. Large chains, in an attempt to emulate or to capitalize upon the success of the globally minded Starbucks Corporation, began to appear and expand in earnest. For one group of businesspeople, Caffè Nero offered a way into London's promising specialty coffee retailing market.

The group of managers who saw Caffè Nero as the foundation for a much larger chain was headed by Gerry Ford. Ford, who earned his B.A. from Stanford University and his Ph.D. from Oxford University, possessed a wealth of business experience, starting his career at Hewlett-Packard. After leaving Hewlett-Packard, Ford spent three years developing a number of small businesses at APAX Partners, an international venture capital firm. Next, Ford served as the chief executive for several companies involved in the food and consumer goods industry. In 1991, he helped start Paladin Associates Ltd., a venture capital group that invested in and managed food, consumer brands, and media businesses. It was through Paladin that Ford and his consortium of investors purchased the five Caffè Neros in operation in 1997. With financial backing from BancBoston, the private equity investment arm of FleetBoston, Caffè Nero Group PLC was formed as the corporate entity Ford would use to expand the small yet established chain. The new management team thoroughly revamped the design of the Caffè Nero units, but kept the name, the coffee, and the espresso shops' signature toasted Italian sandwiches. Once the concept was honed to his liking, Ford pressed forward and began opening additional units.

Company Perspectives:

The Caffè Nero Philosophy is really very simple. Coffee, Atmosphere, Food and Service are the key elements of our business and we put time and energy in to striving for excellence in these four areas. We want all of our customers to enjoy a great cup of coffee and a good Italian snack in an authentic European coffee house atmosphere delivered in a friendly matter.

Caffè Nero nearly tripled in size during its first two years under the control of Ford and his team. Using the capital supplied by BancBoston, which owned a 14 percent stake in Caffè Nero Group, Ford began building a chain of shops, but he was careful to avoid giving his customers the sense of being in a chain. Each company shop operated under the Caffè Nero name and offered the same coffee and same limited food menu, but the stores were designed individually, with each shop endeavoring to incorporate the style of its particular neighborhood. Caffè Neros located in commercial sections of the city were outfitted with stools and tiled floors to reflect customers' preference for a short stay. Company coffee shops in residential areas featured furnishings that were more conducive for a longer stay, with sofas and armchairs replacing stools. Although Ford and his team acknowledged the need to create a single, branded identity, they also eschewed absolute uniformity of the chain's units.

2001 Initial Public Offering Fuels Expansion

By the end of the 1990s, the retail coffee market in London was expanding rapidly. Caffè Nero responded by accelerating its rate of expansion, as the company attempted to keep pace with a handful of other coffee retailers who were saturating London with new espresso shops. By May 1999, the end of Caffè Nero's financial year, there were 13 shops in operation. By this point, Ford was ready to enter markets outside of London for the first time. A Caffè Nero opened in Manchester in October 1999—the company's first step toward expansion throughout the United Kingdom. By mid-2000, the chain had expanded to 30 shops, representing a fraction of what Ford envisioned for the company. He intended to establish 250 stores by 2004, a goal whose fulfillment would require a substantial flow of capital. To help improve its ability to expand, the company completed an initial public offering (IPO) of stock in March 2001, when it had 53 sites in operation, raising £9 million from its debut on the London Stock Exchange.

Caffè Nero's IPO reflected the ambitious expectations of Ford and his executives. The company was planning a major assault on London's specialty coffee retailing market, with longer-range plans calling for similarly aggressive expansion throughout the United Kingdom and across the English Channel. At the time of the IPO, Ford proposed opening 45 shops by the end of 2001. Future expansion also called for a foray into mainland Europe within 12 months of the IPO's completion. Caffè Nero was not alone in articulating bold expansion plans. The company ranked as the fourth largest operator in the U.K. coffee market, trailing Starbucks, Costa Coffee, and Coffee

Republic. Together, the four companies represented the industry elite, with each in a race to capture greater market share than its rivals.

With the capital realized from the IPO, Caffè Nero began expanding with fervor. By May 2001, the company had 75 stores in operation, having opened nearly two dozen new shops in the two months following its IPO. In 2002, Caffè Nero's expansion strategy took on a new dimension, as the company completed its first move on the acquisition front. In March 2002, Caffè Nero acquired Aroma Limited, a chain of coffee shops owned by McDonald's Corporation, "cherry picking 29 of the best sites from Aroma's list of stores," according to Ford in the company's 2002 annual report. Caffè Nero paid £2.3 million for the Aroma shops, giving it a total of 108 shops, or enough to make it the largest independent coffee bar operator in the United Kingdom and the third largest of all types of operators in the United Kingdom. Geographically, the company's presence stretched from Brighton, England, to Glasgow, Scotland.

As Caffè Nero entered its fifth year under Ford's management, the company began to display noticeable financial strength. Although the company had yet to reach a point where its own profits could support its expansion, the growth in revenues was impressive. By the end of its financial year in May 2002, a 70 percent increase in sales was recorded, as Caffè Nero's annual revenue volume swelled from £15.6 million in 2001 to £26.6 million—a figure that largely excluded the influence of the Aroma acquisition. By this point, Caffè Nero and its three rivals controlled approximately 63 percent of the U.K. market. Costa Coffee led the pack with 300 shops, followed closely by Starbucks, which owned 294 sites. Caffè Nero trailed with 108 shops, having passed Coffee Republic and its 85 locations with the acquisition of Aroma. In terms of consumers' preference, however, Caffè Nero outstripped all of its competitors, having been selected as the best coffee house in the United Kingdom in 2002 by coffee research firm Allegra Strategies—the second consecutive year Caffè Nero received the accolade. Ford, encouraged by the success of the company, revealed plans for further expansion in an April 18, 2002 interview with *Leisure & Hospitality Business.* "We will look to Europe once we reach around 140 sites and we're self-financing," he said. "That should be in about half a year."

Ford's advance into mainland Europe did not occur according to his plans, but the company achieved notable progress, nonetheless. The company's pace of expansion was slower than originally planned because of strategic alternatives it was exploring. In August 2002, after securing another £7 million to finance its expansion, the company increased its investment in rival Coffee Republic, whose efforts to compete in the race with Starbucks, Costa Coffee, and Caffè Nero, had begun to result in a number of money-losing shops. Ford increased his company's stake in Coffee Republic from 4 percent to 10 percent in a single transaction in August 2002, sparking speculation that Caffè Nero was attempting a takeover of its competitor. In late 2002, the company decided not to pursue its acquisition of Coffee Republic in the short-term, which allowed it to resume its normal pace of expansion, but the decision did not remove the possibility of a merger between Caffè Nero and Coffee Republic at a later date.

Expansion in the 21st Century

During its 2003 financial year, Caffè Nero applied itself to its ongoing expansion campaign. The company opened 18 new stores and sold five undesirable units acquired in the Aroma transaction, giving it a total of 121 shops by May 2003. The growth achieved during the year typified the company's approach to expansion, reflecting a strategy it intended to embrace as it mapped its future course. The strategy involved expanding either by grouping its stores in clusters in metropolitan markets or by targeting smaller regional towns. In 2003, for instance, the company opened four Caffè Neros in Manchester, giving it a total of nine in the city. Other cities, such as Birmingham, with seven stores, and Leeds, with four stores, were beginning to become the object of Caffè Nero's cluster strategy, but the company was moving into much smaller markets as well. By mid-2003, residents in smaller markets such as Worthing, Maidstone, Durham, and Rickmansworth had become patrons of Caffè Nero.

As Caffè Nero plotted its future expansion, there were encouraging signs that success lay ahead. The retail coffee sector in the United Kingdom continued to show capacity for further growth by all participants in the industry segment. Further, according to Caffè Nero's own estimations, the retail property market offered a wealth of opportunities for those looking to establish additional stores. The company was also strongly positioned financially to continue its march throughout the United Kingdom. Caffè Nero hoped to generate enough profits to finance its expansion by the end of 2004, and thereby eliminate the need for external financing. Once the company achieved financial self-sufficiency, it intended to open between 35 and 40 new Caffè Nero units each year.

Principal Competitors

Coffee Republic PLC; Costa Coffee; Starbucks Corporation.

Further Reading

"Caffè Nero Buys Aroma," *Leisure & Hospitality Business,* April 4, 2002, p. 3.

"Caffè Nero Exit by IPO," *European Venture Capital Journal,* April 2001, p. 36.

"Caffè Nero Float to Push Roll Out," *Leisure Week,* September 21, 2000, p. 1.

"Caffè Nero Likes McDonald's Aroma," *Restaurant Business,* March 15, 2002, p. 15.

"Caffè Nero Ups Its Stake in Rival Chain," *In-Store Marketing,* September 2002, p. 18.

Farthing, Nicolle, "Coffee Shop Operator Looks to Regions As Capital Overflows," *Leisure & Hospitality Business,* September 6, 2001, p. 3.

Frewin, Angela, "Boom Time for Coffee Brands," *Caterer & Hotelkeeper,* May 2, 2002, p. 6.

Gibbons, Neil, "Hot Prospect?," *Leisure & Hospitality Business,* April 18, 2002, p. 25.

Golding, Christina, "Caffè Nero Ups Stake in Coffee Republic," *Caterer & Hotelkeeper,* August 15, 2002, p. 10.

Johnson, Andrew, "Merger Rumours Heat Up As Caffè Nero Raises 7M," *Express,* August 10, 2002, p. 90.

McClary, Samantha, "Caffè Nero Sniffs Out 26 Aroma Purchases," *Caterer & Hotelkeeper,* February 21, 2002, p. 10.

"McDonald's Corp.," *Nation's Restaurant News Daily,* February 20, 2002, p. 1.

—Jeffrey L. Covell

CANNONDESIGN

Cannon Design

2170 Whitehaven Road
Grand Island, New York 14072
U.S.A.
Telephone: (716) 773-6800
Fax: (716) 773-5909
Web site: http://www.cannondesign.com

Private Company
Founded: 1945 as Cannon Corporation
Employees: 550
Sales: $74.4 million (2002)
NAIC: 541310 Architectural Services; 541330
Engineering Services; 541340 Drafting Services;
541490 Other Specialized Design Services

In half a century, Cannon Design has become an international leader in the field of architectural planning. Its award-winning designs grace more than a dozen countries and well-known landmarks dot the American landscape, from innovative commerce centers and sports facilities to medical complexes and schools at all levels of education, both public and private. Cannon is a recognized leader not only for its architectural designs, but for the preservation and renovation of historic buildings as well. Cannon has nine U.S. offices and one in Canada (Vancouver, British Columbia) to serve its growing roster of worldwide clients.

Beginnings: 1940s–80s

Members of the Cannon family had been involved with engineering and architecture as far back as the early 1900s. The family did not come to prominence in the Buffalo area until several decades later when John D. Cannon founded Cannon Corporation in 1945. The Grand Island business was staffed by Cannon family members and the firm landed commercial contracts in the growing Buffalo/Niagara metropolitan area.

Cannon had earned a reputation for excellence by the 1970s with its design work, primarily in the corporate and educational sectors. The firm received widespread recognition when its

work at the University of California at Davis was considered for national merit in the planning/design of sports facilities. When the business climate began weakening Cannon segued into the medical industry, designing hospitals and research facilities.

By the next decade Cannon Corp. was considered the Buffalo area's top design firm, ranked by employees and its growing reputation throughout the United States. In the 1980s Cannon had successfully bid on projects in more than half of the 50 states, as well as work overseas. The firm won contracts in Canada, Germany, and Israel, and had gained prominence for its designs of medical and research complexes. In 1989 Cannon Corp. had reached sales of over $32.9 million with offices in St. Louis, Boston, New York, and Washington, D.C.

End of the Century: 1990s

In 1990 Cannon completed an expansion of its headquarters, adding 20,000 square feet to its Grand Island offices. With 115 employees in Grand Island and another 185 nationwide, the company had become the 12th largest architectural firm in the United States according to *Building Design and Construction* and the 27th largest privately owned firm in the Buffalo area according to *Buffalo Business First*. Cannon finished 1990 with billings just shy of $31.4 million, a healthy showing despite recessionary factors. By this time in its 46-year history, three quarters of the company's commissions came from the healthcare sector, and business was booming.

For the remainder of the decade Cannon hoped to grow both domestically and internationally. The firm parlayed its solid reputation in the medical architecture field into bids for contracts in Belgium, China, Italy, Jordan, Kuwait, Russia, South Korea, and Turkey. On U.S. soil, Cannon was thriving with numerous commissions, including Erie Community College's field house, construction of several area primary and secondary schools, the downtown convention center, the Buffalo Niagara International Airport, and the HSBC Bank Atrium Center (Buffalo); research facilities for the National Institute of Health (Bethesda, Maryland), Cedars Sinai Hospital (Los Angeles), and the National Institute for Occupational Safety and Health (Huntington, West Virginia); a research center and educational

Company Perspectives:

Our mission is to plan and design buildings that enhance the quality of life and contribute value to the built environment. We believe good design is the physical expression of sound ideas, imagination and creativity. We strive to create buildings that are a thoughtful response to their program mission, physical settings and functional purpose. We seek to add value through innovation and creativity, aligning ourselves with our clients' goals, delivering services that meet their quality, schedule and cost objectives.

buildings for Boston University (Boston); a redesign of Zippo Manufacturing Company's corporate headquarters (Bradford, Pennsylvania); and numerous college and university expansions throughout the nation.

Testament to Cannon's design and architectural excellence was an array of awards, both local and national, for such projects as the education center at Washington University in St. Louis; sports facilities at the University of California, University of Miami, and University of Georgia; and the prestigious Energy Star Label from the EPA for its work on Buffalo's Occidental Chemical Center for its energy-saving features.

Despite a turndown in healthcare construction in the late 1990s, Cannon held its own with smaller projects and an upswing in educational and sports-related commissions. By 1999 billings totaled over $47 million, of which an estimated 15 percent was from international contracts. Cannon's workforce had reached 500 worldwide, with eight U.S. offices and ongoing or completed projects in more than a dozen countries.

The New Millennium: 2000s

In 2000, to better reflect the scope of its operations, Cannon Corporation became Cannon Design. Though many had already referred to the company as Cannon Design, the name change made it official by mid-year. Another name conversion came later the same year, when Dworsky Associates was merged into Cannon's West Coast operations. The well established Dworsky, a prominent Los Angeles architectural firm for 47 years, moved from its Wilshire Boulevard offices into shared space with its Cannon counterpart in late 2000. The merged businesses were christened CannonDworsky and took up residence in offices on Avenue of the Stars.

Cannon's first award in the new century came in December 2000 at Constitution Hall in Washington, D.C. In attendance at the ceremony were President and Mrs. Clinton, as Cannon principals received the Presidential Award for Design Excellence, the only federal award recognizing architectural merit. Cannon received the award for its work on the U.S. Port of Entry station buildings on the border of Calexio, California, and Mexico. Cannon's design was one of nine projects throughout the nation to be so recognized.

Cannon continued to win high profile projects and create landmarks rather than simply construct buildings or plazas. Some of the stellar work in 2001 receiving attention included

the $95 million Lloyd P. George Federal Building and Courthouse in Las Vegas (awarded General Service Administration honors from the federal government); the Peace Bridge project in Buffalo; the Shaw Park Plaza project in Clayton, Missouri; and a slew of athletic facilities throughout the country—five dozen in all—underway.

Some of the colleges and universities in line to receive Cannon-designed facilities included Texas Christian University (student recreation center); Rochester Institute of Technology, Ersinus College, and the National Cathedral School (field houses); George Washington University (indoor/outdoor soccer and softball fields); Union College and the University of South Florida (sports complexes); the University of New Hampshire (football stadium); and Boston University (a basketball/hockey arena as well as dorms and a computer lab). Cannon also designed sports-related facilities for municipalities and park districts in many states, including Colorado, Florida, Maryland, New York, and Virginia.

Cannon Design not only set standards in architecture and design, but had an eye on the future of its discipline as well. The firm had established scholarships for secondary school students in a partnership with the Buffalo City Honors School back in 1993, but initiated a new scholarship program in 2001 with the University of Buffalo's School of Architecture and Design to help talented design students cover the costs of graduate level courses.

While 2001 was a year most would never forget due to the terrorist attacks on the World Trade Center and the Pentagon, the events did not devastate the architecture and design industry. Few projects were canceled, though some commissions were slowed and costs reconsidered. Cannon, however, did exceedingly well, ending the year with sales totaling $47.5 million and a seemingly endless roster of projects in the works.

In early 2002 Cannon merged with Johnston Sport Architecture Inc. of Victoria, British Columbia. The Canadian arm of the business was renamed Cannon Johnston Sport Architecture. Gary Miller, Cannon's CEO, commented to *Buffalo Business First*, ''Expanding our international presence is consistent with Cannon Design's vision for the future and with our objective to be a prominent, well-respected force in every geography and market we serve.'' Johnston, which was established in 1985, was well known throughout Canada for its athletic and recreational design services.

The year also marked an important milestone: the opening of Turkey's Sabanci University after three years of design and construction. The campus, which included over two dozen buildings and nearly two million square feet, was a major accomplishment for Cannon. Sabanci University was a marvel and earned the company much respect in the international architectural community; it was sited as one of the major reasons Cannon was awarded the $230 million design/build commission of Ave Maria University in Florida. The new Catholic liberal arts college, located by Naples, Florida, was expected to open in 2006. Sales for 2002 were a robust $74.4 million.

By 2003 Cannon Design had received over 200 honors and awards from local, regional, and national organizations. The company continued to lead the design and architecture field in

Key Dates:

1945: Cannon Corporation is founded by John D. Cannon.
1989: Sales reach $32.9 million with five Cannon offices nationwide.
1990: Cannon is ranked the 12th largest U.S. architectural firm according to *Building Design and Construction.*
1993: Cannon begins offering scholarships to Buffalo City Honors School students.
1999: Sales top $47 million as Cannon's workforce grows to 500.
2000: Company is renamed Cannon Design and merges with the Los Angeles-based Dworsky Associates.
2001: Cannon partners with the University of Buffalo's School of Architecture and Design to offer graduate study scholarships.
2002: The firm merges with Johnston Sport Architecture Inc. of British Columbia.
2004: Cannon is awarded the design contract for Florida's new Ave Maria University.

western New York and was considered one of the industry's finest in the United States and abroad. In 2003 and 2004, like the preceding years, Cannon had dozens of high profile projects underway and commissions encompassing the firm's growing scope of design/build expertise. In addition to designing and constructing new facilities in the healthcare, educational, and commercial sectors, Cannon was also renovating and restoring historic landmarks, providing landscape and horticultural design packages, and even dabbling in interior design and furnishings. For Cannon Design its name change in 2000 was truly representative of the firm's new attitude: to embrace all facets of its craft, though only with the highest demands of excellence.

Principal Subsidiaries

CannonDworsky; Cannon Johnston Sport Architecture.

Principal Competitors

Bechtel Group, Inc.; H + M Company, Inc.; Halliburton Company; Jacobs Engineering Group, Inc.; Parsons Corporation; Washington Group International, Inc.

Further Reading

"Cannon Design, Buffalo, N.Y., Has Merged with Johnston Sport Architecture Inc., Victoria, British Columbia," *Building Design & Construction,* April 2002, p. 12.

"Cannon Design Merges with Canadian Sports and Recreation Firm," *Business First of Buffalo,* December 11, 2001.

English, Dale, "Cannon, City Honors Build a Partnership for Future," *Business First of Buffalo,* November 15, 1993, p. 8.

Fink, James, "Cannon Builds Up Reputation in Medical Field," *Business First of Buffalo,* August 12, 1991, p. 2.

——, "Cannon Designs a New Name to Clarify Identity," *Business First of Buffalo,* May 29, 2000, p. 3.

——, "Cannon Hired to Design New Florida University," *Business First of Buffalo,* February 23, 2004.

——, "Cannon Lands Contract in China for Industrial Park Master Plan," *Business First of Buffalo,* July 10, 1995, p. 2.

——, "International Projects Boost Cannon's Resume," *Business First of Buffalo,* September 20, 1999, p. 4.

——, "Renowned Architect Focuses on Landmarks," *Business First of Buffalo,* February 1, 2001, p. 12.

Hobgood, Cynthia, "D.C. Architects Tackle Array of National Sports Arenas," *Washington Business Journal,* November 9, 2001, p. 58.

"Mizrahi and Cannon Sign Jordan Hospital Deal," *Israel Business Today,* August 31, 1997, p. 13.

Olson, Christopher, "Deft Surgery Creates a Medical Office," *Building Design & Construction,* June 1989, p. 54.

Peinemann, Milo, "Merger Sends Architectural Firm to Century City Digs," *Los Angeles Business Journal,* September 11, 2000, p. 57.

Sommer, Mark, "Building on Talent," *Buffalo News,* February 22, 1996, p. 27.

—Nelson Rhodes

CATERPILLAR®

Caterpillar Inc.

100 Northeast Adams Street
Peoria, Illinois 61629-1425
U.S.A.
Telephone: (309) 675-1000
Fax: (309) 675-1182
Web site: http://www.cat.com

Public Company
Incorporated: 1925 as Caterpillar Tractor Company
Employees: 69,169
Sales: $22.76 billion (2003)
Stock Exchanges: New York Chicago Pacific London
    Paris Euronext Brussels Frankfurt Swiss
Ticker Symbol: CAT
NAIC: 326220 Rubber and Plastics Hoses and Belting
    Manufacturing; 333120 Construction Machinery
    Manufacturing; 333131 Mining Machinery and
    Equipment Manufacturing; 333611 Turbine and
    Turbine Generator Set Units Manufacturing; 333618
    Other Engine Equipment Manufacturing; 333924
    Industrial Truck, Tractor, Trailer, and Stacker
    Machinery Manufacturing; 522220 Sales Financing

Caterpillar Inc. is the world's largest manufacturer of earth-moving machinery. In addition to its tractors, trucks, graders, excavators, scrapers, and other heavy machinery used in the construction, mining, and forestry industries, Caterpillar also makes diesel and gas engines used in Caterpillar machinery, electric power generation equipment, locomotives, and other industrial equipment. With 50 production facilities in the United States and another 60 overseas and more than 200 dealers serving customers in 178 countries, Caterpillar does about 44 percent of its business within the United States and 56 percent abroad. Through Caterpillar Financial Services Corporation and other subsidiaries, the company offers financing and insurance for its customers and dealers.

Roots in Late 19th-Century Endeavors of Best and Holt

In 1859 Daniel Best left his Iowa home for California. After about ten years of working at various jobs, Best observed that many farmers transported their grain to special cleaning stations to make it suitable for market. Best thought there was a way to clean grain by machine at the same time as it was being harvested to avoid the costly step of transporting to another site. By 1871 Best had patented his first grain cleaner, which he manufactured and sold with great success. By the 1880s Best owned manufacturing centers in Oregon and Oakland, California.

Meanwhile, Charles Henry Holt had arrived in California from New Hampshire in 1864. Intending to further the family business of selling hardwood products, Holt founded C.H. Holt and Company with his savings and eventually operated it with his brothers William Harrison and A. Frank, who came west from New Hampshire in 1871. In 1883 younger brother Benjamin Holt arrived in California as well, and the Holt brothers that year set up the Stockton Wheel Company to season woods in a way that would prepare them for use in the arid midlands of California and deserts of the West. This venture was based in Stockton, California, about 80 miles east of San Francisco. Charles and Benjamin soon bought out the other two brothers, and Charles assumed responsibility for the business side of the enterprise, while Benjamin headed up the development of products and their manufacture. As the inventive force behind Stockton Wheel and its successors, Benjamin Holt is most often cited as the founder of Caterpillar Inc.

The Holts poured $65,000 into Stockton Wheel, equipping their factory with the best machinery available. The company manufactured wooden wheels, paving the way for the firm's entrance into the vehicular product market. In the 1880s the combined harvester and thresher, known as the combine, revolutionized the farming industry because of its ability to cut and thresh, and later to clean and sack grain, in vast quantities, using far less time than previously needed for these individual operations. The Holt brothers produced their first combine in 1886. The Link Belt Combined Harvester advanced agricultural technology further by using flexible chain belts rather than gears to transmit power from the ground wheels to the working parts of the machine. This innovation cut down on machine breakage. Meantime, Daniel Best produced his first combine in 1885.

Near the end of the 19th century, the major drawback in large-scale agriculture was the need for animal power. The combine had made large farms profitable, but the cost of housing and feeding large horse teams and the men who drove them cut into earnings. Both the Holts and Daniel Best were interested in solving this problem by using steam-driven engines to supply tractive power.

The Holts built a steam-driven tractor that could haul 50 tons of freight at three miles per hour. The Stockton Wheel Company was then incorporated as Holt Manufacturing Company in 1892. Almost concurrently, Daniel Best refined his steam-engine tractor into one of the finest available during this period, and throughout the 1890s steam-powered tractors were used for hauling freight and plowing fields, as well as for harvesting grain.

In the early 1900s Benjamin Holt turned his ingenuity to another farming problem. The land around Stockton, California, was boggy and became impassable when wet. To overcome this limitation Holt, in 1904, produced the first commercially successful caterpillar-style tractor, or crawler. It was built on tracks instead of wheels, and the "Cat" could negotiate any terrain short of a swamp. It soon allowed planters to reclaim thousands of acres of land previously thought useless. Holt began selling his tractors under the Caterpillar brand; according to lore, the name came about during the first test run of the crawler, when an onlooker commented that the machine moved like a caterpillar. In 1906 a steam-powered crawler was perfected, and caught on quickly because of its ability to work on ground that all but swallowed other machines. In the meantime, Charles Holt had died in 1905, leaving Benjamin Holt firmly in control of the enterprise.

In 1908 Holt Manufacturing produced its first gas-powered crawlers, using gasoline engines made by a newly formed engine division. The engineers who were building the 230-mile Los Angeles Aqueduct used one of the new machines that year to transport materials across the Mojave Desert. The machine worked so well that 25 more tractors were purchased for further work on the aqueduct, thus giving the Holt tractor credibility with the public and a substantial boost to sales.

Also in 1908, after decades of individual success, Daniel Best sold his firm, Best Manufacturing Company of San Leandro, California, to Holt Manufacturing. Best's son, C.L. Best, was taken on as company superintendent, but after two years, he formed his own company, C.L. Best Gas Tractor Company, and advanced the state of tractor technology even further on his own.

In 1909 Benjamin Holt, who had been looking for a new manufacturing plant in the eastern half of the United States, bought the abandoned but relatively new plant of a tractor company that had failed. The new Peoria, Illinois, location offered Holt everything he needed in a manufacturing center, and despite the need to pour capital into retooling the plant, it proved so profitable that by 1911 the factory employed 625 people. At that time Holt Manufacturing began exporting its tractors to Argentina, Mexico, and Canada.

After the Peoria plant opened, Holt continued to improve his tractor and expand its range of applications. He experimented with several different materials for the body design to achieve a heavy-duty tractor that was not excessively heavy. Holt knew that his tractors could be used for even more rugged chores than agriculture or freighting, and fitted adjustable blades onto his tractors. He then hired them out to grade roads or move soil and rocks at construction sites.

Soon after World War I broke out in 1914, thousands of troops were caught in trench warfare. Observing such repeated attacks, a British lieutenant colonel, Ernest Swinton, sought an armored machine to resist automatic weapons that also would be able to negotiate the war-scarred terrain of the battlefield. His requirements resulted in the invention in 1916 of an experimental tank, based on the track-laying tractors designed by Holt and others. A year later the tank was used to such telling effect that it is credited with winning the Battle of Cambrai, in France, for the Allies. Some historians point to this battle as the turning point of the war. Germany had investigated the military applications of the track-laying vehicle well before anyone else and concluded that tractors were without military significance.

Holt tractors themselves served the war effort by hauling artillery and supplies. In all, more than 10,000 Holt vehicles served the Allied forces, and the international exposure that the Holt tractor received during the war did much to popularize the tracked vehicle.

In 1920 Benjamin Holt died at the age of 71. The bankers holding the company's large debt forced the board of directors to accept their candidate, Thomas A. Baxter, a former Boston banker who had joined Holt Manufacturing in 1913 as a business manager, as Benjamin Holt's successor.

In the early 1920s the Holt company faced the problem of going from wartime boom to peacetime bust. Almost overnight the military orders that kept the factories working at capacity seemed to vanish. Holt used this down period to increase efficiency, both mechanical and human; for example, studies were made to determine how to use space and personnel to the best advantage.

Creation of Caterpillar Tractor Company: 1925

In 1925 Holt Manufacturing and C.L. Best Gas Tractor Company merged, this time to form the Caterpillar Tractor Company (Cat). Baxter had been forced out earlier in the year, and C.L. Best was named chairman of Caterpillar, while Raymond C. Force, an attorney and board member, became president and CEO. Caterpillar's first problem was to choose the outlets that would represent the new concern from among the many solid dealerships that Best and Holt had established under

Key Dates:

1883: Brothers Charles Henry Holt and Benjamin Holt found the Stockton Wheel Company in Stockton, California.

1885: Daniel Best produces his first combine.

1886: Stockton Wheel produces its first combine, the Link Belt Combined Harvester.

1892: Stockton Wheel is incorporated as Holt Manufacturing Company.

1904: Holt produces the first commercially successful caterpillar-style tractor, or crawler, which is soon sold under the Caterpillar brand.

1908: Holt Manufacturing produces its first gas-powered crawlers; Daniel Best sells his company to Holt.

1909: Holt establishes an eastern manufacturing operation by purchasing a plant in Peoria, Illinois.

1910: Best's son, C.L. Best, forms his own tractor manufacturing company, C.L. Best Gas Tractor Company.

1925: Holt Manufacturing and C.L. Best Gas Tractor merge to form Caterpillar Tractor Company.

Early 1930s: Remaining production in California is shifted to Peoria, where the company's headquarters are also reestablished.

1931: Caterpillar's Diesel Sixty tractor helps make the diesel the staple engine for heavy-duty vehicles.

1932: Company records its first full-year loss, $1.6 million.

1950: Caterpillar Tractor Company Ltd. was established in Great Britain as the first overseas subsidiary.

1963: Caterpillar and Mitsubishi Heavy Industries, Ltd. form a joint venture to produce Caterpillar-designed vehicles in Japan.

1982: Company suffers first loss since the Great Depression.

1985: A massive factory-modernization program is launched that will eventually cost $1.8 billion and be completed in 1993.

1986: Company is renamed Caterpillar Inc.

1990: Caterpillar reorganizes along product lines and geographic areas.

1991: A lengthy labor dispute begins with a strike at two Caterpillar plants.

1994: Record-long, 17-month strike begins.

1998: LucasVarity PLC's Perkins Engines unit is acquired for $1.3 billion; prolonged labor dispute ends with the signing of a new six-year contract.

2001: Caterpillar exits from the agricultural tractor business.

their respective names. Caterpillar picked only the most successful sites and quickly began to expand by opening dealerships in Australia, the Netherlands, east Africa, and Tunisia. Caterpillar dealerships developed a reputation for keeping their machines running. The firm insisted that the dealers keep a large supply of spare parts available and employ a large service force. Another development in the immediate aftermath of the merger was the shifting of all tractor manufacturing to Peoria; combines continued to be made in Stockton.

In 1929 Caterpillar's sales were $52 million, and the Peoria plant alone employed more than 4,000 workers. The crash of 1929, however, hit Caterpillar hard, but not as hard as it might have, thanks to an increase in sales to the Soviet Union in the early 1930s. In the aftermath of the financial world's collapse, Caterpillar went from sales of $45 million in 1930 to $13 million in 1932, and the company suffered its first full-year loss the latter year, totaling $1.6 million. Salaries were cut, including those of executives, many factories went on a four-day workweek, and the remaining production in California was shifted to Peoria. Yet the company stayed profitable and rebounded in the late 1930s, primarily, again, because of Soviet purchases. The Soviets at that time were forming vast collective farms, some of which approached 400,000 acres in size. Caterpillar products helped make such farms manageable, and the Soviets ordered millions of dollars worth of tractors and combines from Caterpillar. In the early 1930s Caterpillar moved its main office to Peoria, for a more geographically central location.

By 1931, the diesel tractor engine, which had been used before but not widely, was finally perfected for common use by Caterpillar. Previously diesels had been too heavy and undependable for commercial use. The Diesel Sixty tractor, how-

ever, made the diesel the staple engine for heavy-duty vehicles. In 1933 Caterpillar's diesel production was double that of all other U.S. firms combined. This boon gave Cat the impetus to redesign many of its old models, making them more efficient and economical. Sales began to rise and continued to do so throughout the late 1930s, as Caterpillar benefited from the huge road-building projects of President Franklin D. Roosevelt's public works programs. Caterpillar's many innovations in rubber-tired tractors and diesel engines for trucks clearly contributed to revitalizing the firm.

Caterpillar's contributions to World War II were many and varied. Of substantial importance was the conversion of a gasoline airplane engine into a dependable diesel engine. In 1942 Caterpillar unveiled the new RD-1820 radial diesel engine, which was used to power the M-4 tank. The company manufactured other engines, as well, and even artillery shells for the war effort. It set up an aluminum foundry in Decatur, Illinois, to help ease the shortage of this vital material. Caterpillar engineers found that they could make a stronger metal with cheaper, more plentiful raw materials if they used high-frequency electrical induction to harden the steel used in tanks and personnel carriers.

Caterpillar tractors worked in battle zones repairing damaged roads, building new ones, bulldozing tank traps, and constructing pillboxes (gun emplacements). Because the Cat was usually seen doing such roadwork with a bulldozer blade attached, the term "bulldozer" came to be used for Caterpillar products. Caterpillar tractors and road-building equipment were used to build the Burma Road. The makeshift repair shop that was set up to service the machines working on that road by the 497th Heavy Shop Company was dubbed Little Peoria.

Enormous Postwar Growth

In the postwar period, Caterpillar experienced enormous growth rather than recession, because of the massive rebuilding campaigns begun both in Europe and Japan, with the use of Marshall Plan and other funds. In the United States itself, demand seemed limitless. Caterpillar could not get its products to its customers fast enough. Consequently, it launched an expansion program in 1949 that was the first step toward becoming a truly international firm with a major impact on world industry.

The new plant built in 1951 in Joliet, Illinois, was only the beginning of a program to establish manufacturing centers and subsidiaries around the globe. In 1950 Caterpillar announced the formation of its first overseas subsidiary, Caterpillar Tractor Company Ltd. of Great Britain. To further accommodate the postwar need for construction and road-building equipment, Caterpillar opened up subsidiaries in Brazil in 1954, Australia in 1955, and Scotland in 1956. In the 1950s, within the United States, Cat built new factories in Milwaukee, Wisconsin (1951); York, Pennsylvania (1953); Decatur, Illinois (1955); and Davenport, Iowa (1956), and parts distribution centers in Morton, Illinois; and Denver, Colorado.

In the 1960s the continuing boom in the construction of highways, dams, and mines kept sales increasing rapidly. By 1970 employment at Caterpillar was twice that of ten years prior. Caterpillar increased its exports, gaining a rival in the heavy construction industry, Komatsu Ltd. of Japan.

In 1961 Cat suffered the first of many labor conflicts with the United Auto Workers (UAW), when 12,600 workers in Peoria walked off their jobs in a wage dispute. An agreement was reached after only eight days, but this strike was the beginning of a series of increasingly bitter and complex battles between labor and management. Recognizing that industry abroad sometimes operates by rules different from those of the United States, Caterpillar in 1963 formed a joint venture in Japan with Mitsubishi Heavy Industries, Ltd. The venture, initially named Caterpillar Mitsubishi Ltd., began building Cat-designed vehicles in a factory just outside of Tokyo in 1965. It was renamed Shin Caterpillar Mitsubishi Ltd. in 1987.

After the three-year contract extension signed in 1961 was terminated, another strike began in Peoria. Announced as settled as early as February 1964, the strike was off and on until late October. In 1965 Caterpillar exceeded $1 billion in sales for the first time, announced that its stock would be sold on most of the major European stock exchanges, and started Caterpillar Belgium S.A. to build front-loading tractors there.

The year 1966 brought another confrontation with the UAW, this time in the form of a two-month walkout in Decatur. The lawsuit that Cat filed against the union, claiming an illegal strike, was settled out of court, in exchange for an agreement that stipulated that the union would settle all conflicts not relating to contract specifications before going out on strike. During this year Caterpillar of Canada Ltd. announced the construction of a 64,000-square-foot addition to its distribution warehouse.

In March 1968 the U.S. Justice Department moved to block a proposed merger between Cat and Chicago Pneumatic Tool Company, and the merger did not take place. In the same year, Caterpillar was the first company located outside of a major city to enlist in a government-sponsored program to hire and train people considered to be unemployable. This program was directed to persons who had been out of work for extended periods. The hirees would work half of the day at entry-level positions and spend the other half of the day learning job skills for better-paying jobs.

A contract with Ford in 1970 to supply small V-8 truck engines convinced Cat that manufacturing smaller diesels could make money, and the firm spent millions of dollars redesigning and retooling existing plants to build the new engines. Profits earned from an increase in state construction programs helped pay the cost of these investments. By 1972 Cat had announced plans to build a 900,000-square-foot plant in Belgium and a 1.25 million-square-foot production facility in Mossville, Illinois. Sales to the Soviet Union increased during this year.

In 1974 Caterpillar embarked on another dramatic expansion program, announcing plans to build a 650,000-square-foot addition to its Aurora, Illinois, plant, a 1.3 million-square-foot addition to its diesel engine shop in Mossville, a 720,000-square-foot addition to its Peoria plant, and a new 670,000-square-foot manufacturing center in Brazil. In 1975 Caterpillar allocated more funds than ever before for expansion and product development. The company expanded its foreign market at this time by selling pipe-laying equipment to China, cashing in on the thaw in relations between China and the United States.

By 1978 the Cat expansion program was paying off. Sales approached $6 billion and the new manufacturing plants were able to turn out thousands of vehicles. The product line had expanded to the point where Cat offered more heavy-duty agricultural, construction, and material-hauling machines than any other company. In 1978 plans were revealed to build more new plants in York, Pennsylvania; Lafayette, Indiana; and Pontiac, Illinois.

The longest UAW strike against Caterpillar (to that date) occurred in 1979. More than 23,000 workers in Illinois walked out of six of the company's major manufacturing plants. More than 3,500 workers were laid off because of the parts shortages that resulted from the strike. After almost three months of negotiations, a new three-year contract was forged, which offered better wages and a profit-sharing concession.

Deep Downturn in the 1980s

Caterpillar settled an involved lawsuit with Goodyear Tire & Rubber Company in 1981. Three years previously Goodyear had begun selling a radial earthmoving tire that infringed on Caterpillar's beadless-tire technology. The beadless tire lacked the beads, or edges, that attach the tire to wheel rims, and was more durable and economical than previous designs. In the out-of-court settlement Goodyear agreed to pay Caterpillar an amount mutually agreed upon, and become a licensee of Cat, paying the firm royalties for the use of beadless technology in the further manufacture of the tire.

In 1981 the firm won a political battle to be granted the right to sell $90 million in pipe-laying equipment to the Soviet Union, despite stiff opposition from the administration of President Ronald Reagan. That year the firm sold more machines than ever before, with sales in excess of $9 billion for the year. Caterpillar also became the leading supplier of industrial gas turbines that year through the $505 million acquisition of Solar Turbines Incorporated from International Harvester.

The recession of 1982 hit Caterpillar especially hard. The economic downturn caused sales to drop to $6.5 billion that year. Caterpillar laid off almost 12,000 employees at this time, and closed its plant in Mentor, Ohio. Trying to cut overhead, Cat proposed pay freezes and a cut in benefits, prompting a seven-month UAW strike, the firm's longest strike yet. To add to the company's problems, barely six weeks after the 37,500 UAW workers left their jobs, a jury awarded Kast Metals a $9.2 million settlement for Caterpillar's failure to live up to an oral agreement to buy steel castings from Kast if Kast were to build a new plant to make the castings.

Caterpillar began 1983 by announcing the first annual loss in earnings in half a century. Cat started laying off workers, and closed a plant in Newcastle-on-Tyne, England. Sales slumped to a recent history low of $5.4 billion. Yet after the new contract was signed with the UAW, Caterpillar acquired a new direction and strategy that made things look better. Despite the concession of a profit-sharing plan, the wage freeze that the firm won in the contract dispute helped stem rising costs. The anticipation of the bottled-up demand that would create a larger market after the recession made investors think that Cat stock might be a good buy. By committing itself to less expansion, more creative marketing techniques, and reduced costs, Caterpillar intended in late 1983 to ride out the economic slump and position itself to return to profitability in 1984.

Caterpillar's problems continued, however, in 1984. Despite this being the expected comeback year for the firm, the plant closings and layoffs continued. The Burlington, Iowa, parts plant locked its doors to workers and, despite optimistic projections of recalling around 3,200 workers in 1985, Cat actually laid off about 3,000 other workers during that year. Caterpillar continued to cut back operations at its factories, then eliminated cost-of-living allowances in wages, and delayed the completion of its Morton, Illinois, distribution center. The firm blamed its third straight losing year on high interest rates and stiff price competition from other companies; losses for 1992–94 totaled $953 million.

In February 1985 George A. Schaefer was named chairman and CEO of Caterpillar, and Donald V. Fites was named president. Despite a net loss of almost $430 million the year before, Schaefer confidently predicted that Cat would make a profit during his first year as company head. During this year Caterpillar made two key strategic moves, which, despite their controversial nature, would be credited with making the firm once again profitable. Caterpillar first shifted some of its production and purchasing functions overseas. This meant that jobs previously performed in Peoria were moved to Scotland or Japan. The high value of the dollar overseas made such a change necessary for company survival, management argued. Secondly, Caterpillar embarked on a $600 million factory-modernization program. It would reduce permanently the labor force needed to make tractors by automating as many manufacturing processes as possible. Approximately 2,300 workers

were cut from the Caterpillar payroll during 1985. Company executives argued that the firm needed to compete with Komatsu, which had a much greater manufacturing efficiency than Cat because of its highly automated plants.

In 1986 Caterpillar Tractor Company became Caterpillar Inc. and announced that it had made a profit of almost $200 million in the previous year. The firm bounced back from its problems by marketing a new automated lift truck, which had the potential to secure part of a multibillion-dollar market for Caterpillar. The firm even directly challenged Komatsu by expanding Cat's partnership with Mitsubishi Heavy Industries to include the production of hydraulic equipment.

Caterpillar faced, however, another strike during this year. Workers in Joliet walked out for four weeks, but were brought back to work under terms much like those previously rejected. Caterpillar again won a wage freeze, but cash bonuses as well as the firm's promise to lay off other workers as long as the strike continued were enough to get the Joliet workers to settle their grievances.

The weakening of the dollar abroad raised production costs and cut into profits for Caterpillar in 1987. Though the firm improved its sales and earnings over 1986, Caterpillar was still forced to close three factories. Nevertheless, in 1988 Caterpillar again made the kind of large profits it had made in the past, reaping $616 million for the year. In early 1989 Caterpillar's stock took a sharp downturn. The modernization campaign had swelled to a cost of more than $1.8 billion and flattened profits for the year. The cost of the program continued to affect company profits through 1992, while the company also suffered from the effects of the recession of the early 1990s.

A decline in sales in 1991 contributed to Cat's first loss since 1984, $404 million—the worst loss in company history. Sales increased only marginally in 1992, while the firm suffered another loss, this time $218 million. Meanwhile, newly appointed CEO Fites initiated a corporate reorganization in 1990 which moved Cat away from a function-oriented structure to one revolving around product lines and geographic areas.

Bitter Labor Disputes in the 1990s

Labor strife returned to Peoria in late 1991 when Caterpillar tried to alter a pattern agreement that had been agreed to in October at John Deere. When the UAW and Cat workers refused to accept the company's offer, they struck two Cat plants with 2,400 workers in early November. Caterpillar responded by locking out 5,650 more workers. Over the next five months, Caterpillar used managers to fill in at the affected plants, then threatened to permanently replace 15,000 UAW workers. In April 1992 the workers returned to their jobs without a contract and eventually accepted a company-imposed contract. The striking workers, however, returned to what they believed was a hostile environment, where they faced suspension or dismissal for wearing union-supporting T-shirts or buttons. By mid-1994, more than 80 complaints against Caterpillar for such tactics were issued by the National Labor Relations Board.

In 1993 Caterpillar completed the factory modernization program and at the same time began to benefit from its results. The time to process a part from start to finish was reduced by 75 percent and in-process inventories were reduced by 60 percent. Coupled with an overhaul of the new product development process, vast improvements were made in new product introductions. Only 24 new or improved products were introduced in 1991; that figure doubled in 1992 and reached 53 in 1994. Such gains led to record sales of $11.62 billion in 1993 and record profits of $652 million. The next year brought more records: $955 million in profits on sales of $14.33 billion.

In the early 1990s Caterpillar looked to the east and south for its future growth. The company strongly supported both the North American Free Trade Agreement (NAFTA) and the General Agreement on Tariffs and Trade (GATT), concluding that the elimination of trade barriers could add $350 million in Cat sales a year by 2000. By 1994 Caterpillar had already reaped the benefits of NAFTA when it posted $239 million in sales in Mexico, an increase of 59 percent over 1993. Outside North America, Caterpillar formed several joint ventures in Japan (with Mitsubishi), Russia (with AMO-ZiL and with Kirovsky), and China (with Shanghai Diesel and with Xuzhou Construction Machinery Group). New dealerships were also established in Vietnam and the Shanghai region of China in 1994.

On the heels of the firm's improving results came the longest and most bitter strike to hit Caterpillar yet. After sporadic wildcat walkouts following the 1991–92 strike, a full-scale strike began in June 1994 with 10,500 UAW workers honoring picket lines while about 4,000 workers stayed on the job. The issue that precipitated the walkout was Caterpillar's firing of union workers, but the dispute quickly evolved into one concerning a new contract. As with the 1991–92 strike, Caterpillar again shifted managers onto the assembly lines but it also hired temporary workers to fill in. As the strike dragged on into 1995, it was beginning to affect Cat's inventories and operating efficiencies, but its impact was mitigated by the decreasing number of union workers at the company. Caterpillar had been locating its new plants in right-to-work states and foreign countries, and had shifted some production to other manufacturers through outsourcing. While UAW workers made up 45 percent of Cat's workforce in 1980, by 1995 UAW workers numbered only 28 percent.

In early 1995 the two sides agreed to federal mediation for a new round of contract talks. As Caterpillar continued to post record profits and revenues, the company clearly had the upper hand. Even though workers voted to reject a contract offer in early December, the UAW promptly called off the strike and sent the workers back to their jobs without a contract. The rejected contract terms began to be implemented by the company unilaterally, including a two-tier wage system and no overtime pay for days longer than eight hours. Similar to the aftermath of the 1991–92 strike, Cat placed restrictions on what workers could say or display, and by early 1996 at least 50 workers had been suspended or fired for violating what the company called its "standards of conduct." Meanwhile, Caterpillar's board voted to reward Fites for his handling of the strike and for the company's performance with a 1995 compensation package of $3.09 million, an increase of 75 percent over the $1.76 million he received in 1994.

The bitter strike behind it, Caterpillar announced more record results for 1995, with profits exceeding $1 billion for the first time ($1.14 billion) on sales of $16.07 billion. Sales would keep rising during the boom years of the late 1990s, hitting $20.98 billion in 1998, while profits peaked at $1.66 billion in 1997, when Caterpillar enjoyed a profit margin of 8.8 percent (compared to the 1994 figure of 6.7 percent). A key acquisition was completed during this period, the $1.3 billion purchase of LucasVarity plc's Perkins Engines unit in February 1998. Perkins provided Caterpillar a considerable position within the fast-growing market for small diesel engines, which were used in compact construction equipment, such as skid-steer loaders. This deal was well-timed in that Caterpillar was in the process of rolling out its own line of new, small-scale construction equipment. By 1998 engine sales accounted for about 30 percent of annual revenues, aided also by an earlier acquisition, that of MaK Motoren GmbH & Co. KG, a German producer of power generator engines acquired in December 1996.

In March 1998, meantime, Caterpillar and the UAW finally reached an agreement on a new six-year contract, ending the 6½-year labor dispute. Most observers agreed that the company had come out clearly ahead, having largely met most of the goals it had set before the dispute began. The union, however, did manage to force the company to unconditionally recall 160 workers who had been fired for union-related activities during the prolonged and bitter period of strife. In February 1999 Fites, a man despised by many workers for his hardline stance and his threats to permanently replace his employees, retired from the firm. Glen A. Barton, who had been vice-chairman and group president in charge of Caterpillar's forest, mining, and construction equipment operations, was named the new chairman and CEO.

Maintaining Profitability Through the Early 2000s Downturn

Caterpillar began feeling the effects of the early 2000s economic downturn ahead of time, as its customers began cutting back on purchases as early as 1999 in anticipation of the troubled days ahead. Sales fell that year and then stagnated, amounting to only $20.15 billion in 2002. Unlike past recessions, however, Caterpillar remained in the black throughout thanks to its leaner and more diversified operations, which made the company less vulnerable to the cyclical ups and downs of the heavy machinery industry. Caterpillar's worst year came in 2002, when profits amounted to $798 million, which translated into a profit margin of just 4 percent. Barton also initiated additional cost-cutting measures to maintain the company's profitability, announcing in August 2000 a plan to cut annual expenses by more than $1 billion over the succeeding three to five years. He also aimed to increase revenues to $30 billion by mid-decade in part by continuing Caterpillar's diversification drive into engines, compact construction equipment, financial services—mainly loans to its large network of dealers—and rental equipment. Barton also made the difficult decision of exiting from the agricultural tractor business, offloading its tractor line to AGCO Corp. late in 2001. Although this was significant from a historic standpoint given the importance of tractors in Caterpillar's early history, by 2001 agricultural equipment generated only about 4 percent of Cat's total revenues.

Caterpillar rebounded strongly in 2003, posting record revenues of $22.76 billion and profits of $1.1 billion, a 38 percent jump over 2002. Sales were strong in its two largest manufacturing operations, heavy machinery and diesel truck engines. Machinery accounted for 50 percent of the revenues, engines 40 percent, and financial services the remaining 10 percent. During the year, Caterpillar launched its new line of low-emission ACERT engines that complied with U.S. Environmental Protection Agency (EPA) regulations slated to go into effect in 2004 (ACERT stood for Advanced Combustion Emissions Reduction Technology). In February 2003 the company entered into a five-year global alliance with mining company BHP Billiton to supply about $1.5 billion in mining machinery and other equipment.

On the heels of the stellar results for 2003, Barton retired in January 2004. James W. Owens was named his successor, having served as a group president, of various business units, since 1995. Under the new leader, Caterpillar was targeting emerging markets, particularly China, India, and Russia, for future growth. The company was hoping to reach its goal of $30 billion in revenues by 2006.

Principal Subsidiaries

Caterpillar Financial Services Corporation; Caterpillar Insurance Holdings, Inc.; Caterpillar Logistics Services, Inc.; Solar Turbines Incorporated; MaK Deutschland GmbH & Co. KG (Germany); Bitelli S.p.A. (Italy); Caterpillar Overseas S.A. (Switzerland); Perkins Engines Group Limited (U.K.); Turner Powertrain Systems Limited (U.K.).

Principal Divisions

Asia-Pacific Division; Building Construction Products Division; Compact Power Systems Division; Europe, Africa & Middle East Product Development & Operations Division; Global Mining Division; Large Power Systems Division; Latin America Division; Mining & Construction Equipment Division; North American Commercial Division; Track-Type Tractors Division; Wheel Loaders & Excavators Division.

Principal Competitors

Komatsu Ltd.; CNH Global N.V.; Deere & Company; Terex Corporation; Ingersoll-Rand Company Limited; AB Volvo; Hitachi Construction Machinery Co., Ltd.; J C Bamford Excavators Ltd.; Cummins, Inc.

Further Reading

Arndt, Michael, "This Cat Isn't So Nimble: Can Caterpillar's New CEO Reverse Sliding Sales and Profits?," *Business Week,* February 21, 2000, p. 148G.

Benson, Tracy E., "Caterpillar Wakes Up," *Industry Week,* May 20, 1991, pp. 33+.

Bremner, Brian, "Can Caterpillar Inch Its Way Back into Heftier Profits?," *Business Week,* September 25, 1989, pp. 75+.

Byrne, Harlan S., "Track of the Cat: Caterpillar Is Bulldozing Its Way to Higher Profits," *Barron's,* April 6, 1987, pp. 13+.

"Caterpillar: Sticking to Basics to Stay Competitive," *Business Week,* May 4, 1981, pp. 74+.

The Caterpillar Story, Peoria, Ill.: Caterpillar Inc., 1990, 80 p.

Century of Change: Caterpillar Special World Historical Edition, Peoria, Ill.: Caterpillar Inc., 1984.

Deveny, Kathleen, "For Caterpillar, the Metamorphosis Isn't Over," *Business Week,* August 31, 1987, pp. 72+.

Dubashi, Jagannath, "Cat-apult: The Cheap Dollar Helped, but Caterpillar's Turnaround Was Engineered in Peoria," *Financial World,* November 23, 1993, p. 34.

Edgar, George P., "Caterpillar Tractor," *Barron's,* May 18, 1953, pp. 19+.

Elstrom, J.W., "Cat, Union Crawl Toward Settlement: Weary Workers, Pressed Managers Tire of the Fight," *Crain's Chicago Business,* January 16, 1995.

Elstrom, Peter, "This Cat Keeps on Purring," *Business Week,* January 20, 1997, p. 80.

Franklin, Stephen, "Questions Linger As Vote Nears on Caterpillar Pact: Was Strike Worth It? Will Anger Fade?," *Chicago Tribune,* November 27, 1995.

Gibson, Paul, and Barbara Rudolph, "Playing Peoria—to Perfection," *Forbes,* May 11, 1981, pp. 60+.

"The Going May Get Tough for Caterpillar," *Fortune,* May 1972, p. 161.

Gordon, Paul, "Diversification Helping Caterpillar Weather Storm," *Peoria (Ill.) Journal Star,* September 28, 2002, p. E6.

——, "Profiling Highs and Lows of Caterpillar Chairmen," *Peoria (Ill.) Journal Star,* July 23, 2000, p. A18.

Haycraft, William R., *Yellow Steel: The Story of the Earthmoving Equipment Industry,* Urbana: University of Illinois Press, 2000, 465 p.

Henkoff, Ronald, "This Cat Is Acting Like a Tiger," *Fortune,* December 19, 1988, pp. 69+.

Hutchins, Dexter, "Caterpillar Triple Whammy," *Fortune,* October 27, 1986, pp. 91+.

Kelly, Kevin, "Cat Is Purring, but They're Hissing on the Floor," *Business Week,* May 16, 1994, p. 33.

McConville, Daniel J., "Cat's Back: After Four Tough Years on the Road," *Barron's,* April 1, 1985, pp. 36+.

Naumann, William L., *The Story of Caterpillar Tractor Co.,* New York: Newcomen Society in North America, 1977, 23 p.

Payne, Walter A., ed., *Benjamin Holt: The Story of Caterpillar Tractor,* Stockton, Calif.: University of the Pacific, 1982, 102 p.

"A Shaken Caterpillar Retools to Take on a More Competitive World," *Business Week,* November 5, 1984, pp. 91+.

Slutsker, Gary, "What's Good for Caterpillar . . . ," *Forbes,* December 7, 1992, p. 108.

Upbin, Bruce, "Sharpening the Claws," *Forbes,* July 26, 1999, pp. 102–05.

Ward, Sandra, "The Cat Comes Back," *Barron's,* February 25, 2002, pp. 21–22, 24.

Weimer, De'Ann, "A New Cat on the Hot Seat," *Business Week,* March 9, 1998, pp. 56, 61.

Wik, Reynold M., *Benjamin Holt and Caterpillar: Tracks and Combines,* St. Joseph, Mich.: American Society of Agricultural Engineers, 1984, 129 p.

—Wallace Ross
—update: David E. Salamie

:certegy

Certegy, Inc.

11720 Amber Park Drive, Suite 600
Alpharetta, Georgia 30004
U.S.A.
Telephone: (678) 867-8000
Fax: (678) 867-8101
Web site: http://www.certegy.com

Public Company
Incorporated: 1961 as Telecredit, Inc.
Employees: 4,000
Sales: $1.01 billion (2003)
Stock Exchanges: New York
Ticker Symbol: CEY
NAIC: 522320 Financial Transactions Processing,
    Reserve, and Clearinghouse Activities

Certegy, Inc. is a leading provider of check authorization services and credit card, debit card, and merchant card processing. The company provides its services to more than 6,000 financial institutions and to more than 100,000 retailers worldwide. Certegy's business is divided into two main areas, Check Services and Card Services. Certegy helps client retailers such as Wal-Mart and Best Buy by providing risk management and data services that catch bad check writers and verify customers with adequate funds. For its service Certegy receives a percentage of the total dollar amount of checks written to the client. Certegy pioneered this business in the 1960s. Certegy's Card Services unit has prevailed despite competition from larger vendors by concentrating on providing card processing services to small banks and credit unions. The company also has growing international sales, doing business in the United Kingdom, Ireland, and France, in Chile and Brazil, and in Australia and New Zealand. Certegy's card processing unit in Melbourne, Australia, handles multinational and multilingual transactions, allowing Certegy to service customers in Thailand and throughout the Asia Pacific region. Certegy was founded as Telecredit, Inc., and operated under that name through 1990. From 1990 to 2001 the company was the Payment Services unit of Equifax, Inc. Equifax spun off the unit in 2001.

Founding a New Industry in the 1960s

The company that became Certegy was founded in 1961 as Telecredit, Inc. by two men, Ronald A. Katz and Robert Goldman. The Los Angeles company put together existing telephone and computer technology, and patented a quick system of verifying whether a check written to a merchant was good. Telecredit collected data about check writers' habits, and kept it filed by driver's license number. Telecredit kept track of how many checks a person normally wrote a month, what the amounts were, and any instances of bad checks. The company was able to use this databank to assess the merchant's risk of accepting a check from a particular person. At the time, merchants usually monitored bad check writers with a simple system, often a handwritten list kept at the cashier's elbow. If the cashier was in doubt, he or she could call the customer's bank and wait for authorization. Telecredit was the first company to offer a fast and sophisticated automated system. Telecredit compiled many more variables than merchants themselves were able to cover, and the company stored data on a much larger pool of people than the small number of known defaulters that individual stores looked out for.

Telecredit's system had clear technological advantages. Yet it was slow to catch on. Telecredit began by marketing its services to area supermarkets. Business grew gradually, and it was a long time before the company made any money. Telecredit went through 100 consecutive months in the red before finally becoming profitable in 1970. Telecredit's entrepreneurs kept inventing, coming up with a new system for reading and writing codes on the magnetic strips on the backs of credit cards. Ronald Katz went on to hold close to 50 patents for various systems and devices related to computer and telecommunications technology. He continued at Telecredit as its patent licensing administrator, while the business end of the company was run by CEO Lee Ault beginning in 1968. Ault described the early years of the company to *American Banker* (November 7, 1984), saying, "We developed and invented a lot of things that went on to become industry standards. The problem is that they were never commercially successful. The things we had in the '60s never became popular until the '70s. That's the price of being a pioneer."

Yet Ault and his team were patient, and by the mid-1970s Telecredit had sales of $8 million. It collected fees of about 2 percent of the amount of checks it guaranteed. The company also began operating a second business segment, processing credit card transactions. In 1977 Telecredit bought Florida Service Center, a bank card processing company. This was right at the beginning of the era when automated teller machines (ATMs) were being introduced, and plastic cards were being used for new services as well, such as to debit checking accounts. As more and more transactions were done by card, companies including Telecredit made money by processing the data for banks. Bank card servicing became a highly competitive industry, but Telecredit found a niche by working for small banks and credit unions. Bigger competitors such as American Express subsidiary First Data Resources overlooked these smaller financial institutions. This became a growing second line of business for Telecredit. By the early 1980s, some 34 percent of Telecredit's revenue came from its credit card processing division.

Even as credit card, debit card, and ATM card use increased over the 1970s and early 1980s, people continued to write checks and retailers continued to use Telecredit's verification system. As its data banks became larger, Telecredit was able to pursue accounts with national retailers including Toys 'R' Us. By the early 1980s Telecredit was clearly the leader in the check guarantee field, with a market share of about 25 percent. It guaranteed more than $2 billion worth of checks in 1982, and pulled in revenue of $61.5 million. Both sales and earnings grew through the mid-1980s. In 1985 revenue had reached $85 million.

Light Signatures and Other Ventures in the 1980s

Telecredit toiled through the 1960s and finally began earning money in 1970. It began paying dividends to stockholders in 1976, and was able to raise the amount it paid out every year through the mid-1980s. By that time, the company seemed to have arrived. Its technology was widely understood, unlike in its early years, and Telecredit had two viable business units, card processing and check guaranteeing. In the mid-1980s, the company began picking up more large national accounts. By 1985, mall clothier The Gap, the discount department store

Kmart, and the electronics chain Circuit City Stores all used Telecredit's check guaranteeing services. Telecredit had only one major competitor in this business sector, and there seemed to be plenty of room for expansion. Of all checks written to U.S. retailers, only about 3 percent were guaranteed (by Telecredit or other companies), meaning that the potential market for the service was still large. Telecredit's credit card processing business also grew nicely in the early to mid-1980s. Telecredit had an arrangement with the trade group representing the nation's smallest banks, the Independent Bankers Association of America (IBAA). In the mid-1980s Telecredit processed credit cards for 300 of these small banks, and the IBAA estimated that the number would be up to 1,000 in a few years. Telecredit also had an arrangement with a Florida organization called Payment Systems for Credit Unions, in which Telecredit managed credit card payments for the group's 800-plus member credit unions. This was a lucrative niche for Telecredit, providing almost 20 percent of Telecredit's revenue by the late 1980s.

The company had little debt and seemingly strong finances in the mid-1980s. Stock market analysts began to take note of the company. Its two main business areas were sound and expanding, and the company was a leader in its market. In addition, Telecredit revealed that it had another important new technology in the wings. This was an anti-counterfeiting system called Light Signatures. Light Signatures, Inc. was organized in 1981 by Telecredit's founders Katz and Goldman. By 1983, Telecredit owned 51 percent of the company, and it bought the remainder for $14.8 million the next year. Light Signatures used a light beam system to verify the authenticity of paper, plastic, fabric, and other materials. Manufacturers could use Light Signatures' technology to check for counterfeits. Early customers were the blue jeans manufacturer Levi Strauss and the maker of the popular Jane Fonda Workout videotapes. In 1983 Telecredit CEO Lee Ault hired a new president and chief operating officer, Louis Buglioli, and put him in charge of the company's established businesses. Ault gave himself the job of chairman, with the mission of shepherding Light Signatures and seeing to the long-range planning for Telecredit. Ault estimated that the counterfeiting business in the United States, comprising everything from government documents to ripoffs of designer clothes, was worth $50 billion. Thus Light Signatures, a system that could detect many different kinds of fakery, had a potentially enormous market. One analyst from the brokerage firm Raymond James told *American Banker* (November 7, 1984): "Unless I'm missing something, Light Signatures is the next Xerox."

Yet there were problems getting Light Signatures off the ground. The machines were apparently sometimes difficult to use, and it was not clear how the company could establish a viable business by relying on the manufacturers of the often faddish goods that were most often counterfeited. Light Signatures wanted to develop a business detecting fake credit cards. The technology worked best, however, with paper or fiber that already had a slight irregularity in its "signature" when held up to the Light Signatures beam. Thus the company had to manufacture its own plastic cards, which were embedded with a random pattern of extra plastic crystals. This venture apparently went nowhere, while Light Signatures began to fish for customers in the securities industry. Counterfeit stocks and bonds were a real problem, and Light Signatures developed special verification machines called Signa Three. By 1988, Light Signatures had letters of intent from some 20 banks that were interested in buying the Signa Three technology. The major stock exchanges mulled over compelling their members to use the technology. This meant that new stocks and bonds would have to be "signaturized," like the new credit cards, or manufactured with a magnetic strip and certain random elements so that the Signa Three machines could read and code them.

There were many big "ifs" in Light Signatures' future. The stock market crashed in October 1987, and that may have left the securities industry jittery about shelling out for unproven technology. The unit lost money, while Telecredit's core businesses continued to do well. Telecredit had revenue of $133.2 million in 1988, about 60 percent from its check guaranteeing division and most of the rest from credit card processing. Light Signatures had sales of $6.1 million, but at that point it seemed a drain on the parent company. In May 1988, Chairman Ault announced Telecredit would write off more than $25 million in its investment in Light Signatures. This led to a net loss of almost $7 million for Telecredit in 1988. Only a few months later, Telecredit had more bad news to deal with. Payment Systems for Credit Unions, which provided a substantial portion of Telecredit's credit card processing business, announced that it was ending its agreement with the company and moving to a competitor. Telecredit scrambled to set up its own unit, called Card Services for Credit Unions, and it persuaded about half of its former credit union clients to stick with it. Despite these two blows close together, Telecredit managed to do well over 1989. Its revenue came in at $158 million, and profit was about $25 million, which looked impressive compared with the loss of the previous year.

With Equifax in the 1990s

Though Telecredit had shown growth in its core businesses throughout the 1980s, in some ways the company seemed stymied. Revenue was more holding steady rather than bounding along, as the big promise of Light Signatures fizzled out. The company was vulnerable to competitors in its card processing division, as was demonstrated when First Data Resources, a bigger player, took almost half its credit union business away. Nevertheless, Telecredit had strong cash flow, and after writing off Light Signatures, it was free of debt. Analysts expected the company to grow now by acquisition, or to be acquired. Telecredit took the latter choice. It had a firm base on the West Coast, while its competitors were in the East. Therefore, the company hoped it would be a nice acquisition for an Eastern rival looking to build in the other end of the country. In July 1990, Telecredit announced that it was being bought by Atlanta, Georgia-based Equifax, Inc. Equifax had revenue of about $800 million. Equifax was the nation's leading credit bureau, compiling reports and providing information on consumer transactions. The key to both companies was data, and they were in complementary if not overlapping businesses.

As an Equifax subsidiary, Telecredit kept its name for two years, but in 1993 the business became Equifax Payment Services. Equifax Payment Services headquarters were in Tampa, Florida. The division operated two segments, Equifax Card Services and Equifax Check Services. The division attracted large customers, like the growing electronics retailer Best Buy. That firm began to move quickly into new markets in the early 1990s, and it credited Equifax Payment Services with helping it manage check writing risk, especially in unfamiliar urban markets. The Payment Services division also grew by acquisition. In 1996 Equifax bought the card services division of Credit Union National Association (CUNA), the fifth largest credit card processor in the United States. The CUNA unit became part of Equifax Payment Services. The Equifax unit continued to serve small banks through the Independent Bankers Association of America, an arrangement Telecredit had established in the early 1980s.

The parent company also began to grow internationally. Equifax moved into check guaranteeing in Europe beginning in 1992, through a joint venture with regional leader Transax. The arrangement with Transax also led Equifax Payment Services into new markets in Australia and New Zealand. In 1996 Equifax acquired Transax, giving it the leading market share in check guaranteeing in Europe. Equifax also bought First Bankcard Systems, maker of advanced software for credit card processing, and in 1998 bought UNNISA, a large credit card processing firm in Brazil. Over 1999 and 2000 Equifax Payment services moved into markets in England, Ireland, and Chile, and gained a significant contract for credit card processing in its established markets of Australia and New Zealand.

Independent Again in the 2000s As Certegy

Equifax Payment Systems seemed to thrive in the 1990s as Telecredit had never done. It grew quickly through acquisitions, and over the decade the division came to comprise half of Equifax's total revenue. The division's revenue for 1999 came to $680.7 million, with operating income of $135.5 million. The division had worldwide markets, and client retailers in some 300,000 locations. Parent company Equifax decided in 2001 to spin off its payment services division into a separate, publicly traded company to be called Certegy. (The name stood for a combination of "certainty," "technology," and "energy.") Equifax felt that its own stock was undervalued because investors did not fully understand its business. It was known as a credit bureau, yet it had this large and profitable division in a related but separate industry. Equifax's management felt its stockholders would get better value if the payment services unit stood on its own. The company had pursued a similar course in 1997, spinning off ChoicePoint, a division that sold consumer data to insurers. In 2001 Equifax Payment Services, formerly Telecredit, debuted on the New York Stock Exchange as

Certegy. The company operated out of headquarters in Alpharetta, Georgia, with 5,000 employees total.

As a newly independent company, Certegy continued to expand its services at home and abroad, and to grow through acquisition. Shortly after going public, the company hit some bumps, but it seemed to recover well. In late 2002 the company learned it had lost a credit card processing arrangement with a Brazilian bank to rival Electronic Data Systems Corp. The loss of the Brazilian contract cost the company an estimated $46 million. The company also had problems putting in place a check guaranteeing program at a Brazilian discount retailer, causing Certegy to restate its revenue projections. In the United States, Certegy lost its account guaranteeing checks to the online transaction service PayPal when that firm was acquired by eBay. But Certegy moved ahead in other markets, increasing the amount of credit card processing it did in Australia, for example. The company was already a leading player in the Australian market by 2003. The company used its Melbourne, Australia data center to move into new Asian markets. In 2004 it entered an eight-year contract with a Thai credit card company to process transactions and introduce a personal loan program. In 2003 Certegy began offering a payroll check cashing service through the California supermarket chain Safeway. Certegy had begun a payroll check cashing service in 1999 (when it was still Equifax Payment Services). This was possibly a valuable new niche for the company. Also in 2003, Certegy teamed up with the world's largest retailer, Wal-Mart Stores Inc. Certegy began providing Wal-Mart customers with a new service that let them write checks for shopping at Wal-Mart's online catalog. Certegy also let online shoppers write checks for Dell Computers at Dell's company web site, and did the same for Apple Computer.

In 2003, Certegy authorized more than $35 billion in checks and serviced more than 46 million credit cards. Its revenue topped $1 billion, and its services reached about 100 million consumers around the world. Certegy was the world's leading provider of check guaranteeing services. In its second business area, credit card processing, the company continued to focus on small banks and credit unions, and was the leading service provider in that particular niche. In 2004, Certegy made some key acquisitions. It moved into the gaming industry for the first time, purchasing the Game Financial unit of Viad Corporation for $43 million. The unit provided check cashing services and cash advances on credit cards at 60 U.S. casinos. The acquisition was expected to bring Certegy an additional $50 million in revenue. That year Certegy also acquired a smaller rival in the credit card processing field. The company paid $22.5 million for Elkhart, Indiana-based Crittson Financial LLC. Crittson operated in the small bank niche, like Certegy.

Principal Divisions

Card Services; Check Services.

Principal Competitors

Electronic Data Systems Corporation; First Data Corporation; Nova Information Systems Corporation.

Further Reading

"Australia's Suncorp. Metway to Launch New Visa Card in 2003," *AsiaPulse News,* December 17, 2002, p. 5887.

"Best Buy Prizes Equifax Expertise," *Chain Store Age Executive,* September 1994, p. E12.

Breitkopf, David, "In Brief: Certegy Gets Safeway Deal," *American Banker,* April 22, 2003, p. 9.

"Business Saves Big Money with the 'Minitrial,'" *Business Week,* October 13, 1980, pp. 168–72.

"Cashing in on Bank Card Recording," *Business Week,* September 14, 1981, pp. 85–86.

"Certegy Expands Presence in Thai Card Market," *AsiaPulse News,* October 6, 2003.

"Certegy to Buy Viad Unit for $43 Million," *New York Times,* February 21, 2004, p. C4.

Coulton, Antoinette, "Equifax to Buy Credit Union Group's Card Processor," *American Banker,* September 25, 1996, p. 12.

Cox, Rebecca, "Telecredit Posts $25 Million Net for Year," *American Banker,* July 6, 1989, p. 10.

——, "Telecredit Re-Signs 345 Credit Unions," *American Banker,* May 17, 1989, p. 9.

Edgerton, Jerry, and Jordan E. Goodman, "Cash Cows About to Calf," *Money,* November 1985, p. 7.

"Equifax Renames Two Business Units," *American Banker,* October 29, 1993, p. 18.

"Forgery Foiler," *Fortune,* February 29, 1988, p. 14.

Fung, Amanda, "Loss of Revenue Source Spurs Revamp at Equifax," *American Banker,* January 14, 2002, p. 21.

Kutler, Jeffrey, "Telecredit Suffers $6.9 Million Loss, Cites Writeoff in High-Tech Unit," *American Banker,* June 30, 1988, p. 9.

Kuykendall, Lavonne, "Three Strikes Against Certegy," *American Banker,* September 23, 2002, p. 24.

Lazo, Shirley A., "Speaking of Dividends," *Barron's,* September 19, 1988, p. 66.

Mollenkamp, Carrick, "Equifax Hopes to Revitalize Its Stock by Spinning Off Payment-Services Unit," *Wall Street Journal,* October 2, 2000, p. A3.

"More Bad News for Telecredit," *American Banker,* October 26, 1988, p. 8.

Neal, Roger, "Walking the Wire," *Forbes,* November 21, 1983, p. 275.

"Telecredit Inc. Expects Lower Income in Fiscal '85," *Wall Street Journal,* June 19, 1985, p. 1.

"Telecredit Planning Write-Off, Revamp for Unprofitable Unit," *Wall Street Journal,* May 27, 1988, p. 1.

"Telecredit Sticks Out Its High-Tech Neck with a Risky But Promising Innovation," *American Banker,* November 7, 1984, p. 40.

"The Tools for a Risky Business," *Chain Store Age,* April 2002, p. 3A.

Wade, Will, "Wal-Mart Taps ACH As Way to Cut Interchange," *American Banker,* July 23, 2003, p. 1.

Walsh, Jim, "Telecredit Inc.: Knowing When to Fold Is the Key to Growth," *California Business,* October 1990, p. 12.

Welling, Kathleen M., "Up & Down Wall Street," *Barron's,* April 18, 1988, pp. 1, 55–56.

Wiegner, Kathleen K., "What Checkless Society?," *Forbes,* September 21, 1987, p. 8.

Wolfe, Daniel, "Certegy to Buy Game Financial, Crittson," *American Banker,* February 23, 2004, p. 18.

—A. Woodward

ConocoPhillips

600 North Dairy Ashford Street
Houston, Texas 77079-1100
U.S.A.
Telephone: (281) 293-1000
Fax: (281) 293-1440
Web site: http://www.conocophillips.com

Public Company
Incorporated: 2001
Employees: 39,000
Sales: $105.1 billion (2003)
Stock Exchanges: New York
Ticker Symbol: COP
NAIC: 211111 Crude Petroleum and Natural Gas
  Extraction; 211112 Natural Gas Liquid Extraction;
  213111 Drilling Oil and Gas Wells; 324110
  Petroleum Refineries; 325110 Petrochemical
  Manufacturing; 422710 Petroleum Bulk Stations and
  Terminals; 447110 Gasoline Stations with
  Convenience Stores; 447190 Other Gasoline Stations;
  486110 Pipeline Transportation of Crude Oil;
  486210 Pipeline Transportation of Natural Gas;
  486910 Pipeline Transportation of Refined Petroleum
  Products

ConocoPhillips is the third largest U.S. integrated oil company, behind only Exxon Mobil Corporation and ChevronTexaco Corporation. The company was formed in August 2002 from the $15.12 billion merger of Conoco Inc. and Phillips Petroleum Company. ConocoPhillips' main focus is on the upstream side of the petroleum industry. The firm has exploration activities in 29 countries, centering on seven areas: northwestern North America, the Gulf of Mexico, Venezuela, the North Sea, West Africa, the Caspian Sea, and the Asia-Pacific region. Production areas are located in 13 nations: the United States, Canada, Venezuela, the United Kingdom, Norway, Nigeria, Dubai, Russia, China, Indonesia, Vietnam, Australia, and East Timor. Production totals about 1.6 million barrels of oil equivalent per day out of proven reserves of 7.8 billion barrels.

Following the merger, ConocoPhillips began shedding some of its downstream operations, but the company remains the fourth largest petroleum refiner in the world, with 12 refineries in the United States, five in Europe, and one in Asia. Worldwide refinery capacity stands at 2.6 million barrels of crude oil and other feedstock per day. The company's marketing operations include about 14,300 retail fuel outlets in the United States and another 3,000 in Europe and Asia, with the petroleum products sold under several brands: Phillips 66, Conoco, 76, Jet, ProJET, Seca, and Turkpetrol. ConocoPhillips has two other core businesses: the gathering, processing, and marketing of natural gas, an activity conducted through Duke Energy Field Services, LLC, in which ConocoPhillips holds a 30.3 percent stake (with the remainder held by Duke Energy Corporation); and the manufacturing and marketing of petrochemicals and plastics, which is conducted through Chevron Phillips Chemical Company LLC, a 50–50 joint venture between ConocoPhillips and ChevronTexaco.

Conoco's Early History As Continental Oil

Conoco's earliest predecessor, Continental Oil & Transportation Company (CO&T), was founded in Ogden, Utah, in 1875 by Isaac Elder Blake to transport petroleum products from the East Coast for sale in Utah, Idaho, Montana, and Nevada. Operations were later expanded to include Denver and San Francisco, and in 1877 the company was reincorporated in California.

Blake's pioneering use of railroad tank cars to transport oil contributed to CO&T's quick success. By the early 1880s, CO&T was sending modest shipments to Mexico, Canada, the Hawaiian islands, the Samoan islands, and Japan. In the western United States it was competing with Standard Oil Co.

In 1884 CO&T agreed to become a Standard affiliate. The following year CO&T merged with Standard's Rocky Mountain operations, and the company was reincorporated in Colorado as the Continental Oil Company. Blake was named president of the new concern, and headquarters were established in Denver. Continental continued to function much as CO&T had, although operations were consolidated with Standard's in Colorado, New Mexico, Wyoming, Montana, and Utah.

<table>
<tr><td>

Company Perspectives:

Purpose: Use our pioneering spirit to responsibly deliver energy to the world.

</td></tr>
</table>

Continental products were purchased from Standard and other providers in the East and included kerosene refined for lamp oil, lubricating oils, heavy oil for heating fuel, and paraffin used in candlemaking. In 1888 Continental eliminated the need for transporting products from the East Coast by acquiring a minority interest in United Oil Company with production and refining interests in Colorado.

In 1893 Blake resigned, having become bogged down in personal debt due to heavy investments in railroads and other ventures. For the next 14 years, Henry Morgan Tilford served as president. By 1900, Continental was heavily involved in the marketing of kerosene, although its product line had been expanded to include lamps, cooking stoves, ovens, and a variety of household and industrial oils.

Continental continued to grow in its own market under Tilford but did not venture outside of the Rocky Mountain area, where it became the Standard affiliate most closely resembling a monopoly. In 1906 Continental took over Standard bulk stations in Idaho and Montana, and by the end of the year controlled better than 98 percent of the Western market.

In 1907 Continental purchased the Denver office building that housed its sixth-floor headquarters and renamed it the Continental Oil Building. That same year, Edward T. Wilson, who had worked his way up from junior clerk, was named president.

In 1911 the U.S. Supreme Court ordered Standard Oil to divest some of its holdings. Two years later Continental Oil Company became one of 34 independent oil companies formed as a result of the court's antitrust ruling. Continental tapped into the growing market for automobile gasoline in 1914 and built its first service station. Two years later Continental bought out United Oil and officially entered the oil production business.

During World War I Continental worked under the direction of the oil division of the U.S. Fuel Administration, producing airplane fuel for pioneer aircraft and training planes. In 1919 the company adopted a new trademark, a circular emblem with a soldier standing below the word Conoco.

In 1924 C.E. Strong, who had worked his way up through the Continental accounting department, was elected president and chief executive officer. Continental became a fully integrated oil company later that year when it merged with Mutual Oil Company, owning assets in production, refining, and distribution.

By 1926 Continental's assets topped $80 million, including 530 miles of pipeline, six refineries, and marketing operations ranging through 15 states. That year, sales surpassed $50 million for the first time. The following year the company moved into its new $1 million Denver headquarters, and S.H. Keoughan, a former president of Mutual Oil, was named president and chief executive officer of Continental.

Continental's Merger with Marland Oil in 1929

In 1929 Continental merged with Marland Oil Company. The Marland Oil Company had been incorporated in 1920 to combine assets of the Marland Refining Company and Kay County Gas Company, all under the direction of Ernest Whitworth Marland. E.W. Marland, a Pittsburgh attorney turned oil wildcatter, had come to Oklahoma in 1908 and a year later discovered oil on Indian burial grounds near Ponca City. Marland later assembled a staff of geologists who led him to one strike after another, while his young companies paced development of the Oklahoma oil industry and the new group of independent oil concerns. Marland's interests in exploration extended outside of Oklahoma, leaving him in need of additional financing. In 1923, that financing approached Marland when John Pierpont Morgan of J.P. Morgan & Co. offered to become Marland Oil's banker. E.W. Marland agreed and sold Morgan $90 million in company stock.

By 1926 the company owned or controlled 5,000 tank cars emblazoned with Marland Oil's red triangle, operated more than 600 service stations in the Midwest, and was marketing products in every state as well as in 17 foreign countries. Employees shared in the success, receiving high salaries, free medical and dental care, and company loans to buy homes. In 1926 Marland negotiated the right to explore for oil in Canada on land concessions owned by the Hudson's Bay Company of Canada.

While Marland had expanded rapidly, however, so had its liabilities, which had grown to more than $8 million by the end of the year. Marland blamed the company's increasing liabilities on Morgan's bankers, who had forced him to sell oil to Standard, vetoed pipeline plans, and stymied expansion during the mid-1920s. By 1928 those bankers had gained increasing power on the company's board. During an executive committee meeting that year Marland was informed that he would be replaced as president by Dan Moran, former vice-president of the Texas Company. Marland was offered the chairmanship of the company and a pension but was told he would have to leave Ponca City. Marland promptly resigned and left the oil industry altogether shortly thereafter. He was later elected Oklahoma governor and became instrumental in leasing state capital grounds for oil production.

In January 1929 Marland Oil acquired the Prudential Refining Company with a large refinery in Baltimore, Maryland. In June of that year Morgan bankers fostered a merger agreement between Marland Oil and Continental, under which Marland agreed to purchase Continental while the Continental name would be retained. Moran was named president and chief executive officer, Edward Wilson chairman of the board, and Keoughan chairman of the executive committee.

Shortly after the new Continental moved its headquarters from Denver to Ponca City in 1929, the stock market crashed with the company holding a $43 million debt load. During the first full year of the ensuing Depression, Continental lost nearly $11 million. While losses were mounting that year, Moran devised a scheme for a pipeline that would run from Ponca City to Chicago and Minnesota and greatly reduce transportation costs. A partnership was formed called the Great Lakes Pipe Line Company, and Continental subscribed to a 31 percent stake.

Key Dates:

1875: Isaac Elder Blake founds the Continental Oil & Transportation Company in Ogden, Utah.

1885: Standard Oil Co. takes control of Continental, which is merged with Standard's Rocky Mountain operations and reincorporated in Colorado as the Continental Oil Company.

1903: Brothers Frank and L.E. Phillips form the Anchor Oil and Gas Company.

1913: Following the U.S. Supreme Court–ordered breakup of Standard Oil, Continental Oil becomes an independent company once again.

1914: Continental builds its first gas station.

1916: Continental diversifies into oil production with the purchase of United Oil Company.

1917: The Phillips brothers found Phillips Petroleum Company to acquire Anchor Oil and Gas; headquarters are established in Bartlesville, Oklahoma.

1919: Continental adopts a new trademark featuring the word "Conoco."

1927: Phillips Petroleum enters the refining and marketing businesses, opening its first gas station in Wichita, Kansas, under the Phillips 66 brand name.

1929: Continental merges with Marland Oil Company; the new company takes the Continental name but is headquartered in Ponca City, Oklahoma, where Marland had been based.

1948: Phillips Chemical Company is formed as a subsidiary.

1950: Continental relocates its headquarters to Houston.

1969: Phillips Petroleum makes its biggest discovery, the Greater Ekofisk field under the Norwegian North Sea.

1979: Continental Oil changes its name to Conoco Inc.

1981: To fend off hostile takeovers, Conoco agrees to be acquired by E.I. du Pont de Nemours and Company (DuPont) for $7.4 billion.

1983: General American Oil Company is acquired by Phillips; Conoco's headquarters are shifted to Wilmington, Delaware.

1984: Phillips fends off a takeover attempt by T. Boone Pickens, Jr.

1985: Phillips fends off a takeover attempt by Carl Icahn, running debt up to $8.9 billion in the process; massive restructuring commences.

1987: Conoco moves its headquarters back to Houston.

1998: DuPont sells 30 percent of its Conoco stake to the public in a $4.4 billion public offering; Phillips completes Ekofisk II in the Norwegian North Sea.

1999: DuPont divests its remaining 70 percent interest in Conoco.

2000: Phillips' natural gas gathering, processing, and marketing operations are combined with those of Duke Energy Corporation to form Duke Energy Field Services, 30.3 percent owned by Phillips; the company doubles its oil and gas reserves through its biggest acquisition in company history, a $7 billion deal for the Alaskan assets of Atlantic Richfield; Phillips combines its worldwide chemicals businesses with those of Chevron to form a 50–50 joint venture called Chevron Phillips Chemical Company.

2001: Phillips acquires Tosco Corporation, a major U.S. refiner and gasoline retailer, for $7.36 billion; Conoco acquires Calgary-based Gulf Canada Resources Ltd. for $4.33 billion.

2002: Phillips Petroleum and Conoco merge, forming ConocoPhillips in a $15.12 billion deal.

The 1930s and 1940s

In 1932 Continental entered the Midwest through the acquisition of 119 service stations and 43 bulk plants. Meanwhile an emphasis on research resulted in the development of new products, which included Germ Processed Motor Oil and Bronze Gasoline, touted as a high-performance fuel. To reduce company debt, Moran focused the company's attention on domestic operations. In 1933 the Sealand Petroleum Company in the United Kingdom, formed seven years earlier by Marland, was sold and the following year Hudson's Bay's operations were shut down. Continental also withdrew from northeastern states but maintained production at the Baltimore refinery to serve southern markets. By 1937 Continental had eliminated its debt load, and in December of that year 5,000 bonus checks worth a total of $770,000 were awarded to employees.

During the late 1930s Continental expanded its pipeline system by purchasing majority interests in the Rocky Mountain Pipe Line Company and the Crude Oil Pipe Line Company. Refinery operations were expanded in 1941 and a new $4.5 million refinery was opened in Lake Charles, Louisiana. In June of that year, Continental introduced its new lubricant, Conoco Nth Motor Oil, to meet the demand for heavy fuel oils.

During World War II the U.S. government constructed a 100-octane refinery in Ponca City, and Continental's vice-president of manufacturing, Walter Miller, was named to supervise operations. The plant went online in mid-1943 and began producing high-octane jet gasoline. Following the war, Continental focused on areas in which it was fully integrated, namely Texas, Colorado, Oklahoma, Illinois, Kansas, Missouri, and Iowa.

In 1946 a new era of oil exploration was launched when Continental joined with three other oil companies in developing Laniscot I, the world's pioneer offshore exploration boat. The following year Dan Moran resigned because of ill health, and Leonard F. McCollum left Standard Oil Company of New Jersey to become president and chief executive officer at Continental. McCollum's aggressive exploration program soon led to the 1947 acquisition of oil leases for 209,000 acres in the Gulf of Mexico. Hudson's Bay Oil and Gas Company (HBOG) was reactivated about the same time, after oil was discovered in Alberta, Canada. In 1948 Continental joined Ohio Oil Company and Amerada Petroleum Corporation in forming Conorada Petroleum Corporation to explore for oil outside North America.

Continental also initiated a refinery modernization and construction program in the late 1940s, leading to enlarged refineries in Denver and Ponca City and a new refinery in Billings, Montana. Meanwhile, production efforts in Kansas were reduced as the company focused on Texas, Kansas, California, and Wyoming.

Exploration and Diversification at Continental: 1950s–60s

Continental celebrated its 75th anniversary in 1950 by breaking ground for a $2.25 million Ponca City research laboratory and relocating its headquarters from Ponca City to Houston. The company also broke into new business fields during the early 1950s. A synthetic detergent plant was acquired, and Continental Oil Black Company was formed to produce carbon black, used in the production of synthetic rubber.

In 1952 Continental acquired interests in 1,390 miles of pipeline, including the new 1,080-mile line from Wyoming oilfields to an important refining center in Wood River, Illinois. Four years later offshore exploration was revolutionized when Continental, along with the Union, Shell, and Superior oil groups, launched *CUSS I,* the world's first drill ship.

Continental's interest in overseas exploration grew throughout the decade, and by 1957 the company held exploratory concessions for nearly 50 million acres outside the United States, including land in Libya, Guatemala, and Italian Somaliland. HBOG, by 1957, had rights to a total of 700,000 acres in Egypt, Libya, Somalia, British Somaliland, Venezuela, and Guatemala.

During the 1960s, Continental purchased several independent gasoline station chains in Europe to provide a market for its newly found Libyan oil. Included in a string of acquisitions were SOPI, with more than 400 stations in West Germany and Austria; Jet Petroleum, Ltd., with more than 400 stations in the United Kingdom; SECA, with stations in Belgium; Arrow Oil Company, with 70 retail outlets in eastern Ireland; and the Georg Von Opel chain of 155 stations in West Germany.

Continental also strengthened its European presence in the carbon black market by establishing production facilities in Italy, The Netherlands, France, and Japan. The company's presence in North and South America also grew with an expansion of its Montana pipeline system and purchase of the Douglas Oil Company, operating three southern California refineries and more than 300 stations. Continental opened a new refinery near the Atlantic Ocean entrance to the Panama Canal and acquired Mexofina, S.A. de C.V., with exploratory rights in Mexico.

Annual sales topped $1 billion in 1962 and diversification moves followed. In 1963, Continental acquired American Agricultural Chemical Company (Agrico), a major manufacturer of plant foods and agricultural chemicals. About the same time Continental became involved in the production of biodegradable detergents and plastic piping.

In 1964 Andrew W. Tarkington, a former executive vice-president, was named president of Continental. McCollum remained chief executive and was named to the additional post of chairman. By that time, Continental was pumping more crude out of Libya, Canada, Venezuela, and Iran than it was producing in the United States, with Libyan oil having almost by itself made Continental an international dealer. Exploration and production teams also were operating in the Middle East, Mexico, Panama, Argentina, Pakistan, New Guinea, and Australia. With its worldwide presence growing, Continental moved its headquarters from Houston to New York that same year.

In 1966 Continental diversified into minerals and acquired Consolidation Coal Company (Consol), the second largest U.S. coal-producing company. During the late 1960s expansion and diversification continued as the company purchased the Australia pesticides distributor Amalgamated Chemicals, Ltd. as well as Vinyl Maid, Inc., a manufacturer of polyvinyl chloride containers. Continental also entered joint agreements to build a calcined-petroleum coke plant in Japan, a polyvinyl chloride resin plant in the United Kingdom, and Spain's first biodegradable detergent plant.

In 1967 Tarkington assumed the additional duties of CEO while McCollum remained chairman. During the next two years Tarkington spearheaded consolidation efforts and established new policies for gauging financial risks. John G. McLean, another former executive vice-president, was named president and CEO in 1969, replacing Tarkington, who was named vice-chairman of the board.

Leadership Changes and a New Name, Conoco: 1970s

McLean reorganized administrative levels and created a management team with four divisions—Western Hemisphere petroleum, Eastern Hemisphere petroleum, Conoco Chemicals, and Consol. In 1972 he replaced McCollum, who had retired as company chairman. Under McLean's leadership, the company established a policy of focusing on its new mix of natural resources, including coal, uranium, and copper. During the early 1970s the company sold its plastic pipe manufacturing business and interest in Amalgamated Chemicals and closed a petroleum sulfonates plant. Continental stepped up its mineral production during the same period, entering joint ventures to develop uranium prospects in Texas and France. With the onset of the 1973 oil crisis, Continental accelerated its search for oil outside the Middle East, and during the next two years made significant discoveries in the North Sea.

In March 1974, Howard W. Blauvelt was named to fill the post of president, which McLean had left vacant when he assumed the chairmanship. Within two months, however, the responsibilities of chairman and chief executive were also thrust upon Blauvelt, following the untimely death of McLean. During this time of upheaval, John Kircher was named president.

Conoco Coal Development Company, a wholly owned subsidiary, was formed in 1974 to coordinate research and long-range planning for the production of synthetic fuels made from coal. That same year the company signed a ten-year contract for oil and gas exploration for more than two million acres in Egypt.

In 1979 Continental changed its name to Conoco Inc. That year, Ralph E. Bailey was named president, replacing Kircher who remained deputy chairman, a post to which he had been appointed in 1975.

During the late 1970s Conoco entered three major joint ventures, combining with Monsanto Company to manufacture ethylene and related products, with E.I. du Pont de Nemours and Company (DuPont) in a $130 million oil and natural gas exploratory program, and with Wyoming Mineral Corporation, a subsidiary of Westinghouse Electric Corporation, to develop a Conoco uranium deposit in New Mexico. Blauvelt resigned as chairman and CEO in 1979 and was replaced by Bailey in both positions.

The 1980s: Takeover of Conoco by DuPont

Conoco began the 1980s as the ninth largest oil company in the United States with $2 billion dedicated to capital outlays. In 1980 Conoco purchased Globe Petroleum Ltd., with 220 retail outlets in the United Kingdom, and entered into a second exploration venture with DuPont. A facility expansion program was also initiated early in the decade, including a $2 billion upgrade of the Lake Charles refinery, additions to the Lake Charles coke-manufacturing plant, and construction of a Lake Charles detergent chemical plant as well as a St. Louis-based lube-oil plant. In 1981 the company announced that it would build a new world headquarters in Houston for its petroleum and chemical operations.

In May 1981, Dome Petroleum, Ltd. of Canada offered to buy 13 percent of Conoco's common stock for $910 million, in hopes of exchanging the stock for Conoco's 53 percent stake in HBOG. A month later a deal was consummated giving Dome a 20 percent interest in Conoco, which was traded along with $245 million for Conoco's stake in HBOG. The transaction sent a message that Conoco was ripe for a takeover, and a bidding war for the company ensued with Seagram Company and Mobil Corporation participating. With threats of a hostile takeover looming, Conoco went in search of a white knight—a friendly acquirer—and found DuPont a willing participant. By September 1981, DuPont had acquired Conoco for $7.4 billion in the most expensive merger to that date.

Following the takeover, DuPont consolidated Conoco operations and began selling the oil company's interests to reduce a $3.9 billion debt incurred in the purchase. During the first three years after the takeover DuPont closed down some oil and chemical facilities and sold better than $1.5 billion in Conoco assets, including Continental Carbon Company and a variety of chemical, mineral, oil, and gas assets. Conoco Chemicals was absorbed by DuPont's larger petrochemicals departments. DuPont also began utilizing some of Conoco's former chemical assets, including its ethylene business. By 1983 DuPont had increased its output of ethylene, a petrochemical feedstock used in making polyethylene, from 850 million pounds annually to three billion pounds.

In 1983 Constantine S. Nicandros was named president of Conoco, which that same year shifted headquarters to Wilmington, Delaware (where DuPont was based). In the following years, Conoco stepped up offshore exploration and production efforts in the Gulf of Mexico and the North Sea. In 1984 the company began operating the world's first tension leg well platform for deep-sea oil exploration in the North Sea, with capabilities of producing oil under 2,000 feet of water.

During the mid-1980s, Conoco also expanded its oil and gas activities in Canada and Egypt. In January 1985 Conoco joined four other oil companies in a $312 million partnership to produce oil in Alaska. Two years later, however, Conoco pulled out of the partnership, after the price of crude oil dropped.

In 1987 Bailey retired as chairman and his position was eliminated. Edgar S. Woolard was named president of DuPont, with duties to include overseeing Conoco operations. At the same time, Nicandros assumed the additional duties of CEO. Conoco shifted its headquarters yet again in 1987, this time moving back to Houston.

During the late 1980s Conoco made significant oil discoveries in Norway, the United Kingdom, Indonesia, Ecuador, and the United States. In 1989, after a two-year lapse, Conoco reopened its oilfields in Alaska. That same year 64 service stations were purchased in the Denver area in an effort to boost name recognition and sales by branded outlets. In an early 1990 joint venture, Conoco and Calcined Coke Corporation formed a company called Venco to enhance Conoco's ability to meet DuPont's needs for specialty coke products.

Environmental Commitments and High-Risk Prospecting: Early to Mid-1990s

Nicandros would head Conoco from the early 1990s until 1996, a period in which he became widely known both within and outside the international oil industry because of his commitment to the environment and his company's penchant for prospecting in high-risk areas. In 1990 he issued his "nine points for environmental excellence" program as a guide for Conoco's future development in an "earth-friendly" manner. Hailed by environmentalists and anticipative of future U.S. Congressional mandates, the program's most striking commitment was to construct only doubled-hulled tankers in the future in order to prevent oil spills at sea. Industry experts estimated that adherence to the program cost Conoco $50 million a year.

Conoco began the 1990s with exploration teams in 21 countries, and under Nicandros the company aggressively sought new areas of exploration in the early 1990s. With the huge oilfields of North America and the North Sea continuing to be drained, Conoco more than any other oil company reached out to high-risk areas as a long-term strategy of keeping its reserves at an acceptable level. In 1991 the company formed a joint venture in Russia—in that country's largest oil investment by a foreign country to date—to drill oil in the Russian Arctic. By the fall of 1994, the Ardalin oil complex began producing crude oil out of its field of 110 million barrels of recoverable oil beneath the frozen tundra. Conoco also began to see results in 1995 from its 18 percent interest in a $3.9 billion project in the Norwegian Sea, which involved a 288,000-ton tension leg platform installed at a water depth of 1,150 feet through a combined 30 million person-hours of work over a four-year period.

A few of the company's exploration efforts, however, met with some challenges. In March 1995, for example, after three years of negotiations, a $1 billion deal to produce oil in Iran was blocked by the Clinton administration as part of increasingly hostile relations between the United States and Iran. Moreover, in January 1996 a consortium led by Conoco proposed to develop a natural gas field in northern Mexico, a country highly protective of its petroleum industry. Two months later Conoco signed a deal with the state oil company of Taiwan to explore for oil and gas in the Taiwan Strait, an area that had recently been the site of Chinese war games. In April Vietnam's state-owned Petro-Vietnam awarded Conoco rights to develop three million acres of the South China Sea, an area whose sovereignty was in dispute between Vietnam, China, and other southeast Asian countries. China, which had already granted rights to an overlapping area to Denver-based Crestone Energy Corp., issued a warning to Conoco not to proceed, with the company responding that it would leave the issue up to the involved governments.

Meanwhile, also in Asia, Conoco began in 1993 to develop refining and marketing operations as a start toward capturing part of the region's fast-growing petroleum market. That year, the company began by building gas stations in Thailand under the Jet brand name, with a goal of having 260 retail outlets in place by the year 2004. Then in 1994 Conoco entered a joint venture (holding a 40 percent stake) with Petronas, the national oil company in Malaysia, and Statoil of Norway to construct a 100,000 barrel per day, $1.1 billion refinery in Malaysia. This represented Conoco's largest investment outside the United States. Future plans were to spend more than $2.5 billion in Malaysia through 2005, with plans for more than 200 retail outlets in the country. Overall, from 1996 to 1998, Conoco planned to spend 10 to 15 percent of its $2.5 billion capital budget in Asia.

Conoco's overall operating results stagnated during the early 1990s under the pressure of heavy competition. The after-tax operating income as a percentage of sales mark of 6.7 percent in 1990 represented the high level through 1996. A three-year restructuring program that Nicandros initiated helped the company post better results than it would have otherwise. In addition to its exploration efforts and entrance into Asia, neither of which helped in the short term, Nicandros also sought new areas for growth within the broader energy sector, notably the establishment of a Conoco Power business unit that would pursue projects in the worldwide electrical power market. One possible shorter-term aid to company profitability arose in the talks between Conoco and Phillips Petroleum started in late 1995 regarding the combination of the companies' domestic marketing, refinery, and pipeline operations in a 50–50 venture. This would have created the sixth largest refiner of crude oil in the United States and the second largest chain of U.S. gas stations, but talks broke off in June 1996 when the two sides could not reach agreement on "significant commercial issues."

During the 14 years since the DuPont takeover, the parent company's shareholders had not always benefited from the Conoco acquisition, according to some observers. Although about 42 percent of DuPont's revenues were derived from Conoco operations, Conoco contributed only about 17 percent of after-tax operating income to DuPont's overall total. Following the takeover, DuPont had been left with Seagram holding 24 percent of its common stock and a seat on DuPont's board. In the spring of 1995, DuPont paid $8.8 billion to repurchase all the shares Seagram then held, leaving a huge debt load behind. At the same time DuPont announced plans to sell $650 million in Conoco assets. Speculation then arose about the possibility that DuPont would divest itself of Conoco, in particular after Jack Krol replaced Edgar Woolard as chief executive of the

parent company. It was in these difficult and uncertain circumstances that Archie W. Dunham succeeded Nicandros as Conoco chairman, president, and chief executive at the beginning of 1996.

Dunham's leadership stint got off to a stellar start when Conoco posted its second best year ever in 1996, earning $860 million on revenues of $20.2 billion. The improved profits were attributable to higher oil and gas prices and a major restructuring at the firm's Houston headquarters, where the central management staff was cut from around 1,800 to about 150. Also in 1996, Conoco won two of five coveted exploration leases that were open for bidding in Venezuela, which at the time had the hottest exploration and development prospects in the Western hemisphere. In May of the following year, Conoco paid TransTexas Gas Corp. about $900 million to acquire an extensive array of natural gas properties and a 1,100-mile natural gas pipeline, all located in southern Texas. In the North Sea, meantime, Conoco swapped two mature oilfields for Occidental Petroleum Corporation's interest in the Britannia Field, one of the largest natural-gas discoveries in the North Sea. Commercial production at Britannia began in August 1998. Overall, Dunham wanted to take a more focused approach to exploration and development, concentrating on a handful of main areas, including Venezuela, southeast Asia, the Caspian Sea, the North Sea, and the deepwater Gulf of Mexico.

New Era of Conoco Independence: 1998–2001

At this time, Dunham was seeking to gain Conoco's separation from DuPont. He desired to have more financial control over the company in order to pursue the numerous opportunities for foreign asset investments that were arising in the post–Cold War era. Executives at DuPont agreed that the time for a separation had come as they were seeking to transform their firm into a life sciences corporation, shifting focus away from petrochemicals and toward biotechnology. Thus on October 22, 1998, DuPont sold 30 percent of its Conoco stake to the public in what at the time was the largest initial public offering (IPO) in history—nearly $4.4 billion. Conoco emerged as the sixth largest U.S. oil company based on its 1997 revenues of $21.4 billion. The firm employed about 15,000 people worldwide and began its latest stint of independence with about $5 billion in debt. In August 1999 DuPont completed its divestment of Conoco by swapping its remaining Conoco shares (worth about $12.2 billion) for DuPont shares.

Cracks in the OPEC cartel and more efficient energy exploration technologies led to an oil glut and plunging oil prices in 1998 and 1999. Conoco laid off nearly a thousand workers late in 1998 and also reduced its capital budget for 1999 by about $500 million, or 21 percent. Writedowns in the value of reserves, the cost of the workforce reductions, and other special charges pushed the company into the red in the fourth quarter of 1998. Conoco rebounded in 1999 when it earned $774 million (a 65 percent increase over the 1998) on record sales of $27 billion. Meanwhile, the company's joint venture refinery in Malaysia came on line in 1998.

Surging oil and gas prices in 2000 led Conoco to its best year ever: profits of $1.9 billion on revenues of more than $39 billion. The company made major discoveries in Vietnam, the

Gulf of Mexico, and the United Kingdom that year, and it also paid Petro-Canada about $200 million for a broad collection of natural gas liquids operations in the province of Alberta. In July 2001 Conoco completed the largest acquisition in its history, buying Calgary-based Gulf Canada Resources Ltd. for $4.33 billion in cash and the assumption of $2 billion in debt. The deal increased Conoco's worldwide reserves nearly 40 percent, from 2.65 billion barrels to 3.7 billion barrels, and increased production by 32 percent. Gulf Canada had exploration and production operations in western Canada, the North Sea, and Ecuador, and it also owned 72 percent of Gulf Indonesia Resources Ltd., a Jakarta-based company with natural gas production on the island of Sumatra, in the Natuna Sea, and off Java. This proved to be the last major deal for Conoco Inc. as just four months later the company agreed to merge with Phillips Petroleum to form ConocoPhillips.

Early History of Phillips Petroleum

Phillips Petroleum was named after brothers Frank and L.E. Phillips and was organized in 1917 to acquire their original venture in the oil business, Anchor Oil and Gas Company. Raised on an Iowa farm, the Phillips brothers left Iowa after Frank heard rumors of vast oil deposits in Oklahoma, then part of the Indian Territory. Along with others Frank Phillips founded Anchor Oil and Gas in 1903. After a struggle, Frank Phillips, joined by L.E., finally began to make money from oil in 1905. They reinvested their profits, founding a bank. Eventually, the brothers decided to leave the uncertain oil business for good and concentrate on banking. They were forestalled, however, when World War I broke out and the price of crude jumped from 40 cents to more than $1 a barrel. The brothers founded Phillips Petroleum Company in 1917, headquartered in Bartlesville, Oklahoma.

From the very beginning, the Phillips brothers found much natural gas while drilling for oil. Most drillers considered the gas useless and burned it off at the wellhead, but the Phillips brothers sought to turn it into a cash crop. In 1917 Phillips opened a plant near Bartlesville for extracting liquid byproducts from natural gas. The byproducts could be used in motor fuels. The company's research into the uses of natural gas received further impetus in 1926, when it won a patent infringement suit brought against it by Union Carbide over Phillips's process for separating hydrocarbon compounds.

Phillips prospered throughout its first decade. By 1927, it was pumping 55,000 barrels of oil a day from more than 2,000 wells in Oklahoma and Texas. Its assets stood at $266 million, compared with the $3 million it had when it was founded. The company also decided to enter the refining and marketing businesses in 1927, in response to automobile sales and as an outlet for its growing production. In 1927, it began operating a refinery near the Texas town of Borger. It also opened its first gas station, in Wichita, Kansas.

Phillips's entry into retailing presented it with the problem of finding a brand name under which to sell its gasoline. According to company lore, the solution presented itself as a Phillips official was returning to Bartlesville in a car that was road-testing the company's new gasoline. He commented that the car was going ''like 60.'' The driver looked at the speedom-

eter and replied, ''Sixty nothing . . . we're doing 66!'' The fact that the incident took place on Highway 66 near Tulsa only strengthened the story's appeal to Phillips's executives. The company chose Phillips 66 as its new brand name, one that endured and achieved classic status.

In 1930 Phillips added to its refining and retailing capacities when it acquired Independent Oil Gas Company, which was owned by Waite Phillips, another Phillips brother. The Great Depression hit the company early and hard. In 1931 Phillips posted a $5.7 million deficit in its first ever loss-making year. As a consequence, it cut salaries and laid off hundreds of employees. Phillips stock plunged to $3 a share, down from $32. The company quickly regained its profitability, however, posting a modest surplus the next year.

Before the decade was out, Phillips also would make two personnel changes to help secure its future for the longer term. In 1932 a promising young executive named K.S. (Boots) Adams was promoted to assistant to the president, Frank Phillips. Six years later, he succeeded Phillips as president when the company's founder assumed the post of chairman. Boots Adams—a boyhood nickname, inspired by his affection for a pair of red-topped boots—was 38 years old when he became president, and he and Phillips made rather an odd couple at the top of the chain of command. They often disagreed as to how the company should be run, but Phillips seems to have known that the future ultimately belonged to his protégé. ''Mr. Phillips liked me, but not my ideas,'' Adams later recalled. ''He said to me: 'I'm going to object to everything you do, but you go ahead and do it anyway.' ''

Phillips's strength in research and development paid off during World War II. In the late 1930s, the company developed new processes for producing butadiene and carbon black, two key ingredients in synthetic rubber, which became all the more crucial to the United States after Japanese conquests in Indonesia and Indochina cut off the supply of natural rubber in 1941. Phillips also developed high-octane aviation fuels, an early version of which powered British fighters in the Battle of Britain. The fuels were widely used by the Allied air forces.

Postwar Growth and International Expansion

In the years immediately following the war, Phillips began to reap in earnest the harvest of its research and commitment to natural gas. It generated substantial income by licensing its petrochemical patents to foreign companies. At home, the company was eminently positioned to take advantage of the sudden growth of cross-country pipelines in the 1940s and the consequent surge in natural gas prices. By the middle of the next decade, its reserves would total 13.3 trillion cubic feet, worth an estimated $931 million. Phillips also invested heavily in oil exploration, refining, natural gas drilling, and petrochemical plants. In 1948 it formed a new subsidiary, Phillips Chemical Company, and entered the fertilizer business when it began producing anhydrous ammonia.

Although Phillips had the advantage over its competitors in natural gas and chemicals, it fell behind in the postwar foreign oil rush because of Frank Phillips's opposition to overseas ventures. Even though his company had begun drilling in Venezuela in 1944, Phillips was determined to keep the company a mainly domestic enterprise and turned down the exclusive rights to the lucrative concession in the neutral zone between Saudi Arabia and Kuwait in 1947. The company eventually acquired a one-third stake in American Independent Oil, which took the Middle East concession, but it required all of Boots Adams's persuasive powers to get his boss to agree to it.

Frank Phillips died in 1950 and Adams, long his heir-apparent, succeeded him as chairman and CEO. Under Adams, Phillips continued to focus on its interest in natural gas and was the nation's largest producer in the 1950s. Its program of capital expansion was ambitious, with expenditure reaching a peak of $257 million in 1956. Phillips also began to break out of the constricting mold that its late founder had built for it. In 1952 the company started expanding its marketing network beyond the Midwest, opening Phillips 66 stations in Texas and Louisiana. Phillips continued to march through the deep South, then up the Atlantic seaboard, as far as it could extend its supply lines from its refineries. It also was becoming apparent that Frank Phillips had erred in refusing to develop overseas sources of oil, as the cost of finding and pumping crude in the United States increased. Finally, as the decade neared its end, Adams went on an around-the-world fact-finding trip. When he returned, he set a five-year timetable for expanding Phillips's international operations.

In 1951, meanwhile, chemists at Phillips discovered Marlex, a chemical compound that would become a building block for many modern plastics. The first commercial use of the new product was in the manufacture of hula hoops, and the 1950s hula hoop craze fueled demand for the new substance.

Phillips's practice of licensing its patents overseas without acquiring an interest in the new ventures had yielded royalties but no growth; so in 1960 the company took a 50 percent interest in a French carbon black plant using Phillips technology. Petrochemical joint ventures in Asia, Africa, Europe, and Latin America followed. Phillips also acquired drilling concessions in North Africa, the North Sea, New Guinea, Australia, and Iran. These foreign ventures were still not profitable when Adams retired in 1964 and handed the reins to President Stanley Learned, but the company had begun to make up for lost time.

Under Learned, Phillips continued to diversify and expand. In 1964 it acquired packaging manufacturer Sealright Inc. as part of its move into plastics. Two years later, Learned himself broke ground on a petrochemical complex in Puerto Rico that would produce chemical raw materials and motor fuels. Phillips also expanded its domestic oil operations. In 1960, it had tried to break into the California market by acquiring 15 percent of Union Oil Company of California, but litigation by Union Oil and the Justice Department prevented Phillips from pursuing a takeover; in 1963 Phillips sold its stake to shipping magnate Daniel K. Ludwig. Instead, Phillips acquired the West Coast properties of Tidewater Oil Company in 1966 for $309 million. The deal took four months to complete and required great secrecy. When the purchase was announced, the Justice Department filed an antitrust suit to dissolve it, but a U.S. District Court allowed the acquisition to stand, pending an appeal to the Supreme Court. By 1967 there were Phillips 66 stations in all 50 states.

Learned retired in 1967 and was succeeded as CEO by William Keeler. In addition to his career with Phillips, Keeler, who was half Cherokee, was named chief of the Cherokee nation by President Harry S. Truman in 1949. Also known as Tsula Westa Nehi (''Worker Who Doesn't Sit Down''), Keeler used his position as chief to campaign on behalf of Native American causes. Now he assumed responsibility for the eighth largest oil company in the United States, and one in which some serious problems were beginning to manifest themselves. Foremost among these problems was dependence on outside sources of crude oil. For years, Phillips had not pumped enough to supply its refineries, so it had to buy crude from other producers. In 1969 Phillips made an unsuccessful offer to acquire Amerada Petroleum Corporation, a major crude producer with no marketing operations. Phillips was more successful with its new exploration strategy, under which it considerably slowed exploration in the continental United States, the most thoroughly prospected area in the world, and concentrated on Alaskan and overseas locations. This paid off in 1969, when Phillips discovered the massive Greater Ekofisk field under the Norwegian North Sea. Phillips joined with several European partners to develop the field. The discovery of a major field in Nigeria soon followed. In the early 1970s, Phillips joined with Standard Oil Company of New Jersey (later Exxon Corporation), Atlantic Richfield Company, Standard Oil Company of Ohio, Mobil Oil Corporation, Union Oil Company of California, and Amerada Hess Corporation to form Alyeska Pipeline Service Company. Alyeska would build the trans-Alaska pipeline, which allowed the exploitation of the massive deposits in Prudhoe Bay, Alaska.

Turbulent 1970s

During this time Phillips suffered from overexpansion and ailing chemical ventures. Some petrochemical projects fared badly because of falling propane and fertilizer prices. In plastics, Phillips found that it could not compete with smaller companies that had lower capital costs. Keeler addressed these problems by installing tighter controls on corporate planning. Phillips executives also found that having gas stations in all 50 states was no advantage when the company's presence in many markets was too small to ensure a profit. In 1973 Phillips divested most of its stations in the Northeast. A price war in California had drained the 3,000 stations acquired from Tidewater from the start, and it never made money; in 1973 the Supreme Court finally ordered Phillips to divest the Tidewater assets, and two years later the company sold most of its Pacific Coast properties to Oil Shale Corporation.

Keeler retired in 1973 and was succeeded as CEO by President William Martin. The remainder of the 1970s would be turbulent years for Phillips. In 1973 Phillips was one of the first and most prominent U.S. corporations to be accused of making an illegal contribution to President Richard Nixon's reelection campaign. Phillips pleaded guilty and admitted donating $100,000 illegally. Over the course of the next two years, Phillips would admit that the company had made illegal contributions to 65 congressional candidates in 1970 and 1972, as well as to Lyndon B. Johnson's 1964 presidential campaign and Nixon's 1968 campaign. The money came from a secret $1.35 million fund set up by Phillips executives for that purpose and channeled through a Swiss bank account. The company paid $30,000 in fines.

In 1975 the Los Angeles–based Center for Law in the Public Interest filed a class-action suit against Phillips on behalf of several small shareholders. In settling the lawsuit, the company agreed to give up the strong majority that its executives had always held on its board of directors. The board was reconstituted, with nine of the 17 directors coming from outside the company.

In turn, these legal difficulties were followed by even greater disasters. In 1977 Phillips's Bravo platform in the Ekofisk field blew out during routine maintenance and spewed oil into the North Sea for eight days. Two years later, 123 people were killed when a floating hotel for Ekofisk workers capsized in a storm. Also in 1979, an explosion at Phillips's Borger, Texas, refinery injured 41 people. Meanwhile, Keeler's strategy of exploring in foreign lands began to backfire as it produced more dry holes than reserves, while other oil companies were discovering new fields in the Rocky Mountains and in Louisiana.

Fending Off Takeovers in the 1980s

Martin retired in 1980 and was succeeded by William Douce. In 1982 Phillips's fortunes revived somewhat when a joint exploration venture with Chevron found substantial reserves under the Santa Maria Basin, off the coast of California. The company added even further to its crude supplies in the following year, when it acquired General American Oil Company, for $1.1 billion, stepping in as a white knight to thwart a takeover bid from Mesa LP. It would not be Phillips's last encounter with Mesa and its chairman, T. Boone Pickens, Jr. In 1984 Phillips acquired Aminoil, Inc. and Geysers Geothermal Company from R.J. Reynolds Industries for about $1.7 billion. Observers noted that the deal made Phillips, now the subject of takeover rumors, a less attractive buyout candidate because of the debt it would have to assume.

The takeover rumors became reality early in December 1984, when Pickens announced that his company had acquired 5.7 percent of Phillips's stock and intended to try for a majority stake. Douce, though scheduled to retire shortly, had prepared for such an event and was determined to fight. ''Boone Busters'' T-shirts appeared in Bartlesville, which feared for its life should Phillips ever be taken from it, and the company launched a barrage of lawsuits. One suit charged that Mesa was violating a pact it had signed before withdrawing its bid for General American Oil, in which it promised never again to attempt to take that company over. When the dust cleared a month later, Phillips had driven Pickens away and preserved its independence, but Phillips agreed to buy out Mesa's holdings as part of a restructuring that would ultimately cost $4.5 billion, loading itself with debt and requiring the disposal of $2 billion in assets. For his part, Pickens conducted an orderly retreat laden with spoils—$75 million in pretax profits plus an additional $25 million to cover his expenses.

No sooner had Pickens left the field, however, than other attacks began. In January and February 1985, financiers Irwin Jacobs, Ivan Boesky, and Carl Icahn all bought up large blocks of Phillips stock. Then, on February 12, Icahn struck, launching a $4.2 billion offer to buy 45 percent of the company. Combined with the 5 percent he already owned, this would give Icahn a controlling stake. In early March, faced with shareholders willing to sell to Icahn owing to dissatisfaction with the Pickens

deal, Phillips executives came up with a plan to exchange debt securities for half of its outstanding stock, including Icahn's 5 percent, at $62 per share, compared with the $53 per share it had paid Pickens. Icahn accepted and he, too, left with his spoils.

The task of rebuilding the battered company—now saddled with $8.9 billion in debt—was left to C.J. (Pete) Silas, who succeeded Douce as chairman in May 1985. Under Silas, Phillips sold off the necessary $2 billion in assets within 18 months of Icahn's repulse. Among those to go were Aminoil and Geyser Geothermal. The company also cut 9,000 jobs by 1989. As a result of its forced restructuring, Phillips gave up becoming an integrated, worldwide energy company, and refocused on its core oil and gas businesses. In the late 1980s, unexpectedly strong earnings from its petrochemical businesses more than offset the effect of lower oil prices and raised hopes for Phillips's long-term recovery.

These hopes received a setback in October 1989, however, when an explosion occurred at Phillips's plastics plant in Pasadena, Texas, killing 23 people and causing $500 million in damage. The disaster temporarily eliminated Phillips's U.S. capacity to manufacture polyethylene, which is used to make blow-molded containers and other products.

Increasing Exploration and Production Operations in the 1990s

Phillips entered the 1990s still saddled with nearly $4 billion in debt from its battles with corporate raiders. Its debt-to-equity ratio stood at nearly 60 percent. The early 1990s were difficult years for the company as the economic downturn hit the oil and gas industry particularly hard. The company completed additional workforce reductions and asset sales. In 1992 Phillips reorganized its operations into strategic business units, which were given greater autonomy and more profit and loss responsibility. That year also saw Phillips create GPM Gas Corporation, a subsidiary that assumed control of the natural gas gathering, processing, and marketing activities. Phillips planned to sell 51 percent of GPM through an IPO to raise funds to further reduce the debt load, but the poor energy market of early 1992 forced Phillips to cancel the IPO.

Wayne Allen was promoted from president and COO to chairman and CEO in 1994. Under Allen's leadership, Phillips increased its exploration and production operations. The company had already, in 1993, proven the viability of drilling for oil and gas beneath the immense sheets of salt that cover more than half of the Gulf of Mexico. The salt layers had stymied previous attempts to seismically map the deeper layers, but Phillips developed a 3-D seismic technology that enabled it to see clearly beneath the salt. So-called subsalt production in the Gulf began in late 1996. Meantime, international exploration efforts led to the company's first production of oil in China in 1994 and a major gas discovery in the Timor Sea located between East Timor and Australia. Also in 1994 Norway's parliament approved Ekofisk II, a $2.5 billion improvement project involving the replacement of five aging platforms with two new ones, along with the extension of the production license to 2028. Phillips expected that by that year, Ekofisk II will have produced one billion barrels of oil. The construction of Ekofisk II was completed in 1998.

On the marketing side of its operations, Phillips's profits were weaker than those in exploration and production. The company worked to expand its network of gas stations and convenience stores in the mid-1990s. As part of an industry trend toward consolidation and the sharing of costs through joint operations, Phillips and Conoco Inc. in 1996 discussed merging their refining and marketing businesses but failed to reach an agreement. That year Phillips posted net income of $1.3 billion on sales of $15.73 billion, enabling it to reduce its debt load to $3.1 billion and its debt-to-equity ratio to 39 percent.

Pressure to consolidate continued to build in the late 1990s as two megamergers rocked the industry: British Petroleum plc's merger with Amoco Corporation to create BP Amoco p.l.c. and Exxon Corporation's merger with Mobil Corporation to form Exxon Mobil Corporation. The new giants dwarfed Phillips with their revenues in excess of $100 billion. In late 1998 Phillips and Ultramar Diamond Shamrock Corporation reached a preliminary agreement to combine their refineries and gas stations in a joint venture, but the deal fell apart early the following year. Meantime, Phillips in 1998 made its largest discovery since Ekofisk in a field in Bohai Bay, off the northeastern coast of China. At the time, this was the largest find off the shore of China.

Phillips's Rapid Transformation into a Major Integrated Oil Company: 1999–2001

During the second half of 1999 James J. Mulva took over as chairman and CEO from the retiring Allen. Mulva would oversee some of the most dramatic events in the company's history soon after taking over, as Phillips decided to focus even further on exploration and production by either selling or placing into joint ventures its other three units. The company at first planned to sell its GPM Gas unit, but instead in March 2000 Phillips combined GPM with the gas gathering, processing, and marketing operations of Duke Energy Corporation to form a joint venture called Duke Energy Field Services, LLC, with Duke initially holding 69.7 percent of the new entity and Phillips holding the remaining 30.3 percent. In April 2000 Phillips substantially bolstered its exploration and production operations through the acquisition of the Alaskan assets of Atlantic Richfield Company for about $7 billion, the largest acquisition in company history. This deal enabled BP Amoco to complete its $28 billion acquisition of Atlantic Richfield. For Phillips, the addition of the Alaskan assets increased its daily production by 70 percent and doubled its oil and gas reserves. Phillips completed a third major deal in July 2000 when it combined its worldwide chemicals businesses with those of Chevron to form a 50–50 joint venture called Chevron Phillips Chemical Company LLC. Through the new entity, whose annual revenues would be nearly $6 billion, the two companies hoped to reap annual cost savings of $150 million.

Plans to shift the company's refining and marketing operations into another joint venture were abandoned with the announcement in February 2001 that Phillips would acquire Tosco Corporation, a major U.S. petroleum refiner and marketer whose main retail brands included 76 and Circle K. Completed in September 2001 at a price tag of $7.36 billion in stock and about $2 billion in assumed debt, the deal made Phillips the number two refiner in the United States, trailing only Exxon

Mobil, and the number three gasoline retailer, with about 12,400 outlets in 46 states. Phillips now had strong positions in both the upstream and downstream sides of the oil industry. Although Mulva called this acquisition the "final step" in the company's plan to become one of the major integrated oil companies, just two months after its completion Phillips agreed to merge with Conoco in a truly blockbuster deal.

Creation of ConocoPhillips in 2002

In November 2001 Phillips Petroleum and Conoco agreed to merge. The $15.12 billion deal, completed in August 2002, combined two midtier U.S. players into the sixth largest publicly traded oil company in the world and the third largest in the United States. The new corporation, named simply ConocoPhillips (an entity incorporated in 2001), started with 8.7 billion barrels of proven reserves, 1.7 million barrels of daily production, and 2.6 million barrels per day of refining capacity—the latter making the firm the largest U.S. refiner and the number five refiner in the world. The refining capacity would soon be trimmed slightly because the U.S. Federal Trade Commission (FTC), in approving the merger, forced the sale of a Conoco refinery near Denver and a Phillips refinery near Salt Lake City. The FTC also ordered the new company to sell more than 200 gasoline stations in Colorado, Utah, and Wyoming to address antitrust concerns in the Rocky Mountain region. ConocoPhillips nevertheless retained a worldwide network of fuel outlets totaling more than 17,000. Conoco's headquarters in Houston was retained as the base for ConocoPhillips. James Mulva, the head of Phillips, became the CEO and president of the new firm, while Archie Dunham, head of Conoco, served as ConocoPhillips's first chairman.

Upon announcing the merger, the executives cited the potential for annual cost savings of $750 million. By late 2002 they raised their savings goal to $1.25 billion, concentrating primarily on the downstream side of the business. High oil prices were hurting refining and marketing margins at this time, and ConocoPhillips had a higher proportion of downstream assets than most of its major integrated oil company competitors. The company announced that it planned to sell $3 billion to $4 billion of assets by the end of 2004 to rein in costs and to cut the heavy long-term debt load of nearly $19 billion. Late in 2003 ConocoPhillips said it would cut another $1 billion in assets, or approximately $4.5 billion in total, and raised its cost savings goal to $1.75 billion. The biggest divestment came in December 2003 when the company sold Circle K Corp., an operator of more than 1,650 convenience stores/gasoline stations that had come to Phillips through its acquisition of Tosco. Circle K was sold to Montreal-based Alimentation Couche-Tard Inc. for $821 million. In January 2004 ConocoPhillips announced that it would sell 1,180 Mobil-branded gasoline stations in two separate deals. The stations also had come to Phillips through Tosco. These divestments not only fit with the program of asset sales, they also were consistent with two other company aims: reducing the number of stations it owned and operated and focusing the U.S. retail operations on three main brands—Phillips 66, Conoco, and 76. The sales also significantly reduced ConocoPhillips's workforce, which dropped from 55,800 employees to around 39,000.

After reporting a net loss of $295 million during the transitional restructuring year of 2002, ConocoPhillips posted 2003 profits of $4.74 billion on revenues of $105.1 billion. Debt was reduced to $17.8 billion by the end of 2003. For 2004 the company set a capital spending budget of $6.9 billion, more than three-quarters of which was earmarked for the exploration and production operations. This was in line with ConocoPhillips's shift in emphasis away from the downstream and toward the upstream.

Principal Competitors

Exxon Mobil Corporation; BP p.l.c.; Royal Dutch/Shell Group; ChevronTexaco Corporation; TOTAL S.A.

Further Reading

Banham, Russ, *Conoco: 125 Years of Energy,* Lyme, Conn.: Greenwich, 2000.

Barrionuevo, Alexei, "Chevron and Phillips to Form Venture with $5.7 Billion in Revenue," *Wall Street Journal,* February 8, 2000, p. A4.

——, "Phillips Petroleum to Delay Finding Partner for Venture," *Wall Street Journal,* November 16, 2000, p. A6.

——, "Suit Over BP Amoco-Arco Pact Halted: Move Follows Disclosure of Phillips Plan to Buy Arco's Alaskan Assets," *Wall Street Journal,* March 16, 2000, p. A3.

Barrionuevo, Alexei, and Steve Liesman, "Phillips Petroleum, in Strategy Shift, Seeks Sales or Ventures for Some Units," *Wall Street Journal,* September 24, 1999, p. B6.

Biesada, Alexandra, "The Levitation," *Financial World,* June 23, 1992, p. 36.

Blalock, Dawn, "Phillips Petroleum, Long Buried in Debt, Frees Itself," *Wall Street Journal,* April 15, 1996, p. B3.

Blumenthal, Karen, and Christopher Cooper, "Phillips and Ultramar Call Off Plans to Join Refining, Marketing Operations," *Wall Street Journal,* March 22, 1999, p. B8.

Borrego, Anne Marie, "Phillips Petroleum to Cut Staff by 8 Percent, Capital Spending," *Wall Street Journal,* January 7, 1999, p. A4.

——, "Ultramar Diamond Shamrock, Phillips to Combine Refineries and Gas Stations," *Wall Street Journal,* October 9, 1998, p. A3.

Brown, Wesley, and John Stancavage, "Phillips Called Ripe for Merger," *Tulsa World,* August 19, 1998.

"Chevron, Phillips to Form Giant Chemical JV," *Oil and Gas Journal,* February 14, 2000, pp. 24–25.

Conoco: The First One Hundred Years, New York: Dell Publishing, 1975.

"Conoco's Takeover of Gulf Canada Leads Latest Merger Wave," *Oil and Gas Journal,* June 4, 2001, pp. 36–37.

Davis, Michael, "Conoco: How the Leopard Changed Its Spots," *Houston Chronicle,* November 17, 1998.

——, "Oil Firm to Deal Service Stations: ConocoPhillips Selling More Assets," *Houston Chronicle,* January 9, 2003.

Deogun, Nikhil, and Alexei Barrionuevo, "Phillips to Buy Tosco in $7.49 Billion Deal: Move Reflects Strategy Shift for Firm That Set Focus on Output, Exploration," *Wall Street Journal,* February 5, 2001, p. A3.

Deogun, Nikhil, Alexei Barrionuevo, and Tamsin Carlisle, "Conoco Reaches Deal to Buy Gulf Canada for About $4.33 Billion, Debt Assumption," *Wall Street Journal,* May 29, 2001, p. A3.

de Rouffignac, Ann, "Conoco Goes Through a Changing of the Guard," *Houston Business Journal,* December 1, 1995, p. 16.

Finney, Robert, et al., *Phillips: The First 66 Years,* Bartlesville, Okla.: Phillips Petroleum Company, 1983.

Fletcher, Sam, "Merger Done: ConocoPhillips Now Third Largest U.S. Oil Firm," *Oil and Gas Journal,* September 9, 2002, p. 42.

Fletcher, Sam, and David Young, "Phillips, Conoco Plan $35 Billion 'Merger of Equals,'" *Oil and Gas Journal,* November 26, 2001, pp. 26, 28.

Frank, Robert, and Alexei Barrionuevo, "Phillips Petroleum, Conoco Agree to Merge," *Wall Street Journal,* November 19, 2001, p. A3.

Fritsch, Peter, "Conoco Proposes to Develop Gas Field in Mexican Sector Closed to Foreigners," *Wall Street Journal,* January 9, 1996, p. A4.

Gill, Douglas, "Fillip for Phillips: An Exciting New Find Brightens Its Future," *Barron's,* November 1, 1982, pp. 13+.

Gold, Jackey, "Phillips Petroleum: Take a Trip on Route 66," *Financial World,* October 15, 1991, pp. 16+.

Holloway, Nigel, "Conoco Discovers Asia," *Far Eastern Economic Review,* October 26, 1995, p. 78.

"How They Won the West—and More," *Business Week,* January 28, 1967.

Jones, Billy M., "L.E. Phillips: Banker, Oil Man, Civic Leader," Oklahoma City: Oklahoma Heritage Association, 1981.

Kelly, Kevin, "You Got Trouble Right Here in Ponca City: A Bitter Dispute Over Whether Its Conoco Refinery Is a Toxic Hazard," *Business Week,* June 27, 1988, p. 38.

Knowles, Ruth Sheldon, *The Greatest Gamblers: The Epic of American Oil Exploration,* Norman: University of Oklahoma Press, 1978.

Kvendseth, Stig S., "Giant Discovery: A History of Ekofisk Through the First 20 Years," Tananger, Norway: Phillips Petroleum Company Norway, 1988.

Liesman, Steve, "Phillips Petroleum Again Is Hunting for Partner, with Chevron a Possibility," *Wall Street Journal,* September 20, 1999, p. A4.

——, "Phillips Petroleum CEO Says Discovery in China Is Stronger Than Expected," *Wall Street Journal,* February 9, 2000, p. A10.

Mathews, John Joseph, *Life and Death of an Oilman: The Career of E.W. Marland,* Norman: University of Oklahoma Press, 1951.

McWilliams, Gary, Joseph Weber, and Susan Garland, "Why Didn't Conoco See This One Coming?: Washington's Signals on Iran May Have Been Too Subtle," *Business Week,* March 27, 1995, pp. 40–41.

Meyer, Richard, "The Final Straw," *Financial World,* January 26, 1988, pp. 39+.

Norman, James R., "The Sharks Keep Circling Phillips," *Business Week,* February 11, 1985, pp. 24+.

——, "What the Raiders Did to Phillips Petroleum," *Business Week,* March 17, 1986, pp. 102+.

"Phillips Aims at 'Built-in Value,'" *Business Week,* June 27, 1959.

"Phillips, Duke Enter Agreement to Combine Certain Businesses," *Oklahoma City Journal Record,* December 17, 1999.

"Phillips Petroleum: Laying the Groundwork," *Forbes,* February 1, 1965.

"Phillips to Acquire Tosco in Multibillion-Dollar Deal," *Oil and Gas Journal,* February 12, 2001, pp. 33–35.

Plishner, Emily S., "The Dilemma: Will DuPont's New CEO Spin Off Conoco?," *Financial World,* December 5, 1995, p. 34.

Ray, Russell, "Phillips' 'Final Step,'" *Tulsa World,* February 6, 2001.

"Risk and Return," *Economist,* April 27, 1996, p. 66.

Rosett, Claudia, and Allanna Sullivan, "Conoco Tests the Tundra for Oil Profits," *Wall Street Journal,* September 1, 1994, p. A6.

Rublin, Lauren R., "Phillips Pays the Price and T. Boone Pickens Makes Another Big Score," *Barron's,* December 31, 1984, pp. 13+.

Ryan, Christopher, "Phillips Plans Cutbacks," *Tulsa Tribune,* November 21, 1991, p. 1A.

Schein, Chris, "Phillips Has Plans for More Layoffs," *Tulsa World,* November 13, 1991, p. B1.

Smith, Rebecca, "Duke Energy and Phillips Petroleum Form Gas-Gathering, Processing Firm," *Wall Street Journal,* December 17, 1999, p. A4.

Sullivan, Allanna, "Conoco's Dunham Makes Bold Moves to Hit Big Goals," *Wall Street Journal,* June 3, 1997, p. B4.

Tuttle, Ray, ''Deep Drilling: Phillips Believes Mahogany Field May Contain 100 Million Barrels of Oil,'' *Tulsa World,* September 1, 1996, p. E1.

Vogel, Todd, ''Phillips Climbs Up from the Bottom of the Barrel,'' *Business Week,* January 16, 1989.

Wallis, Michael, ''Oil Man: The Story of Frank Phillips and the Birth of Phillips Petroleum,'' New York: Doubleday, 1988.

Warren, Susan, ''DuPont Plans to Shed Conoco Oil Unit,'' *Wall Street Journal,* May 12, 1998, p. A2.

——, ''DuPont, Seeking to Shed Rest of Conoco, Offers $11.65 Billion Swap of Shares,'' *Wall Street Journal,* July 12, 1999, p. A3.

—Roger W. Rouland and Douglas Sun
—update: David E. Salamie

CR England, Inc.

4701 W. 2100 S.
Salt Lake City, Utah 84120-1223
U.S.A.
Telephone: (801) 972-2712
Fax: (801) 977-6736
Web site: http://www.crengland.com

Private Company
Founded: 1920
Employees: 2,700
Sales: $500 million (2003 est.)
NAIC: 484121 General Freight Trucking, Long-Distance, Truckload

CR England, Inc. is a family-owned and operated trucking company based in Salt Lake City, Utah, operating more than 2,600 trucks and 4,000 refrigerated trailers serving the United States, Canada, and Mexico. In addition, England Logistics offers transportation management services and England Transportation Consulting analyzes customers' shipping programs and helps to lower overall freight costs on a ''pay for performance'' basis. CR England boasts a strong safety record, supported by six driving schools located across the United States. For the past two decades the company has been in the vanguard in the trucking industry in the adoption of high technology, among the first to use computers to consolidate and track loads and deploy a satellite communications system that allows management to know the location of all trucks and, thus, be in a position to better manage assets. As a result of these and other changes, revenues have grown from $30 million in 1985 to about $500 million 20 years later.

Beginnings in 1920

The man behind the CR England name was Chester Rodney England, born on a farm in Plain City, Utah, in 1896. Shortly after marrying at the age of 20, England, a devout Mormon, departed on a mandatory church mission, promoting the teachings of the Church of Jesus Christ of Latter-Day Saints in the South. When he returned home 30 months later he turned to

farming, but soon realized that he was not cut out to be a farmer. In order to make a living, he bought a Model T truck in 1920 to haul farm products to the market. He found a ready demand for his service from farmers in Utah's Weber County and Cache Valley. In addition to produce, the industrious England began to haul milk for the Weber Dairy, starting his day at 4 a.m. to serve the dairy and then devote his afternoons to transporting produce to the market. England expanded the territory he served and began to add trucks and drivers. When his sons, Gene and Bill, were growing up they became immersed in the business. During the summers they joined their father on the road, riding along on weeklong runs to Wyoming. When they were old enough to drive, the boys spent their summers driving the several one- and two-ton trucks that the company owned.

After the United States entered World War II in December 1941, Gene and Bill England served in the military. During this time, their father began to buy Mexican bananas in El Paso, Texas, and sold them in Utah. His trucks would then return to Texas with loads of potatoes and pick up more bananas. The business was prosperous enough that after his sons were discharged from the service England was able to buy his first diesel truck, a used 1940 Kenworth. Shortly thereafter, he bought a 35-foot trailer with one of the new mechanical refrigeration units in it. Because the system was unreliable the company continued to utilize an older method employing ice bunkers: The trailer was kept cool by means of a fan and two feet of ice in the front of the trailer.

Coast-to-Coast Capabilities in 1950s

England was always on the lookout for new opportunities. He added more trucks and became involved in Idaho potatoes, with the company eventually operating its own packing shed and a storage facility. During the 1950s, when Mexican bananas were overtaken in popularity by Central American bananas, England switched his focus from Texas to California and Arizona and began to haul produce from these states. In the late 1950s the company made its mark by becoming the first trucking operation to offer 72-hour, coast-to-coast service. The driver of the first shipment of produce from California to Philadelphia was named Robert Gould. Because this new service proved so successful, about a year later a temporary office was set up to serve the Philadelphia area, with Gould hired as the first East Coast terminal manager. (A permanent terminal was later opened in Pennsauken, New Jersey. The East Coast office would then be relocated to Burlington, New Jersey, in 1978, but with the addition of new technology and management the company was able to close the office in 1982 and run all of the East Coast operations out of the Salt Lake terminal.)

In 1977 a third generation became involved in the business when Daniel England, the current chief executive officer, joined the company, just as the trucking industry was about to enter a period of radical change caused by deregulation initiated by the Reagan Administration. CR England like other carriers experienced a significant drop in shipping prices and had a difficult time bringing costs in line with the new reality. As a result, many trucking companies failed, and in 1985 CR England, reduced to about 175 trucks, lost money for the first time in some 60 years. Moreover, the Department of Transportation conducted a safety audit of CR England in 1985 and found it lacking. The company was fined and its status with the DOT was severely compromised. Management decided it had to take steps to aggressively address the company's economics as well as its safety record.

CR England made safety a core value and became diligent about adhering to DOT requirements, such as auditing driver logs, making sure the company followed drive and sleep regulations, and, if need be, curtailing loads if the job took too many hours to drive. A safety management system was implemented and safety managers conferred with drivers on a regular basis. CR England also became much more careful about the drivers it employed, implementing a screening procedure that included drug testing, and raising hiring standards so that eventually only around 30 percent of applicants qualified. In addition, in the late 1980s CR England became one of the first carriers to establish an onsite driver training school. Drivers were also encouraged to be involved in the safety program. They shared driving tips with one another, and the company provided an incentive program, awarding prizes for good driving records. As a result of these changes, CR England won the Truckload Carrier's Association Grand Safety Award three consecutive eligible years.

Management also took steps to improve the company's finances. Accountability tied to incentives and goals was a major part of the company's new strategy. To avoid lapsing into complacency, the goals were revised each quarter. CR England also began to look to high-tech ways to gain a competitive edge. The first step taken in the 1980s was to embrace computers to help in handling logistics and make more profitable use of equipment. The company then leveraged its computer system to digitally image all of its paperwork—invoices, receipts, con-

tracts—to greatly improve accounting operations. Additional costs to the electronic infrastructure were less than $100,000. In the early 1990s, the company installed satellite communications systems in all of its trucks, thus allowing management to know the precise location of drivers and instantly communicate with them, thereby providing even greater control in the management of equipment. Another major improvement was to the phone system. Although the company maintained 150 WATS lines, booking agents might receive 10,000 calls in a day, which meant that many potential customers had to be put on hold. With the trucking industry so competitive, many of these callers, rather than wait, simply hung up and tried a rival firm. The company's phone system was unable to capture the phone number of the abandoned call, resulting in an untold amount of lost business. Rolm, which made the equipment, was hired to upgrade the system to add automatic number identification. Coupled with a computer database of customers, the new system, rolled out in October 1991, allowed booking agents to identify the source of the abandoned call and to promptly call back the shipper to take the order. Customers soon realized that an agent would call back as soon as possible, allowing them to hang up and pursue other tasks rather than track down another carrier. Once the system was established, the company estimated that it captured from 12 to 24 jobs each week that would have previously been lost, representing a considerable amount of increased revenue. The new telephone system also helped the company's telemarketers with a preview dialing feature, which allowed the agent to create a list of customers to call on a frequent basis, whether it be daily or weekly. The preview dialing program would call down the list and when it found a connection, the telemarketer's computer screen would display the customer's record. Once that call was completed, the program would call the next number on the list. As a result, the productivity of the telemarketers virtually doubled. Taken altogether, these changes cut costs, made CR England more competitive, and resulted in annual growth in the 20 percent range. In 1985 revenues totaled $30 million, but by 1993 that amount increased to $160 million. Despite this significant increase in business, the company did not have to hire additional staff in the credit or billing departments, and the savings went straight to the bottom line.

Expansion in 1990s

In the early 1990s CR England expanded in a number of directions. With the passage of the North American Free Trade Agreement (NAFTA), the company quickly began to ship to the Mexico border. CR England forged relationships with a number of Mexican carriers, who would take the trailers at the border and deliver them to their final destination in Mexico. CR England trucks, in turn, could pick up Mexican loads for delivery in the United States. All the Mexican partners also used satellite tracking technology. In addition to adding an international division, CR England began to offer logistical services related to trucking. In 1994 it established England Logistics to offer traffic and transportation management, dedicated contract carriage, contract distribution center services, and fulfillment services to be marketed on a national basis—primarily to food processors and manufacturers. At first, the unit focused on companies that needed refrigerated trucking services, with dry truckload service to follow. A seasoned executive from Chicago-based TNT Contract Logistics, Ronald Wallace, was brought in to serve as president of the new business.

```
┌─────────────────────────────────────────────┐
│                 Key Dates:                    │
│                                               │
│  1920:  Chester Rodney England founds company.│
│  1957:  Company offers 72-hour, coast-to-coast│
│         service.                              │
│  1977:  Third generation becomes involved in  │
│         running company.                      │
│  1985:  First loss in decades leads to major  │
│         changes.                              │
│  1994:  England Logistics is launched.        │
│  2002:  Diversified Division and England      │
│         Transportation Consulting are started.│
└─────────────────────────────────────────────┘
```

By 1997 CR England reached $300 million in annual revenues. Realizing that drivers were a primary asset, the company continued to take steps to retain them, an important consideration since the trucking industry had a high turnover rate. The company had more than 3,000 drivers and in order to continue to expand the business it had to hire as many as 100 new drivers each week. For driver comfort, truck cabs featured beds, a refrigerator, and a television. Family members were also allowed to accompany drivers on trips, helping to alleviate some of the problems associated with drivers being separated from their families for extended periods of time. The company built a driver rest area in Salt Lake City called English Village, which featured overnight accommodations, barber shop, fitness center, video arcade, credit union, theater, and restaurant. To reward senior drivers, CR England launched an effort to create more owner/operators among its drivers as a way to provide further incentives for making a long-term commitment to the company and give employees a greater share of the rewards.

By the end of the 1990s CR England exceeded $400 million in annual revenues and continued to pursue new ways to realize further growth. It took advantage of the Internet to allow customers to book loads as well as to track their shipments. The company also decided to outsource the management of its paperwork. Although it was essentially a breakeven affair, the change speeded up the processing of the paperwork submitted by drivers. To remain competitive, CR England instituted a cost containment initiative, which led to a surprisingly simple, yet highly effective, way to cut nearly $200,000 per month in fuel costs. Traditionally, drivers left their engines running during meals or overnight stops. While the practice kept the cabs warm, it also cost carriers millions of dollars a year. The company's answer was to install Webasto auxiliary heaters and idle-limiting software in each truck.

In 2002 the company formed two new value-added divisions, the Diversified Division to arrange shipping for companies that contract freight hauling, and England Transportation Consulting to offer a range of transportation management services, including transportation cost analysis, carrier selection and rate negotiation, carrier contracting, compliance monitoring, inbound freight management, return goods management, and loss and damage claims filing. ETC offered a no-risk deal to customers, the company's fees generated from the amount of money a customer saved on shipping. There were no upfront charges or consulting fees. Both units operated out of Louisville, Kentucky. In December 2002 the Diversified Division expanded by acquiring one of its competitors, Wisconsin-based Service Transport Inc.

Following the terrorist attacks of September 11, 2001, CR England decided for the first time in 15 years to hold back on growing its fleet. When the company returned to adding drivers, it faced increasing challenges, due in large part to heightened national security provisions that resulted in a more stringent screening process. In addition, the DOT, in the first major change to standards since the 1930s, lowered the maximum number of driving hours from 70 to 60, which meant that carriers had to hire more drivers to make up the difference. When the measures went into effect in 2004, drivers were also allowed to work 11 straight hours as opposed to 10, but they were now required to rest two additional hours between shifts. According to studies conducted by CR England these rules were actually counterproductive, negatively impacting a driver's productivity by 5 to 10 percent. The company was worried that if lower productivity led to lower earnings, the driver shortage would grow even worse.

CR England did not face a shortage in family members to help run what was now a $500-million-a-year business. Scores of relatives were employed at all levels of the company. Gene England told CNNfn in a 1998 interview, "I have 34 grandchildren. And Bill has quite a number. . . . You've got to grow this thing to provide jobs for all of our grand kids; there are so many of 'em. And still growing."

Principal Subsidiaries

Diversified Division; England Logistics; England Transportation Consulting.

Principal Competitors

Central Refrigerated Service, Inc.; Frozen Food Express Industries, Inc.; Stevens Transport Inc.

Further Reading

Adams, Brent, "C.R. England Opens Transportation Management Unit," *Business First,* January 31, 2003, p. 6.

"C.R. England & Sons Launches New Dedicated Logistics Company," *Enterprise,* June 13, 1994, p. 5.

"Dan England," *Utah Business,* January 2001, p. 28.

Glines, Stephen, "ANI Keeps C.R. England Truckin' to Profits," *Communications News,* July 1, 1993, p. 12.

Ophus, Rashae, "Trucking Companies Struggling with Driver Shortage Thanks to Increasing Regulations and Restrictions," *Enterprise,* March 1, 2001, p. S4.

Whisenant, Ben, "Global Positioning Systems, Internet Tracking of Freight Loads Just Some of the High-Tech in Trucking," *Enterprise,* March 25, 2002.

—Ed Dinger

Cresud S.A.C.I.F. y A.

Edificio Inter-Continental Plaza
Calle Moreno 877, 23rd Floor
Buenos Aires, C.F. C1091AAQ
Argentina
Telephone: (54) (11) 4344-4600
Fax: (54) (11) 4344-4611
Web site: http://www.cresud.com.ar

Public Company
Incorporated: 1936
Employees: 245
Sales: ARS 71.95 million ($25.97 million) (2003)
Stock Exchanges: Bolsa de Comercio de Buenos Aires
  NASDAQ
Ticker Symbols: CRES; CRESY
NAIC: 111110 Soybean Farming; 111120 Oilseed
  (Except Soybean) Farming; 111140 Wheat Farming;
  111150 Corn Farming; 112111 Beef Cattle Ranching
  and Farming; 112112 Cattle Feedlots; 112120 Dairy
  Cattle and Milk Production

Cresud S.A.C.I.F. y A. is a corporate farmer and rancher. One of Argentina's largest agriculture and livestock enterprises, it is gambling that the nation's fertile pampas will reach their potential to help meet the world's growing food needs. Much of its vast holdings in eight Argentine provinces is used to produce crops, beef cattle, and dairy products that the company then markets. It also leases land for these purposes. Cresud employs modern farm technology and diversifies its crops to reduce dependence on price fluctuations in the commodity markets.

Cresud's Evolution: 1936–95

Cresud was incorporated in 1936 as a subsidiary of Crédit Foncier, a Belgian company engaged in several activities, including providing rural and urban loans in Argentina. The incorporation had several purposes, including to administer real estate holdings foreclosed by Crédit Foncier. This company was liquidated in 1959. As a part of the liquidation, Cresud's shares were distributed to Crédit Foncier's stockholders and, in 1960, these shares were listed on the Bolsa de Comercio de Buenos Aires. During the 1960s and 1970s Cresud's business shifted exclusively to agricultural activities.

Eduardo S. Elsztain worked for his family's small real estate company in Buenos Aires during the 1980s. After the firm fell victim to the crisis-ridden decade's economic ills, Elsztain took a year off in 1990 to live in New York City. An Orthodox Jew, he spent mornings studying Torah with members of a Brooklyn-based sect and afternoons seeking to convince potential investors that Argentina, under a new presidential administration, was ready to return to prosperity. Elsztain talked his way into the office of George Soros, the fabulously wealthy operator of successful hedge funds, and emerged with a war chest of $10 million earmarked for the purchase of undervalued Argentine stocks and real estate. He purchased a shell company named IRSA Inversiones y Representaciones S.A. and soon turned it into the nation's largest real estate firm.

Real estate, for Elsztain, meant not only holdings in Buenos Aires and other urban areas but also the ample expanses of the nation's plains—or pampas—renowned for their fertility and favorable climatic conditions for agriculture. Argentina's economic decline had left this land undervalued in comparison to similar properties in Australia, Canada, and the United States. The great landed estates on the pampas had been repeatedly subdivided, resulting in holdings that, because of lack of capital, low productivity, and high debt, were on sale at attractive prices. By leasing such properties to others, or by hiring professional managers to enhance production and augment profitability, the purchaser had the opportunity to achieve a high rate of return without making major investments. The reduction of taxes on farm exports in the early 1990s also promised to make an investment in this area more attractive, as did Washington's lifting of barriers against the import of Argentine beef, imposed earlier due to fears of contagion from hoof-and-mouth disease.

To this end, Elsztain started buying shares of Cresud in 1992 and purchased 51 percent of the company in 1994 for $11.2 million. In all, he paid $25 million for the company. His group of investors included Quantum Industrial Partners LDC, a hedge fund whose investment adviser was Soros's company,

Soros Fund Management LLC. Elsztain took the position of chief executive officer but entrusted day-to-day management to his brother Alejandro, a professional agronomist. Soros stayed out of the limelight. "He knows how we're growing, but he doesn't know the name of each cow," a company executive told Peter Hudson, writing for *América economía,* in 1997.

In addition to $61.8 million from Soros's group, Cresud, in 1995, garnered $64 million from a public offering on Bolsa de Comercio de Buenos Aires and, six months later, an additional $26.2 million. As the only publicly traded enterprise of its kind in Argentina, Cresud had the resources other farms and ranches lacked: professional management, ample access to capital and technology, and a low level of debt. Nevertheless, skeptics noted that most of the company's capital had been placed in short-term investments.

Rural Giant: 1996–2002

Cresud's net worth increased from $17.1 million to $89.4 million at the end of 1996 (the year ended June 30, 1996). During this period the company's holdings rose from 20,263 hectares (50,071 acres) with 22,000 head of cattle to 345,410 hectares (853,522 acres) of farms, ranches, and woodlands in six provinces. "Many of the people we buy from are traditional farming and ranching families," Alejandro Elsztain told Ken Warn of the *Financial Times* in 1998. "They have the land but no capital to invest in modernising production." He added, "Food demand will increase. Europe and the US will not subsidise agriculture forever, and the replacement for that will be Argentina." He also noted that, with the establishment of the Mercosur common market, Brazil had become an enormous market for Cresud's products.

Cresud entered the international equity markets in 1997 by a stock offering on the NASDAQ that raised $92 million. The infusion of funds allowed Cresud to purchase, for $25 million, 51,000 hectares (126,000 acres) with 87,000 head of cattle in Santa Fe province from Swift Armour S.A., an acquisition that raised its stock of cattle to 170,000. Also in 1997, Cresud formed a joint venture with Texas-based Cactus Feeders, Inc., the second largest feedlot company in the United States. The partners announced that they would begin fattening 100,000 calves a year on corn, thereby producing the well-marbled cuts of beef preferred by American and Asian palettes in place of traditional lean, grass-fed beef. Their 7,000-hectare (17,500-acre) feedlot opened in 1999 in Villa Mercedes, San Luis. The practice of raising livestock on feed farms was said to lower cost and boost output as well as raise quality. Cresud also was employing biotechnology to increase crop yields and irrigate marginal land extensively.

By now Argentina's agricultural boom was in full swing, making future land acquisitions more expensive. There was a big rise in the nation's grain and meat production between 1992 and 1997, and an even greater increase in such inputs as fertilizer and irrigation equipment. Farmers and ranchers were earning a much higher rate of return than their counterparts in the United States.

Luciano Benetton was the largest landowner in Argentina by 1997. He owned six large ranches in Patagonia covering 900,000 hectares (about 2.25 million acres), on which he raised Merino sheep to yield wool for his family's clothing chain. Benetton even employed satellite images to find out what his flocks preferred to eat. In Patagonia's lake district, such American celebrities as actor Sylvester Stallone and media tycoon Ted Turner bought large spreads—as did Soros himself—to become gentlemen ranchers and enjoy some of the most spectacular scenery in the world.

By the end of 1998 Cresud's land inventory had grown to 26 farms and 475,098 hectares (1.17 million acres), making the company Argentina's leading producer of beef and grain. But in 1999 the company sold, for $16.8 million, Runciman, a dairy and crop farm 380 kilometers (235 miles) northwest of Buenos Aires that it had bought in 1995 for $7.7 million. Cresud was now entering a more difficult period, darkened by a growing economic recession in Argentina and weak commodity prices for the company's products. Soros's fund, which still held 29 percent of Cresud after the 1997 public sale of shares in the United States, eventually sold most of its stock. Elsztain found a new American partner, Michael Steinhardt, in 2001. Steinhardt—like Soros, a former hedge fund operator—took one-quarter of the shares of Inversiones Financieras del Sud S.A., a Uruguay-based investment company controlled by Elsztain and his partners in IRSA and Cresud. This investment company held 30 percent of Cresud's shares, with pension fund managers holding another 28 percent, institutional investors holding 12 percent, and other public investors holding 28 percent.

Although Cresud's sales remained essentially flat between fiscal 2000 and 2003 and below the levels of the two previous years, the company remained profitable except in 2002, when capital flight and the subsequent devaluation of the peso played havoc both with Argentina's economy and that of its busi[-fJ]nesses, including Cresud. Seeking funds to finance its dollar-denominated debts—which grew sizably with the devaluation of the peso—the company sold seven of its farms for a total of $85.8 million between 2001 and 2003. But the devaluation also had some useful effects, reducing Cresud's costs as well as making its products more competitive with those deriving from other countries. In the annual report for 2003 Elsztain declared that agricultural land values in dollars had returned to the levels before devaluation.

Cresud's Prospects in 2003

Of Cresud's properties at the end of 2003, only two were original holdings of the Elsztain-managed company. The larger was Los Pozos in the province of Salta. Purchased in 1995, it

Key Dates:

1936: Cresud is incorporated as a subsidiary of a Belgian company.
1960: The company's shares are listed on the Bolsa de Comercio de Buenos Aires.
1994: Backed by George Soros, Eduardo S. Elsztain purchases a majority stake in Cresud.
1996: Cresud now owns nearly a million acres of farms, ranches, and woodlands.
1997: The company purchases a big ranch from Swift Armour S.A.
1998: Cresud, with 26 farms and ranches, is Argentina's biggest producer of beef and grain.
1999: Cresud opens a cattle feedlot as a joint venture with a Texas-based company.
2002: The company loses money in a crisis-ridden fiscal year.
2003: Cresud has sold seven farms in order to restructure its debts.

consisted of some 262,000 hectares (about 647,000 acres) in a semiarid region, with natural woodland yielding hardwoods for poles and charcoal. More than 15,000 beef cattle had been placed on this tract, and since the sparse rainfall fell mostly in the summer, it was considered to have potential for crops such as cotton, beans, sorghum, and corn. Purchased in 2003 for $9.2 million, El Tigre in La Pampa province was subsequently rated by the company as the most valuable of Cresud's farms. Valued by the company at ARS 26.8 million ($9.67 million), La Suiza in Chaco province was intended for cattle breeding and 21,402 head of beef cattle in 2003. La Juanita, in Buenos Aires province, was Cresud's chief dairy farm, with 1,002 milking cows in mid-2003. Other parts of the farm were being used for crop production and for cattle grazing on sown and natural pastures. San Nicolás, in Santa Fé province, and Las Playas, in Córdoba province, were owned by Agro-Uranga S.A., a company in which Cresud held a 36 percent share in mid-2003. San Nicolás was used for crop production; Las Playas was being used for crop production and the raising of both beef and dairy cattle.

In September 2003 Cresud owned 17 farms and 430,401 hectares (1.06 million acres), of which 139,317 hectares (344,258 acres)—mostly pasture rather than cropland—were under production. The rest was natural woodland. Some 3,093 hectares (7,463 acres) were under irrigation. Cresud hired personnel to manage the farms. Heads of cattle numbered 83,767, and dairy farm stock, 2,768. The company also was leasing 8,489 hectares (20,977 acres) of land, and this leased land accounted for 58 percent of the total sown for crops. Production in 2003 included, in metric tons, corn, 27,508; soybeans, 25,856; wheat, 9,397; and sunflower seeds, 3,074. Beef came to 9,121 metric tons and milk to 6.02 million liters. Some of

Cresud's grain and milk was exported, but none of the beef. Of the company's sales of ARS 71.95 million ($25.97 million), crops accounted for 71 percent, beef cattle for 24 percent, and milk for 3 percent. Operating income was ARS 27.68 million ($9.99 million), a 70 percent gain over the previous year.

Between 2000 and 2002 Cresud purchased 20.3 percent of IRSA's common stock for ARS 127.26 million ($45.4 million) and owned 22.65 percent of the company at the end of 2003, when it also held $49.7 million in IRSA convertible notes. During the same period Cresud also acquired 70 percent of Futuros y Opciones.Com S.A., a business site on the Internet.

Cresud issued $50 million in convertible bonds in 2003 and had outstanding debt of ARS 139.4 million ($50.3 million), all in convertible notes maturing in 2007, at the end of the fiscal year. Eduardo Elsztain owned 34 percent of Cresud's common stock in late 2003 through Inversiones Financieras del Sud. Pension funds owned another 11 percent. Elsztain was president and chairman of the company, while his brother Alejandro was chief executive officer. Cresud's top managers were being paid a 10 percent fee on the company's annual net income, which came to ARS 65.03 million ($23.48 million) in 2003.

Principal Subsidiaries

Cactus Argentina S.A. (50%); Futuros y Opciones.Com S.A. (70%); Inversiones Canaderas S.A.

Principal Competitors

Cooperativa Agricola Regional; Cooperativa Argentina Tres Arroyos; Los Grupos Agropecuaria; Pioneer Argentina; Sociedad Antonio Moreno.

Further Reading

"Argentina: Eduardo Elsztain Plans to Take Control of Cresud," *South American Business Information,* August 3, 2001.
"Argentina Farmed Land Company Poised for Growth," *South American Business Information,* January 9, 2003.
Atance, Christian, "Soros apuesta al campo," *America economia,* December 1995, pp. 17, 20.
"El capitalismo llegó al campo," *Mercado,* March 1998, pp. 22–24, 26.
"Eduardo Elsztain, IRSA," *LatinFinance,* July 1998, p. 191.
Hudson, Peter, "Soros: Cuestión de marca," *América economía,* November 1997, pp. 29, 32.
Krauss, Clifford, "Two Brothers Build an Empire," *New York Times,* April 14, 1998, pp. D1, D4.
Mandel-Campbell, Andrea, "A Stampede on the Pampas," *Business Week,* August 25, 1997, p. 58.
Sims, Calvin, "Wonders of Patagonia Await Clinton," *New York Times,* October 17, 1997, p. A8.
Warn, Ken, "George Soros Joins Cattle Super-League," *Financial Times,* February 11, 1998, p. 30.

—Robert Halasz

Dell Inc.

One Dell Way
Round Rock, Texas 78682-0001
U.S.A.
Telephone: (512) 338-4400
Toll Free: (800) 289-3355
Fax: (512) 283-6161
Web site: http://www.dell.com

Public Company
Incorporated: 1984 as Dell Computer Corporation
Employees: 46,000
Sales: $41.44 billion (2004)
Stock Exchanges: NASDAQ
Ticker Symbol: DELL
NAIC: 334111 Electronic Computer Manufacturing;
    334112 Computer Storage Device Manufacturing;
    334119 Other Computer Peripheral Equipment
    Manufacturing; 454110 Electronic Shopping and
    Mail-Order Houses

Long the world's largest direct-sale computer vendor, Dell Inc. is now also the leading seller of computer systems in the world, capturing a global market share of more than 15 percent. Dell markets desktop personal computers, notebook computers, network servers, workstations, handheld computers, monitors, printers, high-end storage products, and a variety of computer peripherals and software. The firm also has moved into the consumer electronics arena, offering LCD televisions, projectors, and other products. Dell manufactures most of the products it sells, maintaining six production facilities worldwide, located in Austin, Texas; Nashville, Tennessee; Eldorado do Sul, Brazil; Limerick, Ireland; Penang, Malaysia; and Xiamen, China. About two-thirds of revenues are generated in the Americas, with 22 percent originating in Europe, the Middle East, and Africa and with the Asia-Pacific region accounting for the remaining 11 percent. Dell sells its equipment directly to consumers, small to large businesses, government agencies, and healthcare and educational institutions through dedicated sales representatives, telephone-based sales, and online via the company web site. Founder Michael Dell holds 12 percent of the company and will remain chairman of the company after stepping down as CEO in July 2004.

Early History

Dell was founded by Michael Dell, who started selling personal computers out of his dorm room as a freshman at the University of Texas in Austin. Dell bought parts wholesale, assembled them into clones of IBM computers, and sold them by mail order to customers who did not want to pay the higher prices charged by computer stores. The scheme was an instant success. He was soon grossing $80,000 a month, and in 1984 he dropped out of school, incorporating his business as Dell Computer Corporation (though it would initially do business as PC's Limited).

At the time, the PC industry was dominated by such large firms as IBM, while smaller, lesser known mail-order firms sold IBM clones at a steep discount. Dell used low-cost direct marketing to undersell the better known computers being sold through such high-overhead dealer networks. Dell placed ads in computer magazines, gearing his merchandise to buyers who were sophisticated enough to recognize high-quality merchandise at low prices. Customers placed orders to Dell by dialing a toll-free number. As a result of these methods, Dell's computers became the top brand name in the direct-mail market.

Dell achieved sales of $6 million its first full year in business, approaching $40 million the next year. Dell hired former investment banker E. Lee Walker as president in 1986 to help deal with his firm's explosive growth. By 1987 Dell held a dominant position in the mail-order market, but it was clear that the firm had to move beyond mail order if it was to continue growing. To accomplish this goal the firm needed a larger professional management staff, and Dell hired a group of marketing executives from Tandy Corporation, another maker of low-cost PCs. The group built a sales force able to market to large corporations and put together a network of value-added resellers, who assembled packages of computer components to sell in specialized markets.

The Tandy team soon helped raise gross margins to 31 percent, up from 23 percent a year earlier. Rather than merely

122

undercutting the prices of competitors, they set prices in relation to the firm's costs. The new marketing department soon ran into trouble with Michael Dell, however. Battles erupted over advertising budgets and the number of salespeople required for corporations and resellers. While Dell believed that the new team did not understand direct selling and was trying to create a traditional marketing department with an overly large sales force, the Tandy group alleged that Dell lacked the patience to wait for the sales force to pay off. By early 1988, most of the Tandy group had resigned or been forced out.

Regardless, the firm continued growing rapidly, opening a London office that sold $4 million worth of computers during one month in 1988. Dell also formed a Canadian subsidiary. Early in 1988 the firm formed various divisions to raise its profile among corporate, government, and educational buyers. With reported sales of $159 million in 1987, the firm went public in June 1988, selling 3.5 million shares at $8.50 a share.

Increased Competition in the Late 1980s

The firm faced several challenges, however. Announcing their own clone of IBM's new PS/2 computer system well before it was actually ready, Dell later had trouble reproducing important aspects of the PS/2's architecture, and the computers were delayed significantly, embarrassing the young company. Furthermore, Dell faced competition from several Japanese manufacturers, which were offering IBM clones at low prices. Further, having had trouble meeting demand, Dell used money raised from its stock offering to expand capacity and warehouse space, leaving the company with little cash. When it overestimated demand during the fourth quarter of 1988, the firm suddenly had no cash and warehouses full of unsold computers.

Dell responded to the increasing competition by increasing the level of technical sophistication in its computers. Half of its 1988 sales came from PCs using the Intel Corporation's 80386 microprocessor, the most powerful PC chip at the time, and the company began producing file servers using the sophisticated Unix operating system. Dell also hired computer scientist Glenn Henry away from IBM to work on product development. Scrapping the company's first attempts at cloning IBM's PS/2,

Henry initiated new plans for producing clones. Henry built Dell's research and development staff from almost nothing to 150 engineers, who began working on ways to combine the function of several chips onto one chip. When Intel released its 486 microprocessor, Dell began speeding to market the computers that could use it. Another of Henry's goals was high-quality graphics, which required better monitors and special circuit boards. By mid-1989 Dell had finished initial attempts at graphics hardware, giving it inroads into the higher end of the PC market.

Despite these advances, Dell still had a research and development budget of $7 million, compared with the hundreds of millions spent by such larger competitors as IBM. Dell's share of the PC market was only 1.8 percent, but it was still growing rapidly. U.S. sales for 1989 reached $257.8 million, while sales in Britain increased to $40 million and a branch in Western Germany realized the break-even point.

Dell considered itself as much a marketing company as a hardware company, and its sales staff played an important role in its successes. Dell's sales personnel trained for six weeks or more before taking their seats at the phonebanks, and, along with their managers, they held weekly meetings to discuss customer complaints and possible solutions. In addition to fielding questions and taking orders, sales staff were trained to promote products. They helped buyers customize orders, selling them more memory or built-in modems. Orders were then sent to Dell's nearby factory where they were filled within five days. The telemarketing system also allowed Dell to compile information on its customers, helping the firm spot opportunities and mistakes far more quickly than most other PC companies.

In 1990 Dell set up subsidiaries in Italy and France as well as a manufacturing center in Limerick, Ireland, to serve customers in Europe, the Middle East, and Africa. It also began selling some computers through large computer stores, whose high-volume, low-margin strategy complemented Dell's established operations. The firm was making important corporate inroads as well, developing client/server computing systems with Andersen Consulting, for example, and introducing powerful servers using the Unix operating system. As a result, 40 percent of Dell's $546 million in 1990 sales came from the corporate world, up from 15 percent in 1987. Dell became the sixth largest PC maker in the United States—up from number 22 in 1989—and retained a staff of 2,100. Furthermore, the company's emphasis on customer satisfaction paid off, as it was rated number one in J.D. Powers Associates' first survey of PC customer satisfaction.

That year, however, Dell purchased too many memory chips and was forced to abandon a project to start a line of workstations. As a result, 1990 profits fell 65 percent to $5 million, despite the doubling of the firm's sales.

Price Wars in the Early 1990s

Also during this time, the traditional PC market channels were in flux. With a recession dampening sales, PC makers engaged in a furious price war that resulted in slumping profits nearly across the board. Compaq, IBM, and Apple all had profit declines or were forced to lay off employees. Furthermore, Compaq filed a lawsuit against Dell, which it eventually won, claiming that Dell's advertising made defamatory statements against Compaq. Nevertheless, the economic recession actually benefited Dell. While customers had less money, they still needed PCs, and they purchased Dell's inexpensive but technologically innovative IBM clones in record numbers. Consequently, annual sales shot up toward $1 billion.

In the early 1990s, notebook-sized computers were the fastest growing segment of the PC market, and Dell devoted resources to producing its first notebook model, which it released in 1991. The following year it introduced a full-color notebook model and also marketed PCs using Intel's fast 486 microchip.

As the PC wars continued, Compaq, which had been a higher priced manufacturer stressing its quality engineering, repositioned itself to take on Dell, releasing a low-end PC priced at just $899 and improving its customer services. The new competition affected Dell's margins, forcing it to cut its computer prices by up to $1,400 to keep its market share. Dell could afford such steep price cuts because its operating costs were only 18 percent of revenues, compared with Compaq's 36 percent. The competition also forced Dell away from its attempts to stress its engineering. Dell executives began speaking of computers as consumer products similar to appliances, downplaying the importance of technology. Reflecting this increased stress on marketing, Dell began selling a catalogue of computer peripherals and software made by other companies; it soon expanded into fax machines and compact discs. Dell's database, containing information on the buying habits of more than 750,000 of its customers, was instrumental in this effort.

Toward the end of 1992 Dell's product line experienced technological difficulties, particularly in the notebook market. In 1993 quality problems forced the firm to cancel a series of notebook computers before they were even introduced, causing a $20 million charge against earnings. The firm was projected to hold a 3.5 percent share of the PC market in 1993, but Digital Equipment Corporation, whose focus was minicomputers, nevertheless topped Dell as the biggest computer mail-order company. To fight back against Compaq's inexpensive PC line, Dell introduced its Dimensions by Dell line of low-cost PCs. Sales for the year reached $2 billion, and Dell made a second, $148 million stock offering.

During the early 1990s Dell also attempted a foray into retail marketing, the most popular venue with individual consumers. In 1990 Dell placed its products in Soft Warehouse Superstores (later renamed CompUSA) and in 1991 they moved into Staples, a discount office supply chain. Dell agreed to allow the stores to sell the products at mail-order prices, a policy that soon caused Dell a lot of grief. The value of existing computers on store shelves plummeted whenever Dell offered a new computer through its direct sales, and Dell had to compensate retailers for that loss. With its direct sales channel, Dell had never had inventories of old computers that it could not sell, because each of those computers was made specifically to fill a consumer's order. Dell abandoned the retail market late in 1993.

With price wars continuing, Dell cut prices again in early 1993 and extended the period of its warranty. Increased competition and technical errors had hurt Dell, however, and despite growing sales, the firm announced a quarterly loss in excess of $75 million in 1993, its first loss ever. Dell attributed many of the problems to internal difficulties caused by its incredible growth. It responded by writing down PCs based on aging technology and restructuring its notebook division and European operations.

Like most of its competitors, Dell was hurt by an industry-wide consolidation taking place in the early 1990s. The consolidation also offered opportunity, however, as Dell fought to win market share from companies going out of business. Dell moved aggressively into markets outside of the United States, including Latin America, where Xerox began to sell Dell computers in 1992. By 1993, 36 percent of Dell's sales were abroad. That year, Dell entered the Asia-Pacific region by establishing subsidiaries in Australia and Japan.

Late 1990s Expansion

After a loss of $36 million in 1994, Dell rebounded spectacularly, reporting profits of $149 million in 1995. That year, the company introduced Pentium-based notebook computers and a popular dual-processor PC. The company grew by almost 50 percent that year and the next, raising its market share to approximately 4 percent and entering the company into the ranks of the top-five computer sellers in the world.

Expansion continued on many fronts in 1996. Dell introduced a line of network servers and was soon the fastest-growing company in that sector. The company also opened a manufacturing facility in Penang, Malaysia. The most important development that year, however, was Dell's expansion into selling directly to consumers over the Internet. Within three years, Dell was selling $30 million a day over the Internet, which would come to account for 40 percent of the company's overall revenue. Dell achieved enviable efficiencies using the Internet to coordinate the orders of consumers with its own orders of parts from suppliers. The company's web site also provided technical support and allowed consumers to track their orders from manufacturing through delivery.

Dell continued its exponential growth in 1997 and 1998, reaching profits of $944 million in 1998. The company introduced new products and services, including a line of workstations, a leasing program for individual consumers, and a line of storage products under the PowerVault brand. Dell also expanded its manufacturing facilities in the United States and in Europe. In 1998 it established a production and customer center in Xiamen, China, raising the number of its overseas plants to three. By the time Dell sold its ten millionth computer in 1997, it was a close fourth behind IBM, Hewlett-Packard, and Compaq in the computer industry. By mid-1998, it had captured 9 percent of the market and the number two spot.

Following on the success of its direct sales over the Internet, Dell opened an online superstore of computer-related products in 1999. Gigabuys.com offered low-priced computer hardware, software, and peripherals from various companies in the industry, although Dell continued to sell its own products at www.dell.com. The company also expanded its Internet offerings in 1999 with Dellnet, an Internet access service for Dell customers. Two more manufacturing facilities were added to the firm's global production network that year, located in Nashville, Tennessee; and Eldorado do Sul, Brazil. For the fiscal year ending in January 2000, Dell reported net income of $1.86 billion on total revenues of $25.26 billion.

Early 2000s: Surviving Global PC Downturn, Diversifying

When the global PC industry fell into its worst slump ever during 2000, Dell responded by initiating a price war to which its rivals were slow to respond, providing Dell with a chance to further increase its market share. As a result, by 2001 Dell managed to gain for the first time the top spot globally in PC sales, with a 13 percent worldwide share. The downturn also triggered the creation of a more formidable competitor in the form of Hewlett-Packard, which acquired Compaq during this period. Dell also responded to the PC slump by aggressively pushing into the market for Internet servers, a more profitable sector than that of PCs. It launched another price war on the low end of the server market, which cut into its margins somewhat but enabled it to gain share. Dell targeted other higher-margin sectors as well. It continued its push into the storage market in late 2001 by entering into an alliance with EMC Corporation to develop a new line of data-storage systems, and it entered the market for low-end networking gear used by small businesses, launching its PowerConnect line of network switches in 2001. Finally, Dell stayed solidly in the black—while its rivals were losing money—via a major cost-cutting program. The company made the first significant layoffs in its history, slashing 5,700 jobs from the payroll during 2001 and taking nearly $600 million in charges relating to restructuring actions. The charges reduced profits, but Dell still managed to record net income of $1.78 billion on revenues of $31.17 billion for 2002.

Although Michael Dell remained firmly in charge of the company he had founded as chairman and CEO, Kevin B. Rollins was increasingly taking over the day-to-day operations at Dell Computer and had been instrumental in the maneuvers that had enabled the company to gain ground on its rivals during the industry slump. Rollins had consulted for Dell while employed with the consulting firm Bain & Company, before joining Dell in 1996 as a senior vice-president. He was named vice-chairman in 1997 and then became president and chief operating officer in 2001. Rollins's assumption of the operating reins enabled Michael Dell to concentrate more on long-range, strategic planning.

Continuing to seek new avenues for growth—as it aimed to double revenues to $60 billion by fiscal 2007—Dell Computer diversified further. During 2002 the company entered the handheld computer market by launching its Axim line of personal digital assistants (PDAs). Early in 2003 it debuted its own line of printers aimed at both businesses and consumers. Later that year Dell gained a toehold in the cutthroat consumer electronics industry by introducing LCD flat-panel televisions, digital music players, and an online music service. With businesses keeping a tight rein on their PC spending, Dell in 2002 attempted to gain further sales from consumers by setting up kiosks at shopping malls where customers could see and try out Dell computers, printers, and other products before placing their orders online or by phone. Early in 2003, in a trial run, the company set up its first Dell store-within-a-store inside of a Sears, Roebuck & Company outlet.

The corporation's widening interests took a quite concrete form in mid-2003 through the shortening of the firm's name to simply Dell Inc. Dell's diversification, coupled with large increases in shipments of high-profit-margin products such as servers, notebook computers, and storage equipment, propelled the company to new heights in 2004. Net income surged 25 percent that year, hitting $2.65 billion, while revenues jumped 17 percent, to $41.44 billion. Soon after these stellar results were released, Michael Dell, the person with the longest-running tenure as CEO of a major U.S. computer company, announced that he would relinquish his CEO title to Rollins in July 2004 but would remain actively involved in the company as chairman. With a smooth transition in leadership expected, it appeared likely that Dell would maintain its leadership position in computer systems and also continue to pursue its growth ambitions in the wider computer industry and into the realm of consumer electronics.

Principal Operating Units

Dell Americas; Dell Asia Pacific - Japan; Dell Europe, Middle East and Africa.

Principal Competitors

Hewlett-Packard Company; International Business Machines Corporation; Apple Computer, Inc.; Gateway, Inc.; Sun Microsystems, Inc.

Further Reading

''Dell Computer: Selling PCs Like Bananas,'' *Economist,* October 5, 1996.

Dell, Michael, with Catherine Fredman, *Direct from Dell: Strategies That Revolutionized an Industry,* New York: HarperBusiness, 1999.

Forest, Stephanie Anderson, ''PC Slump? What PC Slump?,'' *Business Week,* July 1, 1991, p. 66.

Holstein, William J., ''Dell: One Computer, Two CEOs,'' *CEO Magazine,* November 2003, pp. 30–35.

Jones, Kathryn, ''Bad News for Dell Computer,'' *New York Times,* July 15, 1993, p. C3.

Kelly, Kevin, ''Dell Computer Hits the Drawing Board,'' *Business Week,* April 24, 1989, p. 138.

——, ''Michael Dell: The Enfant Terrible of Personal Computers,'' *Business Week,* June 13, 1988, p. 61.

Koehn, Nancy F., ''Michael Dell,'' in *Brand New: How Entrepreneurs Earned Consumers' Trust from Wedgwood to Dell,* Boston: Harvard Business School Press, 2001, pp. 259–305.

McCartney, Scott, ''Michael Dell—and His Company—Grows Up,'' *Wall Street Journal,* January 31, 1995, p. B1.

McWilliams, Gary, ''Dell Pins Hopes on Services to Boost Profit,'' *Wall Street Journal,* November 11, 2003, p. B1.

——, ''Dell's Founder to Step Down As CEO,'' *Wall Street Journal,* March 5, 2004, p. A10.

——, ''Dell's New Push: Cheaper Laptops Built to Order,'' *Wall Street Journal,* June 17, 1999, p. B1.

——, ''System Upgrade: Dell Looks for Ways to Rekindle the Fire It Had As an Upstart,'' *Wall Street Journal,* August 31, 2000, p. A1.

Morris, Betsy, ''Can Michael Dell Escape the Box?,'' *Fortune,* October 16, 2000, pp. 92–96+.

Park, Andrew, Faith Keenan, and Cliff Edwards, ''Whose Lunch Will Dell Eat Next?,'' *Business Week,* August 12, 2002, pp. 66–67.

Park, Andrew, and Peter Burrows, ''Dell, the Conqueror: Now the King of Cutthroat Pricing Is Looking Beyond PCs,'' *Business Week,* September 24, 2001, pp. 92–93+.

——, ''What You Don't Know About Dell,'' *Business Week,* November 3, 2003, pp. 76–82+.

''Personal Computers: Didn't Delliver,'' *Economist,* February 20, 1999.

Pope, Kyle, ''For Compaq and Dell Accent Is on Personal in the Computer Wars,'' *Wall Street Journal,* July 2, 1993, p. A1.

Roth, Daniel, ''Dell's Big New Act,'' *Fortune,* December 6, 1999, pp. 152–54, 156.

Serwer, Andy, ''Dell Does Domination,'' *Fortune,* January 21, 2002, pp. 70–75.

''You'll Never Walk Alone,'' *Economist,* June 26, 1999.

—Scott M. Lewis
—updates: Susan Windisch Brown, David E. Salamie

Dierbergs Markets Inc.

16690 Swingley Ridge Road
Chesterfield, Missouri 63017
U.S.A.
Telephone: (636) 532-8884
Fax: (636) 532-8759
Web site: http://www.dierbergs.com

Private Company
Founded: 1914
Employees: 4,700
Sales: $575 million (2002 est.)
NAIC: 445110 Supermarkets and Other Grocery (Except Convenience) Stores

Dierbergs Markets Inc., based in Chesterfield, Missouri, operates 21 upscale supermarkets in the St. Louis area, including one in Illinois. Dierbergs is known as an innovator, the first supermarket in the country to establish an in-store cooking school, and the first in the St. Louis market to offer video rentals, a full-service FTD florist outlet, and in-store banking. Dierbergs is well known for the quality of its produce, meat, seafood, and deli departments, and has consistently ranked high in customer satisfaction surveys. The chain is family-owned by the Dierbergs, with a third generation now in charge and a fourth generation assuming leadership positions.

Roots Dating Back to 1854

Dierbergs traces the start of the business to 1854 and the opening of a general store on Olive Street Road in Creve Coeur, a village located near the rapidly growing Mississippi port town of St. Louis. This business would come into the hands of the Dierberg family in 1914 when William Dierberg bought it. He was born around 1880 and originally started out as a blacksmith. After serving his apprenticeship he ran his own shop in the St. Louis vicinity in University City, circa 1900. He then moved his family to a more rural area known as Lake. Here he was situated near a general store owned by a Mr. Zierenberg called the 18 Mile House (many establishments from an earlier period took their name from the distance they stood from the Mississippi River). When Zierenberg decided around 1910 to return home to his native Germany for a year-long visit, Dierberg agreed to give up smithing and take over the management of the general store for him. When Zierenberg returned to the United States, Dierberg did not resume the blacksmith trade. Rather, he moved to Creve Coeur to run the general store, which was owned by a man named H.M. Koch. A few years later, in 1914, Dierberg bought out Koch and laid the roots for today's Dierbergs chain of supermarkets.

The store was located in a building known as ''Creve Coeur House,'' which also included the 14 Mile House hotel and the Creve Coeur Farmer's Bank. Dierberg ultimately bought the hotel and became president of the bank (which would grow from a single rural branch into an institution with $4.2 billion in assets and more than 130 offices spread across four states). In 1929 Dierberg quit the grocery business to pursue other interests and turned over the operation to his sons, William Dierberg, Jr., and Fred. (The elder Dierberg would die in 1945.) A year later the brothers moved the business to an adjacent location on Olive Street Road, opening a 3,500-square-foot store. During the 1930s, like other grocery stores of the day, it made the transition from orders being filled by clerks to self-service, a concept pioneered by Clarence Saunders and his Piggly Wiggly stores. The Dierbergs operated at this new location until 1960, when they moved the business elsewhere in Creve Coeur. A year later a third generation became involved in the business when the son of William Dierberg, Jr., Robert J. Dierberg, went to work for the store. It was not until 1967 that Dierbergs opened a second store, which was built some four miles away from the first. This was a major step for the family business and a harbinger of what was to come: The new store was much admired for its modern design and was named ''Store of the Month,'' by the trade publication *Progressive Grocer*. (It was also during this period that Robert's brother, Jim, took over the presidency of Creve Coeur Farmer's Bank and started to grow that one-location business into First Bank.) In 1969 a cousin, Roger Dierberg, who gave up an engineering career at McDonnell-Douglas, joined the business to help in the expansion of the Dierberg supermarket business.

Company Perspectives:

''What are the needs of our customers?'' Dierbergs contin- ues to ask that question today as the company builds new stores and updates existing ones.

Third Store Opening in 1976

Dierbergs opened its third store in 1976, a 51,000-square-foot unit in Oakville, south of St. Louis. At the time, it was regarded as one of the finest supermarkets in the United States, and would usher in a decade of rapid growth for Dierbergs, which expanded its offerings as well as the number of locations. In 1978 Dierbergs opened its first in-store cooking school at the Manchester site. The concept proved so popular that the company expanded it into a multimedia operation over the years. Eventually there would be four strategically located in-store cooking schools. Not only did Dierbergs hire a staff of professional home economists, it brought in well-known chefs, cookbook authors, caterers, and restaurateurs to teach classes, which were conducted in profes- sionally equipped kitchen classrooms. Topics included such areas as regional cooking style, ethnic foods, appetizers, heart- healthy cooking, and complete meals. Class sizes were also limited to 20 or less, providing ample opportunity for individual attention. Moreover, the schedule offered a lot of flexibility, with day and evening classes, and single sessions or extended courses available. Classes were also available for children, or for groups such as co-workers, birthday parties, and gourmet groups. Out of the cooking school came a quarterly recipe magazine, *Everybody Cooks,* and ultimately a CD that covered 15 years of the publica- tion's most popular recipes, numbering more than 1,900 recipes. In 1986, in a related development, Dierbergs teamed up with the Missouri Baptist Medical Center to launch an information pro- gram, Eat Hearty, to help customers select and prepare heart- healthy foods. In addition, Dierbergs tagged store shelves with a red heart logo, calling attention to products that fell within guideline levels for cholesterol, fat, saturated fat, and sodium. Dierbergs, in 1991, transferred its popular Everybody Cooks concept to television. The company purchased a primetime slot on KMO-TV in St. Louis to broadcast a 30-minute cooking show. Receiving strong ratings, ''Everybody Cooks'' is now broadcast four times a year, offering expert tips, recipes, and food ideas for holidays and entertaining.

Dierbergs continued to add new stores in the St. Louis area, and by 1985 had a slate of ten. In 1978 the company opened a store in Manchester, Missouri, followed a year later by a store in Southroads. Dierbergs was especially active in 1980, adding two new stores as well as relocating the 1960 store that had replaced the original Creve Coeur store bought by the founder in 1914. The Mid Rivers store was opened in 1983 and three more stores followed in 1985: Lemay, Bogey Hills, and Florissant. During this period of expansion, Dierbergs also grew its reputation for high quality and innovation. In 1980 Dierbergs introduced its first pharmacy, which evolved into a significant facet of the company one-stop shopping approach. In the mid-1980s Dierbergs added salad bars and takeout food to all of its locations. The stores also introduced floral shops and a video center that offered movie rentals. To build loyalty, Dierbergs

created its Customer Club, which gave members a check cashing card as well as the right to rent movies. The club also mailed out a quarterly newsletter that included recipes and scores of special coupons. The Creve Coeur store, in 1987, became the first of four locations to feature a European bakery, offering authentic specialties prepared in facilities separate from the regular bakery. Pastries included éclairs, vanilla Na- poleons, Florentine cookies, and fresh fruit tarts, as well as cakes such as ambrosia, Grand Marnier, hazelnut, white choco- late, and raspberry supreme.

Dierbergs reached a turning point in the second half of the 1980s when the company decided to create a new prototypical supermarket, eschewing the successful design features of the previous ten years—homey wallpaper, rustic wooden beams, and chandeliers. In November 1987, Dierbergs opened its 11th store, a 74,000-square-foot unit located in north St. Louis County. According to *Progressive Grocer,* the new store fea- tured ''painted walls, neon lights and modern spotlight fixtures that create a look *Miami Vice* would be proud of.'' In addition, the new store reconfigured certain departments—the deli, bak- ery, and floral shop—in order to accommodate popular services such as video rentals, salad bar, and takeout food. With a leaner look and less ornamental trappings, the new prototype was able to provide more space to value-priced products. In addition, the extra space allowed the new store to offer a seating area in front of the store, a self-service beverage center, and a blood pressure machine in the pharmacy area for customers to use. Moreover, by adding an 11th store Dierbergs now qualified as a chain. Despite being a small chain, Dierbergs was able to flourish in the St. Louis area, where such giants as Kroger and A&P had failed in their attempts to crack the market. To close out the 1980s, Dierbergs added the Market Place store in 1988 and Mackenzie Pointe in 1989. Also in 1989 Dierbergs replaced its third store in Oakville with one in Telegraph.

As Dierbergs moved into the 1990s, the chain, and the family that owned it, approached a watershed moment. According to the *St. Louis Business Journal,* ''The Dierberg family was faced with a difficult problem in 1993, when it had to bring an outside executive into the family-owned grocery chain for the first time. The younger generation was not ready to take on the task of running the company, and the older generation wanted a capable executive to ease the generational transfer.'' In August 1993 Dierbergs hired 43-year-old Darryl Wikoff to succeed Robert Dierberg as president of the chain. Dierberg would stay on as chief executive and chairman, while his cousin Roger assumed a new position, that of vice-chairman. Both continued to be highly involved in the running of the operation. Wikoff had 23 years of experience in the supermarket business, all of which was with the ten-store, Nebraska-based Baker's Supermarket Inc. His ten- ure at Dierbergs, however, would be relatively brief—just three- and-a-half years. In April 1997 he resigned, and Robert Dierberg once again took over the presidency. But by now a fourth generation of the family—Robert Dierberg's son, Greg Dierberg, and his daughter, Laura Dierberg-Padousis—was be- coming more involved in the running of the business.

Unveiling a New Prototype in 1996

In 1996 Dierbergs introduced another new prototype, this one in Brentwood, Missouri. During this period, in an effort to

<table>
<tr><td colspan="2">Key Dates:</td></tr>
</table>

1914:	William Dierberg buys a general store in Creve Coeur, Missouri.
1929:	Brothers William Dierberg, Jr., and Fred Dierberg take over the business.
1967:	A second supermarket opens.
1976:	A third store opens.
1987:	Dierbergs qualifies as a chain with the 11th store opening.
2003:	The first Illinois store opens.

cut down on the volume of intercom pages, Dierbergs experimented with a zone paging system and ultimately settled on a wireless phone system, so that managers and key employees could be contacted immediately, and discretely if necessary. In one case, a store director was able to use her wireless phone to call for help when a customer was struck with a heart attack and she did not have to leave the person's side. The wireless phones would ultimately be rolled out to the entire chain. By September 1998 the chain included 16 stores and was generating estimated sales of $450 million.

As it entered the new century, Dierbergs continued to expand and innovate. Dierbergs added stores in Fenton and Brentwood, which helped the chain realize a substantial growth in sales, from $550 million in 2001 to $575 million in 2002. Dierbergs added the popular Krispy Kreme doughnuts to its bakeries and by 2003 added them to all locations. In that year, all stores also added U-Scan self-serve checkout areas to better serve customer needs. The chain grew to 20 stores and expanded across the Mississippi River in 2003 when Dierbergs opened a store in Shiloh, Illinois, entering St. Louis's Metro East area. Dierbergs and other area supermarkets also faced some labor issues in 2003 as members of the United Food and Commercial Workers Local 655 and management negotiated a new contract, following the June expiration of the previous contract. In September Dierbergs, Schnuck Markets Inc., and Shop 'n Save Warehouse Foods Inc. reached a tentative agreement, only to have union membership decisively reject the deal. The union members then voted to strike on October 7, choosing Shop 'n Save as the immediate target. In response, Schnucks and Dierbergs locked out their union employees. (Dierbergs' Illinois store was not affected.) The two sides were brought back to the negotiating table in late October and by the end of the month they were able to hammer out an agreement that union membership voted to accept.

In 2004 Dierbergs opened its Wildwood store and announced that later in the year it would open a second supermarket in Illinois. With a solid reputation for quality and customer service in the St. Louis market, there was every reason to believe that Dierbergs would continue to make significant inroads east of the Mississippi.

Principal Competitors

IGA, Inc.; Schnuck Markets Inc.; Shop 'n Save Warehouse Foods Inc.

Further Reading

Banstetter, Trebor, "Outsider Helps Family-Owned Dierbergs with Succession," *St. Louis Business Journal,* June 19, 1995, p. 8B.

Lee, Thomas, "Dierbergs Cooks Up a Hit," *St Louis Post-Dispatch,* March 31, 2002, p. E1.

Major, Meg, "Dierbergs Shows 'em," *Progressive Grocer,* August 1, 2002, p. 34.

"150 Largest Privately Held Companies: 21—Dierbergs Markets," *St. Louis Business Journal,* March 28, 2003, p. 34.

Sinsolo, Michael, "Breaking a Successful Mold," *Progressive Grocer,* February 1988, p. 72.

—Ed Dinger

Dobson Communications Corporation

14201 Wireless Way
Oklahoma City, Oklahoma 73134
U.S.A.
Telephone: (405) 529-8500
Fax: (405) 529-8515
Web site: http://www.dobson.net

Public Company
Incorporated: 1936 as The Dobson Telephone Company
Employees: 2,365
Sales: $631.5 million (2002)
Stock Exchanges: NASDAQ
Ticker Symbol: DCEL
NAIC: 517212 Cellular and Other Wireless Telecommu-
    nications; 517110 Wired Telecommunications
    Carriers; 517910 Other Telecommunications; 551112
    Offices of Other Holding Companies

Dobson Communications Corporation is the ninth largest provider of wireless services in the United States, serving 1.6 million subscribers in 16 states. Dobson Communications primarily serves customers residing in rural areas, ranking as the largest independent rural wireless provider in the country. The company also ranks as the largest wireless provider in Alaska. Dobson Communications offers a variety of services, including voice mail and voice messaging, as well as high-speed data functions such as wireless e-mail and Internet access.

Origins

Dobson Communications' role as a provider of wireless services in rural areas was adopted long after the company was founded. The company began operating in 1936 as the Dobson Telephone Company, starting with a single landline telephone exchange more than a half-century before the term "landline" entered the lexicon of telephony. Dobson Communications, at the turn of the 21st century, relied on technological innovations the original founders could not have conceived, but there were two similarities connecting the Dobson Telephone Company to the

modern-day Dobson Communications. The Dobson family controlled the company throughout its existence, presiding over the two eras of its existence. In addition, the geographic orientation of both eras remained focused on providing service to customers residing in rural areas. The Dobson Telephone Company originated in Oklahoma, the home state for the company throughout its existence. Dobson Communications, in its cellular guise, began providing service to customers in Oklahoma, where the Dobson Telephone Company first offered its landline services.

The agent of change in the Dobson enterprise's business scope was Everett R. Dobson, who represented the third generation of the Dobson family's leadership. Dobson joined his family's company in 1980 after earning an undergraduate degree in economics at Southwestern Oklahoma State University. When Dobson joined the company, it was dependent entirely on its wireline business for revenues. Dobson began changing the company's strategic orientation roughly a decade after he joined the firm. In 1989, he formed Dobson Cellular Systems, the entity through which the Dobson family enterprise would navigate its way in the nascent cellular industry. The company's foray into the wireless sector was executed by acquiring cellular systems in clusters, beginning with the original system in Oklahoma and the Texas Panhandle, purchased between August 1989 and September 1991. Through Dobson Cellular Systems, the company commenced wireless operations in 1990.

When wireless service began, Dobson was appointed president and chief operating officer of the company and president of its cellular subsidiaries. Under Dobson's direction, the company executed an acquisition strategy that targeted rural and suburban areas; the underserved markets that provided fertile ground for Dobson Communications' financial and physical growth. The transition to wireless operations, which led to the discontinuation of the company's wireline business by the late 1990s, resulted in exponential financial growth, but the company did not begin to increase its revenue volume meaningfully until it began acquiring cellular systems in earnest. After acquiring the properties in Oklahoma and Texas, the company waited five years before completing its next cellular deal. In March 1996, the company paid $30 million to acquire cellular operations in Kansas and Missouri. The following month, Everett

Company Perspectives:

Dobson has stayed competitive by designing, on a market-by-market basis, rate plans that allow the company to maximize its competitive position. In addition, Dobson is continually introducing new products and services to our customers, which is another important aspect of our success. We provide a variety of cellular services and products to address a range of business and personal needs. The nature of the range of the services we offer varies depending upon the market area. Dobson has been a leader in deploying digital technology to rural and suburban markets. All markets have specialized digital rate plan offers. Our plans are designed to address a range of needs, from high volume to medium, basic, and economy users. Additional targeted plans are available, including our Clear Across America plans that offer no roaming and no long distance on our national network, and our Partner Plan, which lets family members share minutes.

Dobson was named chief executive officer and chairman of the entire Dobson family enterprise, signaling the beginning of the company's rapid expansion in the cellular sector.

Increasing Cellular Interests During the Late 1990s

Dobson Communications' next cellular deal was completed a year after adding subscribers in Kansas and Missouri. Between February and March 1997, the company acquired cellular properties in rural Maryland and Pennsylvania. The acquisition represented a significant geographic leap for the company, taking it beyond its southwestern roots and establishing a presence in the eastern United States. The deal also marked a major expansion for the company, giving it 41,000 subscribers, which more than doubled its customer base. In a separate deal, the company also signed an agreement to acquire controlling interest in a rural Arizona licensee. The transaction was completed in October 1997, when Dobson Communications acquired a 75 percent interest in Gila River Cellular General Partnership, a wireless carrier serving a rural service area with 188,000 potential subscribers between Phoenix and Tucson.

By the end of 1997, the expansion of Dobson Communications' wireless business had fueled an impressive rise in the company's financial growth. The company generated $22.7 million in sales in 1993, a total that increased incrementally to $43.2 million by 1996 before nearly doubling to $85.1 million in 1997. From 1997 forward, Dobson Communications recorded vigorous growth, leveraging its expansion in the wireless sector to greatly increase its financial might.

In 1998, Dobson Communications achieved great strides on the acquisition front. During the year, the company bolstered its presence in Texas and entered the California market for the first time. The most significant addition to the company's portfolio of cellular properties occurred in December, when Dobson Communications paid $337.5 million to acquire Sygnet Wireless, Inc. and its subsidiary Sygnet Communications, Inc. With the assets acquired from the deal, a new subsidiary, Dobson/

Sygnet Communications Company, was created. Through the new subsidiary, Dobson Communications owned and operated cellular systems covering a population of 2.4 million people in northeastern Ohio, western Pennsylvania, and western New York. By the end of 1998, with the assets acquired in the Sygnet purchase included, Dobson Communications' cellular systems covered a population of 5.7 million people in rural areas in Arizona, California, Kansas, Maryland, Missouri, New York, Ohio, Oklahoma, Pennsylvania, and Texas. For the year, the company generated $140.3 million in revenue.

Dobson Communications' tenth anniversary in the cellular business was marked by an acquisition of immense proportions. In February 2000, the company and AT&T Wireless Services, Inc. announced the acquisition of American Cellular Corporation. The joint venture deal, which was equally owned and jointly controlled by Dobson Communications and AT&T Wireless, was valued at $2.4 billion. American Cellular, operating under the Cellular One trade name, provided wireless service to markets in New York, Wisconsin, Minnesota, Michigan, Kentucky, Tennessee, West Virginia, Ohio, Pennsylvania, and Illinois. The company's markets covered a population base of 4.9 million people, of which 431,000 were enrolled as subscribers. In a February 28, 2000, interview with *Cambridge Telecom Report,* Dobson commented on the acquisition, saying, "This acquisition is a significant step in the growth of Dobson. The joint venture acquired one of the largest and fastest growing independent rural cellular operators in the United States and Dobson has expanded its strategic relationship with AT&T." With the addition of American Cellular, Dobson Communications' coverage area included markets in 18 states. Operating revenue by the end of 2000 reached $475 million, more than three times the volume recorded two years earlier.

A Rural Giant Emerging in the 21st Century

As Dobson Communications entered the 21st century, the company continued to record robust growth. Against the backdrop of the company's impressive financial gains, the wireless industry began to consolidate, prompting Dobson and his fellow executives to respond to the changing industry dynamics. In a November 1, 2001 interview with *Mergers & Acquisitions Journal,* Dobson Communications' vice-president of investor relations explained management's mindset. "We believe the industry is getting ready to go through another round of consolidations," remarked Warren Henry. "So basically, we want to be ready to pursue any alternative that's in the best interests of our shareholders." The review of strategic options, which included a possible sale of the company, led to a significant announcement made not long after Henry's comments to *Merger & Acquisitions Journal.* In late 2001, Dobson Communications revealed plans to sell a portion of the company to Verizon Wireless Inc., the nation's leading wireless operator. According to the agreement, Verizon agreed to pay $550 million for Dobson Communications' cellular properties in California, Arizona, Tennessee, Georgia, and Ohio.

As Dobson Communications charted its course during its second decade in the cellular business, significant events on the acquisition front positioned the company among the industry's elite. Although some of Dobson Communications' assets were divested in the deal with Verizon Wireless, a major addition to

---

Key Dates:

1936: The Dobson Telephone Company is founded.
1980: Everett Dobson joins the family-owned company.
1989: Dobson Cellular Systems is formed.
1990: Dobson Communications commences wireless operations.
1997: Cellular properties in Maryland and Pennsylvania are acquired, representing the company's first foray beyond the southwestern United States.
2000: Dobson Communications and AT&T Wireless Services, Inc. form a joint venture to acquire American Cellular Corp.
2003: Dobson Communications becomes the sole owner of American Cellular.

---

the company more than compensated for the loss. In August 2003, Dobson Communications became the sole owner of American Cellular. The transaction, which included a restructuring of American Cellular's debt, vaulted Dobson Communications onto the national stage. In a company press release dated August 19, 2003, Everett Dobson explained the importance of the deal. ''With almost 1.6 million subscribers,'' he said, ''the New Dobson Communications is now the ninth largest wireless operator in the United States and the largest independent rural wireless provider. The combined entity serves markets with a population of approximately 11.1 million. These are among the most strategically attractive markets in the United States with excellent growth potential and relatively low wireless penetration compared to the nation as a whole.''

Dobson Communications' active role in the consolidation of the wireless industry continued after the American Cellular deal was concluded. In January 2004, the company signed an agreement to acquire the assets of NPI-Omnipoint Wireless LLC, a wireless provider with licenses covering northern Michigan. The $28 million deal gave Dobson Communications licenses and a network capable of serving one million subscribers. In 2002, NPI's 38,000 subscribers enabled the company to generate $20 million in revenue.

As Dobson Communications moved forward, the company's unique niche in the cellular industry dictated its acquisition strategy, directing it toward wireless properties in sparsely populated regions. Dobson Communications was expected to bolster its presence in rural markets either through acquisitions or by trading its ownership interests with those controlled by other wireless providers. Acquisitions, such as the purchase of American Cellular, delivered an easily discernible addition to the company's operations, but the benefits of swapping cellular properties with other operators were not to be ignored. In one such transaction, completed in June 2003, Dobson Communications became the largest wireless provider in Alaska by exchanging its properties in California for AT&T Wireless properties in Alaska. In another exchange of properties concluded in February 2004, Dobson Communications swapped its interests

in Maryland for Cingular Wireless interests in Michigan, a deal that complemented the acquisition of NPI one month earlier.

In the future, further acquisitions were expected, as Dobson Communications worked to cement its position as the nation's leading provider of wireless service in rural areas. From the momentum built up during the late 1990s, the company's operating revenue increased at an exponential rate, nearly doubling during a three-year period. The pace of this growth, which saw revenue increase from $331 million in 1999 to $631 million in 2002, transformed Dobson Communications into a formidable national force. To maintain its lead, Dobson looked to flesh out its coverage map and to continue to play the part of a consolidator. By early 2004, Dobson Communications owned wireless operations in 16 states, operating in markets that were populated by 10.6 million people. Of these potential customers, the company served 1.6 million subscribers. In the years ahead, Dobson Communications' objective was to turn potential customers into subscribers and to add to the rural markets under its control.

Principal Subsidiaries

Dobson Cellular Operations Co.; American Cellular Corporation; Dobson Cellular Systems, Inc.; Dobson JV Co.; Dobson Operating Co.; Dobson Tower Co.; Dobson/Sygnet Communications Co.; National Telecom Inc.; Western Financial Services Corporation.

Principal Competitors

AT&T Wireless Services, Inc.; Cellco Partnership; Cingular Wireless LLC.

Further Reading

Appin, Rick, ''Investors Like Dobson's New Deal,'' *Bank Loan Report,* September 15, 2003.
''AT&T and Dobson Communications Complete Acquisition of American Cellular,'' *Cambridge Telecom Report,* February 28, 2000, p. 23.
''The Buzz: February 18, 2002,'' *eWeek,* February 18, 2002, p. 36.
''Dobson to Acquire Michigan Properties,'' *RCR Wireless News,* January 5, 2004, p. 9.
''Dobson Buys Texas Carrier American Telco for $130M,'' *Telecommunications Reports,* March 30, 1998, p. 24.
''Dobson Closes Acquisition of Cellular Carrier Sygnet,'' *Telecommunications Reports,* January 4, 1999, p. 25.
''Dobson Communications,'' *IPO Reporter,* January 31, 2000.
''Dobson Communications Corp.,'' *Telecommunications Corp.,* November 3, 1997, p. 42.
''Dobson of Oklahoma Buys Eastern Cellular Business,'' *Telecommunications Reports,* March 24, 1997, p. 16.
Fitchard, Kevin, ''Dobson Follows Lead of AT&T, Cingular,'' *Wireless Review,* February 2002, p. 61.
Graves, Brad, ''Verizon Wireless Moves into Imperial Company,'' *San Diego Business Journal,* February 25, 2002, p. 9.
Harrison, Joan, ''Dobson Positions Itself for an Expected Merger Wave,'' *Mergers & Acquisitions Journal,* November 1, 2001.

—Jeffrey L. Covell

Domino's, Inc.

30 Frank Lloyd Wright Drive
P.O. Box 997
Ann Arbor, Michigan 48106-0997
U.S.A.
Telephone: (734) 930-3030
Toll Free: (888) 366-4667
Fax: (734) 930-3580
Web site: http://www.dominos.com

Private Company
Incorporated: 1965 as Domino's Pizza, Inc.
Employees: 15,000
Sales: $1.33 billion (2003)
NAIC: 722211 Limited-Service Restaurants; 533110 Lessors of Nonfinancial Intangible Assets (Except Copyrighted Works)

Privately held Domino's, Inc. is the number two pizza chain in the world, trailing only the Pizza Hut division of YUM! Brands, Inc. The company operates a network of more than 7,300 company-owned and franchised stores in all 50 U.S. states and more than 50 other countries. Nearly 90 percent of Domino's more than 4,800 U.S. outlets are franchise stores. Including the employees of franchisees, there are about 145,000 Domino's workers around the world, and global systemwide sales in 2002 totaled $3.96 billion. Domino's was built on simple concepts, offering just delivery or carry-out and an extremely limited menu: for more than 30 years, the company offered only two sizes of pizza, 11 topping choices, and—until 1990—only one beverage, cola. In recent years the company has added salads, breadsticks, and other non-pizza items to its menu in an effort to stave off rivals Pizza Hut, Papa John's International, Inc., and Little Caesar Enterprises, Inc., but has otherwise held fast to its focus on the basics of providing quality pizza and service. The driving force behind Domino's for most of its history was founder Tom Monaghan, who late in 1998 sold control of the company to Bain Capital, Inc., a Boston-based private equity investment firm. Monaghan, however, retained a 27 percent voting stake.

Originating in the 1960s

Monaghan was born in 1937 near Ann Arbor, Michigan. Following his father's death in 1941, Monaghan lived in a succession of foster homes, including a Catholic orphanage, for much of his childhood. His mother, after finishing nursing school and buying a house, made two attempts to have Tom and his brother live at home with her, but she and Tom failed to get along. During these years Monaghan worked a lot of jobs, many of them on farms. His father's aunt took him in during his senior year of high school, but after that he was once again on his own. A quote from Monaghan in his high school yearbook read: "The harder I try to be good the worse I get; but I may do something sensational yet."

For several years Monaghan worked to try to save money for college; he joined the Marines and saved $2,000, but gave it in several installments to a fly-by-night "oil man" he met hitchhiking, who took the money and ran. Monaghan returned to Ann Arbor to live with his brother Jim, who worked for the Post Office and did occasional carpentry work at a pizza shop called DomiNick's. When Jim Monaghan overheard the pizza shop owner discussing a possible sale, he mentioned buying it as a possibility to Tom. With the aid of a $900 loan from the Post Office credit union, in December 1960 Jim and Tom Monaghan were in business in Ypsilanti, Michigan.

Within eight months, Jim Monaghan took a beat-up Volkswagen Beetle as a trade for his half of the partnership. Tom moved in across the street from his shop. The store Monaghan bought had little room for sit-down dining; from the start, delivery was key. The first drivers, laid-off factory workers, agreed to work on commission. After only $99 in sales the first week, profits climbed steadily to $750 a week. Early on, Monaghan made decisions that streamlined work and greatly enhanced profits: on two separate occasions he dropped six-inch pizzas and submarine sandwiches from his menu when he was shorthanded at his shop, reasoning that he and his staff could handle the rush better without making special-sized pizzas or sandwiches in addition to regular pizzas. When he went over the numbers the day after, both times Monaghan found that his volume and profits had increased. Keeping the menu simple made financial sense.

Although his salary rose to $20,000 a year, Monaghan was not satisfied. On the advice of Jim Gilmore, a local chef with some restaurant experience, Monaghan opened a Pizza King store offering free delivery in Mt. Pleasant, near the Central Michigan University campus. Gilmore ran the original DomiNick's as a full partner with Monaghan. By early 1962, although the Ypsilanti store was not doing well, Gilmore persuaded Monaghan to open a Pizza King at a new Ann Arbor location, which Gilmore would oversee while Monaghan whipped the original DomiNick's back into shape. Gilmore convinced Monaghan to continue expanding in a financially dangerous way: because Gilmore had been bankrupt when the partnership began, all papers were in Monaghan's name. By 1964, when Gilmore became ill, he made his differences clear: he liked sit-down stores while Monaghan ran delivery. He asked for $35,000 for his share in the pizzerias. Although Monaghan considered the price preposterous, he did want to separate from Gilmore. He hired lawyer Larry Sperling, who worked out a deal whereby Monaghan would pay Gilmore $20,000. Gilmore would keep two restaurants in Ann Arbor; Monaghan, two pizzerias in Ypsilanti and one in Ann Arbor. Although their partnership was dissolved, Monaghan was still dependent on Gilmore's success in business. In February 1966 Monaghan bought one more shop from Gilmore, but later that year Gilmore filed for bankruptcy, with a total debt of $75,000, in Monaghan's name. Monaghan managed to sell Gilmore's restaurant, leaving him immediately responsible for only $20,000, with the new owner of Gilmore's to pay off related debts on a month-by-month basis.

As Monaghan's operations grew, the original owner of DomiNick's decided to maintain rights to the name. Under deadline for a Yellow Pages ad, driver Jim Kennedy came up with the name Domino's Pizza. The new company incorporated in 1965. Free from the Gilmore-related debts, Monaghan was ready to begin franchising. The first board of directors included Tom, his wife and bookkeeper, Margie, and Larry Sperling. Sperling drafted a franchise agreement in which Domino's would keep 2.5 percent as royalties from sales, 2 percent to cover advertising, and 1 percent for bookkeeping. As Monaghan stated in his autobiography *Pizza Tiger:* "By today's standards, the royalties were far too favorable to the franchisee. But it served our purpose then, and I was not concerned about covering all future contingencies."

The first franchisee, Chuck Gray, was a man visible in local and state politics; he took over an original store on the east side of Ypsilanti. While Sperling and Monaghan hammered out financial matters—the former wanted to control costs, the latter to build sales—Domino's Pizza slowly gathered a base of corporate staff. The second franchisee, Dean Jenkins, was hand-picked by Monaghan to take over the first store to be built from the ground up. By July 1967, when Jenkins's store was up and running, Domino's Pizza moved to East Lansing, home of Michigan State University. Its dormitory population, at approximately 20,000, was the largest in the nation. Dave Kilby, originally hired to do some radio copywriting for Domino's, later bought into a franchise, then began working at company headquarters, located above the Cross Street shop in Ypsilanti. Kilby then worked on franchisee expansion with Monaghan.

In February 1968 a fire swept through Monaghan's original pizza store. Advertising manager Bob Cotman escaped the building just in time, climbing down a fireman's ladder. Although the pizza shop reopened within two days, headquarters was wiped out and Domino's first commissary, with $40,000 of stored goods, was destroyed. The staff pulled together, with each existing store location responsible for producing one pizza item—cheese, dough, chopped toppings—which drivers then ferried from one store to the next to keep operations running.

The biggest challenge for Monaghan was not simply covering the total fire losses of $150,000 (only $13,000 paid for by insurance), but also paying the leases on five new franchises and finding store operators as soon as possible. While Tom worked on his task, Margie Monaghan brought in Mike Paul, her contact at the Ypsilanti bank, who soon joined Domino's to run the commissary. Paul fired half of the staff and cleaned up operations; he introduced caps, aprons, and periodic spot checks for employee neatness.

Monaghan learned a lot in the early years of Domino's, due in part to road trips he took to research business and learn from competitors. When observing the competition did not result in better methods, Monaghan innovated. Looking for equipment ideas at a Chicago convention, he found a meat-grinder that he used to chop cheese as well as mix consistent pizza dough in less than a minute, in contrast to standard mixers, which took eight to ten minutes to mix dough. Dough, once mixed, was stored on oiled pans; although covered by towels, the outside edges of the dough hardened. Monaghan discovered an airtight fiberglass container that stored dough very well, and his practice later became a standard in the industry. Monaghan also was dissatisfied with standard pizza boxes: they were too flimsy to stack, and heat and steam from the pizza weakened them. Monaghan prodded his salesman to work with the supplier and devise a corrugated box with airholes, which also became an industry standard.

Franchising in the 1970s

Plans began in earnest for Midwest expansion as Domino's jumped on the 1960s franchise bandwagon. Although Monaghan had worked on his plan to expand on college campuses, opening a new store a week in late 1968 proved to be the beginning of a nightmare. Monaghan opened 32 stores in 1969 and was hailed as Ypsilanti's boy wonder. Spurred by McDonald's great success going public in 1965, Monaghan planned to do the same. With the aid of loans, he bought a fleet of 85 new delivery cars, and spruced up his personal image; he also hired an accounting

Key Dates:

1960: Tom Monaghan and his brother Jim buy a pizza shop in Ypsilanti, Michigan, called DomiNick's.

1961: Jim Monaghan trades his half of the business for a Volkswagen Beetle.

1965: After briefly partnering with Jim Gilmore, Tom Monaghan gains full control of the company, which is incorporated under the new name Domino's Pizza, Inc.

1967: The first Domino's Pizza franchise store opens in Ypsilanti.

1983: The first international store opens in Winnipeg, Canada.

1984: Headquarters are reestablished at Domino's Farms in Ann Arbor, Michigan.

1989: The company introduces its first new product, pan pizza.

1998: Monaghan sells a controlling 93 percent stake in the company to Bain Capital, Inc.; the company is renamed Domino's, Inc.

1999: Monaghan retires as chairman and CEO and is succeeded by David A. Brandon.

2001: Domino's Pizza International purchases a majority stake in Dutch Pizza Beheer B.V., a franchisee operating 52 Domino's outlets in The Netherlands.

2002: Domino's acquires 82 franchised stores in the Phoenix, Arizona, area in the largest store purchase in company history.

2003: The company announces a multiyear partnership with NASCAR, becoming the "Official Pizza of NASCAR"; Domino's has more than 7,300 stores worldwide by the end of the year.

firm to computerize the company's bookkeeping. When moving information from paper to computer, Domino's lost all its records. Perhaps as a result, the company underpaid the Internal Revenue Service by $36,000. Monaghan was forced to sell his stock for the first time to raise the money to pay the IRS.

Monaghan tried to do too much, too fast. Ohio stores opened before Domino's reputation had spread that far and sales were poor. This was only the beginning of the downturn: on May 1, 1970, Monaghan lost control of Domino's. Dan Quirk, who had bought Monaghan's stock, recommended that he contact Ken Heavlin, a local man known for turning businesses around. Heavlin, in exchange for Monaghan's remaining stock, would run the company, get loans to cover IRS debts, and after two years keep a controlling 51 percent interest in the company, with Monaghan getting 49 percent. In the meantime, Domino's became the target of lawsuits from various franchisees, creditors, and the law firm Cross, Wrock.

In March 1971 Heavlin ended his agreement with Monaghan, who shortly went to speak with each franchisee, persuading them that Domino's would survive the crisis and they would all fare better working with him rather than against him. Their lawsuit was dropped. Monaghan pushed on, and Domino's was back in business, however tight its financial strings.

One man instrumental in the growth of the early 1970s was Richard Mueller. Originally from Ohio, Mueller bought a franchise in Ann Arbor in 1970, during Domino's lowest period. After Mueller ran this store for a year, Monaghan sent him to Columbus to revive an ailing store; within three months, sales shot up from $600 to $7,000 a week. Mueller soon operated ten Domino's franchises and incorporated as Ohio Pizza Enterprises, Inc. Within six-and-a-half years Mueller opened 50 stores. As Domino's grew, Mueller went on to become vice-president of operations in 1978.

Quick to rebuild Domino's, Monaghan encouraged trusted employees and friends to expand. Steve Litwhiler opened five stores in Vermont, while Dave Kilby, who had relocated during the Domino's slump, managed to build a strong base in Florida. A significant hire by Kilby was Dave Black, a top-selling manager who later rose to become president and COO of Domino's Pizza.

The year 1973 was a turning point for Domino's. The company introduced its first delivery guarantee, "a half hour or a half dollar off," as stated in the company newsletter the *Pepperoni Press*. The College of Pizzarology was founded to train potential franchisees. The company decentralized as well: accounting was moved from Ypsilanti headquarters to local accountants, while the commissary was reorganized as a separate company.

Domino's introduced its corporate logo, a red domino flush against two blue rectangles, in 1975. The company was sued the same year by Amstar Corporation, parent company of Domino Sugar, for the right to use the name. After a five-year battle, Domino's won, but not until after more than 30 new stores were opened under the interim name Pizza Dispatch.

Free to expand, Domino's planned to grow by 50 percent each year. By the late 1970s, several acquisitions contributed significantly to company growth. Domino's merged with Pizza-Co Inc., in 1978, gaining 23 open stores plus a handful more under lease. The merger with this Boulder-based company allowed Domino's to move into Kansas, Arizona, and Nebraska. The following year, joining with Dick Mueller's Ohio Pizza Enterprises, Inc., Domino's added 50 stores in Ohio and Texas, for a total of 287 stores. The company ended 1979 by announcing plans to expand internationally. The new non-U.S. store subsequently opened in Winnipeg, Canada, in 1983.

Rapid Growth in the 1980s

The 1980s was a decade of phenomenal growth for Domino's Pizza, but this time the company was prepared. Although Monaghan had always feared that formal budgeting systems promoted bureaucracy, with the advice of Doug Dawson, Monaghan decided to design companywide budgeting procedures, which Domino's continued to use as training tools for potential franchisees. Dawson implemented the new accounting methods and moved on to become vice-president of marketing and corporate treasurer. Instrumental in Domino's surge was John McDevitt, a financial consultant Monaghan met in 1977. Among other accomplishments, he created and became president of TSM Leasing, Inc., a financial services company that loaned money to franchisees who could not find other start-up financing.

To Monaghan, operations was the backbone of the business. When Dick Mueller left the post of vice-president of operations in 1981 to work as a franchiser once again, Monaghan decided to regionalize Domino's operations. Mueller's previous job entailed far too much travel, and changes were necessary. Monaghan set up six geographic regions, with a director fully responsible for each territory. The regional system, as Monaghan stated in *Pizza Tiger,* "gave us the long communication lines with tight controls at the working ends that we needed for rapid but well-orchestrated growth."

At the executive level, Bob Cotman took over as senior vice-president of operations, including marketing. Dave Black advanced from field consultant and regional director to vice-president of operations. Both men (like Dick Mueller and Monaghan himself) had climbed every step of the Domino's ladder, after beginning as delivery driver and pizza maker. In 1981 Black carried Monaghan's favored "defensive management" strategy—whereby each store concentrated on keeping the customers it had—to a new level, by moving the company's focus away from its top-performing stores to its weakest ones. Bringing the lower performers up worked extremely well. As the company added an average of nearly 500 stores each year through the decade, newer, weaker stores were constantly given attention to improve sales.

One other element vital to Domino's 1980s growth spurt was choosing Don Vlcek, formerly in the meat business, to head the eight commissary operations. Vlcek focused on uncovering best practices and disseminating them throughout the organization. When he discovered that one commissary saved on laundry bills by rinsing out the towels used to dry trays, making them last a week before cleaning was necessary, Vlcek made all other commissaries do the same. When he found that another commissary's manager was buying from a local cheese distributor instead of a less expensive national one, the manager reworked his purchasing policies. Vlcek moved sauce-mixing from the commissaries to the company's tomato-packing plant, which resulted in highly consistent, quality pizza sauce. Once Vlcek had taken care of the basics, in one eight-month period he opened a new commissary a month, all with state-of-the-art equipment.

All the support Monaghan received gave him time to fulfill boyhood dreams on a dramatic scale. In 1983 he bought the Detroit Tigers baseball team, which went on to win the World Series in 1984. He followed with the establishment in 1984 of Domino's Farms in Ann Arbor, a $120 million corporate headquarters modeled after architect Frank Lloyd Wright's Golden Beacon tower. Wright advocated the integration of a high-rise building in a rural setting, rather than an urban one. Monaghan also set up a working farm adjacent to the tower.

In 1985, *Advertising Age* placed Domino's "among the fastest-growing money makers in the restaurant industry." The company had to keep pace not only with its own growth but also with that of its competition, including the industry leader, Pizza Hut, which had more than 4,000 units to Domino's 2,300. Domino's stepped up advertising, increasing media spending 249 percent over the previous year. Pizza Hut entered the delivery business in 1986, posing a huge threat to Monaghan's empire.

Domino's systemwide sales reached $1.44 billion by 1987. The company had grown to 3,605 units, spreading to Canada,

Australia, the United Kingdom, West Germany, and Japan. While 33 percent of U.S. stores were company-run, international units were franchised, usually to one operator who could opt to subfranchise. The international marketing challenge was to convince buyers of the need for delivery. Back in the United States, Domino's imitated McDonald's Corporation by tailoring an ad campaign to attract the Hispanic market. Competition in the late 1980s got so tough that Monaghan was quoted in *Advertising Age* as saying, "I want people here in the company to think of it as a war." Unfortunately, with wars come casualties.

By 1989 more than 20 deaths had occurred involving Domino's drivers, calling the company's 30-minute delivery guarantee into question. A Pittsburgh-based attorney representing a couple whose car was broadsided by a driver subpoenaed Domino's for its records. Citizen's groups, major news networks, and the National Safe Work Place Institute joined in the heated criticism. Domino's responded with a national ad campaign and with various tactics at the franchise level. One franchisee hired an off-duty police officer to track his drivers to ensure that they obeyed the law.

Domino's opened its 5,000th store by January 1989, moving into Puerto Rico, Mexico, Guam, Honduras, Panama, Colombia, Costa Rica, and Spain. U.S. sales hit $2 billion. Monaghan named Dave Black as president and chief operating officer, announcing his own intentions to spend more time on community work. In May Domino's introduced pan pizza, its first new product in 28 years. This news was hardly as big, however, as Monaghan's October announcement of his intent to sell the company. After a buyout attempt in the form of an employee stock ownership plan failed, Monaghan went shopping for buyers. By April 1990 Domino's cut its public relations and international marketing departments and continued cutting executive and corporate support staff as part of a companywide effort to improve profitability. Payroll that year decreased by $24 million. Kevin Williams, who made his name as a regional director, replaced Mike Orcutt as vice-president of operations. At the store level, Domino's opened fewer than 300 units in both 1989 and 1990.

Another Comeback in the 1990s

With Domino's sales slipping, and rivals Pizza Hut and Little Caesar's gaining market share, Monaghan returned to Domino's in March 1991 to pull his company back on track. By December he had fired David Black, along with other top executives. Former franchisee Phil Bressler became vice-president of operations. Domino's closed 155 stores, cut regional offices from 16 to nine, and unloaded extravagances such as corporate planes, a three-masted ship, a travel agency, a lavish Ann Arbor Christmas display, and various sports sponsorships. Monaghan made some personal sacrifices, too, leaving his post on the boards of directors of 16 Catholic colleges and organizations. Domino's 1991 systemwide revenues remained flat at $2.6 billion, and the company posted a loss of $67 million.

Adding three new senior executives, the company geared up to battle Pizza Hut, which had aired an ad showing unkempt Domino's drivers buying Pizza Hut products. Domino's moved its advertising accounts to New York's Grey Advertising, Inc., from the local ad agency Group 243. While Monaghan was away, Pepsico's Pizza Hut had converted half of its 7,000 units for home delivery.

Under fire, Monaghan insisted on maintaining Domino's original concept of a simple menu that speeds order preparation, allowing the company to uphold its 30-minute guarantee. In an effort to be flexible—and to compete with Pizza Hut's pan pizza—Domino's offered a new pizza with more cheese and an increased number of toppings. Taking another tip from its rival, Domino's worked on developing a single U.S. phone order number for Domino's customers and a new computer system to track sales, costs, and trends. The company closed the Columbus and Minneapolis offices, with corporate headquarters in Ann Arbor assuming their duties. The overall goal was to decrease debt. Monaghan considered making a public stock offering again in 1992, but too few buyers were forthcoming. The company also worked to lessen the number of company-owned stores.

In November 1992 Monaghan shook up his upper ranks by replacing his longtime adviser and vice-president of finance, John McDevitt, with Tim Carr, another financial executive at Domino's, and hiring Larry Sheehan, a former executive vice-president of Little Caesar's, as vice-president of marketing and product development. Sheehan immediately put his stamp on the turnaround effort, convincing Monaghan to experiment with new strategies and products, including salads, thin-crust pizza, and submarine sandwiches. "Tom Monaghan is now very open about the pizza business," he said. "He believes we need to take a different approach to this business and be willing to change."

The changes seemed to work. Earnings for 1993 picked up, after dropping significantly the two previous years. In yet another change, Domino's dropped its famous 30-minutes-or-less pledge after a jury awarded a $78 million settlement to a woman who had been hit by a Domino's delivery driver in 1989. Monaghan stated that "with our success in home delivery has come a negative public perception that we are not committed to safety." The 30-minute guarantee was replaced with a more general customer satisfaction guarantee.

In January 1994 Larry Sheehan left Domino's, after a dispute with Monaghan over the size of his year-end bonus. Although his departure was widely considered a loss to the company, his changes had taken hold, and Domino's systemwide sales crept upward, to $2.5 billion in 1995. Shortly thereafter Domino's celebrated the opening of its 1,000th international store, in a suburb of Perth, Australia. With a stated goal of having more international than domestic stores, Domino's opened stores in Ecuador, Peru, and Egypt in 1995, and planned to have 3,000 international stores by the year 2,000. By 1996 foreign sales stood at $503 million, and in 1997 Domino's entered its 50th international market. In the meantime, the menu in the U.S. stores expanded yet again, with the introduction of buffalo wings in 1994 and through a limited-time-only promotion of flavored-crust pizzas during 1996.

Sheehan was succeeded as vice-president of marketing and product development by Cheryl Bachelder, a seasoned executive with experience at Planters, Gillette, and Procter & Gamble who brought focus to Domino's efforts. "We're not trying to be fun and wacky and do delivery and carry-out all at the same time," she said. "We're trying to excel single-mindedly on the basics of this business." In March 1997 Domino's announced its previous year results, which dispelled any doubts that the company was back on track. Earnings were a record $50.6 million on systemwide sales of $2.8 billion. "We believe the return to focusing on our core business—pizza delivery—coupled with great new products and strong international growth accounted for our tremendous results in 1996," said CFO Harry Silverman.

Early in 1998 Domino's stores began using a new pizza delivery bag called HeatWave that had been developed by the company. The HeatWave bags, which featured a heating mechanism that was warmed up using electricity prior to use, helped Domino's drivers deliver hotter and crisper pizzas to their customers. The company that year also opened its 6,000th store. But the biggest news came late in the year when Monaghan finally succeeded in selling the company. Seeking to devote his full energies to several Catholic charities, Monaghan sold a controlling 93 percent stake in Domino's to Bain Capital, Inc., a Boston-based private equity investment firm, for about $1 billion and the assumption of about $50 million in Domino's debt. Despite larger offers from other parties, Monaghan took the offer from Bain because the investment firm accepted the existing strategy for growth and did not plan any immediate major changes. As part of the recapitalization, the company's name was shortened to Domino's, Inc., and Monaghan retained a 27 percent voting stake.

Late 1990s and Beyond: The Post-Monaghan Era

After a nationwide search, David A. Brandon was hired as chairman and CEO in March 1999, succeeding Monaghan, who stayed on the company board as chairman emeritus. Brandon was a marketing veteran who had most recently headed up Valassis Communications, Inc., a Livonia, Michigan, firm specializing in the printing and distribution of coupons and newspaper advertising inserts.

Brandon quickly went to work placing his imprint on the company. Within a year of taking over, he completed a store rationalization program in which 146 unprofitable stores were either closed or sold to franchisees, relocated some stores to more visible locations, and cut 100 administration positions at corporate headquarters while simultaneously beefing up such areas as product development and brand management. He also stepped up the expansion pace by opening 340 new stores during 1999 and another 418 in 2000.

On the overseas front, Brandon selected J. Patrick Doyle, formerly senior vice-president of U.S. marketing, to head Domino's Pizza International. Doyle oversaw the opening of the 2,000th Domino's located outside the United States in 2000, and then the following year his division purchased a majority stake in Dutch Pizza Beheer B.V., a Netherlands franchisee that operated 52 Domino's outlets in that country. The acquired firm was subsequently turned into a regional office for managing European franchise expansion and supporting the existing operations in Europe.

Back in the United States, there were several developments in 2001. Two new products were added to the menu: cheesy bread and Cinna Stix, the latter cinnamon breadsticks being the first dessert item to be offered by the chain. The 7,000th Domino's opened its doors. In addition, a new advertising campaign was launched featuring the tag line, "Get the Door. It's Domino's." The corporation ended 2001 with net income of $36.8 million on revenue of $1.26 billion, while systemwide sales totaled $3.78 billion, an increase of 6.8 percent over the preceding year.

During 2001 and 2002 Brandon continued to focus on the bottom line, taking a fairly ruthless approach to shutting down or selling poorly performing stores. As a result unit growth was turned down a notch, and the number of outlets increased only from 6,977 in 2000 to 7,230 in 2002. Consequently, while revenues were fairly flat in 2002, profits nearly doubled, hitting $60.7 million. Also in 2002 the firm acquired 82 franchised stores in the Phoenix, Arizona, area in the largest store purchase in company history, and another new product was launched, Buffalo Chicken Kickers—strips of chicken breast breaded with a buffalo wings–style seasoning.

The new products kept coming in 2003 with the launch of another dessert item, Domino's Dots, balls of dough baked in cinnamon and sugar and served with a vanilla icing glaze. Also introduced that year was the Philly Cheese Steak Pizza. On the advertising and promotion front, the company in February 2003 announced a multiyear partnership with the National Association for Stock Car Auto Racing (NASCAR) through which Domino's became the "Official Pizza of NASCAR." Domino's also began rolling out a new point-of-sale computer system called Pulse that was aimed at cutting errors in making and delivering pizzas, improving customer service efficiency, and enhancing overall communications.

At the time that Monaghan had sold Domino's to Bain, the company had been losing market share in the U.S. delivered pizza sector for several years, and it eventually saw its number one position in that sector taken over by upstart Papa John's. Brandon reversed this trend by focusing on improving the U.S. store portfolio: by 2003, 90 percent of the domestic outlets had either been relocated or remodeled. Improvements on the international side came from the chain's departure from several loss-making markets and a concentration on a handful of the best performing markets: Canada, Mexico, Brazil, the United Kingdom, France, Australia, and Japan. There were more than 7,300 Domino's stores worldwide by the end of 2003, and the company was aiming to eventually have 10,000, with room for at least another 1,000 stores in the United States. Domino's financial position also was improving, as the increased earnings enabled the heavy debt load incurred to fund the 1998 buyout to be gradually reduced; the debt was trimmed even further in mid-2003 through a refinancing. Speculation also was growing about a possible exit strategy for Bain—either a sale of the company to another player in the industry or an initial public offering of stock.

Principal Subsidiaries

Domino's Pizza LLC; Domino's Franchise Holding Co.; Domino's Pizza PMC, Inc.; Domino's Pizza California LLC; Domino's Pizza International, Inc.; Domino's Pizza International Payroll Services, Inc.; Domino's Pizza NS Co. (Canada); Domino's Pizza of Canada; Domino's Pizza of France S.A.S.; Dutch Pizza Beheer B.V. (Netherlands).

Principal Competitors

Pizza Hut Inc.; Papa John's International, Inc.; Little Caesar Enterprises, Inc.

Further Reading

Benezra, Cheryl, "Domino's Bachelder Backs Up to Basics," *Brandweek,* September 2, 1996.

Buckley, Neil, "Domino's Returns to Fast Food's Fast Lane," *Financial Times,* November 26, 2003, p. 14.

Carlino, Bill, "Domino's Launches Safety Ads," *Nation's Restaurant News,* August 14, 1989.

Chaudhry, Rajan, "Domino's Truck Kills 2 En Route to Delivery," *Nation's Restaurant News,* August 29, 1988.

Child, Charles, "New Mood and VP Help Revive Domino's," *Crain's Detroit Business,* November 30, 1992.

"Domino's Delivered $2.8 Billion in Worldwide Sales Last Year," *Detroit News,* March 26, 1997.

"Domino's Pizza: Kevin A. Williams," *Fortune,* April 22, 1991.

Domino's Thirtieth Anniversary, Ann Arbor, Mich.: Domino's Pizza, Inc., 1990.

Driscoll, Lisa, and David Woodruff, "With Tom Monaghan Back, Can Domino's Deliver?," *Business Week,* October 28, 1991.

Garber, Amy, "Operators Across Globe Hungry for Slice of Domino's Pie," *Nation's Restaurant News,* January 19, 2004, pp. 4, 47.

Gibson, Richard, "Bain Capital Pays Estimated $1 Billion for 90%-Plus Stake in Domino's Pizza," *Wall Street Journal,* September 28, 1998, p. B5.

Hume, Scott, and Raymond Serafin, "Domino's Burned Up Over Pizza Hut Spot," *Advertising Age,* January 7, 1991.

Janofsky, Michael, "Domino's Ends Fast-Pizza Pledge After Big Award to Crash Victim," *New York Times,* December 22, 1993.

Kosdrosky, Terry, "Domino's Pizza Is Sold: Founder Monaghan to Retire," *Crain's Detroit Business,* September 28, 1998, p. 1.

Kramer, Louise, "Thomas S. Monaghan (Founder of Domino's Pizza Inc.)," *Nation's Restaurant News,* February 1996.

Lublin, Joann S., "Domino's Reaches Beyond Its Industry to Name Brandon As Chief Executive," *Wall Street Journal,* March 12, 1999, p. B5.

McLaughlin, John, "Is There Life After Thirty?," *Restaurant Business,* March 1, 1994.

Monaghan, Tom, "Domino's Pizza," *Fortune Small Business,* September 2003, p. 58.

Monaghan, Tom, with Robert Anderson, *Pizza Tiger,* New York: Random House, 1986.

Prewitt, Milford, "Domino's Cuts 19 Jobs; More May Follow," *Nation's Restaurant News,* April 30, 1990.

——, "Domino's Franchisees Set Sights on #1," *Nation's Restaurant News,* August 21, 1989.

——, "Domino's Restructures Executive Team," *Nation's Restaurant News,* March 18, 1991.

Schoenberger, Chana R., "Pie in the Sky," *Forbes,* September 17, 2001, p. 70.

Sellers, Patricia, "Getting Customers to Love You," *Fortune,* March 13, 1989.

Serafin, Raymond, "Domino's Pizza Delivers on the Basics," *Advertising Age,* July 8, 1985.

——, "Domino's Pizza Finds Global Going Slow," *Advertising Age,* January 6, 1986.

——, "Domino's Plans Hispanic Push," *Advertising Age,* June 15, 1987.

——, "Making Domino's Deliver," *Advertising Age,* November 28, 1988.

Stopa, Marsha, ''Domino's Stays Focused: Delivery Niche Works for No. 2 Pizza Maker,'' *Crain's Detroit Business,* September 15, 1997, p. 24.

Sympson, Ron, ''Can Monaghan Deliver?,'' *Restaurant Business,* April 10, 1992, pp. 78 +.

Zellner, Wendy, ''Tom Monaghan: The Fun-Loving Prince of Pizza,'' *Business Week,* February 8, 1988, pp. 90 +.

Zuber, Amy, ''Domino's Brandon Keeps Chain on Growth Track with New Product Line,'' *Nation's Restaurant News,* June 5, 2000, p. 8.

——, ''Domino's CEO Search Over, Taps Brandon to Lead Chain,'' *Nation's Restaurant News,* March 22, 1999, pp. 1, 93.

——, ''Domino's New CEO Tackles Growth Goals for Post-Monaghan Era,'' *Nation's Restaurant News,* August 16, 1999, pp. 1, 125.

——, ''1999 Pioneer of the Year: Tom Monaghan,'' *Nation's Restaurant News,* September 13, 1999, pp. 139–40, 144.

—Frances E. Norton
—updates: Paula Kepos, David E. Salamie

Elan Corporation PLC

Lincoln House, Lincoln Place
Dublin 2
Ireland
Telephone: 353 1 709 4000
Fax: 353 1 662 4949
Web site: http://www.elan.com

Public Company
Incorporated: 1969
Employees: 2,000
Sales: $746.0 million (2003)
Stock Exchanges: New York Irish London
Ticker Symbol: ELN
NAIC: 325412 Pharmaceutical Preparation Manufacturing

Founded in a Dublin, Ireland garden shed, Elan Corporation PLC has grown into Ireland's leading pharmaceutical company and a global leader in drug-delivery technologies. Elan operates through two primary divisions. Elan Pharmaceuticals, which conducts discovery, development, and marketing of pharmaceutical preparations under the Elan brand name, focuses on the fields of neurology, oncology, infectious diseases, pain management, and dermatology. The company is currently conducting clinical trials on a number of promising drugs, including preparations for the treatment of Alzheimer's disease, Parkinson's disease, and multiple sclerosis, among others. Elan Pharmaceuticals Technologies, the group's second primary business unit, focuses on developing, licensing, and marketing of drug-delivery technologies, including transdermal patches and other time-release and absorption technologies. A massive acquisition campaign in the mid-1990s allowed Elan to grow into Ireland's largest corporation by market capitalization—valued at more than $22 billion, Elan alone represented some 20 percent of the Irish Stock Exchange's total value. Yet accounting irregularities led Elan, which is also listed on the New York and London Stock Exchanges, into problems with the Securities and Exchange Commission (SEC), and the company's stock value plunged to below $800 million by 2003. In the face of these difficulties, Elan has engaged a companywide "recovery plan," completed at the beginning of 2004, which involved a number of divestments and the slashing of its payroll by more than half. At the end of 2003, Elan posted sales of $746 million, down from more than $1.13 billion the year before.

Delivery Drug Success in the 1960s

Donald E. Panoz was born in Ohio in 1935, but spent most of his childhood in Spencer, West Virginia. Panoz's father was Eugenio Panunzio, a first-generation American who enjoyed some success as a professional featherweight boxer. Panunzio, who began his career at the age of 15, changed the family name because Panoz fit better on the back of his robe—and helped shield him from ethnic slurs from the audience. Yet a broken wrist ended his career at the age of 22.

That event was to mark the young Panoz. As he told the *Van Nuys Journal,* his father "didn't have the word 'quit' in his vocabulary. My father was fighting at Cadillac Gardens in Pittsburgh when he broke his wrist, but he didn't quit like they do nowadays. He started fighting left-handed and won the fight against a tough opponent named Joey Archibald who six months later won the world title."

Donald Panoz appeared to have inherited his father's determination as he began his own career. Panoz attended high school at the Greenbriar Military Academy—learning to play golf under the great Sam Snead—where he met his wife and displayed his first talents as an entrepreneur. Panoz had recognized an opportunity to organize a transportation service for students returning home on weekends and for holidays. This early experience foreshadowed Panoz's later business successes. As Panoz told the *Van Nuys Journal:* "I've always had the ability to identify people's wants and needs."

Panoz joined the army at the age of 19, serving as an intelligence officer during the Korean War. Following the war, Panoz started studies in pharmacy and business at Duquesne University, but left school to buy two drugstores in Pittsburgh in the late 1950s. The retail stores became Panoz's first business success. Yet Panoz's interest turned toward pharmaceutical preparations themselves.

In 1960, after just two years in retail, Panoz took his first gamble, selling off the drugstores and buying a condemned skating rink in Pittsburgh. There, Panoz founded Mylan Pharmaceutical Corporation, later known as Mylan Laboratories. Panoz—who, at the age of 25, became the youngest CEO of a U.S. pharmaceutical company—was backed in the venture by a $20,000 investment from a number of friends on the Pittsburgh Pirates baseball team. Mylan began specializing in packaging generic drugs, selling pills to prisons, orphanages, and other public institutions.

Yet Panoz had recognized the potential of developing expertise in drug delivery methods, and in the early 1960s became one of the first U.S. pharmaceutical companies to begin producing gelatin capsules. Going up against such industry heavyweights as Eli Lilly and Parke Davis, Mylan nonetheless carved a place for itself as a leading producer of gelatin-encapsulated generic pharmaceuticals.

By the end of the 1960s, Panoz had become convinced of the potential for developing new drug delivery technologies. Yet Panoz's idea met with a great deal of resistance from Mylan's board of directors. When they refused to allow Panoz to steer the company into the new direction, Panoz resigned and decided to gamble once again. Selling Mylan for $60,000, Panoz and his family decided to move to Ireland, which boasted lower tax rates and less restrictive bureaucracy, to found a new business based on developing new drug delivery technologies. The new company became known as Elan Corporation.

Building Elan in the 1970s

Panoz installed a laboratory in what was described as a garden shed in Dublin, backed by just four employees, as well as receiving assistance from his wife and five children, Elan began work on its first system for controlling dosage delivery. Into the 1970s, pharmaceutical delivery systems remained relatively primitive, even though dosage was a critical issue in pharmaceutical treatment. Maintaining therapeutic levels—below which a drug became ineffective, above which the same drug risked becoming toxic—represented a particular challenge.

Panoz took up the challenge, developing an idea for controlling delivery, that is, providing a means for the regular release of the active ingredients of a single dose. Panoz initially pitched his idea to Ireland's pharmaceuticals industry. Instead, Elan's first contract came from the British arm of The Netherlands' Organon.

Organon asked Elan to devise a means for improving the delivery of the antibiotic tetracycline, which, while absorbed by the stomach, remained insoluble in the intestines. Elan developed a means of coating the tetracycline dose so that it mimicked the stomach's environment even when in the intestine, thereby improving delivery and reducing by half the number of daily doses normally needed in tetracycline treatment. In 1972, the company licensed its new process as Tetrabid, which became an immediate success for Organon.

Elan adapted Tetrabid's absorption control technology to other antibiotics during the first half of the 1970s. By the middle of the decade, Panoz had recognized the possibility of adapting the technology to other classes of drugs. The company began attracting business from the global pharmaceutical industry—by the early 1980s, Elan had contracts for 25 pharmaceuticals from 16 different companies. Elan itself remained focused on research and development, establishing a new R&D center in Athlone, Ireland, in 1978. In 1981, Panoz reentered the United States, establishing a subsidiary, Elan Pharmaceutical Research Corporation, in Gainesville, Georgia, in 1981. That company took over licensing Elan technology to the U.S. pharmaceutical industry. Panoz himself, however, acquired Irish nationality, renouncing his U.S. citizenship.

In the meantime, Elan benefited from Irish tax law, which did not impose taxes on profits from R&D-based businesses. As a result, the company was extremely profitable, posting profits of more than $900,000 on sales of just $3.1 million in 1983. The company's contracts, and especially the impending launch of a number of new products, made the company's future seem particularly bright. As Panoz told *Forbes:* "We could go fishing tomorrow and within five years we'd earn $10 million a year based on contracts we already have." This optimism led Panoz to float the company's U.S. subsidiary on the NASDAQ, in the form of American Depositary Receipts, in January 1984. The successful stock offering of one million shares reduced Panoz's stake in the company to 57 percent.

Elan benefited especially from a new development in the U.S. pharmaceuticals industry. The patents for a large number of drugs were running out, often before the drug companies were able to recoup their research, development, and marketing investments. The Food and Drug Administration (FDA) ruled, however, that companies would be allowed to extend the lives of their products if they could reformulate the drugs with new therapeutic advantages. This in turn led more and more drug makers to turn to Elan for assistance in developing new preparations.

Among these was Merrill Dow, which contracted with Elan to develop a new delivery system for a treatment for hypertension, which presented the drawback of requiring patients to take the pills four times each day. By 1989, Elan had successfully guided the new formulation through the FDA approval process and the new Cardizem SR quickly became one of the world's most prescribed high blood pressure medications.

While Elan continued to seek contract work for its drug delivery systems, the company's interests increasingly turned toward developing its own integrated operations capable of extending its reach from the research and development stages through the manufacturing and marketing areas as well. In 1985, the company opened a new Institute of Biopharmaceuti-

Key Dates:

1969: Donald Panoz, founder of Mylan Laboratories in Pittsburgh, moves to Ireland and launches Elan Corporation, a specialist in developing drug delivery systems.

1972: The company launches its first product, Tetrabid, developed for The Netherlands' Organon.

1976: Elan begins extending the Tetrabid delivery system to other drug product families.

1978: Elan opens a research and development center in Athlone, Ireland.

1981: A U.S. subsidiary, Elan Pharmaceutical Research Corporation, is launched in Gainesville, Georgia.

1984: Elan floats its U.S. subsidiary on the NASDAQ.

1989: The Food and Drug Administration approves Elan-developed Cardizem SR for Merrill Dow.

1990: Elan absorbs its U.S. subsidiary and launches a full public offering on the New York, London, and Irish Stock Exchanges.

1993: The company acquires a manufacturing operation in Lugano, Switzerland.

1995: The company acquires a manufacturing facility in Israel.

1996: Elan launches a new strategic direction as a full-scale pharmaceuticals company with the acquisition of Athena Neuroscience in the United States; the company establishes its own U.S. sales force.

1997: Elan acquires Sano Corp., in Florida.

1998: Elan acquires GWC Health and Neurex.

2000: Elan acquires the Liposome Co. and Dura Pharmaceuticals.

2002: Elan's stock collapses after the Securities and Exchange Commission launches an investigation into the company's accounting practices; Elan begins a recovery plan, divesting a number of subsidiaries and licenses in an effort to drive down debt.

2004: The company completes its divestiture program, raising more than $2 billion.

cals in its Athlone home base, and also built its first manufacturing facility there. The company's efforts turned toward the development of a new nicotine delivery system based on a transdermal patch—a product that helped revolutionize the market for smoking cessation products. The company became the first to receive FDA approval for its nicotine patch in 1992. Nonetheless, the company turned to a third-party partner for marketing the product, reserving only the Irish and Philippines markets for its own branded sales.

Full-Scale Pharmaceuticals Group in the 21st Century

By then, Elan restructured, taking over its U.S. subsidiary and launching a new public offering for Elan Corporation on the New York Stock Exchange. Elan then became the first Irish company to list its stock on the NYSE, while at the same time the company added listings on the Irish and London Stock Exchanges. The listing enabled Elan to continue to expand its manufacturing

base, with the acquisition of a company in Lugano, Switzerland, in 1993, and another company in Israel in 1995.

Into the mid-1990s, Panoz, whose shares in Elan were reduced to 10 percent, withdrew from active leadership of the company in order to pursue a variety of other interests—including the operation of the Chateau Elan vineyard and golf estate in Georgia and the development of the Panoz sports car. Panoz's spot was filled by Donal Geaney, who led the company into the next phase of its growth—that of becoming a full-scale pharmaceuticals company. Geaney took over a company that relied on just three core products, including Cardizem and Verelan, for the bulk of its $300 million in sales. Under Geaney, however, Elan now sought to broaden its focus; by the end of the 1990s, Cardizem and Verelan represented just 10 percent of company sales, which by then had topped $1 billion.

Elan grew through a two-pronged strategy during the 1990s. On the one hand, the company began an aggressive acquisition drive, buying up a large number of companies through the end of the decade and into the first years of the new century. At the same time, Elan began building a web of strategic partnerships, acquiring minority stakes in a number of companies that in turn paid the company licensing fees for its technology. Yet this practice, which allowed the company to report what were essentially research and development costs as revenue, was to lead to Elan's crash amid SEC investigations in 2002.

In the meantime, Elan lived up to its name, growing rapidly into the new century and transforming itself into a major pharmaceutical company. By 2001, at the height of its boom, Elan's market value had climbed past $22 billion—making it Ireland's largest corporation, and representing some 20 percent of the total value of the Irish Stock Exchange.

A major step in Elan's growth came in 1996 with the merger-acquisition of Athena Neuroscience, a California-based company founded in 1991 that specialized in the treatment of brain diseases and other neurological disorders. The purchase of Athena, valued at $630 million, gave Elan its first branded products operation, and encouraged the company to launch its own U.S. sales force in 1997.

Elan's next major acquisition came at the end of 1997, when it agreed to purchase Sano Corporation, based in Florida, in a stock swap valued at $375 million. Sano gave Elan access to the newly opening market for generic nicotine patches, as this product became available to the over-the-counter market. Yet Sano also held a large number of promising drugs in its own development pipeline, including skin-based delivery systems for treating anxiety, attention deficit disorder, and similar afflictions. The next step in Elan's growth came in 1998, when it paid $150 million in cash to acquire GWC Health and its subsidiary Carnrick Laboratories. That acquisition followed the $700 million purchase of Neurex, another California-based company. The addition of these companies further expanded Elan's range, particularly in the area of pain management.

Elan's growth drive continued into the next decade. In 2000, the company completed several major acquisitions, including the $1.8 billion stock swap purchase of Dura Pharmaceuticals. That purchase doubled Elan's U.S. sales force and also added new specialty areas, including infectious diseases and respiratory ailments. That year also the company picked up New Jersey-based Liposome Co., in a stock swap valued at $575 million. The deal gave Elan access to Liposome's oncology products. By the end of that year, the company's product sales topped $1 billion for the first time, while total sales—which included licensing fees from its "partners"—reached $1.5 billion.

Yet those licensing fees soon brought Elan into conflict with the SEC, which was then tightening its scrutiny of corporations' accounting methods in the wake of the Enron scandal. Worse, the company was already reeling from the cancellation of its Phase IIA trials of a promising new Alzheimer's drug at the end of 2001. When news came out that Elan had come under SEC investigation, the group's stock price plummeted—and Elan's market value plunged from a high of $22 billion to less than $800 million by 2002. The drop in its value came at an especially bad time, as the company faced debt payments of more than $2 billion before the end of 2004.

Elan responded by installing a new executive team, led by Garo Armen as chairman, who was later joined by Kelly Martin as CEO. The company then launched a "recovery plan" designed to restore shareholder confidence and to simplify the group's structure. As such, the company began divesting a number of assets, including much of its European operations and the rights to a number of products, such as the anti-fungal treatment Abelcet, sold to Enzon for $370 million. In 2003, the company sold off its rights to the drugs Sonata and Skelaxin and the rest of its primary care products group to King Pharmaceuticals for $850 million.

By the end of 2003, Elan's divestiture program had succeeded in raising more than $2 billion. While the group's revenues had been reduced to just $746 million, down from more than $1.13 billion the year before, Elan appeared to have emerged from its difficulties with a fresh commitment to regaining its place among the world's top pharmaceuticals groups.

Principal Subsidiaries

Elan International Services Ltd. (Bermuda); Elan Pharmaceuticals, Inc. (U.S.A.); Athena Neurosciences, Inc. (U.S.A.); Elan Pharma International Ltd.; Elan Pharma Ltd.; Elan Transdermal Technologies, Inc. (U.S.A.); Elan Holdings Ltd.

Principal Competitors

Pfizer Inc.; Johnson and Johnson; GlaxoSmithKline PLC; Bayer AG; Merck and Company Inc.; Aventis; Roche Holding AG; F. Hoffmann-La Roche Ltd.; Bristol-Myers Squibb Co.; Idemitsu Kosan Company Ltd.; AstraZeneca PLCB; Abbott Laboratories.

Further Reading

Almond, Siobhan, and Des Crowley, "Elan Chairman Sees Light at End of Tunnel," *Sunday Times,* October 27, 2002, p. 6.
Capell, Kerry, Arlene Weintraub, and Faith Amer, "Elan: One Ailing Celtic Tiger," *BusinessWeekOnline,* September 5, 2003.
Durman, Paul, "Troubled Elan Plans $500m Buyback Bid," *Sunday Times,* May 19, 2002, p. 1.
Hwang, Jeff, "Elan's Happy Pill?," *Motley Fool,* January 8, 2004.
"Laying Foundations for Growth," *Euromoney,* June 2000, p. 222.
MacDonald, Elizabeth, "Elan's Spin," *Forbes,* September 17, 2001, p. 100.
Murdoch, Bill, "Has Martin Got the Mettle for Herculean Task at Elan?," *Irish Times,* July 4, 2003, p. 52.
Murray-Brown, John, "Elan Expands Product Sales to More Than $1 Billion," *Financial Times,* January 30, 2001, p. 29.
Petre, Peter, "Elan's Tasty Dose of the Drug Business," *Fortune,* September 3, 1984, p. 68.
"Shame About the Name, Elan," *Economist,* July 13, 2002.

—M.L. Cohen

The Elder-Beerman Stores Corp.

3155 El-Bee Road
Dayton, Ohio 45439-1919
U.S.A.
Telephone: (937) 296-2700
Fax: (937) 296-4674
Web site: http://www.elder-beerman.com

Wholly Owned Subsidiary of The Bon-Ton Stores, Inc.
Incorporated: 1911 as Elder & Johnston Company
Employees: 6,053
Sales: $670.6 million (2003)
NAIC: 452110 Department Stores

The Elder-Beerman Stores Corp. is one of the largest regional department store retailers in the midwestern United States. It operates a total of 69 department stores, 29 of which are located in Ohio, ten in Indiana, eight each in West Virginia and Michigan, five in Wisconsin, three each in Kentucky and Illinois, two in Pennsylvania, and a single store in Iowa. The company also operates two furniture stores in Ohio. The department stores are generally located in smaller to midsized markets. There, Elder-Beerman is often able to garner an anchor location in medium-sized malls and become each community's primary supplier of soft goods. Elder-Beerman stores range in size from 40,000 to 217,000 square feet, with the median size being 70,000 square feet. Brand name products generate the bulk of the total sales. Prominent brand names include Liz Claiborne, Tommy Hilfiger, Chaps by Ralph Lauren, Estée Lauder, and Wamsutta. The merchandise mix is approximately 78 percent apparel, shoes, and accessories and about 22 percent home furnishings.

Like many department store chains, Elder-Beerman fell on hard times late in the 20th century, primarily because of intensifying competition from non-mall-based discounters. The company was forced to file for bankruptcy protection in October 1995. Elder-Beerman finally emerged from bankruptcy in December 1997 and went public the following February. After recording profits in both 1998 and 1999, the company fell back into the red in 2000, where it stayed into 2003, when a months-

long takeover battle ensued. The Bon-Ton Stores, Inc., a York, Pennsylvania–based operator of 72 department stores in the eastern United States, emerged victorious, purchasing Elder-Beerman for $92.8 million in October 2003.

Histories of the Two Predecessor Firms

The Elder-Beerman Stores Corp. was formed through the 1962 merger of Beerman Stores, Inc., and the Elder & Johnston Company. Known as "The Store with the Friendly Spirit," the Elder & Johnston Company had roots in the pre-20th-century Boston Dry Goods Store located on East Third Street in Dayton, Ohio. William Hunter, Jr., Russell Johnston, and Thomas Elder, who had all worked as traveling salesmen for the venerable eastern retail firm Jordan, Marsh and Company, founded the company in 1883. After scouting the Dayton retail environment, the three partners purchased all the stock and business of a firm that had suffered heavy losses in a fire.

The partners' Boston Dry Goods Store (it was popular in the Midwest to name retail stores after prominent eastern cities) stated its objective in its first advertisement as: "To present to the public good, dependable merchandise at sensible prices." The growing establishment moved into Dayton's first skyscraper, the Reibold Building, in 1896 and incorporated as the Elder & Johnston Company in 1911. In the meantime, Johnston died and Hunter retired, leaving Elder to run the company until his death in 1936. Elder's son Robert had joined the company in 1908 after graduating from Princeton and, upon his father's death, became president. He served as president, and later chairman of the board, until retiring in 1955. Thomas Elder Marshall, a grandson of the founder, joined Elder & Johnston in 1946 and succeeded Robert Elder as president in 1953. He advanced to chairman of the board in 1956. Marshall inaugurated a semi-annual custom of giving each employee of Elder & Johnston a red rose—he had a hobby of cultivating both roses and employee goodwill.

Beerman Stores, Inc., was founded in the late 1930s by Arthur Beerman, who had moved to Dayton from Pennsylvania in 1930 at the age of 22. He went to work for brothers Chester and Raymond Adler at their home furnishings and children's

Company Perspectives:

Our Mission—To be successful we will remain enthusiastically and meticulously focused on three core competencies: Quality, value and selection in our merchandise offerings. Convenient, attractive store locations. Friendly, capable service.

By focusing on our objectives we will create value for our shareholders, customers, associates, and the communities we serve.

clothing stores. But Beerman would not be satisfied with being a mere employee. He founded Beerman Realty Co. in the mid-1930s and would parlay savvy real estate holdings into an Ohio retail empire. During the early 1940s, Beerman opened several neighborhood "Cotton Shops," offering house dresses and aprons. The entrepreneur soon added infants' and children's wear to boost sales in the winter months, and the business incorporated in 1945.

Through his realty venture, Beerman began acquiring and developing neighborhood strip shopping centers in anticipation of the suburban exodus. When a deal to rent a two-story shopping building fell through in 1950, he took advantage of the empty space and established his own Beerman Budget department store. His venture appealed to value-oriented shoppers with its "Beerman's for Bargains" slogan. In 1953, Beerman formed Bee Gee Shoe Corporation, a partnership with Max Gutmann, to operate leased shoe departments within the stores. In 1956, Beerman bought his former employer's Home Store and opened his first shoe store, which later evolved into the El-Bee Shoe Outlet chain. Within three years, he had six stores located at shopping centers around Dayton. By 1961, Beerman had opened two additional stores and expanded into housewares.

Creation of Elder-Beerman Through 1962 Merger

Arthur Beerman acquired a controlling interest in, and the chairmanship of, Elder & Johnston in December 1961. Although he had originally planned to keep the two ventures separate, he merged Elder & Johnston with his own firm early in 1962 and closed the older retailer's flagship downtown store. Thomas E. Marshall, former president of Elder & Johnston, became president and chief executive officer of the newly formed chain, and Max Gutmann became senior vice-president and general manager.

The Elder-Beerman Stores Corp.'s first-year sales were estimated at $30 million. The union facilitated the establishment of branch stores, and the firms' combined buying power helped transform Beerman's bargain image into a more fashion-oriented reputation. Public trading in Elder-Beerman shares began in 1966, but the Beerman family and insiders would continue to hold the vast majority of shares, more than 70 percent.

The new alliance was embroiled in a retail rivalry throughout the 1960s that Arthur Beerman, who was known as "confrontational," took to the courts. In 1961, he filed a $15 million federal antitrust suit against Rike's, which was owned by retail giant Federated Department Stores. Beerman had offered to sell his stores to Rike's in 1959, but was rebuffed by the long-established rival. Although Beerman's stores had initially cultivated a budget orientation by offering lower-priced merchandise, executives hoped to transform the merged chain into a classier operation by offering brand-name goods. Arthur Beerman, however, claimed that Rike's and Federated conspired with suppliers to keep many better quality brand names out of Beerman stores through "exclusive" contracts.

Beerman won a $3.8 million judgment, including triple damages (a stipulation of antitrust law), when the case came to trial in 1969, but the verdict was reversed on appeal. Before the appeal trial, a settlement was reached in which Rike's agreed to pay Elder-Beerman $1.2 million—the original judgment without treble damages. As part of the settlement, the Dayton Mall had to provide direct access from its parking lot to an adjacent Elder-Beerman store. Beerman had accused the mall, its developer Edward J. DeBartolo, and its major tenant, Rike's, of excluding his company from the mall. After defeating Rike's in court, Elder-Beerman supplanted its competitor as the Dayton area's preeminent retailer in the late 1970s.

Dramatic Growth Under Gutmann: 1970s–80s

Elder-Beerman continued to blanket the Dayton area throughout the 1960s and opened its first out-of-town store (in Hamilton, Ohio, north of Cincinnati) in 1968, just two years before Arthur Beerman's death. In 1970, Beerman's longtime partner, Max Gutmann, became president. A native of Germany, Gutmann and his family fled Nazi persecution during World War II. When he ultimately arrived in the United States, the teenager joined the Army and served in Europe. After the war, one of his first jobs was operating the leased shoe department at Dayton's Adler & Childs department store. Gutmann had joined Arthur Beerman to form the Bee Gee Shoe Corp. in the early 1950s and rose in the executive ranks. He became chief executive officer and chairman in 1974, the same year that the chain crossed state lines and established a store in Richmond, Indiana.

Elder-Beerman grew dramatically under Gutmann's guidance. The leader expanded the retail chain internally, building seven local stores before the end of the 1970s, and pursuing an aggressive acquisitions policy. In 1969, Elder-Beerman bought Everybody's Office Outfitters and made it a wholly owned subsidiary, El-Bee Office Outfitters, by 1973. In 1978, Elder-Beerman acquired four of Cincinnati's Mabley & Carew stores, which boasted $20 million in sales the previous year. The 101-year-old Mabley & Carew chain had been acquired previously by national retail powerhouse Allied Stores Corp., which operated the stores from 1961 to 1978.

Elder-Beerman purchased Texas-based Margo's LaMode chain of women's specialty stores from Alexander's Inc. for $7 million in 1981. Founded in the 1930s and owned by Alexander's from 1979 to 1981, Margo's operated 72 stores in Texas, Arkansas, Oklahoma, and New Mexico. The southwestern specialty chain Regan's was acquired in 1984, and its 20 stores were appended to Margo's. After a reorganization, the combined division encompassed 80 stores managed from Dallas. A total of 26 Spare Change discount junior sportswear stores in

Key Dates:

1883: William Hunter, Jr., Russell Johnston, and Thomas Elder open the Boston Dry Goods Store in Dayton, Ohio.

1911: The firm incorporates as Elder & Johnston Company.

Early 1940s: Arthur Beerman begins opening several neighborhood "Cotton Shops" in Dayton.

1945: Beerman incorporates his business as Beerman Stores, Inc.

1953: In partnership with Max Gutmann, Beerman forms Bee Gee Shoe Corporation, operator of leased shoe departments in Beerman Stores outlets.

1956: Beerman forms a shoe store chain that is eventually known as El-Bee Shoe Outlets.

1961: Arthur Beerman acquires a controlling interest in Elder & Johnston.

1962: Beerman Stores and Elder & Johnston are merged to form The Elder-Beerman Stores Corp.

1966: Elder-Beerman stock begins trading publicly, but the Beerman family and insiders continue to own the vast majority of shares.

1968: The first store outside the Dayton area is opened in Hamilton, Ohio.

1970: Beerman dies; Gutmann is named president.

1974: A store is established in Richmond, Indiana, the first outside of Ohio.

1981: Elder-Beerman acquires the Texas-based Margo's LaMode chain of women's specialty stores.

1987: The company is taken private by several executives and members of the Beerman family.

1989: The company acquires Meis of Illiana's ten-store chain, located in Indiana, Illinois, and Kentucky.

1995: Elder-Beerman is forced to file for Chapter 11 bankruptcy protection.

1996: The Margo's chain is closed down and 32 shoe stores are also shuttered.

1997: The company emerges from bankruptcy, mainly owned by creditors.

1998: Elder-Beerman is taken public with a listing on the NASDAQ; the company adds 11 more stores by acquiring the Stone & Thomas department store chain, which is centered in West Virginia.

2000: The company announces plans to concentrate more on smaller stores located in smaller communities.

2003: The Bon-Ton Stores, Inc. acquires Elder-Beerman for $92.8 million.

Ohio, Indiana, Kentucky, and West Virginia were acquired in 1982 and merged into the Margo's chain in 1986. In 1985, Elder-Beerman purchased three R.H. Macy & Co. stores in the Toledo, Ohio, area. Although the company had adopted a policy of avoiding larger urban markets beginning in the early 1980s, it entered Toledo with the assurance that it would begin as the city's number two department store in terms of volume.

Elder-Beerman celebrated its centenary in 1983 with the theme "100 years in the making and still something new every day." The company's sales grew 187 percent from 1975 to 1985, to $312 million, and net profit increased 236 percent to $7.3 million over the same period. Much of this growth was credited to Gutmann's dynamic leadership.

Elder-Beerman was taken private in 1987 by the E-B Acquisition Co., a vehicle of several executives and members of the Beerman family, including Jessie Beerman, Arthur's widow; Barbara Beerman Weprin, their adopted daughter; her husband, William S. Weprin; and Leonard Beerman Peal, a first cousin. The company purchased the remaining 30 percent of Elder-Beerman it did not already own for an estimated $30.7 million, or $33 per share. In 1986, the company posted sales of $380.8 million and net profit of $6.3 million. As consolidation in the retail industry overall accelerated during the 1980s, Elder-Beerman found itself one of the few family-owned, independent department store chains. Local observer James Bohman, of the *Dayton Daily News,* noted that, by 1989, the Beermans ranked among Ohio's 25 wealthiest families.

Elder-Beerman acquired Meis of Illiana's ten-store chain, which operated locations in Indiana, Illinois, and Kentucky, from the Brown Group Inc. in 1989. The chain was founded by the Meis (sounds like "lease") family in 1924 and sold to the

Brown Shoe Co. of St. Louis, Missouri, in 1972. At the time of its sale to Elder-Beerman, Meis was considered one of western Indiana's leading retailers.

Falling into and Emerging Out of Bankruptcy in the 1990s

Gutmann retired in 1991. In addition to the dramatic growth that occurred during his watch, another legacy of Gutmann's leadership was the distinctive blue used in Elder-Beerman's logo—blue was one of the chairman's favorite colors. Gutmann was followed at Elder-Beerman's helm by Herbert O. Glaser, who had served as president of the department store unit from 1984 to 1989, and then as president and chief operating officer. He retained the post of COO only two years before retiring. Glaser was succeeded by Milton E. Hartley, chairman of the board and chief executive officer. The company continued to expand throughout these upper management shifts, opening 11 stores and a distribution center between 1991 and 1994.

By the end of 1994, Elder-Beerman was operating 48 department stores in seven states, having expanded into Michigan, West Virginia, and Wisconsin. In 1993 the company made profits of $15.9 million on sales of $566 million, but the next year Elder-Beerman posted a $1.3 million net loss after writing off its Margo's and El-Bee Shoe Outlet operations. The company decided to place these loss-making businesses on the block and concentrate on its core department stores. The Elder-Beerman department stores, meantime, were facing increasing competition not only from ever expanding retail giant Wal-Mart Stores, Inc. but also from the entrance of discount department store operator Kohl's Corporation into its territory. By September 1995 Elder-Beerman was in serious trouble because of heavy borrowing, slow sales, and a new, high-volume merchandising strategy. Hartley resigned that month, and both Gutmann and Glaser returned to the company to attempt a rescue. Nevertheless, short of funds to buy inventory for the upcoming holiday season, Elder-Beerman was forced to file for Chapter 11 bankruptcy protection in October 1995.

One of the company's first moves under bankruptcy protection was to close down the entire Margo's chain, 32 of its shoe stores, and two outlet stores. These closures were completed in early 1996. The company later closed down another 30 shoe stores and one of its three furniture stores. Elder-Beerman also fended off takeover attempts by two rival department store chains, Milwaukee-based Carson Pirie Scott & Company and Tennessee-based Proffitt's, Inc. The company signaled its intention to remain independent by hiring a new president and CEO in January 1997. Frederick J. Mershad, who had been born in Dayton, had previously been president and chief executive of Proffitt's Stores Division. He replaced Gutmann, who remained chairman. Elder-Beerman also announced a five-year plan that included spending $15 million to open several new stores and renovate several existing ones. Its department stores returned to a merchandise mix offering a broad range of moderately priced to upscale brands, in contrast to the mix that had been introduced shortly before the bankruptcy filing that coupled more expensive brand-name apparel brands with an assortment of low-end merchandise. In December 1997 Elder-Beerman finally emerged from bankruptcy, mostly owned by its creditors but with the Beerman family retaining a small stake. Mershad was named company chairman at this time, succeeding Gutmann. In February 1998 the company was taken public on the NASDAQ through a public offering of more than 12 million shares of common stock at $14 per share. At the time, the company was running 50 department stores, two furniture stores, and 68 El-Bee and Shoebilee! shoe stores.

Elder-Beerman returned to profitability in 1998, reporting profits of $25.5 million on sales of $658 million. Growth was high on the agenda that year. In July 1998 the company paid about $38 million for the 21-store Stone & Thomas department store chain, which operated mainly in Virginia and West Virginia. Eight of the locations in these states, including all those situated in Virginia, were immediately resold. Two others were closed down. Elder-Beerman retained nine stores in West Virginia as well as one each in Ohio and Kentucky. Also in July 1998, Elder-Beerman finally succeeded in opening a store in the Dayton Mall, where it had been barred from becoming a tenant nearly three decades earlier. At 212,000 square feet, it was one of the largest in the chain. Two months later the company expanded into Pennsylvania for the first time, opening a 119,800-square-foot store in Erie. To secure funds for the Stone & Thomas acquisition and to pay down debt, Elder-Beerman in August conducted a secondary offering of common stock that raised more than $61 million.

Dropping Back into the Red in the Early 2000s

Disappointing sales, particularly at the newly acquired outlets, hurt 1999 profits, which fell to $15.2 million. The shoe store chains, which had turned unprofitable again, were sold off in January 2000, allowing management to better focus on the department stores. In an attempt to turn around the department store operations, Elder-Beerman began opening up smaller units in smaller cities. For instance, in October 1999 a 56,000-square-foot store was opened in Warsaw, Indiana, which was located in a county with a population of about 35,000. Similarly, a store of like size opened in Frankfort, Kentucky, in November 1999, targeting a county whose population numbered about 46,000 people. In such towns, Elder-Beerman was less likely to face competition from the top department store retailers.

Around this time, however, Elder-Beerman began facing a fierce uprising among its major shareholders, who were upset with a sharp decline in the firm's stock price. They eventually initiated a proxy fight, nominating their own slate of candidates for the three board positions that would be up for a vote in August 2000. After its stock fell to an all-time low of $4 in June, the company ousted its president and COO, John Muskovich, and then adopted the dissidents' slate of candidates as well as several changes to its corporate governance policies. Also in August 2000, Elder-Beerman announced a major restructuring involving the elimination of 200 jobs, 130 from the headquarters, an acceleration in the development of smaller stores, and changes in the merchandise mix to include more lower-priced items. Three more of the smaller stores opened in time for the 2000 holiday season. They were located in Howell, Michigan; West Bend, Indiana; and Jasper, Indiana. Another four Elder-Beerman outlets opened during 2001, in Alliance, Ohio; Dubois, Pennsylvania; and Plover and Kohler, Wisconsin. All of these new stores were less than 75,000 square feet in size.

Restructuring charges pushed Elder-Beerman to a loss of $6.7 million on revenues of $687.6 million in 2000. The following year the company trimmed its loss to $900,000, but sales fell to $670.3 million. At the end of 2001 Mershad retired. After a brief period of interim leadership under new Chairman Steven C. Mason, former chairman and CEO of the Mead Corporation, a Dayton-based paper firm, Byron Bergren was brought onboard as president and CEO in February 2002. A veteran retailing executive, Bergren had most recently headed up the southern division of Charlotte, North Carolina–based Belk Inc., a privately held department store chain.

The new leader focused on cutting costs and improving the balance sheet during 2002. About 100 jobs were cut from the workforce in April, and then one month later the company made the historic decision to close its downtown store in Dayton. The latter move came after it became increasingly evident that the chain's smaller stores in smaller markets were more profitable than its larger units in midsized cities such as Dayton. As it focused on improving its finances, including trimming its long-term debt by $33.4 million, Elder-Beerman slowed down its expansion program, debuting only one new smaller unit, which opened in March 2002 in Coldwater, Michigan. For the year, the company stayed in the red, but the $14.2 million loss was directly attributable to a $15.1 million charge that was taken for a change in accounting principles.

Takeover by Bon-Ton Stores in 2003

The retail environment remained intensely competitive in 2003, and the consolidation of the department store industry was proceeding apace. Elder-Beerman was vulnerable to a takeover because of its weak financial performance and the continued depressed value of its stock, which dipped below $2 per share early in 2003. In May of that year, the company entered into negotiations with EB Acquisitions Ltd., an Ohio-based investment company, but Elder-Beerman executives soon concluded that the principals behind the potential acquirer were "unqualified." One month later, Elder-Beerman announced that it had agreed to sell the company to Wright Holdings Inc., an acquisition vehicle for Goldner Hawn Johnson & Morrison Inc., a Minneapolis private equity firm. The agreed upon price was $6 per share, or $69 million. In late July, however, The Bon-Ton Stores, Inc. stepped in with an offer to buy Elder-Beerman for $7 per share, or $80 million. Bon-Ton, of York, Pennsylvania, operated 72 department stores in Connecticut, Maryland, Massachusetts, New Hampshire, New Jersey, New York, Pennsylvania, Vermont, and West Virginia—making for an excellent geographic fit with the territory of Elder-Beerman. Bon-Ton's strategy of focusing on smaller, secondary markets was also similar to that of Elder-Beerman. The Bon-Ton offer set off a bidding war, with each party topping the other's offers, until Bon-Ton prevailed in mid-September 2003 with an offer of $8 per share, or $92.8 million. The deal closed in October, the same month that Elder-Beerman opened its 69th store in Muscatine, Iowa, marking the chain's first presence in that state; this was also the 12th smaller format Elder-Beerman store. The 11th such store had debuted earlier in the year in DeKalb, Illinois.

Elder-Beerman became a subsidiary of Bon-Ton, with Bergren initially staying on as president and CEO. The stores also continued to operate under the Elder-Beerman name. In January 2004 Bon-Ton Stores announced plans to eliminate 311 of the 450 jobs at the Elder-Beerman headquarters in Dayton in order to eliminate duplicate staff. More changes were anticipated as Bon-Ton proceeded with the integration of the two companies.

Principal Subsidiaries

The El-Bee Chargit Corp.

Principal Competitors

J.C. Penney Corporation, Inc.; Sears, Roebuck and Co.; Federated Department Stores, Inc.; The May Department Stores Company; Marshall Field's; Wal-Mart Stores, Inc.; Kohl's Corporation; Mervyn's.

Further Reading

"The Beerman Boom," *Dayton Daily News,* March 6, 1989, p. S12.

"Beerman Buying Meis of Terre Haute, IN," *Dayton Daily News,* April 28, 1989, p. B9.

Bohman, James C., "Max Gutmann's Master Plan Is Working Well for Elder-Beerman," *Dayton Daily News,* July 21, 1985, pp. E1, E3.

Bohman, Jim, "Comeback Kid: Elder-Beerman Goes from Near Extinction to Record '98 Profits," *Dayton Daily News,* May 30, 1999, p. 1F.

——, "E-B Sees 'Bright Future': Creditors Must Approve Exit from Bankruptcy," *Dayton Daily News,* August 8, 1997, p. 1A.

——, "Elder-Beerman Hires New Exec," *Dayton Daily News,* January 11, 1997, p. 1A.

Bohman, Jim, Wes Hills, and Jim DeBrosse, "Elder-Beerman Seeks Protection from Creditors," *Dayton Daily News,* October 18, 1995, p. 1A.

Bollinger, Julie, "Elder-Beerman Seeing Red," *Dayton Business Journal,* August 30, 1999.

"A Chronological History of the Elder-Beerman Stores Corp.," Dayton: The Elder-Beerman Stores Corp., 1992.

"Elder-Beerman Stores: Last of a Local Breed," *Dayton Daily News,* March 28, 1988, pp. S1, S2.

"Elder's Diamond Jubilee Birthday Party," *Elder's Store Chat,* Elder Johnston Company: Dayton, February 1958.

Fisher, Doc, "Beerman, Elder's Merge Operations," *Dayton Daily News,* January 30, 1962, p. 1.

Gutmann, Max, *The Elder-Beerman Stores Corp.: A Tradition of Success,* New York: Newcomen Society of the United States, 1986.

"Is Cincy Elder-Beerman's 'Big League' Limit?," *Dayton Daily News,* March 26, 1978, p. 12D.

Kelsey-Jones, Linda, "Elder-Beerman: A Tradition of Success," *Dayton Daily News,* August 4, 1985, p. AA2.

Montgomery, Christopher, "Elder-Beerman Has Faced Series of Challenges," *Dayton Daily News,* May 17, 2003, p. A9.

"Ninety-Year-Old Founder of Store Ill Since August," *Dayton Journal Herald,* November 23, 1936, p. 1.

Roberson, Jason, "Beerman to Lose 311 Moraine Jobs," *Dayton Daily News,* January 6, 2004, p. A1.

——, "Bon-Ton Bids $80M for Elder-Beerman," *Dayton Daily News,* July 30, 2003, p. A1.

——, "E-B Names Bergren President, CEO," *Dayton Daily News,* January 24, 2002, p. 1E.

——, "Elder-Beerman Agrees to $69M Sale," *Dayton Daily News,* June 27, 2003, p. A1.

——, "Elder-Beerman Sold to Bon-Ton for $92.8M," *Dayton Daily News,* September 17, 2003, p. A1.

Roberson, Jason, and Ken McCall, "Elder-Beerman Ends Era by Closing Dayton Store," *Dayton Daily News,* May 3, 2002, p. 1A.

Roberson, Jason, and Shannon Joyce Neal, "Elder-Beerman in Talks to Sell Company," *Dayton Daily News,* May 17, 2003, p. A1.

Sator, Darwin, "Elder-Beerman to Add Four Cincinnati Stores," *Dayton Daily News,* March 20, 1978, p. 21.

Seemuth, Mike, "Elder-Beerman's Share of Dayton Store Sales Grows," *Dayton Daily News,* June 7, 1980.

Sketches of Twelve Dayton Business Firms, Dayton, Ohio: Dayton Area Chamber of Commerce, 1959.

Thau, Barbara, "The States of the (Proposed) Union: Bon-Ton's Elder-Beerman Purchase Puts a New Powerhouse on the Map," *HFN,* September 29, 2003, p. 7.

Tresslar, Tim, "Beerman Ends Board Dispute," *Dayton Daily News,* July 21, 2000, p. 1A.

——, "E-B Chief Announces Retirement," *Dayton Daily News,* August 22, 2001, p. 1A.

——, "Elder-Beerman Under Siege," *Dayton Daily News,* March 12, 2000, p. 1F.

Tresslar, Tim, and Jim Dillon, "Mershad: Overall Plan Is 'Grow,'" *Dayton Daily News,* November 26, 2000, p. 1F.

Tresslar, Tim, Lynn Hulsey, and Laura Bischoff, "E-B Cuts Jobs, Changes Direction," *Dayton Daily News,* August 12, 2000, p. 1A.

Wallack, Todd R., "Beerman Closing 102 El-Bee, Margo's," *Dayton Daily News,* November 25, 1995, p. 1A.

—April Dougal Gasbarre
—update: David E. Salamie

Ermenegildo Zegna SpA

5 Via Forcella
20144 Milan
Italy
Telephone: 39-0258-103-787
Fax: 39-0258-103-921
Web site: http://www.zegna.com

Private Company
Incorporated: 1910
Employees: 5,000
Sales: EUR 661.3 million ($828 million) (2002)
NAIC: 315222 Men's and Boys' Cut and Sew Suit, Coat, and Overcoat Manufacturing; 315223 Men's and Boys' Cut and Sew Shirt, (Except Work Shirt) Manufacturing; 315224 Men's and Boys' Cut and Sew Trouser, Slack, and Jean Manufacturing; 315993 Men's and Boys' Neckwear Manufacturing

Ermenegildo Zegna SpA is the world's leading luxury men's suit maker. Based in the mountain village of Trivero, Italy, near the Swiss border, Zegna is a vertically integrated business, producing more than two million meters of fabric, more than 350,000 finished suits, and another two million shirts, ties, sportswear, and accessories per year. Zegna develops its own fabrics from the world's finest wools—although the company does not itself own sheep herds, it works closely with breeders and farmers in Australia, South Africa, and Mongolia to ensure its supply of top-grade cashmere, mohair, and merino wool. This commitment to top quality enables the company to produce fabrics from threads as fine as just 11 microns. Eschewing the "mass market" approach of rival Armani, which does not produce its own suits, Zegna has developed an exclusive clientele throughout the world. More than 85 percent of the company's sales is achieved outside of Italy, primarily through the company's own store network. Zegna is present in more than 380 shops throughout the world, of which 135 are full-scale retail stores owned by the company, while the others operate as boutiques within department stores. Europe is the company's largest market, at 38 percent of sales, followed by North Amer-

ica, at 33 percent of sales. The company also has a strong presence in the Australasia region, which accounts for 25 percent of its sales and includes China, one of the group's fastest-growing markets. Zegna also has launched an extremely exclusive line of "vintage" clothing, made from the year's finest wool, for which the client chooses his own colors and styles. Ermenegildo Zegna, named for its founder, remains wholly controlled by his family, now represented by its fourth generation, cousins and co-CEOs Ermenegildo and Paolo Zegna. Other members of the Zegna family play active roles in the company.

Top-Quality Fabrics in the 1930s

Ermenegildo Zegna was just 20 years old when he took over his family's small wool-producing business in Trivero, a village in the Biella region of the Italian Alps, in 1910. This region had long been an important center for Italy's fabrics and wool industry, in large part because of the abundance and purity of its water. The low mineral content of the water played a primary role in the important wool finishing process, enabling the creation of softer and finer fabrics.

At the time, the men's luxury suit market was dominated by British wool makers and tailors. Zegna set out to emulate his English counterparts, adopting their production techniques. Nonetheless, Zegna maintained many of the traditional weaving techniques, such as using thistles to comb his wool. Zegna's quest for quality soon brought him to look beyond his own region, and by the 1930s, Zegna himself was traveling around the world in search of the finest wool herds. It was during this period that the company formed relationships with cashmere breeders in such far-flung places as Mongolia, South Africa, and Australia.

By the beginning of the 1960s, Zegna had won recognition for his high-quality and innovative fabrics. Zegna also had displayed an aptitude for wedding new technologies with traditional hand-crafting techniques. In the process, Zegna had expanded the company into a vertically integrated operation. This feature enabled Zegna to maintain control over nearly every aspect of the production process, from the selection and pur-

Company Perspectives:

Dating from 1910, the Ermenegildo Zegna group is a family business that still remains true to the ideals of its founder: our grandfather, Ermenegildo.

All our efforts converge on the attainment of utmost quality, every step of the way, from selection of the finest raw materials to development of innovative customer relations.

Our grandfather built a series of vital infrastructures for his fellow citizens, from roads to schools. He always took a concrete interest in the welfare of his wool mill's work force. And his sense of social responsibility—his commitment to people—endures as a basic principle of our family.

We have assimilated and enlarged upon Ermenegildo's environmental awareness. The group is presently involved in a number of major conservation projects, expression of the good corporate citizenship that has distinguished the company throughout its history.

Inspired by our grandfather's legacy, the new generation of Zegnas is carrying on his work—weaving the future on the loom of the past.

chasing of raw wool through to the marketing of the final finished fabric. At the same time, Zegna contributed greatly to the region, in particular through the planting of more than half a million trees and other plants along the region's barren hillsides. That project, including the building of a panoramic road named after Zegna, later resulted in the establishing of the ''Zegna Oasis'' in 1993.

Zegna, who died in 1966, turned over the leadership of the family business to his sons Angelo and Aldo in the 1960s. The new generation remained committed to their father's tradition of quality, yet became determined to establish the Zegna name beyond the fabrics production. While the company continued to act as a major supplier of high-quality fabric, in the 1960s Zegna began producing its own clothing. The company targeted the men's suit market. Rather than move into the mass consumer categories, Zegna instead became determined to capture a strong share of the rising Italian luxury men's suit sector.

Into the 1970s, Zegna established its own men's collection. By the end of the decade, the company had begun producing a full range of clothing, including knitwear, accessories (including highly prized ties), and sportswear. Zegna also quickly recognized the potential for establishing an international presence to back up its growing export business.

In 1973, Zegna established its first production facility outside of Italy, opening a plant in Spain. The company continued to develop its Spanish presence, creating a number of subsidiaries over the following decades. In the meantime, Zegna also established a manufacturing presence in Switzerland as well, starting in 1977. Zegna also moved to strengthen its supplier relationships, as well as increase the quality of its raw materials, by launching a series of yearly competitions among its breeder suppliers. These efforts helped the company succeed in developing wool threads as fine as silk. At the same time, Zegna began strengthening its international distribution network, add-

ing sales and marketing operations in France, Germany, the United Kingdom, the United States, and elsewhere. These efforts helped introduce the company's brand to a number of the world's high-end department stores and retailers.

By the end of the 1970s, Zegna had begun preparing the next phase in its evolution: that of directly controlling its own retail network. In 1980, Zegna launched its first retail store, in Paris. The success of the format—in which the company claimed that a man could enter the store in his underwear and leave with a complete wardrobe—led the company to expand its network through the 1980s, opening stores in such key cities as Milan in 1985, and in London, before moving to a broader presence. The company's retail development involved the opening of a number of franchised stores, as well as boutique shops in department stores such as Neiman Marcus. Zegna developed a strong network of stores directly owned by the company as well.

High-End Men's Suit Leader in the New Century

Zegna turned toward boosting its U.S. presence at the end of the 1980s. The company established a dedicated subsidiary there, Ermenegildo Zegna Corp., and began scouting for a suitable location, targeting New York City initially. The company succeeded in finding a site, on that city's Fifth Avenue, opening its first U.S. store in 1990. Zegna also had begun producing designer-labeled clothing for other designers. As part of this effort, the company formed a number of partnerships, including those with Romeo Gigli and also Spanish designer Antonio Miro. In 1990 the company formed a joint venture with Versace to produce and distribute a new line of V2 men's sportswear.

The company continued to roll out new stores, including stores in Mexico City, Istanbul, Tokyo, and elsewhere. By the end of 1990, the company already operated 16 stores, in addition to a network of more than 150 in-store boutiques. The following year, the company opened its first store in China, in Beijing. Russia, and particularly Moscow and St. Petersburg, became company targets as well. Zegna by then already claimed a 30 percent share of the world's luxury men's suit market, with sales of more than $350 million per year.

The new generation of the Zegna family, including Aldo and Angelo's nine children, were by then assuming positions of greater importance within the family business. Taking the lead were cousins Ermenegildo, known as Gildo to differentiate him from his grandfather, and Paolo. With business school backgrounds, the cousins now set out to boost production and control costs. Among other initiatives, the company sought to drastically reduce its production lead times. By the mid-1990s, Zegna had succeeded in cutting back its production cycle from eight months to just four—and then set its sights on cutting that in half yet again by the end of the decade. As part of that effort, the company continued to adopt new technologies, such as computerized ordering and cutting systems.

Into the mid-1990s, Zegna developed a new, more aggressively customer-focused strategy, stepping up its level of service. As part of that effort, the company began a new store-opening drive, including plans to open stores in five new U.S. cities, as well as a drive into the South American and Canadian

Key Dates:

1910: Ermenegildo Zegna establishes a textile business in Trivero, Italy, and develops a vertically integrated, luxury fabrics business.

1960: Sons Aldo and Angelo Zegna take over leadership of the business and launch the company's first men's clothing line.

1973: Zegna opens its first international production plant in Spain.

1977: The company opens a production facility in Switzerland.

1980: The first retail store opens in Paris.

1985: The company opens an Italian showroom in Milan.

1990: The company opens its first U.S. retail store in New York; the company forms a joint venture, V2, with Versace.

1992: Two new brands, Zegna Soft and Zegna Sportswear, are launched.

1995: The company acquires Tarsa, a Mexico-based clothing manufacturer and retailer.

1998: A new brand and retail format, Zegna Sport, is launched.

1999: The company acquires luxury womenswear maker Lanerie Agnona SpA, in Italy.

2001: The company acquires majority control of fabric maker Master Loom.

2002: The company acquires majority control of Guida, and its Longhi leather goods brand; a 50/50 joint venture, ZeFer, is established with Ferragamo.

2003: The company acquires 50 percent of Sharmoon, a menswear producer and retailer in China.

2004: The new Z.Zegna youth-oriented brand, slated for the fall season, is launched.

markets. Supporting that effort was the acquisition of Mexico's Tarsa, which produced men's wear and also operated its own retail network, in 1995. While Zegna continued expanding its range of in-store boutiques, its primary retail focus increasingly turned to developing its own Zegna-branded network. In the mid-1990s, the company opened a number of company-owned stores in Lisbon, Vienna, Shanghai, and Barcelona, while also adding franchise stores in Hong Kong, Jakarta, Kuala Lumpur, and elsewhere.

In its push to expand its customer base, Zegna also began designing new clothing lines to attract a younger clientele. In 1992, for example, the company introduced two new lines, Zegna Soft and Zegna Sportswear, which offered more casual clothing styles. The company also introduced its own cologne in 1993. In Japan, in 1997, Zegna launched a new, Japan-only line, E.Z. That brand was also the company's first to be produced outside of Europe and under contract. Then, in 1998, the company introduced a new brand and retail format, Zegna Sport.

For the most part, Zegna had maintained a policy of conservative growth, marked by a low-key marketing program. Yet in the late 1990s, the company found itself in the spotlight when, during the scandal involving President Bill Clinton and Monica Lewinsky, it was revealed that Lewinsky had given the president a Zegna tie as a gift. The controversy helped boost awareness of the Zegna brand, sending sales of its clothing, and especially its ties, soaring in the United States.

As it entered the 2000s, Zegna had built up a strong international sales network, with more than 380 sales points—including 135 directly owned by the company. The company also launched a second retail format, Zegna Sport.

Acquisitions also marked the company's development at the dawn of the 21st century. In 1999, Zegna acquired Lanerie Agnona SpA, a maker of luxury women's wear. That purchase was followed by the acquisition of a controlling stake in Prato, Italy-based Master Loom, a maker of fabrics, in 2001. In 2002, Zegna bought most of Guida, another Italian company, which owned the Longhi brand of leather goods. That year, also, the company continued to extend its range of clothing and accessories with the formation of a joint venture company with Italian footwear group Ferragamo. The new company, called ZeFer, placed the Zegna brand on a line of footwear and leather accessories.

China represented one of the company's fastest-growing markets by then. In 2003, the company strengthened its position in that country through the purchase of a 50 percent stake in Sharmoon, based in Wenzhou, founded by the Chen family at the beginning of the 1990s. That purchase gave Zegna access to three factories, more than 1,000 employees, and an additional ten retail stores, as well as the strong Sharmoon clothing brand.

Zegna meanwhile continued to build its own branded business. In the 2000s, the company launched a new brand concept, called Napoli Couture. The new suits featured the company's exclusive fabric, Vellus Aurem Trophy. The 2003 "vintage" produced just 75 kilos—enough for only 500 suits, at a price of some $7,500 each. At the other end of the spectrum, the company stepped up its efforts to attract a younger, more modern clientele. In October 2003, the company unveiled a new brand, Z.Zegna, with a full-scale rollout slated for the Fall 2004 collection. With more than EUR 680 million in sales in 2003, Zegna remained firmly at the top of the world's luxury menswear market.

Principal Subsidiaries

AGNONA SPA; Artema S.p.A.; Consitex (Switzerland); Ermenegildo Zegna Corporation (U.S.A.); GUIDA; IN.CO. S.p.A; Ismaco (Turkey); Italco (Spain); Italvest (Spain); LANERIE AGNONA S.p.A.; Lanificio Ermenegildo Zegna & F. S.p.A; Master Loom; Matex; Orsini S.p.A.; SAVIT S.p.A; SAVIT S.p.A.; Solteco (Spain); Tarsa (Mexico); ZeFer (50%).

Principal Competitors

RCS MediaGroup; Marzotto S.p.A.; Giorgio Armana S.p.A.; Otavan Trevon A.S.; Cortefiel S.A.; Cantoni ITC S.p.A.; Burberry Ltd.; Miroglio S.p.A.

Further Reading

Conti, Samantha, "Zegna Focusing on Small Details to Woo, Win Customers," *Daily News Record*, June 20, 1997, p. 14.

Forden, Sara Gay, ''Zegna—Leading the Family Toward the Future,'' *Daily News Record,* January 2, 1995, p. 15.

Gellers, Stan, ''Z.Zegna: Younger and Hipper,'' *Daily News Record,* October 27, 2003, p. 20.

Levine, Joshua, ''Armani's Counterpoint,'' *Forbes,* July 4, 1994, p. 122.

Shutt, John, ''Clothier of the Jet Set,'' *International Management,* May 1989, p. 41.

Sullivan, Ruth, ''Family Values Light the Way for Fashion Dynasty,'' *Times,* November 16, 1998, p. 50.

Walsh, Peter, ''Here a Shop, There a Shop, Everywhere a Zegna Shop,'' *Daily News Record,* May 27, 1991, p. 20.

''Zegna Steps Up Asian Focus,'' *Duty-Free News International,* January 15, 2004, p. 9.

—M.L. Cohen

Gateway.

Gateway, Inc.

14303 Gateway Place
Poway, California 92064
U.S.A.
Telephone: (858) 848-3401
Toll Free: (800) 846-2000
Fax: (858) 848-2681
Web site: http://www.gateway.com

Public Company
Incorporated: 1986 as Gateway 2000, Inc.
Employees: 4,000
Sales: $3.4 billion (2003)
Stock Exchanges: New York
Ticker Symbol: GTW
NAIC: 334111 Electronic Computer Manufacturing;
334112 Computer Storage Device Manufacturing;
334119 Other Computer Peripheral Equipment
Manufacturing; 454110 Electronic Shopping and
Mail-Order Houses

Following its March 2004 acquisition of eMachines, Inc., Gateway, Inc. ranks as the third largest personal computer in the United States, trailing only Dell Inc. and Hewlett-Packard Company, with an overall market share of 7 percent as well as a 25 percent share of the U.S. retail PC market. Gateway stands as the eighth largest PC company in the world, with key international markets in the United Kingdom, Western Europe, and Japan. In addition to selling desktop and notebook PCs, Gateway also markets monitors, servers, networking and storage equipment, and accessories and peripherals, as well as a line of consumer electronics products, such as plasma televisions, digital cameras, MP3 players, DVD players and recorders, and home theater systems. Its products are sold via toll-free call centers, Internet web sites, and such retail chains as Best Buy, Circuit City, CompUSA, Costco, Fry's, Sam's Club, and Wal-Mart.

Mid-1980s Beginnings

Gateway was founded in 1985 by Ted Waitt, who had attended two different colleges before returning to his family's cattle farm in Sioux City, Iowa. After spending nine months working at a computer store in Des Moines, Waitt felt that he had learned enough about the business of selling computers to allow him to carve out his own market niche.

Waitt noticed that at the time computers tended to be either inexpensive models with extremely limited capabilities or top-of-the-line models with capabilities that few people would ever need. He decided that a middle path made more sense and devised a ''value equation,'' which stipulated that extra technology should not be added to a computer unless it provided extra value to a customer.

In addition, Waitt observed in his retail job that computers could be sold over the phone by an educated salesperson. This led to the idea that overhead could be virtually eliminated. Because he had no money to invest in his new business, Waitt took over some empty space in a farmhouse that his father's shrinking cattle brokerage business had left empty, and moved in upstairs. Joining him in the business was Mike Hammond, the salesman who had trained him at his computer store job.

In September 1985, aided by a $10,000 loan from Waitt's grandmother, the two started up a mail-order business that they called the TIPC Network. Waitt was 22 years old. Placing advertisements in computer magazines, TIPC sold peripheral hardware and software to people who owned Texas Instrument computers. Because these computers did not conform to the IBM-compatible standard, some considered them obsolete, and many computer stores did not offer additional features for the machines once they had been sold.

Waitt charged each of his customers a $20 membership fee, which gave him start-up capital. Because his costs were so low, he and Hammond could undercut competitors' prices, and within four months, the fledgling business had racked up $100,000 in sales. Six months after they started, Waitt's brother, Norman Waitt, Jr., bought half of the company and began to offer financial advice.

Waitt's goal in starting the company had not been to sell computer accessories, but to sell computers themselves. In 1986 TIPC Network experimented with assembling its own computers, and even sold them to local customers. Nevertheless, these made only a small contribution to the company's first-year revenues of nearly $1 million. Also that year, the company was incorporated as Gateway 2000, Inc.

In mid-1987, however, Gateway was given an opportunity to break into the computer field when Texas Instruments inaugurated a program to let its buyers trade in their old machines for new, IBM-compatible units at a price of $3,500. Waitt and his partners decided that they could offer a similar IBM-compatible machine, put together from parts offered by other mail-order dealers, for less than half as much. Employing Waitt's value equation, and his sense of what customers would be willing to pay for, the company created a machine with two floppy disk drives of different sizes, a color monitor, a large memory, a keyboard with function keys, and a cursor keypad for $1,995. Gateway's competitors offered far fewer features for a similar price.

With the introduction of this computer, Gateway's sales took off. In 1987 the company had revenues of $1.5 million. In the following year, Gateway's sales exploded, hitting $12 million.

In expanding its product line beyond its initial Texas Instrument computer trade-in offer, Gateway eschewed research and development and a staff of designers. Instead, the company relied on Waitt's own sense of what customers would want. "We didn't do a whole lot of market research on it," Waitt told *Inc.* magazine. "A lot of it was instinctive." Hammond elaborated further: "The first question would always be, 'would I buy it,' " he told *Inc.* "Everyone wants smaller, faster, cheaper, so it's a fairly educated guess."

Gateway's clientele of sophisticated users did not make high demands for service or backup support and shopped on the basis of price. Accordingly, despite its rapidly increasing sales, Gateway was not forced to increase its overhead, and the company was able to keep its prices low. With its growth in sales, the company moved from the Waitt family farmhouse to a 5,000-square-foot space in Sioux City's 100-year-old Livestock Exchange building, paying $350 a month in rent. The cow manure was cleaned from the building, and Gateway's new offices were furnished with used furniture. Because of Gateway's rural Midwestern location, Waitt discovered that he could pay his employees $5.50 an hour and experience virtually no turnover. In 1988 the company began to supplement these wages with monthly cash bonuses based on profits.

Gateway's advertising, too, was cut-rate, although effective. Eschewing the services of a professional advertising agency, the company's founders devised their own promotions. Gateway strove to present an image of reliability and trustworthiness to counteract customer fears that their low-priced products were being supplied by a fly-by-night outfit. In the company's first full-page ad, run in computer magazines in 1988, Gateway displayed a picture of Waitt's father's cattle herd, with the

Sioux City water tower looming in the background. Playing on the novelty of the company's midwestern location, the ad asked, "computers from Iowa?" In this way, Gateway was able to remind customers that their products were manufactured in the United States. In addition, the ad stood out in a magazine filled with pictures of computers.

1990: Gateway Moves to South Dakota

Spurred by these promotional efforts, which consumed only 2.5 percent of company revenues, Gateway sales continued their meteoric rise, reaching $70.6 million in 1989. By that time, Gateway had expanded beyond the confines of its second office, and the company moved to North Sioux City, South Dakota, in January 1990. This location was selected in part because South Dakota collected no income taxes.

In 1990 Waitt also hired an advertising manager, a local photographer, and a designer, and produced a series of eye-catching and humorous new Gateway ads that began appearing in computer magazines every few months to keep up momentum in the fast-changing industry. Rather than hiring models, the ads frequently featured company employees, particularly Waitt and his brother. An ad released in July 1990 showed Waitt dressed as an 1890s card shark, flashing a royal flush. Subsequent ads featured other company employees. One showed Gateway staffers standing in a pasture under the slogan, "we're out standing in our field." In a nod to its history, and in an effort to further play up its rural roots, Gateway adopted a cow as its mascot. The company began to ship all its products in white boxes with black spots that looked like the markings on a Holstein. This black-and-white design also kept printing costs low.

By the end of 1990, Gateway's revenues had nearly quadrupled from the previous year, to $275 million. In just five years, the company had grown in value an impressive 26,469 percent. This extremely rapid expansion brought problems of its own, and Gateway was forced to confront some of the consequences of its new size. "The biggest challenge for us right now," Waitt told *Inc.* in 1991, "is figuring out how to add the necessary bureaucracy without becoming slow moving." To expand the company's executive pool, Gateway recruited six vice-presidents from large computer makers and a public accounting firm to help mastermind the company's future growth. In addition, Gateway set up a number of new administrative branches. The company established a 20-member group to investigate new technology, and set up a "Road Map Group" to evaluate choices. Waitt began meeting with ten top assistants, known as the Action Group, every two weeks. Gateway hired a media buyer to systematize its advertising and established a five-member marketing department, which evaluated customer satisfaction by conducting telephone interviews.

To increase productivity in its manufacturing operations, Gateway built a new 44,000-square-foot building down the road from its headquarters in the summer of 1991. In constructing this facility, Gateway stuck to its low-cost, no frills philosophy, to create "the largest metal building I've ever seen," as Waitt told *Marketing Computers.* "It's a big ugly building, but it's very functional," he added. Inside this structure, Gateway reorganized its computer-assembly workers into separate teams. This change was expected to increase output by 30 percent.

Key Dates:

1985: Working out of a Sioux City, Iowa, farmhouse, Ted Waitt and Mike Hammond launch TIPC Network, selling peripheral hardware and software to owners of Texas Instrument computers via mail order.

1986: Company is incorporated as Gateway 2000, Inc.

1987: Gateway begins selling IBM-compatible computer systems, priced lower than competitors.

1990: Gateway relocates to North Sioux City, South Dakota; revenues quadruple that year, reaching $275 million.

1992: Company releases its first notebook computer; revenues reach $1.1 billion.

1993: Gateway establishes a marketing and manufacturing headquarters in Dublin, Ireland; company goes public.

1996: Company begins opening retail showrooms in the United States; customers can now custom configure, order, and pay for a personal computer via the Gateway web site.

1998: Company begins operating as simply Gateway, dropping the "2000"; headquarters are moved to San Diego.

1999: Gateway, Inc. is officially adopted as the corporate name.

2000: Company is hit hard by global PC industry downturn, leading to plunging profits and a net loss during the fourth quarter.

2001: Massive restructuring is launched involving significant consolidation and closures of facilities and the elimination of 9,400 jobs; net loss of $1.03 billion is recorded.

2003: Push into consumer electronics accelerates.

2004: Gateway acquires eMachines, Inc. for nearly $300 million; it announces it will close its remaining retail outlets and begin selling Gateway products through third-party retailers.

Gateway also began an effort in 1991 to expand into lucrative corporate accounts. In the fall of 1991, the company began to run ads that showed a group of conservative executives huddled around a Gateway computer, with the slogan, "because we've stood the test of time."

To further shore up its image as a legitimate computer dealer, Gateway began to divulge some quarterly financial results, in the form of press releases. The company also began to offer the more extensive customer service that corporate clients required, including training programs and troubleshooting procedures. By the end of 1991, Gateway's sales had reached $626 million, and the company was named the fastest-growing private company in America by *Inc.* magazine.

Gateway doubled the pace of its advertising schedule in the following year, releasing new promotions every month. Created by a nine-member in-house team, the ads ran in nine different computer industry magazines, two of which were published weekly. The faster pace was designed to keep up with the company's release of new products and changes in price for old ones.

With the vast increase in the volume of products it sold, Gateway had fallen somewhat behind in technological innovation. "We've been playing catch-up for the last two years," Waitt told *Marketing Computers* in 1992. "We're still not anywhere near where we want to be or need to be, but we're improving our processes continuously and we're learning from our mistakes." As part of its program to regain the lead in technology, Gateway released a notebook computer, called the HandBook, which weighed 2.7 pounds, in 1992. Rather than trying to manufacture this new technology itself, Gateway had the HandBook made by another company.

Gateway also moved to diversify its marketing strategy. Rather than assuming that all customers had the same needs— good value for a good price—the company set out to target the special needs of different segments of the market. "You won't see us introducing separate product lines, but you will see us doing separate sales and marketing efforts and a different level of customization," Waitt told *Marketing Computers.*

By the end of 1992, Gateway's sales had reached $1.1 billion, an increase of 76 percent over the previous year. At a time when other computer makers were reporting losses, Gateway's earnings reached $1.1 million, as the company took the lead in the mail-order computer business.

Gateway's 1,500 employees were supplemented by 200 new hires at the end of 1992. These new workers were assigned to bolster Gateway's sales and support staff in hopes of alleviating some of the company's growing pains. The push to augment Gateway's staff came as the company discovered that finding and training a large number of technical support and computer-assembly workers in the middle of South Dakota was not an easy task.

Growing Pains in the Early 1990s

Starting in late 1992, Gateway found itself deluged by a wide variety of customer complaints, alleging problems ranging from delays in delivery to improperly constructed computers. Gateway buyers complained that the company's quality control had fallen apart, and that its efforts to address complaints were inadequate. The company blamed the shortcomings on extremely high demand for its products in the final quarter of 1992, which made it impossible for all orders to be filled.

Although Gateway's revenues for the first three months of 1993 remained strong, as the company moved to clear its back orders, during the second quarter the company reported its first drop in revenues. The slowdown was attributed to the company's quality control problems, and also to its aging merchandise, which needed to be updated with new products. Gateway responded with a color notebook computer and a sub-notebook based on a new computer chip, which had previously been in limited distribution.

In the fall of 1993, Gateway's competitors began an effort to capitalize on its problems: the Dell Computer Corporation started an ad campaign boasting "performance that blows the gates off Gateway." In addition, the company faced growing competition in the mail-order field from industry giants such as IBM. To protect Gateway's market share, and to insure future growth, the company made plans to move more aggressively into the corporate market, and to enter foreign markets.

To increase the company's corporate sales beyond their 1992 level of 40 percent, Gateway formed a major accounts team, headed by a former IBM employee. The company's technical support staff was doubled to more than 400, and its online technicians were doubled to 14, in order to better service corporate clients. Late in 1993, Gateway inaugurated a separate phone line to provide support services to companies, in which each company was assigned its own personal service representative.

During this time, Gateway also opened its campaign to move into the European market. Previously, foreign sales had accounted for just 3 percent of the company's revenues. In early October, Gateway opened a headquarters in Dublin, Ireland, with sales, marketing, support, and manufacturing facilities. From this base, the company began to sell mail-order computers in Britain. In the future, the company intended to branch out into France and Germany. This plan, however, was complicated by well-established competitors and by the need to customize both machines and marketing programs for each country.

Both Gateway's corporate sales initiative and its expansion into Europe brought with them higher costs than the company had experienced in its South Dakota sales and marketing operations. In an effort to offset the impact of those expenses, Gateway surprised Wall Street by unexpectedly announcing its intention to sell stock to the public in October 1993.

In December 1993, Gateway went public, raising $150 million through the sale of 10.9 million shares, which accounted for 15 percent of the company. Waitt and his brother retained the other 85 percent of Gateway. With this infusion of capital, the company planned to finance current operations, as well as its European push, and also to expand its range of products to include printers, networking products, fax modems, and software. In addition, Gateway announced that it would consider the acquisition of other companies in its field.

In the spring of 1994 Gateway moved to further enhance its corporate marketing effort. The company announced a multifaceted overhaul of its support operations to placate disgruntled customers and win new ones. This program involved a two-year extension of Gateway's one-year warranty, 24-hour-a-day phone lines for technical support, and one-day delivery for replacement parts. In May 1994, the company announced that it would continue to provide technical support free of charge, despite the fact that several of its competitors had begun to charge for this service.

In 1995 Gateway continued to grow, announcing plans to build an $18 million manufacturing plant in Hampton, Virginia, and acquiring 80 percent of an Australian computer maker, Osborne Computer Corporation. Revenues for the year were up again, to $3.7 billion, an increase of $1 billion over 1994. The year 1995 also saw a manufacturing plant opened in Malaysia to serve Far Eastern markets and establishment of the company's web site at gateway.com.

New Marketing Initiatives in the Late 1990s

Early in 1996 the company tried its hand at a new product, the Destination 2000, a combination PC and wide-screen TV. It was designed to be used as a home entertainment center that could also be linked to the Internet. Initial sales were slow, but the company had purposely invested a minimal amount in research and development. After a few months of barely perceptible sales, Gateway announced plans to offer Destinations through such retail outlets as Nobody Beats the Wiz and CompUSA. The price was also dropped by over 20 percent. During this year a small number of Gateway Country Stores were also opened in suburban locations. These stocked no merchandise, but were intended mainly to offer first-hand contact with the company's products. Computers were still ordered over the telephone and shipped directly to the customer. Within the next two years over 140 Country Stores were opened. Also in 1996 Gateway enhanced its web site to allow customers to configure, order, and pay for a personal computer online.

With Gateway's success came increased interest from other companies bent on acquisition. In early 1997 a $7 billion purchase offer from Compaq Computer Corporation was nearly finalized before being rejected by CEO Waitt. In May the company switched its stock listing from the NASDAQ to the New York Stock Exchange. A month later Gateway purchased Advanced Logic Research, Inc., a producer of server computers for business applications, for $196.4 million. This move was part of a newly intensified effort by the company to seek a larger share of the business computer market, as penetration of home PCs reached near-saturation levels. Later in the year, the company announced further measures to increase corporate sales, including removing the ubiquitous cows from its advertising in an attempt to refine its image. Gateway also formed a new subsidiary, Gateway Major Accounts, which focused on sales to business. The company concluded 1997 with record revenues of $6.29 billion and profits of over $1 billion.

During 1998 the company dropped the "2000" from the name it operated under, before the coming millennium made it obsolete (the official corporate name did not change to Gateway, Inc. until May 1999). The firm also moved its headquarters to San Diego, a move taken in part to be closer to the mainstream of the business world, and also because CEO Waitt wanted to live in California. Waitt was able to attract higher profile managers to the company because of the shift, and a slew of new top executives were brought onboard in 1998, including Jeff Weitzen, an AT&T Corp. veteran who was named president and COO. The new management team led an expansion beyond the cutthroat PC market, where brutal competition was steadily ratcheting down profit margins. Gateway pushed deeper into such areas as software, peripherals, services, training, and financing. The company also attempted to get a piece of the Internet pie, launching a new Internet connectivity service, gateway.net, which was made exclusively available to its customers, at prices comparable to America Online and other major services. In June 1998 the company also began to install Netscape Navigator software on its machines along with Microsoft Internet Explorer, which was being bundled with Microsoft's Windows 98. Gateway's Internet service was slow getting off the ground, with only 200,000 subscribers by the beginning of 1999. After a number of problems with the Internet service provider it had chosen, Gateway switched to MCI Worldcom.

Further changes came on the Internet front in 1999. Early in the year Gateway introduced a new offer whereby anyone buying a Gateway PC costing more than $1,000 could get one year of free Internet service via gateway.net. More than a third of Gateway PC buyers were soon signing up for the service, pushing the subscriber base to 600,000 by October 1999. That month, however, Gateway entered into an alliance with America Online, Inc. through which AOL took over the operations of gateway.net and invested $800 million in Gateway for a 5 percent stake. Among the other terms of the deal, Gateway computers began prominently placing the AOL online service on their desktop screens, and AOL began promoting Gateway computers on its various online properties. In December 1999 Waitt stepped down as CEO, remaining chairman, while Weitzen was promoted to president and CEO. For the year, Gateway posted record profits of $427.9 million on record revenues of $9.6 billion.

A Reversal of Fortunes in the Early 2000s

The astounding rise of Gateway came to a crashing halt in 2000 when the global PC industry fell into its worst slump ever. Gateway was hit particularly hard because of its greater reliance on the consumer and small business markets—the hardest hit sectors—and because of questionable management decisions. Soon after taking over, Weitzen began pushing aside old-time Gateway managers and instituted a number of new policies that hurt not only morale but also the bottom line. Weitzen also muddied the company's distribution strategy by launching deals to sell Gateway PCs through such channels as the OfficeMax chain and the QVC home shopping network. He also opened up 100 more Gateway retail stores in the United States. When archrival Dell instituted a price war in an ultimately successful attempt to grab more market share during the PC downturn, Gateway took a heavy blow and ended up suffering a fourth-quarter 2000 net loss of $94.3 million. For the year, net profits fell 26 percent, to $316 million, a figure later revised downward to $241.5 million. Gateway's stock fell 75 percent during 2000, from $72.06 per share to $17.99.

In January 2001 Waitt, a largely hands-off chairman but one who had grown increasingly concerned about the deteriorating situation at the company he had built, reassumed the CEO position, ousting Weitzen and several other top managers. In addition to restating downward the financial results for 2000, Waitt launched a thorough restructuring, brought back a number of old-timers, and adopted a "back to basics" approach reemphasizing Gateway's core business of selling PCs directly to consumers and businesses. Toward the latter end, prices were slashed, in some cases matching Dell's as well as those of the newly bolstered Hewlett-Packard, which acquired Compaq during this period. Cost-cutting initiatives during 2001 were massive. The workforce was reduced from 24,600 to 14,000 as U.S. call center facilities were consolidated; 33 retail stores in the United States and 11 in Canada were closed; manufacturing plants in Lake Forest, California, Ireland, and Malaysia were shut down; and substantially all of the company's international operations were shuttered in order to focus exclusively on the U.S. market. Gateway also moved its headquarters to Poway, a San Diego suburb, during 2001. Special charges for the year totaling $1.1 billion led to a net loss of $1.03 billion. Revenues plunged 38 percent, from $9.6 billion to $5.94 billion.

As the price war and decline in home-PC shipments continued, sales plummeted further in 2002, dropping to $4.17 billion. PC unit sales fell to 2.75 million from the previous year's 3.4 million. Gateway's share of the U.S. PC market dropped to 6.1 percent, down from 9.3 percent at the end of 1999. Gateway fell short in its attempt to counter the PC decline with a push into consumer electronics, such as plasma televisions and digital cameras. The company slashed its payroll by a further 2,500 employees as part of another restructuring that involved the closure of 19 additional stores, two telephone call centers, an engineering operation, and an Internet sales site. Pretax restructuring charges amounted to $109 million, contributing to a net loss for the year of $297.7 million. Gateway's stock ended 2002 trading at just $3.14 per share.

In January 2003 Gateway launched yet another restructuring to close 76 of its remaining 268 retail stores, resulting in the dismissal of 1,900 more employees. In April the company was forced to make another restatement of its past financial results, admitting that it overstated its revenue for 1999 through 2001 by $476 million. The Securities and Exchange Commission (SEC) followed up with a lawsuit filed in November 2003 that accused former CEO Weitzen, former CFO John J. Todd, and former controller Robert D. Manza of fraud, lying to auditors, and other violations of securities law. The three were charged with inflating revenue during 2000, when Gateway began struggling to meet analysts' expectations. The company itself reached a settlement with the SEC on charges of filing false statements and misleading investors, by agreeing to not violate securities laws in the future. No fine was levied on Gateway.

As these accounting machinations were playing out in the background, Gateway was stepping up its push into consumer electronics. During 2003 the firm introduced 118 new products in 22 categories, including DVD players, home theater systems, LCD televisions, digital projectors, personal digital assistants (PDAs), digital music players, and media center PCs that combined the functions of a computer, television, and video recorder. All 192 of Gateway's remaining retail stores were completely remodeled to better display this avalanche of new products. The portion of revenue deriving from consumer electronics and other non-PC products jumped from 19 percent in 2002 to 28 percent in 2003. Gateway also continued its effort to bump up its sales to business customers by enhancing its offerings of servers and storage devices. During the third quarter of 2003, meanwhile, the company restructured yet again, closing down its computer-assembly operation in Hampton, Virginia, and making significant cuts at its PC assembly and refurbishing operations in North Sioux City and Sioux Falls, South Dakota. These and previous closures of manufacturing operations meant that Gateway was increasingly using contractors—mainly Taiwanese—to manufacture the notebook and desktop computers it sold. Job cuts of 1,700 left Gateway with just 7,400 workers by year end, fewer than one-third the total of three years earlier. The net loss of $514.8 million for 2003 reflected in part $148 million in restructuring charges. On a somewhat more positive note, Gateway managed to post a 2003 operating loss of $510.6 million, roughly the same as the 2002 total despite revenues having fallen a further 18 percent, to $3.4 billion. Once the nation's second largest computer seller, Gateway's market share of 3.7 percent was good for only fifth place, behind Dell, Hewlett-Packard, IBM, and upstart eMachines.

The "eMachining" of Gateway, 2004

After three straight years in the red, Gateway shifted gears in 2004. The company announced in January that it had agreed to buy the privately held eMachines for 50 million shares of Gateway stock and $30 million cash. When completed in March 2004 the deal was valued at nearly $300 million. Under the leadership of Wayne Inouye, president and CEO of the low-cost computer marketer since February 2001, eMachines had enjoyed nine straight profitable quarters through relentless cost-cutting and improvements in product quality and customer service. All of eMachines' computers were manufactured by third-party contractors, and they were sold through retail outlets, including Best Buy, Circuit City, CompUSA, Costco, Fry's, Sam's Club, and Wal-Mart stores. By early 2004, eMachines had captured 25 percent of the U.S. retail PC market. The company also distributed its products overseas through retailers in Japan, the United Kingdom, and Western Europe. Founded in 1998 and based in Irvine, California, eMachines had about $1.1 billion in sales in 2003. At the time of its acquisition by Gateway, it employed only about 140 people. By acquiring eMachines, Gateway jumped back up to the number three position among U.S. PC companies—with a market share of nearly 7 percent—and ranked as the eighth largest player in the world market.

Upon completion of the deal, Inouye, who before joining eMachines had served as senior vice-president of computer merchandising at Best Buy from 1995 to 2001, was named president and CEO of Gateway. Waitt remained chairman. Several top executives at eMachines took similar positions at Gateway. Further evidence of the "eMachining" of Gateway came in April 2004 when the company announced that it would close its remaining retail stores, dismiss their 2,500 employees, and shift to selling Gateway computers through third-party retailers— thereby adopting the eMachine approach. Direct selling via call centers and the Internet would nevertheless continue. Coupled with a previously announced cut of 1,000 jobs, mostly in manufacturing and support operations in Iowa and South Dakota, the workforce would thereby be trimmed to about 4,000 workers. Furthermore, Gateway also announced in April that it would close down its head office in Poway and move to California's Orange County, where eMachines was based. Further workforce reductions—perhaps reducing the payroll to around 2,000— seemed imminent as Gateway continued to adopt eMachines's low-cost model in its latest attempt to return to profitability.

Principal Subsidiaries

Advanced Logic Research, Inc.; Cowabunga Enterprises, Inc.; eMachines, Inc.; Gateway Accessory Stores, Inc.; Gateway Asia, Inc.; Gateway Companies, Inc.; Gateway Country Stores LLC; Gateway International Holdings, Inc.; Gateway Japan, Inc.; Gateway Manufacturing LLC; Gateway PC LLC; Gateway Technologies, Inc.; GW Holdings LLC; Nicholas Insurance Company Ltd. (Bermuda); North Merrill Maintenance LLC; Spotware Technologies, Inc.

Principal Competitors

Dell Inc.; Hewlett-Packard Company; International Business Machines Corporation; Apple Computer, Inc.; Sun Microsystems, Inc.

Further Reading

Beatty, Sally, and Evan Ramstead, "Gateway 2000 Plans Shorter Name, Longer Client Talks and No Cows," *Wall Street Journal,* April 28, 1998, p. B6.

Britt, Russ, "Computers & Technology Going Corporate: Gateway Changes Spots," *Investor's Business Daily,* October 30, 1997, p. A1.

Brooker, Katrina, "I Built This Company, I Can Save It," *Fortune,* April 30, 2001, pp. 94–96+.

Brull, Steven V., "A Net Gain for Gateway?," *Business Week,* July 19, 1999, pp. 77–78.

Flynn, Laurie J., "Gateway to Lay Off 2,500 with Closing of 188 Retail Stores," *New York Times,* April 2, 2004, p. C6.

Freeman, Mike, "Former Gateway Execs Accused of Fraud," *San Diego Union-Tribune,* November 14, 2003, p. C1.

——, "Gateway to Buy PC-Maker eMachines," *San Diego Union-Tribune,* January 31, 2004, p. C1.

Graves, Brad, and Andrew Simons, "Gateway's Retooling Begins with Move," *San Diego Business Journal,* April 5, 2004, pp. 1+.

Hesseldahl, Arik, "The McDonald's of Computers," *Forbes,* November 24, 2003, p. 170.

Hyatt, Joshua, "Betting the Farm," *Inc.,* December, 1991.

Impoco, Jim, "Why Gateway Isn't Cowed by the Computer Price Wars," *U.S. News and World Report,* July 26, 1993.

Kasler, Dale, "Will TV-Like Computer Propel Gateway into the Big League?," *Gannett News Service,* June 13, 1996.

Kirkpatrick, David, "New Home. New CEO: Gateway Is Moo and Improved," *Fortune,* December 20, 1999, pp. 44–46.

Krause, Reinhardt, "The New America: Gateway 2000 Adding 'Nuances' to Direct-Selling Strategy," *Investor's Business Daily,* May 29, 1996, p. A4.

Kupfer, Andrew, "The Champ of the Cheap Clones," *Fortune,* September 23, 1991, pp. 115+.

McWilliams, Gary, "Gateway Buys eMachines to Boost Its Own Electronics Sales," *Wall Street Journal,* February 2, 2004, p. B1.

——, "Gateway Inc. Sues to End Contract with Web America," *Wall Street Journal,* January 20, 1999, p. B6.

——, "Under Gateway's Tree, Another Shake-Up," *Wall Street Journal,* January 6, 2003, p. A13.

——, "Waitt List: Gateway Co-Founder Starts Comeback Plan with a Restatement," *Wall Street Journal,* March 1, 2001, pp. A1+.

Palmer, Jay, "Big Moo-ve Ahead? Gateway's Current Woes Don't Dim Its Long-Term Prospects," *Barron's,* December 13, 1999, pp. 28, 30.

Ridgeway, Michael, "Gateway Executives Going Big City," *Gannett News Service,* August 28, 1998.

Smith, Dawn, "Home on the Range," *Marketing Computers,* December 1992.

Therrien, Lois, "Why Gateway Is Racing to Answer on the First Ring," *Business Week,* September 13, 1993.

Turner, Nick, "Gateway's Unusual Move: When Direct Meets Retail," *Investor's Business Daily,* September 29, 1998, p. A10.

Weintraub, Arlene, "Can Gateway Survive in a Smaller Pasture?," *Business Week,* September 10, 2001, p. 48.

——, "Gateway: Picking Fights It Just Might Lose," *Business Week,* September 9, 2002, p. 52.

——, "Powering Up at eMachines: How Did Wayne Inouye Turn a Reviled, Money-Losing PC Maker into a Winner?," *Business Week,* November 17, 2003, p. 77.

Wingfield, Nick, and Gary McWilliams, "AOL to Invest $800 Million in Gateway," *Wall Street Journal,* October 21, 1999, p. A3.

Zimmerman, Michael R., "Gateway Plots New Corporate Program," *PC Week,* April 25, 1994.

——, "Gateway Seizes Moment," *PC Week,* November 1, 1993.

—Elizabeth Rourke
—updates: Frank Uhle, David E. Salamie

imagination at work

General Electric Company

3135 Easton Turnpike
Fairfield, Connecticut 06828-0001
U.S.A.
Telephone: (203) 373-2211
Fax: (203) 373-3131
Web site: http://www.ge.com

Public Company
Incorporated: 1892
Employees: 305,000
Sales: $134.19 billion (2003)
Stock Exchanges: New York Boston London Euronext Paris
Ticker Symbol: GE
NAIC: 325211 Plastics Material & Resin Manuf.; 325413 In-
Vitro Diagnostic Substance Manuf.; 333415 Air-
Conditioning & Warm Air Heating Equip. & Comm. & In-
dustrial Refrigeration Equip. Manuf.; 333611 Turbine &
Turbine Generator Set Units Manuf.; 334510 Elec-
tromedical & Electrotherapeutic Apparatus Manuf.; 334512
Automatic Environ. Control Manuf. for Residential,
Comm., & Appl. Use; 334515 Instrument Manuf. for Mea-
suring & Testing Electricity & Electrical Signals; 335110
Electric Lamp Bulb & Part Manuf.; 335121 Residential
Electric Lighting Fixture Manuf.; 335122 Comm., Indus-
trial, & Institutional Electric Lighting Fixture Manuf.;
335221 Household Cooking Appl. Manuf.; 335222 House-
hold Refrig. & Home Freezer Manuf.; 335224 Household
Laundry Equip. Manuf.; 335228 Other Major Household
Appl. Manuf.; 335311 Power, Distribution, & Specialty
Transformer Manuf.; 335312 Motor & Generator Manuf.;
335313 Switchgear & Switchboard Apparatus Manuf.;
335931 Current-Carrying Wiring Device Manuf.; 336321
Vehicular Lighting Equip. Manuf.; 336412 Aircraft Engines
& Engine Parts Manuf.; 336510 Railroad Rolling Stock
Manuf.; 512110 Motion Picture & Video Prod.; 512120
Motion Picture & Video Distribution; 515120 Television
Broadcasting; 515210 Cable & Other Subscription Pro-
gramming; 522110 Comm. Banking; 522210 Credit Card
Issuing; 522220 Sales Financing; 522291 Consumer Lend-
ing; 522292 Real Estate Credit; 524130 Reinsurance Car-
riers; 532411 Comm. Air, Rail, & Water Trans. Equip.
Rental & Leasing; 532420 Office Machinery & Equip.
Rental & Leasing; 532490 Other Comm. & Industrial Ma-
chinery & Equip. Rental & Leasing; 541710 Research &
Development in the Physical, Engineering, & Life Sciences; 713110 Amusement & Theme Parks

The history of General Electric Company is a significant part of the history of technology in the United States. General Electric (GE) has evolved from Thomas Edison's home laboratory into one of the largest companies in the world, following the evolution of electrical technology from the simplest early applications into the high-tech wizardry of the early 21st century. The company has also evolved into a conglomerate, with an increasing shift from technology to services, and with 11 main operating units: GE Advanced Materials, a specialist in high-performance engineered thermoplastics, silicon-based products, and fused quartz and ceramics used in a wide variety of industries; GE Consumer & Industrial, which is one of the world's leading appliance manufacturers, stands as a preeminent global maker of lighting products for consumer, commercial, and industrial customers, and also provides integrated industrial equipment, systems, and services; GE Energy, one of the largest technology suppliers to the energy industry; GE Equipment Services, which offers leases, loans, and other services to medium and large businesses around the world to help them manage their business equipment; GE Healthcare, a world leader in medical diagnostic and interventional imaging technology and services; GE Infrastructure, which is involved in high-technology protective and productivity solutions in such areas as water purification, facility safety, plant automation, and automatic environmental controls; GE Transportation, the largest producer of small and large jet engines for commercial and military aircraft in the world, as well as the number one maker of diesel freight locomotives in North America; NBC Universal (80 percent owned by GE), a global media and entertainment giant with a wide range of assets, including the NBC and Telemundo television networks, several cable channels, and the Universal Pictures film studio; GE Commercial Finance, which provides businesses, particularly in the mid-market segment, with an array of financial services and products, including loans, operating leases, and financing programs; GE Consumer Finance, a leading financial services provider, serving consumers, retailers, and auto dealer in about three dozen countries; and GE Insurance, which is involved in such areas as life insurance, asset management, mortgage insurance, and reinsurance. The staggering size of General Electric, which ranked fifth in the *Fortune* 500 in 2003, becomes even more evident through the revelation that each of the company's 11 operating units, if listed separately, would qualify as a *Fortune* 500 company. GE operates in more than 100 countries worldwide and generates approximately 45 percent of its revenues outside the United States. Over the course of its 110-plus years of innovation, General Electric has amassed more than 67,500 patents, and the firm's scientists have been awarded two Nobel Prizes and numerous other honors.

Late 19th Century: The Edison Era

Thomas Edison established himself in the 1870s as an inventor after devising, at the age of 23, an improved stock ticker. He subsequently began research on an electric light as a replacement for gas light, the standard method of illumination at the time. In 1876 Edison moved into a laboratory in Menlo Park, New Jersey. Two years later, in 1878, Edison established, with the help of his friend Grosvenor Lowry, the Edison Electric Light Company with a capitalization of $300,000. Edison received half of the new company's shares on the agreement that he work on developing an incandescent lighting system. The major problem Edison and his team of specialists faced was finding an easy-to-produce filament that would resist the passage of electrical current in the bulb for a long time. He triumphed only a year after beginning research when he discovered that common sewing thread, once carbonized, worked in the laboratory. For practical applications, however, he switched to carbonized bamboo.

Developing an electrical lighting system for a whole community involved more than merely developing an electric bulb; the devices that generated, transmitted, and controlled electric power also had to be invented. Accordingly, Edison organized research into all of these areas and in 1879, the same year that he produced an electric bulb, he also constructed the first dynamo, or direct-current (DC) generator.

The original application of electric lighting was on the steamship *Columbia* in 1880. In that same year, Edison constructed a three-mile-long trial electric railroad at his Menlo Park laboratory. The first individual system of electric lighting came in 1881, in a printing plant. But the first full-scale public application of the Edison lighting system was actually made in London, at the Holborn Viaduct. The first system in the United States came soon after when Pearl Street Station was opened in New York City. Components of the system were manufactured by different companies, some of which were organized by Edison; lamps came from the parent company, dynamos from the Edison Machine Works, and switches from Bergmann & Company of New York. In 1886 the Edison Machine Works was moved from New Jersey to Schenectady, New York.

While these developments unfolded at Edison's company, the Thomson-Houston Company was formed from the Ameri-

can Electric Company, founded by Elihu Thomson and Edwin Houston, who held several patents for their development of arc lighting. Some of their electrical systems differed from Edison's through the use of alternating-current (AC) equipment, which can transmit over longer distances than DC systems. By the early 1890s the spread of electrification was threatened by the conflict between the two technologies and by patent deadlocks, which prevented further developments because of patent-infringement problems.

By 1889, Edison had consolidated all of his companies under the name of Edison General Electric Company. Three years later, in 1892, this company was merged with the Thomson-Houston Electric Company to form the General Electric Company. Although this merger was the turning point in the electrification of the United States, it resulted in Edison's resignation from GE. He had been appointed to the board of directors but he attended only one board meeting, and sold all of his shares in 1894, though he remained a consultant to General Electric and continued to collect royalties on his patents. The president of the new company was Charles A. Coffin, a former shoe manufacturer who had been the leading figure at Thomson-Houston. Coffin remained president of General Electric until 1913, and was chairman thereafter until 1922. Meanwhile, also in 1892, GE's stock began trading on the New York Stock Exchange.

In 1884 Frank Julian Sprague, an engineer who had worked on electric systems with Edison, resigned and formed the Sprague Electric Railway and Motor Company, which built the first large-scale electric streetcar system in the United States, in Richmond, Virginia. In 1889 Sprague's company was purchased by Edison's. In the meantime, the two other major electric-railway companies in the United States had merged with Thomson-Houston, so that by the time General Electric was formed, it was the major supplier of electrified railway systems in the United States.

One year after the formation of General Electric, the company won a bid for the construction of large AC motors in a textile mill in South Carolina. The motors were the largest manufactured by General Electric at the time and were so successful that orders soon began to flow in from other industries such as cement, paper, and steel. In that same year, General Electric began its first venture into the field of power transmission with the opening of the Redlands-Mill Creek power line in California, and in 1894 the company constructed a massive power-transmission line at Niagara Falls. Meanwhile the company's electric-railroad ventures produced an elevated electric train surrounding the fairgrounds of the Chicago World's Fair in 1893. Electrification of existing rail lines began two years later.

Early 20th Century: Bolstering Electrification Operations and Moving Beyond Them

By the turn of the century General Electric was manufacturing everything involved in the electrification of the United States: generators to produce electricity, transmission equipment to carry power, industrial electric motors, electric light bulbs, and electric locomotives. It is important to any understanding of the evolution of GE to realize that though it was diverse from the beginning, all of its enterprises centered on the electrification program. It is also worth noting that it operated in

Key Dates:

1878: Thomas Edison establishes the Edison Electric Light Company.

1889: Edison has, by this date, consolidated all of his companies under the name of the Edison General Electric Company.

1892: Edison's company merges with the Thomson-Houston Electric Company to form General Electric Company (GE); company's stock begins trading on the New York Stock Exchange.

1894: Edison sells all his shares in the company, remaining a consultant to GE.

1900: GE establishes the first industrial laboratory in the United States.

1903: Stanley Electric Manufacturing Company of Pittsfield, Massachusetts, a manufacturer of transformers, is acquired.

1906: The first GE major appliance, an electric range, is introduced.

1918: GE merges with Pacific Electric Heating Company, maker of the Hotpoint iron, and Hughes Electric Heating Company, maker of an electric range; company forms Edison Electric Appliance Company to sell products under the GE and Hotpoint brands.

1919: GE, AT&T, and Westinghouse form the Radio Corporation of America (RCA) to develop radio technology.

1924: GE exits from the utilities business following government antitrust action.

1930: Company sells its holdings in RCA because of antitrust considerations.

1938: GE introduces the fluorescent lamp.

1943: General Electric Capital Corporation is established.

1949: Under antitrust pressure, the company is forced to release its light bulb patents to other companies.

1955: The U.S. Navy launches the submarine *Seawolf,* which is powered by a GE nuclear reactor.

1957: GE receives a license from the Atomic Energy Commission to operate a nuclear power plant; an enormous appliance manufacturing site, Appliance Park, in Louisville, Kentucky, is completed.

1961: The company pleads guilty to price fixing on electrical equipment and is fined nearly half a million dollars.

1976: GE spends $2.2 billion to acquire Utah International, a major coal, copper, uranium, and iron miner and a producer of natural gas and oil.

1981: John F. (Jack) Welch, Jr., becomes chairman and CEO.

1986: Company acquires RCA, which includes the National Broadcasting Company (NBC), for $6.4 billion; Employers Reinsurance is also acquired for $1.1 billion, as well as an 80 percent stake in Kidder Peabody.

1987: GE sells its own and RCA's television manufacturing businesses to the French company Thomson in exchange for Thomson's medical diagnostics business.

1994: Company liquidates Kidder Peabody.

1998: Revenues surpass $100 billion.

2000: GE announces a $45 billion deal to take over Honeywell International Inc.

2001: Honeywell deal is blocked by European Commission; Welch retires and is succeeded by Jeffrey R. Immelt; Heller Financial Inc., a global commercial finance company, is acquired for $5.3 billion.

2002: NBC acquires Telemundo Communications Group Inc.

2004: British health sciences firm Amersham plc is acquired for $9.5 billion; in $14 billion deal, GE buys Vivendi Universal Entertainment, which is combined with NBC to form NBC Universal.

the virtual absence of competition. General Electric and the Westinghouse Electric Company had been competitors, but the companies entered into a patent pool in 1896.

In 1900 GE established the first industrial laboratory in the United States. Up to that point, research had been carried out in universities or in private laboratories similar to Edison's Menlo Park laboratory. Initially, the lab was set up in a barn behind the house of one of the researchers, but the lab was moved in 1900 to Schenectady, New York, after it was destroyed in a fire. The head of the research division was a professor from the Massachusetts Institute of Technology. The importance of research at General Electric cannot be underestimated, for GE has been awarded more patents over the years than any other company in the United States.

During the early decades of the 20th century General Electric made further progress in its established fields and also made its first major diversification. In 1903 General Electric bought the Stanley Electric Manufacturing Company of Pittsfield, Massachusetts, a manufacturer of transformers. Its founder, William Stanley, was the developer of the transformer.

By this time GE's first light bulbs were in obvious need of improvement. Edison's bamboo filament was replaced in 1904 by metalized carbon developed by the company's research lab. That filament, in turn, was replaced several years later by a tungsten-filament light bulb when William Coolidge, a GE researcher, discovered a process to render the durable metal more pliable. This light bulb was so rugged and well suited for use in automobiles, railroad cars, and street cars that it was still employed in the early 2000s. In 1913, two other innovations came out of the GE labs: Irving Langmuir discovered that gas-filled bulbs were more efficient and reduced bulb blackening. To this day virtually all bulbs over 40 watts are gas-filled.

The first high-vacuum, hot-cathode X-ray tube, known as the Coolidge tube, was also developed in 1913. Coolidge's research into tungsten had played an important role in the development of the X-ray tube. The device, which combined a vacuum with a heated tungsten filament and tungsten target, has been the foundation of virtually all X-ray tubes produced ever since, and its development laid the foundation for medical technology operations at General Electric.

Perhaps GE's most important development in the early part of this century was its participation in the development of the high-speed steam turbine in conjunction with English, Swedish, and other inventors. Until this invention, all electricity (except hydroelectric) had been produced by generators that turned at no more than 100 rpm, which limited the amount of electricity a single unit could produce. An independent inventor had come up with a design for a very-high-speed steam turbine before the turn of the century, but it took five years of research before GE could construct a working model. By 1901, however, a 500-kilowatt, 1,200-rpm turbine generator was operating. Orders for the turbines followed almost immediately, and by 1903 a 5,000-kilowatt turbine was in use at Chicago's Commonwealth Edison power company.

Such rapid progress led to rapid obsolescence as well, and the Chicago units were replaced within six years. As a result, GE shops in Schenectady were soon overflowing with business. By 1910 the volume of the company's trade in turbine generators had tripled and GE had sold almost one million kilowatts of power capacity. At the same time, General Electric scientists were also researching the gas turbine. Their investigations eventually resulted in the first flight of an airplane equipped with a turbine-powered supercharger.

In the early days of electric power, electricity was produced only during evening hours, because electric lighting was not needed during the day and there were no other products to use electricity. GE, as the producer of both electricity-generating equipment and electricity-consuming devices, naturally sought to expand both ends of its markets. The first major expansion of the General Electric product line was made in the first decade of the 20th century. Before the turn of the century, light bulbs and electric fans were GE's only consumer product. One of the first household appliances GE began to market was a toaster in 1905. The following year the company attempted to market an electric range. The unwieldy device consisted of a wooden table top equipped with electric griddles, pans, toasters, waffle irons, pots, and a coffeemaker, each with its own retractable cord to go into any one of 30 plugs. The range was followed by a commercial electric refrigerator in 1911 and by an experimental household refrigerator six years later.

At the same time two other companies in the United States were producing electric devices for the home. The Pacific Electric Heating Company produced the first electric appliance to be readily accepted by the public: the Hotpoint iron. The Hughes Electric Heating Company produced and marketed an electric range. In 1918 all three companies were prospering, but to avoid competition with one another, they agreed upon a merger. The new company combined GE's heating-device section with Hughes and Pacific to form the Edison Electric Appliance Company, whose products bore either the GE or the Hotpoint label.

GE's first diversification outside electricity came with its establishment of a research staff to investigate plastics. This occurred primarily at the prompting of Charles P. Steinmetz, a brilliant mathematician who had been with the company since the 1890s. All of the initial work by this group was devoted to coatings, varnishes, insulation, and other products related to electrical wiring, so that even this diversification was tied in to electrification.

A more radical branching of GE's activities occurred in 1912, when Ernst Alexanderson, a GE employee, was approached by a radio pioneer looking for a way to expand the range of wireless sets into higher frequencies. Alexanderson worked for almost a decade on the project before he succeeded in creating electromagnetic waves that could span continents, instead of the short distances to which radios had been limited. In 1922, General Electric introduced its own radio station, WGY, in Schenectady. In 1919, at the request of the government, GE formed, in partnership with AT&T and Westinghouse, the Radio Corporation of America (RCA) to develop radio technology. GE withdrew from the venture in 1930, when antitrust considerations came to the fore. General Electric also operated two experimental shortwave stations that had a global range.

Other developments at General Electric contributed to the progress of the radio. Irving Langmuir had developed the electron tube. This tube, necessary for amplifying the signals in Alexanderson's radio unit, was capable of operating at very high power. Other important developments by scientists at General Electric included the world's first practical loudspeaker and a method for recording complex sound on film that is still in use today.

Developments continued apace at GE in the electric motor field. In 1913 the U.S. Navy commissioned General Electric to build the first ship to be powered by turbine motors rather than steam. In 1915 the first turbine-propelled battleship sailed forth, and within a few years, all of the Navy's large ships were equipped with electric power. General Electric also owned several utility companies that generated electrical power, but in 1924 GE left the utilities business when the federal government brought antitrust action against the company.

During the Great Depression the company introduced a variety of consumer items such as mixers, vacuum cleaners, air conditioners, and washing machines. GE also introduced the first affordable electric refrigerator in the late 1920s. It was designed by a Danish toolmaker, Christian Steenstrup, who later supervised mechanical research at the GE plant in Schenectady. In addition, GE introduced its first electric dishwasher in 1932, the same year that consumer financing of personal appliances was introduced.

Also in 1932 the first Nobel Prize ever awarded to a scientist not affiliated with a university went to Irving Langmuir for his work at GE on surface chemistry, research that had grown out of his earlier work on electron tubes. The years that followed witnessed a steady stream of innovation in electronics from the GE labs. These included the photoelectric-relay principle, rectifier tubes that eliminated batteries from home receivers, the cathode-ray tube, and glass-to-metal seals for vacuum tubes. Many of these developments in electronics were crucial to the growth of radio broadcasting.

The broadcasting division of General Electric achieved a breakthrough in the late 1930s. The company had been developing a mode of transmission known as frequency modulation (FM) as an alternative to the prevailing amplitude modulation (AM). In 1939 a demonstration conducted for the Federal Communications Commission proved that FM had less static and noise. GE began broadcasting in FM the following year.

Of course, the light bulb was not forgotten in this broadening of research activity at General Electric. The world's first mercury-vapor lamp was introduced in 1934, followed four years later by the fluorescent lamp. The latter produced light using half the power of incandescent bulbs, with about twice the lifespan. Less than a year after the introduction of the fluorescent light, General Electric introduced the sealed-beam automotive headlight.

Even though production of convenience items for the consumer halted during World War II, the war proved profitable for General Electric, whose revenues quadrupled during the war. The president of General Electric at the time, Charles Wilson, joined the War Production Board in 1942. GE produced more than 50 different types of radar for the armed forces and over 1,500 marine power plants for the Navy and merchant marine. The company, using technology developed by the Englishman Frank Whittle, also conducted research on jet engines for aircraft. The Bell XP-59, the first U.S. jet aircraft, flew in 1942 powered by General Electric engines. By the end of the war this technology helped General Electric develop the nation's first turboprop engine.

Postwar Growth and Difficulties

When production of consumer goods resumed immediately after the war, GE promptly found itself in another antitrust battle. The government discovered that GE controlled 85 percent of the light bulb industry—55 percent through its own output and the other 30 percent through licensees. In 1949 the court forced GE to release its patents to other companies.

In this period the first true product diversifications came out of GE's research labs. In the 1940s a GE scientist discovered a way to produce large quantities of silicone, a material GE had been investigating for a long time. In 1947 GE opened a plant to produce silicones, which allowed the introduction of many products using silicone as a sealant or lubricant.

Meanwhile, as research innovation blossomed and postwar business boomed, the company began an employee relations policy known as "Boulwarism," from Lemuel Boulware, the manager who established the policy. The policy, which eliminated much of the bargaining involved in labor-management relations, included the extension by GE to union leaders of a nonnegotiable contract offer.

During the late 1940s General Electric embarked on a study of nuclear power and constructed a laboratory specifically for the task. Company scientists involved in an earlier attempt to separate U-235 from natural uranium were developing nuclear power plants for naval propulsion by 1946. In 1955 the Navy launched the submarine *Seawolf,* the world's first nuclear-powered vessel, with a reactor developed by General Electric. In 1957 the company received a license from the Atomic Energy Commission to operate a nuclear-power reactor, the first license granted in the United States for a privately owned generating station. That same year GE's consumer appliance operations got a big boost when an enormous manufacturing site, Appliance Park, in Louisville, Kentucky, was completed. The flow of new GE products—hair dryers, skillets, electronic ovens, self-cleaning ovens, electric knives—continued.

Other innovations to come from GE labs during the 1950s included an automatic pilot for jet aircraft, Lexan polycarbonate resin, the first all-transistor radio, jet turbine engines, gas turbines for electrical power generation, and a technique for fabricating diamonds.

Antitrust problems continued to vex the company throughout the postwar years. In 1961 the Justice Department indicted 29 companies, of which GE was the biggest, for price fixing on electrical equipment. All the defendants pleaded guilty. GE's fine was almost half a million dollars, damages it paid to utilities who had purchased price-fixed equipment came to at least $50 million, and three GE managers received jail sentences and several others were forced to leave the company.

During the 1960s and 1970s GE grew in all fields. In 1961 it opened a research center for aerospace projects, and by the end of the decade had more than 6,000 employees involved in 37 projects related to the moon landing. In the 1950s General Electric entered the computer business. This venture, however, proved to be such a drain on the company's profits that GE sold its computer business to Honeywell in 1971.

By the late 1960s, GE's management began to feel that the company had become too large for its existing structures to accommodate. Accordingly, the company instituted a massive organizational restructuring. Under this restructuring program, the number of distinct operating units within the company was cut from more than 200 to 43. Each new section operated in a particular market and was headed by a manager who reported to management just beneath the corporate policy board. The sections were classified into one of three categories—growth, stability, or no-growth—to facilitate divestment of unprofitable units.

When this reorganization was complete, General Electric made what was at the time the largest corporate purchase ever. In December 1976 GE paid $2.2 billion for Utah International, a major coal, copper, uranium, and iron miner and a producer of natural gas and oil. The company did 80 percent of its business in foreign countries. Within a year Utah International was contributing 18 percent of GE's total earnings.

In the meantime, GE scientist Ivar Giaever was a corecipient of the 1973 Nobel Prize in Physics for his discoveries in the area of superconductive tunneling. Giaever became the second GE employee to be honored with a Nobel Prize.

The divestiture of its computer business had left GE without any capacity for manufacturing integrated circuits and the high-technology products in which they are used. In 1975 a study of the company's status concluded that GE, one of the first U.S. electrical companies, had fallen far behind in electronics. As a result, GE spent some $385 million to acquire Intersil, a semiconductor manufacturer; Calma, a producer of computer graphics equipment; and four software producers. The company also spent more than $100 million to expand its microelectronics facilities.

Other fields in which GE excelled were in trouble by the mid-1970s, most notably nuclear power. As plant construction costs skyrocketed and environmental concerns grew, the company's nuclear power division began to lose money. GE's management, however, was convinced that the problem was temporary and that sales would pick up in the future. When by 1980 General Electric had received no new orders for plants in five years, nuclear power began to look more and more like a prime candidate for divestment. GE eventually pulled out of all aspects of the nuclear power business except for providing service and fuel to existing plants and conducting research on nuclear energy.

Though General Electric's growth was tremendous during the 1970s and earnings tripled between 1971 and 1981, the company's stock performance was mediocre. GE had become so large and was involved in so many activities that some regarded its fortunes as capable only of following the fortunes of the country as a whole.

1981–2001: The Jack Welch Era

GE's economic problems were mirrored by its managerial reshuffling. When John F. (Jack) Welch, Jr., became chairman and CEO in 1981, General Electric entered a period of radical change. Over the next several years, GE bought 338 businesses and product lines for $11.1 billion and sold 232 for $5.9 billion. But Welch's first order of business was to return much of the control of the company to the periphery. Although he decentralized management, he retained predecessor Reginald Jones's system of classifying divisions according to their performance. His goal was to make GE number one or two in every field of operation.

One branch of GE's operations that came into its own during this period was the General Electric Credit Corporation, founded in 1943. Between 1979 and 1984, its assets doubled, to $16 billion, primarily because of expansion into such markets as the leasing and selling of heavy industrial goods, inventories, real estate, and insurance. In addition, the leasing operations provided the parent company with tax shelters from accelerated depreciation on equipment developed by GE and then leased by the credit corporation.

Factory automation became a major activity at GE during the early 1980s. GE's acquisitions of Calma and Intersil were essential to this program. In addition, GE entered into an agreement with Japan's Hitachi, Ltd. to manufacture and market Hitachi's industrial robots in the United States. GE itself spent $300 million to robotize its locomotive plant in Erie, Pennsylvania. Two years later GE's aircraft engine business also participated in an air force plant-modernization program and GE later manufactured the engines for the controversial B-1B bomber.

In 1986 General Electric made several extremely important purchases. The largest—in fact, the largest for the company to that date—was the $6.4 billion purchase of the Radio Corporation of American (RCA), the company GE had helped to found in 1919. RCA's National Broadcasting Company (NBC), the leading U.S. television network, brought GE into the broadcasting business in full force. Although both RCA and GE were heavily involved in consumer electronics, the match was regarded by industry analysts as beneficial, because GE had been shifting from manufacturing into service and high technology. After the merger, almost 80 percent of GE's earnings came from services and high technology, compared to 50 percent six years earlier. GE divested itself of RCA's famous David Sarnoff Research Center, because GE's labs made it redundant. In 1987 GE also sold its own and RCA's television manufacturing businesses to the French company Thomson in exchange for Thomson's medical diagnostics business.

GE justified the merger by citing the need for size to compete effectively with large Japanese conglomerates. Critics, however, claimed that GE was running from foreign competition by increasing its defense contracts (to almost 20 percent of its total business) and its service business, both of which were insulated from foreign competition.

In 1986 GE also purchased the Employers Reinsurance Corporation, a financial services company, from Texaco, for $1.1 billion, and an 80 percent interest in Kidder Peabody and Company, an investment banking firm, for $600 million, greatly broadening its financial services division. Although Employer's Reinsurance contributed steadily to GE's bottom line following its purchase, Kidder Peabody lost $48 million in 1987, in part because of the settlement of insider trading charges. Kidder Peabody did come back in 1988 to contribute $46 million in earnings, but the acquisition still troubled some analysts. GE owned 100 percent of Kidder Peabody by 1990.

General Electric's operations were divided into three business groups in the early 1990s: technology, service, and manufacturing. Its manufacturing operations, traditionally the core of the company, accounted for roughly one-third of the company's earnings. Still, GE continued to pour more than $1 billion annually into research and development of manufactured goods. Much of that investment was directed at energy conservation—more efficient light bulbs, jet engines, and electrical power transmission methods, for example.

In 1992 GE signaled its intent to step up overseas activity with the purchase of 50 percent of the European appliance business of Britain's General Electric Company (GEC). The two companies also made agreements related to their medical, power systems, and electrical distribution businesses. Welch said that his aim was to make GE the nation's largest company. To that end, General Electric continued to restructure its existing operations in an effort to become more competitive in all of its businesses. Most importantly, the company launched an aggressive campaign to become dominant in the growing financial services sector.

GE's aggressive initiatives related to financial services reflected the fact that the service sector represented more than three-quarters of the U.S. economy going into the mid-1990s. Furthermore, several service industries, including financial, were growing rapidly. GE's revenues from its giant NBC and GE Capital divisions, for example, rose more than 12 percent annually from about $14.3 billion in 1988 to more than $25 billion in 1994. Encouraged by those gains, GE's merger and acquisition activity intensified. For example, in 1994 the company offered a $2.2 billion bid for Kemper Corp., a diversified insurance and financial services company (it retracted the bid in 1995). GE's sales from services as a percentage of total revenues increased from 30 percent in 1988 to nearly 45 percent in 1994, and neared 60 percent by 1996. The troubled Kidder Peabody unit remained a drag on GE's services operations, leading to the company's late 1994 decision to liquidate the unit. As part of the liquidation, GE sold some Kidder Peabody assets and operations to Paine Webber Group Inc. for $657 million.

In contrast to its service businesses, GE's total manufacturing receipts remained stagnant at about $35 billion. Nevertheless, restructuring was paying off in the form of fat profit margins in many of its major product divisions. Importantly, GE made significant strides with its Aircraft Engine Group. Sales fell from $8 billion in 1991 to less than $6 billion in 1995, but profit margins rose past 18 percent after dipping to just 12 percent in 1993. Reflective of restructuring efforts in other GE divisions, the company accomplished the profit growth by slashing the engineering workforce from 10,000 to 4,000 and reducing its overall Aircraft Engine Group payroll by about 50 percent, among other cost-cutting moves.

Despite a global economic downturn in the early 1990s, GE managed to keep aggregate sales from its technology, service, and manufacturing operations stable at about $60 billion annually. More importantly, net income surged steadily from $3.9 billion in 1989 to $5.9 billion in 1994, excluding losses in the latter year from Kidder Peabody operations. In 1994, in fact, General Electric was the most profitable of the largest 900 U.S. corporations, and was trailed by General Motors, Ford, and Exxon. Revenues reached $70 billion by 1995, the same year that the company's market value exceeded $100 billion for the first time.

The late 1990s saw General Electric reach a number of milestones. In 1996 the company celebrated its 100th year as part of the Dow Jones Index; GE was the only company remaining from the original list. That year, NBC joined with Microsoft Corporation in launching MSNBC, a 24-hour cable television news channel and Internet news service. Overall revenues exceeded the $100 billion mark for the first time in 1998, while the continuing stellar growth at GE Capital led that unit to generate nearly half of GE's revenues by the end of the decade.

Acquisitions in the late 1990s centered on two of the company's growth initiatives: services and globalization. In 1996 the GE Appliances division acquired a 73 percent interest in DAKO S.A., the leading manufacturer of gas ranges in Brazil. GE Capital Services expanded in Japan through the 1996 purchase of an 80 percent stake in Marubeni Car System Co., an auto leasing firm; the 1998 acquisitions of Koei Credit and the consumer finance business of Lake Corporation; and the 1998 formation of GE Edison Life following the purchase of the sales operations of Toho Mutual Life Insurance, which made GE Capital the first foreign company involved in the Japanese life insurance market. In early 1999 GE Capital made its largest deal in Japan to date with the purchase of the leasing business of Japan Leasing Corporation, a business with $7 billion in leasing assets. Then in late 1999 GE Capital agreed to purchase the remaining assets of Toho Mutual for ¥240 billion ($2.33 billion); Toho had collapsed during 1999 after suffering huge losses from the thousands of old, unprofitable policies in its portfolio, and a large portion of its liabilities were to be covered by Japan's life insurance association. Expansion also continued in Europe for GE Capital, highlighted by the 1997 acquisition of Woodchester, one of the largest financial services companies in Ireland. Overall, GE spent some $30 billion during the 1990s in completing more than 130 European acquisitions.

Under Welch's leadership, General Electric in the late 1990s also adopted ''six sigma,'' a quality control and improvement initiative pioneered by Motorola, Inc. and AlliedSignal Inc. The program aimed to cut costs by reducing errors or defects. GE claimed that by 1998 six sigma was yielding $1 billion in annual savings. The company also continued to restructure as necessary, including taking a $2.3 billion charge in late 1997 to close redundant facilities and shift production to cheaper labor markets. During 1999 General Electric adopted a fourth growth initiative, e-business (globalization, services, and six sigma being the other three). Like many longstanding companies, GE reacted cautiously when the Internet began its late 1990s explosion. But once he was convinced of the new medium's potential, Welch quickly adopted e-commerce as a key to the company's future growth. Among the early ventures was a plan to begin selling appliances through Home Depot, Inc.'s web site, a move aimed at revitalizing lagging appliance sales.

In late 1999 Welch announced that he planned to retire in April 2001, but he did not name a successor. At the time, General Electric was one of the world's fastest growing and most profitable companies, and boasted a market capitalization of $505 billion, second only to Microsoft Corporation. Revenues for 1999 increased 11 percent to $111.63 billion while net income rose 15 percent to $10.72 billion. These figures also represented huge gains since Welch took over in 1981, when the company posted profits of $1.6 billion on sales of $27.2 billion.

Welch was not done yet, however. In October 2000 he swooped in to break up a planned $40 billion merger of United Technologies Corporation and Honeywell International Inc. The Honeywell board accepted GE's $45 billion bid, which was set to be the largest acquisition in the company's history. Honeywell was coveted for its aerospace unit, a $9.9 billion business involved in flight-control systems, onboard environmental controls, and repair services. The addition of this unit was expected to significantly boost the GE Aircraft Engines unit, creating a global aerospace giant. Welch agreed to stay on at General Electric through the end of 2001 in order to see the acquisition through to fruition. He did, however, name a successor soon after this deal was announced. In November 2000 Jeffrey R. Immelt won the succession battle and was named president and chairman-elect. Immelt, who joined GE in 1982, had most recently served as president and CEO of GE Medical Systems, a unit with revenues of $12 billion. Immelt's two chief rivals in the race to become only the ninth CEO in GE's long history, W. James McNerney Jr., head of GE Aircraft Engines, and Robert L. Nardelli, head of GE Power Systems, soon left the company to become CEOs of 3M Company and Home Depot, respectively.

Rather than serving as a capstone for a much admired reign of leadership, the Honeywell deal instead provided a sour ending for the Welch era. In the summer of 2001 the European Commission blocked the deal on antitrust grounds as 11th-hour negotiations between the European regulators and GE executives broke down. Welch finally retired soon thereafter, with Immelt taking over as chairman and CEO in September 2001.

The Immelt Era: 2001 and Beyond

Meanwhile, one last major deal was initiated prior to the leadership handover. In July 2001 General Electric's GE Capital unit agreed to pay $5.3 billion for Heller Financial Inc., a global commercial finance company based in Chicago that had total assets of about $19.5 billion. This deal, the second largest in GE history, behind only the 1986 deal for RCA, was consummated in October 2001. Also during 2001, GE Lighting had the largest product launch in its history when it introduced the GE Reveal line of light bulbs, which were touted as providing "a cleaner, crisper light" because the bulbs filtered out the duller yellow rays commonly produced by standard incandescent light bulbs. GE began feeling the effects of the economic downturn that year as revenues fell nearly 3 percent, to $125.68 billion; profits nevertheless increased 7.5 percent, reaching $13.68 billion, though that was a far cry from the yearly 13 to 15 percent increases that Wall Street came to expect from GE during the Welch era.

Immelt began to place his imprint in earnest on GE in 2002 through major restructurings and several significant acquisitions. Midyear he launched a reorganization of GE Capital. The financial services unit was divided into four separate units to streamline management, increase oversight, and improve transparency. The new units were: GE Commercial Finance, GE Consumer Finance, GE Equipment Management (involved in equipment leasing and loans), and GE Insurance. Also during 2002, the GE Appliances and GE Lighting units were combined into a new GE Consumer Products unit. On the acquisitions front, NBC widened its media holdings through the April 2002 acquisition of Hialeah, Florida–based Telemundo Communications Group Inc. for $2.7 billion and the $1.25 billion purchase of the Bravo cable network, completed in December of that year. Telemundo owned the second largest Spanish-language television network, as well as nine U.S. TV stations and the leading TV station in Puerto Rico. NBC hoped to tap into the growing Hispanic market via the deal. Bravo was known for its intelligent, arts-oriented programming such as *Inside the Actors Studio,* and it provided NBC with its first entertainment-oriented cable property. Also during 2002, GE Specialty Materials acquired BetzDearborn, a leading maker of water treatment chemicals, from Hercules Inc. for $1.8 billion. In addition, GE Industrial Systems spent about $777 million for Interlogix, Inc, an Austin, Texas-based manufacturer of electronic security products and systems for commercial, industrial, and residential use. All told, General Electric spent approximately $9 billion on industrial acquisitions alone during 2002. Concerns about whether the company could continue its stellar earnings performance and about its accounting practices sent GE's stock sharply lower in 2002. The stock ended the year trading at $24.35 per share, less than half of the high price for 2001. Once again, profits rose modestly, to $14.12 billion, or about 3 percent.

Taking advantage of the economic downturn to acquire desirable assets from distressed sellers, GE's deal-making appetite grew only larger in 2003. That year was the company's biggest acquisition year yet, with deals worth a collective $30 billion either completed or announced. In August the company agreed to buy Transamerica Finance Corporation's commercial lending business from Aegon N.V. of The Netherlands for $5.4 billion. The deal, which added about $8.5 billion in assets to the GE Commercial Finance unit, closed in January 2004. Also during the summer of 2003 GE sold three of its slower growing insurance businesses: Financial Guaranty Insurance Co., Tokyo-based GE Edison Life Insurance Co., and GE's U.S.-based auto and homeowners insurance unit. About $4.5 billion was raised through these divestments.

As part of its effort to shift emphasis to higher growth fields, General Electric completed two significant acquisitions in healthcare. In October 2003, Instrumentarium Corp. was acquired for $2.3 billion. Based in Finland, Instrumentarium was a major medical-equipment maker with a product line that featured devices for anesthesia, critical care, and patient monitoring. That same month, GE agreed to buy Amersham plc, a British firm specializing in diagnostics agents used during scans of the body for disease, gene-sequencing tools, and protein separation for high-tech drug development. Consummated in April 2004 and valued at about $9.5 billion, the purchase of Amersham stood, very briefly, as the largest acquisition in General Electric history. Following the Amersham acquisition, GE Medical Systems, now a $14 billion business, was renamed GE Healthcare. Based in the United Kingdom—the first GE unit to be headquartered outside the United States—GE Healthcare was headed by Amersham's former chief executive, William Castell; Castell was also named a GE vice-chairman, the first outsider to be so named.

Meanwhile, also in October 2003, General Electric announced an even larger deal, a $14 billion acquisition of Vivendi Universal Entertainment (VUE), the U.S. unit of the French group Vivendi Universal S.A. Among VUE's assets were the Universal Pictures movie studio, the specialty film unit Focus Features, the Universal Television production outfit, cable channels USA Network and Sci-Fi Channel, and theme parks in California, Florida, Japan, and Spain. Upon completion of the deal in May 2004, NBC was merged with VUE to form NBC Universal, which was 80 percent owned by GE and 20 percent by Vivendi. This expansion into entertainment content mimicked earlier combinations involving the ABC and CBS television networks.

Continuing his transformative leadership, Immelt reorganized GE's 13 business units into 11 focused on specific markets and customers. The reorganization, effective at the beginning of 2004, brought similar businesses together in an effort to increase sales and cut costs. The most significant of the changes included combining the firm's aircraft engines business and its rail-related operations in a new GE Transportation unit; merging most of GE Industrial Systems with GE Consumer Products to form GE Consumer & Industrial, which focused on lighting products, appliances, and integrated industrial equipment, systems, and services; and forming GE Infrastructure from certain operations of GE Industrial Systems and GE Specialty Materials. Also in January 2004, GE continued disposing of its insurance operations. That month, General Electric launched an initial public offering (IPO) of about one-third of the stock of the newly formed Genworth Financial, Inc., which consisted of the bulk of GE's life and mortgage insurance businesses. The IPO was planned for completion by mid-2004, after which GE planned to make Genworth fully independent within three years. What was left of GE Insurance was mainly its reinsurance business, which was long rumored to be another candidate for divestment.

Overall, through the myriad moves engineered during just a few years in charge, Immelt was seeking to cut General Electric's reliance on financial services and mature industrial businesses in favor of such higher growth areas as healthcare and entertainment. He was also building operations in fast-growing economies such as China's. By 2005, GE was aiming to outsource $5 billion of parts and services from China and simultaneously grow sales in China to a like figure. Further divestments were also expected, and there had long been speculation that the slow-growing lighting and appliances businesses were prime candidates. Through initiatives such as these, Immelt hoped to return General Electric to double-digit earnings growth by 2005.

Principal Subsidiaries

American Silicones, Inc.; Bently Nevada, LLC; Caribe GE International Electric Meters Corp. (Puerto Rico); Cardinal Cogen, Inc.; Datex-Ohmeda, Inc.; Elano Corporation; GEAE Technology, Inc.; GE CGR Europe (France); GE Drives and Controls, Inc.; GE Druck Holdings Limited; GE Electric Canada, Inc.; GE Energy Europe, BV (Netherlands); GE Energy Parts Inc.; GE Energy Products, Inc.; GE Energy Services, Inc.; GE Energy Services-Dallas, LP; GE Engine Services Distribution, LLC; GE Engine Services, Inc.; GE Fanuc Automation Corporation (50%); GE Gas Turbines (Greenville) L.L.C.; GE Hungary Co., Ltd.; GE Interlogix, Inc.; GE Investment, Inc.; GE Keppel Energy Services Pte., Inc. (Singapore); GE Medical Global Technology Co., LLC; GE Medical Systems Information Technologies, Inc.; GE Medical Systems, Inc.; GE Packaged Power L.P.; GE Petrochemicals, Inc.; GE Plastic Finishing, Inc.; GE Plastics España ScPA (Spain & Canary Islands, Balearic Island); GE Plastics Pacific Pte. Ltd. (Singapore); GE Polymerland, Inc.; GE Power Systems Licensing Inc.; GE Quartz, Inc.; GE Silicones WV, LLC; GE Superabrasives, Inc.; GE Transportation Parts, LLC; GE Transportation Services, LLC; GE Transportation Systems Global Signaling, LLC; GEA Products LP; General Electric International (Benelux) BV (Netherlands); General Electric International, Inc.; Granite Services, Inc.; National Broadcasting Company; Nuclear Fuel Holding Co., Inc.; Nuovo Pignone Holding S.p.A. (Italy); OEC Medical Systems Inc.; PII Limited (U.K.); Reuter-Stokes, Inc.; Sensing Solutions, Inc.; Viceroy, Inc.; General Electric Capital Services, Inc.; General Electric Capital Corporation; GE Global Insurance Holding Corporation.

Principal Operating Units

GE Advanced Materials; GE Commercial Finance; GE Consumer Finance; GE Consumer & Industrial; GE Energy; GE Equipment Services; GE Healthcare; GE Infrastructure; GE Insurance; GE Transportation; NBC Universal (80%).

Principal Competitors

ABB Ltd.; ALSTOM; American International Group, Inc.; AREVA Group; BASF Aktiengesellschaft; CIGNA Corporation; CIT Group Inc.; Citigroup Inc.; AB Electrolux; General Motors Corporation; General Re Corporation; Halliburton Company; Honeywell International Inc.; Household International, Inc.; J.P. Morgan Chase & Co.; Matsushita Electric Industrial Co., Ltd.; Maytag Corporation; MBNA Corporation; The News Corporation Limited; Robert Bosch GmbH; Rolls-Royce plc; Royal Philips Electronics N.V.; Siemens AG; Time Warner Inc.; Toshiba Corporation; Tyco International Ltd.; United Technologies Corporation; Viacom Inc.; The Walt Disney Company; Whirlpool Corporation.

Further Reading

Banks, Howard, "General Electric: Going with the Winners," *Forbes,* March 26, 1984, pp. 97 + .

Berman, Dennis K., and Kathryn Kranhold, "GE to Pay $900 Million to Buy Bomb-Detection Firm InVision," *Wall Street Journal,* March 16, 2004, p. A6.

Bernstein, Aaron, Susan Jackson, and John Byrne, "Jack Cracks the Whip Again," *Business Week,* December 15, 1997, pp. 34–35.

Bongiorno, Lori, "Hot Damn, What a Year!," *Business Week,* March 6, 1995, pp. 98–100.

Brady, Diane, "The Education of Jeff Immelt," *Business Week,* April 29, 2002, pp. 80–84, 86–87.

——, "How GE Locked Up That Boeing Order," *Business Week,* August 9, 1999, pp. 72, 74–75.

——, "Will Jeff Immelt's New Push Pay Off for GE?," *Business Week,* October 13, 2003, pp. 94–96, 98.

Brady, Diane, and Kerry Capell, "GE Breaks the Mold to Spur Innovation," *Business Week,* April 26, 2004, p. 88.

Brown, Ken, and Kathryn Kranhold, "GE's Immelt Faces Hurdles After Acquisitions," *Wall Street Journal,* October 13, 2003, p. C1.

Byrne, John A., " 'Jack': A Close-up Look at How America's #1 Manager Runs GE," *Business Week,* June 8, 1998, pp. 90–95, 98–99, 102, 104–06, 110–11.

Byrne, John A., and Jennifer Reingold, "Who Will Step into Jack Welch's Shoes?," *Business Week,* December 21, 1998, pp. 37–38.

Carley, William M., "Power Ranger: GE Taps Trains Chief in Effort to Shore Up Troubled Energy Unit," *Wall Street Journal,* May 6, 1996, pp. A1 + .

Carlson, W. Bernard, *Innovation As a Social Process: Elihu Thomson and the Rise of General Electric, 1870–1900,* New York: Cambridge University Press, 1991, 377 p.

Colvin, Geoffrey, "The Ultimate Manager," *Fortune,* November 22, 1999, pp. 185–87.

"A Conversation with Roberto Goizueta and Jack Welch," *Fortune,* December 11, 1995, pp. 96–99, 102.

Cox, James A., *A Century of Light,* New York: Benjamin, 1979, 224 p.

Curran, John, "GE Capital: Jack Welch's Secret Weapon," *Fortune,* November 10, 1997, pp. 116–20, 124, 126, 130, 132, 134.

Deogun, Nikhil, and Matt Murray, "GE Capital to Acquire Heller Financial," *Wall Street Journal,* July 30, 2001, p. A3.

Doherty, Jacqueline, "Turning on the Lights," *Barron's,* February 24, 2003, pp. 19 + .

Farrell, John, "GE Cuts Number in Layoff Plans," *Capital District Business Review,* October 31, 1994, p. 5.

Finn, Edwin A., Jr., "General Eclectic," *Forbes,* March 23, 1987, pp. 74 + .

Freudenheim, Milt, "GE, Seeking to Spur Growth, Will Sell Many Insurance Assets," *New York Times,* November 19, 2003, p. C1.

Gapper, John, and Dan Roberts, "Man of the Year: Jeffrey Immelt," *Financial Times,* December 27, 2003, p. 11.

"GE Monkeys with Its Money Machine," *Fortune,* February 21, 1994, p. 81.

"GE: Not Recession Proof, but Recession Resistant," *Forbes,* March 15, 1975, p. 26.

"General Electric: The Financial Wizards Switch Back to Technology," *Business Week,* March 16, 1981, pp. 110 + .

Grant, Linda, "GE's 'Smart Bomb' Strategy," *Fortune,* July 21, 1997, pp. 109–10.

Griffiths, Dave, "GE + RCA = A Powerhouse Defense Contractor," *Business Week,* January 27, 1986, pp. 116 + .

Grover, Ronald, and Mark Landler, "NBC Is No Longer a Feather in GE's Cap," *Business Week,* June 3, 1991, pp. 88 + .

Hammond, John Winthrop, *Men and Volts: The Story of General Electric,* Philadelphia: Lippincott, 1941, 436 p.

Harris, Marilyn A., et al., "Can Jack Welch Reinvent GE?," *Business Week,* June 30, 1986, pp. 62 + .

''The Jack and Jeff Show Loses Its Lustre,'' *Economist,* May 4, 2002, pp. 57–59.

''Jack Welch's Lessons for Success,'' *Fortune,* January 25, 1993, p. 86.

Koenig, Peter, ''If Europe's Dead, Why Is GE Investing Billions There?,'' *Fortune,* September 9, 1996, pp. 114–18.

Kranhold, Kathryn, ''GE, amid Slow Growth, Streamlines,'' *Wall Street Journal,* December 5, 2003, p. A6.

——, ''With New Chief, GE Healthcare Breaks Tradition,'' *Wall Street Journal,* April 8, 2004, pp. B1, B10.

Kranhold, Kathryn, and Charles Fleming, ''GE Agrees to Pay Aegon $5.4 Billion for Finance Units,'' *Wall Street Journal,* August 6, 2003, p. A3.

Laing, Jonathan R., ''Riding into the Sunset: Can Jack Welch's Successor at General Electric Hope to Inherit His Magic Touch?,'' *Barron's,* February 15, 1999, pp. 23–24, 26–27.

Lunsford, J. Lynn, and Kathryn Kranhold, ''GE, Rolls-Royce Gain Boeing Deal,'' *Wall Street Journal,* April 7, 2004, pp. A3, A12.

McClenahen, John S., ''CEO of the Decade,'' *Industry Week,* November 15, 1999, p. 38.

Miller, John Anderson, *Men and Volts at War: The Story of General Electric in World War II,* New York: McGraw-Hill, 1947, 272 p.

Mitchell, Russell, ''Jack Welch: How Good a Manager?,'' *Business Week,* December 14, 1987, pp. 92 + .

Moore, Pamela L., and Nanette Byrnes, ''The Man Who Would Be Welch,'' *Business Week,* December 11, 2000, pp. 94–97.

Moore, Pamela L., et al., ''GE-Honeywell: How Jack Stumbled,'' *Business Week,* April 16, 2001, p. 122.

Morrison, Ann M., ''Trying to Bring GE to Life,'' *Fortune,* January 25, 1982, pp. 50 + .

Murray, Matt, ''GE Capital Is Split into Four Parts,'' *Wall Street Journal,* July 29, 2002, p. A3.

——, ''GE Chairman Sets His Departure Date for 2001: Successor Remains Unclear,'' *Wall Street Journal,* November 3, 1999, p. B12.

——, ''GE Whiz: For Welch's Successor, Filling Legend's Shoes Is Only One Challenge,'' *Wall Street Journal,* November 28, 2000, pp. A1 + .

——, ''Last Conglomerate: Can House That Jack Built Stand When He Goes?,'' *Wall Street Journal,* April 13, 2000, pp. A1 + .

——, ''Late to the Web, GE Now Views Internet As Key to New Growth,'' *Wall Street Journal,* June 22, 1999, p. B1.

Murray, Matt, et al., ''Extended Tour: On Eve of Retirement, Jack Welch Decides to Stick Around a Bit,'' *Wall Street Journal,* October 23, 2000, pp. A1 + .

Norman, James R., ''General Electric Is Stalking Big Game Again,'' *Business Week,* March 16, 1987, pp. 112 + .

O'Boyle, Thomas F., *At Any Cost: Jack Welch, General Electric, and the Pursuit of Profit,* New York: Knopf, 1998, 449 p.

Pare, Terence P., ''GE As a Service Company,'' *Fortune,* April 18, 1994, p. 16.

——, ''Jack Welch's Nightmare on Wall Street,'' *Fortune,* September 5, 1994, p. 40.

Peers, Martin, Bruce Orwall, and John Carreyrou, ''It's Official: Vivendi, GE Make Deal,'' *Wall Street Journal,* September 3, 2003, p. A3.

Petre, Peter, ''What Welch Has Wrought at GE,'' *Fortune,* July 7, 1986, pp. 42 + .

Reich, Leonard S., ''Lighting the Path to Profit: GE's Control of the Electric Lamp Industry, 1892–1941,'' *Business History Review,* summer 1992, pp. 305 + .

Schatz, Ronald W., *The Electrical Workers: A History of Labor at General Electric and Westinghouse, 1923–1960,* Urbana: University of Illinois Press, 1983, 279 p.

Sherman, Stratford P., ''Inside the Mind of Jack Welch,'' *Fortune,* March 27, 1989, pp. 38 + .

Silverman, Rachel Emma, ''GE Goes Back to Future,'' *Wall Street Journal,* May 7, 2002, p. B1.

Slater, Robert, *The New GE: How Jack Welch Revived an American Institution,* Homewood, Ill.: Business One Irwin, 1993, 295 p.

Smart, Tim, ''GE's Money Machine,'' *Business Week,* March 8, 1993, pp. 62 + .

——, ''Jack Welch's Cyber-Czar,'' *Business Week,* August 5, 1996, pp. 82–83.

——, ''Jack Welch's Encore,'' *Business Week,* October 28, 1996, pp. 154–60.

——, ''Just Imagine If Times Were Good,'' *Business Week,* April 17, 1995, pp. 78–79.

Smart, Tim, Pete Engardio, and Geri Smith, ''GE's Brave New World,'' *Business Week,* November 8, 1993, pp. 64 + .

Stewart, Thomas A., ''GE Keeps Those Ideas Coming,'' *Fortune,* August 12, 1991, pp. 40 + .

——, ''See Jack. See Jack Run Europe,'' *Fortune,* September 27, 1999, pp. 124–27, 130, 132, 136.

Tichy, Noel M., and Stratford Sherman, *Control Your Destiny or Someone Else Will: How Jack Welch Is Making General Electric the World's Most Competitive Corporation,* New York: Doubleday, 1993, 384 p.

Useem, Jerry, ''It's All Yours, Jeff. Now What?,'' *Fortune,* September 17, 2001, pp. 64–68.

Vogel, Todd, ''Big Changes Are Galvanizing General Electric,'' *Business Week,* December 18, 1989, pp. 100 + .

Warner, Melanie, ''Can GE Light Up the Market Again?,'' *Fortune,* November 11, 2002, pp. 108–10 + .

Welch, Jack, with John A. Byrne, *Jack: Straight from the Gut,* New York: Warner, 2001, 479 p.

Wise, George, *Willis R. Whitney, General Electric, and the Origins of U.S. Industrial Research,* New York: Columbia University Press, 1985, 375 p.

—Dave Mote
—update: David E. Salamie

GERRY WEBER
INTERNATIONAL AG

Gerry Weber International AG

Neulehenstraße 8
D-33790 Halle/Westphalia
Germany
Telephone: +49 (0) 52 01 18 5-0
Fax: +49 (0) 52 01 10 9-31
Web site: http://www.gerryweber.de

Public Company
Incorporated: 1989
Employees: 1,600
Sales: EUR 350.1 million (2003)
Stock Exchanges: Frankfurt
Ticker Symbol: GWI
NAIC: 315999 Other Apparel Accessories and Other
Apparel Manufacturing; 315232 Women's and Girls'
Cut and Sew Blouse and Shirt Manufacturing; 315234
Women's and Girls' Cut and Sew Suit, Coat, Tailored
Jacket, and Skirt Manufacturing

The union of tennis and fashion propelled Gerry Weber International AG into its position as one of Europe's leading fashion labels. Founded in 1973, the German company gained brand name recognition as a sponsor of tennis champion Steffi Graf during the 1980s. In the 1990s, the company began sponsoring the Gerry Weber Open, a sort of German Wimbledon, which further publicized the label. The company's responsiveness to retailers' needs also helped sales grow, so that Gerry Weber posted increasing sales throughout the 1990s while the fashion industry as a whole was performing poorly. Gerry Weber now designs and sells women's clothing under three main labels. The core Gerry Weber label offers modern clothing with a classical feel for the mid- to high-price market segments and has a market recognition of about 60 percent in Germany. The Taifun label, offering business apparel for younger consumers at mid-range prices, is the company's second strongest label. The third label, Samoon, is a collection of separates in plus sizes and accounts for about 10 percent of sales. In addition, the Gerry Weber name has been licensed for the production of shoes, eyewear, handbags, jewelry, and a fragrance. The company sells most of its apparel through the so-called ''shop-in-shop'' system, in which retailers set aside a minimum amount of floor space for one of the Gerry Weber labels in exchange for advertising and display support from the company. In addition, the company oversees more than 50 ''Houses of Gerry Weber,'' where a full selection from all three labels is available in an exclusive Gerry Weber store. About 40 percent of the company's sales are abroad, mainly in exports to Western Europe, although sales in Eastern Europe, the Middle East, and the Far East are growing. The company is led by cofounders Gerry Weber and Udo Hardieck.

Birth of a Label: 1973–88

Company founder Gerry Weber came from a working-class family and was educated as a textile salesman. At the age of 23, he opened a small fashion shop in the country, which soon expanded into six different locations. In March 1973 he joined with Udo Hardieck to found Hatex KG in their hometown of Halle, a small village in the West German state of Westphalia. Gerry Weber was the personally liable partner and Udo Hardieck was a limited partner. For two years Hatex produced and sold trousers for women. In 1975 the company began producing skirts as well. In order to meet increased production demands, in 1976 Hatex acquired the facilities of a Halle dress manufacturer with approximately 80 employees. The manufacturer became known as ha-we-modelle GmbH and acted as a supply firm for Hatex. Ha-we-modelle moved to Paderborn, a slightly larger town southeast of Halle, in 1979. That same year, Hatex purchased a piece of land for its headquarters in Halle. However, legal provisions held up developments at that site, so the company headquarters moved south to the nearby village of Brockhagen.

Hatex expanded its production to include women's blouses and jackets in 1982. Now the company was able to offer a full set of mix and match coordinates for women. With sales increasing, the company moved about 40 percent of its production to foreign facilities in 1983. Another 20 percent was handled by domestic contractors, and only 35 percent at the company's Paderborn facility. By 1986, annual sales were DEM 72.7 million. That year the brand name Gerry Weber was first created.

Company Perspectives:

Gerry Weber International AG is a globally operating fashion and lifestyle company. Our recipe for success is the perfect blend of innovative power experience and professionalism. Last but not least, it is our added attention to the wishes, needs and demands of our customers that has made so many women delighted with our collections for more than 30 years.

Our brands are individual and unmistakable. Which is exactly what makes them so fashionable.

At the same time, Hatex entered into a sponsoring contract with rising German tennis star Steffi Graf. Graf won her first Grand Slam tournament at the French Open the next year and went on to hold the number one ranking in women's tennis for eight of the next ten years. Her success brought attention to the Gerry Weber brand. The brand was registered as an international trademark in 1987. That year the company also made the decision to build a new factory and headquarters on the piece of property in Halle that had been purchased in 1979. The first segment of the factory, a state of the art shipping facility, warehouse, and forwarding bay, was completed in 1988.

Adding New Brands As a Public Company: 1989–94

In 1989 Hatex changed its name, went public, and launched a second fashion label. Gerry Weber Fashion GmbH was founded as a subsidiary early that year to launch the brand name Taifun. The Taifun collection had a sportswear influence and was meant to appeal to younger women. An East German-born Olympic sprinter, Katrin Krabbe, signed a sponsoring contract to help publicize the new brand. In October 1989, Hatex KG went public and changed its name to Gerry Weber International AG. The company had sales of DEM 103 million that year.

Gerry Weber began production for a third label in late 1989 when it signed a licensing contract with Etienne Aigner, a Munich-based leather goods manufacturer and designer. Gerry Weber was to produce women's clothing for the high end of the market under the Aigner name. The first collection for the new label was presented in 1990. Meanwhile, the company was carrying on with intensive investment in its facilities. The second segment of construction at the Halle site was completed in 1990 and several departments moved operations there. The following year a second warehouse was built. About 80 percent of manufacturing was now handled by foreign subcontractors, mainly in Poland, Yugoslavia, Hungary, and North Africa. In order to ensure a reliable supply of goods, Gerry Weber decided to build a company-owned factory in Portugal after negotiations for a site in East Germany fell through.

The new production and warehouse facilities were needed to keep up with skyrocketing sales. The Taifun label was well received and contributed to a one-year doubling of revenue to DEM 201 million in 1990. In 1992 revenue reached DEM 291 million, 35 percent of which was attributed to the Taifun label. Gerry Weber had about 6,000 retail customers for its three brands and was designing over 600 pieces a season for the core

label, 570 pieces for Taifun, and 200 pieces for Etienne Aigner. The collections, which consisted of mix and match separates built around a central piece, were presented at fashion fairs in Düsseldorf twice a year and were on display year-round at the headquarters in Halle. Gerry Weber gained an edge on competitors by starting the design process earlier and delivering goods ahead of most other labels. Exports had grown to about 40 percent of sales in 1992, mainly to northern Europe, Japan, and the Near East.

The company headquarters was finished in 1992 after an investment of about DEM 45 million. Construction began immediately on another ambitious project. Weber wanted to build on his firm's association with tennis by bringing an internationally known tournament to Halle. With the dynamism and focus he was known for, Weber managed in the course of one year to transform a grassy meadow on the edge of town to a tournament site with ten grass courts and a 9,000-seat stadium. As groundskeeper Weber hired Jim Thorn, who had tended the courts at Wimbledon for a decade. The first Gerry Weber Open was broadcast internationally in 1993 and attracted top-ranked tennis stars. Although the tennis enterprise was not officially part of the firm's operations, Gerry Weber was the number one sponsor. The Open served as a vehicle to further publicize the Gerry Weber brand—the firm noted that brand awareness rose from 14 percent pre-Open to 30 percent after the broadcast of the second Open. Meanwhile, ongoing construction over the next few years transformed the site into an all-around sports resort with a golf course, soccer field, hotel, spa, and fitness center. Weber developed a morning routine where he got up at five o'clock to play a round of golf on his course before heading in to the office nearby.

The company-owned factory in Portugal was finished in 1993, leading to the closing of the manufacturing facility in Paderborn. A small amount of domestic production was still centered in Halle. At the start of 1994 Gerry Weber introduced a fourth label, dubbed ''Samoon'' after an Arabian desert wind. The Samoon collection aspired to provide young-looking, fashionable attire for large sizes. Like the other three labels, it had a distinct identity with its own independent team of designers. The Samoon line sold DEM 31 million in its first year alone.

New Retail Strategies for the Late 1990s

In the second half of the 1990s Gerry Weber turned its attention to finding the optimal retail strategies for its brands. Weber's early experience as a clothing retailer had convinced him that shops needed to offer well-organized, focused collections, rather than trying to cram several different lines into a small space. In order to promote this approach at the stores selling Gerry Weber brands, the company introduced the ''shop-in-shop'' system on a trial basis in 1996. The firm partnered with 50 German fashion houses who agreed to set aside 100 square meters of selling space just for the Gerry Weber label. The company offered its retail partners support in the form of an advertising package, twice yearly training, and a special division devoted to filling the shops' merchandise needs. In another step to accommodate retailers, Gerry Weber began presenting monthly rather than quarterly collections starting in the fall of 1996 for all three labels except Etienne Aigner. Under the motto, ''the right goods at the right time,'' the more

Key Dates:

1973: Gerry Weber founds Hatex KG in Halle (Westphalia), Germany, to make trousers for women.
1982: Manufacturing is extended to a full line of coordinates for women.
1986: The brand Gerry Weber is created and Steffi Graf is signed to promote it.
1989: Taifun brand is created; Hatex goes public as Gerry Weber International AG.
1993: The first Gerry Weber Open tennis tournament is broadcast on television.
1994: Samoon brand is created for plus sizes.
1996: The Gerry Weber shop-in-shop system is introduced at 50 German fashion houses.
1999: The first House of Gerry Weber opens in Bielefeld, Germany.
2003: Company restructures; Court One and Yomanis brands are discontinued.

frequent collections ensured that the shop-in-shops could offer a full, changing selection year-round.

Gerry Weber launched a fifth label, Court One, in the fall of 1997. This was a casual collection created to take advantage of the firm's sporty image, since the Taifun label had evolved into business attire. The next year the shop-in-shop system was extended to the Taifun, Samoon, and Court One brands. By that time, there were about 270 shop-in-shops open in Germany. The company planned to implement the concept internationally as well. In particular, several dozen shops were opened in the Middle East in the late 1990s. The shop-in-shops contributed to ever increasing revenues at Gerry Weber. At a time when the fashion industry as a whole was stagnating, Gerry Weber's annual sales rose to DEM 516.5 million (EUR 297.5 million) for 1998.

With the shop-in-shop network firmly established, Gerry Weber moved its retail engagement to a new level in 1999 when it opened the first House of Gerry Weber in Bielefeld. This store was devoted exclusively to Gerry Weber products and carried a full selection of all the company's brands. The Bielefeld store was located in a former movie theater, which allowed for visually impressive apparel displays. The company also operated a small bistro next to the store. Two more Houses of Gerry Weber opened in Paris and Hamburg over the next year. The fourth House of Gerry Weber was opened in 2001 on the Kurfürstendamm, Berlin's upscale shopping and entertainment street. This store was located on the former site of the famous Café Kranzler, for decades a place to see and be seen after a day of shopping. Gerry Weber planned to sell cake and cocktails next to the historically protected café rotunda. The Gerry Weber Retail GmbH subsidiary was founded to manage all retail activities.

Expansion Despite a Slowdown: 2000–04

The company's next expansion came in the area of licensing. In 2000 the Gerry Weber brand granted licenses for shoes, eyewear, and handbags, with jewelry and watches soon to follow. The idea was for the firm to become a "lifestyle company." The Gerry Weber Open was still an annual destination in the pro tennis tour, and the stadium was used for concerts and other large events as well. Weber's twin sons Ralph and Udo were now active in the family business. Ralph managed the hotel and sports park, while Udo was in charge of marketing the shop-in-shops and Houses of Gerry Weber.

In the fall of 2001 Gerry Weber introduced the Yomanis label. This new brand was intended to replace the Aigner brand in the premium apparel segment. Although Aigner was selling well, Gerry Weber decided not to renew the Aigner licensing contract so that it could create its own exclusive label. Yomanis was the main focus of marketing at that year's Open. Neither of Gerry Weber's two newest labels, however, performed very well. The company's upward trajectory finally hit a bump in 2002 when annual sales remained flat at about EUR 395 million. The following year, as a depression in consumer spending continued, sales were down more than 10 percent. Both the Yomanis and the Court One brands were discontinued after the 2003 spring/summer collection. The Court One label was to be rolled into the core Gerry Weber label. That same year, the firm carried out a critical examination and restructuring of its production processes. About 350 positions were eliminated, many of them related to the closing of factories in Portugal and Tunisia. The company's recently built factory in Romania was now the most important production site.

Despite the slight drop in sales, Gerry Weber planned to go ahead with expansion plans. A Gerry Weber fragrance and line of body care products was expected to be introduced in 2004, based on a licensing contract signed with Cosmopolitan Cosmetics two years earlier. There were now over 50 Houses of Gerry Weber and 600 shop-in-shops. The company planned to increase the number of shop-in-shops to 1,000, concentrating on expansion in foreign markets such as Eastern Europe and China. The core label had been segmented into a "vertically structured" brand that offered clothing for all price brackets under different sublabels, including Gerry Weber Edition, Gerry Weber Sport and the "aggressively priced" G.W., which was expanded to all venues after being available only at the Houses of Gerry Weber for the past two years. The company planned to rely on its established labels and the reputation of its core brand to support growth no matter what economic challenges the future held.

Principal Subsidiaries

Taifun-Collection Gerry Weber Fashion GmbH; ha-we-modelle GmbH; Gerry Weber Life-Style Fashion GmbH; First Class Fashion Bekleidungs-GmbH; SAMOON-Collection Fashion-Concept Gerry Weber GmbH; Gerry Weber Far East Ltd. (Hong Kong); Gerry Weber Fashion Outlet (Spain); Gerry Weber Service International; Gerry Weber Retail GmbH; Gerry Weber Beschaffung Osteuropa GmbH; Gerry Weber France S.A.R.L.; Gerry Weber Tunesia S.A.R.L. (Tunisia); Gerry Weber Dis Ticaret Ltd. (Turkey); Gerry Weber Support S.R.L. (Romania); Hawe Textil SRL (Romania).

Principal Divisions

Gerry Weber; Taifun; Samoon.

Principal Competitors

Hugo Boss AG; Esprit Europe; Marzotto S.p.A.; Calvin Klein, Inc.

Further Reading

Dittrich, Brigitte, "Erster Multimarken-Store eröffnet," *TextilWirtschaft*, December 2, 1999, p. 59.

——, "Gerry Weber: Sublabel G.W. jetzt für alle Kunden," *TextilWirtschaft*, July 31, 2003, p. 12.

"Gegen den Strom geschwommen," *TextilWirtschaft*, February 4, 1993, p. 279.

"Gerry Weber legt stürmisches Wachstum vor," *Süddeutsche Zeitung*, May 28, 1991.

"Gerry Weber schneidert noch mehr im Ausland," *Süddeutsche Zeitung*, May 24, 1993.

"Gerry Weber sieht keine Konkurrenz," *Süddeutsche Zeitung*, March 24, 1998.

"Gerry Weber Signed by Cosmopolitan," *Cosmetics International*, December 15, 2002, p. 5.

"Gerry Weber wird zum Lifestyle-Konzern," *Frankfurter Allgemeine Zeitung*, February 28, 2001, p. 26.

Heidecke, Kerstin, "Eine Cocktail-Bar wird das Sahnehäubchen," *Berliner Morgenpost*, August 30, 2000.

"Modekonzern Gerry Weber Setzt auf Leichte Konsumbelebung," *Die Welt*, December 16, 2003.

Prior, Ingeborg, "Gerry Weber zieht die Frauen an," *Welt am Sonntag*, May 7, 2000.

"Wie der Textilunternehmer Gerry Weber 'Wimbledon in Ostwestfalen' aus dem Boden stampfte," *Frankfurter Allgemeine Zeitung*, June 11, 1993, p. 29.

"Wir denken jetzt in Monaten," *TextilWirtschaft*, March 7, 1996, p. 140.

"Wir haben jetzt viele Möglichkeiten für Expansion," *TextilWirtschaft*, May 18, 1995, p. 70.

"Zwei Jahre der Umstrukturierung," *Frankfurter Allgemeine Zeitung*, February 25, 2002, p. 19.

—Sarah Ruth Lorenz

gevity
people 1st

Gevity HR, Inc.

600 301 Boulevard West
Bradenton, Florida 34205
U.S.A.
Telephone: (941) 741-4300
Toll Free: (800) 243-8489
Fax: (941) 741-4333
Web site: http://www.gevityhr.com

Public Company
Incorporated: 1997
Employees: 934
Sales: $425.8 million (2003)
Stock Exchanges: NASDAQ
Ticker Symbol: GVHR
NAIC: 561330 Professional Employer Organizations

Gevity HR, Inc. is a complete human resources management solutions provider, offering outsourced services for employee recruitment, management, and retention, for payroll processing, benefits administration, and related paperwork, as well as for compliance with government regulations. One of the largest professional employer organizations in the United States, the company serves more than 8,000 clients and 100,000 client employees and operates more than 40 sales and consulting services offices located in Alabama, Arizona, California, Colorado, Minnesota, New Jersey, New York, North Carolina, Tennessee, Texas, and Florida. Gevity HR offers its clients and coemployees the most efficient technological infrastructure for payroll processing, including an online data entry at Gevity HR Central. The Internet portal provides direct access to payroll and benefits information as well as management guidance and ideas.

Founders' Success

In the familiar American tale of the entrepreneur starting a business in the garage, the image is of someone tinkering with a formula or building a better mousetrap. Tom Cooley, William Mullis, Jim Roberts, and Doug Mark diverged from that image when they started a service company in Cooley's garage in 1984. A freshly painted workbench became a shared desk around which the four men tinkered with ideas about how to assist small businesses in handling certain aspects of human resources management. Concerns included payroll processing, state unemployment and other tax issues, workers compensation, health insurance, benefits administration, and a complex array of changing government regulations.

Through the then new concept of employee leasing the company, called Staff Leasing, would become the official employer of client employees, then lease them back to the client for a fee. By pooling employees of many small companies under the umbrella of a professional employer organization (PEO), Staff Leasing would provide insurance benefits to small client companies at costs only available to large businesses. Under this plan the client retained responsibility for hiring, firing, and worksite safety. Service fees covered certain taxes, workers compensation insurance, plus fees for administration. Staff Leasing invoiced clients for paid salaries and wages, and for their portion of costs related to health and retirement benefits plans.

The four founders purchased a photocopier on a payment plan and incurred $20,000 in credit card debt to finance general business expenses while the company established a client base. They began by calling on companies in Bradenton, Florida, street by street. The men approached businesses on one side of the street in the morning, stopped for lunch, and then called on the businesses on the other side. Within six months they attracted enough business and interest to feel assured of success.

Staff Leasing found clients primarily among construction and manufacturing companies who benefited most from low rates for workers compensation insurance. Other client businesses included barber and beauty shops, automotive repair shops, health services, retail stores, restaurants, hotel and lodging services, landscaping companies, and plant nurseries. Clients employed from five to 100 people. In 1988 Staff Leasing posted $26 million in gross sales. The company opened its first branch office in Ocala in 1989, followed by sales offices in St. Petersburg, Orlando, Fort Myers, New Port Richey, Lakeland, Brandon, and throughout the state of Florida. A subsidiary, Total Employee Leasing Services, handled insurance provisions and claims administration.

Company Perspectives:

Vision: Businesses are universally recognizing people as the single most important resource in their endeavors to create value. Sharing in Gevity's expertise, know-how, and technology, specifically designed to leverage human capital, uniquely supports this effort and enhances the ability of business leaders to focus on their core competencies.

Mission: Our mission is to strengthen our clients' human capital by sharing our leading-edge expertise, know-how, and technology to find, develop and retain people, manage all related paperwork, and protect their business.

After eight years of successfully building the business, Roberts and Cooley wanted to retire, so in April 1992 the founders hired an appraiser to evaluate the worth of Staff Leasing. Shortly afterward, Mark became ill, pushing the process forward. As word of the appraisal circulated, Staff Leasing received several unsolicited offers. In November Craig Capital Corporation, an investment group led by Charles Craig, bought the company. Roberts retained his 25 percent interest in the company, while his partners sold for $15 million. Roberts and Mullis stayed with the company for a short time, with Mullis as president and chief executive.

By the time of the acquisition, Staff Leasing had become the largest PEO in the state of Florida, with 25 offices, plus one office in Georgia. Invoices for $450 million generated gross sales of $232 million in 1992; the company employed 30,000 offsite workers and 420 staff members.

Expanding Outside of Florida During the Mid-1990s

Under new ownership Staff Leasing continued to expand, opening offices in Florida and Georgia. In 1993 alone revenues increased 90 percent to $438 million. The company established Staff Leasing in Texas, the second largest employee leasing market, with the September 1994 opening of an office in Irving, near Dallas-Fort Worth. Another four sales offices opened throughout Texas in 1995. By the end of 1995 Staff Leasing operated 35 offices in Florida, Georgia, and Texas.

Other expansion involved partnerships with banks that promoted Staff Leasing services to business customers. Bank of America began to offer the services in 1995. In October 1996 Barnett Bank of Jacksonville experimented by offering Staff Leasing services to small businesses at banks in six counties. Within the first two weeks, six businesses in Manatee County enrolled in the program. Barnett Bank expanded the program statewide and new business generated by Barnett Bank contributed to Staff Leasing's growth by 10 percent that year. A similar promotional arrangement with Dwyer Group, of Waco, Texas, involved Dwyer's franchises, E.K. Williams and General Business Services, which already offered accounting, tax, and counseling services to small businesses. Through Staff Leasing, the franchises began to offer PEO services in Florida, Georgia, and Texas, while Staff Leasing reciprocated with referrals.

Although gross revenues exceeded $1 billion in 1995 and 1996, the company operated at a loss, leading Staff Leasing to

the elimination of health insurance subsidies to client companies. To reduce costs over the long term, Staff Leasing invested in the most advanced computer technology available to process payroll and to facilitate benefits administration for 78,000 leased employees.

To fund further expansion, Staff Leasing became a public company in May 1997, with an initial public offering of 4.6 million shares of stock at $17 per share. The offering grossed $68 million, including approximately $8 million for existing shareholders. Staff Leasing expanded to new states, with two offices in Arizona, one in Mesa, near Phoenix, and the other in Tucson, and one office in Minnesota, in Edina, near Minneapolis. The company chose these markets for their large numbers of small businesses and low unemployment. In addition, the company opened new offices in Savannah, Georgia, and in Corpus Christi and Beaumont, Texas. During 1998 Staff Leasing opened offices in Nashville and Memphis, Tennessee, and Greensboro and Raleigh, North Carolina. By the end of 1998 Staff Leasing operated 44 offices in seven states, serving more than 10,200 clients and 128,000 workers and generating revenues of $2.4 billion.

1999 Insurance Contract Prompting Shift to White-Collar Clientele

Providing blue-collar clients with low-risk workers compensation insurance, Staff Leasing encountered difficulties that prompted a change in its basic business strategy. The change began in 1999 when Liberty Mutual Insurance Company canceled its contract to provide Staff Leasing with workers compensation insurance after losing money on the contract. Staff Leasing negotiated a contract with CNA Financial Corporation, a loss-sensitive agreement that involved a higher level of financial risk than the fixed-rate contract with Liberty Mutual. Under the terms of the contract, the company held $30 million in reserve as collateral, equal to one-third total cash and investments. If premium income invested did not earn 7.5 percent interest during the year, CNA required Staff Leasing to supplement the difference.

To offset the risks of insuring blue-collar employees, who are more likely to be injured at work, Staff Leasing decided to diversify by marketing its services to white-collar businesses. In addition, companies employing higher-paid professionals experienced less employee turnover, reducing unemployment claims as well. Risk management involved an adjustment of fees to account for these differences and termination of contracts with clients that generated minimal profit. During the first three months of 1999, Staff Leasing terminated contracts with 500 clients involving 3,700 employees, maintaining relationships with 10,357 clients and 126,466 employees. The higher cost prompted several clients to end their association with Staff Leasing.

Staff Leasing continued to expand with new office locations in Alabama, Colorado, Georgia, and Tennessee, and a new bank partnership, with Bank One Corporation, but approached sales in a new way. To attract white-collar businesses, as well as to maximize its human and technological administrative infrastructure, Staff Leasing offered existing services individually and added new services. The company offered payroll administration

Key Dates:

1984: Staff Leasing begins operations in the garage of one of its four founders.

1989: The first branch office opens in Ocala, Florida.

1992: Gross sales reach $232 million as the company leases 30,000 employees.

1993: Craig Capital acquires Staff Leasing.

1995: Staff Leasing operates 35 offices in Florida, Georgia, and Texas.

1997: Staff Leasing opens offices in Arizona and Minnesota and initiates a public stock offering.

1999: The company begins a shift from a blue-collar to a white-collar client base.

2001: The company's name change to Gevity HR reflects an emphasis on human resources outsourcing.

2003: Gevity HR opens six offices in California.

and certain kinds of corporate insurance, such as general liability and commercial automobile insurance, separate from its co-employment package. Through the introduction of human resources management outsourcing and consulting services, Staff Leasing provided assistance with employee recruitment and retention and related tasks, such as skills matching, job description, and development of reward and incentive programs.

The new strategy shifted the company's focus of growth, from small businesses in small cities to small and mid-sized companies in major metropolitan areas. Staff Leasing closed some offices and relocated other offices to urban locations. Metropolitan offices opened in Houston, Denver, and Atlanta. Staff Leasing explored opportunities in Philadelphia and Manhattan by sending a sales team to those areas before committing to a permanent office in New York City. In addition, the company intended to attract gray-collar clients, defined as highly skilled workers, though not as highly paid as white-collar workers.

To reflect the change in strategy, Staff Leasing adopted the name Gevity HR in the summer of 2001. The new name suggested the company's mission to help clients develop positive and lasting relationships with their employees.

2001 Setback

Just as Gevity began to see some success through the difficult transition from blue-collar to white-collar clientele, the company experienced a sudden increase in costs due to an unusually high level of workers compensation claims. Fee increases did not adequately cover the costs of CNA's high-risk insurance and Gevity had to draw $22 million from reserve funds to cover the costs. Gevity reported a loss of $15.6 million on revenues of $3.1 billion in 2001.

While many other PEOs closed under similar circumstances, Gevity initiated several cost-cutting measures that would immediately reduce operating expenses. The company eliminated executive bonuses for the year and laid off 120 employees, involving 80 at corporate headquarters and 40 at branch offices. A change in office infrastructure, such as communications

equipment, software, and hardware, also reduced operating expenses. In addition, Gevity raised prices to be more compatible with potential claims, expecting that new business would offset lost clients.

In its attempt to become profitable again, the company faced a difficult economy, which meant lower fees due to high unemployment. The PEO industry experienced slower growth overall and the Florida market for PEO was saturated. From a competitive standpoint, Staff Leasing/Gevity had not advertised much, so the company did not have widespread recognition. Operating the most advanced and efficient technological infrastructure among PEOs, Gevity had a financial and service advantage over the competition, however. Gevity HR Central, the company's new Internet portal, was designed for client convenience, providing customers with online data entry for payroll as well as enhanced information access. The quality of Gevity's technology infrastructure earned the company recognition from *Information Week* as a top innovator.

Factors that served to return Gevity to profitability included an increase in the average employee pay as the company's client base changed. Since fees are based on payroll, the company earned more in fees despite a 10 percent decline in the number of worksite employees. Workers compensation costs declined as a percent of wages as well. The client mix encompassed 24 percent blue-collar, 43 percent gray-collar, and 33 percent white-collar employees.

New Executive Leadership Propelling Gevity to Profitability in 2002–03

In March 2002 Gevity hired Erik Vonk as chief executive officer. Vonk brought a background in international banking and experience as CEO of Randstad North America, a Dutch temporary staffing firm based in Atlanta. Vonk's success at Randstad included the provision of 16,000 temporary workers for the 2000 Summer Olympics in Atlanta. After a rapid succession of four CEOs since 1994, Vonk brought a new level of sophistication and stability to the executive office at Gevity.

Vonk made an immediate impact on the company, as he restructured the branch network in order to improve communication with clients. The function-based structure proved inefficient, requiring a client to speak with different people about different concerns. The new structure provided individual customer relations managers, who could speak with clients about all of their concerns.

Gevity settled issues that improved its financial standing. A new workers compensation insurance contract with American International Group (AIG), effective January 1, 2003, required no investment risk related to premiums. Although Gevity paid a higher premium for coverage through AIG, the increase aligned with marketwide increases. A private placement of $30 million in convertible preferred stock, funded by Frontenac Company LLC, provided funds for expansion and allowed Gevity to repurchase stock from Charles Craig.

In April Gevity announced a change in its accounting procedures. The company began to speak in terms of "net" revenue rather than "gross" revenue. The latter combined salaries, wages, certain payroll taxes, and administration service fees.

Gevity began to separate the fees into net revenues for public disclosure. Thus in 2002 gross sales of $3.4 billion differentiated greatly from net sales of $374.7 million from fees. The corporate accounting scandals of 2002 prompted the accounting change. Gevity led the PEO industry in this move toward transparency and recounted the previous five years of net sales in its 2002 annual report. Gevity reported net income of $4.7 million in 2002.

Vonk addressed the persistent problems in Gevity's sales organization by hiring Robert Minkhorst as senior vice-president of marketing and sales. Throughout the transition to human resources outsourcing, Staff Leasing/Gevity experienced a high turnover in sales representatives as the situation demanded different sales skills, from an appeal based on low-cost insurance to one based on the intangible benefits of human resources outsourcing and consulting services. Initially, Minkhorst's adjustments furthered the turnover, as he sought to reduce competition among Gevity's sales associates by reorganizing the sales structure into five regions, 15 markets, and 330 sales territories. The sales representatives had been accustomed to selling and developing referrals on a national level and the change narrowed the field to smaller, prescribed areas. Minkhorst increased salaries, cut perks, and tied some bonus pay to teamwork. Through psychological testing and intensive, month-long training, Minkhorst ensured that new sales representatives possessed the skills and attitudes that his approach required. Gevity hired more than 100 sales representatives, titled Business Development Managers, seeking candidates with an awareness of the human resource needs of small- to medium-sized companies. Gevity enhanced its consulting services by hiring the same number of human resources consultants.

As the company revived expansion into new markets in 2003, Gevity's offices integrated sales and consulting staff. Growth focused on the New York City area and major metropolitan areas of California. Gevity opened sales and consulting offices in Melville and White Plains, New York, and acquired TeamStaff, Inc., of Somerset, New Jersey, in November. The $9.7 million acquisition involved 1,500 clients and 16,000 client employees and significantly increased Gevity's profits in the fourth quarter. In northern California Gevity opened offices in Concord, San Francisco, and Santa Clara in Silicon Valley, and in southern California in Irvine, Los Angeles, and San Diego. By February 2004 one-third of the 230 sales representatives on Gevity's staff were located in California.

Through alliances with AIG and Transamerica Retirement Services, Gevity enhanced its employee 401K plan benefit to meet the interests of its white-collar and gray-collar clientele. Transamerica provided new investment options, investment consultations, and support materials and services. AIG Advisor Group network offered a variety of finance consultation services.

Gevity succeeded in its strategy to address the human resources requirements of a professional clientele. In addition to attaining more business from legal, computer, and social services, and finance, real estate, and insurance companies, Gevity increasingly contracted with mid-sized companies. New contracts included ComUnity Lending, a California mortgage company, with 1,400 employees, and Financial Service Solutions, a mortgage provider in Charlotte, North Carolina, with 1,000 employees. Contracts with a professional client base provided a higher operating margin, improving profitability. In 2003 revenues increased 13.7 percent to $425.8 million, while net income more than tripled to $15.7 million.

Principal Competitors

Administaff, Inc.; Automatic Data Processing, Inc.; Employee Solutions, Inc.; Kelly Services, Inc.; Paychex, Inc.

Further Reading

"Alliance with AIG and Transamerica Enhances Gevity's 401(k) Plan Services," *DC Plan Investing,* July 29, 2003, p. 10.

"Bradenton. Fla.-Based Staff Leasing Founder Recalls Firm's Beginnings," *Knight Ridder/Tribune Business News,* March 19, 1999.

Braga, Michael, "Five Managers Lose Jobs in Gevity HR Restructuring," *Sarasota Herald Tribune,* July 4, 2002, p. D8.

——, "Gevity Chooses Another New CEO; Erik Vonk Is the Choice of Outgoing CEO James Manning, Who's Been in Charge Only Six Months," *Sarasota Herald Tribune,* March 26, 2002, p. D1.

——, "Gevity HR Signs Deal with Big Carrier; The Bradenton PEO's Stock Rises with News That Clients' Employees Will Have Workers' Comp," *Sarasota Herald Tribune,* October 24, 2002.

——, "Gevity HR to Expand Its Bond with AIG," *Sarasota Herald Tribune,* June 10, 2003, p. D1.

——, "It's a Hard Time for the PEO Industry, and Bradenton's Gevity HR, Formerly Staff Leasing, Is at a Crossroads," *Sarasota Herald Tribune,* December 16, 2001, p. D1.

——, "The Tactician; Gevity HR Has Hired Powerhouse Robert Minkhorst to Reorganize Its Sales Force. If He's Successful, Gevity Will Start Growing Again," *Sarasota Herald Tribune,* May 4, 2003, p. D1.

Cole, Christopher, "Bradenton. Fla.-Based Human Resources Provider to Expand to New Markets," *Knight Ridder/Tribune Business News,* June 20, 2001.

——, "Revenue Reporting Method Changes for Bradenton, Fla.-Based Gevity HR," *Knight Ridder/Tribune Business News,* April 3, 2003.

Devega, Ferdie, "Gevity HR Lays Off 80 Bradenton Workers; The Employees Are Among 120 Let Go Nationwide by the Professional Employer Organization," *Sarasota Herald Tribune,* October 4, 2001, p. A1.

Haber, Gary, "Bradenton, Fla.-Based Staffing Firm Boosts Revenues, Earnings," *Knight Ridder/Tribune Business News,* April 29, 1999.

——, "Bradenton, Fla.-Based Staff Leasing Sees Texas-Size Opportunity in Bank Pact," *Knight Ridder/Tribune Business News,* January 15, 1999.

Heller, Emily, "Founders Sell Florida-Based Staff Leasing, Inc. to Craig Capital Corporation," *Knight Ridder/Tribune Business News,* November 4, 1993.

Horn, Patricia, "Leasing Company Sells Stock for Capital; The $22 Million Raised Will Allow Staff Leasing of Bradenton to Continue Expanding into New States," *Sarasota Herald Tribune,* May 3, 1996, p. 1D.

Keller, Elizabeth, "For Benefits Managers, a Very Good Year," *New York Times,* November 30, 2003, p. 27.

Marsteller, Duane, "Bradenton, Fla.-Based Employer Organization Gevity HR Gets Back in Black," *Knight Ridder/Tribune Business News,* April 26, 2002.

Miille, Margaret Ann, "Florida-Based Staff Leasing Expands North with New Office," *Bradenton Herald,* September 24, 1997.

——, "Taking Market Slump in Stride, Staff Leasing Focuses On Growth; The Company Opens Its Sixth Office This Year and Says It Plans to Continue Building Its Client Base," *Sarasota Herald Tribune,* September 15, 1998.

Pollick, Michael, ''Staff Leasing Decides Stock Price; The Company Will Sell at Least 4 Million Shares to the Public This Summer at $15 to $17 Each. The Proceeds Will Pay Off $19 Million in Debt and Finance Expansion,'' *Sarasota Herald Tribune,* June 3, 1997, p. 1D.

Sauer, Matthew, ''Staff Leasing Hires CEO, But Its President Bows Out,'' *Sarasota Herald Tribune,* June 22, 2000, p. D1.

——, ''Staff Leasing Inks Deal with Dwyer; The Partnership Will Link Dwyer's Small Business Accounting, Tax Work and Counseling with Staff Leasing's Coemployment Services,'' *Sarasota Herald Tribune,* November 2, 1996, p. 1D.

——, ''Stock Falls After Company Maintains Independence,'' *Sarasota Herald Tribune,* April 4, 2000, p. 1D.

Schultheis, Kurt D., ''Gevity HR's Purchase of Former Rival Adds to 2003 Earnings,'' *Knight Ridder/Tribune Business News,* February 18, 2004.

Shopes, Rich, ''Staff Leasing Acquires Dot-com; The Purchase Will Allow the Company to Offer Online Human Resources Services,'' *Sarasota Herald Tribune,* October 4, 2000, p. D1.

——, ''Staff Leasing Begins Major Expansion; The Professional Employer Organization Opens the First of Eight New Offices, in Phoenix and Atlanta,'' *Sarasota Herald Tribune,* April 26, 2001, p. D3.

Watkins, Steve, ''Gevity HR Inc. Bradenton, Florida; White-Collar Customers Have It Seeing Green,'' *Investor's Business Daily,* February 18, 2004, p. A12.

Williams, Tedra T., ''Barnett Bank, Staff Leasing to Help Florida Small Business Owners,'' *Knight Ridder/Tribune Business News,* October 9, 1996.

—Mary Tradii

Grupo Financiero Galicia S.A.

Tte. General Juan D Peron 456
Buenos Aires, C.F. C1038AAB
Argentina
Telephone: (54) (11) 6329 0000
Toll Free: 0-810-444-6655
Fax: (54) (11) 6329 6100
Web site: http://www.gfgsa.com.ar

Public Company
Incorporated: 2000
Employees: 6,229
Total Assets: ARS 22.89 billion ($7.71 billion) (2003)
Stock Exchanges: Bolsa de Comercio de Buenos Aires
    NASDAQ
Ticker Symbol: GGAL
NAIC: 522110 Commercial Banking; 522210 Credit Card
    Issuing; 522291 Consumer Lending; 522310 Mort-
    gage and Other Loan Brokers; 523110 Investment
    Banking and Securities Dealing; 523100 Securities
    Brokerage; 523920 Portfolio Management; 523930
    Investment Advice; 523991 Trust, Fiduciary and
    Custodial Activities; 524113 Direct Life Insurance
    Carriers; 551111 Offices of Bank Holding Companies

Grupo Financiero Galicia S.A. is the holding company for Banco de Galicia y Buenos Aires, S.A., the largest nongovernment bank in Argentina and the only large one that remains in Argentine hands. This bank has a century-long history and offers a full spectrum of financial services for both individual and commercial customers. It has hundreds of branches in Argentina, a subsidiary bank in Uruguay, offices in London, Sao Paulo, Brazil, and Santiago, Chile, and more than 600 correspondents in the world's chief financial centers. Other subsidiaries of Grupo Financiero Galicia include an insurance company.

Rising to the Top in Its Field: 1905–85

The Banco de Galicia y Buenos Aires was founded in 1905 in Buenos Aires by immigrants to Argentina from Spain, espe-

cially businessmen from Galicia, the region of Spain in the northwestern corner of the Iberian Peninsula. Its first offering of stock won it 3,295 shareholders. By the end of the year some ARS 4 million had been deposited in more than 2,500 accounts. The bank's shares were first listed on the Bolsa de Comercio de Buenos Aires in 1907. Soon there were three Buenos Aires branches, and in 1910 a bank office was established in Montevideo, Uruguay. Savings accounts for the small saver were established in 1921. Like other Argentine financial institutions, the Banco de Galicia y Buenos Aires endured a bleak period during the Depression of the 1930s, but—again like others—it experienced a boom in the 1940s, when most of the world outside South America was at war.

One of Banco de Galicia's early presidents was Manuel Escasany, an immigrant from Spain's Catalonia region who established a clock and jewelry retail chain. His son Eduardo, an engineer, became president of the bank in 1948 and remained so until his death in 1972. Eduardo Escasany, in the late 1950s, invited two of Argentina's wealthiest families—the Brauns and the Ayerzas—to become major shareholders in the bank. The Brauns controlled La Anónima, the main retail chain in Patagonia, and the Ayerzas were ranchers. The infusion of their investment provided Galicia with the capital to expand. It became the leading private (that is, nongovernment) Argentine bank in 1965. During this period Galicia began offering mortgage loans, and by 1969 it was issuing an average of 20 such loans a day for residences throughout the Buenos Aires metropolitan area. By the mid-1970s the bank had outgrown its 50-year-old headquarters, and an annex was constructed so that the building could house a staff grown to 1,900 employees. Some 2,000 others were working at 93 branches. By now Galicia held nearly one-fifth of all deposits in Buenos Aires private banks. It also opened an offshore banking subsidiary in Uruguay in 1984.

Surviving and Growing in the 1990s

The 1980s, a rocky period for the Argentine economy, began with repeated currency devaluations and related bank failures in 1981 and ended with hyperinflation of nearly 5,000 percent in 1989. Almost all Argentine money fled to offshore banking centers, and if it returned to Argentina, it was in the form of

Company Perspectives:

The main objective of Grupo Financiero Galicia (GFG) is to be one of Argentina's leading comprehensive financial services companies while continuing to strengthen Banco Galicia's position as one of Argentina's leading banks. Its holding company structure enhances the opportunity to compete more efficiently and to enter into new finance-related businesses such as Internet-based ventures, to profit from the trends in the financial industry worldwide.

equities, Eurobonds, and bank-debt paper. Eduardo Escasany's son Eduardo Jose became president of Banco de Galicia in October of that year. Although some banks found high inflation profitable by handling funds transfers, buying and selling short-term government bonds, and speculative trading, Eduardo Jose Escasany described himself to David Pilling of *Euromoney* in 1995 as a "totally conservative" banker and added, "To live through hyperinflation as a banker is a highly disagreeable experience. . . . What appears to be good business is, in the long term, the very death of banking." He supported the dollarization that restored stability to the nation's currency and provided the basis for economic recovery.

Banco de Galicia was the first Latin American bank to enter, in 1993, both the U.S. and European stock markets with a public offering that raised $60 million in the United States. Also in that year it became the first private Latin American bank to raise funds on the U.S. domestic capital market by floating a $200 million, ten-year Yankee bond. The following year it was the first to issue subordinated convertible negotiable obligations on the international securities market. These initiatives enabled the bank to remain in Argentine hands while its closest rivals were being snapped up by Spanish banks. Also in 1994, Banco de Galicia opened a branch in New York City, the center of international banking, including banking in Latin America. That year as well Banco de Galicia took a one-eighth stake in the consortium that established Correo Argentina S.A., the largest unit of the privatized national postal system. This investment allowed the bank to establish mini-branches in Correo's most desirable locations and corral new customers.

When Spanish banks acquired control of Banco de Galicia's two principal competitors—Banco Río de la Plata S.A. and Banco Francés del Río de la Plata S.A.—in 1994, Galicia remained the only bank among the top nine private financial institutions still controlled by Argentine investors. When a recession blunted Argentina's economic recovery in 1995—the so-called "tequila crisis" that gripped Latin America following Mexico's devaluation of its peso—the bank was already embarked on a major expansion drive while its rivals were still adjusting to the changes in ownership. Galicia also used the slowdown in its business to improve its operating and computer systems. In addition, it benefited from experienced local managers in place who had an intimate knowledge of the market and, as the only remaining large locally owned bank in Argentina, it was the one that foreign institutions consulted in order to tap that knowledge. Indeed, Banco Santander Central Hispano S.A., which had acquired Banco Río de la Plata, accumulated a 10

percent stake in Galicia, but Escasany made it clear that he and his partners had no intention of selling their controlling shares.

Banco Galicia established an insurance company in 1996 as a joint venture with Hartford Life International Ltd. It acquired Banco Sudecor Litoral S.A. and merged it into its operations in 1998. By late 1999, when *LatinFinance* selected it as the best bank in Argentina for the second consecutive year, Galicia had a network of about 300 full-time branches as well as the 100 or so mini-branches in Correo Argentina branches. With the purchase of four credit card companies earlier in the year, the bank now offered consumer banking, credit card, and mortgage services throughout the country. It ranked second to Banco Hipotecario Nacional in generating mortgages. Return on equity was in double digits. About the only negative at this time was the feud between Escasany and his younger sister María Isabel, who demanded—and won—control of her third of the 16.4 percent stake in the bank previously collectively shared by the three Escasany siblings. She also claimed that the bank directors were awarding themselves 15 percent of the profits, and although she did not receive a seat on the board as part of the settlement, her action reduced the share of the bank held by the remaining family partners to 46.34 percent—less than majority control.

Grupo Financiero Galicia: 1999–2003

Control of the bank was the issue that impelled Galicia's management to establish Grupo Financiero Galicia, a holding company for the bank's assets, in 1999. The new entity issued, in 2000, an offer to exchange bank shares for holding company shares in a way that would once again assure management of a voting majority. The ostensible rationale offered was that the new structure would allow Galicia to sidestep regulations that, for example, prevented banks from owning more than one-eighth of insurance companies, but observers noted that the holding company could now raise capital by selling shares in subsidiaries without diluting control of the parent company. As a sweetener, the managers offered a special dividend and said they would reduce their personal take from 12 percent to 6 percent of the profits.

This offer was received poorly by stockholders in both Buenos Aires and New York, some of whom promptly sold their shares. One investment banker told Craig Torres of the *Wall Street Journal* that the directors "are trying to regain control of the bank while only paying a 7% to 13% premium, while bank takeover premiums are around 25% today." No organized opposition emerged, however, in part because Argentine pension funds—who held about 12 percent of the bank's shares—were unsure of their legal right to act together. The offer was accepted by owners of 93.2 percent of the outstanding shares.

As Argentina tottered in late 2001 toward impending default on its public debt and devaluation of its currency, the government placed severe restrictions on cash withdrawals. Banco de Galicia was particularly hard hit by withdrawals because of fears that it could not survive without a foreign owner to bail it out; the bank's deposits fell by 21 percent between September and November alone. Galicia's troubles were compounded by its large holdings of government debt, which was not yielding interest and hence unsalable. When, in January 2002, the gov-

Key Dates:

1905: The Banco de Galicia y Buenos Aires is founded.
1921: The bank begins offering savings accounts.
1960: The Braun and Ayerza families have joined the Escasanys as chief shareholders.
1965: Galicia has become the largest private (that is, non-government) bank in Argentina.
1984: The bank opens a subsidiary in Uruguay.
1989: Eduardo José Escasany becomes president of the bank.
1993: Galicia raises money by selling shares on the U.S. and European stock markets.
1999: The bank has about 300 branches and 100 or so mini-branches in post offices; Grupo Financiero Galicia is established as a holding company for the bank.
2002: The group suffers severe losses amid Argentina's economic crisis.

ernment could no longer support the parity of the peso with the dollar, it fell to less than 30 cents in value. As a result, Galicia's dollar-dominated debt ballooned to $1.8 billion. It began seeking to retire $975 million of the debt in exchange for shares of stock, but without success. In addition, the crisis spread to Uruguay, where the deposits of Banco Galicia Uruguay S.A. were frozen to prevent Argentine clients from closing their accounts. Amid the crisis, Escasany resigned as chairman and chief executive officer of Grupo Financiero Galicia.

During the first half of 2002 Banco de Galicia borrowed billions of pesos from Argentina's central bank, sold holdings from its mortgage and commercial loan portfolios, reduced its branch network by 61, absorbed its mini-branches, and cut its workforce. It showed some signs of improvement in the second half of 2002 but still ended the year with only half the deposits it held at the close of 2000. Galicia reduced its net loss considerably in 2003 and even registered a small gain in deposits but did not succeed in restructuring its debt to creditors abroad and, therefore, still was in default. The Uruguayan bank, however, began making cash payments of 3 percent to its depositors, with the rest to be returned in annual installments over nine years.

The banking services provided by Banco de Galicia y Buenos Aires in 2003 included deposits, checking and savings accounts, automatic teller machines, telephone-operation services, electronic banking, letters of credit, credit and debit cards, residential mortgage financing, foreign currency transactions, investment advisory services, commercial and personal loans, auto loans, electronic collections, mutual fund portfolio management, custody of securities, and travelers' checks. Subsidiaries included the bank in Uruguay, a pension fund management company, a credit card issuing company, and a leasing company. The purchase and sale of real property was available on the bank's web site, e-galicia.com. There were 227 branch offices remaining at the end of 2003. At the end of 2002, Galicia was serving about 2.3 million bank customers and managing more than 1.1 million credit card accounts and more than one million customer deposit accounts. It also maintained 229,000

insurance policies. At the end of 2003, Grupo Financiero Galicia had total assets of ARS 22.89 billion ($7.71 billion) and liabilities of ARS 21.43 billion ($7.22 billion), of which ARS 8.13 billion ($2.74 billion) was owed to the central bank and ARS 5.55 billion ($1.87 billion) was owed to the foreign private sector. Its net loss of ARS 217.06 million ($73.08 million) was much smaller than the 2002 loss of ARS 1.47 billion ($436.2 million). At the end of 2003 the bank held ARS 5.58 billion ($1.88 billion) in deposits. Its revenue for the year was ARS 2.11 billion ($710.43 million).

Net Investment S.A. was the group's incubator for investing and developing Internet-related businesses. By means of its subsidiary B2agro S.A. it was engaged in serving the agriculture and livestock-raising sector, offering help by means of having assembled a network of more than 500 producers and more than 30 providers of goods and services. It was implementing a program that ranged from the search for materials to the sale of grains by means of participation in the Buenos Aires futures market. In addition, B2agro had implemented an alliance with José Manuel Díaz Herrera S.A. to sell farms and ranches. Net Investment was also evaluating other areas of electronic commerce, including wideband and wireless communications.

Sudamericana Holding S.A. was the holding company for life insurance and life-related retirement insurance subsidiaries. It became the sole proprietor of these firms in 2002, following the 2001 purchase of the shares held by Hartford Life Insurance Corp. and Hartford Life Ltd. (Bermuda). In 2003 Sudamericana held nearly 3 percent of the Argentine life insurance market and eighth place among such companies. It was also developing a health plan combining indemnification with medical loans and was pursuing the sale of personal accident policies and others to be sold by independent agents. Galicia Warrants S.A. was offering custodial services to more than 600 enterprises, mainly in the agricultural, industrial, and export sectors.

EBA Holding S.A.—its initials standing for the Escasany, Braun, and Ayerza families—held 26 percent of Grupo Financiero Galicia's Series A shares of common stock in 2003 and 63 percent of its voting capital.

Principal Subsidiaries

Banco de Galicia y Buenos Aires S.A.; Galicia Warrants S.A.; Net Investment S.A.; Sudamericana Holding S.A.

Principal Operating Units

Retail Banking Group, including Customer Contact Center, Galicia Office, and Private Banking; Wholesale Banking Group, including Commercial Department, Corporate Banking Division, International Division, Investment Banking Division, and Treasury Division.

Principal Competitors

Banco Río de la Plata, S.A.; Banco Francés Río de la Plata S.A.

Further Reading

Casey, Michael, "Argentina's Biggest Private Bank Survived Crisis, Shows Some Life," *Wall Street Journal*, November 5, 2003, p. B4J.

''Como la familia dejo de estar unita,'' *Mercado,* June 1999, pp. 100–03.

Evans, Judith, ''Galicia Goes Postal,'' *LatinFinance,* October 1994, pp. 52–53, 56.

Kandall, Jonathan, ''The Open Door,'' *Institutional Investor,* May 1998, p. 123.

Kraus, James B., ''Argentine Bank Opens a Beachhead in N.Y. to Support Growth Abroad,'' *American Banker,* February 6, 1994, p. 4.

''La nueva imagen del Banco de Galicia,'' *Mercado,* December 4, 1975, pp. 37–38, 40.

Pilling, David, ''The Clockmakers of Galicia,'' *Euromoney,* March 1995, pp. 83–84.

Rich, Jennifer L., ''Best Bank in Argentina: Banco de Galicia,'' *Latin-Finance,* October 1999, pp. 31–32.

Torres, Craig, ''Big Argentine Bank Plans Major Revamp,'' *Wall Street Journal,* May 18, 2000, p. A23.

——, ''Holders Wield Little Clout in Latin Deal,'' *Wall Street Journal,* July 21, 2000, p. A9.

Wallin, Michelle, ''Argentina's Galicia Bank Turns to Private Creditors for Help,'' *Wall Street Journal,* February 26, 2002, p. A19.

——, ''An Argentine Bank Struggles with Rumor,'' *Wall Street Journal,* January 17, 2002, p. A10.

—Robert Halasz

Harmony Gold Mining Company Limited

Harmony Farm 222, Private Road
Glen Harmony, Virginia, Free State
South Africa
Telephone: 27-11-684-0140
Fax: 27-11-684-0188
Web site: http://www.harmony.co.za

Public Company
Incorporated: 1950
Employees: 50,718
Sales: $1.2 billion (2003)
Stock Exchanges: Johannesburg New York
Ticker Symbols: HAR; HMY
NAIC: 212221 Gold Ore Mining; 331419 Primary
    Smelting and Refining of Nonferrous Metal (Except
    Copper and Aluminum)

Harmony Gold Mining Company Limited is the largest gold producer in South Africa, accounting for about one-third of all gold produced in the country; the company is among the largest gold producers in the world. Harmony specializes in transforming mature gold mines of marginal profitability by applying low-cost methods of extraction and refining for low-grade gold ore. The company's properties in South Africa are located in the Free State, Evander, Randfontein, and West Rand region of the Witwatersrand basin and the Kraaipan Greenstone Belt in the North West Province. Foreign operations included the Bisset mine in Manitoba, Canada, and the Hill 50 and New Hampton mines in Western Australia. The company has investment interests also, in Abelle Limited in Papua New Guinea and Highland Gold Ltd. in Russia. At the gold mines where Harmony is involved in operations, the company owns 22.2 million ounces of proven gold reserves at a grade rate of 0.12 ounces per ton and 39.8 million of probable reserves at a grade of 0.17 ounces per ton. Harmony sells its gold within South Africa and on international markets and prefers to remain unhedged, believing that hedging results in lower gold prices. Harmony is the only major gold producer to market its own brand of gold bars. The company uses the name Pure Gold, representing 999.9 percent purity. Other gold products include gold medallions and jewelry designed at a jewelry school established by the company to develop a national style.

Becoming a Specialist in Low-Grade Gold in the Mid-1990s

Named for its first gold mine in the Free State province of South Africa, Harmony operated as a subsidiary of Randgold & Exploration until it became an independent company in 1997. Discontented shareholders initiated changes at Randgold in 1994, after a sludge dam burst, damaging the town of Merricspruit and killing 17 people. That year a consortium of British banks took control of Randgold and hired a new management team, including Peter Flack as chairman of Randgold and Bernard Swanepoel as managing director of Harmony.

A marginally profitable, mature mine, in which the premium grade ore had been extracted over several years of underground mining, the Harmony mine was on the edge of closure in 1995. The new management implemented methods to make the property productive and profitable through low-grade ore mining and refining techniques. One dimension of this plan involved a series of acquisitions in 1996 that increased gold production and achieved economies of scale through integration into existing operations. The acquisitions included mineral rights to Farm Vermeulenskraal Noord (FVN), an adjacent, undeveloped property with an estimated 12 million ounces of recoverable gold, and Unisel properties adjacent to FVN, which extracted gold from the same mineral reef. The acquisitions raised Harmony's annual production to 580,000 ounces of gold.

In late 1996 Harmony initiated a pilot project to test a new solvent-extraction method of gold refining that sharply reduced operating costs. Designed for small-scale smelting and refining projects, the technique processed gold to 99.9 percent purity. After successfully completing the test, Harmony began construction of a commercial scale plant with a refining capacity of two tons per month. Operations began in the fall of 1997, only the second such refinery in South Africa. The savings generated by the refining process exceeded the cost of construction within the first year.

High-quality refined gold from low-cost low-grade ore opened new marketing opportunities for Harmony. The company decided to expand its revenue base by selling gold to jewelry manufacturers and by offering branded gold bars on the international market. In January 1997 South Africa's Reserve Bank granted Harmony permission to sell one-third of its gold production in international markets and the following year Harmony became the first gold producer to sell its own brand of gold bars, under the name Pure Gold. LG International, a South Korean conglomerate, purchased the first consignment.

Harmony became an independent company in September 1997 when Randgold separated four mature mines and placed them under two independent companies, Durban Roodepoort Deep and Harmony Gold Mining Company. To Harmony's operations Randgold added East Rand Properties, which included the Grootvlei and Consolidated Modderfontein mines, and Saaiplaas No. 3 shaft near the Harmony mine, the last purchased by Randgold in early 1997.

Harmony's debut as an independent company occurred at a turbulent time. During its first quarter as an independent company, the grade of gold ore declined, reducing gold output; coupled with weak gold prices, low output reduced revenues. An operating profit at the Free State properties was offset by an operating loss at East Rand Properties (despite government subsidies) and at Saaiplass. Other problems included sporadic illegal strikes, leading to the dismissal of 4,600 mine workers. As economic difficulties continued due to weak gold prices, Harmony laid off an additional 770 mine workers, plus supervisory personnel, reducing overall employment from 18,600 workers in September to 11,700 in December.

Late 1990s Acquisitions Leading to Profitability

Despite low gold prices, Harmony continued to acquire new properties or mineral rights in order to expand production. The company focused on marginal, mature properties that it could transform into highly productive and profitable operations by implementing its low-grade ore mining and refining methods. In addition to expanding ore reserves, acquisitions provided harmony with flexibility in operations, to produce gold from the highest-grade ore available within the context of low-grade ore mining. In April 1998 Harmony acquired the mineral rights, equipment, and infrastructure of the Steyn Shafts #5, 6, 7, and 8 from Free State Consolidated Gold Mines, adding 237,000 ounces to annual production. The company acquired Bisset Gold Mining Company in Manitoba, Canada, including infra-

structure, equipment, a 16-year mineral lease, and environmental permits. The small mine produced 60,000 ounces of gold per year, and held reserves of 670,000 ounces. In South Africa Harmony acquired the Maasimong Mine at Freegold 3 and Free State 3 Gold Plant at Saaiplaas.

In August Harmony acquired an 86 percent interest in Evander Gold Mines, a consolidation of four mines. Harmony paid ZAR 250 million cash plus nine million new shares of stock for the properties. With production at 400,000 ounces of gold per year, the Evander properties increased Harmony's total production to more than one million ounces per year. Within nine months Harmony improved cash operating costs, from $340 per ounce, to $196 per ounce, well below the $250 per ounce industry standard for profitability. The improvement increased the ore reserve that could be mined profitably from 10.4 million ounces to 15.1 million ounces.

Harmony surpassed its goal to produce one million ounces of gold during the fiscal year ended June 30, 1999. The company met its goal in April, and produced a total of 1.2 million ounces of gold, representing a 66 percent increase over 1998. The February 1999 sale of the troublesome East Rand Properties supported profitability, but gold prices continued to be rather weak in 1999, particularly after May 7, when the British Treasury announced its intention to sell more than half of its gold reserves during the next few years. Although Harmony did not maintain hedges, believing that hedging lowered gold prices, the company expected to remain profitable as long as gold prices did not drop to less than $250 per ounce. That year the average price received was $288 per ounce, a decline from $316 per ounce. After a loss in 1998, the company earned a net profit of $28 million (ZAR 171 million) in 1999.

Harmony continued to expand its mining operations, seeking diverse opportunities, primarily in South Africa. On July 1, 1999, Harmony completed a merger with West Rand Consolidated Mine (WRCM) and Kalahari Goldridge Mining Company (Kalgold). WRCM owned mining operations at the Kraaipan Greenstone Belt, while Kalgold was involved in open pit mining, a low-cost method of extracting gold from low-grade ore. The merger provided Harmony with an opportunity to diversify into exploration and open pit mining and brought experienced management in both areas. In practice, Harmony acquired the companies for ZAR 300 million, adding 100,000 ounces of gold to annual production.

In January 2000 Harmony made a $128 million (ZAR 780 million) cash and stock offer for Randfontein Estates. Completed the following April, the acquisition increased the company's production by 560,000 ounces of gold per year and Harmony became the third largest gold producer in South Africa, and the sixth largest worldwide. Harmony planned to transform the mature gold mining properties from a high-cost operation, to a profitable, low-cost operation.

In January 2001 Harmony completed a ZAR 1 billion ($131 million) acquisition of Elandsrand and Deelkraal mining operations in the Free State from AngloGold. With ore grades declining, yet still of higher grade than other Harmony properties, the mines were prime prospects for Harmony's skills in transforming mature mines into productively profitable mines.

Harmony funded expansion by offering stocks and corporate bonds. In June 2001 the company issued 27 million new shares of stock plus nine million warrants, listed on the Johannesburg Securities Exchange (JSE) and the New York Stock Exchange (NYSE). Harmony raised ZAR 1.2 billion from the offering and an additional ZAR 1.2 billion through the company's first issue of corporate bonds. The sale of stocks and bonds allowed the company to continue to expand despite weak gold prices in the U.S. market. With gold prices at a 16-month low, Harmony hedged one million ounces of gold put in options, at $260 per ounce, in order to assure financers of the AngloGold mines acquisition. During fiscal 2000–01 Harmony produced 1.6 million ounces of gold at a cost of $234 per ounce. The company generated a cash operating profit of $88 million (ZAR 673 million).

Early 2000s Expansion Involving Domestic and International Acquisitions

After investigating mining opportunities in Australia, Harmony began to make investments in gold properties there in 2000. The company started with a 23 percent interest in Goldfields Ltd., involving gold mines located near Kalgoorlie and in Tasmania, as well as in Papua New Guinea, then turned around and sold the stake to bid on New Hampton Goldfields. In December the company made a cash offer for New Hampton Goldfields Ltd., which operated the Big Bell and Jubilee gold mines in Western Australia. By April 2001 Harmony increased its holding to 90 percent. The company sold its interest in Goldfields in order to purchase Hill 50 Ltd. in December 2001. The acquisition provided Harmony an opportunity to combine operations of the New Hampton properties with Hill 50's nearby Murchison Belt property. Hill 50 included New Celebration mine south of Kalgoorlie and the Maud Creek property in the Northern Territory, then in an advanced stage of exploration. The company obtained higher quality ore reserves as well. Harmony invested AUD 50 million for a 31.3 percent interest in Bendigo Mining in Victoria, to fund a renewal of mining in the prospect area.

In November 2001 Harmony entered into a joint venture agreement with African Rainbow Minerals Pty Ltd. (ARM

Gold) to acquire the mature Joel, Tshepong, Matjhabeng, and Bambanani mines in the Free State from AngloGold. The ZAR 2.7 billion acquisition included infrastructure and mineral rights. With combined production of the four mines at more than one million ounces of gold per year, Harmony's share, at 500,000 ounces of year, increased the company's total output to three million ounces per year.

Actions in the international marketplace involved a stock offering and investment acquisitions. Harmony made an international public offering of 8.5 million shares of stock, which sold on the JSE at $13.20 per share in April 2002. Of the $112 million in net proceeds, Harmony applied $95 million to off-shore debt. Investments during 2002 included a minor share in Placer Dome located in Manitoba, Canada, and a 32 percent interest in Highland Gold, with assets in Russia. In November Harmony purchased a 21 percent interest in High River Gold Mines Ltd. from Jipangu, Inc. for $14.5 million. High River owned and operated gold mining properties in Russia, Canada, and West Africa.

Harmony introduced new Pure Gold brand gold bars and coins to the South Africa and international markets in April. Gold products included the Elephant Ten Tola, a 116.7 gram bar designed especially for sale in India (the elephant being a significant emblem in both South Africa and India). Wrought gold bars and medallions for sale in South Africa were produced in 28-gram, 15-gram, and 8-gram weights.

Harmony benefited from increased interest in gold as an investment alternative to volatile investments. Average price received per ounce of gold increased 15 percent, to $329 per ounce. A stronger rand value offset the stronger U.S. dollar price in gold in real terms, however. During fiscal 2002–03 Harmony's gold production increased to 2.9 million ounces, compared to 2.6 million ounces the previous year. Operating costs declined from $192 per ounce to $242 per ounce due to high-cost acquisitions, specifically St. Helena in South Africa and Hill 50 in Australia. Operating profit increased slightly, however, from $254 million in 2002 to $260 million (ZAR 2.4 billion) in fiscal 2003. The September 2003 spot price of gold at $392 per ounce promised to maintain a significant level of profitability.

Investment and divestment activities during late 2003 included an offer for a 20 percent interest in Abelle Limited, with properties in Australia and Papua New Guinea. In October Harmony sold its High River Gold and the following month the company sold Kalgold operations for ZAR 275 million, but retained an interest in mineral rights in a platinum discovery on the property.

2003: Fulfillment of National Black Empowerment Requirements

Durng 2003 Harmony took steps to meet the South African Mining Charter, which requires the country's mining companies to expand black ownership of assets in South Africa to 26 percent. The intent of the Mining Charter is to correct the historical injustices of apartheid. Toward that end, Harmony formed a joint venture with Africa Vanguard Resources (AVR), a new black empowerment company, to manage the Doornkop

South Reef Project at Randfontein. AVR acquired a 26 percent share in the mineral rights for $29 million and would share in 16 percent of the profits.

In January 2003 Harmony announced its decision to expand the project by deepening existing mine shafts. With an estimated gold content of 6.6 million ounces of gold, Harmony expected the project to have a 20-year lifespan and to optimize production in six years, producing 330,000 ounces per year. To raise funds for development, Harmony sold its Placer Dome interest for $87 million, obtaining a substantial profit. In addition, the company sold eight million shares of common stock for $15.50 per share in January 2003.

A merger agreement between Harmony and ARM Gold, announced in May, met the South African Mining Charter as well. Renamed Harmony, the new company combined Harmony's 319.9 million ounce resource base and ARM Gold's 90.2 million ounce resource base, creating the world's largest resource base at 410 million ounces. In conjunction with the merger agreement, Harmony and ARM Gold acquired a 35 percent interest in Anglovaal Mining Ltd. (Avmin) from Anglo American, specifically to obtain the Target mine in Free State province, with annual production of 350,000 ounces of gold. The Target North project, then in development, was estimated to contain 59.6 million ounces.

The company's Social Plan Framework Agreement, signed by the National Union of Mineworkers in July 2003, corrected the last vestiges of historically discriminatory practices as it applied to mine employees. Changes involved re-grading employee categories with appropriate pay increases, providing retirement benefits, and improving employee housing.

Upon completion of the merger in September, Harmony increased its ownership interest in Avmin to 53.7 percent through the purchase of a 42.4 percent interest in Avgold, a subsidiary of Avmin. In conjunction with the stock exchange, Avmin changed its name to African Rainbow Minerals. With the additional resources of the ARM Gold merger and the Anglovaal acquisitions, Harmony expected production to exceed four million ounces of gold in 2004.

Principal Subsidiaries

Abelle Limited (Australia; 20%); Bendingo Mining; Bisset Gold Mining Company; Evander Gold Mines Ltd.; Highland Gold Ltd. (Russia; 32%); New Hampton Goldfields Ltd. (Australia); Hill 50 Ltd. (Australia); Randfontein Estates (74%).

Principal Competitors

AngloGold Limited; Barrick Gold Corporation; Newmont Mining Corporation.

Further Reading

Abboud, Joseph B., ''S. Africa's Gold Miners Dig In,'' *American Metal Market,* July 22, 1999, p. 4.

''African Gold Miners Swap Ownership,'' *Daily Deal,* November 14, 2003.

''Anglogold to Sell Mines to Harmony Gold for 127 Mln Rand,'' *Extel Examiner,* September 10, 1998.

Ashurst, Mark, ''Randgold Completes Unbundling Process,'' *Financial Times,* October 28, 1997, p. 35.

Bell, Terry, ''Liability Found in Harmony Case,'' *American Metal Market,* April 14, 1995, p. 5.

Burgert, Philip, ''Harmony, Baird Teaming Up to Sell New Gold Bar Online,'' *American Metal Market,* April 27, 2000, p. 9.

Curtin, Matthew, ''Production Setbacks Hit Randgold Mines,'' *Financial Times,* January 14, 1994, p. 28.

Damsell, Keith, ''Rea Gold Sells Bissett Mine,'' *Financial Post,* April 9, 1998, p. 4.

Gooding, Kenneth, ''Branded Gold Bars Generate Interest,'' *Financial Times,* March 2, 1998, p. 24.

——, ''Randgold Plans Low Cost Refining Experiment at Its Harmony Mine,'' *Financial Times,* July 19, 1996, p. 25.

''Goldfields, Delta Merger Gets Greenlight,'' *Australasian Business Intelligence,* September 18, 2001.

Graulich, Ilja, ''Gold Mines Consolidating,'' *Business Day,* February 7, 1999, p. 16.

Hagopian, Arthur, ''Harmony Chases Aussie Firm,'' *American Metal Market,* December 20, 2000, p. 7.

''Harmony Acquires Stake in High River Gold Mines Ltd.,'' *Canadian Corporate News,* November 11, 2002.

''Harmony/Arm Joint Venture Acquires Anglogold's Free State Mines,'' *E-M-J – Engineering & Mining Journal,* January 2002, p. 17.

''Harmony Gold Allowed to Market 1/3 of Gold Production Internationally,'' *Extel Examiner,* January 9, 1997.

''Harmony Gold Buys Steyn Shafts from Freegold for 85 Mln Rand,'' *Extel Examiner,* April 8, 1998.

''Harmony Gold Makes Takeover Bid for Australia's Hill 50,'' *AsiaPulse News,* December 11, 2001, p. 0500.

''Harmony Gold Mining – 4th Quarter & Final Results,'' *Regulatory News Service,* July 19, 1999.

''Harmony Gold Mining Co. Plans Further Acquisitions in Australia,'' *AsiaPulse News,* April 10, 2001, p. 0594.

''Harmony Gold to Set Up Commercial Scale Gold Refinery,'' *AFX News,* November 7, 1996.

''Harmony in Pursuit of Randfontein,'' *Africa News Service,* January 10, 2000.

''Harmony Puts in $50m to Mine Old Bendigo Gold Field,'' *Australasian Business Intelligence,* September 25, 2001.

Innocenti, Nicol Degli, ''Harmony Offers 'More Than $128m' for AngloGold Mines,'' *Financial Times,* November 28, 2000, p. 38.

McKay, David, ''Harmony Posts a Modest Profit,'' *Business Day,* January 22, 1998, p. 13.

——, ''Saaiplaas Losses Hit Harmony's Results,'' *Business Day,* October 21, 1997, p. 18.

Pisculli, Alysson, ''Harmony Gold Switching to NYSE to Reduce Volatility, Broaden Base,'' *American Metal Market,* November 20, 2002, p. 5.

——, ''Harmony Offers Gold Coins, Bars in Move to Dazzle Global Investors,'' *American Metal Market,* April 16, 2003, p. 6.

Roberts, Adrienne, ''Hedge Plans Push Gold to 16-Month Low,'' *Financial Times,* February 10, 2001, p. 21.

Ross, Priscilla, ''Harmony on Song,'' *African Business,* June 1999, p. 3.

''S. African Firm Picks Up 20% in Australia's Goldfields,'' *AsiaPulse News,* February 8, 2000, p. 0652.

—Mary Tradii

Harte-Hanks, Inc.

200 Concord Plaza Dr.
San Antonio, Texas 78216
U.S.A.
Telephone: (210) 829-9000
Fax: (210) 829-9403
Web site: http://www.harte-hanks.com

Public Company
Incorporated: 1928
Employees: 7,026
Sales: $944.6 million (2003)
Stock Exchanges: New York
Ticker Symbol: HHE
NAIC: 754186 Direct Mail Advertising Services; 541870
    Advertising Material Direct Distribution Services

Harte-Hanks, Inc. is a diversified direct marketing company offering a host of services to customers worldwide. The company's specialties include data analysis, strategic planning, and market research. Originally a newspaper business cofounded by Houston Harte and Bernard Hanks, over the years the company acquired additional interests in television and radio stations. In the 1970s it established a direct marketing segment, which became responsible for targeted mailings, advertising shoppers, telemarketing, and web sites featuring searchable databases of shopper ads. In the 1990s, as growth in the newspaper industry stalled, the company began to shift more of its resources to its direct marketing division, until it finally sold off its remaining newspaper and other media outlets to the E.W. Scripps Company in 1997. Today, Harte-Hanks, Inc. serves a range of clients in the retail, financial, pharmaceutical, technology, and health industries.

Partnership Between Rivals in the 1920s

Houston Harte, owner of the *San Angelo Standard,* and Bernard Hanks, owner of the *Abilene Reporter,* met for the first time at a publishers' meeting in Dallas in the early 1920s. Their papers, located only 90 miles apart, had for years competed fiercely in the primarily rural areas where their territories over-

lapped. That rivalry, which continued throughout their partnership, did not prevent the two from taking a liking to each other. When Harte heard about an opportunity to purchase a weekly in Lubbock, Texas, he joined with Hanks and another investor to purchase it. The partnership might have ended with the sale of that paper six years later; however, a new purchase by Harte and Hanks, of the *Corpus Christi Times,* sealed their relationship.

By then, both men had several decades of newspaper experience. Born in 1883 in Knob Noster, Missouri, Harte worked as a reporter for the *Los Angeles Examiner* while studying at the University of Southern California. In 1913, while finishing a journalism degree at the University of Missouri, Harte bought his first newspaper, the *Knob Noster Gem.* Three years later, Harte took over the *Central Missouri Republican,* based in Boonville. The U.S. entry into World War I briefly interrupted Harte's newspaper career; by 1920, however, Harte had returned to civilian life, selling his Missouri paper and moving to Texas, where he began publishing the *San Angelo Standard,* a paper founded in 1884. Harte worked to expand the paper's circulation, slowly widening its reach into 40 west Texas counties. In 1922 Harte purchased two more papers. Soon after that, he and Hanks formed their partnership.

Hanks, born in 1884, began his newspaper career as a horseback carrier for the *Abilene Reporter* when he was 12 years old. When Hanks's father moved to another town, Hanks moved in with *Reporter* publisher George Anderson. In 1907 Anderson incorporated his newspaper and allowed Hanks to purchase shares in the new company. In 1923 the company separated into two parts: Anderson took over the printing operation, while Hanks became the newspaper's publisher and owner.

After selling the Lubbock weekly, Harte and Hanks decided to remain partners. Harte had heard that the owner of a Corpus Christi paper, the *Times,* was having financial problems. Hanks and Harte took out an option to buy the paper, and went down to Corpus Christi to inspect it. As reported in a company publication, Harte recalled: "The *Times* was printed on an old flatbed press on a vacant lot in back of its building. . . . It was under a tarpaulin. It was quite a feat to print the paper out in the open in the South Texas rain." The partners nevertheless bought the paper.

Company Perspectives:

Our Business Philosophy: We operate select marketing-related businesses in markets where we can sustain a competitive advantage by adding value and meeting customer needs better than our competitors. We are innovative, flexible, and focused to respond proactively to opportunities and challenges in the market environment. We are results oriented—setting aggressive goals and improving our performance through hands-on management and active individual participation.

The *Corpus Christi Times* was then the number two paper in town; a dismal first year brought Harte-Hanks Newspapers only $2,800. Instead of fighting a newspaper war, the young partnership took a different approach: they formed a new partnership, called Texas Newspapers, Inc., with two other investors, and bought out the rival paper. Texas Newspapers would go on to buy several more Texas papers over the next three years, but moving into the Depression the partnership proved unprofitable and was disbanded. Harte-Hanks took control of the *Corpus Christi Times* and a second paper, the *Paris News,* in Paris, Texas. By then, Harte-Hanks had also added the *Big Spring Herald* to its newspaper chain. Nevertheless, the Harte-Hanks partnership remained a more or less informal arrangement, with no written contract. Harte tended to handle the operational and editorial end, while Hanks focused on the partnership's finances. Newspapers were primarily bought on credit, with the former publisher holding the note, and often a share in the newspaper as well. Harte-Hanks generally retained a newspaper's former management. Purchases usually involved buying a town's second paper, which often would suffer from poor circulation and operations.

Harte-Hanks added several more newspapers, all based in Texas, during the 1930s and 1940s. In 1945 the partners took on their first corporate employee, Bruce Meador, who would later become trustee of Hanks's estate. Bernard Hanks died in 1948. By then, the second generation—Houston H. and Ed Harte, and Andrew Shelton—were already learning the newspaper trade. The company continued adding newspapers to its fold. One acquisition, of the *Greenville Daily Banner,* sparked a bitter newspaper war that led Harte-Hanks to purchase and then consolidate the rival *Greenville Herald.* The owners of that paper took Harte-Hanks to court, charging them with unfair competition, but Harte-Hanks was acquitted of this charge.

Expanding into New Markets and New Media: 1960s–70s

During the 1960s, Harte-Hanks acquired a number of newspapers, including its largest to date, the *San Antonio Express-News.* By the end of the decade, Harte-Hanks controlled a 13-paper empire. In 1962 the company moved beyond newspapers for the first time with the purchase of KENS-TV, a CBS affiliate based in San Antonio. Prior to the Harte-Hanks acquisition, that station had been understaffed and underbudgeted and was consistently ranked last in its market. Under Harte-Hanks, however, the station's fortunes improved, and it quickly captured its

market's top rating, a position it would hold until the 1990s. The company moved its corporate headquarters from Abilene to San Antonio in 1968.

As the company moved into the 1970s, however, the family faced the future with uncertainty. Harte's health was failing, and the chain—made up of 27 family-owned corporations—offered no clear line of succession. New technology was also entering the newspaper industry, and the company worried about its ability to keep pace. Meador, who by then was running the company, approached outside consultants. They proposed three options for the company: do nothing, which might lead the company to break up; sell out; or go public. Over Harte's objections, the family chose the last option. Their first step, in 1971, was to consolidate the 27 corporations into a single entity, called Harte-Hanks Newspapers, Inc. Their next step was to find the person to lead the company into its initial public offering (IPO).

At about the same time, Robert G. Marbut, a graduate of the Harvard Business School and a former corporate director with Copley Newspapers, was making plans to start his own publishing company. Marbut approached Harte-Hanks for financial backing for his venture; instead, the Harte family proposed that Marbut lead their company instead. Harte-Hanks went public on March 13, 1972. Houston Harte died six days later.

Marbut set about transforming the company, instituting a modern control system, a budgetary process, market research, and, as a first for the company, a system of long-range planning. Marbut also took Harte-Hanks outside of Texas, beginning in 1971, by buying the *Journal-News* (Hamilton, Ohio). Other new markets included Ypsilanti, Michigan; Anderson, South Carolina; and Yakima, Washington. Funds raised in the IPO allowed the company to step up its expansion: by the end of 1972, the chain had more than doubled, to 27 newspapers. Importantly, Marbut began to transform the character of the newspapers themselves, adding lifestyle and other service features to the newspapers to boost their circulation, and turning at least some of the papers into what *Forbes* described as "aggressive marketing vehicles tailored for advertisers."

While adding new papers, Marbut also began shedding others. Harte-Hanks focused its chain on smaller markets where its newspapers could hold monopoly positions. The average circulation of these papers was 10,000 to 30,000. Larger papers—such as the *San Antonio Express-News,* bought by Rupert Murdoch for $19 million in 1973—were sold, with the exception of the Corpus Christi paper, which had a circulation of about 85,000. By 1974, the company's revenues had reached $79 million, with profits of $6.5 million, compared to income of around $1.5 million at the time of the company's IPO.

The number of available small-market papers was shrinking, however. To continue expanding company revenues, Marbut took Harte-Hanks deeper into other communications areas. In 1975 Harte-Hanks bought a second television station, WTLV in Jacksonville, Florida, an NBC affiliate. Two more stations were added by the end of the decade in Greensboro, North Carolina, and Springfield, Missouri. The company also moved into radio with the 1978 purchase of Southern Broadcasting's AM and FM station holdings. By then, Harte-Hanks had also begun to build its advertising shopper empire. While newspapers remained the

Key Dates:

1913: While finishing a journalism degree at the University of Missouri, Houston Harte buys his first newspaper, the *Knob Noster Gem.*

1923: Bernard Hanks becomes publisher and owner of the *Abilene Reporter.*

1928: Harte and Hanks establish a partnership.

1945: The partners take on their first corporate employee, Bruce Meador.

1948: Bernard Hanks dies.

1962: The company moves beyond newspapers for the first time with the purchase of KENS-TV, a CBS affiliate based in San Antonio.

1968: The company moves its corporate headquarters from Abilene to San Antonio.

1971: The family-owned network of 27 corporations is consolidated into a single entity, called Harte-Hanks Newspapers, Inc.; Robert G. Marbut takes over leadership of the company, extending its business interests outside Texas for the first time.

1972: Harte-Hanks goes public on March 13; Houston Harte dies six days later.

1977: The company changes its name to Harte-Hanks Communications, Inc. to reflect its diversified interests.

1978: The company moves into radio with the purchase of Southern Broadcasting's AM and FM station holdings.

1984: To avoid a hostile takeover, Marbut, Houston and Ed Harte, Andrew Shelton, and other corporate directors take the company private in a leveraged buyout.

1993: The company goes public for the second time.

1997: Harte-Hanks sells off remaining newspaper, television, and radio outlets in order to focus exclusively on direct marketing.

1998: The company changes its name to Harte-Hanks, Inc. to reflect a new focus on targeted marketing.

company's chief revenue source, its growing diversity prompted a name change, to Harte-Hanks Communications. Revenues jumped to $243 million in 1979. Income topped $19 million.

Radical Restructuring in the 1980s

By 1980, the company's holdings included 29 daily newspapers, 68 weekly newspapers, four VHF television stations, 11 radio stations, four cable television systems, and three trade publications. Its fastest-growing division was its Consumer Distribution Marketing (CDM) unit, which consisted of its advertising shoppers, three market research firms, and three direct mail distributors. Also included in CDM were electronic publishing and video entertainment software businesses. Moving into the recession of the early 1980s, Harte-Hanks's emphasis fell more heavily on CDM. As one analyst told the *New York Times,* "Harte-Hanks is much less newspaper-oriented than the other newspaper companies. It's more interested in information transfer. It's much more financially oriented." Marbut confirmed this, telling the *New York Times,* "Our job is not just to produce newspapers. Our job is to meet people's needs for information."

By 1983, CDM represented 28 percent of the company's revenues. Holdings had expanded to include 23 direct mail systems, seven research companies, a cable television shopping channel, seven delivery systems and a trucking service, and nine shoppers. Harte-Hanks' revenues neared $445 million, with earnings over $33 million, placing it on the *Fortune* 500 list. But the emphasis on CDM, as well as Harte-Hanks's plans to invest aggressively in cable television, had begun to make investors nervous: by 1984, the company's stock was trading below $20 per share, despite being valued as high as $30 per share. The company was becoming a potential target for a hostile takeover. To prevent this, Marbut, along with Houston and Ed Harte, Andrew Shelton, and other corporate directors, took the company private in a leveraged buyout (LBO).

The LBO, executed in 1984, saddled the company with $1 billion in debt, just as the Texas economy, crippled by the oil crash of the 1980s, was going sour. The company began streamlining its operations, quickly shedding 56 of its 113 units, including three of its four television stations, its cable television systems, and all of its radio stations. Sales of these units, of which all but three were profitable, brought $200 million to pay down debt. The company also traded seven of its Texas, Washington, Ohio, and Michigan papers for 19 papers in Dallas and Boston. By 1988, revenues had grown to $450 million, with operating income of $70 million. The company had reduced its debt to just $375 million in zero coupon debentures, bringing its interest payments down from $81 million paid in 1986 to $20 million.

By 1990, the company had reinvented itself. The company's restructuring had turned its focus to three key areas—the shoppers, by then zoned into 465 separate editions, reaching 5.8 million households, which made Harte-Hanks the largest distributor of advertising shoppers; direct marketing; and the company's nine newspapers. KENS-TV also continued to contribute a small share to the company's revenues. Marbut retired in 1991, turning the company over to Larry Franklin, his longtime chief operating officer and executive vice-president. By 1992, the company had reduced total long-term debt to less than $220 million. Yet, with stock divided among the Harte and Shelton families, the company once again faced a problem of succession. In 1993, the company went public for the second time.

Revenues grew to $463 million in 1993. But problems with Harte-Hanks's 14-paper Boston chain drove the company to a $52 million net loss that year. The company sold off the Boston papers in 1995. In the meantime, the company acquired Select Marketing, a high-tech industry marketer, and Steinert & Associates, another marketing group. With revenues topping $532 million in 1995, the company continued to shore up its marketing and high-technology industry capacities; its efforts included purchasing a minority interest in the SiteSpecific Internet ad-placement firm.

A New Direction for a New Century: The End of a Newspaper Business

By the mid-1990s, Harte-Hanks began to develop a new strategy tailored to the changing face of the news and marketing businesses. In recent years the newspaper industry had begun to stall, with distribution rates hitting a plateau in the 1980s, and the market over-saturated with competitors; under these circumstances, the company's newspaper business seemed to promise limited profitability for the foreseeable future. On the other hand, revenues in the direct marketing segment had demonstrated a consistently high rate of growth over the past several years. Circulation trends reinforced these conclusions: between 1986 and 1996, nationwide daily newspaper readership actually declined, dropping from 60.9 million to 58.6 million; over a similar period, the country's 3,000 shoppers saw circulation increase from 42 million to 51 million.

In order to capitalize on these developments, the company began to seek out strategic alliances and acquisitions in the late 1990s, in the hope of bolstering its profitable direct marketing division. In February 1996, the company announced its intention to purchase DiMark, Inc., a Pennsylvania-based direct marketing firm serving the pharmaceutical, telecommunications, and healthcare industries. Prior to the merger, Harte-Hanks specialized in providing marketing services to high-tech firms and financial institutions. With the addition of DiMark, the company saw a golden opportunity to expand its client base into new areas. That same year, Harte-Hanks acquired the Lead Management Group, a response-management company specializing in the high-tech sector, further bolstering its nationwide response-management network.

These acquisitions forecasted major changes for Harte-Hanks. The company's increased emphasis on marketing had already begun to pay off in the spring of 1997, when second quarter net earnings surpassed those from the previous year by 26.2 percent; by itself, the direct marketing business saw net earnings increase by nearly 37 percent. Meanwhile, the company had watched its newspaper revenues drop steadily between 1995 and 1997. Now firm in its belief that its future success lay in direct marketing, in May 1997 the company entered into a preliminary agreement with E.W. Scripps Company to sell off its remaining media outlets—six daily newspapers, 25 non-daily papers, a television station, and a radio station—for $775 million. With this sudden infusion of capital, Harte-Hanks planned to pay down its debt, as well as seek strategic acquisitions to bolster its direct marketing division. Although the Scripps deal did not become finalized until the end of the year, Harte-Hanks wasted no time executing its new strategy. The company's first purchase came in July 1997, when Harte-Hanks agreed to acquire four shoppers from The Walt Disney Company, for $104 million. The transaction raised the company's nationwide shopper circulation to 9.5 million, a 33 percent increase.

Toward the end of the decade, the company also found itself confronting new technological challenges. Facing the increasing complexity of communication in the information age, the company needed to develop a marketing strategy that utilized the potential of the Internet to transport data in a rapid and cost-effective manner. Harte-Hanks took one of its first steps toward achieving this goal in December 1998 when it acquired Spectral Resources Inc., a pharmaceutical data provider that specialized in Internet and CD-ROM technology. During this period the company also established a new subsidiary, Harte-Hanks Data

Technologies, which became responsible for developing a range of new products to address the company's growing electronic marketing needs. One of the key elements of the new subsidiary was its Trillium Software Division, which was soon creating innovative software solutions for a number of high-profile clients worldwide. In February 2004, Harte-Hanks acquired the British software company Avellino Technologies Ltd., integrating its product line into the Trillium Division.

Although Harte-Hanks was clearly positioning itself to remain competitive in an increasingly technological world, market fluctuations in the high-tech industry, combined with the costs of transforming the company's core business, delivered an initial blow to the company's revenues. Although profits rose 12.3 percent between 1999 and 2000, from $72.9 million to $81.9 million, in 2001 net earnings actually declined by 2.7 percent from the previous year, dropping to $79.7 million. With the American economy in turmoil, financial and technology sectors stalled, and the retail industry slashing marketing budgets, it remained to be seen whether or not Harte-Hanks would eventually emerge as a major player in the direct marketing industry.

Principal Subsidiaries

Harte-Hanks Market Research; Harte-Hanks Direct; Harte-Hanks Data Technologies; Harte-Hanks Logistics.

Principal Competitors

Acxiom Corporation; Experian Information Solutions Inc.; Valassis Communications, Inc.

Further Reading

Barrett, William P., "I'm Real Happy About the Way It's Turning Out," *Forbes*, April 18, 1988, p. 44.
Cropper, Carol Marie, "Harte-Hanks Sees the Future, and It's Marketing," *New York Times*, August 25, 1997, Section D, p. 9.
"The Education of Bob Marbut," *Forbes*, December 15, 1976, p. 53.
"Harte-Hanks Acquires Data Profiling Leader Avellino Technologies Ltd.," *Business Wire*, February 27, 2004.
Jones, Alex S., "A Media Industry Innovator," *New York Times*, April 30, 1984, p. D1.
Kleinfeld, N.R., "Rise of an Information Empire," *New York Times*, October 30, 1980, p. D1.
O'Donnell, Thomas, "Forget Glamour, He Will Deliver the Mail," *Forbes*, April 11, 1983, p. 166.
Phelps, Christi, "Harte-Hanks Charts Post-Divestiture Path," *San Antonio Business Journal*, March 2, 1987, p. 1.
Poling, Travis E., "San Antonio, Texas-Based Direct Marketing Firm Records Big Profit Increase," *San Antonio Express-News*, February 1, 2001.
Valentine, Tammy, "Harte-Hanks: The First 50 Years," *Harte-Hanks Commemorative Series*, San Antonio: Harte-Hanks Communications, Inc.
Williams, Norma Joe, and Dick Tarpley, "Harte-Hanks: The Founders," *Harte-Hanks Commemorative Series*, San Antonio: Harte-Hanks Communications, Inc.

—M.L. Cohen
—update: Stephen Meyer

Hutchinson Technology Incorporated

40 West Highland Park N.E.
Hutchinson, Minnesota 55350-9784
U.S.A.
Telephone: (320) 587-3797
Toll Free: (800) 689-0755
Fax: (320) 587-1810
Web site: http://www.htch.com

Public Company
Incorporated: 1965 as Hutchinson Industrial Corporation
Employees: 3,446
Sales: $498.9 million (2003)
Stock Exchanges: NASDAQ
Ticker Symbol: HTCH
NAIC: 334419 Other Electronic Component Manufacturing

Hutchinson Technology Incorporated (HTI), a high-tech firm located in the middle of rich farmland just west of Minneapolis, Minnesota, holds 60 percent of the worldwide market for hard disk drive suspension assemblies. Most personal computers contain its primary product, a thin metal spring that holds the recording head in position a few millionths of an inch from the disk. HTI designs and manufactures the close-tolerance components by using chemical, mechanical, and electronic technologies. The company shipped 526 million suspension assemblies in 2003, with more than 80 percent of revenues coming from five Asia-based manufacturers: SAE Magnetics, Ltd./TDK; Alps Electric Co., Ltd.; Seagate Technology LLC; Hitachi Global Storage Technologies; and K.R. Precision Co. In spite of the predominance of these Asian customers, HTI has remained an American manufacturer. All of its production is completed at four plants, which are located in Hutchinson; Sioux Falls, South Dakota; Eau Claire, Wisconsin; and Plymouth, Minnesota. HTI also maintains service offices in Singapore, Japan, China, Thailand, and the Netherlands.

Early Years As a Custom Component Maker

HTI developed out of the collaboration between Jon Geiss and Jeffrey Green. The men met in the early 1960s; they were neighbors in a Minneapolis apartment building. Geiss, an engi-

neer for Minnco Products, asked Green, a Sperry technical writer, to help with a manual for a photoetching process. The men became friends and shared an interest in photoetching. Thus when Geiss later suggested they develop a manufacturing business using the technology, Green agreed.

The men looked for a suitable, low-rent building in the metropolitan area of Minneapolis-St. Paul, but instead their first site became a chicken coop in Geiss's hometown of Hutchinson, 60 miles west of the Twin Cities. In 1965 the men established Hutchinson Industrial Corporation. Low on personal funds, they depended largely on private investors for financial backing, and paid rent and some other bills with company stock. Geiss moved to Hutchinson but Green stayed on at Sperry.

Their original idea was to use the photoetching technology to manufacture a lower-cost heater for gyroscopes in rocket guidance systems. That first venture failed to get off the ground, but they continued to look for new product ideas and business opportunities. A set of events opened up a door for the fledgling business, and they found their first customer: Green's employer, Sperry. By sending specifications and materials back and forth by bus between Hutchinson and Minneapolis, they put their photoetching and laminating equipment to its first real test. But the company's first big break came when Geiss persuaded a Control Data Corporation (CDC) buyer to allow the Hutchinson company to make a sample disk drive component. CDC liked what they saw, and Geiss and Green began manufacturing ferrite tracks. The down side of the deal was that CDC's disk drive manufacturing process was unique and therefore not marketable to other disk drive makers.

During the first decade of its existence Hutchinson Industrial produced a variety of components—mainly in small lots—for computer, satellite, medical, and even fake fur manufacturers. In 1972 the company began construction on a new building, eventually converting the chicken coop into a maintenance and equipment fabrication shop. The company continually reworked its photoetching processes: by the mid-1970s the company was using fourth generation equipment. They also added tool and die capabilities and laser welding. The upgraded facilities and technology helped the company finally land work with IBM in 1974. By 1975 Hutchinson employed 70 people and achieved revenues of $2.3 million.

Company Perspectives:

We will be the leader among all suppliers serving the disk drive market. As a leader we recognize that our people are the source of our strength and we will treat them with the highest regard. We will promote creativity, efficiency and vitality by encouraging involvement, teamwork and the development of our people.

We will expand our market opportunities and enhance our value by enabling disk drive manufacturers to advance their technology and capability. We will achieve this through cooperative product design with customers and by developing processes and product features that meet anticipated market needs.

We will fundamentally understand, develop, improve and leverage our competencies and technologies through product, process and system design to set the industry standard of performance and quality excellence.

We will maintain our market standing through delivery of products and services that provide the most value at the lowest total cost in the least amount of time. We will accomplish this by consistently achieving unequaled levels of quality, reliability, productivity, and flexibility. We will assure that the value delivered to our customers will be reflected in the return to our shareholders.

Catching the Early 1980s Wave of Personal Computer Production

The late 1970s brought an end to the majority of Hutchinson Industrial's small quantity production runs. The company refocused its energy on the disk drive market and brought on more technical people. Growth magnified the differences between founders Geiss and Green. In the early 1980s Geiss, who was CEO, tried and failed to convince the board of directors to accelerate business diversification in order to increase revenues. In 1982, Geiss decided to leave the company and sought a buyout for his 35 percent of the company stock. A struggle ensued between a Geiss faction and a newly organized Green faction. A resulting lawsuit was decided in Green's favor. Eventually, Geiss and other original shareholders accepted a buyout offer. Green became CEO, and Wayne Fortun took over as company president. Also in 1982, the business was renamed Hutchinson Technology Incorporated (HTI).

The early 1980s personal computer boom sent disk drive manufacturing into high gear. HTI grew rapidly, adapting and adding equipment, and hiring new employees to meet the demand for rigid disk drive components. HTI delivered its first thin-film suspension assemblies in 1983. High start-up costs and delays related to fine-tuning the new manufacturing processes kept profit margins low, but HTI proceeded to work on another new product, flexible circuits. The company ended the 1983 fiscal year with a net loss. Increased thin-film suspension assembly sales and revived suspension component shipments to a major customer pushed net sales for 1984 to $31.4 million, 95 percent higher than the previous year; net income was $3.2 million.

The addition of complex assembly manufacturing in 1985 helped boost net sales another 68 percent, to $52.7 million.

Fifty-five percent of that year's sales were in a volatile segment of the computer market. The components and assemblies HTI manufactured for the makers of small-and medium-sized computer systems were subject to rapid price and technology changes. The majority of HTI's remaining sales were in the large computer market, which was more stable. HTI also sold some flexible circuits to Honeywell, Teledyne, Hewlett Packard, and Textronix for use in military applications.

HTI offered its stock to the public for the first time in August 1985 for $10 per share. The newly issued stock lost as much as half of its value shortly after the offering of 1.6 million shares. In February 1986, Clinton H. Morrison of Dain Bosworth said the drop resulted from the combination of IBM order cutbacks and ''an unfavorable recommendation by one of the underwriters.'' But Morrison pointed out that HTI had developed and implemented difficult to duplicate manufacturing technologies, which were well respected by the industry, as evidenced by its market share. In spite of the setback, HTI remained profitable by implementing a production slowdown and employee layoffs.

Focus on Engineering and Expansion in the Late 1980s

The vertically integrated HTI adapted and combined high-tech processes including photoetching, laminating, and laser welding in order to keep pace with the rapidly changing disk drive industry. The company also implemented quality control programs and management systems designed to meet the expectations of its biggest customer. According to a September 1986 *Corporate Report Minnesota* article, direct sales to IBM accounted for about 50 percent of HTI revenues, and indirect sales by way of original equipment manufacturers boosted the figure even higher. In the same article an IBM procurement manager, Hud Sherlock, said of HTI, ''They continue to have a good record in terms of reliability, quality, and durability. We demand zero defects from our vendors, and Hutchinson Technology has done a lot to achieve that goal.'' Steve Marshall of Seagate said, ''Their reliability and pricing can't be beat. We had our own flexure assembly plant, but shut it down. We found we couldn't put them together for what they can do it for.''

In 1988 HTI's Green sparked a public controversy when he announced that the Minnesota business climate was a factor in the decision to open a plant in South Dakota. Newspaper columnists and editors, officials of the State of Minnesota, and other business leaders exchanged public barbs regarding the contention that workers' compensation laws, taxes, and the propensity of state government to involve itself in business matters were driving employers from the state. Regardless of the reason for choosing Sioux Falls, South Dakota, HTI needed the new facilities. The company turned out 1.9 million suspension assemblies a week, while the demand was for 2.2 million. In another move to increase available capacity, HTI began to phase out its low-margin complex assemblies.

The small-town company had expanded its horizons considerably under Green's leadership. In May 1988, Dave Peters described the company as being ''in the forefront of high-tech manufacturing techniques,'' which involved such things as maintaining low inventory, using worker clusters rather than assembly lines, and sharing volume and quality statistics with employees on a daily basis. In 1988 HTI opened sales and

Key Dates:

1965: Jon Geiss and Jeffrey Green found Hutchinson Industrial Corporation, working out of a chicken coop in Hutchinson, Minnesota; company spends first several years as a custom component maker.

Late 1970s: Company refocuses on the disk drive market.

1982: Geiss leaves the company, Green becomes CEO, and Wayne Fortun is named president; company changes its name to Hutchinson Technology Incorporated (HTI).

1983: HTI delivers its first thin-film suspension assemblies.

1985: Company goes public.

1988: HTI opens a second plant in Sioux Falls, South Dakota; sales and technical support offices are opened in Singapore and South Korea.

1995: Production begins at a third plant in Eau Claire, Wisconsin.

1996: Fortun is promoted to CEO, with Green staying on as chairman.

1999: Rapid adoption of trace suspension assemblies (TSAs) leads to record revenues of $580.3 million for the fiscal year; falling demand toward the end of the calendar year sets off a major restructuring that will involve the elimination of thousands of jobs from the workforce.

2003: Increasing demand for suspension assemblies and the previous years' cost-containment efforts yield record profits of $64.5 million.

technical support offices in Singapore and Seoul, South Korea; at that point, 40 percent of HTI products were sent to the Far East by either direct or indirect sales. The company also looked to the future by delving into production of detector cells for nuclear research and cancer treatment.

HTI began its 1989 fiscal year with its first quarterly loss since becoming a publicly held company; employee layoffs and cost-cutting measures were implemented. The company had just experienced an interval of heavy start-up expenditures and high employment and overtime costs, while the disk drive market weakened. In addition, consumers were showing a strong preference for 3.5-inch rather than 5.25-inch disk drive computer systems. Consequently, HTI was left with an inventory of the larger format components and retooling costs.

In February 1989 the company announced that it was holding acquisition talks with a Japanese company, Minebea Co. Ltd. HTI stock climbed to $15 per share, but fell to $9 after the company rejected the Minebea purchase bid as "grossly inadequate." In the second quarter of 1989, HTI was hit by more big losses and the criticism of financial analysts, some of whom maintained that with its dominance over its much smaller competitors, the company should be able to control pricing and be less susceptible to industry downturns. Fortun, HTI president, countered that their prices were already higher than competitors, and the trend in the disk drive market was for falling, not rising, prices. HTI ended 1989 with a loss of $5.7 million.

Fluctuations in the Early to Mid-1990s

HTI acted quickly to stop its downslide and entered the 1990s on an upswing. The disk drive industry backlog of inventory was down; orders for the smaller disk format were rising; and the low-profit complex assemblies were phased out of HTI's product mix. Although the company had lost some of its market share, it still held 60 percent of the suspension assembly market. Technology stocks as a whole were gaining strength, and HTI's price per share rose 42 percent within the first three months of 1990. Analyst Clinton Morrison noted in *Corporate Report Minnesota* that HTI's slump the previous year had pushed management to improve efficiencies and implement cost-cutting measures that had a positive effect on its profit margins. The company ended fiscal 1990 with record profits of $5.3 million on sales of $122 million.

HTI's stock price remained linked to the ups and downs of the industry and its own profit margins throughout the next year. Then, in spite of a decline in yearly profits, HTI stock skyrocketed. Dick Youngblood asserted in the *Minneapolis Star Tribune* that a number of long-term changes in the market and the company were behind the newly found investor confidence: the disk drive market was more stable because of a drop in the number of manufacturers; a line of HTI-designed suspension assemblies was well-received by the market; and the company was automating its manufacturing processes, spending $35 million over the previous three years and planning to spend an additional $18 million.

But HTI stock fell to less than half its 52-week high following a projected drop in third-quarter revenues and earnings. Technical problems had slowed production just as demand was rising, and efficiency and productivity had been hampered by a move to around-the-clock production. The bad news came on the heels of a $27.75 per share secondary stock offering in March. Morrison noted in the *Minneapolis Star Tribune* that some of the slide was due to the reaction of new investors who were unfamiliar with HTI's history of ups and downs. HTI stock recovered and climbed above the $40 mark in December, when the company announced expansion plans for both its Hutchinson and Sioux Falls plants.

Stock price volatility continued to hound HTI in 1993 as familiar problems related to growth and demand drove down earnings. Once again, HTI had to make rapid manufacturing adjustments as disk drive manufacturers flocked to buy the newly developed nano-sized suspension assembly. HTI was the only producer of suspension assemblies for the smaller, cheaper heads.

The company caught up with the demand for its nano-sized suspension assemblies by the end of the second quarter of its 1994 fiscal year. Suspension assemblies accounted for 97 percent of HTI's business in 1994; the remaining 3 percent was from etched and stamped components, welded assemblies, and laminated components. Eighty-five percent of all business came from its largest customers: Seagate Technology, Read-Rite Corp., Yamaha Corporation, IBM, and SAE Magnetics Ltd.

In 1995 HTI began work on a new plant in Eau Claire, Wisconsin, where production began in December. The firm also entered into a technology-sharing agreement with IBM to develop trace suspension assemblies (TSAs); this type of assembly included embedded copper electrical leads, allowing for more automation and more accuracy. The company shipped nine million suspension assemblies a week in the final quarter of the year. The nano-sized suspension assemblies accounted for nearly 90 percent of HTI suspension production for 1995. In addition, an even smaller suspension assembly—pico-sized—was put into production, anticipating future trends in the disk drive industry. Stock prices ranged from $27 to $91 in 1995. Net sales were $300 million, with net income of $21.1 million.

HTI stock continued to ride the highs and lows of the technology sector in 1996. Once again, company earnings were subject to production problems related to growth. HTI had nearly doubled its total number of employees during the most recent expansion drive. Wayne Fortun succeeded Jeffrey Green as CEO in 1996, but Green stayed on as chairman of the board. Fortun had already been acting as CEO without the title for the previous two or three years, and the leadership change marked the company's evolution from an entrepreneurial firm into what Fortun called "a larger, more methodical, systemic kind of company." Early in 1997, with the company stock trading at an all-time high, HTI announced a three-for-one stock split. For the fiscal year ending in September 1997, HTI posted record profits of $41.9 million on record sales of $453.2 million.

Lagging Demand, Staggering Losses, and Massive Restructuring: Late 1990s and Early 2000s

During 1998 HTI suffered from a serious decline in demand for disk drives and from start-up costs related to the new TSA assemblies. As a result, the firm lost $48.4 million and revenues fell to $407.6 million. HTI returned to profitability the following year, and its revenues reached a new high of $580.3 million thanks to the rapid adoption of the TSA assemblies, which sold for a much higher price than conventional assemblies. The TSA line represented 42 percent of total products shipped that year and 64 percent of overall revenues.

This turn of events proved short-lived, however. In the late 1990s advancements in disk drive technology were beginning to reduce the number of suspension assemblies required for each drive. Between 1997 and 2003, the average number of assemblies per drive fell from 6.7 to 2.3. This latest decline in demand sent HTI back into the red in 2000 and into a massive effort to cut costs and restructure. A series of six large staff reductions reduced the workforce from 7,701 to 4,729 employees during 2000. A $63.3 million charge for asset impairment and severance costs, along with an operating loss, added up to a net loss for the year of $73.6 million. Sales fell 21 percent that year, and the company stock fell below the $10 mark during the year, having traded as high as $51.25 the preceding year.

The slump continued in 2001, which saw a further drop in revenues as well as additional cost-cutting. The workforce was cut to fewer than 3,500 employees, and a $27.9 million charge was taken for asset impairment and restructuring. For the year, HTI suffered a net loss of $56.3 million.

HTI eked out a modest profit in 2002 but saw sales bottom out at $390.7 million. The real rebound came in fiscal 2003 when HTI shipped 526 million suspension assemblies, a 32 percent increase over the 2002 level. Revenues jumped more

than 27 percent, amounting to $498.9 million. Most impressive was the record net income figure of $64.5 million, which also translated into the company's best ever profit margin, 12.9 percent. Increased manufacturing productivity and higher use of manufacturing capacity aided the profit figure, as did the steadily increasing sales of more lucrative TSA assemblies. By 2003, 86 percent of the suspension assemblies sold by HTI were of the TSA variety. During the year, HTI also improved its share of the worldwide suspension assembly market from 55 percent to 60 percent. Nevertheless, with virtually all of the company's revenues deriving from the sale of suspension assemblies or the components of such assemblies (which were sold to competing makers of suspension assemblies), Hutchinson Technology was likely to remain extremely vulnerable to the volatility of the disk drive industry.

Principal Subsidiaries

Hutchinson Technology Asia, Inc.; Hutchinson Technology Service (Wuxi) Co., Ltd. (China).

Principal Divisions

BioMeasurement Division.

Principal Competitors

K.R. Precision Co.; Magnecomp International Limited; Nihon Hatsujo Kabusikigaisha; Fujitsu Limited; Suncall Corporation.

Further Reading

Alexander, Steve, "Big Cuts at Hutchinson Tech: Company Planning 950 Layoffs at Four Sites," *Minneapolis Star Tribune,* April 19, 2000, p. 1D.

Beal, Dave, "Corporate Survivor," *St. Paul Pioneer Press,* November 16, 2003.

Broderick, Richard, "Big Hutch on the Prairie," *Corporate Report Minnesota,* September 1986, p. 60.

Carideo, Anthony, "Computer Parts Maker Expects a Turnaround," *Minneapolis Star Tribune,* January 22, 1990, p. 1D.

——, "Local Computer-Related Firms Getting Deserved Recognition," *Minneapolis Star Tribune,* December 31, 1990, p. 1D.

——, "Stock of Hutchinson Technology Hurt by Slowdown in Disk Drive Market," *Minneapolis Star Tribune,* April 3, 1993, p. 2D.

Desilver, Drew, "Two Firms Square Off over Suspension Systems," *Minneapolis/St. Paul Business Journal,* March 17, 1997.

Feyder, Susan, "Riding Roller Coaster on Way to Top," *Minneapolis Star Tribune,* December 11, 1995, p. 1D.

Fiedler, Terry, "Driving Force: New CEO Fortun Keeps Steady Grip on the High-Flying Hutchinson Tech," *Minneapolis Star Tribune,* February 28, 1997, p. 1D.

Fredrickson, Tom, "Hutchinson in Overdrive As Staff, Plants Expand," *Minneapolis/St. Paul CityBusiness,* January 21, 1994, p. 6.

——, "Hutchinson Spends $2 Million to Build New Training Center," *Minneapolis/St. Paul CityBusiness,* October 7, 1994, p. 2.

——, "Minnesota Growth 40," *Minneapolis/St. Paul CityBusiness,* July 21, 1995, p. 7.

Grover, Mary Beth, "Keep Them in Suspension," *Forbes,* January 26, 1998, pp. 85–86.

McCartney, Jim, "Acquisition Offer Is Rejected by Hutchinson Technology," *St. Paul Pioneer Press Dispatch,* March 23, 1989.

——, "Hutchinson Technology Reports Heavy Losses," *St. Paul Pioneer Press Dispatch,* March 21, 1989.

Meyers, Mike, ''Hutchinson Technology Selects Eau Claire,'' *Minneapolis Star Tribune,* March 21, 1995, p. 1.

Morrison, Clinton H., ''Periscope—Hutchinson Technology, Inc.,'' *Corporate Report Minnesota,* February 1986, p. 111.

Past . . . Present . . . Future . . . , Hutchinson, Minn.: Hutchinson Technology Incorporated, July 1994.

Peters, Dave, ''He Makes Business Climate His Business,'' *St. Paul Pioneer Press Dispatch,* May 9, 1988, p. 1.

——, ''Tech Firm Picks S.D. Site,'' *St. Paul Pioneer Press Dispatch,* March 10, 1988.

Peterson, Susan E., ''Hutchinson Technology Plans to Expand Two Plants,'' *Minneapolis Star Tribune,* December 10, 1992, p. 3D.

Phelps, David, ''Hutchinson Technology Confidence Crisis Called Blip,'' *Minneapolis Star Tribune,* March 4, 1996, p. 1D.

Reilly, Mark, ''Hutchinson Defies Slump As Sales, Stock Price Climb,'' *Minneapolis/St. Paul Business Journal,* December 16, 2002.

Youngblood, Dick, ''CERN Buys Hutchinson Firm's Cells,'' *Minneapolis Star Tribune,* August 22, 1988, p. 1D

——, ''What's Behind Big Run-up in Hutch Tech's Stock?'' *Minneapolis Star Tribune,* February 10, 1992, p. 2D.

Yu, Roger, ''Hutchinson Tech Will Eliminate 500 Jobs,'' *Minneapolis Star Tribune,* August 5, 1999, p. 1D.

—Kathleen Peippo
—update: David E. Salamie

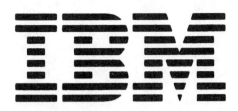

International Business Machines Corporation

New Orchard Road
Armonk, New York 10504
U.S.A.
Telephone: (914) 499-1900
Toll Free: (800) 426-3333
Fax: (914) 765-4190
Web site: http://www.ibm.com

Public Company
Incorporated: 1911 as Computing-Tabulating-Recording
  Company
Employees: 316,303
Sales: $89.1 billion (2003)
Stock Exchanges: New York
Ticker Symbol: IBM
NAIC: 334111 Electronic Computer Manufacturing;
  334112 Computer Storage Device; 334113 Computer
  Terminal Manufacturing; 334119 Other Computer
  Peripheral Equipment Manufacturing; 333313 Office
  Machinery Manufacturing; 334210 Telephone
  Apparatus Manufacturing; 334290 Other
  Communications Equipment Manufacturing; 334613
  Magnetic and Optical Recording Media
  Manufacturing; 333315 Photographic and
  Photocopying Equipment Manufacturing; 339944
  Carbon Paper and Inked Ribbon Manufacturing;
  541511 Custom Computer Programming Services;
  511210 Software Publishers; 541512 Computer
  Systems Design Services; 518210 Data Processing
  and Related Services; 518111 Internet Service
  Providers; 541513 Computer Facilities Management
  Services; 532420 Office Equipment Rental and
  Leasing; 811212 Computer and Office Machine
  Repair; 541519 Other Computer Related Services;
  541613 Marketing Consulting Services; 541612
  Human Resource Consulting Services

International Business Machines Corporation (IBM) is the largest computer maker in the world. Because of its enormous size, power, and success, and because it sells that most modern of tools, the computer, IBM has come to symbolize modern life itself for many. The company's nickname—Big Blue—is a phrase that may have been originally suggested by IBM's army of uniformly dressed salesmen, whose dark suits and white shirts were required by the firm's leader, Thomas Watson, Sr., who transformed the Computing-Tabulating-Recording Company (CTR) into a world leader in information technology.

Company Origins

CTR was formed in 1911 by Charles Runlet Flint. The so-called "father of trusts" merged two of his earlier creations, International Time Recording Company and Computing Scale Company of America, with a third, unrelated entity known as Tabulating Machine Company. The latter had been founded some years before by Herman Hollered, an engineer who invented a machine that would sort and count cards based on the pattern of holes punched in each.

Hollered had supplied the U.S. Census Bureau with these machines for use in the 1890 and 1900 censuses, and the device was quickly adopted by other organizations in need of rapid computation. As perfected, the tabulator operated in a simple three-step manner. Small cards were punched in a variety of patterns, each one representing a different category of the subject under survey; the assembled cards were run through a sorting machine, set to distribute them according to relevant categories; at the same time an accounting machine kept track of the results, and, in the later, more sophisticated models, performed any number of calculations based on those results.

Such a machine found increasing use in a society evolving rapidly into a largely urban, commercial matrix, where the ability to monitor and analyze large sums was critical to business profitability. Flint was less interested in Tabulating Machine Company than in the other two members of his new creation, which in any case got off to a slow start and threatened to stay that way.

In 1914 Flint hired a new general manager for CTR. Thomas Watson was already a well-known, if not notorious, figure in U.S. business. Watson had gone to work for John Patterson at National Cash Register (NCR) in 1895 and quickly proven himself a quintessential "NCR man"; bright, aggressive, and loyal, he rose to the position of general sales manager for the entire company in 1910. At Patterson's order, Watson then set up a company whose supposed purpose was to compete with NCR. The company's real purpose, however, was to eliminate NCR's competitors. In 1912, along with John Patterson, his former employer at NCR, Watson was convicted of violating the Sherman Antitrust Act on behalf of the company. Shortly after Watson and Patterson were convicted, Patterson fired Watson. Watson was then hired by Charles Flint. Watson never admitted any wrongdoing, and in 1915 the government dropped its case against NCR after the company became famous for its help during a catastrophic flood in its hometown of Dayton, Ohio. The threat of a jail sentence now past, Watson was made president of CTR.

Watson understood immediately that his company's future lay in its tabulating division, and it was there that he committed most of his energy and resources. Scales and clocks were useful items, but the United States would soon be a nation of office workers in need of basic office tools like the tabulator. Watson hired many ex-NCR men and patterned his own well-disciplined sales force along NCR lines—intense competition was combined with equally intense corporate loyalty, and salespeople were courteous, spotlessly dressed, and, above all, understood that CTR sold not a product but a service. A completed sale was just the beginning of the salesman's job; in effect, he had to become a partner in the customer's business, and together they designed a tabulating system for that particular organization.

As was the case at NCR, Watson's sales force became a key factor in his company's success. In a pattern that still holds today, many customers remained loyal because they trusted and to an extent relied upon the CTR salesman's knowledge of their business. Numerous, well-trained, devoted, and well-paid, the CTR sales staff actually dominated the company, ensuring that new technology followed upon the needs of customers and not the reverse. Throughout IBM's history (the company's name was changed to International Business Machines Corporation in 1924) massive and talented sales energy, rather than technological leadership, kept the company ahead of competitors.

Watson pushed hard in the late 1910s to make CTR the industry leader in tabulating design. He gradually turned back all boardroom challenges to his plans, and by 1925, was both chief executive officer and chief operating officer. In the ten years following Watson's arrival, CTR sales shot up from $4.2 million to a temporary peak of $13 million in 1919, weathered a minor crisis in the early 1920s, and stood poised to ride the booming U.S. economy. The newly named IBM faced some formidable competitors—Remington Rand, Burroughs, and NCR, among others—but from the beginning Watson steered clear of mass-produced, low-priced office products like typewriters and simple adding machines, concentrating instead on the design of large tabulating systems for governmental and private customers. With superior products and a more dedicated sales force, by 1928 IBM was the clear leader in its specialized field and a force in office technology as a whole.

Booming Sales: 1920s–50s

The company was remarkably profitable. In 1928, for example, its profit of $5.3 million was nearly as great as that of giant Remington Rand, though the latter more than tripled IBM's sales of $19.7 million. In 1939, IBM's profit of $9.1 million exceeded that of the next four companies combined, and held an impressive 23 percent of sales.

IBM's business was particularly profitable for several reasons: the company focused on large-scale, custom-built systems, an inherently less competitive segment of the business; IBM's policy of leasing, rather than selling, its machines to customers was very profitable; and IBM maintained cross-licensing agreements dating back to the mid-1910s with its chief competitor, Remington Rand, preventing the two leaders from falling into competitive squabbles. The company required its customers to buy IBM cards for their IBM tabulators. The cards could not be read by any other machine. This last condition made it almost impossible for IBM customers to try other products. With literally millions of such cards already punched, IBM's clients tended to stay put.

The U.S. government filed a suit in 1932 alleging that the IBM-Remington Rand cross-licensing agreement and IBM's exclusive punch card design were anti-competitive. In 1936, after learning that IBM sold nearly 85 percent of all keypunch, tabulating, and accounting equipment in the United States, the Supreme Court ordered IBM to release its customers from all such card restrictions. The Court's decision had little impact on the company's growth, however. Even the Great Depression did not check IBM's progress, as most cash-pressed companies needed more numerical information, not less.

In addition, President Franklin D. Roosevelt's New Deal had created a large federal bureaucracy in need of the very calculating machines IBM manufactured. In 1935, at the same time the Justice Department was pursuing its case against IBM, the newly formed Social Security Administration placed an order with the company for more than 400 accounting machines and 1,200 keypunchers. The pattern was clear; modern society rested on massive organizations that required machines capable of massive calculations, which were made by IBM. By the end of the 1930s Thomas Watson was enjoying praise for his enlightened employee relations as well as for his "thinking machines."

Key Dates:

1900: The International Time Recording Company (ITR) is formed.

1901: Computing Scale Company of America is incorporated.

1910: Charles R. Flint organizes the merger of ITR, Computing Scale Company, and Tabulating Machine Company to form Computing-Tabulating-Recording Company (CTR), IBM's predecessor.

1914: Thomas J. Watson is hired as CTR's general manager; within a year, he is promoted to president.

1920: CTR introduces the first complete school time control system, the lock autograph recorder.

1924: Company develops Carroll Rotary Press to produce cards at high speed, doubling punched card capacity; CTR's name is officially changed to International Business Machines Corporation (IBM).

1944: IBM completes the Automatic Sequenced Control Calculator, also called the Mark I; it is the first machine to automatically complete long computations.

1949: Company introduces the 604 Electronic Calculating Punch, the first IBM product designed specifically for computation centers.

1952: Company introduces the IBM 701, the first vacuum-tube based large computer; Thomas J. Watson retires as IBM's president, allowing his son, Thomas J. Watson, Jr., to take over (he becomes CEO upon his father's death in 1956).

1957: Company introduces the IBM 305 Random Access Method of Accounting and Control (RAMAC), the first computer disk storage system.

1965: IBM introduces the System/360, the first large grouping of computers to use interchangeable software.

1971: Thomas J. Watson, Jr., steps down as CEO; T. Vincent Learson takes over temporarily, until Frank T. Cary steps in (1973); IBM introduces the floppy disk.

1973: Company sells a laser device to supermarkets, which is used to automatically read product prices at checkout stands; company introduces the IBM 3614 Consumer Transaction Facility, an early form of the Automatic Teller Machine.

1981: The IBM personal computer (PC) is introduced; John R. Opel becomes CEO.

1985: John F. Akers takes over as CEO, leading IBM to four Nobel Prizes in physics.

1993: After struggling with changes in the PC world, IBM's net losses exceed $8 billion; Louis V. Gerstner, Jr., becomes IBM's CEO, the first to be hired outside of the company's ranks.

2002: Samuel J. Palmisano becomes IBM's CEO.

During World War II both private and governmental demand for IBM tabulators increased. The machines were needed to monitor the manufacture and movement of vast resources. Sales boomed, more than tripling to $141.7 million in five years. The war offered IBM another opportunity, less immediately exciting but in the long run of far greater importance. The armed forces needed high-speed calculators to solve a number of military problems relating to ballistics and, later, the development of the atomic bomb. Partly as a result, IBM helped build what might be called the world's first computer, the Mark I. This machine was similar to the first electromechanical calculators built a few years earlier, which used IBM punch cards to work out long arithmetic sums; the Mark I was also capable of retaining a set of rules which could be applied to any later input. Such a memory is one of the essential differences between the calculator and the computer, and the Mark I represented a great step forward. With 765,000 parts and 500 miles of wire, the Mark I still delivered less power than today's hand-held calculator.

Entering the Early Computer Market

Computer design evolved rapidly during the war. IBM joined the partnership building the new Electronic Numerical Integrator and Calculator (ENIAC) at the University of Pennsylvania. ENIAC was useful to the military and gave IBM the experience it needed to precede with its own electronic machine. When the war ended in 1945, interest in ultra-high-speed calculators died down quickly; few outside the Army needed a room-sized machine designed to analyze howitzer trajectories. Only a handful of scientists continued refining the advances won by ENIAC, eventually creating a more saleable machine called UNIVAC around 1948. When IBM's old rival, Remington Rand, began to market UNIVAC in 1951, it took a significant lead in the new computer business. IBM continued its typically cautious approach. IBM waited until the new product proved its lasting appeal before leaping into the fray. Since it controlled 85 percent of the market for which computers were targeted, and because even electronic computers then still used IBM punch cards, Watson was not especially alarmed by Rand's success.

Heir apparent Thomas Watson, Jr., strongly favored an all-out push into the computer market. By the time he became president in 1952, he had won the power struggle with his father and led IBM into an immense research program designed to surpass Rand. The new president staked his reputation—as well as a significant portion of IBM's assets—on the computer campaign, which had paid off by 1955 with the success of IBM's new 705 general purpose business computer. By the following year Remington Rand had already lost its lead. It was no surprise that IBM came to dominate in computers so quickly, since at that time the computer business was only a small segment of the office products market, which IBM continued to control. The 85 percent of offices using IBM tabulating equipment simply switched over to IBM computers.

In 1949 Thomas Watson's younger brother, Dick Watson, was also brought into the business. The 30-year-old Dick Watson was named president of IBM World Trade Corporation, the parent company's new subsidiary for international sales. In 1949 World Trade had sales of only $6.3 million but operated in 58 countries. In the more prominent of these countries World Trade set up a subsidiary to market IBM products and even do additional research and development. As the world's industrial powers awoke to the computer age, they found themselves greeted by IBM. It was not unusual for local IBM units to achieve market domination comparable to that of the parent company in the United States. Only in Japan and the United Kingdom were local competitors able to match IBM's presence, forcing the latter to settle for around 33 percent of the market. Barely on the sales map in 1949, World Trade eventually surpassed IBM domestic in total revenue.

Meanwhile, the U.S. computer business filled up with potential rivals. Some of these, like RCA, General Electric, and the newly merged Sperry Rand, were as large as or larger than IBM and should have been able to mount a serious challenge. In every case, however, competitors either lacked an adequate sales organization or were not fully committed to the commercial computer business. RCA, for example, made important contributions to computer technology, but mainly with an eye toward possible applications in its growing television business. Sperry Rand, on the other hand, still controlled the successful UNIVAC machine but was hopelessly behind IBM in sales experience and customer loyalty.

In 1952 the government filed a second, more ambitious antitrust suit against IBM. In 1956 IBM entered into a consent decree, which ordered it to divest many of its card-production facilities, sell its machines as well as lease them, submit to certain cross-licensing agreements, and create a subsidiary to compete with itself in the service end of the business. None of these injunctions limited IBM's success, but the 1957 appearance of a small company called Control Data did.

IBM Computer Dominance Through the 1970s

Control Data Corporation (CDC) was a pioneer in niche specialization in the computer world. This tactic seemed to be the only way to compete successfully with IBM. The newcomer made very large, very fast computers for scientific and governmental users in need of maximum crunching power, and after a brief battle, IBM largely ceded the field to CDC. IBM's bread and butter remained the medium to large business computer.

In 1958 Sperry Rand and Control Data brought out the first second generation computers, which used transistors instead of vacuum tubes. No sooner had IBM met this challenge with its own line of transistorized machines, than it faced the arrival of the industry's third generation—integrated circuitry. Once again IBM lagged in technological change as Honeywell and CDC brought out the first integrated circuit units in the early 1960s, but this time Big Blue's response necessitated a companywide revolution. Integrated circuitry was clearly destined to become the industry standard, and IBM decided to bring out a complete line of such computers. After an unprecedented capital-spending program involving six new plants and many thousands of new workers, the company introduced its 360 line in April 1965. Small, fast, and accompanied by a new set of exclusive software, the 360s were an immediate and lasting success, remaining the worldwide computer leader for more than a decade.

Sperry Rand, GE, Burroughs, RCA, Honeywell, NCR, and Control Data were unable to close the gap between themselves and IBM, which now delivered 65 percent of all U.S. computers. Control Data filed yet another antitrust suit in 1968, charging that IBM had sold "phantom" computers to its customers to keep them from placing orders for superior CDC products. The government filed its own suit the following year, supporting CDC's claims and alleging other monopolistic practices. Encouraged by these efforts, IBM's competitors, big and small, filed 22 similar lawsuits in the next few years. IBM beat back every one of them, however, with one exception. The U.S. Justice Department continued its battle for 13 years, until President Ronald Reagan's administration dropped the suit shortly before a ruling was expected.

Niche specialization was clearly the only way to survive in the face of IBM's power. In 1960 Digital Equipment Corporation (DEC) brought out a relatively small, inexpensive computer designed for researchers, effectively creating the microcomputer business. Micros were only a further step in the evolution of the computer, but IBM chose not to enter the market. DEC was soon joined by a host of other micro manufacturers offering a wide range of computers for ever smaller tasks, culminating years later in Apple's marketing of the personal computer for home use. IBM failed to join this race until 1980, at which late date it was unable to dominate the market, as it did mainframes and minicomputers.

In 1971 Tom Watson retired from IBM after suffering a heart attack. His successor, Frank Cary, remained in charge until 1981, at which time John Opel was named CEO. Under these men and IBM's present chairman, John Akers, the 360 line of computers grew into the 370, sales continued to climb, and in the golden year of 1984 corporate earnings reached a staggering $6.6 billion on revenue of $46 billion. With a return on shareholders' equity of 25 percent, IBM was the unchallenged favorite of Wall Street and perceived by many in Washington as the only U.S. company able to hold its own against Japanese competition. The firm was profiled in a bestselling book as a paradigm of business excellence.

Losing Ground in the 1980s

The years following were not nearly so kind to IBM. A drop in earnings for 1985 was dismissed as inevitable after the glory year of 1984, but by the end of the decade financial analysts were convinced that IBM was in need of an overhaul. Revenue growth was slow and earnings weak by IBM standards, resulting in a long decline in the company's stock price, and its share of the worldwide computer market had fallen from 36 percent to 23 percent. Chairman Akers responded by cutting his workforce by 32,000 (from a 1985 peak of 405,000) and urged a return to IBM's traditional strength in marketing and customer relations. After a good year in 1990, however, revenue in 1991 fell for the first time since the 1940s and Akers was widely quoted as saying that the company faced a crisis.

By historical standards, he was correct: Big Blue was losing ground. The dip in revenues could be explained as part of the severe 1990–91 recession that took its toll on the entire computer industry, but clearly IBM was no longer the juggernaut it had been during most of its history. Underlying its sluggish growth was a fundamental change in the nature of the computer industry, and that was change itself—the continually accelerating rate of technological breakthrough in the world of data processing. So long as computers had remained primarily large and very expensive machines designed for number crunching (mainframes), it was possible for IBM to keep its dominant position by simply building bigger and faster machines.

The increasing power of semiconductor chips changed all of that, however; computers became smaller and were applied to a greatly broadened range of tasks. The mini, micro, and workstation technologies all tended to undercut the value of monolithic mains, and independent breakthroughs now tended to focus on software and the crucial problem of networks, the means by which computers communicate with each other and with other forms of data transmission such as telephone and video. Sheer computing power remained important, of course, but it became available in a far greater range of machines at prices that dropped every week.

Given these changes, IBM faced a vastly more complex marketplace both in terms of niches and in the number of its competitors around the world. A wide consensus of observers agreed that IBM's enormous size was a drawback in the quicksilver markets of the 1990s, and in November 1991 Chairman Akers announced the dawn of a new era at the company. Each division of IBM would become a semi-detached business, responsible for its own decisions and bottom-line results. The details of this centrifugal structure transformed IBM into becoming a type of holding company with possibly dozens of discrete operating units under its loose administration. It was hoped that IBM's PC (personal computer) division, for example, would be better able to respond to customer needs and a changing marketplace than when it was forced to take its decisions to company headquarters before acting; and similarly with IBM's mains, minis, software, maintenance, and the many other parts of this $70 billion-per-year corporation.

New Management in the Mid-1990s

Akers had sold the copier division to Kodak in 1988 and followed up in 1991 with the sale of Lexmark, IBM's typewriter, personal printer, keyboard, and supplies business. The divestiture plan had not progressed far, however, when Akers was fired in 1993 and replaced by Lou Gerstner, former CEO of RJR Nabisco. Gerstner scrapped the plan and set about revitalizing the company.

Turning IBM's size and diversity to its advantage, Gerstner expanded the company's small services division, making it a place customers could come for network solutions. By recommending products appropriate for each customer rather than simply pushing IBM goods, Global Services grew rapidly. By 1995 it surpassed Electronic Data Systems (EDS) to become the largest computer services business in the world.

One of the divisions slated to be sold in the divestiture plan was IBM Research, notorious for its long-term research into technologies that never were translated into saleable products. With an $8.9 billion loss in 1993, IBM was searching for costs to cut. Gerstner, however, refused to sell off the division, although he did trim the $6 billion budget by $1 billion. Researchers were also instructed to spend more time working directly with customers, focusing on solutions for real customer problems. The changes led to the resignation of many of the company's scientists. Despite the new focus on the bottom line, the research division continued to lead the industry in patents each year through the 1990s.

By 1994 Gerstner's turnaround strategy was already bearing fruit: The company posted a profit for the first time since 1990. IBM was helped in its recovery in the mid-1990s by the massive growth of the Internet. Although the company abandoned its browser and sold its Prodigy online service, the company benefited from the Internet boom through sales of the big servers needed to run it. IBM also began helping customers move onto the Internet by creating web sites and establishing e-commerce.

In the mid-1990s IBM moved into new areas of the computing industry. In 1994 it signed an agreement with Cyrix to manufacture its computer chips. The following year it purchased Lotus Development, a software company best known for its office software, for $3.5 billion. IBM saw the company's Notes groupware, designed to help a company's staff communicate more effectively, as helpful in its foray into networked desktop computing. Remaining at its Boston headquarters, Lotus continued as an independently run subsidiary, with very little interference from IBM. With IBM's resources and distribution network supporting Lotus, Notes users rose from two million in 1995 to 22 million by 1998. IBM benefited by including the Lotus software in a package of applications called eSuite. In 1996 IBM gave a boost to its software planning for networks by purchasing Tivoli Systems Inc., which specialized in creating tools for network management.

By 1996 IBM's recovery seemed solid, with a $50 billion rise in its market value since 1993. The company's image got a boost in 1997 when its computer Deep Blue won a six-game chess match against World Class Champion Garry Kasparov. The computer, which used huge amounts of parallel processing, could evaluate 200 million chess moves a second, a processing capability the company hoped could be used in such endeavors as weather forecasting and modeling financial data.

Difficult Times in Late 1990s Leading to Prosperity in 2000s

IBM continued to expand via new product development and acquisitions through the late 1990s. In 1997 the company bought Unison Software, which specialized in managing computer systems, and in 1998 purchased CommQuest Technologies, a designer and manufacturer of wireless communications chips. Other smaller purchases included a majority holding in site development software company NetObjects in 1998 and NUMA systems expert Sequent Computer Systems in 1999.

The company's shift to providing services had progressed well by the late 1990s. Services accounted for 29 percent of IBM's revenues in 1998 and 39 percent of pretax profits. By 1999, e-business service revenue alone exceeded $3 billion, a

60 percent increase from 1998. Also in 1999, IBM acquired two new technology companies—Sequence Computer Systems and Whistle Communications—and signed contracts exceeding $15 billion with several other technology companies: Dell Computer Corporation, Acer Incorporated, Cisco Systems, Inc., and Nintendo Company, Ltd.

Y2K, the fear that all computer-related systems would malfunction upon entering the year 2000, caused financial difficulties for IBM in 1999, decreasing server revenue 17.9 percent from 1998. In 2000, with financial distress lingering, IBM focused on strict management of costs and expenses. It also continued to concentrate on service. In the year, demand for services and products dramatically increased (as fears of Y2K subsided), so much that IBM could not always meet customer needs. But by 2000's end, while IBM's earnings rose 16 percent, the value of stock decreased 21 percent, from $108 to $85. This decline partly reflected the state of the stock market, as 2000 watched nearly all information technology stocks decrease in value.

In 2001 the financial situation for IBM turned gloomy, as the company lost nearly $3 billion in overall revenue, decreasing net income from $8 billion to $7.7 billion. IBM's CEO V. Gerstner, Jr., attributed the losses to a sluggish technology economy and a decline in personal computers and hard disk drives. Still, IBM continued to perform relatively well in the areas of services, software, zSeries servers, and high-end storage. The company continued its focus on cutting costs, but 2002 did not fare any better for IBM.

Gerstner was replaced as CEO by the company's president, Samuel. J. Palmisano, but the new CEO would not immediately improve IBM's finances. Under new leadership, the company invested heavily in the areas of research and development, capital expenditures, and acquisitions. For one, IBM acquired PricewaterhouseCoopers' global business consulting and technology services unit, PwC consulting, for $3.5 billion in cash and stock. As a result, IBM created a new global business unit, IBM Business Consulting Services, which became part of IBM Global Services. In the same year, IBM introduced a number of new products, including the eServer z800, an entry-class mainframe and eServer p650, which immediately became the world's most powerful eight-way UNIX server. Innovation aside, IBM ended 2002 with an earnings decrease of 35 percent, to $5.3 billion.

Palmisano turned focus on an on-demand business management technique, a strategy IBM pegged "e-business on demand." The strategy, according to IBM, would help to further meet customer demands, as well as to take better advantage of market opportunities and to ward off external threats. The strategy proved sound, as 2003 total revenue improved by 10 percent, or nearly $8 billion, from 2002, with global services contributing close to $6 billion of this. In addition, gross profits rose almost $3 billion from 2002.

The year 2003 also witnessed further innovation at IBM, including the introduction of the world's most advanced server, the eServer z Series 990; the eServer p690 system, offering 65 percent more speed than its predecessor; and two new high-end iSeries servers: iSeries 825 and 870. IBM concluded 2003 with

the sale of the 20 millionth ThinkPad since introducing the ThinkPad line of laptops in 1992.

Success followed IBM into 2004. To begin the year, IBM and Unica Corporation signed a lucrative contract with BJ's Wholesale Club for a new marketing platform that would personalize interactions with BJ's members. At the same time, IBM broke the record for patents received in a single year, with 3,415 for new products. One such product, introduced in 2004, was the IBM eServer Blade Center HS40, the most powerful and flexible (and smallest) 4-way blade server available.

With continually increasing revenues and a recovering economy, IBM looked toward growth, including plans to acquire Candle Corporation, which specialized in infrastructure management information. Further innovation was anticipated, specifically concerning IBM's semiconductor manufacturing facility, for which IBM accepted a $325 million investment from Sony Group for the use of chip production.

Principal Subsidiaries

IBM Credit LLC.; IBM International Foundation; IBM International Services Corp.; IBM Business Transformation Center, SRL; Tivoli Systems, Inc., IBM World Trade Corp.; IBM Plans Management Corp; IBM Foreign Sales Corp.; WTC Insurance Corporation, Ltd. (Bermuda); IBM Canada Credit Services Co.; IBM Canada Limited-IBM; IBM Argentina Sociedad Anonima (99.99%); IBM de Bolivia SA (99.98%).; IBM Brasil-Industria, Maquinas E Servicos Limitada (Brazil; 99.99%); IBM de Chile SA (99.99%); IBM de Columbia SA (90%); IBM Del Ecuador; Grupo IBM Mexico S.A. de C.V. (99.99%); IBM del Peru SA (99.99%); IBM Del Uraguay SA; IBM de Venezuela SA; IBM A/NZ Holdings Pty, Ltd. (Australia); IBM Australia Ltd.; IBM New Zealand Ltd; IBM India Ltd (99.99%); PT IBM Indonesia (99%); YK IBM AP Holdings; IBM Japan, Ltd; IBM Korea, Inc.; IBM Malaysia SDN BHD; IBM Philippines, Inc. (99.99%); IBM Thailand Company Ltd (99.99%); IBM Israel Ltd (99.99%); IBM Turk Limited (Turkey; 98%); IBM South Africa Group Ltd.; IBM China Company Ltd.; IBM Central Holding GMBH (Germany); IBM Ireland Ltd.; IBM Nederland NV (Netherlands); IBM United Kingdom Holdings Ltd; IBM United Kingdom Ltd.; IBM Europe Holding BV (Netherlands); Compagnie IBM France SA; International Business Machines SA (Spain; 99.99%); IBM Danmark As (Denmark).

Principal Divisions

Global Services; Hardware Systems Group; Personal Systems Group; Technology Group; Software; Global Financing; Enterprise Investments.

Principal Competitors

Accenture; Dell Computer Corporation; Hewlett-Packard Company; Microsoft Corporation; Toshiba Corporation; Xerox Corporation.

Further Reading

"Blue Is the Colour," *Economist,* June 6, 1998.
DeLamarter, Richard Thomas, *Big Blue: IBM's Use and Abuse of Power,* New York: Dodd, Mead & Company, 1986.

Henriques, Diana B., ''Off the Shelf: The Insecurities and Iron Fist That Built I.B.M.,'' *New York Times*, May 11, 2003, section 3, p. 5.

Kirkpatrick, David, ''IBM: From Big Blue Dinosaur to E-Business Animal,'' *Fortune,* April 26, 1999, pp. 116–27.

Lohr, Steve, ''Technology: IBM Will Collaborate Somewhat More on Chip Design,'' *New York Times*, April 1, 2004, section C, p. 8.

Maney, Kevin, *The Maverick and His Machine: Thomas Watson, Sr. and the Making of IBM:* John Wiley & Sons, 2003.

''The New IBM,'' *Business Week,* December 16, 1991.

Sobel, Robert, *IBM: Colossus in Transition,* New York: Times Books, 1981.

Watson, Thomas J., Jr., *Father, Son, and Company: My Life at IBM and Beyond,* New York: Bantam Books, 1990.

—Jonathan Martin
—updates: Susan Windisch Brown, Candice Mancini

Intrado Inc.

Intrado®

Informed Response.®

1601 Dry Creek Drive
Longmont, Colorado 80503
U.S.A.
Telephone: (720) 494-5800
Toll Free: (877) 856-7504
Fax: (720) 494-6600
Web site: http://www.intrado.com

Public Company
Incorporated: 1979 as Systems Concepts of Colorado Inc.
Employees: 716
Sales: $124.65 million (2003)
Stock Exchanges: NASDAQ
Ticker Symbol: TRDO
NAIC: 511210 Software Publishers; 541512 Computer Systems Design Services; 514210 Data Processing Services

Intrado Inc. is the leading supplier of 911-related support services in the United States. The company produces technology to inform emergency dispatchers of potentially lifesaving information, such as the identity and location of 911 callers. It serviced 221 million of 252 million 911 records in the United States in 2003, according to *Investor's Business Daily.* The company supports 200 million 911 calls a year.

Wire-based 911 services accounted for two-thirds of revenues in 2003. Intrado has developed Enhanced 911 systems for mobile phones to instantly inform emergency personnel of the location of 911 callers. Intrado also supplies emergency notification systems allowing public safety authorities to broadcast warning messages to residents of a specific geographic area. A project in development in late 2003 automatically alerts authorities in the event of a motorist becoming incapacitated.

Colorado Origins

Intrado was launched by George K. Heinrichs and Stephen M. Meer in 1979 as a part-time consulting business called Systems Concepts of Colorado Inc. (SCC). The founders were just 21 years old at the time. Meer was a former paramedic who also managed 911 technology for the Boulder County Sheriff's Department. Heinrichs was also a deputy there. The two turned in their badges to work for SCC full time in 1985. Heinrichs would become the company's chairman, president, and chief executive officer, while Meer served as vice-president and chief technology officer.

The original focus of the business was systems integration. An early product was jail management software. SCC launched a vitally important new product in 1986: database software for storing names and addresses of phone users for the purpose of informing emergency personnel. Enhanced 911, or E911, automatically displayed this information to dispatchers during 911 calls.

Changing Focus in 1993

In 1990, SCC landed its first venture capital backing, from Hill-Carman Ventures of Boulder. The company was renamed SCC Communications Corp. in 1993. It had 110 employees, and ended the year with $15.3 million in revenues. *Inc.* magazine put SCC on its list of fast-growing small companies.

According to the *Denver Post,* about this time, the company shifted to the business of managing data for its clients, rather than simply selling them computer platforms. SCC landed its first $100 million, ten-year contract in 1994. Chicago-based Ameritech and BellSouth were early clients. In 1996, SCC won a ten-year contract to maintain the E911 database for US West (later Qwest) of Englewood, Colorado, throughout a 14-state region.

Revenues were $27.1 million in 1996. By early 1997, reported the *Rocky Mountain News,* 100 million phone numbers were in E911 databases developed by SCC. The company's employment then stood at 240.

A war room called the SCC National Data Services Center monitored but did not directly handle incoming calls. It was located at SCC headquarters and backed up by 15 remote locations.

SCC then developed, in partnership with SignalSoft of Boulder, a system to identify the number and location of mobile

Key Dates:

1979: Systems Concepts of Colorado starts as a consulting company.
1986: Enhanced 911 software is launched.
1993: The company is renamed SCC Communications Corp.
1998: SCC goes public on NASDAQ.
2001: Lucent Public Safety Systems is acquired; SCC is renamed Intrado Inc.
2004: Intrado buys bmd wireless.

phone callers. Providers, under an FCC mandate, had until April 1998 to install the technology, though they succeeded in getting this deadline extended. The first phase system used the position of cell phone towers to identify the location of callers. In early 1997, Meer told the *Denver Post* mobile phones accounted for 20 to 40 percent of 911 calls. AT&T Wireless Services, with more than seven million customers, contracted with SCC to provide E911 in 1997. SCC launched E911 cell phone service in Clark County, Washington, in April 1998. It caught on more slowly than expected. Only 2 percent of wireless phone users had enhanced 911 service in 1999, reported the *Denver Post*.

SCC also had developed the Computer Aided Dispatch system for tracking the location of emergency personnel. In July 1997, SCC sold this unit, which employed 50 people, to Anaheim, California-based Printrak International Inc.

1998 Initial Public Offering

SCC went public on the NASDAQ National Market System in June 1998 under the ticker symbol SCCX; 3.3 million shares were offered at $12 each. Part of the proceeds was earmarked to pay down a $4.6 million debt. By this time, the company had added MCI and Sprint PCS to its client list.

An Enhanced 911 system for wireless phones developed by SCC with SignalSoft and SnapTrack Inc. was tested in Colorado in August 1998. SnapTrack, based in San Jose, California, supplied the global positioning system (GPS) used to identify the precise location of the handset making the call. This was the second phase of E911. (The first phase traced callers to within a few hundred feet of a cell phone tower.)

SCC developed a new product, the IntelliCast Notification Service, to allow public safety authorities to broadcast warning messages to residents in a particular geographic area. The system helped evacuate parts of Boulder County, Colorado, during a series of forest fires in 2000.

Investor's Business Daily reported that SCC management brought in a Denver investor relations consultant, Genesis Select, in April 2000 to help gain some attention for the com-

pany's languishing stock among institutional investors. It worked; within two-and-a-half years, eight analysts were following Intrado shares, and institutional ownership rose from 9 percent to more than 80 percent. Improved financials would help, though SCC posted a net loss of $9.5 million on revenue of $43.1 million in 2000. The company had 680 employees, most of them in Colorado.

Turning the Corner in 2001

In May 2001 SCC acquired Lucent's Public Safety Systems wireless 911 unit for $29.1 million, mostly in stock, plus future performance-based payments. There was little overlap, SCC CEO George Heinrichs told the *Boulder County Business Report*, and the assimilation of the new unit, whose 85 employees remained based in Chicago, went smoothly. The Lucent deal made SCC the undisputed market leader in 911 services. SCC was then renamed Intrado Inc. in June 2001; its NASDAQ ticker symbol became TRDO.

The September 11, 2001 terrorist attacks on the United States gave a new sense of urgency to the development of E911 to enhance mobile phones' potential as safety devices, as one FCC official described it to *Investor's Business Daily*. Phone number portability provided another market for Intrado, which developed products to spare long-distance carriers the costly mistake of billing the wrong local phone companies.

The company ended 2001 with about 700 employees. Revenues rose 81 percent to $78.2 million, and the company was again posting quarterly profits after nearly three years of losses. Investors noticed; Intrado had Colorado's best-performing stock in 2001, reported the *Denver Post*. Its 911 products were used by nearly 205 million subscribers. Intrado's sparkle was all the more dramatic against the backdrop of failed tech companies.

By the end of 2002, Intrado's IntelliCast Target Notification system was being used in more than 30 cities. In addition to warning residents of fire and weather emergencies, it was being used to broadcast instant alerts following child abductions. Intrado charged a setup fee between $25,000 and $200,000 depending upon the size of the city, reported the *Rocky Mountain News*, plus 20 to 25 cents per completed call.

In 2003, Intrado was beginning to offer the capacity to include callers' medical conditions in its E911 databases. Sales rose nearly 16 percent to $124.7 million in 2003, while net income was up 3.6 percent to $10.7 million.

Going into 2004, the company was working on technology to automatically inform authorities when the driver of a vehicle became incapacitated. Intrado was testing the system with the Houston Police Department.

In February 2004, the company went global by buying bmd wireless, a ten-year-old network messaging infrastructure firm based in Switzerland. Intrado paid $4.2 million in cash and 735,000 shares of stock for bmd, plus an additional amount of stock based on future performance.

Principal Subsidiaries

bmd wireless AG (Switzerland); Intrado Communications Inc.; Intrado Communications of Virginia Inc.; Intrado International Limited (Ireland).

Principal Divisions

Competitive Local Exchange Carrier (CLEC); Direct; Incumbent Local Exchange Carrier (ILEC); Wireless.

Principal Operating Units

Wireline; Wireless; New Markets.

Principal Competitors

HBF Group, Inc.; Independent Emergency Services, LLC; Openwave Systems Inc.; Sigma Communications Incorporated; TeleCommunication Systems, Inc.

Further Reading

Aguilar, John, "New Warning Technologies Add to Intrado's 911 Revenue Base," *Boulder County Business Report,* December 25, 2003, p. 4B.

Angell, Mike, "Intrado Connecting with 911; Better Service to Come," *Investor's Business Daily,* November 19, 2001, p. A9.

——, "9-1-1 Provider Intrado Dials Up New Markets," *Investor's Business Daily,* September 30, 2003, p. A6.

Beauprez, Jennifer, and Kris Hudson, "Phone Product Cool in Crisis," *Denver Post,* June 16, 2002, p. K3.

Branaugh, Matt, "Summit County, Utah, Picks Colorado Firm's Emergency-Notification Technology," *Daily Camera,* January 15, 2002.

Cantwell, Rebecca, "SCC Is Largest 911 Services Provider; Boulder Firm Signs Contract to Help Public Safety Agencies," *Rocky Mountain News* (Denver), August 25, 1997, p. 1B.

Couch, Mark P., "Lease Boosts Northwest Market; Intrado Signs Deal on Longmont Space," *Denver Post,* March 8, 2002, p. C2.

Dutta, Mahua, "SCC Calls for IPO," *IPO Reporter,* June 22, 1998.

Forgrieve, Janet, "Intrado's Successful Connection," *Rocky Mountain News* (Denver), July 20, 2001, p. 4B.

——, "Proactive Approach; Intrado's Reverse 911 Technology Helps Law Enforcement to Alert Public When Children Go Missing," *Rocky Mountain News* (Denver), November 18, 2002, p. 1B.

Gannon, Michael, "SCC Communications Inc.," *Venture Capital Journal,* August 1, 1998.

Greim, Lisa, "Enhanced 911; System Tested to ID Location of Wireless Calls," *Rocky Mountain News,* August 20, 1998, p. 1B.

Hudson, Kris, "Intrado Gaining Believers; Stocks Reflect Momentum of 911 Services Firm," *Denver Post,* September 28, 2001, p. C1.

Kelleher, Elizabeth, "Making Its Mark in the 911 Phone Market," *New York Times,* Sec. 3, Bus. Sec., August 17, 2003, p. 7.

Locke, Tom, "Boulder, Colo., 911 Services Company Sells Unit to California Firm," *Daily Camera,* July 22, 1997.

Luzadder, Dan, "CEO of Boulder, Colo.-Based Emergency Communications Firm to Accept Award," *Denver Post,* February 21, 2002.

Menezes, Bill, "US West Makes Deal on 911 Management," *Rocky Mountain News* (Denver), February 24, 1996, p. 51A.

Narvaes, Emily, "Boulder Firm's Software Helps Track 911 Calls," *Denver Post,* March 17, 1997, p. C1.

Parker, Penny, "First Day of Trading Good for SCC Stock," *Denver Post,* June 25, 1998, p. C2.

Shinkle, Kirk, "Investor Relations Firms Can Be Pipelines to Investors, Analysts; One Denver-Based Firm Helped Intrado Get the Attention of 10 Analysts," *Investor's Business Daily,* Leaders & Success Sec.: Managing a Successful Company, November 6, 2002, p. A4.

Thomas, Jeff, "Assimilation of Lucent Team Went Smoothly," *Boulder County Business Report,* November 30, 2001, p. A5.

Vuong, Andy, "Stock Surges on Profit at Boulder, Colo.-Based Intrado," *Denver Post,* February 11, 2002.

Yamanouchi, Kelly, "Cellular Phones to Get 911 Boost; Senate OKs National Number Setup," *Denver Post,* August 7, 1999, p. C2.

—Frederick C. Ingram

Inverness Medical Innovations, Inc.

51 Sawyer Road, Suite 200
Waltham, Massachusetts 02453
U.S.A.
Telephone: (781) 647-3900
Fax: (781) 647-3939
Web site: http://www.invernessmedical.com

Public Company
Incorporated: 1992 as SelfCare Inc.
Employees: 1,190
Sales: $296.4 million (2003)
Stock Exchanges: American
Ticker Symbol: IMA
NAIC: 325413 In-Vitro Diagnostic Substance
   Manufacturing

Inverness Medical Innovations, Inc. is a leading manufacturer of home pregnancy test kits and fertility monitors. The company's major brands include its ClearBlue home pregnancy test and the ClearPlan Easy fertility monitor. The company also develops and markets other products relating to women's health, such as prenatal vitamins. Inverness sells an array of other medical diagnostic products, such as tools to detect osteoporosis, mononucleosis, and sexually transmitted diseases. Inverness also sells the Smartcare brand of dietary supplements. The company's focus on women's health issues comes following the sale of its business in home blood glucose monitoring test kits to medical giant Johnson & Johnson in 2001. A sister company, Inverness Medical, is now a wholly owned subsidiary of Johnson & Johnson. Ron Zwanziger founded Inverness Medical Innovations under the name SelfCare in 1992.

Founder's First Venture in the 1980s

Inverness Medical Innovation's founder, Ron Zwanziger, grew up in Cyprus and was educated in England. He earned a degree in engineering from Imperial College at London University, and then moved to the United States to attend prestigious Harvard Business School. In 1981, Zwanziger and three other Harvard Business School students banded together to form MediSense, a biotechnology company. The new company planned to come up with ten different possible products. The executives hoped at least one of these ten ideas would prove to be a good one.

After three years of research and development, MediSense started focusing on one product. This was a device that detected blood sugar levels. Diabetics needed to test their blood sugar (glucose) levels daily, and the disease was gaining ground, with millions afflicted in the United States and hundreds of thousands more people diagnosed with the disease each year. Existing blood test kits were bulky, and required a relatively large drop of blood to give accurate results. MediSense developed a blood sugar test device that was only about the size of a credit card and used a pinprick-sized drop of blood. It was potentially a real advance in the home test industry, and investors funneled money into the company. MediSense raised some $60 million from investors within a few years of bringing its first blood test to market in 1988. MediSense had sales of $30 million in 1989, and worked on recruiting a worldwide sales force. In 1990, the business magazine *Inc.* picked MediSense as one of the fastest-growing private companies in the United States. Zwanziger told *Inc.* that the company had been close to running out of cash at several points, but that things looked good for the future.

Starting Over with SelfCare

Despite the optimism surrounding its improved diagnostic kits, MediSense ran into difficulty. Although its product had clear merits over existing test kits, the company's sales force was not able to make the headway it had hoped against larger competitors such as Johnson & Johnson and Boehringer Mannheim and Miles. MediSense lost money in both 1990 and 1991, and its directors disagreed over whether or not to broaden the company's offerings into other areas. At that point Zwanziger left to start a new company.

Zwanziger's new firm, also headquartered near Boston, was called SelfCare. It focused on the other major part of the home medical diagnostics industry, home pregnancy tests. The home health products industry was growing quickly. Overall drugstore sales in 1992 were estimated at $1 billion, with analysts predict-

Company Perspectives:

Inverness Medical Innovations is a leading provider of women's health and other consumer and point-of-care health products and a developer of advanced technologies for both the consumer and professional diagnostic marketplaces.

ing sales of more than $2 billion by 1995. More than 90 percent of home diagnostic kits were for either blood glucose or to detect pregnancy. MediSense had been developing pregnancy tests, but it had put all its marketing muscle behind its diabetes tests. Zwanziger and other investors started SelfCare with $2 million, buying rights to 11 diagnostic products from MediSense. SelfCare started out small, employing only 17 people by 1993. Revenue was less than $1 million that year, and the firm was not yet profitable. However, SelfCare was developing products for an expanding market, as the bigger manufacturers touted their existing test kits. The company's first products were a pregnancy test and an ovulation predictor, and it also began developing a home test for vaginal yeast infections. The Food and Drug Administration (FDA) had allowed drug manufacturers to sell treatments for yeast infections without a prescription beginning in December 1990, and SelfCare thought this might signal a greater need for diagnostic kits for the condition.

While SelfCare developed various products for women's health, it also began working on blood glucose diagnostic tests. By the mid-1990s, Zwanziger's old firm MediSense had managed to do well with its diabetes monitoring products. That company was profitable again, and held the number three spot in the home blood sugar monitoring market niche, with an estimated 10 percent of the U.S. market. It also had raised more than $50 million in an initial public stock offering in 1994. The example of MediSense showed that it was possible for a small company to do well in the diabetes self-test market. SelfCare developed a new blood glucose monitoring system that it called The New System. The FDA approved The New System in late 1996, and SelfCare began selling the product within a few months. Instead of handling marketing of its new device itself, though, SelfCare worked out an agreement with LifeScan Inc., a subsidiary of healthcare giant Johnson & Johnson. LifeScan was already the leader in the blood sugar detection kit segment, with about 35 percent of the market. The New System offered advantages over LifeScan's products because it used an electro-chemical analysis. The electrochemical method was both faster and less invasive than older diagnostic methods, requiring a smaller amount of blood. LifeScan hoped to gain market share by promoting SelfCare's new product; SelfCare would also benefit, gaining the larger company's established marketing presence and distribution channels.

Healthcare analysts expected the blood glucose monitoring market to continue to rise, growing from overall sales of around $1.8 billion in the mid-1990s to more than $3 billion by 2000. SelfCare's prospects seemed rosy. The company had sales of $7.2 million in 1995, and operated at a loss, yet it confidently expected revenue of close to $200 million by 2000. SelfCare went public in August 1996. By that time it had expanded internationally, with offices and manufacturing plants in Inverness, Scotland, and in Galway, Ireland, and a European sales office in Munich, Germany. The company continued to promote its pregnancy tests and ovulation predictors, and it developed home test kits for other conditions as well. By 1996 SelfCare had developed or was working on products for the detection of Lyme disease, the tick-borne illness endemic in much of the eastern United States, and for hepatitis, chlamydia, and HIV, as well as for H. pylori, an organism associated with both stomach ulcers and stomach cancer.

Name Change and a Sale in the 2000s

SelfCare prospered, with sales of $170.3 million for 2000. This was not far from company estimates made in 1995, which had projected extravagant growth. The company opened a new manufacturing facility in Israel, and sold its diabetes monitoring products and pregnancy tests in major mass market outlets in the United States, including the drug chains Walgreens and CVS and mega-retailer Wal-Mart. Its diabetes monitoring products were the real engine of the company's expansion. The strips for the glucose detection kits were manufactured in Inverness, Scotland, where SelfCare was one of the area's leading employers. In 2000 SelfCare changed its name to Inverness Medical Technology. Company headquarters remained in Waltham, Massachusetts, but the new name reflected the importance of the products made in Inverness. The year 2000 was a banner year for the company, which saw sales of its blood sugar testing strips double.

Inverness continued to pour money into research and development. The blood sugar monitoring market was growing quickly, yet competition was intense. Rivals for the market included German aspirin maker Bayer AG, Abbott Laboratories, which had acquired MediSense in 1995, and subsidiaries of the multinational drug firm Roche Holding Ltd. LifeScan Inc., which marketed Inverness's diabetes care products, reinforced its agreement with the company in 2000, signing a new global distribution contract that year. LifeScan began phasing out its own diabetes test kits, as the ones made by Inverness were much faster. Inverness brought out the One-Touch Ultra blood sugar test kit in 2000, which gave results in only five seconds. Older test kits took two minutes to perform their analysis.

LifeScan was more dependent on Inverness as it let its own products go by the wayside. Its market share was squeezed by competitors, and it lost ground. In 2001 LifeScan purchased the diabetes monitoring business of its supplier, Inverness. The deal was worth $1.33 billion, paid for with Johnson & Johnson stock. The way the sale worked, Johnson & Johnson bought Inverness Medical Technologies for its subsidiary, LifeScan. But since Johnson & Johnson wanted the glucose monitoring business only, part of the acquired firm was then spun off as a new entity, called Inverness Medical Innovations. This company remained headquartered in Waltham, with Zwanziger in charge. It included the pregnancy and fertility testing business and the other diagnostic testing businesses of the old firm.

Inverness was now a much smaller company with a new market focus. The company looked at ways to build on its existing strength in women's health. Inverness's main consumer products were its pregnancy tests and ovulation predictors. It

Key Dates:

1981: Ron Zwanziger founds MediSense.
1991: Zwanziger leaves MediSense; starts SelfCare.
1996: SelfCare goes public.
2000: The name is changed to Inverness Medical Technology.
2001: The company sells its diabetes diagnostic business to Johnson & Johnson; the company re-forms as Inverness Medical Innovations.
2002: The company acquires Ostex International and the medical diagnostics unit of Medpointe, Inc.
2003: The company purchases the pregnancy test and illicit drug test divisions of Abbott Laboratories; the company agrees to supply Pfizer's Warner-Lambert subsidiary with a digital version of Warner-Lambert's E.P.T. brand pregnancy tests.

also manufactured some vitamins and nutritional supplements. In 2001 Inverness began exploring cross-marketing of its product lines, for example, packaging prenatal vitamins with its pregnancy tests. The company spent at least $10 million on advertising in 2002, sending its account for two of its leading pregnancy test kits to the New York ad agency Kirshenbaum Bond + Partners.

The company seemed to be repeating the strategy that had worked for it in the blood glucose monitoring market earlier. Inverness made several acquisitions, giving it clout in the women's health arena, and also building its portfolio of diagnostic tools for various conditions. Inverness bought Ostex International in 2002, a company that made tests for osteoporosis. It also bought the medical diagnostics unit of Medpointe, Inc. in 2002, spending $70 million for the division. While broadening its product mix, the company also brought out a new and improved version of the home pregnancy test. As it had brought out a faster and easier blood glucose test, Inverness came out with a pregnancy test that was significantly easier to use. Whereas existing pregnancy test kits relied on the user interpreting a colored line on the test strip, Inverness's new digital test spelled out the word "pregnant" for a positive test, and "not pregnant" for a negative. Although the home pregnancy test market was very competitive and sales were relatively flat for the first half of 2003, sales of the new Inverness ClearBlue Easy digital kits spiked, hitting $1 million after only a few months on the market.

Other manufacturers hastened their own digital tests to market. Inverness strengthened its position in the home pregnancy test market by buying the pregnancy test and illicit drug test divisions of Abbott Laboratories in 2003. The company paid $92.5 million for the businesses. Due to its substantial acquisitions, Inverness Medical Innovations saw its revenue rise rapidly after it sold its diabetes business to Johnson & Johnson. Revenue was only $49.4 million in 2001, down from more than $170 million in 2000, as Inverness was much smaller. Sales for 2002 rose to $207.9 million, a huge increase over a year earlier. Yet Inverness operated at a loss in both 2001 and 2002. For 2003, sales climbed to close to $300 million, and Inverness was back in the black, with a net income of $12 million.

As Inverness had worked earlier with the much larger Johnson & Johnson to market its diabetes diagnostic tests, Inverness made a similar arrangement in 2003 with the large drug manufacturer Pfizer Inc. Inverness agreed to supply Pfizer's Warner-Lambert subsidiary with a digital version of Warner-Lambert's E.P.T. brand pregnancy tests. At the same time, Inverness planned to continue to market its own ClearBlue brand digital test. Inverness seemed to be reproducing its success with diabetes test kits in the pregnancy and fertility test kit market.

Principal Subsidiaries

Ostex International, Inc.; Orgenics, Ltd.

Principal Competitors

Wyeth Pharmaceuticals; Abbott Laboratories; Roche Group.

Further Reading

Aoki, Naomi, "Diabetes Tests Drive Growth," *Boston Globe,* May 22, 2001, p. E25.

Benevides, Lisa, and Julie Carrick Dalton, "Home Diabetes Test Kits Open New Market for Selfcare," *Boston Business Journal,* October 7, 1996.

Brokaw, Leslie, "Rank 89: Ron Zwanziger, MediSense," *Inc.,* December 1990, p. 74.

Convey, Eric, "Abbott to Buy MediSense," *Boston Herald,* March 30, 1996, p. 12.

Glasser, Jeff, "A Turnaround, and Wariness of Competitors," *Boston Globe,* July 2, 1995, p. 65.

"Inverness and Pfizer End Dispute with Five-Year Deal," *New York Times,* June 10, 2003, p. C4.

"Inverness Expands with Purchase from Abbott Labs," *New York Times,* October 2, 2003, p. C4.

"Inverness Medical Innovations to Acquire Ostex International," *Women's Health Weekly,* October 31, 2002, p. 20.

"Inverness Medical Technology," *Investor's Business Daily,* December 13, 2000, p. A12.

Johnsen, Michael, "Digital Pregnancy Test Kit Launches May Trigger Category Sales," *Drug Store News,* November 17, 2003, p. 37.

Mack, Ann M., "KB + P Picks Up Inverness Brands," *Adweek,* April 8, 2002, p. 8.

Marcial, Gene, "Is Inverness Being Fattened Up for Market?," *Business Week,* December 2, 2002, p. 122.

"Medical Corporation Purchases Waltham, Mass.-Based Glucose Monitoring Business," *Knight Ridder/Tribune Business News,* May 24, 2001.

Michaels, Adrian, "J&J in Talks to Buy Diabetes Products," *Financial Times,* May 10, 2001, p. 32.

Morse, Andrew, "Inverness Buys MedPointe Unit," *Daily Deal,* August 9, 2002.

Pham, Alex, "Abbott Labs' Acquisition of MediSense Pays Off for Investors," *Knight Ridder/Tribune Business News,* March 31, 1996.

Powell, Jennifer Heldt, "Inverness Buying Three Abbott Tests for $92.5M," *Boston Herald,* October 2, 2003, p. 39.

Rosenberg, Ronald, "How Patients Make House Calls," *Boston Globe,* June 2, 1993, p. 42.

Timmerman, Luke, "Massachusetts Firm Buys Seattle Osteoporosis Diagnostic Kit Maker," *Seattle Times,* September 10, 2002.

Yonkin, John, "Q & A," *Drug Store News,* December 17, 2001, p. 70.

—A. Woodward

(i)nvestor

Investor AB

Arsenalsg 8c
Stockholm
S-103 32
Sweden
Telephone: 46 8 614 20 00
Fax: 46 8 614 21 50
Web site: http://www.investorab.com

Public Company
Incorporated: 1916
Employees: 320
Total Assets: SEK 163.65 billion ($14.27 billion) (2003)
Stock Exchanges: Stockholm
Ticker Symbol: INVE
NAIC: 551112 Offices of Other Holding Companies

Investor AB is the flagship of the Wallenberg financial empire—the family has long dominated northern Europe's financial sector and, through Investor and other investment vehicles, owns as much as 40 percent of the value of companies listed on the Stockholm Stock Exchange (as well as a share of the exchange itself). Once an offshoot of the family's core banking business—now known as SEB—Investor AB has itself become the family's largest business, with more than SEK 163 billion ($14 billion) in assets at the end of 2003. Investor is the holding vehicle for the Wallenberg's primary investments, many of which date back to the beginning of the 20th century. As such the company holds major and often controlling stakes in much of Swedish industry, including Atlas Copco, Electrolux, Ericsson, Gambro, SEB, and WM-data. Together, these six companies represent the vast majority of the company's total assets. At the turn of the 21st century, Investor began seeking to reduce its reliance on ''old-fashioned'' industrial investments, launching a thrust to increase its number of ''New Investments,'' and especially the high technology sector. Among the group's recent acquisitions is a controlling stake in Hi3G, one of Sweden's high-speed mobile telephone licenses. More than a simple investment group, Investor plays an active role in the operation of the companies in which it invests, appointing CEOs, taking seats on the board of the directors, and steering mergers and acquisitions. With its own listing on the Stockholm Stock Exchange, the company has nonetheless been under pressure from its own shareholders to reduce its large-scale investments in favor of smaller, more flexible, and more short-term stakes. The company is led by CEO Marcus Wallenberg, the fifth generation of the Wallenberg family to oversee its financial empire.

19th-Century Financial Empire

Founded in 1916, Investor AB already represented some 60 years of the Wallenberg family's influence in Sweden's financial and industrial communities. By then, too, the family had already cemented its position as one of the most influential family dynasties in Scandinavia—and in the whole of Europe. Yet, into the 18th century, the Wallenbergs, or Persson, as the family was originally known, remained rooted in Sweden's peasant class.

Upward mobility began for the family, originally from Skärkinds parish, near Norrköping, when Jacob Persson was named constable of the parish in the early decades of the 18th century. Persson later married the daughter of a member of the Swedish clergy—a mark of his improved social standing—and changed his name to the more upwardly mobile name of Wallberg. Jacob Wallberg died in 1758. The influence of the church remained strong in Swedish society through the second half of that century, and both of Wallberg's sons, Jacob and Marcus, entered the clergy themselves, signifying the family's growing prominence. Both Jacob and Marcus then adopted the family name of Wallenberg.

The next generation of Wallenbergs carried on the family's ascension, when Marcus Wallenberg, born in 1774, became Bishop of Linköping in 1819, signaling the family's arrival near the top of Swedish social life. Yet it was the following generation that was to found the family's financial empire. Born in 1816, André Oscar Wallenberg was the youngest son of Marcus Wallenberg. When the elder Wallenberg died in 1833, André left school and began working as a deck hand on a ship trading between Sweden and the United States. Wallenberg then attended the Swedish Naval Academy, graduating in 1835. Yet,

Company Perspectives:

Vision: To deliver superior returns to shareholders by establishing Investor AB as a globally recognized entrepreneurial and active owner of companies with high growth and profit potential. Goal: To grow net asset value in excess of market cost of capital over a business cycle.

with no opening for an immediate appointment into the Navy's officer ranks, Wallenberg returned to the United States, gaining experience on merchant shipping lines.

Wallenberg, however, had already begun developing his business and financial interests, helping to set up Sweden's first steam boat company, and, in 1837, cofounding the Ostergötlands Enskilda Banken. Wallenberg later led that bank's extension, forming branches in Härnosand and Sundsvall in the 1850s, before founding his own bank, Stockholms Enskilda Banken (SEB), in 1856. The following decade, Wallenberg backed the formation of Sweden's first joint-stock limited liability bank, Skandinaviska Enskilda Banken. In the meantime, Wallenberg continued to develop his influence in Sweden's political, social, and economic circles, joining the country's parliament.

André Wallenberg was joined by eldest son Knut, born in 1853. Although Knut Wallenberg was made a member of the family bank's board of directors in 1874, he went to work overseas, namely for Credit Lyonnais in France, where he deepened his banking experience before joining SEB full-time at the end of the decade—in time for the financial crisis that nearly caused the bank's collapse. Yet the bank was able to rebuild in the 1880s, in part by using Knut Wallenberg's French connections in order to place SEB in position as acting broker for foreign capital investments in Sweden. The country's financial crisis had also given the company the opportunity to take significant shares in a number of Sweden's fledgling industrial companies. These shareholdings became the basis of the future Investor AB.

André Wallenberg died in 1986, and Knut Wallenberg took over as leader of the family's financial and industrial empire, which included among other interests a growing shipping business. In 1892, Wallenberg was joined by one of his younger brothers, Marcus Wallenberg, who was named the bank's vice-president that year. Wallenberg, who held a legal degree from Uppsala University, took charge of restructuring and then building up the group's industrial shareholding. Together, Knut and Marcus Wallenberg developed SEB into a two-pronged powerhouse, building up its financial arm while putting together a diversified web of industrial holdings. By the turn of the century, the Wallenberg family was already the most powerful in Sweden, dominating its industrial sector.

Named Sweden's foreign minister, Knut Wallenberg transferred his CEO position to Marcus Wallenberg in 1911. Despite the Wallenberg family's dominant position in Swedish life, SEB was confronted with new legislation, enacted during World War I, which severely restricted the ability of the country's banks to hold long-term shares in Swedish industrial companies. In response to the new legislation, the Wallenbergs set up Investor AB in 1916, transferring its vast industrial shareholdings to the new holding company. From the start, therefore, Investor held majority positions in a number of Sweden's oldest and most prominent industrial companies, such as Scania, Atlas Copco, and others.

Wallenberg Flagship: 1970s

Marcus Wallenberg's growing political commitments led him to step down from the bank's leadership toward the end of World War I. His place was temporarily filled by an outsider to the family, Joseph Nachmanson, who had nonetheless served on the bank's board of directors since 1909 and had become a close confidant of Marcus Wallenberg. Nachmanson was credited with helping to guide the bank through the turbulent economic period after World War I, conducting a conservative investment strategy that prepared SEB for the economic collapse of the late 1920s and early 1930s.

By then, the third generation of the Wallenberg family had taken the leadership of the family empire. Jacob Wallenberg, eldest son of Marcus Wallenberg (Knut Wallenberg had died childless), had spent his early career working for foreign banks before joining SEB as a junior officer in 1918. After Nachmanson died in 1927, Jacob Wallenberg became the bank's president, joined by younger brother Marcus as the bank's vice-president. Nonetheless, Marcus, Sr., remained a strong presence in the family concern until his death in 1943.

As their father and uncle before them, the new generation of Wallenbergs proved complementary partners, with Jacob Wallenberg taking charge of leading the family's banking business, while Marcus Wallenberg developed its industrial holdings, helping to steer the company's growing range of businesses. Indeed, the bank's sound financial health during the Depression era allowed it to gain significant shareholding positions in many of Sweden's most important industrial companies. The family also took advantage of Sweden's acceptance of preferential share levels, in which certain classes of shares were accorded a stronger proportion of voting rights than others. As such, the Wallenberg's were able to parlay an investment stake into majority control of a company—for example, the group's 4 percent equity stake in Electrolux gave it control of nearly 94 percent of the company's voting rights.

While the Wallenberg family became world renowned for the heroic action of Raoul Wallenberg during World War II, the family's financial dealings led it into difficulties at the end of the war. In 1939, the Bosch company had approached SEB, offering to sell its American subsidiary to the bank in order to prevent it being taken over by the U.S. government—and turned over to Bosch's American competitors—in the event of the U.S. entry into the war. Jacob Wallenberg agreed to the transaction. At the end of the war, however, the bank was accused of having acted as a front for Bosch's continued ownership of its U.S. subsidiary. Threatened with SEB becoming blacklisted in the United States, Jacob Wallenberg agreed to step down from the bank's presidency, and instead was named chairman of both Investor and a newly formed family investment vehicle, Providentia, established in 1946. Marcus Wallenberg then became SEB president—which, in keeping with banking legislation, barred him from active involvement in the family's industrial investment companies.

Key Dates:

1856: André Oscar Wallenberg founds Stockholms Enskilda Banken (SEB).

1863: Wallenberg backs creation of Skandinaviska Enskilda Banken.

1916: Investor AB is formed after new legislation restricting direct ownership by banks of shares in industrial companies.

1946: Wallenbergs form second investment vehicle, Providentia.

1971: Merger of SEB and Skandinaviska Enskilda Banken creates S-E Banken but reduces Wallenbergs to minority ownership; Investor now becomes family flagship, joined by new investment company, Export-Invest.

1992: Investor acquires Providentia.

1994: Investor acquires Export-Invest.

1995: Investor forms start-up investment specialist, Novare Kapital.

1999: Marcus Wallenberg is named president and CEO of Investor.

2002: Company increases shareholding in most of its long-term investments, including ABB, Electrolux, Ericsson, SEB, and WM-data.

2003: Company acquires stake in Hi3G, joint-owned by Hutchison Whampoa.

2004: Investor AB becomes candidate to re-acquire control of Scania after European Commission directs Volvo to sell off its stake in that company.

Nearly 50 years later, the Wallenberg family's conduct during World War II was once again called into question, when it was revealed that SEB had accepted gold and securities stolen by the Germans from Dutch Jews during the war. At the same time, however, observers recognized that the importance of SEB and Sweden itself—as Germany's sole export market during the war—had played a role in providing the leverage needed to save tens of thousands of lives, not only through Raoul Wallenberg's efforts in Hungary, but also within Sweden itself.

The fourth generation of Wallenbergs joined the family business in 1953, including heir apparent Marc Wallenberg, eldest son of Marcus, Jr., who became an assistant director at SEB in 1953, before taking over as president after his father resigned the position in 1958. Marcus, Sr.'s decision meant that he was now eligible to take a position on the boards of the family's investment companies, Investor and Providentia, leading to a power struggle between him and Jacob Wallenberg.

Marcus Wallenberg ultimately triumphed over his brother, who resigned in 1969, opening his seat on the bank's board of directors to Peter Wallenberg. With Jacob Wallenberg out of the picture, Marcus Wallenberg pushed through a merger agreement between SEB and rival Skandinaviska Enskilda Banken in 1971. Soon after, however, tragedy struck the Wallenberg family when Marc Wallenberg committed suicide—observers suggested that the act came possibly because Wallenberg felt himself inadequate to the task of guiding what was to become the Scandinavian banking giant S-E Banken. The merger went through in 1972.

As a result of the merger, the Wallenberg family lost its majority control of the bank, including control of the bank's voting rights. Instead, Marcus Wallenberg, and younger son Peter, focused their interests on the family's investment companies, including Investor, Providentia, and a new investment vehicle created at the time of the bank merger, Export-Invest. Investor now became the family's flagship business, and, under Marcus Wallenberg's leadership began actively promoting the restructuring of most of the industrial companies under its control, replacing board members and promoting younger CEOs and other management.

Peter Wallenberg took over after Marcus Wallenberg's death in 1982. For many outsiders, the change in leadership marked a final moment in the family's more than 100-year dominance of the Swedish banking and industrial sectors. Indeed, the Wallenbergs were coming under increasing pressure to reform their shareholdings as a new range of foreign investors took significant stakes in former ''Wallenberg'' companies. Yet Peter Wallenberg rose to the challenge, guiding Investor—and Sweden's industry—into a new era.

Refocusing in the New Century

Investor under Peter Wallenberg drew back from the direct control over the operations of its holdings—in this sense, Wallenberg's strategy was more akin to uncle Jacob Wallenberg's leadership than his father's. The company also developed new competence in administration, market research, and finance, as well as a dedicated mergers and acquisitions team, and other competencies in order to provide support services to its corporate holdings.

Investor now pushed through a steady stream of mergers and acquisitions among its core holdings, resulting in the ultimate creation of the Stora Enso paper giant; the Swedish-Swiss ABB (Asea Brown Boveri), considered the first major cross-border European group; and the creation of Saab-Scania through a merger with GM. The company also divested parts of its long-time holdings, such as Kema Nobel. In 1991, Investor bought out GM's share of Saab-Scania. Meanwhile, the company split off parts of ABB as a new, publicly listed holding company, Incentive, which later developed into medical equipment group Gambro—itself controlled by Investor.

In 1992, Investor became the Wallenberg family's primary investment vehicle, through the takeover of Providentia. In 1994, the company also took over Export-Invest, then formed a new investment subsidiary, EQT, in partnership with SEB. The following year, the company created another investment subsidiary, Novare Kapital, part of its Investor Growth Capital division, which focused on investing in start-up companies.

Investor began a program of reducing its shareholding position in many of its long-term investments. After splitting Saab and Scania into two separate companies in 1995, Investor sold a 55 percent stake in Scania in a public listing on the Stockholm and New York Stock Exchanges. The following year, the company sold a stake in Saab to British Aerospace, then listed the automaker in a public offering. That year also saw the merger of Stora with Finland's Enso, creating Stora Enso, and the launch of the merger between Investor-held Astra with Zeneca, completed in 1998.The following year, the Wallenberg family regained control of S-E Banken, which was then renamed SEB.

Peter Wallenberg stepped down from leadership of Investor in 1997, replaced by Percy Barnevik, who had previously served as chairman of ABB, seconded by another longtime Wallenberg associate, Claes Dahlback. The latter gave up his position in 1999, however, as a new generation—the fifth—prepared to take over the reins of the company. Marcus Wallenberg, then 43, took over as company CEO, and set out to lead Investor—and the Wallenberg financial empire with it—into the new century. Investor now began to concentrate on building up a portfolio of shorter-term "New Investments," such as its purchase in 2003 of a major stake in Hi3G, part owned by Hutchison Whampoa, one of the winners of a high-speed mobile telephone license for the Swedish market. At the same time, Investor moved to solidify its positions in many of its core long-term holdings, including the acquisition of additional shares in ABB, Electrolux, Ericsson, SEB, and WM-data in 2002.

By 2004, Investor's commitment to long-term positions gave it a lift, as a strong performance by Ericsson during the previous year lifted Investor's own value. The company was also buoyed by a decision by the European Commission directing Volvo to sell off its stake in Scania—a move that opened the opportunity for Investor to regain its control over another of its oldest investments. Investor appeared to be a worthy flagship to carry the Wallenberg family empire into a new century.

Principal Subsidiaries

Atlas Copco AB (15%); Electrolux (6%); Ericsson (5%); Gambro AB (20%); Saab Automobile AB (20%); SEB (20%); WM-data (19%).

Principal Competitors

Dioss Holding spol S.R.O. ; Mitsubishi Tokyo Financial Group Inc.; Nissei Sangyo Company Ltd.; Barclays Bank Plc; American International Group Inc.; AXA UK PLC; Tomoegawa Paper Company Ltd.; General Electric Capital Services Inc.; Aviva plc; KBC Bankverzekeringsholding; Prudential Public Limited Co.

Further Reading

Gumbel, Peter, "Putting on Heirs: A New Generation Is Leading Europe's Biggest Family Firms Toward New Profits—and Risks," *Time*, March 24, 2003, p. A10.

Hopkins, Nic, "Wallenbergs Will Go Back to the Future," *Times*, October 18, 2003, p. 59.

Kochan, Nick, "Drawing a Bead on a Swedish Dynasty," *Euromoney*, September 2001, p. 200.

——, "No Longer a Family Affair," *Business Week*, December 17, 2001, p. 22.

Lindgren, Hakan, *Succession Strategies in a Large Family Business Group: The Case of the Swedish Wallenberg Family*, paper prepared for the 6th European Business History Association Annual Congress in Helsinki, August 22–24, 2002.

Rubin, Dana, "Old Wine, New Bottle?," *Institutional Investor International Edition*, October 1999, p. 42.

Shearlock, Peter, "Trim the Empire," *Banker*, March 1996, p. 22.

—M.L. Cohen

IRSA Inversiones y Representaciones S.A.

Edificio Inter-Continental Plaza
Moreno 877, 22nd Floor
Buenos Aires, C.F. C1091AAQ
Argentina
Telephone: (54) (11) 4344-4600
Fax: (54) (11) 4344-4611
Web site: http://www.irsa.com.ar

Public Company
Incorporated: 1943
Employees: 1,696
Sales: ARS 212.94 million ($76.87 million) (2003)
Stock Exchanges: Bolsa de Comercio de Buenos Aires
   New York
Ticker Symbols: IRSA; IRS
NAIC: 531110 Lessors of Residential Buildings and
   Dwellings; 531120 Lessors of Nonresidential
   Buildings; 531312 Nonresidential Property Managers;
   531210 Offices of Real Estate Agents and Brokers

In the space of less than a decade—the 1990s—IRSA Inversiones y Representaciones S.A. became the largest and most diversified real estate company in Argentina. Its principal activities consist of the acquisition, development, and operation of office, retail, and shopping center properties; the acquisition and development of residential properties; and the acquisition and operation of luxury hotels. IRSA's portfolio includes many of the most prestigious shopping centers, office towers, and luxury hotels in Buenos Aires. The company also acquires undeveloped land reserves for future developments or sale.

Buying Cheap and Selling Dear: 1991–96

Eduardo S. Elsztain, a college dropout, went to work in 1981 for the small real estate company established by his grandfather in Buenos Aires. The decade proved to be disastrous, with Argentina lurching from crisis to crisis and culminating in hyperinflation. The family-owned company went into bankruptcy, and Elsztain came to New York City in 1990. An Orthodox Jew, he spent his mornings seeking guidance from the Brooklyn-based Lubavitcher sect and his afternoons seeking to convince investors that Argentina, under its recently elected president, Carlos Menem, was about to embark on a new era. He talked his way into the office of George Soros, the fabulously wealthy Hungarian-American hedge fund operator, and persuaded Soros to give him $10 million to invest in beaten-down Argentine stocks. "George and I make a good combination," Elsztain later said, according to Jonathan Friedland of the *Wall Street Journal.* "He likes to take risks, while I believe a certain amount of fear is a precondition to any successful deal."

Argentina stopped inflation in its tracks by tying its currency to the dollar and stimulated foreign investment by privatizing state-owned enterprises. Back in Buenos Aires, Elsztain and his partner, Marcelo Mindlin, purchased IRSA Inversiones y Representaciones, a shell company—but one with a Buenos Aires stock exchange listing—for $120,000, and began assembling a portfolio of stocks. As the stock market soared in 1991 and 1992, Elsztain plowed his profits into the business he knew best, real estate, acquiring office buildings that, purchased cheaply, were yielding 18 to 20 percent a year in profit. Soros continued to provide capital and at one point owned almost half the shares. After IRSA entered the international equity markets in late 1994, raising $110 million, it bought three large office buildings in the heart of Buenos Aires for $61 million. These were landmark properties that the new owners carefully restored.

Also in 1994, IRSA began development of a shopping center in Abasto, a neglected but conveniently located Buenos Aires neighborhood. Before the end of the year the company had sold half of this enterprise to a Chilean firm for $11.5 million. The art-deco shell of the Abasto warehouse, formerly the site of the city's primary fresh produce market, subsequently became the facade of a structure housing a major retail commercial complex with 180 stores as well as movie theaters, a museum, and restaurants (including the only kosher McDonald's outside Israel). By late 1995 IRSA also had taken a stake in Brazilian and Venezuelan real estate ventures through IRSA International Ltd., a company registered in the British Virgin Islands. By late 1997 IRSA International also had holdings in Chile, and its investments in the three countries constituted one-quarter of IRSA's total portfolio.

In the wake of the Mexican peso devaluation of late 1994, foreign investment in Latin America slumped, and IRSA's net sales fell 40 percent in 1996 (the year ended June 30, 1996) from the previous year. The company reacted by halting development and property sales and acquiring existing buildings to increase its cash flow through rentals. It also used the crisis to buy back some of its bonds and stocks at significant discounts, thereby supporting its share price and reducing its outstanding debt. In addition, the company made money by purchasing Argentine government bonds cheaply, then selling them as the economy improved. IRSA's fast footwork enabled it to maintain its profit level despite the drop in sales. Twenty percent of its assets were in cash at the end of 1996, and much of this money was used to buy prime office properties cheaply during the next fiscal year, just before the Argentine economy recovered from Mexico's so-called "tequila effect."

During its first five years, IRSA had reinvested all its profits, but in 1996 it began returning a percentage of its rental income to shareholders in order to attract pension funds as investors. By the end of the year its 13 office buildings, renting to blue-chip tenants, had occupancy rates averaging 97 percent. The remaining 55 percent of the company's portfolio was divided evenly between retail and residential properties. The retail properties were concentrated in supermarkets and shopping centers as well as the Mercado de Abasto. Residential properties included the 312 hectare (771 acre) suburban Barrio Abril development that IRSA began organizing in 1995 in partnership with Alto Palermo S.A., the real estate subsidiary of the family-owned Perez Companc conglomerate. The planned development called for a private residential community with 1,320 house lots, sports facilities, shops, and a school.

Expansion, Then Retrenchment: 1997–2002

In 1997 IRSA paid $115.4 million for a 63 percent interest in Alto Palermo, whose holdings included a Buenos Aires shopping center by the same name. This acquisition brought the company's portfolio to one-third of all shopping center sales in Buenos Aires. Also that year, the company acquired the Llao-Llao luxury hotel near Bariloche in Argentina's alpine lake district and 51 percent of the Inter-Continental Hotel on the Buenos Aires riverfront. IRSA paid $13.3 million for Llao-Llao, which continued to be a white elephant often less than half-occupied.

By mid-1998 IRSA was managing assets valued at $1.2 billion and had taken in $453 million of capital between 1991 and 1997. Its shopping centers now included the prestigious

downtown Galerias Pacifico, Patio Bullrich, and 51 percent of Buenos Aires Design, plus commercial centers in Rosario, Salta (80 percent), and Mendoza (25 percent). The Maple and Pirelli buildings had been added to its roster of Buenos Aires office towers. The company had paid $54.3 million for 71 hectares (175 acres) earmarked for residential development in the city's gritty La Boca neighborhood and had purchased two waterfront docks in the up-and-coming Puerto Madero area adjoining the business center, a project inspired by Battery Park City in downtown Manhattan. IRSA also had added another Buenos Aires hotel, the Libertador, giving it one-quarter of the five-star hotel rooms in the Argentine capital. (It subsequently sold a 20 percent share in the renamed Sheraton Libertador to an affiliate of Sheraton Hotels.)

Not all IRSA's tenants were enchanted with the company. The owner of one firm told Diego Ardiara of *Mercado,* "They seek a very high rate of return. They established as their objective a return of 17 percent, and that is expressed in the down payment and rents we have to pay. Our return from locations in the shopping centers is so low that sometimes it's necessary to attribute the investment to the advertising account, since it's no longer a question of making money but of marketing." Elzstain responded, "I'm not going to cry, especially for the worst businessmen in Buenos Aires." He added that a much higher rate of return was needed in Argentina than in a nation like the United States because of the much higher rate of risk. "When a tenant closes shop here, Argentine law doesn't impose a penalty after six months, while a North American contract obliges him to pay rent over the full period of the lease," he continued. "Besides, here the developer has to wait eight to ten years to recover his investment. . . . There, six months after a complex is completed, he presents the contracts and recovers his money."

About this time Argentina began sinking into a new recession that would worsen until the government defaulted on its debts in early 2002. Meanwhile, Soros Fund Management LLC was cashing out its holdings, which by September 1999 had dropped to about 7 percent. Other shareholders expressed dissatisfaction with the 10 percent of after-tax profits that Elzstain, Mindlin, and other IRSA managers had been collecting in lieu of salary as compensation for running the company. Accordingly, in 1999 the four top executives agreed to accept salaries instead. In exchange for foregoing their management contract, however, they won the right to buy up to 20.9 million shares of the company for $1 apiece, a huge discount from the current price of $2.92 a share. "We like to see management incentivized by stock, especially in emerging markets," a Wall Street mutual fund manager told Craig Torres of the *Wall Street Journal.* "But this is a little excessive." Investors also were angered because Elsztain and his partners exercised an option to buy 20 percent of Alto Palermo from IRSA, then sold millions of these shares back to IRSA for a $4.8 million profit.

As the new millennium dawned, IRSA became ensnared in the ever worsening Argentine economy. Revenue fell in 2000, and the company suffered the first of three consecutive years of net losses. It sold its Venezuelan interests for $67 million, and its remaining half-share in Llao-Llao; the deal also included Galerias Pacifico. IRSA paid $50 million, however, for a 10 percent share of Corporación Financiera Hipotecaria, a new mortgage bank similar to Fannie Mae in the United States. This

Key Dates:

1991: Eduardo Elsztein and Marcelo Mindlin purchase IRSA for $120,000.

1994: IRSA buys three large Buenos Aires office buildings for $61 million.

1996: The company begins acquiring shopping centers and developing apartment complexes.

1997: Holdings in Brazil, Chile, and Venezuela account for one-fourth of IRSA's portfolio; company's properties account for one-third of Buenos Aires shopping center sales.

1998: Work has begun on a residential community south of Buenos Aires.

2000: IRSA suffers the first of three consecutive years of net losses.

2002: The company has sold all its non-Argentinian holdings to refinance its debts.

2003: IRSA records a profit again as Argentina's battered economy improves.

investment became a loser when Argentina's banking system collapsed under the weight of unpaid debt. Through Alto Palermo, the company launched a virtual shopping center named Altocity.com as a joint venture with Telefónica de Argentina S.A., offering an initial 150,000 products from 70 retailers in 12 categories. IRSA pledged to spend $36 million on developing and marketing the site in 2000 alone and expected sales through the web site to reach $100 million within four years. By the end of the year, however, Altocity was combined with other e-commerce ventures that IRSA controlled, and it was still in the red in 2003.

After the Argentine peso lost more than two-thirds of its value in 2002, IRSA's dollar-denominated debt rose proportionately. It sold its Brazil holdings—which had been accounting for nearly one-quarter of its sales—for $44.2 million and liquidated IRSA International. Fifty-four percent-owned Alto Palermo S.A. was consolidated into the parent company in that year as APSA. During 2003 IRSA converted most of its outstanding debt from short-term to long-term liabilities. Despite its setbacks, Mindlin said that as soon as the economy recovered, IRSA was ready to begin construction on new projects.

IRSA in 2003

IRSA, either directly or through subsidiaries and joint ventures, held significant interests in 59 properties in Argentina in 2003, mainly in Buenos Aires. Its net sales during the fiscal year came to ARS 212.94 million ($76.87 million), and its operating income to ARS 20.1 million ($7.26 million). Net income came to ARS 286.4 million ($103.39 million), mainly because of financial transactions such as the sale of the company's Brazilian interests. Of IRSA's net sales, its seven remaining shopping center properties (five in Buenos Aires) accounted for 53 percent. Residential properties accounted for 22 percent and luxury hotels for 16 percent. The 17 office and non-shopping-center properties—all in Buenos Aires—accounted for 8 percent. IRSA's real estate portfolio was valued at ARS 2.12 billion

(about $757 million) at the end of March 2004, of which shopping centers accounted for 55 percent; land reserves, 21 percent; offices and others, 16 percent; hotels, 7 percent; and residential, 1 percent.

Among IRSA's office buildings in Buenos Aires was Inter-Continental Plaza, a 24-story structure next to the IRSA-owned hotel. Its shopping centers in the city included Alto Palermo, a 153-store complex opened in 1990; Paseo Alcorta, a 121-store complex opened in 1992; and Abasto Shopping, which opened in 1999 with 180 stores. Residential buildings included Torres de Abasto, a four-building high-rise complex completed in 1999; Palacio Alcorta, consisting of 191 residential lofts converted from a former Chrysler Corp. factory; and Alto Palermo Park and Alto Palermo Plaza, twin 34-story apartment buildings. Some 566 homes had been completed in Barrio Abril, and 92 percent of them had been sold. Another IRSA residential development, Villa Celena, on the southeast edge of Buenos Aires, was 99 percent sold.

Elsztain owned 25 percent of IRSA's common stock in late 2003. Templeton Investment Counsel owned 15 percent and various pension funds a combined 10 percent. Between late 2000 and the end of 2003 a sister company, Cresud S.A.C.I.F. y A., invested about ARS 133.6 million ($48.23 million) to purchase approximately 22.65 percent of IRSA's outstanding shares.

Principal Subsidiaries

Abril S.A. (83%); APSA (54%); Baldovinos S.A. (83%); Es. As. Trade & F.C.; Hoteles Argentinos (80%); Inversiones Bolivar (67%); Nuevas Fronteras (51%); Palermo Invest Inc. (67%); Pereirnola S.A. (83%); Ritelco S.A.

Principal Operating Units

Communications Department; Hotel Department; Office Department; Residential Department; Shopping Center Department; Technical Department; Treasury Department.

Principal Competitors

El Fondo de Inversión Directa Argentina Real Estate.

Further Reading

Ardiaca, Diego, "Otro patio en el edificio," *Mercado,* August 1998, pp. 159–60, 162.

Bachelet, Pablo, "Espiritu de riesgo," *América economía,* December 28, 2000, pp. 42–43.

Benechi, Mario, "El fin del maleficio?," *Mercado,* May 1999, pp. 63–64.

"Eduardo Elsztain, IRSA," *LatinFinance,* July 1998, p. 191.

Friedland, Jonathan, "Financier Soros, Argentine Developer Ride Latin American Real-Estate Boom," *Wall Street Journal,* June 19, 1996, p. A16.

"From the Mall to the Cybermall," *Business Week,* July 10, 2000, p. 29.

Gascoigne, Clare, "IRSA Finds Room for Growth," *Financial Times,* December 4, 1996, p. 36.

Hahn, Tamar, "Argentina Readies Its Own Version of Fannie Mae," *Investment Dealers' Digest,* February 28, 2000, p. 13.

Hudson, Peter, "Soros: Cuestión de marca," *América economía,* November 1997, pp. 28–29, 32–35.

Kilby, Paul, "Hot Property," *LatinFinance,* November 1996, pp. 46, 48–49.

Krauss, Clifford, "Two Brothers Build an Empire," *New York Times,* April 14, 1998, pp. D1, D4.

Morales, Leonardo, "El sur también existe," *Mercado,* October 1998, pp. 90, 92.

Torres, Craig, "Argentine Small Holders Get No Respect," *Wall Street Journal,* August 31, 1999, p. A17.

——, "George Soros to Sell Argentine Stake to U.S. Investors," *Wall Street Journal,* August 10, 1999, p. A19.

Warn, Ken, "George Soros Joins Cattle Super-League," *Financial Times,* February 11, 1998, p. 30.

—Robert Halasz

Johnsonville Sausage L.L.C.

950 Woodlake Road
Kohler, Wisconsin 53044
U.S.A.
Telephone: (920) 459-6800
Toll Free: (888) 556-2728
Fax: (920) 459-7148
Web site: http://www.johnsonville.com

Private Company
Incorporated: 1945
Employees: 1,000
Sales: $200 million (2003 est.)
NAIC: 311612 Meat Processed from Carcasses; 311611
 Animal (Except Poultry) Slaughtering

Johnsonville Sausage L.L.C. is a leading manufacturer of bratwurst, dinner sausage, and breakfast sausage. The company sells its products nationwide through retail outlets and to food processors, institutional customers, and food services. Johnsonville bratwurst (brats) are the official brats of Lambeau Field, home field of Wisconsin's Green Bay Packers, and the brand is also sold seasonally at more than 4,000 McDonald's restaurants. The company has plants in Johnsonville, Sheboygan Falls, and Watertown, Wisconsin, and in Momence, Illinois. The company is owned and run by members of the Stayer family. Johnsonville achieved national prominence in the 1990s for its unique management style. Many traditional management roles at the company have been replaced by worker-run teams, and workers control their compensation, hiring and firing, quality control, and near- and long-term goals for the company. CEO Ralph C. Stayer initiated this system in the 1980s, as the company grew from a small regional player to a national marketer.

Early Years

Johnsonville Sausage was founded in 1945 by Ralph and Alice Stayer. The couple bought a small market and slaughterhouse in Johnsonville, Wisconsin, and named the business after the town. Johnsonville is a small community near Sheboygan, north of Milwaukee near the western edge of Lake Michigan. The Stayers were of German and Austrian descent, and they began making sausages according to an old family recipe traced to 19th-century Austria. Their sausages grew popular, and within a year the Stayers had added on to their business. Apparently their bratwurst was a big hit from the very beginning. Founder Ralph Stayer recalled in company documents an early customer requesting ten pounds of bratwurst and 40 pounds of hamburger. "On his next visit," Stayer went on, "he ordered 40 pounds of bratwurst and 10 pounds of hamburger." Stayer knew the young company must have been doing something right.

Johnsonville Sausage expanded throughout the postwar years. In the 1950s and 1960s, the company began selling in more nearby Wisconsin communities. By the 1970s, the company had bought its own fleet of trucks and was making deliveries throughout Wisconsin. The Stayers' son Ralph C. Stayer graduated from Notre Dame, where he studied business and finance, in 1965. He then went to work for the family business. He had worked on the production floor since high school, and his academic training led him to imagine big things for the company. Annual sales were about $1 million when Ralph C. joined Johnsonville full time. Ralph C. got his parents to agree to let him develop the manufacturing and wholesale business, while they remained in control of the retail operations. In 1978, Ralph C. Stayer became president of Johnsonville Sausage. The company also broke ground for a new production facility that year. Stayer began moving the company's products into markets beyond Wisconsin, pushing first into nearby Michigan, Minnesota, and Indiana. As Johnsonville expanded in the 1970s, sales grew at around 20 percent annually. Johnsonville was changing from a small local producer into a leading regional sausage company.

Management Odyssey in the 1980s

By all conventional markers, Johnsonville Sausage was a successful and growing company by 1980. Sales were strong, the company was profitable, and the Johnsonville brand was making inroads into more midwestern markets. Nevertheless, Ralph C. Stayer was deeply dissatisfied with the way things were going, and he pushed the company into a massive change in structure and attitude. Several factors led Stayer to take the company in a new direction. One was fear of competition. Although Johnsonville was doing well, Stayer felt that its success might be tenuous. The sausage industry was dominated by a few national players like Armour and Oscar Mayer, who were able to spend far more on advertising and promotion than Johnsonville could. On the other end, small sausage producers that sold only in their nearby communities had intense customer loyalty. Stayer felt that Johnsonville was too big to be a small producer but not big enough to fight off the national brands, if it came to a battle over market share. The second major factor that set Stayer on his management odyssey was his perception that Johnsonville's workers did not care about the company or their work. This led to many avoidable mistakes. Workers mislabeled products, spiced the meat wrong, wasted time and materials, and even caused physical damage to the plant unintentionally. The product was good, quality control was okay, but Stayer was sure the company could do better, if only the employees cared more about their results. Stayer began reading management books, looking for a solution. He beefed up the company's quality control department, and he began meeting with groups of workers to find out about problems at the plant. But things failed to change at Johnsonville.

Eventually Stayer was sparked by a consultant from the University of Wisconsin, Lee Thayer, who specialized in communication. Thayer pushed the CEO to let Johnsonville's employees solve the company's problems themselves. In 1982, Stayer sent a six-page letter to all his employees, along with a $200 bonus. In the letter, he explained that Johnsonville's workers could become the best paid in the industry as they shared in the profits of the growing company. But they needed to figure out how to make the plant work better. Over the next decade, Stayer completely turned the structure of Johnsonville Sausage around. Workers took control of many aspects of production, the hierarchy of the company simplified, and everyone was compensated in relation to their ability to meet performance goals.

The changes began small, and gradually encompassed the entire way of doing business. For example, workers had complained to Stayer that they did not like the food in the factory's vending machines. Stayer had them research competitors and find a new vending machine company. Ordinarily, Stayer or another manager would have dealt with this. But Stayer felt that

it was not his problem, and he trusted the people who used the vending machines to make the best decision about them. Next came more complex problems. The sausage makers often had to work weekends in order to meet delivery dates, and they resented this. Stayer prodded the workers and plant managers to figure out how they could avoid weekend work, and soon equipment downtime was revealed as the problem. Slipshod work practices had led to a lot of stalled time on the production line. When it was up to them to change it, the Johnsonville workers made many improvements that kept the plant going, and soon they were able to get their weekends free. The workers eventually took responsibility for traditional human resources roles, hiring, firing, and training. Lateness, absence, and maintenance problems declined, and the plant became much more efficient. Workers were compensated for new roles they took on, and they also earned a share of the company's profits. Stayer put 28 percent of profits into a pool that was divvied up every six months. This greatly increased motivation at Johnsonville.

Quality control had been a major issue at the company. Though Stayer had hired more quality control people since 1980, he found that quality had actually gone down. Finally he took a crucial step. He decided that top management would no longer taste the sausage. He asked the people who made the sausage to taste it in a daily session. This seemed to make all the difference. Quality went up as the line workers got to eat and critique what they made. Eventually customer complaint letters were funneled directly to the production workers. They responded to customers and used customer input to find ways to make the sausage better. The quality control department became a new animal at Johnsonville. Instead of checking the quality of the sausage, the quality control department began providing technical support to the line workers who wanted to improve quality. Terminology also changed throughout the company. Workers became ''members,'' and managers became ''coordinators'' or ''coaches.''

This radical change was not easy, yet Stayer was adamant in ceding more and more of his control to Johnsonville's members. Between 1980 and 1985, the company became more efficient, raising its return on assets, and it improved quality and profit margins. Sales climbed to $50 million by 1985, up from $15 million in 1982. That year, the company had the opportunity to take on a big new chunk of business, making private-label sausage for a large competitor who was closing one of its own plants. It was a great chance for Johnsonville to gain more business, but it carried some clear risks. The company would have to run weekend shifts to handle the increased production, but the competitor could cancel the order at any time on only 30 days' notice. Johnsonville could invest in a new plant to handle the increased production, but might have to swallow those costs and lay off workers if the contract was canceled. Stayer's own instinct was to turn down the offer. But instead of making the decision himself or with his senior managers, he called a meeting of the entire workforce, laid out the problem, and asked for input. Workers met in groups, and representatives got back to Stayer with plans. The workers were in favor of taking on the new business, as long as they could continue to improve quality enough to keep their large customer happy. The venture was a success, with expanded sales and a new, efficient production plant completed in 1987.

Stayer wrote in *Harvard Business Review* (November-December 1990), "Everyone at Johnsonville discovered they could do considerably better and earn considerably more than they had imagined. Since they had little trouble meeting the accelerated production goals that they themselves had set, members raised the minimum acceptable performance criteria and began routinely to expect more of themselves and others." He went on, "Our greatest enemy now is our success. Our sales, margins, quality, and productivity far exceed anything we could have imagined in 1980." The company, and Stayer, became media darlings, to the point where Johnsonville began hosting day-long management seminars for executives from other industries curious to learn about the "Johnsonville Way."

Changes in the 1990s and After

Although the company had already turned around, Johnsonville did not stand still. In 1991 Johnsonville held a company-wide meeting and discussed its compensation and profit-sharing systems. Johnsonville changed from offering a six-month performance bonus to allocating a monthly share of profits, dubbed GPS, for Great Performance Shares. This allowed members to be compensated more quickly for meeting goals. The Great Performance Shares came to 20 to 25 percent of an individual's total compensation. Stayer credited Johnsonville's growing sales to improved employee performance. By 1994, sales had climbed to $120 million, and increased to around $165 million the next year. By 1998, sales had grown to $200 million. The company was still a model for its management style, which it had not given up on. A management consultant told the *Business Journal-Milwaukee* (April 17, 1998) that it had been a challenge at Johnsonville both "to give autonomy and maintain structure." The company had swung between poles of chaos and rigidity, but by the late 1990s it was well balanced.

In 1998, Johnsonville entered a venture with leading fast-food restaurant McDonald's to offer Johnsonville brats on the McDonald's menu at selected regional stores. The Johnsonville brats appeared under the Johnsonville brand name at close to 300 McDonald's restaurants in Wisconsin, Illinois, and Michigan's Upper Peninsula. This was the first time McDonald's had offered another company's brand-name product on its menu. The initial rollout was a success, and over the next five years, McDonald's sold Johnsonville brats in more than 4,000 of its restaurants.

Ralph C. Stayer had been president of the company since 1978. His sister Laura had been directing Johnsonville's sales force since 1984. In 2000 the Stayer family agreed to sell 20

percent of the company to the Chicago-based conglomerate Sara Lee . Sara Lee had begun as frozen foods manufacturer, but by 2000 was a huge company that marketed a variety of consumer goods worldwide, from Kiwi shoe polish to the Wonderbra. It acquired a chunk of Johnsonville in 2000 with the aim of strengthening its core packaged food business. Sara Lee's chief executive believed that with the big company's distribution networks, Johnsonville would increase its sales by 6 percent a year under the deal. The arrangement allowed for Sara Lee to purchase the remaining shares in the company at a later time.

The next year, Johnsonville moved to a new advertising agency, the Minneapolis firm Kerker and Associates. Kerker put together a $10 million campaign to elevate Johnsonville to a national brand. The Wisconsin company was well known for its brats, but Kerker hoped to also raise consumer awareness of Johnsonville's other sausages. Television ads highlighted Johnsonville's ties to the football team the Green Bay Packers. These aired during nationally and regionally broadcast games. In 2002, Johnsonville Sausage began airing new commercials on national television. These featured the small town of Johnsonville. The next year, Johnsonville co-sponsored a car on the popular Nascar race circuit. Not only did the car feature the Johnsonville logo, but it had a grill strapped to its hood. The company aimed to bring awareness of brats to markets beyond the Upper Midwest, where they were already established summer grill food.

The market for sausage as a whole grew substantially in the early 2000s. Johnsonville was one of the fastest growing brands in the industry. Between 2000 and 2003, the company found demand for its product growing by almost 20 percent annually. By 2003, Johnsonville employed more than 1,000 people, and put out some 100 million pounds of sausage annually. It broke ground that year for a new plant in Sheboygan Falls, Wisconsin, investing $34 million in the 70,000-square-foot facility. A few months after starting work on the new factory, the Stayer family announced that it had bought back the 20 percent of the company that Sara Lee had bought in 2000. Brother and sister Ralph and Laura Stayer said they had decided to keep the company private.

Principal Competitors

ConAgra Foods, Inc.; Kraft Foods North America, Inc.; Klement's Sausage Co., Inc.

Further Reading

Baar, Aaron, "Johnsonville Looks Beyond Brats," *Adweek,* April 2, 2001, p. 5.
——, "Kerker Builds Sausage Brand," *Adweek,* April 22, 2002, p. 5.
——, "Kerker Kicks Off Johnsonville Effort in Lambeau," *Adweek,* August 27, 2001, p. 6.
Bowe, Christopher, "Stripping Down to Reveal a More Vital Set of Statistics," *Financial Times,* June 7, 2000, p. 34.
Brokaw, Leslie, and Curtis Hartman, "Managing the Journey," *Inc.,* November 1990, p. 44.
Byrne, John A., "Management Meccas," *Business Week,* September 18, 1995, pp. 122–32.
"Family Repurchases Interest in Johnsonville," *Feedstuffs,* September 15, 2003, p. 8.
"Johnsonville Sausage Breaks Ground on Plant," *Wisconsin State Journal* (Madison), June 27, 2003, p. D9.

Lublin, Joann S., "My Colleague, My Boss," *Wall Street Journal,* April 12, 1995, pp. R4, R12.

Lundin, Diana E., "Sausage Executive Finds New Recipe for Success," *Los Angeles Times,* February 24, 1997, p. SS4.

Mullins, Robert, "Johnsonville Workers Test Sausage, Management," *Business Journal-Milwaukee,* April 17, 1998, p. 22.

"Selling Sausage," *National Provisioner,* July 2003, pp. 40–41.

Smith, Rod, "Johnsonville, PSF Form Sausage Venture," *Feedstuffs,* April 14, 2003, p. 6.

Stayer, Ralph, "How I Learned to Let My Workers Lead," *Harvard Business Review,* November–December 1990, pp. 66–74, 80–83.

Stingl, Jim, "Fast Brats," *Milwaukee Journal Sentinel,* December 2, 1998, p. 1.

—A. Woodward

KAWASAKI

Kawasaki Heavy Industries, Ltd.

**Kobe Crystal Tower, 1-3, Higashikawasaki-
cho 1-chrome, Chuo-ku, Kobe 650-8680
Japan
Telephone: (078) 371-9530
Fax: (078) 371-9568
Web site: http://www.khi.co.jp**

Public Company
Incorporated: 1896 as Kawasaki Dockyard Co., Ltd.
Employees: 29,651
Sales: $10.3 billion (2003)
Stock Exchanges: Tokyo Osaka Nagoya
Ticker Symbol: KWHIY
NAIC: 336412 Aircraft Engine and Engine Parts
Manufacturing; 333611 Gas Turbines (Except
Aircraft) Manufacturing; 541330 Industrial
Engineering Services; 336611 Ship Building and
Repairing; 336510 Railroad Rolling Stock
Manufacturing; 336991 Motorcycles and Parts
Manufacturing; 336312 Gasoline Engine and Engine
Parts Manufacturing; 332312 Fabricated Structural
Metal Manufacturing; 331111 Iron and Steel Mills;
234930 Industrial Nonbuilding Structure Construction

Kawasaki Heavy Industries, Ltd. was one of a handful of firms that helped propel Japan into the modern industrial world, playing a major role in the automobile, aircraft, power plant, and heavy-machinery industries as well as in shipbuilding. It was one of the world's leading shipbuilders for much of the 20th century, although in the latter half of the century it developed an equally strong reputation for its motorcycles and lawnmower engines. Long a diversified company, Kawasaki has survived numerous challenges to its shipbuilding business over the course of its history, from the drastic and apparently permanent slump that overtook the shipbuilding industry after the 1973 oil embargo, to the emergence of intense competition from South Korean shipbuilders. The company has managed to stay afloat amid these trends by continually evolving into a multifaceted manufacturer of rolling stock, aircraft, and industrial plants.

Late 19th-Century Company Origins

Shipbuilding gave Kawasaki its start in the world of heavy industry. When Japan emerged from two centuries of isolation in the mid-1800s, its first need as an island nation was to develop a modern shipbuilding industry. The Meiji government at first attempted to run its own shipping lines, but when that effort failed, the government offered considerable subsidies and favorable leasing terms to anyone who cared to try to imitate the sleek Western steamship designs. Shozo Kawasaki was only too eager to accept the challenge. Born in 1836, Kawasaki had survived two maritime disasters as a young man. He attributed his survival to the technical superiority of Western ships in which he had been sailing, and decided to devote his life to bringing such innovations to Japanese shipping. In April 1878, he accordingly borrowed ¥30,000 and leased harbor land in Tokyo from the Japanese government to begin his own shipbuilding company. Kawasaki hired a bright young engineer and opened for business, but he soon discovered that Japanese shipping lines were reluctant to abandon their ancient sailing vessels and traditional style of doing business. After a long wait the new firm finally received its first order, for the 80-ton Hokkai Maru, and Kawasaki invited thousands of business and government leaders to view its christening. This early venture succeeded in announcing the company's arrival in the burgeoning Japanese industrial sector.

Before long Kawasaki had as much work as he could handle. When the Meiji government began divesting major shipbuilding facilities, it offered one to Kawasaki, who happily moved his operations from Tokyo to Hyogo in 1886 and named the company Kawasaki Dockyard. With the Sino-Japanese War of 1894 spurring demand for ships, Kawasaki went public in 1896 as Kawasaki Dockyard Co., Ltd. Its first president was 31-year-old Kojiro Matsukata, and Kawasaki himself remained with the company only as an adviser. Matsukata immediately ordered the construction of a new, vastly larger dry dock, which, upon completion in 1902, solidified Kawasaki's position as one of Japan's leading shipbuilders. At the same time, Matsukata bought up adjacent land and began a series of larger construction slips, increasing the company's building capacity from 6,000 to 31,000 gross tons. Both moves enabled Kawasaki to take advantage of various state subsidies with which the Japanese government encouraged industrial growth, but in a country lacking an industrial economy, it remained difficult for Kawasaki to get materials and parts. In most cases company engineers had to manufacture whatever they needed themselves, an inefficient but educational method of building modern steamships.

Expansion and Diversification in the Early Decades of the 20th Century

In 1906 Kawasaki opened a new factory to produce a variety of rolling stock—railroad cars, locomotives, and related parts. This was only the first of a series of such diversifications. The firm was soon not only building ships and railroad cars but also supplying its own steel plates and castings, as well as taking orders for large civil-engineering projects such as bridges. By the end of World War I, Kawasaki had, in addition, established itself as a maker of airplanes and automobiles, as it sought to keep pace with its heavy-industry rival, Mitsubishi. Kawasaki turned the relative backwardness of the Japanese economy to its advantage: it used the government's enforced education in the industrial arts to expand into new technologies as they found their way to Japan. This process accounts for the breadth of Kawasaki's current interests, and is similar to the development of other Japanese heavy-industry giants.

In the meantime, Kawasaki's shipbuilding business flourished. In 1907 the company introduced its first marine turbine engine, and shortly thereafter adopted German diesel technology. A chunk of the company's business involved naval contracts, like the 1905 construction of Japan's first submarine and the 1910 delivery of a 5,000-ton cruiser. These projects solidified Kawasaki's relationship with the Japanese navy, and in particular its role as a leading builder of submarines and anti-submarine aircraft. After weathering a brief recession, Kawasaki and Japanese shipbuilding as a whole enjoyed a boom during World War I, when the Allies turned with increasing frequency to the Japanese for their shipping requirements. The jump in orders raised production to 12 times the prewar high, with Kawasaki finishing 35 ships in 1918 alone and creating an entirely new class of standardized freighters weighing between 6,000 and 9,000 tons each. These stock boats were highly successful.

The postwar recession in shipbuilding proved to be unusually harsh. In addition to the natural decline in orders, an Allied-sponsored arms-limitation agreement of 1921 forced the cancellation of several large warships still in Kawasaki docks. Perhaps worst of all was the company's failure to cut production of stock boats quickly enough. The excess boats were unsold, and despite rapidly expanding business in its steel, aircraft, and civil-engineering divisions Kawasaki was soon in serious financial trouble. A 1927 bank run left the company without working capital and forced a major restructuring: the rolling stock division was spun off as a separate entity; about 20 percent of the company's 16,000 employees were permanently laid off, and longtime President Matsukata retired to be replaced by Fusanosuke Kojima. These decisions had no sooner been reached than the Depression struck in 1929, necessitating a second round of bank negotiations and corporate reductions.

War pulled Japan out of the Depression in 1931, when that country invaded Manchuria. Along with plentiful government subsidies, the growing need for warships quickly reinvigorated Kawasaki. Between 1937, when China was invaded, and the 1945 Japanese surrender, Kawasaki's employees produced 109 warships, including four aircraft carriers and 35 submarines. Midway through the war the Japanese government essentially took control of the shipbuilding industry, establishing a set of six standard warships to be built under their direction as needed. It was a period of intense productivity at Kawasaki, which also supplied the war effort with aircraft from the newly founded Kawasaki Aircraft Company. Merchant shipping picked up as well. Japan's need for oil spurred the introduction of what would later grow into the supertanker. Kawasaki had built 21 of these by the end of the war in August 1945.

Rapid Growth in the Postwar Era

Losses suffered by Kawasaki at war's end amounted to more than ¥1.7 billion, and the company once again required a major restructuring. It shed its steel division—which, as Kawasaki Steel Corporation, remains one of the country's foremost steel producers—and wrote off much of its debt. At this juncture Kawasaki was composed only of the shipbuilding, engine, and electrical machinery divisions of the original entity, with rolling stock, aircraft, and steel all operating as separate companies.

Employment at Kawasaki had immediately dropped to less than 25 percent of its wartime peak, and the company was saddled with unpaid-for ships. The Kawasaki docks were still largely in one piece and functioning, however, and the company achieved prodigious postwar growth. For the first few years little was built, but with the growing perception of Communist China as a threat, the Allies encouraged Japan to rebuild its economy.

In August 1947 the Japanese government adopted the Programmed Shipbuilding Scheme, by which it directed the construction of new ships as needed while providing funds to the shipping lines to help them cover the purchase price. The scheme, which remains in effect, gave the shipbuilding industry the capital needed to restore productivity.

Thus fortified, Kawasaki resumed operations at all of its plants. Japan's shattered infrastructure promised work for a

Key Dates:

1878: Shozo Kawasaki opens Kawasaki Tsukiji Shipyard in Tokyo to build Western-type oceangoing steel.

1886: Kawasaki moves operations to Hyogo and incorporates the company as Kawasaki Dockyard Co., Ltd.; Kojiro Matsukata is appointed as the first president of the new company.

1896: Company goes public as Kawasaki Dockyard Co., Ltd.

1906: Kawasaki opens a new factory, Hyogo Works, to produce a variety of rolling stock—railroad cars, locomotives, and related parts.

1950: The company spins off its steel division as part of a broad restructuring.

1969: Kawasaki Aircraft Heavy Industries is created by the reintegration of Kawasaki Aircraft and Kawasaki Rolling Stock with the original parent, Kawasaki Dockyard.

1975: Kawasaki becomes the first Japanese motor vehicle producer to produce motorcycles in the United States.

2002: Kawasaki Shipbuilding Corporation and Kawasaki Precision Machinery Ltd. are established as wholly owned subsidiaries.

company with Kawasaki's construction capabilities, and its machinery, steel, and engine divisions were soon operating at full throttle. In particular, the Kawasaki steel division opened three new works and took the lead in Japanese sheet steel production. The shipbuilding business was flooded with more orders than it could handle.

Beginning with the Korean War in 1950 and continuing through to the oil embargo of 1973, Kawasaki and the rest of Japan's shipbuilders enjoyed nearly unbroken success. By the mid-1950s Japan had become the world's leading shipbuilder—a remarkable achievement for a country broken by war only ten years earlier—and as the national economy surged toward eventual world leadership, Kawasaki flexed its muscle in several fields. Growing oil dependence of industrialized countries created a lucrative market for supertankers, and Kawasaki was soon expert in building these largest of all ships. At the same time, Kawasaki was also filling construction orders for everything from a cement plant in Malaysia to a baseball stadium in Koshien, Japan, while improving its technical expertise in engine and machinery design. Many of the latter improvements were the results of working agreements with leading European and U.S. firms, as Kawasaki pursued its policy of international cooperation. The company early formed alliances with Escher Wyss of Switzerland and IMO Ltd. of Sweden, and later worked with aeronautical giants Lockheed, Boeing, Hughes, and Messerschmidt on a wide variety of civil and military projects.

Withdrawing from Shipbuilding in the 1970s

In 1969 the present Kawasaki Aircraft Heavy Industries was created by the reintegration of Kawasaki Aircraft and Kawasaki Rolling Stock with the original parent, Kawasaki Dockyard.

The newly formed conglomerate suffered a blow in 1973 when the Arab oil embargo brought supertanker orders to an abrupt halt. In the years that followed, Japanese companies began a steady withdrawal from the shipbuilding field, and Kawasaki and the other big makers began shifting their energy to more promising, and less competitive, endeavors. The diversity of Kawasaki's portfolio at the time was one result of this massive shift. By the mid-1970s, shipping accounted for less than 10 percent of the company's revenue, lower than sales of leisure products such as motorcycles and jet skis. Its shipbuilding business began primarily to involve military and more exotic varieties of commercial vessels, as Kawasaki sought to avoid direct competition with Korea, the new price leader in merchant shipping.

In contrast, Kawasaki's machinery and construction division grew into the company's largest. Here Kawasaki built everything from factory robots to an ethylene plant in Bulgaria, and also offered bridges, tunnel-boring machines, and breeder-reactor research. Almost as large was the aircraft division, which undertook a significant number of projects for the Japanese Defense Agency and the national space program. In rolling stock, Kawasaki supplied the New York subway system with a set of stainless steel, graffiti-proof cars, while continuing to deliver some of Japan's fastest railroad trains. Add to these three divisions the company's old standby, as well as its newest addition—ships and leisure products—and investors saw a corporation capable of supplying modern civilization with most of its industrial needs.

New Strategies for Evolving Economies: 1980s–90s

In the 1980s, to counteract the negative impact of the declining yen on its export business, Kawasaki shifted its emphasis to the domestic market. By the early 1980s revenues from exports had dropped from 50 percent to 25 percent of the company's total sales. This shift in focus eventually paid off, and by 1990 Kawasaki was enjoying profit levels it had not seen in almost 15 years, with net earnings exceeding ¥20 billion for the first time since 1977, a 25 percent increase over earlier expectations. One major reason for the company's success was the surprising turnaround in its shipbuilding segment. In the face of a marked increase in global demand for new ships, the division had secured more than ¥100 billion worth of new contracts in the past year alone. Overall, Kawasaki Heavy Industries received more than ¥900 billion in new orders in the first three months of 1990, a 20 percent increase over the previous year.

Although the global shipping industry fell into a major slump in the mid-1990s, Kawasaki's shipbuilding division managed to remain profitable. Indeed, in 1994 Kawasaki Heavy Industries was the only leading Japanese shipbuilder to see a net earnings increase for the first half of the fiscal year. The company took further steps to firm up its market position in January 1995, when it struck a major agreement with its longtime strategic partner in China, the China Ocean Shipping Co. Under the terms of the contract, the largest in Kawasaki's history, the company would build six containerships worth more than $83 million apiece. Among the largest vessels of their kind ever built, the containerships would each span nearly 1,000 feet in length, and have a cargo capacity of more than 5,000 20-foot containers.

Still, the long-term profitability of new shipbuilding contracts remained in doubt. The industry-wide trend toward overcapacity, combined with aggressive competition from shipbuilders in South Korea, left Kawasaki struggling to earn consistent profits with its ships. The company once again announced higher than expected profits in mid-1996, but its shipbuilding sector saw an overall loss. Although market fluctuations briefly drove the shipbuilding line into profitability in the second half of 1996, by the following year it had entered a definitive, prolonged slump, forcing the company to ponder a more radical approach to the problem.

A New Business Model for the 21st Century

The company incurred losses in fiscal years 1999 and 2000, much of these connected to restructuring costs, as well as to slumping revenues in its aerospace and general machinery divisions. By May 2000, with its shipbuilding segment in serious debt, Kawasaki began to consider whether or not it should spin off the division. At the same time, the early years of the 21st century witnessed a growing trend toward consolidation in the Japanese shipping industry. Clearly, the company had several routes it could take.

In April 2001, hoping to preserve some stake in its shipbuilding operations, the company entered into an agreement with Ishikawajima-Harima Heavy Industries Co., to form a joint shipping venture by May of the following year. Under the terms of the deal, the companies planned to reduce operating costs by between ¥7 billion and ¥8 billion per year, with an eye toward achieving profits of ¥4 billion to ¥5 billion by 2004. By the fall of that year, however, the companies abruptly terminated the deal, citing difficulties coming to acceptable terms.

For 2001, higher sales and reduced operational costs helped Kawasaki earn ¥6.28 billion, its first profit in four years. Perhaps more significant, the company's shipbuilding division enjoyed net gains of ¥5.6 billion, compared to losses of ¥1.7 billion the previous year. Part of the turnaround came from increased demand for the company's liquefied natural gas carriers. Although Kawasaki saw another significant profit increase in 2002, it fell back into the red the following year. While much of this abrupt turnaround came as a result of a cut in the company's deferred tax assets, the slide was in part due to the continued volatility of the global shipbuilding industry. With the future of this time-honored division in question, in 2004 it remained to be seen how the company would come to a long-term resolution of the problem.

Principal Subsidiaries

Kawasaki Shipbuilding Corporation; NIPPI Corporation; Kawasaki Thermal Engineering Co., Ltd.; Kawasaki Motors Corporation Japan; Kawasaki Precision Machinery Ltd.; Kawasaki Safety Service Industries, Ltd.; Kawaju Shoji Co., Ltd.; Kawasaki Setsubi Kogyo Co., Ltd.; Kawasaki Heavy Industries (U.S.A.), Inc.; Kawasaki Rail Car, Inc.; Kawasaki Robotics (U.S.A.), Inc.; Kawasaki Motors Corp., U.S.A.; Kawasaki Motors Manufacturing Corp., U.S.A.; Kawasaki Construction Machinery Corp. of America; Canadian Kawasaki Motors Inc.; Kawasaki do Brasil Industria e Comercio Ltda.; Kawasaki Aeronautica do Brasil Industria Ltda.; Kawasaki Heavy Industries (U.K.) Ltd.; Kawasaki Precision Machinery (U.K.) Limited; Kawasaki Robotics (UK) Ltd.; Kawasaki Heavy Industries G.m.b.H.; Kawasaki Gas Turbine Europe G.m.b.H.; Kawasaki Robotics G.m.b.H.; Kawasaki Heavy Industries (Europe) B.V.; KHI Europe Finance B.V.; Kawasaki Motors Europe N.V.; Kawasaki Machine Systems Korea, Ltd.; Wuhan Kawasaki Marine Machinery Co., Ltd.; Shanghai Cosco Kawasaki Heavy Industries Steel Structure Co., Ltd.; Nantong Cosco KHI Ship Engineering Co., Ltd.; Kawasaki Heavy Industries (H.K.) Ltd. (Hong Kong); Kawasaki Motors Enterprise (Thailand) Co., Ltd.; KHI Design & Technical Service Inc. (Singapore); Kawasaki Motors (Phils.) Corporation; Kawasaki Heavy Industries (Singapore) Pte. Ltd.; P.T. Kawasaki Motor Indonesia; Kawasaki Motors Pty. Ltd. (Australia).

Principal Competitors

Deere and Company; Mitsubishi Heavy Industries, Ltd.; Toyota Tsusho Corporation.

Further Reading

Chida, Tomohei, and Peter N. Davies, *The Japanese Shipping and Shipbuilding Industries,* London: The Athlone Press, 1990.

Flynn, Matthew, "Kawasaki Heavy Yard Spin-Off Plan Welcomed," *Lloyd's List,* May 11, 2000.

"Kawasaki Heavy Bullish in Spite of Stronger Yen," *Nikkei Weekly* (Japan), July 15, 2002.

"Kawasaki Heavy Only Shipbuilder with Profits, Sales Up," *Japan Economic Newswire,* October 28, 1994.

Magnier, Mark, "Kawasaki Heavy Industries Lands $500 Million Cosco Deal," *Journal of Commerce,* January 4, 1995.

—Jonathan Martin
—update: Stephen Meyer

Key Safety Systems, Inc.

7000 Nineteen Mile Road
Sterling Heights, Michigan 48314
U.S.A.
Telephone: (586) 726-3800
Web site: http://www.keysafetyinc.com

Private Company
Incorporated: 1987 as Breed Automotive Corp.
Employees: 10,000
Sales: $1.1 billion (2003)
NAIC: 334519 Other Measuring and Controlling Device
   Manufacturing; 336399 All Other Motor Vehicle Parts
   Manufacturing; 421120 Motor Vehicle Supplies and
   New Parts Wholesalers

Key Safety Systems, Inc. is a leading producer of automotive equipment such as airbags, seat belts, steering wheels, and interior trim parts. Key Safety was known as Breed Technologies before 2003, when it was acquired by Carlyle Management Group (CMG). It is an affiliate of Carlyle's Key Automotive Group.

Origins

Key Safety Systems, Inc. was founded in 1987 as a spinoff of Breed Corp. Breed Corp. had been started in 1961 as a producer of ammunition components, including mortar fuses.

Company founder Allen K. Breed was born in 1927 in Chicago. According to *Inc.*, his father was an oncologist credited with pioneering radiation therapy. Allen Breed would himself become an acclaimed innovator.

Breed graduated from Northwestern University in 1950. Five years later, after working for RCA as an engineer, he launched a defense-oriented joint venture, Waltham Engineering, with Gruen Watch Company, a maker of gears. Breed left that company in 1961 after a falling out with investors.

Breed developed an electromechanical airbag sensor using his fuse technology in 1968. However, the auto industry did not embrace the airbag concept until prompted by a mid-1980s federal mandate to develop passive restraint systems. Breed delivered its first automotive crash sensor in 1984.

The airbag sensor business was spun off as Breed Automotive Corp. in 1986. Within a couple of years, Breed would be supplying airbag sensors for most Ford and General Motors automobiles.

Sales were $27 million in 1989, noted a retrospective in *Florida Trend.* Breed Automotive lost $8 million. Allen Breed recalled that he and his wife were personally responsible for the company's debt of $43 million.

Public in 1992

In 1991, Congress decreed that all new cars for sale in the United States be equipped with airbags by 1997. During the year, the company's name was changed to Breed Technologies, Inc. Breed went public on the New York Stock Exchange in November 1992 (ticker symbol: BDT). The public offering raised $67 million, most of which went to pay off bank debt of $48.4 million. Sales for 1992 were $88.6 million. Breed accounted for 59 percent of the airbag sensor market for U.S.-built vehicles in the 1993 model year.

Breed relocated its headquarters from Boonton Township, New Jersey, to Lakeland, Florida, in 1993. It had begun to shift manufacturing there three years earlier to a former Sooner Defense plant. The rural location on a 488-acre campus was suited to the company's new business of making airbag inflators, which incorporated small amounts of explosives.

In 1995, the company more than doubled the size of its facilities in Florida to 382,000 square feet. Breed also had three plants in Mexico, one in Turin, Italy, and sales and engineering sites near Detroit, Dayton, Ohio, and Coventry, England.

In the mid-1990s, Breed offered airbag-equipped replacement steering wheels as retrofits for 16 different car models made between 1987 and 1994. Breed tapped Midas Muffler as a retail distribution partner, starting with a test run in Florida. The aftermarket airbags were priced at $900.

Unlike most airbag systems, the retrofits included the crash sensor in the steering wheel itself, rather than up front in the engine compartment. Jaguar, Fiat, and Toyota used this system as original equipment on certain models; Jeep began using this all-mechanical, self-contained airbag system in its Cherokees during the 1995 model year.

Mid-1990s Acquisition Drive

In 1995, Breed had sales of $401 million, up from $278 million in 1994. The company had 4,800 employees and net income was $72.3 million, both figures up roughly 50 percent from the previous year. Breed airbag sensors were found in many brands of vehicle, including Ford and General Motors (which together made up 72 percent of Breed's sales), Mazda, Nissan, Fiat, Toyota, Chrysler, and Jaguar. Not only were airbags becoming more prevalent among passive restraint systems (the other main type being automated seat belts), but the market for cars and trucks was booming in the United States. *Inc.* magazine named Allen Breed its Entrepreneur of the Year in 1995.

However, the market was becoming more competitive, with Ford and GM developing their own electronic airbag sensors to replace Breed's electromechanical ones. Breed had developed its own electronic sensor, and was working on the next generation of inflators as well.

Breed set out on an acquisition drive in order to become a supplier of complete automotive safety systems. In August 1994, the company acquired Hamlin, Inc., a Lake Mills, Wisconsin producer of reed switch products, including airbag crash sensors. Founded in 1949, Hamlin had 1,300 employees and sales of $46 million in 1994. The Finnish Company VTI Hamlin Oy, another maker of sensors, was acquired in June 1995.

The next year, Breed bought circuit board manufacturer Italtest, S.r.l. and MOMO S.p.A. and G. Holding, S.r.l. (MOMO), a maker of steering wheels and alloy wheels. Gallino Plasturgia S.r.l., which produced trim and plastic parts, was also acquired. Gallino, purchased from IAO Industrie Riunite S.p.A., had annual sales of about $250 million.

Sensor producer Force Imaging Technologies, Inc. (FIT) was added in May 1996, as was the steering wheel business of

United Technologies. Breed bought a small crash pulse technology company, Artistic Analytical Methods, Inc., in November.

Breed acquired BTI Investments Inc., the holding company for Custom Trim Group, in February 1997. Custom Trim produced leather-wrapped steering wheels at plants in Canada and Mexico. That October, Breed paid $710 million for SRS, AlliedSignal's airbag and seat belt units, which had sales of $900 million a year. The buy, the company's largest, made Breed the leading safety belt producer in the United States; Breed was also billed as the world's largest steering wheel producer. The firm had about 11,000 employees in 1997, when sales were $795 million. Finally, HS Technik and Design, a seatbelt technology developer, was acquired in May 1998.

BSRS Restraint Systems International, a 50–50 joint venture with the Automotive Systems Group of German electronics firm Siemens AG, was created in 1998. As part of the arrangement, Siemens took a 13 percent share in Breed Technologies (the Breed family owned 46 percent).

Siemens was one of several electronics companies looking for a piece of the airbag sensor business. The future of airbag development, according to automakers, seemed to be in electronic "smart bags" that could adjust to the size and weight of passengers. Breed was also studying inflatable seat belts, designed for minivans and SUVs, as well as curtain walls and other next-generation restraint devices.

Johnnie Cordell Breed, wife of company founder Allen Breed and a successful entrepreneur in her own right, had become Breed's CEO in 1997 when Allen Breed retired from the position. There were serious challenges to face at the time. Breed was on its way to posting a massive loss for fiscal 1998. Extensive layoffs followed. Breed had spent $1.1 billion, most of it borrowed, in accumulating 11 companies between 1994 and 1998; total debt was $1.6 billion.

The company filed for Chapter 11 bankruptcy protection in September 1999. The bankruptcy discharged half of Breed's $1 billion debt; the rest was converted to equity, turning ownership of the company to the company's lenders. Auto components suppliers Harvard Industries and EGI Corp. had submitted unsuccessful takeover offers.

Company founder and Chairman Emeritus Allen Breed died in December 1999, having patented more than 90 inventions during his life. His wife, Johnnie Breed, and President and COO Charles Speranzella would leave Breed Technologies during the reorganization. John Riess, former head of Gates Rubber Co., became the firm's new CEO.

Revenues were about $1.4 billion in 2000 and 2001 and fell to $1.1 billion in 2002 and 2003. The number of employees, which peaked at 16,000 after the acquisition drive, dropped to 10,000 in 2003.

New Owners, New Name in 2003

Carlyle Management Group (CMG), an affiliate of the Washington, D.C. area investment firm, bought Breed on April 27, 2003, for a reported $300 million to $315 million. Analysts considered the acquisition a good sign for the company's

Key Dates:

1961: Defense contractor Breed Corp. is formed.
1968: Allen Breed develops electromechanical airbag sensor.
1984: First airbag sensor is delivered to auto industry.
1986: Breed Automotive is spun off from Breed Corp.
1991: Company name is changed to Breed Technologies, Inc.
1992: Breed goes public on the New York Stock Exchange.
1993: Headquarters are relocated from New Jersey to Florida.
1998: Eleven companies are acquired in mid-1990s acquisition drive.
1999: Breed undergoes Chapter 11 reorganization.
2003: Company is acquired by Carlyle Management Group, renamed Key Safety Systems.

long-term survival. Carlyle Management specialized in turning around troubled companies. CMG CEO Bernie Edward Ewing, a former turnaround specialist with General Dynamics and Lockheed Martin, was named CEO and chairman of Breed.

Ewing noted that Breed had been losing $50 million a year since emerging from bankruptcy. In May 2003, a restructuring was announced that aimed to cut costs by $200 million a year. Overhead was slashed, about 3,500 jobs were cut worldwide, and the company worked with suppliers to lower its material costs. Breed was reorganized into four divisions according to region and product lines: North America; Europe; Asia; and Hamlin, Inc. The Lakeland, Florida home office, which had employed 230 people, was soon closed and administrative operations moved to a suburb of Detroit. Sixty management employees were relocated.

Breed changed its name to Key Safety Systems, Inc. in October 2003, reinforcing its identity as part of Carlyle's Key Automotive Group LLC, which also included Key Plastics LLC, acquired two years earlier during its own bankruptcy. Key Automotive Group had 14,000 employees and sales of $1.7 billion.

Projects in development included a dual-stage airbag inflator and inflatable knee cushions. Breed was also working on a seat belt using a special Honeywell International fiber, Securus, designed to stretch somewhat in the event of an accident.

Principal Operating Units

North America; Europe; Asia; Hamlin, Inc.

Principal Competitors

Autoliv Inc.; Takata Corp.; TRW Automotive Inc.

Further Reading

"Allen Breed (Entrepreneur of the Year)," *Inc.,* December 1995, p. 43.

Backmann, Dave, "You Can Teach an Old Car New Tricks," *News* (Kenosha, Wisconsin), November 6, 1994, p. E1.

Bouffard, Kevin, "Automotive Company Breed Technologies Inc. in Lakeland, Fla., Gets New Name," *Ledger* (Lakeland, Florida), October 2, 2003.

"Breed Makes European Move," *Automotive Components Analysis,* July 1996, p. 3.

Brewer, Bill, "AlliedSignal Gone; Jobs Stay," *News Sentinel* (Knoxville), February 22, 1998, p. D1.

Casey, Jerry, "When Clients Become Competitors," *Florida Trend,* June 1994, p. 76.

Dorfman, John R., "Shares of Breed, a Maker of Air-Bag Gear, Enjoy Nice Run, But Some Fear They Are Overblown," *Wall Street Journal,* May 2, 1994, p. C2.

Gates, Max, "Retrofit Air Bags Are on the Way for 20 Top-Selling Vehicles," *Orlando Sentinel,* July 1, 1993, p. F3.

Gilpin, Kenneth N., "Allied Signal Agrees to Sell 2 Auto Units," *New York Times,* September 3, 1997, p. D4.

Hale, Fraser, and Kim Norris, "A Driving Force in Air Bag Technology," *St. Petersburg Times* (Florida), May 22, 1994, p. 1H.

Johnston, Jo-Ann, "A New Breed," *Tampa Tribune,* Bus. Sec., March 24, 2003, p. 10.

"Kettering's EGI Corp. Fails in Bid for Breed," *Dayton Daily News* (Ohio), June 15, 2000, p. 1E.

Konrad, Rachel, "Lakeland, Fla.-Based Auto Safety-Equipment Maker Files for Bankruptcy," *Detroit Free Press,* September 29, 1999.

"A Long, Slow Haul Ahead," *Automotive Components Analyst,* April 1, 1999.

Norris, Kim, "Air-Bag Pioneer Races Rivals to Smarter Safety Systems," *St. Petersburg Times* (Florida), February 9, 1997, p. 7H.

Petrimoulx, John, "Lakeland, Fla.-Based Auto Parts Firm Breed Technologies Gets New Lease on Life," *Ledger* (Lakeland, Florida), May 18, 2003.

Sasso, Michael, "Investment Firm to Buy Lakeland, Fla.-Based Breed Technologies," *Ledger* (Lakeland, Florida), March 5, 2003.

Simonian, Haig, "Siemens to Take 10% Breed Stake," *Financial Times* (London), October 17, 1997.

Stockfisch, Jerome R., "Breed Has Plan, Rejects Buyout," *Tampa Tribune,* Bus. Sec., September 29, 2000, p. 1.

——, "Troubled Breed Entertains Offer by Harvard Industries," *Tampa Tribune,* Bus. Sec., June 14, 2000, p. 1.

Toothman, Mary, "Automotive Equipment Firm to Pull 290 Jobs Out of Lakeland, Fla., Headquarters," *Ledger* (Lakeland, Florida), May 28, 2003.

Trigaux, Robert, "Midas Steers Toward Air Bags," *St. Petersburg Times* (Florida), October 6, 1995, p. 1E.

Wald, Matthew L., "Retrofitting Old Cars with Driver's-Side Air Bags," *New York Times,* February 2, 1994, p. D5.

Wilkening, David, "For Your Protection," *Florida Trend,* November 1, 1997, p. 28.

Wilson, Amy, "Honeywell Buckles Down to Work on Seat Belt Fiber," *Orlando Sentinel,* April 12, 2001, p. F2.

—Frederick C. Ingram

KIRIN

Kirin Brewery Company, Limited

2-10-1 Shinkawa
Chuo-ku
Tokyo 104-8288
Japan
Telephone: (03) 5540-3411
Fax: (03) 5540-3547
Web site: http://www.kirin.co.jp

Public Company
Incorporated: 1907
Employees: 23,070
Sales: ¥1.60 trillion ($14.91 billion) (2003)
Stock Exchanges: Tokyo Osaka Nagoya Fukuoka
   Sapporo London
Ticker Symbol: 2503
NAIC: 312120 Breweries; 422810 Beer and Ale
   Wholesalers; 312111 Soft Drink Manufacturing;
   312112 Bottled Water Manufacturing; 312130
   Wineries; 312140 Distilleries; 422820 Wine and
   Distilled Alcoholic Beverage Wholesalers; 325412
   Pharmaceutical Preparation Manufacturing; 551112
   Offices of Other Holding Companies

Longtime leader of the Japanese beer market, Kirin Brewery Company, Limited in the early 2000s was overtaken by its archrival, Asahi Breweries, Ltd. Kirin nevertheless continues to sell two of the most popular beers in Japan, Kirin Lager (the country's oldest beer brand) and Ichigan Shibori. In the burgeoning *happoshu* (low-malt) category, Kirin Tanrei is the top seller. In addition, Kirin handles domestic distribution for several foreign brands, including Budweiser and Heineken. Kirin's brewery operations also extend overseas, through strategic alliances, subsidiaries, and affiliates, to China, Taiwan, Australia, the Philippines, Europe, and the United States. The company holds a 46 percent stake in Lion Nathan Limited, a consolidated subsidiary that is based in Australia but has particularly important operations in China. Kirin has also invested a 15 percent stake in San Miguel Corporation, the dominant brewer in the Philippines. With more than 100 years of experience in the brewing business,

Kirin now applies its fermentation technology to areas such as plant genetics, pharmaceuticals, and bioengineering. Although brewing and related businesses remain the core of Kirin's activities, the company is also involved in several other sectors: hard liquor, wine, soft drinks, and food products.

Early History

William Copeland, a naturalized U.S. citizen of Norwegian descent, arrived in Yokohama in 1864. Japan had recently reopened its ports to Western commerce, and Copeland hoped to make his fortune there. He first established a drayage (cart-hauling) business and later a dairy firm; both of these ventures were modestly successful. In 1869, however, responding to the large foreign contingents' demand for domestically brewed beer (Japan had no brewing industry to speak of at this time), Copeland opened the Spring Valley Brewery. In 1872 Copeland left Yokohama temporarily to search for a bride in Norway; later, he returned with his wife, but she died in 1879. Shortly thereafter Copeland, who seemed dogged by misfortune, found that he lacked the necessary capital to improve and expand the business. By 1884 he had closed the brewery and sailed for the United States.

A year later W.H. Talbot and E. Abbott, both foreign entrepreneurs, entered into partnership with two Japanese businessmen, Yonosuke Iwasaki and Eiichi Shibusawa, to reopen Copeland's brewery. With sound financial backing, the newly formed Japan Brewery Company, Ltd. soon became a profitable enterprise. By 1888, all of its beer carried the ''Kirin'' label. According to ancient Chinese legend, the Kirin, which is half horse and half dragon, heralds good fortune to those able to catch a glimpse of it.

Although Copeland's association with the company that would one day control a major share of the Japanese beer market was relatively short and difficult, he is credited with founding the only Yokohama brewery that has survived until the present with some degree of continuity. Copeland returned to Yokohama during the late 1880s to open the Spring Valley Beer Garden next door to his old brewery. He operated his establishment with a new wife, but it was not a success and he again left Yokohama. He returned once more in 1901 and died a

Company Perspectives:

Long-Term (2010) Group Vision: Deliver enjoyment and pleasure through food and health as a trusted partner of consumers. Become a leading alcohol beverage and soft drink company in Asia and Oceania, utilizing leading technology in fermentation and biotechnology.

year later. To this day, however, employees pay tribute to the founder by leaving cans of Kirin beer at his grave.

Initially, many foreigners were involved with the company: Americans and Englishmen filled the executive ranks and German technicians supervised the brewing process. Over the years, however, their presence gradually diminished. By 1907, when the firm was incorporated as Kirin Brewery Company, Limited, management had been taken over entirely by the Japanese; the company was purchased that year by the Mitsubishi family, marking the beginning of Kirin's affiliation with the Mitsubishi *keiretsu*. It was not long before Kirin began to expand rapidly; in 1918 the company constructed a brewery in Amagasaki and later built another facility to house the operations of the Toyo Tozo Company, which Kirin had taken over.

In 1923 the Great Kanto Earthquake destroyed most of the company's facilities in Yokohama, including its main brewery. Kirin, however, soon built a new brewery at a different site in Yokohama. In 1929 Kirin opened its own bottling factory, the Yokohama Bottle Plant. It was clear by this time that the novel attraction of beer had developed into a large market demand; Kirin achieved record sales figures during the mid-1930s.

Postwar Ascendancy

With the start of World War II, the government imposed strict controls over the entire brewing industry. Sales of Kirin beer dropped drastically. Despite a reduction in operations, Kirin established the foundation for its future research and development efforts. In January 1943 the company created the science laboratory at the Yokohama brewery and the research department at the Amagasaki brewery.

Over the years, Kirin's research and development activities outgrew the original facilities. Consequently, to coordinate long-term projects and centralize its scientific investigations, the firm built a new laboratory in Takasaki. The General Research Laboratory, completed in 1967, placed Kirin in the forefront of brewing technology. At Kirin's Takasaki laboratory scientists offered the first explanation for the mechanics of diacetyl formation in the brewing process. Based on this discovery, Kirin devised a way to control metabolism during the period of fermentation. Another noteworthy research effort included the development of the "Amagi-Nijo" strain of malting barley, which eventually commanded more than a 50 percent share of the worldwide market. More recently, company bacteriologists learned how to control a virus known to destroy the bitter flavor of hops.

Sales improved dramatically after the war; during the 1950s the average increase was 17 percent a year. In 1954 Kirin became the number one brewer in Japan, with a market share of 37.1 percent (Kirin had been aided in this by U.S. occupation forces who in 1949 broke the giant Dai Nippon Brewery into two regional companies—Asahi Beer, Ltd. [later Asahi Breweries, Ltd.] and Nippon Breweries, Ltd. [later Sapporo Breweries Limited]—leaving Kirin, temporarily at least, as the only national brewery). By the end of the 1950s, beer had replaced sake as Japan's most popular beverage, fueling additional Kirin growth.

A little more than ten years later, Kirin's sales figures were exceeded by only one other brewery in the world—the St. Louis-based Anheuser-Busch Company, Inc. Much of Kirin's success was attributed to its controlling more than 60 percent of Japan's beer market, which was itself growing by an annual rate of 8 percent. To keep up with this growth, Kirin opened several more breweries in the 1960s and early 1970s. The Nogoya Brewery was completed in 1962, the Takasaki Brewery in 1965, the Fukuoka Brewery in 1996, the Toride Brewery in 1970, the Okayama Brewery in 1972, and the Shiga Brewery in 1974.

Beginning to Diversify in the 1970s

During the early 1970s Kirin's management decided to diversify into new areas. In 1971 a partnership was announced with Joseph E. Seagram & Sons Inc., the U.S. subsidiary of the Montreal-based liquor company; Kirin-Seagram Ltd. operated a distillery in Japan to produce Robert Brown scotch whisky. The company also launched a variety of new soft drinks, and Kirin's Lemon Fizz and Orangeade were generating large sales. Later, dairy items and fruit juices were added to its product line. In 1977 Kirin established a U.S. subsidiary, KW, Inc. (later known as The Coca-Cola Bottling Company of Northern New England, Inc.), to bottle and sell Coca-Cola in New England. In addition, using its expertise and knowledge acquired from years of developing fermentation technology, Kirin introduced new drugs to the health care field.

Kirin's beer sales reached a record high in 1977. But, threatened with an antitrust suit, the company president, Yasusaburo Sato, initiated a temporary program of self-imposed regulation. The plan was to control production, ration distribution, and tone down the advertising campaign. By the following year, Kirin achieved a stabilization in beer sales and still increased revenues because of its successful diversified businesses.

Kirin suffered a setback in the fiscal year of 1979–80. Following the yen's depreciation, import costs for barley and fuel reduced the company's operating profits by 22.2 percent. Moreover, the increased price of domestic barley and wheat, which Japanese brewers were forced to use by government decree, contributed to Kirin's unimpressive performance. The company had to raise the price of its beer; two years later Kirin reported an increase in operating profits.

Making Further Moves Overseas in the 1980s

Kirin had been deterred from selling its beer in foreign markets because of high transportation costs. But in 1984 a licensing contract was arranged with Heineken N.V., the Netherlands-based brewing company, whereby Kirin produced Heineken for the Japanese market and Heineken produced Kirin for the Dutch market.

Key Dates:

1869: William Copeland establishes the Spring Valley Brewery in Yokohama, Japan.
1884: Copeland closes his brewery.
1885: A group of foreign and Japanese businessmen reopen Copeland's brewery as Japan Brewery Company, Ltd.
1888: All of Japan Brewery's beer carries the "Kirin" label.
1907: Firm is incorporated as Kirin Brewery Company, Limited; Mitsubishi family has purchased the company, making it an affiliate of the Mitsubishi *keiretsu*.
1918: Second brewery is established in Amagasaki.
1954: Kirin becomes the number one brewer in Japan.
1962: Another brewery is opened in Nogoya; several more follow over the next dozen years.
1967: General Research Laboratory is completed in Takasaki.
1971: Partnership with Joseph E. Seagram & Sons Inc. is created to produce Robert Brown scotch whisky in Japan.
1984: Alliance with the Dutch brewer Heineken N.V. is established, whereby Kirin begins producing Heineken in Japan and Heineken begins making Kirin in the Netherlands.

1990: Company introduces the draft beer Kirin Ichiban Shibori.
1993: Kirin begins distributing Budweiser beer in Japan through joint venture with Anheuser-Busch Companies, Inc.
1996: Kirin and Anheuser-Busch establish Kirin Brewery of America, LLC to produce and distribute Kirin brands in the United States; Kirin enters the Chinese beer market through a licensing agreement and a joint venture with local partners.
1998: Company enters the *happoshu* (low-malt beer) segment with the launch of Kirin Tanrei; a 45 percent stake in Lion Nathan Limited is acquired.
2000: Anheuser-Busch dissolves its joint venture with Kirin in Japan, replacing it with a licensing agreement between the two firms.
2001: Kirin enters the Japanese market for *chu-hi* low-alcohol drinks; the company loses its position as the top brewer in Japan to Asahi Breweries, Ltd.
2002: A 15 percent interest in San Miguel Corporation is acquired.

As Japanese cuisine became popular with Americans, the demand for Kirin beer increased. The firm established the Cherry Company Ltd., a wholly owned subsidiary in Hawaii, to supervise Kirin's U.S. market distribution. Kirin USA, Inc. was then established in New York in 1983 to promote sales.

By 1986 Kirin's international operations encompassed Europe, North America, South America, Asia, and Australia. In West Germany, Kirin contracted Krones A.G. to market empty bottle inspection machinery. (This equipment marked the introduction of intelligent robots to the brewing industry.) In Brazil, Kirin held a majority interest in a food and beverage company; in China, the company constructed a soft drink production factory; in Australia, the Kirin Australia Pty. Ltd. subsidiary manufactured and supplied Kirin products to the Australian market. In 1987 the company entered into an agreement with Molson Companies Ltd. (later known as Molson Breweries of Canada Limited) whereby Molson would brew Kirin beer in Canada for sale in Canada and the United States. The following year Kirin bought Raymond Vineyard and Cellars, Inc., a winery in California's Napa Valley.

In the 1980s, management initiated major changes in Kirin's research and development program. The company's laboratory was divided and reorganized along three major fields of investigation—brewing science, pharmaceuticals, and plant bioengineering. New departments were also added at the administrative level to coordinate fund-raising activities for research projects.

A number of joint ventures with American companies established in the 1980s increased Kirin's participation in the field of biotechnology. In 1984 Kirin completed a 50–50 venture—known as Kirin-Amgen, Inc.—with Amgen Inc., a California-based company, to develop and market a synthetic human hormone to treat anemia. This pharmaceutical, called Erythropoietin, was created to help patients undergoing kidney dialysis. In the past, many patients commonly became anemic and required blood transfusions during treatment. Another potential application was as a drug for cancer patients suffering blood cell reduction from chemotherapy. Kirin also combined its resources with an agricultural biotechnology company, Plant Genetics Inc., to develop synthetic seeds for a variety of agricultural products.

A successful chain of beer pubs called Kirin City was started in the Roppongi district in 1983, eventually growing to 11 pubs across Japan. Similarly, the Kirin Food Service Co., Ltd. was established to operate a restaurant franchise. Kirin also constructed a number of health clubs and sports complexes across the nation. Another addition to Kirin's list of subsidiaries was Flower Gate Inc., which produced African violets developed by an innovative tissue culture process.

Facing Heightened Domestic Competition in the Late 1980s and 1990s

In the mid-1980s Kirin maintained a domestic market share in beer of about 60 percent, with Sapporo holding 20 percent, Asahi at 10 percent, and Suntory Ltd., a whiskey distiller that had entered the beer market in 1963, at 8 to 9 percent. Asahi then made an extraordinary leap starting in the late 1980s, catching Kirin more or less flat-footed, with Asahi's most important move coming in March 1987 when Asahi Super Dry, Japan's first dry beer, was introduced. Super Dry, a cold-filtered draft beer, quickly became popular with younger drinkers who liked its lighter, less bitter taste. Just a year after Super Dry's introduction, Asahi increased its domestic market share to 17 percent. By 1996 Super Dry became the top-selling beer in

Japan, displacing Kirin Lager, and Asahi's market share had increased to 35 percent while Kirin's had fallen to 47 percent.

During this period Kirin faced not only stiffened competition but also changes in consumer tastes and distribution, to which the company failed to react quickly enough. Japanese consumers wanted lighter, less bitter beers—Super Dry delivered this; Kirin Lager did not. Kirin eventually, somewhat belatedly, in early 1996, gave in to consumer preferences and changed Kirin Lager to a less bitter, draft beer. In the intervening years, Kirin was not idle, however, having introduced, in 1990, the successful Kirin Ichiban Shibori (meaning "first pressing"), which quickly became the country's number three beer brand. Kirin Light also debuted in 1989. Nevertheless, Kirin was certainly slow to adapt to changes in beer distribution in Japan. For decades, beer had been sold in small liquor stores by the bottle, and Kirin had built a nationwide distribution network of special contract wholesalers who sold to the liquor stores. The emergence in Japan of convenience stores and discounters in the late 1980s marked a major shift in the way consumers purchased beer, and by the mid-1990s as much beer was sold through these new outlets as through the traditional liquor stores. With its long-established distribution network and with most of its beer still bottled rather than canned (the new outlets preferred the easier-to-stock cans), Kirin was unable to shift quickly to the new outlets. By the mid-1990s, Kirin had gone a long way toward adapting to the new environment—offering more canned beer and shifting more of its stock to the convenience stores and discounters. But the firm's belated moves only slowed the steady decline of its market share, and in late 1997 Kirin was forced to restructure. It closed three aging breweries located in Tokyo, Kyoto, and Hiroshima, shifting production to its remaining 12 plants, and began a process to reduce its workforce by 20 percent, or about 1,000 employees, through attrition by 2000.

At the same time that it was defending itself at home, Kirin was aggressively expanding its foreign brewing ventures. In 1989 the company established a brewing operation in Hong Kong called Kirin Brewery (H.K.) Co., Ltd. The following year Kirin entered into an agreement with South Korea's Oriental Brewery Co., Ltd. whereby Kirin would sell OB Beer, South Korea's top beer, in Japan. In 1992 Kirin entered into a joint venture with Charles Wells Ltd. through which the U.K. brewer began making and selling Kirin beer in Europe. That same year the company's joint venture with Molson ended, and it began distributing its products in the United States. Kirin and Anheuser-Busch Companies, Inc. in 1993 entered into a joint venture, Budweiser Japan Co., for the distribution of Budweiser beer in Japan. Three years later the two companies established Kirin Brewery of America, LLC to produce and distribute the Kirin Lager, Kirin Ichiban (equivalent to Kirin Ichiban Shibori), and Kirin Light brands in the United States at an Anheuser-Busch facility in the Los Angeles area; Kirin invested an initial $8 million in this venture, which began production in April 1997. In addition to solidifying its position in the world's number one beer market—the United States—Kirin also aimed to grab a share of the Chinese market, number two in the world in the mid-1990s but predicted to surpass the United States in beer consumption in the early 21st century. In April 1995 Kirin signed a licensing agreement with China Resources (Shenyang) Snowflake Brewery Co. (the second largest brewer in China), through which Kirin beer would be brewed on a consignment

basis for sale in seven large cities in northern China. Production began in June 1996. A few months later, Kirin entered into a joint venture called Zhuhai Kirin President Brewery Co., Ltd., which operated in China's Guangdong province, where it began brewing Haizhu Beer and Ichiban Shibori for the Chinese market.

Late 1990s and Early 2000s: Losing Market Share at Home, but Gaining Ground Overseas

In the late 1990s and into the early 2000s, the overall beer market in Japan was stagnant (in part because of the shrinking number of young people), but there was a significant shift occurring in the types of beers that Japanese people were consuming. Rapidly growing in popularity were low-malt beers known as *happoshu*. Starting in 1994, some Japanese brewers decided to take advantage of the Japanese tax system, which taxed beer according to its malt content. The tax on low-malt beers was significantly lower, resulting in a retail price about two-thirds that of a regular beer. Budget-conscious consumers, wracked by the lengthy Japanese recession, snapped up the lower-priced beer in increasing numbers, such that by 2000 the *happoshu* segment accounted for 22 percent of the overall beer market. (To maintain a beer-like taste, producers of *happoshu* used various types of malt substitutes.) Kirin joined the *happoshu* bandwagon in February 1998 when it launched Kirin Tanrei. The new brew quickly captured the top spot in its sector, grabbing half of the *happoshu* market.

Amid the increasing competition at home, Kirin announced in September 1997 its intention to seek mergers and acquisitions to increase its presence overseas. Its first step in this direction came in April 1998 when it revealed it had purchased a 45 percent stake in Lion Nathan Limited for NZD 1.33 billion ($746.1 million). Lion Nathan operated two breweries in New Zealand, where it had a 54 percent market share, and four in Australia, where its share was 42 percent. Its brands included Castlemaine XXXX, Swan, Tooheys, Steinlager, and Lion Red. Also attractive to Kirin was Lion Nathan's significant presence in China, where it had a joint venture brewery in Wuxi and a wholly owned brewery at Suzhou, both located in the Chang (Yangtze) River Delta area.

At the start of 2000 Anheuser-Busch dissolved its six-year-old joint venture with Kirin in Japan, Budweiser Japan Co., after the venture fell victim to the highly competitive market and turned loss-making. The venture was replaced by a licensing agreement between the two companies, whereby Kirin took over production and distribution of the Budweiser brand in Japan. Later in 2000, as part of its ongoing cost-containment efforts, Kirin closed another of its aging Japanese breweries, this one located in Takasaki. In January 2001 Kirin adopted a holding company structure to oversee its group companies' operations; each business sector—including brewing, soft drinks, distilled liquor, food, and pharmaceuticals—gained more independence. Also in 2001, Kirin entered another growing low-alcohol market in Japan, *chu-hi* drinks, canned mixtures of distilled liquor and fruit juices. Through the combined talents of Kirin's brewing, liquor, and soft drinks businesses, Kirin Chu-hi Hyoketsu had a strong debut and was offered in several varieties, including lemon, grapefruit, orange, plum, and lime. The liquor used was *shochu*, a local spirit similar to vodka but specially distilled to remove all harsh flavors.

In February 2001 arch-rival Asahi Breweries launched its first *happoshu* beer, and despite being the last of the major Japanese brewers to enter the segment, Asahi Honnama captured 22.3 percent of the *happoshu* market for 2001. This strong debut finally knocked Kirin from its perch as the top Japanese brewer—a position it held for nearly 50 years—as Asahi grabbed 38.7 percent of the market in 2001, compared to Kirin's 35.8 percent.

Early in 2002 Kirin acquired the global rights to the Four Roses brand of bourbon whisky. The company completed its second acquisition of a stake in a major Asia-Pacific brewer in February of that year when it spent PHP 27.88 billion ($544 million) for a 15 percent stake in San Miguel Corporation, the overwhelmingly dominant beer maker in the Philippines, where it held a 90 percent market share. In addition to its five breweries in the Philippines, San Miguel also operated breweries in China, Vietnam, Indonesia, and Australia. Meantime, Kirin and Lion Nathan joined forces in May 2002 to launch a new product in Taiwan called Kirin Bar Beer, the first low-priced beer sold outside of Japan under the Kirin name. In November 2002 Kirin Brewery's Kirin Beverage Corporation subsidiary, Groupe Danone of France, and Mitsubishi Corporation established a joint venture called Kirin MC Danone Waters Co., Ltd. with the explicit aim of creating the leading mineral water company in Japan.

In 2003, despite an unusually cool summer in Japan and an increase in the tax on *happoshu,* which made the low-malt beers more expensive but still cheaper than regular brews, Kirin Brewery managed to eke out a small increase in sales while seeing net income fall very slightly. Despite the tax increase, sales of *happoshu* kept growing, accounting for more than 40 percent of the overall beer market in Japan by 2003; Kirin predicted that during 2004 it would, for the first time, sell more *happoshu* than traditional beer. Nevertheless, sales of *chu-hi* drinks were growing even faster, and Kirin saw its revenues in that sector jump 44 percent in 2003. Overseas, Kirin and Lion Nathan continued to collaborate on new products, launching Kirin Pure and Light in Shanghai and Kirin Ichiban—First Press Beer in Australia and New Zealand. In April 2004 Kirin's Chinese affiliate Zhuhai Kirin President Brewery introduced Haizhu Draft Beer into its market area in Guangdong province. Kirin may have been dethroned from the top spot in Japanese brewing, but its aggressive pursuit of faster growing markets overseas boded well for the future.

Principal Subsidiaries

ALCOHOLIC BEVERAGES BUSINESS: El Sho Gen Co., Ltd.; Kirin Distillery Co., Ltd.; Kirin Australia Pty. Ltd.; Lion Nathan Limited (Australia; 46%); Zhuhai Kirin President Brewery Co., Ltd. (China); Kirin Europe GmbH (Germany); Taiwan Kirin Company, Ltd.; Four Roses Distillery LLC (U.S.A.); Kirin Brewery of America LLC (U.S.A.); Raymond Vineyard & Cellar, Inc. (U.S.A.). SOFT DRINKS BUSINESS: Hokkaido Kirin Beverage Corp.; Kirin Beverage Corporation; Kirin MC Danone Waters Co., Ltd.; Vivax Co., Ltd.; The Coca-Cola Bottling Company of Northern New England, Inc. (U.S.A.). PHARMACEUTICALS BUSINESS: Kirin Kunpeng (China) Bio-Pharmaceutical Co., Ltd.; Kirin Pharmaceuticals (Asia) Co., Ltd. (Hong Kong); Jeil-Kirin Pharmaceutical Inc. (South Korea); Kirin Pharmaceuticals Co., Ltd. (Taiwan); Gemini Science, Inc. (U.S.A.). OTHER BUSINESSES: Kirin Dining Co., Ltd.; Kirin Engineering Co., Ltd.; Kirin International Trading Inc.; Kirin Lease Co., Ltd.; Kirin Logistics Co., Ltd.; Kirin Techno-System Corp.; Kirin Well-Foods Company, Limited; Nagano Tomato Co., Ltd.; Takeda-Kirin Foods Corporation; Yokohama Akarenga, Inc.; Yokohama Arena Co., Ltd.; Indústria Agrícola Tozan Ltda. (Brazil); Qingdao International Seed Co., Ltd. (China); Germicopa S.A. (France); Fides Holding B.V. (Netherlands); Kirin Agribio EC B.V. (Netherlands); Barberet & Blanc, S.A. (Spain); Southern Glass House Produce Ltd. (U.K.); Twyford International, Inc. (U.S.A.).

Principal Competitors

Asahi Breweries, Ltd.; Sapporo Breweries Limited; Suntory Limited; Takara Holdings Inc.; Mercian Corporation.

Further Reading

Agnew, Joe, " 'Japanese Beer from Canada': Kirin Pushes for Larger U.S. Market Share," *Marketing News,* January 18, 1988, pp. 1, 2.

"Asahi Flattens Kirin's King of Beers," *Nikkei Weekly,* July 8, 1996, p. 9.

Bassiri, Houtan, "Kirin Gains Controlling Interest in Lion," *Asian Wall Street Journal,* April 28, 1998, p. 11.

"How Kirin Lost Its Sparkle," *Economist,* September 14, 1996, pp. 66–67.

"Japan's Beer Wars," *Economist,* February 18, 1998, p. 68.

Kato, Hiroyuki, "Focus or Diversify? Top Brewers Have Different Recipes for Success," *Daily Yomiuri,* January 25, 2002.

Keck, Barbara, "Kirin Yokohama: Japan's Super-Brewery Built on Cooperation, Technology, Discipline," *Beverage Industry,* January 1993, p. 1.

Kuramitsu, Yumi, "Brewers Step Up Fight for Market Share," *Daily Yomiuri,* September 18, 1997.

Larano, Cris, "San Miguel Shareholders Approve Kirin Buy-In," *Asian Wall Street Journal,* February 28, 2002, p. M3.

Murakami, Fumika, "Kirin Brews Up Formula to Restore Health," *Nikkei Weekly,* October 6, 2003.

Ono, Yumiko, "Anheuser Scraps Kirin Venture, Citing Low Sales," *Asian Wall Street Journal,* November 3, 1999, p. 4.

Rahman, Bayan, "Japan Strengthens Its Brew: Asahi and Kirin Breweries Are Tapping China's Soft Drinks Market to Life Sales," *Financial Times,* January 7, 2004.

——, "Kirin Eyes Expansion As Beer Market Goes Flat," *Financial Times,* July 29, 2002, p. 13.

"A Right Old Brewhaha in Japan," *Economist,* February 24, 2001, p. 67.

Robinson, Gwen, and Bethan Hutton, "Japanese Group Eyes Lion's Share," *Financial Times,* April 28, 1998, p. 31.

Sato, Makoto, "Brewers Belly Up to Burgeoning China Market," *Nikkei Weekly,* December 4, 1995, p. 8.

Tanzer, Andrew, "Beer Wars from Across the Pacific," *Forbes,* April 18, 1988, pp. 33–35.

Yamamoto, Yuri, "In Beer Battle, Kirin Goes Flat While Asahi Barrels Ahead," *Nikkei Weekly,* March 3, 1997, pp. 1, 19.

——, "Japan's Brewers Tapping Chinese Market," *Nikkei Weekly,* October 7, 1996, pp. 1, 21.

—update: David E. Salamie

*Pioneering Medicines
for a Better Life®*

Kos Pharmaceuticals, Inc.

1001 Brickell Bay Drive
Miami, Florida 33131
U.S.A.
Telephone: (305) 577-3464
Fax: (305) 577-4596
Web site: http://www.kospharm.com

Public Company
Incorporated: 1996
Employees: 726
Sales: $293.9 million (2003)
Stock Exchanges: NASDAQ
Ticker Symbol: KOSP
NAIC: 325412 Pharmaceutical Preparation
    Manufacturing

Kos Pharmaceuticals, Inc. specializes in the development of proprietary pharmaceutical products for the treatment of cardiovascular and respiratory disease through the reformulation of existing, government-approved medicines. By reformulating approved medications into different forms of delivery, such as a time-release pill, a skin patch, or an inhalation device, Kos seeks to improve the safety and effectiveness of these products, as well as to make them easier for patients to use.

Kos markets two proprietary cholesterol modulation products, reformulated with its patented time-release technology. Niaspan is a once-a-night tablet of a niacin compound prescribed for reducing low-density lipoprotein (LDL), or bad cholesterol, and raising high-density lipoprotein (HDL), or good cholesterol. Advicor, a combination of time-release niacin and lovastatin in once-a-night dosage, provides stronger cholesterol modulation by increasing HDL cholesterol and lowering LDL, triglycerides (TG), and lipoprotein (a). For the treatment of asthma, Kos owns and markets Azmacort Inhalation Aerosol, an inhaled corticosteroid manufactured by Aventis Pharmaceuticals. Kos takes its name from the Greek island where Hippocrates originated the science of medicine.

Company's Founding by Successful Team of Executives in 1988

Before forming Kos Pharmaceuticals, Michael Jaharis, with then partner Dr. Phillip Frost, owned and operated Key Pharmaceuticals. The two men acquired Key in 1972 for $50,000 as the company neared bankruptcy. Under the direction of Jaharis and Frost, Key became profitable, first marketing the company's cough and cold medicines, then a best-selling asthma product, Theo-Dur. The product originated with a 50-year-old asthma medicine, theophylline, which Jaharis and Frost revived by applying time-release technology to resolve problems associated with the drug. During Jaharis and Frost's ownership of Key, revenues increased from less than $1.5 million in 1972 to $200 million in 1986. That year Key merged with Schering-Plough, with Schering-Plough acquiring Key for $826 million. Jaharis gained $90 million from the transaction and reinvested the funds to start Kos Pharmaceuticals.

Jaharis founded Kos in 1988 along with two other former Key executives, Daniel Bell, the chief operating officer, and David Bova, director of product development. Taking the positions of chairman, chief executive, and director of product development, respectively, Jaharis, Bell, and Bova formed Kos Pharmaceuticals to take advantage of medicine reformulation opportunities. Because existing medications have withstood the rigors of research and development, as well as regulatory scrutiny, newly reformulated products could potentially be developed at a significantly lower cost. In addition, a product created with a new delivery system is considered proprietary and, therefore, patent protected from generic imitations for a period of time.

From the start Kos focused on the development of pharmaceutical products for the treatment of chronic cardiovascular and respiratory diseases. The company's most promising product involved a time-release version of niacin, a B-vitamin, known to reduce LDL and increase HDL. Niacin has an uncomfortable side effect, a prickly flushing sensation, and is potentially damaging to the liver, however. Existing time-release niacin products did not address these problems adequately and delivered the niacin too slowly.

Company Perspectives:

Kos is committed to being a leading provider of specialty pharmaceuticals.

Our Company will improve human health and quality of life through our innovation in drug-delivery systems, product development and commercialization.

The Kos culture, rich in spirit, fosters peak performance for the benefit of patients, health-care practitioners, customers, shareholders, and employees.

To support the development of respiratory products, Kos acquired Aeropharm Technology, Inc. and IEP Group, Inc. in 1993. Aeropharm developed asthma medicine, and IEP designed and engineered proprietary, ergonomically correct inhalation devices that deliver the medicine into the lungs. In 1996 Kos signed an agreement to collaborate on hypertension products with Fuisz Technologies, Ltd., a specialist in controlled release formulations of pharmaceuticals. Lower-cost products became available, however, and Kos ended the program in 1998.

Research and development on time-release niacin took several years, during which time Jaharis provided incremental loans to support the process. As a development stage company, Kos lost $42 million during the three years from 1994 through 1996. The losses increased progressively as Kos completed the four phases of clinical trials on Niaspan, its time-release niacin product, as required by the Food and Drug Administration (FDA). Phase I and Phase II proves the efficacy and safety of a product, Phase III initiates human clinical trials, and Phase IV involves a wider sample of patients.

Kos filed for related patents as research proved its claims. In 1995 the company filed a patent claim for method-of-use in the composition of niacin and hydroxypropyl methylcellulose as a once-a-night sustained-release treatment of hyperlipidemia (high cholesterol). Two patents made additional claims for the niacin composition. One, filed in March 1997, established claims for safety, involving lower elevations of uric acid and glucose and reduced liver toxicity; the other patent, filed in October, asserted claims for reducing flushing.

1997 Transition from Development Stage to Marketing Stage

Kos took a number of steps to prepare for the public introduction of its sustained-release niacin, named Niaspan. First the company hired another Key executive to develop a marketing strategy, Robert E. Baldini, formerly senior vice-president of sales and marketing, and, later, president of Key as a division of Schering-Plough. Baldini joined Kos as vice-chairman and chief sales and marketing officer and began to develop a sales organization.

In March 1997 Kos made an initial public offering of 3.6 million shares of stock at $15 per share. Although Kos had not made the transition from a development stage company to a marketing company, and held $60 million in debt, investors expressed confidence in an experienced management team with a record of success. Kos applied proceeds from the offering to fund its marketing efforts.

In late July Kos received final FDA approval to market Niaspan for lowering LDL cholesterol, triglycerides (TG), and ApoB in patients with hypercholesterolemia (high cholesterol) and mixed dyslipidemia (mixed lipid disorder). A few days later Kos hired a staff of 85 sales representatives experienced in cardiovascular medical products to promote Niaspan. The initial market involved 70,000 specialists in coronary heart disease, including cardiologists, endocrinologists, and internists, as well as general practice physicians. On August 15, the company shipped its first orders to wholesalers, meeting its promise to shareholders to bring a new product to market in a timely manner.

With a new product bringing income to the company, Kos made a secondary offering of 3.6 million shares of common stock at $42.75 per share, including 2.15 million shares owned by Jaharis, reducing his ownership in the company from 69.7 percent to 52.5 percent. The company's net proceeds of $44.1 million, from 1.1 million primary shares sold, were used to expand its sales and marketing staff, as well as production, and to fund research and development for eight other products.

Initial sales of Niaspan progressed slowly for several reasons. Competition from a plethora of new cholesterol modulating products hindered sales. Pfizer introduced a cholesterol-reducing product, Lipitor, five months before Kos introduced Niaspan. Pfizer, as well as other large pharmaceutical companies with similar products, had the advantage of a large sales force and an established presence. In addition, Kos did not advertise or market the product prior to FDA approval and did not advertise directly to consumers. Kos reported revenues of $2.8 million in 1997, and a net loss of $40.6 million.

Throughout 1998 Kos expanded its sales force to 200 representatives, provided more sales training, and narrowed its market to 25,000 high prescribers in large cities. The retail prescription rate increased steadily, an average 20 percent per month. Kos executives considered this successful growth given the size of the company's sales organization. In 1998 sales of Niaspan reached $13 million.

In July 1998 Kos filed an application with the Medicines and Healthcare Products Regulatory Agency to market Niaspan in the United Kingdom, the first step toward expanding distribution throughout Europe. The United Kingdom acts as a reference member state. After approval there, the next step is to gain approval in individual countries through the European Union Mutual Recognition Procedure.

To expand its revenue base and to make fuller use of its sales staff, Kos signed an agreement with Knoll Pharmaceuticals Company in July 1999 to co-promote Knoll's once-a-day, anti-hypertension drugs, Mavik (trandolapril) and Tarka (trandolapril/extended release verapamil). Kos and Knoll shared the costs of promotions, using Kos's sales force, which specialized in marketing to cardiovascular physicians. Kos obtained the right to market Mavik and Tarka for five years and to receive an increasing percentage of revenues as sales grew. Kos expected $5 million in revenues the first year, and $25 million by 2004.

Kos received a boost for potential sales of Niaspan in October when the FDA approved a supplemental application of the product for increasing HDL cholesterol in patients with dyslipidemia, the second product to obtain approval for HDL treatment. Advanced clinical studies showed that Niaspan raised HDL up to 26 percent while it lowered LDL up to 17 percent, and TG up to 35 percent.

Niaspan sales potential increased with the approval of several healthcare services extending coverage for the product. By the end of 1999 eight of the ten largest health maintenance organizations and nine of the ten largest pharmacy benefits managers provided reimbursement for Niaspan prescriptions. Niaspan won approval for reimbursement by state Medicaid agencies in California and Tennessee, where standards were the most stringent. Thus coverage was automatically extended to Medicaid agencies in all 50 states. In January 2000 the U.S. Veterans Affairs Department extended coverage to Niaspan, adding it to the national formulary at 170 hospitals serving more than 3.5 million military veterans.

During 2000 Kos obtained approval of patents filed for components of Niaspan technology in 1995 and 1997. These included the composition and method-of-use patent for once-a-night dosage and the patent related to additional claims on safety and formulation. The two patents extended patent protection for Niaspan to 2017, as well as to other products, not yet on the market, which contained a once-a-night dosage of time-release niacin, alone or in combination with another compound.

Aeropharm Technology obtained two patents in November 2000 for formulations of non-ozone depleting propellants for use in pressurized metered-dose inhalation devices, with patent protection expanded to 2017 and 2018. This brought Kos's total patents to 20, with another 38 patents pending. In July 2001 the Aeropharm subsidiary received a patent for a non-ozone depleting formulation that used water as the stabilizing component to deliver aerosolized protein through an inhaler.

2002 Launch of Second Proprietary Product: Advicor

In September 2000 Kos filed a New Drug Application for a new product, then named Nicostatin, which integrated the benefits of Niaspan with lovastatin, a drug known to reduce cholesterol. In preparation for product launch Kos signed a marketing agreement with DuPont Pharmaceuticals to market Nicostatin. DuPont agreed to invest up to $80 million in Kos, beginning with an initial equity investment of $30 million plus $20 million for product development. Kos and DuPont agreed to share equally in promotional costs as well as profits, less initial royalties paid to Kos.

Bristol-Myers Squibb acquired DuPont Pharmaceuticals in late 2001, however, and terminated the agreement. In December Kos received a $45 million cash settlement from Bristol-Myers Squibb, which brought Kos to profitability for the first time. Without the settlement Kos would have recorded a net loss of $36.6 million in 2001, but instead recorded net income of $2.4 million. Revenues reached $91.4 million in 2001, including about $7 million in royalties from the sale of Knoll products.

Kos applied funds from the settlement to the launch of Nicostatin, renamed Advicor, after Kos received FDA approval in late 2001 to begin marketing the product. Advicor became the first dual-component treatment for cholesterol modulation to be approved by the FDA, as clinical trials showed that Advicor increases HDL cholesterol up to 30 percent while it lowers LDL up to 42 percent, TG up to 44 percent, and lipoprotein (a) up to 22 percent. Kos launched Advicor in January 2002 with a staff of 300 sales representatives. The company allocated more than five times the resources for marketing than it did for Niaspan, expanding its market base to primary care physicians and incorporating a medical education program. A two-year marketing agreement with Quintiles Transnational added 150 sales representatives specially trained in cardiovascular health to Kos's sales efforts. Sales of Advicor reached $27 million in 2002 and seemed to benefit sales of Niaspan, which rose 73 percent to $146 million.

Overcoming Hurdles to International Distribution in 2003

With patents in place and a second product on the market, Kos focused on international distribution of its products. In June 2001 Kos hired Adrian Adams as chief operating officer. Formerly chief executive officer of Novartis-UK, the Swiss pharmaceuticals giant, Adams brought international experience to Kos just as the company prepared for overseas expansion. Adams became chief executive of Kos in January 2002; Bell became chairman and Jaharis, chairman emeritus.

Initial international expansion focused on Europe and Canada. Kos applied to the European Union to market Advicor in July 2002 and, a few months later, signed an agreement with Merck KGaA to market Niaspan and Advicor outside of North America and Japan. Kos received an initial payment of $15 million to be supplemented with licensing and milestone fees, expected to add up to $46 million in revenues, as well as royalties of 25 percent of net sales. In August 2003 Kos signed an agreement with Oryx Pharmaceuticals to market Niaspan and Advicor in Canada, granting Oryx exclusive rights. Kos expected the drugs to be approved by late 2005.

Kos continued to advance its sales efforts within the United States. Kos signed a comarketing agreement with Takeda Pharmaceuticals-North America (TPNA) to market Niaspan and Advicor to 48,000 physicians. More than 1,000 TPNA sales representatives sold the products as a complement to TPNA's ACTOS, a pioglitazone HCI used by patients with type 2 diabetes, which is associated with cardiovascular disease. Kos expected 10 percent revenue growth from the association with TPNA during 2004.

In order to better compete with large pharmaceutical companies, Kos continued to approach health insurance providers to advocate for coverage of Niaspan and Advicor. Kos emphasized its role as a specialty manufacturer providing a lower-priced option. Price comparisons illustrated the difference. For instance, a bottle of 60 tablets of 500 mg Niaspan sold at Walgreens for $79.99, while 30 tablets of 40 mg of Pfizer's Lipitor sold for $95.99; 500 mg Advicor was priced at $55.99. Comparatively, the daily dose was $1.70 for Niaspan, $1.97 for Advicor, and $2.42 for Lipitor.

Merck began to market Niaspan in the United Kingdom in November 2003, a few months after receiving approval. The United Kingdom approved the Niaspan label for the treatment of dyslipidemia and mixed hyperlipidemia, as an adjunct to healthy diet and exercise. In February 2004 the European Mutual Recognition Procedure approved the label by a consensus of 13 countries. Merck awaited marketing authorization pending price negotiations, to be followed by a national license in each country.

New Products and New Product Applications Leading to the Future

Unable to bring a proprietary respiratory product to market, in March 2004 Kos acquired Azmacort Inhalation Aerosol, an inhaled corticosteroid used by asthma patients, from Aventis Pharmaceuticals for $200 million. Global sales of Azmacort reached $88 million in 2003. The product acquisition included global rights to Azmacort, which is a CFC propellant product, as well as an environmentally safe hydrofluoroalkane (HFA) propellant still in development; Kos agreed to pay royalty fees once the HFA technology was used in a marketed product. In addition to increasing revenues, Kos viewed the acquisition as an entry into the respiratory pharmaceuticals market and expected to create new and differentiated products by combining its own respiratory technologies with Azmacort and the HFA propellant. Kos considered it possible to combine the HFA propellant with other products in the formulation stage, such as an inhaled insulin then in the proof of concept phase of human clinical study.

Kos sought to expand medical applications for its products. An independent study of Advicor proved it to be an effective treatment for cholesterol modulation in patients with metabolic syndrome. Metabolic syndrome involves more than one contributing factor in coronary heart disease, including obesity, high blood pressure, and high blood sugar, in combination with

a high level of bad cholesterol and a low level of good cholesterol. Kos awaited FDA approval to expand usage of Niaspan to reduce the risk of stroke and for lipid disorders related to type 2 diabetes, which contributes to coronary heart disease.

Principal Subsidiaries

Aeropharm Technologies, Inc.

Principal Competitors

Abbott Laboratories; Bristol-Myers Squibb Company; Merck & Co., Inc.; Pfizer, Inc.; Schering-Plough Corporation; Sepracor, Inc.

Further Reading

Broder-Singer, Rochelle, ''Kos Fires Up: How Does a CEO Respond When Sales Jump from $36 Million to $170 Million in Three Years? Kos Pharmaceuticals' Adrian Adams Is Expanding R&D in South Florida—and Pushing Expansion Overseas—to Maintain the Pace,'' *South Florida CEO,* February 2003, p. 24.

Chandler, Michele, ''Marketing Matters for Miami-Based Pharmaceutical Firm,'' *Knight Ridder/Tribune Business News,* May 5, 1998.

——, ''Miami-Based Drug Company Sees Increasing Sales, Lands DuPont Marketing Deal,'' *Knight Ridder/Tribune Business News,* October 31, 2000.

''Companies Enter Strategic Commercialization Agreement for Niaspan, Advicor,'' *Biotech Week,* March 6, 2002, p. 32.

''Companies Report European Mutual Recognition Procedure for Niaspan Completed,'' *Health & Medicine Week,* February 23, 2004, p. 248.

''DuPont to Invest $80 Million in Drug Maker,'' *Chemical Week,* May 10, 2000, p. 5.

''Key Pharmaceuticals Owes Its Growth to Timed Drugs,'' *New York Times,* July 5, 1982, p. 33.

''Kos Pharmaceuticals Inc.,'' *Going Public IPO Reporter,* February 3, 1997, p. 14.

''Kos Shares Plunge on News of Slow Sales of Drug,'' *New York Times,* November 13, 1997, p. D4.

''Kos Takes Two Shots in the Arm,'' *Business Week,* February 14, 2000, p. 153.

''Miami-Based Kos Pharmaceuticals Is Building Business with Cheaper Drugs,'' *Knight Ridder/Tribune Business News,* October 16, 2003.

''Miami-Based Kos Pharmaceuticals Seeks Niaspan Approval for Diabetes,'' *Knight Ridder/Tribune Business News,* July 23, 2002.

Miller, Susan R., ''A Healthy Dose of Cash; Kos Pharmaceuticals Set to Raise Additional $36 Million; Kos Pharmaceuticals Is Losing Money, But Wall Street Success Means Profits for Its Founders and $36 Million to Build Growth,'' *Palm Beach Daily Business Review,* September 23, 1997, p. A1.

Mowatt, Twig, ''After Respite from the High-Profile '80s, Drug Company Executive Returns to Public Eye; Michael Jaharis Got $90 Million from the Sale of Key Pharmaceuticals, Started His Own Company in Miami and Now Plans a $428 Million IPO,'' *Palm Beach Daily Business Review,* January 31, 1997, p. A6.

Seemuth, Mike, ''Debt Conversion Would Mean Big Payoff for Kos Shareholder,'' *Miami Daily Business Review,* October 30, 2003, p. A1.

—Mary Tradii

the road to success

LANDSTAR®

Landstar System, Inc.

13410 Sutton Park Drive South
Jacksonville, Florida 32224
U.S.A.
Telephone: (904) 398-9400
Fax: (904) 390-1437
Web site: http://www.landstar.com

Public Company
Incorporated: 1991
Employees: 1,230
Sales: $1.6 billion (2003)
Stock Exchanges: NASDAQ
Ticker Symbol: LSTR
NAIC: 484121 General Freight Trucking, Long-Distance,
Truckload; 484230 Specialized Freight (Except Used
Goods) Trucking, Long-Distance

Landstar System, Inc. is a top U.S. trucking firm. Landstar operates on a "variable cost non-asset based business model," which means rather than having the company buy and maintain its own trucks, Landstar hires owner-operators as subcontractors. The carrier segment of Landstar's business is manned by 7,300 owner-operators, whom the company refers to as "business capacity owners" (BCOs), supplying 8,400 tractors and 14,300 trailers. They are dispatched by 1,000 agents, most of them independent contractors as well. Landstar also contracts with third party truck, rail, and air providers.

Landstar has two other business segments: multimodal and insurance. Landstar Logistics and Landstar Express America make up the multimodal segment, the capacity of which is provided by more than 300 independent contractors. Signature Insurance Company and RMCS form the insurance segment.

Landstar was formed through the acquisition of several trucking firms, some of whose names are reflected in operating companies Landstar Gemini, Landstar Inway, Landstar Ligon, and Landstar Ranger. These and other units are owned through Landstar System, Inc. subsidiary Landstar System Holdings, Inc.

The U.S. military is a major customer. Landstar also specializes in serving the automotive and construction industries, and counts many well-known corporations among its client list.

Origins

NEOAX, an industrial services company based in Stamford, Connecticut, acquired IU International Corp. through a hostile takeover in 1988. IU, based in Philadelphia, had acquired several different trucking companies. Major customers included auto makers and the Department of Defense.

NEOAX then sold one of IU's seven trucking companies and closed another. This left five carriers in the Truckload Group, each with its own specialty: Ranger Transportation Inc. of Jacksonville, Florida (just-in-time delivery); Independent Freightway Inc. of Rockford, Illinois (flatbed); Gemini Transport Inc. of Greensburg, Pennsylvania (intermodal containers drayage); Ligon Nationwide Inc. of Madisonville, Kentucky (heavy hauls); and Poole Truck Lines Inc. of Evergreen, Alaska (high-density short and medium hauls). They had combined sales of $579 million in 1987. Of these, Ranger was unionized. Poole was the only unit that owned its own trucks; the others were manned by owner-operators.

According to the *Fairfield County Business Journal,* truckers received 75 percent of gross revenues (later upped to more than 80 percent), leaving 7 percent for the independent agents and 18 percent for the company. Landstar offered a buying coop to save its drivers on purchases of fuel, tires, and lodging.

Landstar System Inc. was formed in October 1988 to purchase the IU Truckload Group from NEOAX Inc. in a management buyout. Landstar paid $94 million in cash plus $16 million in stock for the unit. NEOAX retained a 49 percent interest.

The Truckload Group's head, John B. Bowron, became chairman and CEO of the new Landstar System. Jeffrey C. Crowe, formerly head of Independent Freightway, was named president and CEO of Landstar in 1989.

Management Buyout in 1991

EnviroSource Inc., formerly NEOAX, sold its interest in Landstar System to Landstar Holding Corp. in March 1991 for $12 million in cash plus the assumption of more than $70 million in debt. Kelso & Co., a group whose interests ranged from American Standard to International House of Pancakes, was the controlling shareholder of Landstar Holding. Kelso also controlled a dozen other trucking companies. Other investors included 48 senior Landstar System managers. CEO Jeffrey Crowe became board chairman after the deal.

According to *Industry Week,* Crowe placed a heavy emphasis on safety, and the company tried a number of innovative approaches. For example, in 1990, Landstar began adding reflective tape to the sides of trucks to increase their night-time visibility. This reduced the number of cars driving into the sides of the trucks by 75 percent. Safety was stressed in the corporate culture through regular weekly and monthly meetings, mandatory safety programs for new drivers, and recognition programs. In the mid-1990s, the company became an early user of onboard collision avoidance radar.

Revenues exceeded $620 million in 1990. Landstar bought a number of small to midsized truckload carriers in the early 1990s. Revenues were $672 million in 1992. Landstar's headquarters moved from Stamford to Shelton, Connecticut, during the year.

Public in 1993

Landstar completed an initial public offering (IPO) on NAS-DAQ in March 1993. The IPO took in $30.3 million before expenses, earmarked to pay down debt. The offering freed Landstar management to focus more on operations and acquisitions, rather than finance. Landstar was focusing on the automotive, steel, chemicals, and refrigerated segments of the trucking business.

Landstar acquired three companies in 1994 and 1995, increasing the range of its transportation offerings. T.L.C. Lines of St. Clair, Missouri, specialized in long hauls, including refrigerated. Two Dublin, California firms were being acquired: Intermodal Transport Co. (ITCO) and LDS Truckline Inc.

Intermodal Transport was renamed Landstar ITCO Inc., and the name was changed again to Landstar Logistics Inc. in 1996. Another subsidiary, Landstar Express America Inc., was formed in 1995 to acquire Express America Freight Systems Inc. of Charlotte, North Carolina. The operations of Landstar T.L.C. were merged with those of Landstar Inway in a 1997 restructuring, and T.L.C.'s company-owned trucks were sold off.

The five original subsidiaries were prefixed with the parent company's name in January 1995. Independent Freightway, Inc., also known as Inway, became Landstar Inway, Inc. Landstar System had three other subsidiaries: Landstar Intermodal, Inc., Landstar Transportation Services, Inc., and Landstar Expedited, Inc.

Landstar invested more than $12 million in upgrading its IT and communications systems during this time. The company used various means to communicate with its drivers, including pagers, cell phones, and satellite links, and operated a network of 750 field stations.

The company was working on computer and marketing systems to help its subsidiaries work together better. Smaller accounts made up 75 percent of Landstar's business; the company created a new subsidiary, Landstar Transportation Services Inc., to offer national accounts convenient access to Landstar's variety of services. Another new subsidiary, Landstar Expedited Inc., was also added.

Driver turnover was between 60 and 70 percent a year in the mid-1990s, a rate far superior to the 100 to 200 percent turnover some truckload carriers reported. With 10,500 drivers, Landstar was the third largest truckload carrier at this point, behind J.B. Hunt Transport Services Inc. and Schneider National, Inc. J.B. Hunt, however, operated mostly in the retail shipping market, not one of Landstar's specialties.

The trucking industry was booming. At the time, Landstar was the third largest truckload firm in the United States. A trend toward outsourcing of transportation helped Landstar throughout the 1990s. The company's mass and breadth of services benefited it as customers trimmed the number of different trucking companies they hired. Landstar earned a record $25 million on revenues of $1.2 billion, also a record, in 1995.

The figures would be even better, reasoned management, if the company could get rid of its lowest performing unit. In 1998, Landstar sold Landstar Poole, which owned its own trucks and classified its drivers as employees, in contrast to the other Landstar operations. Schneider National paid $41 million for Poole.

Relocating to Jacksonville in 1997

Revenues were $1.2 billion in 1997. In June of that year, Landstar's headquarters was relocated to Jacksonville, Florida, where three of its subsidiaries (Landstar Ranger Inc., Landstar Gemini Inc., and Landstar Logistics Inc.) were already based.

The company had 1,000 agents and 8,000 drivers, all of them independent contractors, plus another 1,300 regular employees. Landstar was the only publicly traded trucking company to rely on independent owner-operators. As Crowe told *Forbes,* "We want to manage assets, not own them."

Landstar used the Internet to communicate with its drivers. It was difficult to obtain Internet access on the road, however, and satellite systems were prohibitively costly. In 2000, Landstar and PhoneOnline.com unveiled a system designed to use the tiny text screens of web-enabled mobile phones.

Key Dates:

1988: Landstar System is formed from the IU Truckload Group.
1991: Landstar System is sold to a management group.
1993: Landstar goes public on the NASDAQ.
1995: Multimodal companies ITCO and Express America are acquired.
1997: The Signature Insurance Company subsidiary is formed; headquarters are relocated to Jacksonville.
1998: Landstar Poole is sold to Schneider National.
1999: Landstar moves into a new headquarters building.
2003: Revenues reach $1.6 billion, despite a weak economy.

Same Model, New HQ for 2000 and Beyond

Landstar moved to a new five-story headquarters in Jacksonville, Florida, in late 1999. The 180,900-square-foot building also housed head offices for several subsidiaries. While most of Jacksonville's publicly traded companies were taking a beating, Landstar was poised to ride its business model to future success, reported the *Florida Times-Union.* At least investors thought so. Although revenues and earnings fell slightly in the weakened economy of 2001, share price rose 31 percent during the year.

Driven by the strength of the BCO business model, Landstar's revenues passed $1.5 billion in 2002 as the rest of the trucking industry struggled in a weak economy. Landstar achieved net income of $50.7 million on sales of $1.6 billion in 2003. The company was consistently finding itself a spot on *Forbes* magazine's Platinum 40 List of America's Best Big Companies.

Principal Subsidiaries

Landstar System Holdings, Inc.

Principal Divisions

Carrier; Multimodal; Insurance.

Principal Operating Units

Landstar Express America; Landstar Gemini; Landstar Inway; Landstar Ligon; Landstar Logistics; Landstar Ranger; Risk Management Claim Services, Inc.; Signature Insurance Company.

Principal Competitors

J.B. Hunt Transport Services; Schneider National, Inc.; Swift Transportation Co., Inc.; U.S. Xpress Enterprises; Werner Enterprises, Inc.

Further Reading

Barker-Benfield, Simon, "Jacksonville, Fla.-Based Transportation Company to Move Jobs from Kentucky," *Florida Times-Union,* March 29, 2000.

Basch, Mark, "Cloud Hung Over Public Companies Headquartered in Jacksonville, Fla., in 2001," *Florida Times-Union,* May 13, 2002.

——, "Jacksonville, Fla.-Based Firm Keeps Trucking Along with Record Earnings," *Florida Times-Union,* January 29, 2004.

——, "Landstar Shifting Gears; Trucking Firm's Restructuring Seen As 'Positive Step,' " *Florida Times-Union,* December 21, 1996, p. C9.

——, "Landstar Trucking in Headquarters," *Florida Times-Union,* December 19, 1996, p. C7.

——, "A Model That Keeps Landstar Trucking Along," *Florida Times-Union,* Bus. Sec., June 5, 2000, p. 12.

——, "New Landstar HQ Planned; Kroger to Build Five-Story Building at Windsor Parke," *Florida Times-Union,* May 6, 1998, p. B6.

Brown, Geoffrey H., "Kelso Gets Final Nod to Acquire Five Carriers," *Journal of Commerce,* April 3, 1991, p. 2B.

"CEO Interview: Jeffrey Crowe—Landstar System Inc. (LSTR)," *Wall Street Transcript,* November 26, 2001.

D'Orio, Wayne, "Landstar Puts Rough Road Behind, Maps a Brighter Future," *Fairfield County Business Journal,* November 15, 1993, p. 8.

Douglas, Merrill, "Hit the Road, Jack—And Take Your Wireless Phone with You," *Frontline Solutions* (Duluth), November 2000, pp. 24 +.

Fleischer, Jo, "Landstar in Driver's Seat As Trucking Industry Enjoys Economic Boom," *Fairfield County Business Journal,* December 5, 1994, p. 7.

Gerdel, Thomas W., "System Scuttled; But Work on Collision-Avoidance Devices Is Continuing at Two Local Companies," *Plain Dealer* (Cleveland, Ohio), September 14, 1994, p. 1C.

Goudreau, Priscilla, "Business Journal 50: Jeff Crowe; All in a Day's Work for Crowe," *Business Journal* (Jacksonville), August 1, 2003, p. 18.

Green, Heather, "Landstar," *Business Week,* The Web Smart 50—Customer Service, November 24, 2003, p. 92.

Higgins, Stephen, "Landstar Becomes a Big Wheel: Trucking Firm Benefits from Owner/Operators," *New Haven Register,* January 22, 1995, p. 1.

Holusha, John, "Tech Notes: Rigged Up to Glow in the Dark," *New York Times Abstracts,* July 28, 1991, p. 11.

Johnson, Gregory S., "Core Carrier Concept Is Profitable Strategy for Landstar," *Journal of Commerce,* October 17, 1995, p. 2B.

"Landstar Restructures Operations," *New Haven Register,* January 16, 1996, p. 3.

Martinez, Barbara, "Jeffrey Crowe, Chairman and CEO of Landstar," *Dow Jones Investor Network,* February 16, 1996.

Norman, James R., "A Fleet of Entrepreneurs," *Forbes,* January 2, 1995, p. 194.

Schulz, John D., " 'BCO' Model Still Works," *Traffic World,* February 17, 2003, p. 1.

——, "Truckload 'Seller's Market,' " *Traffic World,* August 11, 2003.

"Trucking Firm Uses Variety of Technologies While Waiting for 'Perfect' One," *En Route Technology,* December 19, 1994.

Tyner, Christopher L., "Landstar System's Jeffrey Crowe—His High-Tech Network of Truckers Lets Them Ride High," *Investor's Business Daily,* May 2, 2000, p. A4.

Verespej, Michael A., "Better Safety Through Empowerment," *Industry Week,* November 15, 1993, p. 56.

Wastler, Allen R., "Trucking Giant Landstar Bolstered by Niche Units Working Together," *Journal of Commerce,* March 1, 1994, p. 1A.

Watson, Rip, "Landstar, Continuing Its Buying Spree, Plans to Acquire Two Motor Carriers; Company Broadens Transport Options," *Journal of Commerce,* November 18, 1994, p. 2B.

—Frederick C. Ingram

Le Chateau Inc.

5695 Ferrier Street
Montreal, Quebec H4P 1N1
Canada
Telephone: (514) 738-7000
Fax: (514) 577-7419
Web site: http://www.le-chateau.com

Public Company
Incorporated: 1959 as Le Chateau Men's Wear
Employees: 2,400
Sales: $142.4 million (2003)
Stock Exchanges: Toronto
Ticker Symbol: CTU.A
NAIC: 448110 Men's Clothing Stores; 448120 Women's
   Clothing Stores; 448130 Children's and Infants'
   Clothing Stores; 448150 Clothing Accessories Stores;
   315223 Men's and Boys' Cut and Sew Shirt (Except
   Work Shirt) Manufacturing; 315233 Women's and
   Girls' Cut and Sew Dress Manufacturing

Le Chateau Inc. is one of Canada's leading clothing retailers. The chain operates more than 160 stores, mostly in Canada, with a cluster of stores in the northeastern United States. Le Chateau sells almost exclusively its own branded clothing, in lines for women, men, and preteen girls. It also sells shoes and accessories. Its retail formula has been likened to The Gap in that both chains rely primarily on their store brand. Le Chateau designs and manufactures most of its store brand goods. Le Chateau made its mark as a store catering to youth, featuring moderately priced faddish designs that often changed from week to week. The chain evolved to include clothes for more mature shoppers, and it defines its core customer base as people between the ages of 15 and 35. Le Chateau is an innovative marketer, using music, film, and television events to promote its lines. The company began a push into U.S. markets in the late 1990s, with the goal of setting up as many as 300 new stores across the country. With an impressive rise in sales and profits in the early 2000s, the chain was one of the brightest lights in a generally sluggish North American retail clothing market.

Bringing Carnaby Street to Canada in the 1960s

The Le Chateau chain was founded in Montreal in 1959 by Herschel Segal. Segal was born in Montreal in 1931, and grew up working in his family's clothing business, Peerless Clothing Manufacturing Ltd. Segal studied economics and political science at McGill University, then returned to work at Peerless after graduating with honors. But Segal was unhappy working in the family business, where he felt trapped by the expectations of his elders and uninterested in the fashions the company purveyed. Segal resigned his position at Peerless in the early 1950s and moved to New York City. He enrolled at the New School for Social Research and soaked up the burgeoning art and music scene of New York's radical hotbed, Greenwich Village.

After a few years in New York, Segal returned to his hometown. Following his father's death in 1955, Segal again went to work for Peerless Clothing. Segal apparently liked the company even less in this second stint, and he began to plan to go into business for himself. Segal had inherited money from his father, and he sank this into a store in Montreal's Victoria Square, on St. Catherine's Street. He called it Le Chateau Men's Wear, a name that played up the francophone feelings budding in Quebec at the time. The Victoria Square neighborhood was a bustling shopping district, but at first Le Chateau was not much of a fashion-forward store. Segal sold overstock from Peerless. In an interview with *Canadian Business* (February 17, 2003), Segal described a core group of his early customers as "blue-haired ladies." Le Chateau did well at first, and Segal was able to open three more shops. But Segal overreached, and was forced to close down the new stores. By the early 1960s, he had only the original store left, he had spent his inheritance, and his new business was close to bankruptcy.

At this point, Segal changed the fashion concept behind Le Chateau completely. The company became a vanguard for youthful fashions, bringing in the very latest in English and European trends. The transformation came when Segal, in trouble with his lenders, was letting loose at a fashionable party. There he encountered a woman wearing something he had never seen before, a leather dress. The woman informed him that he had not seen much leather yet because it was new, but it was all the rage in certain circles. Curious, Segal got the address of the partygoer's tailor, and the next day bought a leather coat from him. Segal put the leather coat in the front window of Le Chateau, and promptly sold it for $135. This was more than four times the going price for a similar jacket made of cloth. For the next eight months, Segal sold all kinds of leather goods out of Le Chateau, and did brisk business.

After his success with leather, Segal took a trip to Europe to find other new fashion trends. He was enchanted with London's Carnaby Street, an old-time tailoring district that by 1965 had become the epicenter of youth-oriented fashion. Segal imported French suits, Italian turtlenecks, and all the latest goods from the London scene. Segal claimed he introduced bell bottoms, the era's ubiquitous wide-bottomed pants, to Canada, and that Le Chateau sold fashions direct from Europe that had not even arrived in New York yet. Le Chateau became a mecca for youth, while for a time Segal continued to stock his traditional fashions from Peerless. The Le Chateau store was for a time an odd mix of the outrageously fashionable young and sedate old people looking for bargains. Segal decided to drop the kinds of clothes that had appealed to his older customers, and focus entirely on youth. This was a wise decision, and Segal was able to move into more locations. By 1972, Le Chateau had ten stores, all in metropolitan shopping areas.

Expansion in the 1970s and 1980s

Le Chateau grew in fits and starts. It had started with one store, expanded to three, went back down to one, and then grown to a small chain of ten retail outlets. Over the mid-1970s, Le Chateau had another growth spurt, and it opened stores rapidly in shopping malls and suburban areas. By the end of the decade, Le Chateau had more than 50 stores across the country. Its fashions became somewhat more mainstream and moved more toward women's clothing. The company had been steadily profitable until 1977. That year, the company registered its first loss. Determined to get Le Chateau back on track, Segal hired an executive assistant to help him plan. Jane Silverstone had been a sales clerk and understood the business from the inside. Segal eventually married her. (In 2001 Silverstone was named the company's vice-chairman.) Together they brought the company back to financial health. In 1983 they took Le Chateau public. The initial public offering raised some $7.3 million for the company.

Le Chateau continued to expand across Canada, and now in the mid-1980s it moved into the United States as well. Beginning in 1985, Le Chateau opened stores in Boston, New York, Chicago, Baltimore, and other U.S. cities, until it had 26 U.S.

locations. Segal admitted that the company's southern foray was badly planned. The stores were in badly chosen locations, and the fashions were not adequately adjusted for the tastes of U.S. consumers. The push into U.S. markets did not work the first time around, and Le Chateau quietly closed the U.S. stores as their leases expired. The only one it left in operation was a store on Houston Street and Broadway in Manhattan, a heavily trafficked shopping district.

The number of Le Chateau stores in Canada continued to grow, until by the early 1990s the company had approximately 160 locations. Le Chateau was vertically integrated, doing all its design and most of its manufacturing in its own facilities. This allowed the company to hold down costs and to turn out new designs quickly. These were competitive advantages, but the company nevertheless had problems, and the late 1980s and early 1990s were difficult times. Poor economic conditions overall made the retail sector difficult. Consumer confidence sank in Canada through the early 1990s as a prolonged recession kept people out of stores. A headline from Canada's *Financial Post* newspaper (August 15, 1992) declared, ''Clothing Sector in Tatters.'' The industry struggled with sluggish sales, while some prominent chains, such as Town & Country (owned by huge retailer Dylex Ltd.) and Ayre Ltd., filed for bankruptcy. In 1997, Canada's venerable department store chain Eaton's, which had been in business since 1869, filed for bankruptcy and quickly disappeared from the retail scene.

Le Chateau blamed the recession for poor sales, and also acknowledged mistakes handling inventory. The quality of some of Le Chateau's goods slipped in the 1990s. Le Chateau's clothes had always been moderately priced, and the chain emphasized the very latest trends, bringing in new collections every two or three weeks. An article in *This Magazine* (November-December 2002) characterized Le Chateau's specialty as ''cheap, trendy, disposable clothes.'' This in itself was not pejorative. The chain had thrived on selling faddish goods that by definition went quickly out of style. But by the late 1990s, the formula had perhaps become overdone, and the stores earned the nickname ''Le Crapeau.'' In 1999, Le Chateau designers miscalculated what their youthful customers wanted, and the company took a large and unexpected quarterly loss. The company's stock fell to its lowest point since the early 1990s.

New Directions in the 2000s

Galvanized by the serious misstep in 1999, Segal began instituting changes in top management. Jane Silverstone became vice-chairman, while the vice-president for finance, Emilia Di Raddo, became the firm's president. Le Chateau beefed up its quality control process, improved store design, and made changes to the mix of merchandise. Then the company began building its brand image. The firm needed to change consumers' perception that Le Chateau's goods were only for wearing to nightclubs. Le Chateau hoped to bring back more mature customers, men and women in their 20s and 30s who were appreciative of cutting edge style. In the early 2000s the company began a series of innovative marketing campaigns. In 2003 the company designed an entire collection around the movie *Down with Love,* a Renee Zellweger vehicle set in the 1960s. The collection premiered with a star-studded party at Le Chateau's Montreal flagship store, and much media attention

<table>
<tr><td colspan="2">Key Dates:</td></tr>
<tr><td>1959:</td><td>Herschel Segal opens the first Le Chateau store.</td></tr>
<tr><td>1972:</td><td>The chain grows to ten stores.</td></tr>
<tr><td>1983:</td><td>The company goes public.</td></tr>
<tr><td>1985:</td><td>The company begins its first push into the U.S. market.</td></tr>
<tr><td>1999:</td><td>Quarterly losses spark a company turnaround.</td></tr>
<tr><td>2002:</td><td>Company doubles its fourth-quarter profits over the same period in 2001; same-store sales rise over 19 percent; holiday sales increase by almost 14 percent.</td></tr>
<tr><td>2003:</td><td>The company's stock price climbs to a high of $11.</td></tr>
</table>

drew shoppers in droves. The "Down with Love" collection sold out in six weeks. Le Chateau also tied its brand to the popular television show *Canadian Idol.* The show's top contestants all wore Le Chateau goods as they competed to be Canada's next musical star. Le Chateau put fashion, film, and music together in these promotions.

Although Le Chateau instituted many changes in its management, inventory process, and quality control in the early 2000s, it also reconsidered the U.S. market. Le Chateau had stepped back from its expansion into the United States in the 1980s, leaving in place only a store in lower Manhattan. That store had done well, and in 1997 Le Chateau began opening several new stores in Manhattan and New Jersey. The plan this time around was for the company to cluster stores in one geographical area. In the 1980s, the stores had opened in many metropolises, from Boston to Chicago. Le Chateau now planned to concentrate on the northeastern United States, beginning with the New York metropolitan area. The New York area stores were a little different from the Canadian stores, offering more goods from other brands. This was because of difficulties importing some lines, such as sweaters. Le Chateau opened a New York office to coordinate the U.S. market push. By 2003, the company had five stores in the United States. But the company told the fashion weekly *WWD* (November 2, 2000) that it planned to open as many as 300 stores in the United States.

By the early 2000s, Le Chateau had recovered from the problems that plagued it in the 1990s, and it was growing at a time when the North American retail market remained difficult overall. For its final quarter of 2002, Le Chateau doubled its profits over the same period a year earlier. In addition, its same-store sales (a key indicator of retail growth, measuring sales of stores that have been open at least one year) were up over 19 percent for the same period. Its 2002 holiday sales rose almost 14 percent over the year previous, yet for the retail sector overall, 2002 was one of the worst holiday sales seasons ever. Le Chateau was now doing very well, while many competitors were still stymied. The company's stock price rose, from a low of $2.10 in 2000 to a high of $11 in early 2003. Sales continued to climb over 2003, at a modest 4.2 percent, while earnings climbed more than 40 percent. The company seemed to have found its footing. Now industry analysts wondered if founder Herschel Segal, who had turned 70 in 2001, would sell the chain.

Principal Competitors

Reitmans (Canada) Ltd.; Les Boutiques San Francisco, Inc.; La Senza Corporation.

Further Reading

Evans, Mark, "Clothing Sector in Tatters," *Financial Post,* August 15, 1992, p. 6.

Giese, Rachel, "Consuming Passion," *This Magazine,* November-December 2002, p. 23.

Kletter, Melanie, "Le Chateau's American Dream," *WWD,* November 2, 2000, p. 8B.

"More 34th Street Changes," *WWD,* March 13, 1997, p. 30.

Olijnyk, Zena, "Retail Sector Shudders in Eaton's Shock Wave," *Financial Post,* March 1, 1997, p. 4.

Starr, Ryan, "The Clothes That Made the Man," *Canadian Business,* February 17, 2003, p. 36.

Vogl, Cara, "Quitting the Club," *Marketing Magazine,* September 29, 2003, p. 16.

—A. Woodward

Levenger Company

420 South Congress Avenue
Delray Beach, Florida 33445-4696
U.S.A.
Telephone: (561) 276-4141
Fax: (561) 272-1643
Web site: http://http://www.levenger.com

Private Company
Incorporated: 1987
Employees: 400
Sales: $70 million (2003 est.)
NAIC: 454110 Electronic Shopping and Mail-Order
   Houses

A fast-growing, family-owned business, Levenger Company markets a unique array of goods via catalog, Internet, and retail outlets. The company offers branded and private-label home and office lighting products and other reading tools, desk accessories and clocks, stationery, luxury leather goods, fine writing instruments, globes, timepieces, briefcases and bags, specialty books and journals, home-to-office furniture systems, and storage solutions. More than 80 percent of its products are either originally designed or proprietary. Levenger's upscale products are intended for long-term use and are constructed from quality materials such as leathers, woods, and papers. Since 1989, the company has operated a 5,200-square-foot flagship store within Levenger's corporate headquarters, which also houses a warehouse, merchandising, and design center, and a call center. The company also has expanded to a separate 2,300-square-foot store within a store, inside Marshall Field's State Street store in Chicago. The founders were recognized in Ernst and Young's 1994 Entrepreneur of the Year awards, representing owner/managers who created substantial new jobs, impressive sales growth, business experience, development, and community involvement.

Founding by Bibliophiles in 1987

The concept for Levenger was born of personal necessity. It originated when bibliophiles Lori Granger Leveen and husband Steven Leveen became frustrated at not having adequate reading lights in their living room. Both were detaching from their computer industry jobs and both had dreamed of starting a business, preferably a business involving products rather than one offering a service. Lori Leveen, who did her undergraduate studies at Vassar College and earned her master's degree in international business from Georgetown University, had taken a maternity leave from IBM, where she worked in research and marketing. Steven Leveen earned a doctorate in sociology at Cornell University and had worked until he was laid off as a marketing executive at a Boston software company. They found themselves at home together with time enough for reading but lacking bright enough lighting. The couple began investigating possible lighting options by thoroughly researching what was then available. Steven Leveen read about halogen lighting in *The International Design Yearbook.* The Leveens were sparked by what they then discovered to be a revolution in lighting technology, a technology widely available in European markets but less accessible domestically. Impressed by the quality of light from their own halogen fixture, the Leveens interviewed lighting engineers and reasoned that halogen light bulbs could be marketed as an excellent source of lighting for professional readers and writers.

Steven Leveen explained in a December 1994 *Chain Store Age* interview, "We were the first to identify serious readers as a group to be marketed to for something other than reading materials." Convinced that a mail-order company would be the best option for a home-based business, the couple combined the surnames of Granger and Leveen and cofounded Levenger Company.

Initially, the cofounders attracted sales with a one-inch advertisement in the *New Yorker* magazine, captioned, "Serious Lighting for Serious Readers." They produced a small four-page brochure with simple black-and-white photos including descriptions, and purchased lists of mail-order customers. The couple began building a small inventory from a "fulfillment center" in their den and inventory was stored in the foyer of their condominium.

The new company received more than 400 subscriptions before the first catalog was sent from the founders' Belmont,

Company Perspectives:

Whether it be reading, writing, or some other pursuit, Levenger helps customers create their own productive and pleasing environments by giving them thoughtfully designed, carefully made products of high quality that have real value. Levenger makes the functional beautiful, and the beautiful that will last for generations. As serious as the construction may be, the product is a delight to use.

Massachusetts home. Funded by $8,000 brought in from the sale of their car, the 5,000 catalogs featured a literary tone with detailed descriptions and black-and-white depictions of halogen floor and desk lamps. The high-end merchandise tended to attract lawyers, business people, professors, writers, scientists, and other professionals who read substantially for their work as well as for pleasure. Prompted by a positive reception to their merchandise, the Leveens then cashed in $13,000 in retirement funds and accessed almost $80,000 in other savings to advance further growth. With prospects aglow, the business soon required more space and a move to a neighbor's garage. A baby monitor served as the communications system between "departments." Due to customer requests, the lamps and reading-product line expanded to include reading chairs, magnifying glasses, briefcases, dictionary stands, ergonomic devices, bookends, and related bookworm items. As the volume of their buying increased, the company from which Levenger was purchasing advised the Leveens to go directly to the manufacturer, a Danish company, for future orders.

Encompassing more than strong entrepreneurial instincts, Steven and Lori Leveen, acting as company president and vice-president, respectively, displayed a talent for design. When a desired product was unavailable, the founders designed it and produced prototypes. As the business evolved, most of the products for manufacture were designed in-house by the Leveens and supplemented by a close-knit design team. The team members constituted a diverse group with eclectic backgrounds that included museum work, retail, antiques, and academia. With an eye to satisfaction and future sales the Levenger motto came to light: "under-promise and over-deliver." According to Steven Leveen, "Our goal is to make products that look absolutely beautiful in the catalog but look even better when they show up at home" (*Knight Ridder/Tribune Business News*, July 1997).

Traveling widely, the Leveens found inspiration for their products in foreign antique stores and novelty shops. A substantial portion of their merchandise ended up mirroring historic travel bags, "barrister" bookcases, Mission-style furnishings, and other designs either no longer being manufactured or in relative neglect. Termed by the Leveens as "industrial archaeology," according to *Entrepreneur* (January 1997), new ideas were gleaned from the old items and modified for contemporary use. They began purchasing items at auctions or antique stores to bring home for their designers to study and re-introduce as replicas or as updated interpretations of older items. Once the specifications for a new product were determined, an appropriate vendor was found to produce it.

Relocating to Florida in 1989–90

By 1989, the need for a permanent business location became apparent. Sales had grown to almost $700,000 annually. Fostered in part by a desire to be nearer Steven Leveen's father and the desire to live in a warmer climate where commercial real estate was attractively priced, the Leveens moved from the Boston area to Delray Beach, Florida. The following year, they were fortunate to meet Rick Leichtung, an accomplished businessman who was to become their future mentor. Leichtung sought them out after noticing a Levenger advertisement in a *Smithsonian* magazine. A retired CEO, Leichtung had by then become a millionaire through his Leichtung Workshops Catalog business, a Cleveland-based mail-order tool company. Once aware that the Levenger catalog company was headquartered just ten minutes from his home, Leichtung drove to Delray Beach to introduce himself to the company owners. Following his meeting with Steven Leveen, Leichtung offered to review for him the 16-page catalog of Levenger reading tools.

Leichtung's credentials included recognition as a three-time recipient of *Inc.*'s annual list of recognized CEOs in the United States. Since retirement he had considered business counseling a hobby, often refusing fees for his services. Following their initial meeting, he provided the Leveens with several single-spaced typewritten pages of criticism regarding their catalog. According to *Inc.* (Fall 1994), Steven Leveen's response was receptive: "I felt like the Karate Kid, or like Luke Skywalker getting the force." Further crediting Leichtung's influential role, Steven Leveen said in an August 1993 *South Florida Business Journal* article, "He took us under his wing and taught us about the catalog business." He added, "I know we couldn't have done it without his help." According to Leveen, Leichtung's advice covered every aspect of the business. The two men quickly established a rapport that included daily exchanges via phone conversations and letter faxing. As an overriding principle for steering their venture, Leichtung told the Leveens that almost anything could be sold via mail order, but to succeed, each approach to the market would need to be different from everyone else's, and the line of items would need to make sense as a whole. Steven Leveen displayed an aggressive competitive instinct and considered every mail-order company as among Levenger's competitors since they all vied for a portion of the home-shopping market. The company's first color catalog was issued in 1990. In the interests of quantity and in controlling the quality of their advertising, the Leveens created their own in-house facilities for the design, layout, and photography of their catalogs.

Company sales soared and the Leveens applauded Leichtung for helping to grow their business to $29 million by 1994, just a year after breaking ground on a new 220,000-square-foot facility. With 118 people on its payroll, Levenger continued to expand, and its customer base grew to about 2,000 people nationally, including famous actors, writers, and winners of Nobel and Pulitzer prizes.

Corporate headquarters were established in Congress Park South, housing merchandise, offices, and a showroom floor, sited on acreage that allowed room for future expansion. In its new outlet store, the company began offering catalog merchandise at a discount, as well as overstocked and slightly damaged closeout items. The retail site was conceived as a testing ground for future expansion possibilities and offered pricing that allowed less affluent customers access to Levenger merchandise. Items at the retail store ranged in price from $10 to $1,000, with average orders at approximately $130. The Leveens were concerned that their merchandise be considered tools for all readers and writers, rather than catering solely to the rich. Steven Leveen's August 1993 *South Florida Business Journal* interview expressed their dilemma: "We are looking for products that are well made and are not expensive. But the fact is that most products that are made well cost a lot."

In 1993, Levenger placed eighth on *Inc.* magazine's 500 list of top privately held companies. Throughout the 1990s, Levenger continued to be recognized as one of the nation's top success stories, with its name and products appearing in national publications such as *House Beautiful, Forbes FYI,* the *Wall Street Journal,* and *House and Garden,* among others. Several Levenger items, including a mouse pad, Best & Lloyd Bestlite lamp, and Page Point were used as props in the film *You've Got Mail,* starring Tom Hanks and Meg Ryan. The company concept had evolved from being primarily a provider of reading lights to one offering organizational tools adapted for readers and writers.

Reaching Its One Millionth Sale in 1995

Levenger filled its one millionth order in 1995 following the introduction of the company's first Professional and Corporate Sales catalog, adding educational institutions, media companies, law firms, and laboratories to its customer list. Overall during this period, the company distributed 12 catalogs that encompassed 20 million copies annually. Simmons Market Research bureau reported that 132 million people made purchases from home in 1996 and that catalog purchases were expected to increase at an annual rate of 6 percent over the next several years as people increasingly appreciated the convenience of mail order. The catalog industry as a whole began emphasizing no-hassle returns, quantity pricing on shipping, and improving customer service as a means of satisfying consumer confidence in the medium.

Levenger's presence was further expanded in 1996 with the introduction of its virtual store and the doubling in size of the

Delray Beach outlet. The company concentrated efforts at broadening its appeal overseas, and translated its order forms into Japanese, where the merchandise was particularly well received. Due to foreign consumers' discomfort with the idea of distance ordering, only 5 percent of its business came from overseas in 1997. Steven Levenger explained, "Being Americans, we take the notion of a 100 percent refund for granted, but it does not exist in other countries, and because of that people are reluctant to buy expensive things by mail" (*Knight Ridder/ Tribune Business News,* July 9, 1997).

The company's trial-and-error approach to the market continued. It seemed fitting that a company geared for bibliophiles would eventually turn a new page and enter the publishing industry. Levenger added 700 book titles and a coffee bar at its Delray Beach headquarters. Studiously avoiding stock that included bestsellers as offered by such mega-bookstores as Barnes & Noble, Levenger kept to its niche-marketing scheme and stocked a selection of biographies on historical figures and nonfiction books on topics relating to art, photography, and architecture. Among the intriguing titles included on the Levenger online-catalog site, consumers might find *Painting As a Pastime: An Account of Finding One's Muse in Midlife,* by Sir Winston Churchill, or helpful references such as *Rare Words and Ways to Master Them.*

The Leveens continued to look forward. Several options were considered in anticipation of funding Levenger's future growth strategy. A team was hired to concentrate on corporate sales and it attracted further sales by customizing products with monograms, engraving, and embroidery. In 2000, CFO Greg Driscoll left Levenger for a CFO spot at Vermont Country Store, another catalog company. The search for a new CFO focused on finding someone with rapid growth experience in a multi-channel retail setting to coincide with plans for growing through the addition of retail outlets, nationally and domestically. Larry Jenkins filled the void as the Leveens considered a pubic offering as one possibility for raising major expansion capital. They held off, however, on that decision.

2003 and Beyond: Launching a Store Within a Store

The new millennium brought opportunity knocking at Levenger's door. The company was courted by Marshall Field's, one of the preeminent retail enterprises in the country. Interested in developing a new downtown shopping Mecca for State Street in Chicago, Marshall Field offered Levenger the opportunity to open a store inside the landmark Marshall Field's department store in Chicago. Levenger's acceptance marked the opening of its first store outside the Delray Beach headquarters. The company began establishing its ground-floor presence by defining an appropriate ambiance, consisting of a 2,300-square-foot space designed in stone, metal, and glass to reflect the quality and solidity of its merchandise. Steven Leveen commented in a company press release: "Marshall Field's has a long and notable history of pleasing guests, and giving a guest what she or he wants." He added, "We've followed a parallel path at Levenger and see this as an ideal partnership." Trendy British shirt tailor Thomas Pink, New York-based home designer Thomas O'Brien, and the London-based Designer's Guild were invited as companion businesses in the flagship Marshall Field's store.

The company continued to reach milestones as Levenger entered the first decade of the twenty-first century. It was listed on Oprah.com as a source for office makeovers and it was featured on the 2004 HGTV Program called ''Mission: Organization,'' which highlighted a Levenger ''Johnson Chair'' and other Levenger products. Despite the heightened visibility, the company joined the ranks of other retailers affected by the dimming economic environment. The company was forced to cut costs and lay off 8 percent of its workforce in 2001. Higher postage costs had a negative impact on the catalog business, and the Internet business—costly to support—was slow to attract new customers, although it offered an alternative form of ordering for existing ones. Steven Leveen told *Knight Ridder/ Tribune Business News* (February 15, 2001), ''Direct marketing is being redefined by the Internet. There's no choice but to become very proficient at e-mail marketing and Web site information.'' He added that one approach is to target e-mails of furniture and other defined specials to reach customers who tend to buy particular types of items. Their strategy is to improve quality and focus on novel products that complement the core business of reading and writing tools. In Leveen's words, ''People respond to products that have meaning for them. One of the problems in retailing today is that there's a lot of sameness in it; it's all very boring, homogenized and un-inspirational. A mall is a mall whether you're in South Florida or Southern California'' (*South Florida Business Journal*, August 1993).

Principal Competitors

Brookstone Company, Inc.; Sharper Image Corporation; Williams-Sonoma, Inc.

Further Reading

''Catalog Company Looks to Grow,'' *Corporate Financing Week,* February 28, 2000, p. 3.

''Delray Beach, Florida-Based Catalogue Company to Cut 24 Jobs,'' *Knight Ridder/Tribune Business News,* February 15, 2001.

Ellerson, Amy, ''Florida-Based Levenger Catalog Company Continues to Grow,'' *Knight Ridder/Tribune Business News,* July 9, 1997.

Greenlaw, Dawn, ''A Well-Read Workflow,'' *Publishing and Production Executive,* June 2000, p. 34.

Gruner, Stephanie, ''One Success Breeds Another,'' *Inc.,* Fall 1994, p. 152.

Leveen, Lori Granger, ''Levenger VP Follows Serious Approach,'' *South Florida Business Journal,* July 27, 2001, p. 11.

Lunsford, Darcie, ''Levenger's New Chapter,'' *South Florida Business Journal,* April 24, 1998, pp. 1A+.

''Serious Reader Tools: Firm Builds Headquarters, Outlet in Delray,'' *South Florida Business Journal,* August 27, 1993, pp. 1A+.

Sherberg, Ellen, ''A Closer Look,'' *St. Louis Business Journal,* February 9, 2001, p. 56.

Stodder, Gayle Soto, ''Read All About It,'' *Entrepreneur,* January 1997, pp. 144+.

—Terri L. Mozzone

The Macallan Distillers Ltd.

The Macallan Distillery
Craigellachie
Banffshire AB38 9RX
United Kingdom
Telephone: +44 (0) 1340 871471
Fax: +44 (0) 1340 871212
Web site: http://www.themacallan.com

Wholly Owned Subsidiary of Edrington Group
Incorporated: 1824
Sales: £269 million ($363.10 million) (2003 Edrington
   Group)
NAIC: 312140 Distilleries

The Macallan, made by The Macallan Distillers Ltd., is one of the world's top selling Scotch whiskey brands, typically ranking in the top three in terms of global sales. The Macallan is also considered by many to be the world's finest single-malt whiskey, earning monikers such as "the Rolls Royce of single malts" and "the Dom Perignon of Scotch." Safeguarding the company's reputation for quality is its adherence to traditional distillery techniques, including the use of small, hand-crafted brass stills, high quality "Golden Promise" barley, and Spanish oak sherry casks for aging at its Craigellachie, Scotland base. The Macallan single malt whiskey comes in a variety of ages. The company also releases Cask Strength and "replica" bottles of 1841 and 1861 single malt whiskeys. Macallan pioneered the trend for laying down stock in the 1950s and 1960s, allowing it to create a new vintage class of single malt whiskeys. The company's vintage range includes its Fine & Rare Vintage collection, featuring bottles from each year between 1926 and 1973. The full collection, available at per glass prices ranging from $50 to $3,500, was presented for the first time at the Borgata Hotel Casino & Spa in Atlantic City, New Jersey, in 2004. The company also sells a 60-year Scotch—at prices ranging to more than $22,000 per bottle. The Macallan is one of the five core brands owned by Scotland's Edrington Group, which also owns the brands The Famous Grouse, Cutty Sark, and Highland Park, among others. In 2003, the Edrington

Group, a private company, reported total sales of £269 million ($363 million).

Origins of Whiskey Legend in the 19th Century

Although whiskey had been distilled in Scotland for many centuries, it remained under English domination into the early 19th century. Steady increases in tax duties drove most whiskey makers underground—also serving in part as an act of defiance against the British crown. As a result, hundreds of distillers operating thousands of illegal stills sprang up throughout the country. Stills were often cleverly disguised, hidden among the rocks and brush of the wild northern country. Many of these sites were to remain important locations for Scottish distilleries.

In the rush to produce their whiskey before being discovered, the clandestine distillers tended to produce a clear alcohol that bore little relation to later Scotch whiskey fame. Nonetheless, the whiskey produced in the area known as Glenlivet, in the Speyside region, became recognized for its higher quality—and even became the favorite of King George IV.

Pressure began to build to banish the tax duties and introduce a less burdensome licensing system. The Duke of Gordon became the champion of this cause, and in 1823 promulgated the Excise Act. Under that legislation, distillers were provided a license to operate, in exchange for an annual fee of £10, and a smaller per-gallon duty. The first distiller to take advantage of the new license was George Smith, who founded what became known as The Glenlivet distillery. Smith was to win the exclusive right to the "The" in its name, yet it remained common practice for distillers from the Glenlivet area to include "Glenlivet" in their own distillery names into the 1970s.

Another distillery emerged from the underground in 1824, when Alexander Reid obtained the license to operate on a small hill overlooking the River Spey in the village of Craigellachie. Distilling had most likely taken place on the hill since the early 1700s and the introduction of the first punitive whiskey duties. The following year, Reid formed his own company, Alexander Reid & Co., remaining head of the distillery, known as Macallan, until his death in 1847. Reid was succeeded by his son, also named Alexander, who led the company until his own death in 1858.

246

In the meantime, Reid took on partners, James Davidson and James Shearer Priest, who entered the company starting in 1848. James Davidson, who had made his fortune as a corn merchant, eventually emerged as sole owner of the distillery. Davidson was credited with instituting a policy of purchasing only high-grade barley for use in distilling its whiskey, then known as The Craigellachie. After Davidson's death in 1868, operation of the distillery was taken over by James Stuart under a tenant arrangement. Stuart, who went on to own and operate a number of distilleries in the region, purchased the Macallan distillery outright in 1886. A prolonged recession brought Stuart, further preoccupied with building a new distillery in Glen Rothes, into financial difficulties in the 1870s. Help came from an unexpected source, however. In 1879, French vines were struck by the phylloxera pest, which destroyed most of the country's vineyard. For more than ten years, brandy remained unavailable in the United Kingdom, leading to a surge of interest in Scottish whiskey.

Single Malt Boom in the 1970s

Macallan's modern period began with the arrival of Roderick Kemp as the new owner of the Macallan distillery in 1892. After buying the distillery, Kemp renamed the company as R. Kemp Macallan-Glenlivet in order to emphasize its location in the by then world famous Glenlivet area. Kemp then set to work rebuilding the Macallan distillery, adding new warehouse facilities, and improving the company's stills and other buildings. Kemp continued to make improvement through to the end of the century, expanding Macallan's production. Kemp also developed most of the company's quality standards, which included aging its whiskeys only in unbroken Spanish oak sherry casks. Although Kemp died in 1909, the Kemp family remained in control of the distillery into the 1990s.

For the most part, the Scotch whiskey market remained dominated by blended whiskeys. Blenders purchased whiskey stock from distillers, and a typical bottle often blended various types of whiskey. Macallan became a highly sought after commodity by blenders, who used it to provide a top note to their blends. While distillers also produced a limited range of single malts—so-called because the whiskey in a given bottle came from a single cask—these were almost entirely consumed by the domestic population.

This situation was to change in the 1960s and especially in the 1970s, as consumers over the world began discovering the more subtle flavors of single malts. The surge in interest caught most distillers off-guard as the "laying down" of stock for the long periods of time needed to produce properly aged single malt whiskeys had long been a luxury avoided by most distillers. The Macallan distillery, however, had already instituted a policy of keeping back a significant proportion of its whiskey in the 1950s

and 1960s, and even earlier—among the company's possessions were casks filled as early as 1926. Nonetheless, the majority of its production, as much as 93 percent, was sold on to blenders.

The rise in interest in single malt whiskey, and a slump in blended whiskey sales, encouraged Macallan-Glenlivet to step up production in the mid-1960s. The company nonetheless maintained its commitment to its traditional distilling methods, including the use of small, hand-crafter brass stills. Instead of converting to larger, industrial-sized stills, the company began adding new stills to its property, doubling the number of stills to 12 in 1965. The company's further expansion plans required financial backing. In 1968, the company went public, a move meant to finance the laying down of stock, as well as to continue its expansion drive. Among the investors in the company over the next decades were fellow Scottish group Highland Distillers, France's Remy Cointreau, and Japan's Suntory. The proceeds of the public offering helped Macallan-Glenlivet add a new still to its No. 1 still house, a move that helped it top more than one million gallons of production for the first time. The company ended 1968 with sales of more than £822 million.

After changing its name to Macallan-Glenlivet in 1970, the company began construction of a new generation of stills, adding another six stills in 1974. The following year, the company added three more to reach a total of 21 stills. By the end of 1975, the company's sales had topped £1 million for the first time. In response to rising demand, Macallan-Glenlivet arranged loans, enabling it to reserve yet more of its stock, even as it stepped up production. By then, the company's whiskey had already begun to attract a global audience, helping to push sales past £2 million by 1977.

The surge in interest in Scottish single malts led the company to restore an old manor house located on its estate as a reception center for visitors and as an office complex for its growing international distribution. That center opened in 1977. By then, the Macallan distillery had already earned international recognition for its whiskey. In order to capitalize on its growing renown, the company decided to launch its first official, branded single malt, called The Macallan.

The launch was an immediate success and The Macallan became one of the single-malt category's major ambassadors around the world. By the mid-1980s, the growth in single malt sales had even inspired a collectors' market. The Macallan promptly became one of the most sought after labels, especially with the release of the first bottles of the group's prized 60-year label.

Core Brand in the New Century

The drinks world meanwhile entered a new era of consolidation, and by the early 1990s the beverage market had become dominated by a handful of major groups. Macallan-Glenlivet stayed out of the consolidation fray for the most part. Nonetheless, the company took advantage of the growing clout of the major players. In 1994, for example, the company signed a distribution agreement with Highland Distillers. Toward the mid-1990s, however, the industry trend toward the building of strong brand portfolios caught up with the company. By then, the Kemp family's interest in the company had dropped to around 20 percent.

Key Dates:

1824: Alexander Reid obtains license to open distillery in Craigellachie, Scotland, which later becomes the Macallan distillery.

1847: Alexander Reid dies and is succeeded by his son.

1848: James Davidson and James Pierce become partners in distillery.

1868: James Stuart takes over distillery, first as tenant operator, then as owner.

1892: Distillery is sold to Roderick Kemp, who rebuilds its warehouse and distillery facilities, renaming company as R. Kemp Macallan-Glenlivet.

1968: Company goes public in order to finance expansion and laying down of single-malt stock.

1970: Company changes name to Macallan-Glenlivet.

1980: The Macallan single-malt brand is introduced.

1986: Exclusive 60-year-old label debuts.

1996: Highland Distillers, in partnership with Japan's Suntory, acquires control of Macallan-Glenlivet.

1999: Edrington Group acquires Highland, and designates The Macallan as one of its five core brands; launch of 15-year and 30-year labels.

2003: Company launches 1841 and 1861 ''replicas,'' as well as Fine & Rare Vintage Collection.

2004: Complete Fine & Rare Vintage Collection is offered per glass for the first time.

Highland Distillers began maneuvering for a larger stake in Macallan-Glenlivet. In January 1996, Highland acquired the 26 percent in Macallan it had turned over to Remy Cointreau during a 1990 cross-shareholding arrangement between the two fast-growing drinks groups. By July 1996, Highland had worked out a second agreement, this time with Japan's Suntory, to place its own 26 percent and Suntory's 25 percent in Macallan into a new joint venture, HS Distillers. Highland maintained a controlling stake in HS Distillers, while Suntory agreed to act as a silent partner and ensure distribution of The Macallan in Japan. The new venture, with 51 percent of Macallan, immediately launched a buyout of the minority 49 percent stake in Macallan. Macallan, already one of the world's top single malts, joined Highland's Famous Grouse, the top-selling blended whiskey brand in the United Kingdom.

Highland Distillers itself appeared to become the object of takeover speculation at the end of the decade. In response, that company agreed to be acquired by the Edrington Group, a privately held Scottish company with operations ranging from distilling to blending to bottling. In particular, Edrington was the source of the grain whiskey stocks needed to blend Highland's Famous Grouse, and the two companies already had substantial cross-shareholding interests.

Although Highland itself disappeared into Edrington, The Macallan emerged as one of the new Edrington's core brands. Under Edrington, The Macallan moved to take full advantage of its prestigious reputation. The company released a number of new labels, including a 15-year-old and a 30-year-old bottle in 1999. That launch was followed in 2000 with the release of a new 50-year label. In the meantime, demand for the group's limited 60-year-old Scotch continued to build, prompting company-held auction prices to top $20,000 per bottle. In 2003, the company debuted two new single malts, the 1841 and 1861 ''replicas,'' said to be copies of two rare bottles of single-malt found in the company's own collection.

In 2003, The Macallan released a new collection of single malts. Dubbed ''The Macallan Fine & Rare Vintage Collection,'' the offering featured bottles spanning a range of vintages from 1926 to 1973, valued at $170,000. In 2004, the newly opened Borgata Hotel Casino & Spa located in Atlantic City, New Jersey, became the first in the world to offer the full collection for sale by the glass—with prices per glass ranging up to $3,500. Under the Edrington Group's guidance, The Macallan seemed certain to retain its place at the top of the world's whiskey hill.

Principal Competitors

Diageo PLC; Seagram Company Ltd.; Asahi Breweries Ltd.; Asahi Kasei Corp.; Fortune Brands Inc.; Jim Beam Brands Worldwide Inc.; Brown-Forman Corp.; Irish Distillers Group PLC; Remy Cointreau; Allied Distillers Ltd.

Further Reading

Baker, Lucy, ''Highland Distillers to Be Taken Private,'' *Independent*, September 11, 1999, p. 18.

Givens, Ron, ''Spirits: One for the Ages,'' *Newsweek*, November 24, 2003, p. 89.

Mason, Tania, ''The Whisky Generation Game,'' *Marketing*, September 25, 2003, p. 17.

Murry, Alasdair, ''Macallan Yields to Highland,'' *Times*, July 11, 1996, p. 24.

''To the Dark Side,'' *Financial Times*, October 20, 2003, p. 12.

Wattie, Alec, ''Edrington to Swallow Highland Distillers,'' *Sunday Times*, August 15, 1999, p. 2.

—M.L. Cohen

Malt-O-Meal Company

80 South 8th Street, Suite 2600
Minneapolis, Minnesota 55402-2297
U.S.A.
Telephone: (612) 338-8551
Toll Free: (800) 328-4452; (800) 743-3029
Fax: (612) 339-5710
Web site: http://www.malt-o-meal.com

Private Company
Incorporated: 1919 as Campbell Cereal Company
Employees: 1,000
Sales: $520 million (2003 est.)
NAIC: 311230 Breakfast Cereal Manufacturing

Malt-O-Meal Company is the fifth largest cereal manufacturer in the United States, holding slightly more than 7 percent of the $7.1 billion U.S. cereal market. Best known as a manufacturer of hot wheat cereals for the majority of its years in business, Malt-O-Meal has evolved into a leader in the value-priced, bagged ready-to-eat U.S. cereal market while still selling its mainstay products; it also makes four varieties of instant oatmeal. The low-profile company produces and markets cereals under its own and private-label names, distributing its products in more than 70 percent of the nation's retail grocery stores. Its facilities include two manufacturing plants in Northfield, Minnesota, and one in Tremonton, Utah, as well as distribution centers in Grove City, Ohio; Coppel, Texas; and Salt Lake City, Utah. The firm remains privately owned by members of the Brooks and Fort families, descendants of the founder.

The Early Years: 1910s–50s

Malt-O-Meal Company founder John S. Campbell's first job was in his father's grain milling company. After serving in World War I, Campbell returned home to Owatonna, Minnesota, and invested $800 (poker earnings, according to a 1969 *Minneapolis Tribune* article by Charles B. McFadden) in his own business venture. "My idea was to make a cereal that tasted better and cooked quicker than the top-selling wheat farina product, Cream of Wheat, which then took about 30 minutes to cook.

Malt gave me the flavor I wanted and toasting reduced the cooking time of my finished product to two or three minutes."

In 1919 Campbell Cereal Company began operating out of an old creamery building rented for $11 per month. Initially a one-man venture, Campbell processed the malt and wheat in an iron cylinder with a gas burner, then packaged and sold the cereal he named Malt-O-Meal. He quickly found there was an art to selling a new product and hired a salesman, who offered free customer samples to retail grocers. Distribution was limited to southern Minnesota and northern Iowa during the first few years.

Campbell experimented with radio promotion in 1925 on WLS in Chicago. Kids were offered the chance to win a free toy by sending in a joke and Malt-O-Meal box top to the *Steamboat Bill* show. Grocers were swamped with requests for the cereal, and Malt-O-Meal began gaining shelf space. The WLS promotion, which began as a two-week trial, ran for more than a year. Additional promotions were aired on stations in the Midwest, Southwest, and West.

With business booming, Campbell moved the company into the Simpson Mill, which had once been operated by his father and an uncle. In 1927 the company relocated to Northfield, Minnesota, in the Ames Mill, which had been built in 1869. The southwestern market opened up in the late 1920s thanks to a Texas businessman named C.C. Lindley. Campbell established a Minneapolis sales and marketing office in 1932 and began working with an advertising agency. In 1936 the corporate headquarters also were shifted to Minneapolis.

Campbell's Corn Flakes was introduced in 1939. Because of stiff competition from the Kellogg Company, the ready-to-eat cereal was dropped in 1942. Meanwhile, Malt-O-Meal sales climbed steadily. Box sizes changed in the late 1940s, but the product itself remained the same. In 1953 Campbell Cereal Company was renamed Malt-O-Meal Company. Sales by the privately held business nearly doubled from 1948 to 1958.

Changing Marketplace: 1960s–70s

Competitor Cream of Wheat was purchased by the National Biscuit Company in 1961, the year Malt-O-Meal added a sec-

Company Perspectives:

We've provided excellent quality and value in breakfast cereals for over 75 years!

ond flavor. Chocolate Flavored Malt-O-Meal kept the company's momentum going as industrywide sales began to drop off. Also in 1961 Malt-O-Meal expanded its manufacturing space in Northfield with the purchase of the Carnation Creamery building, which was renamed the Campbell Mill. John Campbell was succeeded as president of Malt-O-Meal by his son-in-law Glenn S. Brooks in 1966. Brooks had joined the company in 1956 and had been appointed vice-president and general manager in 1965.

Malt-O-Meal sales flattened out in the mid-1960s. U.S. consumers were buying more and more convenience and sweetened foods. In 1966, Malt-O-Meal began producing State Fair brand Puffed Wheat and Puffed Rice at its new plant site. The next year, Malt-O-Meal entered the snack food market with Soy Town roasted and salted soybeans. The purchase of Profile Extrusion Company marked the first major diversification for the 46-year-old company. The 20-employee, vinyl plastic subsidiary produced component parts for other manufacturers.

Malt-O-Meal employed a total of 55 people in its two Northfield plants and Minneapolis office by 1969. Malt-O-Meal 100 Plus, which the company touted as the first hot cereal with 100 percent of the established daily minimum requirements of vitamins and iron, was added to the hot cereal line in 1969 but discontinued four years later. Pophitt Cereals, Inc., purchased in 1970, bolstered Malt-O-Meal's ready-to-eat cereal segment with its Whiffs and Sunland Puffed Wheat and Puffed Rice line.

Chairman and CEO John Campbell died in 1971. The company he founded had extended its reach throughout the western two-thirds of the country. Yet Malt-O-Meal remained a relatively small independent company holding less than 3 percent of the hot cereal market versus the 64 percent held by the Quaker Oats Company.

Malt-O-Meal took another bite into the ready-to-eat cereal market in the early 1970s, when the company began to box private-label cereals for grocery store chains such as Super Valu and Kroger. In 1975 Malt-O-Meal introduced Toasty O's, a lower-cost, bagged version of General Mills, Inc.'s Cheerios. A second major brand imitation, Sugar Puffs, hit the market in 1980. The push into the ready-to-eat market helped revenues double between 1975 and 1980.

Accelerating Expansion in the 1980s

During the first half of the 1980s, the company introduced several more national brand knockoffs: Raisin Bran, Corn Flakes, Crispy Rice, Sugar Frosted Flakes, and Honey & Nut Toasty O's. In 1985 the ready-to-eat cereal segment of the business contributed about two-thirds of the year's estimated $50 million in revenues. Malt-O-Meal's revenues had doubled again between 1980 and 1985. John W. Lettmann, who worked in the marketing department at General Mills before coming on

board as Brooks's assistant in 1971, was named president in 1986, the same year that the firm opened a distribution center in Northfield.

Malt-O-Meal increased the size of its package in 1982. With the exception of instant products, the hot cereal market had continued to stagnate. Malt-O-Meal introduced an instant hot cereal in 1987, but the latecomer never gained significant market share and was discontinued in 1990. Malt-O-Meal Plus 40% Oat Bran was manufactured between 1988 to 1992. The company divested itself of two other business ventures in the 1980s: the snack food business was sold, and Profile Extrusion became an independent company.

Chair and CEO Brooks died in 1988. During his tenure the company had grown from 20 to 300 employees and revenues reached an estimated $77 million. The company was producing approximately 150 cereal items, including its own brands, private-label brands, and bulk or single-serving cereals for the food-service operations of major cereal companies.

Price increases by the top-of-the-line, ready-to-eat cereal makers had opened a window of opportunity for Malt-O-Meal in the 1980s. Budget-conscious consumers balked at paying upward of $4 a box for national brands. By foregoing expensive advertising and packaging, Malt-O-Meal offered a comparable product for about half the price of the high-profile cereals: limited magazine, radio, and television ads emphasized that message. Selling through food brokers instead of staffing a large internal sales force also helped Malt-O-Meal keep prices down.

Malt-O-Meal's strategy paid off on the bottom line. In a September 1990 *Forbes* magazine article, John Harris estimated 1989 profits to be $4 million. Harris wrote, "Only a handful of regional and independent cereal companies remain in a business in which a new product introduction can easily cost $15 million." Despite purchase offers, Malt-O-Meal continued to be held by members of the founding family.

Challenges of the 1990s

Revenues reached an estimated $137 million in 1991. Malt-O-Meal sales had grown at a compound annual rate of just less than 17 percent since 1975, according to a May 1992 *Minneapolis Star Tribune* article by Dick Youngblood. The company added to its production facilities nine times during that same period. The well-trained employees, numbering more than 450, were divided into production teams.

Malt-O-Meal had pumped in about $100 million on plant and equipment during the 1980s and first few years of the 1990s, according to Youngblood. But while its laboratories could copy the ingredients of big name cereals—only trademarks, names, and technologies could be patented—they still faced some marketing barriers. Time-crunched consumers tended to buy familiar brands, and many potential customers viewed Malt-O-Meal as only a hot cereal maker.

So with about a dozen different flavors in its bagged cereal lineup, Malt-O-Meal began experimenting with additional advertising. General Mills quickly complained that the firm's TV ad comparison of Toasty O's to Cheerios was misleading in terms of taste and price. The National Advertising Division of

Key Dates:

1919: John S. Campbell founds the Campbell Cereal Company in Owatonna, Minnesota, producing a new cereal he calls Malt-O-Meal.

1927: The company relocates to Northfield, Minnesota, in the Ames Mill.

1936: Company headquarters are moved to Minneapolis.

1953: Campbell Cereal is renamed Malt-O-Meal Company.

1961: Manufacturing space in Northfield is expanded with the purchase of the Carnation Creamery building, which is renamed the Campbell Mill.

Early 1970s: Malt-O-Meal begins boxing private-label cereals for grocery store chains.

1975: The company introduces Toasty O's, a lower-cost, bagged version of Cheerios.

1993: A distribution center in Salt Lake City is opened.

1995: A Grove City, Ohio, distribution center is opened.

1996: The company opens a distribution center in Coppel, Texas.

1998: An outbreak of salmonella poisoning forces Malt-O-Meal to recall about three million pounds of its toasted oat cereals; the company breaks ground on a new plant and distribution center in Tremonton, Utah.

2000: Construction of the Tremonton plant is halted because of a cereal price war; Big Bowl brand of instant oatmeal debuts.

2002: Malt-O-Meal acquires Quaker's U.S. bagged cereal line and announces that construction of its Utah plant will resume.

2003: Balance with Berries is introduced as the first in a new Malt-O-Meal Originals line of unique cereals.

2004: Production begins at the Tremonton plant.

the Better Business Bureau agreed, and Malt-O-Meal pulled the 1992 ad.

Sales topped the $200 million mark in 1993, two years ahead of Lettmann's target date, according to a March 1994 *St. Paul Pioneer Press* article by Dave Beal. Malt-O-Meal celebrated its 75th anniversary in 1994 with the groundbreaking for a three-year expansion estimated by Beal to cost about $80 million. The 70 percent increase in space would boost the facility to 860,000 square feet and make it one of the largest manufacturing plants in Minnesota.

While Malt-O-Meal bagged cereal sales were growing, the private-label boxed cereals continued to bring in about half the ready-to-eat cereal revenues. Malt-O-Meal held an estimated 25 percent share of the U.S. private-label market. Ralston Purina (later Ralcorp Holdings, Inc.) held about 60 percent. But, according to the Beal article, market analysts believed Ralston's share was falling while Malt-O-Meal was on the rise.

The value end of the cereal business was growing at a faster pace than the overall industry and both small and large companies wanted to tap into the market. Minnesota-based Grist Mill

Inc., which packaged granola cereal under its own name and private labels, began offering several more cereal varieties in 1993. Quaker Oats, which held 15 percent of the bagged cereal market through its Stokely Van Camp subsidiary's Popeye brand, began putting its own name on the lower-cost bags in 1994. Malt-O-Meal held about 75 percent of the bagged cereal market.

Malt-O-Meal moved to increase consumer awareness of bagged cereals through a new take on its advertising. Laurie Freeman wrote in a July 1995 *Advertising Age* article, "The 'Walk This Way' spot shows regular folks doing a duck walk—squatting down and waddling by the lower shelves of the cereal aisle, where Malt-O-Meal cereals are usually found." The humorous television ad aired in 13 key markets, including Minneapolis, Seattle, and Phoenix, and on network cable. But Malt-O-Meal's ad budget remained minuscule compared with those of the national brands.

Production commenced on five more ready-to-eat cereals, Tootie Fruities, Apple Cinnamon Toasty O's, Coco Roos, Marshmallow Mateys, and Corn Bursts, between 1989 and 1994. Malt-O-Meal added Apple & Cinnamon to the hot cereal offerings in 1995. Original and chocolate-flavored cereals, and Maple & Brown Sugar Malt-O-Meal, which had been produced since 1992, completed the line that produced about 15 percent of total company sales of about $250 million.

Sales grew to an estimated $275 million by 1996, aided by the opening of three distribution centers located around the country: Salt Lake City in 1993; Grove City, Ohio, in 1995; and Coppel, Texas, in 1996. Also in 1996 Malt-O-Meal was the first value-priced cereal maker to lower its prices in response to price cuts by Kellogg, General Mills, and Philip Morris Companies Inc., owner of Post and Nabisco brands. The companies were trying to halt market share erosion caused by the value-priced offerings. Although Malt-O-Meal had not raised its prices in five years, an average of 12 percent was knocked off ten of its cereals to maintain an 80 cents to $1.00 price differentiation.

Malt-O-Meal continued introducing new products—all knockoffs of other brands—in the late 1990s. These included Berry Colossal Crunch (1996), Honey Buzzers and Frosted Mini Spooners (1997), Apple Zings (1998), and Cocoa Dyno-Bites and Fruity Dyno-Bites (1999). In addition, the packaging for Malt-O-Meal's bagged cereals began featuring zip-off tops with resealable pour spouts in 1998, an innovation that the company touted as a way for consumers to keep the product fresher after opening.

In June 1998 Malt-O-Meal recalled about three million pounds of its Toasty O's, Toasted Oats, and private-label plain toasted oat cereals after finding that some of its toasted oat cereal was the likely culprit in an outbreak of salmonella poisoning that at the time had reportedly sickened more than 200 people in 12 states in the Midwest and Northeast, sending nearly 50 of them to the hospital. A class-action lawsuit was soon filed against Malt-O-Meal on behalf of those affected. Final approval of a settlement was granted in 2002, whereby the company, without admitting any liability or wrongdoing, agreed to pay $2 million to the plaintiffs, which by then numbered more than 1,000.

By 1998, despite the recall, Malt-O-Meal had captured 4 percent of the overall U.S. cereal market, more than doubling its share of five years earlier. Revenues reached about $350 million that year. Late in the year the company broke ground in Tremonton, Utah, for a new 200,000-square-foot manufacturing plant as well as a new western distribution center that would replace the one in Salt Lake City. Seeking a town in the West similar to Northfield—small but within a reasonable distance to a major metropolitan area—Malt-O-Meal officials settled on Tremonton, a town of about 5,000 in northwestern Utah, located in Box Elder County about 70 miles north of Salt Lake City. Cost of construction was estimated at about $90 million.

Growth Initiatives in the Early 2000s

This plant, however, fell victim—at least temporarily—to the cereal price wars. The cereal market took a sharp turn for the worse in 2000, leading competitors such as Post and Kellogg to slash their prices by as much as 20 percent. Forced to cut its own prices, Malt-O-Meal saw its revenues fall and its margins squeezed. It halted construction of the Tremonton plant just short of completion.

As its potential new plant sat idle, Malt-O-Meal moved forward with several new products. In 2000 it introduced a new line of instant oatmeals under the Big Bowl brand. The following year the company debuted two more bagged cereals: Toasted Cinnamon Twists, a knockoff of General Mills' Cinnamon Toast Crunch, and Honey Graham Squares, a knockoff of Golden Grahams, yet another General Mills product.

In December 2002 Malt-O-Meal announced that it had bought the U.S. bagged cereal business of Quaker, which had been purchased by PepsiCo, Inc. two years earlier. Malt-O-Meal gained a line of 40 bagged cereals marketed under the Quaker brand, including Frosted Flakes, Marshmallow Safari, Apple Zaps, and Cocoa Blasts. Quaker agreed to continue manufacturing the line for up to two years, during which time Malt-O-Meal could use the Quaker name under license.

The deal breathed new life into the Tremonton plant. Knowing that it would eventually need more manufacturing capacity to produce the acquired products on its own, Malt-O-Meal restarted work on the plant. It finally opened in January 2004, producing Toasted Cinnamon Twists and Golden Puffs. Additional products were slated to be produced at the plant over the next two to three years, during which time the firm also planned to move its distribution center from Salt Lake City to Tremonton. Also by early 2004, the company had completed its conversion of the Quaker bagged cereals to the Malt-O-Meal brand.

Meantime, Malt-O-Meal took its bagged cereal line in a new direction in 2003 with the introduction of Balance with Berries. Featuring wheat flakes and freeze-dried strawberries, this new cereal was not a knockoff but the first in what the company said would be a Malt-O-Meal Originals line of unique cereals. Balance with Berries also targeted the fast-growing "cereal with fruit" segment of the market. Aided by this new introduction and the acquired Quaker line, Malt-O-Meal reported a sales increase for 2003 of 28.8 percent, compared with flat sales for cereals industrywide. This pushed sales up to

about $520 million, translating into a market share of about 7.3 percent. Through its most recent moves, Malt-O-Meal had clearly strengthened its position in the highly competitive cereal market.

Principal Competitors

Kellogg Company; General Mills, Inc.; Kraft Foods Inc.; PepsiCo, Inc.; Ralcorp Holdings, Inc.

Further Reading

Barnes, Sam, "Mill in Northfield That Made History Still Makes Breakfast," *Minneapolis Star Tribune,* December 17, 2003, p. 1S.

Beal, Dave, "Malt-O-Meal Heats Up," *St. Paul Pioneer Press,* March 28, 1994, pp. 1B, 3B.

Egerstrom, Lee, "Malt-O-Meal of Minneapolis Cuts Prices on Its Breakfast Cereals," *St. Paul Pioneer Press,* July 9, 1996.

Fiedler, Terry, "Cereal Recall Expands," *Minneapolis Star Tribune,* June 6, 1998, p. 1A.

"Founder of Cereal Company Dies at 83," *Minneapolis Star,* November 2, 1971.

Fredrickson, Tom, "Rivals Could Milk Gain from Kellogg Price Hike," *Minneapolis/St. Paul CityBusiness,* February 18, 1994.

Freeman, Laurie, "Malt-O-Meal Stirring Up the Competition," *Advertising Age,* July 17, 1994, p. 4.

"Glenn Brooks Is Named President of Malt-O-Meal," *Minneapolis Tribune,* April 20, 1966.

"Good Ideas," *Twin Cities Business Monthly,* April 1997, p. 11.

Groeneveld, Benno, "Firms Look Beyond the Family for CEOs," *Minneapolis/St. Paul Business Journal,* May 24, 2002.

Harris, John, "Your Taste Buds Won't Know, Your Pocketbook Will," *Forbes,* September 3, 1990, pp. 88, 90.

Jones, Gwenyth, "Firm Says Hot Cereal Sales Gain," *Minneapolis Star,* May 9, 1958.

Kennedy, Tony, "Battle of the Cereals," *Minneapolis Star Tribune,* October 28, 1992, p. 6D.

——, "Grist Mill Is Expanding to Private-Label Cereals," *Minneapolis Star Tribune,* December 18, 1992, p. 5D.

——, "Quaker to Put Its Brand on Bagged Cereals in Bid for Larger Share of the Budget Market," *Minneapolis Star Tribune,* January 24, 1995.

Kratz, Gregory P., "Malt-O-Meal Plans to Build $90 Million Plant in Box Elder," *Deseret News* (Salt Lake City, Utah), August 8, 1998, p. B5.

Kurschner, Dale, "Cold Cereals Are Hot Sellers in Strategy by Malt-O-Meal," *Minneapolis/St. Paul CityBusiness,* July 23–29, 1990, pp. 1, 18.

Leonhardt, David, "Cereal-Box Killers Are on the Loose," *Business Week,* October 12, 1998, p. 72.

Lo Bosco, Maryellen, "Malt-O-Meal Co. Recalls Plain Toasted-Oat Cereals," *Supermarket News,* June 15, 1998, p. 61.

"Malt-O-Meal," *Minneapolis Tribune,* January 17, 1971.

"Malt-O-Meal Co. Acquires Vinyl Plastics Firm," *Minneapolis Star,* November 17, 1967.

"Malt-O-Meal: 75 Years of Tradition and Progress," *Northfield (Minn.) News,* Special Section, 1994.

McFadden, Charles B., "Malt-O-Meal Began As $800 Gamble," *Minneapolis Tribune,* September 21, 1969.

Mitchell, Lesley, "Malt-O-Meal Pulls Out of Plant in Tremonton As Result of 'Cereal Wars,' " *Salt Lake Tribune,* September 4, 2002, p. D6.

——, "Malt-O-Meal Reclaims Tremonton Facility," *Salt Lake Tribune,* January 22, 2004, p. E1.

Peterson, Susan E., "Malt-O-Meal's New Chief Takes Over in Era of Change," *Minneapolis Star Tribune,* February 10, 1986, p. 2M.

Smith, M.L., "Executive Glenn Brooks Dies at 61," *Minneapolis Star Tribune,* June 14, 1988, p. 6B.

Tellijohn, Andrew, "Malt-O-Meal Acquires Quaker Bagged Cereal," *Minneapolis/St. Paul Business Journal,* December 4, 2002.

Wallace, Brice, "Cereal Deal to Aid Tremonton Plant," *Deseret News* (Salt Lake City, Utah), December 4, 2002, p. C3.

——, "Malt-O-Meal Plant to Start Up," *Deseret News* (Salt Lake City, Utah), October 17, 2002, p. B12.

Youngblood, Dick, "Malt-O-Meal Story a Series of Cereals," *Minneapolis Star Tribune,* May 4, 1992, p. 2D.

—Kathleen Peippo
—update: David E. Salamie

Marshall Field's

700 Nicollet Mall
Minneapolis, Minnesota 55402-2040
U.S.A.
Telephone: (612) 375-2200
Fax: (612) 375-2795
Web site: http://www.marshallfields.com

Division of Target Corporation
Incorporated: 1901 as Marshall Field & Company, Inc.
Employees: 26,000
Sales: $2.58 billion (2003)
NAIC: 452110 Department Stores; 454110 Electronic
    Shopping and Mail-Order Houses

Marshall Field's, a division of Target Corporation, is a major mid-market to upscale department store chain operating in eight states in the Upper Midwest: Illinois, Indiana, Michigan, Minnesota, North Dakota, Ohio, South Dakota, and Wisconsin. Of the 62 Marshall Field's stores, more than half of them are located in three major metropolitan areas: Chicago, Detroit, and Minneapolis/St. Paul. This geographic range is a reflection of the Chicago-founded Marshall Field's having absorbed the Minneapolis-based Dayton's and the Detroit-based Hudson's department stores following the 1990 purchase of Marshall Field's by Dayton Hudson Corporation (now Target Corporation). Target's three department store chains were united under the Marshall Field's banner in 2001. With roots dating back more than 150 years, Marshall Field's is one of the oldest and most venerated names in American retailing.

Laying of the Foundation by Potter Palmer: 1852–65

Although the early history of Marshall Field's is most often associated with the company's namesake, Marshall Field, it was Potter Palmer who actually launched the business, which would eventually develop into the world's leading retailer. Palmer arrived in Chicago from Lockport, New York, in 1852, at the young age of 26 but already with eight years experience as a clerk and country merchant. Chicago, incorporated only in 1833, still had the appearance of a frontier town at the time of Palmer's arrival—complete with largely unpaved roads and wooden sidewalks—but it was in the midst of a boom fueled by Easterners seeking their fortune in the West and by the hundreds of towns being founded in the surrounding prairies. Chicago's growth was ignited by several other factors as well, including its central location, its position at the foot of Lake Michigan (making it a natural port), and its development into a main hub for the burgeoning system of railroads. The population growth of Chicago was astounding: from less than 30,000 in 1850 to nearly 300,000 in 1870 to almost 1.1 million in 1890 to 1.7 million in 1900. This environment created a ready opportunity for merchants of both the wholesale and retail variety.

Palmer came to this boomtown with $5,000 as seed capital for a new venture, and he soon rented out the first floor of a four-story frame building on Lake Street, then known as ''the street of merchants,'' and opened a retail dry goods store called P. Palmer & Company. From his modest first-year gross sales of $73,000 in 1852, Palmer fairly rapidly created a thriving enterprise. Key to his success were several innovations. After first centering his merchandise inventory on the less refined needs of the many pioneer settlers passing through town, Palmer added to his stock higher quality, fashion-conscious goods—such as silks, velvets, laces, and fine carpeting—arranging them into inviting displays. This attracted the more well-to-do into the store—particularly women. According to Tony Jahn, Marshall Field's corporate archivist and historian, ''[Palmer] created the store as a sanctuary for women. It was a place where they could be treated well, could see some of the finest things available in the day and be treated with dignity and respect'' (quoted in *Women's Wear Daily,* October 9, 2003). Palmer's innovative approach went well beyond his unique inventory. In place of the haggling over price then prevalent, he instituted fixed pricing, placing price tags on every piece of merchandise. This practice irritated his competitors, as did his undercutting the prices his rivals charged for certain items. Palmer also allowed his customers to buy on credit. Perhaps playing the biggest role in securing loyal customers was Palmer's ''no questions asked'' return and exchange policy—unheard of at the time. Cementing his goal of making ''respectable'' women comfortable browsing his establishment was the absence of the spittoons and whiskey barrels common in rival stores of the day.

Company Perspectives:

At Marshall Field's stores, the guest is always first. This guest-focused approach has inspired millions of shoppers across the Midwest and beyond to look to Marshall Field's for fashion leadership, superb guest service and a commitment to community involvement.

Palmer's formula proved highly successful. In October 1857 he moved his store out of its original cramped quarters into the building next door, taking all four floors. That same year he placed his first newspaper advertisement. In September 1858 Palmer moved his store one block east, into an even larger, newly built, five-story marble-fronted building. Around this same time, Palmer branched out into wholesaling. He thrived at this endeavor as well, particularly by avoiding as much as possible having to deal with Eastern importers and jobbers. He made his own buying trips abroad and also dealt directly with manufacturers in New England. By 1865 his enterprise was able to post a $300,000 profit on sales of $8 million—with wholesaling revenues now outstripping retail sales. P. Palmer & Co. was now the largest enterprise of its kind in Chicago.

From Partnership Between Marshall Field and Levi Leiter to Marshall Field & Company: 1865–81

During this period when Palmer was developing his business, Marshall Field was arriving in town to find his fortune. Field moved to Chicago from Pittsfield, Massachusetts, in 1856, having been raised in a strict New England farm family. He had spent four years as a clerk in a country store in Pittsfield, before heading west in 1856 at the age of 21 with his savings of less than $1,000. He gained employment as a clerk at what was then the leading wholesale dry goods house in Chicago, Cooley, Wadsworth & Company, at the starting salary of $400 per year. Finding his métier, Field progressed quickly, becoming a junior partner in the firm (by then known as Cooley, Farwell & Company) in 1860. Four years later, senior partner Francis Cooley retired, and the company was reorganized as Farwell, Field & Company, with John V. Farwell a senior partner and Levi Z. Leiter a junior partner. Leiter, who several years earlier had moved to Chicago from Springfield, Ohio, was the company bookkeeper.

Personal disagreements and differing ideas about how to run the business led Field to seek a way out of his partnership with Farwell. Coincidentally, Palmer began suffering from ill health, and his doctor in 1864 strongly urged him to retire from business. Seeking partners outside his firm, Palmer approached Field and Leiter, whom Palmer had admired for their obvious merchanting acumen, and the parties agreed to a deal. In January 1865, then, P. Palmer & Company was reorganized as Field, Palmer & Leiter. Field and Leiter were now in charge of Palmer's very successful business, although Palmer had agreed to leave $330,000 in the firm as a silent partner. Potter Palmer's brother Milton, a salesman at the company, signed on as a junior partner, contributing $50,000. Field and Leiter signed notes that would come due in two years for their respective shares of the initial capital, $250,000 and $120,000. (During the brief time that the company operated as Field, Palmer & Leiter, in 1866 to be exact, Aaron Montgomery Ward briefly clerked for the firm before founding his famous mail-order business early the following decade.)

With some further financial assistance from Potter Palmer, Field and Leiter were able to survive a rough beginning as the boom prices of the Civil War era came to a sudden end. The company's new leaders also helped themselves by continuing the innovative ways of their predecessor. For instance, a new notions department was set up featuring such items as combs, brushes, spools of thread, scissors, and sun umbrellas. Three female clerks were hired to help make women more comfortable buying items such as skirts, frocks, and lingerie. Field and Leiter also wisely continued Palmer's still unusual money-back guarantee policy. By January 1867 Field and Leiter were secure enough to buy out the Palmers in large part (though Potter retained part of his original investment). They renamed the firm Field, Leiter & Company.

Potter Palmer still had one last major influence on the company he had founded. In the mid-1860s he began buying up a string of properties on Chicago's State Street, seeking to turn a nondescript street into a new retail center. Palmer spent more than $2 million on his State Street project, which eventually included an eight-story hotel—the first Palmer House—as well as a six-story marble-fronted building, complete with Corinthian columns, at the corner of State and Washington. Upon its completion in late 1868, Field, Leiter & Co. promptly took a lease on the new building, which became known as the "Marble Palace." The company was thus able to expand its retail business and place itself in the center of what indeed developed into Chicago's new trade center, just as Palmer had envisioned; competitors soon followed Field, Leiter to State Street. Further expansion came in 1871 when Marshall Field sent his older brother Joseph to England to set up a buying office in Manchester. Field, Leiter thus became the first U.S. retailer to open a European buying office.

As it turned out, the firm's palatial new store would last only three years. In October 1871 the Great Chicago Fire burned down nearly the entire central business district, including the Field, Leiter & Co. store. More than $2.5 million in Field, Leiter merchandise was destroyed. The partners acted quickly to find a new location, hoping to get a jump on their competitors. Just three weeks after the fire, they reopened at a temporary location, an old trolley barn at Twentieth and State Streets. Simultaneously, a decision was made to physically separate the retail and wholesale divisions for the first time. In March 1872, then, the company's wholesale side moved into a newly constructed building on Madison Street just west of the modern-day Loop. That same year, the retail side continued its innovative ways by introducing free, same-day delivery service to customers' homes via a horse and wagon. The firm's wagons eventually featured the company logo painted in green, the color that eventually would become synonymous with Marshall Field & Company.

For a short while, Field, Leiter & Co. operated retail stores at both the converted trolley barn and the wholesale site, but Field and Leiter soon decided to return to State Street. To finance the building of a new Palmer House (what would become the first wholly fireproof hotel in the nation), Potter Palmer had sold much of his Chicago property holdings. Field, Leiter & Co.'s

Key Dates:

1852: Potter Palmer opens a retail dry goods store called P. Palmer & Company on Lake Street in Chicago, soon finding success creating an upscale emporium catering to women.

1865: Marshall Field and Levi Z. Leiter buy into Palmer's enterprise, which is renamed Field, Palmer & Leiter.

1867: Field and Leiter buy out Palmer, renaming the firm Field, Leiter & Company.

1868: Field and Leiter move their store to State and Washington Streets.

1871: The store is destroyed in the Great Chicago Fire; three weeks later, it reopens at a temporary site.

1873: The retail store reopens in a new building at State and Washington.

1877: Another fire burns the store to the ground, forcing another temporary relocation.

1879: Field, Leiter & Company returns once again to State and Washington.

1881: Field buys out Leiter and renames the firm Marshall Field & Company.

1885: Field's retail store opens its bargain basement area.

1901: The company is incorporated as Marshall Field & Company, Inc.

1906: Marshall Field dies, leaving ownership of his company to a complex family trust; John G. Shedd takes over as president.

1917: Field family trustees sell 90 percent of their company shares to the firm's officers and managers.

1929: The Frederick & Nelson department store in Seattle, Washington, is acquired.

1930: The company finishes construction of the mammoth $35 million Merchandise Mart, new home of the wholesale and manufacturing divisions; Marshall Field & Co. offers shares to the public for the first time; the Field family retains a 10 percent stake.

1932: At the height of the depression, Marshall Field & Co. posts a net loss of $8 million.

1935: James O. McKinsey is brought in from the outside as chairman and CEO to direct the liquidation of the wholesale division.

1945: The Merchandise Mart is sold to Joseph P. Kennedy for $12.9 million.

1953: Marshall Field completes the divestment of its manufacturing operations, selling Fieldcrest Mills.

1956: The company leads the development of Old Orchard, a new shopping center in Skokie, Illinois, featuring a Marshall Field's store.

1965: The Field family sells its last remaining holdings in Marshall Field & Co.

1976: Water Tower Place, half-owned by the company, is completed on Chicago's North Michigan Avenue and includes a new Marshall Field's store.

1977: Carter Hawley Hale Stores, Inc. launches a takeover bid that is rejected by Marshall Field's board.

1979: The first Marshall Field store outside the Midwest opens in Houston, Texas.

1982: To fend off a takeover bid led by Carl Icahn, Marshall Field sells itself to BATUS Inc., a division of B.A.T. Industries PLC, for $367.6 million.

1987: A $110 million, five-year renovation of the flagship State Street store is launched.

1989: To fend off a hostile takeover led by James Goldsmith, B.A.T. Industries announces that it will sell off its U.S. retailing operations.

1990: Dayton Hudson Corporation acquires Marshall Field's for $1.04 billion.

1996: Marshall Field's exits from the Texas market, selling its four stores there.

2000: Dayton Hudson changes its name to Target Corporation.

2001: Target rebrands its Dayton's and Hudson's department stores under the Marshall Field's banner.

2004: Target announces that it will explore a possible sale of Marshall Field's.

---

old site at State and Washington was sold to Singer Sewing Machine Company, which soon built a new five-story structure featuring a large glass dome in the middle of its mansard roof. Field, Leiter signed a three-year lease on the building, which had 30 percent more square footage than its predecessor, and reopened their retail store there in October 1873. More than 500 employees worked in the new store.

Nearly concurrent with this latest reopening, the United States entered a severe depression (the "panic of 1873") that endured for six years. Field, Leiter & Co. nevertheless flourished during this period, averaging nearly $1 million in annual profits—despite the further calamity of another fire, this one burning the new State Street store to the ground in November 1877. The store was temporarily moved to two locations before finally—and permanently—returning to the corner of State and Washington in April 1879. Singer had built a six-story French Renaissance building topped by another mansard-style roof as well as eight cupolas. Among the notable features inside were

the store's first lavatories as well as electrical lighting fixtures. In addition, after lengthy and contentious negotiations, Field and Leiter bought the building from Singer for $700,000 and leased it themselves to Field, Leiter & Co.

By 1880 Field, Leiter & Co. was able to post profits of $1.8 million on revenues of $23.7 million; retail sales contributed $3.6 million of the total. This was the best year yet for the Field–Leiter partnership, but it would also be the last. The relationship between the two became increasingly strained, in part because Leiter never cared much for the retail side of the business, whereas Field felt that retail was the engine driving the firm's success, despite the larger profits and sales generated by the wholesale division. Field also believed that Leiter's brusque personality was losing them customers. Gaining the support of the firm's junior partners, Field essentially forced Leiter to accept a buyout of about $2.7 million. As a result, in early 1881 Field owned most of the company (with the junior partners owning a small percentage). He renamed the firm Marshall Field & Company.

The Field, Shedd, and Selfridge Era: 1881–1906

Aside from Marshall Field himself, two other figures came to prominence at the company in the late 19th century. John G. Shedd had joined the company in 1872, having followed Field to Chicago from the East. Shedd started out as a stock boy on the wholesale side, making $10 per week, before progressing rapidly to salesman and then to general merchandise manager of the wholesale division in 1885. His scientific approach to planning inventories and making seasonal purchases helped the division achieve steadily increasing sales. The wholesale operation grew so large that in 1887 it moved into a new 500,000-square-foot building that covered the entire block bounded by Adams, Quincy, Wells, and Franklin Streets in North Chicago. Shedd was promoted to head of the wholesale division in 1890 (when annual wholesale revenues had reached $26 million) and three years later was made a junior partner of Marshall Field & Co.

On the retail side, it was Harry Selfridge who made a lasting mark. Selfridge hailed from Jackson, Michigan, and started at the company in 1879 at age 21, in the same job and with the same salary that Shedd had begun with. He shifted to the retail division four years later and just four years after that was its 29-year-old general manager. Selfridge, nicknamed "Mile-a-Minute Harry," was full of ideas, many of which he implemented with Field's approval. Early moves included the installation of more electric lighting to better illuminate the merchandise, the use of modern displays of piece goods arrayed on tables to give customers easy access to them, and the institution of annual sales in order to clear the shelves and tables for new goods. In 1885 he transformed the store's cellar into a widely copied "bargain basement" that was eventually dubbed the Budget Floor. By 1900 sales in the basement reached $3 million, or nearly one-quarter of the total retail revenues. Selfridge also is given credit for transforming the retail division from a dry goods store into a modern full-line department store. Among the departments added were ones stocking children's clothing, "fine shoes," furniture, Japanese bric-a-brac, cut glass, and stationery. The number of departments grew steadily from 42 in 1884 to 74 in 1898 to more than 100 by 1902. In addition, after several years of cajoling, Selfridge finally, in 1890, persuaded Field to allow him to open up a formal restaurant in the store, the elegant Tea Room. It quickly became famous for its food, service, and decor and was serving more than 1,200 people per day just two years after opening. In 1895 Selfridge and his staff began creating lavish displays in the store's windows as lures to potential customers. As these changes were made over the years, the store maintained its emphasis on superior customer service, centered around its mainly female clientele; the store's reputation in this regard was forever enshrined through the motto, "Give the Lady What She Wants," which was said to have been coined by Marshall Field himself in 1890.

Selfridge's innovations helped the retail side grow rapidly—and at a much faster clip than the wholesale. By 1900—the same year that Selfridge was made a Marshall Field & Co. junior partner—the retail division generated 27 percent of overall sales, up from just 16 percent in 1883. Retail sales surged from $4.4 million to $12.5 million during this period. This rapid

growth created a need for more space, so in 1893 construction was completed on a new nine-story building at the corner of Washington and Wabash. In 1897 Field ordered the installation of a large clock, visible for blocks, mounted above the corner entrance at State and Washington. It quickly became a famous Chicago landmark and a popular meeting place (and was immortalized via a Norman Rockwell drawing that appeared on the cover of the November 3, 1945, *Saturday Evening Post*).

By the early 1900s, the Marshall Field store was firmly established as the premier department store in Chicago. Its reputation for high quality, status, and fashion particularly grew out of the company's buying decisions—most notably, the goods imported from overseas. By 1900 the business had established a string of buying offices in Britain, Germany, Belgium, France, and Japan. Marshall Field bought $6 million in foreign goods abroad in 1906, making it the largest importer in the United States. As a further way to supply high-quality goods to its ever-growing retail division, the company in the last two decades of the 19th century created a fairly extensive network of manufacturing operations consisting of large workshops and offsite factories. Most of these goods were produced solely for the store and were marked with the company name, an increasingly famous brand.

In 1901 the company was incorporated as Marshall Field & Company, Inc. During the early years of the new century, Field began giving Shedd more responsibility for running the company. Selfridge grew increasingly unhappy, eventually becoming determined to run his own business. (One legend had it that Selfridge wanted the company to be renamed Field, Selfridge & Company.) In 1904 he sold his shares in the company for $1 million. Five years later he landed in London, where he brought American-style department store retailing to the British, establishing the famed Selfridge's emporium.

In 1906, just two years after Selfridge's departure, Marshall Field died as the wealthiest person in Chicago, leaving behind an estate totaling $118 million ($2.1 billion in 2002 money). His lasting mark on the city of Chicago went well beyond his namesake company, whose sales would reach a record $72.6 million in 1906. His philanthropic pursuits helped create the Art Institute of Chicago and the original campus of the University of Chicago. He also donated millions of dollars for the construction of a natural history museum for the 1893 Columbian Exposition world's fair. This became the core of the eponymous Field Museum of Natural History. His company would later give $3 million to build the John G. Shedd Aquarium, located adjacent to the Field Museum.

Steady Expansion of the Retail Side: 1906–29

Shedd took over as president of Marshall Field & Co., with the principal owner now being a complex family trust. In 1917, however, the trustees sold 90 percent of their shares in the company to its officers and managers. The company went public in 1930, with the Field family retaining their 10 percent interest.

Meantime, between 1893 and 1914 Field or his estate acquired the entire block bounded by State, Wabash, Washington, and Randolph. New buildings were added gradually during this period, until in 1914 the Marshall Field store occupied the entire block. A 1902 expansion made it the largest retail store in the world, with more than half a million square feet spread over three buildings. A six-day "grand opening" that year attracted more than half a million people. A workforce of 7,000 was needed to man the mammoth store. Another major expansion occurred in 1907, when the 1878-built structure at State and Washington was replaced with a more modern building. The most noteworthy feature of this building was the Tiffany Dome, designed by acclaimed artist Louis Comfort Tiffany. It is the largest glass mosaic of its kind, containing about 1.6 million pieces, and was the first dome ever built in iridescent glass. Another highlight of the 1907 building was the inclusion of the Walnut Room, an elegant restaurant that quickly became a Chicago restaurant landmark. The installation of a giant Christmas tree in the atrium of the Walnut Room during that year's holiday season started an annual tradition.

The company's Store for Men opened on Washington Street across from the main store in 1913. One year later, the main store added a book department and began featuring in-store book signings by authors. That same year, it began publishing its own quarterly magazine called "Fashions of the Hours," which continued to be produced until 1978. By the mid-1920s sales at the retail store exceeded those of every other single department store in the world.

During Shedd's tenure, the company significantly enlarged its manufacturing operations, eventually owning around 30 mills, most of which concentrated on producing or converting textiles. The output from these mills was primarily sold to the firm's wholesale operation, which marketed sheets, towels, bedspreads, and blankets under the Fieldcrest label. The textile mills, located in North Carolina and Virginia, were operated through a Marshall Field & Co. subsidiary called the Thread Mills Co. This subsidiary also launched the highly successful Karastan line of oriental rugs in 1928.

In addition to overseeing the vast expansion of the company's main retail store, Shedd also engineered the 1923 purchase of the A.M. Rothschild department store on South State Street for $9 million. This was renamed the Davis Store and headed by Arthur Davis, a department head in the wholesale division. It was positioned as a low-price store, the impetus for its creation being company officials' increasing concern about losing customers to lower-priced competitors.

Shedd retired from active management in 1923, though he served as chairman for three more years. Taking over as president and CEO was James Simpson, who had started as an office boy and later became Marshall Field's personal secretary. The company expanded its retailing side further under the new leader, opening up three small department store branches in suburban Chicago in the late 1920s, in Evanston, Oak Park, and Lake Forest. In 1929 Marshall Field & Co. gained its first retail presence outside of the Chicago area when it purchased Frederick & Nelson in Seattle, Washington, the leading department store in the Pacific Northwest, for $6 million. Frederick & Nelson had been established in 1890 by D.E. Frederick and Nels Nelson, who modeled their store on that of Marshall Field & Co. Sales for the Seattle store reached $12 million by 1929, compared with the $179.7 million achieved by Marshall Field that year.

There was one important Frederick & Nelson product that was quickly imported to Chicago: Frango chocolates and mints, which were probably first made in Seattle in the late 1910s. Soon after the purchase of the Seattle department store, the candy kitchen at the flagship Marshall Field store on State Street began producing their own line of Frango chocolates with the help of the store's new candy-making colleagues. It was hoped that the new line could help revive sales, which were slumping because of the Great Depression—and would amount to only $150.7 million for all of 1930.

Divestment of Wholesaling and Manufacturing Operations: 1930–53

While the retail side was expanding, the firm's wholesale operations had entered a period of precipitous decline in the early 1920s. There were numerous reasons for the general fall of the great wholesale houses, most notably the rapid growth of chain stores and the increasing number of merchants and retailers who were buying directly from manufacturers. To stem the mounting wholesale losses, Simpson launched the construction of the mammoth Merchandise Mart, believing that this huge new building could do for the wholesale operations what State Street had done for the retail side. Construction began in August 1928, while the 1920s boom was still progressing, but was not finished until 1930, when the Great Depression had taken firm hold of the country. Marshall Field & Co. spent $35 million constructing the Mart, which at five million square feet was the largest building in the world at that time. The company's wholesale division and the sales headquarters of its manufacturing operations took about half of the space, and Simpson had envisioned other jobbers and manufacturers' representatives taking the remainder.

John McKinlay, yet another executive who had worked his way up through the ranks, took over as president in the inopportune year of 1930. The depression and the poorly timed construction of the Mart sent the wholesale and manufacturing operations into the red, where they would stay for eight straight years. The collapsed economy even forced the retail side into a $900,000 loss in 1932, a year in which Marshall Field & Co. posted a total net loss of $8 million and paid no dividends for the first time since its incorporation some three decades earlier. McKinlay tried to turn the tide by cutting the wholesale departments that were showing the largest losses, but the red ink continued to flow.

Board member Marshall Field III, grandson of the first Marshall Field (who would later found the *Chicago Sun* newspaper—which evolved into the *Chicago Sun-Times*), forced the board to hire an outside management consultant, James O. McKinsey, in 1935 to make recommendations on turning the firm around. After three months of study, McKinsey (the founder of the McKinsey & Company consulting firm) advocated the rapid liquidation of the wholesale operations, and the board of directors gave him the responsibility to carry out this plan as the new chairman and CEO. This marked the first time in the company's history that an outsider had been placed in charge.

McKinsey directed the liquidation of the wholesale division in late 1935. He also disposed of some of the mills, with the remainder reorganized as part of Marshall Field's manufacturing division, whose headquarters was shifted to New York City. The loss-making Davis Store also was sold. McKinsey, however, clashed with many of the top managers, including McKinlay, who quit in June 1936. Frederick D. Corley was named president, having previously served as vice-president of retail merchandising. When McKinsey died suddenly in late 1937, Corley became CEO. That year Marshall Field & Co. achieved overall net profits of $3.5 million, a huge improvement over the previous year's loss of $1.6 million.

Corley's reign proved rather short, but it produced two important developments. In 1939 the company purchased the land on which its downtown Chicago department store rested, having previously bought the buildings themselves in 1924. The seller in both cases was the Field estate. In 1941, a month before Pearl Harbor, the downtown store opened the 28 Shop, an upscale fashion store-within-the-store and one of the first exclusive women's salons to be created within a U.S. department store. It was hoped that the shop—named for the store's private elevator entrance at 28 East Washington and for its 28 dressing rooms—could return Field's to its position as the home of feminine elegance. By 1944 sales at the 28 Shop reached $1.2 million. Other special shops soon were added, including a bridal salon called the Brides' Room.

The 28 Shop was the brainchild of Hughston M. McBain, who was in charge of all retail operations in the early 1940s. In 1943 he took over management of Marshall Field & Co. upon Corley's retirement. During the war years, the company's factories produced large quantities of war goods, such as parachute cloth, camouflage netting, wool blankets, and uniforms. The firm's increasing prosperity was evident in 1944, when it earned profits before taxes of $20 million on total revenues of $152 million. The balance sheet improved immensely the following year when the Merchandise Mart was sold to Joseph P. Kennedy for $12.9 million. (The subsequent profits earned by the Kennedy family from operating the Mart helped finance John F. Kennedy's successful 1960 presidential campaign.) Selling the Mart aided Marshall Field & Co. in the retirement of its long-term debt, which had totaled $25 million at the beginning of 1943.

In the years immediately following the end of World War II, Marshall Field & Co. spent millions of dollars improving and modernizing its flagship store in Chicago as well as the Frederick & Nelson store in Seattle. The latter was enlarged from six stories to ten stories in 1952. In 1946 a second, smaller Frederick & Nelson store was opened east of Seattle, in Bellevue. It was replaced by a much larger store ten years later. The Marshall Field stores in Chicago made a concerted push into selling hard goods such as refrigerators and other major appliances in the postwar period.

Meantime, the manufacturing division, which had generated about $30 million of the 1944 revenues, had been reduced to only ten mills. To enhance brand identity, the mills began operating under the name Fieldcrest Mills in 1947. McBain was named chairman and CEO in 1949, and James L. Palmer—no relation to the company founder—was promoted from head of retailing to president. McBain and Palmer directed the final transformation of Marshall Field & Co. into a pure retailer by divesting the last of the manufacturing operations. Funds from

the sale of the mills were slated to be used to fund store expansion, particularly in the emerging suburban landscape of the postwar era. The final chapter of the company's manufacturing side came in 1953 when Fieldcrest Mills was sold to Amoskeag Company, a Boston Investment trust. Fieldcrest Mills would later evolve into the powerful Fieldcrest Cannon, Inc., which was acquired by Pillowtex Corporation in 1997. The latter firm, however, went bankrupt in the early 2000s, another victim of the decline in U.S. manufacturing.

Postwar Decline and the End of Independence

By 1951 the company's revenues had grown to a record $225 million. The retail environment in the United States was changing, however, as shopping centers started popping up in the burgeoning suburbs and consumers began a shift in their shopping habits from downtown to the suburbs. Marshall Field & Co. followed this trend. In 1955 a new Marshall Field's store was opened in Park Forest, south of Chicago. The following year a larger store opened northwest of downtown Chicago in a new shopping center in Skokie. Marshall Field & Co. took a lead role in developing the entire center, which was called Old Orchard. In 1959 the firm entered the Milwaukee market by opening a store in the new Mayfair shopping center in Wauwatosa. Another new shopping center, Oakbrook Center, opened in the western suburbs of Chicago in 1962 with a Marshall Field's outlet as one of the anchors. In 1959, in the midst of this expansion spree, McBain retired and Palmer assumed the CEO position.

During the 1960s the company acquired the small Crescent department store chain, which operated in Spokane, Washington. Following the death of Marshall Field IV in 1965, the Field family sold its last remaining holdings in Marshall Field & Co., thus breaking the bonds between the family and the company 100 years after the first Marshall Field had bought into the enterprise that Potter Palmer had founded.

The fortunes of Marshall Field & Co. were on the decline in the 1960s and into the 1970s. As it expanded into suburban malls, Marshall Field lost much that had distinguished it when most of its revenues came from its flagship store in downtown Chicago. The company's share of the Chicago metro area market fell as competitors moved in, such as Lord & Taylor, owned by Associated Dry Goods Corporation, and Neiman-Marcus, owned by Carter Hawley Hale Stores, Inc. Specialty stores began outdoing Marshall Field in key areas, such as fashions for young women. In general the company gradually gained a reputation as a dowdy retailer—not keeping up with changing tastes and lifestyles, and failing to appeal to younger consumers. At the same time, acquisitive large companies such as Federated Department Stores, Inc. and the May Department Stores Company were creating nationwide entities operating several different chains.

Outside of Chicago, the company had been very conservative about expansion over the decades; its only Marshall Field's store outside its core market remained the one in Milwaukee, and its only acquisitions had been those of Frederick & Nelson and the Crescent. In 1970, however, the company completed an acquisition as a defensive measure. Fearing a possible takeover by Associated Dry Goods, whose holdings included stores in Cleveland, Ohio, and Erie, Pennsylvania, Marshall Field purchased the Cleveland-based Halle's department store chain, which had nine stores in Ohio and Pennsylvania. The move succeeded in thwarting any takeover attempt by Associated, because it now faced antitrust obstacles. The deal also unfortunately saddled Marshall Field with an operation that consistently lost money throughout the 1970s, mainly because of the poor performance of the 600,000-square-foot Halle's store located in economically depressed downtown Cleveland.

In 1974 Joseph A. Burnham became president of Marshall Field, having worked up through the ranks, joining the firm as a staff assistant in 1948. Burnham oversaw the completion of Water Tower Place, which was half-owned by the firm's real estate subsidiary. Located on North Michigan Avenue, known in Chicago as ''The Magnificent Mile,'' Water Tower Place was a 74-story complex that included a shopping center, offices, condominiums, and an elegant Ritz-Carlton hotel. Completed in early 1976, it included a new Marshall Field's store that was only one-twelfth the size of the State Street store but was easily as opulent—a store that quickly became immensely successful. The company was now operating a total of 15 Marshall Field's stores.

Revenues for Marshall Field & Co. were increasing steadily but moderately during this period, reaching $611 million by 1976, when it ranked as the largest of the remaining U.S. independent department store operators. Earnings, however, had been stagnant for nearly a decade, amounting to about $18 million in 1976.

The following year, Angelo R. Arena was hired as president of Marshall Field, lured away from his position as head of Carter Hawley Hale's Dallas-based Neiman-Marcus. The board selected an outsider because it wanted a leader who could build the company into more of a national firm. Plans began to be laid for the expansion of the Marshall Field chain into Texas. Chairman and CEO Burnham, however, died suddenly of a heart attack that October, thrusting Arena into the CEO post. Seeing an opening with the change at the top, Carter Hawley Hale almost immediately contacted Marshall Field, offering to take over the company—an ambition it had had for more than a decade. In December 1977 Carter Hawley Hale made a $36 per share, or $325 million, bid. Although this represented a significant premium over what the company's stock had been trading at, the Marshall Field board unanimously rejected the offer. They wanted to keep the company independent and also contended that the deal could not pass antitrust muster given the two firms' overlapping markets of operation. Arena pushed ahead with expansion plans in early 1978. He reached an agreement to acquire two Liberty House stores in Tacoma, Washington, and three in Portland, Oregon, all of which were subsequently converted into Frederick & Nelson outlets. In addition, he formally announced plans to open five new Marshall Field's stores in the faster-growing South, attending the groundbreaking for the first one, to be located in Houston's Galleria shopping center. Although Carter Hawley Hale bumped its price up to $42 per share, the offer was withdrawn in February 1978 when it was clear that Marshall Field would continue to fight the takeover and after the Federal Trade Commission began investigating the deal's antitrust implications. Shareholders subsequently filed class-action lawsuits against Marshall Field claiming that the board had not acted in the interest of the shareholders, but these suits were quickly dismissed.

Its independence at least temporarily secured, Marshall Field proceeded with its expansion. In 1978 and 1979 it acquired John Breuner Company, operator of 14 home furnishings stores and 11 furniture rental outlets in California, Arizona, and Nevada. Six Lipmans stores in Oregon were acquired from Dayton Hudson Corp. and melded into the Frederick & Nelson unit. A deal to buy Hess's Inc., a Pennsylvania-based department store chain, fell through in early 1979, the same year that a new Marshall Field's opened in Joliet, Illinois. The huge new Marshall Field store in Houston opened for business that year as well. One year later, Marshall Field bought J.B. Ivey & Co., a department store chain specializing in women's fashions, for $30 million in stock. Ivey operated 12 stores in North Carolina, one in South Carolina, and ten in northern Florida. Marshall Field attempted to revive its ailing Halle's chain by buying six Union Stores in Columbus, Ohio. This latter endeavor proved short-lived, however, as the company pulled the plug on the loss-making Halle's, selling it in late 1981 to Schottenstein Bros. (which early in 1982 announced it was shutting the Ohio chain down). Also in 1982, the second new Marshall Field's store in Texas opened in the upscale Galleria shopping center in Dallas.

The BATUS Era: 1982–90

By early 1981 Arena had tripled the number of stores owned by the company to 93—only 19 of which were Marshall Field's outlets. Revenues just topped $1 billion for the fiscal year ending in January 1981, though the profits of $20.7 million were below the peak of $21.5 million in 1972, when revenues were less than half that of 1981. Marshall Field's inconsistent earnings and low stock price meant that it continued to be vulnerable to a takeover. Corporate raider Carl Icahn stepped into the picture in early 1982, gradually buying large chunks of the company's stock, eventually gaining a nearly 30 percent stake, and apparently determined to take the firm over. Resigned that its days as an independent were numbered, but not wanting to be bought by Icahn, Marshall Field began casting about for a friendlier acquirer. Talks were held with May Department Stores, Dayton Hudson, and even the previously spurned Carter Hawley Hale, but it was BATUS Inc. that emerged with a successful white knight offer. In June 1982 BATUS bought Marshall Field & Co. for about $367.6 million in cash, or $30 per share. BATUS was the U.S. division of B.A.T. Industries PLC, a U.K. tobacco firm that had diversified into retailing. Among BATUS's holdings were the Gimbels and Saks Fifth Avenue department store chains.

Almost immediately after the BATUS takeover, the Marshall Field company was dismantled, with the various chains going their separate ways. Frederick & Nelson subsequently went into a steady decline, going through three more ownership changes before closing for good in 1992. (The founding store in downtown Seattle was later remodeled and turned into the flagship store of Seattle-based Nordstrom, Inc.) The Crescent too was sold off and eventually went out of business. At Marshall Field's, George P. Kelly initially served as CEO, having previously headed the company's Chicago division. Kelly resigned in mid-1993, however, and Philip B. Miller was brought onboard as the new chief executive. Miller had been president of Neiman-Marcus.

Under Miller's leadership, Marshall Field's attempted to recapture some of its lost glory. Miller wanted to target a more youthful but still upscale, fashion-conscious customer. The merchandise mix was overhauled and began featuring more contemporary, upscale merchandise. The stores began offering a larger selection of special products that could be found only at Marshall Field's. Many of these products were featured in newly launched in-store boutiques. These included Angela Cummings fine jewelry boutiques and several designer accessories boutiques featuring such brands as Bottega Veneta, Louis Vuitton, Fendi, Gucci, and Chanel. More space also was given to quality apparel, cosmetics, and gourmet and specialty foods. Tens of millions of dollars were spent on store remodeling, and Miller also moved quickly to improve customer service. The new management also instituted stringent expense controls to improve the retailer's profitability. Initial results were encouraging: For 1984, revenues increased 8 percent to about $750 million, and pretax profits jumped 12 percent to approximately $52 million.

Of the 1984 revenue total, 10 percent was generated in Texas, where there were now three stores following the opening of a second store in Houston in 1983. A fourth Texas store opened in 1986 in San Antonio. That same year, Marshall Field's expanded in Wisconsin, acquiring five stores from sister company Gimbels (which BATUS was in the process of divesting in a piecemeal fashion). Three of the stores were located in Milwaukee, including a 601,000-square-foot unit located downtown on Grand Avenue; the other two were in Madison and Appleton. Further changes to the mix of stores occurred in the late 1990s. Two of the older stores in Chicago—the Oak Park and Evanston units—were closed down in 1987; the company also had planned to shut down the Park Forest store, but reversed course after residents objected. In 1989 two underperforming stores in Milwaukee were sold off; only the downtown and the Mayfair locales remained in that city. That August, Marshall Field's returned to Ohio, opening a 200,000-square-foot Marshall Field's store in Columbus. The firm thus ended the decade with 24 stores, 15 in Illinois, four in Wisconsin, four in Texas, and one in Ohio. For the fiscal year ending in January 1989, Marshall Field's posted strong results—pretax profits of $90.7 million on sales of $1.09 billion—that indicated that Miller's efforts were paying off.

Late in 1987, Miller announced a massive $115 million, five-year renovation of the flagship State Street store, a revamp billed as the largest such undertaking in U.S. history. The centerpiece of the ambitious makeover was the installation of an 11-story, glass-covered atrium and an elaborate indoor fountain in the center of the store. The new design made the huge store much more accessible as the Wabash Avenue and State Street sides of the first floor—previously separated by an alley—were united by the atrium. Escalators also were installed, and nearly 6 percent more selling space was added. The lower level was changed from the "bargain basement" to a sort of late 19th-century Chicago streetscape with a food court and boutiques. As this renovation progressed, ownership of Marshall Field's changed hands once again.

The Dayton Hudson/Target Era: 1990–2004

This latest turn of events started with another hostile takeover bid. In July 1989 an investor group led by maverick Anglo-French financier James Goldsmith launched a $21.7 billion leveraged buyout of B.A.T. Industries. For Marshall Field's, the proposal contained a real twist. One of the investors in the proposed takeover was Frederick "Ted" Field, son of Marshall Field IV and great-great-grandson of the first Marshall Field, and a man better known for racing cars and producing Hollywood movies. But the return of a Field to even partial ownership of the namesake company was not to be. B.A.T. Industries rejected the bid led by "Sir James," and in September the firm launched a major restructuring in order to preserve its independence. B.A.T. placed up for sale its entire U.S. retailing operation, including Marshall Field's, Saks, J.B. Ivey, and John Breuner. All four were sold in 1990. Saks was bought by an investment group and later taken public before being acquired in 1998 by department store consolidator Proffitt's, Inc., which later changed its name to Saks Incorporated. Dillard Department Stores, Inc. bought the Ivey's stores, which were converted to Dillard's stores. John Breuner would eventually become part of the privately held, Lancaster, Pennsylvania–based Breuners Home Furnishings Corporation.

Marshall Field's ended up in the hands of Dayton Hudson Corporation, named for its Dayton's department stores in Minneapolis and its Hudson's stores in Detroit but increasingly better known for its fast-growing discount chain, Target. Dayton Hudson, which also ran the Mervyn's moderately priced department store chain, bought Marshall Field's for $1.04 billion in June 1990, besting offers from May Department Stores and Dillard, as well as a bid from management that was led by Miller. The Miller era came to an immediate end with his resignation upon completion of the deal. (Ironically, Miller would later become CEO of Saks, Marshall Field's former sister company.) Finally, in a blow to the city that had nurtured Marshall Field's and that had been influenced in so many ways by the company, Dayton Hudson made Marshall Field's part of its Department Store division, which was managed out of Minneapolis. Some 850 Chicago-based staff, including buying, sales promotion, accounting, and public relations personnel—and the staff of the in-house advertising agency—lost their jobs via this centralization. Gary Witkin was named Marshall Field's president after the takeover. But in December 1991 he took over management of all three of Dayton Hudson's department stores, and Daniel J. Skoda became the president of Marshall Field's. Skoda was a former senior vice-president at Neiman-Marcus.

Marshall Field's was taken down market in the early 1990s as part of an efficiency drive that saw the three Dayton Hudson department store chains become more alike (Marshall Field's had always been more upscale than the Dayton's and Hudson's chains). The product mix was shifted to emphasize moderately priced products. A heavy emphasis on promotions also was instituted. Critics complained that what had once been a very distinctive group of stores was becoming indistinguishable from numerous other chains. Many longtime customers, particularly those in Chicago, reacted negatively to the changes, which also included the replacement of Marshall Field's signature green shopping bag with "environmentally friendly" beige packaging. In 1995 the company reversed course, cutting down on promotions, taking the merchandise back upscale, hiring more local buyers, improving customer service, and bringing back the green shopping bags. Sales were aided by new advertising campaigns launched in the late 1990s featuring the tag line,

''Where else? Marshall Field's,'' as well as some of the cheekiness for which Target's ads were known.

On the store openings and closings front, a 280,000-square-foot Marshall Field's store was opened at Northbrook Court in the North Shore suburbs of Chicago in September 1995. Shortly thereafter, a second Marshall Field's store in Columbus, Ohio, opened. The company moved into Indiana for the first time in 1997 when three Hudson's stores located in South Bend and Fort Wayne, Indiana, and Toledo, Ohio, were converted to Marshall Field's stores. Citing the inefficiencies of running such a far-flung operation, and seeking to reallocate resources in its core Midwest market, Marshall Field's sold off its four stores in Texas late in 1996. Several other Marshall Field's stores were closed during this period, including the last two remaining stores in Milwaukee and the Park Forest store in Chicago.

Although Marshall Field's prospects were on the upswing thanks to the mid-1990s strategic reversal, the decade ended on a sour note. In March 1999 Dayton Hudson announced that it would close the Frango candy kitchen at its State Street store after nearly 70 years of operation and begin outsourcing production of the mints and chocolates to a confectioner in Dunmore, Pennsylvania, Gertrude Hawk Chocolates, Inc. This caused an uproar in Chicago among citizens and politicians alike, incensed with this break with tradition and with the further blow to civic pride. Despite the negative publicity and intense pressure from local officials, including Mayor Richard M. Daley, who urged the company to shift Frango production to a local candymaker, Dayton Hudson stood its ground and proceeded with its plan as announced. Coincidentally or not, shortly after this fiasco, Skoda resigned from his role as Marshall Field's president—a position that was promptly eliminated. Marshall Field's regional directors assumed Skoda's duties and began reporting directly to Ertugrul Tuzcu, executive vice-president of the Department Stores division.

In another break with tradition Dayton Hudson changed its name to Target Corporation in January 2000, adopting the name of its largest and fastest growing division. By this time, the Target Stores division was generating nearly 80 percent of the parent company's revenues, whereas the department stores were contributing only about 10 percent. Speculation that the corporation would divest either the department stores or Mervyn's or both, already rife for some time, began heating up. The performance of Marshall Field's was becoming increasingly incidental to the overall results of its parent company.

Marshall Field's gained a larger profile exactly one year later when Target Corporation announced that it would change the names of its Dayton's and Hudson's department stores to Marshall Field's. Marshall Field's was chosen for several reasons: It was the most widely known of the three names; its base of Chicago was bigger than both Minneapolis and Detroit and was a major travel hub; and it was the largest chain, with 24 stores, compared with 19 Dayton's and 21 Hudson's. In addition, Target was planning to launch an online gift registry for its department stores during 2001 and wanted to do so under a unified name. There were now 64 Marshall Field's stores in eight states, and the well-known name now appeared for the first time in four of the states: Michigan, Minnesota, North Dakota, and South Dakota. Marshall Field's also secured significant shares of three major Upper Midwest cities: Chicago, Detroit, and Minneapolis. Linda L. Ahlers, who had served as president of the Department Stores division since 1996, became president of Marshall Field's.

Marshall Field's and the entire department store sector struggled during the early 2000s under the weight of intense competition and the poor economy. Revenues for the newly enlarged operation fell from $2.97 billion in the fiscal year ending in January 2001 to $2.78 billion the following year and to $2.69 billion one year after that. Pretax profits slumped from $190 million to $135 million during this same period. During early 2003 two underperforming Marshall Field's stores in Columbus, Ohio, were sold to May Department Stores, reducing the store count to 62.

Marshall Field's celebrated its 150th anniversary in 2002, having served more than two billion customers at its flagship State Street store in Chicago alone. It was fitting, therefore, that the company in 2002 and 2003 was busy with another major renovation of its State Street store, where it hoped to recapture its lost glory. Marshall Field's launched a plan to lease out about 10 percent of the store's 800,000 square feet to outside vendor partners, who were able to set up their own boutiques stocked with merchandise of their own choosing. (In a historic twist, this concept was adopted from Selfridge's, the U.K. department store that Harry Selfridge established after leaving Marshall Field & Co.) The first of these was an upscale Thomas Pink menswear boutique, which was set up in the second half of 2002. By October 2003 the store had introduced 30 such boutiques, including Mimi Maternity, Creative Kidstuff, Australian Homemade Ice Cream, Levenger upscale writing supplies, and Wrigleyville Sports. Many of these boutiques could be found nowhere else in the Midwest, which provided the store with a way to differentiate itself from the competition. The plan was to use the State Street store as a sort of lab to test out these boutiques for possible rollout to other Marshall Field's stores. The new stores-within-a-store concept was backed by an ad campaign featuring the flexible slogan, ''Marshall Field's &'' (which also played off the department store's original name: Marshall Field & Co.). Most of the ads were very simple, such as one that showed a stack of baseball caps along with this copy: ''Marshall Field's & Wrigleyville Sports.'' In addition, Marshall Field's aimed to emulate the great success that the Target chain had achieved through its red bull's-eye branding campaign. Marshall Field's began talking about ''owning'' the color green, and the retailer began using bar code-style green stripes in its advertising, on its shopping bags, and on its Sunday circulars.

It was unclear whether this latest attempt to rejuvenate the fortunes of the ''grande dame'' of Chicago retailing would succeed, but the possibility of another change in ownership was becoming ever more certain. Sales at stores open more than a year fell 2.6 percent in the fiscal year ending in January 2004, though they grew in both January and February 2004, signaling a possible turnaround. In addition, the ongoing rapid growth of the Target chain meant that Marshall Field's revenues of $2.58 billion in fiscal 2003 comprised only 5.4 percent of the $48.16 billion total for the parent company. As pressure from Target Corporation shareholders unhappy with the performance of Marshall Field's and Mervyn's mounted, Target announced in March 2004 that it had hired Goldman Sachs Group, Inc. to review "strategic alternatives" for the two divisions, including possible sales. Analysts believed that the two most likely buyers of Marshall Field's were Federated Department Stores and May Department Stores, and they speculated that a sale of the venerable department store retailer could fetch more than $1.8 billion.

Principal Competitors

Federated Department Stores, Inc.; The May Department Stores Company; Carson Pirie Scott & Company; Dillard Department Stores, Inc.; Nordstrom, Inc.; Saks Incorporated; Neiman-Marcus Co.; J.C. Penney Corporation, Inc.; Sears, Roebuck and Co.

Further Reading

Baeb, Eddie, "Field's a Smaller Department for Target: As Chain Grows, Local Retailer Becomes Less Important," *Crain's Chicago Business*, July 24, 2000, p. 1.

Barmash, Isadore, "BATUS Bid Is Accepted by Field," *New York Times*, March 17, 1982, p. D1.

Berg, Eric N., "Marshall Field Deal by Dayton," *New York Times*, April 20, 1990, p. D1.

Berner, Robert, "Dayton Hudson's Once-Fashionable Stores Tread Water," *Wall Street Journal*, August 1, 1996, p. B4.

Blackburn, Tom F., "Hard Times Nurtured Marshall Field," *Nation's Business*, February 1932, p. 55.

Chandler, Susan, "Target Corp. Makes Field's Day: Renaming Ends Era of Dayton's, Hudson's Stores," *Chicago Tribune*, January 13, 2001, p. 1.

——, "Under the Gun at Dayton Hudson," *Business Week*, May 20, 1996, pp. 66+.

Dayton, George Draper, II, *Our Story: With Histories of the Dayton, McDonald, and Winchell Families*, Wayzata, Minn., 1987.

Fallon, James, "Now It's Saks and Field's Up for Sale," *Women's Wear Daily*, September 27, 1989, p. 1.

Fass, Allison, "Marshall Field's Decides It's Time for a Big Branding Effort," *New York Times*, September 11, 2001, p. C8.

"Field's and Its Foe Go Their Own Ways," *Business Week*, March 6, 1978, p. 33.

Gallun, Alby, "The Targeting of Field's," *Crain's Chicago Business*, April 15, 2002, p. 1.

Gill, Penny, "Macke Maps Plan for Dayton Hudson," *Stores*, November 1991, pp. 28+.

Goff, Lisa, "Bringing Back Field's Glory Days," *Crain's Chicago Business*, December 15, 1986, p. 1.

Griffin, Dick, "Marshall Field: Is Independence Worth It?," *Fortune*, February 12, 1979, pp. 106–09.

Heller, Laura, "Frango Fracas Peeves Chicago," *Discount Store News*, April 5, 1999, pp. 3, 47.

Hull, Hamilton, *Marshall Field & Company: The World's Greatest Merchandiser*, Chicago: Marshall Field & Co., 1907.

Jones, Sandra, "Pressure to Dump Field's," *Crain's Chicago Business*, November 17, 2003, p. 3.

——, "Target: Fresher Field's," *Crain's Chicago Business*, November 3, 2003, p. 3.

Koehn, Nancy F., "Marshall Field, 1834–1906," in *Brand New: How Entrepreneurs Earned Consumers' Trust from Wedgwood to Dell*, Boston: Harvard Business School Press, 2001, pp. 91–130.

Levy, Melissa, "An Old Firm, a New Name: Target Corp.," *Minneapolis Star-Tribune*, January 14, 2000, p. 1A.

Madsen, Axel, *The Marshall Fields: The Evolution of an American Business Dynasty*, New York: Wiley, 2002.

"Marshall Field & Co.," *Fortune*, October 1936, pp. 78–87+.

"Marshall Field: Seeking New Markets in the South and West," *Business Week*, March 23, 1981, p. 125.

"Marshall Field, the Store," *Fortune*, December 1945, pp. 142–47+.

Merrick, Amy, "Field's Lures New Brands to Polish Image," *Wall Street Journal*, July 8, 2003, p. B1.

Moin, David, "Marshall Field's Newest Dream," *Women's Wear Daily*, October 9, 2003.

Moore, Janet, "The Store Formerly Known As Dayton's: Dayton's and Hudson's Department Stores to Use Marshall Field's Name," *Minneapolis Star-Tribune*, January 13, 2001, p. 1A.

Nazem, Susie Gharib, "Marshall Field's Too Successful Strategy," *Fortune*, March 22, 1982, pp. 81–82, 84.

Palmer, James L., *The Origin, Growth, and Transformation of Marshall Field & Company*, New York: Newcomen Society in North America, 1963.

"Professor's Purge," *Time*, December 27, 1937, p. 42.

Prokesch, Steven, "British Conglomerate to Sell Off Saks and Marshall Field Chains," *New York Times*, September 27, 1989, p. A1.

"Putting Some Pizazz into Marshall Field's," *Business Week*, August 22, 1983, p. 87.

Rutberg, Sidney, "Dayton Hudson Win Marshall Field's," *Women's Wear Daily*, April 20, 1990, p. 1.

Salmans, Sandra, "Behind the Slippage at Marshall Field," *New York Times*, March 17, 1982, p. D1.

Tebbel, John William, *The Marshall Fields: A Study in Wealth*, New York: Dutton, 1947.

Turner, Melissa, "Field's Hopes Restructuring Will Pay Off," *Women's Wear Daily*, July 8, 1995, pp. 1+.

Twyman, Robert W., *History of Marshall Field & Co., 1852–1906*, Philadelphia: University of Pennsylvania Press, 1954.

——, "Potter Palmer: Merchandising Innovator of the West," *Explorations in Entrepreneurial History*, December 1951.

Veverka, Mark, "The Battle Field's: Fighting for a Focus," *Crain's Chicago Business*, November 28, 1994, p. 1.

——, "A Down Field's Heads Upstream," *Crain's Chicago Business*, November 13, 1995, p. 1.

Webber, Oscar, *J.L. Hudson: The Man and the Store*, New York: Newcomen Society in North America, 1954.

Wendt, Lloyd, and Herman Kogan, *Give the Lady What She Wants! The Story of Marshall Field & Company*, Chicago: Rand McNally, 1952.

"Why Profits Shrink at a Grand Old Name," *Business Week*, April 11, 1977, pp. 66+.

Wieffering, Eric J., "Refashioning Dayton's," *Corporate Report Minnesota*, April 1994, pp. 60+.

Williams, Alfred Harry, *No Name on the Door: A Memoir of Gordon Selfridge*, London: W.H. Allen, 1956.

Wilson, Anamaria, "Through the Years," *Women's Wear Daily*, October 9, 2003.

Wilson, Beth, "Dreams of Field's: Famed Chicago Store Embarks on Overhaul," *Women's Wear Daily*, June 30, 2003, p. 1.

Zuckerman, Gregory, and Ann Zimmerman, "Target Indeed: Unhappy Investors Take Aim," *Wall Street Journal*, February 4, 2004, pp. C1, C3.

—David E. Salamie

VERMOUTH

Martini & Rossi SpA

Corso Vittorio Emmanuele 11 42
Torino I-10123 TO
Italy
Telephone: +39 11 81081
Fax: +39 011 8108200
Web site: http://www.martini.com

Wholly Owned Subsidiary of Bacardi-Martini
Incorporated: 1847 as Distilleria National di Spirito di
   Vino
Employees: 400
Sales: EUR 290 million ($320 million) (2002)
NAIC: 312130 Wineries; 312140 Distilleries

Martini & Rossi SpA has been producing its world-famous vermouth for nearly 150 years. The company also has been the world's top-selling vermouth brand for more than a century, and its name has become synonymous with the famed martini cocktail. Martini & Rossi produce four main varieties of its vermouth: Martini Rosso, its earliest vermouth recipe, which is available in "simple" and "quinquina" versions; Martini Bianco, a white, more aromatic vermouth; and Martini Extra Dry, a less sweet variation of the original recipe. Martini & Rossi vermouth is 75 percent wine blended with a botanical mix of herbs, spices, and fruits—including ginger, cinnamon, mint, raspberry, coriander, cardamom, but also lungwort, lungmoss, speedwell, and some 20 other ingredients—in a recipe kept secret by the company. Although production of the group's vermouth occurs in a number of subsidiary facilities around the world, the botanical mix itself is prepared at Martini & Rossi's main Turin, Italy-area facility. In addition to its vermouth, Martini & Rossi also produces its own sparkling wine, the best-selling Asti Spumante brand. Martini & Rossi has been part of the Bacardi-Martini drinks empire since 1992—the group, which includes labels such as Bacardi rum, Bombay Sapphire vodka, William Lawson whiskey, and others, ranks among the top five drinks groups in the world. Martini & Rossi's sales reach more than EUR 290 million ($320 million) per year. The company is headed by Managing Director Peter Heilbron and Chairman Luigi Combetto.

Making Drinks History in the 19th Century

While Italy had been a leading center for the creation of "aperitivo" beverages, including liqueurs and other alcoholic drinks since the 16th century, these drinks were used typically for medicinal purposes, and were often quite bitter to the taste. By the 18th century, fortified and blended wines became popular and acceptable as beverages themselves, and were often used to stimulate the appetite before meals, launching a European tradition. Drink makers now began developing more palatable blends and mixes, which led to the development of a number of regional specialties. Vermouth, a blend of wine with alcohol, sugar, herbs, spices, fruits, and other ingredients, became an increasingly popular aperitivo at the turn of the 19th century. A specialty of the Piedmont region, and especially Turin, vermouth became increasingly important to the regional economy in the early decades of the century. This importance was recognized in 1840, when then King Carlo Alberto called for the creation of a register of certified vermouth makers in the region surrounding Turin.

In 1840, four local wine producers—Clemente Michael, Carlo Re, Agnelli, and Baudino—joined together to form a new business, Distilleria National di Spirito di Vino, which was added to the King's list in 1847. The new company produced and sold wine, liqueurs, and vermouth and other alcoholic beverages. Growing quickly, the Distilleria National added a new distillery in San Salvatore Monferrato, and branch facilities in the towns of Genoa, Narbonne, and Cagliari.

In 1850, the company brought in three new partners. Alessandro Martini, a commercial agent, also had been operating his own small Turin-area vineyard, purchased from the Agnelli family (of later Fiat fame) in 1830. Joining the company with Martini were Teofilo Sola, who became the company's accountant, and Luigi Rossi, who came to play the primary role in the company's lasting success.

Rossi combined winemaking knowledge with a talent as an herbalist, and began developing his own vermouth recipe. The success of that recipe in the early 1850s put the company on the map, and Rossi was made one of the company's directors at the end of the decade. The death of Carlo Re in 1860, followed by

Key Dates:

1840: Distilleria National di Spirito di Vino is registered as a producer of vermouth in the region of Turin, Italy.

1850: Alessandro Martini, Teofila Sola, and Luigi Rossi enter the company, where Rossi develops a new vermouth recipe.

1863: Martini, Sola, and Rossi take over leadership of the company, which is renamed Martini, Sola & Cia.

1865: The company begins exports, and wins its first international competition at the Dublin exhibition.

1879: Teofila Sola dies and Martini and Rossi acquire full control, changing the company's name to Martini & Rossi.

1884: First international branch opens in Buenos Aires.

1900: The company launches a new vermouth variant, Martini Extra Dry.

1910: The company launches Martini Bianco, a white vermouth.

1922: The company registers Martini as a trademark in Europe.

1950s: William Lawson distillery and brand is acquired as part of a portfolio expansion.

1960: Saint-Raphaël, a quinquina liqueur brand, is acquired.

1966: The company acquires the port wine brand Offley.

1971: French dry vermouth brand Noilly Prat is acquired.

1977: A new central company, General Beverage Corporation, based in Geneva, is created.

1988: The company acquires the La Benedictine liqueur brand.

1991: The company acquires the Otar cognac brand.

1992: The Bacardi family acquires Martini & Rossi for a reported $1.4 billion.

1997: Martini & Rossi vermouth is repackaged with a new bottle and label.

2003: A new single-serve packaging concept is launched for the Asti sparkling wine brand.

Clemente Michael's retirement in 1863, placed Martini, Sola, and Rossi in charge of the company, which changed its name to Martini, Sola & Cia at that time.

The following year, the company moved its production and headquarters to the village of Pessione di Cheri, giving the company a link to the new railroad connecting Turin with the port in Genoa. This access to the shipping routes linking Italy to the rest of the world encouraged the company to attempt to bring its vermouth recipe to an international market.

Building a Global Brand in the 20th Century

The company's efforts met with immediate success. In 1865, for example, its vermouth won first medal at the Dublin Exhibition. Two years later, Rossi's vermouth recipe was honored with the prize at the prestigious Paris Exhibition. The year 1867 also marked the company's arrival in the United States, with a shipment of the first 100 cases of its vermouth. Other awards

followed, in Vienna, Philadelphia, and again in Paris. At the same time, the vermouth became the favorite among European royalty. In 1868, King Victor Emmanuel II authorized the company to place the House of Savoy's arms on its label. This honor launched a trend, and by the beginning of the next century the vermouth label sported the royal crests of Portugal and Spain, as well as the crests of the British parliament and the cities of Melbourne, and Antwerp, among others.

Teofila Sola died in 1879, and his sons sold their share of the company to Martini and Rossi, leading to the company's permanent name, Martini & Rossi. By then, the company had added to its line, producing its own sparkling wine, originally called Vino Canelli Spumante, but later made world famous under the Asti Spumante brand name. Martini & Rossi vermouth was already one of Italy's top-selling vermouth brands, and the company had become the Piedmont region's largest wine and spirits company.

Martini & Rossi began expanding their international reach in the 1880s, adding a number of international sales branches. Among the first of these was an office in Buenos Aires in 1884. This office was followed by the opening of an office in Geneva in 1886, and in Barcelona in 1893.

By the dawn of the 20th century, Martini & Rossi had not only conquered Italy, but had become a bestseller in such far-flung markets as the United States, Brazil, Argentina, Greece, Portugal, Belgium, Switzerland, Turkey, and Egypt. By then, a new generation prepared to guide the company. Luigi Rossi's four sons, Teofilo, Cesare, Enrico, and Ernesto took over as leaders of the company; the Rossi family became the company's sole owners after Alessandro Martini's death in 1905.

Martini & Rossi now began building itself as one of the first truly global brand names of the 20th century. As part of this effort, the company became an early example of industrial globalization as well. In the opening decades of the century, the company decided to extend its production and distribution range by opening a series of foreign subsidiaries. Backed by their own capital, each subsidiary operated more or less autonomously, adapting their sales and distribution efforts to their local markets and consumer preferences. Meanwhile, the parent company retained control of production of the botanical mix at the heart of the popular drink. By the outbreak of World War II, the company's network of production subsidiaries stretched to Geneva, Barcelona, Buenos Aires, Brussels, Paris, Sao Paulo, London, Hamburg, Casablanca, Santiago, and The Hague. The company also opened branch offices in the United Kingdom and the United States.

Martini & Rossi also began expanding its brand range. The first addition to its vermouth line came in 1900, with the launch of Martini & Rossi Extra Dry, a move made to counter the increasing popularity of rival French "sec" vermouths. The company began offering two variations of its Martini Rosso, one with quinquina, the other without, dubbed "simple." In 1910, the company launched a fourth vermouth type, Martini Bianco, a "white" vermouth.

The brand's fame only grew with the invention of a new cocktail: the Martini. While some dispute exists about who actually invented the cocktail—one story even claims that the cocktail was named after a rifle—the mixture of gin and vermouth quickly caught on in the pre-Prohibition United States. The popularity of the cocktail had become so great that, in 1922 when the company trademarked the Martini name, it was nonetheless forced to label its brand as Martini & Rossi in the United States. Even so, Martini & Rossi's vermouth became synonymous with the martini. Overseas, vermouth drinkers tended to consume the beverage unmixed, as an aperitif. Yet, when U.S. bartenders, forced out of their jobs by Prohibition legislation, found new jobs behind the bars at Europe's great hotels, they introduced the martini to a highly receptive foreign market as well.

Martini & Rossi backed up its growing sales with a knack for advertising. The company's Art Deco advertisement quickly set a standard and came to represent an entire trend in graphic design in the 1920s and 1930s. The company also became an early sponsor of a wide range of events, from motor racing to opera.

Forming a Global Drinks Giant for the New Century

The company weathered the years of World War II, under the leadership of the next generation of the Rossi family, who took over in the 1930s. Rebuilding after the war, Martini & Rossi launched a new wave of advertising initiatives that repositioned the drink as a sophisticated, more youthful product—launching a trend that culminated in the adoption of the martini as the favorite drink of cinema hero James Bond in the 1960s.

At the same time, Martini & Rossi moved to reduce its reliance on its core vermouth and sparkling wine brands. The company now began a push to acquire scale through the acquisition of other brands. In the 1950s, the company bought up the William Lawson distillery and brand. In 1960, the company added Saint-Raphaël, a quinquina-based aperitif.

Other brands followed. In 1966, the company acquired its own port brand, Offley, then took over the famed French dry vermouth brand Noilly Prat. In 1988, the company bought up La Benedictine, a liqueur based on a recipe stemming from 1510. Three years later, Martini & Rossi acquired Otar cognac, one of the oldest and most exclusive cognac brands.

By then, Martini & Rossi had moved toward its modern corporate form. Amid growing competition on the international market, and faced particularly with the growth of a small number of giant beverage companies, Martini & Rossi abandoned its network of independently operating affiliates. Instead, the company moved to a centralized organizational model, absorbing its international subsidiaries, which were then regrouped under a newly created body, General Beverage Corporation, based in Geneva, in 1977.

At the beginning of the 1990s, however, the company's relatively small size left it at a distinct disadvantage in the market—now dominated by a handful of far larger, globally operating beverages conglomerates. Martini & Rossi had already developed a partnership with the Bacardi family, forming a distribution agreement in 1987 that gave Bacardi control of Martini & Rossi's distribution in the United States.

In 1992, the Rossi family, now in its fifth generation with the company, agreed to sell Martini & Rossi to the Bacardi family. The purchase, reportedly at a price of $1.4 billion, placed the newly created Bacardi-Martini group in the top ten among the world's alcoholic beverages groups.

While sales of Martini & Rossi's vermouth remained strong, the brand—particularly the cocktail—had lost much of its luster. Yet the late 1990s marked a resurgence in interest in the martini, and the company moved to capitalize on the new trend by revamping its advertising to promote a more youthful, yet sophisticated, image. At the same time, the company—in part to thwart imitations from competitors—redesigned its flagship product's bottle for the first time in more than a century, adopting a more distinctive shape. The company also began developing new packaging concepts for its sparkling wine brand as well, and in 2003 debuted a new single-serve Asti, complete with a straw. In the meantime, the rising demand for the company's vermouth helped push its sales near the EUR 300 million mark. One hundred fifty years after Luigi Rossi developed the original recipe, Martini & Rossi remained the world's leading vermouth brand.

Principal Competitors

Allied Domecq Netherlands BV; Diageo Plc; Seagram Company Ltd.; Fortune Brands, Inc.; Jim Beam Brands Worldwide Inc.; Brown Forman Corp.; Davide Campari Milano SpA.

Further Reading

"Bacardi & Co. Ltd.," *Euromonitor,* April 2003.

Kercheval, Nancy, "The Martini Re-emerges As Popular Drink," *Daily Record,* March 7, 2002.

Kiley, David, "Shaking Up Vermouth," *Brandweek,* March 23, 1998.

"Martini & Rossi," *Beverage Dynamics,* May-June 2002, p. 37.

Masciaga, Marco, "Martini, America's Classic Cocktail Has an Italian name," *Italy Life,* January 13, 2004.

Watin-Augouard, Jean, "Martini, l'apéritif qui ne manque pas d'appétit," *Prodimarques,* 2004.

—M.L. Cohen

Masonite International Corporation

1600 Britannia Road East
Mississauga, Ontario L4W 1J2
Canada
Telephone: (905) 670-6500
Toll Free: (800) 663-3667
Fax: (905) 670-6520
Web site: http://www.masonite.com

Public Company
Incorporated: 1982 as Premdor, Inc.
Employees: 12,000
Sales: $1.77 billion (2003)
Stock Exchanges: New York Toronto
Ticker Symbol: MHM
NAIC: 321999 All Other Miscellaneous Wood Product
  Manufacturing

Masonite International Corporation is a leading manufacturer of doors and door components, based in Mississauga, Canada. Approximately two-thirds of sales come from interior doors. All told, the company each day produces some 120,000 doors, which it sells to more than 50 countries. The North American market accounts for close to 85 percent of sales. Masonite sells to a variety of customers, including distributors, jobbers, big box home center chains, and wholesale and retail building supply dealers.

Appropriating the Masonite Name in 2002

Masonite International Corporation is the result of the 2001 acquisition of the Masonite business from International Paper by Premdor, Inc. Taking advantage of Masonite's brand recognition, Premdor assumed the name starting in 2002. The legacy of the Masonite name can be traced to engineer and inventor William H. Mason, who apprenticed under Thomas A. Edison. Mason married into a Wisconsin lumber family and became interested in finding a way to make commercial use of the mountains of wood chips cast off by milling operations. With timber becoming depleted, lumbermen were willing to back his

efforts as a way to find a secondary use for their waste. Mason moved to Laurel, Mississippi, where his wife's family owned saw mills that could supply all the waste he needed for his experiments. He soon developed a way to extract turpentine from lumber, simultaneously reducing weight and improving quality, but his preoccupation was to convert wood chips into fibers that could in turn be used to make quality paper products. To make wood fibers, he fashioned a gun of sorts. Wood chips and water were packed into a steel tube, which was then sealed with a plug. After a blowtorch heated the tube, creating a tremendous amount of pressure, the plug was pulled, and the wood chips exploded into individual wood fibers.

Mason now turned his attention to making a salable product out of the fibers. To his disappointment, the fibers he produced did not make for very good paper, and so he began to think of making a lumber replacement that would be an improvement over plywood. He tried pressing the slurry produced from mixing wood fibers and water, at first using presses designed to make paper. The results were not satisfactory, leading Mason to try other presses. He had limited success in his efforts until chance intervened one day when he took a break from his experiments to have lunch. He was unaware that a pressure valve on his press was leaking, which allowed high-pressured steam to react with the fibers. Before going to lunch, he forgot to release the pressure on the press, and as a result the steam was allowed to interact with the fibers until he returned to the laboratory some time later. When he saw the smoldering press, he quickly released the steam, opened the press and was surprised to discover the fibers had turned into a hard, grainless particleboard. With further experimentation he was able to produce thin sheets of the materials, well suited for the construction industry. He named the new substance after himself, calling it Masonite.

Forming the Mason Fiber Company in 1924

Wisconsin and Laurel lumber companies funded Mason to establish the Mason Fiber Company in 1924; four years later it would adopt the Masonite Corporation name. In October 1925 construction was started on the company's first plant, located in Laurel, to produce insulation board and hardboard. It began operations in 1926. Mason continued to improve Masonite, creating attractive finishes and increasing the strength through a tempering process. With the advent of the Great Depression of the 1930s, Masonite thrived because of its cheap price, and because of its quality and strength it would remain a standard construction product even after the economy rebounded. Mason was awarded a string of patents connected to Masonite before his death in 1940.

Masonite licensed plants in Australia, Canada, Italy, and Sweden to produce its hardwood. In 1934 the company went public, becoming listed on the New York Stock Exchange, and a year later moved its headquarters from Laurel to Chicago. During the first half of the 1940s Masonite, like most businesses, concentrated on defense contracts; its materials were used to make airplane dies, trailers, field kitchens, barracks, shell carrying cases, and a myriad of other uses. In the decade following the war, Masonite looked to broaden the uses of hardboard, which gradually became an acceptable raw material for making toys, play pens, television cabinets, and furniture. Along the way, to ensure a steady supply of materials, Masonite acquired some 500,000 acres of land. Not only did the company benefit from timber sales, it also made money from producing oil wells on its property. During the 1950s Masonite faced increased competition, resulting in lower prices for its products. As a result, it cut expenses, to the detriment of the flagship Laurel plant, which was no longer upgraded on a regular basis, and management began to focus on selling pre-finished hardboard and specialties.

Masonite remained a prosperous company through the 1970s, but a housing slump early in the 1980s had an adverse impact. Weakened, Masonite found itself the target of corporate raiders of the 1980s who realized the breakup value of the company. To thwart a takeover, management sold off hundreds of thousands of acres of timberland, taking in $80 million, but being cash rich only made Masonite an even more attractive target. Faced with a takeover attempt by General Felt Industries Inc., management decided to accept a buyout offer from building-materials manufacturer United States Gypsum Co. (USG), which paid $380 million to acquire about 95 percent of the company. It was a time of change for the company in other ways as well. Mason's method of producing hardboard was superceded by a new, cheaper technology—oriented strand board, OSB. It was rushed into the marketplace without proof that in outdoor applications it could absorb moisture after years of exposure to rain and snow, a fact that would later come back to haunt the company.

Under USG ownership Masonite dropped some product lines and added others, but remained a very profitable business. In 1987 it generated $529 million in sales and a pretax profit of $58 million. But Masonite would change corporate parents in 1988 when USG was itself threatened by a hostile takeover bid. As part of a recapitalization and restructuring plan, USG

sold Masonite to International Paper Company for approximately $400 million. International Paper hoped that Masonite would complement efforts to improve its wood-products and laminated-panels businesses.

In 1995 a class-action lawsuit was filed against Masonite, alleging that its exterior siding, made using the OSB process, failed to stand up to moisture, "that it will rot, buckle, discolor, deteriorate . . . after only a few years." Masonite countered that the siding, which carried a 20- to 25-year warranty, either had not been installed correctly or had not been properly maintained by homeowners. A state court jury in Mobile, Alabama, found in September 1996 that the siding was defective. Before the next phase of the trial was to begin, and rather than prolong the matter through the court system, International Paper agreed to a $197.5 million settlement in July 1997.

Merger of Premdor and Century Wood Door in 1989

During the 1990s Masonite forged an alliance with Premdor, so that the two companies were working together on a global basis. Premdor became Masonite's largest customer, and Masonite became Premdor's largest supplier. Premdor was launched in 1979 by Saul Spears, who was president of the door-making business of Seaway Multicorp Ltd. and led a buyout of the unit. The Toronto-based company was known as Premium Forest Products Ltd. until 1986, when it changed its name to Premdor and went public. The Canadian door market became highly competitive in the late 1980s with Premdor and its chief rival, Century Wood Door Ltd., finding themselves in a difficult bind, facing a lengthy and costly fight over market share. Instead, the two companies decided to join forces, and in 1989 they merged under the Premdor banner. Spears became chairman of the company, and Century's president, Philip Orsino, took over as president and chief executive officer. Orsino would be instrumental in the rapid growth of Premdor in the 1990s and in the eventual acquisition of Masonite.

Orsino, a Toronto native, earned an undergraduate degree from the University of Toronto in 1976 and went to work for the accounting firm of Hilborn Ellis Grant. Three years later he became a certified public accountant and a partner in his firm. Many of his clients were builders and contractors, and some of his in-laws were also involved in the building-products industry. Because he had always wanted to run a business, it was not surprising that he seized upon an opportunity to become directly involved in building products. During a recession in the early 1980s there was a fallout in the door industry so that only one door company was left operating in eastern Canada. In November 1982, while still an accountant, he and a small group of investors launched Century with less than $1 million. By 1984, when a new investor entered the picture, he quit the accounting firm to take over as Century's president. "By then," he recalled in a 2003 interview, "I was convinced that we could grow it to any size we wanted, that the opportunities were unlimited."

After Century and Premdor merged, Orsino's ambitions were given free reign. He looked to the south, eyeing the large and lucrative U.S. market, and restructured Premdor into two divisions, one devoted to the Canadian market and the other to the U.S. market. The next three years were challenging, as Premdor had to spend a great deal of money to consolidate the

Key Dates:

1924: Mason Fiber Company is formed.
1928: Mason Fiber is renamed Masonite Corporation.
1979: Premdor, Inc. is formed.
1988: International Paper acquires Masonite.
1989: Premdor and Century Wood Door Ltd. merge.
2001: International Paper acquires Masonite.
2002: Premdor changes its name to Masonite International Corporation.

20 plants and distribution centers joined together in the merger, as well as the purchase of U.S. door companies. As a result, Premdor lost $3.7 million in 1989, $1.9 million in 1990, and another $1.7 million in 1991. But Orsino had doubled the size of the company during this period and was making significant inroads in the U.S. market. Because the cost of shipping doors was such a major factor in price, it was important, to be competitive and gain significant market share in the United States, for Premdor to buy local doormaking operations. Another major step in the company's growth came in 1993 when Premdor, in addition to having its stock traded on the Toronto and Montreal Stock Exchanges, became listed on the New York Stock Exchange, a move that provided greater exposure to the investment community and led to increased funding for its ongoing expansion plans. At this point, approximately 70 percent of Premdor's facilities and personnel were operating in the United States. But the company was still in acquisition mode. All told, between 1989 and 2000, Premdor completed 43 acquisitions, mostly of manufacturers.

The Masonite sale made sense to both International Paper and Premdor. After International Paper merged with Union Camp Corporation in 1999 and acquired Champion International Corporation the following year, it sought to focus on its main business of making paper products. As part of a long-term strategy, International Paper decided to shed more than $3 billion in noncore assets, including Masonite. Premdor, on the other hand, was interested in expanding internationally and becoming more vertically integrated, and the addition of Masonite could forward both of these goals. An agreement was reached in September 2000 for International Paper to sell Masonite to Premdor for $523 million, but a year would pass before the two sides were able to gain regulatory approval and the deal was completed. In the meantime, the price of Premdor's stock fell to an eight-year low before slowly rebounding, as many investors were afraid that the company would take on an excessive level of debt to finance the acquisition. During the regulatory process, however, the deal was refined, including the divestiture of some assets as required by the U.S. Justice Department and a lowering of the purchase price. In the end, Premdor paid $427.3 million for Masonite.

Masonite became involved in the door business in the 1970s when it began making wood-composite moulded door facings, but was not readily associated with doors. Nevertheless, from the very beginning of the Masonite acquisition, Orsino planned to adopt the Masonite name. Premdor, though well known in Canada, was not widely recognized in the United States. The Masonite name, on the other hand, had international scope and was essentially a generic term for hardboard itself. As Orsino explained to the *Financial Post*, "It was a name that consumers recognized and builders recognized. What we did was to try to take advantage of the fact that people knew the name and consumers knew the name. Then we repositioned it and initiated a marketing strategy to associate the name with a beautiful line of interior and exterior doors. So we changed the logo, we changed the name of the company from Masonite Corp. to Masonite International Corp., and we came up with the tag line, 'Masonite: The Beautiful Door.' "

Premdor's name change to Masonite took effect on January 1, 2002. As the company continued its rebranding efforts, it shifted from a growth-by-acquisition strategy to one dominated by the pursuit of organic growth opportunities. Masonite would look to enter new geographic markets around the world, in some cases by just selling wood-composite moulded door facings to other door manufacturers. The company also pursued an all-product strategy. "The idea," according to Orsino, "is to look at all our customers, some who are only buying interior doors or some that are only buying entry doors, and try to get them to buy the full product line." Nevertheless, if a suitable acquisition candidate emerged, Masonite was willing to take advantage of an opportunity. In a deal completed in March 2004, Masonite paid $160 million to acquire the residential entry door division of The Stanley Works, a business that contributed about $200 million in annual sales.

Principal Subsidiaries

Premdor U.S. Holdings, Inc.; Premdor Corporation; Premdor Mouldings, Inc.; Europa Door Limited.

Principal Competitors

Atrium Companies, Inc.; International Aluminum Corporation; Pella Corporation.

Further Reading

Cohen, Laurie P., "International Paper Plans to Buy USG's Masonite," *Wall Street Journal,* October 3, 1988, p. 1.
Gates, Bruce, "U.S. Opportunity Knocks for Canadian Doormaker," *Financial Post,* November 30, 1991, p. U7.
Jones, Kevin D., "The Making of a Dinosaur," *Mississippi Business Journal,* July 1989, p. 14.
"Opportunity Knocked," *Financial Post,* November 1, 2003.
"That Wonderful Leaky Valve," *Nation's Business,* February 1972, p. 84.

—Ed Dinger

Material Sciences Corporation

2200 E. Pratt Boulevard
Elk Grove Village, Illinois 60007
U.S.A.
Telephone: (847) 439-8270
Fax: (847) 439-0737
Web site: http://www.matsci.com

Public Company
Incorporated: 1971
Employees: 740
Sales: $266.8 million (2003)
Stock Exchanges: New York
Ticker Symbol: MSC
NAIC: 332812 Metal Coating, Engraving (Except Jewelry and Silverware), and Allied Services to Manufacturers

Material Sciences Corporation (MSC) is a publicly traded company based in Elk Grove, Illinois. It designs, manufactures, and markets materials-based solutions for electronic, acoustical/ thermal, and coated metal applications. MSC's metal laminate product, NRGDamp, is used in the electronics industry to reduce noise and vibrations in hard disk drives. The company also produces Quiet Steel, used by the auto industry to reduce noise and vibration. The material has been applied primarily in dash panels but is also being used in an increasing number of other applications such as wheel wells and floor pans. In addition, MSC's high-speed coated metal operation produces painted and electrogalvanized sheet metal for use in building and construction products, automobile exterior panels, and appliances such as refrigerators and freezers. MSC also makes sensors and switches, relying on its patented field effect technology, for the automotive, recreational vehicle, marine, and consumer electronics markets.

Founding the Company in 1971

MSC was founded in 1971 as a holding company to acquire businesses involved in advanced materials technologies. The most important of these companies, and the only one in the fold when the company went public in 1984, was Pre Finish Metals. It was originally known as All Weather Steel Products, founded in Chicago in 1951 by Roy Crabtree. The company started out applying protective aluminum paint to sheets of metal, used to make air ducts for heating and air conditioning systems. The demand for the product grew so rapidly that All Weather soon dropped sheet processing in favor of continuous coil coating. In 1954 the operation was transferred to a converted mushroom barn in Des Plaines, Illinois, where new coil processing equipment was installed to meet ever increasing demand. Then, in May 1958, sawdust insulation in the roof ignited spontaneously and the subsequent explosion and fire completely destroyed the building. All Weather's management took immediate steps to establish a new production facility and preserve the company's customer base. Three competitors agreed to fill outstanding orders, with All Weather's personnel dispatched to oversee production. A new 16,000-square-foot building was quickly constructed in Elk Grove, Illinois—just 40 days after ground was broken, the roof of the structure was being completed. In the meantime, other All Weather personnel were combing the country for a coil line that was available for sale. A two-year-old 18-foot line was found in Tampa, Florida, bought for $75,000, and then dismantled and shipped to Elk Grove, where it was assembled even as the construction of the building was underway. As a result of these efforts, All Weather was able to retain about 95 percent of its customers, and less than three months after the fire, the company was once again producing its own coils of coated metal.

All Weather continued to prosper in its new plant, so much so that another 16-foot coating line and a 20-foot slitting line were added. Because the company was now able to broaden its product offerings, the board of directors in March 1959 decided to change the name to Pre Finish Metals Incorporated. Moreover, the new name was more in keeping with the direction that the metal coating industry was taking in general. Two-coat equipment was becoming more prevalent in order to handle printing, the embossing of heavy plastics, and film laminating. To keep pace, the Elk Grove plant was expanded in 1960 to accommodate a new 48-foot slitting line, which was soon joined by a 48-foot tandem coating line, the first wide two-coat line in the United States.

Throughout the 1960s Pre Finish added production capacity to fuel even greater growth in sales and profits. A new 28-foot coating line was added in 1965, followed by the introduction of a cut-to-length line and square shear line, which allowed the company to make and sell pre-coated steel sheet for use in the manufacture of small appliances. In 1966 Pre Finish expanded to the West Coast by opening a new plant in Vernon, California, where the company's original 18-foot coating line was installed, plus a 48-foot slitter. Two years later, a new high-speed tandem 54-foot line was installed in a new building located in Cucamonga, California, and the equipment in the Vernon plant was subsequently relocated here. Back in Elk Grove, in the meantime, Pre Finish began construction on a second plant, where in 1967 a 54-foot high-speed tandem coating line was installed (followed several months later by a 48-foot electro-galvanizing line, which was in fact owned and operated by CM Products Company). In 1968 a high-speed 54-foot slitter was added to the new facility.

Pre Finished Metals was acquired by MSC in November 1971, and as part of the deal the California operation was sold off. Crabtree would remain in charge of the business until his death later in the decade. The new corporate parent added to the technical as well as marketing departments to spur further growth. As part of a 42,500-square-foot addition to Plant #2 in 1973, a 5,000-square-foot laboratory facility was built. A year later, warehouse and office space were also added, so that this plant now boasted 162,500 square feet of occupied space. Beginning in 1975 Pre Finish invested $2 million to boost the production of its 54-foot coating line by 65 percent. It was during this period that parent company MSC began receiving greater funding from the venture capital fund owned by E.F. ''Ned'' Heizer, who became a director in 1976 and whose fund became the principal owner.

After graduating from Northwestern University, Heizer went to work for Allstate Insurance in 1962, where over the course of the next seven years he built up the company's private placement division, ultimately overlooking $100 million in investments in more than 70 early stage companies. In 1969 he formed a venture capital firm, Heizer Corporation, becoming a pioneer in the venture capital industry by attracting institutional investors in a major way for the first time. He would go on to found the National Venture Capital Association, serving as its first chairman.

Upon Crabtree's death, Heizer was instrumental in bringing in an outside chairman and chief executive officer to head Pre Finish. Although MSC bought a number of cutting edge companies during the 1970s, by 1983 Pre Finish remained the only subsidiary. During that year, MSC was reincorporated in Delaware in preparation for spinning off the business from Heizer Corp. Before then, the company expanded eastward, in the fall of 1983 acquiring coating facilities in Morrisville and Fairless Hills, Pennsylvania. At this point, MSC was generating in excess

of $71 million a year in revenues, after posting sales of $26.2 million in 1981, $30 million in 1982, and $43.4 million in 1983.

Going Public in 1984

MSC was spun off from Heiser Corp. in November 1984, as the company was on its way to topping the $100 million sales mark for 1985 (which ended February 28, 1985). Prospects appeared promising for the newly independent public company, which now traded on the American Stock Exchange, as management followed a three-pronged approach to ongoing growth. First the company looked for internal development of the business, spurred by investments in research and development, spending two cents on every sales dollar, which led to the development of lucrative specialty products. It was during the early 1980s, for example, that the company's engineers developed Quiet Steel by spreading a polymer, .001 in thickness, between two sheets of thin metal. The resulting laminate was able to absorb vibrational energy, dissipate heat, and muffle sound. It was discovered to be highly suited to the automotive industry, especially in removing the squeal from disk brakes. It also proved useful in damping the hum of computer disk drives. Another R&D success of the 1980s was the development of Specular, a fluorescent light fixture reflective laminate. The second prong of MSC's strategy for growth was a joint venture it formed with Bethlehem Steel and Inland Steel to provide electrogalvanized steel to the auto industry for making exposed car parts. Finally, MSC was in the market for outside acquisitions, primarily interested in companies involved in constrained-layered composites, laminates, and specialty adhesives.

In January 1986 MSC completed the first in a pair of acquisitions for the year when it bought San Diego-based Deposition Technology Inc. for nearly $20 million in convertible notes. Deposition was in the business of sputter depositing metals on flexible plastics films, primarily used to produce solar control window films. In July 1986 MSC spent $13.8 million in cash, notes, and stock to acquire Schaar Industries, the nation's largest independent vapor metallizing firm to the packaging and graphics arts markets.

By 1988 MSC was looking to strike a balance between its coating and electroplating sheet metal and laminates business and specialty products such as Speculart and laminates used in microwavable prepared-food packaging (thin sheets of foil or metallized film laminated to cardboard, used to crisp microwave foods). Business appeared to be on the rise, but in 1989 such key industries as automobile and appliances entered into down cycles and drastically cut their orders for MSC products. As a result, MSC lost more than $30 million in 1989, mostly due to writedowns. In February 1990, Schaar was sold for $3 million, more than $10 million less than what MSC paid for the subsidiary three years earlier. Moreover, coil coating caused $5 million in cleanup costs at two Superfund sites in Indiana. The board of directors decided to retain the services of William Blair & Co. to consider all options, including the sale of the business. Likely suitors included joint venture partners Bethlehem Steel or Inland Steel. But nearly a year would pass and the board was unable to sell the company. Instead, new management was installed in the form of turnaround specialist G. Robert Evans, who in February 1991 was named president, chief executive officer, and chairman. Evans had some 40 years of experience,

Key Dates:

1951: All Weather Steel Products is formed.
1959: All Weather is renamed Pre Finish Metals Inc.
1971: Material Sciences Corporation (MSC) is formed; the company acquires Pre Finish.
1984: MSC becomes a public company.
1991: Turnaround specialist G. Robert Evans is named president, CEO, and chairman.
1992: The company's stock is listed on the New York Stock Exchange.
1997: MSC moves into a new 210,000-square-foot headquarters in Elk Grove, Illinois; Evans steps down as CEO and is replaced by Gerald G. Nadig.
2002: Sales fall by nearly 50 percent; CEO Nadig resigns and is replaced by Michael J. Callahan.
2003: MSC wins the Innovation Award at the International Boatbuilder Exhibition and Conference for its Solidswitch field effect switch developed for the marine market.
2004: Callahan steps down as president and CEO, replaced by Ronald L. Stewart.

serving in a number of management positions during a 16-year career at United States Gypsum Company, and various stints as a chief executive officer for Arcata Corporation; Southwall Technologies, Inc.; Allstell Inc.; Bemrose Group USA; and Corporate Finance Associates Illinois, Inc.

In a matter of just 18 months, Evans was able to return MSC to fiscal health. In truth, although investors bid down the price of the company's stock, MSC retained the foundation of a very strong business, especially in its Quiet Steel and Speculart products. With some positive developments, the company looked to build on its momentum. The company was able to complete a secondary offering of stock and moved to the New York Stock Exchange. Then, in June 1993, the company once again attempted to grow through acquisitions, paying $14.5 million in cash for Armco Steel Company's coil coating facility in Middletown, Ohio. MSC also was beginning to think internationally, hiring its first international sales executive during this period. In a matter of three years the company grew its international sales from less than 1 percent of revenues to around 10 percent. The company was moving aggressively into Europe and South America, and even shipping its brake dampers to Japanese automakers.

External Growth in the 1990s

MSC completed additional acquisitions during the 1990s. In 1995 it paid approximately $8 million for Solar Gard International Inc. The company completed a pair of purchases in 1997, adding Richmond, California-based Pinole Point Steel, a hot-dipped galvanizing operation, and affiliated Colorstrip, Inc., a coil coating paint facility. It was also during 1997 that MSC moved into a new 210,000-square-foot headquarters in Elk Grove. In addition, Evans stepped down as CEO, although he stayed on as chairman. Replacing him was Gerald G. Nadig, who had been hired by Evans's predecessor in 1989 with the

intention of one day running the company. Because of the difficult period the company suffered in 1989–90, this plan was abandoned. Nevertheless, Nadig remained with MSC and worked his way up, becoming president, chief operating officer, and chairman of the board.

Nadig was quickly faced with an unexpected challenge. On March 31, 1997, the controller for one of the company's subsidiaries announced that he would not be coming into work, saying that "he had been doing things and that it would be discovered." What management soon learned was that net income for fiscal years 1995, 1996, and 1997 was overstated by nearly 10 percent, or some $5 million. Piecing the situation together, it became apparent to management that the controller in late 1995 was unable to reconcile his books, and made some irregular adjustments in order to make a quick fix that he hoped to clean up later. But matters only grew worse, and he ultimately had no choice other than to reveal the problem. Although the management team was not at fault, investors punished the company's stock.

This downturn, however, did not dissuade the company from completing the acquisition of Pinole Point and Colorstrip, although in retrospect MSC would have been better off not making the deal. California suffered through torrential rains, which hurt the construction industry, Pinole Point's primary customers. To make matters worse, Pinole Point locked into raw steel prices that were subsequently undercut by the dumping of Asian steel, putting the subsidiary at a severe competitive disadvantage. MSC replaced the management team, but matters did not improve significantly. More positive developments were the increased usage of Quiet Steel by U.S. automakers and the 2000 acquisition of Goldbach Automobile Consulting, which paved the way for the company's Quiet Steel products being sold in Europe.

In April 2001 Nadig announced that MSC would focus on its businesses with the greatest potential, moving away from such mature businesses as metal coating, which accounted for two-thirds of the company's total sales, to smaller yet faster-growing businesses. As a result the MSC Specialty Films division was cut loose, sold to Bekaert Corp. for $122 million in cash. MSC also began looking for a buyer for Pinole Point, while management initiated a reorganization and cost reduction plan. Finally in June 2002 Pinole Point was sold to a Mexican holding company, Grupo IMSA.

But with the manufacturing sector struggling, MSC continued to struggle. In 2002, the company lost $27 million, with reported sales falling almost 50 percent. The well-known investment fund manager Mario J. Gabelli began to pressure MSC to make changes. In April 2002, Nadig resigned, according to the company, to "spend more time with his family and pursue other opportunities." New independent directors, including a Gabelli ally, were named to the board. The company's new president and CEO, Michael J. Callahan, promised to make a "systemic change in the way we do business." But much of the company's fortunes depended on the increased use of its Quiet Steel product. According to a November 2003 *Forbes* profile, "If automakers don't clamor for more quiet metal soon, Callahan may be forced to bust up the company. Shares went for a recent $9.80—down 23% in the last year, compared with a 19% run-up in the S&P 500. Gabelli Asset Management, which owns 13% of the stock, thinks all the pieces sold separately—including a unit that makes electronic sensors for liquid-crystal displays—could fetch a total of $15 a share. 'We're examining all alternatives,' says Callahan. Beyond that, he's keeping quiet.''

Aside from the potential of Quiet Steel, MSC also had high hopes for its field effect switch technology, which produced an electronic field in front of and behind a panel. Because a finger entering the field triggered the switch, there was less wear and tear on the switch. Moreover, the technology could be fine-tuned for a number of applications. Toshiba, for instance, decided in January 2003 to use field effect touch switches in new television sets. Later in 2003 MSC won the Innovation Award at the International Boatbuilder Exhibition and Conference for its SolidSwitch field effect switch, which was impervious to the elements and developed for the marine market.

Further management changes occurred in February 2004 when Callahan stepped down as president, CEO, and board member, replaced by Ronald L. Stewart, who had been working with the company as a manufacturing consultant since June 2003. He brought with him more than 30 years of experience with such major companies as Chrysler Motor Corporation, J.I. Case, and Volkswagen of America.

Principal Subsidiaries

Electronic Materials and Devices Group, Inc.; MSC Laminates and Composites Inc.

Principal Competitors

Ameron International Corporation; Industrial Coatings Group, Inc.; Kasle Steel Corporation.

Further Reading

Arndorfer, James B., ''Gabelli Groups Turn Up Heat on Metal Firms,'' *Crain's Chicago Business,* June 2, 2003, p. 3.

Keefe, Lisa M., ''Metal Firm Is Up for Sale,'' *Crain's Chicago Business,* July 2, 1990, p. 70.

Murphy, H. Lee, ''Bad Timing Snarls Material Sci. Deal,'' *Crain Chicago Business,* July 19, 1999, p. 36.

Nelson, Brett, ''Shhh!,'' *Forbes,* November 24, 2003, p. 84.

Savitz, Eric J., ''A Fresh Shine,'' *Barron's,* November 4, 1991, p. 14.

Setton, Dolly, ''Steel Deal,'' *Forbes,* October 18, 1999, p. 190.

Troxell, Thomas N., Jr., ''Tripod for Growth,'' *Barron's,* July 1, 1985, p. 33.

—Ed Dinger

Mazda Motor Corporation

3-1 Shinchi, Fucho-cho
Aki-gun
Hiroshima 730-8670
Japan
Telephone: (082) 282-1111
Fax: (082) 287-5225
Web site: http://www.mazda.com

Public Company
Incorporated: 1920 as Toyo Cork Kogyo Company, Ltd.
Employees: 36,184
Sales: ¥2.36 trillion ($19.7 billion) (2003)
Stock Exchanges: Tokyo
Ticker Symbol: 7261
NAIC: 336111 Automobile Manufacturing; 336112 Light
 Truck and Utility Vehicle Manufacturing

Mazda Motor Corporation is the number five Japanese automaker, behind Toyota Motor Corporation; Nissan Motor Co., Ltd.; Honda Motor Co., Ltd.; and Suzuki Motor Corporation. Mazda produces sedans, sport wagons, station wagons, minivans, sports cars, light trucks, and commercial vehicles, selling them in Japan under such names as the Demio, Axela, Atenza, Roadster, RX-8, MPV, and Tribute. Among the company's U.S. brands are the Protegé, Mazda3, Mazda6, Miata, RX-8, MPV, and Tribute. During fiscal 2003, Mazda sold more than one million vehicles, 294,000 in Japan and 723,000 overseas. The company operates two main production facilities in Japan and 15 overseas and is also involved in two production joint ventures with Ford Motor Company located in Michigan and Thailand. Ford took a substantial equity stake in Mazda in 1979, and after 1996, when it gained a controlling 33.4 percent stake of a Mazda verging on bankruptcy, Ford spearheaded a turnaround at the company based on cutting costs, restructuring, and introducing a string of successful new models.

Early History

Mazda was organized by Jugiro Matsuda in 1920 as the Toyo Cork Kogyo Company, Ltd., or East Sea Cork Manufacturing Company. The small enterprise, located in Hiroshima in southern Japan, was initially involved in the manufacture of cork products. In the mid-1920s, however, it expanded its product line to include several machined products. Reflecting this diversification, Matsuda dropped the word *Cork* from its name in 1927, and in 1929 the company began production of machine tools. Matsuda believed that the enterprise could remain successful only if it had a truly unique product. To this end, Toyo Kogyo began design work on an unusual three-wheeled truck that proved commercially successful after its introduction in 1931.

The company was also an early supplier of products to a family of closely linked firms operating under the Sumitomo industrial conglomerate, with whom Toyo Kogyo maintained a close relationship. In 1935 the company began turning out rock drills and gauge blocks, which were of particular interest to Sumitomo, then one of Japan's largest mining concerns. The company supplied Sumitomo—and other companies involved in the exploitation of resources in Taiwan, Korea, and later Manchuria—with machine tools.

After the seizure of the Japanese government by right-wing militarists in the mid-1930s, Toyo Kogyo was drawn into military production. The company produced a variety of products for the Japanese Army, including automotive parts and machinery. The company's management was placed under government authority after the United States declared war on Japan in 1941. Although an important and capable supplier, Toyo Kogyo was not considered a target for strategic bombing. Its operations remained intact until the last days of the war, although they were somewhat limited by the increasing lack of access to raw materials.

Recovery After World War II

On August 9, 1945, the entire city of Hiroshima was destroyed by an American atomic bomb. Toyo Kogyo was Hiroshima's largest employer, and while the factory was located far enough from the city center to avoid serious damage, many of Toyo Kogyo's employees were not; 400 workers died. Soldiers who had worked for Toyo Kogyo before the war returned to Hiroshima skeptical as to whether the city and its businesses could be rebuilt. Nevertheless, by December 1945 Toyo Kogyo was back in business, again turning out the three-wheeled trucks

Company Perspectives:

Mazda's raison-d'être is to make cars that are fun to drive—cars that enthuse but are also affordable. The brand message "Zoom-Zoom" aims to capture this feeling, expressing the passionate spirit of motoring enjoyment that drives Mazda forward.

that were the core of its business. With a large commercial operation back in business, and a thriving local economy, Hiroshima was quickly reconstructed. Many workers felt a personal debt to Toyo Kogyo for its role in reviving the war-torn city.

During this time, Jugiro Matsuda retired, designating his son, Tsuneji, as his successor. Tsuneji Matsuda proved to be an extremely capable manager, exemplifying many of the qualities that would come to define the company as a whole: patience, diligence, and dedication to quality and efficiency. Early in his tenure, Tsuneji Matsuda became interested in the manufacture of automobiles, which he saw as essential to modern life in Japan. Indeed, with personal incomes increasing in Japan, automobile production had the potential to generate tremendous profit and lift the company to even greater heights.

In 1954 Toyo Kogyo established a technological agreement with Acme Resin that enabled the company to begin using a new shell molding method. After several years of development, Toyo Kogyo established plans for its first mass-produced automobile, the two-door "Mazda" R360 coupe, introduced in 1960. Matsuda reportedly chose the car's name for its association with Ahura Mazda, the ancient Zoroastrian god of light, as well as for its similarity to the name Matsuda. The R360 made Toyo Kogyo a competitor in the growing consumer automobile market. Nevertheless, while the company had introduced a viable product, the Mazda lacked one thing: it was not unique.

Production of the Wankel Engine in the 1960s

Matsuda had long known of a virtually abandoned engine technology developed in Germany by the inventor Felix Wankel. Wankel's pistonless engine worked on a revolutionary principle in which a single triangular rotor circulated around a large combustion chamber with a gear at its axis. The rotor, moving orbitally around the gear, compressed air and fuel on one side, where a spark plug ignited the mixture. This drove the rotor around the axial gear, expelling exhaust fumes while setting up the next face of the rotor for another combustion. As the rotor wound its way around the combustion chamber, the gear at its axis was forced to spin. This gear was attached to a clutch and transmission, and from there to a drive shaft. The Wankel engine offered more than mere novelty; by eliminating the in-out, in-out motion of pistons, the Wankel would operate more smoothly and with better performance than a conventional engine.

While successful in a laboratory, the Wankel engine was overlooked by engine makers because no one believed that it could be accurately machined in mass production. Matsuda, however, had great faith in his company's machining techniques, and his engineers assured him that such an engine could be built on a massive scale. Matsuda reached an agreement with

NSU/Wankel, the German firm that held a patent for the Wankel Engine, and in 1961 he won an exclusive agreement to develop the engine. Design work commenced, but it took several years to develop a suitable model.

In the meantime, Toyo Kogyo introduced a four-door automobile, the Carol 600, in 1962, and the following year the company's one millionth vehicle rolled off its assembly line. In 1965 Toyo Kogyo produced another new model, the Mazda 800/1000, and completed work on a proving ground at Miyoshi. Also that year, the company established a diesel engine technology agreement with Perkins Services. Branching into the market for light-duty trucks, Toyo Kogyo introduced the Mazda Proceed B-series compact pickup truck.

In 1966 the company completed construction of a new passenger car plant at Hiroshima. The following year, this plant began manufacturing the Mazda Cosmo Sports 110S automobile, the first Toyo Kogyo vehicle to be powered by a Wankel rotary engine. This model placed Toyo Kogyo in a truly unique position in the market. The rotary-powered engine gave the company an exclusive product that was smooth riding, quiet, and fast. Nothing produced by Toyo Kogyo's competitors, industry giants Nissan and Toyota, could match it.

Expanding the Product Line and Refining the Wankel Engine

Other introductions to the company's automobile line during this time included the Mazda 1000/1200; the rotary-powered R100 Mazda Familia Coupe; the RX-2 Capella; the RX-3 Savanna; and the RX-4 Luce. In 1972, Toyo Kogyo completed manufacture of its five millionth vehicle, nearly one million of which had been exported; exports to Europe had begun in 1967 and to the United States three years later. As worldwide sales increased, Toyo Kogyo set up sales organizations in the United States, Canada, Belgium, West Germany, Australia, and Malaysia.

In 1972 Henry Ford flew to Hiroshima to negotiate a license that would allow the Ford Motor Company to begin building rotary engines. Sure that Toyo Kogyo was onto something unique and profitable, however, Matsuda flatly refused to share the Wankel technology. Subsequently, Matsuda launched a bold worldwide marketing campaign in which the rotary engine was touted as the answer to high fuel prices. Consumers showed strong interest in the Mazda product line. To finance an expansion of production capacity, Toyo Kogyo made a huge public equity offering.

The OPEC oil embargo sent a shockwave through the world economy in 1973. With petroleum prices skyrocketing, consumer demand for energy efficient automobiles increased dramatically. The Mazda's highly efficient rotary engine seemed the perfect alternative to conventional piston-engined automobiles.

Emissions from the rotary engine, however, exceeded clean air standards in California, the company's largest export market. Adjustments made to clean up the engine came at the expense of fuel economy, which fell to ten miles per gallon. Furthermore, the rotary model was prone to breakdown. Production continued while Toyo Kogyo technicians launched an emergency reengineering of the Wankel design.

Key Dates:

1920: Jugiro Matsuda forms Toyo Cork Kogyo Company, Ltd. in Hiroshima, Japan, as a manufacturer of cork products.
1927: After expanding the product line to include machined products, the company drops the word *Cork* from its name.
1929: Company begins production of machine tools.
1931: Toyo Kogyo introduces an unusual three-wheeled truck.
1945: Following a wartime shift to military supply production, the company resumes production of its three-wheeled truck.
1960: Company introduces its first passenger car, the two-door Mazda R360 coupe.
1961: Toyo Kogyo enters into an agreement with NSU/Wankel to develop the German firm's rotary engine.
1967: The Mazda Cosmo Sports 110S debuts and is the first company vehicle to be powered by a Wankel rotary engine; exports to the European market begin.
1970: Mazda starts exports to the U.S. market.
1979: Affiliation with Ford Motor Company is formalized when the U.S. automaker purchases a 25 percent stake in Toyo Kogyo.

1984: Company changes its name to Mazda Motor Corporation.
1987: Mazda establishes a U.S. production facility in the Detroit suburb of Flat Rock, Michigan.
1989: The Mazda MX-5 Miata sports car is introduced in the U.S. market.
1992: Company sells Ford a 50 percent interest in its Flat Rock, Michigan, plant, creating the joint venture AutoAlliance International, Inc.
1994: Mazda posts a net loss for the year, the first of five straight years in the red.
1996: Ford sinks an additional $481 million into Mazda, increasing its interest to a controlling 33.4 percent; former Ford executive Henry D.G. Wallace is named president of Mazda, becoming the first non-Japanese to head a Japanese corporation.
1999: Mazda posts its first full-year net profits in six years.
2002: The midsize Atenza/Mazda6 debuts.
2003: RX-8 sports car and the subcompact Axela/Mazda3 are introduced.

By 1974, amid increasing pressure from the OPEC embargo, Toyo Kogyo managed to stretch the Mazda's mileage rating to 16 miles per gallon, and then 20. But by this time, Honda, Ford, General Motors, and Curtiss-Wright had begun development of stratified charge engines that promised greater efficiency than conventional and rotary engines. Moreover, Nissan and Toyota began an all-out war for market leadership in Japan, squeezing out smaller competitors such as Toyo Kogyo and Suzuki Motor Co., Ltd.

As consumer interest in the rotary waned, Toyo Kogyo began searching for ways to keep its factories operating nearer capacity. Matsuda negotiated a deal with Ford in which Toyo Kogyo would manufacture Ford's Festiva model at its facilities. Strapped for cash, Toyo Kogyo finally agreed to license its rotary technology to Suzuki, which used the engine for a new motorcycle. Sumitomo Bank also assisted Toyo Kogyo in getting out of financial danger.

When the oil embargo was lifted, oil prices and consumer interest in fuel-efficient engines declined rapidly. Improvements in the rotary design were finally perfected, giving Toyo Kogyo the efficient, environmentally friendly engine it needed—about two years too late. While U.S. fuel economy regulations kept Toyo Kogyo in the American market, the company had lost two years in fixing the rotary engine, during which time Honda, Ford, and GM had developed their own improved engines, leaving Toyo Kogyo in the middle of a crowded pack.

With nothing other than the rotary engine to distinguish its product line, Toyo Kogyo was forced to quickly develop new models and concentrate on product quality as a competitive factor. The Mazda Familia and Capella/626 were introduced in 1977, followed by the Savanna RX-7 in 1978. By this time Toyo Kogyo had turned out more than ten million vehicles, one million of which were rotary-powered.

Amidst the company's efforts to recover from the debacles of the 1970s, Tsuneji Matsuda retired, leaving his son Kohei Matsuda in charge. The younger Matsuda initially made great progress in shoring up the company's balance sheet. But in the opinion of the Sumitomo interests, which owned most of Toyo Kogyo's shares and bankrolled its earlier failures, the turnaround was not good enough. Sumitomo Bank officers felt that Kohei Matsuda was not adequately preparing the company for the future, and they disagreed strongly with his plans for restructuring the company, which included a wider product line and greater autonomy from Sumitomo management. Eventually, Matsuda was forced to resign his presidency to Yoshiki Yamasaki, a director favored by Sumitomo. The abdication formally ended the Matsuda dynasty at Toyo Kogyo.

The company enjoyed a jump in sales in 1979, when the Iranian Revolution caused a brief oil crisis. Also helping boost sales was the fact that Toyo Kogyo and other Japanese manufacturers had become known in the United States for the high quality of their products; American cars, by contrast, had become known as poorly designed, carelessly built, and overpriced.

Growing Affiliation with Ford in the 1980s

In 1979 Ford Motor Company began negotiations to acquire a large stake in Toyo Kogyo, hoping to merge it with its own Japanese subsidiary, Ford Industries. The $135 million deal, completed in November, left Ford with a 24.5 percent share of Toyo Kogyo. The merger paved the way for several new joint ventures between Ford and Toyo Kogyo, in which the Japanese company built small cars and trucks under the Ford nameplate and distributed Ford products in Japan.

In 1980, shedding the last of its failures with the rotary engine, Toyo Kogyo settled a class-action suit charging design flaws with early models. Also that year, the Mazda FWD Familia was named car of the year in Japan. Unable to match Nissan and Toyota's large sales staffs, Toyo Kogyo established a string of showrooms across Japan under the name Autorama. In 1981, as it exported its five millionth vehicle, the company set up sales organizations in the United States and Europe. In 1982 Toyo Kogyo established another production plant at Hofu, and in 1983 turned out its 15 millionth vehicle. The following year, Toyo Kogyo formally changed its name to Mazda Motor Corporation, reflecting the tremendous popularity of its main product line.

Mazda introduced several new automobiles in 1985, 1986, and 1987, including the new versions of the Mazda RX-7 and 626. By 1987 the company had produced 20 million vehicles. Mazda also entered into several joint ventures, including one with Ford and Matsushita for the production of air conditioning systems. Under a second partnership, Mazda manufactured microcars for Suzuki, and under a third, it imported Citroën cars to Japan.

Mazda Motor continued to be led by a committee of Sumitomo bankers, who received input from Ford and the South Korean automaker Kia Motors Corporation; Mazda had acquired an 8 percent interest in Kia in 1983. In 1987, however, Norimasa Furuta, a former official of the Ministry of International Trade and Industry, assumed the presidency of the company.

Under Furuta, Mazda sharpened its focus, developing several new vehicles for specific markets. The Persona and Proceed were developed specifically for the Japanese market, joining the company's mainstay, the 323 Sedan. The MPV minivan, initially intended for sale only in the United States, was later introduced in Japan. Of the company's new vehicles, the MX-5 Miata, introduced in 1989, was undoubtedly the most successful. A small sports car reminiscent of the MGB and Triumph Spitfire, the Miata was marketed in the United States, where it found an appreciative market particularly among young, affluent males. In designing the Miata, Mazda engineers borrowed liberally from the British Lotus and Elan, which they admitted disassembling for reference. Miata sales were brisk and did much to revive the reputation of Mazda in the United States.

While Nissan, Toyota, and Honda created luxury car divisions to compete with American Buicks, Lincolns, and Cadillacs, Mazda continued to specialize in smaller cars and trucks. With Ford as its largest shareholder, Mazda found its marketing niche operating informally as a small car subsidiary of Ford. In 1987 Mazda established a U.S. production facility in the Detroit suburb of Flat Rock, Michigan, employing American union labor. The company also established a massive sales and research organization in the United States, employing thousands of Americans.

Nevertheless, 80 percent of the vehicles Mazda sold in foreign markets were produced in Japan, saddling the company with extra transportation costs and subjecting it to foreign import restrictions, particularly in Europe. In addition, Mazda maintained five separate dealerships in Japan for Mazda, Ford, and Citroën.

Yoshihiro Wada succeeded Furuta as president of Mazda in 1990. Furuta was given a ceremonial position on the board, joining Chairman Kenichi Yamamoto, who had headed Toyo Kogyo's rotary development during the 1960s. As it entered the 1990s, Mazda occupied a unique niche in the market, producing a relatively narrow line of midsize cars and small trucks.

1990s: Falling Production, Flowing Red Ink, and a Ford-Engineered Turnaround

The Miata's successful introduction in 1989 led Mazda to introduce five new vehicles in the United States, including the 626, in the hopes of becoming a full-line car maker. With at least three-quarters of its parts manufactured in the United States, the 626 was the first Japanese vehicle to be classified as a U.S. car under federal law. Despite these advances, Mazda's U.S. market share remained low, at between 2.2 percent and 2.6 percent from 1988 to 1993. In 1992 Mazda sold a 50 percent interest in its Flat Rock, Michigan, facility to Ford, creating a joint venture called AutoAlliance International, Inc. The next year, the company laid off 25 percent of its U.S. headquarters workforce, bringing Mazda's American headquarters staff to 400.

The company was not faring any better domestically. Between 1990 and 1996 Mazda's market share had dropped from 7.6 percent to 4.1 percent. Actual vehicles made and sold had declined also, from a peak of 1.4 million manufactured and 600,000 sold in Japan to 800,000 manufactured and 400,000 sold in 1996. Such a decline meant massive overcapacity in Mazda factories. Still, Mazda refused to combat the shrinkage by laying off employees; instead it used several piecemeal approaches that were only somewhat effective in cutting costs. First, it stopped replacing retirees to reduce head count, then it decreased bonuses and stopped production at its Hofu and Hiroshima factories for a few days each month. According to the *Economist* in 1996, Mazda had lost its unique edge, which it had hoped to recover with the Miata: "Most of Mazda's output is dull, fairly mainstream and fairly expensive. There is a market for boring, reliable cars, but customers tend to prefer those produced by bigger names, such as Toyota. Mazda's one hope of outsmarting bigger car makers is to be nimbler than they are, guessing trends ahead of time."

Sumitomo Bank had its own idea of how to bolster the company, which at times teetered on the brink of bankruptcy and which was in the midst of five straight years in the red, a streak that began with the fiscal year ending in March 1994. In 1996 it again exerted its power over Mazda by setting up a cash infusion and, in effect, a takeover by Ford. By putting up $481 million in cash, Ford brought its investment to 33.4 percent of the company, the legal line in Japan for a controlling interest. Soon thereafter, Henry D.G. Wallace, a former Ford executive, became president of Mazda Motor Corp., the first non-Japanese to head a Japanese corporation.

For approximately 20 percent below the market price for Mazda shares, Ford vastly increased its access to Japanese and other southeast Asian markets. It also hoped to integrate Mazda into its global reorganization, Ford 2000, intending to use Mazda's small-car and engineering expertise to benefit other Ford operations and, at the same time, to create economies of scale for Mazda. Ford's small-car operations in Europe, however, threatened to make Mazda production redundant.

Mazda made some headway in the fiscal year ending in March 1998. Sales of its new Demio model, a subcompact wagon, proved strong in Japan, and the consolidated net loss of ¥6.8 billion ($51.1 million) for the year was less than half of the ¥17.55 billion ($141.8 million) loss reported for the previous year. At the end of 1997, Wallace retired from the presidency and was replaced by another former Ford executive, James Miller. That same year, as its U.S. market share continued to fall, Mazda restructured in North America. Four U.S. subsidiaries were consolidated into the Irvine, California-based Mazda North American Operations, resulting in the trimming of 400 jobs from its North American workforce of 1,630. Mazda also found success that year introducing new models, including a new version of the Capella/626 sedan and station wagon, a new Familia/323 three-door hatchback, an all-new third-generation version of the Protegé sedan (Protegé was a more recently used U.S. name for the 323), and, also in the United States, the first redesigned version of the MX-5 Miata. These initiatives, coupled with a weaker yen, which made the firm's imports more competitive, helped return Mazda to profitability in the fiscal year ending in March 1999, when net income totaled ¥38.7 billion ($321.1 million). This turn of events was achieved despite the economic turmoil in southeast Asia in 1997 and 1998 that had threatened Mazda's nascent turnaround. The company had been expanding its operations in southeast Asia in the mid-1990s, hoping to reduce the negative effect of the rising yen on its car prices. In 1993 Mazda had opened another production company in the Philippines, and two years later it began a joint venture with Ford called AutoAlliance (Thailand) Company Limited. This venture began production of pickup trucks for sale in Thailand in May 1998 and then began exporting both Mazda- and Ford-badged trucks that December; it also enabled Mazda to close its existing plant in Thailand.

As part of its turnaround strategy, Mazda aimed to shrink its asset base, cut down on its heavy debt, and improve profitability. Toward these ends, Mazda in 1999 sold its stake in Ford Sales Japan, the former Autorama chain of showrooms, to Ford of Japan, and its stake in Mazda Credit, Mazda's finance arm, to Ford Credit. Mazda also worked to rein in its sprawling dealership network in Japan, shutting down more than 100 sales outlets, leaving 60 consolidated sales subsidiaries, in addition to 695 independent dealers. Mazda also sold to Nissan its 34 percent stake in JATCO Corporation, a joint venture with Nissan that produced automatic transmissions. The company also announced its intention to sell its stake in Kia. In December 1999 Miller retired from Mazda and Ford for health reasons, and he was replaced as Mazda president by Mark Fields. The 38-year-old Fields had been sent to Mazda by Ford in August 1998 as a senior adviser and had led the streamlining of Mazda's Japanese dealerships. He became the youngest executive to head a Japanese automaker.

Further Restructuring, New Models, and a Stronger Recovery in the Early 2000s

During 2000 Mazda introduced into the U.S. and Japanese markets the Tribute, a compact sport-utility vehicle (SUV) that had been jointly developed with Ford. Sales of the Tribute in the United States were strong, but they were disappointing in Japan. In November of that year, as Mazda began losing money again, primarily because of the impact of a stronger yen, Fields announced plans to step up the pace of restructuring. He launched

an early-retirement plan that led to the elimination of 2,200 jobs, and he also closed an assembly line in Japan that was capable of producing 266,000 cars per year, representing a cut in Japanese production of 25 percent. A portion of the production was shifted to a Ford plant in Valencia, Spain, where 100,000 Mazda vehicles would begin to be produced annually. For the fiscal year ending in March 2000, Mazda posted a net loss of ¥155.24 billion ($1.29 billion), because of a combination of falling sales in Japan and Europe, ¥40 billion in restructuring charges, and a ¥155 billion charge to offset an expected shortage in retirement-benefit funds. The company returned to modest profitability the following year based on further cost-cutting and a more favorable currency-exchange environment.

As its efforts to cut costs were enacted, Mazda concentrated as well on getting additional new cars to market as part of Fields' plan to overhaul and jazz up an aging model lineup. Ironically, Fields would not be onboard to see his efforts come to fruition because in June 2002 he was appointed head of Ford's luxury division. Lewis Booth was the successor, becoming the fourth Ford-dispatched executive to lead Mazda since the U.S. automaker acquired its controlling stake in 1996. Booth had most recently headed Ford's Asia-Pacific and African operations.

Late in 2002 the new models began their rollout. The Atenza, a sporty midsize sedan sold in Europe and North America as the Mazda6, was introduced as a replacement for the Capella/626. In addition to the sedan version, the Atenza/Mazda6 was eventually also available in a sport wagon and a five-door hatchback. Also debuting was a new version of the subcompact Demio; in Europe this car was sold as the Mazda2, and production of the Mazda2 took place at the Ford plant in Valencia, Spain, starting in January 2003. These introductions were supported by a marketing campaign that featured the slogan "Zoom-Zoom." Even though the new models did not affect the full-year results, they nevertheless aided Mazda's strong performance for the fiscal year ending in March 2003. The number of cars sold jumped 7.2 percent, to 1.02 million, and revenues advanced 12.9 percent, to ¥2.36 trillion ($19.7 billion); net income more than tripled, hitting ¥24.13 billion ($201.1 million). Also during 2002 Mazda announced that it would stop manufacturing trucks in Japan and would shut down its Fuchu truck plant in Hiroshima Prefecture in order to concentrate more of its energies and resources on its core passenger automobiles. The company planned to continue to sell Mazda-badged trucks that would be produced by other companies and by the Ford-Mazda joint venture in Thailand.

Mazda next introduced during the later months of 2003 the RX-8 sports car and the Axela subcompact, sold in Europe and North America as the Mazda3. The RX-8 was a successor to the popular RX-7, which had been discontinued in 1996. It featured a new compact rotary engine, could seat four adults, and had a unique four-door design in which the rear doors opened toward the rear and the frame had no side pillars separating the doors. Though it was not expected to sell as briskly as the lower-priced cars that Mazda was also debuting, company executives hoped the RX-8's snazzy design would woo consumers back into Mazda showrooms and could serve as the centerpiece of its strategy of attracting young families through cars featuring better road performance—road performance having been identified as the quintessential component of the Mazda brand. By

March 2004 *Nikkei Weekly* was reporting that the Atenza/Mazda6, the Demio/Mazda2, the RX-8, and the Axela/Mazda3 had won a total of 129 awards worldwide. Strong sales of the cars was expected to result in record pretax profits for the fiscal year ending in March 2004 of ¥57 billion ($523 million), double the previous year's figure.

In August 2003 Ford selected Booth to take over European operations. The string of Americans in charge of Mazda ended with the appointment of the company's number two man, Hisakazu Imaki, to the presidency. In December 2003, in a certain sign of Mazda's comeback, Ford selected the Japanese automaker to take a leading role in the development of a new subcompact slated to reach the market in 2007. Ford also planned to develop up to ten models for its three North American brands—Ford, Lincoln, and Mercury—based on the Atenza/Mazda6. Also on the agenda for Mazda was to build a much larger presence in the burgeoning market in China. By March 2004 Mazda was involved in three joint ventures with China FAW Group Corp., the nation's leading automaker, for the production of several Mazda models. The company hoped to increase sales in China from 80,000 vehicles to 200,000 by 2007.

Principal Subsidiaries

Kansai Mazda Co., Ltd.; Kanto Mazda Co., Ltd.; Kurashiki Kako Co., Ltd.; Kyushu Mazda Co., Ltd.; Malox Co., Ltd.; Mazda Autozam Inc.; Mazda Car Rental Corporation; Mazda Chuhan Co., Ltd.; Mazda Parts Kanto Co., Ltd.; Tokai Mazda Hanbai Co., Ltd.; Toyo Advanced Technologies Co., Ltd.; Mazda Australia Pty., Ltd.; Mazda Motor Logistics Europe N.V. (Belgium); Mazda Canada Inc.; Compañía Colombiana Automotriz S.A. (Colombia); Mazda Automobiles France; Mazda Motors (Deutschland) GmbH (Germany); Mazda Motor Europe GmbH (Germany); Mazda Motor Italia S.p.A. (Italy); Mazda Motors of New Zealand Ltd.; Mazda Motor de Portugal Lda.; Mazda Automobiles España S.A. (Spain); Mazda Swisse S.A. (Switzerland); Mazda Sales Thailand Co., Ltd.; Mazda Motors UK Limited; Mazda Motor of America, Inc. (U.S.A.).

Principal Competitors

Toyota Motor Corporation; Nissan Motor Co., Ltd.; Honda Motor Co., Ltd.; Suzuki Motor Corporation; Mitsubishi Motors Corporation; Yamaha Motor Co., Ltd.; Fuji Heavy Industries Ltd.; General Motors Corporation; DaimlerChrysler AG; Volkswagen AG.

Further Reading

Armstrong, Larry, Keith Naughton, and Emily Thornton, "The Struggle for Mazda's Soul: Is the Carmaker Mapping Its U.S. Recovery—or Is Ford?," *Business Week,* July 21, 1997, p. 98.

Beauchamp, Marc, "A Third Miracle?," *Forbes,* December 15, 1986, pp. 108+.

Bremner, Brian, Kathleen Kerwin, and Larry Armstrong, "Will the RX-8 Put Mazda Back in the Race?," *Business Week,* July 14, 2003, p. 52.

Dawson, Chester, "Will Mazda Ever Be Anything but a Headache for Ford?," *Business Week,* June 25, 2001, pp. 88–89.

"Family Operation Ends in Toyo Kogyo Shuffle," *Automotive News,* January 30, 1978, pp. 15–16.

"A Ford Acquisition," *Business Week,* July 23, 1979, p. 72.

Horton, Cleveland, "Mazda's Drive for Full-Line Image Stalls As Automaker Retrenches," *Advertising Age,* August 30, 1993, p. 2.

"Japan's Underworked Marvel," *Economist,* July 13, 1996, pp. 66–67.

"Kenichi Yamamoto: Leading by Courageous Example," *Automotive Industries,* February 1986, pp. 46–49.

"Mazda Fine-Tunes Performance," *Nikkei Weekly,* March 8, 2004.

Rapoport, Carla, "Mazda's Bold New Global Strategy," *Fortune,* December 17, 1990, pp. 109–11.

"The Rotary Turnabout," *Forbes,* March 1, 1975, p. 46.

Schreffler, Roger, and Mack Chrysler, "Will Wankel Work Wonders? Mazda Looks to Rotary Engine to Spur Revival," *Ward's Auto World,* May 2001, pp. 67–69.

"They Too," *Economist,* March 16, 1991, p. 70.

Thornton, Emily, "Mazda Learns to Like Those Intruders," *Business Week,* September 14, 1998, p. 172.

"Toyo Kogyo Agrees to Court Settlement on Mazda Complaints," *Wall Street Journal,* February 25, 1980, p. 18.

Updike, Edith Hill, and Keith Naughton, "Ford Has a Long Haul at Mazda," *Business Week,* October 7, 1996, pp. 108–14.

"When I Was a Lad," *Economist,* December 23, 1989, p. 70.

Williams, Michael, and John Bussey, "Mazda Ponders Its Route Through a Bumpy Future," *Wall Street Journal,* September 8, 1993, p. B4.

Zaun, Todd, "Mazda Retools, As Its President Gets More Calls for a Quick Fix," *Wall Street Journal,* November 20, 2000, p. A16.

——, "Mazda's Chief Hopes Revamped RX-7 Engine Will Be Rx for Growth," *Wall Street Journal,* April 26, 2001, p. B1.

——, "Shifting Gears: Mazda Near Turnaround," *Wall Street Journal,* December 31, 2002, p. A11.

Zino, Ken, "Economies of Sale," *Road and Track,* July 1996, p. 73.

—John Simley
—updates: Susan Windisch Brown, David E. Salamie

McDonald's Corporation

McDonald's Plaza
Oak Brook, Illinois 60523-2199
U.S.A.
Telephone: (630) 623-3000
Fax: (630) 623-5004
Web site: http://www.mcdonalds.com

Public Company
Incorporated: 1955
Employees: 413,000
Sales: $17.14 billion (2003)
Stock Exchanges: New York Chicago Euronext Paris
    German Swiss
Ticker Symbol: MCD
NAIC: 722211 Limited-Service Restaurants; 533110
    Lessors of Nonfinancial Intangible Assets (Except
    Copyrighted Works)

Since its incorporation in 1955, McDonald's Corporation has not only become the world's largest quick-service restaurant organization, but has literally changed Americans' eating habits—and increasingly the habits of non-Americans as well. On an average day, more than 46 million people eat at one of the company's more than 31,000 restaurants, which are located in 119 countries on six continents. About 9,000 of the restaurants are company owned and operated; the remainder are run either by franchisees or through joint ventures with local business-people. Systemwide sales (which encompass total revenues from all three types of restaurants) totaled more than $46 billion in 2003. Nine major markets—Australia, Brazil, Canada, China, France, Germany, Japan, the United Kingdom, and the United States—account for 80 percent of the restaurants and 75 percent of overall sales. The vast majority of the company's restaurants are of the flagship McDonald's hamburger joint variety. Two other wholly owned chains, Boston Market (rotisserie chicken) and Chipotle Mexican Grill (Mexican fast casual), along with Pret A Manger (upscale prepared sandwiches), in which McDonald's owns a 33 percent stake, account for about 1,000 of the units.

Early History

In 1954 Ray Kroc, a seller of Multimixer milkshake machines, learned that brothers Richard and Maurice (Dick and Mac) McDonald were using eight of his high-tech Multimixers in their San Bernardino, California, restaurant. His curiosity was piqued, and he went to San Bernardino to take a look at the McDonalds' restaurant.

The McDonalds had been in the restaurant business since the 1930s. In 1948 they closed down a successful carhop drive-in to establish the streamlined operation Ray Kroc saw in 1954. The menu was simple: hamburgers, cheeseburgers, french fries, shakes, soft drinks, and apple pie. The carhops were eliminated to make McDonald's a self-serve operation, and there were no tables to sit at, no jukebox, and no telephone. As a result, McDonald's attracted families rather than teenagers. Perhaps the most impressive aspect of the restaurant was the efficiency with which the McDonald's workers did their jobs. Mac and Dick McDonald had taken great care in setting up their kitchen. Each worker's steps had been carefully choreographed, like an assembly line, to ensure maximum efficiency. The savings in preparation time, and the resulting increase in volume, allowed the McDonalds to lower the price of a hamburger from 30 cents to 15 cents.

Believing that the McDonald formula was a ticket to success, Kroc suggested that they franchise their restaurants throughout the country. When they hesitated to take on this additional burden, Kroc volunteered to do it for them. He returned to his home outside of Chicago with rights to set up McDonald's restaurants throughout the country, except in a handful of territories in California and Arizona already licensed by the McDonald brothers.

Kroc's first McDonald's restaurant opened in Des Plaines, Illinois, near Chicago, on April 15, 1955—the same year that Kroc incorporated his company as McDonald's Corporation. As with any new venture, Kroc encountered a number of hurdles. The first was adapting the McDonald's building design to a northern climate. A basement had to be installed to house a furnace, and adequate ventilation was difficult, as exhaust fans sucked out warm air in the winter, and cool air in the summer.

Company Perspectives:

McDonald's is the world's leading food service organization. We generate more than $40 billion in Systemwide sales. We operate over 30,000 restaurants in more than 100 countries on six continents. We have the benefits that come with scale and a strong financial position. We own one of the world's most recognized and respected brands. We have an unparalleled global infrastructure and competencies in restaurant operations, real estate, retailing, marketing and franchising. We are a leader in the area of social responsibility. We actively share our knowledge and expertise in food safety and are committed to protecting the environment for future generations. Yet, we have not achieved our growth expectations for the past several years. So, our challenge is to leverage our strengths to profitably serve more customers more ways more often.

Most frustrating of all, however, was Kroc's initial failure to reproduce the McDonalds' delicious french fries. When Kroc and his crew duplicated the brothers' method—leaving just a little peel for flavor, cutting the potatoes into shoestrings, and rinsing the strips in cold water—the fries turned into mush. After repeated telephone conversations with the McDonald brothers and several consultations with the Potato and Onion Association, Kroc pinpointed the cause of the soggy spuds. The McDonald brothers stored their potatoes outside in wire bins, and the warm California breeze dried them out and cured them, slowly turning the sugars into starch. In order to reproduce the superior taste of these potatoes, Kroc devised a system using an electric fan to dry the potatoes in a similar way. He also experimented with a blanching process. Within three months he had a french fry that was, in his opinion, slightly superior in taste to the McDonald brothers' fries.

Once the Des Plaines restaurant was operational, Kroc sought franchisees for his McDonald's chain. The first snag came quickly. In 1956 he discovered that the McDonald brothers had licensed the franchise rights for Cook County, Illinois (home of Chicago and many of its suburbs) to the Frejlack Ice Cream Company. Kroc was incensed that the McDonalds had not informed him of this arrangement. He purchased the rights back for $25,000—five times what the Frejlacks had originally paid—and pressed forward.

Kroc decided early on that it was best to first establish the restaurants and then to franchise them out, so that he could control the uniformity of the stores. Early McDonald's restaurants were situated in the suburbs. Corner lots were usually in greater demand because gas stations and shops competed for them, but Kroc preferred lots in the middle of blocks to accommodate his U-shaped parking lots. Since these lots were cheaper, Kroc could give franchisees a price break.

McDonald's grew slowly for its first three years; by 1958 there were 34 restaurants. In 1959, however, Kroc opened 67 new restaurants, bringing the total to more than 100.

Kroc had decided at the outset that McDonald's would not be a supplier to its franchisees—his background in sales warned

him that such an arrangement could lead to lower quality for the sake of higher profits. He also had determined that the company should at no time own more than 30 percent of all McDonald's restaurants. He knew, however, that his success depended upon his franchisees' success, and he was determined to help them in any way that he could.

In 1960 the McDonald's advertising campaign "Look for the Golden Arches" gave sales a big boost. Kroc believed that advertising was an investment that would in the end come back many times over, and advertising has always played a key role in the development of the McDonald's Corporation—indeed, McDonald's ads have been some of the most identifiable over the years. In 1962 McDonald's replaced its "Speedee" the hamburger man symbol with its now world-famous Golden Arches logo. A year later, the company sold its billionth hamburger and introduced Ronald McDonald, a red-haired clown with particular appeal to children.

Phenomenal Growth in the 1960s and 1970s

In the early 1960s, McDonald's really began to take off. The growth in U.S. automobile use that came with suburbanization contributed heavily to McDonald's success. In 1961 Kroc bought out the McDonald brothers for $2.7 million, aiming at making McDonald's the number one fast-food chain in the country.

In 1965 McDonald's Corporation went public. Common shares were offered at $22.50 per share; by the end of the first day's trading the price had shot up to $30. A block of 100 shares purchased for $2,250 in 1965 was worth, after 12 stock splits (increasing the number of shares to 74,360), about $1.8 million by the end of 2003. In 1985 McDonald's Corporation became one of the 30 companies that make up the Dow Jones Industrial Average.

McDonald's success in the 1960s was in large part due to the company's skillful marketing and flexible response to customer demand. In 1965 the Filet-o-Fish sandwich, billed as "the fish that catches people," was introduced in McDonald's restaurants. The new item had originally met with disapproval from Kroc, but after its successful test marketing, he eventually agreed to add it. Another item that Kroc had backed a year previously, a burger with a slice of pineapple and a slice of cheese, known as a "hulaburger," had flopped. The market was not quite ready for Kroc's taste; the hulaburger's tenure on the McDonald's menu board was short. In 1968 the now legendary Big Mac made its debut, and in 1969 McDonald's sold its five billionth hamburger. A year later, as it launched the "You Deserve a Break Today" advertising campaign, McDonald's restaurants had reached all 50 states.

In 1968 McDonald's opened its 1,000th restaurant, and Fred Turner became the company's president and chief administrative officer. Kroc became chairman and remained CEO until 1973. Turner had originally intended to open a McDonald's franchise, but when he had problems with his backers over a location, he went to work as a grillman for Kroc in 1956. As operations vice-president, Turner helped new franchisees get their stores up and running. He was constantly looking for new ways to perfect the McDonald's system, experimenting, for example, to determine the maximum number of hamburger patties one could stack in a box without squashing them and pointing out that seconds could be saved if McDonald's used buns that were presliced all the way through and were not stuck together in the package. Such attention to detail was one reason for the company's extraordinary success.

McDonald's spectacular growth continued in the 1970s. Americans were more on-the-go than ever, and fast service was a priority. In 1972 the company passed $1 billion in annual sales; by 1976, McDonald's had served 20 billion hamburgers, and systemwide sales exceeded $3 billion.

McDonald's pioneered breakfast fast food with the introduction of the Egg McMuffin in 1973 when market research indicated that a quick breakfast would be welcomed by consumers. Five years later the company added a full breakfast line to the menu, and by 1987 one-fourth of all breakfasts eaten out in the United States came from McDonald's restaurants.

Kroc was a firm believer in giving "something back into the community where you do business." In 1974 McDonald's acted upon that philosophy in an original way by opening the first

Ronald McDonald House, in Philadelphia, to provide a "home away from home" for the families of children in nearby hospitals. Twelve years after this first house opened, 100 similar Ronald McDonald Houses were in operation across the United States.

In 1975 McDonald's opened its first drive-thru window in Oklahoma City. This service gave Americans a fast, convenient way to procure a quick meal. The company's goal was to provide service in 50 seconds or less. Drive-thru sales eventually accounted for more than half of McDonald's systemwide sales. Meantime, the Happy Meal, a combo meal for children featuring a toy, was added to the menu in 1979.

Surviving the 1980s "Burger Wars"

In the late 1970s competition from other hamburger chains such as Burger King and Wendy's began to intensify. Experts believed that the fast-food industry had gotten as big as it ever would, so the companies began to battle fiercely for market share. A period of aggressive advertising campaigns and price slashing in the early 1980s became known as the "burger wars." Burger King suggested that customers "have it their way"; Wendy's offered itself as the "fresh alternative" and asked of other restaurants, "where's the beef?" But McDonald's sales and market share continued to grow. Consumers seemed to like the taste and consistency of McDonald's best.

During the 1980s McDonald's further diversified its menu to suit changing consumer tastes. Chicken McNuggets were introduced in 1983, and by the end of the year McDonald's was the second largest retailer of chicken in the world. In 1987 ready-to-eat salads were introduced to lure more health-conscious consumers. The 1980s were the fastest-paced decade yet. Efficiency, combined with an expanded menu, continued to draw customers. McDonald's, already entrenched in the suburbs, began to focus on urban centers and introduced new architectural styles. Although McDonald's restaurants no longer looked identical, the company made sure food quality and service remained constant.

Despite experts' claims that the fast-food industry was saturated, McDonald's continued to expand. The first generation raised on restaurant food had grown up. Eating out had become a habit rather than a break in the routine, and McDonald's relentless marketing continued to improve sales. Innovative promotions, such as the "when the U.S. wins, you win" giveaways during the Olympic Games in 1988, were a huge success.

In 1982 Michael R. Quinlan became president of McDonald's Corporation and Fred Turner became chairman. Quinlan, who took over as CEO in 1987, had started at McDonald's in the mailroom in 1963, and gradually worked his way up. The first McDonald's CEO to hold an M.B.A. degree, Quinlan was regarded by his colleagues as a shrewd competitor. In his first year as CEO the company opened 600 new restaurants.

McDonald's growth in the United States was mirrored by its stunning growth abroad. By 1991, 37 percent of systemwide sales came from restaurants outside the United States. McDonald's opened its first foreign restaurant in British Columbia, Canada, in 1967. By the early 1990s the company had established itself in 58 foreign countries and operated more than 3,600 restaurants outside the United States, through wholly owned subsidiaries, joint ventures, and franchise agreements. Its strongest foreign markets were Japan, Canada, Germany, Great Britain, Australia, and France.

In the mid-1980s, McDonald's, like other traditional employers of teenagers, was faced with a shortage of labor in the United States. The company met this challenge by being the first to entice retirees back into the workforce. McDonald's placed great emphasis on effective training. It opened its Hamburger University in 1961 to train franchisees and corporate decision-makers. By 1990, more than 40,000 people had received ''Bachelor of Hamburgerology'' degrees from the 80-acre Oak Brook, Illinois, facility. The corporation opened a Hamburger University in Tokyo in 1971, in Munich in 1975, and in London in 1982.

Braille menus were first introduced in 1979, and picture menus in 1988. In March 1992 Braille and picture menus were reintroduced to acknowledge the 37 million Americans with vision, speech, or hearing impairments.

Quinlan continued to experiment with new technology and to research new markets to keep McDonald's in front of its competition. Clamshell fryers, which cooked both sides of a hamburger simultaneously, were tested. New locations such as hospitals and military bases were tapped as sites for new restaurants. In response to the increase in microwave oven usage, McDonald's, whose name is the single most advertised brand name in the world, stepped up advertising and promotional expenditures stressing that its taste was superior to quick-packaged foods.

McRecycle USA began in 1990 and included a commitment to purchase at least $100 million worth of recycled products annually for use in construction, remodeling, and equipping restaurants. Chairs, table bases, table tops, eating counters, table columns, waste receptacles, corrugated cartons, packaging, and washroom tissue were all made from recycled products. McDonald's worked with the U.S. Environmental Defense Fund to develop a comprehensive solid waste reduction program. Wrapping burgers in paper rather than plastic led to a 90 percent reduction in the wrapping material waste stream.

1990s Growing Pains

It took McDonald's 33 years to open its first 10,000 restaurants—the 10,000th unit opened in April 1988. Incredibly, the company reached the 20,000-restaurant mark in only eight more years, in mid-1996. By the end of 1997 the total had surpassed 23,000—by that time McDonald's was opening 2,000 new restaurants each year—an average of one every five hours.

Much of the growth of the 1990s came outside the United States, with international units increasing from about 3,600 in 1991 to more than 11,000 by 1998. The number of countries with McDonald's outlets nearly doubled from 59 in 1991 to 114 in late 1998. In 1993 a new region was added to the empire when the first McDonald's in the Middle East opened in Tel Aviv, Israel. As the company entered new markets, it showed increasing flexibility with respect to local food preferences and customs. In Israel, for example, the first kosher McDonald's opened in a Jerusalem suburb in 1995. In Arab countries the restaurant chain used ''Halal'' menus, which complied with Islamic laws for food preparation. In 1996 McDonald's entered India for the first time, where it offered a Big Mac made with lamb called the Maharaja Mac. That same year the first McSki-Thru opened in Lindvallen, Sweden.

Overall, the company derived increasing percentages of its revenue and income from outside the United States. In 1992 about two-thirds of systemwide sales came out of U.S. McDonald's, but by 1997 that figure was down to about 51 percent. Similarly, the operating income numbers showed a reduction from about 60 percent derived from the United States in 1992 to 42.5 percent in 1997.

In the United States, where the number of units grew from 9,000 in 1991 to 12,500 in 1997—an increase of about 40 percent—the growth was perhaps excessive. Although the additional units increased market share in some markets, a number of franchisees complained that new units were cannibalizing sales from existing ones. Same-store sales for outlets open for more than one year were flat in the mid-1990s, a reflection of both the greater number of units and the mature nature of the U.S. market.

It did not help that the company made several notable blunders in the United States in the 1990s. The McLean Deluxe sandwich, which featured a 91 percent fat-free beef patty, was introduced in 1991, never really caught on, and was dropped from the menu in 1996. Several other 1990s-debuted menu items—including fried chicken, pasta, fajitas, and pizza—failed as well. The ''grown-up'' (and pricey) Arch Deluxe sandwich and the Deluxe Line were launched in 1996 in a $200 million campaign to gain the business of more adults, but were bombs. The following spring brought a 55-cent Big Mac promotion, which many customers either rejected outright or were confused by because the burgers had to be purchased with full-priced fries and a drink. The promotion embittered still more franchisees, whose complaints led to its withdrawal. In July 1997 McDonald's fired its main ad agency—Leo Burnett, a 15-year McDonald's partner—after the nostalgic ''My McDonald's'' campaign proved a failure. A seemingly weakened McDonald's was the object of a Burger King offensive when the rival fast-food maker launched the Big King sandwich, a Big Mac clone. Meanwhile, internal taste tests revealed that customers preferred the fare at Wendy's and Burger King.

In response to these difficulties, McDonald's drastically cut back on its U.S. expansion—in contrast to the 1,130 units opened in 1995, only about 400 new McDonald's were built in 1997. Plans to open hundreds of smaller restaurants in Wal-Marts and gasoline stations were abandoned because test sites did not meet targeted goals. Reacting to complaints from franchisees about poor communication with the corporation and excess bureaucracy, the head of McDonald's U.S.A. (Jack Greenberg, who had assumed the position in October 1996) reorganized the unit into five autonomous geographic divisions. The aim was to bring management and decision-making closer to franchisees and customers.

On the marketing side, McDonald's scored big in 1997 with a Teenie Beanie Baby promotion in which about 80 million of the toys/collectibles were gobbled up virtually overnight. The chain received some bad publicity, however, when it was discovered that a number of customers purchased Happy Meals just to get the toys and threw the food away. For a similar spring 1998 Teenie Beanie giveaway, the company altered the promotion to allow patrons to buy menu items other than kids' meals. McDonald's also began to benefit from a ten-year global marketing alliance signed with Disney in 1996. Initial Disney movies promoted by McDonald's included *101 Dalmatians, Flubber, Mulan, Armageddon,* and *A Bug's Life.* Perhaps the most important marketing move came in the later months of 1997 when McDonald's named BDD Needham as its new lead ad agency. Needham had been the company's agency in the 1970s and was responsible for the hugely successful "You Deserve a Break Today" campaign. Late in 1997 McDonald's launched the Needham-designed "Did Somebody Say McDonald's?" campaign, which appeared to be an improvement over its predecessors.

A Failed Turnaround: Late 1990s and Early 2000s

Following the difficulties of the early and mid-1990s, several moves in 1998 seemed to indicate a reinvigorated McDonald's. In February the company for the first time took a stake in another fast-food chain when it purchased a minority interest in the 16-unit, Colorado-based Chipotle Mexican Grill chain. The following month came the announcement that McDonald's would improve the taste of several sandwiches and introduce several new menu items; McFlurry desserts—developed by a Canadian franchisee—proved popular when launched in the United States in the summer of 1998. McDonald's that same month said that it would overhaul its food preparation system in every U.S. restaurant. The new just-in-time system, dubbed "Made for You," was in development for a number of years and aimed to deliver to customers "fresher, hotter food"; enable patrons to receive special-order sandwiches (a perk long offered by rivals Burger King and Wendy's); and allow new menu items to be more easily introduced thanks to the system's enhanced flexibility. The expensive changeover was expected to cost about $25,000 per restaurant, with McDonald's offering to pay for about half of the cost; the company planned to provide about $190 million in financial assistance to its franchisees before implementation was completed by year-end 1999.

In May 1998 Greenberg was named president and CEO of McDonald's Corporation, with Quinlan remaining chairman; at the same time Alan D. Feldman, who had joined the company only four years earlier from Pizza Hut, replaced Greenberg as president of McDonald's U.S.A.—an unusual move for a company whose executives typically were long-timers. The following month brought another first—McDonald's first job cuts— as the company said it would eliminate 525 employees from its headquarters staff, a cut of about 23 percent. In the second quarter of 1998 McDonald's took a $160 million charge in relation to the cuts. As a result, the company, for the first time since it went public in 1965, recorded a decrease in net income, from $1.64 billion in 1997 to $1.55 billion in 1998.

McDonald's followed up its investment in Chipotle with several more moves beyond the burger business. In March 1999 the company bought Aroma Café, a U.K. chain of 23 upscale coffee and sandwich shops. In July of that year McDonald's added Donatos Pizza Inc., a midwestern chain of 143 pizzerias based in Columbus, Ohio. Donatos had 1997 revenues of $120

million. Also in 1999, McDonald's 25,000th unit opened, Greenberg took on the additional post of chairman, and Jim Cantalupo was named company president. Cantalupo, who had joined the company as controller in 1974 and later became head of McDonald's International, had been vice-chairman, a position he retained. In May 2000 McDonald's completed its largest acquisition yet, buying the bankrupt Boston Market chain for $173.5 million in cash and debt. At the time, there were more than 850 Boston Market outlets, which specialized in home-style meals, with rotisserie chicken the lead menu item. Revenue at Boston Market during 1999 totaled $670 million. McDonald's rounded out its acquisition spree in early 2001 by buying a 33 percent stake in Pret A Manger, an upscale urban-based chain specializing in ready-to-eat sandwiches made on the premises. There were more than 110 Pret shops in the United Kingdom and several more in New York City. Also during 2001, McDonald's sold off Aroma Café and took its McDonald's Japan affiliate public, selling a minority stake through an initial public offering.

As it was exploring new avenues of growth, however, McDonald's core hamburger chain had become plagued by problems. Most prominently, the Made for You system backfired. Although many franchisees believed that it succeeded in improving the quality of the food, it also increased service times and proved labor-intensive. Some franchisees also complained that the actual cost of implementing the system ran much higher than the corporation had estimated, a charge that McDonald's contested. In any case, there was no question that Made for You failed to reverse the chain's sluggish sales. Growth in sales at stores open more than a year (known as same-store sales) fell in both 2000 and 2001. Late in 2001 the company launched a restructuring involving the elimination of about 850 positions, 700 of which were in the United States, and some store closings.

There were further black eyes as well. McDonald's was sued in 2001 after it was revealed that for flavoring purposes a small amount of beef extract was being added to the vegetable oil used to cook the french fries. The company had cooked its fries in beef tallow until 1990, when it began claiming in ads that it used 100 percent vegetable oil. McDonald's soon apologized for any "confusion" that had been caused by its use of the beef flavoring, and in mid-2002 it reached a settlement in the litigation, agreeing to donate $10 million to Hindu, vegetarian, and other affected groups. Also in 2001, further embarrassment came when 51 people were charged with conspiring to rig McDonald's game promotions over the course of several years. It was revealed that $24 million of winning McDonald's game tickets had been stolen as part of the scam. McDonald's was not implicated in the scheme, which centered on a worker at an outside company that had administered the promotions.

McDonald's also had to increasingly battle its public image as a purveyor of fatty, unhealthful food. Consumers began filing lawsuits contending that years of eating at McDonald's had made them overweight. McDonald's responded by introducing low-calorie menu items and switching to a more healthful cooking oil for its french fries. McDonald's franchises overseas became a favorite target of people and groups expressing anti-American and/or antiglobalization sentiments. In August 1999 a group of protesters led by farmer José Bové destroyed a half-built McDonald's restaurant in Millau, France. In 2002 Bové, who gained fame from the incident, served a three-month jail sentence for the act, which he said was in protest against U.S. trade protectionism. McDonald's was also one of three multinational corporations (along with Starbucks Corporation and Nike, Inc.) whose outlets in Seattle were attacked in late 1999 by some of the more aggressive protesters against a World Trade Organization (WTO) meeting taking place there. In the early 2000s McDonald's pulled out of several countries, including Bolivia and two Middle Eastern nations, at least in part because of the negative regard with which the brand was held in some areas.

Early in 2002 Cantalupo retired after 28 years of service. Sales remained lackluster that year, and in October the company attempted to revive U.S. sales through the introduction of a low-cost Dollar Menu. In December 2002, after this latest initiative to reignite sales growth failed—and also after profits fell in seven of the previous eight quarters—Greenberg announced that he would resign at the end of the year. Cantalupo came out of retirement to become chairman and CEO at the beginning of 2003.

Launching of Revitalization Plan Under New Leadership in 2003

Cantalupo started his tenure by announcing a major restructuring that involved the closure of more than 700 restaurants (mostly in the United States and Japan), the elimination of 600 jobs, and charges of $853 million. The charges resulted in a fourth-quarter 2002 loss of $343.8 million—the first quarterly loss in McDonald's 38 years as a public company. The new CEO also shifted away from the company's traditional reliance on growth through the opening of new units to a focus on gaining more sales from existing units. To that end, several new menu items were successfully launched, including entree salads, McGriddles breakfast sandwiches (which used pancakes in place of bread), and white-meat Chicken McNuggets. Some outlets began test-marketing fruits and vegetables as Happy Meal options. Backing up the new products was the launch in September 2003 of an MTV-style advertising campaign featuring the new tag line, "I'm lovin' it." This was the first global campaign in McDonald's history, as the new slogan was to be used in advertising in more than 100 countries. It also proved to be the first truly successful ad campaign in years; sales began rebounding, helped also by improvements in service. In December 2003, for instance, same-store sales increased 7.3 percent. Same-store sales rose 2.4 percent for the entire year, after falling 2.1 percent in 2002.

In December 2003 McDonald's announced that it would further its focus on its core hamburger business by downsizing its other ventures. The company said that it would sell Donatos back to that chain's founder. In addition, it would discontinue development of non-McDonald's brands outside of the United States. This included Boston Market outlets in Canada and Australia and Donatos units in Germany. McDonald's kept its minority investment in Pret A Manger, but McDonald's Japan was slated to close its Pret units there. These moves would enable the company to concentrate its international efforts on the McDonald's chain, while reducing the non-hamburger brands in the United States to Chipotle and Boston Market, both of which were operating in the black.

McDonald's continued to curtail store openings in 2004 and to concentrate on building business at existing restaurants. Much of the more than $1.5 billion budgeted for capital expenditures in 2004 was slated to be used to remodel existing restaurants. McDonald's also aimed to pay down debt by $400 million to $700 million and to return approximately $1 billion to shareholders through dividends and share repurchases. Cantalupo also set several long-term goals, such as sustaining annual systemwide sales and revenue growth rates of 3 to 5 percent. In a move to both simplify the menu and make its offerings less fattening, McDonald's announced in March 2004 that it would phase out Super Size french fries and soft drinks by the end of the year.

Principal Subsidiaries

McDonald's Deutschland, Inc.; McDonald's Restaurant Operations Inc.; McG Development Co.; Chipotle Mexican Grill, Inc.; Boston Market Corporation; McDonald's Franchise GmbH (Austria); McDonald's Australia Limited; McDonald's France, S.A.; MDC Inmobiliaria de Mexico S.A. de C.V.; McDonald's Restaurants Pte., Ltd. (Singapore); Restaurantes McDonald's S.A. (Spain); McKim Company Ltd. (South Korea); Shin Mac Company Ltd. (South Korea); McDonald's Nederland B.V. (Netherlands); Moscow-McDonald's (Canada); McDonald's Restaurants Limited (U.K.).

Principal Competitors

Burger King Corporation; Wendy's International, Inc.; CKE Restaurants, Inc.; Jack in the Box Inc.; Sonic Corporation; Checkers Drive-In Restaurants, Inc.; White Castle System, Inc.; Whataburger, Inc.; YUM! Brands, Inc.; Doctor's Associates Inc.

Further Reading

Alexander, Delroy, "McDonald's Chief to End Rocky Tenure Years Early," *Chicago Tribune,* December 6, 2002.
——, "McDonald's Focus Flips Back to Fast," *Chicago Tribune,* March 16, 2003.
Arndt, Michael, "Did Somebody Say McBurrito?," *Business Week,* April 10, 2000, pp. 166, 170.
Bigness, Jon, "Getting McDonald's Sizzling Again," *Chicago Tribune,* August 30, 1998.
Branch, Shelly, "McDonald's Strikes Out with Grownups," *Fortune,* November 11, 1996, pp. 157+.
——, "What's Eating McDonald's?," *Fortune,* October 13, 1997, pp. 122+.
Burns, Greg, "Fast-Food Fight," *Business Week,* June 2, 1997, pp. 34–36.
Byrne, Harlan S., "Welcome to McWorld," *Barron's,* August 29, 1994, pp. 25–28.
Canedy, Dana, "McDonald's Burger War Salvo," *New York Times,* June 20, 1998, pp. D1, D15.
Chiem, Phat X, "Putting the Sizzle Back in McDonald's," *Chicago Tribune,* April 16, 2000.
Cohon, George, with David Macfarlane, *To Russia with Fries,* Toronto: M & S, 1997.
David, Grainger, "Can McDonald's Cook Again?," *Fortune,* April 14, 2003, pp. 120–24+.
Donlon, J.P., "Quinlan Fries Harder," *Chief Executive,* January/February 1998, pp. 45–49.
Forster, Julie, "Thinking Outside the Burger Box," *Business Week,* September 16, 2002, pp. 66–67.

Gibson, Richard, "McDonald's Makes Changes in Top Management," *Wall Street Journal,* May 1, 1998, pp. A3, A4.

——, "Some Franchisees Say Moves by McDonald's Hurt Their Operations," *Wall Street Journal,* April 17, 1996, pp. A1, A10.

——, "Worried McDonald's Plans Dramatic Shifts and Big Price Cuts," *Wall Street Journal,* February 26, 1997, pp. A1, A6.

Gibson, Richard, and Bruce Orwell, "New Mission for Mickey Mouse, Mickey D," *Wall Street Journal,* March 5, 1998, pp. B1, B5.

Gogoi, Pallavi, and Michael Arndt, "Hamburger Hell," *Business Week,* March 3, 2003, pp. 104–06, 108.

Kroc, Ray, with Robert Anderson, *Grinding It Out: The Making of McDonald's,* Chicago: H. Regnery, 1977.

Leonhardt, David, "McDonald's: Can It Regain Its Golden Touch?," *Business Week,* March 9, 1998, pp. 70–74, 76–77.

Leonhardt, David, and Ann Therese Palmer, "Getting Off Their McButts," *Business Week,* February 22, 1999, pp. 84, 88.

Leung, Shirley, "McDonald's Makeover," *Wall Street Journal,* January 18, 2004, pp. B1, B10.

Leung, Shirley, and Kevin Helliker, "As McDonald's Braces for Loss, CEO Has a Plan," *Wall Street Journal,* January 20, 2003, p. B1.

Love, John F., *McDonald's: Behind the Arches,* rev. ed., New York: Bantam, 1995.

Machan, Dyan, "Polishing the Golden Arches," *Forbes,* June 15, 1998, pp. 42–43.

Papiernik, Richard L., "Mac Attack?," *Financial World,* April 12, 1994, pp. 28–30.

Racanelli, Vito J., "Recipe for Growth," *Barron's,* December 11, 2000, pp. 19–20.

Sachdev, Ameet, and Jim Kirk, "No Retreat for Greenberg," *Chicago Tribune,* August 26, 2001.

Sellers, Patricia, "McDonald's Starts Over," *Fortune,* June 22, 1998, pp. 34, 36.

Serwer, Andrew E., "McDonald's Conquers the World," *Fortune,* October 17, 1994, pp. 103+.

Stires, David, "Fallen Arches," *Fortune,* April 29, 2002, pp. 74–76.

Watson, James L., ed., *Golden Arches East: McDonald's in East Asia,* Stanford: Stanford University Press, 1997.

—Tom Tucker
—updates: Anne C. Hughes, David E. Salamie

McJunkin Corporation

835 Hillcrest Drive
Charleston, West Virginia 25311
U.S.A.
Telephone: (304) 348-5211
Fax: (304) 348-4922
Web site: http://www.mcjunkin.com

Private Company
Incorporated: 1951
Employees: 1,600
Sales: $830 million (2002 est.)
NAIC: 421840 Industrial Supplies Wholesalers

Located in Charleston, West Virginia, McJunkin Corporation is a major distributor of carbon steel; stainless steel and corrosion-resistant pipe, valves and fittings; instrumentation and controls; tubular goods and other drilling supplies; mining supplies; and electrical supplies. Originally established to serve the oil and gas industry, the privately held company now offers 70,000 products to a range of industries, including automotive, chemical and petrochemical, construction, food and beverage processing, mining, pharmaceutical, power companies, pulp and paper, and refining processes. In addition, McJunkin offers its customers value-added solutions such as storeroom management; systems engineering; the rebuilding, cleaning and actuation of valves; project services to determine the optimal amount of materials needed for a job; integrated supply services; and portable material distribution facilities for use in shutting down plants or other special projects. McJunkin maintains 100 locations in 28 states and operates in Mexico and Latin America through the joint venture Trottner-McJunkin. McJunkin is still owned by the founding families and is now headed by a third generation.

Forming the Company in 1921

Brothers-in-law Jerry McJunkin and H. Bernard Wehrle established McJunkin Supply Co. in Charleston, West Virginia, in 1921 to serve the oil and gas industry in the Appalachian Mountains. They set up shop in a corner of the town's Arcade building. After two years, another brother-in-law, George Her-

scher, joined the business. According to company lore, the founders were enamored with the color red, constantly wearing red ties, painting the fenders of company vehicles fire-engine red, and going so far as to require the two women working for the company to have red hair. One, Lillian Mairs, was a natural blonde, who had to dye her hair red to keep her job.

Through the prosperous 1920s, McJunkin thrived and expanded its operations. A branch was opened in Paintsville, Kentucky, in 1924, the same year that sales topped the $1 million mark. By the end of the decade the company added a machine shop and blacksmith shop. But with the stock market crash in October 1929 the good times came to an end, the country was soon mired in the Great Depression, and like most businesses McJunkin faced some difficult years.

Sales dipped to $700,000 by 1934, but McJunkin was fortunate that Union Carbide came into being in Clendenin, West Virginia. McJunkin expanded into the chemicals industry and Union Carbide became a major customer. With business once again on an upswing, McJunkin was able to grow sales to $1.2 million by 1938, and by the end of the decade, the company was able to add branches in Hamlin and Grantsville, West Virginia, and Allen, Kentucky. McJunkin decided to share its prosperity with its employees. In 1941 the company made the first contribution to what would become one of the most generous profit-sharing plans in the United States.

Second Generation Becoming Involved in the Postwar Years

Like many companies during World War II, McJunkin did what it could to support the war effort. The company's shops were converted to turn out amphibious vehicles as well as 500-pound bomb casings. With the close of the war, McJunkin grew at an even greater pace, spurred by a booming economy. A second generation also became involved in the running of the business. In 1946 Henry D. Wehrle, Jr., went to work for the company, after serving in the U.S. Navy following his 1943 graduation from Princeton University, in New Jersey. He would later be joined by his brother, Russell Wehrle. The company's first industrial supply branch opened in Marietta, Ohio, in 1947, a move that also marked the first time that McJunkin expanded beyond the Appalachian region of West Virginia and Kentucky. By the end of the decade the company also had built a new facility in Charleston, a combination headquarters and warehouse, allowing McJunkin to escape the Arcade building, which had been shabby some 30 years earlier when the company was launched.

The 1950s and 1960s brought further changes to the business. In March 1951, McJunkin Supply Company became McJunkin Corporation. The following year, branches were opened in Columbus, Ohio; Louisville, Kentucky; and Atlanta, Georgia, bringing the total number of branches to 12. In addition to other greenfield operations the company would open in the ensuing years, McJunkin also expanded through acquisitions. In 1957, it moved into the Pittsburgh market by purchasing Chandler-Boyd Supply. Additional sales from this operation helped McJunkin to reach $26 million in total revenues. In 1964 there was a turnover in leadership when Henry D. Wehrle, Jr., became president and CEO of the company. A year later the company opened a branch in Beaumont, Texas, to serve the state's all-important oil and gas industry. Now operating 18 branches, the company enjoyed a significant growth spurt to close out the 1960s. Branches were opened in Philadelphia and Chicago, and McJunkin became involved in electrical supplies by acquiring Charleston Electrical Supply. By the close of the decade, the company boasted 29 branches located in 18 states.

At the start of the 1970s annual sales exceeded the $75 million level and the company had 900 employees. During the 1970s McJunkin became increasingly committed to the refining and petrochemical industries. To support this sector new branches were opened in the Gulf Coast Region and on the West Coast. During this period, McJunkin also moved into the mining sector by designing, developing, and manufacturing light products suitable for mining purposes. The company also looked overseas for the first time. In 1976 McJunkin opened a sales office in Brussels, Belgium.

Because of McJunkin's dependence on oil and gas customers, a major slump in the oil and gas industries in the 1980s had an adverse impact on the company's fortunes for much of the decade. As a result McJunkin had to cut staff and implement other cost-saving initiatives. But by the late 1980s the company was once again looking to expand. In 1987 McJunkin acquired Grant Supply Co., adding 11 branches in the Southwest. Also of note, in 1989 the company merged its oil and gas division with Appalachian Pipe, creating McJunkin Appalachian Supply Co. Despite a difficult stretch, by the end of the 1980s McJunkin, with estimated annual sales in the $500 million range, cracked the *Forbes* list of the 400 largest privately owned companies in the United States. The decade also was marked by the death of Russell Wehrle in 1987, an event that led to the installation of a

third generation into leadership positions. W.B. "Bernie" Wehrle III became president of the company and his cousin Michael Wehrle was named chief financial officer.

McJunkin grew on a number of fronts during the 1990s. In January 1992 it made a major acquisition, buying Republic Supply Co. of California. Republic was older than McJunkin, formed in 1910. It distributed industrial supplies, valves, pipe and fittings, and oilfield specialty items to oil, energy, and natural resources companies. Republic generated $96 million in annual sales in 1988, the last public estimate before it was brought together with two other companies in 1990 to form Earle M. Jorgensen Co. Reportedly, due to difficult economic conditions, Jorgensen concluded that Republic, the smallest of three operations, was expendable, and its sale would help to pay down debt incurred in the buyout. For McJunkin, picking up Republic added 18 centers, of which 14 were located in California and 15 were new markets. Existing McJunkin branches in Bakersfield, Los Angeles, and San Francisco were incorporated into Republic operations, which possessed larger warehouses.

McJunkin and Rival Firm Joining Forces in 1994

McJunkin also achieved growth in the 1990s by way of joint ventures. In 1994 the company joined forces with rival Charleston distributor Cameron & Barkley Company to form McJunkin-Cambar. The new company distributed electrical and electronic products and industrial mill supplies, the goal being to pursue markets where the parent companies were not operating. In addition, McJunkin and Cameron & Barkley established a distributor consortium, International Supply Consortium, dedicated to selling integrated supply and systems contracts for MRO (maintenance, repair, and operations) and construction products. The venture was soon supplemented by the addition of Bearings, Inc., adding more than 300 locations. In 1998 McJunkin established another 50-50 joint venture, this time to do business south of the U.S. border. McJunkin's partner was Mexico City-based Casa Trottner, which led a group of Mexican partners. The resulting company, Trottner-McJunkin SA de CV, would help McJunkin on more than one level. Finding a cultural partner like Trottner allowed McJunkin to better serve customers with Mexican and Latin American operations. Moreover, the parent companies looked to combine their complementary inventories and reputations to enter new Latin American markets through the joint venture, rather than going it alone. In addition to spurring growth through partnerships during the 1990s, McJunkin also added automated products to its slate, creating McJunkin Process Automation Controls to handle the business.

The pipe and valve business entered a period of consolidation, with larger distributors swallowing smaller operations. In order to keep pace, McJunkin completed several acquisitions in the early years of the new century, four in 2001 alone. In that year, McJunkin in alliance with Cameron & Barkley and the McJunkin-Cambar joint venture acquired 18 Fairmont Supply Co. sites. For its share, McJunkin added locations in the eastern and southwestern United States. Also in 2001 McJunkin acquired Toledo, Ohio-based M.P. Wilkins Supply Co., the leading PVF (pipes, valves, and fittings) distributor in northwest Ohio with more than 50 years in business. As part of the deal, the Wilkins Supply management team agreed to stay on to run the company, which would now be known as "Wilkins-

Key Dates:

1921: The company is founded as McJunkin Supply Company.
1941: A profit-sharing program is launched.
1951: The company's name is changed to McJunkin Corporation
1964: Henry D. Wehrle, Jr., is named CEO.
1992: Republic Supply Co. is acquired.
2002: Michael Wehrle is named chairman, and Bernie Wehrle is named CEO.

McJunkin Supply, a Division of McJunkin Corporation.'' Furthermore, in 2001 McJunkin augmented its Controls Division (the devices and instruments that remotely activate and monitor the performance of valves used by oil refineries, chemical plants, and paper mills), by purchasing virtually all of the assets of Automation & Controls Specialists Inc., a Dublin, California, company that served northern California and western Nevada. Finally, in 2001 McJunkin acquired Joliet Valves Incorporated, based in Minooka, Illinois. Joliet Valves was founded in 1971 and had evolved into a leading PVF distributor in the Midwest and Great Plains markets. The company brought with it 17 locations in Illinois, Indiana, Iowa, Minnesota, and North Dakota. As had been the case with Wilkins Supply, the management team would stay on after closing. The business would operate under the name ''Joliet Valves-McJunkin, a Division of McJunkin Corporation.''

McJunkin underwent some management changes in 2002. In May of that year Henry B. Wehrle, Jr., essentially retired, although he retained the title of chairman of the board emeritus. He was replaced as chairman by his nephew, Michael Wehrle, who also served as senior vice-president and chief financial officer. His son, Bernie Wehrle, in the meantime, was re-elected as president and chief executive officer. Also of note in 2002, McJunkin bought out its Mexican partner to acquire a 100 percent interest in Trottner McJunkin Venezuela. In addition, McJunkin sold its interest in McJunkin-Cambar to its joint venture partner Cameron & Barkley, which in the years since the business was launched had been purchased by Hagemeyer North America. Because of its acquisitions, Hagemeyer had emerged as a competitor to its partially owned subsidiary. It made sense to both parties that McJunkin sell out to Hagemeyer and allow the joint venture, renamed Hagemeyer/CamBar, to continue in business with a single corporate parent. By all accounts, the split was amicable and integrated contracts were fulfilled.

In 2003 McJunkin completed a pair of acquisitions. First, it bought Valvax, Corp., a Cincinnati-based valve products distributor and fabricator, focusing on the chemical process, food, HVAC, pharmaceutical, power, and pulp and paper industries. Valvax had offices in Columbia, Ohio; Charleston, West Virginia; Evansville and Indianapolis, Indiana; and Pittsburgh, Pennsylvania. The addition of Valvax fortified McJunkin's ability to provide a wide range of valve solutions to its customers. Several weeks later, McJunkin reached another agreement, this time to purchase virtually all of the assets of Indianapolis-based Cigma, LLC, a major provider of industrial pipe, pipe fittings, meters, regulators, valves, and related products to the natural gas industry. Cigma also brought with it sales offices in the Cincinnati area and Kansas City. The addition of Cigma strengthened McJunkin's growing gas products segment.

After more than 80 years in business, McJunkin was generating in excess of $800 million in annual sales. With a large number of descendants from the founding families involved at all levels of the organization, the company was positioned to remain a private, family-run company for the foreseeable future, one that was likely to enjoy continued growth.

Principal Subsidiaries

McJunkin-Appalachian; McJunkin Controls; McA Target Oil Tools.

Principal Competitors

American Cast Iron Pipe Company; Cooper Cameron Corporation; Tyco International Ltd.

Further Reading

Haflich, Frank, ''Jorgensen Selling Republic,'' *American Metal Market,* January 9, 1992, p. 1.

O'Connor, Marjie, ''McJunkin and Mexican Firm Form Group for Latin America Market,'' *Supply House Times,* December 1997, p. 25.

''A Proud Past and a Solid Future,'' *The Piper – A Newsletter for the McJunkin Employees,* September/October 1999.

Schweizer, John, ''Eight Decades of Growth and Leadership Put McJunkin in PVF Hall of Fame,'' *Wholesaler,* May 2003.

Stadelman, Chris, ''Always in the Family,'' *Charleston Daily Mail,* February 20, 1996, p. 1D.

—Ed Dinger

MDC Partners Inc.

45 Hazelton Avenue
Toronto, Ontario M5R 2E3
Canada
Telephone: (416) 960-9000
Toll Free: (800) 387-0825
Fax: (416) 960-9555
Web site: http://www.mdccorp.com

Public Company
Incorporated: 1980
Employees: 4,700
Sales: $312.71 million (2003)
Stock Exchanges: Toronto
Ticker Symbol: MDZA
NAIC: 541990 All Other Professional, Scientific and
Technical Services

MDC Partners Inc. is a leading marketing communications firm that owns interests in roughly 20 marketing agencies. MDC operates more than 30 offices, serving high-profile clients such as AOL, Sprint, Xerox, and Purina. The company generally acquires between 51 percent and 80 percent of advertising agencies, giving each agency control over the day-to-day operation of its business.

Origins

The history of MDC was the story of the entrepreneurial ventures and diverse investments made by Miles Nadal, MDC's founder, chairman, chief executive officer, and president. Nadal exerted comprehensive influence over the development of MDC, guiding the company through a divergent corporate life that saw a small photography business develop into a leader in the secure transaction business before becoming an entity charged with overseeing dozens of loosely affiliated marketing agencies. MDC, as it existed in the early 21st century, represented the former communications and marketing division of MDC Communications Corp., a company that garnered the bulk of its revenues from the secure transaction business for most of the 1990s. The individual behind the various incarnations of the MDC enterprise was Nadal, who started his maturation into a multimillionaire in 1980, when he formed a photography business while in his early 20s.

Nadal joined Canada's wealthy elite by turning his photography business into a leader in the secure transaction business, a rise that did not begin until the mid-1990s. During the mid-1990s, Nadal's company was operating as MDC Communications Corporation, which was divided into two divisions: secure transaction products and communications and marketing services. The secure transaction products division recorded exponential growth during the second half of the 1990s, increasing its sales from CAD 39 million in 1995 to CAD 361 million by 1998. The division, which produced products such as checks, credit and debit cards, airline and event tickets, and postal stamps, achieved its revenue growth in large part through acquisitions, although the company recorded substantial internal growth, particularly in its check-producing business. In 1996, MDC acquired Canadian check producer Davis + Henderson, which boasted a 40 percent share of the country's market. During the ensuing two years, the company doubled Davis + Henderson's revenues and its market share. MDC's secure transaction division also made other ground during the mid-1990s, entering the global card services business in 1996 with the acquisition of an Australian company named Placard Security Pty Ltd. The following year, the company acquired a Canadian company, Bicybec Ltee, and the card-production unit belonging to Canadian Imperial Bank of Commerce. Further expansion of MDC's secure transaction business occurred in 1996, when the company acquired Data Imaging, an electronic printing and mail service bureau catering to financial institutions and the retail industry.

The growth of MDC's secure transaction business was complemented by strides achieved in the company's other business segment, its communications and marketing services division. While MDC's secure transaction division increased its revenue volume, the company's communications and marketing services division was recording growth as well, eclipsing the CAD 100 million mark in 1998, when the division was renamed Maxxcom Inc. The name change was significant, signaling Nadal's intention to spin the division off as a separate, publicly traded company in the near future. The division, which recorded a CAD 35 million increase in sales to slip past CAD 100 million in sales in 1998, had been built up in large part in Canada by this point. Nadal had purchased roughly a dozen Canadian marketing companies to give the division its foundation. The exceptions to the native profile of the division arrived in 1998, and they were telling additions. Although his plans were not publicly broadcast by 1998, Nadal intended to create a network of advertising agencies and marketing companies with a global reach. He began to aim toward this goal in earnest in 1998, and he directed his efforts toward the United States.

Entering the United States in 1998

MDC's foray into the United States reflected Nadal's desire to build a global competitor in the advertising and marketing industry. The company completed its first U.S. acquisition in May 1998, when it purchased a Portland, Oregon-based Internet marketing firm named CyberSight. MDC also acquired Source Marketing, a Westport, Connecticut-based sales promotion firm. The most significant acquisition of the year was the company's investment in a New York City-based consumer agency named Margeotes/Fertitta & Partners (MFP). MFP's clients included MediaOne, United Distillers & Vintners, and Hearst Corp. The acquisition represented MDC's foundation for its aggressive expansion into U.S. marketing communications.

The investment in MFP was a model of Nadal's acquisition strategy in the United States. Although MDC did not disclose the amount of the investment, industry observers estimated the company spent between $25 million and $35 million for an 80 percent stake in MFP. In the years ahead, MDC typically purchased between 51 percent and 80 percent of an acquisition target. Once its investment was made, the company left the day-to-day operation of the acquired agency to the firm's executives, who generally retained a stake in their business's profitability. Nadal's hands-off approach created a loose and mostly autonomous collection of marketing firms, a federation of agencies that occasionally referred clients to each other but otherwise operated independently. MDC, as Maxxcom's owner, represented what *ADWEEK,* in the trade publication's March 22, 2004 issue, referred to as an "antiholding company," an arrangement that promoted creativity and encouraged an entrepreneurial spirit throughout the organization. "Large holding companies go at it in a backwards manner," an industry analyst remarked in a March 22, 2004 interview with *ADWEEK*. "They buy a company and focus on cost cutting. Miles [Nadal] buys a company and focuses on expanding revenue."

Nadal's partnership model appealed not only to industry pundits, but also to the management of acquisition candidates.

Agency owners generally readily agreed to Nadal's solicitations, attracted by the independence they would retain and the access to financial resources they would gain by affiliating themselves with MDC's Maxxcom. In 1999, when MDC changed its name from MDC Communications Corp. to MDC Corporation Inc., Nadal completed his next major U.S. acquisition. In April, he paid an estimated $19 million for an 80 percent stake in Colle & McVoy Inc. (the remaining percentage was acquired later). Founded in 1935, Minnesota-based Colle & McVoy provided advertising, public relations, market research, and other services to clients such as 3M Co., Caterpillar, and Winnebago. The reaction of Jim Bergeson, Colle & McVoy's chairman and chief executive officer, typified the response of executives whose agencies joined Maxxcom's fold. "It was appealing to us from a standpoint that MDC is truly a holding company," Bergeson explained in an April 1, 1999 interview with *Business Marketing.* "They don't want to run our business on a day-to-day basis. They're very hands-off. Their model of perpetual partnership is unique in the industry. It's a much more appealing way to get access to capital that we need to grow our business."

As MDC concluded its second decade of existence, its Maxxcom division was shaping into the company's most valuable asset, although the company continued to generate the majority of its revenue from its secure transaction division. The acquisition of Colle & McVoy was one of seven acquisitions completed by Maxxcom in 1999, helping the division to more than double its revenue volume during the year to CAD 214 million. The gap separating the two divisions' revenue totals promised to narrow in the near future, as Nadal placed increasing emphasis on acquiring marketing and communications companies. "We will look in Europe," Nadal said in an April 1, 1999 interview with *Business Marketing,* referring to the company's search for acquisition candidates in the marketing field. "We will look in Asia. We will look in Latin America. We will look in Eastern Europe."

Nadal's expansionist mood reflected the importance he was placing on Maxxcom's role within MDC. The communications and marketing division was driving the company's revenue growth at the start of the new decade. MDC surpassed CAD 1 billion in sales for the first time in its history in 2000, a year that also marked the first time the company generated more revenue from communications and marketing services than from secure transactions. For the year, Maxxcom recorded CAD 605 million in sales, while the secure transaction division posted CAD 561 million in sales. During the year, Maxxcom acquired nine companies, most notably a London, England-based company named Interfocus Network Limited. The year's most significant event occurred in March, when Maxxcom completed its initial public offering (IPO) of stock, raising CAD 62.4 million from the offering. After the IPO, MDC remained Maxxcom's majority owner, retaining a 76 percent interest in the company.

Restructuring in 2001 Increasing the Role of Marketing Communications

MDC was beset by difficulties in the wake of Maxxcom's IPO. Recessive economic conditions caused a slowdown in the advertising, marketing, and communications sector throughout North America. Further, the company was hobbled by more

Key Dates:

1980: Miles Nadal starts a photography business, the fore-runner to MDC.
1998: MDC's communications and marketing services division is renamed Maxxcom; Maxxcom begins acquiring marketing agencies in the United States.
1999: Maxxcom acquires Colle & McVoy Inc.
2000: Maxxcom completes its initial public offering of stock.
2001: Maxxcom acquires a 49 percent interest in Crispin Porter + Bogusky.
2003: MDC returns Maxxcom to the private sector.
2004: MDC acquires stakes in Kirshenbaum Bond + Partners and Cliff Freeman and Partners.

than $500 million in debt, a consequence of its aggressive acquisition campaign. Nadal stopped his acquisition activities in the fall of 2001 and initiated a companywide restructuring program that greatly reduced MDC's involvement in the secure transaction industry, but before he retrenched his acquisition campaign, several significant investments were made. During the first half of 2001, Maxxcom acquired a majority interest in Grange Advertising, ranked as one of the leading five business-to-business agencies in the United Kingdom. Maxxcom also invested between $10 million and $15 million for a 49 percent interest in a well-known, Miami, Florida-based advertising agency named Crispin Porter + Bogusky (CP + B).

Nadal began to restructure MDC in September 2001, when the company's stock plunged to below CAD 2 per share. As part of the restructuring efforts, MDC's check-printing businesses were divested, greatly reducing the revenue obtained from its secure transaction division. Another aspect of the restructuring program involved the privatization of Maxxcom, a process completed in July 2003, when MDC acquired all the Maxxcom stock it did not already own. By the end of 2003, the company was ready to begin building again, with Nadal announcing that he was prepared to invest $100 million in the advertising business. The promise to expand was fulfilled in early 2004, when the company, which adopted the name MDC Partners Inc. in January 2004, completed several high-profile acquisitions.

The investments completed in 2004 greatly expanded the awareness of MDC in the United States, leading Nadal to comment in a March 22, 2004 interview with *ADWEEK* that MDC "took 24 years to build and six months to get recognized." After several months of negotiations, MDC spent between $50 million and $75 million for a 60 percent interest in Kirshenbaum Bond + Partners (KB + P), a firm that an MDC

executive referred to as "one of the two best independent agencies of significant size left in America," as quoted in the February 2, 2004 issue of *ADWEEK.* The New York City-based agency claimed more than $500 million in billings and nearly $50 million in annual revenue, serving clients such as Target Stores, Snapple, and Hennessey. While the deal with KB + P was being concluded, Nadal was in the midst of negotiations with another high-profile agency, Cliff Freeman and Partners. MDC spent between $3 million and $5 million for a 20 percent stake in Cliff Freeman, completing the deal in March 2004.

By the spring of 2004, MDC's prospects were far brighter than two years earlier. The company's stock value had increased significantly, trading around CAD 20 per share in April. Additional investments were expected in the future, as Nadal sought to fulfill his pledge of devoting $100 million to fuel MDC's growth. In the March 22, 2004 issue of *ADWEEK,* a research analyst expressed his confidence in MDC enjoying a successful future. "The Procter & Gambles and DaimlerChryslers of the world are always going to want and need a global network like the big guys," the analyst said. "There is plenty of business for MDC to win on a slightly smaller scale, and that's where they are focused right now."

Principal Subsidiaries

Maxxcom, Inc.

Principal Competitors

Omnicom Group Inc.; Havas; American Banknote Corporation.

Further Reading

Callahan, Sean, "Canadian Firm Builds Stable of Agencies," *Business Marketing,* April 1, 1999, p. 3.
Cardona, Mercedes M., "Margeotes Goes North to Find Buyer," *Advertising Age,* August 10, 1998, p. 1.
Dini, Justin, "Margeotes Sells to MDC," *ADWEEK Eastern Edition,* August 10, 1998, p. 2.
Koelln, Georgann, "Communications Firms Based in Minneapolis, Toronto to Merge," *Knight Ridder/Tribune Business,* March 10, 1999.
Levy, Melissa, "Toronto Firm to Acquire 80 Percent of Colle & McVoy," *Star Tribune,* March 10, 1999, p. 3D.
" 'Who Is This Guy?,' " *Forbes,* February 16, 2004, p. 108.
Zammit, Deanna, "A Little-League Holding Co. Gets a Bigger Profile," *ADWEEK,* March 22, 2004, p. 16.
——, "MDC Acquires Majority Stake in Kirshenbaum," *ADWEEK Eastern Edition,* January 29, 2004, p. 5.
——, "With KB&P Bought, MDC Could Soon Turn to Startups," *ADWEEK,* February 2, 2004, p. 12.

—Jeffrey L. Covell

Microsoft®

Microsoft Corporation

1 Microsoft Way
Redmond, Washington 98052-6399
U.S.A.
Telephone: (425) 882-8080
Fax: (425) 936-7329
Web site: http://www.microsoft.com

Public Company
Incorporated: 1981 as Microsoft, Inc.
Employees: 56,104
Sales: $32.19 billion (2003)
Stock Exchanges: NASDAQ
Ticker Symbol: MSFT
NAIC: 511210 Software Publishers; 511130 Book
Publishers; 334111 Electronic Computer
Manufacturing; 334119 Other Computer Peripheral
Equipment Manufacturing; 423990 All Other Durable
Goods Merchant Wholesalers; 443120 Computer and
Software Stores; 551112 Offices of Other Holding
Companies; 541613 Marketing Consulting Services;
541618 Other Management Consulting Services

With annual revenues of more than $32 billion, Microsoft Corporation is more than the largest software company in the world: it is a cultural phenomenon. The company's core business is based on developing, manufacturing, and licensing software products, including operating systems, server applications, business and consumer applications, and software development tools, as well as Internet software, technologies, and services. Led by Bill Gates, the world's wealthiest individual and most famous businessman, Microsoft has succeeded in placing at least one of its products on virtually every personal computer in the world, setting industry standards and defining markets in the process.

Origins of an Empire

Bill Gates was born in Seattle in 1955, the second of three children in a well-to-do family. His father, William H. Gates II, was a lawyer, while his mother, Mary Gates, was a teacher, a regent of the University of Washington, and member of several corporate boards. Gates was first exposed to computers at school in the late 1960s with his friend Paul Allen, the son of two Seattle librarians. By the time Gates was 14, the two friends were writing and testing computer programs for fun and profit.

In 1972 they established their first company, Traf-O-Data, which sold a rudimentary computer that recorded and analyzed traffic data. Allen went on to study computer science at the University of Washington and then dropped out to work at Honeywell, while Gates enrolled at Harvard. Inspired in 1975 by an issue of *Popular Electronics* that showed the new Altair microcomputer kit just released by MITS Computer, Gates and Allen wrote a version of BASIC for the machine. Later that year Gates left college to work full time developing programming languages for the Altair, and he and Allen relocated to Albuquerque, New Mexico, to be near MITS Computer, where Allen took a position as director of software development. Gates and Allen named their partnership Micro-soft. Their revenues for 1975 totaled $16,000.

A year later, Gates published "An Open Letter to Hobbyists" in the Altair newsletter, in which he enjoined users to avoid illegally copied software. Arguing that software piracy prevented "good software from being written," Gates wrote prophetically, "Nothing would please me more than being able to hire ten programmers and deluge the hobby market with good software." In November 1976 Allen left MITS to devote his full attention to Microsoft, and the company's tradename was registered. In 1977 Apple and Radio Shack licensed Microsoft BASIC for their Apple II and Tandy computers, with the Apple license going for a flat fee of $21,000. As Apple sold a million machines complete with BASIC, Microsoft's unit revenues dropped to two cents a copy.

That same year Microsoft released its second programming language, Microsoft FORTRAN, which was followed in 1978 by a version of COBOL. Both were written for the CP/M operating system, one of many available in the rapidly expanding but still unstandardized microcomputer market. As CP/M was adopted by computer manufacturers including Sirius, Zenith, and Sharp, Microsoft became the leading distributor for microcomputer languages. By the end of 1978 Microsoft had 13 employees, a sales subsidiary in Japan, and $1 million in revenues. The following year Gates and Allen moved the company to Bellevue, Washington.

The Early 1980s: Associations with IBM and Apple

Microsoft's big break came in 1980 as IBM began developing its Personal Computer, or PC. While IBM contracted Microsoft to develop languages for the PC, IBM's first choice to provide an operating system was the leader in the field, Digital Research; however, IBM and Digital Research were unable to agree on terms, so the contract for the operating system was awarded to Microsoft. As Microsoft was under a tight deadline and did not have an operating system of its own, the company purchased the rights to one from Seattle Computer Products for $75,000. Originally dubbed Q-DOS (for ''Quick and Dirty Operating System''), the product was renamed MS-DOS (for ''Microsoft Disk Operating System'') and modified for IBM's purposes. Under the terms of the agreement, Microsoft retained the right to sell the operating system to other companies and to consumers, while IBM could not. Neither company could have foreseen the value of this arrangement: as other manufacturers developed hardware compatible with the IBM PC, and as personal computing became a multibillion-dollar business, the fast and powerful MS-DOS became the industry's leading operating system, and Microsoft's revenues skyrocketed.

The year 1980 also saw the arrival of Steve Ballmer, a close friend of Gates from Harvard, who was hired to organize the non-technical side of the business. Ballmer later recalled the company's stormy beginnings under Gates's leadership: ''Our first major row came when I insisted it was time to hire 17 people. He claimed I was trying to bankrupt him.'' Conservative in his spending, Gates dictated that the company must always have enough money in the bank to operate for a year with no revenues. Nearly 20 years later that policy still stood—in 1999 Microsoft had cash reserves of more than $13 billion and no long-term debt—while Ballmer, who had by then become Microsoft president, remained Gates's closest friend and adviser.

In 1981 the company was incorporated as Microsoft, Inc., with Gates as president and chairman and Allen as executive vice-president. The company closed the year with 128 employees and revenues of $16 million. Two years later Allen left Microsoft after being diagnosed with Hodgkin's disease. He remained on the board of directors and continued to hold more than 10 percent of the company's stock. Also in 1983 Microsoft launched a word processing program, Word 1.0, in an effort to supplant the category leader, WordStar. Simpler to use and less expensive than WordStar, Word used a mouse to move the cursor and was able to display bold and italic type on the screen. Nevertheless, some users felt that the product was too complex—designed for software engineers rather than business users—and it was quickly surpassed in the market by WordPerfect, released by the Word-

Perfect Corporation. Word did not become a success until its greatly improved version 3.0 was released in 1986, whereupon the application became Microsoft's best-selling product.

Throughout its history, Microsoft has been known for releasing products that were initially unsuccessful but eventually grew to dominate their categories. Many reviewers have been harsh in their criticism: David Kirkpatrick, writing in *Fortune,* described the first release of one product as a ''typically unreliable, bug-ridden Microsoft mess,'' while Brent Schlender noted in the same magazine that ''from its beginnings, Microsoft has been notorious for producing inelegant products that are frequently inferior and bringing them to the market way behind schedule.'' These critics note that the success of Microsoft has been based not only—or even principally—on the company's technological prowess, but also on Bill Gates's business acumen, which combined dogged perseverance, strategic marketing, powerful alliances, and, increasingly as the years went on, highly aggressive competitive tactics.

Microsoft worked closely with Apple during the development of Apple's Macintosh computer, which was introduced in 1984. Revolutionary in its design, the Mac featured a graphical user interface based on icons rather than the typed commands used by the IBM PC, making its programs simple to use and easy to learn, even by computer novices. Microsoft introduced Mac versions of BASIC, Word, and the spreadsheet program Multiplan, and quickly became the leading supplier of applications for the Mac. Revenues jumped from $50 million in 1983 to nearly $100 million in 1984.

Convinced that the Mac's graphical user interface represented the future of end-user applications, Gates sought to develop an interface manager to work on top of MS-DOS that would convert the operating system to a graphical model that would be user-friendly and provide a single method for interacting with the many non-standardized programs designed to run on the system. Because other companies, including IBM, were working to develop similar interface managers for MS-DOS, Gates solicited support from hardware manufacturers and software publishers who were concerned about IBM's continued dominance of the PC market. Compaq, Hewlett-Packard, Texas Instruments, Digital Equipment Corporation, and others announced their support for the project, called Microsoft Windows, while IBM, in the face of this opposition, threw its weight behind VisiOn, a similar product already being marketed by VisiCalc, while working to develop its own program, called TopView. Plagued by delays in development, the release of Windows was repeatedly rescheduled throughout 1984 and 1985, causing tensions at Microsoft and with other software publishers who were forced to delay releases of the applications they were designing for the system. Finally released in November 1985, after some 110,000 hours of frantic work by programmers, Windows faced a disappointing reception. The system was slow, few applications were available to run on it, and customers delayed purchase decisions while waiting for the introduction of TopView.

In 1985 Microsoft also introduced Excel 1.0, a Mac spreadsheet product. Based on the earlier and less successful Multiplan, Excel gradually took hold against its principal competitor, Lotus 1-2-3, and eventually came to account for more than

Key Dates:

1975: Microsoft is founded by Bill Gates and Paul Allen; they sell BASIC, the first PC computer language program to MITS Computer, Microsoft's first customer.

1981: Microsoft, Inc. is incorporated; IBM uses Microsoft's 16-bit operating system for its first personal computer.

1982: Microsoft, U.K., Ltd. is incorporated.

1983: Paul Allen resigns as executive vice-president but remains on the board; Jon Shirley is made president of Microsoft (he later becomes CEO); Microsoft introduces the Microsoft Mouse and Word for MS-DOS 1.00.

1985: Microsoft and IBM forge a joint development agreement.

1986: Microsoft stock goes public at $21 per share.

1987: The company's first CD-ROM application, Microsoft Bookshelf, is released.

1990: Jon Shirley retires as president and CEO; Michael R. Hallman is promoted in Shirley's place; the company becomes the first PC software firm to surpass $1 billion of sales in a single year.

1992: Bill Gates is awarded the National Medal of Technology for Technological Achievement.

1993: The company introduces Windows NT.

1995: Bill Gates publishes his first book, *The Road Ahead.*

1996: The company acquires Vermeer Technologies and its software application, FrontPage.

1997: The Justice Department alleges that Microsoft violated a 1994 consent decree concerning licensing the Windows operating system to computer manufacturers.

1998: The U.S. Department of Justice files two antitrust cases against Microsoft, alleging the company had violated the Sherman Act.

2000: The company acquires Visio Corporation, its largest acquisition to date.

2001: Microsoft Windows XP is released internationally.

2003: Microsoft launches Windows Server 2003.

$1 billion of Microsoft's annual revenues. That same year Microsoft began collaborating with IBM on a next-generation operating system, called OS/2.

The Late 1980s: Emergence of a Corporate Culture

In early 1986 Microsoft moved to a new 40-acre corporate campus in Redmond, Washington, near Seattle. Designed to provide a refuge free of distractions for those whose job was, in Gates's words, to "sit and think," the campus was nestled in a quiet woodland setting and reflected huge expenditures for tools, space, and comfort. Buildings were designed in the shape of an X to maximize light, with each programmer given a private office rather than a cubicle. The buildings featured many small, subsidized cafeterias, as well as refrigerators stocked with juice and caffeinated beverages. The self-contained, collegiate surroundings were carefully designed to promote the company's distinctive culture, which one commentator described as a close approximation of "math camp." Like most software companies, Microsoft had no dress code (although company lore recounts that in 1988 senior management did express a preference that employees not go barefoot indoors). Employees were hired on the basis of sheer intelligence, with the company selecting only a small fraction of applicants from the more than 100,000 resumes it received each year, and were expected to work brutal schedules to bring products to market as quickly as possible. Microsoft paid salaries that were distinctly lower than elsewhere in the industry, even to their senior executives, but compensated with generous stock options that made thousands of Microsoft employees millionaires. At the same time, the company tried to maintain a small company mentality, in which executives traveled coach class, the necessity of additional staff positions was closely scrutinized, and other unnecessary expenditures were vigilantly avoided.

In March 1986 Microsoft held an initial public offering (IPO) of 2.5 million shares which raised $61 million. Within a year the stock had risen from $25 to $85, making Bill Gates a billionaire at the age of 31. The following year Microsoft released its first CD-ROM product, *Microsoft Bookshelf,* a collection of ten reference works, as well as Excel for Windows, its first application for the new operating system. Microsoft also purchased Forethought, Inc., for $12 million, thereby acquiring that company's PowerPoint presentation graphics program, and released OS/2 in collaboration with IBM. In November 1987 Microsoft introduced Windows 2.0, a greatly improved version of the operating system, and by the end of the year Windows had sold more than one million copies. As Windows began to take hold, more software companies were convinced to develop applications for the operating system, which brought it increased usefulness and further sales momentum. In 1988 Microsoft surpassed Lotus Development Corporation as the leading software vendor, with more than $500 million in sales. The company was accused of copyright infringement by Apple, which alleged that Microsoft had copied the "look and feel" of the Macintosh, in a lawsuit that was finally dismissed after five years of litigation. In 1989 the company introduced Microsoft Office, a "suite" of programs that eventually came to dominate the market and become Microsoft's best-selling application product. While the initial release of Office was a discount package, later versions incorporated standard, shared features and included Word, Excel, PowerPoint, and the e-mail program Mail, with the Access database management program included in the Office Professional version.

Before 1990 Microsoft was primarily a supplier to hardware manufacturers, but after 1990 the bulk of the company's revenues came from sales to consumers. That year Microsoft became the first software company to reach $1 billion in revenues, closing the year with 5,600 employees.

Product Development in the 1990s

In 1993 Microsoft introduced *Encarta,* the first multimedia encyclopedia on CD-ROM, as well as the first version of Windows NT, an operating system for users on corporate networks. While the initial acceptance of Windows NT was disappointing, an upgrade shipped in September of the following year as NT 3.5 was a dramatic success: winning the *PC Magazine* award for technical excellence in system software and named the best operating system product of 1994, the upgrade boosted sales of NT to more than one million copies by the end of the year. Microsoft announced an agreement to purchase Intuit, the producer of the leading package of personal financial software, called Quicken; however, after the U.S. Department of Justice filed suit to prevent the takeover on the basis of antitrust concerns, Microsoft withdrew its offer. Revenues for 1994 exceeded $4 billion.

In August 1995 Microsoft launched its next version of Windows, called Windows 95, which sold more than one million copies in the first four days after its release. For the rest of the decade Microsoft expanded aggressively into new businesses associated with its core franchise. Its projects included two joint ventures with the National Broadcasting Company under the name MSNBC: an interactive online news service and a cable channel broadcasting news and information 24 hours a day. The company's web-based services included the Microsoft Network online service, a travel agency, local events listings, car buying information, a personal financial management site, and a joint venture with First Data that allowed consumers to pay their bills online. Microsoft purchased 11 percent of the cable television company Comcast for $1 billion and cut a licensing deal with the largest U.S. cable operator, TCI Communications, to put Windows into at least five million set-top boxes. The company also purchased WebTV, whose core technology allowed users to surf the Internet without a PC. Microsoft's latest generation of Windows, Windows CE, was designed to expand the franchise into computer-like devices including mobile phones, point-of-sale terminals, pocket organizers, digital televisions, digital cameras, handheld computers, automobile multimedia systems, and pagers. By early 1999 the company had secured more than 100 licensing agreements with manufacturers of these "intelligent appliances."

Legal Challenges and Competition in the Future

Microsoft's many critics believed that the company's goal in this widespread expansion was to control every delivery channel of information, thereby providing the means to control the content. According to Scott McNealy of rival company Sun Microsystems, "By owning the entry points to the Internet and electronic marketplace, Microsoft has the power to exercise predatory and exclusionary control over the very means for people to access the Internet and all it represents."

The U.S. government apparently agreed. After an intensive investigation of Microsoft's competitive practices that had gone on for much of the decade, in 1998 the U.S. Department of Justice and a group of 20 state attorneys general filed two antitrust cases against Microsoft alleging violations of the Sherman Act. The government sought to prove a broad pattern of anticompetitive behavior on Microsoft's part by demonstrating an array of claims, including the following: that Microsoft had a monopoly on the market for operating systems; that the company used that monopoly as a means of preventing other companies from selling its competitors' products (most notably Netscape's Internet browser); that it was illegal for Microsoft to bundle its own browser into the operating system Windows 98 as a means of precluding customers from purchasing Netscape's product; that the company sought to divide markets with competitors; that Microsoft sought to subvert the Java programming language, developed by Sun Microsystems, which it viewed as a threat to Windows; and, finally, that Microsoft's business practices were detrimental to consumers. The case was conducted under a flurry of media attention, with all parties agreeing that the stakes were extremely high: should Microsoft win, its brand of extremely aggressive capitalism would secure a legal blessing; should the company lose, the company could be forced to license the source code for Windows to competitors, thus destroying its monopoly, or could be broken up into smaller components, crippling its hold over the marketplace.

The fear and resentment that Microsoft and its founder Gates engendered were testament to the company's mythic status and Gates's role as the embodiment of the digital era. Gates's extreme wealth (in early 1999 he was worth $50 billion) made him the subject of constant scrutiny, while the Internet was rife with Bill Gates "hate pages," named, for example, "The Society for the Prevention of Bill Gates Getting Everything." Resentment and legal action notwithstanding, with more than $14 billion in sales in 1998, Microsoft showed no signs of slowing down.

Microsoft continued to grow rapidly, increasing its net revenue by 29 percent, to $19.7 billion, in 1999. Additionally, net income rose to $7.79 billion, a dramatic 73 percent increase over 1998. While the antitrust suit against Microsoft showed threats of a forced breakup of Microsoft, innovations in the company continued. Encarta Africana, the first complete encyclopedia of black history and culture, was launched, as well as Shop, Microsoft's first online store.

Unprecedented Growth in 2000 and Beyond

In 2000 Microsoft acquired Visio Corporation, the top supplier of business diagramming and technical drawing software. The transaction, at approximately $1.3 billion, became the largest acquisition in Microsoft history. Also in 2000, Microsoft invested $135 million in the software publisher Corel. Apparently, Corel negotiated the investment, offering to drop "certain legal actions" it had against the company, even as it had no legal claims filed against Microsoft. Another transaction—in Microsoft's desire to expand into the television market—involved a $56 million investment in Intertainer Inc, a provider of video-on-demand service. In the same year, Microsoft increased its employee base by nearly 9,000, from 39,170 to 48,030. The total expenditures took a temporary toll on Microsoft's net income, which dropped 22 percent, to $7.35 billion, in 2001. At the same time, net revenue continued to increase, up 10 percent from 2000.

The release of Windows 2000, while causing a stir, was overshadowed by the highly anticipated debut and worldwide release of Microsoft Windows XP. So confident was Microsoft in the product, and in its ability to boost worldwide sales of computers (which had declined 11.3 percent since the September 11 attacks just a month before), they launched a $250 million ad campaign for the product. The software did not represent a brand new development, as much of the technology came from that of its predecessor, Windows 2000. But as Paul Thurrott, writer for *Network Windows* magazine, wrote, "There's no doubt that we'll eventually look back on Windows XP as one of the key OS releases of all time."

Meanwhile, the Department of Justice ruled that they would not enforce a breakup of Microsoft. By the end of 2002, the U.S. District Court approved the settlement Microsoft reached with the Justice Department. The settlement included preventing Microsoft from benefiting from exclusive deals that could hinder competition; uniform contract terms for computer manufacturers; the required ability of customers to remove icons from certain Microsoft features; and a requirement that Microsoft release specific innovational technical information to its rivals, in order to enforce competition.

Microsoft's net revenue increased to $28.37 billion in 2002, while net income rebounded, gaining 6 percent from the previous year. In 2003, Microsoft saw an impressive 28 percent jump in net income, to reach just below $10 billion. The launching of Windows Server 2003, the largest software development project in the company's history to date, contributed to the growth. According to Microsoft, Windows Server 2003 would be a more reliable, more manageable, and more collaborative piece of software. Security would also be tighter, especially due to a newly built IIS (Internet Information Server) Web Server.

By 2004, with more than 56,000 employees and anticipated year-end revenues of up to $38 billion, Microsoft continued to hold a strong lead in the computer software industry. With an emphasis on continuous innovation—including such business products as the BizTalk Server 2004—further success seemed ensured. Still, resentment toward Microsoft was omnipresent. In April 2004, the company was fined by the European Union for abusing its monopoly on computer operating systems. The fine, at EUR 497 million ($596 million), was not likely to be the last for Microsoft.

Principal Subsidiaries

Microsoft Asia, Ltd. (Nevada); Microsoft Business Solutions Aps (Denmark); Microsoft Capital Group, L.P.; Microsoft E-Holdings, Inc.; Microsoft Finance Company Ltd. (Ireland); Microsoft Ireland Capital Ltd.; Microsoft Ireland Operations Ltd.; Microsoft Licensing, Inc.; Microsoft Manufacturing BV (Netherlands); Microsoft T-Holdings, Inc.; MSLI, GP; Round Island, LLC; Round Island One Ltd.

Principal Divisions

Client; Server & Tools; Information Worker; Business Solutions; MSN; Mobile and Embedded Devices; Home and Entertainment; Other.

Principal Competitors

Apple Computer, Inc.; Hewlett-Packard Company; International Business Machines Corporation; Logitech International SA; Novell, Inc.; Sony Corporation; Sun Microsystems, Inc.; Time Warner Inc.; Yahoo! Inc.

Further Reading

Consuming, Michael A., *Microsoft Secrets: How the World's Most Powerful Software Company Creates Technology, Shapes Markets, and Manages People,* New York: Free Press, 1995, 512 p.

Desmond, Edward W., "Microsoft's Big Bet on Small Machines," *Fortune,* July 20, 1998, pp. 86–90.

"EU, Microsoft Clash Over Monopoly Ruling," *Associated Press,* April 29, 2004.

Evers, Joris, "Ballmer: Windows Server 2003 Does More with Less," *IDG News Service* (San Francisco Bureau).

France, Mike, "Microsoft: The View at Halftime," *Business Week,* January 25, 1999, p. 78.

Hamm, Steve, "No Letup—And No Apologies: Antitrust Scrutiny Hasn't Eased Microsoft's Competitiveness," *Business Week,* October 26, 1998, p. 58.

Higgins, David, "The Man Who Owns the Future," *Sydney Morning Herald,* March 14, 1998, p. 1.

Iceboat, Daniel, and Susan L. Knepper, *The Making of Microsoft: How Bill Gates and His Team Created the World's Most Successful Software Company,* Rocklin, Calif.: Prima Publishing, 1991, 304 p.

Isaacson, Walter, "In Search of the Real Bill Gates," *Time Magazine,* January 13, 1997, pp. 44+.

Kirkpatrick, David, "He Wants All Your Business—And He's Starting to Get It," *Fortune,* May 26, 1997, pp. 58+.

——, "Microsoft: Is Your Company Its Next Meal?," *Fortune,* April 27, 1998, pp. 92–102.

Krantz, Michael, "If You Can't Beat 'Em . . . Will Bill Gates' Bailout Save Apple—Or Just Strengthen Microsoft's Hand in the Web Wars?," *Time Magazine,* August 18, 1997, pp. 35+.

Manes, Stephen, and Paul Andrews, *Gates: How Microsoft's Mogul Reinvented an Industry—And Made Himself the Richest Man in America,* New York: Doubleday, 1993.

Mardesich, Jodi, "What's Weighing Down Microsoft?," *Fortune,* January 11, 1999, pp. 147–48.

McKenzie, Richard B., *Trust on Trial: How the Microsoft Case Is Reframing the Rules of Competition,* Perseus Publishing, 2000.

Moody, Fred, *I Sing the Body Electronic: A Year with Microsoft on the Multimedia Frontier,* New York: Viking, 1995, 311 p.

Nocera, Joseph, "High Noon," *Fortune,* November 23, 1998, pp. 162+.

Pollock, Andrew, "Media; Microsoft Makes Another Interactive TV Investment," *New York Times,* January 24, 2000.

Schlender, Brent, "What Bill Gates Really Wants," *Fortune,* January 16, 1995, pp. 34+.

Stross, Randall E., *The Microsoft Way: The Real Story of How the Company Outsmarts Its Competition,* Reading, Mass.: Addison-Wesley Publishing, 1996, 318 p.

Wallace, James, and Jim Erickson, *Hard Drive: Bill Gates and the Making of the Microsoft Empire,* New York: Wiley, 1992, 426 p.

—Scott Lewis
—updates: Paula Kepos, Candice Mancini

Mohawk Industries, Inc.

P.O. Box 12069
160 South Industrial Boulevard
Calhoun, Georgia 30703
U.S.A.
Telephone: (706) 629-7721
Fax: (706) 625-5271
Web site: http//www.mohawkind.com

Public Company
Incorporated: 1902 as Shuttleworth Brothers Company
Employees: 33,000
Sales: $5.0 billion (2003)
Stock Exchanges: New York
Ticker Symbol: MHK
NAIC: 314110 Carpet and Rug Mills; 442210 Floor
    Covering Stores; 423990 All Other Durable Goods
    Merchant Wholesalers

With three of the industry's most recognized brands—Karastan, Mohawk, and Bigelow—Mohawk Industries, Inc. ranks second among the largest carpet and rug makers in the United States. As one of the carpet industry's oldest players, Mohawk has a history that echoes that of its trade, from its foundation in 19th-century New England to its move to Georgia in the 1980s. A period of intense growth through acquisition sextupled Mohawk's sales from $280 million in 1991 to nearly $1.8 billion by 1996. In 1995, it held 17 percent of the $9.8 billion wholesale carpet and rug market, compared to leader Shaw Industries' 26 percent share. Mohawk's acquisition spree gave it a family of more than a dozen brands and made it the nation's largest manufacturer of machine-made rugs, a key segment of the maturing, consolidating market. By the mid-1990s, the company had a presence in virtually every segment of the industry, from mass-produced area rugs sold at promotional prices to custom-made wool carpets.

19th-Century Origins

The company was founded in 1878 by four brothers in the Shuttleworth family. That year, the family shipped 14 used Wilton looms from Great Britain to Amsterdam, New York, and launched their own carpet mill. At the time, New England, with its corresponding emphasis on textile mills, was the carpet capital of the nation. For most of its history, Mohawk and its competitors wove floor coverings from wool, a naturally water-repellent and insulating fiber. In fact, little about the industry changed from the time of the invention of the power loom in the mid-19th century until after World War II. Even with mechanization, carpetmaking was a highly labor-intensive prospect using massive, complicated machinery. Manufacturers' dependence on unpredictable wool production added another variable to the equation, making for steep fluctuations in expenses. For most families, carpeting was an expensive luxury, so costly that per household shipments peaked at four square yards in 1899 and did not exceed that mark until the mid-1960s.

The Shuttleworth family business was not incorporated until a generational shift in leadership probably precipitated the move in 1902, when the company became known as Shuttleworth Brothers Company. The firm's reputation grew substantially after 1908, when it introduced the Karnak carpet pattern. This new style was so popular that a company history noted: "Weavers worked four and five years without changing either the color or the pattern on their looms."

Three generations of Shuttleworths dominated the carpet mill's first century in business. In 1920, they guided the first of what would become many mergers and acquisitions. That year, the family combined its firm with carpetmakers McCleary, Wallin and Crouse to form a leading force in the then fragmented industry. Renamed Mohawk Carpet Mills, Inc., the company was the country's only weaver with a full line of domestic carpets, encompassing the Wilton, Axminster, Velvet, and Chenille weaves. Mohawk did not rest on its laurels, creating the industry's first textured design, Shuttlepoint; the first sculptured weave, Raleigh; and Woven Interlock, "the first successful application of the knitting principle to the manufacture of carpet."

Postwar Era Brings Rapid Change

Several trends converged in the 1950s to reshape the carpet industry drastically. Wartime restrictions on the use of wool

Company Perspectives:

The key to growth is not only to establish effective strategies, but also to follow through on them. By taking sound strategic action, we have created opportunity—opportunity to grow.

fueled research into alternative fibers, especially petrochemical-based synthetics including nylon and, later, acrylics. These man-made materials were much cheaper to produce and the supply was much more consistent than that of wool. At the same time, a revolution in the main weaving methods was underway. The new technique found its origins in Dalton, Georgia, which boasted a thriving cottage industry in tufted coverlets. In the late 1940s, housewives there had built up something of a tourist-trap industry in tufted bedspreads. Machines were soon developed to tuft carpets by the same process—inserting loops of fiber into a jute backing. These broadlooms could manufacture carpet many times faster than previous methods. Faster manufacturing methods, combined with the new materials developed in the ensuing decades, made the now familiar tufted carpets inexpensive and popular. By 1968, tufted carpeting accounted for 90 percent of all carpet sales.

In 1956, Mohawk merged with Alexander Smith, Inc. to form Mohasco Industries. Though the acquisition made Mohasco the world's largest carpet company, it proved to be poorly timed. The troubled Alexander Smith brought with it a high level of debt and a large inventory of outdated carpeting at a time when competition from imports was gaining steam. Tariff relaxations during the 1950s increased importers' share of the U.S. industry from 2 percent to 25 percent by the end of the decade. At the same time, Mohasco was compelled by industry imperatives to consolidate its mills in the South. Notwithstanding these problems, Mohasco President Herbert L. Shuttleworth II, the third and last of the family to lead the business, was able to stabilize the business enough to purchase high-ranking Firth Carpet in 1962.

Diversification into Furniture in the 1960s

Dreaming of "a home furnishings empire," Shuttleworth turned his attention to the furniture industry in 1963, acquiring nine furniture makers by 1970. Two years later, Mohasco ranked number two in the overall home furnishings market and second only to Bassett in furniture; carpet contributed only about one-fourth of sales. *Forbes* dubbed the company the "GM [General Motors] of the living room."

But Shuttleworth did not forsake the core carpet business. He launched a joint venture carpet plant in Belgium as well as subsidiaries in West Germany and Mexico in the 1960s and invested more than $100 million in production capacity from 1963 to 1973. Baby boomers, who by this time had grown to marrying and house-buying age, fueled the rapid expansion of the carpet industry in the late 1960s and early 1970s. Carpet volume increased from 138 million square yards in 1955 to 430 million square yards in 1965, surpassing one billion square yards in 1973. In the early 1970s, Mohasco's sculptured, brightly colored "Canyon Paradise" carpet, in such classic 1970s color

schemes as orange and gold, became the carpet industry's "all-time best-seller." But when tastes changed and more muted colors came into style, Mohasco failed to pick up on the trend. *Forbes* compared the mill to "those clothing companies that were caught with warehouses of polyester leisure suits."

When combined with a mid-decade recession and price controls, Mohasco's lack of fashion savvy proved to be a major misstep; by 1975, Burlington Industries had surpassed it in carpet production. Perhaps more telling, its earnings were declining precipitously. Furthermore, carpet industry shipments peaked in 1979 over the one billion square yard mark, then entered a steep and ongoing decline. In the wake of this decline was a mature industry burdened with overcapacity and facing ferocious competition.

Reorganization in the 1980s Leading to LBO

In 1980, Mohasco hired David Kolb, an attorney who had served as comptroller and director of the nylon carpet fibers division at Allied Fibers, as CEO. Kolb was charged with turning the then unprofitable company around. The new chief undertook a five-year modernization program that encompassed plant and systems modernizations, cost reductions, and development of new managers. He even moved the company's headquarters from Amsterdam, New York, to Atlanta, Georgia, to be nearer to what had become the "carpet capital of the world," Dalton, Georgia. He also shifted the company to higher margin products and increased direct distribution to retailers (thereby cutting out the middleman). Having achieved his profit goals, Kolb took the carpet division private via a $120 million leveraged buyout (LBO) in 1988.

Public Stock Offering, Acquisition Binge During Early 1990s

Mergers and acquisitions reduced the number of carpet producers from more than 300 in 1980 to 100 by the mid-1990s, with vertically integrated—and, in Mohawk's case, well-diversified—"mega-mills" emerging at the top of the heap.

Kolb used the $38 million proceeds of Mohawk's 1992 public stock offering to reduce the company's LBO debt in preparation for a rapid-fire series of acquisitions funded in part by new debt. Four key acquisitions from 1992 to 1994 catapulted Mohawk from 11th in the industry to second, increased its sales from less than $300 million to nearly $1.5 billion, and multiplied its market share from less than 4 percent to 17 percent. In addition, Mohawk's growth rate ranked it second among the *Fortune* 500's fastest growing companies in 1993.

The first purchase came in October 1992. Although larger than Mohawk, Horizon Industries was vulnerable because of back-to-back losses in the early 1990s. Less than eight months later, Kolb engineered the acquisition of American Rug Craftsmen (ARC), a ten-year-old manufacturer of area rugs. ARC made Mohawk the nation's leading producer of mass-market rugs. Hoping to capitalize on fragmentation within the area rug segment, the new parent boosted ARC's manufacturing and distribution capacity. Under the care of its doting new parent, ARC's sales burgeoned from $50 million in 1993 to $150 million in 1996.

The August 1993 purchase of Karastan Bigelow from Fieldcrest Cannon added two of the industry's best known and most valuable brands. In fact, Bigelow was named for Erastus B. Bigelow, the 19th-century "Father of the Modern Carpet Industry," so named for his invention of the power loom. The addition of Karastan Bigelow pushed Mohawk past competitor Beaulieu of America to become the United States' second largest carpet company.

But Mohawk's most important acquisition was yet to come. In 1994, the carpetmaker merged with highly profitable and privately held Aladdin Mills Inc. via a $430 million "pooling-of-interests." Mohawk paid a premium price for Aladdin but felt justified by the target's comparatively high profitability. Aladdin's compound sales growth had averaged 20 percent from 1988 to 1993, and after the merger, the "subsidiary" contributed 40 percent of sales and 50 percent of net income. Because Aladdin was more profitable than Mohawk, the privately held company's owners, the Lorberbaum family, ended up with a controlling 39 percent stake in Mohawk.

In 1995, Jeffrey Lorberbaum, son of Aladdin founder Alan Lorberbaum, was appointed president and chief operating officer. Lorberbaum was charged with boosting profitability. He planned to "rationalize" the corporation's manufacturing capacity along product lines, closing several mills over the ensuing years and consolidating their operations at the most efficient plants. He also expected to expand Aladdin's existing warehousing and distribution system to service all of Mohawk's operations. A more dynamic marketing program emphasized the strength of the company's core brands. Meanwhile, ongoing industrywide difficulties included declining wholesale prices

and rising raw material costs. Mohawk's high debt load, the legacy of the acquisition spree, did not help matters. Debt service ran at $40 million in 1995, cutting a large chunk of cash flow.

Nevertheless, Mohawk continued to eye acquisition candidates mid-decade. In 1995, it purchased Galaxy Carpet Mills Inc. for $43.3 million. The new subsidiary added $200 million in sales of higher-margin residential carpets. In 1997, Mohawk acquired Diamond Rug & Carpet Mills, a bankrupt manufacturer of inexpensive cut pile polypropylene rugs. These two additions exemplified Mohawk's continuing quest to add capacity in all price and quality ranges, from mass to class. That year, the company proudly trumpeted its highest ever sales and earnings, at $2.4 billion and $84 million, respectively. The latter amount was a particularly large jump from the previous year's net income of $55 million.

Steady Growth Continuing: Late 1990s and Early 2000s

Mohawk's sales and earnings continued to climb; again, in 1998, net income shot up dramatically, to $130 million. The nearly 60 percent increase was especially impressive given the number of acquisitions Mohawk completed that year. The first was Newmark & James, specialists in high-quality cotton bath area rugs, a company with previous annual sales around $35 million. The second, America Weavers, was a leader in throws, tabletop linens, and coordinated textiles. The third acquisition, of World Carpets, helped Mohawk to hold an approximate 24 percent of the carpet market. At the same time, Mohawk concentrated on expanding into hard surfaces for flooring. Such products included Insignia, Mohawk's laminate product, and Mohawk Ceramic brand tile. With an ever increasing demand for tile, Mohawk began seeking ways to expand upon its tile holdings.

The next few years brought four more acquisitions for Mohawk. The 1999 acquisitions of Image Carpets and Durkan Patterned Carpets further increased Mohawk's hold in the carpet market. In 2000 Mohawk acquired Crown Crafts wovens division, making the company a leader in the markets of the woven throw, bedspreads, and coverlets. At the same time, Mohawk was selected by Congoleum Corporation to become a national distributor of its hard-surface products. While these developments helped to enhance the company as a whole, it was the 2001 merger with Dal-Tile that made the biggest splash.

In the agreement, Mohawk paid approximately $1.66 billion for Dal-Tile. The acquisition—Mohawk's 14th since 1992— was expected to add $1 billion to Mohawk's already substantial $3.3 billion in 2002 sales. Dal-Tile lived up to its expectation, as 2002 sales reached an incredible $4.5 billion. This was especially noteworthy given the faltering economic environment of 2002. President and CEO Jeffrey Lorberbaum credited the success to the implementation of a "big-picture view" of the company's business.

By 2003, Mohawk's net sales reached $5 billion, with net income of $310 million. With such sturdy financial success, Mohawk looked into further expansion, acquiring Lees Carpet, for approximately $346 million, at the end of the year. But while the company was expanding in some areas, it was cutting back in others. A month after the Lees Carpet acquisition, Mohawk announced that it would permanently close its yarn-manufacturing facility in Talladega, Alabama. The closure left 125 workers unemployed.

The first quarter of 2004, meanwhile, brought record numbers for Mohawk. At more than $66 million, 2004's first quarter earnings were an astounding 59 percent higher than that of 2003. With its long history of steady, and at times enormous, growth, Mohawk expected to continue on its path of expansion and productivity.

Principal Subsidiaries

Aladdin Manufacturing Corp.; Alladin Carpet Mills; American Rug Craftsmen; American Weavers LLC; Dal-Tile Corp.; Diamond Carpet Mills; Durkan Patterned Carpets; Fiber One; Galaxy Carpet Mills; Horizon Industries; Image Carpets; Karastan Bigelow; Lees Carpet, Inc.; Mohawk Carpet Corp.; Mohawk Carpet Distribution; Mohawk Factoring, Inc.; Mohawk Resources, Inc.; Newmark & James; World Carpet.

Principal Competitors

Interface, Inc.; The Dixie Group, Inc.; Burlington Industries.

Further Reading

''Acquisition Adds Luster to Outlook of Mohasco,'' *Barron's,* January 21, 1963, p. 21.

Allison, David, ''Mohawk Weaves a Carpet Giant: Atlanta Company Threads Acquisitions into a Growing Business,'' *Atlanta Business Chronicle,* April 9, 1993, pp. 1B.

''Clean Sweep at Mohasco,'' *Forbes,* December 15, 1958, pp. 27–28.

Dorral, Cecile B., ''Mohawk Grows Top Line with Dal-Tile,'' *Home Textiles Today,* November 26, 2001.

Elliott, J. Richard, Jr., ''Carpet Magic,'' *Barron's,* March 16, 1959, pp. 3, 15–16.

Feldman, Andy, ''A Slippery Rug,'' *Forbes,* May 22, 1995, pp. 68–69.

''From Rugs to Riches,'' *Forbes,* March 15, 1973, p. 31.

''Georgia-Based Floorcovering Maker Mohawk Industries Posts Record Profits,'' *Chattanooga Times,* April 22, 2004.

''GM of the Living Room?,'' *Forbes,* February 15, 1966, p. 38.

Greene, Joan, ''Wall-to-Wall; Carpet Makers Are Piling Up Handsome Gains,'' *Barron's,* February 16, 1976, pp. 11, 53–54.

Hussey, Allan F., ''Mohasco—It's Spinning Bright Earnings Pattern,'' *Barron's,* May 24, 1976, pp. 34, 36.

Joyce, Amy, ''American Rug Craftsmen's Plans,'' *HFD-The Weekly Home Furnishings Newspaper,* March 22, 1993, p. 30.

Kaye, Michael, ''The Best of the Brightest Sectors,'' *Business Week online,* February 20, 2003.

Kolb, David L., ''The Metamorphosis of Mohawk from LBO to Big Acquirer,'' *Mergers & Acquisitions,* November–December 1994, pp. 47–50.

McCurry, John, ''Mohawk Signs Letter of Intent to Buy Assets of Diamond Rug,'' *Textile World,* November 1996, p. 26.

''Mohasco Industries Benefits from Stake in Home Furnishings,'' *Financial World,* November 17, 1971, p. 18.

''Mohawk Buys Aladdin Mills,'' *Textile World,* January 1994, p. 23.

''Mohawk in Deal for Karastan-Bigelow,'' *Textile World,* August 1993, p. 23.

Mohawk Industries, Inc.: International Competitive Benchmarks and Financial Gap Analysis, Icon Group International, Inc., 2000.

''Mohawk to Buy Galaxy Carpet for $42.4 M,'' *HFD-The Weekly Home Furnishings Newspaper,* December 19, 1994, p. 24.

Montero, Santiago, and Julie Naughton, ''Walking Away with the Rug Business: Karastan Bigelow Buy Gives Mohawk Industries Commanding Market Share,'' *HFD-The Weekly Home Furnishings Newspaper,* July 12, 1993, pp. 16–17.

Naughton, Julie, ''Mohawk Acquires American Rug Craftsmen,'' *HFD-The Weekly Home Furnishings Newspaper,* May 17, 1993, p. 26.

——, ''Mohawk Continues Buying Spree,'' *HFD-The Weekly Home Furnishings Newspaper,* July 26, 1993, p. 24.

——, ''Mohawk's Tribe Increases,'' *HFD-The Weekly Home Furnishings Newspaper,* June 21, 1993, p. 20.

——, ''Mohawk to Shut Tufting Mill in S.C., Ga., Yarn Spinning Unit,'' *HFN-The Weekly Newspaper for the Home Furnishing Network,* May 8, 1995, p. 19.

''New Lines Furnish Lift to Mohasco Industries,'' *Barron's,* December 27, 1965, p. 18.

''No Turn in Sight for Carpet Makers,'' *Financial World,* March 26, 1958, pp. 11, 27.

Pacey, Margaret D., ''Flying Carpets,'' *Barron's,* December 16, 1963, pp. 11, 20, 22–23, 25, 32.

''Prosperous Carpet Makers,'' *Financial World,* May 15, 1968, pp. 10, 22.

''Roll Out the Carpets!,'' *Forbes,* March 15, 1964, p. 42.

Saltzman, Cynthia, ''Make Mine Beige,'' *Forbes,* May 28, 1979.

Schonbak, Judith, ''New Horizons for Mohawk Industries,'' *Business Atlanta,* October 1992, p. 10.

Wyman, Lissa, ''American Rug: The Big Payoff,'' *HFN-The Weekly Newspaper for the Home Furnishing Network,* May 13, 1966, pp. 13–14.

—April Dougal Gasbarre
—update: Candice Mancini

Montupet S.A.

202 quai de Clichy, BP 77
Clichy
F-92112 Cedex
France
Telephone: 33 1 47 56 47 56
Fax: 33 1 47 39 77 93
Web site: http://www.montupet.fr

Public Company
Incorporated: 1894 as Fonderies Montupet—Primet et Cie
Employees: 1,700
Sales: EUR 434.7 million ($500 million) (2003)
Stock Exchanges: Euronext Paris
Ticker Symbol: MON
NAIC: 336399 All Other Motor Vehicle Parts
   Manufacturing

Montupet S.A. is one of Europe's leading manufacturers of aluminum-based components for the automotive and other industries. The company, based in Clichy, France, focuses on a number of core product lines, including cylinder heads, aluminum wheel rims, engine blocks, and other engine parts including intake manifolds, fuel-injection part housing, and cylinder heads; and braking system components, including the master cylinder, divider, and ABS body. The company also produces structural components, such as chassis—replacing the traditional cast iron and steel components with aluminum alloys permits automobile manufacturers to build lighter vehicles. Montupet counts among its customers Renault, accounting for more than 25 percent of sales; Ford and Volvo, which provide more than 20 percent of sales; General Motors (GM) and Saab, which add another 17 percent of sales; PSA, accounting for 16 percent of sales; and other car makers including Audi and Volkswagen. Montupet also produces components for other industries, including aerospace and heavy vehicles. The company operates three production plants in France, and plants in Spain, Canada, Northern Ireland, and Mexico. Montupet also operates its own tooling business, which enables it to design and fabricate its production machinery in collaboration with its

customers. The company, which posted EUR 434 million ($500 million) in sales in 2003, is listed on the Euronext Paris stock exchange. Stephane Magnan is company CEO.

Early 20th-Century Parts Producer

The development of the automobile industry began in earnest at the dawn of the 20th century with the invention of new technologies, production techniques, and materials. By 1883, De Dion and Bouton had built the first automobile made of metal, replacing the wood parts that had been common features on the earliest automobiles. The demand for components inspired the development of an entire support industry, in France and elsewhere. Among the many new companies that appeared at the end of the 19th century was a small foundry business in Nogent-sur-Oise, just north of Paris.

Founded by Pierre Montupet, the Nogent foundry at first focused on producing components based on copper alloys. By the end of the century, however, Montupet had begun experimenting with a relatively new metal type: aluminum. Large-scale production of aluminum metal had become possible through the development of the electrolytic smelting process introduced in the late 1880s. France's rich bauxite deposits—a primary source of aluminum—gave Montupet a steady and widely available source of raw materials.

Montupet began exploring means of adapting aluminum for use in automobiles. Into the new century, the company began developing new alloys to meet the steadily increasing mechanical demands of the new generations of larger and more powerful engines. Montupet was soon joined by a number of other companies that began producing aluminum components for France's buoyant automobile industry. Among these was the Debard, founded by Paul Debard, an industrialist based in Paris. In 1905, Debard built an aluminum foundry in Chateauroux, in the Indre region south of Paris, and began producing components for the automobile industry as well as for the aviation and marine industries.

By the 1930s, Montupet had perfected its aluminum alloys, helping it become a major producer of automobile components, and especially engine parts, to the French automobile industry.

More than a simple supplier, Montupet became a primary partner in the development of many of France's most popular cars. For example, in 1953, Citroen debuted its famed DS series—featuring components designed in conjunction with and produced by Montupet, including the arms for the DS's revolutionary air suspension system.

Expansion in the 1960s

The 1960s marked a new era for the French automobile industry. The booming economy had made purchasing automobiles accessible for a wider range of the population. The automotive industry responded by producing a broad array of models and automotive classes. To meet the rising demand for its components, Montupet began preparing for its own expansion. In 1966, the company made its first acquisition, that of Société de Fonderie d'Aluminum et d'Alliages Légers. To fund the acquisition and to further its own expansion, Montupet went public that year. The public offering also marked the gradual exit of the Montupet family from company ownership.

By the 1970s, Montupet was already one of France's leaders in its component category. A major rival appeared in Dedard, which had been acquired by another company, Virax, in 1964. Originally specialized in the manufacture of machine tools and industrial pumps, Virax had begun a diversification drive during the 1960s. In 1970, Virax moved the Dedard plant from its original location to a new, larger facility outside of Chateauroux. The 20,000-square-meter plant became one of the largest and most modern aluminum foundries in France. The new facility became known as Fonderie de la Precision-Virax.

By the late 1970s, however, Virax decided to abandon the automotive market. In 1977, it sold its Fonderie de la Precision to Montupet, which then restructured, creating a new holding company with the name of Société Industrielle et Financière Montupet. Both the company's original foundry operation and the former Virax foundry were placed under the holding firm that year. The following year, Montupet created a new sales division overseeing marketing and distribution for both subsidiaries. Then, in 1980, Fonderie de la Precision was fully merged into Fonderie Montupet.

By then, Montupet had launched a new expansion branch. In 1978, the company joined with Ford to begin development of the first aluminum cylinder heads for the North American market. These were then used in constructing the successful Ford Escort and other models. The collaboration with Ford led Montupet to begin planning a wider entry into North America.

Montupet continued to focus on expansion into the 1980s. In 1981, the company diversified its business, acquiring wheel rim manufacturer Sudrad, which became Sudrad Montupet.

That year, also, the company acquired a stake in Aluminoy y Aleaciones S.A., or Alumalsa, founded in 1946 and located in Saragosa, Spain. Montupet continued to build up its share of Alumalsa, acquiring majority control in 1987. That year marked a new restructuring of the group, as a result of a management buyout led by Stephane Magnan. After merging the Fonderies Montupet into its holding parent, the company changed its name to Montupet S.A.

International Leader in the New Century

Montupet had meanwhile been scouting for new international opportunities. By 1988, the company had settled on Canada for its first expansion into the U.S. automobile component market, and construction began on a new foundry in Riverie Beaudette that year. The company also opened a sales office close to the heart of the U.S. automotive industry, in Michigan.

In 1989, Montupet launched a new international operation when it took over the Belfast factory built by the failed DeLorean company in the early 1980s. The new facility helped Montupet meet the rising demand, and placed it in a strong position as car manufacturers prepared the launch of new engine designs for the 1990s. As part of that effort, the company also acquired its own tooling business, BS Tooling, also in Northern Ireland, in order to be able to design and build machinery specifically for customers' products.

In the early 1990s, Montupet sought to step up its presence in North America. Already considered the European leader, Montupet entered merger talks with Teksid, a subsidiary of Italy's Fiat. Teksid complemented Montupet, adding not only a strong European position but also serving as one of North America's largest components suppliers. Yet, as the global automotive industry entered an extended crisis, the two sides were forced to call off merger talks, explaining that the resulting combination would prove unprofitable.

The mid-1990s saw a return to growth in the automotive market. Montupet took advantage of the expanding market, signing up a new customer, General Motors, to produce aluminum cylinder block castings for the Pontiac Firebird and Chevrolet Camaro V-8 engines, starting in 1997. The following year, Montupet received another major new order, this time to produce cylinder heads for the Ford Motor Company. As part of that purchase, Montupet agreed to build a new foundry in Torreon, Mexico.

The expanding automotive market in Europe enabled Montupet to increase its capacity at home as well, and in 2000 the company opened a new facility in Laigneville, near the original Nogent foundry. The company's next expansion effort came as a result of a request from the Ford Motor Company, which asked it to take over operations of Ford's own production plant in Northern Ireland in order to produce up to 500,000 cylinder heads per year for Ford's own Explorer model. The new site was then renamed Calcast.

Into the 2000s, Montupet found itself burdened by debt and by a new slump in automobile demand. The company began a new restructuring effort to cut costs amid slipping revenues, which dropped some 8.5 percent over 2003 to EUR 435 million ($500 million). Nonetheless, the company remained confident for the future, in part because it expected to launch production of several new series of components for DaimlerChrysler and Renault, among others, for 2005.

Principal Subsidiaries

ALUMALSA (Spain); CALCAST Ltd. (Northern Ireland); MFT Sarl; MFT-MONTUPET Snc (Belgium); MONTIAC SA de CV (Mexico); MONTUPET GmbH (Germany); MONTUPET Inc. (U.S.A.); MONTUPET Ltd. (Canada); MONTUPET UK Ltd.

Principal Competitors

Dana Corporation; Textron Inc.; TRW Automotive; Grundfos GmbH; American Standard Companies Inc.; FASA Renault S.A; Mondragon Corporacion Cooperativa; Eaton Corporation.

Further Reading

"French Foundry Uses Power of Simulation," *Foundry Trade Journal,* December 2000, p. 4.

"Montupet affiche un CA annuel en baisse," *LesInfos.com,* February 24, 2004.

"Montupet Forges Ahead," *Europe Intelligence Wire,* October 10, 2002.

Saint-Seine, Sylviane de, "New Megane Boosts Montupet Sales," *Automotive News Europe,* January 27, 2003, p. 20.

Wrigley, Al, "GM Taps Montupet for Parts," *American Metal Market,* December 16, 1996, p. 5.

—M.L. Cohen

Newpark Resources, Inc.

3850 N. Causeway Boulevard, Suite 1770
Metairie, Louisiana 70002
U.S.A.
Telephone: (504) 838-8222
Fax: (504) 833-9506
Web site: http://www.newpark.com

Public Company
Incorporated: 1932 as New Park Mining Company
Employees: 1,121
Sales: $373.2 million (2003)
Stock Exchanges: New York
Ticker Symbol: NR
NAIC: 333132 Oil and Gas Field Machinery and
     Equipment; 213112 Support Activities for Oil and
     Gas Operations; 562211 Hazardous Waste Treatment
     and Disposal

Newpark Resources, Inc. provides integrated environmental and drilling fluid services to oil and gas drillers, including fluid processing and recycling on site at rigs. The company supplies prefabricated work sites and temporary access roads made of interlocking hardwood or composite mats for use in oil and gas exploration and commercial, industrial, and military applications, and sells these mats to commercial concerns. It also sells lumber and wood byproducts. Newpark processes and disposes of oilfield waste by injecting this waste underground, and processes and disposes of nonhazardous industrial waste in similar fashion.

From Old-Line Metal Mining to Oilfield Waste Servicing: 1932–70s

In 1932, New Park Mining Company formed as the consolidation of three mining companies: Star of Utah Mining Company, Mayflower Mines Corporation, and Park Galena Mining Company. For the next three decades, the publicly owned, old-line mining company expanded through acquisitions of similar companies, until, by the late 1960s, the mining of metals as an industry fell on hard times.

To survive, Newpark bought two Louisiana companies in 1968 and got into the oil service business. The first of these, SOLOCO Inc., built roads to swampy well sites. The second company, Louisiana Oilfield Rentals, or LOR, was an oilfield tool manufacturing and rental company that later spun off as Triumph LOR in the 1986 restructuring of the company. The SOLOCO acquisition provided Newpark with the foundation for its Mat and Integrated Services segment. In 1972, the company changed its name to Newpark Resources, Inc. to reflect the change in its core business and moved its corporate headquarters to New Orleans, Louisiana.

In 1976, James Cole joined the company as its chief executive officer, and, in 1977, Newpark listed on the New York Stock Exchange. Cole brought with him a California-based oil service company, called ELPAC Inc., that he had helped to found. The following year, Newpark created a new operating unit, Newpark Drilling Fluids, to develop its oilfield waste business, an industry it helped to pioneer. The company participated in the drilling fluids business from 1977 to 1985, during which time it became the third largest drilling fluids company in the United States. From 1982 to 1984, capitalizing on the oil boom of the early 1980s, it added ten drilling fluids supply locations on the Gulf of Mexico to provide drilling fluids to the offshore petroleum exploration industry. During this period, its stock sold for as much as $33 a share.

Industry Downturn Leading to New Directions in Site Construction and Cleanup: 1980s to Early 1990s

The oil industry downturn of the early to mid-1980s led to overcapacity, price-cutting, and consolidation among oil companies, and to difficult times for Newpark. From 1982 to 1987, Newpark did not turn a profit. As a result, in 1986, the company, which had traded on the New York Stock Exchange since 1977, was delisted and moved to the NASDAQ.

Others in the industry were having difficulties as well. From the end of 1983 to the end of 1985, there were more than a dozen oil patch mergers among former competitors to save individual companies from going under. In 1985, Newpark merged its Drilling Fluids segment into a joint venture with a subsidiary of

Company Perspectives:

Newpark Resources is a niche provider of high performance, environmentally focused services and products to the explorations and production industry. Newpark seeks to differentiate itself from competitors through the application of unique products and technology to its customers' projects.

Key Dates:

1932: New Park Mining Company incorporates.
1972: The company changes its name to Newpark Resources, Inc. and moves its corporate headquarters to New Orleans, Louisiana.
1977: The company lists on the New York Stock Exchange; founds Newpark Drilling Fluids.
1985: Newpark Resources, Inc. consolidates its Drilling Fluids division with Milchem, Inc. to form Milpark Drilling Fluids, Inc.
1986: Newpark divests its interest in Milpark and is delisted from the New York Stock Exchange.
1988: Company reincorporates in Delaware.
1991: Company acquires George R. Brown services; completes its initial public offering on NASDAQ.
1995: Newpark moves to the New York Stock Exchange.
1996: Company acquires the marine-related nonhazardous oilfield waste collection operations for Campbell Wells, Ltd.
1997: Company purchases SBM Drilling Fluids Management and reenters the drilling fluids business as Newpark Drilling Fluids.
2001: Company purchases Ava Drilling Fluids.

Baker Hughes International Corp., Milchem, to form Milpark. In 1985, it combined its Louisiana Oilfield Rentals (LOR) with Triumph Drilling Tools, jointly owned by Galveston-Houston and National Lead to form Triumph LOR, Inc. It exited the drilling fluids business when it traded its ownership of Milpark to its banks in exchange for the majority of its outstanding indebtedness. Baker Hughes later acquired all of Milpark.

Newpark also began a process of restructuring in 1986, after being delisted from the New York Stock Exchange. That process culminated in a private financing transaction in 1987, after which only a small public shareholder base remained. Newpark also reincorporated in Delaware in 1987, and began trading on the NASDAQ in 1991. It conducted a secondary stock offering in 1996.

Facilitated by its financing transaction and improving operations, Newpark expanded its oilfield construction operations into Texas with the acquisition of Mallard & Mallard in 1990 and the purchase of George R. Brown Services, Inc. in 1991. Also in 1991, Newpark invested in its environmental cleanup operations. It relocated its principal oilfield waste transfer facility to a site near Port Arthur, Texas, and increased its capacity to process and dispose of nonhazardous oilfield waste (NOW) by 50 percent. Oilfield waste comes from the cuttings removed from the wellbore during drilling, from drilling fluids, and from the pits that handle drilling muds during the drilling process. Newpark introduced a process whereby it could inject such wastes into secure geological formations underground, or process the waste to yield a material to cover landfills.

A pickup in gas drilling in south Louisiana in the early 1990s helped turn Newpark around. The company had 1990 revenues of $46.1 million and 1991 revenues of $60.1 million. But 1993 was another bad year for Newpark. With drilling by oil and gas companies way down, both of Newpark's oilfield service businesses, building drilling sites, and oilfield cleanup, were down as well.

The showpiece of the company's new services was its disposal of oilfield "naturally occurring radioactive materials," known as NORM, which were not suitable for recycling or reuse. NORM are not drilling-related, but accumulate during the productive life of a well and include some radioactive materials from deep in the earth's crust. Newpark extended its waste disposal technology to dispose of NORM underground in the same manner as NOW.

Building a Niche Market Position in North America: Late 1990s

Newpark's NOW and NORM disposal business kept steadily growing, and the company's revenues continued to increase.

In 1994, sales reached $79.5 million, and, in 1996, $100 million. In 1995, the company completed two additional NOW injection wells in Texas and moved to the New York Stock Exchange. In 1996, assisted by a secondary equity offering, it purchased the nonhazardous oilfield waste collection operations of Campbell Wells Ltd., a subsidiary of Sanifill Inc. It also received a license to inject NORM-contaminated oilfield waste directly into disposal wells in east Texas. In 1997, it reentered the drilling fluids business as Newpark Drilling Fluids, an extension of its waste disposal business, when it purchased SBM Drilling Fluids Management of Houston. SBM was a supplier of drilling fluids for specialized wells, such as horizontal drilling and deepwater Gulf of Mexico drilling.

Newpark also sought to build a niche market position for itself within North America by marketing its water-based Deep-Drill system as an environmentally neutral substitute for conventional drilling fluids. This system of proprietary fluid products substitutes food-grade products for the salt and diesel or synthetic oils typically employed in oil-based systems, eliminating the need for the elements that can cause environmental damage.

The company's profits increased to $38 million in 1997. Then in 1998, oil patch drilling began to dry up, and Newpark suffered a loss of $64 million. In 1999, low oil prices resulted in a 50 percent cut in spending plans and the loss of 100 jobs at Newpark. The drilling market remained depressed through the first years of the next decade; yet Newpark continued to expand in new, but related directions. In 1999, it formed Newpark Performance Services Inc., a new operating unit to provide onsite processing, fluid recycling, and waste management as well as drilling fluids. In some cases, these services were provided in combination with site services. It also received a permit in 1999 to enter the industrial waste business.

By 2000, the company was receiving five million barrels of waste a year, and new EPA rules calling for reduced discharges into federal waters were boosting demand for Newpark's services. Declines in rig activity after July 2001 reduced Gulf Coast activity, however, and these volumes retreated to 3.6 million barrels per year shortly thereafter. Newpark also began selling its composite mats late in 2000 and shipped over 21,000 units in 2001. Sales slowed in 2002 and 2003 to approximately 5,000 units annually. The company also expanded geographically in 2001 and began serving the Mediterranean basin and North Africa with the purchase of Ava Drilling Fluids of Italy.

Although revenues took another 21.4 percent dip to $321 million in 2002, they rebounded in 2003 to $373 million. As the company looked to the future, it determined to continue to seek out niche markets in which to offer those products and services that distinguished it from its competitors. As the oil industry turned to focus on oil and gas exploration in foreign markets Newpark sought to position itself to make use of its expertise in working in difficult environmental conditions. In Canada, for example, where much of the primary exploration area has difficult soil conditions with drilling possible only when the soil is frozen from November to March, Newpark's mat system could enable a change to a year-round pattern of operation. Newpark also believed itself well positioned to benefit from expected increases in drilling activity in the Gulf Coast and from continuing regulatory pressure restricting discharges of drilling fluid waste into the surface waters of the United States.

Principal Subsidiaries

Newpark Drilling Fluids, LLC; Ava S.P.A. Drilling; Newpark Canada, Inc.; SOLOCO, LLC; Newpark Environmental Services, LLC.

Principal Competitors

Halliburton (Baroid division); Schlumberger and Smith International (MI Drilling Fluids); Varco International.

Further Reading

Blouin, Keith, "A Muddy Future for Newpark," *New Orleans City Business,* May 13, 1985, p. 1.

Hall, John, "Newpark's Changes Lead to Success As Mining Firm Evolves," *Times-Picayune,* May 21, 1995, p. 114.

Hosch, Andrew, "Industry, DEQ Work to Resolve Differences on Cleanup Regulations," *New Orleans City Business,* July 12, 1993, p. 21.

Judice, Mary, "Newpark Reborn: Oilfield Cleanup Company Sees Profit Below the Surface," *Times-Picayune,* August 24, 1994, p. C1.

Norman, James R., "Matt Simmons: Doctor to the Oil Fields' Walking Wounded," *Business Week,* November 4, 1985, p. 82.

—Carrie Rothburd

Nippon Oil Corporation

1-3-12 Nishi Shimbashi
Minato-ku
Tokyo 105-8412
Japan
Telephone: (03) 3502-1131
Fax: (03) 3502-9862
Web site: http://www.eneos.co.jp

Public Company
Incorporated: 1893 as Nippon Oil Company, Limited
Employees: 13,882
Sales: ¥4.19 trillion ($34.89 billion) (2003)
Stock Exchanges: Tokyo Osaka Nagoya Fukuoka
Sapporo
Ticker Symbol: 5001
NAIC: 324110 Petroleum Refineries; 211111 Crude
Petroleum and Natural Gas Extraction; 324121
Asphalt Paving Mixture and Block Manufacturing;
324191 Petroleum Lubricating Oil and Grease
Manufacturing; 325110 Petrochemical Manufacturing;
422710 Petroleum Bulk Stations and Terminals;
422720 Petroleum and Petroleum Products
Wholesalers (Except Bulk Stations and Terminals);
447110 Gasoline Stations with Convenience Stores;
447190 Other Gasoline Stations; 454311 Heating Oil
Dealers; 454312 Liquefied Petroleum Gas (Bottled
Gas) Dealers

Nippon Oil Corporation is Japan's largest importer and distributor of petroleum products, controlling about 25 percent of the market. The company's main petroleum products include gasoline, naphtha, kerosene, diesel fuel, jet fuel, heavy fuel oil, lubricants, and asphalt. Nippon owns seven crude oil refineries in Japan that have a total daily capacity of about 1.22 million barrels. It operates a network of nearly 11,700 service stations throughout the country, approximately 2,750 of which are company-owned; all of the stations operate under the ENEOS brand. Nippon Oil also is engaged in a number of related activities, including oil and natural gas exploration and production, natu-

ral gas distribution, electric power generation, and the manufacture of petrochemicals. Oil and natural gas production is centered in Vietnam, the U.K. North Sea, the Gulf of Mexico, Canada, Papua New Guinea, and Myanmar. Nippon Oil shares a broad alliance with Cosmo Oil Company, Limited involving crude-oil procurement, refining, and distribution, and is also active in several alliances with Idemitsu Kosan Co., Ltd.

Origins During Japanese Oil Industry Infancy

Nippon Oil Company was founded in 1888 during the Meiji restoration, which lasted from 1867 to 1912. This was a time of extraordinary changes in Japan. The government transformed Japan into a world power and sought to model the country's development on that of the West. Western technology, especially that of the United States, was used to modernize the Japanese economy. A parliamentary system of government was introduced in 1885, modeled on that of Germany.

While the Japanese oil industry was itself in its infancy, many entrepreneurs—*yamashi*—capitalized on the growing demand for oil created by Japanese industrialization. In 1888, 21 *yamashi* founded Nippon Oil. All were wealthy landowners at a time when most Japanese were landless peasants. Control of Nippon Oil rested with these shareholders, who owned 66 percent of the stock. Yet most decisions were made by two men, Gonzaburo Yamaguchi and the man who became the first company president, Hisahiro Natio. Almost immediately after the company was formed, successful drilling for crude oil began at Amaze, north of Tokyo. Within a year drilling also took place off the Japanese coast, and Nippon became the first Japanese company to drill offshore for oil.

A key to the company's initial success was its willingness to obtain technology from abroad. In particular, Nippon Oil looked to the United States, which had already pioneered technological innovations in the oil industry. In 1889 Yamaguchi visited the United States to obtain information on the latest advances in oil drilling. Impressed by the sophistication of U.S. technology, Yamaguchi, on his return, persuaded his colleagues to purchase an advanced drilling machine from the Pierce company of New York. Yamaguchi hired a Texan to instruct Nippon Oil employees in the operation of the new equipment.

Profits in the infant oil company were small. The salary of the American drilling equipment expert amounted to 12 percent of total company expense; yet Nippon Oil was determined to master Western technology. The financial depression of 1897, which led to the collapse of many of Japan's smaller oil companies, left Nippon Oil with an ever increasing share of Japanese oil production and refining.

Key Acquisitions of International Petroleum and Hoden Oil in the Early 20th Century

In 1900 Nippon Oil experienced stiff competition from the newly arrived International Petroleum. This company had been founded in Japan but was operated by the American Standard Oil Company. In 1907 Nippon Oil overcame this domestic competition by purchasing all the Japanese assets of International Petroleum. By so doing, Nippon Oil became one of the largest oil companies in Japan. Its major competitor was now another Japanese company, Hoden Oil.

From 1908 onward, Nippon Oil's output of oil gradually decreased as wells became exhausted. Nippon Oil, again relying on U.S. technology, introduced a rotary drill that enabled existing wells to be deepened. Other Japanese companies soon followed Nippon Oil's example, leading to increased oil production throughout Japan.

In World War I, Japan concentrated its activities against the German colonial empire in the Far East. Following Germany's defeat, Japan not only acquired former German colonial possessions in the Pacific but also gained important commercial concessions in China. The war too led to the rapid development of Japanese industry as well as an increase in the demand for oil. In 1921, three years after the end of the war, Nippon Oil merged with its former competitor, Hoden Oil, and controlled 80 percent of domestic crude oil production.

The interwar period in Japan witnessed not only industrial expansion but also an increase in living standards. As the number of automobiles on Japanese roads grew, Nippon Oil established a network of gasoline-storage depots throughout the country. In 1919 the company set up its first hand-pump gasoline service station with an underground storage tank, in Tokyo. By the late 1920s more than 160 stations were in operation.

By the late 1920s also Japan's oil reserves were insufficient to meet the needs of a growing industrialized economy. Imported oil, therefore, became vital for the continued growth of the Japanese economy, and Nippon Oil, like most other Japanese oil refineries, increasingly relied on imported oil. In 1923 Nippon Oil imported only 170,000 kiloliters of oil. The ratio of domestic oil to imported oil was 63 percent to 23 percent. By 1937 only 20 percent of Nippon Oil's crude oil supply came from domestic sources. The remaining 80 percent had to be imported, mainly from the United States. As domestic oil production lessened, importing and refining gradually became Nippon Oil's principal business activity.

Loss of Independence During World War II

During the 1930s, Japan, like other industrialized countries, suffered the effects of the worldwide Great Depression. The Japanese government, under pressure from its army and navy chiefs, sought new markets on the Chinese mainland through military aggression. In 1931 the Japanese military seized Manchuria, forcing Chinese troops to withdraw from the area. In 1937 war had broken out with China. By this time, the military had gained control of the Japanese government and had begun to regulate the Japanese economy to the needs of the war effort. All important industries came under state control. In 1937 Nippon Oil lost all of its independence, coming under the control of a state-run monopolistic organization known as Oil Co-operative Sales.

Japan's role in World War II had a devastating impact on the economy. Japan's reliance on imported oil and other raw materials meant that the country was vulnerable to an Allied blockade. U.S. submarines operating close to the Japanese coast inflicted heavy losses on Japanese oil tankers carrying supplies to the mainland. Slowly the Japanese economy ground to a halt.

Because of the blockade, Nippon Oil's supply of imported oil almost totally dried up. In 1941, in an attempt to encourage domestic production of oil under embargo conditions, the Japanese government merged Nippon Oil with Ogura Oil. Yet, under the weight of heavy bombing attacks on oil installations, little could be done to remedy Japan's acute oil shortage.

Reestablishment of Nippon Oil in the Postwar Period

Japanese defeat in 1945 was followed by a lengthy period of reconstruction under the Allied occupation authority, the objective of which was the reestablishment of a peacetime industrial economy. The old state monopolies were broken up and competition between smaller economic units was encouraged. Nippon Oil Company was reestablished as a wholesaler in 1949 and occupied a much smaller role in the Japanese postwar economy than it had had for decades. Its main activity continued to be the importing and refining of mostly imported oil.

The Korean War, which broke out in 1950, transformed Japan into an important ally of the United States in the Far East and led to closer economic ties between the two countries. In 1951, recognizing the importance of the U.S. connection, Nippon Oil established Nippon Petroleum Refining Company, Limited, as a joint venture with Caltex Petroleum Corporation of the United States—Caltex itself being a joint venture of Standard

Key Dates:

1888: Twenty-one *yamashi* (entrepreneurs) form Nippon Oil Company; almost immediately the firm successfully drills for crude oil at Amaze, north of Tokyo; Nippon soon becomes the first Japanese company to drill offshore for oil.

1907: Nippon buys the Japanese assets of International Petroleum, becoming one of the nation's largest oil companies.

1919: The company sets up its first hand-pump gasoline service station, in Tokyo.

1921: Through a merger with Hoden Oil, Nippon Oil now controls 80 percent of domestic crude oil production.

1937: Nippon Oil loses its independence, coming under control of a state-run monopolistic organization known as Oil Co-operative Sales.

1941: The Japanese government merges Nippon Oil with Ogura Oil.

1949: A much smaller Nippon Oil is reestablished, with its main activity being the importing and refining of oil.

1951: Nippon Oil forms Nippon Petroleum Refining Company, Limited as a joint venture with Caltex Petroleum Corporation.

1955: The company enters the petrochemical and gas industries.

1984: Nippon Oil and Mitsubishi Oil Company, Limited enter into an alliance involving cooperation in wholesale and retail operations and in the use of facilities.

1996: Deregulation of Japan's oil industry begins; Nippon buys Caltex's 50 percent interest in Nippon Petroleum Refining for $1.98 billion.

1998: The company's first self-service station and first Dr. Drive service station are opened.

1999: Nippon Oil and Mitsubishi Oil merge to form Nippon Mitsubishi Oil Corporation, the largest oil company in Japan; Nippon Mitsubishi and Cosmo Oil Company, Limited enter into a wide-ranging alliance involving cooperation in crude-oil procurement, refining, and distribution.

2001: Two majority owned, publicly traded refinery affiliates, Koa Oil Company, Limited and Tohoku Oil Co., Ltd., are made into wholly owned subsidiaries; conversion of service stations to the new ENEOS brand begins.

2002: Koa and Tohoku are merged into the company's main refinery subsidiary, Nippon Mitsubishi Petroleum Refining Company (soon renamed Nippon Petroleum Refining); Nippon Mitsubishi Oil Corporation changes its name to Nippon Oil Corporation.

Oil Company of California (later Chevron Corporation) and the Texas Company (later Texaco Inc.). Most of Nippon's crude oil supply was subsequently purchased from Caltex and refined by Nippon Petroleum. Also in 1951, a further subsidiary, Tokyo Tanker Co., Ltd. was established to transport oil to Japan. In 1955 Nippon Oil entered the petrochemical and gas industry through the establishment of two subsidiaries, Nippon Petrochemicals Company, Limited and Nippon Petroleum Gas Company, Limited.

In 1960 Nippon Oil established an overseas office in the United States, incorporated in Delaware. The 1960s witnessed a period of sustained growth at Nippon Oil. In 1961 operating profits for the year stood at ¥2.13 billion. For 1970 Nippon Oil declared a profit of ¥10.76 billion. This trend of increased profitability was interrupted by events in the Middle East early in the 1970s. Since the end of World War II, Japan had increasingly relied on Middle East oil. The Yom Kippur War of 1973 between Israel and its Arab neighbors interrupted the oil supply. The Arab-dominated Organization of Petroleum Exporting Countries (OPEC) cut production and raised prices. Within a year of the war, prices had quadrupled. These increases might have been passed on to the Japanese consumer, but in 1974 the Japanese government froze retail gas prices. After-tax profit fell at Nippon Oil to ¥902 million, less than one-tenth of what it had been in 1970.

Maneuvering Through an Industry in Flux in the 1980s and 1990s

By 1977 Nippon had recovered from the energy crisis through the growing strength of the Japanese economy and the high appreciation of the yen on world money markets. In 1980 profits reached an all-time high of ¥45.67 billion. The early 1980s, however, witnessed a slump in the oil industry because of an abundance of supply and too much refining capacity. The Japanese Ministry of International Trade and Industry sought to rationalize the oil industry by encouraging cooperation among the large companies. In November 1984 Nippon Oil and Mitsubishi Oil Company, Limited reached an accord on the sharing of marketing and facilities. This pact gave both companies joint command of 25 percent of Japan's oil market. Under the agreement, the two companies cooperated in wholesale and retail operations and use of tanker and storage facilities. Mitsubishi Oil had been 50 percent owned by the U.S. Getty Oil Company until earlier in 1994 when Getty was acquired by Texaco; as part of that buyout, Getty sold its interest to members of the Mitsubishi group and other Japanese buyers for $335 million.

Under the leadership of its chairman, Yasuoki Takeuchi, Nippon Oil during the 1980s took steps to reduce its dependence on Middle East oil. In 1985 alone, Nippon Oil set aside $100 million for the development of oilfields in the United States, and in 1986, Nippon Oil found promising oilfields in North Dakota. The company also reached an agreement with Texaco of the United States for joint development of Alaskan oilfields. Another joint exploration deal with Chevron led to the discovery of two gas fields in the Gulf of Mexico.

This policy of developing alternative sources of supply somewhat reduced dependence on Middle East oil. In 1989 while 56.6 percent of Nippon Oil imports came from the Middle East, 37 percent came from Southeast Asia, and the remaining 6.4 percent from other regions, mainly Mexico.

Japanese oil refiners and distributors were hit hard by the prolonged economic stagnation that afflicted Japan in the wake of the bursting of the bubble economy of the late 1980s. Demand for petroleum products fell sharply in the 1990s, hampering an industry already struggling with overcapacity. Under pressure from the Japanese government, Nippon Oil and two other Japanese refiners in 1991 entered into a joint venture with Saudi Arabian Oil Company and Caltex to build a new export refinery in Saudi Arabia and to turn a mothballed refinery in Japan owned by Nippon Oil into a state-of-the-art plant. The Japanese government hoped to establish a stable procurement route through the venture, but late in 1993, as the economic environment continued to deteriorate, the Japanese refiners pulled out. Meantime, in mid-1992 Hidejiro Osawa was promoted to president, replacing Kentaro Iwamoto, with Takeuchi remaining chairman.

In the fiscal year ending in March 1995, Nippon Oil ceded its number one position in the Japanese oil industry to Idemitsu Kosan Co., Ltd. Competition in the industry—already fierce because of refinery overcapacity and the economic travails—was about to intensify as a result of deregulatory moves initiated by the government. In April 1996 a law limiting oil imports to 29 refiners and distributors was repealed, opening the door for supermarkets, trading companies, and even farm cooperatives to begin importing petroleum products for direct distribution in Japan. In anticipation of this sea change, Caltex elected to partially exit from the Japanese refinery industry, having concluded that it could more profitably import into Japan petroleum products that had been refined elsewhere in Asia, where production costs were cheaper. Caltex, therefore, sold its 50 percent interest in Nippon Petroleum Refining to Nippon Oil for $1.98 billion in April 1996. Caltex held onto a 50 percent interest in Koa Oil Company, Limited, a Japanese oil refiner that supplied almost all of its output to Nippon Oil. In May 1996 Takeuchi stepped down from his post of chairman, which was subsequently made vacant.

The newly competitive environment led to lower prices for petroleum products, sending profits at Nippon Oil and other Japanese refiners on a steadily downward path during the late 1990s. Cost-cutting came to the fore, and Nippon announced in 1996 that it would cut its workforce from 4,200 to 3,600 by decade's end. The company closed 6 of 18 branch offices and also began seeking alliances as an additional way of cutting costs. During 1996 Nippon Oil and Idemitsu Kosan began jointly supplying kerosene and fuel oil, and then the following year the two firms reached an agreement to merge some of their oil tank stations that supplied gasoline to service stations. In November 1997 Nippon announced that it would close its refinery in the city of Niigata in another cost-cutting move. The Niigata refinery was the smallest of Nippon's three wholly owned refineries, with a capacity of just 26,000 barrels per day. A further consequence of lower prices at the gas pump was that many Japanese gas stations were no longer operating profitably. Nippon Oil, along with the other Japanese refiners, began shuttering underperforming outlets. Between March 1997 and September 1998, for example, Nippon reduced the number of stations in its network by nearly 500.

Further roiling the industry was the late 1990s debut in Japan of self-service gasoline stations, after they had long been banned because of an arcane fire regulation. In April 1998 Nippon Oil opened its first self-service station in Kobe through a joint venture with McDonald's Company (Japan) Ltd., an affiliate of McDonald's Corporation. This service station complex included a drive-through McDonald's restaurant and a video rental shop. Additional complexes were subsequently opened in cooperation with McDonald's, the Kentucky Fried Chicken restaurant chain, and other partners. Through these multipurpose outlets, Nippon aimed to reduce labor costs and increase sales of gasoline. Toward similar goals, the company opened its first Dr. Drive service station, also in April 1998. In addition to gasoline, these stations offered a wide range of auto-related products and services, with the latter including vehicle checkups, maintenance and repairs, government-mandated vehicle inspections, and car washing and waxing. By March 2000, Nippon was operating 20 service station complexes incorporating other shops and restaurants and 44 Dr. Drive service stations.

1999 Merger with Mitsubishi, Alliance with Cosmo, Restructuring

In October 1998 Nippon Oil announced that it had agreed to merge with Mitsubishi Oil in a marriage of the second and sixth largest Japanese oil companies. The stock-swap deal, completed in April 1999, created the biggest oil company in Japan, which took the name Nippon Mitsubishi Oil Corporation. It also saved Mitsubishi from possibly severe financial trouble as that company had been beset by mounting losses in the difficult environment in which Japanese oil companies had been operating, ultimately posting a net loss of ¥20.2 billion in 1999. Nippon Oil was the surviving company in the merger, and Osawa served as president of Nippon Mitsubishi. The newly enlarged company wholly or partially owned nine refineries with a total capacity of 1.35 million barrels per day. It controlled about 25 percent of Japan's market for petroleum products, surpassing the previous leader, Idemitsu Kosan. Its retail network included some 14,000 stations, which at least initially continued to operate under the Nisseki and Mitsubishi Oil names. The firm also had a much stronger upstream side, having gained Mitsubishi Oil's exploration and production operations in Vietnam and Papua New Guinea, as well as Mitsubishi's interest in a liquefied natural gas venture in Malaysia.

The new Nippon Mitsubishi moved quickly to achieve its stated goal of cutting annual costs by ¥70 billion ($574 million) over a three-year period. During 2000, its refinery operations were streamlined through several strategic measures. The Mizushima refinery, formerly operated by Mitsubishi Oil, was transferred to Nippon Mitsubishi's main refining subsidiary, the newly renamed Nippon Mitsubishi Petroleum Refining Company. Mitsubishi's refinery in Kawasaki, near Tokyo, a smaller facility with a capacity of 75,000 barrels per day, was shut down. Nippon Mitsubishi also spent ¥26.1 billion ($224 million) to buy out Caltex's remaining stake in Koa Oil. Nippon thus gained majority control of the publicly traded Koa Oil, which operated refineries in Marifu and Osaka with a refinery capacity of 252,000 barrels a day.

In October 1999, in its most significant alliance yet—one that stopped just short of a full merger—Nippon Mitsubishi reached an agreement with Cosmo Oil Company, Limited, the number three Japanese oil firm, to cooperate in a number of areas, including crude oil procurement, tanker allocation, oil refining, petroleum product distribution, lubricant manufacturing, and distribution. The alliance did not extend into the firms' service station operations. The companies hoped to save at least ¥15 billion ($140 million) from synergies by the third year of the partnership. Yet another alliance was entered into in February 2000 with Teikoku Oil Co., Ltd., a firm that had particular strength on the upstream side of the oil business. Nippon Mitsubishi subsequently became Teikoku's largest shareholder, increasing its stake to 16.5 percent.

For the fiscal year ending in March 2000, Nippon Mitsubishi reported a net loss of ¥4.86 billion ($45.8 million) because of a ¥23.3 billion ($220 million) charge it took to change the way it accounted for retirement benefits. About ¥50 billion ($470 million) in cost savings was achieved that year, representing 60 percent of the three-year target. Revenues for the year totaled ¥3.59 trillion ($33.91 billion). In June 2000 Osawa retired and was replaced as president by Fumiaki Watari, who had been vice-president and had joined the former Nippon Oil in 1960.

A main focus for Nippon Mitsubishi over the next two years was the further restructuring of its refinery operations. During 2001, refinery capacity was reduced to 1.23 million barrels per day, increasing the company's capacity utilization from 76 percent to 84 percent. In October 2001 Nippon Mitsubishi bought the minority stakes in two of its majority-owned, publicly traded oil refining affiliates, Koa Oil and Tohoku Oil Co., Ltd.; the latter operated a 145,000-barrel-per-day refinery in the northern Japanese city of Sendai. Then in April 2002 Koa and Tohoku were merged into Nippon Mitsubishi Petroleum Refining Company, which now had refining capacity of 1.17 million barrels per day, or 95 percent of the parent company's total capacity, through the six refineries it operated. Nippon Mitsubishi's seventh refinery, located in Toyama, was operated by the majority-owned Nihonkai Oil Co., Ltd.

At the same time that the integration of the refining operations was nearing completion, integration also was occurring on the retailing side. The company's Nisseki and Mitsubishi Oil service stations were united under a new brand, ENEOS, a process completed in March 2002. The new name was a combination of the words *energy* and *neos,* meaning ''new energy.'' Over the previous three years, Nippon Mitsubishi had gradually trimmed its service station network, so that by the time the name change was effected, it ran about 12,000 stations. Of this total, about 1,300 were Dr. Drive stations.

In June 2002 the company dropped ''Mitsubishi'' from its name, becoming simply Nippon Oil Corporation. Likewise, the refining subsidiary was renamed Nippon Petroleum Refining Company, Limited. In December 2002 Nippon Oil entered into an oil refining alliance with Idemitsu Kosan that would enable the latter firm to close its Hyogo refinery. Nippon agreed to supply Idemitsu with 40,000 barrels per day of petroleum products, including gasoline, kerosene, jet fuel, diesel fuel, and fuel oil. Nippon simultaneously cut its refinery capacity by 10,000 barrels per day. Although the Japanese economy remained sluggish during 2003, Nippon Oil managed a 6 percent increase in net sales, to ¥4.19 trillion ($34.89 billion), while net income increased one-third, jumping from ¥24.01 billion to ¥32.28 billion ($269 million).

In August 2003 Nippon Oil temporarily shut down two of its refineries after discovering that it had falsified inspection reports during a four-year period starting in 1998. Nippon issued an apology for this scandal, but that did not preclude Japan's Ministry of Economy, Trade, and Industry from launching an investigation to determine what penalties, if any, should be imposed on the company. Nippon reduced its profit forecast for 2004 because of the shutdowns.

Looking to the future, Nippon was likely to continue to seek opportunities for streamlining its refining and marketing operations and to pursue further alliances and perhaps mergers. The company also wanted to achieve a better balance between its upstream and downstream operations by expanding its capacity to produce oil and gas from the 2003 level of 50,000 barrels of oil equivalent per day (BOED) to 150,000 BOED within a few years. Nippon Oil was also likely to continue another initiative: using its remaining refineries as bases for expanding into related energy fields, such as electric power generation and liquefied natural gas storage and supply. It was making a concerted effort to become a more comprehensive energy enterprise, lessening its dependence on the troubled Japanese oil refining and distribution sector.

Principal Subsidiaries

OIL REFINING AND WHOLESALING: Nippon Petroleum Refining Company, Limited; Nippon Petroleum Processing Company, Limited; Nihonkai Oil Co., Ltd. (66%); Wakayama Petroleum Refining Co., Ltd. (50%). OIL STORAGE AND TRANSPORT: Nippon Oil Staging Terminal Company, Limited; Nippon Oil Tanker Corporation; Okinawa CTS Corporation (65%). GAS BUSINESS: Nippon Petroleum Gas Company, Limited (95.2%). OIL DEVELOPMENT AND OVERSEAS OPERATIONS: Nippon Oil Exploration Limited; Nippon Oil Exploration U.S.A. Limited; Nippon Oil Exploration and Production U.K. Limited; Japan Vietnam Petroleum Co., Ltd. (53.1%). OVERSEAS OIL MARKETING: Nippon Oil (U.S.A.) Limited (U.S.A.); Nippon Oil (Asia) Pte. Ltd. (Singapore). PETROCHEMICALS BUSINESS: Nippon Petrochemicals Company, Limited. CONSTRUCTION AND ENGINEERING: Nippon Oil Engineering and Construction Co., Ltd.; Nippon Hodo Co., Ltd. (56%). OTHER: Nippon Oil (Australia) Pty. Limited; Nippon Oil Finance (Netherlands) B.V.; Nippon Oil Real Estate Company, Limited; Nippon Oil Trading Corporation; Nippon Oil Information Systems Company, Limited.

Principal Competitors

Exxon Mobil Corporation; Idemitsu Kosan Co., Ltd.; Showa Shell Sekiyu K.K.; Nippon Mining Holdings, Inc.

Further Reading

Abrahams, Paul, ''Oil Groups Reveal Big Merger Deal,'' *Financial Times,* October 29, 1998, p. 27.
Aoto, Maki, ''Nippon Mitsubishi Merges Units,'' *Asian Wall Street Journal,* February 8, 2002, p. M7.
——, ''Nippon Oil, Idemitsu to Team in Crude-Refining Operations,'' *Asian Wall Street Journal,* December 11, 2002, p. M3.
''Nippon-Mitsubishi Merger Speeds Overhaul of Japanese Refining-Marketing Industry,'' *Oil and Gas Journal,* March 1, 1999, pp. 23–26.

''Nippon Oil, Mitsubishi Oil Agree to Merge,'' *Oil and Gas Journal,* November 2, 1998.

''Refineries Strike Deal to Trim Capacity,'' *Nikkei Weekly,* December 16, 2002.

Timmermans, Jeffrey, ''Chevron, Texaco to Sell Refinery Stake to Nippon Oil for Total of $1.98 Billion,'' *Wall Street Journal,* December 7, 1995, p. A11.

Uyehara, S., *The Industry and Trade of Japan,* London: P.S. King & Son, 1936.

Watanabe, Mika, ''Alliance Should Boost Oil Firms' Profit: Nippon Mitsubishi, Cosmo Will Integrate Most Operations to Cut Cost,'' *Asian Wall Street Journal,* October 13, 1999, p. 4.

——, ''Nippon Mitsubishi to Purchase Caltex's Remaining Koa Oil Shares,'' *Asian Wall Street Journal,* July 29, 1999, p. 4.

—Michael Doorley
—update: David E. Salamie

Norske Skogindustrier ASA

PO Box 329
Lysaker
N-1326
Norway
Telephone: 47 67 59 90 00
Fax: 47 67 59 91 81
Web site: http://www.norske-skog.com

Public Company
Incorporated: 1962
Employees: 9,213
Sales: NOK 24.07 billion ($3.97 billion) (2003)
Stock Exchanges: Oslo
Ticker Symbol: NSG.OL
NAIC: 322110 Pulp Mills; 322121 Paper (Except Newsprint) Mills

Norske Skogindustrier ASA (the name literally means Norwegian Paper Industry) has repositioned itself at the beginning of the 21st century as the world's second largest producer of publication papers, including newsprint and magazine quality paper. The company produces more than eight million tons of paper each year, with newsprint paper accounting for approximately two-thirds of the group's total activity. In a little more than a decade, Norske Skog has transformed itself from a relatively minor player wholly focused on the Norwegian market to one of the paper industry's global giants. The company owns wholly or in partnership more than 50 paper production facilities in 24 countries worldwide. Europe remains the group's biggest market, with mills in Austria, France, The Netherlands, the Czech Republic, Germany, and the United Kingdom, in addition to several plants in Norway. The company is also highly present in the Australasian market, with mills in Australia and New Zealand, and in South America, with mills in Chile and Brazil. The company also holds a 36 percent stake in Canadian paper giant Norske Canada, and a 50 percent stake in the Pan Asia Paper joint venture with partner Abitibi. In 2003, Norske Skog sold off the last of its forestry holdings in its drive toward refocusing itself exclusively around paper production. The company has exited a number of other fields, such as pulp production and power generation. The company's sales topped NOK 24 billion ($4 billion) in 2003.

Norwegian Forestry Consolidator in the 1960s

In the late 1950s, a group of forest owners from Norway's central region began exploring the possibility of grouping together in an effort to create a reliable outlet for their forestry products. Their talks led to the creation of a new company, Norske Skog—pronounced closer to "skoog" in English, the word means "paper"—in 1962. Major financial backing for the venture came from the Norwegian Forest Owners' Federation, which became the new company's majority shareholder at 50 percent. The company initially targeted the newsprint sector.

Observers were skeptical about the new company's chances of success, as the founding group had little industrial experience among them. Moreover, Norske Skog had to overcome other obstacles, including low cash reserves—the company's startup capital stood at just NOK 49 million—and a lack of marketing experience. Nonetheless, the company pushed ahead with plans to build its own mills and begin newsprint production.

Despite its small size, the company decided to build a mill with two newsprint machines, at a total investment cost of some NOK 300 million—a move credited with giving Norske Skog the production capacity it needed to survive its early years. The first newsprint machine at the company's Skogn mill was completed in 1966; the second machine was in production the following year.

By the early 1970s, Norske Skog was a profitable and expanding business. The company's shareholders had agreed to plow profits back into the company—the company was to pay dividends for the first time only in 1983—and Norske Skog now began a diversification effort, becoming a driving force behind the restructuring of the Norwegian forestry and paper and pulp sectors. In 1972, Norske Skog reached a cooperation agreement with Follum Fabrikker, one of Norway's oldest paper producers founded in 1873, in which each company acquired shares in the other. At the same time, the two companies agreed to form a joint marketing and logistics program for their newsprint production.

Norway's small size—and the risks that competition among the country's paper and pulp producers might result in the collapse of the domestic industry—brought new impetus for consolidation of the pulp, paper, and forestry sectors in the 1980s. Norske Skog had continued its expansion and diversification, in part by building up its shareholding in Follum as well as by gaining a majority share in Skien, Norway-based newsprint producer Union, and in part by diversifying its holdings. By the late 1980s, Norske Skog, along with its forest holdings and newsprint production, had added lumber and wood products, packaging, printing, retail book and stationery operations, and even power generation facilities. The company also became a leading Norwegian wood pulp producer through a controlling stake in Tofte Industrier.

Norske Skog completed its hold over Follum in 1989, forming the basis of a three-way merger, together with Tofte, that created Norway's dominant newsprint group. Shortly after the merger, the enlarged group took over another paper producer, Saugbrugsforeningen, a company with operations dating back to the late 1850s. As a result of that acquisition, and including the group's stake in Union, Norske Skog emerged with control over nearly all of Norway's newsprint production. The company also used the Saugbrugs plant as the springboard for its launch into the magazine paper sector, investing NOK 3 billion to build a new paper machine at the site in 1990.

European Leadership in the 1990s

Norske Skog now began a long, two-pronged process. On one side, the group began to refocus itself as a dedicated paper producer, while on the other Norske Skog began plans to expand its operations internationally for the first time. The company began selling off its noncore holdings in 1990, starting with the shutdown of its Otto Langmoen sawmill, followed by the winding up of a cellulose mill and a laminates plant in 1991. That year, as well, the company sold off its retail book- and stationery-store network and its wholesale and retail printing operations. The company also exited the packaging sector with the sale of three subsidiaries.

In the meantime, the company had made its first overseas purchase. In 1990, the company bought up 49 percent of France's Papeteries de Golbey SA. Following that purchase, Norske Skog began construction of a first newsprint mill at the French facility, spending more than NOK 3 billion. That machine came on-stream in 1992, boosting the group's total capacity by more than 250,000 tons per year. Soon after, the company brought its new Saugsbrugs magazine paper machine online, adding another 550,000 tons per year of capacity.

Divestments continued into the mid-decade, including the sale of the group's 50 percent stake in Olaf Norlis Bokhandel, and paper products distributor Ad. Jacobsen, in 1993, and the group's building materials supply division in 1997. The company also began seeking buyers for its forest holdings—a move that highlighted the group's transformation into a dedicated paper producer.

Norske Skog took full control of Papeteries de Golbey in 1995. The company began plans to expand the French site's capacity again, launching construction of a new, NOK 2.8 billion machine in 1997. The new machine, launched in 1998, added another 335,000 tons per year to the group's production in France.

At the same time, Norske Skog sought a deeper penetration into the European paper industry. In 1996, the company bought a mill in Bruck, Austria. The site added some 220,000 tons per year of magazine paper and 115,000 tons per year of newsprint to Norske Skog's total. The company remained in Central Europe for its next purchase, buying up a newsprint mill in Steti, in the Czech Republic, adding 100,000 tons per year of newsprint capacity in 1997. By the end of that year, Norske Skog's total production had topped two million tons.

Global Newsprint Leader in the 2000s

The late 1990s marked a new turning point in the company's history. Norske Skog now began targeting expansion beyond Europe in an effort to join the ranks of top global publication paper producers. In 1998, the company bought 90 percent control of a newsprint mill in Korea, boasting 180,000 tons per year, as well as a mill in Thailand, adding an additional 120,000 per year to the group's Asian capacity. Both mills had previously been owned by Korea's Shin Ho Paper.

The company's Asian ambitions became clearer at the end of 1998, when the company agreed to a form a joint venture with Canada's Abitibi Consolidated and Korea's Hansol Paper Co. to form Pan Asia Paper. The new company, owned at one-third each by the partners, then acquired Hansol's Korean and Chinese newsprint operations for $1 billion. Pan Asia then bought up Norske Skog's Korean and Thai holdings as well.

Norske Skog completed its ownership of Union in 1999. The company then began a new phase in its restructuring, shedding still more of its noncore holdings, including a merger of its sawn timber business into Moelven Industrier that year. The company also sold off its Fibo-Trespo laminate products business in 1999. By 2001, the company had sold off nearly 20 noncore operations. Instead, the group turned its attention to the South American market, acquiring a 50 percent stake in the newsprint operations of Brazil's Industrias Klabin de Papel e Cellulose. At the same time, Norske Skog announced its intention to seek out a major international acquisition.

That opportunity came the following year, when Norske Skog reached an agreement to acquire New Zealand newsprint and magazine paper group Fletcher Challenge Paper. The purchase, worth NOK 21 billion ($2.5 billion) nearly doubled Norske Skog's size, adding mills in New Zealand, Australia, Canada, Brazil, Chile, and Malaysia. The move gave Norske Skog control of some 13 percent of the global publication papers market.

The new paper giant continued to seek acquisition opportunities. The company's next target came in Canada, where it agreed to merge Pacifica Papers into its Norske Skog Canada subsidiary in a deal worth CAD 900 million. Following the merger, Norske Skog's stake in the Canadian operation was reduced to just 36 percent, and accordingly the company changed its name to Norske Canada.

By the end of 2002, Norske Skog had expanded its production capacity past eight million tons, while boosting revenues to more than NOK 24 billion ($4 billion). The company now took a break from acquisitions as it worked to integrate its newly expanded global operations. At the same time, however, Norske Skog continued in its drive to shed its noncore holdings. In 2002, the company sold off its 13 hydropower electric generating plants for NOK 1.4 billion. By the end of 2003, it also had found a buyer for the last of its forest holdings, a 330,000-acre tract.

By then, too, Norske Skog once again began plotting for further expansion, now eyeing the Asian region. In 2001, Hansol had exited the Pan Asia Paper joint venture, enabling Norske Skog to increase its share to 50 percent. That company now prepared to step up its presence in the massive Chinese market, forming a joint venture with Hebei Longteng Paper Corporation to form Hebei Pan Asia Long-Teng Paper Co. The move, which included construction of a new paper mill expected to be completed in 2005, was slated to double Pan Asia's Chinese production and confirm its position as the largest paper producer in Asia, excluding Japan. In just 40 years, Norske Skog had grown from a tiny Norwegian company to a major player in the worldwide paper sector.

Principal Subsidiaries

Nornews AS, Lysaker; Norske Treindustrier AS; Lysaker Invest AS; Norske Skog Holding AS; Norske Skog Flooring Holding AS; Embretsfos Fabrikker AS; Union Paper & Co. AS; Wood and Logistics AS; Oksenøyveien 80 AS; Norske Skog Golbey (France); Pan Asia Paper Company Ltd. (Singapore; 50%); Norske Skog Bruck GmbH (Austria); Norske Skog Steti (Czech Republic); Norske Skog Osterreich GmbH (Austria); Markproject Ltd. (England); Norske Skog Deutschland GmbH (Germany); Norske Skog (UK) Ltd.; Norske Skog Holland B.V.; Norske Skog Belgium NV; Nornews Portugal (75%); Norske Skog Espana S.A. (Spain); Norske Skog (Ireland) Ltd.; Norske Skog (Schweiz) AG; Norske Skog Danmark ApS; Norske Skog Italia S.R.L.; Norske Skog France S.A.R.L.; Norske Skog Japan Co. Ltd.; Norske Skog AB (Sweden); Norske Skog Polska Sp. z.o.o. (Poland); Norske Skog Hungary Trading and Service Limited; THP Paper Company (Canada).

Principal Competitors

Marubeni Corporation; International Paper Co.; Georgia-Pacific Corporation; Perm Timber Producers Joint Stock Co.; Mondi Ltd.; Weyerhaeuser Co.; Zaklady Celulozy i Papieru CELULOZA SWIECIE S.A.; VENEPAL SACA; Krasnoyarsk Pulp and Paper Mill Joint Stock Co.; Stora Enso Oyj; Orkla ASA; Jefferson Smurfit Group PLC.

Further Reading

"Change of Leadership in Norske Skog," *Australasian Business Intelligence,* January 28, 2004.

Criscione, Valeria, "Expansion Extends Grip on Global Imprint," *Financial Times,* April 5, 2001, p. 16.

——, "Norske Skog Near to Deal on Sell-off," *Financial Times,* July 1, 2002, p. 27.

——, "Norske Skog Set for More Growth," *Financial Times,* January 11, 2001, p. 28.

"Norske Skog Sells Forest for NOK 153 Million," *Nordic Business Report,* November 13, 2003.

"Norske Skog to Buy New Zealand's Fletcher Challenge Paper," *European Report,* April 21, 2000.

Rosenberg, Jim, "Is Norske the Next No. 1 in Newsprint?," *Editor & Publisher,* April 2, 2001, p. 24.

—M.L. Cohen

Oceaneering International, Inc.

11911 FM 529
Houston, Texas 77041
U.S.A.
Telephone: (713) 329-4500
Fax: (713) 329-4951
Web site: http://www.oceaneering.com

Public Company
Incorporated: 1969
Employees: 3,500
Sales: $639.25 million (2003)
Stock Exchanges: New York Pacific Philadelphia
Ticker Symbol: OII
NAIC: 213112 Support Activities for Oil and Gas
    Operations; 234920 Power and Communication
    Transmission Line Construction; 234930 Industrial
    Nonbuilding Structure Construction; 235990 All Other
    Special Trade Contractors; 334511 Search, Detection,
    Navigation, Guidance, Aeronautical, and Nautical
    System and Instrument Manufacturing; 541330
    Engineering Services; 541370 Surveying and Mapping
    (Except Geophysical) Services; 541710 Research and
    Development in the Physical, Engineering, and Life
    Sciences

Oceaneering International, Inc. (OII) provides an array of services and equipment to customers operating in various forbidding environments, including deepwater and space. Activities include underwater drilling support and inland environmental inspection services. Hardware includes remotely operated diving vessels (ROVs) and robotic devices for the space program and amusement parks.

About half the company's revenues come from outside the United States. Oceaneering is active in the deepwater oil fields in the North Sea and off the coasts of West Africa and Brazil as well as in the Gulf of Mexico. It is a world leader in the market for umbilicals, or undersea connectors. The company is active during the exploration, development, and production phases of the oil and gas life cycle.

The company's Advanced Technologies Group applies tools and techniques from the offshore drilling support business to non-oil related industries. This unit is often called in to search for debris after high-profile air accidents over water, such as the ValuJet crash over the Everglades and the downed TWA Flight 800. It also filmed footage of the RMS *Titanic* at a depth of 12,500 feet. "This is a real-life Jules Verne operation," CEO John Huff told *Investor's Business Daily.*

Oceaneering Origins

Oceaneering International, Inc. grew from a Gulf of Mexico diving business founded in 1964. Combined with two other diving outfits, the company was incorporated in 1969. According to *Investor's Business Daily,* most of the company's work in its first four decades involved inspecting the legs of oil rigs in the Gulf of Mexico.

Oceaneering relocated its headquarters from Santa Barbara, California, to Houston in March 1980. A merger with the French firm Comex S.A. was planned in 1981 but never consummated.

Oceaneering completed a number of acquisitions during the 1980s. The Canadian offshore surveying company Marinav Corp. was acquired in 1982 for $3 million. A $37 million stock swap in 1984 gave OII a new underwater services unit, Solus Ocean Systems Inc., which was formerly owned by Enserch Corp. of Dallas.

An important acquisition was made in 1983. That year, Oceaneering acquired Steadfast Marine Inc., a marine search firm employed by the U.S. Navy. Steadfast was derived from Seaward Inc., a partnership formed in 1972. It was named Oceaneering's East Coast Division after the acquisition; it had operations in McLean, Virginia, and Fort Lauderdale, Florida.

J. Wesley Rogers was promoted to the CEO position in 1982, succeeding Edward A. Wardwell. D. Michael Hughes, one of the company's founders, was chairman from 1970 to 1978 and took the post again in 1984. Rogers died in a plane crash in 1986, and was replaced by John R. Huff, who had been chairman and president of oilfield services firm Western Oceanic, a unit of the Western Co. of North America, from 1980 to early 1986. He was elected chairman of Oceaneering in 1990.

Huff had studied civil engineering and played football at Rice University and Georgia Tech, and later attended Harvard Business School. Other early jobs included assignments with The Offshore Co. (later Sonat Offshore) and Zapata Offshore.

Revenues were $120 million in fiscal 1986 and, reports *Forbes,* the company had a loss of $45 million in the previous three years. During the fiscal year, the company had begun applying project management and other services and equipment to non-oilfield related markets though its Oceaneering Technologies division.

Late 1980s Recovery

Oceaneering lost $70 million between 1982 and 1987. Huff led the company through a recapitalization program in 1987. The offshore oilfield supply business was experiencing severe competition in the last half of the 1980s. The company bid for more U.S. Navy work to get by.

Oceaneering was the Navy's global contractor for marine searches. The firm conducted some high-profile underwater searches in the 1980s, seeking the wreckage of the Space Shuttle Challenger and Korean Air Lines Flight 007. Record depths of more than 17,000 feet were breached in other cases. Such searches called for state-of-the-art gathering and analysis of sonar data, and Oceaneering developed a reputation as the best of the best.

Revenues were $183.4 million in the 1990 fiscal year, producing net income of $10.3 million—nearly nine times the previous year's figure. Business benefited from large undersea construction projects in the North Sea. Oceaneering had 1,500 employees at the time, and trained divers at its own College of Oceaneering near Los Angeles. OII bought the school in 1981 and owned it until 1995. It had been launched in 1967 as the Commercial Dive Center.

In 1991, Oceaneering acquired its first tanker for gathering and storing from well off the coast of Africa. This represented the start of the company's Mobile Offshore Production Systems (MOPS) division. Oceaneering shares migrated from the NASDAQ to the New York Stock Exchange in December 1991.

Two new divisions, Oceaneering Technologies and Oceaneering Space Systems, were created to cater to non-oilfield customers. Oceaneering Technologies, based in western New York, handled such chores as inspecting bridges and aboveground structural inspections.

OII acquired Eastport International Inc., a Maryland-based producer of robotic systems, through a $10 million stock deal in August 1992. Eastport had 200 employees, revenues of about $25 million a year, and had billed itself as the world's leading undersea search and recovery firm.

Eastport was a pioneer in the development of ROVs, or remotely operated diving vessels (these were the size of small automobiles). Renamed Oceaneering's Advanced Technologies Group (ATG), this unit also was breaking into the entertainment business. One of its higher visibility projects was a leaping robotic shark for the Jaws ride at the Universal Studios theme park in Orlando. OII's revenues were $168 million in fiscal 1992. The company was profitable again, with earnings of $16 million.

Shooting for the Stars in 1993

OII acquired the assets of ILC Dover Inc.'s Space Systems division in 1993. OII already had been designing robotic tools for space applications on a small scale for several years. Space Systems also manufactured thermal protection blankets used in aircraft and space vehicles. The ILC buy brought with it important contracts with major aerospace suppliers including Lockheed. ILC Space Systems had 120 employees and revenues of $11 million.

In March 1994, OII acquired Multiflex, a leading producer of umbilicals, or connectors, for the offshore petroleum industry. It had been founded in 1977 and was acquired from Edisto Resources Corp. for $12 million.

OII employed about 2,000 people in the mid-1990s. It had 46 offices in 37 countries around the world. With 60 ROVs, the company operated the second largest fleet in the world. Utilization was increasing as oil companies turned increasingly to deepwater oil production. Sales were $290 million in the fiscal year ended March 31, 1996, producing earnings of $12.4 million.

OII's Advanced Technology Group also laid fiber optic cable on the sea floor. The division had revenues of about $25 million a year in the late 1990s.

Late 1990s Capital Projects

In 1998, the parent company had revenues of $358 million and a net income of $22 million. It employed 2,600 people in 30 countries. The company had just started a five-year capital improvement plan. From 1997 to 2002, Huff told the *Wall Street Transcript,* OII invested $450 million in capital projects, most of it to support its oilfield-related business.

The Multiflex umbilical operations were expanded by doubling the size of its U.K. subsidiary's facilities and established manufacturing in Brazil. Multiflex's operations also were upgraded.

The company's largest single capital investment was $90 million to build a MOPS unit off the coast of western Australia. In 2002, Oceaneering had three such units.

OII also invested in developing its ROV business. AUVs, or autonomous underwater vehicles, accounted for only $2 million in sales in 2000, but were growing in importance. These could perform preprogrammed tasks without being tethered by control cables.

Key Dates:

1969: Oceaneering is formed from three diving companies.
1980: Headquarters are relocated from Santa Barbara to Houston.
1983: Navy search contractor Steadfast Marine is acquired.
1991: The first MOPS unit is acquired.
1992: ROV pioneer Eastport International is acquired.
1993: ILC Space Systems is acquired.
1994: Multiflex umbilicals supplier is acquired.
1997: Five-year, $450 million capital improvement plan is launched.
2003: Rotator AS is acquired.
2004: ROV holdings are acquired from Stolt Offshore.

By 2002, Oceaneering dominated the ROV market with a 30 percent share. Deepwater—sometimes more than 5,000 feet deep—was becoming an attractive area for oil companies to explore. In 2000, the Advanced Technology Group was called in to lift the *Hunley,* a downed Confederate submarine that had been located five years earlier.

Rotator AS, a Norwegian outfit that produced valves for offshore oil and gas use, was acquired from Houston-based Grant Prideco in September 2003. It had revenues of about $16 million a year.

Oceaneering reported revenues of $639.25 million in 2003, with net income of $29.3 million. Booming oil prices in early 2004 meant more interest in exploring for oil, and great prospects for support companies such as Oceaneering. The company was relocating its Multiflex USA division from Houston to Panama City, Florida.

In early 2004, OII acquired 44 ROVs and other assets from Stolt Offshore S.A. for $48.4 million. These ROVs were based in western Africa, Brazil, and Norway.

Principal Subsidiaries

Consolidated Launcher Technology, Inc.; Eastport International, Inc.; Gulf Coast International Inspection, Inc.; Ian Murray Engineering Ltd. (U.K.); Marine Production Systems do Brasil Ltda.; Marine Production Systems Ltd.; Marine Production Systems Servicos Ltda.; Multiflex, Inc.; Ocean Systems Engineering Ltd.; Ocean Systems Engineering, Inc.; Oceanteam UK Limited; Oil Industry Engineering, Inc.; Specialty Wire and Cable Co., Inc.; Steadfast Oceaneering, Inc.; P.T. Calmarine (50%); Smit Oceaneering Cable Systems, L.L.C. (50%); Pro-Dive Oceaneering Co. (49%); Rotator AS (Norway).

Principal Divisions

Advanced Technologies; Offshore Oil and Gas.

Principal Operating Units

Remotely Operated Vehicles (ROVs); Subsea Products; Mobile Offshore Production Systems; Other Services.

Principal Competitors

Alcatel S.A.; Global Industries, Ltd.; Halliburton Company; Kvaerner Oilfield Products; Saipem; Technip-Coflexip; Thales S.A.

Further Reading

Alva, Marilyn, "Oceaneering International Inc.: Houston, Texas Support to Oil Drillers Has Deep-Sea Expert Swimming in Profits," *Investor's Business Daily,* May 9, 2002, p. A9.

Boisseau, Charles, "Company Thriving on Diving; Oceaneering, Finding Calmer Waters, Continues Focus on Underwater Services Business," *Houston Chronicle,* The Chronicle 100/Houston's Leading Companies, May 23, 1993, p. 6.

Coghlan, Keely, "Analysts Paint Bright Picture for ROVs, But Oceaneering Takes More Cautious View," *Oil Daily,* May 23, 2000.

D'Oliveira, Stephen, "No Ocean Too Deep for Them; Team Takes on Jobs to Do Survey Work," *Sun Sentinel* (Fort Lauderdale), July 7, 1991, p. 1B.

Durgin, Hillary, "Becoming Clearer: Oceaneering Sinks Money into Services; Unit's Growth Gives Strategy New Focus," *Houston Chronicle,* Bus. Sec., August 31, 1996, p. 1.

Fletcher, Sam, "Oceaneering to Double Manufacturing Capacity," *Oil Daily,* September 10, 1997, p. 4.

——, "Offshore Oil Platform Technology Blasts Off," *Houston Post,* September 25, 1992, p. C1.

Gallagher, Kathleen, "Demand for Gas Is Factor: Oceaneering May Offer Investment Worth Exploring," *Milwaukee Journal Sentinel,* Bus. Sec., May 20, 1996, p. 12.

Hamilton, Carl, "Expert Survives Swamp; The Rescue and Recovery Technician Said the ValuJet Crash Site Assignment Was His Hardest," *York Daily Record* (Pennsylvania), June 1, 1996, p. 1.

Harnett, Dwayne, "Oceaneering International to Bring High-Paying Jobs to Bay County, Fla.," *News Herald* (Panama City, Florida), December 23, 2003.

Kelly, Andrew, "Oceaneering Can Ride Oil-Price Storm—CEO," *Reuters News,* August 21, 1998.

Liberante, Carrie A., "Oceaneering's Inland Unit Thriving on Diving," *Buffalo News,* Bus. Sec., May 29, 1994, p. 7.

Mack, Toni, "Underwater Rescue," *Forbes,* November 9, 1992, pp. 190+.

Mintz, Bill, "Oceaneering Says It's Now on Course to Bigger Profits," *Houston Chronicle,* December 18, 1995, p. B6.

Neuberger, Christine, "Firm Gets to the Bottom of All Things Lost at Sea," *Richmond Times-Dispatch,* Bus. Sec, January 19, 1992.

Petty, John Ira, "Oceaneering's Huff Making Drive to Paydirt," *Houston Post,* July 2, 1990, p. C16.

Redden, Jim, "Huff Examines Diving Industry," *Offshore,* October 1986, pp. 32+.

Schlegel, Darrin, "Underwater Firm Goes Airborne Via Space Acquisition," *Houston Business Journal,* June 7, 1993, pp. 1+.

Shelsby, Ted, "Undersea Search Company OKs Takeover; Texas Rival to Buy Eastport," *Sun* (Baltimore), July 15, 1992, p. 9C.

Swoboda, Frank, "Getting to the Bottom of It All," *Washington Post,* September 21, 1998, p. F10.

—Frederick C. Ingram

Phillips Foods, Inc.

1215 East Fort Avenue
Baltimore, Maryland 21230
U.S.A.
Telephone: (443) 263-1200
Toll Free: (888) 234-2722
Fax: (410) 837-8526
Web site: http://www.phillipsfoods.com

Private Company
Incorporated: 1914 as A.E. Phillips & Sons
Employees: 1,200
Sales: $200 million (2002 est.)
NAIC: 311712 Fresh and Frozen Seafood Processing;
    114112 Shellfish Fishing; 722110 Full-Service
    Restaurants; 722210 Limited-Service Eating Places

Phillips Foods, Inc. is the world's largest manufacturer of blue swimming crabmeat and products, operating 13 processing plants in the United States and abroad. A family- owned and operated company, Phillips Foods is the processing and wholesale side of the Phillips family's involvement in the seafood industry. The family also operates seven restaurants in the eastern United States that are controlled by Phillips Seafood Restaurants. Phillips Foods and Phillips Seafood Restaurants share the same management. Phillips Foods' processing facilities are primarily located overseas, scattered throughout southeast Asia and South America. The company has plants in Baltimore, Maryland, Vietnam, Thailand, the Philippines, Indonesia, East Malaysia, India, and Ecuador. Phillips Foods produces crab and other seafood products for Phillips Seafood Restaurants and for sale to retailers and other restaurants. More than a half-dozen regional sales offices serve more than 11,000 accounts in the United States, selling a range of value-added seafood products made by Phillips Foods.

Origins

For multiple generations of the Phillips family, the production and sale of crabs defined their lives. "The story is the growth of a small family-run company into a monolith," an industry observer noted in a November 30, 2002 interview with *Daily Record*, referring to the rise of the Phillips family in the seafood industry. The company began operating in 1914, when the patriarch of the family, A.E. Phillips, opened a crab packing plant on Hooper's Island in Maryland's Chesapeake Bay. Phillips, the great-grandfather of the generation in charge of Phillips Foods in the 21st century, made his livelihood processing blue crab, a species found in abundance along the Atlantic and Gulf coasts of North America. Phillips's company, A.E. Phillips & Sons, thrived on Hooper's Island, becoming a fixture in the area. For four decades, the extent of the Phillips family enterprise consisted solely of the packing plant established in 1914. The business's development into a "monolith," began modestly 42 years after A.E. Phillips began processing crab. A second generation of Phillips family members, led by Shirley and Brice Phillips, were responsible for the business' first diversification, an offshoot that eventually became a multimillion-dollar-in-sales component of the Phillips's seafood conglomerate.

The Phillips family's entry into the restaurant business began with a $2,000 investment. The initial aim of the diversification was to create sideline business. "We just wanted to sell off some of the crab from our packing house in Hopper's Island," Brice Phillips was quoted as saying on the company's web site. In 1956, Brice and Shirley Phillips moved to Ocean City, Maryland, settling in the small, resort town at a time when businesses were only open in the summer. Brice and Shirley Phillips aspired to live a leisurely paced life selling surplus crab from the family's processing plant while they raised their two sons, Steve and Jeffrey. They paid $2,000 to establish a carryout shop, a four-seat crab stand they built in the north end of Ocean City. The popularity of the crab shack soon demanded more time than Shirley and Brice Phillips anticipated, as tourists flocked to the location, prompting the Phillipses to open a dining room in time for the second season of business. This first restaurant, known as Phillips Crab House, became the foundation for a small chain of restaurants operated by the Phillips family, eventually expanding into a 1,200-seat dining facility.

The family's packing plant served as the source of the crab used by Phillips Crab House, as it would serve for additional restaurants opened by the family. A second dining establishment was opened in 1973, when Phillips-By-The-Sea, also located in Ocean City, debuted. A third Ocean City restaurant opened four years later, an establishment called Phillips Seafood House, which featured three dining rooms, two kitchens, and seating for 350 patrons. After 20 years of exposure in Ocean City, where three restaurants served to broadcast the association of the Phillips name with crab, the family was ready to expand outside of Ocean City. Many of the visitors to Ocean City were tourists from nearby metropolitan areas such as Baltimore, Philadelphia, and Washington, D.C. The family made the natural deduction that those who frequented its restaurants in Ocean City might enjoy the Phillips brand of seafood in their home cities. Accordingly, in 1980 the family opened Phillips Harborplace in Baltimore's newly revamped Inner Harbor. In 1985, the family opened Phillips Flagship in Washington, D.C. Shortly after the Washington, D.C. restaurant opened, the processing side of the family business—in operation for more than 70 years by that point—was about to undergo significant changes, making its development the highlight of the Phillips family's business activities in the 1990s and the early 21st century.

Processing Capabilities Increase During the 1990s

Shirley and Brice Phillips were responsible for leading the family into the restaurant business. Their son, Steve, was responsible for leading the family in a new direction on the processing front. By the late 1980s, when the company's restaurant business was steadily expanding and enjoying increasing business, Steve Phillips was becoming worried about the supply of crabs. The family's restaurants received all their crab from the family's processing activities, but Phillips foresaw the day when the family would not be able to feed its restaurants with a sufficient supply of crab. "The problem," Phillips reflected in an August 2000 interview with *Seafood Business,* "was that I couldn't get crab in the wintertime. I needed a supply for the crab product that we are famous for." During the late 1980s, he began searching for a solution to the problem, and found one overseas, in southeast Asia, where the blue swimming crab was found in abundance. In 1990, Phillips Foods opened its first overseas processing plant in the Philippines, the first of a string of foreign processing plants that extended Phillips Foods' presence into Thailand, Indonesia, east Malaysia, India, and Ecuador.

Phillips Foods Entering Retail Business: 1996

Between 1990 and 2000, Phillips Foods opened ten overseas processing facilities. Eventually, nearly all of the company's raw product came from Asia and South America. The expansion made the company the largest producer of blue swimming crabmeat in the world, providing an abundant supply of product that would be needed during the decade, as Phillips Foods began to record an unprecedented, exponential rate of growth. The spark that ignited the company's growth was its foray into the retail business, a move made possible by its innovative work in developing a way to pasteurize fresh crabmeat and quick-freeze it, enabling the company's signature crab cakes to retain their freshness, consistency, and taste for up to a year. For the first time, the company could entertain the idea of shipping its seafood products great distances, something it began to do when it entered the retail business in 1996. The company relied on a sales force comprising chefs and managers from its restaurants to promote Phillips Foods' seafood products to a national audience. By 2000, the company had established six regional sales offices in the United States and one office in London, England.

The impact of Phillips Foods' entry into the retail sector was enormous, causing an explosive rise in annual sales. In 1996, the year the company began selling its crab cakes to retailers, Phillips Foods posted $7 million in sales, a figure that excluded revenue generated by Phillips Seafood Restaurants, the restaurant arm of the Phillips enterprise. During the ensuing five years, the company's revenue volume swelled by nearly 1,000 percent, eclipsing $130 million in 2001. As the company's involvement in the retail sector increased, it looked toward expanding its line of value-added products, or those products whose sale price—their value—was increased by applying manufacturing processes to a raw material. Crab cakes, for instance, commanded a higher price than raw crab. By the beginning of the 21st century, Phillips Foods' roster of value-added products included crab and spinach dip, crab cakes, and crab slammers, which were a mixture of crabmeat, cream cheese, and spices. Steve Phillips intended to expand the company's offering of value-added products, believing such diversification offered an important avenue of revenue growth. As the company entered its ninth decade of existence, plans were underway to introduce a full line of fish, lobster, and scallop products, as well as pre-grilled or stuffed tuna, mahi mahi, grouper, and snapper.

The desire to introduce more value-added products combined with the growth of the family's restaurant business—there were seven restaurants operating by the beginning of the 21st century, forced Phillips Foods to look for a new, larger headquarters and manufacturing complex. "We're shoulder to shoulder at our plant (in Baltimore)," the company's president, Mark Sneed, said in an April 4, 2002 interview with *Daily Record.* "We can't introduce any new products." After a two-year search, the company settled for the site of a former Coca-Cola syrup manufacturing plant in south Baltimore. The $20 million facility, slated to open in the fall of 2002, was expected eventually to triple the company's daily output of crab cakes, replacing its existing 80,000-square-foot facility with a 270,000-square-foot office, manufacturing, and freezer complex. The new facility, once a third line was added, would be capable of producing 600,000 crab cakes per day and preparing 2,000 gallons of soup. The company expanded overseas in 2002 as well, purchasing a 25,000-square-foot processing plant in Vietnam, Phillips Foods' 13th production facility.

Key Dates:

1914: A.E. Phillips & Sons begins processing crab.
1956: The Phillips family opens a carryout shop in Ocean City, Maryland.
1977: A third Ocean City restaurant is opened.
1980: Phillips Harborplace, located in Baltimore, is opened.
1985: Phillips Flagship, located in Washington, D.C., is opened.
1990: Phillips Foods opens a processing plant in the Philippines, its first overseas facility.
1996: Phillips Foods enters the retail market.
2002: Phillips Foods opens a new headquarters and manufacturing complex in Baltimore.
2004: Phillips Foods announces plans to open a chain of small foodservice outlets under the name Phillips Famous Seafood.

As Phillips Foods prepared for its 100th anniversary, the company was gearing up for expansion. Plans were unveiled in early 2004 for a new breed of restaurants to operate in what was known as the "fast-casual" segment of the restaurant industry. The format for the new units, to be operated under the name Phillips Famous Seafood, was a smaller version of the company's full-service restaurants. The fast-casual units occupied 2,500 square feet and were designed to seat 125 patrons. (The company's full-service restaurants served between 600 and 1,200 diners). The company had one Phillips Famous Seafood unit, located in a shopping mall in Rockville, Maryland, in operation by 2004, with plans calling for five more units by the beginning of 2005 and as many as 500 units by 2014. The company was using its longstanding branding partnership with HMSHost Corp., a Maryland-based airport and travel concessionaire, to test the market viability of the concept. As part of its relationship with HMSHost, Phillips Foods also was planning to market its seafood products to restaurants in more than 30 airports by the end of 2004.

Phillips Foods second century of business promised to bring continued growth if its plans to expand came to fruition. Growth in one area of the company's business fueled growth in other areas of its business, with expansion of the company's restaurant business necessitating the expansion of its processing business. One aspect of its business not under its control was the supply of crabs, the one crucial unknown with the potential to influence future growth. The company sales were somewhat limited by the lack of crabmeat. It was not uncommon for the company to be fulfilling less than 50 percent of its orders. Provided its was supported by a sufficient supply of crabs, Phillips Foods appeared destined to enjoy a lucrative future.

Principal Subsidiaries

Phillips Foodservice, Inc.

Principal Competitors

Bumble Bee Seafoods, L.L.C.; Bui Family Crab Company; Landry's Restaurants, Inc.

Further Reading

Cecil, Andrea, "Businesses Flourishing in Baltimore's Inner City," *Daily Record,* July 15, 2003, p. 7.

Kercheval, Nancy, "Phillips Foods Relocates; Ups Crab Cakes Output," *Daily Record,* April 4, 2002, p. 8.

King, Paul, "Phillips to Expand, Wade into Fast-Casual Waters," *Nation's Restaurant News,* February 16, 2004, p. 8.

"Phillips Expands Operations," *Seafood Business,* March 2002, p. 8.

"Phillips Foods," *Seafood Business,* November 2002, p. 6.

Robinson, Fiona, "Phillips Foods Solves Crab Supply Problem In-House," *Seafood Business,* August 2000, p. 38.

Sherman, Christopher, "Phillips Foods Plans to 'Reinvent' the Selling of Crab Cakes," *Daily Record,* November 30, 2002, p. 5.

—Jeffrey L. Covell

REUTERS ⋮⋮⋮⊃

Reuters Group PLC

85 Fleet Street
London EC4P 4AJ
United Kingdom
Telephone: (44) 20-7250-1122
Fax: (44) 20-7542-4064
Web site: http://www.reuters.com

Public Company
Incorporated: 1865 as Reuter's Telegram Company
    Limited
Employees: 16,744
Sales: £3.2 billion (2003)
Stock Exchanges: London NASDAQ
Ticker Symbols: RTR; RTRSY
NAIC: 514110 News Syndicates; 514191 On-Line
    Information Services; 523110 Investment Banking and
    Securities Dealing

Reuters Group PLC has from its inception employed any and all means at its disposal to achieve timely dissemination of news and information. From the founder's mid-19th-century use of carrier pigeons to scoop the competition to the late 20th-century exploitation of satellites and global computer networks to provide round-the-clock data, the company has remained at the forefront of its industry. With the establishment of an Internet presence in the late 1990s, the company's profile began to evolve, from a behind the scenes news wholesaler to a leading source for late-breaking stories, one with emerging brand-name recognition. As Reuters confronted the many challenges facing news agencies in the years after the attacks of September 11, 2001, it set out to reinvent itself as a web-savvy, diversified information company, with the aim of becoming the preferred source for first-hand news and financial data in the new millennium.

Mid-19th-Century Origins

Reuters is named for its founder, Julius Reuter. A native of Germany, Reuter was born Israel Beer Josaphat in 1816. He converted from Judaism to Christianity and adopted his new name while on a brief trip to London in the 1840s. After working as a publisher in Berlin, he fled the city during the revolution of 1848 and arrived in Paris. Here he is said to have worked for Charles Havas, the French news agency pioneer, before setting up in business himself. In 1849 Reuter started his own newssheet, translating information taken from French newspapers into German and sending this data to provincial papers in his homeland. The business failed after a few months. Reuter left for Germany to establish a service in Aachen, supplying financial and general news from the major centers of Paris, Brussels, and Berlin to the merchants and bankers in Cologne and elsewhere. The enterprising Reuter used carrier pigeons to bridge the gap in the telegraph line then existing between Aachen and Brussels, thereby achieving a seven-hour jump on the local mail train.

By the end of 1850 the gap in the telegraph line was closed and Reuter moved to London. In response to the laying of a cable across the English Channel, linking the stock exchanges of London and Paris, he opened an office near the London Stock Exchange in October 1851. In addition to being the financial center of the Victorian world, London was becoming the communications center for the growing world telegraph network. Free trade and a free press added to the atmosphere Reuter needed to succeed in his new venture. He had long been impressed by the potential of telegraphic communication and the profits to be derived from the sale of news and information via this medium. Twice a day, for a fixed-term payment, his Submarine Telegraph office provided London and Paris brokers and merchants with opening and closing prices in both capitals. He gradually widened his geographic range and in 1857 made a contract with the recently established telegraphic news agency in Russia.

The repeal of the newspaper stamp duty—a tax on the sale of newspapers—in 1855 was to transform the British press, making way for the penny daily papers and the rise of popular journalism. Newspapers had more space for news, and their readership extended rapidly. The *London Times* already had its own network of correspondents in Europe, the Near East, India, China, and the United States, and refused to make any contract with Reuter. In 1858, despairing of the *Times,* Reuter approached several other London daily papers and persuaded them to subscribe to his news service. This was a breakthrough. The *Times* eventually softened its attitude and made a contract for telegrams.

Reuter was by this time offering general and political news, received by telegraph from all over Europe, as well as financial information. Reuter pioneered the information embargo and foreshadowed real-time transmission of information in 1859, when he persuaded Napoleon III to give him an advance copy of a speech. Reuter held the address until the French leader began speaking, then transmitted it to the newspapers via telegraph. The speech heralded the war of Italian liberation.

After several unsuccessful attempts to lay a cable across the Atlantic, a transatlantic line was finally laid in 1866. By this date Reuter was already receiving news from agents in many parts of the world beyond Europe. His correspondent in the United States reported the Civil War and was two hours ahead of rivals in announcing the news of the assassination of President Abraham Lincoln in 1865.

Julius Reuter was a businessman, collecting and selling news, rather than a journalist. The first editor was Sigismund Engländer, a Viennese revolutionary, who had fled to Paris at the same time as Reuter in 1848. Engländer was one of several emigrés employed in the early years of the business. His great knowledge of the politics and culture of Europe opened many doors. When the Russo-Turkish War broke out in 1877, he went to Constantinople as chief correspondent.

Incorporation in 1865

In 1865 Julius Reuter's private business became Reuter's Telegram Company Limited. The new company was incorporated with a nominal capital of £250,000. Reuter was appointed managing director. One reason for the restructuring was to raise capital to pay for a cable from England to Norderney on the north German coast. This cable became the link in the first telegraph to India in 1866. In pursuing his grand design of creating a world news agency, Reuter was ready to become a cable owner as well as a cable user. In 1869 he and Baron Émile d'Erlanger, a Paris banker, financed a French cable across the Atlantic. This company was absorbed by its rival, the Anglo-American Telegraph Company, in 1873. After this, Reuters became less exposed to the charge of seeking to monopolize news supply.

In the 1860s Reuters faced two main news agency rivals, Charles Havas in Paris and Bernard Wolff in Berlin. From this period until the 1930s Reuters, Havas, and Wolff divided most of the news of the world outside North America between themselves. The leading member of the ''ring combination'' was Reuters. The company's exclusive territories were the most extensive, and its network of offices and agencies, correspondents and stringers made it the largest news contributor to the pool. This activity, and Britain's prominence within the world telegraph system, made the Reuters office—by now in Old Jewry, London—the international clearing center for news. Reuters had established an enviable reputation for speed, accuracy, and impartiality in news collection and distribution.

In 1865 Reuters opened an office in Alexandria, its first office outside Europe. Offices were established in Bombay and other Indian cities from 1866. India became an important territory for Reuters. As the world's communications network spread to India and the East, the company followed the cable to China and Japan in 1871 and on to Australia in 1872. The prestige of Reuters—and also its profitability—came to depend heavily upon the growing British Empire. Reuters was to report the many wars which accompanied imperial expansion. From the 1870s the transmission of private telegrams for both businesses and individuals within the empire became a major Reuters activity. This was especially successful in the East where the substitution of code words for common phrases saved words and thus money. The revenue from this enterprise helped to pay for the news services, which increasingly lost money.

In 1878 Reuter retired as managing director. He had been granted a barony in 1871 by the Duke of Saxe-Coburg-Gotha, a title recognized by Queen Victoria in 1891. His son Herbert succeeded him as managing director. Baron Herbert de Reuter did not possess the same business acumen as his father, but he raised the standard of journalism within Reuters, meeting the public demand for more popular news in the 1890s. He introduced the latest technology to Reuters, but he also led the company down some dangerous paths. Forays into advertising and banking very nearly led to financial ruin. The formation of a Reuters bank was his final mistake. Business worries and the death of his wife contributed toward his suicide in 1915.

Reuters Taken Private in 1916

The Boer War of 1899 to 1902 had been a great drain on the company's resources, but it had been well reported and enhanced the reputation of Reuters for impartiality. It had placed correspondents on the Boer side as well as the British. From this scene of operations came the new head of Reuters. Soon after Herbert's death, Roderick Jones, manager in South Africa, became the first non-family managing director. To escape a hostile takeover bid, the company returned to private ownership in 1916. Jones and Mark Napier, the company's chairman, formed a group to buy the entire shareholding. Reuter's Telegram Company now became Reuters Limited. Napier died in 1919, leaving Roderick Jones as the principal proprietor and executive head, a post which he held until 1941.

World War I was a difficult time for the company. The cost of reporting was high both in terms of profits and of the independence that Reuters strove to achieve in all its business and news transactions. The private telegram business was no longer so profitable, since the censors would not allow the use of codes. Reuters was accused of being in the pay of the British

Key Dates:

1851: Julius Reuter opens the Submarine Telegraph Office in London.

1865: Reuter incorporates Reuter's Telegram Company Limited; first office outside of Europe opens in Alexandria, Egypt.

1916: Roderick Jones, managing director of the company, and Mark Napier, chairman, form group to buy entire shareholding of Reuters Telegraph, forming a new, private company, Reuters Limited.

1925: The Press Association acquires majority stake in Reuters.

1941: The Reuter Trust is formed, a joint company owned by the Press Association and the Newspaper Proprietors' Association.

1947: The Australian Associated Press and the New Zealand Press Association join the Reuters Trust.

1973: Reuter Monitor Money Rates service is formed; Reuters creates Information, Dissemination and Retrieval Inc., a U.S.-based subsidiary.

1993: Reuters New Media Inc. is formed.

1997: Reuters establishes Global Technical Centre in Geneva.

2003: Reuters launches the Fast Forward Programme.

government, and this was a difficult charge to deny. Roderick Jones was also head of the Department of Propaganda at the Ministry of Information, work for which he was knighted.

As head of Reuters between the two world wars, Roderick Jones ran the business as an autocracy. Reuters found it hard to keep its lead over the other international news agencies, especially the Associated Press and the United Press, both U.S. agencies. Jones thought that Reuters could seek to work *with* the British government, so long as it was not seen to be working *for* it. Reuters badly needed government subscriptions. Jones was careful not to ask for subsidies.

In 1920 Reuters set up a trade department to expand the distribution of business news. This was followed three years later by a service of price quotations and exchange rates sent in Morse code by long-wave radio to Europe. This became the company's chief commercial service in Europe, later reaching other parts of the world via more powerful radio transmitters. In 1927 Reuters started using teleprinters to distribute news to London newspapers. In 1934 the company began news transmission to Europe by Hellschreiber, a forerunner of the radio teleprinter.

Takeover by Newspaper Cartel in 1925

In 1925 the Press Association (PA) had taken a majority shareholding in Reuters. It followed this in 1930 by purchasing the remainder of the Reuters shares, except for 1,000 retained by Roderick Jones. In 1941 the PA directors forced Jones to resign, believing he had compromised the agency in his dealings with the British government. The government itself helped to ease Jones out. The Reuter Trust was now established to ensure the independence of the agency. From 1941 the company was jointly

owned by the PA and the Newspaper Proprietors' Association (NPA). A commonwealth dimension was added when the Australian Associated Press (AAP) and the New Zealand Press Association (NZPA) joined the partnership in 1947. The Press Trust of India joined in 1949, only to leave four years later.

Christopher Chancellor was general manager during the 1940s and 1950s. Under his leadership Reuters did not crumble along with the British Empire, despite the growing ascendancy of the U.S. news agencies. The range of economic services expanded, and Reuters assisted in the establishment of news agencies in postwar Europe, and later in the Third World. In Chancellor's day, the newspaper owners of Reuters were not adventurous. They were aiming at little more than balancing the books. They expected to pay the minimum annual contribution towards the running of Reuters and to get their news cheap.

Computerized Information, Rapid Expansion: Late 20th Century

Walton Cole, who succeeded Chancellor in 1959, had strengthened the news file during the later stages of World War II as managing editor. Cole died in 1963. His successor, Gerald Long, sought to make Reuters an aggressive and profitable international news organization. Notably, he persuaded a reluctant Reuters board to enter the market for computerized information. This initiative was eventually to transform the company's character and to earn it huge profits. Long encouraged Michael Nelson, the manager of Reuters Economic Services, to lead Reuters into price reporting via computer terminals. In partnership with Ultronic Systems Corporation of the United States, Reuters started a desktop market-quotation system called Stockmaster in 1964. It served Reuters clients throughout the world outside North America. In just ten years the profits from Stockmaster and its successor Videomaster amounted to £4 million.

In 1971 the collapse of the Brenon Woods Agreement, which had regulated rates of exchange, encouraged Reuters to undertake another daring yet calculated initiative. This was the introduction of the Reuter Monitor Money Rates service in 1973. Catering to the needs of the decentralized money markets, Monitor was the first of a number of contributed data products designed to serve the international business community. The Reuter Monitor Dealing service followed in 1981. This enabled dealers in foreign currencies to conclude trades over video terminals. These innovations gradually made Reuters more profitable than ever before. In 1963 the company had made a profit of £51,000; in 1973 profits reached more than £709,000; and in 1981 profits were more than £16 million.

On the news front, there were similar technological advances. In 1968 an Automatic Data Exchange (ADX)—a computerized message-switching system for faster handling and distribution of news throughout the world—went into operation in the London editorial offices. This was the first of its kind to be used by an international news organization. In 1973 Reuters formed a U.S. subsidiary, Information, Dissemination and Retrieval Inc. (IDR), to develop and manufacture systems and equipment for the company's use in cable television news and retrieval services. For the first time in 1973 Reuters journalists in New York began to use video display units for writing and sending news.

1984 IPO Presages Rapid Growth

Glen Renfrew, a 32-year veteran of Reuters, became managing director in 1981. Charged with the development of Reuters' computer services since their inception in 1964, Renfrew would be hailed as the architect of the media firm's spectacular growth throughout the 1980s. A key to his strategy was the 1984 flotation of Reuters Limited as a public company, Reuters Holdings PLC. As part of the restructuring, the composition of the board was broadened to make it more international, and the number of directors was increased to include the first representatives from outside the newspaper world. A separate company, Reuters Founders Share Company, was formed to maintain the Reuter Trust principles. Through this company the trustees and their chairman retained a single share with the power to outvote all other shares to prevent a takeover bid. Sir Christopher Hogg, chief executive of Courtaulds plc, became chairman of Reuters in 1985.

The flotation raised about £52 million of new capital which was available for investment in new products and new technology. Reuters Monitor quickly expanded to become the agency's largest operation. The company went into the international news picture business in 1985 when it purchased the United Press International picture service, and launched a news picture terminal in 1987. In 1985 Reuters acquired control of Visnews Ltd., the international television news agency in which it had held a stake since 1959. Revenues more than doubled from less than $1 billion in 1986 to over $2.7 billion by the time Renfrew retired in 1991. Net income nearly quadrupled from $119 million to $430 million during that same period, while earnings per share tripled. In line with this remarkable financial performance, Reuters' stock price shot from $8.25 at issue to nearly $29 at the close of 1991. Worldwide staff numbers more than tripled from less than 3,000 in 1980 to more than 10,000 by 1991.

A 1989 reorganization categorized Reuters' services under five areas—real-time information, transaction products, trading room systems, historical information, and media products. The related products were named with a view to the 21st century—Equities 2000, Money 2000, Dealing 2000, and Triarch 2000. That same year, Reuters' geographical divisions were organized according to three time zones—Reuters Asia; Reuters America; and Reuters Europe, Middle East, and Africa.

The 1990s and Beyond

Former foreign correspondent Peter Job was selected to succeed Renfrew as managing director in March 1991. Though Reuters made a number of significant acquisitions in the early 1990s, Job emphasized the internal development of new products to serve emerging information needs over the purchase of market share in existing segments. Key to this strategy was Reuters New Media Inc., a division created in 1993 to foster fresh markets. Andrew Nibley, executive vice-president of the new operation, told *Editor & Publisher*'s Jodi Cohen that New Media's chief objective was "to be the number one news application in cyberspace." In doing so, the company placed a strong emphasis on the Reuters brand, transforming it from a behind-the-scenes role to a distinct image as the leader in "the business of information."

Reuters launched the next-generation versions of its core product lines—Markets 3000, Treasury 3000, Securities 3000,

and Money 3000—in 1996. The company continued to grow vigorously in the early 1990s, increasing revenues from $2.7 billion in 1991 to $4.2 billion by 1995. Though net income grew more slowly, from $430 million to $642 million, the company boasted a $1.4 billion stockpile by the end of 1996.

However, by the end of the decade it became increasingly clear that the company's 3000 products would not be enough to ensure substantial growth in the information age. For one, persistent operational problems with the new products stalled the full implementation of the new systems, in addition to delaying the company's marketing campaign, leaving sales far below original projections. At the same time, the continued, rapid development of the Internet, where countless new rivals had begun to offer much cheaper financial services to a range of clients, threatened to render the company's business strategy obsolete. Although Reuters did devote resources to repairing the glitches in its 3000 products, it was clear that it would also need to develop an Internet strategy of its own in order to remain competitive. It took its first step in this direction in October 1997, when it earmarked £50 million for the establishment of a "Global Technical Centre." Based in Geneva, the new division would be responsible for creating Internet-related products for Reuters. In the same year, the company launched its first web site.

Reuters suffered a more damaging setback in early 1998, when reports emerged that its U.S. subsidiary, Reuters Analytics Inc., may have hired a consulting firm to steal financial information from one of the company's primary U.S. rivals, Bloomberg L.P. The controversy revolved around Bloomberg's highly touted analytic systems, which enabled financial managers to analyze business transactions, study company histories, and track bond issues. The precision and ease of Bloomberg's system made it difficult for Reuters, who had no similar product, to compete in the U.S. financial market. The company eventually released a statement declaring its innocence, explaining that it had directed the subsidiary to evaluate the Bloomberg product, not steal it; in the end the charges were dropped. However, its slow, somewhat clumsy response to the allegations did a great deal to undermine market confidence, and the company watched its overall stock value plummet more than £1.6 billion in the immediate wake of the scandal.

The Bloomberg controversy also underscored a glaring weakness in the Reuters business model: By not offering detailed analysis to go with its financial information services, the company's products simply could not compete with the more comprehensive offerings of its competitors. At the same time, it was becoming clear that the Internet, while still lagging behind the larger data-providers in terms of speed and reliability, would pose an increasingly larger challenge, as well as opportunity, as technology improved. While Reuters attempted to address this mounting challenge with a series of minor acquisitions at decade's close, it was becoming clear that a more radical reshaping of the company's strategy might be essential to its future growth.

Entering the New Millennium: New Challenges in a Changing World

By the year 2000, Reuters had become firmly enmeshed in the intricate web of strategic alliances and mergers that formed the backbone of the Internet, forging joint ventures with software and financial groups such as Multex and Aether, and acquiring the Yankee Group, an up-and-coming e-business specialist based in the United States. On one hand, this aggressive approach stoked the company's stock valuation, driving shares up to £12.58 by late July 2000, and attracting a host of new high-powered clients, among them Merrill Lynch. However, the flurry of acquisitions also seemed to lack a specific direction, giving the company a host of new products that were not unified according to a single guiding business philosophy. By late 2001, in the wake of the dot-com crash, terrorist attacks in the United States, and significant market fluctuations, it had become apparent that Reuters needed to get itself back onto solid footing.

To address these concerns, in 2001 new CEO Tom Glocer launched a major reorganization project, dubbed the "business transformation program." The restructuring called for approximately 4,000 job cuts over the next three years, and aimed to streamline operations into four discrete business segments. In June 2003 Reuters introduced Fast Forward Programme, an effort to simplify the company's product line. The following month brought signs of improvement. On July 22, Reuters entered into contracts with two leading brokerage firms: Goldman Sachs—a longtime Bloomberg client—and Lehman Brothers. At the same time, results for the first two quarters of the year exceeded original expectations.

The new millennium posed unique challenges to Reuters. As a news wholesaler, Reuters was for most of its history accustomed to working behind the scenes of the major news outlets it served. Now that it had a strong web presence, however, the company had to adapt to its new, public role as a news source. At the same time, the company had the task of providing up-to-the-minute global news in a world deeply divided by conflict. Since Reuters delivered the same information to all its markets, whether in the United States or the Middle East, its traditional standard of objectivity would become more crucial than ever.

Principal Subsidiaries

Dow Jones Reuters Business Interactive LLC (U.S.A.); Instinet Group Incorporated (U.S.A.; 63%); TIBCO Software Inc. (U.S.A.; 49%); The Yankee Group (U.S.A.)

Principal Divisions

Reuters SA (Switzerland); Reuters America; Reuters Asia (Singapore).

Principal Competitors

The Associated Press; Bloomberg L.P.; Dow Jones & Company, Inc.

Further Reading

Boyd Barrett, Oliver, *The International News Agencies,* London: Constable, 1980.

Chen, Jodi B., "Invasion of the Body Snatchers," *Editor & Publisher,* May 25, 1996, pp. 28–30.

Collins, Henry M., *From Pigeon Post to Wireless,* London: Hodder and Stoughton, 1925.

Desmond, R.W., *The Information Process: World News Reporting to the Twentieth Century,* Iowa City: University of Iowa Press, 1978.

Eichenwald, Kurt, "Memos Said to Detail Reuters Effort to Obtain Bloomberg Data," *New York Times,* February 2, 1998.

Fenby, Jonathan, *The International News Services (A Twentieth Century Fund Report),* New York: Schocken Books, 1986.

Grande, Carlos, "Ugly Duckling Reuters Awaits Change: Investors Are Hoping for Quick Results from the Electronic Information Group's Restructuring," *Financial Times* (London), April 4, 2002.

Hayes, John R., "Acquisition Is Fine, But Organic Growth Is Better," *Forbes,* December 30, 1996, pp. 52–55.

Jones, Roderick, *A Life in Reuters,* London: Hodder and Stoughton, 1951.

Lawrenson, John, and Lionel Barber, *The Price of Truth: The Story of the Reuters Millions,* London: Sphere, 1986.

Malkani, Gautam, "Reuters Basks in the Warmth of Summer Sun," *Financial Times* (London), July 23, 2003.

Price, Christopher, "Reuters to Invest £50m on Internet Technology," *Financial Times* (London), October 2, 1997.

Read, Donald, *The Power of News: The History of Reuters,* Oxford: Oxford University Press, 1994.

Six Drown Saving Chicken: And Other True Stories from the Reuters "Oddly Enough" File, New York: Carroll & Graf Publishers, 1996.

Storey, Graham, *Reuters Century,* London: Max Parrish, 1951.

—Justine Taylor
—updates: April Dougal Gasbarre, Stephen Meyer

Richtree Inc.

111 Richmond Street West, Suite 1600
Toronto, Ontario M5H 2G4
Canada
Telephone: (416) 366-8122
Fax: (416) 366-1934
Web site: http://www.movenpickcanada.com

Public Company
Incorporated: 1996
Employees: 2,400
Sales: CAD 53.83 million (2003)
Stock Exchanges: Toronto
Ticker Symbol: MOO.b
NAIC: 722110 Full-Service Restaurants; 311920 Coffee
and Tea Manufacturing; 722410 Drinking Places
(Alcoholic Beverages)

Richtree Inc. operates restaurants in Canada and the United States under licensing agreements with Movel Restaurants Holdings A.G., a subsidiary of Zurich, Switzerland-based Mövenpick Holdings. Richtree operates four Marché restaurants and six Marchélino restaurants. The company's Marché restaurants are designed as combination restaurants and markets with separate counters featuring made-to-order gourmet meals. Richtree operates two Marchés in Toronto, one unit in Montreal, and another restaurant in Boston, Massachusetts. Richtree's Marchélino restaurants are designed as smaller versions of the company's Marché format. There are six Marchelino restaurants in Canada: four in Toronto and one each in Ottawa and Montreal. Richtree also operates a Marchélino in Boston.

Origins

The Mövenpick organization traces its roots to 1948, when Ueli Prager opened his first Mövenpick restaurant in Zurich. The son of a Swiss banker, Prager spent the next four decades expanding upon the success of his first restaurant, whose name, in German, was meant to convey the image of a gull snatching a meal while in flight. The first restaurant's popularity—it touted itself as a provider of high-quality food to people in a hurry—led to a series of additional restaurant openings, as Mövenpick restaurants opened in Bern, Geneva, and Lugano. Propelled by the success of his Mövenpick concept, Prager began to build a conglomerate around his highly successful restaurant properties. He founded a purchasing and import company in 1960, launched a line of Mövenpick branded merchandise, and in 1970 opened a chain of wine cellars—called Caves Mövenpick—in Germany and Switzerland. In 1972, Prager began making Mövenpick Premium Ice Cream, and he opened his first two hotels. Meanwhile, Mövenpick restaurants had crossed Swiss borders for the first time in 1963, when Prager opened a unit in Munich. By the end of the following decade, Prager was focused on advancing the Mövenpick banner across the globe. He expanded his restaurant and hotel holdings into Africa, Asia, and North America. As part of this expansion, he laid the foundation for Richtree, opening the first Mövenpick restaurant in Canada in 1980.

The first Mövenpick restaurant opened in Toronto, offering its signature casual and fine dining experience to a North American audience for the first time. The restaurant was managed by the Canadian division of Swiss-based Mövenpick Holdings. In 1982, two years after it opened, the Toronto restaurant fell under the new management of Jörg and Marianne Reichert, the husband-and-wife team who later founded Richtree. Jörg Reichert, who held the titles of president and chief executive officer, had served the Mövenpick organization in Switzerland and Germany before being selected to head the holding company's Canadian operations. The Toronto restaurant thrived under the managerial control of the Reicherts, convincing the couple to commit their future to the promotion of the Mövenpick concept. In 1985, they took a stake in their success, purchasing a 25 percent interest in Mövenpick Holdings' Canadian operations.

Shortly before the Reicherts became equity owners, Prager unveiled a new Mövenpick format that would become one of the primary vehicles driving the growth of Richtree. In 1984, Mövenpick Holdings, through a subsidiary company named Movel Restaurant Holding A.G., opened a combination restaurant and market named Mövenpick Marché. The first Marché debuted in Stuttgart, a springboard for a spate of openings to follow. Marchés were designed to emulate open-air French markets, featuring separate counters, or stations, where cus-

Company Perspectives:

Richtree Inc. presently owns 14 restaurants and food service outlets in Canada, and operates and owns jointly with a major Canadian supermarket company, an additional 10 outlets. The Company has announced plans to expand through Canada and the United States with its innovative Marché and Marchélino concepts. The expansion plans call for the addition of flagship Marchés in Canada and the United States, as well as Marchélino Restaurants and Take Me! Marché (Canada only) outlets. The company's plans do not provide for franchising in the near future, but franchising will be an option to be considered once the Marché and Marchélino brands are established in the U.S.

tomers selected ingredients to be prepared by chefs in open view. There were separate stations for meats, pasta, vegetables, soups, cakes and pastries, salads, desserts, coffee, and wine and alcohol, each featuring daily specials made with only fresh ingredients. Marchés never used canned or frozen food or ingredients containing additives and preservatives. The format proved to be an immediate success, prompting the expansion of Marchés to Hanover, Dusseldorf, Stuttgart, and West Berlin within four years of the Stuttgart debut.

Back in Canada, the Reicherts presided over the growth of Mövenpick's Canadian operations. A second Mövenpick restaurant was opened in Toronto during the second half of the 1980s. In 1991, Toronto gained another Mövenpick restaurant concept, when the first Marchélino restaurant opened. Marchélino, the fast-food version of Mövenpick Holdings' approach to the restaurant business, was described by a Mövenpick Holdings executive as the company's riposte to McDonald's. Featuring pasta, pizza, salad, sandwiches, muffins, and bagels, Marchélinos represented a scaled-down version of Marchés.

The early 1990s also witnessed the opening of the first Marché in North America, adding a powerful asset to the Reichert's operations in Canada. In May 1992, a 20,000-square-foot Marché opened in Toronto. Like its European counterparts, the Toronto Marché allowed station managers to operate independently, an arrangement that spread out the responsibility for purchasing and producing food and fostered beneficial competition among the various stations, much like the personal incentive driving vendors competing in a farmer's market. Unlike European-based Marchés, the Toronto store offered takeout sales to position itself as a specialty food store as well as a restaurant. Inside the store, the space was divided into a variety of separate stations, each vying for customers' business. The stalls operated as: Grill & Rotisserie, Seafood & Raw Bar, Salad & Produce Bar, Mamma's and Pap's Pasta, Pizzeria Angelo, Max and Moritz Bakerie, and Bistro de Vin, featuring a 450-bottle wine cellar. Once customers made their selections, receiving a stamp from each station visited, they had the option of five dining rooms, each designed with a particular theme: La Brasseries du Nord resembled a Parisian tavern; La Poterie aped a pottery-making cottage; L'Orangeries featured a gazebo; Café Pergoal emulated a coffee and espresso bar; and Place de la Fontaine was reminiscent of an indoor garden.

The Toronto Marché was enormously successful. The restaurant attracted between 3,000 and 4,000 customers a day, a parade of patrons who flocked to the restaurant between 7:30 a.m. and 2:00 a.m. Because of the store's high volume of business, Jörg Reichert was able to offer Mövenpick's gourmet food at reasonable prices, featuring, among a slew of other items, a half-dozen oysters for less than $6, a bowl of salmon pasta for $4.98, and green salads with freshly sautéed chicken for $1.99.

Formation of Richtree: 1996

While executives in Switzerland enjoyed the successful global expansion of the Mövenpick brand, the Reicherts decided to assume greater control over the success of their efforts in Canada. In December 1996, the couple acquired the exclusive rights in Canada and the United States for Mövenpick restaurants, Marché restaurants, and Marchélino restaurants, forming Richtree to take on a 100 percent equity position in Mövenpick Holdings' North American operations. In February 1997, the Reicherts executed Richtree's initial public offering on the Toronto Stock Exchange, raising sufficient capital to pay Movel Restaurant Holding A.G. for the licensing rights.

As the Reicherts accustomed themselves to their new roles as Richtree's owners, they could count on the revenue generated by a fourth Mövenpick restaurant concept. By the fall of 1997, there were four units of what the company called Take Me! Marchés in operation, restaurants that were positioned in the home-meal-replacement segment of the restaurant industry. The four Take Me! Units, serving as prototypes for further expansion, were located at the entrance of four supermarkets operated by Loblaws Cos., a leading supermarket chain in Canada. Ranging in size from 2,000 square feet to 3,000 square feet, the Take Me! Units featured chefs who prepared meals using ingredients selected by customers, offering a merchandise mix of seafood, soups, sandwiches, grilled vegetables, meats, pasta, salads, and breads and pastries. In November 1997, Richtree and Loblaw agreed to open two more Take Me! units by the end of the year, with plans calling for the establishment of several additional units in 1998.

By the end of 1997, Jörg Reichert was also hatching expansion plans far more ambitious than those involving the establishment of additional Marchélino units. The company announced it intended to open restaurants in five major North American markets by the end of 2000, an expansion plan that included the introduction of the Mövenpick brand of restaurants into the United States. As the company set out on its expansion campaign, it intended to focus on the Marché, Marchélino, and Take Me! concepts to actualize its plans. There were no plans to increase the number of its traditional, full-service Mövenpick restaurants.

By the beginning of 1998, Richtree had sites selected for expansion in New York City's World Trade Center and in Boston. The company's first steps outside the province of Ontario were taken in August 1998, when the company opened a Marché and Marchélino in Montreal, Quebec. The 33,000-square-foot Marché featured a separate wine caveau, a running stream, an operating water wheel, and seating for 825 diners. Near the Marché, located in Montreal's Place Ville Marie, the company's Marchélino occupied 3,000 square feet. The company's first location in the United States opened in Boston in November 1998, when a 2,800-square-foot Marchélino opened in Boston's Prudential Center. The following month, an 18,000-square-foot

Marché opened in the Prudential Center, offering seating for 600 patrons. One level below the Marché, a 200-seat wine-bar, called Caveau, offered wines by the glass or by the bottle.

Richtree recorded more than CAD 50 million in sales in 1998, a total that promised to increase substantially in the coming years. The figure excluded the expansion completed in 1998 (the company's fiscal year ended in July) and it could not account for the growth expected to be realized by Richtree's expansion in 1999. The company announced plans to open its collection of restaurant formats in several U.S. cities, including New York, San Diego, and Chicago. Richtree's promise of further expansion did not materialize, however, with the repercussions from the aborted expansion plans delivering a serious blow to the company's finances.

Expansion Plans Scuttled in 1999

The suspension of Richtree's expansion plans marked the beginning of contentious times at the company's Toronto headquarters. The company was forced to halt its expansion efforts in New York, where it had secured a lease in late 1997, and in San Diego because it was not able to secure the necessary financing. As a result of abandoning these two expansion efforts, the company recorded write-down costs of CAD 9.9 million, and sought to reposition itself for an immediate future without further expansion. Jörg Reichert pointed the blame for Richtree's failure to expand directly at his former employer, Mövenpick Holdings, filing a lawsuit against the Swiss company in 2001. The complaint filed by Richtree cited Mövenpick's unlawful behavior resulting from breaches of contract, breaches of fiduciary duty, and breaches of good faith and fair dealing, among other accusations. Reichert, in a November 20, 2001 interview with *Market News Publishing*, chastised Mövenpick Holdings' management for its lack of support. "Mövenpick has done absolutely nothing to support Richtree in the United States since we entered into the franchise and license agreements with them," he said. "In fact, as our suit alleges, their failure to fulfill their obligations and their pattern of constant interference has damaged Richtree and our company's value very significantly."

Richtree was forced to rethink its strategy after failing to execute its expansion plans. Its partnership with Loblaws, which had produced 11 Take Me! units by the beginning of the decade, ended in May 2001 when the Take Me! units were integrated into Loblaws and placed under the full control of the supermarket company. Once the Take Me! units were removed from Richtree's operations, the company's assets comprised four Marché restaurants, six Marchélino restaurants, and three full-service Mövenpick restaurants. By mid-2002, the company had decided to concentrate exclusively on the Marché and Marchélino formats and discontinue operation of the full-service restaurants. In November 2002, Richtree closed the Mövenpick restaurant it operated on Yorkville Avenue in Toronto, which had opened during the 1980s. Meanwhile, the company continued to press its case in courts against Mövenpick Holdings.

As Richtree prepared for its future, the uncertainty of its future relationship with Mövenpick Holdings continued to be a cause for concern. In April 2003, Richtree filed another suit against its Swiss franchiser, seeking to recover between CAD 200 million and CAD 336 million in damages. The following month, Mövenpick Holdings filed a damage claim against Richtree, seeking damages of CAD 100 million. The resolution of the court cases promised to factor heavily in determining Richtree's future. Richtree's first decade of business was highlighted by encouraging success and pocked by a forced retreat from its growth strategy. In the years ahead, Reichert and his management team hoped to achieve greater consistency, as they sought to transform their company into a perennial success story.

Principal Subsidiaries

Richtree U.S. Inc; Richtree Markets Inc.

Principal Competitors

Darden Restaurants, Inc.; Brinker International, Inc.; McCormick & Schmick Management Group.

Further Reading

Gatlin, Greg, "Red Tape Scorches Movenpick Debut," *Boston Herald,* December 2, 1998, p. 51.
Kapner, Suzanne, "Movenpick's Marche Takes on Canadian Palates," *Nation's Restaurant News,* January 11, 1993, p. 7.
Luca, Anna, "Movenpick's Carrotti Chops Through Clutter," *Marketing Magazine,* June 29, 1998, p. 2.
"Richtree Files Claim of Damages by Master Franchisor Movenpick," *Canadian Corporate News,* April 7, 2003.
"Richtree Inc.—Seeks Damages from Movenpick in U.S.," *Market News Publishing,* November 20, 2001.
Robertiello, Jack, "Loblaw Set to Serve Up More Stores with Richtree," *Supermarket News,* November 3, 1997, p. 25.
——, "Movenpick Marche Format Picks Manhattan for U.S. Move," *Supermarket News,* December 29, 1997, p. 19.
Sanders, Lisa, "World Trade Ctr. Lures Shoppers with New Retail," *Crain's New York Business,* December 15, 1997, p. 3.
Schneider, Madelin, "Movenpick's New Winner: Caveau," *Hotels,* June 1992, p. 79.

—Jeffrey L. Covell

Rite Aid Corporation

30 Hunter Lane
Camp Hill, Pennsylvania 17011-2400
U.S.A.
Telephone: (717) 761-2633
Toll Free: (800) 748-3243
Fax: (717) 975-5871
Web site: http://www.riteaid.com

Public Company
Incorporated: 1958 as Rack Rite Distributors, Inc.
Employees: 72,000
Sales: $16.54 billion (2004)
Stock Exchanges: New York Pacific
Ticker Symbol: RAD
NAIC: 446110 Pharmacies and Drug Stores

Rite Aid Corporation, which ranks as the third largest retail drugstore chain in the United States, operates about 3,380 drugstores in 28 states across the nation and in the District of Columbia. Rite Aid's stores average 12,750 square feet and offer a professional pharmacy service, a full selection of health and personal care products, an assortment of general merchandise, and more than 1,900 Rite Aid brand products. Through an alliance with General Nutrition Companies, Inc. (GNC), a leading retailer of specialty vitamins and supplements, more than a quarter of Rite Aid outlets include a GNC "store-within-the-store." Prescription drug revenue accounts for about 63 percent of total sales. Over-the-counter medications and personal care products generate 10 percent; health and beauty aids, 5 percent; and general merchandise, 22 percent. More than half of the company's stores are freestanding outlets, nearly 40 percent have a drive-through pharmacy, and close to 70 percent include a one-hour photofinishing department. To keep its stores supplied, Rite Aid maintains 12 distribution centers and overflow storage facilities.

Company Origins

Although Rite Aid Corporation was not formally incorporated until 1968, it got its start a few years earlier through Rack

Rite Distributors, Inc., developed by Alex Grass, Rite Aid's founder and later chairman and chief executive officer. Grass had founded Rack Rite in 1958 to provide grocery stores with health and beauty aids, as well as other nonfood products. In 1962 U.S. federal legislation repealed the fair trade laws that fixed minimum retail prices on most products, opening up the door to discount stores, price wars, and vigorous competition. Quick to take advantage of the situation, Rite Aid opened its first discount drugstore in 1962 in Scranton, Pennsylvania. Called the Thrif D Discount Center, this was the forerunner of the modern Rite Aid drugstores.

By Christmas 1962 Thrif D was taking in $25,000 each week. It tripled its first-year projected sales of $250,000, pulling in $750,000. While the company continued to develop Rack Rite distributors, Thrif D's sales results proved that discount drugstores were truly profitable. In 1963 Rite Aid opened five more drugstores, extending its market area to New York.

By 1964 Rite Aid's market territory included New Jersey and Virginia. Its store count doubled, bringing the total to 12. The number of employees had grown to 200. Expansion did not stop there; in 1965 Rite Aid penetrated Connecticut, and its store count rose to 25.

In 1966 Rite Aid continued to expand. Its number of stores reached 36. The growth of both the retail chain and the "rack-jobbing" portion of the business, Rack Rite Distributors, generated the need for more space, so Rite Aid began to construct a new corporate headquarters and distribution center. It also opened the first Rite Aid pharmacy in one of its drugstores in New Rochelle, New York. The following year Rite Aid introduced 70 of its own private-label products. The results of the Rite Aid pharmacy's first year were so positive that the company planned to continue installing pharmacies throughout its drugstore chain.

Acquisitions and Change in the Late 1960s and 1970s

The following years brought many changes and firsts for the company. Rite Aid made its first acquisition when it bought the Philadelphia-centered 11-store Martin's chain. Its store count

Company Perspectives:

Our Mission: To be a successful chain of friendly, neighborhood drugstores. Our knowledgeable, caring associates work together to provide a superior pharmacy experience, and offer everyday products and services that help our valued customers lead healthier, happier lives.

rose to 60, and its market share began to grow in Baltimore, Maryland; Newark, New Jersey; and Rochester and Buffalo, New York. In 1968 Rite Aid made its first public stock offering, issuing 350,000 shares at $25 per share on the American Stock Exchange, as well as formally changing its name to Rite Aid Corporation.

In 1969 Rite Aid acquired the 47-store Daw Drug Co. of Rochester, New York, bringing Rite Aid's store count to 117. The company also acquired Blue Ridge Nursing Homes along with Immuno Serums, Inc., and Sero-Genics, Inc., incorporating them into the company's medical services division. Offering more than 260 of its own private label products also contributed to Rite Aid's growth. The company increased its mechanical efficiency, installing material-handling equipment, such as conveyers, in its drug warehouse. It hooked up a telephone-order transmission system between the warehouse and drugstores to move orders swiftly. In addition, Rite Aid installed electronic data-processing equipment to produce price tags. That year expansion was so visible that Rite Aid declared a two-for-one stock split.

On January 20, 1970, Rite Aid was admitted to the New York Stock Exchange and began trading on the big board at $25 per share with 2.8 million shares outstanding. Although the U.S. economy moved into a recession, Rite Aid was among the discount stores that flourished. Also in 1970 Rite Aid acquired the 16-store Fountain Chain in Clarksburg, Virginia. By that time the company offered more than 300 of its own products bearing the Rite Aid logo, prompting the addition of 100,000 square feet to its main distribution center in Shiremanstown, Pennsylvania. In November 1971 Rite Aid sold 250,000 new shares of common stock to the public.

In 1971 the company acquired Sera-Tec Biologicals, Inc., of New Jersey, which was combined with the company's prior acquisitions of Immuno Serums and Sero-Genics to comprise the company's medical services division. Rite Aid also purchased a 50 percent equity in Superdrug Stores, Ltd., of the United Kingdom. During this period of rapid growth, Rite Aid pharmacies were filling more than five million prescriptions a year. To consolidate management and increase efficiency of the rapidly growing number of stores, Rite Aid separated its market area into five divisions and 20 supervisory districts.

In 1972 Rite Aid focused on internal efficiency in preparation for additional expansion. Also in 1972, Sera-Tec Biologicals, Biogenics, Inc., and Immuno Blood Services, Inc., were merged to form what would become known in the early 1990s as Sera-Tec. When 1972's Hurricane Agnes wrought severe damage on the company's stores in Wilkes-Barre, Pennsylvania, and Elmira, New York, it also damaged the phone and water service at corporate headquarters. Teams worked around

the clock to make the necessary repairs, and stores were reopened fairly rapidly. In fact, Rite Aid handled the disaster so impressively that it still was able to report filling more than 6.25 million prescriptions that year.

In 1973, despite the Middle East oil embargo and ensuing recession, Rite Aid again began making acquisitions. It acquired the 49-store Thomas Holmes Corp. chain and the 50-store Warner chain, both in greater Philadelphia. The company also set about creating distribution centers that could handle the rapidly multiplying number of Rite Aid stores. It expanded its Shiremanstown distribution center by 71,000 square feet, enabling the facility to supply up to 500 stores. The company also built an automated distribution center in Rome, New York, to handle the growing northeastern market. Rite Aid's accounting and data processing departments moved to a separate building in Shiremanstown, which became the hub of the Rite Aid complex.

Further activity during this time included reducing its holdings in Superdrug PLC, the successor to Superdrug Stores, Ltd., to 42.5 percent, selling a 7.5 percent interest. The number of private-label products that appeared bearing the Rite Aid logo climbed to 700. In addition, Rite Aid became one of the first drugstore chains in the United States to implement a senior citizen discount cardholder program.

By 1974 the Rome distribution center was supplying 131 Rite Aid stores. Rite Aid also created a fifth Sera-Tec center in Pittsburgh, just as the Dow Jones Industrial Average was falling to 663—the lowest since 1970—and worldwide inflation set in. Over the next year Rite Aid focused on internal organization and increased its security department in an effort to reduce shoplifting.

By 1976 Rite Aid resumed acquisitions, purchasing the 52-store Keystone Centers, Inc. of Pennsylvania and New Jersey. The following year, it acquired 99 more stores by buying the Read's, Inc. drug chain in Baltimore. This $18 million purchase led to Rite Aid's garnering the largest market share in Baltimore. In 1977 Rite Aid's private-label products, with almost 900 different items, accounted for 9 percent of its retail sales.

Although the value of the dollar plunged in 1978, Rite Aid's momentum did not. Rite Aid acquired 11 stores from Red Shield in Pittsburgh and the four-store Quality Drugs chain of greater Philadelphia. By focusing on providing value in the most efficient manner possible, Rite Aid gained substantial market share in the major metropolitan markets of Buffalo, Rochester, and Syracuse, New York; Charleston, South Carolina; Baltimore; and Philadelphia. The company also added 11,500 square feet to its executive space in Shiremanstown, where it bought a 79,000-square-foot building to house the growing finance, advertising, store engineering, and construction departments. Then, focusing on its central businesses, Rite Aid sold the Blue Ridge Nursing Homes in Camp Hill and in Harrisburg, Pennsylvania, for an after-tax profit of $1.8 million.

In 1979 Rite Aid acquired six U-Save stores in North Carolina and eastern Tennessee, as well as nine Shop Rite stores in the Hudson Valley. It redesigned its company logo and updated its store interiors, using mirrored canopies and bright colors throughout, while streamlining checkout counters in the process. In order to save time and money on West Virginia store openings and transportation costs among 140 of its existing stores, Rite Aid started up a 210,000-square-foot distribution center in Nitro, West Virginia. Moreover, the company set ambitious goals, such as increasing store count by 10 percent every year and continuing to open higher-margin pharmacies throughout its drugstore chain.

New Strategies, Including Diversification, in the 1980s

In 1980 Rite Aid adopted some new tactics in its growth plan. Its board of directors agreed tentatively to buy back as many as one million shares of Rite Aid common stock. These shares would be retained as treasury shares to provide liquid assets that could be quickly translated into cash for acquisitions,

funds for the employees' stock option plan, or any other corporate purposes. That year Rite Aid acquired the six-store Schuman Drug of Lansdale, Pennsylvania, and the four-store Lane drugstores in Youngstown, Ohio, establishing a new prescription division for Ohio and western Pennsylvania. To expedite the processing of third-party claims, Rite Aid installed a scanning system in its data processing department. The company opened a 43,000-square-foot addition to its finance and accounting building. Also in 1980 Rite Aid became one of the nation's largest suppliers of plasma with the opening of its ninth plasmapheresis center.

By 1981 Rite Aid had become the third largest retail drug chain. It acquired the 31-store South Carolina division of Fays Drug and made its third stock split since its initial public offering in 1968, issuing additional common stock contingent on the four-for-three stock split. The company also formed a new division to handle its business in West Virginia and western Pennsylvania.

In 1982 Rite Aid became the largest U.S. drug chain as measured by the number of stores and market share in New York, Pennsylvania, New Jersey, Maryland, and West Virginia. Rite Aid continued to expand its market area westward, acquiring the four-store Cochran Drugs in Columbus, Ohio; the 16-store Lomark Discount Drug Stores Inc., in Cincinnati, Ohio; and the 26-store Mann Drugs of High Point, North Carolina. In addition to these drugstores, Rite Aid acquired the fifth largest toy store in the nation, the 128-store Circus World Toy Stores, Inc., for $11.1 million. Rite Aid also expanded its Nitro, West Virginia, distribution center. The company now had total distribution capacity for 1,200 stores, which was essential and timely; Rite Aid opened its 1,000th store in Durham, North Carolina.

Rite Aid's sales exceeded $1 billion in 1983. It was listed among *Forbes* magazine's top 500 companies in both sales volume and number of employees. It issued a three-for-two stock split, its fourth stock split since it became listed and its second in two years. The value of Rite Aid's holdings in Superdrug PLC increased when that company went public and began trading its shares on the London Stock Exchange—at which point Rite Aid sold one-third of its interest in Superdrug, bringing its holdings down to 28.2 percent of the company's outstanding shares. Partially because of this, Rite Aid was able to offer a new employee stock purchase plan; to acquire the four-store Beagle chain in West Virginia and Ohio; to open its first Heaven novelty shop; and to integrate a point-of-purchase and pharmacy computer system. All of this helped to establish Rite Aid as the largest drugstore chain in the Northeast.

By 1984 Rite Aid started expanding beyond its core business. It bought American Discount Auto Parts (ADAP), a 32-store chain based in Avon, Massachusetts. It also purchased Encore Books, Inc., a 19-store deep-discount bookstore chain in Philadelphia. In addition to these departures from the company's core business, Rite Aid acquired the three-store Nifty Norm's, Inc. of Philadelphia, the six-store Herrlich Drugstores, the five-store Remes Drug Stores, the 13-store Lippert Pharmacies, three State Vitamin stores of Michigan, the three-store Jay's Drugstores in western New York, and the 24-unit Muir Drug Store chain based in Grand Rapids, Michigan. In 1984 Rite Aid also spun off its subsidiary wholesale and grocery division, Super Rite, as an autonomous public company, selling a partial interest in its holdings for $22 million.

In 1985 Rite Aid focused less on acquisitions than on internally generated growth. While Rite Aid that year acquired four Midland Valley Drug stores in Midland, Michigan, and eight State Vitamin discount stores in Lansing, Michigan, it opened five stores of its own, moving into the deep-discount drug market with the company's Drug Palace. Rite Aid further penetrated new markets by opening video rental departments in more than 160 of its drugstores. It also installed point-of-purchase scanning registers and more computerized pharmacy equipment. The newly spun-off Super Rite took its first step into retail grocery with its purchase of the 47-store Food-A-Rama supermarket chain in Baltimore and Washington, D.C. Rite Aid's subsidiary, Sera-Tec, opened two new plasma centers, bringing the count to 11. That year, Rite Aid sold Circus World Toy Stores for $28.8 million cash and 185,000 common shares. In addition, Rite Aid bought 1.1 million shares of its own common stock at $19 per share.

Rite Aid did not experience major expansion in 1986. It acquired only two Revco stores in Buffalo and opened six more Drug Palaces, bringing its deep-discount drugstore total to 11. The year was nevertheless notable in that two of Rite Aid's corporate officers received prestigious positions. Preston Robert Tisch of Rite Aid's board of directors was appointed Postmaster General of the United States, and company President Alex Grass was named chairman of the board and president of the National Association of Chain Drug Stores.

Adding More Than 1,000 Stores: 1987–91

In 1987 Rite Aid acquired the nine-store Harris Drug in Charleston, South Carolina; 113 SupeRx stores in Florida, Georgia, and Alabama, and a 200,000-square-foot distribution center in Florida from the Kroger Co. (in a $57 million deal); and 94 Gray Drug Fair, Inc. stores in Florida and Maryland, from the Sherwin-Williams Company. These acquisitions substantially expanded Rite Aid's southern market area. Because of the success of its pilot video departments in 1986, Rite Aid added 429 more video departments to its drugstores in 1987, bringing the total to 971. Rite Aid also continued to install pharmacy and point-of-purchase automated systems throughout the chain. That year *Dun's Business Month* ranked Rite Aid 25th among all publicly traded companies for consistent dividend advances. In 1987 Rite Aid was the largest employer in the retail drug industry.

The following year Rite Aid purchased from Sherwin-Williams the balance of Gray Drug Fair, consisting of 356 stores in Delaware, the District of Columbia, Indiana, Maryland, New York, Ohio, Virginia, West Virginia, North Carolina, and Pennsylvania. This purchase brought Rite Aid's store count to more than 2,100 and greatly expanded the company's market penetration in these states. That year, in Winnsboro, South Carolina, Rite Aid opened its fifth distribution center. This 265,000-square-foot distribution center enabled Rite Aid to supply up to 450 more stores in the Southeast. In April 1988 Rite Aid acquired the Begley Company, consisting of 39 drugstores in Kentucky and 140 dry cleaners in ten states, for about $20 million.

In 1989 the company continued to expand and enhance the technology available to its stores. Moreover, Rite Aid finalized a deal with Super Rite Foods Holding Corporation in March 1989 to sell its 46 percent interest in Super Rite Foods, Inc. Rite Aid also acquired 99 People's Drug Stores and 18 Lane Drug units. In September of that year, it disposed of its 46.8 percent equity in Super Rite Foods for $18.37 million, with a positive cash flow in excess of $40 million. That same year showed record sales for Rite Aid; its revenues of $2.87 billion for this 53-week fiscal year represented a 15.4 percent increase from the previous 52-week fiscal year. Company earnings, however, continued to absorb the cost of the enormous acquisitions the company made in 1987.

The company in 1990 continued to focus on the integration of both its past and present acquisitions. Rite Aid added 1,754 store computer systems, and it enhanced 2,279 pharmacy terminals. The pharmacy terminals enabled drug interaction analysis and cumulative tax information, all of which resulted in speedier prescription service. Prescription sales for 1990 advanced 17.8 percent from the previous year, and then represented a full 43 percent of store revenues. Rite Aid's computerization also propelled the company toward greater efficiency, enabling it to cut back on unnecessary corporate staffing in spite of the fact that the company's store count had continued to grow.

From 1987 to 1991, Rite Aid acquired more than 800 drugstores and opened 276 new stores, closing only 103 units. Within this period, Rite Aid's store count grew by nearly 60 percent. In 1991 Rite Aid added 68 stores and bought prescription records from 65 drugstores in Washington, D.C.

A Growing Appetite for Acquisitions in the 1990s

While some organizations viewed the recession of the early 1990s as a bleak period, Alex and Martin Grass, the father-and-son team then running Rite Aid, said it was a good time to buy, according to a January 13, 1992, *Business Week* article. The recession brought opportunities to acquire vulnerable companies, and Rite Aid bid for the bankrupt Revco D.S., Inc. chain in early 1992. Although the deal later fell through, Rite Aid had demonstrated its ability to move decisively and quickly. Significant acquisitions included 34 Whelby Super Drug Stores in Maine and New Hampshire in 1993, and 72 La Verdiere Enterprises, Inc. drugstores and 16 Revco drugstores, both in 1994. Rite Aid completed its largest acquisition yet in March 1995, spending $132 million for the 224-unit Perry Drug Stores, Inc., the largest drugstore chain in Michigan, with annual revenues of $735 million. This deal pushed Rite Aid's store count near the 3,000 mark.

Beginning in 1994 Rite Aid opened 50 state-of-the-art drugstores in New York City, boosting the total to 67 within the city. Rite Aid planned to bring more stores into all of New York's boroughs later in the decade. In fiscal 1994 Rite Aid acquired Pharmacy Car, Inc. and Intell Rx Inc., a drug review company with proprietary software that reviewed physicians' prescription patterns. From these two purchases emerged the subsidiary Eagle Managed Care Corp.

Martin Grass succeeded his father, Alex Grass, as Rite Aid's chairman and CEO in March 1995. In July of that year, Rite Aid bolstered its presence in the New York metropolitan region by purchasing the 30-store Pathmark Stores, Inc. chain. In October, 20 stores in Maine were bought from Brooks Pharmacy. Also that year, the company shed four unrelated businesses in order to focus on its pharmaceutical operations: Encore Books, Concord Custom Cleaners, Sera-Tech Biologicals, and ADAP, the auto parts dealer. Proceeds from these divestments totaled about $142 million. By midyear Rite Aid appeared well positioned. Market value, once $1.3 billion in 1993, reached about $2.5 billion. Rite Aid set out to open, renovate, or expand 1,000 more stores over a three-year period.

In 1996 Rite Aid continued to restructure its business to operate larger, higher-volume, and more profitable drugstores. In June the company purchased Taylor Drugs, a chain of 34 stores operating in Louisville, Kentucky. Rite Aid, already the largest drugstore operator in the state, entered Louisville with a major share of the market. At the same time, the company divested operations in certain areas where its market share was weak. During 1996 Rite Aid sold 37 drugstores and the assets of 72 more stores in Florida, as well as 33 drugstores and the assets of 21 others located in Massachusetts and Rhode Island. In October 1996 the company reached an agreement to sell 190 stores in North and South Carolina to J.C. Penney Company, Inc.'s Thrift Drug chain, which would soon merge with and into Eckerd Corporation.

In November 1996 the company entered into a joint venture to provide mail-order pharmacy services with Smith Kline Beecham's Diversified Pharmaceutical Services, a leading pharmacy benefit manager. This move was seen as another channel of distribution to offer prescriptions to select managed care customers.

Another attempt was made by the company in 1996 to buy its rival, Revco, but when the Federal Trade Commission rejected the $1.8 billion deal, Rite Aid moved on to other prospects. (Revco was subsequently acquired by CVS Corporation in 1997.) December 1996 marked the largest acquisition in Rite Aid history—a merger with Thrifty PayLess Holdings, Inc., which had sales of $4.4 billion in 1,007 stores in the western United States. The price tag was $1.4 billion in stock and the assumption of almost $900 million in debt. Thrifty was the largest chain drugstore operator in California, Oregon, Washington, and Idaho.

In 1997 Rite Aid integrated this West Coast operation into the chain, installing new computer hardware in all Thrifty PayLess stores. Then, having just abandoned most of the South, Rite Aid reentered the region in August 1997 when it spent about $340 million for two privately held companies, New Orleans–based K&B, Incorporated and Tuscaloosa, Alabama–based Harco, Inc. K&B operated 186 stores in Louisiana, Texas, and four other southern states and had 1996 sales of $580 million. Harco ran 146 stores in Alabama, Mississippi, and Florida and had $258 million in revenues in 1996. In addition, in 1997 Rite Aid opened 369 new, 10,500-square-foot prototype stores, which seemed to pay off. These new stores generated more than $3 million compared with the $2 million average of older, smaller stores, thanks to added space and innovative design. The new format placed a greater emphasis on so-called front-end merchandise (i.e., nonprescription items), particularly

health and beauty care items and cosmetics. The siting of the new stores reflected an evolving emphasis on freestanding outlets over those located within strip shopping centers. Rite Aid now operated more than 3,600 stores, and revenues for 1998 reached $11.38 billion.

During 1997 and 1998 the more than 1,300 Thrifty, PayLess, K&B, and Harco stores were converted to the Rite Aid banner. Many of the acquired stores were older, outdated stores, sorely in need of a remodeling. The company began a multiyear process of converting the units to the Rite Aid format. Some were expanded, while others were relocated—often shifting from a strip mall to a freestanding locale. In addition, Rite Aid opened a number of its new prototype stores; the chain wished to continue growing, but there were few opportunities left for large acquisitions. The corporation also bolstered its advertising in 1998, spending $200 million that year, a 35 percent increase over the ad spending from a few years earlier.

A Host of Troubles and the Beginnings of a Turnaround: 1999 and Beyond

Continuing its acquisitions spree, Rite Aid in November 1998 reached an agreement to acquire PCS Health Systems, Inc. from Eli Lilly and Company. The $1.5 billion deal, financed through short-term borrowing, was completed in January 1999. PCS was a leading pharmacy benefits manager, or PBM, involved in handling the administrative, paperwork side of prescription-drug services for health maintenance organizations (HMOs) and large employers and attempting to secure lower overall drug costs for them. Rite Aid's existing PBM, Eagle Managed Care, was subsequently melded into PCS. Also in January 1999 Rite Aid entered into an alliance with General Nutrition Companies, Inc. (GNC), a leading retailer of specialty vitamins and supplements. The firms agreed to place 1,500 GNC outlets within Rite Aid stores over the next three years. In February, Rite Aid spent about $25 million to purchase Edgehill Drugs, Inc., a 25-store chain operating in Maryland and Delaware. In July, the company allied with drugstore.com, acquiring a 25 percent stake in the online pharmacy; through this partnership, customers were soon able to order prescriptions online through drugstore.com and then pick them up later that same day at a Rite Aid outlet.

During these same months of 1999, however, Rite Aid was simultaneously in the process of going seriously off-track. Investigations conducted by *Business Week* magazine and the *Wall Street Journal* began delving into allegations of dealings between Rite Aid and companies whose owners included members of the Grass family—dealings that the company had not disclosed. The company soon launched an internal investigation, which indeed uncovered undisclosed holdings in Rite Aid suppliers by Grass family members. At the same time, Rite Aid began running into serious financial problems, in part because of difficulties integrating the recent acquisitions, particularly that of Thrifty PayLess, but also because of the heavy debt it had accrued to fund the growth spurt; the total debt load reached as high as $6.7 billion. In March, Rite Aid announced that its fiscal 1999 fourth quarter earnings would fall far short of expectations, sending its stock plunging 39 percent. Shareholder lawsuits were soon filed. In June, after uncovering accounting irregularities, the company made its first downward adjustment in its earnings for the previous three fiscal years; in October it went further, adjusting earnings for these years down by $500 million. Late that month, Rite Aid faced a huge debt payment that it was not going to be able to make. The company's bankers agreed to a one-year extension of the credit, but not before forcing the ouster of Martin Green. After a short period of interim leadership, Robert G. Miller was named chairman and CEO of Rite Aid in December 1999. Miller had been CEO of Fred Meyer, Inc. from 1991 until the acquisition of the Portland, Oregon–based grocery retailer by the Kroger Co. in May 1999. Miller brought with him three other former Fred Meyer executives, including Mary F. Sammons, who was named president and chief operating officer. By the time the new executive team was in place, Rite Aid's stock was trading well under $10 per share, down from the 52-week high of $51.13 in January 1999.

Miller and company quickly brought Rite Aid's store expansion program to a halt and launched a rigorous review of the existing store portfolio, targeting underperforming units for closure. In 2001 alone, 144 stores were shuttered. Sammons also slashed prices on Rite Aid's 1,500 top-selling products by 20 percent to get customers back into the stores and worked with vendors to repair supply-chain problems. In June 2000 the new management team completed a $1 billion refinancing plan, providing some breathing room for a company on the verge of a bankruptcy filing. Then in July, after months of poring over the books for the previous three-plus years, Rite Aid revealed even larger losses: an additional $1.06 billion in losses for 1998 and 1999, turning what had been $450 million in profits for those years into losses of $600 million. The $1.6 billion restated earnings total amounted to the largest accounting restatement in U.S. history—a dubious distinction that soon would be erased by the wave of accounting scandals that shook the country in 2000. In addition, the company reported a $1.14 billion loss for 2000. In a move to further reduce debt, Rite Aid also unveiled the sale of PCS Health Systems to Advance Paradigm, Inc. for about $910 million plus equity securities in the resulting firm, AdvancePCS, Inc. The deal closed in October 2000. The following March, Rite Aid sold its stake in AdvancePCS for $284.2 million.

Meanwhile, litigation connected to the accounting scandal and the former managers of Rite Aid proliferated. In November 2000 the company agreed to pay at least $200 million to settle the class-action suits brought by shareholders contending that the firm's stock had been inflated by falsified bookkeeping. While Miller said, "This is a major step in putting the past behind us," several former top Rite Aid officials still had to contend with the legal consequences of their past actions, as formal investigations had been launched by the Securities and Exchange Commission (SEC) and federal prosecutors. In June 2002 a federal grand jury in Pennsylvania issued a 37-count indictment, charging Martin Grass and three other former Rite Aid executives with masterminding an illegal accounting scheme. One year later, on the eve of his trial, Grass pleaded guilty to conspiracy to defraud and conspiracy to obstruct justice. He faced as many as eight years in prison. In all, six former Rite Aid executives either pled guilty to or were convicted of criminal conduct in connection with the accounting fraud. They included the top four administrators at the firm during the late 1990s. The SEC also launched a suit seeking civil penalties against the former executives that potentially could amount to millions of dollars.

Outside the courtroom, Rite Aid continued its turnaround efforts. A $3.2 billion loan refinancing completed in June 2001 further strengthened the firm's financial footing, helping reduce total debt to about $3.7 billion and easing it back from the brink of bankruptcy. Additional funds were raised through the sale of the firm's stake in drugstore.com between January and May 2002. Drugstore.com continued to function as Rite Aid's exclusive online pharmacy. During 2002 and 2003 an additional 156 underperforming stores were closed, further reducing the store count to about 3,400. For the year ending on March 1, 2003, Rite Aid trimmed its net loss to $112.1 million, compared with the $827.7 million loss of the preceding year. Perhaps most impressively, Sammons's efforts at turning around the performance at the stores were clearly beginning to pay off: Same-store sales (sales at stores open more than one year) were up 6.7 percent for the year. Sammons was rewarded by being promoted to president and CEO in June 2003, with Miller remaining chairman.

By the third quarter of 2004, Rite Aid was on the verge of a return to steady profitability. Net income of $22.5 million that quarter reduced the net loss for the first nine months of the year to $26.9 million. Another signal of the firm's recovery came in February 2004 when it was reported that Rite Aid had entered the bidding for the Eckerd chain, which J.C. Penney was attempting to sell. Rite Aid reportedly offered as much as $4 billion for the chain, which operated almost 2,800 stores, mostly in the East and South. Given the nascent nature of Rite Aid's recovery, analysts were doubtful that the firm's bid would prevail against competing offers from arch-rival CVS and the Jean Coutu Group Inc., a Canadian firm that owned the Brooks Pharmacy chain in the Northeast. It was nevertheless certain that Rite Aid had entered a new growth phase: In June 2003 the company announced plans to build 175 new stores in its strongest markets over the next two fiscal years. With a keen eye on controlling costs and keeping its books clean, Rite Aid was poised for a full recovery from its black days in the late 1990s.

Principal Competitors

Walgreen Co.; CVS Corporation; Wal-Mart Stores, Inc.; Eckerd Corporation.

Further Reading

"Bar Codes and RFDC Fill the Information Gap at Rite Aid," *Modern Materials Handling,* October 1993.

Barrett, Amy, and Karen Stevens, "Rite Aid Tells All—After the Storm Breaks," *Business Week,* February 22, 1999, pp. 36, 38.

Berner, Robert, and Mark Maremont, "Lost Heir: As Rite Aid Grew, CEO Seemed Unable to Manage His Empire," *Wall Street Journal,* October 20, 1999, pp. A1+.

Brookman, Faye, "Grass Leaves a Mixed Legacy at Rite Aid," *Women's Wear Daily,* October 22, 1999, p. 9.

Campanella, Frank W., "Recovery Room: Rite Aid Finds It in Its High-Margin Pharmacy Operation," *Barron's,* January 19, 1987, pp. 35+.

Coleman, Calmetta Y., "Rite Aid's Rapid Expansion Poses Problem for Chain," *Wall Street Journal,* September 3, 1998, p. B4.

Condon, Bernard, "Like Father, Like Son. Sort Of," *Forbes,* June 1, 1998, pp. 90, 92.

Dochat, Tom, "Rite Aid Keeps Its Focus on Building 'on Good Results,' " *Harrisburg (Pa.) Patriot-News,* June 22, 2003, p. A1.

——, "Stockholders to Settle Rite Aid Lawsuit," *Harrisburg (Pa.) Patriot-News,* October 16, 2002, p. D6.

——, "Under New Team, Rite Aid Changes Its Ways," *Harrisburg (Pa.) Patriot-News,* June 22, 2002, p. A5.

"Eagle Managed Care: A Wrong Way and a Rite Way," *Drug Topics,* September 5, 1994.

Fried, Lisa I., "Rite Aid Keeps Getting Bigger and Bigger," *Drug Store News,* April 27, 1998, pp. 133+.

Gerber, Cheryl, "High Tech Pain Killer," *Forbes ASAP,* December 4, 1995, pp. 108–10.

"Groomed for Success," *Chain Store Age Executive,* April 1995, pp. 25–28.

Hannon, Kerry, "The Doctor Is In," *Forbes,* July 13, 1987, p. 426.

Harris, Gardiner, "Rite Aid to Sell Its PCS Unit for $800 Million," *Wall Street Journal,* July 12, 2000, p. B2.

Hussey, Allan F., "Prescription at Rite Aid Calls for Profits Rebound," *Barron's,* November 17, 1975, p. 63.

Johnsen, Michael, "On Steadier Ground, Rite Aid Sets New Goals," *Drug Store News,* July 21, 2003, pp. 51, 61.

Kilman, Scott, "Rite Aid Ex-Officials Charged in Accounting-Fraud Probe," *Wall Street Journal,* June 24, 2002, p. A2.

Lipin, Steven, "Rite Aid to Pay $1.4 Billion for Thrifty," *Wall Street Journal,* October 14, 1996, p. A3.

Lipin, Steven, and Robert Berner, "Rite Aid to Buy Lilly Business for $1.5 Billion," *Wall Street Journal,* November 17, 1998, p. A3.

Longo, Don, "The Maestro of Rite Aid's Recovery," *Retail Merchandiser,* February 2004, pp. 19+.

"Lost in Space," *Financial World,* November 21, 1995, pp. 46–47.

Maremont, Mark, "Call to Account: Rite Aid Case Gives First View of Fraud on Trial," *Wall Street Journal,* June 10, 2003, pp. A1+.

Maremont, Mark, and Robert Berner, "Family Affairs: Rite Aid Does Business with Firms Linked to CEO Martin Grass," *Wall Street Journal,* January 29, 1999, pp. A1+.

Murray, Matt, and Bryan Gruley, "Rite Aid Corp. Abandons Revco Deal, Blaming FTC for Aggressive Opposition," *Wall Street Journal,* April 25, 1996, p. A3.

Nelson, Brett, "Looking Up—Maybe," *Forbes,* March 4, 2002, pp. 64–66.

"Rite Aid Sees a Future in Capitated Managed Care," *Drug Topics,* November 1993, p. 52.

"Rite Aid's Softer Side," *Chain Store Age Executive,* April 1995, p. 28.

Sherrid, Pamela, "Rite Place, Rite Price," *Forbes,* November 23, 1981, pp. 87+.

Spurgeon, Devon, and Mark Maremont, "Rite Aid Posts $1.14 Billion Loss for Year," *Wall Street Journal,* July 12, 2000, p. A3.

Tosh, Mark, "Pushing Recovery's Boundaries," *Drug Store News,* April 29, 2002, pp. 74, 127.

Weber, Joseph, et al., "Seizing the Dark Day," *Business Week,* January 13, 1992, pp. 26–28.

—Maya Sahafi
—updates: Catherine Hamrick, David E. Salamie

The Rouse Company

Rouse Company Building
10275 Little Patuxent Parkway
Columbia, Maryland 21044-3456
U.S.A.
Telephone: (410) 992-6000
Fax: (410) 992-6363
Web site: http://www.therousecompany.com

Public Company
Incorporated: 1954 as James W. Rouse & Company, Inc.
Employees: 3,169
Sales: $1.17 billion (2003)
Stock Exchanges: New York
Ticker Symbol: RSE
NAIC: 236220 Commercial and Institutional Building
    Construction; 531120 Lessors of Nonresidential
    Buildings (Except Miniwarehouses); 531190 Lessors
    of Other Real Estate Property; 721110 Hotels (Except
    Casino Hotels) and Motels (pt)

One of the largest publicly held real estate development and management firms in the United States, The Rouse Company has a reputation for innovation. Under the direction of founder and "industry prophet" James W. Rouse, the company was in the vanguard of suburban enclosed-mall construction in the 1950s, the planned community movement in the 1960s, and the proliferation of urban "festival marketplaces" in the 1970s and early 1980s. The saturation of the retail development market in the early 1990s led the company into the construction and management of more office and mixed-use projects. By the early 21st century, The Rouse Company—now operating as a Real Estate Investment Trust (REIT)—owned and/or operated more than 150 retail, residential, and office properties nationwide.

Leading the Postwar Exodus
to the Suburbs: 1939–69

The Rouse Company traces its roots to the Moss-Rouse Company, a Baltimore mortgage banking firm owned by James W.

Rouse and Hunter Moss in 1939. The partners, who had borrowed $20,000 to start their business, originated Federal Housing Administration loans for several years. When World War II drew Rouse and other key employees into military service the firm lapsed. But the company flourished in the postwar era when there was a boom in government-funded veterans' housing.

Hunter Moss left the partnership in 1954, when it was renamed James W. Rouse & Company, Inc. Rouse expanded the scope of his financing activities to commercial real estate projects, including the new strip shopping centers that were springing up on the outskirts of cities. After conducting pre-construction market research, arranging financing, leasing space to merchants, and directing construction for the owners of the Mondawmin Shopping Center in Baltimore, Rouse decided to enter the real estate development business. To conduct these endeavors, he created Community Research and Development (CRD), a real estate development subsidiary, in 1956. CRD opened Rouse's first enclosed large shopping center, Harundale Mall, two years later. By the early 1960s, James Rouse was one of the United States' busiest and most prosperous mortgage bankers and shopping center executives. His company acted as a mortgage correspondent for 50 lenders, had a loan portfolio of over $500 million, and was famous for uniting esthetics and profitability in retail centers.

The Rouse Company, as it finally became known, experimented with community development through the creation of The Village of Cross Keys, a Baltimore townhouse development. Then, in 1963, Rouse formed a partnership with Connecticut General Life Insurance Company to create Howard Research and Development Corporation. The lofty goal of this new venture was to plan and create the entire city of Columbia, Maryland. Rouse set his "total city concept" in motion by anonymously accumulating more than 14,000 acres in Howard County, Maryland, between Baltimore and Washington, D.C. The 165 separate parcels cost less than $1,500 per acre, in compliance with a stipulation of Connecticut General, which provided the majority of the funding for the project. Rouse surprised Howard County's commissioners when he revealed in a meeting that he owned 10 percent of the region they governed and requested rezoning of the area. Although the commissioners had a mandate to keep the county rural, Rouse's ensuing public relations campaign convinced them and their electorate that they would be better off planning for (and exercising some control over) the inevitable urbanization of the strategic corridor between two of the East Coast's most vital cities.

Rouse assembled a coterie of planners, sociologists, educators, religious groups, and cultural and medical institutions to advise and support the creation of the new city. When it was launched in 1967, Columbia featured 11,000 residences (including low-cost housing jointly sponsored by the three primary religious denominations); schools within walking distance of elementary and junior high students; Howard County's first hospital; public transportation; and a shopping center. By 1975, when the city boasted 38,000 residents, it had become "suburban Baltimore," and within a decade it would be, according to *Financial World* (1986), "one of the hottest developing territories in the country."

Rouse's stock soared from $2 per share in the early 1960s to $30 by 1972. But during the 1974–75 real estate slowdown, the company lost Housing and Urban Development funding for a major low-income housing project. This, in turn, effected a $7 million loss and compelled Rouse to pull out of two engineered communities in Tennessee and Maryland, resulting in additional losses of $4.2 million. Connecticut General even had to purchase most of Rouse's share of the Columbia project during this difficult time. Short-term debt stood at $80 million, while equity was at $6 million. From 1974 to 1976, the company retrenched by selling 50 percent stakes in 7 of 24 retail centers, reaping a total of $24 million cash. It also eliminated half the headquarters staff and wrote off $30 million in bad investments.

During the company's difficult years, Rouse invented his own method of accounting. He pioneered a new accounting figure dubbed "current value." During this decade of economic uncertainty, Rouse claimed that current value gave a fairer, more accurate estimation of the company's assets than depreciation under generally accepted accounting standards. At the time, both *Business Week* and the Securities and Exchange Commission praised the outside-auditor-certified figures as "more realistic." The use of such estimates would come under fire in the early 1990s, however.

Urban Development Projects: 1970s and Early 1980s

Rouse did not rely on number-crunching alone to improve his company's financial prospects. After leading the postwar exodus to suburbia in the 1940s and 1950s, Rouse defied conventional wisdom by starting urban development projects in the late 1970s and early 1980s. His first, and definitive, undertaking transformed three virtually abandoned 150-year-old, block-long Greek revival buildings in Boston's warehouse district into an enticing complex

of food markets, restaurants, offices, and retail shops. Rouse was approached by architect Benjamin Thompson with his idea for the project. After overcoming his own initial skepticism, the developer convinced the city of Boston to join him in a 99-year partnership wherein the city received 25 percent of the project's gross rentals. Rouse added funding from local and regional financiers to the municipal contributions.

Named for Mayor Josiah Quincy and opened August 26, 1976 (150 years after its namesake had originally dedicated it), the retail center hosted 100,000 shoppers on its first day. By the end of its first year, Quincy Market had attracted as many consumers as Disneyland had attracted tourists, and its average per-square-foot sales more than doubled comparable department store figures. In 1978, it won an Honor Award from the American Institute of Architects. Rouse hoped that his revival of the "spirit of festival" embodied in this project would satisfy the "yearning for life at the heart of the city," according to *Fortune*.

The developer applied his festival marketplace concept, with appropriate adaptations, in Philadelphia, Santa Monica, New York City, Milwaukee, St. Louis, and San Francisco. By the end of the decade, Rouse managed about 30 shopping centers in ten states and two Canadian provinces, claiming $479 million in assets. The company's mortgage banking subsidiary ranked among the largest in the United States, with a $1.4 billion loan portfolio. Columbia's population had risen to 50,000 and had rebounded from recession-related indebtedness. With his company back on track, Rouse retired the presidency and chief executive office in 1979 (but retained the chairmanship) to devote himself more fully to the social welfare activities he had long espoused.

Unlike other real estate mavens who had trouble engineering the transfer of power, Rouse had groomed a successor. He convinced Mathias DeVito to relinquish his partnership in the prestigious Baltimore law firm of Piper & Marbury and create an in-house legal department for Rouse in 1968. DeVito advanced from general counsel to vice-president and chief operations officer later that year. He also played a vital role in the company's survival of the 1974–75 recession, and gradually assumed Rouse's responsibilities over the ensuing five years.

Change of Leadership and Focus: Mid- to Late 1980s

With many traditional suburban markets saturated with malls by the 1980s, DeVito took a more conservative tack than his intrepid predecessor. He eschewed the middle markets that many developers targeted to concentrate on what he described as "expensive, high-amenity urban projects," according to *Forbes*. He continued to pursue Rouse's one-of-a-kind renovations, however, leveraging the company's talent and reputation with relatively small capital investments. In Milwaukee, for example, municipal and federal governments combined with two major department stores, local businesses, and a large insurance company to invest $70 million in the Grand Avenue Mall, while Rouse's cash contribution was only $500,000. In spite of its comparatively small cash outlay, Rouse was able to command half the excess cash flow and a share of residual values as its share of the profits. The new CEO also made strategic alliances with investment groups to renovate and manage older malls. Institutional investors contributed the capital necessary to purchase 21 malls from

Key Dates:

1939: Moss-Rouse Company is formed.

1954: Having terminated his partnership with Hunter Moss, James W. Rouse renames his mortgage-banking firm James W. Rouse & Company, Inc.

1956: Rouse creates a subsidiary, Community Research and Development (CRD), to enter the business of commercial real estate development.

1963: Rouse forms a partnership with Connecticut General Life Insurance Company to create Howard Research and Development Corporation, with the lofty goal of planning and building the entire city of Columbia, Maryland.

1967: Rouse's urban development project, Quincy Market, opens for business in Boston, Massachusetts.

1979: Rouse retires from the presidency and chief executive office (still retaining the chairmanship) to devote himself more fully to social welfare activities; Mathias DeVito is his successor.

1984: DeVito sells the company's founding business, Rouse Real Estate Finance, to PaineWebber for $50.5 million.

1985: After a decade of minority ownership, Rouse re-acquires the planned community of Columbia, Maryland.

1996: James W. Rouse dies at the age of 81.

1998: The Rouse Company converts from a standard corporation to a Real Estate Investment Trust (REIT).

1979 to 1983, while Rouse brought its esthetic and managerial expertise to the joint ventures.

James Rouse retired as the company's chair in 1984 to give his full attention to the Enterprise Foundation, a nonprofit organization he began in 1981 to improve housing, healthcare, and job programs in the nation's poorest neighborhoods. Rouse's social sensitivity was evidenced early in his career. In the late 1940s, he led an attempt to rehabilitate Baltimore slums without gentrifying them. In 1953 Rouse was appointed to President Eisenhower's Task Force on Housing, which crafted the Urban Renewal Administration. But as the developer began to believe that "government programs . . . tend to be costly in relation to their benefits," he increasingly employed his own resources for societal improvement.

A subsidiary of the Foundation, Enterprise Development Company, was formed to build festival marketplaces for smaller cities. Its profits were intended to fuel the charity's endeavors, a tangible product of Rouse's belief that "the free enterprise system should have the capability to produce profits for the poor as well as for the rich." The nonprofit also accepted donations from corporations, foundations, and individuals, with $1 million donated from Rouse. By the time he fully retired, the Enterprise Foundation had formed relationships with 22 neighborhood groups in 12 cities.

In the meantime, DeVito sold the company's founding business, Rouse Real Estate Finance, to PaineWebber for $50.5 million in 1984. The 45-year-old, mid-sized mortgage company was

getting squeezed out in an industry increasingly dominated by giants. The following year, however, Rouse regained one of its most celebrated projects. After a decade of minority ownership, Rouse re-acquired the planned community of Columbia, Maryland, by adding CIGNA's 80 percent stake of Howard Research and Development Corporation to its 20 percent. The purchase increased Rouse's debt to $120 million, but DeVito hoped that income from mixed-use projects, combining hotel, office, and retail spaces, would provide new sources of cash flow. By 1986, the company's holdings were valued at $1.6 billion.

Facing Uncertainty in the Early 1990s

But in the absence of headline-grabbing new development projects that had characterized James Rouse's tenure, Mathias DeVito's term came under increasing scrutiny. In October 1989, *Forbes* reporter Tatiana Pouschine characterized Rouse's future as "cloudy" and its $29 per share stock as "overvalued." She also criticized the company's current value statistics (used virtually unchallenged since 1976) as particularly high when compared to traditional valuations. In addition, she noted that Rouse had negative cash flows that were not improving.

In the early 1990s, Rouse became embroiled in a debate pitting its "current value" asset estimates against generally accepted accounting principles (GAAP). In 1991, for example, GAAP figures set its assets at $2.4 billion, compared to the company's current value calculation of $4 billion. It was not merely an academic dispute, however. Based on conventional data, Rouse's stock was trading around $14 per share, but based on its own figures, the company thought it should be selling closer to $26 per share. That year, DeVito commissioned the highly respected firm of Landauer Associates Real Estate Counselors to corroborate its current valuation. As a result, Rouse acknowledged the early 1990s real estate slump by lowering its current value in 1990, 1991, and 1992.

From 1990 to 1993, Rouse recorded a cumulative net loss of $11.56 million (according to GAAP). The company's only year of profitability during the period was 1991. Rouse contended that, since it was not valid to depreciate its earnings in a conventional way, it was more telling to examine the company's earnings before depreciation and deferred taxes from operations (EBDT). Rouse reported that its EBDT rose from $50.29 million in 1990 to $78.28 million in 1993. Rouse also increased its current value in 1993.

Even Adrienne Linsenmeyer-Hardman, an analyst with *Financial World* who was critical of Rouse's accounting methods, conceded that Rouse was "a powerhouse in its industry" in 1992. She cautioned, however, that as retail sales shifted from department stores and regional malls to discounters, specialty shops, and strip malls, Rouse would be forced to adapt its holdings and construction plans. James Rouse had met such a challenge in the 1970s with his pioneering festival marketplaces. Whether DeVito could meet the challenges of the 1990s in the same way would determine the company's future.

Surviving the Collapse: New Opportunities in the 21st Century

Although the early 1990s was a rough period for the real estate sector, Rouse emerged from the prolonged downturn relatively intact. True, the company suffered some heavy losses, with its revenues in consistent decline, and its stock price hitting a low of roughly $10 a share during the slump. However, in spite of the temporary loss of profitability, and the absence of any real growth over a seven-year period, Rouse did manage to remain solvent, without losing any of its holdings to foreclosure or takeover. Much of the credit for the company's survival belonged to its business model, widely acknowledged as one of the most professional in the industry. Rather than risking its future by pouring money into new acquisitions, Rouse instead devoted its resources to maintaining and improving its existing properties, doing everything it could to ensure that income from leases remained constant. As a result, while many of the company's competitor's did not survive, Rouse appeared to be in good shape heading into the next upswing in the real estate market.

The turnaround began in May 1994, when Rouse announced plans to construct two new shopping centers, in Spartanburg, South Carolina, and Orlando, Florida, the company's first new projects since 1987. The move sparked a flurry of new building projects and acquisitions for the company over the next several years. In the spring of 1996, Rouse embarked on one of the most ambitious projects in the company's history when it purchased the Las Vegas-based Howard Hughes Corporation for $520 million. With the merger, Rouse acquired more than three million square feet of office space, predominantly in Las Vegas, as well as the Fashion Show Mall on the famed Las Vegas Strip, which boasted some of the highest sales figures among nationwide shopping centers. The centerpiece of the acquisition was the Summerlin development, a ''master-planned'' community covering 22,500 acres in suburban Las Vegas. Although only 20 percent completed at the time of the merger, Summerlin had consistently proven to be the top selling master-planned community in the nation over the previous five years. Upon its completion, Summerlin was projected to have a population of well over 100,000 people.

In January 1998, Rouse officially became a Real Estate Investment Trust, or REIT. Since REITs were exempt from federal income tax if they funneled all their profits into stockholder dividends, they proved exceptionally popular among investors, and generally enjoyed share values roughly double those of standard companies. Although Rouse had initially resisted becoming a REIT, primarily because of restrictions imposed on REITs by tax regulations, in the end the company determined that raising its market value was the key to long-term growth. Ultimately, the strategy did result in a major boost to the company's stock. By April 1998, its share price rose to $32; in February 2004, the value exceed $50 a share.

Meanwhile, the company's aggressive growth campaign continued. In April 1998, Rouse purchased $1.1 billion worth of shopping centers from Toronto-based TrizecHahn Corp. The acquisition gave Rouse new upscale shopping malls in several states, including New Jersey, Nevada, Colorado, and Iowa. In July 1998 Rouse purchased more than 4.5 million square feet of office space in the Washington and Baltimore area from Teach-

ers Properties Inc., a deal worth $375 million. In 2003, Rouse acquired controlling interests in two major master-planned communities: The Woodlands, a community on the outskirts of Houston, Texas, and Mizner Park in Boca Raton, Florida. Overall, master-planned communities accounted for $123 million in revenues that year.

The company did weather some sad news during this period of unprecedented growth, when its philanthropic founder, James Rouse, died in April 1996, at the age of 81. In his last years Rouse devoted his energy to helping run the Enterprise Foundation, which had developed more than 60,000 low-income homes in its 14-year existence. In the fall of 1995 President Bill Clinton presented Rouse with the Presidential Medal of Freedom, while a biography of Rouse, *Better Places, Better Lives*, was published by Maryland native Joshua Olson in 2004. The biography appeared at a time when The Rouse Company was enjoying record earnings on sales exceeding $1.1 billion in 2003. Although Rouse did not live to witness this unprecedented prosperity, it was clear that his legacy was well in place as his company forged ahead in the 21st century.

Principal Competitors

General Growth Properties, Inc.; JMB Realty Corporation; Simon Property Group, Inc.

Further Reading

''Back to Earth,'' *Forbes*, October 1, 1974, p. 26.

Bivins, Jacquelyn, ''James Rouse: Enterprise for the Public Good,'' *Chain Store Age Executive*, September 1986, pp. 45–51.

Breckenfeld, Gurney, ''The Rouse Show Goes National,'' *Fortune*, July 27, 1981, pp. 49–54.

''An Equitable Distribution,'' *Financial World*, May 2–15, 1984, p. 93.

Haggerty, Maryann, ''Getting Back to Building; Rouse Emerges from Real Estate Collapse with Plans for New Malls, Housing Development,'' *Washington Post*, May 30, 1994.

——, ''Hughes May Deal Rouse Huge Stake in Las Vegas; Billionaire's Heirs Ready to Sell Properties,'' *Washington Post*, January 10, 1996.

James, Ellen L., ''The Sure Touch of The Rouse Co.,'' *Financial World*, July 10–23, 1985, pp. 44–46.

Linsenmeyer-Hardman, Adrienne, ''Value Judgment,'' *Financial World*, July 21, 1992, pp. 34–35.

Luebke, Cathy, ''The Rouse Co.,'' *Business Journal—Serving Phoenix & the Valley of the Sun*, June 25, 1993, p. 107.

''Master Builder with a New Concept,'' *Business Week*, August 20, 1966, pp. 106–110.

Olsen, Joshua, *Better Places, Better Lives: A Biography of James Rouse*, Independent Publishers Group, 2004.

Peirce, Neal, ''Urban Developer James Rouse: The Great Oak Falls,'' *Times-Picayune* (New Orleans, LA), April 22, 1996.

Pouschine, Tatiana, ''Malled,'' *Forbes*, October 30, 1989, pp. 46, 49.

''Rouse,'' *Financial World*, July 22, 1986, pp. 50–51.

Rudnitsky, Howard, ''Make Room, Disney World, Federated and Gimbels,'' *Forbes*, May 9, 1983, pp. 100–04.

—April Dougal Gasbarre
—update: Stephen Meyer

Safety Components International, Inc.

41 Stevens Street
Greenville, South Carolina 29605
U.S.A.
Telephone: (864) 240-2600
Fax: (864) 240-2728
Web site: http://www.safetycomponents.com

Public Company
Incorporated: 1994
Employees: 2,800
Sales: $244.3 million (2003)
Stock Exchanges: OTC
Ticker Symbol: SAFY
NAIC: 314999 All Other Miscellaneous Textile Product
Mills; 336399 All Other Motor Vehicle Parts
Manufacturing

Safety Components International, Inc. (SCI) is a major supplier of components for automotive airbags. SCI sells airbag fabric in the United States and sells cushions to airbag module integrators around the world. The company's products, which include cushions for passenger, driver, and side impact airbags and knee protection curtains, are found in over 200 models of cars and trucks. Airbag products account for about 90 percent of sales.

The company also produces a variety of specialized synthetic fabrics for use in defense, aerospace, oil, and other industries. Applications include filtration, military tents, high-end luggage (used in Hartman and Tumi brands), and clothing for firefighters.

U.S. manufacturing facilities account for half of sales; Safety Components also has plants in Mexico, the United Kingdom, Germany, and the Czech Republic, and farms out some work to contractors in Germany and Romania. It produces about two million airbag cushions per month. The company maintains technical centers in South Carolina, Mexico, and Germany. Safety Components underwent a prearranged Chapter 11 bankruptcy in 2000, selling off ammunition supplier Valentec Systems, Inc.

Origins

Safety Components International, Inc. (SCI) was formed on January 12, 1994, as a wholly owned subsidiary of Valentec International Corporation, a contractor for the defense, aerospace, and automotive industries. Valentec CEO Robert A. Zummo became SCI's first chairman, president, and CEO.

Zummo had in 1993 bought Valentec International Corp. from Insilco Corp., a Big Board-listed U.S. defense contractor based in Meriden, Connecticut, that had acquired Valentec eight years earlier. Based in St. Louis with subsidiaries in Florida and Ohio, Valentec produced metal components such as ammunition cartridges, link belts, and projectiles used by the military, mostly for target practice.

Valentec also made miniature parachutes for ordnance. This experience led to a contract supplying TRW with fabric for automotive airbags. After Zummo acquired the company, the airbag business was spun off as Safety Components International. The company completed an initial public offering on the NASDAQ (ticker: ABAG) in May 1994.

SCI was based in Costa Mesa, California. It produced projectiles and other ammunition components at a factory in Galion, Ohio. In September 1994, SCI won a two-year, $65 million contract to supply the U.S. Army with 120 mm mortar cartridges as a prime contractor.

SCI grew rapidly. Eventually the company began sewing the airbag fabric into airbag cushions itself. Sales were $7 million in 1992. For an 11-month fiscal year ended March 31, 1994, they were up to $22.4 million. Sales reached $51.8 million in 1995, with net income of $2.1 million. Sales for the automotive division nearly tripled to $43 million.

Although SCI faced increasing competition, demand for airbags was growing considerably in world markets. The introduction of side impact airbags produced more demand for SCI's components. TRW was the company's only automotive airbag customer until September 1995, when SCI won a large contract to supply airbag material to Delphi Interior and Lighting for passenger side airbags in GM trucks. Neither of these were

Key Dates:

1994: Safety Components International (SCI), a subsidiary of defense contractor Valentec, is spun off in an initial public offering.
1996: SCI buys Germany's Phoenix Airbag GmbH.
1997: JPS Automotive airbag unit, as well as Valentec International, are acquired.
2000: SCI divests non-automotive units during prearranged bankruptcy reorganization.
2004: Zapata Corporation acquires controlling interest in SCI.

exclusive arrangements; both TRW and Delphi supplied a portion of their own airbag fabric.

Growing Globally in the Mid-1990s

The company's Mexican plant was producing 2.6 million airbag cushions a year. A research and development center was set up there in 1995. A joint venture was established in China in 1995 but was ended after four years. SCI also had a U.K. facility in Gwent, Wales, which subcontracted work to a plant in the Czech Republic; these operations produced 800,000 airbags a year.

In 1996 the company established its own direct sales force. It had retained an outside marketing firm, Champion Sales & Service Co., since 1992. At this time, SCI had nearly 800 employees in the Automotive Division and 100 in the Defense Division.

An 80 percent share of Phoenix Airbag GmbH, based in Hildesheim, Germany, was acquired in 1996 for about $22 million, plus up to an additional $7.5 million if it met certain financial targets. The remaining shares were to be acquired later. Phoenix had sales of $30 million a year.

The deal made SCI Europe's leading independent airbag producer. Building its low cost manufacturing capacity, in April 1996 the company began work on a 100,000-square-foot office and manufacturing facility in the Czech Republic.

Valentec International Corporation, SCI's largest shareholder since its founding, was acquired in May 1997. Valentec made stamped and machined metal parts used in airbag inflators as well as in ammunition for the military.

Later in 1997, SCI bought the airbag fabrics business of Collins & Aikman Corp.'s JPS Automotive L.P. Unit for $56.3 million plus assumption of $650,000 in debt. Collins & Aikman had acquired JPS only a few months earlier. JPS's Air Restraint and Technical Fabrics Group dominated the airbags fabric business in North America, with 40 percent of the market; chief customers included TRW (which accounted for 47 percent of fiscal 1997 sales), AlliedSignal, and AutoLiv Inc. It was renamed Safety Components Fabric Technologies after the purchase.

SCI also bought a 350,000-square-foot building next to the JPS site in Greenville, South Carolina, for about $1.25 million. The company also relocated its headquarters to Greenville from Costa Mesa, California.

Bolstered by the JPS buy, SCI's sales rose from $84 million in 1997 to more than $200 million in 1998. SCI claimed about 50 percent of the North American market for both outsourced airbag fabric and outsourced airbag cushions.

Research firm Tier One reported that 87.7 million airbag modules were sold worldwide in 1997, versus 3.6 million in 1991. Increasing airbag use in Europe and Asia was expected to push demand to 158 million modules by 2000. In addition, U.S. legislation required the installation of driver and passenger side airbags in all new passenger cars by model year 1998, and in light trucks and other vehicles by model year 1999.

The market was also growing increasingly competitive, however, and the company began to lose money—$48.7 million in the 1999 and 2000 fiscal years. SCI's common stock was delisted from the NASDAQ in February 2000. The company then began trading shares over the counter.

Reorganized 2000

Safety Components filed for bankruptcy protection in April 2000 and emerged from the prearranged Chapter 11 reorganization six months later. In September 2000, the company sold defense contractor Valentec Systems, Inc. to an investor group led by its president, Victor Guadagno, for $4.15 million. Valentec Systems, picked up in the 1997 purchase of Valentec International, had been SCI's only non-automotive unit.

SCI resolved to dispose of its metal and defense businesses in October 2000. Valentec Wells, LLC, a metal belt link business, was sold to an Alliant Techsystems ((ATK) subsidiary in September 2001 for about $5 million. Valentec Wells had earlier in the year relocated from Costa Mesa, to plants in Ohio and Missouri, partly due to problems with California's power supply. Galion, Inc., an Ohio-based defense business, was sold to an affiliate of The Diversified Group Incorporated in December 2002 for $454,000.

In November 2001, Safety Components, through its U.K. subsidiary Automotive Safety Components International Limited, acquired Woodville Airbag Engineering from Smiths Group plc subsidiary TISPP UK Limited in November 2001. SCI paid £3 million for it. Woodville, based in South Derbyshire, England, was losing more than £1 million a year but had a large backlog. SCI soon transferred much of Woodville's work to the Czech Republic and other locations with lower wage costs. A plan to close SCI's plant in Crumlin, Wales, was announced in August 2002.

SCI then had two main divisions. The North American Automotive Group was made up of Safety Component Fabric Technologies, Inc. (SCFTI) and Automotive Safety Components International, Inc. (ASCI). The European Automotive Group included Automotive Safety Components International Limited (Wales, U.K.), Automotive Safety Components International GmbH & Co. KG (Hildesheim, Germany), and Automotive Safety Components International s.r.o. (Jevicko, Czech Republic).

SCI reported sales of $244.3 million for the fiscal year ended March 31, 2003. Holding company Zapata Corporation accumulated an 83 percent interest in Safety Components in 2004. SCI subsequently changed its fiscal year to coincide with that of Zapata, ending December 31.

Principal Subsidiaries

Automotive Safety Components International Inc.; Automotive Safety Components International Limited (U.K.); Automotive Safety Components International RO S.R.L. (Romania); Automotive Safety Components International S.A. de C.V. (Mexico); Automotive Safety Components International sro (Czech Republic); Automotive Safety Components International Verwaltungs GmbH (Germany); Safety Components Fabric Technologies, Inc.

Principal Operating Units

European Automotive Group; North American Automotive Group.

Principal Competitors

Autoliv, Inc.; Highland Industries, Inc.; Key Safety Systems, Inc.; Milliken & Company Inc.

Further Reading

Apodaca, Patrice, "O.C. Air Bag Maker to Buy Fabric Supplier for $56 Million," *Los Angeles Times,* July 2, 1997, p. D1.

Couretas, John, "Collins & Aikman Corp. Sells Airbag Fabric Operations," *Automotive News,* July 7, 1997, p. 26.

"First Safety Deal Soon," *High Yield Report,* July 7, 1997, p. 1.

Gowrie, David, "Sewing Up the Air Bag Business," *Record* (New Jersey), October 30, 1998.

Hinman, Catherine, "Contractor Wins Air Force Project; Valentec to Boost Employment After Receiving Contracts," *Orlando Sentinel,* September 5, 1988, p. 10.

"Insilco Corp. to Acquire Valentec International," *PR Newswire,* January 7, 1985.

McGhie, Tom, "British Official Fights to Stop Carolina Firm from Shutting Airbag Factory," *Daily Mail,* November 18, 2001.

——, "U.S. Company Announces Job Cuts After Buying British Airbag Business," *Daily Mail,* November 11, 2001.

O'Dell, John, "Safety Components Acquires Shareholder," *Los Angeles Times,* June 2, 1997, p. D9.

Robertson, Joe, "New Company Creates Jobs at Lake City," *Kansas City Star,* May 4, 2001, p. C3.

"Safety Components Closes JPS Airbag Unit Purchase," *Autoparts Report,* August 1, 1997.

"Safety Components Gets GM Delphi Airbag Contract," *Autoparts Report,* October 3, 1995.

"Safety Components International Inc. Announces Initial Public Offering," *Wall Street Transcript,* May 16, 1994.

"Safety Components Sets Acquisition of Air Bag Unit," *New York Times,* Bus. Sec., July 26, 1997, p. 35.

"Safety Components Stock Gets Delisted from Nasdaq," *Dow Jones Business News,* February 2, 2000.

"38 Jobs Lost As Airbag Maker Ceases Production," *Western Mail* (Cardiff, Wales), Bus. Sec., August 13, 2002, p. 12.

Vyas, Rajiv, "Power Proves Final Straw for Some," *Orange County Business Journal,* July 9, 2001, p. 1.

—Frederick C. Ingram

St. Mary Land & Exploration Company

1776 Lincoln Street, Suite 700
Denver, Colorado 80203
U.S.A.
Telephone: (303) 861-8140
Fax: (303) 861-0934
Web site: http://www.stmaryland.com

Public Company
Incorporated: 1908 as St. Mary Parish Land Company
Employees: 226
Sales: $393.9 million (2003)
Stock Exchanges: New York
Ticker Symbol: SM
NAIC: 211111 Crude Petroleum and Natural Gas

Operating out of Denver, Colorado, St. Mary Land & Exploration Company is a publicly traded independent oil and gas company involved in the acquisition, exploration, exploitation, and development of natural gas and oil bearing properties. The company is involved in five core areas of the United States: the Mid-Continent region of Oklahoma and northern Texas; the ArkLaTex area that includes parts of Arkansas, Louisiana, Texas, and Mississippi; the Gulf Coast region; the Rocky Mountain region that includes the Williston Basin in eastern Montana and western North Dakota, and Wyoming's Powder River, Green River, and Wind River basins; and the Permian Basin of west Texas and eastern New Mexico. St. Mary also maintains offices in Tulsa, Oklahoma; Billings, Montana; Shreveport, Louisiana; and Houston, Texas.

Incorporating in 1908

The origins of St. Mary date back to 1900 when Chester Congdon and four men—Guilford Hartley, David Adams, A.L. Ordean, and A.S. Chase—paid $11,000 to acquire 17,700 acres of Gulf Coast marshland in St. Mary Parish (the equivalent of a county) of Louisiana, located about 85 miles southwest of New Orleans. Congdon, who resided in Duluth, Minnesota, had already made a fortune from Minnesota iron mines and Arizona copper mines. His partners in the Louisiana venture were also mining

men, and although they planned to drain the land for agricultural development, they were wise enough to obtain the mineral rights in addition to the surface rights. Given that the land proved wholly unsuited to agriculture, this decision was key to the success of the investment. In 1908 the venture was incorporated as the St. Mary's Parish Land Company. It would be reincorporated in Delaware in 1915. Congdon and Adams also bought another 7,200 acres of land in the area, which they held under a company they named Tidal Wave Land Company. The two companies would be merged under the St. Mary name in 1935.

Oil was discovered on the Texas Gulf Coast in 1901 in an area known as the Spindletop salt dome. St Mary land abutted the Belle Isle salt dome, where it was hoped that oil would eventually be found. The land may not have been a good investment in terms of farming, but it was worth holding onto to see what developed. During the 1920s Louisiana experienced a boom in oil and gas exploration, which gradually spread toward St. Mary, Louisiana. Some attempts were made to discover oil on the property, but no one had succeeded until the predecessor of Texaco, which took a lease on the land in 1933 and began exploration efforts. On May 6, 1938, the St. Mary No. 1 well, dug to the depth of 9,910 feet, became operational, producing 335 barrels of oil per day. It became the anchor of the Horseshoe Bayou Field, one of the country's great oilfields. St. Mary then leased some 4,000 acres to Atlantic Richfield, the predecessor to Vastar, which in 1941 discovered the Bayou Sale Field. It was also in 1941 that St. Mary began to pay cash dividends, distributing essentially all of the company's income from royalties to shareholders.

To support the United States' efforts in World War II, the exploitation of the two St. Mary oilfields was greatly accelerated. Natural gas was a byproduct but there was no way to capitalize on it until the postwar years when a network of gas pipelines was developed, in many cases converting oil pipelines to the purpose. Gradually, U.S. gas companies began to switch from ''town gas'' made by reducing coal to coke in local plants to natural gas. Sun Oil Company, now known as Oryx, had actually discovered gas at Belle Isle in 1941 but it was not until 1950 that it took a lease on St. Mary's adjacent land to look for the commodity. In 1955 the company completed its first well on the property.

Company Perspectives:

Our primary objective is to invest in oil and gas producing assets that provide a superior return on equity while preserving underlying capital, resulting in a return on equity to stockholders that reflects capital appreciation as well as the payment of cash dividends.

St. Mary's business relied exclusively on lease payments and royalties, which were distributed almost completely to shareholders until the mid-1960s when it became clear that the company had to invest some of that predictable cash flow to prepare for the day when the lands were depleted of oil and gas. In 1966, Thomas E. Congdon, the grandson of Chester Congdon and a Yale and Harvard graduate, was named president of St. Mary. The headquarters of the company was moved to Denver, Colorado, and with a small staff he began a diversification effort, looking for opportunities in the Rocky Mountains and Mid-Continent region with partners through both drilling and acquisition. In 1971 Congdon established a long-term relationship with George Anderson, a man who would one day be named "Wildcatter of the Year" by the Independent Petroleum Association of the Mountain States. Like Congdon, Anderson was an Ivy Leaguer, graduating from Princeton University in 1957 with a doctorate in geology. After a brief academic career he started his own company in Oklahoma's south Anadarko basin. Although, according to Congdon, Anderson had only a moderate level of revenue from his few wells, "he was very instinctive and aggressive. When a play was in the making, he was on it—bang. He could recognize an opportunity and grab it quickly." With Anderson's assistance, St. Mary broadened its portfolio to include large holdings in the Anadarko Basin in Oklahoma and smaller holdings in the Permian Basin of west Texas and southeast New Mexico, Williston Basin of Montana and North Dakota, and properties in the ArkLaTex Basin. In 1983 Anderson and St. Mary formalized their relationship to pursue drilling operations.

Looking Overseas in the 1980s

In the late 1980s St. Mary and Anderson's company, Anderson/Smith Inc., began to look for overseas opportunities and acquired target drilling properties in Argentina, Chile, Papua New Guinea, the Philippines, and Russia. Their involvement in Russia began in 1990 when officials from that country brought data packages to the United States showing a great deal of promise in properties that had just become privatized in the wake of the breakup of the Soviet Union. According to Congdon, "We bought a couple of those data packages and went over in spring 1990 to look at some projects. But they were well beyond our capability, so they offered us a third project to do." This project was the development of a 127,000-acre site in the Chernogorskoye field in western Siberia. St. Mary bought in, along with Itochu Corporation of Japan, which arranged to buy the production. With St. Mary providing support personnel, Russian partners handled operational control. In late December 1992, drilling began on the site and in 1993 production began and Itochu began to take delivery.

In 1992 St. Mary went public, taking advantage of a period of time when Wall Street was interested in energy companies. St.

Mary had enjoyed strong growth in the previous three years, with revenues increasing from $20.3 million to $27.8 million. It also boasted an enviable record of having paid a cash dividend for 52 consecutive years. The company's domestic portfolio of oil and gas properties was impressive and its prospects in Russia inviting. (The company also was involved in some domestic mining projects.) Moreover, St. Mary had little debt, just $4.9 million, as opposed to $44 million in equity. The initial offering of stock, with Denver's Hanifen, Imhoff serving as lead underwriter, was oversubscribed. In the end, St. Mary netted $23.1 million. In connection with the offering, the company shortened its name, dropping the word "Parish," to avoid the possible misconception that the company was a nonprofit, religious organization.

As part of St. Mary's transformation, experienced executives were brought in to help run the business. In September 1991 Mark A. Hellerstein was hired as chief financial officer and several months later, in May 1992, he became president and within the year was named a director of the company. (Congdon became chief executive officer, a new position.) Hellerstein graduated from the University of Colorado in 1974 with a degree in accounting. From 1980 to 1986 he served as CFO for Worldwide Energy Corporation. He then went to work for CoCa Mines Inc., a St. Mary affiliate headed by Congdon that was involved in mining. The business was sold in 1991, leading Hellerstein and other CoCa Mines executives to transfer to St. Mary. Some of them would launch some modest copper mining ventures with St. Mary. But with Congdon approaching 70 years of age, Hellerstein was singled out to be groomed as the future head of the company. He would succeed Congdon as chief executive officer in 1995, and upon Congdon's retirement in September 2002, he became chairman of the board.

St. Mary posted uneven results in the first half of the 1990s. The company reported sales of $50.7 million in 1992 and net income of $15.6 million, but the next year sales fell to $38.6 million and net income dropped to $3.7 million. In 1994, sales rebounded to $4.8 million, while net income held steady at $3.7 million, and then in 1995 revenues dipped again, to $38.6 million, and profits eroded further, dipping to $1.7 million. One area of disappointment was the company's foreign investments, which failed to pan out, prompting a change in direction in the mid-1990s as St. Mary's management decided to focus on five core domestic operating areas. The Argentine and Chilean interests were sold in 1994. In 1996 the company sold Wyoming gas properties that no longer fit with its strategy. Then, in early 1997, the company sold its working interest in the Chernogorskoye oilfield in Russia. In the meantime, St. Mary began a judicious program to acquire properties in its core areas, generally making buys of less than $10 million. Larger opportunities were more competitively priced and eliminated the advantages that St. Mary could bring to a property. In 1994 the company completed four acquisitions at a total cost of $12.4 million. A year later, it spent $8.1 million for six properties, and spent $21 million in 1996 to acquire 11 properties in the Permian Basin of New Mexico and west Texas. The largest of these transactions was the $10 million purchase of a 90 percent interest in the oil and gas properties of Siete Oil and Gas Co. St. Mary enjoyed a strong year in 1996, when sales topped $59.5 million and net income improved significantly, to $10.3 million. Whereas much of this success was attributed to recent acquisi-

Key Dates:

1900:	Chester Congdon and partners buy land in St. Mary Parish, Louisiana.
1908:	St. Mary Parish Land Company is incorporated.
1938:	The first major oil find is made on company properties.
1966:	Congdon's grandson, Thomas E. Congdon, is named president and launches a diversification effort.
1992:	The company goes public, and drops ''Parish'' from its name.
2002:	Thomas Congdon retires as chairman; the company is listed on the New York Stock Exchange.

tions, St. Mary also was able to take advantage of 3-D seismic data to squeeze out further oil and gas in older properties.

Secondary Stock Offering in 1997

To fund its exploration and development activities as well as to pay for further acquisition, St. Mary made a secondary offering of stock in February and March 1997, selling 2.18 shares of stock and netting $51.3 million. The company used some of this cash during the course of 1997 to continue adding to its reserves. For the year, St. Mary paid $27.3 million for five separate acquisitions. Of that amount, $20.3 million was spent to supplement the company's interests in the Anadarko Basin, $3.8 million for properties in Louisiana, and $3.2 million for properties in the Permian and Williston Basins. In addition, to support Gulf Coast operations, St. Mary opened an exploration office in Lafayette, Louisiana, in 1997.

St. Mary sold off some nonstrategic interests in Oklahoma and Canada in 1998, realizing net proceeds of approximately $23.2 million. During the year, the company also invested $4.2 million to complete six acquisitions, spending $3.4 million for properties in the Permian and Williston basins and another $800,000 for producing properties in Louisiana and the Anadarko Basin. Revenues jumped to $91 million in 1997 and net income more than doubled over the previous year, totaling $23.1 million. The following year, however, sales fell to $78.7 million and the company posted an $8.8 million net loss, a large portion of which, $4.5 million, was a charge taken on the Russian joint venture.

St. Mary completed two important acquisitions in 1999. In June of that year, it added Nance Petroleum Corporation and Quanterra Alpha L.P. in an $8.2 million stock transaction. As a result, St. Mary picked up 25.85 percent of a partnership that it did not previously own and added properties in the Williston Basin of Montana and North Dakota. Then, in December 1999, St. Mary used its stock to acquire King Ranch Energy, Inc., which owned properties in the Gulf of Mexico and the onshore Gulf Coast. It was subsequently renamed St. Mary Energy Company. St. Mary barely returned to profitability in 1999, earning just $82,000 on $73.3 million in sales, but the company was poised for an exceptional year in 2000, when sales improved to more than $195.6 million and net income soared to

$55.6 million, results that landed St. Mary on *Fortune* magazine's list of fastest-growing companies, ranked at number nine. Although a surge in energy prices was attributed for much of the gain, the company also took advantage of the situation because it was able to improve its oil and gas production by 69 percent over the previous year.

In the first years of the new century, St. Mary continued to acquire properties and add to its reserves. In 2001 it branched into coalbed methane development by acquiring properties of Caribou Land & Livestock Montana, located in the Hanging Woman Basin of Montana and Wyoming. In December 2002 St. Mary paid $69.5 million in cash to acquire oil and gas properties in the Williston Basin of Montana and North Dakota from Burlington Resources Oil and Gas Company. Later in that month, in a deal that would close in 2003, St. Mary acquired oil and gas properties in the Williston, Powder River, and Green River basins of the Rocky Mountains from Flying J Oil and Gas and Big West Oil and Gas. In 2001 and 2002, St. Mary posted revenues of $207.5 million and $196.4 million, respectively, and net income of $40.5 million and $27.6 million. Also in 2002, the company received permission to be listed on the New York Stock Exchange, a move that management hoped would improve investor recognition of the company's stock.

St. Mary enjoyed another outstanding year in 2003, recording revenues of nearly $394 million and net income exceeding $95.5 million. The company also was well positioned for continued growth. The venture into coalbed methane was now in the development stage and on the verge of beginning production. Moreover, the company expected to soon receive 3-D seismic data on its original 25,000 acres in St. Mary Parish, Louisiana, which during its history had already produced some 200 million barrels of oil and 3.5 TCF of natural gas, and held the potential to provide even more profits to St. Mary shareholders.

Principal Subsidiaries

St. Mary Minerals Inc. Parish Corporation; St. Mary Operating Company; Nance Petroleum Corporation; St. Mary Energy Company.

Principal Competitors

Abraxas Petroleum Corporation; BP p.l.c.; Burlington Resources Inc.

Further Reading

Hoffman, Ryan, ''St. Mary's Three-Year Growth, Astounding 40,400 Percent,'' *Denver Business Journal,* October 2, 2002.

Raabe, Steve, ''Denver-Based Oil, Gas Firm's Success Isn't Flashy, But Steady,'' *Denver Post,* August 26, 2001.

Rule, Rick, and Jeff Howard, ''Sailing with the Independents,'' *Oil & Gas Investor,* November 1992, p. 34.

Svaldi, Aldo, ''St. Mary Land & Exploration Going Public,'' *Denver Business Journal,* November 6, 1992, p. 3.

Toal, Brian A., ''Seizing the Day,'' *Oil & Gas Investor,* February 1993, p. 34.

—Ed Dinger

Scheels All Sports Inc.

3218 13th Avenue Southwest
Fargo, North Dakota 58103
U.S.A.
Telephone: (701) 232-3665
Fax: (701) 232-3735
Web site: http://www.scheelssports.com

Private Company
Incorporated: 1969
Employees: 2,000
Sales: $170 million (2003 est.)
NAIC: 451110 Sporting Goods Stores

Hunters, cyclists, golfers, runners and nearly all other sports and outdoor enthusiasts can find the gear they need at the stores operated by Scheels All Sports Inc. Centered in Fargo, North Dakota, Scheels has nearly 25 retail locations in mid-size Midwestern cities. Its stores span seven states: North Dakota, South Dakota, Minnesota, Wisconsin, Nebraska, Montana, and Iowa. The first Scheels store, opened over a century ago, was a general merchandise and hardware store. The company added a line of sporting goods to its stores in the mid-1950s and steadily expanded across the Midwest over the next several decades. As sales of sporting goods grew, hardware sales were gradually phased out. Scheels' newest locations are two-level Scheels All Sports superstores of over 100,000 square feet, organized as "boxes" containing several separately managed specialty shops. The company is owned by store managers, employees, and the Scheel family and is led by Steve Scheel, great-grandson of the founder.

A Chain of General and Hardware Stores: 1902–64

In the early years of the 20th century, Frederick A. Scheel, a German immigrant, moved to northwestern Minnesota from Chicago with his wife, Augusta. The couple gave their children, Frederick M., age 10, and Margaret, age 8, the job of planting and tending a three-acre potato plot. The field produced 300 bushels of potatoes, which the family sold for $300. The proceeds were used as the down payment for the first Scheels store,

a hardware and general merchandise store in the tiny town of Sabin, Minnesota, near the North Dakota border. The total cost of the store was $600.

Frederick M. Scheel, son of the founder, bought the business in 1919 after returning from service with the U.S. Navy in World War I. At the time, the store was selling hardware and farm implements. The farm implement line was dropped in 1925. In 1927 Carl "Charlie" Buth and Chris Kuehl took over management of the Sabin store.

Frederick M. stayed in the hardware business, moving to the Fargo-Moorhead area on the North Dakota/Minnesota border. He bought the Moorhead Hardware Co. in 1928 with his partner Memfred Nelson and the Swanson Hardware Co. in downtown Fargo the following year. Both stores were converted to Scheels hardware stores.

Between 1940 and 1946, Scheel opened hardware stores in Casselton, Hillsboro, and Fairmount, North Dakota, all small communities in the Fargo area. The Fargo store also moved to a new downtown location. Frederick M.'s son Fred B. joined the family business in 1946 after a stint as a Marine fighter pilot in World War II. A second son, Charles, became active in the business the next year.

Several new stores opened in the early 1950s: first in Wheaton and Breckenridge, Minnesota, both communities a short distance from the Fargo-Moorhead area, then a few years later in Jamestown, North Dakota, about 100 miles west of Fargo, and finally, in a great leap west, a Scheels store opened in Billings, Montana, in 1955.

In a propitious move, Scheels added a small selection of sporting goods to its hardware stores in 1954. More and more sports lines were added over the following years in response to customer interest. In 1962, the company opened a second Fargo location, a hardware and sporting goods store at the Southside Shopping Center. That year Scheels also relocated its Moorhead store, doubling its size, and shortly thereafter moved the downtown Fargo store to a location about a block away. Robert Scheel, a third son of Frederick M., joined the business in 1964.

Expanding the Sporting Goods Line: 1965–88

Scheels store managers found that sporting goods were easier to sell than hardware, and sporting goods sales drove the steady expansion of the Scheels chain over the next four decades. In 1965 the first Scheels store to be located in a mall opened in St. Cloud, Minnesota. Another store started operations that year in Bismarck, North Dakota, followed by a store in Great Falls, Montana, in 1968. In 1969 Scheels was incorporated in North Dakota. It opened stores in Mankato, Minnesota, and Waterloo, Iowa, that year as well.

Athletic shoes and clothing were introduced at Scheels stores in 1972. That year the company opened a third store in Fargo, at the West Acres Shopping Center. The West Acres store was a small 7,700-square-foot shop almost entirely devoted to sporting goods, particularly athletic apparel. Meanwhile, hardware lines were being cut back at most Scheels stores.

In 1974 the Scheels partnerships were converted into a corporation with Charles Scheel, grandson of the founder, acting as president. Rapid expansion continued: stores opened in Minot, North Dakota, in 1974; on the north side of Fargo in 1975; in Cedar Falls, Iowa, and Sioux Falls, South Dakota, in 1977; and in Sioux City, Iowa, in 1981. The Minot store moved to a mall location, the Dakota Square Mall, in 1980.

Although the Scheels corporate offices were in Billings, Montana, in the 1980s, most of the corporate control came from Fargo. A central advertising office coordinated direct mailings and newspaper ads for the Fargo-Moorhead area and offered advertising support for more far-flung locations. To a great extent, however, individual stores were allowed to function independently. Each store took care of its own buying and the corporation pooled orders for price negotiations. Store managers determined benefits for their own employees. Managers were allowed to buy into the company up to a point depending on their store's size and were also allowed to reserve a certain percentage of profits for distribution to employees.

By 1984, sporting goods accounted for about half of the chain's business. The Southside Fargo store, for example, operated like two stores under one roof: the awning on one side of the storefront advertised a sports shop while the other half of the 24,000-square-foot site was a hardware store. By the mid-1980s, Scheels was operating 15 Hardware and Sports Shops in five states. Several of the early hardware locations, including those in Casselton, Hillsboro, Fairmount, Wheaton, Breckenridge, and Jamestown, had closed. The hardware store in Bismarck, North Dakota, had also closed, but a new store opened there in 1984. It was the first Scheels store devoted exclusively to sporting goods.

Opening Sports-Only Superstores: 1989–94

In the late 1980s, Scheels began opening a series of sports-only superstores. The company was getting ready to leave hardware behind and market its sporting goods lines on a much larger scale than previously. The first Scheels All Sports Superstore opened in Grand Forks, North Dakota, in 1989. The 30,000-square-foot store was larger than any of the company's existing sites, and none of the space was needed for hardware. But as the sporting goods displays started to be installed, the company found it had no problem using up the floor space. Steven Scheel told the Fargo *Forum* a decade later, "We looked at it when it was done and thought, 'How are we going to fill this up?' And then it was full!"

Scheels also introduced an employee stock ownership plan in 1989. The company was interested in attracting high achievers with a personal interest in sports and the outdoors. Scheels paid employees more than many retailers and offered full-time associates the opportunity to become involved in product display, buying, and management, thus developing a long-term career at the company. Sales associates took part in Scheels "universities," where they went directly to the outdoors to test and become experts in the products they were selling.

In 1990 Charles Scheel stepped down after a 15-year tenure as company president. His position was filled by Steve D. Scheel, a son of Frederick B. Scheel. Frederick B. had become well known as an amateur photographer but remained involved with the family business in an advisory capacity for another decade. In 1991 Scheels opened a store in Sioux Falls, South Dakota, its second in that city. The company moved its existing Mankato location to the River Hills Mall in 1993 and opened new stores in two new cities in 1994: Rapid City, South Dakota, and Appleton, Wisconsin. The Appleton Scheels store was the company's first foray into Wisconsin.

Another Scheels All Sports Superstore opened in 1994 on 13th Avenue in south Fargo. The Grand Forks superstore that had been opened five years earlier had filled up so easily with merchandise that the company was ready to make another leap forward in terms of size. With 45,000 square feet of retail space and 30,000 square feet of office and warehouse space, the 13th Avenue site was about three times as large as an average Scheels store. The company spent an estimated $750,000 to $1 million to renovate the building, which formerly held a Best store. With the opening of the new superstore, Scheels planned to close the nearby Southside Scheels Hardware and Sports. However, area residents said they still wanted to be able to buy hardware from a Scheels store, so former store managers Bob Scheel and Bob Alin took over the site as partners and converted it to a hardware-only store. As a result, Scheels closed its north side Fargo store instead. The West Acres site in Fargo continued operating as a small neighborhood store with a focus on shoes and apparel. The new 13th Avenue store proved to be very popular. Another large store—50,000 square feet—opened at the Oakwood Mall in Eau Claire, Wisconsin, a year later.

Ever Larger Megastores: 1994–2004

Now that the superstore model had been tested and proven profitable, Scheels moved ahead with new locations that

1902: Frederick A. Scheel opens a general store in Sabin, Minnesota.

1928: Frederick M. Scheel acquires hardware stores in Fargo and Moorhead.

1954: A small selection of sporting goods is added to the stores. New stores open across the Midwest over the next decades.

1972: Athletic shoes and clothing are introduced as sales of sporting goods rise.

1989: The first Scheels All Sports superstore opens in Grand Forks, North Dakota.

1998: Scheels opens a two-level megastore near Iowa City.

2004: Three megastores totaling 470,000 square feet are scheduled to open.

dwarfed the original superstores. The company had touted the size of the 13th Avenue store in Fargo, but in 1998 a site twice that size opened near Iowa City. The 105,000-square-foot two-level store would be one of six anchors at the new Coral Ridge Mall near the intersection of interstate highways 80 and 380. In the center of the store was a realistic looking 66-foot-high Sequoia tree. The new Scheels superstores were operated as ''boxes'' that housed a number of independently managed specialty shops for everyone from bowlers to baseball players. Special merchandise areas within the Iowa City store included small shops set up by adidas and Nike, a section devoted to University of Iowa Hawkeye gear, and a part of the gun department featuring premium guns costing $10,000 to $30,000.

Scheels began expanding and relocating some of its older stores as well, moving many of them to mall locations. The Cedar Falls, Iowa store moved to the College Square Mall and the Billings, Montana store moved to the Rimrock Mall in 1999. The Eau Claire store was expanded to 80,000 square feet in 2001. In addition, a new two-level 80,000-square-foot superstore opened at Southpointe Pavilions in Lincoln, Nebraska. This was the first Scheels site in that state.

With grandiose superstores opening up around the Midwest, the 13th Avenue store in Scheels' home town no longer seemed so impressive. Even though the site had been open less than a decade, Scheels made plans to replace it with a true superstore. The company acquired land in a southwest area of the city that was expected to become a retail destination in the coming years. The plan was to construct a $19 million, two-story, 140,000-square-foot building at the site. The Moorhead and West Acres sites would still remain open to serve the customers in their respective areas.

Scheels celebrated its 100th anniversary in 2002. That year it consolidated its two Sioux Falls, South Dakota stores into a single 109,000-square-foot superstore. In 2003 the company opened its fifth double-decker megastore in the Fox River Mall in Appleton, Wisconsin, replacing the existing 16,000-square-foot store in the same mall. The site also featured a 65-foot artificial tree in the middle and carried goods ranging from fishing poles to fudge to running shoes to Northwoods gifts in a log cabin lodge. Later that year the Sioux City, Iowa store was moved to a new location at the Southern Hills Mall and expanded to 65,000 square feet.

Three store openings were planned for 2004. In March a 128,000-square-foot store opened in St. Cloud, Minnesota, after relocating within the Crossroads Center mall. A 177,000-square-foot store was scheduled to open in Omaha in May and a 179,000-square-foot store was expected to open in August at the Jordan Creek Development in Des Moines. This would be the largest Scheels All Sports store in the United States.

Principal Competitors

Gander Mountain, Inc.; Cabela's Inc.

Further Reading

Gilmour, Gerry, ''Scheels Plans Fargo Superstore,'' *Forum* (Fargo, ND), August 21, 2000.

Knutson, Jonathan, ''From Nuts and Bolts to Sporting Goods Giant,'' *Forum* (Fargo, ND), August 14, 1999.

——, ''Largest Scheels Store Opening in Iowa City,'' *Forum* (Fargo, ND), April 4, 1998.

——, ''Scheels Planning to Close North Fargo Store,'' *Forum* (Fargo, ND), April 27, 1994, p. A1.

''Scheels Hardware & Sports: Changing with the Times,'' *DIY Retailing*, November 1984, p. 84.

Wallenfang, Maureen, ''Scheels Tries to Reel in Families,'' *Post-Crescent* (Appleton, WI), June 19, 2003, p. 8D.

—Sarah Ruth Lorenz

Serologicals Corporation

5655 Spalding Drive
Norcross, Georgia 30092
U.S.A.
Telephone: (678) 728-2000
Fax: (678) 728-2247
Web site: http://www.serologicals.com

Public Company
Incorporated: 1994 as Serologicals Holdings, Inc.
Employees: 677
Sales: $146.9 million (2003)
Stock Exchanges: NASDAQ
Ticker Symbol: SERO
NAIC: 325414 Biological Product (Except Diagnostic)
    Manufacturing

Serologicals Corporation is a Norcross, Georgia, company that, on a global basis, provides biological products and enabling technologies to life sciences companies for use in the research, development, and manufacture of new drugs and other life sciences products. Originally involved in running plasma collection centers, the publicly traded company now concentrates on three growth areas: cell culture supplements, for use in producing diagnostic and therapeutic recombinant proteins; molecular reagents and assays, for use in cell biology research and molecular discovery; and diagnostic antibodies. Serologicals' products and technologies have applications in such disciplines as cardiology, hematology, infectious diseases, immunology, molecular biology, and oncology. Domestically, the company maintains facilities in Massachusetts, Illinois, and California, and internationally in Australia, Canada, Scotland, and the United Kingdom. Serologicals also maintains a global sales force, supplemented by more than 30 international distributors. Customers include life science companies as well as academic and private research institutions.

Founding the Company in 1971

Serologicals was founded by North Carolina native Samuel A. Penninger, Jr. After graduating from Catawba College, he became a helicopter pilot in the U.S. Marine Corps and then served as a legislative aide for the Secretary of State in Florida. In 1971 he established Serologicals Corporation in Pensacola, Florida, as a single plasma donor center. The company had one product, Anti-D antibodies drawn from human plasma, which since 1968 had been added to immunoglobulin to prevent the death of infants susceptible to Hemolytic Disease of Newborns. Penninger added a handful of donation centers over the next 15 years, but the company only began to grow beyond its narrow confines in the 1980s when he recognized two significant developments: the need for a range of anti-D vaccines and a rise in the blood-typing diagnostics business. Penninger began to move Serologicals into these areas.

In 1989 Serologicals took a major step in its transformation when it acquired Bioscot, Ltd., an Edinburgh, Scotland, company that could clone and produce antibodies. To help finance growth, the company turned to venture capitalists and in 1990 raised $3.5 million. Annual revenues topped $14 million in 1991 and approached $18 million a year later, but the company remained a minor player in its field, operating just eight donation centers. At this point Penninger brought in new management talent to take the company to the next level. Russ Plumb was named vice-president of finance and in March 1993 Harold Tenoso was tabbed to be the company's president and chief executive officer. Tenoso was uniquely qualified for the job. He held a doctorate in immunology and microbiology from UCLA and boasted 30 years of experience in the healthcare field, including ten years at pharmaceutical Unimed, Inc., where he became CEO and chairman before joining Serologicals.

Under Tenoso's leadership, Serologicals began to add donation centers at a steady clip, while also increasing the kinds of antibodies that each center collected. In December 1994 the company acquired assets from Acadiani Group, paying $29.5 million. Tenoso also prepared to take the company public. In preparation for this move, the company's headquarters was relocated to Clarkson, Georgia, and in November 1994 Serologicals Holdings, Inc. was incorporated in Delaware. Several weeks later this entity acquired Serologicals Inc. and Bioscot, then in May 1995 it became Serologicals Corporation, the company's current name. Underwritten by Smith Barney Inc., Lehman Brothers Inc., and Volpe, Welty & Company, Serologicals completed its public offering in June 1995, selling 2.4 million shares of common stock at $11.50 per share, which resulted in a net of $24.6 million. The money was used to pay off debt.

Acquiring Donor Centers in the Mid-1990s

Serologicals enjoyed strong growth under Tenoso, with revenues improving from $22.9 million to $30.1 million in 1994 and more than $52.1 million in 1995. During this period, net income totaled $1.2 million, $3.46 million, and $3.4 million, respectively. To fuel further growth, Tenoso aggressively pursued acquisitions in what was a highly fragmented field. There were more than 400 plasma centers in the United States, mostly mom-and-pop operations or small chains that were hard pressed to keep pace with increasing demands imposed by the Food and Drug Administration. Hence, Serologicals was presented with an opportunity to gain size quickly. In October 1995 Serologicals paid $2.5 million for Allegheny Biologicals, Inc., picking up two specialty donor centers in Jacksonville, Florida, and Pittsburgh, Pennsylvania. A few months later, in February 1996, the company added Am-Rho Laboratories at the cost of $1.7 million, gaining a specialty antibody donor center in Washington, D.C., along with other assets located in Jacksonville, Florida. A month later, Serologicals added nine nonspecialty donor centers by acquiring Southeastern Biologics, Inc., Plasma Management, Inc., and Concho Biologics, Inc. for approximately $4.75 million.

Serologicals' balance sheet at the end of 1996 reflected the company's growth in facilities. Net sales improved to $65.6 million and net income more than tripled, totaling $8.25 million. More than half of those sales were to Bayer Corporation, and about 87 percent came from just ten accounts. Moreover, two-thirds of all sales were domestic. At this stage, Serologicals maintained a network of some 40 donor centers, many of them located close to medical schools, where the company was well positioned to receive donor referrals. Gone were the days of plasma centers receiving walkup traffic of college students and winos. Now, donor recruitment was an important task, as Serologicals sought out donors who had high concentrations of certain specialty antibodies. Donor candidates were thoroughly screened and given a physical examination before being approved. To stimulate the development or increase the quantity of the specialty antibodies, accepted donors were hyperimmunized. The company also maintained a donor management program to make sure that visits were comfortable and safe, especially important because specialty donors might donate once or twice per week and retention of their services was important to profitability. A major key in retaining donors, of course, was the payment of high rates and incentive programs. Serologicals offerings were divided between specialty therapeutic products and specialty diagnostic products. The first segment included

the company's first product, Anti-D Immune Globulin, as well as Anti-Rabies Immune Globulin, Anti-Hepatitis Immune Globulins, and Intravenous Immune Globulin. Specialty diagnostic products included antibodies for blood typing reagents and clinical diagnostic antibodies.

Serologicals continued its acquisition spree over the next two years. In March 1997, it bought Nations Biologics, Inc. and its affiliates, collectively the Nations Group, paying $10.2 million in cash and a $4 million convertible note. As a result, Serologicals added 16 donor centers that specialized in the collection of nonspecialty IVIG antibodies. In August 1997 the company swapped some donor centers with Los Angeles-based SeraCare Inc., exchanging facilities in Reno, Nevada, and Fort Smith, Arkansas, for three plasma collection centers in Colorado. Then, in September 1997, Serologicals paid $8.5 million to acquire Bio-Lab Inc. and Med-Lab, Inc., adding two specialty donor centers. The company added four nonspecialty donor centers and a clinical trial site in two separate transactions in 1998, paying some $5.5 million. At the close of 1998, Serologicals completed a major acquisition in picking up the Pentex Blood proteins business from Bayer Corporation at the cost of $27.5 million. Located in Kankakee, Illinois, Pentex was a leader in the area of purified blood proteins. Serologicals posted strong results in both 1997 and 1998. Revenues improved to $97.5 million in 1997 and more than $123 million in 1998, while net income during this time grew to $12 million and $16.3 million, respectively. As a result of this strong performance, Serologicals made *Forbes* magazine's list of America's best 200 small companies.

Suffering a Difficult 1999

The boom times for Serologicals would come to an abrupt end in 1999, caused by a number of factors. Both Serologicals and important European customers were hampered by new, tougher quality control standards, which forced the shutdown of some facilities. Thus the Europeans were unable to ship products and canceled orders of raw materials from Serologicals. To make matters worse, later in the year Serologicals discovered problems at its Atlanta testing laboratory, which caused shipping delays and recalls on products that passed through the Atlanta facility. A new director of the laboratory was ultimately installed. The company also endured accounting errors in 1999 that required a restatement of results during the first three quarters of the year, and a canceled software development project led to a write-off that adversely impacted the balance sheet. Although sales improved slightly, to $129.7 million, the company suffered a net loss of $15.5 million in 1999. In the midst of this difficult period, in September 1999, after the price of Serologicals stock fell from $30 to just $3 per share, Tenoso resigned. Director Desmond H. O'Connell, Jr., stepped in to serve as acting president and CEO. By the end of 1999 Penninger also announced that he would step down as chairman by the time the company held its annual shareholders meeting in May 2000.

At the 2000 shareholders meeting, Serologicals underwent several management changes. As promised, Penninger resigned. He was replaced as chairman by O'Connell, who was in turn to be replaced as president and chief executive officer on June 1 by David Dodd, hired away from Solvay Pharmaceuticals, where he had been president and CEO since 1995. Dodd, a

Key Dates:

1971: The company is founded by Samuel A. Penninger, Jr., in Pensacola, Florida.
1989: Bioscot, Ltd. is acquired.
1993: Harold Tenoso is named CEO.
1995: The company completes its initial public offering.
1999: Tenoso resigns.
2003: The company exits the therapeutic plasma business.

Harvard Business School graduate, had 25 years of experience in the life sciences industry. In addition to his tenure at Solvay, he also held executive positions at U.S. Pharmaceuticals, Wyeth-Ayerst Laboratories, Bristol-Myers Squibb, and Abbott Laboratories. Even before Dodd officially took over, Serologicals began to make significant changes. In May 2000, the company sold its Seramed, Inc. subsidiary, which operated 47 nonspecialty donor centers, to Aventis Bio-Services, Inc. for a net cash consideration of more than $20 million. As a result, Serologicals, with its 17 specialty centers, would now concentrate on its specialty, diagnostic, and bioscience businesses. Dodd also took steps to build the company's infrastructure, establishing a global regulatory and quality compliance group, and adding steps to its quality control process as well as automating some procedures to lower the chance of human error, improve efficiency, and aid in inventory management. A new software system now linked the company's donation centers so that if a customer needed a rare antibody, it would be able to be located quickly. Dodd also began to look for ways for Serologicals to take advantage of the revolution in genomics and leverage its expertise to do upfront work for biotech companies.

Most of 2000 was devoted to restructuring operations. Because of the sell-off of its nonspecialty centers, Serologicals saw revenues recede to $45.3 million, but it returned to profitability, recording net income of $12.9 million. More important, the company was retooled for ongoing growth. In 2001 it acquired Intergen Company for $45 million in cash, a deal that not only added to Serologicals' business in purified blood proteins but also helped the company to enter the research reagent sector. Revenues grew to $53.6 million in 2001, and net income improved to $17.1 million. A year later, revenues virtually doubled, approaching $100 million, while the company recorded net income of $14 million.

Serologicals reached a significant turning point in 2003. First it completed a major acquisition, buying Chemicon International, Inc., a Temecula, California company for approximately $95 million. The addition of Chemicon was important because it added to Serologicals' product lines, in particular cell culture and molecular biology. Chemicon also created a platform that permitted Serologicals to add other acquisitions and pursue product licensing opportunities in the biotechnology market. Management believed that its interests in biotechnology were so promising, in fact, that a few months later it announced that it planned to exit the therapeutic plasma business altogether. In January 2004 Serologicals sold its ten plasma collections centers and central testing laboratory to an Australian company, Gradipore Limited. The company had now completely severed its ties to its past, the plasma business that grew out of a single Florida donor center.

Principal Subsidiaries

Chemicon International, Inc.; Serologicals Proteins, Inc.; Serologicals Discovery Products, LLC; Serologicals Research Products, Inc.

Principal Competitors

Aventis Behring L.L.C.; TECHNE Corporation.

Further Reading

Bryant, Julie, "Serologicals Mounts Comeback," *Atlanta Business Chronicle,* November 3, 2000, p. A1.

Ebeling, Ashlea, "Mining Antibodies," *Forbes,* November 3, 1997, p. 170.

Haupt, Wyatt, "Temacula, Calif., Biology Firm to Be Purchased by Atlanta Bio-Manufacturer," *North County Times,* February 13, 2003, p. 1.

Luke, Robert, "Shipment Woes Hurt Atlanta-Based Blood-Products Company," *Atlanta Journal and Constitution,* July 30, 1999.

McNaughton, David, "Norcross, Ga.-Based Antibody Firm Finds Success in Niche Business," *Atlanta Journal and Constitution,* May 20, 2001.

Robbins, Roni B., "Serologicals Didn't Skip a Beat Despite 'Upheavals,'" *Atlantic Business Chronicle,* October 30, 1998, p. 14A.

Sumner, Gary, "Blood Antibodies Bolster Serologicals' Growth," *Atlanta Business Chronicle,* April 17, 1998.

—Ed Dinger

State Bank of India

State Bank Bhavan, Madame Cama R
Mumbai
400 021
India
Telephone: 91 22 2202 2426
Fax: 91 22 2285 2708
Web site: http://www.statebankofindia.com

Public Company (60% Government-Owned)
Incorporated: 1921 as the Imperial Bank of India
Employees: 220,000
Total Assets: $104.81 billion (2003)
Stock Exchanges: Mumbai Kolkata Chennai
   Ahmedabad Delhi New York London
Ticker Symbol: SBI
NAIC: 522110 Commercial Banking

State Bank of India (SBI) is that country's largest commercial bank. The government-controlled bank—the Indian government maintains a stake of nearly 60 percent in SBI through the central Reserve Bank of India—also operates the world's largest branch network, with more than 13,500 branch offices throughout India, staffed by nearly 220,000 employees. SBI is also present worldwide, with seven international subsidiaries in the United States, Canada, Nepal, Bhutan, Nigeria, Mauritius, and the United Kingdom, and more than 50 branch offices in 30 countries. Long an arm of the Indian government's infrastructure, agricultural, and industrial development policies, SBI has been forced to revamp its operations since competition was introduced into the country's commercial banking system. As part of that effort, SBI has been rolling out its own network of automated teller machines, as well as developing anytime-anywhere banking services through Internet and other technologies. SBI also has taken advantage of the deregulation of the Indian banking sector to enter the bancassurance, assets management, and securities brokering sectors. In addition, SBI has been working on reigning in its branch network, reducing its payroll, and strengthening its loan portfolio. In 2003, SBI reported revenue of $10.36 billion and total assets of $104.81 billion.

Colonial Banking Origins in the 19th Century

The establishment of the British colonial government in India brought with it calls for the formation of a Western-style banking system, if only to serve the needs and interests of the British imperial government and of the European trading houses doing business there. The creation of a national banking system began at the beginning of the 19th century.

The first component of what was later to become the State Bank of India was created in 1806, in Calcutta. Called the Bank of Calcutta, it was also the country's first joint stock company. Originally established to serve the city's interests, the bank was granted a charter to serve all of Bengal in 1809, becoming the Bank of Bengal. The introduction of Western-style banking instituted deposit savings accounts and, in some cases, investment services. The Bank of Bengal also received the right to issue its own notes, which became legal currency within the Bengali region. This right enabled the bank to establish a solid financial foundation, building an interest-free capital base.

The spread of colonial influence also extended the scope of government and commercial financial influence. Toward the middle of the century, the imperial government created two more regional banks. The Bank of Bombay was created in 1840, and was soon joined by the Bank of Madras in 1843. Together with the Bank of Bengal, they became known as the "presidency" banks.

All three banks were operated as joint stock companies, with the imperial government holding a one-fifth share of each bank. The remaining shares were sold to private subscribers and, typically, were claimed by the Western European trading firms. These firms were represented on each bank's board of directors, which was presided over by a nominee from the government. While the banks performed typical banking functions, for both the Western firms and population and members of Indian society, their main role was to act as a lever for raising loan capital, as well as help stabilize government securities.

The charters backing the establishment of the presidency banks granted them the right to establish branch offices. Into the

Key Dates:

1806: The Bank of Calcutta is established as the first Western-type bank.
1809: The bank receives a charter from the imperial government and changes its name to Bank of Bengal.
1840: A sister bank, Bank of Bombay, is formed.
1843: Another sister bank is formed: Bank of Madras, which, together with Bank of Bengal and Bank of Bombay become known as the presidency banks, which had the right to issue currency in their regions.
1861: The Presidency Banks Act takes away currency issuing privileges but offers incentives to begin rapid expansion, and the three banks open nearly 50 branches among them by the mid-1870s.
1876: The creation of Central Treasuries ends the expansion phase of the presidency banks.
1921: The presidency banks are merged to form a single entity, Imperial Bank of India.
1955: The nationalization of Imperial Bank of India results in the formation of the State Bank of India, which then becomes a primary factor behind the country's industrial, agricultural, and rural development.
1969: The Indian government establishes a monopoly over the banking sector.
1972: SBI begins offering merchant banking services.
1986: SBI Capital Markets is created.
1995: SBI Commercial and International Bank Ltd. are launched as part of SBI's stepped-up international banking operations.
1998: SBI launches credit cards in partnership with GE Capital.
2002: SBI networks 3,000 branches in a massive technology implementation.
2004: A networking effort reaches 4,000 branches.

second half of the century, however, the banks remained single-office concerns. It was only after the passage of the Paper Currency Act in 1861 that the banks began their first expansion effort. That legislation had taken away the presidency banks' authority to issue currency, instead placing the issuing of paper currency under direct control of the British government in India, starting in 1862.

Yet that same legislation included two key features that stimulated the growth of a national banking network. On the one hand, the presidency banks were given the responsibility for the new currency's management and circulation. On the other, the government agreed to transfer treasury capital backing the currency to the banks—and especially to their branch offices. This latter feature encouraged the three banks to begin building the country's first banking network. The three banks then launched an expansion effort, establishing a system of branch offices, agencies, and sub-agencies throughout the most populated regions of the Indian coast, and into the inland areas as well. By the end of the 1870s, the three presidency banks operated nearly 50 branches among them.

Funding National Development in the 20th Century

The rapid growth of the presidency banks came to an abrupt halt in 1876, when a new piece of legislation, the Presidency Banks Act, placed all three banks under a common charter—and a common set of restrictions. As part of the legislation, the British imperial government gave up its ownership stakes in the banks, although they continued to provide a number of services to the government, and retained some of the government's treasury capital. The majority of that, however, was transferred to the three newly created Reserve Treasuries, located in Calcutta, Bombay, and Madras. The Reserve Treasuries continued to lend capital to the presidency banks, but on a more restrictive basis. The minimum balance now guaranteed under the Presidency Banks Act was applicable only to the banks' central offices. With branch offices no longer guaranteed a minimum balance backed by government funds, the banks ended development of their networks. Only the Bank of Madras continued to grow for some time, supplied as it was by the influx of capital from development of trade among the region's port cities.

The loss of the government-backed balances was soon compensated by India's rapid economic development at the end of the 19th century. The building of a national railroad network launched the country into a new era, seeing the rise of cash-crop farming, a mining industry, and widespread industrial development. The three presidency banks took active roles in financing this development. The banks also extended their range of services and operations, although for the time being were excluded from the foreign exchange market.

By the beginning of the 20th century, India's banking industry boasted a host of new arrivals, and particularly foreign banks authorized to exchange currency. The growth of the banking sector, and the development of indigenous banks, in turn created a need for a larger "bankers' bank." At the same time, the Indian government had outgrown its colonial background and now required a more centralized banking institution. These factors led to the decision to merge the three presidency banks into a new, single and centralized banking institution, the Imperial Bank of India.

Created in 1921, the Imperial Bank of India appeared to inaugurate a new era in India's history—culminating in its declaration of independence from the British Empire. The Imperial Bank took on the role of central bank for the Indian government, while acting as a bankers' bank for the growing Indian banking sector. At the same time, the Imperial Bank, which, despite its role in the government financial structure remained independent of the government, carried on its own commercial banking operations.

In 1926, a government commission recommended the creation of a true central bank. While some proposed converting the Imperial Bank into a central banking organization for the country, the commission rejected this idea and instead recommended that the Imperial Bank be transformed into a purely commercial banking institution. The government took up the commission's recommendations, drafting a new bill in 1927. Passage of the new legislation did not occur until 1935, however, with the creation of the Reserve Bank of India. That bank took over all central banking functions.

The Imperial Bank then converted to full commercial status, which accordingly allowed it to enter a number of banking areas, such as currency exchange and trustee and estate management, from which it had previously been restricted. Despite the loss of its role as a government banking office, the Imperial Bank continued to provide banking services to the Reserve Bank, particularly in areas where the Reserve Bank had not yet established offices. At the same time, the Imperial Bank retained its position as a bankers' bank.

Into the early 1950s, the Imperial Bank grew steadily, dominating the Indian commercial banking industry. The bank continued to build up its assets and capital base, and also entered a new phase of national expansion. By the middle of the 1950s, the Imperial Bank operated more than 170 branch offices, as well as 200 sub-offices. Yet the bank, like most of the colonial government, focused primarily on the country's urban regions.

By then, India had achieved its independence from Britain. In 1951, the new government launched its first Five Year Plan, targeting in particular the development of the country's rural areas. The lack of a banking infrastructure in these regions led the government to develop a state-owned banking entity to fill the gap. As part of that process, the Imperial Bank was nationalized and then integrated with other existing government-owned banking components. The result was the creation of the State Bank of India, or SBI, in 1955.

The new state-owned bank now controlled more than one-fourth of India's total banking industry. That position was expanded at the end of the decade, when new legislation was passed providing for the takeover by the State Bank of eight regionally based, government-controlled banks. As such the Banks of Bikaner, Jaipur, Idnore, Mysore, Patiala, Hyderabad, Saurashtra, and Travancore became subsidiaries of the State Bank. Following the 1963 merger of the Bikaner and Jaipur banks, their seven remaining subsidiaries were converted into associate banks.

In the early 1960s, the State Bank's network already contained nearly 500 branches and sub-offices, as well as the three original head offices inherited from the presidency bank era. Yet the State Bank now began an era of expansion, acting as a motor for India's industrial and agricultural development, that was to transform it into one of the world's largest financial networks. Indeed, by the early 1990s, the State Bank counted nearly 15,000 branches and offices throughout India, giving it the world's single largest branch network.

SBI played an extremely important role in developing India's rural regions, providing the financing needed to modernize the country's agricultural industry and develop new irrigation methods and cattle breeding techniques, and backing the creation of dairy farming, as well as pork and poultry industries. The bank also provided backing for the development of the country's infrastructure, particularly on a local level, where it provided credit coverage and development assistance to villages. The nationalization of the banking sector itself, an event that occurred in 1969 under the government led by Indira Gandhi, gave SBI new prominence as the country's leading bank.

Even as it played a primary role in the Indian government's industrial and agricultural development policies, SBI continued to develop its commercial banking operations. In 1972, for example, the bank began offering merchant banking services. By the mid-1980s, the bank's merchant banking operations had grown sufficiently to support the creation of a dedicated subsidiary, SBI Capital Markets, in 1986. The following year, the company launched another subsidiary, SBI Home Finance, in a collaboration with the Housing Development Finance Corporation. Then in the early 1990s, SBI added subsidiaries SBI Factors and Commercial Services, and then launched institutional investor services.

Competitor in the 21st Century

SBI was allowed to dominate the Indian banking sector for more than two decades. In the early 1990s, the Indian government kicked off a series of reforms aimed at deregulating the banking and financial industries. SBI was now forced to brace itself for the arrival of a new wave of competitors eager to enter the fast-growing Indian economy's commercial banking sector. Yet years as a government-run institution had left SBI bloated—the civil-servant status of its employees had encouraged its payroll to swell to more than 230,000. The bureaucratic nature of the bank's management left little room for personal initiative, nor incentive for controlling costs.

The bank also had been encouraged to increase its branch network, with little concern for profitability. As former Chairman Dipankar Baku told the *Banker* in the early 1990s: "In the aftermath of bank nationalisation everyone lost sight of the fact that banks had to be profitable. Banking was more to do with social policy and perhaps that was relevant at the time. For the last two decades the emphasis was on physical expansion."

Under Baku, SBI began retooling for the new competitive environment. In 1994, the bank hired consulting group McKinsey & Co. to help it restructure its operations. McKinsey then led SBI through a massive restructuring effort that lasted through much of the decade and into the beginning of the next, an effort that helped SBI develop a new corporate culture focused more on profitability than on social and political policy. SBI also stepped up its international trade operations, such as foreign exchange trading, as well as corporate finance, export credit, and international banking.

SBI had long been present overseas, operating some 50 offices in 34 countries, including full-fledged subsidiaries in the United Kingdom, the United States, and elsewhere. In 1995 the bank set up a new subsidiary, SBI Commercial and International Bank Ltd., to back its corporate and international banking services. The bank also extended its international network into new markets such as Russia, China, and South Africa.

Back home, in the meantime, SBI began addressing the technology gap that existed between it and its foreign-backed competitors. Into the 1990s, SBI had yet to establish an automated teller network; indeed, it had not even automated its information systems. SBI responded by launching an ambitious technology drive, rolling out its own ATM network, then teaming up with GE Capital to issue its own credit card. In the early 2000s, the bank began cross-linking its banking network with its ATM network and Internet and telephone access, rolling out "anytime, anywhere" banking access. By 2002, the bank had succeeded in networking its 3,000 most profitable branches.

The implementation of new technology helped the bank achieve strong profit gains into the early years of the new century. SBI also adopted new human resources and retirement policies, helping trim its payroll by some 20,000, almost entirely through voluntary retirement in a country where joblessness remained a decided problem.

By the beginning of 2004, SBI appeared to be well on its way to meeting the challenges offered by the deregulated Indian banking sector. In a twist, the bank had become an aggressor into new territories, launching its own line of bancassurance products, and also initiating securities brokering services. In the meantime, SBI continued its technology rollout, boosting the number of networked branches to more than 4,000 at the end of 2003. SBI promised to remain a central figure in the Indian banking sector as it entered its third century.

Principal Subsidiaries

Bank of Bhutan (Bhutan); Indo Nigeria Merchant Bank Ltd. (Nigeria); Nepal SBI Bank Ltd. (Nepal); SBI (U.S.A.); SBI (Canada); SBI Capital Market Ltd.; SBI Cards & Payments Services Ltd.; SBI Commercial and International Bank Ltd.; SBI European Bank plc (U.K.); SBI Factors & Commercial Services Ltd.; SBI Funds Management Ltd.; SBI Gilts Ltd.; SBI Home Finance Ltd.; SBI Securities Ltd.; State Bank International Ltd. (Mauritius); State Bank of Bikaner & Jaipur; State Bank of Hyderabad; State Bank of Indore; State Bank of Mysore; State Bank of Patiala; State Bank of Saurastra; State Bank of Travancore.

Principal Competitors

ICICI Bank; Bank of Baroda; Canara Bank; Punjab National Bank; Bank of India; Union Bank of India; Central Bank of India; HDFC Bank; Oriental Bank of Commerce.

Further Reading

Chatterjee, Debojyoti, "The Great SBI Makeover," *Business Today,* August 4, 2002.
Chowdhury, Neel, "Privatizing in India: Bank's Thorny Path," *International Herald Tribune,* August 16, 1996, p. 17.
Guha, Krishna, "State Bank of India Faces a Bumpy Ride," *Financial Times,* January 14, 1998, p. 38.
Merchant, Khozem, "SBI Close to Finding Partner," *Financial Times,* February 2, 2004, p. 24.
"SBI's Technology Blueprint," *India Business Insight,* November 30, 2003.
"SBI to Launch 100th ATM in Kerala Today," *Asia Africa Intelligence Wire,* March 26, 2004.
Thaur, B.S., *The Evolution of the State Bank of India,* London: Sage Publications, 2003.
Verma, Virenda, "SBI Stays a Star Performer," *Business Line,* January 10, 2004.

—M.L. Cohen

Steel Technologies Inc.

15415 Shelbyville Road
Louisville, Kentucky 40245
U.S.A.
Telephone: (502) 245-2110
Fax: (502) 245-3821
Web site: http://www.steeltechnologies.com

Public Company
Incorporated: 1971 as Southern Strip Steel, Inc.
Employees: 1,039
Sales: $512.7 million (2003)
Stock Exchanges: NASDAQ
Ticker Symbol: STTX
NAIC: 331221 Rolled Steel Shape Manufacturing

With its headquarters located in Louisville, Kentucky, Steel Technologies Inc. is a publicly traded intermediate steel processor. The company produces flat-rolled steel to the precise specifications of industrial customers: thickness, width, shape, temper, and finish. Steel Technologies' product line includes cold-rolled strip, one-pass cold-rolled strip, high-carbon and alloy strip and steel, cold-rolled sheet, high-strength low-alloy strip and sheet, hot-rolled pickled and oiled sheet, coated strip and sheet, and tin plate. Special capabilities include pickling (steel cleaning), slitting, oscillating, edging, precision rolling, annealing, cut-to-length, blanking, custom steel fabrication, and engineered products. Automotive supply is the company's largest market, accounting for 43 percent of all revenues, followed by agricultural/lawn and garden, and appliance/HVAC, each with an 11 percent share. The automotive direct market accounts for an additional 8 percent of the company's business. Steel Technologies operates 21 facilities, some through joint ventures, in 21 strategic locations in the United States and Mexico.

Founder's Involvement in the Steel Industry in the 1950s

Steel Technologies was founded by Merwin J. Ray, who was raised in the steelbelt of northeastern Ohio. For two years in the early 1950s he studied industrial engineering at the Ohio State University and Kent State University, but dropped out because he found the experience "not practical enough." He then spent two years in the Army during the Korean War, serving in Seoul, South Korea. Upon returning home he took a job as a car salesman in Warren, Ohio, but by his own estimation he was "a lousy car salesman—an absolute, utter failure." Reflecting on this time, he would later explain, "I couldn't bring myself to do the things and say the things needed to sell cars. I didn't believe in it." He would soon, however, discover a product in which he did believe. In 1954 he took a sales job with Shenango Steel and after two years moved on to Worthington Industries Inc., an intermediate steel processor to which he would devote the next 15 years of his life. Starting out in sales, Merwin worked his way up through the ranks at Worthington, ultimately becoming an executive vice-president. One of his stops during his tenure at Worthington was overseeing the company's operation in Louisville, a city he would grow fond of.

Merwin left Worthington in 1970 to launch his own steel processing company. He decided to locate the business in the Louisville area because he recognized its strategic location. Not only could he ship to the North, primarily to Detroit automakers, he would also be in a position to serve the emerging southern markets. Merwin settled on the outlying town of Eminence, Kentucky, because of reasonably priced land and the willingness of the town's Farmers Deposit Bank to provide credit and assist him in obtaining a major loan from First National Bank of Louisville. Merwin was considered a good risk because he possessed strong contacts in the steel industry and was willing to risk all of his personal assets in launching his company, which he named Southern Strip Steel Inc.

Southern Strip Steel began business in 1971. After losing money its first year, the company began a three-decade-long string of profitable years. A major key to the company's success was Merwin's willingness, unlike many U.S. competitors, to invest in state-of-the art machinery, which was matched by an increasing demand for higher quality steel products by automakers. The years after World War II saw the introduction of statistical process control (SPC), used to produce highly precise products in a number of mediums, including steel. While American steel processing companies disregarded the technology, their Japanese counterparts embraced it. Because the Japanese could now produce higher quality steel parts, other Japanese manufacturers were able to produce higher quality goods, giving them an edge that was instrumental in Japan's economic rise. Because of Merwin's decision to invest in high technology, Southern Strip Steel created a profitable niche in SPC in the United States.

By the end of the 1970s, sales at Southern Strip Steel had grown to $22 million. Merwin proved to be strong in sales and promotion, building an aggressive sales team, but where the company fell short during this period was in its accounting. The company had grown large enough that it needed more than a mere bookkeeper. In 1979 Merwin hired his auditor at Coopers & Lybrand, Timothy M. Graven. It was a major step for Graven to leave a well established accounting firm for a young niche company, but he accepted the position as corporate controller. He was a key addition to the management team and proved especially adept at dealing with the company's banks. In 1981 he was named a director of the corporation and would take on an increasing level of responsibility.

Going Public in 1985 As Steel Technologies

In 1985, after years of steady growth, Southern Strip Steel changed its name to Steel Technologies—more in keeping with the company's expanded capabilities—and was taken public. By this point the company was generating some $50 million in annual sales. It had moved its headquarters to Louisville, and in addition to the plant in Eminence, it also operated facilities in Peru, Indiana, and Madison Heights, Michigan. It was also in 1985 that Merwin turned over the presidency to Daryl Elser, part of a young executive team Merwin had assembled. Elser actually started out as a policeman, then went to work as a scheduler at Southern Steel's Indiana plant in 1978 and two years later transferred to the Eminence facility to become involved in purchasing. Merwin recognized Elser's abilities and promoted him through a series of management positions. Although Steel Technologies was now a public company, it remained essentially a family business. Merwin's sons—Bradford, the eldest, and Stuart—both worked for the company but were in their 20s and in the process of being groomed to one day take over. In 1990 Graven would replace Elser as president, a position he would hold for four years, at which point Bradford Merwin would succeed him.

After going public, Steel Technologies expanded plants and added facilities at a steady rate over the next several years. In 1986 the Michigan plant was expanded from 28,000 square feet to 40,000 square feet. A year later the company entered into a joint venture—Mi-Tech Steel Inc.—with the Japanese firm of Mitsui & Co. to operate processing plants in the United States to serve both Japanese and American automobile and appliance-parts makers. The first plant opened in Murfreesboro, Tennessee, in the fall of 1987. Also during that year, Steel Technologies opened a new plant in Portage, Indiana. In 1989 the company

opened a plant in Elkton, Maryland. The Madison Heights plant was replaced by a new 130,000-square-foot plant in Canton Township, Michigan, in 1991, producing such automotive steel products as safety-belt buckles, door locks, and steering column components. Sales during this period grew from $85.9 million in 1987 to $140 million in 1990, at which point a recession hurt auto production and Steel Technologies' sales dipped to $129 million. But the company remained profitable, recording net income of $3.5 million in 1991, and it continued to invest in new plants and equipment, positioning itself to take advantage of a rebound in the economy. All told, from 1987 to 1991 Steel Technologies invested $50 million in this endeavor. In 1992 the company was able to resume its growth: Sales improved to $154.4 million and net income to $6 million.

Steel Technologies continued to expand in the mid-1990s. In June 1994 the company moved beyond the U.S borders for the first time, gaining a presence in Mexico by acquiring 80 percent of the common stock of Transformadora y Comercializadora de Metalels, S.A. de C.V., which was then renamed Steel Technologies de Mexico, and brought with it a facility located in Monterrey. Within a matter of months, the venture began to add equipment to increase the plant's capabilities. By having a plant in Mexico, Steel Technologies was looking to serve longtime customers who were taking advantage of cheap labor and opening plants south of the border. Domestically, in 1995 the company opened its first plant with pickling capabilities, the facility located in Ghent, Kentucky.

External Growth in the Late 1990s

During the latter years of the 1990s, Steel Technologies looked to fuel growth by external means. In 1997 it acquired Atlantic Coil Processing, Inc. in a deal worth an estimated $19.6 million in cash, notes, and assumption of debt. As a result, the company added three processing plants in North Carolina. In 1998, Steel Technologies bought Roberts Steel Co. in a deal worth $14.8 million. Based near Cleveland, Roberts, which generated $25 million in annual sales, processed flat-rolled steel, creating value-added products for use by metal stampers, fabricators, and a range of manufacturers. The addition of the company helped Steel Technologies to service the northern Ohio market.

Expansion, complemented by attention paid to reducing expenses and a rising demand for its products, helped Steel Technologies to post strong results in the late 1990s. Revenues in 1997 reached $345 million, then improved to $383.9 million the following year and $411.4 in 1999. Net income during this period grew from $8.5 million in 1997 to a record $15.6 million in 1999. It was also in 1999 that Merwin Ray took the next step in a planned management succession program by turning over the CEO's duties to his 41-year-old son, Bradford Ray, who also assumed the newly created role of vice-chairman. The elder Ray remained as chairman of the company, electing to focus his efforts on strategic growth, management structure, and organizational development. In addition, another younger executive, Michael J. Carroll, who had devoted 20 years to Steel Technologies, was named president and chief operating officer.

Steel Technologies continued to open new plants. In 1999 a steel processing facility became operational in Berkeley

County, South Carolina, a move that complemented the Atlantic Coil acquisition. In Mexico in 2000, the Steel Technologies' majority owned subsidiary opened a $6.5 million plant in Matamoros, Mexico, across the border from Brownsville, Texas, as part of a plan to double business to $60 million by 2003. The company was also on the lookout for acquisition opportunities and considering the possibility of further greenfield sites in order to further expand the Mexican business.

As Steel Technologies entered the new century it continued to pursue acquisitions stateside. In January 2000 the company bought Custom Steel Inc. and Custom Steel Processing Corp., known collectively as Custom Steel, which generated annual sales of $33 million. Steel Technologies paid $13.35 million in cash plus conditional payments and the assumption of $5.8 million in liabilities to gain steel processing plants in Kennett, Missouri, and Wurtland, Kentucky. A year later, Steel Technologies bought a minority stake, 49 percent, in Ferrolux Metals Co., a Wayne, Michigan, auto sheet processor with additional facilities in Ohio and Mississippi. Ferrolux specialized in the production of exposed auto panels. Steel Technologies' partnership with Ferrolux expanded what the company could offer the marketplace. Ferrolux looked to benefit from Steel Technologies' willingness to invest money in expanding its capabilities and growing the business. Early in 2003 Steel Technologies paid approximately $10 million in cash to acquire a cold-rolled strip facility and other assets owned by bankrupt Cold Metal Products Company. The plant, located in Ottawa, Ohio, had been expanded in recent years and offered a wide range of rolling, annealing, and oscillating capabilities. The only setback for the company during these years was the closing of a Decatur, Alabama, pickle line operated by the Mi-Tech joint venture, due to a weak steel market.

In June 2001, 72-year-old Merwin Ray announced that he would retire at the end of the year and turn over the chairmanship to Bradford Ray. His youngest son, Stuart Ray, would continue to serve as the president of the Mi-Tech venture, a position he had held since 1996. Ray continued to serve in an advisory capacity to the company, holding the honorary title of founding chairman, but in essence the succession of power was now complete. The elder Ray had presided over 29 consecutive years of profitability, and despite the adverse effects of a slumping economy in 2001, exacerbated by the terrorist attacks of September 11 of that year, Steel Technologies posted a modest profit. In 2001 Steel Technologies experienced a significant decrease in sales over the previous year, dipping from $461.3 million to $436.8 million. Net income fell from $10.2 million to just $800,000 in 2001. But the company rebounded over the next two years, recording sales of $475.4 million in 2002 and $512.7 million in 2003, with net income during this period totaling $15.8 million and $9.2 million, respectively. There was every reason to believe that the second generation of the Ray family to head Steel Technologies was in line to enjoy continued growth for the foreseeable future.

Principal Subsidiaries

Steel Technologies de Mexico (90%); Custom Steel Corp.; Mi-Tech Steel Inc. (50%).

Principal Competitors

AK Steel Holding Corporation; Gibraltar Steel Corporation; Shiloh Industries, Inc.; Worthington Industries, Inc.

Further Reading

Benmour, Eric, "Steel Driver: Graven's Hard Work Started Early," *Business First-Louisville*, October 12, 1992, p. 20.
——, "Steel Technologies Tempers Right Mix for Record Earnings," *Business First-Louisville*, October 29, 1999, p. 9.
King, Angela, "Ready for Good Times: Steel Firm Builds Plant in Canton," *Crain's Detroit Business*, June 1, 1992, p. 3.
Osman, Karen, "Strong As Steel," *Louisville*, November 1988, p. 56.
Rayburn, Ray, "Steel Tech Chairman Is 'Straight Shooter,' " *Business First-Louisville*, June 2, 1986, p. 10.
Sacco, John E., "Steel Technologies Names CEO," *American Metal Market*, November 17, 1999, p. 3.

—Ed Dinger

Stefanel SpA

Via Postumia 85
Ponte di Piave
I-31047 TV
Italy
Telephone: +39 0422 8191
Fax: +39 0422 8193
Web site: http://www.stefanel.it

Public Company
Incorporated: 1959 as Maglificio Piave
Employees: 1,250
Sales: EUR 649 million ($800 million) (2003)
Stock Exchanges: Borsa Italiana
Ticker Symbol: STEF
NAIC: 315232 Women's and Girls' Cut and Sew Blouse and Shirt Manufacturing; 315233 Women's and Girls' Cut and Sew Dress Manufacturing; 315234 Women's and Girls' Cut and Sew Suit, Coat, Tailored Jacket, and Skirt Manufacturing; 315999 Other Apparel Accessories and Other Apparel Manufacturing

Stefanel SpA is an Italian clothing designer, manufacturer, and retailer, producing fashions for the men's and women's segments under its own Stefanel and Stef in Time brands, as well as clothing under license for French design duo Marithé and François Girbaud, including their jeans collection and the SPQRCITY sportswear collection. The company's Interfashion subsidiary produces its licensed clothing. Stefanel's sales come primarily through its international retail network of both company-owned and franchised stores, operating under the Stefanel name and, in Germany, under subsidiary Hallhuber's name. Altogether there are some 750 stores under the Stefanel umbrella, including outlets throughout Europe, and in North America, the Middle East, and Asia. Italy, however, remains the group's primary retail and clothing market, accounting for more than half of its stores. Hard-pressed by strong competition at the dawn of the 21st century, including from Italian rivals Benetton and Diesel, Stefanel has diversified its operations. In 2002, the company acquired a 50 percent stake (together with partner and Italian hard-discounter PAM) in the Nuance Group, the world's leading operator of retail duty-free stores with nearly 400 outlets worldwide. Nuance now accounts for more than 70 percent of Stefanel's revenues, which neared EUR 650 million ($800 million) in 2003. Stefanel, listed on the Borsa Italiana since the mid-1980s, remains controlled by the Stefanel family, under the leadership of Guiseppe Stefanel, son of the company's founder. In October 2003, Guiseppe Stefanel raised his shareholding position in the company to more than 57.5 percent; the company's other major shareholder is Delta Erre, with 27.5 percent.

Village Origins in the 1950s

The Treviso region near Venice became the home of one of Italy's—and the world's—most important fashion and design centers, providing the birthplace for such internationally known brand names as Benetton and Diesel. Yet Stefanel was one of the first of the design houses to come from the region.

Carlo Stefanel was born in the village of Ponte di Piave in 1925 and began working at his aunt's spinning mill, in Oderzo, at a young age. Following World War II, Stefanel became determined to go into business for himself. As he recalled in 1986: "I had lots of ideas and I was able to start out on my own thanks to the faith and financial support of a friend whom I will never thank enough."

Stefanel started out producing his own wool blend, which he sold at stalls in a number of local marketplaces. At first, Stefanel transported his goods by bicycle. Before long, his growing business enabled him to buy a small car, which he converted into a truck.

Stefanel continued to build his wool business through the 1950s. Yet Stefanel was eager to move on to the next phase, that of the production of textiles and clothing designs. At last, in 1959, he had the opportunity to buy four knitting machines, which he installed in his home in Oderzo. Stefanel founded his own company, Maglificio Piave, and began producing knitwear for the wholesale market.

The company grew strongly through the 1960s, yet remained exclusively a supplier to wholesalers. The late 1960s and especially the 1970s marked a new period of designer and brand name consciousness, giving rise to a new breed of textile groups in Italy.

By then, Stefanel had been joined by son Guiseppe, born in 1952. At the end of the 1960s, Guiseppe Stefanel had begun working for the company, taking responsibility for its production of yarn and textiles. During the 1970s, however, the younger Stefanel recognized the potential for launching the company's own clothing designs—under its own brand name.

The company began producing a range of knitwear in the mid-1970s, selling its clothing collections directly to other retailers. The Stefanel-branded line quickly captured the interest of Italian consumers, and before the end of the decade the company began to enjoy national recognition and success.

International Retailing Empire in the 1980s

Guiseppe Stefanel took over as company managing director in 1979 in order to lead it into the next phase in its development. In that year, the company began developing its own retail concept, originally along a franchise model. The initial success of the retail concept encouraged the company to begin opening a number of stores under its direct control, starting with a shop in Siena in 1980.

Adopting a new corporate name, Stefanel, the company began a period of rapid expansion. By 1982, the company made the bold decision to expand beyond Italy, opening its first international store in Paris that year. Stefanel posted impressive growth into the middle of the decade, inspired in part by its decision in 1983 to begin selling clothing exclusively through its own rapidly growing retail network.

By the middle of the 1980s, that network had grown to nearly 800 company-owned and franchised stores throughout the world. Fueling the company's growth was its public offering in 1986. In that year, the company's sales topped the equivalent of $128 million. Just two years later, Stefanel's revenues had already passed the $200 million mark. Italy remained the company's primary market, backed by a network of more than 550 stores by the end of the decade. With little room for further growth at home, however, the company stepped up expansion of its international network.

Guiseppe Stefanel became company chairman and CEO following his father's death in 1987. By then, the company had begun eyeing a new and potentially huge market—North America, especially the United States. The company opened its first

franchised stores in New York and Bermuda that year, and announced its intention to add another 40 to 60 stores—with ultimate plans to boost its North American presence to as many as 200 stores by the 1990s.

Yet success in the United States proved elusive for the company. By 1989, it had succeeded in opening only 18 stores in the United States, with a further eight operating in Canada. Stefanel had been unable to position itself as a true brand name in the United States, and was forced to reduce its objectives in the U.S. market, lowering its sights to just 100 stores. Even this goal proved optimistic—by 1992, the company's presence in the United States had shrunk back to just four stores.

Despite its difficulties in North America, Stefanel's growth remained impressive into the start of the 1990s. By the beginning of that decade, Stefanel boasted more than 1,100 franchise boutiques in its retail network, producing sales of nearly $400 million. Among the company's successes was winning the right to form a joint venture with the city of Leningrad (later renamed Saint Petersburg) to open two stores, and operate two factories, supplied by textiles from Stefanel's home base, starting from 1988. In 1989, the company moved into Japan, forming a joint venture with Onward Kashiyama. That business grew rapidly, topping 100 stores in the early 1990s, including 40 stores in Japan, and stores in South Korea, Taiwan, and China.

Finding New Focus for the New Century

Stefanel, which had concentrated its efforts on its core mid-range knitwear line, now began seeking to extend the range of its retail offering. In 1989 the company expanded its manufacturing base through the acquisition of Compagnia Finanziaria Moda, which produced clothing under license, including the clothing manufacturing license for the Converse All-Star brand. With its expanded production capacity, Stefanel began looking for new licensing partners.

In 1990 it entered two licensing partnerships. The first was with Italian designer Romeo Gigli, with an agreement to launch and distribute the new mid-priced G Gigli collection, inspired by the designer's ready-to-wear clothing. The two companies strengthened their relationship in 1992, forming a joint venture company to take over design and production of the G Gigli line. In the meantime, Stefanel was enjoying success through another design partnership, formed with France's Marithé and François Girbaud, designers of a successful jeans line, as well as their own ready-to-wear collection. The licensing deal gave Stefanel the European retailing rights to Girbaud jeans and other clothing.

Stefanel's licensing deals came as part of an overall effort to drive its retail offering into a higher-priced category—a strategy that came as much in reaction to the huge success then being enjoyed by Italian rivals Benetton and Diesel, among others. Yet Stefanel was outpaced by these groups, which had captured international attention through bold advertising campaigns.

By 1995, with an international network approaching 1,500 stores, Stefanel appeared to have run out of steam. In that year, the company slipped into the red. Losses continued into 1996, despite the company's effort to cut costs and refocus its retail network. As part of that process, the company slashed the number of shops, dropping some 500 stores. Many of these were

Key Dates:

1947: Carlo Stefanel begins producing and selling wool and fabrics in local markets in the Treviso region of Italy.

1959: Stefanel buys four knitting machines and establishes his own clothing company, Maglifico Piave, supplying wholesalers in Italy and Europe.

1970s: Joined by son Guiseppe, Stefanel begins designing and selling clothing under the Stefanel brand directly to retailers.

1979: Stefanel develops its own retail store concept and begins franchise operations.

1980: The first company-owned store is opened in Siena; the company changes its name to Stefanel.

1982: The first international Stefanel store opens in Paris.

1983: Stefanel decides to restrict sales to its own retail network.

1987: Stefanel enters the North American market with stores in New York and Bermuda; by then, the company already operates 800 stores.

1989: Stefanel forms a joint venture with Onward Kashiyama to open stores in Japan, South Korea, Taiwan, and China; the company acquires Compagnia Finanziaria Moda to begin producing clothing under license.

1990: The company acquires licenses for Marithé and François Girbaud jeans; a joint venture is formed to launch the new mid-range G Gigli collection in partnership with Romeo Gigli.

1995: Stefanel forms a joint venture with Calvin Klein to develop the CK retail chain in Europe.

2000: The CK joint venture is abandoned; the company acquires Germany's Hallhuber.

2002: Stefanel acquires 50 percent of the Nuance Group, which triples the company's revenues.

2003: Guiseppe Stefanel boosts his stake in the company past 57 percent and begins efforts to revitalize the Stefanel brand.

smaller stores, closed in favor of a new and far larger "superstore" concept. The company also attempted to broaden its consumer base by introducing a new Stefanel Kids collection.

Stefanel also turned to a new partner to restore its momentum. In 1995, the company reached an agreement with American designer Calvin Klein, then making an attempt to enter the European market. The two companies agreed to form a joint venture, SKY Co., held at 73 percent by Stefanel, to open as many as 150 CK stores in Europe by the end of the decade.

Yet CK failed to inspire European shoppers. By the end of the decade, the costs of developing the CK network had begun to weigh heavily on Stefanel, which once again slipped into losses. As a result, the company abandoned the CK partnership. At the same time, it ended its struggling Stefanel Kids line.

Stefanel was once again faced with finding new growth avenues. The company now began targeting acquisitions of existing businesses as a means forward. In 2000, the company turned to Germany, paying $17.5 million to acquire that country's Hallhuber group. Hallhuber operated 44 stores throughout the country, selling its own brands, as well as clothing from Marithé and François Girbaud and Calvin Klein. The company expected to build up its presence in Germany, both through its own 23 Stefanel stores in that country, and through the expansion of the Hallhuber chain.

Stefanel continued to seek other expansion possibilities. The next opportunity came in 2002, when the company was offered an option to acquire 50 percent of the Nuance Group, then being acquired by Italian hard-discounter PAM from Swissair. Nuance had been formed in 1992 through the combination of the duty-free business of Swissair and Crossair. By the beginning of the 2000s, after a number of acquisitions, Nuance had emerged as the worldwide leader in the retail duty-free market, with nearly 400 shops. The addition of its Nuance stake transformed Stefanel's balance sheet, tripling its revenues. Nuance also gave Stefanel a new outlet for its own clothing fashions. Leading the company's new charge was Guiseppe Stefanel, who, after delegating direction in the 1990s, decided once again to oversee the company's day-to-day operations in order to restore its former glory. As part of that effort, Stefanel increased his own direct ownership in the company, stepping up his shareholding to more than 57.5 percent in October 2003. Stefanel hoped to become once again one of Italy's fastest-growing design and retail groups in the 2000s.

Principal Subsidiaries

Fordan S.L. (Spain); Genfico Holding B.V. (Netherlands); Hallhuber GmbH (Germany); Interfashion S.p.A.; Interpool S.p.A.; Lara Stefanel S.a.s. (France); Nuance Group; Retail S.r.l.; S.T.ARIE' Lda (Portugal); Sfk Ltd. (Korea); Stefanel Fashion Turkey A.S.; Stefanel GmbH (Germany); Stefanel International Holding N.V. (Netherlands); Stefanel Romania S.r.l.; Stefanel Universal S.r.l. (Romania); Stefburg Mode GmbH (Austria); Stefpraha S.r.o. (Czech Republic); Stout S.p.A.; Swiss Factory Outlet S.A.; Tindareo S.r.l.; Victorian S.r.l.

Principal Competitors

Marzotto S.p.A.; Cortefiel S.A.; ESCADA AG; Quiksilver Inc.; Benetton SpA; Diesel S.p.A.

Further Reading

Conti, Samantha, "Stefanel's Booster Shot," *WWD,* August 26, 1997, p. S54.

Galbraith, Robert, "Life in the Global Fast Lane," *International Herald Tribune,* September 29, 2001, p. 13.

"Guiseppe Stefanel Ups Stake in Family Firm to 57.2%," *FWN Select,* October 15, 2003.

Forden, Sara Gay, "Restructuring and Cutting Costs Return Stephanel to Profitability," *WWD,* March 18, 1998, p. 18.

"Stefanel Buys Hallhuber Chain," *WWD,* March 22, 2000, p. 19.

"Stefanel to Purchase 50% Nuance Stake," *Duty Free News International,* May 15, 2002, p. 5.

—M.L. Cohen

Swift Energy Company

16825 Northcase Drive, Suite 400
Houston, Texas 77060
U.S.A.
Telephone: (281) 874-2700
Toll Free: (800) 777-2412
Fax: (281) 874-2726
Web site: http://www.swiftenergy.com

Public Company
Incorporated: 1979
Employees: 241
Sales: $211.1 million (2003)
Stock Exchanges: New York
Ticker Symbol: SFY
NAIC: 211111 Crude Petroleum and Natural Gas
   Extraction

Swift Energy Company is a Houston-based independent oil and natural gas company with a dual geographical focus: the onshore and inland water areas of the Texas and Louisiana Gulf Coast, and onshore properties in New Zealand. The publicly traded company owns interests in nearly 1,000 wells, evenly balanced between oil and gas. Of Swift's proven reserves, 40 percent is located in Louisiana, 37 percent in Texas, and 21 percent in New Zealand. A. Earl Swift is chairman of the company, and his son, Terry E. Swift, serves as president and CEO.

Founding the Company in 1979

Earl Swift grew up in Oklahoma, part of a family well versed in the oil business. His grandfather worked as a muleskinner moving drilling equipment from site to site, and his father worked in the Oklahoma oilfields at $1 a day. According to his own recollections Swift encountered his first oil rig at the age of three. At the time, such rigs were steam-powered, and the child made the mistake of backing up against the hot metal with his bare legs. As a result, the oil industry made a vivid, if not searing, first impression on him. He grew up fascinated with the oil business, but at the insistence of his parents, who had no formal education past the eighth grade, he delayed the start of

his working life until after college. He would more than exceed his parents' expectations. After receiving a petroleum engineering degree from the University of Oklahoma, he went on to earn an M.B.A. from Pepperdine University. Still not satisfied, he took a law degree from South Texas College of Law. In 1955 he went to work as a petroleum engineer for Humble Oil Company, Exxon's predecessor. He then joined American Natural Resources Co. and worked for their affiliates, ultimately rising to the post of vice-president of Exploration and Production for Michigan-Wisconsin Pipe Line Company. But after 17 years of working for others, Swift, at the age of 45, decided he wanted to start his own oil business and in 1979 he tendered his resignation and formed Swift Energy.

Earl Swift accepted some consulting jobs in the early months as he became organized, and then began to assemble limited partnerships to purchase producing properties. He took the company public in 1981, at which point he was joined in the business by his oldest brother, Virgil N. Swift, who was also a professional petroleum engineer and well seasoned in the oil industry. Over the course of 28 years he held a number of positions with Gulf Oil Corporation and its subsidiaries. Before joining Swift Energy, he served as general manager of drilling for Gulf Canada Resources, Inc. Because the brothers had many years of accumulated wisdom between them, they were well aware of the cyclical nature of the oil and gas business, but they were also willing to employ new tools to help in making decisions. The company came to rely heavily on computer programs that mapped long-term energy trends. Because of these factors, Swift Energy proved to be especially effective in determining when the industry was in a down cycle and properties could be bought on the cheap and when the cycle was peaking and the company was better off sitting on the sidelines.

During the late 1970s oil prices surged to unprecedented levels, prompting many in the industry to take on massive debt in order to buy up reserves and producing properties at what proved to be inflated prices. In its early years, Swift Energy stayed out of the market, opting instead to make money drilling development and exploration wells for others. In 1983 the Swift brothers recognized that conditions in the market were changing and they felt it was a more opportune time to acquire producing oil and gas properties. As a result, the company shifted into acquisition mode and prepared to manage these purchases through limited partnerships. The first property was bought in 1984, a year in which the company was successful in raising approximately $4.5 million. The next year it raised another $9.5 million. Although the limited partnerships were saddled with time-consuming paperwork, which caused many competitors to cease their involvement in such endeavors, the Swifts believed that partnerships were an excellent investment vehicle and a better alternative than taking on excessive debt in a highly cyclical industry. At the close of fiscal 1985 Swift Energy had just $23,000 in long-term debt. Many others, who had assumed too much debt during the boom times of the late 1970s, would soon be ruined.

Quickening Acquisition Pace in 1986

In 1986, many in the industry predicted that oil prices, which were in the $10 to $12 a barrel range, would dip even further, to as low as $5 a barrel, making the acquisition of oil and gas reserves a foolhardy act. But Swift Energy defied conventional wisdom and picked up its rate of making acquisitions, acting on the belief that oil prices would rise beyond $20 by the early 1990s. In 1986 the company picked up $35 million in new investments. Time would also prove management right about the trajectory of oil prices. At this point, the company was involved in three basic areas: operating and developing properties, performing joint venture work with larger partners, and acting as fund managers for the limited partnerships. In addition to the acquisition of producing properties, the company bought some leases, and also delved into some side areas, such as the marketing of a blowout preventer through subsidiary Pet-Tech Tools Inc. While others in the industry struggled, and many failed, Swift Energy from 1983 to 1988 enjoyed a 47 percent annual rate of growth. It was also at the close of this period that Earl Swift's son, Terry, joined the business after earning a degree in chemical engineering and an M.B.A.

In 1988, on behalf of its limited partners, Swift Energy spent $55.9 million on oil and gas interests. In 1989 Swift Energy continued to acquire oil and gas interests at discounted prices. In conjunction with chief partner Denver-based Manville Corp., the company paid about $52.1 million to acquire assets in oil and gas wells located in Arkansas, Kansas, Louisiana, New Mexico, Oklahoma, and Texas. To fuel ongoing growth without adding debt, Swift Energy made a secondary offering of stock in October 1989, netting $6.1 million. But primarily the company continued to acquire properties through joint ventures and limited partnerships, generally taking on a 25 percent ownership stake. Not only did this approach keep down debt, it also

provided the economies of scale associated with a company four times its size. As a result, Swift Energy would be able to maintain in-house 3-D seismic and horizontal drilling capabilities that would prove highly beneficial when the company returned its focus to drilling and exploration. Early in 1990 Swift and its partnerships paid another $42.5 million to add oil and gas producing properties in Oklahoma, Louisiana, and Texas in five separate acquisitions.

Again responding to changing conditions, Swift Energy in 1991 began to transition away from the acquisition of producing properties, choosing instead to return to its roots and concentrate on drilling and development activities. From 1991 to 1995 the company production grew by 180 percent, while at the same time proved oil and gas reserves increased by more than 260 percent. In addition, revenues almost doubled, from $14.9 million in 1991 to nearly $29 million in 1995. Net income in 1991 totaled $2.5 million, improving to $4.9 million in 1995. Cash flow from operating activities also increased more than 140 percent during this period. It was during this time that Swift Energy first became involved in the Giddings Field of Central Texas, part of the well-known Austin Chalk trend, infamous for its many fractures that proved frustrating for traditional vertical wells. While oil might flow fast in the beginning, wells in this region were notorious for going dry very quickly. Horizontal drilling techniques used later in the 1990s would finally solve this problem, making Swift's investment in the region pay off handsomely.

In addition to its U.S. activities, Swift also began to look for opportunities overseas. In 1993 the company reached an agreement with Senega, one of the privately held Russian oil and gas companies that emerged after the breakup of the Soviet Union. The deal called for Swift to provide technical and managerial assistance to develop and produce reserves in two Western Siberia sites, near the Arctic circle and close to the largest natural gas field in the world, work for which it was slated to receive at least 5 percent of net profits. Swift also paid $300,000 for a 1 percent net profit interest. The company then formulated a $325 million plan to develop the properties and arranged the investment of the federal Overseas Private Investment Corp., as well as forging an alliance with McDermott International, Hungary's national oil company, to help with the work. It was a high-risk venture that, if successful, promised a high reward. Swift kept its investment modest, and with good reason: Conducting business in the new Russia was fraught with unforeseen difficulties, including currency problems and political uncertainties. At the close of 1997, after spending $10 million on the project, Swift terminated its agreement with Senega. Although the company retained a minimum 6 percent net profit interest in the fields, the fate of the project was now out of its hands and it relied on the eventual success of outside parties to recover its investment.

New Zealand Venture in 1995

Swift also looked to Venezuela, in 1993 forming a subsidiary in order to bid on a contract to construct and operate a methane pipeline. As with the Russian venture, this project failed to come to fruition, costing the company nearly $3 million. Officially, both investments were relegated to the unproved properties section of the company's portfolio.

```
┌─────────────────────────────────────────────┐
│              Key Dates:                       │
│                                               │
│ 1979:  Swift Energy Company incorporates.     │
│ 1981:  Company goes public.                   │
│ 1991:  Company returns to a focus on drilling.│
│ 1995:  Company enters New Zealand market.     │
│ 1998:  Terry Swift succeeds his father as     │
│        president.                             │
│ 2002:  Further New Zealand assets are acquired.│
└─────────────────────────────────────────────┘
```

Swift, however, enjoyed much better success with its investment in New Zealand, where it established a presence in 1995 by obtaining the first of two petroleum exploration permits for the country's North Island. New Zealand was certainly a worthwhile risk. It was one of the few remaining areas of untapped promise in the world. Despite the potential for hydrocarbons, only around 500 exploration wells were drilled in the country throughout the 20th century, primarily because of New Zealand's remote location, which increased service costs, and its small economy, which offered a modest local market for the gas and oil the wells might produce. As a result, even though New Zealand shared the same geological features of other area countries, oil and gas companies elected to set up drilling operations in Australia, Indonesia, and the South China Sea. In essence, New Zealand lacked investment more than it lacked hydrocarbons. For such American companies as Swift, New Zealand offered obvious advantages, namely the language spoken was English, the laws familiar, the political situation stable, and the government friendly. Late in 1999 the company completed its first exploratory well. Further tests followed in 2000, during which Swift announced that it believed that it had discovered a new oilfield, one that could contain 500 million barrels. Furthermore, the company believed that it had only intersected the edge of the field. More wells were scheduled to be drilled later in the year.

In the meantime, Swift began boosting its profile stateside, increasing its domestic drilling activity to gain the attention of investors. In 1995 the company was able to raise $46.2 million with the issuance of 5.8 million new shares of common stock, 70 percent of the money promised to be spent on the development of reserves in the Giddings Fields and the AWP Field in Texas. A further benefit of the offering was that Swift topped the $100 million threshold in total market capitalization, meaning that large institutional investors would now give the stock consideration. In 1997 Terry Swift replaced his father as president of the company, part of a succession program that would soon make him chief executive officer; his father remained chairman of the board.

Swift suffered a minor setback in 1998 when an article in the *Wall Street Journal* claimed that the company was inflating its reserves in Texas. The company's stock was adversely impacted at a time when similar companies were enjoying a surge in stock prices, triggering an aggressive response from management, which maintained that the negative report was based on information produced by short-sellers of its stock. Management threatened to sue in order to depose the engineer responsible for the study of its drilling program and reserves. More important, the company hired an independent consultant to review its holdings. The resulting study was within 10 percent of the information Swift had submitted to the SEC, silencing critics. Swift further demonstrated its belief in its Austin Chalk interests in 1998 by paying $87 million in cash for Sonat Exploration Company, which brought with it 156 wells, interests in two gas plants, and 355,000 acres in the region. It was considered a gamble, but Swift soon drilled some high-producing wells, all in excess of a million barrels.

With two solid drilling programs in the United States and New Zealand, Swift saw its stock price increase 227 percent in 2000. For the year, the company recorded revenues of $191.6 million and income of $59.2 million. In 2001 the company added important properties in Louisiana, located in the Lake Washington Field, where management focused much of its domestic drilling activities in 2002 and into 2003. Swift also acquired assets to bolster its New Zealand position, spending more than $55 million. Following two years of declining numbers, Swift rebounded in 2003 with revenues of $211 million. As the company embarked on 2004, its 25th anniversary, management was pleased with the diversification of its drilling activities and fully expected record-setting performance.

Principal Subsidiaries

Swift Energy International, Inc.; Swift Energy New Zealand Limited; Southern Petroleum (NZ) Exploration Limited.

Principal Competitors

Apache Corporation; BP p.l.c.; Exxon Mobile Corporation.

Further Reading

De Rouffignac, Ann, "Independent Thinker," *Houston Business Journal,* October 30, 1998, p. 14A.

"Swift Energy Company," *Oil & Gas Investor,* June 1995, p. 32.

Van Levy, C., and Brad L. Beago, "Swift Energy Co.: Growth Through the Drill Bit," *Oil & Gas Investor,* April 1996, p. 40.

——, "Swift Takes Legal Action Over Report," *Houston Business Journal,* April 17, 1998, p. 1A.

Weeden, Scott L., "Houston Firm Thrives by Following Long-Term Energy Development," *Oil Daily,* March 3, 1987, p. 4.

—Ed Dinger

Taco John's International, Inc.

808 W. 20th Street
Cheyenne, Wyoming 82001-3404
U.S.A.
Telephone: (307) 635-0101
Toll Free: (800) 854-0819
Fax: (307) 638-0603
Web site: http://www.tacojohns.com

Private Company
Incorporated: 1969 as Taco John's
Employees: 160
Sales: $20 million (2003 est.)
NAIC: 722211 Limited-Service Restaurants; 533110
Lessors of Nonfinancial Intangible Assets (Except
Copyrighted Works)

Taco John's International, Inc. franchises and serves a chain of Mexican-style fast-food restaurants. The privately owned firm supports around 400 outlets—only a handful of which are company owned—in 24 states, centered in the upper Midwest and West. Average annual sales for a Taco John's unit in 2002 was about $490,000, which translated into total systemwide sales of approximately $200 million. Through an emphasis on food seasonings, generous portions, good service, and fair prices, the company has come to rival Del Taco, Inc. as the second largest Mexican quick-service chain in the United States. (The Taco Bell chain, owned by YUM! Brands, Inc., is by far the largest player in this sector.) Taco John's has generally concentrated on rural areas and smaller towns but began targeting major urban areas, such as Denver and Kansas City, in the early 2000s.

Early History: From Taco Stand to Taco John's Chain

The sprawling restaurant chain dubbed Taco John's was born as a single, tiny taco stand. The "Taco House" as it was called, opened in 1968 in Cheyenne, Wyoming. It was started by a high-plains cowboy rancher named John ("Taco John") Turner and his wife. The Taco House was a big hit with the locals in Cheyenne because it offered good-tasting Mexican food, fast. An important ingredient in the taco stand's success was the spice that the Turners used in the food. They ground various spices and prepared all of the seasonings in their basement and garage. They used the seasonings to flavor traditional Mexican fare, including tacos and burritos.

Intrigued by the success of the bustling taco stand, Cheyenne businessmen Harold Holmes and Jim Woodson purchased the franchise rights to the fledgling venture in 1969. They believed that they could transport the concept to other cities in the region and, if the new restaurants were as popular as the first Taco House, profit handsomely. They realized that the special seasonings developed by the Turners were important to the chain's success. In fact, the Turners' seasonings became a closely guarded trade secret that continued to be used by Taco John's restaurants throughout the 1980s and into the 1990s.

Holmes and Woodson immediately began franchising restaurants based on the Taco House concept. They changed the name of the outlets to "Taco John's," but left many other elements the same, including much of the menu. They opened their first franchised stores in Rapid City, South Dakota; Scottsbluff, Nebraska; and Torrington, Wyoming. Like the first Taco House, the new Taco John's outlets were a big success. Holmes and Woodson knew that they were onto something. During the 1970s, then, they expanded throughout the upper Midwest and West, franchising Taco John's outlets primarily in small towns.

The decision to target small towns evidenced a new strategy that became characteristic of the Taco John's organization. The franchising concept was relatively new at the time, and most companies up to that period had focused on opening franchise outlets solely in larger urban areas. In contrast, Holmes and Woodson decided to open their stores in small towns, which were often devoid of competition. Their goal was to bring to those small towns a unique eating experience, including good-tasting Mexican food, served fast, at reasonable prices. The overall strategy was ultimately a big success. Each Taco John's eatery developed a loyal customer base in its town, and also managed to attract regular patrons from outlying regions that would become desperate for a Taco John's "fix."

Company Perspectives:

The Taco John's Brand Position: To adult Mexican food lovers who use fast food restaurants and are willing to pay a bit more to get larger portions, more variety, and fresh preparation, Taco John's offers higher quality, more authentic-tasting Mexican food than Taco Bell, served in a more personal and comfortable environment.

Growth Fueled by Franchisees in the 1970s and 1980s

In fact, Taco John's loyal fans played an important role in the company's growth during the 1970s and 1980s. Many customers in outlying areas would write to the Cheyenne headquarters, begging the company to open an outlet closer to them. In some cases, those same customers became franchisees, owning and operating their own store. Likewise, some Taco John's fans who relocated to other regions, realizing that no Taco John's existed in their area, would open their own Taco John's franchise. The result was that the company gradually blanketed many parts of the upper Midwest—South Dakota, Minnesota, Nebraska, Wisconsin, Iowa, Wyoming—with Taco John's outlets.

Taco John's prospered during the 1970s and 1980s by cultivating a win-win partnership with its franchisees. Franchisees paid Taco John's a franchise fee, plus royalties on income from their stores. In return, they got complete support from Taco John's. In the early years, Taco John's would ship a prefabricated 12- by 30-foot taco stand from Wyoming; the stand was complete with kitchen appliances and other necessary fixtures. Later, the company built or outfitted larger structures with seating, rather than shipping prebuilt units. (One of the original prefabricated units was still operating in 1995 in Des Moines, where it had been a lunchtime favorite with high school students since 1973.) Taco John's would then work to ensure that its franchisees were given the training and support they needed to make their stores prosper. When the franchisees profited, so did Taco John's. As the word got out that a Taco John's franchise was a good investment, the company found a steady supply of franchisee candidates.

Thus it was the enterprising franchisees that became the engine for Taco John's growth. Those entrepreneurs typically toiled long hours to make their restaurants successful, and often opened other Taco John's outlets in their areas. Representative of the franchisees who helped to grow Taco John's during the 1970s and 1980s were Bill Byrne and Dean Neese, owners of one of Taco John's largest franchise groups. Byrne, who was in his late 20s when he opened his first Taco John's, was working as a branch manager of a Dain Bosworth Inc. stock brokerage in the early 1970s. He became interested in the emerging Taco John's concept, and convinced 38-year-old Neese to join him in investing $39,500 to open the first Taco John's outlet in Des Moines, Iowa (one of the first Taco John's opened in a larger urban area).

Byrne and Neese labored to make their first Taco John's a success. Once the store was up-and-running and the Taco John's name began to catch on in Des Moines, they added a second outlet. They added one restaurant at a time, making sure that each store was a success before they opened another unit. In 1978 they opened the first Taco John's that sported both a drive-up window and indoor seating. The unit became a model for the next generation of Taco John's stores. They also helped to pioneer Taco John's mall stores. Over time, Byrne gravitated toward the finance and operations end of the business, while Neese focused on real estate and site location. Both partners also became involved with Taco John's International in Cheyenne, helping to formulate and implement corporate strategy. By the late 1980s, Byrne and Neese were operating ten Taco John's outlets in Des Moines, compared with six units operated by their nearest competitor. Those ten outlets consumed ten tons of beef and two tons of cheese each month.

Also demonstrating the importance of Taco John's franchisees were husband-and-wife team Charles and DeMaris Mathison, the owners and operators of one of Taco John's International's most successful stores. Charles grew up in Rapid City, South Dakota, where his parents operated a diner. After getting a degree in engineering and working in sales for a few years, he and DeMaris purchased a Taco John's franchise in 1976 for the city of Marshalltown, a small city in Iowa. They set up shop in an A-frame building and went to work. The first three years were "tough, real tough," DeMaris recalled in the March 14, 1994 *Des Moines Register*. "We were both exhausted for three years. One of us was there all the time. He would close one night, and I would close the next."

Despite various setbacks, the Mathisons managed to get the store off the ground by focusing on quality food and good service. They also worked to develop a loyal customer base, and were known for being able to greet more than half of their customers by name. Over time, the Mathisons' Taco John's developed a regular clientele that spanned all socioeconomic groups, from businessmen to laborers whose ethnic heritage ranged from German and Swedish to Hispanic. The couple moved their store to a larger space in 1985, and in 1988 added an atrium that boosted seating capacity to 114. With help from a professional restaurant manager, they were able to grow their Taco John's into one of the most successful units in the history of the company. In 1994, in fact, the Marshalltown Taco John's, after leading all other units in sales volume for four straight years, became the first unit to generate more than $1 million in receipts during a single year.

The efforts of franchisees, with support from headquarters staff in Cheyenne, allowed Taco John's to post big gains. By the end of the 1980s, in fact, Taco John's consisted of a network of approximately 400 units, most of which were located in the upper Midwest and West. Those stores were generating annual sales approaching $150 million. States with the greatest number of restaurants included Minnesota, Wisconsin, Iowa, the Dakotas, Nebraska, and Wyoming. But the chain also had extended into both large and small towns in Missouri, Montana, Illinois, and other states in those regions. At the same time, Taco John's was branching out with units in other parts of the nation, including (by the early 1990s) Tennessee, Florida, Arkansas, and New York.

Taco John's managed to sustain its growth during the 1980s, despite an onslaught of competition that knocked many of its

Key Dates:

1968: A high-plains cowboy rancher named John Turner and his wife open a tiny taco stand in Cheyenne, Wyoming, known as the ''Taco House.''

1969: Cheyenne businessmen Harold Holmes and Jim Woodson buy the franchise rights to the Turners' venture; they begin franchising restaurants based on the founders' concept, changing the name to Taco John's, concentrating on smaller towns, starting with Rapid City, South Dakota; Scottsbluff, Nebraska; and Torrington, Wyoming.

1978: The first Taco John's to sport both a drive-up window and indoor seating opens in Des Moines, Iowa; this unit becomes the model for the next generation of Taco John's stores.

1989: The Taco John's chain consists of about 400 units, generating annual sales of nearly $150 million.

1997: Paul Fisherkeller is named president and CEO; ''A Whole Lot of Mexican'' is adopted as the company slogan; a new prototype store for small towns is introduced.

2003: The chain unveils a new, more contemporary store design as it begins targeting major urban areas for growth.

competitors out of the industry. Notable was the threat posed beginning in the 1980s by Mexican-style fast-food behemoth Taco Bell, which at the time was a subsidiary of the giant PepsiCo, Inc. (The beverage firm spun off its restaurant holdings in 1997 as Tricon Global Restaurants, Inc., which later changed its name to YUM! Brands, Inc.) Taco Bell used its parent's deep pockets to fund an aggressive expansion drive, often penetrating markets where Taco John's had long been established. Taco John's executives realized that its franchisees could not compete with Taco Bell on price. Instead, they chose to buck the industry trend toward ''value pricing'' and stick with Taco John's proven strategy of offering larger portions of high-quality food in an attractive, friendly setting. Taco John's nacho chips, for example, were made fresh in each store, daily. ''We'll leave it to the other guys to sell the bite-sized items,'' said Taco John's president, Pieter Roelofs, in the March 14, 1994 *Des Moines Register*.

Early 1990s: Rewarded for Franchisee Relations; Changes to Menu and Image

Taco John's also retained its longtime philosophy of establishing win-win relationships with its franchisees. For example, to confront increased competition, the company stepped up its advertising efforts, introducing the new tag line, ''More than you imagined,'' in the fall of 1991, and began working more closely with franchisees to develop multimedia campaigns. Taco John's reputation for treating its franchisees fairly was rewarded in 1994, when Taco John's received the first-ever ''Fair Franchising Seal of Approval'' from the America Association of Franchisees and Dealers. At the same time, Taco John's was named by Dow Jones's *National Business Employment Weekly* as one of the best franchise buys in the country.

By 1994, Taco John's was operating 430 units in 30 states. It was still privately owned, and the original founders remained active in the company, although they had handed control of day-to-day operations to restaurant industry veteran Roelofs. Under Roelofs' direction, Taco John's initiated a number of changes in the early 1990s. For example, its menu was broadened to incorporate a variety of new items, including several ''Heart Smart'' items that used low-fat ingredients. In addition to those newer items were Taco John's more traditional, popular features, such as the Beef Burrito, Taco, Taco Burger, Mexican Style Rice, and various platters and combos. Taco John's also was moving to grow through new distribution channels, such as ''Mexpress'' kiosks and small food court units.

Going into the mid-1990s, Taco John's was updating its image. Among other moves, the company replaced its longtime logo and character, Juan, a cartoon-like Mexican with a big hat. The new character, dubbed John, was less representative of the stereotypical Mexican image, and ''more of a contemporary person who probably has a broader agenda, if you will,'' according to Byrne. The logo change was part of Taco John's ''Image 2000'' program, which also included updating the chain's stores with new, brighter colors and completely remodeling the stores. The first franchisee to renovate his stores under the new program was Byrne, who by 1994 was operating 12 units in Des Moines.

New Initiatives Under New Leadership: Late 1990s and Early 2000s

Paul Fisherkeller became president and CEO of Taco John's International in 1997. One of the many initiatives that the new leader implemented—and perhaps the most important—was to promote greater consistency across the chain. Fisherkeller told *QSR* magazine in November 2000 that when he took the job he found that Taco John's was ''the most un-chain-like chain [I'd] ever seen. Changing that has been my mission around here.'' Under the new CEO, a core menu was developed for the whole chain, and a concerted effort was made to make sure that specific items on the menu tasted the same across the chain. One way to do so was to begin using single suppliers for certain ingredients, such as taco meat or cheese sauce, when in the past two or more suppliers may have been used. On the marketing side, the chain was united around a new slogan, ''A Whole Lot of Mexican,'' which was introduced in 1997. All of these changes were made in close consultation with the chain's franchisees to maintain the good relations that had characterized Taco John's since its founding.

Also in 1997, Taco John's adopted a new prototype for units located in small towns. Traditional Taco John's units ranged from 1,700 to 1,900 square feet, included about 60 seats, and had two drive-through lanes. The new small-town prototype was around 1,200 square feet in size and had less than 30 seats and a single drive-through lane. Designed specifically for communities of 10,000 or less, the new prototype could be situated either as a freestanding unit or in the end-cap location of a strip mall.

Over the next several years the Taco John's chain did not grow in unit terms—in fact the number of stores fell from around 440 in the late 1990s to about 400 by early 2004. Systemwide sales, however, did increase, reaching around $200 million by 2003. This advance through contraction was achieved through the closure of underperforming units and the abandonment of some marginal markets. Taco John's outlined a core area in which it planned to concentrate its growth consisting of 15 states: Colorado, Idaho, Illinois, Iowa, Kansas, Kentucky, Minnesota, Missouri, Montana, Nebraska, North Dakota, South Dakota, Washington, Wisconsin, and Wyoming. Although the chain continued operating elsewhere, it concentrated its resources in this core territory. Given that sales at fast-food restaurants are driven by advertising, a more concentrated growth strategy would enable Taco John's to get the maximum return possible from its advertising efforts.

Working in tandem with this growth strategy was a shift in the makeup of Taco John's franchisees. Whereas the chain had been built, in large part, on the backs of single-unit franchisees, who might eventually open an additional unit or two, Taco John's increasingly sought out partnerships with multi-unit operators. Many of these new partners were veteran operators of quick-service restaurants who were seeking a new vehicle for growth. So, for example, in mid-1999 Simmonds Restaurant Management Inc., operator of 68 Burger King outlets in Nebraska and Iowa, signed an agreement to develop 15 Taco John's in Omaha, Nebraska, and along Interstate 80 between Omaha and Des Moines. In 2000 several more such deals were reached, such as one with Doug Day, a Wichita-based owner of 16 Burger King franchises, who agreed to develop ten Taco John's in Wichita and Hutchinson, Kansas.

Another important development at Taco John's came in 1999, when Brian Osborn was brought onboard as the chain's first executive chef. Osborn previously served as corporate chef for Frisch's Restaurants, Inc. and the Hardee's hamburger chain. At Taco John's he spearheaded an effort to shift from the use of off-the-shelf products to ones that were proprietary to Taco John's, such as refried beans and tortillas. He also helped develop a new upscale platter line, which included chicken enchiladas, beef enchiladas, and a beef and bean chimichanga, with each entrée accompanied by nacho chips, Mexican rice, and refried beans. In May 2001 Taco John's marked the sale of its billionth taco.

During the early 2000s Taco John's joined the industry trend of cobranded outlets, in which two restaurants occupy a single location. The chain explored this strategy as a possible way to accelerate its expansion, particularly into new markets contiguous to existing ones. Among these were Taco John's operating alongside Noble Roman's, a pizza concept, in Illinois, Kentucky, and Iowa; MaggieMoo's, an ice cream eatery in Omaha, Nebraska; and Steak Escape in Minnesota, Colorado, and South Dakota. In March 2004 Good Times Restaurants Inc. entered into an agreement with Taco John's to develop a cobranded test store in Cheyenne that would include both a Taco John's and a Good Time Burgers & Frozen Custard outlet.

As it prepared to expand by about 25 units in 2004, the year of its 35th anniversary, Taco John's in late 2003 unveiled a new, more contemporary store design that it hoped would facilitate a push into major urban areas, such as Denver and Kansas City. The new design replaced the stucco typically used by most Mexican fast-food restaurants (including Taco John's) with natural stone, did away with other clichéd elements, such as what many called the "Alamo arch," and incorporated new colors. Part of a "reimaging" program for the chain, the new design also was accompanied by the rollout, on a test basis, of new, more authentic Mexican items, such as a shredded beef quesadilla, grilled burritos, a shredded beef soft-shell taco, and new salads. A prototype of the new design was built by the company in Cheyenne, and this was then followed by the first franchise store to feature the new look, located in Pierre, South Dakota. According to Fisherkeller, Taco John's was "putting a fresh face on everything from our building design to our food in order to position ourselves for continued growth in a market filled with generic Mexican fast-food and emerging 'fresh-Mex' quick-service restaurants." Building a niche between these two approaches to fast Mexican food was to be the company's goal moving forward.

Principal Competitors

Taco Bell; Del Taco, Inc.; Chipotle Mexican Grill, Inc.

Further Reading

Davis, Lea, "Standing Tall," *QSR,* November 2000.

Elbert, David, "Big Success in a Small Town," *Des Moines Register,* March 14, 1994, p. 1B.

Howard, Theresa, "Sandwich Rollout Positions Taco John's a Step Above the Competition," *Nation's Restaurant News,* May 11, 1992, p. 12.

Jost, Rick, "Welcome to the New Taco John, A New Age, '90s Fellow," *Des Moines Register,* Sec. B, September 26, 1994.

Lacher, Lisa, "Franchise Partners Make a Hot Combo," *Business Record,* February 22, 1988, p. 12.

LaHue, Polly, "A Whole Lot of Mexican at Taco John's," *Restaurant Hospitality,* September 2000, p. 140.

Luckett, Bill, "A Whole New Look of Mexican," *Casper (Wyo.) Star-Tribune,* December 6, 2003.

Taco John's: Working Together for Quality, Cheyenne, Wyo.: Taco John's International, Inc., 1994.

Zuber, Amy, "Brian Osborn: Spicing Up Taco John's with New Creations," *Nation's Restaurant News,* October 25, 1999, p. 34.

——, "Taco John's Adopts 'Small-Town Mentality' with New Prototypes," *Nation's Restaurant News,* August 25, 1997, p. 18.

—Dave Mote
—update: David E. Salamie

TDC A/S

Norrgade 21
Copenhagen C
DK-0900
Denmark
Telephone: 45 33 43 77 77
Fax: 45 33 43 76 19
Web site: http://www.tdc.dk

Public Company
Incorporated:
Employees: 22,263
Sales: DKK 50.26 billion ($8.34 billion) (2003)
Stock Exchanges: Copenhagen New York
Ticker Symbol: TLD
NAIC: 517110 Wired Telecommunications Carriers;
515112 Radio Stations; 515210 Cable and Other
Subscription Programming; 517212 Cellular and Other
Wireless Telecommunications; 517910 Other
Telecommunications

TDC A/S—formerly Tele Danmark, itself created from the former state-owned telephone monopoly—is Denmark's top telecommunications provider, with more than three million fixed line subscribers and more than two million mobile telephone customers. In addition to its core telephony services, TDC is also the leading Danish Internet services provider, with more than 830,000 subscribers. In addition, the company is a leading provider of cable television services in Denmark, with nearly 900,000 subscribers. Yet since the early 2000s, TDC has been restructuring itself as an international telecommunications group—by 2004, more than 55 percent of the company's revenues come from outside of Denmark. For its international expansion, TDC has focused in large part on the mobile telephone sector in central and Eastern Europe, acquiring stakes in companies in Lithuania (Bité GSM), the Czech Republic (Ceske Radiokomunikace), Poland (Polkomtel), Hungary (Hungarian Telephone & Cable Corp.), and Austria (Connect Austria and one). Switzerland is the company's most important foreign market, where its TDC Switzerland subsidiary is that market's

second leading provider of mobile telephony, Internet, and other telecommunications services. In Germany, the company owns Talkline, the third largest mobile telephone company in that market, and TDC is also present in the Benelux market through its stake in Belgacom. TDC's restructured operations are now conducted under seven core divisions: TDC Tele Danmark; TDC Mobil International; TDC Switzerland; TDC Internet; TDC Cable TV; TDC Directories; and TDC Services. In 2003, TDC posted revenues of more than DKK 50 billion ($8.3 billion). SBC of the United States owns more than 41 percent of the publicly listed company.

Building the Danish Telecommunications Market in the 20th Century

Although the economies of the Scandinavian countries remained modest in the mid-19th century, the region proved highly receptive to newly developing technologies. In particular, the region was among the earliest adopters of the new telecommunications services, starting with the telegraph, invented in that era.

Denmark itself played an important role in the development of telecommunications technologies. In 1829, a Danish physicist, Christian Oestrad, had pioneered the principle of electromagnetism. Using a live electric wire, Oestrad was able to push the dial of a compass, proving that an electric current was capable of producing a magnetic field. The discovery, which in turn led to the use of magnetic fields to create electricity, became a cornerstone of the development of the telegraph and especially the telephone, patented by Alexander Graham Bell in 1875.

Bell's company soon began marketing its technology worldwide, but also began setting up its own telephone networks in a large number of foreign markets. Such was the case in Denmark, where Bell established the country's first telephone exchange in Copenhagen in 1881. Observers at the time looked on the telephone as a novelty destined primarily for the consumer market, yet the Bell company found its first customers chiefly among the business sector, connecting 22 subscribers that year.

By then, however, governments had begun to recognize the strategic importance of the new telecommunications technol-

Company Perspectives:

It is TDC's vision to be the best provider of communications solutions in Europe. TDC will strive to be a company that always provides excellent service, always offers new innovative and interesting services—and a company that always takes good care of its customers and offers outstanding customer care.

TDC is for people who want communications tools that work and will enrich their lives. Busy people do not necessarily want the very latest gadgets, but just proven technology that can help them manage their lives better.

That is why the companies in the TDC group bring all the latest communications technology together in a simple and reliable way.

ogy. Foreign ownership of the telephone networks was banned in many countries. In Denmark, the Bell company was placed under Danish ownership in 1882, and renamed as Kjøbenhavns Telefon-Aktieselskab (KTAS). That company remained focused building Copenhagen's telephone network. Meanwhile, a number of new, primarily local companies sprang up throughout the country. By the end of the century, Denmark already counted some 25,000 telephone subscribers.

The early years of the new century saw the adoption of the telephone intensify. By 1910, KTAS alone numbered nearly 50,000 subscribers—and reached 250,000 subscribers by the end of World War II. Like most European countries, the country's telephone sector was placed under government control following the PTT model—bundling the country's post office, telegraph, and telephone services into one central organization. Nonetheless, the telephone sector remained fragmented among a large number of local companies until the early 1950s.

Breaking the Model in the 1980s

At that time, the PTT moved to reorganize the telephone sector into three larger regional companies, including KTAS, Jydsk Telefon, and Fyns Telefon, while the PTT itself directly operated the telephone networks in Southern Jutland and the island of Møn. The PTT also became responsible for radio-based telecommunications, as well as radio and television transmission, and telegraph and international telephone connections.

The restructuring, coupled with the booming Danish economy in the postwar years, led to the increased penetration in the telecommunications sector. By the early 1960s, KTAS, the largest of the regional telephone groups, already boasted more than 500,000 subscribers, and topped the one million mark by the late 1970s.

In the mid-1980s, however, Denmark became one of the first of the European markets to begin the long deregulation and privatization process that was to last through much of the rest of the century. In 1986, the country took the unusual step of abandoning the PTT model. Instead, the government created a fourth regional telecommunications provider, Tele Sønderjylland. At the same time, a new company, Telecom A/S, was established to provide international telecommunications services.

Denmark's small size in the face of the impending internationalization of the European and global telecommunications markets led to a further restructuring of the country's telecom sector. While many countries were in the process of breaking up their domestic telecommunications monopolies, the Danish government instead appeared to take the opposite direction. In 1990, the government merged the four regional telecommunications companies, together with Telecom A/S, under a new umbrella entity, Tele Danmark.

At first acting as a holding company for its five subsidiaries, Tele Danmark quickly began a move toward direct control of the national telecommunications network. In 1991, Tele Danmark acquired Tele Sønderjylland and Fyuns Telefon. The company also took control of Telecom A/S at this time. The following year, Tele Danmark acquired full control of KTAS and Jydsk Telefon, both of which had already been partially privatized, as well.

Restructuring for the New Century

These moves paved the way to the first stage in Tele Danmark's privatization. In 1994, the Danish government launched a public offering of nearly 49 percent of Tele Danmark. The share issue, a large percentage of which was issued in the United States through American Depositary Receipts, raised more than DKK 18.5 billion ($3 billion), marking the world's largest international share issue at the time.

Following the public offering, Tele Danmark began to reorganize its operations ahead of the deregulation of the Danish market, scheduled for 1996, and in preparation for the completion of its privatization slated for later in the decade. The company now merged all of the former regional telephone companies, together with its other subsidiaries, including its growing Internet and data communication operations, under a single corporate entity, Tele Danmark.

With its home market opened for competition in 1996, Tele Danmark began looking elsewhere for growth. In 1996, the company joined in an investment group to acquire 49.9 percent of Belgium telecommunications company Belgacom. Tele Danmark's own stake in Belgacom came to 16.5 percent; partner Ameritech acquired 17.5 percent.

That deal set into motion a closer relationship with the U.S. telecom giant. In 1997, Tele Danmark and Ameritech agreed to form a strategic partnership as part of Ameritech's efforts to enter the European telecommunications market. As part of the agreement, Ameritech agreed to acquire an initial 34 percent stake in Tele Danmark, later raising its shareholding to nearly 42 percent.

Tele Danmark continued forging its own path into the European market, buying up German mobile telephone group Talkline, which grew into that market's third largest player. At the same time, Tele Danmark targeted growth in the central and Eastern European regions, buying up stakes in telecom—especially mobile telephone—and Internet companies in Lithuania, Hungary, Poland, the Czech Republic, and the Ukraine, as well as in Sweden.

Key Dates:

1881: The Bell company installed the first telephone exchange in Copenhagen, with 22 subscribers.

1882: The Copenhagen exchange is placed under Danish control and becomes Kjøbenhavns Telefon-Aktieselskab (KTAS).

1945: KTAS numbers 250,000 subscribers.

1950: PTT establishes control over the telephone market, regrouping local telephone companies into four regional telephone companies.

1986: PTT abandons control of the telephone market in the first step toward deregulation, creating Telecom A/S to take over international phone connections.

1990: Tele Danmark is created as a holding company for four regional telephone companies and Telecom A/S.

1992: Tele Danmark completes acquisitions of regional telephone companies.

1994: Tele Danmark is privatized with a public share offering, reducing the government's stake to 51 percent.

1995: Tele Danmark merges with its subsidiaries.

1996: The Danish telecommunications market is deregulated; Tele Danmark begins international expansion with the acquisition of a 16.5 percent stake in Belgacom.

1997: Tele Danmark and Ameritech form a strategic partnership, giving Ameritech a 34 percent (later 42 percent) stake in Tele Danmark.

1998: Tele Danmark acquires the remaining share from the Danish government, completing its privatization.

1999: SBC Communications becomes the primary shareholder after its merger with Ameritech.

2000: The company changes its name to TDC; the company acquires sunrise and diAx in Switzerland, which are merged to form the primary international subsidiary TDC Switzerland; the company completes a restructuring into the holding company TDC and seven primary subsidiaries.

2003: TDC announces its intention to sell off its stake in Belgacom; the company joins Deutsche Telekom in a bid for the Czech Republic's Radiokom.

2004: SBC announces its intention to sell off its stake in TDC as part of a pullout from the European market.

The partnership with Ameritech provided the company with the clout needed to take on its far larger competitors in France, Germany, the United Kingdom, and elsewhere. As the company's chairman told *Telecommunications Reports:* "In an international context we are small. The company has already actively and successfully participated in the highly competitive international telecom market on our own and in various partnerships. In that process the advantages of a strong and well-placed strategic partner have become clear."

With its growing success at penetrating the European market—particularly the development of a web of alliances, such as its partnership with Belgacom to launch a mobile telephone network in The Netherlands in 1998—Tele Danmark moved to complete its privatization. In January 1998, Tele Danmark bought out the majority control of its shares that had been held by the Danish government. The following year, Ameritech merged with SBC, forming SBC Communications, which now took over Ameritech's former stake in Tele Danmark.

Tele Danmark changed its name to TDC in 2000, a move that served to underscore its transformation from a small, domestic market-focused telephone monopoly into a full-fledged European telco with far-reaching international ambitions. Yet not all of TDC's expansion efforts came to fruition—its attempt to dominate the Scandinavian telecom market met with strong resistance from rivals Telia, Telenor, and Sonera.

More successful for the group was its entry into Switzerland in 2000, with the purchases of Internet and mobile telephony providers sunrise and diAx. These companies were then merged into a single operation, TDC Switzerland. Meantime, TDC had been engaged in a new restructuring of its operations, converting to a holding company overseeing seven primary subsidiaries, including TDC Teledanmark, TDC Mobile International, and the company's primary foreign subsidiary, TDC Switzerland.

Yet TDC remained a relatively minor player in the international market, despite backing from its primary shareholder SBC. Merger talks between Telia and TDC failed to find agreement in 2001, ending hopes for the company's participation in the emergence of a single Scandinavian telecom powerhouse. Instead, the company turned its focus more firmly on the central and Eastern European market, where the company acquired Austrian mobile telephone group one, and a stake in Poland's Polkomtel. The company also joined with Deutsche Telekom in 2003 in a bid to acquire control of the Czech Republic's Ceske Radiokomunikace, or Radiokom, the country's second largest telecom company. As part of that process, the company announced its interest in selling off its stake in Belgacom.

TDC emerged from the crisis affecting the global telecommunications sector in the early 2000s with solid operations. The company had transformed itself from a tiny domestic operation to a fast-growing international telco, with stakes in more than a dozen countries—including majority control of nearly a dozen major domestic players in the mobile telephone and Internet sectors. Yet TDC itself was widely seen as a candidate for acquisition by one of its larger rivals—a possibility that took on greater likelihood with SBC's announcement in late 2003 of its intention of pulling out of the European market. Nonetheless, for the near future at least, TDC expected to continue its drive to become a major player in its target markets.

Principal Subsidiaries

TDC Solutions; TDC Mobile International; TDC Switzerland; TDC Directories; TDC Cable TV.

Principal Competitors

Turk Telekomunikasyon End A.S.; Verizon Communications Inc.; Vivendi Universal S.A.; Vodafone Group Plc; France

Telecom S.A.; Deutsche Telekom AG; Telecom Italia S.p.A.; Telefonica S.A.; Telia AB.

Further Reading

''CEO of TDC A/S Says That It's Time for the Company to Grow,'' *Nordic Business Report*, January 15, 2004.

Criscione, Valeria, ''Warning for TeleDanmark,'' *Financial Times*, July 28, 2000, p. 31.

George, Nicholas, Valeria Criscione, and Claire MacCarthy, ''Telenor, Telia and TDC Vie for Top Dog Position,'' *Financial Times*, May 17, 2001, p. 33.

Koza, Patricia, ''DB, TDC's Buyout Plan Blocked,'' *Daily Deal*, September 17, 2003.

Ratner, Juliana, ''Telia Making Eyes at TeleDanmark,'' *Financial Times*, May 24, 2001, p. 28.

''TDC Wants to Dominate in North and Central Europe,'' *Europe-Media*, February 8, 2002.

—M.L. Cohen

Telecom Argentina S.A.

Alicia Moreau de Justo 50
Buenos Aires, C.F. C1107AAB
Argentina
Telephone: (54) (11) 4968-4000
Fax: (54) (11) 4313-5842
Web site: http://www.telecom.com.ar

Public Company
Incorporated: 1990
Employees: 11,157
Sales: ARS 3.75 billion ($1.26 billion) (2003)
Stock Exchanges: Bolsa de Comercio de Buenos Aires
    New York
Ticker Symbols: TECO; TEO
NAIC: 511140 Database and Directory Publishers;
    513310 Wired Telecommunications Carriers; 513322
    Cellular and Other Wireless Companies; 514191 On-
    Line Information Services

Telecom Argentina S.A. is one of the two enterprises that dominate telecommunications services in Argentina (the other being Telefónica de Argentina S.A. and its affiliated companies) and one of the nation's biggest businesses. It vies with Telefónica for leadership in fixed-line services, including local, long-distance, and international telephone service, and is the nation's leading operator in cellular telephone services and access to the Internet.

Serving Half of Argentina: 1990–95

A Belgian company and an American company provided the first commercial telephone service in Argentina in 1881. Both were acquired the following year by a British company that formed Unión Telefónica del Río de la Plata Ltd. This company merged with a British rival, Compania de Telefono Gower-Bell, in 1886. In 1929 it was acquired by the U.S.-based multinational International Telephone & Telegraph Corp. The Argentine government purchased Unión Telefónica in 1946 and renamed it Empresa Nacional de Telecomunicaciones (ENTel) in 1956, by

which time telephone service was virtually a government monopoly. Under government control ENTel was a deficit-ridden, poorly administered behemoth. By 1990 the bloated workforce of 47,000 had been under 28 chief executives in the last 30 years. People were waiting as long as 15 years to obtain a phone line, and installation cost as much as $1,500. One journalist called ENTel the most corrupt telephone company in the world, "served" by staffers who took bribes and kickbacks.

As part of a vast privatization program, 60 percent of ENTel was offered for sale in 1990 to private investors in two parts. One concession, serving southern Argentina, including 57 percent of the access lines in metropolitan Buenos Aires, was purchased by Telefónica de España S.A. The other, serving the northern part of the country and the remaining Buenos Aires lines, was sold to Nortel Inversora S.A., a consortium whose shareholders included the Italian telecommunications company Stet-Societá Finanziaria Telefónica S.p.A. (which later became Telecom Italia S.p.A.); France Telecom S.A.; the Perez Companc group, an Argentine holding company; and the U.S. investment bank J.P. Morgan & Co. Inc. Nortel paid $2.31 billion in government bonds and $100 million in cash for the concession. Another 30 percent was sold to public investors in 1992 on the Buenos Aires and New York stock exchanges for $1.23 billion, and the remaining 10 percent went to ENTel employees through a stock participation program.

The new company was named Telecom Argentina Stet-France Telecom S.A. The concession gave Telecom Argentina the exclusive right to provide basic public telephone service in its designated area for a period of seven years, with an extension of three years if terms and conditions were met. Stet and France Cables et Radio S.A., a subsidiary of France Telecom, were awarded the management contract. Prices were linked to the dollar by a regulatory agency, with periodic adjustments based on the U.S. consumer price inflation index.

Telecom Argentina adopted a five-year plan to spend $3.3 billion in order to achieve a 60 percent, 1.1 million increase in the existing lines (only one-ninth digitalized) in its concession area. The company had to revise the architecture of the network because of apparent sabotage by employees who opposed privatization. It reduced employment from 19,234 to 16,101 in its

Company Perspectives:

The strategies and politics of the distinct companies of the Group are aligned in order to generate a synergy both in business matters and in the development of network technology.

first 13 months of operation (and 9,275 by late 1999) and increased productivity by 18 percent in that time. By 1994 some 300,000 new lines had been connected and even more replaced, raising the proportion of digitalized lines to more than half of the total. Demand for new lines remained heavy, with the waiting list totaling 215,000 by the end of 1993. Telecom and Telefónica were equal partners in three other companies: Telintar, which had a monopoly on international long-distance calls; Startel S.A. for domestic value-added services such as telex, telegraph, videoconferencing, data transmission (including Internet service), and ship-to-shore radio communication; and Movistar (later Miniphone S.A.) for cellular mobile telephone and paging services. Telintar installed the first optic fiber cable in Latin America.

Further Progress: 1995–2000

After several years of double-digit earnings growth, both Telecom Argentina and Telefónica de Argentina developed problems in the mid-1990s. The companies had met unfulfilled demand for new lines and were slashing fees to connect poor people and those living in sparsely settled rural areas. The most profitable part of their business, long-distance services, was meeting competition from credit cards issued by foreign telephone companies and U.S.-based providers offering call-back for overseas calls. Telecom downgraded its commitment to Movistar, the joint cellular company, by establishing Telecom Personal S.A. to operate this mobile service in its concession area. By late 1998 Telecom Personal had signed up 490,000 customers—64 percent of the Argentine market. As with the parent company's fixed lines, however, the growth in cellular customers was reaching a point of diminishing returns, especially in view of competition from CTI Holdings, S.A., the Argentine subsidiary of Verizon Communications Inc., and Moviecom, another rival formed by a consortium led by Bell-South Corp. To keep its impetus, Telecom Personal purchased 75 percent of a new company competing for such service in neighboring Paraguay.

These problems did not keep Telecom Argentina from increasing its revenues 37 percent and its profit 44 percent between 1996 and 1998. By 1997 it had connected 1.3 million new customers and 800 remote areas, installed 22,000 public telephones, laid more than 4,000 kilometers (2,485 miles) of optic fiber, and digitalized 95.6 percent of its network. It also offered a state-of-the-art special support service for businesses and a "smart network" incorporating such features as call credit, universal number, and virtual private networking. By late 1999 the number of lines in service had grown from the original 1.4 million to 3.4 million. The company, which also restructured its organization into autonomous business units, recorded double-digit profits on sales every year between 1992 and 1999.

Foreign investors, who originally paid top dollar for Telecom Argentina and Telefónica de Argentina shares, tended to consider the latter to be the stronger company because it was controlled by a single parent rather than a consortium and because of slightly larger market share. This was reflected in the higher price for Telefónica stock. By 1998, however, Telecom was the favored company, because it was perceived to have remained on firmer ground; Telefónica, by contrast, was spending money to enter the highly competitive field of cable television. In addition, projecting forward into the era of fixed-line competition, analysts saw Telecom as better placed than its rival. Because its concession took in the central business district of Buenos Aires, Telefónica held three-quarters of the corporate market, meaning it had more to lose from competition. In addition, many of this company's other large customers were on the frontier with Telecom, while Telecom's customers in industrial and commercial centers such as Córdoba, Rosario, and Santa Fé were far from Telefónica's base in southern Argentina.

Shortly before the Telecom Argentina and Telefónica de Argentina concessions were due to lapse in October 1999, Telecom was serving 3.2 million telephones, fully digital and based on the most advanced technologies. Telecom Personal obtained licenses to compete for cellular business not only in Buenos Aires—thereby dissolving Miniphone—but also in Telefónica's bailiwick, southern Argentina. Telintar also was dissolved, with Telecom establishing a new subsidiary, Telecom Internacional S.A., to handle international long-distance calls. At the end of 1999 Startel was dissolved, and Telecom Internet S.A. was established. The consortium that held the majority stake in Nortel Inversora now consisted only of Telecom Italia and France Telecom, Perez Companc and J.P. Morgan having agreed in July 1999 to sell their shares for EUR 522 million (about $530 million).

To survive in the new millennium of competition, Telecom Argentina pledged to invest $4.3 billion in the next five years. It was planning not only to lure big corporate customers away from Telefónica but to attract smaller subscribers unable to invest in large networks by offering to link up personal computers with software and connections for $300 a month per workstation. Data communications, including Internet, was providing Telecom with only 3 percent of its revenues, but the company was hoping to win more customers by updating its technology to yield faster connections. (Telecom Internet was absorbed by the parent company in 2001.)

Tougher Road in the New Millennium

As the Argentine recession that began in 1998 deepened, Telecom Argentina suffered reduced earnings. Rates fell because of deregulation, and customers tightened their belts, especially when it came to mobile phones. In 2001 the company tried to reduce its costs by about 4 to 5 percent, or about $85 million, partly by laying off employees. Like most large Argentine companies, Telecom had assumed its debt mostly in dollars, and when, in early 2002, the government found itself unable to maintain its currency—the peso—on a par with the dollar, the value of the peso fell below 30 cents, and dollar-denominated debts ballooned correspondingly. Telecom Argentina suspended payments on its debt of about $3.2 billion in April 2002, putting the company into default. Its losses

Key Dates:

1990: Telecom is founded to provide telephone service in the northern half of Argentina.
1994: Telecom Argentina has connected 300,000 new telephone lines since its inception.
1997: The company has digitalized nearly 96 percent of its network.
1998: Telecom Personal has signed up 490,000 customers for its cellular service.
1999: Telecom Argentina's 3.2 million fixed telephone lines are fully digitalized.
2002: Following devaluation, the company defaults on its debts by suspending payments.
2003: France Telecom sells its stake in the company to a private Argentine group.

mounted because, while the inflation rate was 41 percent in 2002, the government would not allow utilities to raise their rates. Telecom incurred a loss of ARS 4.39 billion ($1.38 billion) in 2002.

While Telefónica de Argentina's Spanish parent put up enough cash to keep its subsidiary from defaulting on its debts, Telecom Argentina's French and Italian partners were squabbling among themselves and not inclined to invest a single peso to save the enterprise. Instead they—along with a dozen or so other multinational companies—sought compensation for an alleged breach of bilateral investment treaties before a special panel of the World Bank. France Telecom sources said the action was intended to allow Telecom Argentina to increase its rates in order to catch up with inflation. The claims presented by the partners, along with those made by Telefónica, could cost the Argentine government as much as $17 billion, according to one source.

But in September 2003 France Telecom shed its half-interest in Nortel Inversora, selling it to W de Argentina–Inversiones S.L. for $125 million. W de Argentina was owned by the Wertheim Group, a leading Argentine investment company. According to the terms, France Telecom and Telecom Italia (through subsidiaries) would contribute their shares of common stock in Nortel Inversora (totaling 67.8 percent) to a company created for this purpose, Sofora Telecomunicaciones S.A. The France Telecom subsidiaries would then sell 48 percent of this company's share capital to W de Argentina, along with an option for the purchase of the remaining 2 percent, exercisable between 2008 and 2013. Telecom Italia became the new exclusive operator of Telecom Argentina, in which Nortel continued to hold a 54.74 percent stake. The company's name was shortened to Telecom Argentina S.A.

Telecom Argentina was able to report positive results for 2003, earning a net profit of ARS 351 million ($118 million) on net sales of ARS 3.75 billion ($1.26 billion). Of its net sales, voice, data, and Internet transmission accounted for 68 percent, cellular for 31 percent, and its printing and publishing subsidiary for telephone directories and other such material, along with the sale of advertising in these publications, for 1 percent. Telecom's debt was just short of ARS 10 billion ($3.2 billion) at the end of 2003. The company had about 3.2 million fixed-line subscribers at the end of 2002, some 2.2 million wireless subscribers in Argentina (and 519,000 in Paraguay), about 177,000 Internet subscribers (36 percent of the Argentine market), and 79,812 pay telephones.

Principal Subsidiaries

Nucleo, S.A. (Paraguay; 67.5%); Publicom S.A.; Telecom Argentina USA Inc.; Telecom Personal S.A.

Principal Competitors

CTI Movil; Movicom Bell South; Telefónica de Argentina S.A.

Further Reading

Abeles, Martin, et al., *El oligopólio telefónico argentino frente a la liberalización del mercado,* Bernal, Buenos Aires: Universidad Nacional de Quilmes Ediciones, 2001.

Bachelet, Pablo, "El día después," *America economía,* October 21, 1999, pp. 32–34.

Doman, Matthew, "Trying to Come in Line with Foreign Callers," *Financial Times,* September 20, 1995, p. 33.

Druckerman, Pamela, "Telecom Argentina Plans to Suspend Debt Payments," *Wall Street Journal,* April 3, 2002, pp. A16, A18.

"France Telecom and Telecom Italia Increase Stake in Telecom Argentina," *Cambridge Television Report,* August 2, 1999.

Friedland, Jonathan, "Many Are Called to Argentina's Phone Stocks But Gains May Be Fewer Than Risks Involved," *Wall Street Journal,* September 25, 1995, p. C2.

"Goldman Helps France Telecom Sell Latam Stakes," *Financial News,* September 9, 2003.

Henni, Jamal, "Telecoms Groups Push for Redress in Argentina," *Financial Times,* July 18, 2003, p. 31.

Hickman, Matthew, "Telecom Argentina," *LatinFinance,* January/February 1994, pp. 74–75.

Hudson, Peter, "El discreto encanto de Telecom," *América economía,* May 7, 1998, p. 29.

——, "Y ahora, qué?," *América economía,* December 31, 1998, pp. 27, 30.

Krauss, Clifford, "Argentina to Hasten End of Phone Monopoly," *New York Times,* March 11, 1998, p. D4.

Luxner, Larry, "Argentine telco sale causes uproar," *Telephony,* April 23, 1990, pp. 9–10.

Moyano, Julio, ed., *The Argentine Economy,* Buenos Aires: J. Moyano Communicaciones, 1997, pp. 426–27.

Smith, Joanne C., "Telecom Argentina," *LatinFinance,* April 1992, pp. 66–67.

Voorhees, Richard, "Out of Step," *LatinFinance,* September 1992, pp. 66–67.

—Robert Halasz

Telecom Italia Mobile S.p.A.

Via Luigi Rizzo 22
Roma
I-00136
Italy
Telephone: +39 06 39001
Fax: +39 06 39002111
Web site: http://www.tim.it

Public Company
Incorporated: 1995
Employees: 12,000
Sales: EUR 11.78 billion ($9 billion) (2003)
Stock Exchanges: Borsa Italiana
Ticker Symbol: TIT
NAIC: 517212 Cellular and Other Wireless Telecommunications; 334220 Radio and Television Broadcasting and Wireless Communications Equipment Manufacturing

Telecom Italia Mobile S.p.A., or TIM, is not only Italy's leading mobile communications company—with more than 26 million lines in Italy alone, it is also the largest mobile telecommunications group in Europe. In Italy, the company remains the dominant mobile player, in a market that, with more than 97 percent penetration, has achieved one of the world's highest subscriber rates in the world. Yet TIM has positioned itself as an international mobile telephony provider, targeting in particular the Mediterranean basin and the South American markets. The company's foreign operations are focused especially on Brazil, where the company holds stakes in Brasil Telecom and two other mobile telephone providers, as well as its own mobile telephone license for a 16-state area. Other South American markets for the company include Venezuela, Chile, and Peru. In Europe, TIM holds more than 81 percent of Stet Hellas, which won one of Greece's high-speed UTMS licenses. In 2003, TIM merged its share of the IsTIM joint venture with Turk Telecom's Aycell, giving it 20 percent of one of Turkey's largest mobile telephone companies. TIM is also present in the Czech Republic. TIM's international operation adds nearly 20 million more subscriber lines to its customer base. The company has

joined The Netherlands' KPN and Japan's NTT DoCoMo, to roll out the DoCoMo mobile Internet platform. At the same time, TIM is part of a pan-European alliance, including Orange, T-Mobile, and Telefonica Moviles, which together controls more than 170 million subscriber lines throughout Europe.

Mobile Telephone Spinoff in the Mid-1990s

The problems that long plagued the Italian fixed-line telephone sector prepared the country for the mobile telephone revolution of the 1990s. After decades of industry fragmentation, lagging technology, high taxes, government corruption, and anemic investment, the Italian phone system was in disarray. For much of its history, the Italian telephone sector had been dominated by the STET (Societa Italiana L Esercizio Telecom), established by the Mussolini government in the 1930s.

STET had grown into a vast conglomerate during the 1960s and 1970s, with operations from telecommunications to satellite and data communications. The state-owned company later developed into a five-headed organization: SIP, which controlled domestic telecommunications; Iritel, which handled long-distance services; Italcable, which controlled international long-distance connections; Telespazio, governing satellite communications; and SIRM, for maritime communications. STET itself came under control of the Institute for Industrial Reconstruction, the government-run organization that controlled most of Italy's industrial economy.

In the late 1980s and early 1990s, most of Europe began preparing for the abolition of trade barriers within the European Union (EU), slated for 1992, and the ultimate emergence of a single monetary unit, the euro, scheduled to be completed in 2001. The liberalization of a number of sectors, including the energy, utility, and telecommunications markets, formed a key feature of the trade reforms enacted by the EU. Telecommunications, viewed as a strategic industry, had long been dominated by government-run monopolies in each market. Yet by the mid-1990s, nearly all European countries had begun the process of privatization and deregulation.

Italy's planned telecommunications deregulation became mired in a series of delays, but finally resulted in the merger of

Key Dates:

1990: SIP, the Italian government-owned domestic telephone monopoly, launches mobile telephone services.

1995: Telecom Italia Mobile is spun off as a public company from the newly formed Telecom Italia; GSM technology is launched in Italy.

1997: SMS service is launched.

1999: The company integrates its own network into the European GSM system.

2000: The company forms IsTIM in Turkey, which acquires a mobile telephone license; the company acquires a Greek UTMS license through its stake in Stet Hellas; the company acquires a controlling stake in Digitel in Venezuela.

2001: The company launches cellular phone service in Peru; the company gains a major position in the Brazilian market through the purchase of two licenses, including one covering Sao Paulo state.

2002: The company begins national coverage in Brazil.

2003: The company acquires Blu, the holder of Italy's fourth mobile telephone license.

2004: The company agrees to merge IsTIM with Turk Telekom's Aycell.

the five state-owned telecommunications companies operated by STET into a new, unified body, Telecom Italia. That company nonetheless retained its near-monopoly on the country's telecommunications network. In particular, Telecom Italia controlled all of the country's mobile telephone network.

Italy had begun developing its mobile telephone services in the early 1990s. That service, run by SIP, had been launched in 1990. Based on the TACS analogue network, the mobile telephone service benefited from the widespread problems in the fixed-line sector—where long waiting times for telephone lines, high prices, and intermittent service remained problems into the 1990s. Whereas mobile telephony operations represented a relatively minor part of most markets, serving chiefly the corporate sector, the Italian market proved fertile ground for its early and massive adoption. At the same time, the company recognized the need for competitive rates. Already in 1993, the company launched an innovative Family rate.

Telecom Italia spun off its fast-growing mobile telephone business as a separate, publicly listed company in 1995, reducing its holding to just 60 percent. The new company, Telecom Italia Mobile, or TIM, retained a near monopoly on the Italian mobile telephone market. Indeed, into the middle of the decade, the sector had operated without even a licensing system, remaining entirely controlled by the government's telecommunications company. Complaints about the government's monopolistic policies led to the opening of the market in the later part of the decade, with the country's first nongovernment mobile telephone license granted to Olivetti subsidiary Omnitel Pronto Italia.

By then, the European Market countries had agreed on a new mobile telephony standard, GSM, in an effort to create a single European-wide technology standard. TIM adopted the GSM standard in 1995. The improvements in technology offered by the new standards were to lead to the first great boom in consumer demand across Europe at the end of the decade. TIM's large subscriber base placed Italy at the forefront of this trend. The success of the new digital standard—which enabled, among other features, a drastic reduction in the size of the telephone units themselves—was particularly evident in the mobile telephony penetration rate across Italy. By the turn of the century, more than 90 percent of the consumer market already owned a mobile telephone.

TIM continued to innovate into the dawn of the 21st century. In 1996, the company launched a new prepaid, rechargeable phone card. The new service was an instant hit, winning over the large consumer segment that had been unwilling or unable to commit to a subscription-based service. Less than six months later, the company had already sold more than one million cards. From 5.7 million subscribers at the end of 1996, the company's base leapt to more than nine million by the end of 1997, making it Europe's largest mobile telephone operator.

International Mobile Telephony Leader in the 21st Century

By the end of 1998, TIM counted more than 14 million subscriber lines under its control. The company had managed to head off competition from Omnitel Pronto, which launched its own service at the beginning of 1997, in part by launching new high-use pricing packages. The company also continued to innovate, such as its launch of short messaging service (SMS) capability in 1997. That technology, akin to e-mail, quickly became a primary driving force behind cellular phone adoption. At the same time, the company benefited from the delay in awarding a third mobile telephone license (later awarded to WIND).

TIM began preparing for the highly touted next generation of mobile telephones at the end of the 1990s. The company began implementing services based on WAP (Wireless Access Protocol) technology, offering a limited form of Internet access through telephone handsets, in 1999. The following year, TIM won one of Italy's high-speed UTMS licenses, and began preparing its own rollout of the so-called 3G technology.

While parent Telecom Italia was battling—ultimately unsuccessfully—the hostile takeover attempt by Olivetti, TIM began plotting its future expansion. With its growth in Italy more or less assured—the company topped 26 million subscriber lines at home in 2003—TIM's attention turned to the international market. In 1999, the company integrated its own network into the European mobile system, and the company began seeking alliances with other European groups. As part of that effort, also, TIM began acquiring minority stakes in a number of European companies, such as Bouygues in France, Auna in Spain, and Mobilkom in Austria (Mobilkom).

One of TIM's main expansion targets became the Mediterranean basin. In 2000, the company joined with Turkish bank Isbank to win a mobile phone license for that country. The partners then launched the IsTIM mobile phone service. The company also entered Greece, taking a stake in Stet Hellas, backing its bid for a UTMS license there. TIM continued to increase its stake in Stet Hellas, acquiring more than 80 percent by the end of 2003.

In the meantime, the company had turned its attention to the fast-growing South American market, then actively undergoing its own deregulation process at the beginning of the 21st century. In late 2000, TIM bought a controlling share of Venezuela's Digitel, the country's third largest mobile phone provider. Although Digitel had just 110,000 subscribers, its coverage area included Caracas, giving TIM access to expansion in the capital city. The company then began negotiating for stakes in two other regional mobile phone operators in order to establish a national footprint in Venezuela.

TIM now focused on the lucrative Brazilian market, acquiring a license to launch a mobile service in two southern states. That service, called Tele Celular Sul, came online by the end of 2000. By the beginning of 2001, TIM decided to move more aggressively into the Brazilian market. In February of that year, TIM paid BRL 1.5 billion ($778 million) to acquire two regional licenses covering 15 states—including the highly prized Sao Paulo state. As part of that agreement, TIM agreed to sell off Tele Celular Sul. Instead, the company announced its intention to spend as much as BRL 3 billion ($1.5 billion) implementing its two new mobile networks.

TIM continued building out its Brazilian operations, and in 2002 the company began offering national coverage. The company meanwhile had continued its South American expansion, launching mobile services in Peru in 2001. By the end of its first full year, the company had succeeded in attracting nearly 200,000 customers—a number that passed 500,000 in 2003. TIM stepped up its investment in that market, achieving national penetration by the beginning of 2004.

By then, TIM had revised its growth strategy, focusing on the Mediterranean and South American markets. As such, the company sold off its minority stakes in Europe, and instead concentrated on forming strategic alliances with other major telecommunications players. As part of that effort, TIM joined an alliance with The Netherlands' KPN Telecom and Japan's NTT DoCoMo to roll out NTT's third-generation DoCoMo service in Europe. The company also joined with Orange, T-Mobile, and Telefonica Moviles, in an alliance that together controlled more than 170 million subscriber lines throughout Europe.

Rollout of UTMS service hit a snag across Europe as the telecommunications market collapsed in the early 2000s. Nonetheless, TIM maintained its level of investment, and despite setbacks—including postponing its launch for more than a year—the company became one of the first to implement the new high-speed system in a soft launch at the end of 2003. Although the full-scale launch was slated only for 2004, TIM provided a taste of the mobile telephony market of the future when it debuted a live television service adapted to the tiny mobile telephone screen in October 2003.

Meanwhile, TIM continued its expansion. In 2003, the company took control of Italy's Blu, the failing holder of the country's fourth mobile telephone license. At the beginning of 2004, TIM increased its position in Turkey, when it agreed to merge IsTIM with Turk Telekom's Aycell. Following the merger, TIM's share of the new company, trading under the Aria and Aycell brands, stood at 40 percent. The merger added some 4.5 million customers to TIM's international base of 43 million. Now the world's largest mobile telephone provider, TIM had taken the industry driver's seat at the beginning of the 21st century.

Principal Subsidiaries

Tele Celular Sul Participaçoes S.A. (Brazil).

Principal Competitors

Verizon Communications Inc.; Siemens AG; Sumitomo Corporation; Turk Telekomunikasyon End A.S.; Vivendi Universal S.A.; France Telecom S.A.; SBC Communications Inc.; Telefonica S.A.

Further Reading

Boulton, Leyla, "IsTIM to Merge with Aycell," *Financial Times,* May 14, 2003, p. 32.

Budden, Robert, "TIM to Push Ahead with 3G Launch in Italy," *Financial Times,* November 6, 2002, p. 29.

Colitt, Raymond, "TIM Wins Brazilian Mobile License," *Financial Times,* March 14, 2001, p. 18.

"Italy's TIM Says Merger Has Been Completed Involving GSM Operator in Turkey," *America's Intelligence Wire,* February 20, 2004.

Nicholson, Christopher, "Telecom Italia Readies for Cellular Expansion in Brazil," *LatinFinance,* October 2002, p. 8.

Proctor, Darrell, "Live TV Comes to Cell Phones," *Rocky Mountain News,* October 6, 2003, p. 2B.

Sylvers, Eric, "Player in Cellular Phone Market in Europe Predicts Consolidation," *New York Times,* April 8, 2003, p. W1.

"Telecom Italia Media Once Again Outshines the Rest," *Irish Times,* September 18, 2003, p. 18

"TIM Stands Alone As Results Jump," *Utility Week,* September 12, 2003, p. 11.

—M.L. Cohen

Telefonos de Mexico S.A. de C.V.

Parque Via 198
Col. Cuauhtemoc
Mexico City, DF 06599
Mexico
Telephone: 52-55-5703-3990
Fax: 52-55-5545-5550
Web site: http://www.telmex.com.mx

Public Company
Founded: 1947
Employees: 63,775
Sales: $10.4 billion (2003)
Stock Exchanges: New York Bolsa Mexicana de Valores
*Ticker Symbol*s: TMX; TELMEX
NAIC: 517212 Cellular and Other Wireless
    Telecommunications; 517310 Telecommunications
    Resellers; 517211 Paging; 517110 Wired
    Telecommunications Carriers

Telefonos de Mexico S.A. de C.V. (Telmex) is one of the largest companies in Mexico. It provides local and long-distance telecommunication services throughout Mexico and abroad to both residential and commercial customers. Telmex operated as a government-owned utility until the early 1990s, when the Mexican government began to privatize the organization. Under private ownership, Telmex was rapidly expanding and improving going into the mid-1990s.

Merger Creates Telecommunications Ownership for Mexico

Telefonos de Mexico was created in 1947 to purchase two telephone companies that were operating in Mexico: L.M. Ericsson, of Sweden, and the U.S.-based International Telegraph Corporation. Both companies had pioneered the telephone industry in Mexico and had succeeded in bringing basic services to larger cities in Mexico. Telmex was created to make the dominant phone service provider in Mexico a domestic company. The newly created organization acquired the Mexican division of L.M. Ericsson in 1947 before buying the Mexi-

can subsidiary of International Telegraph in 1950. In effect, the merger gave Telmex a monopoly on the long-distance telephone industry in Mexico, although a number of smaller phone companies continued to provide local services. L.M. Ericsson and International Telephone managers continued to operate the Mexican enterprise.

From the start, the Mexican telephone service industry, like telephone industries in most other countries, was heavily influenced by the national government. That influence intensified during the 1950s and 1960s when the government decided that it needed to push the development of a national phone system that would keep Mexico from falling too far behind the United States and Europe in communications capabilities. Importantly, in the 1960s the government imposed a telephone service tax on all long-distance calls. The money was earmarked for investment in the telephone sector, namely to help supply the billions of dollars needed to add telephone lines and switching stations throughout the country. Thus, throughout the 1950s and 1960s Telmex operated as a private enterprise that cooperated with the Mexican government to deliver phone services to the nation.

Under Government Control: 1970s

The Mexican government's role at Telmex continued to expand until 1972, when Mexico actually took control of the enterprise by purchasing 51 percent of Telmex's voting shares; the remainder of the shares in the company were owned by Mexican citizens and institutions as well as foreigners. From that point forward, Telmex in effect operated as a government-owned utility. The government regulated the prices that the company could charge, influenced its operating budget, and made other management decisions. However, Telmex still maintained some of its private-company flavor; government appointees shared seats on Telmex's board with private individuals, and the government even retained most of Telmex's management after it took control of the company.

Throughout most of the 1970s Telmex operated much as it had as a private company. The chief executive of the company, a highly respected manager, served as head of Telmex throughout the 1970s and even during most of the 1980s. For much of that time, Telmex expanded its services at a rate of approxi-

Company Perspectives:

Since its privatization in 1990, TELMEX has risen to become Latin America's telecommunications leader.

mately 6 percent annually. At the same time, older parts of the system were gradually modernized. By 1980, close to 100 percent of Telmex's exchanges were automatic (not controlled by an operator), and the company was preparing to launch an ambitious plan to install only digital, rather than electromechanical, lines. Furthermore, Mexico's telephone service in comparison to other developing nations at the time ranked well in such categories as average number of inoperable lines or amount of time required to install a new line.

Telmex also performed well in comparison to other state-owned companies in Mexico during the 1970s and early 1980s, largely because it was still partly a private company. At the same time, Telmex began to suffer from many of the problems that afflicted other state enterprises, including political interference, inefficiency, labor union strength, and fiscal mismanagement. Indeed, although the utility had expanded service at a rate of about 6 percent annually, it could have grown at a much faster clip. A prime example of the problems the company faced was the telephone service tax that had been created in the 1960s. Over the years the government had raised the long-distance tax at a dizzying pace to the point that more than 50 percent of Telmex's revenues were eventually coming from the tax. At the same time, the government began drawing from the funds generated by the surcharge to pay for unrelated government programs. The unfortunate result was that Telmex, by the 1980s, had become a financing vehicle for the Mexican government.

Telmex Service Under Scrutiny: 1980s

The effects of bureaucratic influence at Telmex were undeniable by the mid-1980s. The company's overpaid workforce had become bloated, yet service was barely improving. Although the Mexican telephone network compared positively with phone systems in Venezuela, Argentina, or Indonesia, for example, its performance was dismal when compared to the systems in the United States, the European Community, and other wealthy regions. A customer that requested a telephone line from Telmex had to wait, on average, about three years for a hookup. That compared to eight years in Venezuela, but just a few days in the United States, Japan, and most of Europe. In addition, the hookup fee for a single business line could cost $500 or more. Furthermore, at any one time about 10 percent of all the phone lines in Mexico were out of service. To make matters worse, the government had been increasing long-distance prices (through the tax) at a rapid pace, to the point where the cost of a call had become prohibitive for many customers.

Telmex's problems reflected lackluster national leadership. Between 1976 and 1982, for example, Mexico suffered under the inept direction of the Jose Lopez Portillo administration. Telmex remained profitable and always paid dividends because it was protected by the state, but it fell behind during the early 1980s in adopting such key technologies as toll-free service and

fiber optic transmission. Portillo was removed in 1982 and was followed by the Miguel de la Madrid administration. Madrid, realizing the urgency of the situation, took several drastic steps to improve the economy and decrease the nation's debt. Among his initiatives was a program designed to privatize many of Mexico's 1,155 state-owned enterprises, one of the largest of which was Telmex.

Both Mexico's economy and Telmex improved under the new administration. For instance, between the early and late 1980s the percentage of phone lines that were digital increased from zero to more than 20 percent. Toll-free 800 service was added in the late 1980s and even extended to calls to and from the United States. Throughout the period, Telmex continued to post profits and to pay dividends on its stock. At the same time, however, long-distance rates continued to rise. By the late 1980s a seven-minute phone call to the United States, for example, cost about $10. By that time the telephone tax was making up 60 percent of all of Telmex's revenues, and about half of the total tax proceeds were being consumed for other government programs. Furthermore, Telmex's powerful labor unions remained entrenched, making for an increasingly bloated and inefficient company.

Improving Service in the Early 1990s

The turning point for Telmex came in the early 1990s, shortly after Carlos Salinas was elected president of Mexico. Salinas had worked for the previous administration as the secretary of budget and planning, during which time he also served as government director on the board of Telmex. Salinas had supported the privatization program that had reduced the number of state-owned companies by more than half by the time he took office in the late 1980s. However, Salinas believed that Mexico was in need of much more radical economic changes. To that end, he announced plans in 1989 to make Telmex a private company again. The plan was to get Telmex operating on its own and then gradually allow other companies to begin competing for long-distance customers.

The reasons behind Salinas's decision to take Telmex private were multifold. Importantly, by privatizing giant Telmex soon after being elected, he would be sending a message to the global investment community that Mexico was serious about making its economy more competitive and free. A second reason for privatizing Telmex was to increase its efficiency. Indeed, having served on the company's board, Salinas knew that Telmex's potential for growth and profit were enormous but were being hampered by politics. By freeing the company from political strings, he hoped to markedly improve Telmex's performance and to enhance the country's communication infrastructure. Finally, Salinas knew that the sale of the government's 51 percent voting share—it represented about 20 percent of the company's total equity—could help cut Mexico's debt by as much as $2 billion.

Mexico began decentralizing the bureaucratic Telmex organization in 1989, in preparation for privatization. Then, in 1990, Telmex began accepting bids from investors who wanted to purchase the 20 percent equity stake in Telmex. Easily winning the bid contest was a consortium of three companies that, by outbidding their closest rival by more than $70 million, purchased the

Key Dates:

1947: Telefonos de Mexico (Telmex) is created.

1972: The Mexican government purchases 51 percent of Telmex's voting shares, taking control of the company.

1990: Telmex is sold to a consortium of three companies—Southwestern Bell, France Telecom, and Mexico's Grupo Carso—and becomes privatized.

1995: Telmex launches the TELCARD, a prepaid calling card.

1997: The company loses its monopoly over Mexico's long-distance phone market.

1998: The company acquires 18.9 percent of the capital stock of Prodigy Communications Corporation and over 55 percent of Topp Telecom.

2002: SBC sells off 0.6 percent of its 8.1 percent stake in Telmex.

2004: Carlos Slim Helu steps down as CEO, handing the reins to his son, Carlos Slim Domit.

controlling interest in Telmex for $1.76 billion. The three partners were Southwestern Bell (of the United States), France Telecom, and Mexico's Grupo Carso. Grupo Carso put up half of the $1.76 billion and received a leading 10 percent equity stake in Telmex, while its partners financed the other half and shared the other 10 percent interest. The group agreed that Grupo Carso would have operating control of the company, Southwestern Bell would be responsible for improving operations and developing paging and cellular divisions, and France Telecom would concentrate on line expansion and modernization.

The head of Grupo Carso, Carlos Helu ("Slim"), headed Telmex's new management team. After hearing about the privatization plan in 1989, Slim had approached executives at Southwestern Bell and France Telecom about teaming up to get control of Telmex. He reasoned that those two companies had the technological and management tools necessary to whip Telmex into shape and he had the political and economic clout. Indeed, at the time of the buyout, Slim's Grupo Carso was Mexico's sixth largest company, with a market value of about $2.4 billion and only $300 million in long-term debt. Known as unassuming and publicity shy, the 50-year-old Slim had amassed a $1.9 billion personal fortune through his varied interests in mining, manufacturing, paper products, retailing, insurance, tourism, and other businesses. Incredibly, Slim, the son of a Lebanese immigrant, had started a small construction company that he built into the Grupo Carso empire.

When Telmex went private it was generating net profits of about $1.1 billion from sales of roughly $3.8 billion. Despite those impressive numbers, the government-supported monopoly was in serious need of repair. There were only six lines for every 100 Mexican citizens, for example, which compared to more than 50 lines per 100 citizens in the United States. More than 1.5 million people were on a waiting list to get service, and the typical wait was at least 18 months. The company was only generating revenues of about $400 per line (compared to nearly twice that in the United States). Furthermore, about 10 percent

of Telmex's lines were inoperable on a regular basis, despite a bloated workforce by world telephone industry standards.

As part of the purchase agreement between the Grupo Carso consortium and the Mexican government, the new controllers of Telmex had to agree to rapidly increase and improve long-distance telephone service in Mexico. Specifically, the government designed a three-year plan for improvement that began in 1991 and directed Telmex to install about 8,500 miles of fiber optic lines, replace 500,000 electromechanical lines with digital analog technology, bring phone service into all rural towns with a population of more than 500, and significantly reduce the waiting time to get new service installed. Furthermore, by 1996 Telmex was expected to interconnect with other carriers offering long-distance service, which would open the door for long-distance competition.

Telmex made significant progress toward its goals during the early 1990s. By late 1994, in fact, Telmex had replaced most of its obsolete lines and had converted old switching systems to 75 percent digital switching, one of the highest levels in the world. Furthermore, between 1992 and 1994 the company managed to increase the number of phone lines on its network at an average annual rate of 12.6 percent, bringing the number of phone lines per 100 citizens to ten. As a result, Telmex's sales rose to about $6.6 billion in 1992 before jumping to $7.9 billion in 1993. Although revenues declined to about $6 billion in 1994, the company netted income of about $1.6 billion. About 45 percent of Telmex's revenues came from local services, with the other portion attributable to domestic long-distance and international calls. Furthermore, Telmex invested about $2.3 billion in its phone system in 1994 as part of an ongoing drive to improve service and prepare for competition in the long-distance market, which was scheduled to commence in 1997.

Troubled Times for Telmex: Mid-1990s

In 1995 Telmex added 308,509 lines in service to total 8.8 million lines, a 3.6 percent increase over 1994. Additionally, they launched the prepaid calling card TELCARD, as well as various digital services. But even as both domestic and international long distance traffic improved since 1994, by 8 percent and 15 percent, respectively, total revenues for the year dropped from approximately $8.8 billion to $8.2 billion. Net income suffered a greater percentage loss, over 22 percent, from roughly $2.4 billion to $1.85 billion. Increasing competition, which was being pushed by the government, largely accounted for the drop. Still, Telmex, which held a monopoly in long-distance service lines, had the clear competitive advantage. In order for other telephone companies to offer long-distance service in Mexico, they were required to pay Telmex an interconnection fee. But the structure would soon change, as the Mexican government was making steps to eliminate Telmex's monopoly on the market. Still, Telmex's innovations continued and by 1995, Telmex's first 120 cellular public telephones had been installed within Mexico City and its main highways.

Revenues and net income dropped slightly further in 1996, and then again in 1997. To increase revenue flow, Telmex placed new advertising media on its Ladatel "Smart Cards." Meanwhile, after Telmex and its eight competitors failed to reach an agreement concerning the interconnection fee, the federal government stepped in to do so. The final decision decreased the fee so that competitors would pay Telmex an average 5.32 cents a minute for domestic and international long-distance service in 1997, which would drop to around 4.69 cents in 1998 and be capped at 3.15 cents between 1999 and 2001. As of January 1, 1997, Telmex lost its monopoly over Mexico's long-distance phone market.

Roller-Coaster Effect in Late 1990s to 2000s

After three lag years, Telmex's numbers rebounded in 1998. Total revenues jumped to approximately $11.4 billion from $7.6 billion in 1997. During the year, Telmex increased its service lines by 7.3 percent. They also boosted sales of digital services, including three-way calling, call waiting, call forwarding, caller ID, and voice mail, so that 12.6 percent of all customers' lines used one or more of these services. The company's cellular company, TELCEL, also had reason to boast, as it expanded its customer base by over one million, an impressive 89.9 percent leap from 1997.

Reaching beyond telephone service, TELMEX acquired 18.9 percent of the capital stock of U.S. Internet services provider Prodigy Communications Corporation. By the end of 1998, it was present in 600 cities and boasted a customer base of 671,000. Other acquisitions included a contract with Guatemala's telecommunications company, Telecomunicaciones de Guatemala, S.A., which allowed TELMEX the option to acquire 49 percent of the company by 2003. Also in 1998 TELMEX acquired more than 55 percent of U.S. cellular telephone company Topp Telecom.

TELMEX revenue continued to grow steadily, exceeding around $11 billion in 2000 and over $13 billion in 2001. But net income had been dropping, from roughly $3.1 billion in 2000 to $2.8 billion in 2001. By 2002 both revenue and income dropped. While revenue returned to approximately where it had been in 2000, income dipped below $2 billion. Uncertainty about Telmex ensued and U.S.-based SBC Communications, which had an 8.1 percent stake in the Mexican telephone company, sold off enough stocks to scale back its holdings to 7.5 percent. Still, Telmex underwent further growth. In 2002, for instance, it added over one million service lines and 252,000 internet users.

The year 2003 was challenging for Telmex, witnessing an approximate $1 billion drop in revenues. The U.S. recession, as well as the low economic growth rate, largely contributed to the prolonged difficulties. Innovation continued, with broadband service access, for instance, reaching 58.9 percent of the Mexican population. The 2004 first quarter showed a glimmer of

promise for Telmex, with a 0.5 percent increase in revenues over the same period in 2003, and a 5.9 percent increase in net income. Also, total debt decreased 4.6 percent from 2003. Still, difficulties loomed for Telmex, even as it underwent huge expansion projects, including plans to expand its long-distance service into Brazil. The deal included the sale of Brazil's largest long-distance carrier, Embratel, to Telmex for $400 million. While the potential for profit was present for Telmex, fierce Brazil competition was expected. The deal would be overseen by a new CEO for Telmex, Carlos Slim Domit, son of Carlos Slim Helu.

Principal Subsidiaries

Red Uno; Seccion Amarilla (Yellow Pages); Telbip; Telnor; Uninet.

Principal Competitors

Alestra; Avantel.

Further Reading

Barrera Diaz, Cyntia, "Mexico's Telmex to Face Fiercer Brazil Competition," *Reuters, UK*, April 30, 2004.

Dabrowski, Andrea, "Mexico's Privatization Plan Under Pressure," *Washington Post*, September 3, 1991, p. E1.

DePalma, Anthony, "Once a Monopoly and Still a Threat," *New York Times*, October 26, 2000.

Dukcevich, Davide, "Around-the-Globe: Telmex Opens Its Wires," *Forbes.com*, January 3, 2001.

Gilpin, Kenneth N., "Market Insight; In Mexico, Stocks Rise As Growth Slows," *New York Times*, June 3, 2001.

LaFranchi, Howard, "Competition Lines Up for Long Distance Opening in Mexico," *Christian Science Monitor*, October 4, 1994, p. 9.

Lowe, Sandra, "Party Line: Telefonos de Mexico Braces for More Competition," *San Antonio Business Journal*, November 4, 1994, p. B1.

Luxner, Larry, "Special Report: Mexico Reaches for New Telecom Heights," *Telephony*, February 3, 1992, p. 22.

"Mexico Stocks Take Beating on News Report," *Reuters News Service*, January 12, 1996.

Poole, Claire, "El Conquistador," *Forbes*, September 16, 1991, p. 68.

Ramamurti, Ravi, "Telephone Privatization in a Large Country: Mexico," *North-South Agenda*, May 1994, pp. 1–20.

Tagliabue, John, "Telefonica to Expand in Cellphones in Mexico," *New York Times*, March 8, 2002.

Wills, Rick, "World Business Briefing: The Americas; Mexico Phone Rates," *New York Times*, June 22, 1999.

—Dave Mote
—update: Candice Mancini

Tenaris SA

13, rue Beaumont
L-1219 Luxembourg
Luxembourg
Telephone: 352-26-47-89-78
Fax: 352-26-47-89-79
Web site: http://www.tenaris.com

Public Company
Incorporated: 2001
Employees: 13,841
Sales: $3.2 billion (2003)
Stock Exchanges: Bolsa de Comercio de Buenos Aires
Bolsa Mexicana de Valores Bolsa Italiana New York
Ticker Symbols: TS; TEN
NAIC: 331210 Iron and Steel Pipe and Tube
Manufacturing from Purchased Steel

As a manufacturer and supplier of steel pipe products, Tenaris SA is the leader in world production of seamless steel pipe, carrying 20 percent of the world trade in seamless steel pipe and 30 percent of world trade in oil country tubular goods (OCTG). At Tenaris's manufacturing facilities, located in Argentina, Brazil, Canada, Italy, Japan, Mexico, and Venezuela, annual production exceeds three million tons of seamless pipe and 850,000 tons of welded pipe. Tenaris engineers collaborate with customers in research and development to create pipe and tubular products that tolerate the requirements of unique utilization situations. With offices in more than 20 countries, Tenaris facilitates a streamlined procurement process, offering project and supply chain management from product design and manufacturing through product handling, inventory, and distribution anywhere in the world. Tenaris customers include multinational companies in the oil and gas, automotive, and mechanical industries. In South America Tenaris is the primary supplier of welded steel pipes used for gas pipelines. Techint Group owns approximately 60 percent of Tenaris stock; Tenaris is part of an integrated product services strategy for Techint's operations in industrial engineering, supply, and infrastructure construction worldwide.

Early History: 1900s–80s

Tenaris formed through the consolidation of three geographically disparate, but not unrelated, steel pipe manufacturers: Dalmine SpA of Italy, Siderca SAIC of Argentina, and Tubos de Acero de Mexico SA (Tamsa) of Mexico. Dalmine began manufacturing seamless steel tubes in 1909. Though it listed on the Borsa Italiana in 1924, the company was nationalized under Mussolini's dictatorship. Agostino Rocca, a prime mover in the Italian steel industry during the 1930s, became managing director of Dalmine in 1935. Along with his son Roberto, in 1945 Rocca founded Compagnia Tecnica Internazionale, later renamed Techint, providing engineering and construction for industrial development. Techint's South American Division, formed after Agostino emigrated from Italy to Argentina, built the production plants for Siderca, in Campana, Argentina, and Tamsa, in Veracruz, Mexico. Operations at both factories began in 1954. Techint held ownership interests in both companies and managed the Siderca facility. Tamsa listed on the Bolsa Mexicana de Valores in 1953 and Siderca on the Bolsa de Comercio de Buenos Aires in 1958. Tamsa became the first Mexican company to be listed on an exchange in the United States in 1967, through the New York Stock Exchange's American Depository Receipts (ADR) program.

Roberto Rocca, who became president of Techint in 1978, initiated the consolidation of the three steel pipe manufacturers as part of a long-term plan to integrate steel and steel product manufacturing with its construction activities, especially pipeline construction, which occurred on a global basis. During the mid-1980s Techint developed Siderca's operations, expanding the steel mill facilities at Campana and acquiring Siat, an Argentine welded pipe manufacturer, in 1986. Under Roberto's direction Siderca invested in product research and development, and Siderca became known worldwide as a low-cost producer of seamless steel pipe and tube. Through Siderca, Techint acquired a controlling interest in Tamsa in 1993 and began to manage that operation, known for its electric-furnace pipe and tube mill, with Paolo Rocca as president. When Italy privatized industry, Siderca obtained a controlling interest in Dalmine in 1996.

Formation of DST Alliance: 1990s

Through the consolidation of the three steel pipe companies, Techint formed a new company, DST Alliance, the world's largest producer of seamless steel pipe. DST formed a $2 billion entity, with Dalmine valued at $400 million, Siderca at $1 billion, and Tamsa at more than $600 million. Dalmine, Siderca, and Tamsa continued to operate autonomously, but in a coordinated manner, with all three companies using the DST trademark. Production at each company tended towards different kinds of pipe, with little overlap or competitive disadvantages. Siderca produced welded and seamless pipe, casings, tubings, and line pipe for the oil and gas industry. In addition to these products, Tamsa produced mechanical and structural seamless pipe, primarily used by the automotive industry. Dalmine produced seamless steel pipe applied to automotive, mechanical, and machinery uses. While each company maintained a significant hold on local markets, they exported a significant amount of product as well, with Siderca and Tamsa exporting about 80 percent of production and Dalmine about 50 percent of production. As president of DST, Rocca intended to exploit these varying strengths in the international marketplace to create an efficient steel pipe supply line to industrial projects worldwide, particularly by integrating management services with product supply.

Through alliances with several steel pipe manufacturers worldwide, DST improved its base of product and technology. In 1996 Tamsa and Corporacion Venezolana de Guayana formed Tavsa to acquire control of the Sidor seamless steel tube mill. A 1997 supply and licensing agreement with NKK Corporation of Japan gave Siderca access to carbon steel products as well as to advanced technology for premium pipe used in deepwater oil and gas recovery; in turn Siderca supplied NKK with steel pipe. In 2000 Siderca expanded its relationship with NKK, forming NKKTubes. The new entity, 51 percent owned by Siderca, managed the Keihin Works, NKK's seamless tube manufacturing facility. Siderca expanded an existing association with Brazil's Confab, a manufacturer of welded steel tubes and industrial equipment, acquiring a controlling interest in Confab in 1999. An agreement with Algoma Steel of Canada established a seamless steel tube manufacturing facility in Sault Ste. Marie, Ontario, which operated under the name Algoma Tubes; Siderca managed the plant and DST handled marketing and distribution.

DST changed its name to Tenaris in April 2001 and announced its new corporate identity at the Houston Offshore Technology Conference. Tenaris took its name from the Latin word *tenax,* the root of tenacious, which means to hold a firm grip. The name reflected the company's international standing, in that the word could be understood in many languages. An advertising campaign followed, emphasizing Tenaris's position as a global network of integrated steel pipe manufacturing and supply management operations. Through global and local trade publications, Tenaris introduced the brand along with the company's eight steel mills, offering a variety of services that utilized the combined capacities of the mills.

2001–03: Establishing Presence in International Service and Supply

With production and technology in place, DST began to offer project and supply chain management services, from product design through distribution and inventory. One of the company's first major successes involved collaboration with Shell Canada, to meet the needs of extracting heavy oil at the Peace River oilfield in Alberta. Through intensive study and experimentation at the Tamsa and Dalmine mills, Tenaris Pipeline Services provided Shell Canada with line pipe capable of handling steam injection underground, necessary to thin heavy oil for easier extraction. The new grade of pipe, ranging from 10 to 14 inches in diameter, withstood temperatures up to 698 degrees Fahrenheit and pressure up to 11,700 pounds per square inch. Tenaris delivered the pipe in January 2001. The successful implementation of that technology earned the company orders from other companies requiring high-grade line pipe for steam injection methods of heavy oil extraction.

Tenaris's technological capabilities attracted business from companies involved in offshore oil and gas extraction. Tenaris designed and produced pipe for the shallow water portion of an oil and gas export pipeline at Horn Mountain in the Gulf of Mexico. The pipe had to meet specifications of the American Petroleum Institute (API) as well as British Petroleum (BP). Engineers from BP determined the metallurgical conditions for ''sour service,'' a balance of a high level of corrosion resistance and reduced metal hardening, and Tenaris engineers determined how to produce it; API inspectors collaborated on its specifications as well. Collaboration occurred in face-to-face meetings and through video conferencing. Once production specifications were finalized, Tenaris produced the pipe at its Siderca and Dalmine mills within five weeks and delivered it in June 2001, earlier than scheduled.

In June 2002 Tenaris Global Services signed a five-year, $80 million agreement with ChevronTexaco, to supply well casing and oil production tubing for international affiliates in Argentina, Canada, Europe, Nigeria, and Venezuela. Tenaris managed the supply chain, beginning with pipe design and manufacturing through delivery and inventory management, and accommodated the unique needs of each affiliate.

In its research center in Argentina, Tenaris developed pipe for deepwater oil and gas production which occurred at increasing depth offshore. As pipe supply and project manager for the TotalFinaElf E&P USA's Canyon Express project in the deepwater Gulf of Mexico, Tenaris developed a low-carbon steel pipe that met the requirements of a hydrogen sulfide environment and intense water pressure, at a depth of 7,200 feet and temperatures as low as minus 21 degrees Fahrenheit. In addition to providing over 30,000 tons of pipe for the 118-mile line, produced at its Tamsa and Dalmine plants, Tenaris color coded joints for efficient, economical welding at sea.

Tenaris provided 10,000 tons of pipe for Pioneer Natural Resources' Falcon project in the deepwater Gulf of Mexico. The specific requirements of that project involved solving delivery and welding problems that would allow gas and oil to be extracted economically. Pioneer used the reel-laying process, flexible pipe spooled in 5,400-ton increments, placed vertically and welded at sea. The oversized length of the double-jointed pipe required special handling procedures as the product was transported from the Siderca facility to Mobile, Alabama.

In 2003 Tenaris introduced a new connective technology, TenarisBlue, a dopeless pipe thread for applications where worker safety and environmental sensitivity were primary concerns. A metal-to-metal seal through premium pipe threading, TenarisBlue Dopeless offered a more effective enclosure for gas and liquid than using an absorbent material as a secondary seal. ConocoPhillips used the technology at its Ekofisk X50 offshore oil well in Norway, the first application of dopeless pipe offshore.

Continuing Worldwide Expansion: 2003–04

Though Techint had united its steel pipe operations under Tenaris, the company did not have complete ownership of those operations; Tenaris owned 71.3 percent of Siderca, 50.8 percent of Tamsa, and 47.2 percent of Dalmine. Consolidation of ownership occurred in 2002 and 2003, with Tenaris reorganizing from a base in Luxembourg. The process involved obtaining approval for exchange offers, of Tenaris stock for Siderca, Dalmine, and Tamsa stock, with the exchanges in Italy, Argentina, Mexico, and the United States, and then making exchange offers to shareholders. Exchange transactions took several months to complete. The three companies were delisted in 2002, then Tenaris relisted as a single company on the New York Stock Exchange, and on the Italian, Buenos Aires, and Mexican stock exchanges. The board of directors elected Roberto Agostino chairman and his son, Paolo Agostino, chief executive officer; however, after Roberto's death, Paolo became

chairman as well. Exchange offers continued in 2003, and by the end of the year Tenaris owned 99.9 percent of Tamsa, 99.9 percent of Siderca, and 88.4 percent of Dalmine.

Tenaris operated profitably at this time, earning net income of $194 million in 2002 and $210 million in 2003, with revenues at $3.2 billion both years. An unusually large sales volume for welded pipe delivered to large pipeline projects in Ecuador, Peru, and Brazil in 2002 and seamless pipe for projects in the deepwater Gulf of Mexico delivered in 2003 maintained stable sales volume, though war in Iraq significantly impacted sales to the Middle East and Africa. With production plants operating at 95 percent capacity in 2003, Tenaris invested $120 million in production, technology, safety, and environmental standards at its facilities worldwide. Tenaris and Confab built a new casing processing plant in Sao Paolo, Brazil, and planned to add production of pumping equipment for the oil industry in late 2004.

Alliances continued to play a significant role at Tenaris, in expanding its worldwide product base. Through an agreement with Sandvik Materials Technology of Sweden, Tenaris began to distribute Sandvik's seamless stainless steel downhole production tubing for the oil industry. The companies agreed to collaborate on the development of new products, with Sandvik to handle manufacturing and technology and Tenaris to handle marketing and distribution. Tenaris formed a five-year alliance with Socotherm in Italy, to share technology on pipe coating. Through Confab Tenaris already operated a joint venture with Socotherm, as pipe-coating contractor with plants adjacent to Tenaris mills in Argentina. Active industrial development in China prompted the formation of an alliance with Tianjin Pipe Corporation in December 2003. With Tenaris holding majority ownership, the joint venture planned to build a pipe threading plant and oil production accessories facility in Tianjin, China.

Tenaris opened a service center in Francisco de Orellana, Ecuador, near oil and gas drilling activity in the eastern part of the country. The center offered product design, material requirement planning, maintenance, inspections, tube preparations, and administration services.

Tenaris sought to increase its holdings in 2004, acquiring the assets of Algoma Tubes from Algoma Steel for $9.6 million. Tenaris signed a letter of intent for the acquisition of a controlling interest in S.C. Silcotub SA of Romania. That company produced small-diameter, seamless pipe for OCTG and other industrial uses. Facilities included a steel pipe mill, finishing plant, and cold-drawing plant. In April Tenaris announced an agreement with Sidor, a steel producer in Venezuela with ties to Techint, to purchase a production facility for prereduced hot briquetted iron from Posven, another Venezuelan company. A joint venture with Sidor, in which Tenaris would hold a 55 percent interest, would acquire the plant for $120 million. The plant would supply Tenaris with low-cost, high quality ferrous raw material.

Principal Subsidiaries

Algoma Tubes, Inc. (Canada); Confab (Brazil); Dalmine SpA (Italy; 88.4%); NKKTubes (Japan; 51%); Siat (Argentina); Siderca SAIC (Argentina; 99.9%); Tavsa (Venezuela); Tuberos de Acero de Mexico SA (Mexico; 99.9 %).

Principal Competitors

IPSCO, Inc.; JFE Holdings, Inc; Lone Star Technologies, Inc.; Maverick Tube Corporation; Sumitomo Metal Industries Ltd.; United States Steel Corporation; Vallourec SA.

Further Reading

"Argentina: Siderca to Associate with Algoma Steel in Canada," *South American Business Information,* December 17, 1999.

Barham, John, "Techint Instigates a 30-Year-Old Plan—The Argentine Group's Expansion Strategy," *Financial Times,* July 20, 1993, p. 20.

"Company News, Mergers & Acquisitions," *Pipeline & Gas Journal,* June 2002, p. 81.

"NKK Forms Tube, Distribution and Maintenance Partnerships," *Steel Times International,* July 2000, p. 6.

"Pipe Dope Eliminated from Offshore Supply Chain: ConocoPhillips Turns to TenarisBlue for Ekofisk Operations," *World Oil,* January 2004, p. S24.

Robertson, Scott, "Global Alliance to Tap OCTG Pipeline," *American Metal Market,* July 9, 2003, p. 1.

——, "Three Tube Makers Join Forces; $2.1B Group Will Control 12% of World Seamless Market," *American Metal Market,* May 10, 1996, p. 1.

"Steel Tubes: Making the Grades: Tenaris Mills Met the Custom Order for Horn Mountain's Export Line Pipe Ahead of Schedule," *Oil and Gas Investor,* January 2003, p. S86.

"Techint's Rocca Wins Steel Vision Award," *American Metal Market,* February 15, 1999, p. 16.

"Tenaris Announces Its New Board of Directors," *Canadian Corporate News,* December 16, 2002.

"Tenaris Announces Successful Conclusion of Its Exchange Offer," *Canadian Corporate News,* December 16, 2002.

"Tenaris—Chmn. & CEO Interview," *CEO Wire,* March 26, 2004.

"Tenaris Develops Tubular Solution for High Pressure, Deepwater," *Pipeline & Gas Journal,* September 2003, p. 8.

"Tenaris Group of Tube Makers Launches Advertising Campaign," *American Metal Market,* October 9, 2001, p. 3.

"Tenaris in Deal on China Ventures," *American Metal Market,* December 4, 2003, p. 5.

"Tenaris Introduces a New Concept in Tubular Goods: Service," *Oilweek,* September 1, 2003, p. 38.

"Tenaris Steaming Ahead in Canada," *Pipeline & Gas Journal,* July 2002, p. 63.

—Mary Tradii

TRIBUNE

Tribune Company

435 North Michigan Avenue
Chicago, Illinois 60611-4066
U.S.A.
Telephone: (312) 222-9100
Fax: (312) 222-1573
Web site: http://www.tribune.com

Public Company
Incorporated: 1861
Employees: 23,800
Sales: $5.59 billion (2003)
Stock Exchanges: New York Chicago Pacific
Ticker Symbol: TRB
NAIC: 511110 Newspaper Publishers; 512110 Motion
   Picture and Video Production; 515112 Radio Stations;
   515120 Television Broadcasting; 515210 Cable and
   Other Subscription Programming; 516110 Internet
   Publishing and Broadcasting; 519110 News
   Syndicates; 711211 Sports Teams and Clubs

Tribune Company is one of the largest media companies in the United States. Its diversified businesses are arranged within two main operating units: Tribune Publishing, generator of 72 percent of overall revenues, and Tribune Broadcasting and Entertainment, which accounts for the remaining 28 percent. Tribune Publishing publishes 13 leading daily newspapers, including papers in each of the three largest U.S. markets: the *Chicago Tribune,* the *Los Angeles Times,* and *Newsday* (Long Island, New York). Other newspapers include the *South Florida Sun-Sentinel* (Fort Lauderdale), the *Orlando Sentinel,* the *Baltimore Sun,* and the *Hartford Courant,* as well as three Spanish-language newspapers in New York, Chicago, and Los Angeles, all called *Hoy.* Tribune Publishing also manages the web sites for both the company's newspapers and its television stations; operates CLTV, a 24-hour local cable news channel serving the Chicago area; runs the Tribune Media Services syndication service; and owns various community newspapers, niche magazines, and classified advertising–based publications. Tribune Broadcasting and Entertainment owns and operates 26 televi-

sion stations, the national cable superstation WGN, and Chicago radio station WGN-AM; develops and syndicates television shows, such as *Gene Roddenberry's Andromeda* and *Mutant X,* through Tribune Entertainment Company; owns the Chicago Cubs major league baseball team; and holds a 22 percent stake in The WB Television Network and a 31 percent interest in the TV Food Network. Eighteen of the firm's television stations are WB affiliates.

Starting with the Chicago Daily Tribune *in 1847*

The company originated with the first publication of the *Chicago Daily Tribune* on June 10, 1847. The newspaper's founders were James Kelly, who also owned a weekly literary newspaper, and two other journalists, John E. Wheeler and Joseph K.C. Forrest. At the time, the paper was one of three major dailies published in Chicago.

The founders soon parted company, however, and the *Chicago Daily Tribune* had gone through several changes in ownership and editorial policy by 1855, when it was sold to a man who would be influential in its history, former Cleveland, Ohio, newspaperman Joseph Medill. His associates in the purchase were Charles Ray, a physician, journalist, and political activist in Springfield and Galena, Illinois, and John Vaughan, a coproprietor of Medill's Cleveland paper. Under Medill's leadership, the *Tribune* maintained a strong antislavery stand but abandoned the antiforeign, anti-Catholic, and antisaloon campaigns that the paper had led previously. It also reorganized its presentation of news, establishing separate departments for local, national, and international stories.

Coming out of the economic panic of 1857, the *Tribune* was having financial problems, but so was a competitor, the *Democratic Press.* The two papers merged in 1858, resulting in the *Chicago Daily Press and Tribune.* Active in the partisan journalism common in its day, the paper was allied with the recently formed Republican Party. It supported Abraham Lincoln in his unsuccessful campaign to unseat U.S. Senator Stephen Douglas in 1858 and in his successful campaign for the presidency in 1860.

In 1860 the paper's name was returned to the *Chicago Daily Tribune.* The following year the Tribune Company was incor-

Company Perspectives:

Mission: Build businesses that inform and entertain our customers in the ways, places and at the times they want.

porated and the paper became the *Chicago Tribune.* That year, 1861, also brought the start of the Civil War, during which the *Tribune* gained national fame for its excellent wartime news coverage and its support of the Union cause. The paper's Sunday edition appeared during the war, disappeared for a while, and was resumed after the war, to the chagrin of local ministers. In October 1871 came a disaster against which the *Tribune* had warned—the Great Chicago Fire—which devastated the city, filled as it was with wooden buildings and suffering a lack of firefighting equipment and regulations. As the city rebuilt, Joseph Medill was elected mayor on the Union-Fire-proof ticket. Medill declined to run for a second term in 1873. In 1874 he emerged victorious in a struggle with Managing Editor Horace White for editorial control of the *Tribune*; Medill borrowed money from department store owner Marshall Field to gain full control of the company's stock.

The *Tribune* grew and prospered, as did Chicago itself, in the years after the fire. As it entered the last decade of the 19th century, the paper was attractive, vocal, and profitable, reporting annual income of $1.5 million a year. In 1895 the *Tribune* lowered newsstand prices and increased circulation. Medill's son-in-law, Robert W. Patterson, became increasingly important to the *Tribune*; he was named general manager in 1890, after having been managing editor for seven years. At Medill's death at age 76 in 1899, Patterson assumed the titles of editor-in-chief of the newspaper and president of Tribune Company. Medill's last words reportedly were, "What is the news this morning?"

In 1900 a formidable competitor came to Chicago, as William Randolph Hearst began publishing the *Chicago American,* a paper with a Democratic political alliance and a sensational reporting style. It was an evening paper but later added a morning edition as a direct competitor to the *Tribune.* The *Tribune* and the Hearst papers engaged in a circulation war that lasted 20 years, marked at times by physical violence among newspaper vendors.

The early part of the century also was marked by the rise to power by two of Joseph Medill's grandsons, Robert R. McCormick and Joseph Medill Patterson. Their mothers, Katherine Medill McCormick and Elinor Medill Patterson, battled frequently over *Tribune* affairs after Medill's death. Katherine McCormick's eldest son, Medill McCormick, made a mark on the *Tribune* as a reporter and later business executive, but left the paper in 1910; he had been plagued by psychiatric illness and, upon recovery, opted for a career in politics. Meanwhile, Robert Patterson, Joseph Patterson's father, had died in 1910. In 1911 Joseph Patterson was elected chairman of Tribune Company and Robert McCormick was named president. Their immediate accomplishments were Patterson's upgrading of the Sunday paper and McCormick's initiation of a paper mill to produce newsprint for the *Tribune.*

According to their biographers, Patterson and McCormick had many differences, including political ones—McCormick was a staunchly conservative Republican, while Patterson was far more liberal. Still, under their leadership Tribune Company expanded and diversified, and both became well-known public figures, retaining titles from their World War I military service—Colonel McCormick and Captain Patterson. During the war, the *Tribune* had more correspondents at the front than any other Chicago morning daily, and McCormick and Patterson themselves were among these correspondents. After the war, the *Tribune* pulled off a major publishing coup with early publication of the Treaty of Versailles. By 1920 the *Tribune* had the largest circulation of any Chicago newspaper.

Diversifying in the Early 20th Century

By then, the parent company also had expanded beyond Chicago, with Patterson's opening of the *New York News*—formally the *Illustrated Daily News* and later known as the *Daily News*—in 1919. Eventually, the New York paper, a lively tabloid, became the largest circulation newspaper in the United States. In 1924 Tribune Company formed a subsidiary to publish a weekly national magazine, *Liberty,* designed to compete with the *Saturday Evening Post* and *Collier's.* It passed *Collier's* in circulation, but did not attract adequate advertising, so was sold in 1931.

Also in 1924, Tribune Company launched a more enduring venture, with the leasing of Chicago radio station WDAP, whose call letters it changed to WGN—standing for World's Greatest Newspaper, a nickname the Tribune had given itself. Two years later, Tribune Company bought the entire station. The station's early programming included coverage of the 1925 Scopes trial and a comedy show called *Sam 'n' Henry,* which eventually went network as *Amos 'n' Andy.* It was also the first station to broadcast the World Series, the Indianapolis 500, and the Kentucky Derby.

The year 1925 was marked by the Tribune Company's opening of its new headquarters, Tribune Tower, a 36-story Gothic tower that is still a Chicago landmark, and the company's decision to provide funds to a journalism school at Northwestern University in Evanston, Illinois, just north of Chicago. The school became known as the Joseph Medill School of Journalism, one of the most prestigious in the United States.

The 1920s provided many political and crime stories that made the decade a lively one for newspapers, but the 1920s ended with the worst stock market crash in history, ushering in the Great Depression. Tribune Company weathered the economic downturn by cutting unprofitable and marginal ventures, such as *Liberty* and the *Tribune's* European edition, which had begun during World War I. There was one new venture, however, the Chicago Tribune–New York News Syndicate, which was formed in 1933 and was the forerunner of the Tribune Media Services news syndicate. Editorially, McCormick's *Tribune* was vociferously opposed to President Franklin Roosevelt's New Deal programs, while Patterson's *Daily News* generally was sympathetic to them. Later, however, the cousins joined in opposition to Roosevelt over U.S. entry into World War II. After the bombing of Pearl Harbor, though, the papers supported the war effort.

Key Dates:

1847: James Kelly, John E. Wheeler, and Joseph K.C. Forrest begin publishing the *Chicago Daily Tribune* newspaper.

1855: Joseph Medill and associates purchase the paper.

1858: The paper is merged with the *Democratic Press,* forming the *Chicago Daily Press and Tribune.*

1860: The paper's name returns to the *Chicago Daily Tribune.*

1861: Tribune Company is incorporated; the paper is renamed the *Chicago Tribune.*

1874: Medill gains full control of Tribune Co.

1911: The company falls under the control of two grandsons of Medill, Robert R. McCormick and Joseph Medill Patterson.

1919: Patterson launches the *New York News* (later the *Daily News*).

1924: The company expands into radio with the launch of the Chicago station WGN.

1925: The company's new headquarters, Tribune Tower, is opened.

1933: The Chicago Tribune–New York News Syndicate is formed and is the forerunner of the Tribune Media Services syndication service.

1948: WGN-TV begins broadcasting in Chicago, and WPIX-TV in New York City.

1963: Tribune acquires the *Sun-Sentinel* newspaper in Fort Lauderdale, Florida.

1965: The *Orlando Sentinel* newspaper is added to the fold.

1978: WGN-TV becomes a nationwide cable television "superstation."

1981: The company buys the Chicago Cubs baseball team from William Wrigley for $20.5 million; Tribune Broadcasting Company is established.

1982: Tribune Entertainment Company is established.

1983: Tribune Company goes public.

1985: Los Angeles station KTLA-TV is acquired for $510 million.

1991: Following a protracted strike, the company divests itself of the *New York Daily News.*

1993: CLTV News, Chicago's first 24-hour, local news cable channel, is launched; an educational publisher arm, Tribune Education, begins to be built through acquisitions.

1995: Tribune acquires a 12.5 percent stake in the upstart Warner Bros. (WB) Television Network.

1997: The company acquires Renaissance Communications Corp. and its six television stations for $1.1 billion.

2000: Tribune acquires the Times Mirror Company for $8.3 billion, gaining the *Los Angeles Times, Newsday,* the *Baltimore Sun,* and several other newspapers; Tribune Education is sold off, as are three units acquired as part of the Times Mirror deal: Jeppesen Sanderson, Inc., AchieveGlobal, and Times Mirror Magazines.

2002: The company trades two of its Denver radio stations for two television stations in Indiana; *Chicago* magazine is acquired for $35 million.

2003: Tribune exchanges its last Denver radio station for a television station in Portland, leaving the company with one remaining radio station, WGN-AM in Chicago; a fourth television station, KPLR-TV in St. Louis, is purchased for $200 million; Dennis FitzSimons takes over as president, CEO, and chairman.

Joseph Patterson died in 1946. Briefly, McCormick took over the management of the *Daily News,* but concluded it was in good hands with Patterson's widow, Mary King Patterson, and other top executives. In 1948 came the death of Joe Patterson's sister, Eleanor (Cissy) Patterson, who had owned the *Washington Times-Herald.* Tribune Company acquired the paper and operated it until 1954, when it was absorbed by the *Washington Post.*

Entering TV Broadcasting in 1948

In 1948 the *Tribune* made one of the most famous mistakes in journalistic history: going to press early because of a printers' strike, the paper published the headline "Dewey Defeats Truman" in the 1948 presidential election. The strike ended the following year with no other comparable disasters. The year 1948 also brought a happier milestone in the company's history, the commencement of broadcasting by WGN-TV. This station would become a "superstation" in 1978, when it began reaching a nationwide audience via cable television. Also launched in 1948 was WPIX-TV in New York City (the PIX call letters referring to its founder, the *Daily News,* New York's first picture newspaper).

Robert McCormick died in 1955 and Chesser Campbell succeeded him as president of Tribune Company. The following year, the company bought Hearst's *Chicago American.* In 1963 Tribune Company acquired Gore Newspapers Company of Fort Lauderdale, Florida, publisher of the *Fort Lauderdale News* and the *Pompano Sun-Sentinel.* Later that year, the *New York Daily News* acquired certain assets of the *New York Mirror,* which had folded. In 1965 Tribune Company bought the Sentinel-Star Company, the Orlando, Florida, publisher of the *Orlando Sentinel.* Tribune Company also purchased New York radio station WQCD-FM in 1964 and KWGN-TV, an independent television station in Denver, in 1965.

In 1967 the *Chicago Tribune* responded to suburban growth by beginning to publish a tabloid aimed at suburban readers. The *Suburban Trib* continued until 1983, when the *Tribune* opted for zoned editions of the main paper to handle suburban coverage and appeal.

In 1968 there came a major corporate reorganization, with Tribune Company dropping its Illinois incorporation and reincorporating in Delaware, which provided a better climate for companies planning expansion and diversification. The company also split its privately held stock by a ratio of four for one and set up a separate subsidiary to publish the *Chicago Tribune.* The Chicago newspaper opened 1969 by abandoning the policy of partisan slanting of news, while it remained conservative on the editorial page. Also in 1969, the *American* was revamped as the tabloid *Chicago Today. Today,* however, operated at a deficit and ceased publication in 1974, with the *Tribune* going to all-day editions to replace the afternoon tabloid.

In 1974 Tribune Company shareholders approved changes in bylaws that were widely perceived to be paving the way for taking the company public. Two dissident shareholders, Josephine Albright—Joseph Patterson's daughter—and her son, Joseph Albright, challenged the bylaw changes in a lawsuit that was dismissed in 1979. In 1975 company officials denied any immediate plans to go public, which, indeed, the company did not do until 1983.

In the 1970s the company continued its acquisitive ways, buying a Los Angeles shopper in 1973 and changing it into the *Los Angeles Daily News* and purchasing the *Times-Advocate* in Escondido, California, in 1977. The *New York Daily News* was beset with strikes by pressmen, deliverers, and editorial personnel in 1978, but the parent company still had a record profitable year. Photoengravers also struck the paper briefly in 1979. An afternoon edition of the *Daily News* began publishing in 1980 to go up against the *New York Post*; the edition, however, did not succeed in terms of circulation or profits, so it closed the following year. Also in 1980, the company launched a longer-lived venture, the Independent Network News, an alternative to the three major television networks' news programs, originating in the studios of Tribune Company's New York television station, WPIX. The venture was discontinued in 1990.

Purchase of Chicago Cubs in 1981

In August 1981 Tribune Company acquired the Chicago Cubs baseball team from William Wrigley for $20.5 million. The Cubs turned in some good seasons for their new owners, winning the National League Eastern Division title in 1984 and 1989. In 1988, once a city ban was lifted, the company installed lights in Wrigley Field and began Cubs night games; the park had been the last in the major leagues with day baseball only.

Also in 1981, Tribune Company began seeking buyers for the *New York Daily News,* which had experienced declines in circulation and advertising and rises in costs and competition. When a proposed sale to Texas financier Joe Allbritton fell through, the company opted to revitalize the *Daily News,* taking a charge of $75 million in the second quarter of 1982 to do so. The paper won concessions from its unions that were expected to result in savings of $50 million a year.

Two key subsidiaries were formed in the early 1980s, highlighting the growing importance of non-newspaper operations to the company. In 1981 Tribune Broadcasting Company was established as an umbrella subsidiary for the television stations. Tribune's original programming activities, which dated back to the syndication of the *U.S. Farm Report* in 1975, were amalgamated within the 1982-formed Tribune Entertainment Company, which was charged with developing, producing, and distributing television programming for both Tribune and non-Tribune stations.

Purchase of Additional TV Stations in the Mid-1980s

The year 1983 brought the Tribune Company's $21 million purchase of WGNO-TV in New Orleans, as well as the public

stock offering that had been the subject of speculation for so long. In October, 7.7 million shares of Tribune Company stock went up for sale to the public at $26.75 each.

Tribune Company acquired two key employees from the *Chicago Sun-Times* in 1984 after the *Sun-Times* was sold to Rupert Murdoch, the controversial publisher of the *New York Post.* James Hoge, who had been publisher of the *Sun-Times,* moved into that post at the *Daily News,* and popular columnist Mike Royko switched to the *Chicago Tribune* from the *Sun-Times.*

The company also continued acquiring broadcast operations, buying Atlanta independent WGNX-TV in 1984 for $32 million and, the following year, buying Los Angeles station KTLA-TV for $510 million, the largest price ever paid for a TV station. The move also made Tribune Company the fourth largest broadcaster in the United States, just behind the three major networks. Because of the KTLA purchase, Tribune Company had to divest itself of the *Los Angeles Daily News* to comply with Federal Communications Commission (FCC) rules; Jack Kent Cooke, whose other business interests included cable television, real estate, and professional sports, was the buyer. The price was $176 million; Tribune Company had paid $24 million for the paper.

In 1985 three production unions went on strike against the *Chicago Tribune,* a labor conflict that ended in the company's favor. With the strike, the *Tribune* discontinued its afternoon edition, a move it had planned anyway, with newspaper circulations slumping around the United States.

Production of television programs became a major business for Tribune Company in the 1980s; most significant during the decade was Tribune Entertainment's launch of the *Geraldo Rivera Show,* a syndicated daytime talk show, in 1987. The company also continued acquiring print properties, buying Daily Press Inc., a Newport News, Virginia publisher, in 1986 and reselling Daily Press's cable TV operations; in 1988 Tribune Company bought five weekly newspapers in Santa Clara County, California.

Mindful of the rash of unfriendly corporate takeovers in the 1980s, Tribune Company enacted shareholder-rights plans as defenses against such possibilities; a 1987 plan gave shareholders a right to acquire a new series of preferred shares in the event of a potential buyer obtaining 10 percent of the company's common shares or making a tender offer for the company. In 1987 shareholders ratified a two-for-one stock split.

In 1988 the *Chicago Tribune* replaced its system of independent distributors with a more centralized system. The change resulted in legal challenges by the distributors, with one awarded $1.9 million by an arbitrator.

In August 1990 company veteran Charles T. Brumback became Tribune president and CEO. That year, the company encountered more labor relations problems. Nine of the ten unions at the *Daily News* went on strike in October; the newspaper struggled to publish with replacement workers and eventually, as the strike dragged into 1991, Tribune Company announced that the paper would close unless it was sold. British publisher Robert Maxwell came to the newspaper's rescue, reaching agreements with the unions that allowed him to take over. In March 1991 the company paid Maxwell $60 million to assume the *Daily News'* liabilities. Tribune Company had been forced to take a *Daily News*-related charge of $255 million in 1990, leading to a net loss for the year of $63.5 million.

Expanding into Interactive Media and Education Publishing in the 1990s

The early and mid-1990s were a time of enormous change across all media-related industries. Cable television continued to grow, the consolidation and diversification of media companies—aided by the relaxation of federal regulations governing ownership of media properties—became commonplace, and the Internet emerged as a new format with which to contend and within which to compete. Tribune Company placed itself at the center of all of these changes. The company, which traditionally had been managed fairly conservatively, grew bolder as the decade progressed under Brumback's leadership and that of his successor, John Madigan, who became president in 1994, added the CEO slot in 1995, and then tacked on the chairmanship as well in early 1996.

The company's newspaper publishing unit, known as Tribune Publishing, was scaled back some during this period to focus on its most profitable papers, with several weeklies and smaller dailies being divested. By 1997, only four daily newspapers remained in the fold—*Chicago Tribune,* the Fort Lauderdale *Sun-Sentinel,* the *Orlando Sentinel,* and the Newport News, Virginia–based *Daily Press.* Starting in 1995, online versions of each of these papers began to be developed, with the Internet edition of the *Chicago Tribune* debuting on the World Wide Web the following year. Also in 1996, a joint venture with America Online (AOL) called Digital City, Inc.—80 percent owned by AOL and 20 percent owned by Tribune—led to the creation of a series of Digital City web sites, which provided local, interactive news and information. Tribune Company also formed a unit called Tribune Ventures to invest in various emerging media businesses. By mid-1997, $100 million had been spent to purchase stakes in various interactive services and cyberspace businesses, including AOL (4 percent), electronic payment specialist CheckFree Corporation (5 percent), Internet search company Excite, Inc. (7 percent), e-mail service Mercury Mail, Inc. (13 percent), transaction software company Open Market, Inc. (6 percent), and online grocery shopper Peapod LP (13 percent).

Meanwhile, the company's broadcasting and entertainment sector, known as Tribune Broadcasting, entered cable programming for the first time in 1993 with the launch of CLTV News, Chicago's first 24-hour, local news cable channel; a similar channel was launched in 1997 in central Florida through a joint venture of the *Orlando Sentinel* and Time Warner Cable. Tribune Company also purchased a 31 percent stake in TV Food Network, a 24-hour basic cable channel covering food, nutrition, and fitness, which by the end of 1996 could be seen in more than 19 million cable households.

The loosening of federal regulations on radio and television ownership enabled Tribune's group of television broadcast stations to grow dramatically in the 1990s. The company began the decade with just six stations but added ten more by 1997. WPHL in Philadelphia was purchased in 1992, WLVI in Boston

in 1994 for $25 million, KHWB in Houston in 1996 for $102 million, and KSWB in San Diego also in 1996 for $71 million. In March 1997 Tribune Company became the number two television group in the United States by acquiring Renaissance Communications Corp. for $1.1 billion in cash. The deal brought six more stations to the Tribune fold—KDAF in Dallas, WBZL in Miami, KTXL in Sacramento, WXIN in Indianapolis, WTIC in Hartford, and WPMT in Harrisburg—bringing the total to 16. Ten of the stations were affiliated with the relatively new Warner Bros. Television Network, better known as the WB. This fit in well with Tribune Company's 21.9 percent equity stake in the WB; the company had acquired an original 12.5 percent interest in August 1995, then invested an additional $21 million in the fifth U.S. television network in March 1997.

Already possessing strong positions in two business sectors, Tribune Company quickly added a substantial third leg to its operations with the beginnings of Tribune Education in 1993. From that year through 1996, the company spent more than $400 million to acquire several prominent publishers of supplemental education materials, including Contemporary Books, Inc.; The Wright Group; Everyday Learning Corporation; Jamestown Publishers, Inc.; Educational Publishing Corporation; NTC Publishing Group; and Janson Publications. In just three years, Tribune Education was the number one publisher of supplemental education materials, a publishing sector growing rapidly because of increasing school enrollment while also providing high profit margins. In 1997 Tribune Education spent $80 million for an 80.5 percent stake in Landoll, Inc., a leading publisher of children's books for the mass market, thus providing entrée into the consumer market.

Tribune closed out the decade by acquiring a handful of additional television stations. In June 1998 the company exchanged its WQCD radio station in New York for two television stations: KTZZ (later KTWB) in Seattle and WXMI in Grand Rapids, Michigan. Then in March of the following year, Tribune traded WGNX-TV in Atlanta for KCPQ-TV in Seattle. Two more WB stations were acquired later in 1999: WEWB in Albany, New York, for $18.5 million and WBDC in Washington, D.C., for $125 million. Also in 1999 the company created a subsidiary called Tribune Interactive, Inc. to manage the web sites of its newspapers, television stations, and publishing operations. Gains from the strategic sales of some of the Internet investments helped Tribune Company earn a stunning $1.47 billion in profits in 1999 on total revenues of $2.92 billion.

Blockbuster Times Mirror Acquisition in 2000

Tribune started out 2000 by acquiring the 67 percent of Qwest Broadcasting LLC it did not already own for $107 million in February. Qwest owned television stations WATL in Atlanta and WNOL in New Orleans. Tribune's 22 television stations (15 of which were affiliates of the WB) now reached 27 percent of the country. It was the newspaper operations of Tribune Publishing, however, that gained center stage later in the year. In June 2000 the company acquired the Times Mirror Company in a blockbuster cash and stock deal valued at about $8.3 billion—the largest acquisition in newspaper industry history. Tribune thereby gained seven newspapers, four major papers—the *Los Angeles Times, Newsday* (Long Island, New

York), the *Baltimore Sun,* and the *Hartford Courant*—along with smaller papers the *Morning Call* (Allentown, Pennsylvania), the *Advocate* (Stamford, Connecticut), and *Greenwich Time* (Greenwich, Connecticut). Also included in the deal was *Hoy,* the leading Spanish-language daily newspaper in New York City, which had been launched in 1998. With overall daily circulation of 3.6 million subscribers, Tribune Company became the number three U.S. newspaper company, trailing only Gannett Co., Inc. and Knight-Ridder, Inc. This increased scale, which was also more spread out nationally, positioned Tribune to compete more effectively for national newspaper advertising revenues, and the company created a national sales arm called Tribune Media Net, Inc. to pursue these opportunities. The deal also returned the newspaper side back to its more traditional place of prominence. Whereas only about 55 percent of revenues came from Tribune Publishing in 1999, the Times Mirror deal bumped this figure up to 73 percent by 2001. Revenues reached $5.25 billion in 2001.

To pay down debt taken on to acquire Times Mirror and to focus the company more sharply on market-based media, several divestments were completed in the wake of the deal, including three units acquired along with the Times Mirror newspapers—Jeppesen Sanderson, Inc., AchieveGlobal, and Times Mirror Magazines. Flight information provider Jeppesen Sanderson was sold to the Boeing Company for $1.5 billion in October 2000. AchieveGlobal, a provider of soft skills training and consulting for domestic and international businesses, was sold to the Institute for International Research for about $100 million, also in October 2000. Finally, Times Mirror Magazines, which published such titles as *Field & Stream, Popular Science,* and *GOLF Magazine,* was sold to Time, Inc. for $475 million in November 2000. In September 2000, meantime, the company sold Tribune Education to the McGraw-Hill Companies for about $686 million. These divestments left Tribune Company with long-term debt of about $4 billion. Also during 2000, Tribune joined with Knight-Ridder in forming CareerBuilder Inc., an online recruitment company. Two years later, Gannett Co. bought into CareerBuilder, becoming an equal partner with Tribune and Knight-Ridder.

In July 2001 Dennis FitzSimons was named president and chief operating officer of Tribune Company. As head of Tribune Broadcasting, FitzSimons was the driving force behind the series of acquisitions that had made Tribune the largest non-network owner of television stations in the United States. That year, the media industry suffered from a severe advertising slump brought on by the poor economic climate, which was exacerbated post-9/11. CEO Madigan called it ''the worst advertising environment since the Depression.'' Tribune announced in June that it would cut its companywide staff by 10 percent, eliminating more than 2,000 positions. It took a restructuring charge of $151.9 million to effectuate the cuts, leading to a net income figure for the year of just $111.1 million, compared with $224.4 million for 2000.

During 2002 and 2003 Tribune boosted its television station count to 26, and the percentage of U.S. households reached by its broadcast stations surpassed 30 percent. In July 2002 the company traded two of its Denver radio stations for WTTV-TV in Indianapolis and its sister station in Kokoma, Indiana, WTTK-TV. Then in March 2003 Tribune exchanged its last Denver radio station for KWBP-TV in Portland, Oregon. These moves left the company with just one remaining radio station, WGN-AM in Chicago. The fourth television station acquired was KPLR-TV in St. Louis, which was purchased for $200 million in March 2003. On the print side, Tribune Company spent $35 million in August 2002 to acquire *Chicago* magazine from Primedia, Inc. This monthly publication provided information about entertainment, dining, shopping, and real estate in the Chicago metro area. Attempting to create a national brand, Tribune Publishing launched a Chicago edition of the Spanish-language newspaper *Hoy* in September 2003, followed by an edition for Los Angeles, which debuted in March 2004. Tribune Publishing also attempted to reach young adults, many of whom were not regular readers of traditional newspapers, through commuter tabloid publications *RedEye* (Chicago) and *amNewYork,* both of which debuted in 2003. The Chicago Cubs, meantime, won the National League Central Division in 2003 and then proceeded to win their first postseason series in 95 years. The team came within one victory of reaching the World Series, losing the National League Championship Series in heartbreaking fashion thanks in part to an overenthusiastic fan who interfered with a Cub player attempting to make a catch in foul territory.

FitzSimons took over as president and CEO of Tribune Company in January 2003, becoming the first person to attain that position without first serving as publisher of the company's flagship newspaper, the *Chicago Tribune.* At the end of 2003 Madigan retired from the company after a 28-year career, as FitzSimons took on the chairmanship as well. Although an improved advertising environment helped the company achieve stellar profits of $891.4 million on record revenues of $5.59 billion in 2003, the new leader faced one major challenge involving federal government regulations of media ownership. Tribune lobbied hard for changes to these rules to loosen even further the rules regarding cross-ownership of newspapers and television stations in one market and concerning limits on the number of broadcast stations that one company may own. In June 2003 the FCC voted to relax the rules in both these areas. Crucial for Tribune was the easing of cross-ownership prohibitions, because the Times Mirror acquisition had placed Tribune in violation of federal regulations as a result of its ownership of both a newspaper and a television station in three markets: Los Angeles, New York, and Hartford; its holdings in the Fort Lauderdale/Miami market also violated the rules but had been granted a temporary waiver pending completion of the proposed regulatory overhaul. (The firm's Chicago holdings predated the regulations, so they were exempt.) Without changes to the regulations, Tribune would need to make divestments to place itself into compliance as the licenses for the television stations come up for renewal, which would begin in 2005 with the Miami station. The FCC vote to relax the rules ignited a firestorm of public protest, court challenges, and legislative proposals to overturn or modify the new rules, lending a real measure of uncertainty to Tribune Company's future.

Principal Subsidiaries

PUBLISHING: Tribune Publishing Company; The Baltimore Sun Company; Chicago Tribune Company; The Daily Press, Inc.; E Z Buy & E Z Sell Recycler Corporation; Forum Publishing Group, Inc.; The Hartford Courant Company; Hoy Publications, LLC; Orlando Sentinel Communications Company; The Morning Call, Inc.; Southern Connecticut Newspapers, Inc.; Sun-Sentinel Company; TMD, Inc.; Newsday, Inc.; Tribune Classifieds, Inc.; Tribune Los Angeles, Inc.; Los Angeles Times Communications LLC; Los Angeles Times Newspapers, Inc.; Tribune Manhattan Newspaper Holdings, Inc.; Tribune Media Services, Inc.; Tribune Media Net, Inc.; Tribune National Marketing Company. BROADCASTING AND ENTERTAINMENT: Tribune Broadcasting Company; ChicagoLand Microwave Licensee, Inc.; ChicagoLand Television News, Inc.; KHWB Inc.; KSWB Inc.; KPLR, Inc.; KTLA Inc.; KWGN Inc.; Oak Brook Productions, Inc.; Tower Distribution Company; Tribune Broadcasting News Network, Inc.; Tribune Broadcast Holdings, Inc.; Tribune Entertainment Company; Tribune (FN) Cable Ventures, Inc.; Tribune Network Holdings Company; Tribune Television Company; Tribune Television Holdings, Inc.; Tribune Television New Orleans, Inc.; Tribune Television Northwest, Inc.; WATL, LLC; WBDC Broadcasting, Inc.; WEWB, L.L.C.; WGN Continental Broadcasting Company; Chicago National League Ball Club, Inc.; Diana-Quentin, Inc.; Tribune California Properties, Inc.; Tribune Interactive, Inc.

Principal Operating Units

Tribune Publishing; Tribune Broadcasting and Entertainment.

Principal Competitors

Gannett Co., Inc.; Hollinger Inc.; The New York Times Company; Knight-Ridder, Inc.; Cox Enterprises, Inc.; The Hearst Corporation; Dow Jones & Company, Inc.; The News Corporation Limited; Daily News, L.P.

Further Reading

Alkin, Michael, "The Tribune Company: Batter Up," *Financial World,* March 18, 1997, pp. 24, 26.
Borden, Jeff, "Merger Heat for Trib Co.: Big Media Combines Make It Also-Also Ran," *Crain's Chicago Business,* August 7, 1995, pp. 3, 34.
——, "Trib CEO Shuns Headlines: Ad Slump, Daily News Woes Test Low-Key Style," *Crain's Chicago Business,* July 9, 1990, p. 1.
——, "Trib Co. Buys Low, Flies High with Shrewd Internet Buys," *Crain's Chicago Business,* August 30, 1999, p. 4.
——, "Trib's Blessing and Curse: Cash," *Crain's Chicago Business,* May 6, 1996, pp. 1, 78.
——, "Tribune Rewrites Corporate Future," *Crain's Chicago Business,* January 20, 1992, pp. 1, 45.
——, "With News an Old Story, Trib Is in a Mood to Shop," *Crain's Chicago Business,* May 20, 1991, p. 3.
Byrne, Harlan S., "Thank You, Geraldo Rivera: Tribune Co. Is Full of Good News," *Barron's,* November 21, 1988, pp. 36–37+.
Copple, Brandon, "Paper Tiger," *Forbes,* March 19, 2001, p. 66.
Fawcett, Adrienne, "Tribune's Vision Goes Well Beyond Online Newspapers," *Advertising Age,* June 2, 1997, pp. S-8, S-10.
Fitzgerald, Mark, "Broadcasting Dominant," *Editor and Publisher,* July 13, 1996, p. 17.
Fitzgerald, Mark, and Todd Shields, "Tribune Taps Broadcast's Fitz-Simons As New Head," *Editor and Publisher,* December 9, 2002, p. 3.
Gelfand, M. Howard, "Tribune Fine-Tunes Plans by Unloading Cable," *Crain's Chicago Business,* October 27, 1986, p. 22.
Kinsley, Philip, *The Chicago Tribune, Its First Hundred Years* (3 vols.), New York: Knopf, 1943–46.
Kogan, Rick, "Down to Business: Tribune Company," *Chicago History,* March 1993, pp. 20–25.
Lazare, Lewis, "Flush Tribune Fine-Tunes Broadcast Unit's Signals," *Crain's Chicago Business,* April 25, 1988, p. 2.
Littleton, Cynthia, "Renaissance Buy Should Boost Tribune Entertainment," *Broadcasting and Cable,* July 8, 1996, p. 9.
McCarthy, Michael J., and Matthew Rose, "Media Owners See Few Benefits of Bundling Ads," *Wall Street Journal,* May 14, 2003, p. B1.
McCormick, Brian, "Meet Trib's Next CEO: Broadcast Vet Fitz-Simons a Break from Print Past," *Crain's Chicago Business,* May 6, 2002, p. 4.
Miller, James P., "How Tribune Grabbed a Media Prize: With a $5.9 Billion Deal, Tribune CEO's Strategy Is Put to High-Stakes Test," *Wall Street Journal,* March 14, 2000, p. B1.
Milliot, Jim, "Tribune Spends $97 Million on Publishing Acquisitions," *Publishers Weekly,* July 12, 1993, p. 12.
Milliot, Jim, and Bridget Kinsella, "Tribune Acquires EPC, NTC for Total of $282 Million," *Publishers Weekly,* February 12, 1996, p. 10.
Moore, Thomas, "Why Tribune Co. Is Feeding the Chicago Cubs," *Fortune,* June 28, 1982, pp. 44+.
Mullman, Jeremy, "Media Muscle: No Longer a Mere Newspaper-Broadcast Concern, Tribune Co. Intends to Get Bigger," *Crain's Chicago Business,* June 2, 2003, p. A75.
——, "Trib Triumph at Risk: Firm Could Win or Lose Big As Congress Revisits FCC Rules," *Crain's Chicago Business,* August 4, 2003, p. 1.
Rathbun, Elizabeth A., "Tribune's Renaissance," *Broadcasting and Cable,* July 8, 1996, pp. 4, 8–9.
Rowan, Roy, "Secrets of the Tribune Tower," *Fortune,* April 5, 1982, pp. 66+.
Santoli, Michael, "Widening Net: Tribune's National Reach Offers Potential Overlooked by Wall Street," *Barron's,* September 18, 2000, pp. 18, 20, 22.
Smith, Richard Norton, *The Colonel: The Life and Legend of Robert R. McCormick, 1880–1955,* Boston: Houghton Mifflin, 1997.
Squires, James D., *Read All About It!: The Corporate Takeover of America's Newspapers,* New York: Times Books, 1993.
Sturm, Paul W., "Is There an Exorcist in the House?," *Forbes,* September 1, 1977, p. 61.
Teinowitz, Ira, "Taking Charge at Tribune Co.: New President Madigan Sees Growth Ahead," *Advertising Age,* June 6, 1994, p. 11.
——, "Tribune Looks Forward with Latest Acquisitions," *Advertising Age,* August 2, 1993, p. 20.
Weber, Joseph, "Ad Slump? What Ad Slump?," *Business Week,* March 12, 2001, pp. 78–79.
Weiner, Steve, "It's a Changing World," *Forbes,* October 3, 1988, pp. 88+.
Wendt, Lloyd, *Chicago Tribune: The Rise of a Great American Newspaper,* Chicago: Rand McNally, 1979.
"What Turned Tribune Co. into a Penny Pincher," *Business Week,* June 22, 1981, pp. 111+.

—Trudy Ring
—update: David E. Salamie

TriQuint Semiconductor, Inc.

2300 Northeast Brookwood Parkway
Hillsboro, Oregon 97124
U.S.A.
Telephone: (503) 615-9000
Fax: (503) 615-8900
Web site: http://www.tqs.com

Public Company
Incorporated: 1985
Employees: 2,046
Sales: $312.27 million (2003)
Stock Exchanges: NASDAQ
Ticker Symbol: TQNT
NAIC: 334413 Semiconductor and Related Device
    Manufacturing

TriQuint Semiconductor, Inc. is a leading designer and manufacturer of semiconductor products, using gallium arsenide instead of silicon as the base material for its circuits. TriQuint operates four manufacturing facilities, in Oregon, Florida, Texas, and Costa Rica. The company derives the bulk of its business from sales to wireless communications companies.

Origins

TriQuint was born within the corporate structure of another company, its mission to serve its parent by turning nascent technology into market viability. TriQuint's earliest roots were traced to a research project undertaken by Tektronix Inc. in 1978. In their Beaverton, Oregon-based laboratories, Tektronix engineers experimented with developing high-speed semiconductors, using an exotic material called gallium arsenide, or GaAs, as the base material for their integrated circuits. In 1985, when Tektronix's sales eclipsed $1 billion, the company used its venture capital firm, Tektronix Development Corp., to provide the funding for a new independent subsidiary, TriQuint Semiconductor, Inc. Tektronix, a company known for electronic design and engineering tools, hoped to use the high-speed semiconductors developed by TriQuint in its own instruments.

When TriQuint first began operating as Tektronix's independent subsidiary, the prospects were high for the market potential of gallium arsenide semiconductors. Although Tektronix never revealed how much it originally invested in TriQuint, industry observers estimated that the company's venture capital arm provided TriQuint with at least $20 million in start-up capital. With this initial investment, Tektronix management hoped TriQuint's engineers could develop a way of producing gallium arsenide chips in large volumes and at a price low enough to attract customers. Gallium arsenide possessed superior qualities to silicon—by far the most common base material used to manufacture semiconductors—but it was also much more costly to produce, particularly in large volumes. Gallium arsenide allowed for much faster computing than silicon, carrying an electronic charge faster than silicon could while consuming less power than silicon. The advantage came at a price, however. Gallium arsenide typically cost as much as $200 per wafer, ten times the price for a silicon wafer. Further, manufacturing techniques for producing gallium arsenide chips in bulk at a price acceptable for the commercial market had yet to be developed. As such, there was great promise for gallium arsenide, but much work was required to turn the material's promise into reality. As TriQuint set out, it was positioned as a pioneer in the development of gallium arsenide technology, with industry observers and Tektronix management waiting to see if the company could deliver on the promise of the next-generation material.

TriQuint's first years in business were spent trying to unlock the potential of gallium arsenide by improving production methods. At a 20,000-square-foot facility leased from Tektronix, TriQuint engineers worked on increasing commercial acceptance of gallium arsenide chips, which many industry pundits believed would ignite sales. In the mid-1980s, the U.S. military was the primary purchaser of gallium arsenide integrated circuits, accounting for two-thirds of the gallium arsenide market, a $50-million-in-sales business. By the 1990s, some experts believed the gallium arsenide market could reach $2 billion in annual sales, but only if the commercial sector was persuaded to choose gallium arsenide over silicon in greatly increased numbers. TriQuint, itself, was hoping to reach $50 million in annual sales by the late 1980s, but it would take roughly a decade before the company met its financial objec-

Company Perspectives:

We are a global supplier to the communications industry with a focus on media interface applications of RF and optical communications systems. Our mission is, "Connecting the Digital World to the Global Network," and we accomplish this through a diversified product portfolio. We strive to be a premier supplier of solutions based on complex materials such as GaAs, InP and other compound semiconductor materials and SAW-based products.

tive. Instead, the first five years of TriQuint's existence proved to be a financial struggle, as the company racked up successive annual losses throughout the latter half of the 1980s.

Although TriQuint was a money-loser during its first half-decade of business, profitability was not the sole measure of the company's success. By the beginning of the 1990s, TriQuint ranked as the largest manufacturer of gallium arsenide semiconductors in the United States. The gallium arsenide market, as a whole, had developed into a $200 million business by the beginning of the 1990s, with TriQuint keeping pace with the industry's growth by registering compounded annual sales increases of between 30 percent and 50 percent. Much of the company's focus was on developing its commercial business, particularly in telecommunications where gallium arsenide's properties were useful for converting sound waves into digital signals.

As TriQuint sought to exploit the technological advantages of gallium arsenide in the telecommunications sector, the company also searched for a partner in the gallium arsenide industry. TriQuint occupied the leadership position in the market and had recorded strong sales growth, but profits eluded the company. Further, the slower-than-expected growth of the gallium arsenide industry exacerbated the costly nature of gallium arsenide production, forcing the company to seek help in navigating its course as an industry pioneer. The addition of a partner, specifically a partner willing to invest, promised to alleviate the financial demands of gallium arsenide production, to open new marketing opportunities, and to better the chances of achieving profitability. By the beginning of the 1990s, TriQuint was negotiating with three companies, attempting to secure an investment to better its chances and to assuage the growing impatience of its 90 percent owner, Tektronix.

TriQuint entered the 1990s facing a critical juncture in its development. The gallium arsenide market was growing, but not at the pace predicted in the mid-1980s. TriQuint was recording steady sales growth, but not at the pace forecasted at its inception. Most disconcerting, the company was proving to be a perennial money-loser, its ability to turn a profit hampered by the difficulties in manufacturing gallium arsenide chips in volume at an acceptable market price. To improve its situation the company sought a partnership, negotiating with aerospace giant McDonnell Douglas Corp. in 1990. As part of the talks, TriQuint proposed producing advanced computer chips for McDonnell Douglas's military needs. Aside from providing a new source of revenue, the joint effort with McDonnell Douglas promised to help TriQuint establish new product lines. "I think you're going

to see more and more of this happening," a TriQuint marketing executive commented to *Business Journal-Portland* in an April 9, 1990 interview. "The gallium arsenide business is a very expensive one, and there's not enough demand out there at this point to justify the duplication of capacity."

1991 Merger Bringing in New Management

The pressing nature of TriQuint's financial condition led to a corporate maneuver far more profound than a joint venture agreement. The event also signaled the arrival of a new leader, an individual who would guide the company into the 21st century. In January 1991, a merger was arranged between TriQuint and a California-based gallium arsenide chip producer named Gigabit Logic. Within months, another merger was arranged, adding Gazelle Microcircuits, another California-based gallium arsenide chip producer, to the combination of TriQuint and Gigabit Logic. In the fall of 1991, a new leader was hired to manage the merged companies, a veteran of the semiconductor industry named Steven J. Sharp. Before joining TriQuint in September 1991, Sharp spent nine years at Texas Instruments and 14 years working for Signetics Corp. After leaving Signetics, Sharp founded Power Integrations, Inc. and Silicon Architects.

With Sharp at the helm serving as president and chief executive officer (he was named chairman in May 1992), TriQuint embarked on a new era. Sharp made severe cuts after he arrived, closing several facilities and trimming the company's workforce by a significant amount. Following the merger with Gigabit Logic and Gazelle, TriQuint's payroll swelled to 330, which Sharp reduced to 185 within months after his arrival, leaving TriQuint with a smaller workforce than it had before the merger. Sharp also oriented the company's strategic focus toward communications applications such as fiber optic telecommunications, satellite communications, and, most important, wireless communications. In the years ahead, the demand from cellular companies for gallium arsenide technology would increase robustly, making Sharp's decision to place an emphasis on wireless applications an astute one.

Following the mergers and Sharp's arrival, TriQuint began to exhibit unprecedented financial vitality. By mid-1992, the company had recorded its first six months of profitability, ending six years of successive losses. By the end of 1992, as the profits continued to roll in, TriQuint had collected $29 million in revenue. The sales total was less than TriQuint's original management would have expected for the company by the early 1990s, but for Sharp and his new management team, the financial results for the year were cause for celebration. Further cause for joy arrived in 1993, as TriQuint began to shine for the first time in its history.

Not long after TriQuint recorded its string of six profitable months, Sharp began negotiating with AT&T Microelectronics. The talks carried on for nearly a year before industry observers were apprised of what precisely the two companies were discussing. In August 1993, AT&T announced it had acquired a substantial stake in TriQuint, an investment that was part of a product development deal with TriQuint. According to the terms of the agreement, TriQuint began manufacturing most of the gallium arsenide semiconductors for AT&T Microelectronic's wireless telecommunications equipment. Also, the partnership called for both companies to jointly develop a new manufacturing process related to technology developed by AT&T Microelectronics. With this process, TriQuint hoped to be able to develop gallium arsenide integrated circuits for higher power wireless devices and next-generation fiber-optic communications systems.

Following the announcement of the deal with AT&T Microelectronics, Sharp, in a September 6, 1993 interview with *Business Journal-Portland,* declared, "With this investment, we have no need to go public." Before the end of the year, however, TriQuint completed an initial public offering of stock, raising roughly $17 million in a December 1993 debut on NASDAQ. TriQuint appeared to be destined for a successful 1994, having brokered a pivotal deal with AT&T Microelectronics, shown itself able to post consistent profits, and made its public debut. The company faltered, however, making 1994 "the year from hell," according to Sharp in a February 1995 interview with *Electronics Business Buyer.*

TriQuint's run of success ended in the spring of 1994, a point at which the company had reported ten consecutive profitable quarters. The downward slide began when the company's largest customer, Northern Telecom Ltd., announced slower than expected sales of some of its transmission equipment. For TriQuint, which relied on Northern Telecom for 30 percent of its total sales, the announcement meant a substantial reduction in orders for the rest of the year. Negative reaction to the news was swift, causing TriQuint's stock price to plummet 48 percent in one day, which led to a shareholder lawsuit. The company lost money for each of the final three quarters of the year, including a $7.5 million loss in the company's third quarter as sales dropped by one-third.

Sharp responded quickly to TriQuint's anemic condition. The company's facility in Santa Clara, California, obtained in the merger with Gazelle, was closed, which reduced the company's overhead. "We also focused on speeding up our product introduction cycle," Sharp explained in his February 1995 interview with *Electronics Business Buyer.* "We got more new products out in the third quarter than in any quarter in our history, and had 17 design wins of over $100,000 last year," he added. Although the company found itself in a precarious financial position, it did not reduce research and development spending. In fact, TriQuint increased its funding of product development for the wireless market, which Sharp viewed as "probably the single biggest opportunity we can identify over the next 10 years," as quoted in his February 1995 interview with *Electronics Business Buyer.*

Rapid Growth in the Late 1990s

Following a disastrous inaugural year as a publicly traded company, TriQuint rebounded well, setting the stage for the company's explosive rise during the second half of the 1990s. Sales increased 50 percent to $46 million in 1995, as its focus on the wireless market began to pay dividends. In 1997, the company left Beaverton and moved to Hillsboro, Oregon, where it constructed a 32-acre corporate campus anchored by a 160,000-square-foot complex. By the end of the following year, sales had eclipsed $100 million for the first time.

By the end of the 1990s, TriQuint exuded strength, its commitment to gallium arsenide production at last delivering substantial financial gains. The commercial demand for gallium arsenide chips enabled the company to garner a greater portion of the multibillion-dollar semiconductor market, as telecommunications companies, and cellular telephone manufacturers in particular, provided a foundation for growth. In the February 18, 2000 issue of *Business Journal-Portland,* Dan McMillan wrote: "TriQuint appears to have a solid strategy and a management team that is focused on executing that strategy. The company is focused on the telecommunications market and it's tough to find any sort of industry expert who doesn't think that's a good strategy." Other industry observers, particularly investors, saw the soundness of TriQuint's strategic focus as well. In a three-month period in 1999, the company's stock price soared, jumping from $90 per share to more than $220 per share. Sales reached $164 million in 1999 before climbing to $300 million in 2000.

TriQuint entered the 21st century recording robust growth and deepening its involvement in the wireless market. The first years of the new century saw the company forge several important deals that increased its capabilities to attract customers from the wireless sector. In May 2001, TriQuint announced it had signed a cooperative agreement with San Jose, California-based Atmel Corp. to design, manufacture, and market cellular telephone components using Atmel's silicon-germanium technology. In July 2001, TriQuint completed another merger, absorbing the assets of $160 million-in-sales Sawtek Inc., an Orlando, Florida-based manufacturer of surface acoustic wave-based signal processing components for the wireless communications industry.

As TriQuint charted its course for the future, the company anticipated bolstering its involvement in the wireless sector and adding new technological capabilities to its portfolio. For the years ahead, TriQuint would rely on a new leader to oversee the day-to-day management of the company. In October 1991, after a decade in charge of the company, Sharp announced his desire to reduce his corporate responsibilities. His decision to lessen his involvement in the company led to the appointment of Ralph Quinsey in July 2002 as president and chief executive officer. Sharp retained his title as TriQuint's chairman. Before joining TriQuint, Quinsey spent 20 years working for Motorola, where he served in various capacities developing both silicon and gallium arsenide technologies for wireless telephone applications. Under Quinsey's stewardship, TriQuint entered a new business area in January 2003, when the company acquired

Agere Systems Inc.'s optoelectronics business for $40 million. The addition of the optoelectronics business, which contained components that carried data and voice traffic over optical networks, added further strength to TriQuint's operations. As the company pushed forward, nearing its 20th anniversary, it promised to explore other strategic opportunities in the telecommunications and networking markets.

Principal Subsidiaries

Sawtek Inc.; TriQuint Optoelectronics, Inc.; TriQuint Semiconductor GmbH (Germany); TriQuint Semiconductor Texas L.P.

Principal Competitors

Infineon Technologies AG; Skyworks Solutions, Inc.; Vitesse Semiconductor Corporation.

Further Reading

Anderson, Michael A., "Fast Wafers Power TriQuint's Pursuit of Profits," *Business Journal-Portland,* July 14, 1986, p. 9.

"Big 'T,'" *Orlando Business Journal,* May 18, 2001, p. 2.
Chin, Spencer, "TriQuint Ventures into Turbulent Waters—Acquires Agere's Wounded Optical Components Unit for $40M," *EBN,* October 28, 2002, p. 4.
DeTar, Jim, "AT&T Takes More Equity in TriQuint Semiconductor," *Electronic News,* January 2, 1995, p. 10.
Law, Steve, "TriQuint Joining Chip Plant Boom," *Business Journal-Portland,* October 6, 1995, p. 1.
Manning, Jeff, "Six Months of Profits Bolstering TriQuint Initial Stock Offering," *Business Journal-Portland,* June 15, 1992, p. 3.
——, "TriQuint Gets Cash, New Product Development Deal from AT&T," *Business Journal-Portland,* September 6, 1993, p. 6.
——, "TriQuint Tries for Chip Linkup with McDonnell Douglas," *Business Journal-Portland,* April 9, 1990, p. 4.
McMillan, Dan, "Exciting Times at TriQuint, RadiSys and InFocus," *Business Journal-Portland,* January 21, 2000, p. 14.
——, "TriQuint Stock's Meteoric Rise Has Been Stunning," *Business Journal-Portland,* February 18, 2000, p. 19.
Ristelhueber, Robert, "TriQuint Tries to Bounce Back from Rocky Start," *Electronic Business Buyer,* February 1995, p. 28.

—Jeffrey L. Covell

Tyco International Ltd.

The Zurich Centre
Second Floor
90 Pitts Bay Road
Pembroke HM 08
Bermuda
Telephone: (441) 292-8674
Fax: (441) 295-9647
Web site: http://www.tyco.com

Public Company
Incorporated: 1962 as Tyco, Inc.
Employees: 258,000
Sales: $36.8 billion (2003)
Stock Exchanges: New York Bermuda
Ticker Symbol: TYC
NAIC: 322221 Coated & Laminated Packaging Paper &
   Plastics Film Manuf.; 322291 Sanitary Paper Product
   Manuf.; 325520 Adhesive Manuf.; 326199 All Other
   Plastics Product Manuf.; 332911 Industrial Valve
   Manuf.; 332912 Fluid Power Valve & Hose Fitting
   Manuf.; 332919 Other Metal Valve & Pipe Fitting
   Manuf.; 332996 Fabricated Pipe & Pipe Fitting Manuf.;
   334290 Other Communications Equipment Manuf.;
   334417 Electronic Connector Manuf.; 334418 Printed
   Circuit Assembly; 334513 Instruments & Related
   Product Manuf. for Measuring, Displaying, &
   Controlling Industrial Process Variables; 335929
   Communications Wire & Cable; 335931 Current-
   Carrying Wiring Device Manuf.; 339112 Surgical &
   Medical Instrument Manuf.; 339113 Surgical
   Appliance & Supplies Manuf.; 339999 All Other
   Misc. Manuf.; 421610 Electrical Apparatus &
   Equipment, Wiring Supplies, & Construction Material
   Wholesalers; 561621 Security Systems Services
   (Except Locksmiths)

Tyco International Ltd. is a diversified manufacturing and service company, with five main operating groups. Tyco Fire and Security (generating 31 percent of total revenues) is the world leader in the design, manufacture, installation, monitoring, and service of fire detection, protection, and suppression systems, as well as being the world leader in electronic security services. Tyco Electronics (28 percent of revenues) is one of the world's largest suppliers of electronic components, with a leading position in passive electronic components, and is also one of the world's leading providers of undersea fiber-optic networks and services. Tyco Healthcare (23 percent of revenues) manufactures and distributes a wide variety of medical devices and supplies, including sutures and surgical staplers, needles and syringes, laparoscopic instruments, electrosurgical devices, minimally invasive surgical instruments, and adult incontinence products. Tyco Engineered Products and Services (13 percent of revenues) is the world's leading maker of industrial valves and controls, serving the petroleum, chemical, petrochemical, power generation, water management, pharmaceutical, pulp and paper, food and beverage, commercial construction, and other industries. Tyco Plastics and Adhesives (5 percent of revenues) is the number one producer of plastic trash bags in the United States, is one of the largest extruders of plastic film in the country, and holds world-leading positions in both plastic garment hangers and duct tape. Domiciled in Bermuda for tax purposes, Tyco International maintains its operational headquarters in West Windsor, New Jersey.

Tyco grew tremendously in the 1990s and early 2000s, with revenues increasing from $3.07 billion in 1992 to $34.04 billion in 2001; an aggressive program of acquisition during this period saw the company spend an estimated $62 billion to purchase more than 1,000 companies. But the engineer of this ascent, L. Dennis Kozlowski, resigned in June 2002 under a cloud, and he and Mark H. Swartz (former Tyco CFO) later faced criminal charges for allegedly stealing $600 million from the company and its shareholders. Tyco subsequently struggled to rid itself of the taint of scandal with which it became associated, leaving it lumped in with such firms as Enron Corporation and WorldCom, Inc. as the prime symbols of the excesses and greed of the 1990s bubble economy.

Beginnings in 1962 in High Tech

In 1960, with a science Ph.D. from Harvard, Arthur J. Rosenburg opened a research laboratory in Waltham, Massachusetts, and did experimental work for the government. Two years later

Company Perspectives:

Our mission: to increase the value of our company and our global portfolio of diversified brands by exceeding customers' expectations and achieving market leadership and operating excellence in every segment of our company.

Rosenburg incorporated Tyco, Inc. and branched into the commercial sector. He assembled a team of top researchers and Tyco developed high-tech products for the marketplace.

Tyco's early technological breakthroughs included a silicon carbide laser. This laser was the first blue-light laser and the first to fire a nonstop beam, all at room temperature. Other successful research projects led to the marketing of the Dynalux battery charger, a device that would never overcharge a battery. It had many industrial applications. Other advances came in fluid controls, microcircuitry, and fuel cell catalysts. In 1964 Tyco went public.

Rosenburg established an ambitious growth schedule for his company. To fill the gaps in its development and distribution network, Tyco began to acquire other companies. In 1965—the same year that the company changed its name to Tyco Laboratories, Inc.—Tyco began a spree of acquisitions that drastically changed the makeup of the company. In 1966 the company bought Industrionics Control, Inc., adding to other recent purchases of Mule Battery Manufacturing Company and Custom Metal Products, Inc. The next year, Tyco acquired the North American Printed Circuit Corporation, General Nucleonics Corporation, and Bytrex, Inc. In 1968 Electralab Electronics Corporation; Air Spec, Inc.; Explosive Fabricators Corporation; Dynaco Inc.; Coating Products, Inc.; and Digital Devices, Inc. were acquired. Accurate Forming Company, CBM Realty Corporation, Linear Corporation, Micro-Power Corporation, and Custom Products Inc. were added to the group in 1969. Tyco's sales increased from less than $1 million in 1963 to more than $41 million for all of its companies by 1969.

This dazzling growth, however, did not occur without complications. By the end of the 1960s, Tyco Laboratories needed a major reorganization to put its new units in order. The price of company stock had dropped dramatically from its peak in the mid-1960s, as Wall Street became disillusioned with high-tech companies. Tyco divested a number of unprofitable units in 1969, and assessed its corporate direction.

In 1970 the Tyco board quietly eased out founder Rosenburg, replacing him temporarily with Joshua M. Berman, a partner in the law firm Goodwin, Proctor, and Hoar, and a director of Tyco Laboratories. In September 1971 Ralph W. Detra took over as president, while Berman remained chairman and CEO. Detra resigned one year later, and Tyco was without a president until April 1973, when the Tyco board appointed Joseph P. Gaziano chairman, president, and CEO.

Acquisitions of Simplex and Grinnell in the Mid-1970s

Gaziano, a graduate of the Massachusetts Institute of Technology, had held a number of positions at the Raytheon Company before leaving in 1967 to run Prelude Corporation, a lobster-fishing concern. Gaziano launched a new era for Tyco Laboratories. During his tenure the company became much larger and more diverse, making acquisitions on a much grander scale than earlier. In January 1974 the stock of Tyco Laboratories was listed on the New York Stock Exchange, and four months later Gaziano completed Tyco's most ambitious acquisition thus far, the $22 million cash purchase of the Simplex Wire and Cable Company, a firm specializing in undersea cable. While Simplex competed with such manufacturing giants as Western Union and Anaconda Wire and Cable in the conventional wire and cable markets, it had a lead in the underwater cable market. This specialization was one of the factors that made it attractive to Tyco Laboratories.

In September 1975 Tyco purchased the Grinnell subsidiary of International Telephone and Telegraph (ITT). Grinnell was the market leader in automatic sprinklers. ITT had been ordered by federal courts to divest the fire-protection-equipment and piping manufacturer on antitrust grounds. Tyco President Gaziano took the opportunity to purchase a well-established company at a reasonable price. Tyco paid $14 million and agreed to pay ITT 40 percent of Grinnell's net earnings for the next ten years, with a minimum payment of $28.5 million. At the time of the acquisition, Tyco's total sales were $58 million, overshadowed by its new subsidiary, Grinnell, whose turnover was $107 million.

Failure to Acquire Leeds & Northrup in the Late 1970s

Tyco began its third major acquisition in November 1976 when it bought 13 percent of the Philadelphia-based process-control designer and manufacturer Leeds & Northrup Company. Through a press release Tyco announced its intention to buy more of Leeds & Northrup's stock. Leeds & Northrup filed suit in federal court, claiming that Tyco's press release was in effect an illegal tender offer and that Tyco had not filed the necessary documents with the Securities and Exchange Commission (SEC). Tyco agreed to halt its purchase of the stock temporarily, but over the next two years President and CEO Gaziano waged one of the most convoluted hostile takeover battles in corporate history.

Tyco's agreement to stop buying Leeds & Northrup stock was dependent on the latter company's continued independence. Leeds & Northrup President David Kimball began issuing new shares, and arranged for the Milwaukee-based Cutler-Hammer Inc. to buy 9 percent of Leeds & Northrup stock as a hedge against further encroachment from Tyco. Gaziano protested, but could do little; Tyco was prevented by a court-approved agreement from gaining more than 19 percent of Leeds & Northrup until March 1978. In January 1978, Tyco gave up its attempt to acquire Leeds & Northrup, and sold its 19 percent interest to Cutler-Hammer for a $9.2 million profit.

Two months later Tyco bought 8.5 percent of Cutler-Hammer Inc., which now controlled 33.5 percent of Leeds & Northrup. By June, Tyco had 28.4 percent of the Cutler-Hammer shares. Gaziano then raised $25 million through debentures in the Eurodollar market, and increased Tyco's holding in Cutler-Hammer to 32 percent. Meanwhile, Koppers Inc., a chemical and engineering firm, accumulated 21 percent of the

Key Dates:

1960: Arthur J. Rosenburg opens a research laboratory in Waltham, Massachusetts, doing experimental work for the government.

1962: Rosenburg incorporates Tyco, Inc. and changes the focus to high-tech products for the commercial sector.

1964: The company goes public.

1965: Mule Battery Manufacturing Company is the firm's first acquisition; the company changes its name to Tyco Laboratories, Inc.

1970: Rosenburg is eased out by the board of directors.

1973: Joseph P. Gaziano is appointed chairman and CEO.

1974: Tyco stock is listed on the New York Stock Exchange; Simplex Wire and Cable Company is acquired.

1975: The Grinnell subsidiary of International Telephone and Telegraph (ITT) is acquired.

1979: Tyco acquires Armin Corporation.

1981: Ludlow Corporation is acquired.

1982: Gaziano dies suddenly; John F. Fort succeeds him; the new leader soon divests peripheral units and reorganizes the remaining operations into three divisions: fire protection and plumbing, electronics, and packaging.

1986: Grinnell Flow Control is purchased from ITT.

1987: The acquisition of Allied Pipe & Tube Corporation is completed.

1988: Tyco purchases Mueller Company.

1990: Australia-based Wormald International Limited is acquired.

1992: L. Dennis Kozlowski succeeds Fort as CEO.

1993: The company changes its name to Tyco International Ltd.

1994: Kendall International is acquired.

1997: Tyco acquires the undersea cable-laying and maintenance operations of AT&T Corp., Keystone International Inc., and Bermuda-based ADT Limited; Tyco merges into the latter, becoming a Bermuda-domiciled firm.

1998: Acquisitions include American Home Products' Sherwood-Davis & Geck division and United States Surgical Corporation.

1999: AMP Incorporated is acquired for $11.3 billion; Raychem Corporation is also acquired.

2000: Tyco acquires the global electronics connectors business of Thomas & Betts Corporation, Lucent Technologies Inc.'s power-systems division, and Mallinckrodt Inc.

2001: CIT Group, Inc. is acquired for $9.5 billion.

2002: Tyco announces plans to split into four separate publicly traded companies but soon reverses course, splitting off only CIT Group through a public offering; Kozlowski resigns under a cloud of suspicion; Edward D. Breen is brought in from outside as the new chairman and CEO; Tyco reports a net loss of $9.41 billion; New York prosecutors indict Kozlowski and Mark H. Swartz (former Tyco CFO) on numerous counts of grand larceny, securities fraud, and enterprise corruption.

2003: Restructuring is launched that involves the divestiture of more than 50 noncore businesses, the elimination of about 7,200 jobs, and the closure of 219 facilities worldwide.

2004: The trial of Kozlowski and Swartz ends in a mistrial.

---

stock, erecting a formidable roadblock to Tyco's gaining a majority interest in Cutler-Hammer.

Joseph Gaziano responded by selling Tyco's 32 percent holding in Cutler-Hammer at a profit to the Eaton Corporation, a heavy equipment manufacturer that planned to merge with Cutler-Hammer, stipulating that Eaton would spin off the Leeds & Northrup shares to Tyco.

Eaton quickly made a tender offer of $261 million for the remaining Cutler-Hammer shares, a bid its board could not refuse, but at the last minute Cutler-Hammer sold the coveted 33.5 percent holding in Leeds & Northrup to General Signal Corporation. General Signal immediately announced its plan to merge with Leeds & Northrup. After a 20-month effort Gaziano failed to acquire Leeds & Northrup. "It just wasn't meant to be," he told *Forbes* magazine in 1978. Nevertheless, Tyco netted $12.9 million from the transactions.

Entering Packaging Through 1979 Purchase of Armin and 1981 Purchase of Ludlow

Gaziano continued to pursue his goal of making Tyco a $1 billion company by 1985. In September 1979 Tyco bought the Armin Corporation for $27 million. Armin was a leader in the production of polyethylene films, products used primarily in packaging.

Armin Corporation proved a profitable acquisition for Tyco Laboratories, and Gaziano increased the company's share of the lucrative packaging market through the 1981 acquisition of the Ludlow Corporation, a manufacturer of packaging and other materials, for $97 million. When Tyco purchased Ludlow, the latter needed some streamlining. The company sold unprofitable units producing furniture, jute backing, textiles, and bags. Its specialty paper units enjoyed strong markets in medical applications and other technologically advancing fields.

Increasing Efficiency Under Fort in the 1980s

In 1982 Gaziano died suddenly at the age of 47. During his decade at the helm, Tyco Laboratories' sales increased from $34 million to more than $500 million. The company entered a new period under the leadership of John F. Fort. Fort had risen through the ranks of the Simplex Wire and Cable Company, and was president of that firm at the time of the Tyco takeover. His style differed markedly from Gaziano's.

Fort disposed of Tyco's corporate jets and apartments, and trimmed the corporate staff to 35. Reining in the somewhat unwieldy conglomeration of businesses his predecessor had brought together, he divested such peripheral units as lawn furniture and latex. Fort organized Tyco's remaining subsidiaries into three main units: the fire protection and plumbing division, which consisted of Grinnell Corporation; the electronics division, made up of Simplex Wire and Cable and the Tyco Printed Circuits Group; and the packaging division, made up of Armin and Ludlow. Concentrating on making Tyco's existing businesses more profitable, Fort instituted a compensation program under which employees were rewarded in proportion to the profits their units generated.

Tyco made smaller acquisitions in the mid-1980s, including Micro-Circuit, Inc.; Hersey Products, Inc.; a water meter manufacturer, Atcor, Inc.; a pipe manufacturer; and 48 ITT production and distribution facilities worth $220 million. Following any such acquisition, Fort was ruthless about making the purchased firm more profitable, searching for ways to eliminate excess overhead and cut out unnecessary fat.

In 1987 Tyco's sales passed the $1 billion mark. Tyco paid $350 million in 1988 for the Mueller Company, a 132-year-old water and gas pipe manufacturer. The acquisition made Tyco a strong player in the area of flow control products, and this area soon became the company's fourth main unit, with the fire protection and plumbing division changed to a focus only on fire protection and the plumbing operations being subsumed into the new flow control division. This acquisition also built upon the 1986 purchase of Grinnell Flow Control from ITT. Sandwiched between these acquisitions was another important flow control buy, that of Allied Pipe & Tube Corporation, which was consummated in 1987. Another important deal came in 1990 when Tyco significantly bolstered its fire protection division through the purchase of Australia-based Wormald International Limited for $642.5 million in cash, stock, and a warrant. Wormald's marketing presence encompassed Australia, New Zealand, Asia, and Europe, heightening Tyco's international sales.

Escalating Pace of Acquisition Under Kozlowski in the Mid- to Late 1990s

The early 1990s were a difficult period for Tyco thanks to the recession. Earnings were down despite the focus on cost containment, and the 1993 fiscal year saw the company post net income of a mere $1 million. Amidst these doldrums, the company leadership shifted in mid-1992 from Fort to L. Dennis Kozlowski, who had been with Tyco since the mid-1970s.

Kozlowski retained Fort's penchant for cost control but he slowly began to take a more aggressive approach to acquisitions—without ever pursuing a hostile bid and with two tough additional rules: an acquisition had to be immediately accretive to earnings and twice as accretive as a stock buyback. The new leader also worked to build up Tyco's operations outside the area of fire and security services, its largest sector but one subject to the ups and downs of the U.S. construction market. At the same time, acquisition targets had to be complementary to an existing Tyco operation, however subtle that synergy might be. With this approach—and through spending $28 billion to acquire 110 companies from 1992 through 1998—Kozlowski was able to transform Tyco into a $12 billion-plus revenue giant with market leading positions in four areas: disposable and

specialty products, fire and security services, flow control products, and electrical and electronic components. In reflection of an increased emphasis on the international market, the company changed its name to Tyco International Ltd. in 1993.

The first major acquisition of the Kozlowski era came in 1994 when Tyco paid $1.4 billion for Kendall International, a maker of disposable medical products with annual sales of $800 million. It was this purchase that transformed the packaging division into the disposable and specialty products division. This division was further bolstered in 1996 with the addition of five more companies, including Professional Medical Products, Inc., another disposable medical products maker, and Carlisle Plastics, a maker of plastic film and plastic garment hangers. Also in 1996 Tyco added Thorn Security Group, a U.K. fire alarm and security system company.

In January 1997 Tyco abandoned a $4 billion bid to take over American Standard, a maker of air conditioners and bathroom fixtures. American Standard would have fit in well with Tyco's flow control division, but Tyco, keeping to its no-hostile-bids policy, walked away after the target's board rejected the offer. Undeterred, Tyco completed four major acquisitions over the remainder of 1997, adding one company to each of its divisions. Acquired in the area of disposable and specialty products was INBRAND, bought for $320 million, and a maker of disposable personal products such as adult incontinence products, feminine hygiene products, and baby diapers. By spending $850 million, Tyco secured the undersea cable-laying and maintenance operations of AT&T Corp. As part of the electrical and electronic components division, the AT&T unit was combined with Simplex to form Tyco Submarine Systems Ltd. In flow control, Tyco acquired Keystone International Inc. for $1.2 billion in stock. Houston-based Keystone was a world leader in the manufacture of valves, pipes, and other equipment used in the chemical, power, food/beverage, and petroleum industries. Tyco's largest acquisition to date was consummated in July 1997, when the company merged with ADT Limited, a Bermuda-based home security company, in a $5.4 billion transaction—a white knight deal that fended off a hostile takeover bid from Western Resources Inc. In this complicated transaction, a wholly owned subsidiary of ADT merged with Tyco International Ltd.; ADT thereupon changed its name to Tyco International Ltd.; and the wholly owned subsidiary that had merged with the former Tyco was renamed Tyco International (US), Inc. and became the U.S. headquarters for the new Tyco, which was now domiciled in Bermuda for tax reasons. Tyco also added stock listings on the London and Bermuda exchanges to its NYSE listing. In addition to the number one electronic security service in North America and the United Kingdom, the ADT merger also brought Tyco, through ADT Automotive, the new area of vehicle auction services; this peripheral unit, which was small relative to other Tyco activities, was placed within the disposable and specialty products division.

In February 1998 Kozlowski turned down an offer to become president and eventual CEO of Raytheon Company. In April of that year Kozlowski told the *Financial Times* that he aimed to increase Tyco's non-North American revenue from 40 to 60 percent of the total within three years. Meantime, the Tyco executive did not slow down his company's pace of acquisition. In March 1998 Tyco closed on a $1.8 billion purchase of the

Sherwood-Davis & Geck division of American Home Products. Sherwood-Davis was a leading maker of disposable medical products, including surgical sutures, catheters, and feeding tubes, and had annual revenues of about $1 billion. Three months later Tyco snapped up the Wells Fargo Alarm unit of Borg-Warner Corporation for $425 million. In October 1998 the company acquired United States Surgical Corporation (USSC) for about $3.17 billion in stock. USSC's complementary product line included disposable medical sutures, staples, and surgical items for minimally invasive operations. Yet another maker of disposable medical products was added in November 1998 when Tyco paid $460 million in cash for Graphic Controls Corporation. This spate of medical deals led Tyco to change the name of its disposable and specialty products division to healthcare and specialty products.

Tyco expanded its electronic security unit through the early 1999 purchases of Alarmguard Holdings, Inc. and Entergy Security Corporation, the latter paid for with $237 million in cash. In April of that year came Tyco's largest acquisition to date, that of AMP Incorporated, the world's leading manufacturer of electrical, electronic, fiber-optic, and wireless connection devices and interconnective systems. This was another white knight maneuver for Tyco, in that the $11.3 billion stock swap fended off AlliedSignal Inc.'s hostile bid to take over AMP. In August 1999 Tyco acquired Raychem Corporation for nearly $3 billion in cash and stock, plus the assumption of $400 million in debt. Raychem, maker of electric and electronic components used in appliances, telecommunications, motor vehicles, and the aerospace industry, was seen as a good follow-on to the AMP deal. The AMP and other acquisitions helped to nearly double Tyco's revenues, which increased from $12.31 billion in 1998 to $22.5 billion in 1999. During 1999, in keeping with an increased focus on businesses with strong recurring sales streams and low cyclicality, Tyco divested the Mueller Company and portions of Grinnell Supply Sales and Manufacturing.

Peak of Acquisitions Activity, Then Precipitous Fall, in the Early 2000s

Analysts had occasionally expressed concerns about the way in which Tyco was accounting for its myriad acquisitions. The Securities and Exchange Commission (SEC) launched an inquiry into the matter in 1999 but did not take any action. The deals, meantime, continued in 2000 with two major takeovers involving the electronics division. In July the global electronics connectors business of Thomas & Betts Corporation was acquired for $750 million. In December, Tyco bought Lucent Technologies Inc.'s power-systems division for $2.5 billion. The acquired unit, which generated $1.6 billion in annual revenues, specialized in providing power supplies and backup power systems to telecommunications companies and operators and data networks. Also acquired in October 2000 was Mallinckrodt Inc. in a deal that expanded the healthcare division. Mallinckrodt, a firm with annual sales of about $2.6 billion, produced such medical products as ventilators and other respiratory care equipment, blood-analysis products, and analgesics, including opium-based narcotics, synthetic narcotics, and peptides used in various pharmaceuticals. Tyco sold its ADT Automotive vehicle auction business to Cox Enterprises, Inc. for $1 billion in October 2000.

The fiscal year ending in September 2001 evolved into Tyco's most acquisitive year yet. The company reported laying out $19.55 billion on acquisitions for the year, including not only the aforementioned Lucent power-systems division and Mallinckrodt but also Simplex Time Recorder Co., CIT Group, Inc., and the electronic security systems operations of Cambridge Protection Industries, L.L.C. The fire and security services division was enlarged through the January 2001 purchase of Simplex for $1.15 billion. Simplex, producer of fire and security products and systems, had annual revenues of $870 million. The $9.5 billion purchase of CIT Group, completed in June 2001, surprised many given that it fell outside of Tyco's core industrial area of focus: with $50 billion in assets, CIT was the largest independent commercial-finance company in the United States. But Kozlowski, who told *Business Week* in May 2001, ''Hopefully, we can become the next General Electric,'' evidently envisioned CIT becoming Tyco's financial arm, similar to the role played by GE Capital Corporation at General Electric Company. Tyco wrapped up fiscal 2001 with the $1 billion Cambridge Protection deal, completed in July 2001, which gave Tyco the SecurityLink line of electronic security systems. For the fiscal year, Tyco reported net income of $3.97 billion on total revenues of $36.39 billion.

In November 2001 Tyco spent about $2.2 billion for Sensormatic Electronics Corp., thereby giving the fire and security services division entrée into the market for theft-detection and video-surveillance equipment for retailers. Then in January 2002 Tyco spent about $650 million for Paragon Trade Brands, Inc., providing the healthcare division with a worldwide supplier of disposable diapers and other absorbent personal-care products. Meantime, a deal to acquire medical products supplier C.R. Bard Inc. for $3.1 billion, announced in May 2001, fell apart in early 2002. This turn of events coincided with an abrupt strategy reversal for Kozlowski, whose dealmaking had earned him the nickname ''Deal-a-Day Dennis.'' The dizzying string of acquisitions that had created a huge if unwieldy conglomerate ended with astonishing speed, and events at Tyco overtook even the seemingly unflappable Kozlowski.

The backdrop for Tyco's—and Kozlowski's—precipitous fall was the wave of corporate scandals that followed the end of the bubble economy of the 1990s. In particular, the collapse of Enron Corporation in 2001 produced a great deal of skepticism among investors regarding any company with a complex accounting structure—something that Tyco certainly had thanks to its torrid acquisitions pace. The previous concerns about the company's accounting practices resurfaced and multiplied, and investors reacted by pummeling the stock. Late in January 2002, Kozlowski put acquisitions on hold and announced a radical plan to boost shareholder value by splitting the firm into four separate publicly traded companies—concentrating on security and electronics, fire protection and flow control, healthcare, and financial services—and selling off the plastics business. But Wall Street reacted extremely coolly to this plan, and just three months later, Kozlowski shifted course again, vowing to keep the company together, retain the plastics division, and sell off only CIT Group through an initial public offering (IPO). By May Tyco's stock was trading at less than $20 per share, down 66 percent since the beginning of the year; the firm's market capitalization, which in December 2001 had been higher than that of General Motors Corporation, Ford Motor Company, and DaimlerChrysler AG combined, had plummeted by about $80 billion.

It was ironic, then, that when Kozlowski resigned in June 2002 the reason given for the action was not related to his management of Tyco but rather concerned a personal matter: he had become the subject of a criminal probe into his possible evasion of New York sales tax on the purchase of expensive artwork. Just one day after his resignation, Kozlowski was indicted on charges of conspiring to evade $1 million in sales tax. Tyco named Kozlowski's predecessor, Fort, as interim CEO before bringing Edward D. Breen onboard in late July as its new chairman and CEO. Breen had been president and chief operating officer at Motorola, Inc. Also in July, Tyco completed the CIT Group IPO, raising $4.6 billion—less than half of what it had paid for the company. For the fiscal year ending in September 2002, Tyco recorded a net loss of $6.28 billion related to CIT. Coupled with a host of other charges and expenses, the company suffered an overall net loss for the year of $9.41 billion.

Breen quickly cleaned house at Tyco, overhauling the entire top management team over the course of his first several months in office and replacing two of the firm's five division presidents (the plastics and adhesives division was created in January 2003). He also engineered a complete turnover of the company board, even ousting Fort. Kozlowski's chief financial officer, Mark H. Swartz, was cashiered in August 2002 and replaced by David J. FitzPatrick, who had been CFO at United Technologies Corporation. In September 2002 New York prosecutors indicted Kozlowski and Swartz on numerous counts of grand larceny, securities fraud, and enterprise corruption, accusing them of stealing more than $170 million from the company and pocketing $430 million from illegal stock sales. The case went to trial one year later and lasted six months. In March 2004 the judge threw out the enterprise corruption charge, but the remaining counts went to the jury. After several weeks of jury deliberation, however, the judge was forced to declare a mistrial, citing outside pressure that had been brought to bear on one of the jurors. The jury was apparently on the verge of returning guilty verdicts on several felony counts when the mistrial was declared. Prosecutors promised to retry the case.

Meanwhile, Breen was busy with his turnaround effort. One of his key moves was to transform the corporate culture, tightening the accounting procedures and replacing the company's opulent U.S. operational headquarters in New York City with much more modest digs in an office park in West Windsor, New Jersey. Thorough internal reviews of the accounting for the previous several years revealed some aggressive accounting tactics and resulted in the restatement of more than $2 billion in earnings but did not uncover any instances of outright fraud. Breen also had to contend with the staggering $26 billion debt load the company was burdened with thanks to Kozlowski's hyper-acquisitiveness. Through efficiency initiatives and the freeing up of cash, Breen was able to trim the total to $18.5 billion by early 2004, and he improved cash flow by refinancing this remainder. In November 2003 Tyco announced a wider restructuring program involving the shedding of more than 50 low-margin, noncore businesses, including the money-losing Tycom undersea optical-fiber network. About 7,200 jobs would be slashed from the payroll as a result, and 219 facilities worldwide would be closed. Through this and other streamlining initiatives, Breen aimed to achieve $3 billion in savings by 2006. In December 2003 Tyco canceled the listing of its shares in London because of low trading volume on that exchange, retaining the listings on the New York and Bermuda exchanges.

By March 2004, Tyco's stock had recovered somewhat, trading at around $28 per share, a huge improvement over the less than $8 per share nadir of July 2002 but still less than half of the $63 peak of mid-2001. Breen had earned kudos from the press for turning around the company's image and for instituting a wide-ranging corporate governance program. Still, a serious hangover remained from the Kozlowski era. The debt load—though smaller—remained huge, the firm's credit ratings were poor, and more than two dozen shareholders suits were pending against Tyco. The company also faced an Internal Revenue Service audit for the years 1997 to 2000 and an SEC investigation into accounting irregularities. The pending retrial of Kozlowski and Swartz loomed as well, promising another dredging up of Tyco's infamous past, and Tyco itself had civil suits pending against Kozlowski and Swartz, as well as other former executives, in attempts to recover some of the money allegedly looted from the firm. It seemed likely that Breen and Tyco's new management team faced several more years of work dealing with the mess left behind by the once-revered Kozlowski and company.

Principal Operating Units

TYCO FIRE AND SECURITY SERVICES: ADT Limited; Ansul; Scott; Sensormatic Electronics Corporation; SimplexGrinnell; Total Walther; Wormald International Limited. TYCO ELECTRONICS: AMP Incorporated; Elo TouchSystems; M/A-COM; Potter & Brumfield; Raychem Corporation. TYCO HEALTHCARE: Auto Suture; Kendall International; Mallinckrodt Inc.; Nellcor; Puritan Bennett; United States Surgical Corporation; Valleylab. TYCO ENGINEERED PRODUCTS AND SERVICES: Allied Pipe & Tube Corporation; Earth Tech; Grinnell Corporation; Keystone International Inc.; Tracer. TYCO PLASTICS AND ADHESIVES: A&E Products; Ludlow Coated Products; Tyco Adhesives; Tyco Plastics.

Principal Competitors

Molex Incorporated; 3M Company; Ingersoll-Rand Company Limited; Kidde PLC; Cooper Industries, Ltd.; ITT Industries, Inc.; Chubb plc; Johnson & Johnson; Becton, Dickinson and Company; Flowserve Corporation; Murata Manufacturing Co., Ltd.; Kyocera Corporation; C.R. Bard, Inc.

Further Reading

Bianco, Anthony, William Symonds, and Nanette Byrnes, "The Rise and Fall of Dennis Kozlowski," *Business Week,* December 23, 2002, pp. 64–69+.

Byrne, Harlan S., "One Hungry Tyke," *Barron's,* April 8, 1996, pp. 22–23.

Campanella, Frank W., "Tyco's Taint: It Ignores Solid Operating Gains," *Barron's,* December 31, 1979, pp. 31+.

Chakravarty, Subrata N., "Deal-a-Month Dennis," *Forbes,* June 15, 1998, pp. 66, 68.

"Clean Breen," *Economist,* June 14, 2003.

Deogun, Nikhil, Steven Lipin, and Mark Maremont, "Tyco to Acquire CIT for About $9 Billion," *Wall Street Journal,* March 13, 2001, p. A3.

Deutsch, Claudia H., "As Its Ex-Bosses Await Their Fate, Tyco Continues Comeback," *New York Times,* March 22, 2004, p. C1.

——, "Finding the Profits (and Fun) in Mergers," *New York Times,* November 29, 1998, Sec. 3, p. 4.

Green, Leslie, and J. Richard Elliot, Jr., "Cause for Alarm: The Story of the Anti-Trust Suit Against Grinnell Corp.," *Barron's,* May 30, 1966.

Jereski, Laura, "Synergy, Synergy, Synergy," *Forbes,* November 14, 1988, pp. 194+.

Johannes, Laura, "American Standard Rejects Tyco International's Offer," *Wall Street Journal,* January 14, 1997, pp. A3, A11.

——, "Tyco Aims to Boost Shareholder Value with Breakup," *Wall Street Journal,* January 23, 2002, p. A4.

——, "Tyco International Isn't Playing, It's Out on the Prowl," *Wall Street Journal,* January 17, 1997, p. B4.

——, "Tyco Plans to Acquire for $850 Million AT&T's Undersea Cable-Laying Unit," *Wall Street Journal,* April 14, 1997, p. B4.

——, "Tyco to Pay Cash and Stock for Raychem," *Wall Street Journal,* May 20, 1999, p. A3.

——, "Tyco Will Acquire Alarm-System Unit of Borg-Warner," *Wall Street Journal,* April 21, 1998, p. B9.

Johannes, Laura, and Steven Lipin, "Tyco International, ADT in Merger Pact," *Wall Street Journal,* March 18, 1997, pp. A3, A14.

Johannes, Laura, and Thomas M. Burton, "Tyco Agrees to Buy Mallinckrodt Inc. for $4.2 Billion," *Wall Street Journal,* June 29, 2000, p. A4.

Laing, Jonathan R., "The New Tyco," *Barron's,* December 15, 2003, pp. 17–18.

——, "Tyco's Titan," *Barron's,* April 12, 1999, pp. 27+.

Lewis, William, "Tyco to Shift Focus Outside N. America," *Financial Times,* April 28, 1998, p. 32.

Lipin, Steven, "Tyco to Acquire Keystone International," *Wall Street Journal,* May 21, 1997, pp. A3, A6.

Lipin, Steven, and Gordon Fairclough, "Tyco Reaches Agreement to Buy AMP in Stock Swap Valued at $11.3 Billion," *Wall Street Journal,* November 23, 1998, pp. A3, A8.

Lublin, Joann S., and Jon G. Auerbach, "Tyco's CEO Refuses to Run Raytheon Co.," *Wall Street Journal,* March 5, 1998, p. A4.

Lublin, Joann S., and Mark Maremont, "A CEO with a Motto: 'Let's Make a Deal!,' " *Wall Street Journal,* January 28, 1999, pp. B1, B2.

Maremont, Mark, "Tyco Agrees to Buy Sherwood Division from American Home for $1.77 Billion," *Wall Street Journal,* December 22, 1997, pp. A3, A6.

——, "Tyco Posts Loss, Will Cut 7,200 Jobs," *Wall Street Journal,* November 5, 2003, p. A3.

——, "Tyco's Deal-a-Month Man," *Business Week,* January 27, 1997, p. 36.

Maremont, Mark, and Laurie P. Cohen, "Executive Privilege: How Tyco's CEO Enriched Himself," *Wall Street Journal,* August 7, 2002, pp. A1+.

Maremont, Mark, and Jesse Drucker, "Tyco Lures Breen from Motorola to Become CEO," *Wall Street Journal,* July 26, 2002, p. A3.

Maremont, Mark, et al., "Tainted Chief: Kozlowski Quits Under a Cloud, Worsening Worries About Tyco," *Wall Street Journal,* June 4, 2002, pp. A1+.

Maremont, Mark, and Gordon Fairclough, "Accord with AMP Caps Months of Deal Making by Tyco," *Wall Street Journal,* November 24, 1998, p. B4.

Maremont, Mark, and Ross Kerber, "Tyco to Buy U.S. Surgical for $3.3 Billion in Stock," *Wall Street Journal,* May 26, 1998, p. A3.

Maremont, Mark, and Jerry Markon, "Former Tyco Executives Are Charged: New York Prosecutors Say Ex-CEO, Finance Officer Ran 'Criminal Enterprise,' " *Wall Street Journal,* September 13, 2002, p. A3.

Maremont, Mark, Kara Scannell, and Charles Forelle, "Mistrial Scuttles Possible Guilty Verdicts in Tyco Case," *Wall Street Journal,* April 5, 2004, pp. A1, A8.

Pasztor, Andy, "Water-System Gear Suit Draws Attention," *Wall Street Journal,* December 22, 1998, p. B7.

Symonds, William C., "The Most Aggressive CEO," *Business Week,* May 28, 2001, pp. 68–72, 74, 77.

Thackray, John, "Tyco: The Operator," *Across the Board,* November 1991, pp. 21–23.

"Tyco: Pursuing Profits As Relentlessly As It Once Pursued Growth," *Business Week,* March 5, 1984, pp. 96+.

Warner, Melanie, "Exorcism at Tyco," *Fortune,* April 28, 2003, pp. 106–08, 110.

Waters, Richard, "ADT Agrees to Takeover by US Conglomerate," *Financial Times,* March 18, 1997, p. 27.

——, "Low-Tech But Riding High," *Financial Times,* March 18, 1997, p. 36.

Woolley, Scott, "The Conglomerator Wants a Little Respect," *Forbes,* October 16, 2000, pp. 150–57.

—Thomas M. Tucker
—update: David E. Salamie

Unit Corporation

1000 Kensington Tower
7130 S. Lewis
Tulsa, Oklahoma 74136
U.S.A.
Telephone: (918) 493-7700
Fax: (918) 493-7711
Web site: http://www.unitcorp.com

Public Company
Incorporated: 1986
Employees: 1,291
Sales: $302.6 million (2003)
Stock Exchanges: New York
Ticker Symbol: UNT
NAIC: 211111 Crude Petroleum and Natural Gas
Extraction

Unit Corporation is a publicly traded Tulsa, Oklahoma, energy company with two complementary business segments. A subsidiary, Unit Drilling Company, maintains a fleet of 88 onshore rigs, mostly used for the production of natural gas and primarily serving customers in the Gulf Coast, midcontinent, and Rocky Mountain regions. Unit's exploration and production subsidiary, Unit Petroleum Company, often relies on its sister drilling operation in its exploration and production efforts. Unit concentrates on natural gas projects in the Anadarko and Arkoma basins, located in Oklahoma and Texas. The company owns proved reserves of 294.5 billion cubic feet of natural gas reserves and 7.84 million barrels of oil, and operates or owns an interest in more than 3,300 wells. Because customers of the drilling unit may be competitors of the production unit, Unit maintains what it calls a "Chinese firewall" between the operations. Results of third parties' drilling efforts are kept confidential, and the producing unit is charged competitive rates when using Unit's drilling rigs. This two-sided approach to the oil and gas business offers a number of advantages. The production arm can plan its activities around the availability of Unit drilling rigs, which are only contracted out on a short-term basis. Moreover, the two units provide diversity: When one business is in a down cycle, the other is generally able to keep Unit prosperous. When both units are thriving, Unit has proven to be a highly profitable concern.

Kirchner and Bodard: Acquiring Unit Drilling in 1963

Unit Corporation was cofounded by King Pouder Kirchner and Don Bodard in 1963 when they purchased Unit Drilling Company from Woolaroc Oil Company and moved the operation from Bristow, Oklahoma, to Tulsa. Born in 1927 in Kansas City, Missouri, Kirchner was named after his grandfather, Harry Pouder, an oilman who during his amateur boxing days received the nickname "King." While growing up on a farm near Perry, Oklahoma, Kirchner became aware that the truly prosperous farmers had oil and gas wells on their properties—unlike his family's spread. His interest in the business was further sparked by visits to his grandfather in Tulsa, which was an oil boom town of the period. His grandfather traded oil and gas well properties and introduced Kirchner to the city's famous oil tycoons. The young man was determined to become involved in the industry despite the warnings of his grandfather and father, who believed the best days of the business were in the past. In 1950 Kirchner earned an engineering degree from Oklahoma A&M University, and following a two-year stint in the Army, earned a second degree at the University of Oklahoma. In 1954 he went to work for Unit Drilling as a petroleum engineer. He became partners with Don Bodard, and the two men co-signed bank notes to borrow the $150,000 needed to buy Unit Drilling. Unit's corporate parent, Woolaroc, was founded by John Phillips, the nephew of Frank Phillips, founder of Phillips Petroleum Company.

Unit Drilling consisted of just three drilling rigs and three employees when Kirchner, serving as both CEO and chairman, relocated the operation to the Petroleum Club Building in downtown Tulsa. From the outset, Kirchner was determined to take a conservative approach to the business and maintain debt at a manageable level. Another bedrock principle he would repeat over the years was "Hire people who know more than you do." According to Kirchner's recollections, the company drilled around 30 wells and took in less than $10,000 in the first year. Demand was strong enough, however, to justify the addition of four more rigs in 1964, purchased from Falcon Seaboard

Drilling Company. Unit Drilling remained a seven-rig operation for the next decade. It was not until 1974, in response to an increased demand for its services, that the company bought four more rigs from Leaben Drilling Company.

Moving into Production in 1979

Because the drilling business was prone to deep cycles, Unit Petroleum Company was formed in 1979 to become involved in production, which was less volatile than drilling. The drilling and exploration units were then packaged under Unit Drilling & Exploration Co. and taken public, its shares traded on an over-the-counter basis. The basic concept, which the company has called turning iron into oil, called for cash flow from the drilling operation to be invested in the production side, which started modestly enough. In the beginning Unit Petroleum had just two billion cubic feet of natural gas reserves and 12 operational wells. Also starting in 1979, Unit Petroleum, acting as managing partner, formed limited partnership drilling programs to fund its activities.

Unit benefited from steep increases in the price of natural gas and oil in 1980, which resulted in a high demand for contract drilling rigs. To keep pace, Unit bought five rigs from Barrett Drilling Company. Unit was so prosperous that in 1981 its stock began trading on the New York Stock Exchange. At this point Unit had 28 rigs in its fleet and had a market capitalization of $168 million. But the boom would soon come to an end. Kirchner recognized that the market was beginning to tighten in 1981–82, and the company took immediate steps to cut costs to the bone in order to weather the coming storm. Kirchner even slashed his own salary by two-thirds and sold off the company plane, 30 company cars, and other equipment deemed unnecessary. Kirchner did not, however, reduce headcount, preferring instead to retain his experienced people by giving them a chance to stay on by accepting reduced salaries. Given the plight of other energy companies, many of which went bankrupt, keeping a job at a lower salary was an enticing offer. The down cycle in oil and gas proved to be deep and enduring. According to Oklahoma City's *Journal Record,* Unit was ''one of the 20 biggest losers on the stock market between 1982 and 1986, falling 92.5 percent during that period.'' Nevertheless, Unit was able to survive, mostly due to Kirchner's conservative fiscal approach that limited debt.

In 1986 the business was reorganized. Limited partnerships in drilling programs that Unit sponsored from 1980 to 1983 were acquired in exchange for stock in a new company—Unit Corporation—incorporated in Delaware in September 1986. In all, six partnerships agreed to the stock swap—but the partners in a 1979 program rejected the offer, leaving that partnership intact. When all the maneuvering was finished, Unit Corporation became the parent of Unit Drilling and Exploration Company, replacing it on the New York Stock Exchange. Two years later, in 1988, the structure would be modified further, resulting in the company's current operating units: Unit Drilling Company and Unit Petroleum Company.

Business slowly began to pick up in the late 1980s. The company drilled only 22 wells in 1986, but that number would more than double to 46 wells in 1987. Moreover, the company's stock rebounded in 1987, regaining about 16.7 percent of its price. Revenues slowly improved as well, growing from $26.4 million in 1986 to $28.9 million in 1987 and $31.6 million in 1988. Although the company was still losing money, the hemorrhaging had stopped. The company lost $35.6 million, mostly due to writedowns, in 1987. A year later the net loss would total just $1.6 million.

Unit experienced steady improvement during the early years of the 1990s and was able to add significantly to its reserves. In 1990 the company acquired Roundup Resources, Inc. for $1.3 million, as a result doubling its proved reserves and bolstering Unit's presence in the Texas Panhandle region, which was an important area of concentration. In 1994 Unit took a major step in its development, acquiring producing properties in Louisiana, New Mexico, Oklahoma, and Texas, allowing the company to enter the Permian Basin in east Texas and the Gulf Coast regions. A regional office in Houston also was added. Unit added to its drilling fleet in 1995, paying $4.2 million for Willis Drilling Co. Inc., a subsidiary of Di Energy Inc. At the same time, the company's production subsidiary continued to add to the reserves, which in 1995 reached the 120 billion cubic feet level. As a result of these developments and improving financial results, Unit once again hit the radar screens of investors, and several research analysts began to tout the stock.

Cofounder's Death in 1997

Unit maintained its growth through the second half of the 1990s. In 1997 the company added ten drilling rigs by acquiring privately owned Hickman Drilling Company in a cash and stock deal valued at nearly $24 million. But 1997 also marked the passing of one of Unit's cofounders, Don Bodard, who died in September at the age of 77. Unit added to its rig fleet in 1999 by acquiring 13 diesel-electric deep drilling rigs from Parker Drilling Company at a cost of $40 million in cash and stock worth more than $8.1 million. This transaction also allowed Unit to enter a new market, the Rocky Mountain region. It was paid for by a secondary offering of stock that netted $50.4 million. Despite a drop in commodity prices in 1999, Unit was able to increase revenues to $97.5 million, compared with $93.3 million in 1998, although net income dropped off, from $2.2 million in 1998 to $1.5 million in 1999.

The production business was bolstered in 2000 by the acquisition of Questa Oil and Gas Co., financed by a stock exchange. As a result, Unit's proved reserves reached 240.7 billion cubic feet. With the help of the Questa acquisition and unusually high oil and natural gas prices, Unit was able to achieve record results in 2000, posting total revenues of $201.3 million, almost double the previous year's results. In addition, the company enjoyed net income of $34.3 million.

Key Dates:

1963: The company is founded by King Kirchner and Don Bodard.
1979: The company arms its production unit and goes public.
1981: The company's stock begins trading on the New York Stock Exchange.
1986: The business is reorganized as Unit Corporation.
1997: Bodard dies.
2003: Kirchner retires as chairman.

In 2001 the drilling fleet was expanded once again, bringing the total to 55 rigs. It was also in July 2001 that Kirchner stepped down as CEO, although he retained the chairmanship until August 2003. Replacing him as chief executive—and eventually as chairman—was the company's president, John Nikkel, a seasoned executive as well as a trained geologist. He had been with Unit since 1983, when he was named the president and a director. Prior to his tenure at Unit, he had worked 18 years for Amoco Production Company, rising to the level of Division Geologist for the Denver division. In 1976 he cofounded Nike Exploration Company, and from 1979 until 1983 he served as president and a director for Cotton Petroleum Corporation. Working under Kirchner for nearly 20 years, Nikkel was already wedded to the conservative approach that had served the company well for so many years. It was due to these principles that Unit was able to continue to grow during 2001, a year in which the economy slowed, the United States suffered terrorist attacks, and the weather was unseasonably warm. All of these factors created a difficult environment for many energy companies. Nevertheless, Unit was able to improve total revenues to $259.2 million and net income to $62.8 million.

Unit's drilling fleet grew to 75 rigs following the August 2002 acquisition of assets from Cactus Drilling Company in exchange for 7.5 million shares of stock, worth an estimated $133 million. The company was eager to drill more wells but its activity was curtailed somewhat by partners concerned about the state of the economy and fluctuating commodity prices. All

in all, Unit enjoyed what management described as an acceptable year in 2002: revenues of $187.7 million and net income of $18.2 million. In 2003, the company would experience a year more in keeping with the results of 2001. Revenues reached record levels, to $302.6 million, and net income rebounded to $50.2 million.

Unit's steady expansion continued in 2003 when it paid $35 million in cash for Serdrilco Incorporated and subsidiary Service Drill Southwest LLC. The deal added 12 drilling rigs under contract in the Anadarko Basin in the Texas Panhandle, as well as a 12-truck moving fleet and other equipment. It also increased Unit's drilling fleet to 88 rigs. Unit also made a significant purchase on the production side, paying $182 million in cash and stock to acquire PetroCorp in early 2004. PetroCorp was another Tulsa company, and one that Unit's management had been eyeing for several years. PetroCorp brought with it 40.26 billion cubic feet of natural gas and 2.74 million barrels of oil, its properties located in the Mid-Continent and Gulf Coast regions and nicely complementing Unit's current holdings. PetroCorp was simply too small to compete efficiently, and by adding it to the fold Unit was now much stronger and ready to take on larger competitors.

Principal Subsidiaries

Unit Drilling Company; Unit Petroleum Company.

Principal Competitors

BP p.l.c.; Grey Wolf, Inc.; Nabors Industries Ltd.

Further Reading

Robinson, Robin, "Unit Corp. Eyes Long-Term Improvement," *Journal Record,* May 10, 1988.
Russell, Ray, "King Kirchner Builds Royal Legacy," *Tulsa World,* September 10, 2003, p. E1.
Tippee, Bob, "Unit's Nikkel: US Onshore Drilling Remains Attractive," *Oil & Gas Journal,* August 4, 2003, p. 29.
"Tulsa, Okla.-Based Oil-Drilling Firm Focuses on New Assets, Low Debt," *Daily Oklahoman,* October 28, 2001.

—Ed Dinger

United National Group, Ltd.

Walker House, 87 Mary Street
P.O. Box 908GT
George Town, Grand Cayman
Cayman Islands
Telephone: 345-949-0000
Web site: http://www.ungl.ky

Three Bala Plaza, East, Suite 300
Bala Cynwyd, Pennsylvania 19004
U.S.A.
Telephone: (610) 664-1500
Fax: (610) 660-8882
Web site: http://www.unitednat.com

Public Company
Incorporated: 1960 as United National Insurance
    Company
Employees: 260
Total Assets: $2.84 billion (2003)
Stock Exchanges: NASDAQ
Ticker Symbol: UNGL
NAIC: 524126 Direct Property and Casualty Insurance
    Carriers (pt)

United National Group, Ltd. (UNG) was formed as a holding company by investment firm Fox Paine to acquire the United National group of insurance companies. Cornerstone United National Insurance Company ranks among the largest surplus line insurers in the United States. The company offers specialty insurance products in areas that standard insurers generally do not cover.

Growing from Philadelphia Roots:
1960s to Mid-1990s

The original UNG company, United National Insurance Company (UNIC), was established in 1960 to write specialty personal and commercial lines of insurance in the Philadelphia area. In 1972, one of the founders, Raymond L. Freudberg, established

American Insurance Service, Inc. (AIS), which took ownership of United National. Seven years later, a group of private trusts controlled by Philadelphia's Ball family acquired AIS.

Additional insurance companies joined United National in the 1980s. Diamond State Insurance Company (DSIC) was formed in 1981. United National Specialty Insurance Company (formerly Hallmark Insurance Company) was acquired in 1985. Freudberg served as president and CEO from 1960 until 1986, when he moved to the position of chairman. Seth D. Freudberg succeeded him as president and CEO.

In the early 1990s, United National was writing on a non-admitted basis in all states but Pennsylvania, where its subsidiaries Diamond State and Hallmark were approved non-admitted insurers, according to *Business Insurance*. The company provided coverage for risks that might be viewed as too large, difficult, or unusual by companies licensed to do business in a particular state.

In 1995, the umbrella and excess casualty insurance line brought in the majority of non-admitted premiums, followed by primary liability and property and miscellaneous lines. Overall, non-admitted premiums fell to $173.9 million from a record $260.7 million in 1994. According to the company, business backlogged from 1993 drove up 1994 figures, while a procedural accounting change in 1994 had a downward impact on 1995 numbers.

The loss of some program business also contributed to the 1995 drop-off. A trucking program and a contractors liability program ended when the reinsurer discontinued its backing. But, a positive environment in the investment market allowed United National to post a gain in net income of 15 percent to $19.9 million.

The insurance business experienced increased softness during the year. Property casualty premiums, which had been growing, fell off, joining the premium slide in general liability and excess liability insurance. Umbrella insurance was even weaker.

During 1995, United National reduced its number of brokers. They had found that 80 percent of the business generated in

---

---

this way was produced by 20 percent of the brokers. Concurrently, the company established relationships with an increased number of managing general agencies (MGAs). In addition to new business, the MGAs brought in new programs.

United National financed new program business through its relationship with reinsurance companies. Mergers among reinsurers had created larger companies with more capital to offer but cut down on the number of reinsurance options for companies such as United National.

New program business helped boost United National's nonadmitted premiums to $195.8 million in 1996. *Business Insurance* ranked the company as eighth largest among surplus line insurers. New products included a habitational program, for buildings such as condominiums and apartments; two product liability programs; and one employment practices program. Generally, United National was adding a number of smaller programs and in a variety of areas. The company's largest program was for hospitals, nursing homes, and other healthcare facilities, which had limits of $35 million. Umbrella and excess casualty had the next largest limit, $10 million.

Like the primary insurance market, the reinsurance market had been softening, giving United National less costly and more flexible financing. But, the door also opened to others seeking to expand their capacity. In addition, some competitors had been writing policies at rates below what United National would consider. United National had dropped policyholders wanting large rate cuts, leaving the company in search of replacement accounts. Admitted insurers had also increasingly entered the surplus lines markets, placing more pressure on the market.

Moving to Meet Marketplace Challenges: 1997–2000

To increase business in challenging market conditions, United National bolstered its marketing department in 1997 and made plans to acquire managing general agencies. To further strengthen the company, the underwriting department was reorganized into Eastern, Central, and Western regions.

Non-admitted gross premiums rose in 1998 aided by the expanded marketing department, underwriter generated activity, and business coming from newly established offices. Moreover, programs added the prior year had come up to speed. The company brought on seven new programs and dropped five that were not profitable, leaving a total of 88 specialty programs by the end of 1998. A total of 15 binding authorities also got the ax. Agents cut included those who had other binding authorities of greater priority than those to United National. In addition, in response to the movement of admitted insurers into the surplus

market, Diamond State and Hallmark units were seeking admitted status on a state-by-state level in order for the company to compete on that level.

In 1999, American Re Corp. moved to buy AIS, the holding company for the United National Group of insurance companies. American Re, the largest reinsurer of program business for United National, was a part of one of the world's leading reinsurance groups, Germany-based Munich Re.

The Ball family's decision to sell all outstanding AIS shares to American Re was prompted by its desire to diversify its portfolio, according to *National Underwriter Property & Casualty.* The deal was estimated at slightly less than $300 million, the approximate book value of the company.

The company would continue to operate as an independent operation, with Seth Freudberg remaining in place as president and CEO. The insurance group included United National, the main excess and surplus line unit; admitted insurers Diamond and Hallmark; an inactive offshore insurer in Barbados; an in-house claims adjuster; and three managing general agencies.

By purchasing excess and surplus companies, such reinsurers as American Re could embark on new areas of business without encroaching directly on their clients. United National would be on the receiving end of new business from American Re and probably would not lose the business of American Re competitors because of its sound reputation in such a specialized area of insurance.

In December 1999, American Re received approval in both Wisconsin and Indiana to proceed with the purchase of United National. But, the Pennsylvania insurance commissioner withheld action on the request due to concerns over the payment of Holocaust-era claims by Munich Re subsidiaries.

The commissioner was an alternative member of the International Holocaust Commission, a group of insurers and regulators working on resolution of unpaid claims. Munich Re had joined a different group, the German Foundation Initiative. Ultimately, the issue killed the American Re deal. After more than ten months of delays in the Pennsylvania application process, marked by legal action by both the state insurance commissioner and American Re, AIS terminated the purchase agreement in August 2000.

Ups and Downs: 2001–03

Double-digit rate increases helped boost non-admitted premiums by 54.1 percent to $382.3 million in 2001, putting United National in the number six spot in *Business Insurance* rankings. Three-quarters of the year's growth came from existing customers buying more policies and paying the higher rates.

United National dropped out of residential contracting coverage in 2001, citing the increasing risk of litigation in the sector. ''We believe in writing tough risks and finding creative ways of underwriting them,'' Seth Freudberg told *Business Insurance* in August 2002. ''We don't want to run out of a line of business when everyone else is, unless the volatility is so unpredictable that you're purely rolling the dice.''

Key Dates:

1960: United National Insurance Company begins writing specialty personal and commercial lines of insurance in the Philadelphia area.

1972: American Insurance Service, Inc. (AIS) is formed as a holding company.

1979: AIS is acquired by private related trusts of Philadelphia's Ball family.

1981: Diamond State Insurance Company (DSIC) is formed.

1985: Hallmark Insurance Company, Inc. is acquired and later called United National Specialty Insurance Company (UNSIC).

1994: A record level of $260.7 million in non-admitted premiums is reached.

2000: A deal in which United National would be acquired by American Re falls through.

2001: United National Casualty Insurance Company (UNCIC) is formed.

2003: Fox Paine becomes the majority owner.

In 2002, United National experienced a net loss—the first in a half decade. Although the company's premium numbers were up, a huge increase in reserves for prior accident years plus costs related to a canceled reinsurance agreement drove net losses past the $50 million mark.

A federal court ruling in early 2003 gave United National the right to pursue fraud charges against a former managing general agent, whose binding activities left United National and others with large claims related to weather derivative policies. Enron Corp. was among the companies covered against such losses. United National subsidiary Diamond State claimed the agent had exceeded his authority and hid unauthorized business from the company. In January 2004, the company paid the Bank of America $17.9 million to settle claims related to one of those contracts.

An ownership change was placed on the table again, when the longtime owners of United National agreed to sell majority interest to funds managed by Fox Paine & Company, L.L.C. The firm, which managed investment funds in excess of $1.5 billion, was founded in 1997 by Saul A. Fox, former general partner in Kohlberg Kravis Roberts & Co. (KKR), and W. Dexter Paine III, former general partner in Kohlberg & Co. In the proposed deal, the Ball family would retain a minority interest in the company they had held for more than two decades.

The players in this transaction were connected through previous business transactions. The AMC Group L.L.C. Management Co., which oversaw Ball family interests in United National and other businesses—such as manufacturing, real estate development, and franchising—had, as a private investor, backed a fund managed by Fox Paine. Saul Fox, in turn, had managed the $1.5 billion acquisition of American Re by KKR in 1992. Munich Re bought American Re from KKR four years later.

California-based Fox Paine embarked on restructuring United National beginning in August 2003. United National Group, Ltd. (UNG) was established in the Cayman Islands as a holding company to acquire United National's U.S. operations. A non-U.S. operation was formed in Barbados to offer insurance products to third parties and reinsurance to its U.S. operations. The offshore entity planned to specialize in property and casualty insurance for social service agencies, equine mortality risks, and insurance for vacant property risks.

Fox Paine made a $240 million investment on September 5 in exchange for ten million Class B common shares and 14 million Series A preferred shares. UNG used $100 million of the capital infusion to buy out Wind River Investment Corp., controlled by a group of Ball family trusts, which also received a combination of common and preferred shares and notes. As for the balance of the new money, $80 million went to U.S. operations, $43.5 million to capitalize non-U.S. operations, and the remainder to fees and expenses connected to the acquisition. Fox Paine was scheduled to receive an initial management fee of $13.2 million plus annual sums of $1.2 million.

UNG filed for an initial public offering (IPO) under the ticker symbol UNGL in September 2003. The company was among a throng of financial service companies making IPOs during the year. The insurance industry was experiencing an upswing in premiums that fueled capital investment. Previous surges in equity financing for the insurance industry took place in 1985–86 and 1993. The most recent flow of funds actually began following the attacks on New York and Washington, D.C., when new reinsurers entered the marketplace to meet the demands of a changing environment.

The majority of the proceeds from the IPO were earmarked for redeeming all outstanding preferred shares: Fox Paine held 83 percent and the Ball family 17 percent. Because of the weighting of shares, following the IPO, Fox Paine would actually increase its control over the board of directors.

In December, 9.75 million Class A common shares were offered for $17 per share on the NASDAQ. When completed the IPO brought in $166 million in net proceeds.

In February 2004, UNG announced a pro forma net operating income for 2003 of $27 million, reversing the net operating loss of $54.1 million a year earlier. The company benefited from another year of favorable pricing in commercial, property, and casualty insurance sectors and from the shedding of unprofitable business. Net retention grew year over year despite the increase in premiums.

Principal Subsidiaries

United National Insurance Company; Diamond State Insurance Company; United National Specialty Insurance Company; United National Casualty Insurance Company.

Principal Competitors

American International Group, Inc. (AIG); Nationwide Mutual Insurance Co.; W.R. Berkley Corp.

Further Reading

Howard, Lisa S., "Holocaust-Era Claims Dispute Kills Re Deal," *National Underwriter Life & Health—Financial Services Edition,* August 21, 2000, p. 1.

"Insurers Queue Up at the IPO Trough," *Investment Dealers' Digest,* October 20, 2003.

"Late News; California Court Oks 'Play or Pay' Referendum," *Business Insurance,* January 26, 2004 p. 1.

Lonkevich, Dan, "Am RE Agrees to Buy United National Group," *National Underwriter Property & Casualty,* September 6, 1999.

MacFadyen, Ken, "Fox Paine's United National Files for IPO," *Buyouts,* October 6, 2003.

McLeod, Douglas, "United National to Sell Majority Stake," *Business Insurance,* March 24, 2003, p. 4.

——, "Weather Risk Deals Create Legal Whirlwind," *Business Insurance,* January 20, 2003, p. 1.

McMorris, Frances A., "Fox Paine Exits UNG, Highland Cuts Debt," *Daily Deal,* December 17, 2003.

Moreira, Peter, "Cayman Insurer Drops IPO Price," *Daily Deal,* December 1, 2003.

——, "PE-Backed Insurer to Go Public," *Daily Deal,* September 18, 2003.

"6: United National Insurance Co.," *Business Insurance,* August 19, 2002, p. 15.

Souter, Gavin, "8: United National Insurance Co.," *Business Insurance,* October 4, 1999, p. 20.

——, "United National Insurance Co.," *Business Insurance,* September 16, 1996, pp. 26+.

——, "United National Insurance Co.," *Business Insurance,* September 15, 1997, pp. 32+.

——, "United National Insurance Co.," *Business Insurance,* September 7, 1998, p. 29.

——, "United National Insurance Co.," *Business Insurance,* August 30, 1999, p. 2.

"United National Calms Partner Reinsurers' Fears," *Reactions,* December 1999.

—Kathleen Peippo

United Parcel Service, Inc.

55 Glenlake Parkway, N.E.
Atlanta, Georgia 30328-3474
U.S.A.
Telephone: (404) 828-6000
Toll Free: (800) 742-5877
Fax: (404) 828-6562
Web site: http://www.ups.com

Public Company
Incorporated: 1907 as American Messenger Company
Employees: 357,000
Sales: $33.49 billion (2003)
Stock Exchanges: New York
Ticker Symbol: UPS
NAIC: 492110 Couriers

Known in the industry as "Big Brown," United Parcel Service, Inc. (UPS) is the world's largest package delivery company. The Atlanta-based business delivered approximately 3.4 billion items throughout more than 200 countries and territories in 2003. In addition to its fleet of 88,000 vehicles, the company operates the ninth largest airline in North America by virtue of its nearly 600 company-owned and chartered aircraft. Although UPS's global reach has been steadily expanding, it is the firm's U.S. operations that are its most impressive asset. Its door-to-door delivery system reaches every residential and business address in the country, and UPS estimates that its system carries goods that are valued at more than 6 percent of the U.S. gross domestic product. More than 83 percent of UPS's revenues is generated in the United States, where the firm has a market share of about 60 percent in ground shipping and about 35 percent in air shipping. Although UPS sold a 10 percent stake in the company to the public in November 1999 through newly created Class B shares, the Class A shares, which control 99 percent of the voting rights in the company, remain in private hands, mostly those of employees and retirees.

Roots in the Early 20th Century

UPS was founded in 1907 in Seattle, Washington, by 19-year-old Jim Casey as a six-bicycle messenger service called American Messenger Company. He set the future tone of the company by mandating that it be employee-owned. Casey delivered telegraph messages and hot lunches and sometimes took odd jobs to keep his struggling business going. In 1913 Casey merged his company with Evert McCabe's rival firm, Motorcycle Delivery Company, creating Merchants Parcel Delivery. The "fleet" at this point consisted of a few motorcycles and one Model T Ford. In 1915, by which time the fleet had expanded to four cars and five motorcycles, the company began painting its delivery vehicles brown. It was Charlie Soderstrom, one of Casey's partners, who urged that brown be adopted, noting that the color hid dirt well—a fact that had earlier led the Pullman company to paint its railroad cars that same hue.

With Casey's tacit approval, company drivers joined the International Brotherhood of Teamsters in 1916. In 1918 three Seattle department stores hired the service to deliver merchandise to purchasers on the day of the purchase. Department store deliveries remained the center of the firm's business until the late 1940s. In 1919, meantime, Merchants Parcel Delivery made its first move outside its home market, buying a delivery firm in Oakland, California. Because there was a similarly named firm already operating in San Francisco, another name change was in order. The moniker chosen was United Parcel Service. During the 1920s, UPS expanded to Los Angeles, San Francisco, San Diego, and Portland, Oregon. An expansion drive on the East Coast began in 1930 with the start of delivery service in New York City. UPS moved its headquarters to New York that same year.

In 1929 UPS began air delivery through a new division, United Air Express, which put packages on to passenger planes. The Great Depression ended plans for an overnight air service, and UPS terminated United Air Express in 1931; the company did not resume air service until 1953, when UPS Air was launched as a two-day service connecting major cities on the East and West Coasts. In the late 1940s the urban department stores that UPS serviced began following their clients to the new suburbs. More people owned cars and picked up their own parcels. UPS's revenue declined.

Casey decided to change direction and expand the common-carrier parcel business, picking up parcels from anyone and taking them to anyone else, charging a fixed rate per parcel. The company's initial customers were primarily industrial and commercial shippers, although the firm also serviced consumers. The company had offered common-carrier service in Los Angeles since 1922, and in 1953 UPS extended it to San Francisco, Chicago, and New York. UPS delivered any package meeting weight and size requirements to any location within 150 miles of these bases. After this initial expansion, UPS frequently appeared before the Interstate Commerce Commission (ICC) to expand its operating rights.

UPS scaled its operations to fit its market niche, refusing packages weighing more than 50 pounds or with a combined length and width of more than 108 inches, limitations that would increase in concert with the company's capabilities. Its average package weighed about ten pounds and was roughly the size of a briefcase, making sorting and carrying easy. UPS competed with scores of regional firms but most had not limited the size and weight of their packages. They ended up with the heavier packages, higher overheads, and lower volumes.

A New Generation of Leadership for the 1960s

Casey resigned as chief executive officer in 1962, when UPS achieved annual revenues of about $141 million. He was succeeded by George D. Smith. UPS more than doubled its sales and profits between 1964 and 1969, when the company made $31.9 million on sales of about $548 million. The company remained privately owned, its stock held by several hundred of its executives. UPS in 1969 served 31 states on the East and West Coasts. It had just gotten ICC approval to add nine midwestern states and soon got approval for three more states. Only the lightly populated states of Arizona, Alaska, Hawaii, Idaho, Montana, Nevada, and Utah were without UPS service. The firm kept a low profile, avoiding publicity, and refusing interviews of its chief executives. UPS officials believed only one parcel shipping company could exist in the United States, and it hoped that keeping a low profile would prevent anyone from copying its methods.

The firm's secrecy policy was possible because it was closely held. Its 3,700 stockholders (a number raised to 23,000 by 1991) were its own top and middle managers and their families. Stockholders wanting to sell sold their stock back to the company. Because management owned UPS, the company could make long-range plans without the pressure for instant

profits faced by many publicly owned firms. Most managers started as UPS drivers or sorters and came up through the ranks, creating great loyalty. The company's management structure was relatively informal, stressing partnership and the involvement of management at all levels.

In 1970 Congress considered a reform of the United States Postal Service that would allow it to subsidize its parcel post operations with profits from its first-class mail. This would allow it to lower prices and compete more directly with UPS. UPS hired a public relations firm and for the first time officially announced its earnings, trying to build a case that it was an integral part of the U.S. economy and that the postal reform would be disruptive. UPS handled 500 million packages in 1969 for 165,000 regular customers. The company claimed that 95 percent of all deliveries within 150 miles were delivered overnight. The company centered operations around a five-day-a-week cycle. Drivers made deliveries in the morning, made pickups in the afternoon, and returned to operations centers around 6 p.m. Their packages were immediately sorted and transferred for delivery.

UPS trucks, which were cleaned every night, were assigned to specific drivers, who the company treated as future managers and owners. The company had 22,000 drivers in 1969, and most were kept on the same route to develop a relationship with customers. Some drivers, however, found UPS management inflexible, resulting in occasional local strikes.

In 1976 UPS tried to replace, gradually, all of its full-time employees who sorted and handled packages at warehouses with part-time workers. Teamsters locals in the South, Midwest, and West accepted the idea, but 17,000 UPS employees from Maine to South Carolina went on strike. The strike caused chaos for East Coast retailers as their suppliers were forced to send Christmas goods through the overburdened U.S. Postal Service. UPS eventually reached agreement with the Teamsters, but its labor relations continued to be spotty. Because management owned the business, it tended to drive its employees hard, and many drivers complained of the long hours and hard work. To maximize driver performance, the company kept records of the production of every driver and sorter and compared them to its performance projections. Drivers' routes were timed in great detail.

In 1975, meantime, UPS achieved a long coveted goal when it became the first package delivery firm to serve every address in the continental United States. That same year, the company expanded outside the country for the first time, launching delivery service in Ontario, Canada, and also relocated its headquarters to Connecticut. In 1976 UPS launched service in West Germany with 120 delivery vans. It quickly ran into trouble because of cultural and language differences. UPS eventually adapted by hiring some German managers and accepting the German dislike of working overtime. George C. Lamb, Jr., succeeded Harold Oberkotter as UPS chairman in 1980.

Intensifying Competition in the 1980s

UPS continued to grow rapidly, aided by trucking deregulation in 1980. By 1980 UPS earned $189 million on revenues of $4 billion, shipping 1.5 billion packages. Federal Express Corporation (FedEx), however, which began operations in 1973, was siphoning off a growing amount of UPS's business.

Key Dates:

1907: Jim Casey founds a six-bicycle messenger service called American Messenger Company in Seattle, Washington.

1913: American Messenger merges with Motorcycle Delivery Company, creating Merchants Parcel Delivery, which has a "fleet" of a few motorcycles and one Model T Ford.

1915: The company begins painting its delivery vehicles brown.

1916: The company drivers join the International Brotherhood of Teamsters.

1918: Three Seattle department stores hire the firm to deliver merchandise to their customers.

1919: After buying a delivery firm in Oakland, California, the company changes its name to United Parcel Service (UPS).

1930: Operations are expanded to New York City, which also becomes the location of the company's new headquarters.

1953: UPS begins a steady expansion of its common-carrier parcel business, through which it picks up parcels from anyone and takes them to anyone else; UPS Air is launched as a two-day air express service connecting major cities on the East and West Coasts.

1962: Casey ends his long reign as CEO.

1975: UPS becomes the first package delivery firm to serve every address in the continental United States; the first international expansion begins with the launch of delivery service in Ontario, Canada; the company moves its headquarters to Connecticut.

1976: UPS enters the European market through the start-up of a delivery service in West Germany.

1982: UPS Next Day Air, an overnight air delivery service, debuts.

1985: The company begins offering international air service between the United States and Europe.

1991: Headquarters are relocated to Atlanta.

1999: The company raises $5.47 billion through an initial public offering; the official name of the company is changed from United Parcel Service of America Inc. to United Parcel Service, Inc.

2001: UPS acquires the Mail Boxes Etc. chain of 4,300 franchised shipping and mail services stores and Fritz Companies, Inc., which specializes in freight forwarding, customs brokering, and logistics.

2002: The company's supply-chain management operations are merged to form a new unit, UPS Supply Chain Solutions.

2003: Most of the U.S. locations of Mail Boxes Etc. change their names to the UPS Store.

FedEx shipped packages overnight by air, and many businesses began shipping high-priority packages with FedEx. UPS had the resources to challenge FedEx, but it meant taking on significant debt, something the conservatively run UPS was reluctant to do. In 1981 it had only $7 million in long-term debt and a net worth of $750 million. To compete with FedEx, UPS bought nine used 727 airplanes in 1981 from Braniff Airlines for $28 million. It opened an air hub in Louisville, Kentucky, but was hesitant about directly challenging FedEx because of the huge cost of building an air fleet. It decided to stick with two-day delivery rather than overnight delivery, hoping that many businesses would be willing to let packages take an extra day if it meant savings of up to 70 percent. It called its two-day delivery Blue Label Air and spent $1 million in 1981 to promote it—a large sum for UPS, which had rarely advertised. In 1982 UPS ran its first-ever television ads, trying to convince executives that two-day service was fast enough for most packages.

The recession of the early 1980s helped UPS because many companies shifted to smaller inventories, shipping smaller lots more frequently and demanding greater reliability. Package volume grew by 6 percent in 1981. Because of the recession, the Teamsters accepted a contract in 1982 that limited wage increases to a cost-of-living adjustment, which then was diverted to pay the increased cost of medical benefits. When UPS then released information showing its net income rose 74 percent in 1981, labor relations worsened. Bitterness continued between UPS management and drivers as company profits swelled 48 percent to $490 million in 1983. UPS and the Teamsters secretly negotiated for two months in 1984 and reached a three-year agreement providing for bonuses and increased wages. The

move averted a probable strike by 90,000 employees. Despite this labor tension, UPS's employee turnover remained remarkably low at 4 percent. Many workers were recruited as part-time employees while college students and were offered full-time positions after graduation.

In 1982 UPS decided to offer overnight air service (UPS Next Day Air), charging about half of FedEx's rate. By 1983 its second-day and next-day services were shipping a combined 140,000 packages a day. In 1982 UPS earned $332 million on $5.2 billion in sales. It had a fleet of more than 62,000 trucks. Mail-order firms and catalog houses were the fastest growing part of UPS's business. Jack Rogers became UPS chairman in 1984. In 1985 UPS began offering international air service between the United States and six European countries.

Despite labor troubles, a *Fortune* survey found UPS's reputation the highest in its industry every year from 1984 to 1991. It was by far the most profitable U.S. transportation company, making more than $700 million in 1987 on revenue of $10 billion. FedEx, however, had 57 percent of the rapidly growing overnight package business; UPS had only 15 percent. FedEx was highly automated and used electronics to track packages en route and to perform other services. UPS still did most jobs manually, but was rapidly switching to the use of electronic scanners at its sorting centers and to computers on its trucks. UPS introduced technology methodically, buying a software firm and a computer design shop to create the necessary equipment. It then field-tested its new gear at a 35-car messenger service it owned in Los Angeles. It launched a $1.5 billion five-year computerization project, trying to create a system that tracked packages door-to-door, which FedEx was doing already. UPS's healthy river of cash flow enabled it to pay $1.8 billion for 110 aircraft in 1987. The purchase made it the tenth largest U.S. airline. The company launched its first wide-range television advertising campaign in 1988, spending $35 million to publicize the slogan, "We run the tightest ship in the shipping business." Despite these expenses, the company still had only $114 million in long-term debt and continued to finance large projects out of its cash flow.

By 1988 UPS's ground service was growing by 7 to 8 percent per year, and air service was growing by 30 percent per year. UPS handled 2.3 billion packages per year, compared with 1.4 billion for the U.S. Postal Service. The 300-plane fleet of the UPS overnight service handled 600,000 parcels and documents per day, making $350 million on $2.2 billion in sales in 1988. UPS continued building an overseas air network, but in West Germany, where it had 6,000 employees, it delivered only on the ground. The company shipped eight million packages overseas in 1988, losing $20 million in the process. UPS bought its Italian partner, Alimondo, in 1988, hoping to use it and its German base to expand through Europe. The company also bought nine small European courier companies to expand air service. Its overseas acquisitions cost UPS less than $100 million. UPS and rival FedEx both were losing money on overseas operations, but UPS had an advantage: FedEx could not match its $6.5 billion in assets and $480 million in cash with minimal debt. UPS hoped this would give it greater staying power as the two companies struggled to build a global delivery network. Meanwhile, UPS slowly won some FedEx customers by giving volume discounts, which it previously had refused to do. The overseas shipping war escalated as FedEx bought Tiger International, Inc., a major international shipper that UPS used for some of its foreign deliveries.

Invigorated Through New Leadership in the 1990s

Kent C. Nelson succeeded Jack Rogers as chairman and CEO in 1989. Nicknamed "Oz" for 1940s-era band leader Ozzie Nelson, the 52-year-old had spent his entire working life at UPS, starting with the company only two days after graduating from college. The new leader undertook a gradual, but complete transformation of UPS that extended from its innermost workings to its public image.

Challenged by competitors large and small, UPS launched a plethora of new services in the early 1990s. These ranged from timed and same-day deliveries to less expensive two- and three-day services. The company's Worldwide Logistics subsidiary (formed in 1993) offered clients everything from inventory management to warehousing and, of course, delivery. Powerful and costly technical systems, often developed internally by a 4,000-member staff, backed up these expanded operations. UPS's DIAD (delivery information acquisition device), for example, combined a barcode scanner, electronic signature capture, and cellular tracking network in a single handheld tool. By 1992, the corporation was investing more money in computers than in ubiquitous brown vehicles. These internal changes reflected the company's traditional focus on super-efficiency as well as its newfound emphasis on customer satisfaction.

In 1991, meanwhile, UPS relocated its corporate headquarters from Greenwich, Connecticut, to Atlanta, Georgia. Another important development during this period came in 1995, when the corporation introduced a new stock purchase program that was open to all UPS employees—both full- and part-time; previously, only management was given the opportunity to buy the stock.

In contrast to its secretive early years, the UPS of the 1990s was a bold global marketer. The company embarked on the largest advertising campaign in its history in 1996, spending an estimated $100 million in conjunction with its sponsorship of the Centennial Olympics held in its new base of Atlanta. UPS hoped that the worldwide recognition enjoyed by the Olympic rings would rub off on its brown trucks, which were not well known outside the United States.

That recognition was vital to the success of UPS's international operations, which continued to lose money into the mid-1990s. By 1995, in fact, losses on the company's European assault totaled nearly $1 billion. But backed by its patient and confident employee/stockholders and a hefty bank account, UPS was able to wait out publicly held FedEx, which had limited its European service to intercontinental deliveries by mid-decade. In stark contrast, UPS had expanded its international network to include 200 countries and territories worldwide. Undaunted by its massive losses, UPS announced plans to invest more than $1 billion in its European operations from 1995 to 2000, and it infused another $130 million into its Asian operations. The company hoped to profit on its piece of the $25 billion European parcel post market by the end of the century.

This global push fueled a 69 percent increase in sales over the course of Nelson's first six years at the helm of UPS. At the same time, however, it played a significant role in the reduction of the company's overall profit margin from 8 percent in 1987 to 4.8 percent in 1995.

In January 1997 James P. Kelly succeeded Nelson as chairman and CEO. Kelly had worked his way up through the ranks, having joined UPS in 1964 as a package car driver. His first year at the company turned into a rough one as the 190,000 Teamsters employees at UPS went on strike for 15 days in August before agreeing to a new five-year pact. In addition to wage increases, the new agreement called for the creation of 10,000 new full-time jobs and the shifting of 10,000 part-time workers into full-time jobs as such jobs became available through attrition and growth. The strike cost UPS $700 million in lost revenue, resulting in less than 1 percent sales growth for the year and a decline in profits to $909 million from the 1996 figure of $1.15 billion.

UPS shook off any lingering effects from the strike by 1998 when its domestic shipping revenues jumped 9.4 percent, reaching $20.65 billion. UPS continued to reap benefits from the ever-growing e-commerce section, which was fueling demand for shipping services. During the year, the company rolled out a money-back guarantee for on-time delivery for all of its ground business-to-business shipments. Other good news came in the form of the first-ever annual profits for the company's international operations, which now generated nearly 13 percent of overall revenues.

In 1999 company executives determined that UPS needed the added flexibility of publicly traded stock in order to pursue some larger acquisition targets. Thus in November, UPS completed what was then the largest initial public offering (IPO) ever conducted in the United States. The company raised $5.47 billion by selling 109.4 million shares of newly created Class B shares at $50 per share on the New York Stock Exchange. The Class A shares, which controlled 99 percent of the voting rights at the company, remained in the private hands of employees and retirees. The newly public company (whose official name was shortened from United Parcel Service of America Inc. to United Parcel Service, Inc.) was immediately confronted with a new challenge from FedEx. The arch-rival had bought a truck-based shipping company earlier in the year and then in 2000 launched two new truck-based delivery services: FexEx Ground, specializing in business-to-business deliveries, and FedEx Home Delivery, concentrating on deliveries to residences.

Acquisitions at Center Stage in the Early 2000s

UPS's post-IPO acquisition spree began with the 2000 purchase of Challenge Air Cargo, a Miami-based freight carrier operating in Latin America. That same year, the firm gained the right to fly directly to China from the United States; the following April, UPS began making six weekly freight flights to Shanghai and Beijing. Also in April 2001, UPS spent about $185 million in cash for Mail Boxes Etc., a U.S. franchise-based chain of stores providing packing, shipping, and mail services. There were more than 4,300 Mail Boxes Etc. locations throughout the United States as well as overseas, and the chain was expected to expand UPS's services to small and home-based businesses and to consumers as well. In May 2001, as part of the company's aggressive move into global supply-chain management, UPS acquired Fritz Companies, Inc. in a $456 million stock swap. Fritz, which specialized in freight forwarding, customs brokering, and logistics, was subsequently renamed UPS Freight Services. Then in late 2002 UPS Freight Services was merged with UPS Logistics Group to form UPS Supply Chain Solutions, a streamlined unit operating out of 120 countries and offering freight forwarding, international trade management, logistics and distribution, and other specialized supply-chain services.

At the beginning of 2002 Michael L. Eskew succeeded the retiring Kelly as chairman and CEO. Eskew had joined the company in 1972 as an industrial engineering manager and had risen to become executive vice-president by 1999. Also in 2002, UPS extended its money-back guarantee for on-time ground-delivered packages to include residential shipments within the continental United States, and it also launched an advertising campaign featuring a new slogan, ''What can Brown do for you?''

In early 2003 most of the 3,300 Mail Boxes Etc. outlets in the United States began operating under a new name, the UPS Store, in the hope of capitalizing on the well-known UPS brand. Simultaneously, the corporation revamped its logo for the first time since 1961. The new logo kept the shield that had been part of the logo since 1919, though the shield was modernized with a more three-dimensional look. The previous logo's bow-tied package was removed, however, as the company wanted to emphasize that it was involved in more than just shipping. Likewise, the phrase ''Worldwide Delivery Service,'' which had appeared on its 88,000-vehicle fleet, was replaced with ''Synchronizing the World of Commerce,'' thereby reflecting UPS's expanded activities in the wider supply-chain industry.

Brown remained the company's principal color. Also during 2003, UPS attempted to fend off the inroads that FedEx and other competitors had made into its core domestic ground shipping business by shaving at least one day off the amount of time it needed to ship items between more than half of the largest U.S. metropolitan areas.

Despite the implosion of numerous e-commerce companies, and the package deliveries that died along with the companies, UPS managed to continue to grow during the recessionary early 2000s. Total revenues reached $33.49 billion by 2003, with faster growth in international package deliveries and nonpackage operations (including the extended supply-chain activities and the UPS Store) making up for shortfalls in the U.S. package delivery sector. As it neared its 100th anniversary in 2007, UPS remained one of the most respected companies in its industry and a formidable competitor. One concern going forward was the aggressive move of Deutsche Post AG, the German postal agency, into the U.S. cargo market through its acquisitions of DHL Worldwide Express and Airborne Inc.

Principal Subsidiaries

United Parcel Service of America, Inc.; United Parcel Service General Services Co.; United Parcel Service Co.; UPS Worldwide Forwarding, Inc.; UPICO Corporation; UPS Capital Corporation; UPS Supply Chain Solutions, Inc.; UPS Re Ltd. (Bermuda); UPS International, Inc.; United Parcel Service Deutschland Inc. (Germany); C.C. & E. I, L.L.C.

Principal Competitors

United States Postal Service; Federal Express Corporation (FedEx); Deutsche Post AG; DHL Worldwide Express; TPG N.V.

Further Reading

Barron, Kelly, ''Logistics in Brown,'' *Forbes,* January 10, 2000, pp. 78–83.

''Behind the UPS Mystique: Puritanism and Productivity,'' *Business Week,* June 6, 1983, pp. 66 + .

Blackmon, Douglas A., ''UPS, Feeling Boxed In, Stages Its Own Coming Out,'' *Wall Street Journal,* September 17, 1996, p. B4.

——, ''UPS Plans to Sell 10 Percent Stake to the Public,'' *Wall Street Journal,* July 22, 1999, p. A3.

——, ''UPS Still Fails to Wrap Up Its Recovery from Strike,'' *Wall Street Journal,* December 8, 1997, p. B4.

Blackmon, Douglas A., et al., ''UPS Faces Huge Rise in Annual Labor Costs,'' *Wall Street Journal,* August 20, 1997, p. A3.

Bonney, Joseph, ''UPS Bets a Billion,'' *American Shipper,* January 1993, p. 26.

Brooks, Rick, ''New UPS Delivery Service Sends Packages Through the Post Office,'' *Wall Street Journal,* November 6, 2003, p. A1.

——, ''UPS Cuts Ground-Delivery Time,'' *Wall Street Journal,* October 6, 2003, p. A3.

Credeur, Mary Jane, ''Painting the World Brown: International Growth Drives UPS,'' *Atlanta Business Chronicle,* July 21, 2003.

Curtis, Carol E., ''The Brown Giant Tries Wings,'' *Forbes,* October 26, 1981, pp. 62 + .

Day, Charles R., Jr., ''Shape Up and Ship Out,'' *Industry Week,* February 6, 1995, pp. 14, 17–20.

''Delivering in Tough Times,'' *Chief Executive,* March 2003, pp. 32–33.

Duffy, Caroline A., "UPS Toes the Line with Its Package-Tracking Technologies," *PC Week,* June 28, 1993, p. 211.

Gillam, Carey, "Delivering the Dream," *Sales and Marketing Management,* June 1996, pp. 74–78.

Greenwald, John, "Hauling UPS's Freight," *Time,* January 29, 1996, p. 59.

"Ground Wars," *Business Week,* May 21, 2001, p. 64.

Guilford, Roxanna, "UPS Reinvents Itself As International Company," *Atlanta Business Chronicle,* November 12, 1999.

Hirschman, Dave, "UPS Boxes Competition," *Atlanta Journal-Constitution,* March 11, 2001, p. Q1.

——, "UPS Moves to Extend Brand Mail Boxes Chain to Adopt Name," *Atlanta Journal-Constitution,* February 11, 2003, p. D1.

"James E. Casey," *Puget Sound Business Journal,* April 2, 1993, p. 2A.

Labich, Kenneth, "Big Changes at Big Brown," *Fortune,* January 18, 1988, pp. 56+.

Lukas, Paul, "UPS: The Whole Package," *Fortune Small Business,* April 12, 2003.

Lyne, Jack, "UPS COO Jim Kelly: Bold Days for 'Big Brown,' " *Site Selection,* August 1995, pp. 53–54.

Martin, Neil A., "A New Ground War," *Barron's,* April 21, 2003, pp. 21–22, 24, 26.

Molis, Jim, "On a Roll, UPS Gearing Up for an E-Commerce Future," *Atlanta Business Chronicle,* April 12, 1999.

O'Reilly, Brian, "They've Got Mail!," *Fortune,* February 7, 2000, pp. 100–04+.

"The Quiet Giant of Shipping," *Forbes,* January 15, 1970.

Rocks, David, "UPS: Will This IPO Deliver?," *Business Week,* November 15, 1999, p. 41.

"Why United Parcel Admits Its Size," *Business Week,* July 18, 1970.

Williams, John D., "The Brown Giant: UPS Delivers Profits by Expanding Its Area, Battling Postal Rates," *Wall Street Journal,* August 25, 1980, p. 1.

"The Wizard Is Oz," *Chief Executive (U.S.),* March 1994, pp. 40–43.

—Scott M. Lewis

—updates: April Dougal Gasbarre, David E. Salamie

VINTON STUDIOS

Vinton Studios

1400 NW 22nd Avenue
Portland, Oregon 97210
U.S.A.
Telephone: (503) 226-1130
Fax: (503) 226-3746
Web site: http://www.vintonstudios.com

Private Company
Incorporated: 1975
Employees: 80
Sales: $16 million (2003 est.)
NAIC: 512110 Movie Picture and Video Production

Vinton Studios is one of the largest producers of animated commercials in the world and one of the only producers of prime-time network television series using stop-motion animation. Vinton's commercial work includes many award-winning commercials and campaigns for regional, national, and international clients, including: M&M Mars, Kraft, Samsung, Clorox, 3Musketeers, Chili's Restaurants, Nabisco, Gateway Computers, Cadbury, Wrigley's, NFL on Fox, Nestlé, Sony Playstation, Nissan, ESPN, Orkin, Raid, Levi's, Pacific Bell, Domino's Pizza, and The California Raisin Board. The studio also employs computer animation, cel animation, and some live action.

1975–95: The Early Years—A Focus on Advertising

Will Vinton began toying with clay animation while he was an architecture student at UC-Berkeley. After his graduation in 1971, he took a series of jobs at small film production companies while continuing to develop his Claymation techniques in his Portland, Oregon basement. Claymation works by modeling characters and background settings from colored clay. Animators move these by painstakingly small increments and record the "motion" frame by frame on film. There can be as many as 50 different changes between frames and 24 individual frames per second of film. Although Vinton did not make a living at Claymation for at least seven years, he enjoyed pioneering a new art form, as he recalled in a 1988 *Wall Street Journal* article. "What kept me going is that I really had a following at film festivals."

Vinton's first big break came in 1975, when he and Bob Gardiner won the Academy Award for Best Animated Short Film for "Closed Mondays," a film about a wino who finds himself in a closed museum in which the characters in the paintings come to life. Shortly afterward, Vinton founded Vinton Studios in Portland, Oregon. Other awards followed, and, by 1986, when the studio created a group of singing and dancing raisins for The California Raisin Board, Vinton had won every major international film award, except for Cannes. The huge success of the California Raisins brought Vinton Studios increased attention, along with offers to create television commercials and other projects using Claymation.

In the 1980s, Vinton and his team produced some of the most memorable advertising spots on television—ads for Domino Pizza, Kraft Foods, Levi Strauss, Nickelodeon, and the California Raisins. By the time David Altschul joined the company as president of its advertising division in 1982, the company was famous for its characters—and for their edge. Even in its commercials, the studio tried ". . . to understand what kind of world that characters live in, who the other characters are, and most important, what conflicts exist between them," Altschul explained in a 2000 *FastCompany* article. "What are their flaws, their vulnerabilities? Without knowing those things, it's hard to tell a story that engages the audience." Some of Vinton's characters, such as the California Raisins, became very well known; actors dressed in raisin costumes marched in Macy's Thanksgiving Day parade in New York, and a raisin congo line danced at the White House tree lighting ceremony during the Reagan years.

By the late 1980s, Vinton Studios had 60 employees drawn from the sculpture departments of art schools and was experimenting with full-length films. In 1985, it produced and directed *The Adventures of Mark Twain,* the first feature-length Claymation film, an undertaking that took three and a half years to complete. There was also a half-hour Claymation Christmas Celebration in 1987 on CBS that ranked fifth in the Nielsen ratings.

But despite the studio's creative success, Claymation had become so thoroughly associated with the California Raisins that other companies were reluctant to hire Vinton to work for them. Ad executives feared that as soon as consumers saw a Claymation commercial, they would think of raisins instead of the product advertised. Thus in 1991, Vinton visited Madison Avenue agencies to try to convince them that Claymation was not overexposed. "The important thing when you get pigeonholed, as we did with the raisins and Claymation, is to show the range of what else is possible," he said in a *Wall Street Journal* article in 1994.

That range included evolving beyond the studio's hallmark characters and creatures to develop a complicated animation technique that melded three forms of production—Claymation, stop-motion animation, and computer animation—to create a three-dimensional effect on screen and to enable its artists to achieve desired results in less time than it took to achieve them entirely in clay. "Claymation served us well for a very long time. . . . But now we have something new that we desire to show to other ad agencies," Vinton announced in the *Wall Street Journal*. Vinton Studios employed this new technique for the first time in a 1994 Chips Ahoy! commercial in which the brand's signature punctuation mark leaps off the package. In 1996, Vinton Studios wowed the ad world again with its innovative approach to advertising in a spot for Nissan cars that featured Barbie-type dolls making a getaway in a Nissan Z car. But while the ad won Best spot of 1996 by *Time* magazine and *Rolling Stone,* sales at Nissan fell.

By the mid-1990s, animation had become the hot new way to make movies, and there were box office hits such as *Toy Story* and *The Lion King* and television shows such as *The Simpsons.* But despite success on Madison Avenue and with award juries, Vinton Studios was still making mostly commercials. Vinton desired to branch out into feature-length productions, but two things prevented this. There was, first, as he explained in *FastCompany*, the fact that the studio ". . . didn't have the efficiency required to make larger projects. . . . In terms of talent, we genuinely felt that we were the best company in the works. But we didn't have the management chops to produce high-quality work on a low enough budget." Secondly, "[t]here was a stigma attached to dimensional animation," according to Vinton in a *Forbes* article in 1994. Vinton Studios had been relegated largely to film festivals, and Vinton's dream of breaking into feature-length films seemed unattainable.

Becoming a Force in the Entertainment Industry

However, by the time Vinton Studios hit the 20-year mark, Vinton was determined to build the infrastructure necessary to do longer projects in film. In 1997 the company, which by then had more than 100 employees and a roster of blue-chip clients, recruited and hired Tom Turpin, a Harvard M.B.A. and former Goldman Sachs banker, as its president and CEO. Turpin's role was to build the business practices that would support the company's artistic goals. Under Turpin's lead, between 1997 and 2000, the company chalked up an enviable financial record; revenues grew at a compound annual rate of 50 percent, and the company began to see its first profits.

Hollywood producer Ron Howard also called Vinton in 1997 to pitch an idea for a Foamation (a more realistic version of Claymation) television series created by Eddie Murphy. The studio partnered with Imagine Entertainment, Eddie Murphy Productions, and Touchstone Television in 1998 to produce the first-ever stop-motion series for prime-time network television, *The PJs.* The series premiered on the Fox network to record-breaking ratings. After two seasons, it had won three Emmy Awards, and director Mark Gustafson had won an Annie Award for Outstanding Individual Achievement for Directing. "What we're doing with *The PJs* is really the first step in where we want to be going," announced Turpin in the *Los Angeles Times* in 1998. "Our core strength is in character development and creation, and we really want to be into original programming." Each episode of *The PJs* took about 28 weeks to produce.

Vinton Studios and Big Ticket Television partnered to produce the studio's second prime-time television series, titled *Gary and Mike,* which aired on Fox in 1999 at a cost of slightly more than $1 million per episode. To support the company's shift into prime-time entertainment, the studio hired an additional 150 people, boosting its payroll to 400. In addition, the studio formulated a strategic plan that involved looking for private investment money. Vinton still held his studio's majority stock interest, with minor interests belonging to longtime employees and members of the board of directors. In 1998, Phil Knight, cofounder of Nike, joined the company's list of investors, when he purchased a minority share of its stock.

The new millennium brought new challenges for independent studios such as Vinton as consolidation became common in the industry. Vinton still earned 70 percent of its revenues as the largest provider of animation and effects for commercials in the United States, but it encountered hard times as both *The PJs* and *Gary and Mike* were placed on hiatus. Warner Brothers Network eventually picked up *The PJs* for its third season, and UPN picked up *Gary and Mike* from Fox, but, in the interim, the studio enforced its first staff cutbacks in six years. Still, determined to see itself on prime-time and in film, Vinton Studios went ahead with plans to open a Los Angeles office to handle productions, sales, and interaction with television networks.

The studio also began making strides in another area in the late 1990s. In 1998, it had opened its Character Development Lab as part of its advertising division with the aim of helping agencies and advertisers update aging brand symbols and create new personas for commercials. In 2000, the Character Development Lab handled five development projects for Kellogg's, Nabisco, and a brand in the Dr. Pepper/7Up Line. In 2001, it reworked the lonely Maytag repairman into more of a can-do sort of guy, who set out to bring perfection to realms other than washing machines and dryers. In 2001, when Jeff Farnath, a former Disney Animation executive, took over the reins at Vinton Studios from Turpin, he began to position the studio for major growth in its Character Development Lab and for a much bigger focus on feature-length animation films.

Key Dates:

1975: Will Vinton founds Vinton Studios in Portland, Oregon.

1986: Vinton Studios develops the California Raisins.

1997: Tom Turpin joins the company as its president and CEO.

1998: Vinton Studios produces the first-ever stop-motion series for prime-time network television, *The PJs*; opens its Character Development Lab.

1999: Vinton Studios produces the *Gary and Mike* series for television.

2002: The company acquires Celluloid Studios; Philip Knight becomes the studio's majority shareholder and a member of the board.

2003: Will Vinton is fired and sues Knight for inappropriate control of the board.

In 2002, Vinton Studios acquired Celluloid Studios, known for its cel animation and for a variety of hand-rendered and digital media, which it used to create a broad range of animation styles. As a leader in cel animation for more than 20 years, Celluloid had produced spots for national and international broadcast and was responsible for such character icons as the Raid Roaches, Cap'n Crunch, Tony the Tiger, Toucan Sam, the Keebler Elves, Lucky the Leprechaun, and Hawaiian Punch's Punchy. Celluloid had produced the pilot episode of *South Park* as well as the earlier ''Jesus vs. Santa'' short upon which it was based. It became a fully integrated division of the Vinton Portland facility.

Battle for Control

Also in late 2002, the company issued additional stock for Knight to purchase as a means of improving its finances. Knight became the studio's majority shareholder and a member of the board and appointed his son, a Vinton employee, and two others to the board of directors. Farnath had begun meeting with Knight upon his arrival at Vinton Studios in 2001 to propose that Knight become more involved in the company financially.

In March 2003, Farnath again turned to Knight for a cash infusion to help Vinton Studios through hard times. Vinton objected to the terms of the additional financing, and when the company implemented additional layoffs, Will Vinton was among them. Vinton sued Knight and other members of the board of directors after he was dismissed, claiming that his firing had been orchestrated by Knight. Knight's lawyers argued that Farnath had fired Vinton per the terms of an agreement Vinton had with the studios that specified that he could be fired without cause. In September 2003, Knight's Phight LLC became the sole shareholder and director of Vinton Studios. A county judge dismissed Vinton's claims that Knight had improperly induced his termination.

Under Knight and Farnath's direction, Vinton Studios continued to plan for its future in feature-length animation. In 2004, in addition to its full slate of commercial work, Vinton Studios was hard at work producing the animated feature film, *Corpse Bride,* in association with Tim Burton and Warner Brothers. The film was due for a Halloween 2005 release.

Principal Competitors

Aardman Animations Ltd.; Light and Magic; Pixar Animation Studios; Pacific Data Images.

Further Reading

Braxtin, Greg, ''Puppetz N the Hood,'' *Los Angeles Times*, August 1, 1998, p. F1.

Brenneman, Kristina, ''Vinton Studios' Latest TV Show Is Fox's Answer to *South Park*,'' *Portland Business Journal*, September 17, 1999, p. 3.

Darlin, Damon, and Joshua Levine, ''Stars Who Don't Throw Hissy Fits,'' *Forbes*, February 28, 1994, p. 94.

Goldman, Kevin, ''Claymation's Creator Develops New Wizardry for Chips Ahoy!'' *Wall Street Journal*, February 9, 1994, p. B1.

Hauser, Susan, ''Everything's Coming Up Raisins,'' *Wall Street Journal*, May 17, 1988, p. 1.

Liever, Ron, ''Feat of Clay,'' *FastCompany*, April 2000, p. 230.

Manning, Jeff, ''Portland, Oregon-Based Animation House Will Vinton Studios Goes to Nike Chief,'' *Knight Ridder Tribune Business News*, September 7, 2003, p. 1.

—Carrie Rothburd

The Wackenhut Corporation

4200 Wackenhut Drive, Suite 100
Palm Beach Gardens, Florida 33140-4243
U.S.A.
Telephone: (561) 622-5656
Fax: (561) 691-6423
Web site: http://www.wackenhut.com

Wholly Owned Subsidiary of Group 4 Falck A/S
Incorporated: 1958
Employees: 40,000
Sales: $2.8 billion (2001)
Stock Exchanges: New York
NAIC: 561610 Investigation, Guard, and Armored Car
Services; 561612 Security Guards and Patrol Services;
561210 Correctional Facility Operation on a Contract
or Fee Basis; 541690 Security Consulting Services;
922160 Fire Protection

Headquartered in Palm Beach Gardens, Florida, The Wackenhut Corporation is a wholly owned subsidiary of Group 4 Falck A/S, a Danish security firm. It is a longtime leader in the security services industry, providing highly trained armored security forces for nuclear power plants, airports, and embassies. The company also offers a range of other services, including security consulting, management, training, emergency support, and fire deterrence. Throughout the 1980s and 1990s Wackenhut also established a strong presence in the private prison and employer services industries. However, the company's merger with Group 4 Falck in 2002 forced it to shed many of its subsidiaries and streamline its operations considerably.

Company Origins: 1950s

Wackenhut was founded in Miami in 1954 as Special Agent Investigators, Inc. by George R. Wackenhut, a former special agent of the Federal Bureau of Investigations (FBI), and three other former FBI agents. The company's initial focus was in investigative services; by 1955, however, the company began to provide physical security services as well, winning a contract

with National Airlines of Miami, which lasted for the next 20 years. In 1958, George Wackenhut bought out his partners and incorporated the company as The Wackenhut Corporation, moving the company to Coral Gables, Florida. In that same year, Wackenhut received its first major contract from the Martin Company (later known as Martin Marietta) to provide security and protection services; later contracts with Martin, in 1961 and 1963, brought Wackenhut security guards to Martin's Titan missile sites.

By 1959, the company was posting revenues of more than $1 million, and by 1961 the company employed more than 1,300 people. The acquisition of General Plant Protection Company in 1962 allowed Wackenhut to expand its operations beyond Florida, into California and Hawaii. One of the company's first government agency contracts followed in 1963, when the company, through its Wackenhut Services, Inc. (WSI) division, was hired to guard NASA's Lewis Research Center in Cleveland. The next year, Wackenhut won a $44 million, seven-year contract at the Kennedy Space Center. WSI began a contract for the Nevada nuclear testing site of the Atomic Energy Commission (later the Department of Energy) in 1965, with renewals through 1997. There, WSI deployed "a paramilitary operation," as noted by its vice-president of Nevada Operations in *Security Management,* comprising "a very heavily armed force of individuals who receive specialized SWAT-type training, and armored vehicles and helicopters."

Expansion and Diversification: 1960s–80s

Wackenhut went public in 1966, listing initially with the American Stock Exchange, and, since 1980, on the New York Stock Exchange. That same year Wackenhut went international, opening an office in Venezuela, followed over the next several years by offices in Columbia, Ecuador, and Brazil. By 1971, Wackenhut had opened offices in Italy, France, and the Dominican Republic as well. This same period saw the company continuing to expand through acquisitions of other security services-related firms.

When construction on the 800-mile Alaska pipeline began in 1974, Wackenhut, through its subsidiary Ahtna AGA Security,

Company Perspectives:

Year after year, The Wackenhut Corporation delivers unrivaled business services to a growing list of commercial, industrial and government organizations. The company was included in Fortune*'s list of "America's Most Admired Companies" in 2001, and* Forbes*'s most recent "Platinum 400" list of "America's Best Big Companies." These distinctions are testament to Wackenhut's reputation for excellence and its continuing pursuit of quality and professionalism.*

Inc., provided guard and security services, and later, with the completion of the pipeline, continued to guard the pipeline and nearby oil reserves and facilities through the 1990s. In 1976, another division, Wackenhut International Inc., won a contract for providing the security design and installation at Jeddah (Saudi Arabia) International Airport, then the largest airport in the world. During this time Wackenhut sold off its U.S. divisions specializing in "central-station" security, where guards monitored properties from a centrally located office, a market that had proved unprofitable.

By the early 1980s, Wackenhut had grown to include more than 20,000 employees and over $200 million in revenue. At this time, the company sought to diversify its services, in part because of the low margins available through its guard and security services. Increasing competition, with over 10,000 security firms operating in the United States, were another factor in Wackenhut's efforts to diversify. Although the guard services would remain the company's core business, the company expanded to include strike support services, in which Wackenhut provided security and other services to allow companies to continue to operate while their workers were on strike. Another area Wackenhut attempted to develop was the privatization of emergency, police, and fire services, replacing communities' publicly funded services with its own trained personnel; however, this effort met with only limited success. In addition, Wackenhut continued to market its airport crash, fire, and rescue teams. Further acquisitions, in 1979 of Stellar Systems, Inc. in California, and in 1980 of Indentimat Corp. in New York, enabled Wackenhut to expand its high-technology security operations as well.

Wackenhut won several major government contracts in the 1980s. Its 1983 three-year, $81 million contract at the Savannah River Site in South Carolina was the largest paramilitary security contract ever awarded by the U.S. government. A $5 million, three-year contract in 1984 to create and manage the Department of Energy's Central Training Academy in Nevada continued to be held by the company through 1995, when it was renewed through the year 2000 for $58.6 million. Another significant, and lasting, contract began in 1986, when Wackenhut was awarded $25.3 million for security services at the DOE's Strategic Petroleum Reserve.

During the 1980s, financial pressures, as well as overcrowding, led to the privatization of increasing numbers of state and federal corrections facilities. Wackenhut ventured into this new market when WSI was hired to design, construct, and operate an Immigration and Naturalization Service detention center in Colorado in 1987. In the next year, Wackenhut formed Wackenhut Corrections Corporation (WCC) as a wholly owned subsidiary and received contracts for two 500-bed facilities in Texas. WCC went public in 1994, selling approximately 26 percent of its stock, with the remainder under Wackenhut Corp.'s control. By the end of 1994, the number of prison beds under its direction had totaled 14,000. With annual revenues of $105 million, consultant and construction fees generating an additional $80 million, and profit margins as high as 10 percent, corrections became one of the most successful areas of Wackenhut's business. Facilities under WCC's control included prisons in Australia, England, and Puerto Rico, as well as in six states in the United States, with ten facilities in Texas alone. A contract in December 1994 for the construction and management of a 1,300-bed medium-security prison in Florida provided WCC with $50 million, its largest contract as of that date.

Maintaining a Focus on Long-Term Growth in the 1990s

Despite continued rises in revenues, Wackenhut's profit margin decreased at the beginning of the 1990s to 1.3 percent, a decline from the 2.5 percent in the early 1980s. *Florida Trend* ascribed this decline to Wackenhut's focus on long-term, rather than short-term, opportunities as it entered new markets and new services. In contrast to its chief competitors, where the security guard market accounted for 90 percent of their business, Wackenhut had diversified to the extent that its security services generated only 43 percent of its revenues. Government services, including airport and municipal fire and rescue, accounted for 35 percent, with an additional 10 percent of revenues arising from its DOE and corrections contracts. Wackenhut had become less dependent on the traditionally low-margin guard business, while supporting its newer projects with this core. Accordingly, Wackenhut's emphasis on diversification has been praised by Find/SVP of New York as "a conscious decision to forego short-term profits in favor of long-term gains." During this time, also, Wackenhut sold off two of its less profitable divisions, Stellar Systems, Inc. in 1991, and, in 1994, Wackenhut Monitoring Systems, which had lost $1.5 million in 1993.

Additional difficulty for Wackenhut came in 1992 when it was named in a lawsuit, along with the Alyeska Pipeline Service Company, the consortium of oil companies operating the Alaska pipeline, for illegally spying on an environmental activist. A government report prepared by Democratic members of the House Interior and Insular Affairs Committee further charged Wackenhut and Alyeska with attempting to interfere with the congressional investigation into their activities. However, the report's conclusions were challenged by Republican House members, and the lawsuit was settled for undisclosed terms and with neither Alyeska nor Wackenhut admitting guilt. Apart from the bad publicity and a $10,000 fine from the State of Virginia, the incident was described, in *Florida Trend,* as a "short-term problem for a company whose thinking is slanted toward the long term."

By the mid-1990s, Wackenhut's organizational structure comprised three main components: domestic operations; government services; and international operations. Domestic operations provided—in addition to the traditional uniformed guard and

Key Dates:

1954: Wackenhut Corporation is founded in Miami as Special Agent Investigators, Inc. by George R. Wackenhut, a former special agent of the Federal Bureau of Investigations (FBI), and three other former FBI agents.

1958: George Wackenhut buys out his partners and incorporates the company as The Wackenhut Corporation, moving the company to Coral Gables, Florida.

1962: The acquisition of General Plant Protection Company allows Wackenhut to expand its operations beyond Florida, into California and Hawaii.

1964: Wholly owned subsidiary Wackenhut Services, Inc. (WSI) is formed specifically to handle the company's government contract business

1966: Wackenhut goes public, listing shares on the American Stock Exchange; company opens its first international office in Venezuela.

1985: Company begins first Job Corps Centers operations.

1987: Wackenhut enters the growing private correctional facilities business, forming Wackenhut Corrections Corporation (WCC) as a wholly owned subsidiary.

1994: WCC goes public, selling approximately 26 percent of its stock, with the remainder under Wackenhut Corp.'s control.

1997: Wackenhut Corporation launches Oasis Outsourcing, a professional employer organization (PEO).

2002: Wackenhut Corporation becomes a subsidiary of Group 4 Falck, a Danish security firm.

other physical security services—such services as loss prevention analysis and system design, employee and prospective employee screening, and insurance inspections, fraud investigations, strike support, and transportation of assets. The rise in airplane hijackings in the 1970s and the continued threat of terrorism brought Wackenhut into the country's airports, where their guards were charged with screening passengers prior to boarding. The Nuclear Services Division of Domestic Operations were providing physical services to 16 nuclear power generating plants by 1995. The Domestic Operations Group also oversaw Wackenhut's Alaska Pipeline activities. With the increasing privatization of corrections facilities, Wackenhut Support Services and Creative Food Management, which offered specialized foodservices to correctional institutions, increased revenues from $3 million in 1989 to $25 million in 1994.

Wackenhut's Government Services Group included the wholly owned subsidiaries Wackenhut Services, Inc. (WSI), which was formed in 1964 specifically for Wackenhut's government contract business; and Wackenhut Education Services, Inc., through which Wackenhut operated Job Corps Centers for the U.S. Department of Labor. Wackenhut Corrections Corp.'s activities were also included under the Government Services Group. In addition to the Nevada Nuclear Test Site, the Savannah River Site, the Strategic Petroleum Reserve, and the nuclear manufacturing plant in Rocky Flats, Colorado, WSI expanded beyond the Department of Energy to other government agencies, particularly the U.S. Army, for which WSI provided security, maintenance, hazardous waste disposal, and fire protection at three ammunition plants. WSI continued to provide private police, fire, and emergency services to municipalities as well as in major airports; a July 1995 contract with the state of Hawaii awarded Wackenhut nearly $35 million for security at eight airports over the next three years. The trend toward privatization included education as well. In 1984, the DOE contracted WSI to establish and then operate its Central Training Academy in New Mexico, and in 1985 the company began its first Job Corps Centers operations.

The International Operations Group of Wackenhut, through its subsidiary Wackenhut International Incorporated, extended Wackenhut's domestic services to six continents and more than 50 countries, including placing security guards at 18 U.S. embassies and missions. New markets opened for Wackenhut in the 1990s with the fall of the Berlin Wall and the increasing normalization of relations with China. Wackenhut opened offices in Russia and in the Czech Republic and began to develop contacts with mainland China through its Hong Kong office. Additional expansion came as the company entered India and Pakistan and gained new embassy security contracts with the U.S. State Department. The 1994 acquisition of 60 percent ownership in SEGES extended Wackenhut into the Ivory Coast, described in the company's 1994 annual report as a "strategic move." Other services offered by the International Operations Group included central alarm station services, executive protection, armored car services, vehicle location and recovery, and privatized forestry, toll collection, corrections, and police and fire support.

As late as 1995, The Wackenhut Corporation remained under the control of George R. Wackenhut, its founder, who functioned as chairman of the board and chief executive officer and held 50 percent of the company's stock. In the early 1990s, however, George Wackenhut turned the presidency of the company over to his son, Richard R. Wackenhut, who also functioned as the company's chief operating officer. The company had also seen a shift in management, away from a personnel traditionally recruited from among retired police and military officers, to those with business school and established business backgrounds, with an average age in the mid-40s. The privatization of corrections facilities remained an important Wackenhut market, and the company continued to look to the privatization of government functions for new markets for its services. With a reduction in its long-term debt, from $57 million in 1993 to $39 million in 1994, and a credit agreement allowing the company as much as $60 million in new loans, Wackenhut was poised to continue its program of expansion and diversification.

Into the 21st Century: Diversification, Consolidation, and a Major Merger

In the mid-1990s, the private prison industry seemed on the verge of explosive growth. With national inmate populations at all-time highs, and most states feeling the pinch of rising incarceration costs, the privatization lobby, notably Wackenhut Corrections and its principal competitor, Corrections Corporation of America, appeared to offer a cheaper, and ultimately more rehabilitative, alternative to the traditional prison system. In mid-1996, prison officials in several states, including Florida, California, Texas, and New Mexico, conducted studies to determine whether or not prison privatization made economic sense. The preliminary findings in Florida were particularly encouraging for Wackenhut: in a report filed in November 1996, the Florida Corrections Commission estimated that the state would need to devote $200 million to expanding its prison capacity, and that privatization was the most cost-effective way to address this increased demand. In response to the report, Wackenhut Corrections produced a 28-page proposal outlining its plan to systematically privatize all of the state's prisons, region by region. At around this time, Wackenhut entered into a contract with New Mexico to build 3,400 new prisons in the state.

However, this potential business opportunity abruptly evaporated the following year. By mid-1997, most studies showed that the cost-efficiency of privatization remained undetermined, and that the push for more private prisons might be premature. In Florida, new data revealed a growing pattern of leniency in the state's judicial system, resulting in a slower increase in the state's prison population; at the same time, new laws allowed for an increase in the state's existing prison capacity to 150 percent, obviating the need for the construction of new facilities. Florida legislators were also daunted by the scope of Wackenhut's proposal, which struck most as too large an investment for an unproven business model. Florida's position reflected a nationwide trend; even New Mexico scaled back its original contract with Wackenhut by nearly a third. This sudden shift delivered a major hit to the subsidiary's stock, which dropped to $15.50 in November, down from $45 the previous June. The parent company's market value suffered as well; share prices of Wackenhut Corporation fell below $15 during the same period.

Still, these setbacks proved to be temporary, and overall The Wackenhut Corporation enjoyed consistent profitability throughout the late 1990s. For the third quarter of 1996, the company saw its profits increase by 50 percent, from $2 million to $3 million, over the previous year. Equally encouraging, by mid-1997 the private prison industry had rebounded, boosting shares in Wackenhut Corrections more than 80 percent. In early 1997, Wackenhut Corporation also took steps toward entering the burgeoning field of employer services by establishing a professional employer organization, or PEO, in Denver, Colorado. In April of that year Wackenhut launched a new subsidiary, Oasis Outsourcing, in south Florida. The company further expanded its new niche with the purchase of Jim King Cos., a Jacksonville, Florida-based PEO, in May 1997 for $11.5 million. Eventually, the company hoped to develop similar businesses in Texas and California. Meanwhile, Wackenhut Corrections continued to flourish into the new century, winning $140 million in federal grants in 2000, and entering into a contract to build a maximum-security prison in South Africa. By 2002, The Wackenhut Corporation had roughly 68,000 employees worldwide.

In March 2002, after decades as an independent company, The Wackenhut Corporation announced its intention to enter into a merger with Group 4 Falck, a Danish security company. Under the terms of the deal, Group 4 Falck acquired all of Wackenhut's common stock for $573 million. The merger had its share of messes. Two shareholders filed suit against the company, charging that company insiders, who mainly possessed "Series B" stock in the corporation, stood to enjoy a much larger return than "Series A" shareholders. Even company founder George Wackenhut expressed ambivalence about the transaction, despite receiving a parting compensation package worth roughly $124 million; "it's like giving up your baby," he told reporters for the *Palm Beach Post* in May 2002, after shareholders finally approved the deal. As part of the merger, Group 4 Falck decided to unload its new stake in Wackenhut Corrections. To this end, in July 2003 Wackenhut Corrections entered into a share repurchase agreement with Group 4 Falck, relinquishing its rights to the Wackenhut name and paying $126 million, thereby becoming an independent company. Meanwhile, Wackenhut Corporation remained the U.S.-based subsidiary of Group 4 Falck, continuing to provide security services throughout the United States, with a staff of more than 40,000 in 2004. Although scandals concerning security failures at key nuclear facilities in the United States, which first surfaced in April 2004, threatened to undermine The Wackenhut Corporation's continued growth, it seemed a safe bet that the company would remain a leading name in the American security industry—which had grown exponentially since the September 11 terrorist attacks—well into the 21st century.

Principal Subsidiaries

Wackenhut Services, Inc.

Principal Competitors

Guardsmark, Inc.; Securicor plc; Securitas AB.

Further Reading

Bork, Robert H., Jr., "Big George Wackenhut," *Forbes,* November 21, 1983, pp. 203–6.

Bryce, Robert, "Prison Business Booms in the US," *Christian Science Monitor,* August 12, 1993, p. 8.

"Critic Settles Suit Against Alaska Pipeline," *New York Times,* December 21, 1993, p. 23.

DeGeorge, Gail, "Wackenhut Is Out to Prove That Crime Does Pay," *Business Week,* December 17, 1990, pp. 95–96.

Dorfman, John R., "Caught Flat-Footed," *Forbes,* April 12, 1982, pp. 74–78.

Hersch, Valerie, "The Gumshoes Are Gone," *Florida Trend,* June 1992, pp. 65–67.

Keller, Larry, "Good Deal? Lawsuits Say Wackenhut's Planned Sale to Danish Company Would Shortchange Most Shareholders," *Miami Business Daily Review,* March 14, 2002.

Kenworthy, Tom, "Alaska Oil Pipeline Company and Security Firm Criticized," *Washington Post,* July 24, 1992, p. 2.

Millman, Joel, "Captive Market," *Forbes,* September 16, 1991, p. 190.

Ottolenghi, Hugo, "Wackenhut Unbound; Wackenhut Corrections Share Price Jumps with Better Industry Numbers," *Miami Daily Business Review,* July 2, 1997.

Parker, Susie T., "Targets of Probe File Suit Against Alyeska Pipeline," *Oil Daily,* July 28, 1992, pp. 1, 8.

Pounds, Stephen, "Danish Company Likely to Sell Prison Spinoff After Acquiring Wackenhut Corp.," *Palm Beach Post,* May 3, 2002.

Seemuth, Mike, "Wackenhut Corrections Buys Freedom with Name," *Miami Daily Business Review,* July 17, 2003.

Sullivan, Allanna, "Congressional Report Urges Prosecution of Wackenhut and Alyeska Over Spying," *Wall Street Journal,* July 24, 1992, p. 12.

—M.L. Cohen
—update: Stephen Meyer

Wal-Mart Stores, Inc.

702 Southwest 8th Street
Bentonville, Arkansas 72716-8611
U.S.A.
Telephone: (501) 273-4000
Fax: (501) 273-6850
Web site: http://www.walmartstores.com

Public Company
Incorporated: 1969
Employees: 1,500,000
Sales: $256.68 billion (2004)
Stock Exchanges: New York Pacific
Ticker Symbol: WMT
NAIC: 445110 Supermarkets and Other Grocery (Except
Convenience) Stores; 452910 Warehouse Clubs and
Superstores; 452990 All Other General Merchandise
Stores; 454110 Electronic Shopping and Mail-Order
Houses

Wal-Mart Stores, Inc. is not only the largest retailer in the world, it now also ranks as the largest corporation in the world. The retail giant dwarfs its nearest competition, generating three times the revenues of the world's number two retailer, France's Carrefour SA. Domestically, Wal-Mart has more than 1.2 million workers, making it the nation's largest nongovernmental employer. U.S. operations include 1,478 Wal-Mart discount stores (located in all 50 states); 1,471 Wal-Mart Supercenters, which are combined discount outlets and grocery stores (and which make Wal-Mart the country's top food retailer); 538 Sam's Clubs, the number two U.S. warehouse membership club chain (trailing Costco Wholesale Corporation); and 64 Wal-Mart Neighborhood Markets, smaller food and drug outlets also offering a selection of general merchandise. International operations, which commenced in 1991, include Wal-Mart discount stores in Canada and Puerto Rico; Wal-Mart Supercenters in Argentina, Brazil, China, Germany, Mexico, Puerto Rico, South Korea, and the United Kingdom; and Sam's Clubs in Brazil, China, Mexico, and Puerto Rico. In Mexico, Wal-Mart also operates Bodegas discount stores, Suburbias specialty department stores, Superamas supermarkets, and Vips restaurants. In addition, the company runs Todo Dias supermarkets in Brazil, Neighborhood Markets supermarkets in China, ASDA combined grocery and apparel stores in the United Kingdom, and Amigo supermarkets in Puerto Rico. Wal-Mart also holds a 36 percent stake in The Seiyu, Ltd., a leading Japanese retailer. In all, more than one-quarter of Wal-Mart's stores are located outside the United States, and international operations generate about 18.5 percent of total revenues. The heirs of founder Samuel Walton continue to own about a 38 percent interest in the company.

Development of a "Good Concept" in the 1960s

Founder Walton—who at his death in 1992 was among the richest people in the United States—graduated from the University of Missouri in 1940 with a degree in economics and became a management trainee with J.C. Penney Company. After two years he went into the army. Upon returning to civilian life three years later, he used his savings and a loan to open a Ben Franklin variety store in Newport, Arkansas. In 1950 he lost his lease, moved to Bentonville, Arkansas, and opened another store. By the late 1950s, Sam and his brother J.L. (Bud) Walton owned nine Ben Franklin franchises.

In the early 1960s Sam Walton took what he had learned from studying mass-merchandising techniques around the country and began to make his mark in the retail market. He decided that small town populations would welcome, and make profitable, large discount shopping stores. He approached the Ben Franklin franchise owners with his proposal to slash prices significantly and operate at a high volume, but they were not willing to let him reduce merchandise as low as he insisted it had to go. The Walton brothers then decided to go into that market themselves and opened their first Wal-Mart Discount City in Rogers, Arkansas, in 1962. The brothers typically opened their department-sized stores in towns with populations of 5,000 to 25,000, and the stores tended to draw from a large radius. "We discovered people would drive to a good concept," Walton later recalled in a 1989 article in *Financial World.*

Wal-Mart's "good concept" involved huge stores offering customers a wide variety of name-brand goods at deep discounts

Company Perspectives:

Sam Walton built Wal-Mart on the revolutionary philosophies of excellence in the workplace, customer service and always having the lowest prices. We have always stayed true to the Three Basic Beliefs Mr. Sam established in 1962: 1. Respect for the Individual. 2. Service to Our Customers. 3. Strive for Excellence

that were part of an "everyday low prices" strategy. Walton was able to keep prices low and still turn a profit through sales volume as well as an uncommon marketing strategy. Wal-Mart's advertising costs generally amounted to one-third that of other discount chains; most competitors were putting on sales and running from 50 to 100 advertising circulars per year, but Wal-Mart kept its prices low and ran only 12 promotions a year.

By the end of the 1960s the brothers had opened 18 Wal-Mart stores, while still owning 15 Ben Franklin franchises throughout Arkansas, Missouri, Kansas, and Oklahoma. These ventures became incorporated as Wal-Mart Stores, Inc., in October 1969.

The 1970s held many milestones for the company. Early in the decade, Walton implemented his warehouse distribution strategy. The company built its own warehouses so it could buy in volume and store the merchandise, then proceeded to build stores throughout 200-square-mile areas around the distribution points. This practice cut Wal-Mart's costs and gave it more control over operations; merchandise could be restocked as quickly as it sold, and advertising was specific to smaller regions and cost less to distribute.

Wal-Mart went public in 1970, initially trading over the counter; in 1972 the company was listed on the New York Stock Exchange. By 1976 the Waltons had phased out their Ben Franklin stores so that the company could put all of its expansion efforts into the Wal-Mart stores. In 1977 the company made its first significant acquisition when it bought 16 Mohr-Value stores in Missouri and Illinois. Also in 1977, based on data from the previous five years, *Forbes* ranked the nation's discount and variety stores, and Wal-Mart ranked first in return on equity, return on capital, sales growth, and earnings growth.

In 1978 Wal-Mart began operating its own pharmacy, auto service center, and jewelry divisions, and acquired Hutcheson Shoe Company, a shoe-department lease operation. By 1979 there were 276 Wal-Mart stores in 11 states. Sales had gone from $44 million in 1970 to $1.25 billion in 1979. Wal-Mart became the fastest company to reach the $1 billion mark.

Establishment of Sam's Clubs in 1983

Wal-Mart sales growth continued into the 1980s. In 1983 the company opened its first three Sam's Wholesale Clubs and began its expansion into bigger city markets. Business at the 100,000-square-foot cash-and-carry discount membership warehouses proved to be good; the company had 148 such clubs by 1991, by which time the name had been shortened to Sam's Clubs.

The company continued to grow rapidly. In 1987 Wal-Mart acquired 18 Supersaver Wholesale Clubs, which became Sam's

Clubs. The most significant event of that year, however, was the opening of a new Wal-Mart's merchandising concept—taken from one originated by a French entrepreneur—that Walton called Hypermart USA. Hypermart USA stores combined a grocery store, a general merchandise market, and such service outlets as restaurants, banks, shoe shine kiosks, and videotape rental units in a space that covered more area than six football fields. Prices were reduced as much as 40 percent below full retail level, and sales volume averaged $1 million per week, compared with $200,000 for a conventional-sized discount store.

Making customers feel at home in such a large-scale shopping facility required inventiveness. The Dallas store had phone hot lines installed in the aisles for customers needing directions. Hypermart floors were made of a rubbery surface for ease in walking, and the stores offered electric shopping carts for the disabled. To entertain children, there was a "ball pit" or playroom filled with plastic balls—an idea taken from Swedish furniture retailer Ikea.

Evolution of Hypermart into the Wal-Mart Supercenter in 1988

There were also wrinkles to work out. Costs for air conditioning and heating the gigantic spaces were higher than expected. Traffic congestion and limited parking proved a drawback. Customers also complained that the grocery section was not as well-stocked or maintained as it needed to be to compete against nearby grocery stores. Wal-Mart began addressing these problems by, for example, redesigning the grocery section of the Arlington, Texas, store. In 1988 Wal-Mart also opened five smaller "supercenters"—averaging around 150,000 square feet—featuring a large selection of merchandise and offering better-stocked grocery sections, without the outside services such as restaurants or video stores. These stores, dubbed Wal-Mart Supercenters, proved much more successful than the Hypermart format, which was eventually abandoned. Hundreds of Supercenters were subsequently opened during the 1990s.

Wal-Mart received some criticism during this period for its buying practices. One analyst, according to an article in the January 30, 1989, edition of *Fortune,* described the treatment sales representatives received at Wal-Mart: "Once you are ushered into one of the spartan little buyer's rooms, expect a steely eye across the table and be prepared to cut your price." Wal-Mart was known not only for dictating the tone with its vendors, but often for only dealing directly with the vendor, bypassing sales representatives. In 1987, 100,000 independent manufacturers representatives initiated a public information campaign to fight Wal-Mart's effort to remove them from the selling process, claiming that their elimination jeopardized a manufacturer's right to choose how it sells its products.

During this time, however, Wal-Mart's revenues kept going up, and the company moved into new territory. Wal-Mart enjoyed a 12-year streak of 35 percent annual profit growth through 1987. In 1988 the company operated in 24 states—concentrated in the Midwest and South—1,182 stores, 90 wholesale clubs, and two hypermarts. David D. Glass, who was named president and CEO in 1988 but who had been with the company since 1976, was a key player in Wal-Mart's expansion.

Key Dates:

1962: Samuel Walton and his brother J.L. (Bud) Walton open their first Wal-Mart Discount City in Rogers, Arkansas.

1969: The brothers are operating 18 Wal-Mart stores in Arkansas, Missouri, Kansas, and Oklahoma; they incorporate these ventures as Wal-Mart Stores, Inc.

1970: Wal-Mart stock begins trading over the counter.

1972: The company's stock is listed on the New York Stock Exchange.

1979: Revenues surpass $1 billion; the company is the fastest to reach this milestone.

1983: The first Sam's Wholesale Clubs are opened; they are later renamed Sam's Clubs.

1988: The company opens its first Wal-Mart Supercenters, combined discount outlets and grocery stores.

1990: Wal-Mart becomes the largest retailer in the United States.

1991: Foreign expansion begins with the creation of a joint venture with Cifra, S.A. de C.V., Mexico's largest retailer.

1994: The company enters the Canadian market through the purchase from Woolworth Corporation of 122 Woolco stores.

1997: Revenues surpass $100 billion; Mexican joint ventures are merged into Cifra, and then Wal-Mart acquires a controlling stake in Cifra; the company enters Europe through acquisition of the 21-unit Wertkauf hypermarket chain in Germany.

1998: The first Wal-Mart Neighborhood Markets are opened in the United States; 74 Interspar hypermarkets are acquired in Germany.

1999: ASDA Group plc, third largest U.K. supermarket operator, is acquired for about $10.8 billion.

2000: After Wal-Mart increases its stake in Cifra to about 63 percent, Cifra is renamed Wal-Mart de México S.A. de C.V.

2002: Wal-Mart takes a 35 percent interest in The Seiyu, Ltd., a leading Japanese retailer.

2003: Fiscal 2003 revenues of $244.52 billion make Wal-Mart the world's largest corporation.

In a move motivated by good business sense and public relations efforts, Wal-Mart sent an open letter to U.S. manufacturers in March 1985 inviting them to take part in a "Buy-American" program. The company offered to work with them in producing products that could compete against imports. "Our American suppliers must commit to improving their facilities and machinery, remain financially conservative and work to fill our requirements, and most importantly, strive to improve employee productivity," Walton told *Nation's Business* in April 1988. Product conversions—arranging to buy competitively priced U.S.-made goods in place of imports—were regularly highlighted at weekly managers' meetings. William R. Fields, executive vice-president of merchandise and sales, estimated that Wal-Mart cut imports by approximately 5 percent between 1985 and 1989. Nonetheless, analysts estimated that Wal-Mart still purchased between 25 and 30 percent of its goods from overseas, about twice the percentage of competitor Kmart Corporation.

Criticism for Small Town Impact in the 1990s

Wal-Mart also came under criticism for its impact on small retail businesses. Independent store owners often went out of business when Wal-Mart came to town, unable to compete with the superstore's economies of scale. In fact, Iowa State University economist Kenneth Stone conducted a study on this phenomenon and told the *New York Times Magazine* (April 2, 1989): "If you go into towns in Illinois where Wal-Mart has been for 8 or 10 years, the downtowns are just ghost towns." He found that businesses suffering most were drug, hardware, five-and-dime, sporting goods, clothing, and fabric stores, while major appliance and furniture businesses picked up, as did restaurants and gasoline stations, because of increased traffic.

Nevertheless, Wal-Mart developed a record of community service. The company began awarding $1,000 scholarships to high school students in each community Wal-Mart served. At the same time, the company's refusal to stock dozens of widely circulated adult and teen magazines, including *Rolling Stone,* had some critics claiming that Wal-Mart was willfully narrowing the choices of the buying public by bowing to pressure from conservative special interest groups.

In 1990—the year in which Wal-Mart became the number one retailer in the United States, passing both Sears, Roebuck and Co. and Kmart—stores were added in California, Nevada, North Dakota, Pennsylvania, South Dakota, and Utah. The company also opened 25 Sam's Clubs, of which four were 130,000-square-foot prototypes incorporating space for produce, meats, and baked goods. In mid-1990, the company acquired Western Merchandise, Inc., of Amarillo, Texas, a supplier of music, books, and video products to many of the Wal-Mart stores. Late in 1990 Wal-Mart acquired the McLane Company, Inc., a distributor of grocery and retail products based in Temple, Texas, for about $275 million. Early in 1991, in a $162 million transaction, The Wholesale Club, Inc. of Indianapolis merged with Sam's Clubs, adding 28 stores that were to be integrated with Sam's by year-end. In addition, Wal-Mart agreed to sell its nine convenience store-gas station outlets to Conoco Inc.

Wal-Mart's expansion continued, and by 1992 the company opened about 150 new Wal-Mart stores and 60 Sam's Clubs, bringing the total to 1,720 Wal-Mart stores and 208 Sam's Clubs. Some of these stores represented a change in policy for the company, opening near big cities with large populations. Another policy change was instituted by the company when it announced that it would no longer deal with independent sales representatives.

In 1991 Wal-Mart introduced its new store brand, Sam's American Choice, whose first products were beverages including colas and fruit juices. The beverages were made by Canada's largest private-label bottler, Cott Corp., but the colas were supplied from U.S. plants. Future plans called for the introduction of many different types of products that would match the quality of national brands, but at lower prices.

Beginning of Foreign Expansion in 1991

Also in 1991 Wal-Mart ventured outside the United States for the first time when it entered into a joint venture with Cifra, S.A. de C.V., Mexico's largest retailer. The venture developed a price-club store called Club Aurrera that required an annual membership of about $25. Shoppers could choose from about 3,500 products ranging from fur coats to frozen vegetables. Within the year, the joint venture operated three Club Aurreras, four Bodegas discount stores, and one Aurrera combination store.

Expansion in the United States also continued, and from 1992 to 1993, 161 Wal-Mart stores were opened, while only one was closed. Another 48 Sam's Clubs and 51 Bud's Warehouse Outlets also were opened. Expansions or relocations took place at 170 Wal-Mart stores and 40 Sam's Clubs. By 1993 the 2,138 stores included 34 Wal-Mart Supercenters and 256 Sam's Clubs.

Founder Sam Walton died on April 5, 1992, of bone cancer. A fairly smooth management transition at Wal-Mart ensued, because Walton had already hand-picked his successor, David Glass, who had served as CEO since 1988. S. Robson Walton, eldest son of the founder, was named chairman of the board.

In January 1993 Wal-Mart's reputation was shaken when a report on NBC-TV's *Dateline* news program reported on child laborers in Bangladesh producing merchandise for Wal-Mart stores. The program showed children working for five cents an hour in a country that lacked child labor laws. The program further alleged that items made outside the United States were being sold under ''Made in USA'' signs as part of the company's Buy American campaign instituted in 1985. Glass appeared on the program saying that he did not know of any ''child exploitation'' by the company, but did apologize about some of the signs incorrectly promoting foreign-made products as domestic items.

In April 1993 Wal-Mart introduced another private label, called Great Value. The brand was initially used for a line of 350 packaged food items for sale in its Supercenters. The proceeds from the company's other private label, Sam's American Choice, were to be channeled into the Competitive Edge Scholarship Fund, which the company launched in 1993 in partnership with some vendors and colleges. In the same year, Wal-Mart spent $830.5 million to purchase 91 Pace Membership Warehouse clubs from Kmart, which had decided to shut down the Pace chain. Wal-Mart subsequently converted the new units into Sam's Clubs. The Sam's Club chain was thereby solidified—particularly in California, where it gained 21 stores—soon after the emergence of a rival, PriceCostco Inc. The product of the October 1993 merger of Price Co. and Costco Wholesale Corp., PriceCostco—later renamed Costco Cos. and then Costco Wholesale Corporation—would within a few years overtake the Sam's Club chain as the nation's top warehouse membership club. Overall, Wal-Mart posted profits of $2.33 billion on revenues of $67.34 billion in 1993. The company workforce now exceeded half a million people.

Mid-1990s Growth Slowdown

In the mid-1990s Wal-Mart continued to grow in the United States, but at a slower pace than previous years. Whereas the company had always posted double-digit, comparable-store

sales increases, starting in fiscal 1994 these sales increases had fallen to levels closer to the retail industry average—4 to 7 percent. Furthermore, overall net sales typically had risen 25 percent or more per year in the 1980s and early 1990s. For fiscal years 1996, 1997, and 1998, however, net sales increased 13 percent, 12 percent, and 12 percent, respectively. The company was beginning to reach the limits of expansion in its domestic market. This was reflected in the scaling back of the Wal-Mart discount store chain, which reached a peak of 1,995 units in 1996 before being reduced to 1,921 units by 1998. The company staked its domestic future on the Wal-Mart Supercenter chain, which was expanded from 34 units in 1993 to 441 units in 1998. Most of the new Supercenters—377 in total—were converted Wal-Mart discount stores, as the company sought the additional per-store revenue that could be gleaned from selling groceries. Meanwhile, the Sam's Club chain was struggling and was not as profitable as the company overall. As it attempted to turn this unit around, Wal-Mart curtailed its expansion in the United States; there were only 17 more Sam's Clubs in 1998 than there were in 1995.

Another vehicle for company growth was aggressive international expansion. Following its earlier move into Mexico, Wal-Mart entered into the other NAFTA market in 1994 when it purchased 122 Woolco stores in Canada from Woolworth Corporation in a $335 million deal. Over the next few years Wal-Mart entered Argentina, Brazil, and China through joint ventures. By 1997 Wal-Mart had set up several joint ventures with its Mexican partner, Cifra. That year, these joint ventures were merged together and then merged into Cifra. Wal-Mart then took a controlling, 51 percent stake in Cifra for $1.2 billion. The company thereby held a majority stake in the largest retailer in Mexico, whose 402 stores included 27 Wal-Mart Supercenters, 28 Sam's Clubs, and 347 units consisting of several chains, including Bodegas discount stores, Superamas grocery stores, and Vips restaurants.

In December 1997 Wal-Mart entered Europe for the first time when it acquired the 21-unit Wertkauf hypermarket chain in Germany for an estimated $880 million. The Wertkauf format was similar to that of the Wal-Mart Supercenter. The profitable Wertkauf chain had annual sales of about $1.4 billion and was the eighth largest hypermarket operator in Germany. Also in December 1997 Wal-Mart bought out its minority partner in its Brazilian joint venture, which by that time ran five Wal-Mart Supercenters and three Sam's Clubs. By early 1998 the company also operated nine Wal-Mart Supercenters and five Sam's Clubs in Puerto Rico. Later that year Wal-Mart announced plans to triple its retail base in China by the end of 1999, aiming for a total of nine stores at that time. Moreover, in July 1998 the company announced that it had purchased a majority stake in four stores and six additional development sites in Korea, extending its expansion in Asia. Around this same time, however, a Wal-Mart expansion into the troubled nation of Indonesia under a franchise agreement failed.

During fiscal 1997 Wal-Mart's international operations were profitable for the first time. By 1998 international sales had reached $7.5 billion, an impressive figure given that the company had begun its foreign expansion only in 1991; still this figure represented just 6.4 percent of overall sales. Although growth in sales at home were slowing down, Wal-Mart managed to exceed the $100 billion mark in overall revenues for the first time during fiscal 1997 and that year also gained further prestige through its selection as one of the 30 companies on the Dow Jones Industrial Average, a replacement for the troubled Woolworth. The firm also became the largest nongovernmental employer in the United States, with 680,000 domestic workers.

As another possible outlet for shoring up its top position in retailing in the United States and for increasing sales amid its nearing the saturation point for its Supercenters, Wal-Mart in late 1998 began testing a new format, the Wal-Mart Neighborhood Market. In an attempt to compete directly with traditional supermarkets and with convenience stores, this new concept consisted of a 40,000-square-foot store offering produce, deli foods, fresh meats, other grocery items, and a limited selection of general merchandise. The new store also featured a drive-through pharmacy. The company hoped that the Neighborhood Market would allow it to penetrate markets unable to support the huge 100,000-square-foot Supercenters, such as very small towns and certain sections within metropolitan areas.

Reaching New Heights in the Early 2000s

By 1999 Wal-Mart was the world's largest retailer (and the largest nongovernmental employer in the world, with 1.14 million employees) and was also the leading retailer in both Mexico and Canada. But it was Europe that was at the forefront of the corporation's international expansion in the late 1990s. In December 1998 Wal-Mart bolstered its German operations through the purchase of 74 Interspar hypermarkets from SPAR Handels AG. Then in July 1999 the company entered the U.K. market for the first time by acquiring ASDA Group plc for about $10.8 billion. Ranking as the third largest supermarket operator in the United Kingdom, ASDA operated 229 stores at the time of its acquisition and generated about $13.2 billion in annual revenues. Its stores were run in a fashion similar to that of Wal-Mart Supercenters: they were large-format units offering food, apparel, and general merchandise at everyday low prices, with an emphasis on private-label brands and an avoidance of promotions. The stores acquired in the United Kingdom continued to operate under the ASDA name, whereas the German units were eventually rebadged as Wal-Mart Supercenters.

In January 2000 H. Lee Scott, Jr., a 20-year company veteran, was promoted from chief operating officer to president and CEO. Scott succeeded Glass, who remained on the board of directors as chairman of the executive committee. The new leader had played an important role in reversing the declining results at Wal-Mart's domestic operations. One key to the turn-around was the adoption of a more aggressive approach to controlling bloated inventories at the stores and warehouses. Making better use of technology led both to significant decreases in inventory levels and to improved performance in keeping store shelves better stocked. Also during 2000 Wal-Mart spent $587 million to purchase another 6 percent of Cifra, which was subsequently renamed Wal-Mart de México S.A. de C.V. Wal-Mart held a stake of approximately 62 percent in this subsidiary.

During 2001 Wal-Mart became the largest food retailer in the United States as its grocery sales reached $56 billion. This milestone was reached in large measure through the aggressive rollout of the Wal-Mart Supercenter format. By early 2002 there were about 1,050 Supercenters in the United States, while the number of Wal-Mart discount stores had declined to fewer than 1,650. In fiscal 2002 alone, 178 Supercenters were opened, whereas there was a net reduction in discount units of 89 (121 had been converted to Supercenters, one was closed, and 33 were opened). At the same time, the Wal-Mart Neighborhood Markets format had grown to include 31 stores, providing a further base for the ever rising grocery revenue.

Despite some setbacks in its attempt to penetrate the very difficult German retail market, Wal-Mart kept up its steady international expansion. In 2001 the first Wal-Mart Supercenter in Puerto Rico opened for business. Then in December 2002 the firm paid approximately $242 million for Supermercados Amigo, Inc., the leading supermarket chain in Puerto Rico, with 37 outlets. Next on the expansion roster was Japan. In May 2002 Wal-Mart acquired a 6.1 percent interest in The Seiyu, Ltd. for about $51 million. Seiyu operated about 400 stores in Japan of various formats but mainly of the food-and-clothing variety. It ranked as Japan's fifth largest supermarket chain. In December 2002 Wal-Mart spent another $459 million to expand its stake in Seiyu to 35 percent, and it also had the right to increase it to nearly 67 percent by 2007. By 2003 Wal-Mart had more than 330,000 workers outside the United States, and its international operations produced $40.7 billion in sales that year, representing a 15 percent increase over the preceding year as well as about 17 percent of total revenues. International operating profits for 2003 jumped nearly 56 percent, hitting $2.03 billion. In May 2003 Wal-Mart, seeking to focus solely on retailing, sold its McLane wholesale distribution subsidiary to Berkshire Hathaway Inc. for $1.5 billion.

Overall fiscal 2003 revenues of $244.52 billion made Wal-Mart Stores, Inc. the world's largest corporation. Its achievement of becoming the first nonmanufacturing company to top the *Fortune* 500 was fitting as the company increasingly had become a symbol of both the positive and negative aspects of the U.S. economy of the early 2000s. In an October 6, 2003 article titled "Is Wal-Mart Too Powerful?," *Business Week* suggested a number of ways in which to view the power of Wal-Mart, such as: its drive to keep costs and prices down being at least partly responsible for the low rate of inflation in the late 20th and early 21st centuries; its cost-cutting focus also being a contributing factor in the shifting of factories outside the United States; and its 2002 imports from China of $12 billion representing 10 percent of total U.S. imports from that country. Furthermore, Wal-Mart had always taken a hard line on labor costs, particularly by resisting efforts to unionize its workforce. Two consequences of this were the company's extraordinarily high turnover rate of 44 percent per year for its hourly workers and the fact that in 2001 the average Wal-Mart sales clerk made less than the federal poverty level. As another way of looking at the power of Wal-Mart, *Fortune* in a March 3, 2003 issue estimated that the company's share of the U.S. gross national product (GNP) in 2002 was 2.3 percent. This approached the levels reached by General Motors Corporation (3 percent in 1955) and U.S. Steel Corp. (2.8 percent in 1917) when these firms were at their respective peaks. *Fortune* estimated that Wal-Mart's share of the nation's economy would become the biggest ever by around 2006, assuming the continuation of its then current growth rate.

As it continued to be dogged by detractors opposed to its business practices, Wal-Mart launched a PR offensive in 2003 to counter the relentless criticism it faced. But the retail giant had to contend with much more than just the attacks of journalists and social critics; it was facing a barrage of potentially damaging lawsuits. These included a host of class-action lawsuits involving employee claims that they were asked to work off the clock and to not take scheduled breaks. A sex discrimination lawsuit that potentially could involve 1.5 million current and former female employees alleged that Wal-Mart engaged in a pattern of discrimination against women in pay and promotion. In addition, in the fall of 2003 a federal investigation was launched into the company's use of a cleaning contractor that employed illegal immigrants.

Notwithstanding these legal battles, Wal-Mart Stores, Inc. was placing no brakes on its drive to become ever larger. During 2004 the company planned to open at least 220 new Supercenters, while its discount store chain would be reduced by a net of about 90 units. This would mean that for the first time there would be more Supercenters than Wal-Mart discount stores in the United States. The Neighborhood Market chain was scheduled to grow by between 25 and 30 units, and Sam's Club would add about 15 stores. The international store count would likewise increase, by about 100 units. It seemed clear that Wal-Mart intended to aggressively defend its position as the largest retailer of all time.

Principal Subsidiaries

Wal-Mart Stores East, LP; Wal-Mart Property Company; Wal-Mart Real Estate Business Trust; ASDA Group plc (U.K.).

Principal Divisions

Wal-Mart Discount Stores; Wal-Mart Supercenters; Wal-Mart Neighborhood Markets; Sam's Club.

Principal Competitors

Target Corporation; Kmart Corporation; Costco Wholesale Corporation; The Kroger Co.; Albertson's, Inc.; Walgreen Co.; CVS Corporation; Carrefour SA; Royal Ahold N.V.; Toys 'R' Us, Inc.

Further Reading

Bianco, Anthony, and Wendy Zellner, ''Is Wal-Mart Too Powerful?,'' *Business Week,* October 6, 2003, pp. 100–04+.

Bowermaster, Jon, ''When Wal-Mart Comes to Town,'' *New York Times Magazine,* April 2, 1989.

Capell, Kerry, et al., ''Wal-Mart's Not-So-Secret British Weapon,'' *Business Week,* January 24, 2000, p. 132.

Daniels, Cora, ''Women vs. Wal-Mart,'' *Fortune,* July 21, 2003, pp. 78–80, 82.

Donlon, J.P., ''A Glass Act,'' *Chief Executive,* July/August 1995, pp. 40+.

Fitzgerald, Kate, ''Suppliers Rallying Against Negative 'Dateline' Report,'' *Advertising Age,* January 4, 1993, pp. 3, 38.

Friedland, Jonathan, and Louise Lee, ''The Wal-Mart Way Sometimes Gets Lost in Translation Overseas,'' *Wall Street Journal,* October 8, 1997, pp. A1, A12.

Kahn, Jeremy, ''Wal-Mart Goes Shopping in Europe,'' *Fortune,* June 7, 1999, pp. 105–06+.

Kelly, Kevin, ''Wal-Mart Gets Lost in the Vegetable Aisle,'' *Business Week,* May 28, 1990.

Koepp, Stephen, ''Make That Sale, Mr. Sam,'' *Time,* May 18, 1987.

Laing, Jonathan R., ''Super-Saviors,'' *Barron's,* May 6, 1996, pp. 17–19.

Lee, Louise, ''Discounter Wal-Mart Is Catering to Affluent to Maintain Growth,'' *Wall Street Journal,* February 7, 1996, pp. A1, A8.

——, ''Facing Superstore Saturation, Wal-Mart Thinks Small,'' *Wall Street Journal,* March 25, 1998, pp. B1, B8.

Loomis, Carol J., ''Sam Would Be Proud,'' *Fortune,* April 17, 2000, pp. 130–36+.

Malkin, Elisabeth, ''Warehouse Stores Move into Mexico,'' *Advertising Age,* January 18, 1993, p. 13.

Nelson, Emily, ''Why Wal-Mart Sings, 'Yes, We Have Bananas!,' '' *Wall Street Journal,* October 6, 1998, pp. B1, B4.

Ortega, Bob, *In Sam We Trust: The Untold Story of Sam Walton and How Wal-Mart Is Devouring America,* New York: Times Business, 1998.

Ortega, Bob, and Christina Duff, ''Kmart Will Sell 91 Warehouse Clubs to Wal-Mart, Shut Rest of Pace Chain,'' *Wall Street Journal,* November 3, 1993, p. A4.

Quinn, Bill, *How Wal-Mart Is Destroying America (and the World) and What You Can Do About It,* rev. ed., Berkeley, Calif.: Ten Speed Press, 2000.

Saporito, Bill, ''And the Winner Is Still . . . Wal-Mart,'' *Fortune,* May 2, 1994, pp. 62+.

——, ''David Glass Won't Crack Under Fire,'' *Fortune,* February 8, 1993, pp. 75+.

——, ''Is Wal-Mart Unstoppable?,'' *Fortune,* May 6, 1991, pp. 50–59.

Schwartz, Nelson D., ''Why Wall Street's Buying Wal-Mart Again,'' *Fortune,* February 16, 1998, pp. 92+.

Sellers, Patricia, ''Can Wal-Mart Get Back the Magic?,'' *Fortune,* April 29, 1996, pp. 130+.

Slater, Robert, *The Wal-Mart Decade: How a New Generation of Leaders Turned Sam Walton's Legacy into the World's #1 Company,* New York: Portfolio, 2003.

Sparks, Debra, ''Life After Sam,'' *Financial World,* December 6, 1994, pp. 52, 54.

Trimble, Vance H., *Sam Walton: The Inside Story of America's Richest Man,* New York: Penguin, 1990.

Useem, Jerry, ''One Nation Under Wal-Mart,'' *Fortune,* March 3, 2003, pp. 64–68+.

Vance, Sandra S., and Roy V. Scott, *Wal-Mart: A History of Sam Walton's Retail Phenomenon,* New York: Twayne, 1994.

''Wal-Mart: Will It Take Over the World?,'' *Fortune,* January 30, 1989.

Walton, Sam, with John Huey, *Sam Walton, Made in America: My Story,* New York: Doubleday, 1992.

''Walton's Mountain,'' *Nation's Business,* April 1988.

Whitsett, Jack, ''Ten Years After Walton's Death, Wal-Mart Reflects His Vision,'' *Arkansas Business,* April 15, 2002, pp. 1+.

Zellner, Wendy, ''A Grand Reopening for Wal-Mart,'' *Business Week,* February 9, 1998, pp. 86, 88.

——, ''The Sam's Generation,'' *Business Week,* November 25, 1991, pp. 36–38.

Zellner, Wendy, et al., ''How Well Does Wal-Mart Travel?,'' *Business Week,* September 3, 2001, pp. 82, 84.

——, ''Wal-Mart Spoken Here,'' *Business Week,* June 23, 1997, pp. 138–41, 143–44.

—Carole Healy
—updates: Dorothy Kroll, David E. Salamie

The Walt Disney Company

500 South Buena Vista Street
Burbank, California 91521
U.S.A.
Telephone: (818) 560-1000
Fax: (818) 840-1930
Web site: http://www.disney.com

Public Company
Incorporated: 1938 as Walt Disney Productions
Employees: 117,000
Sales: $27.06 billion (2003)
Stock Exchanges: New York Pacific Midwest Tokyo
Ticker Symbol: DIS
NAIC: 515120 Television Broadcasting; 515112 Radio
Stations; 713110 Amusement and Theme Parks;
512110 Motion Picture and Video Production; 511120
Periodical Publishers; 423990 All Other Durable
Good Merchant Wholesalers; 511210 Software
Publishers; 512110 Motion Picture and Video
Production; 711510 Independent Artists, Writers, and
Performers

A colossal force in the entertainment industry, The Walt Disney Company (Disney) is best known for bringing decades of fantasy and fun to families through its amusement parks, television series, and many classic live-action and animated motion pictures. Beginning in 1984, Disney enjoyed an enormous creative and financial renaissance, due to the leadership of CEO Michael Eisner; the success of such subsidiaries as Touchstone Films, Hollywood Pictures, The Disney Studios, Buena Vista Distribution, The Disney Channel, and Buena Vista Home Video; the sales of Disney consumer products through The Disney Stores and a multitude of licensing arrangements; and a recommitment to excellence in the making of original feature-length animated films. Under Eisner's reign, Disney acquired Capital Cities/ABC in 1996, a $19 billion deal that increased the company's stature enormously. Adding to the theme parks, cruise ships, professional sports teams, and dozens of other businesses owned by the company, the acquisition of Capital Cities/ABC gave Disney the power of broadcasting and the ability to meld entertainment content with programming. During the late 1990s, the company was aggressively building a presence on the Internet and adopting a concerted approach to international expansion.

The Birth of a U.S. Icon

Walt Disney, the company's founder, was born in Chicago in 1901. His appeal to the greater United States is said to have had roots in his humble, middle-class upbringing. Disney's father, Elias, moved the family throughout the Midwest seeking employment. Young Disney grew up in a household where hard work was prized: feeding the family's five children left little pocket change for amusement. Walt Disney began working at the age of nine as a newspaper delivery boy. His father instructed him and his siblings in the teachings of the Congregational Church and socialism.

Drawing provided an escape for Disney, and at the age of 14 he took his work on the road and enrolled at the Kansas City Art Institute. His art was temporarily put on hold when he joined the Red Cross at age 16 to serve as an ambulance driver at the end of World War I. In 1919 he returned to the United States and found work as a commercial artist. Together with Ub Iwerks, another artist at the studio, Disney soon formed an animated cartoon company in Kansas City.

In 1923, following the bankruptcy of this company, Disney joined his brother Roy O. Disney in Hollywood. By the time he arrived on the West Coast, word came from New York that a company wanted to purchase the rights to a series of Disney's live-action cartoon reels, ultimately titled *Alice Comedies*. A distributor named M.J. Winkler offered $1,500 per reel, and Disney joined her as a production partner.

A series of animated films followed on *Alice*'s heels. In 1927 Disney started a series called *Oswald the Lucky Rabbit,* which met with public acclaim. The distributor, however, had the character copyrighted in its own name, so Disney earned only a few hundred dollars. It was while pondering the unfairness of this situation on a California-bound train that Disney first thought of creating a mouse character named Mortimer. He changed the name to Mickey Mouse, drew up some simple sketches, and went on to make several Mickey Mouse films with his brother Roy, using their own money.

On the third Mickey Mouse film, Disney decided to take a bold step and add sound to *Steamboat Willie*. The cartoon was synchronized with a simple musical background. The process provided some of the first technical steps in film continuity: music was played at two beats a second and the film was marked every 12 frames as a guide to the animator, and later an orchestra.

Film distributors laughed at Disney's idea. Finally one, Pat Powers, released *Steamboat Willie* in theaters. Audiences loved what they saw and heard, and suddenly Disney was a hit in the animation business. In 1935 the *New York Times* called Mickey Mouse ''the best-known and most popular international figure of his day.'' Meanwhile, Disney suffered criticism from observers who judged him to be a cartoonist of only mediocre ability. (Iwerks was responsible for the actual design of Mickey Mouse and the other characters.) Disney was, however, given credit for his ability to conceptualize characters and stories.

The Mickey Mouse projects brought in enough cash to allow Walt Disney to develop other projects, including several full-length motion pictures and advances in Technicolor film. Disney's first full-length film, *Snow White and the Seven Dwarfs,* opened in 1937 to impressive crowds and led to a string of Disney hits, including *Pinocchio* and *Fantasia* in 1940, *Dumbo* in 1941, *Bambi* in 1942, and *Saludos Amigos* in 1943.

Around 1940 Disney decided to tackle live-action films, first with *The Reluctant Dragon* and to a greater extent with 1946's *Song of the South*. Meanwhile, during World War II, Disney lent his characters to the war effort, making shorts, including one in which Minnie Mouse showed U.S. homemakers the importance of saving fats. After the war, Walt Disney Productions was back in business with live-action features including *20,000 Leagues Under the Sea. The Living Desert* was released in the early 1950s by Disney's new distribution company, Buena Vista, to tremendous box office success.

Taking on Television: 1950s

During the 1950s, as Americans began to spend more time at home watching television for entertainment, Disney's studio took full advantage of the small screen revolution. In 1954, the ''Disneyland'' television series premiered. The show included an introduction by Walt Disney and incorporated film clips from Disney productions with live action and coverage of Disneyland. Some four million people tuned in each week. Disney also made a national folk hero out of Davy Crockett when he devoted a three-part program to coverage of his life. Within a matter of weeks, U.S. boys could not live without coonskin caps and other

Crockett merchandise, all of which earned Disney a fortune. Crockett's popularity led to the era of the Disney live-action adventures that included the 1950s hits *The Great Locomotive Chase, Westward Ho, Old Yeller,* and *The Light in the Forest.*

In October 1955 *The Mickey Mouse Club* debuted on the ABC television network. The hour-long show aired at 5 p.m. weekdays and made television history. Six years later, his groundbreaking Sunday night color TV show *Walt Disney's Wonderful World of Color* (later changed to *The Wonderful World of Disney*), began its 20-year run on NBC. At the same time, Disney was making stars out of Fred MacMurray, Hayley Mills, and Dean Jones in such movies as *The Shaggy Dog, The Absent-Minded Professor, Pollyanna,* and *The Parent Trap.* In 1964 Disney's *Mary Poppins* became one of the top-grossing films of all time.

Disney required professionalism of his staff and demanded the highest-quality Technicolor available, and as a result his live-action films topped competitors in both creativity and technical standards. He also had his hand in several other projects, including Audio-Animatronics (automatically controlled robots) and a Florida amusement complex that eventually became Walt Disney World, complementing California's vacation hot spot, Disneyland.

On December 15, 1966, Walt Disney died of lung cancer. Shortly after Disney's death, his brother Roy issued an optimistic statement pledging that Walt Disney's philosophy and genius would be carried on by his employees.

But no one could match Walt Disney's keen story sense or enthusiasm, and the studio floundered through most of the 1970s despite several strong CEOs, including E. Cardon ''Card'' Walker, who had joined the company as a traffic boy in 1938. The studio did manage a few successes during this period, including *Blackbeard's Ghost,* with Dean Jones and Suzanne Pleshette, and the 1969 release *The Love Bug,* which became the year's biggest box office hit. Other popular releases of the late 1960s and early 1970s included *The Jungle Book, The Aristocats, Bedknobs and Broomsticks,* and several live-action features.

But a run of box office disappointments followed in the mid-1970s before *The Rescuers* proved successful. *Pete's Dragon,* an experimental film combining human and animated characters, followed. Progress was slow but steady for the Disney studio in the late 1970s and early 1980s as well. The studio released three new live-action movies: *The World's Greatest Athlete, Gus,* and *The Shaggy D.A. Return from Witch Mountain,* a sequel to the popular mystery-fantasy *Escape to Witch Mountain,* premiered in 1978. A risky science fiction venture titled *The Black Hole* cost $20 million to produce but was lost in the amazing success of *Star Wars,* an all-time box office record-breaker. CEO Ron Miller brought in new directors and younger writers who produced such films as *Watcher in the Woods* and the computer-generated *Tron,* but achieved only mild success in the face of competition from other movie studios.

In 1983, beginning with the release of *Mickey's Christmas Carol,* Disney's fortunes finally began to look up. A string of successful movies followed, including the Arctic adventure *Never Cry Wolf* and a production of Ray Bradbury's *Something Wicked This Way Comes.* That same year the company also began marketing a family-oriented pay-TV channel called the

Key Dates:

1901: Walt Disney, the company's founder, is born.
1919: With Ub Iwerks, Disney forms Iwerks-Disney Commercial Artists.
1923: The distributor M.J. Winkler purchases Disney's *Alice Comedies* for $1,500 per reel; Disney creates Disney Bros. Studios with his brother Roy.
1924: M.J. Winkler Productions debuts the Alice Comedy Series, with the film *Alice's Day at Sea*, in theaters.
1928: Mickey Mouse is ''born''; Disney releases *Steamboat Willie*, its first film with sound.
1937: *Snow White and the Seven Dwarfs*, Disney's first full-length animated film, debuts.
1940: *Pinocchio* and *Fantasia* are released.
1955: The *Mickey Mouse Club* debuts; Disneyland opens in Anaheim, California.
1966: Walt Disney dies of lung cancer.
1971: Walt Disney World opens near Orlando, Florida; Roy O. Disney dies.
1982: EPCOT Center opens on the grounds of Walt Disney World.
1983: The first foreign Disneyland, Tokyo Disneyland, opens.
1984: Michael Eisner is named Disney's new CEO; Disney releases *Splash* under its new label, Touchstone Pictures.
1989: Disney-MGM Studios Theme Park opens near Orlando, Florida.
1992: Euro Disney (later named Disneyland Paris) opens.
1996: Disney acquires television station Capital Cities/ ABC for $19 billion; Radio Disney debuts.
1998: Animal Kingdom opens in Walt Disney World, Florida.
1999: Disney Cruise Line begins operations with the *Disney Magic*.
2001: Disney's California Adventure opens next to Disneyland; Disney acquires Fox Family Worldwide for $5.3 billion.
2003: Roy E. Disney—son of Roy O. Disney, last of the founding family associated with the company—and Stanley Gold quit the Disney board and start Save Disney.com in an attempt to oust CEO Michael Eisner.

Disney Channel, which quickly became the fastest-growing channel on cable television.

Corporate raider Saul Steinberg attempted a hostile takeover of the company in 1984. Disney ultimately bought Steinberg's 11.1 percent holding in the company for $325.4 million. A number of lawsuits were filed by shareholders against both Disney and Steinberg's Reliance Group Holdings, charging that Disney's managers had attempted to secure their positions and had lowered the value of the stock. The suits were settled in 1989 when the two companies jointly agreed to pay shareholders $45 million.

The Eisner Era Begins: 1984

Shortly after its purchase of 18.7 percent of Disney's stock, the Bass family of Texas supported the Disney board's hiring of Michael Eisner from Paramount Pictures to be Disney's new CEO and Frank Wells to be president.

Eisner, responsible for such Paramount blockbusters as *Raiders of the Lost Ark* and *Beverly Hills Cop,* immediately began to emphasize Touchstone Films, a subsidiary devoted to attracting adult movie audiences. Commentators began to note that Eisner, like Walt Disney, had the ability to predict and deliver movies people wanted to see. The 1985 release of *Down and Out in Beverly Hills* helped Touchstone build momentum, which it increased with *Outrageous Fortune, Tin Men, Ruthless People,* and other hits. In Eisner's first four years as CEO, Disney surged from last place to first in box office receipts among the eight major studios.

Eisner also set out to take full advantage of expanding markets such as cable television and home video. Disney signed a long-term deal with Showtime Networks, Inc., giving the cable service exclusive rights to Touchstone and other Disney releases through 1996. In addition, Eisner bought KHJ, an independent Los Angeles TV station; sought new markets for old Disney productions through television syndication; and began to distribute such TV shows as *The Golden Girls.*

Certain Disney classics, including *Lady and the Tramp* and *Cinderella,* were released on videocassette during the late 1980s. Eisner protected the value of the films by limiting the availability of the tapes. He also scheduled the re-release of many other films for the late 1980s and early 1990s, by which time a new generation of children would be ready to see the films in the theater once again. Disney's revenues soon began to increase, averaging an improvement of approximately 20 percent annually during the second half of the 1980s.

In 1989 Disney-MGM Studios Theme Park opened near Orlando, Florida, on the grounds of Walt Disney World. Despite its name, the park was not a collaboration between the two studios; Disney purchased the rights to include attractions based on MGM films. Euro Disney, of which Disney owned 49 percent, opened outside of Paris, in Marne-la-Vallée, on April 12, 1992; and Tokyo Disneyland, licensed though not owned by Disney, regularly drew phenomenal crowds in a powerful consumer market. Plans were made to open a second Disney-MGM Studios park, on a site adjacent to Euro Disney, in the mid-1990s.

In the early 1980s the parks were responsible for about 70 percent of the company's revenue. Although they continued to be a crucial part of the company, the theme parks found competition with Disney's newer projects, including hotel expansions, home video distribution, and Disney merchandising, which together in 1991 garnered an impressive 28 percent of fiscal revenues. Virtually as important, perhaps more so given their unrealized potential, were Disney's international operations— evident not only in Japan and France, but throughout much of Europe, the former Soviet Union, South America, and China— which contributed 22 percent of total revenues in 1991.

Meanwhile, Touchstone remained healthy. Hollywood Pictures, Disney's newest film-producing arm, also began making more films in the late 1980s. Disney continued to score hits with *Three Men and a Baby, Good Morning Vietnam, Who Framed Roger Rabbit,* and others. Most importantly, production costs, though constantly rising, were held by Disney in 1989 to an average of $15 million per movie, compared to an industry average of more than $23 million.

Taking a Roller-Coaster Ride: 1990s

The 1990s, termed the "Disney Decade" by the company, promised to witness perhaps the most dramatic changes and accomplishments of Disney's more than half-century history. The combined talents of Eisner, President Frank Wells, and studio Chairman Jeffrey Katzenberg caused a rush of excitement as the decade began. By the second quarter of 1991, the studio, under Katzenberg's strong leadership, had surpassed the theme parks in profitability, leading the company to commit to a record-high 25 new films in 1992. By far the greatest highlight of 1991 was Disney's 30th feature-length animated film, *Beauty and the Beast.* Amid a troubled year and a depressed economy, during which corporate net income plummeted by 23 percent and Disney, despite the success of its studio, experienced its first year with no growth since 1984, this film—nominated for best picture and winner of Academy Awards for best original score and best original song—provided much welcomed relief. *Beauty,* like its 1989 Oscar-winning predecessor *The Little Mermaid,* shattered previous records for the most successful opening of an animated film. It quickly became the highest-grossing picture of its genre.

Although Disney was notorious for undercutting its Hollywood competitors, it, too, was forced to pay exorbitant amounts for top creative talent. Both Bernard Weinraub, in a *New York Times* article, and Eisner, in the company's 1991 annual report, reported that Disney was going to try to stem the flow of high production costs for big-budget films and instead offer films with appealing storylines and engaging characters. According to Ron Grover, Katzenberg himself began pushing for such a redirection in early 1991. Presumably, films like the modestly budgeted 1990 sleeper *Pretty Woman* were expected in the future.

Disney's next forays—its creation, for example, of Hyperion Press and Hollywood Records for stakes in the publishing and adult music industries—were expected to further strengthen its reputation as an entertainment giant. Yet, here too, it became increasingly cautious. In August, the company revealed that its Imagineering division, responsible for theme park design, was laying off up to 400 of its employees. Further news that Euro Disney's profitability for its first year was in serious doubt indicated to some that Disney might be struggling. However, Disney's overseas investment was less than $200 million, "a fraction of the total," according to Stewart Toy. "And whether or not there's a profit, Walt Disney gets 10 percent of ticket sales and 5 percent of merchandise sales."

During the latter half of the 1990s, Disney grew at a prolific rate, but by the decade's end there was little cause to celebrate. The remainder of the Disney Decade was pocked with troubling developments that shook the foundation of the Disney empire, prompting some experts to suggest the previously unimaginable: that the omnipotent Disney name was losing its market appeal. The tumultuous period began with tragedy, when Frank Wells died in a helicopter crash in 1994. The fatal accident left Eisner without his most trusted aide and left Disney without a president, a title Katzenberg reportedly coveted. Two days after the helicopter crash, Katzenberg approached Eisner about the job, but

his bid to become president was rebuffed. Katzenberg responded by leaving Disney, departing on decidedly unfriendly terms. An acrimonious feud between Eisner and Katzenberg erupted that became litigious. Upon his departure, Katzenberg was given the equivalent of ten year's pay, but the former studio head wanted considerably more cash. He filed a lawsuit against Disney, demanding $580 million in compensation.

Against the backdrop of a sordid legal battle, whose ugly details became the stuff of headlines, Eisner prepared to add a new dimension to Disney's operations. In 1994, Eisner attempted to buy the NBC television network from General Electric Company, but the deal fell through because General Electric reportedly wanted to retain ownership of 51 percent of the network. Eisner pressed ahead, determined to buy a television network. His search ended in 1995 when Disney announced its head-turning merger with Capital Cities/ABC, a $19 billion deal that gave Disney control over television stations, radio stations, cable networks, and legions of other properties. Applauded by industry pundits as a strategically sound move, the acquisition of Capital Cities/ABC married the vast content collection controlled by Disney to the expansive broadcasting capabilities of the ABC network, exponentially increasing the might of what, after the transaction was completed in 1996, stood as a more than $20 billion entertainment conglomerate.

The late 1990s saw Eisner steer Disney in several other strategically important directions. The growth of the Internet presented the company's chairman and CEO with another opportunity to disseminate Disney's entertainment content to the public. In 1998, Disney acquired Starwave, which maintained ESPN.com and Mr. Showbiz, as well as other web sites, and purchased 43 percent of Infoseek, acquiring the rest of the Internet search engine company in 1999. In January of that year, the company launched the GO Network Web portal. Other additions to the company's operations included the opening of the 540-acre Animal Kingdom park in Florida, the Disney version of a zoo, and the launching of an 875-stateroom cruise ship christened the *Disney Magic,* to be followed by the debut of a sister ship, the *Disney Wonder.* Eisner also acquired two professional sports clubs, the Mighty Ducks of Anaheim, a professional hockey team, and Major League Baseball's Anaheim Angels. Concurrent with the numerous acquisitions he presided over, Eisner endeavored to expand Disney's geographic reach. During the late 1990s, the company collected roughly 20 percent of its revenue from overseas business—too low of a percentage from Eisner's viewpoint. China and India were considered to be high-growth markets.

The scope and scale of Disney's properties by the late 1990s represented an impressive list of businesses that few companies in the world could equal. The additions to the Disney portfolio during the latter half of the decade turned an already sprawling empire into a multifaceted entertainment conglomerate of mindboggling proportions, but no matter the size of a company, success depended on execution. As it became evident during the court proceedings to resolve Katzenberg's lawsuit, Disney's massive revenue-generating, profit-making engine was sputtering inefficiently. The details delineating the company's problems were divulged because of the nature of the Katzenberg case. Eisner, who had the opportunity to settle his former studio chief's compensation claim for $100 million, decided not to give in without a fight, believing the demand for as much as $580 million was preposterously high. It was a decision he later regretted. In court, Eisner learned that Katzenberg had negotiated a contract with Wells during the 1980s. A passage in the contract, as published by the *Financial Times* on June 4, 1999, read: "It is, of course, obvious but nonetheless worth pointing out that many of these pictures still have substantial revenues forthcoming from ancillary markets which continue to accrue to Jeffrey's benefit. ... Of course, some of these will continue 'forever' in the sense that even if he should leave one day, there would be an arbitrated amount as to future income from the pictures." The inclusion of the word "forever" in the contract struck a crippling blow to Eisner's hope of leaving the courtroom victorious.

Because the amount of Katzenberg's claim depended on the future profit potential of certain facets of the Disney enterprise, company lawyers were inclined to paint a bleak picture of the company's financial health at the end of the 1990s and its prospects for the years ahead. Despite the incentive to underestimate the company's financial might, it became obvious to onlookers that all was not right in the Magic Kingdom. The theme parks were performing well, but nearly every other aspect of the company's business suffered from disappointing results. ABC was at the top of the list, hobbled by low ratings and rising costs, including the $9.2 billion spent for ABC and ESPN to acquire the rights for the NFL through 2008. Internationally, the company was not making headway, notoriously evident in two cinematic failures. *Mulan,* the Chinese-themed animation film, generated a paltry $1.3 million during its run in China. The release of *Hercules* in India fell decidedly flat and actually led to a loss of $14,000. On the whole, the last year of the decade signaled a depressing end to the 20th century for Disney. For the first nine months of 1999, excluding the income gained from an asset sale, operating income was down 17 percent, net income dropped 26 percent, and earnings per share fell 27 percent.

The Katzenberg compensation claim was settled for a reported $200 million, although both parties refused to divulge the amount. More significant to industry observers than the exact dollar amount of the settlement was the information revealed during the proceedings, prompting some analysts to cast a wary eye toward the entertainment behemoth. Some critics charged that Eisner's autocratic leadership inhibited efficiency and progress, but the most threatening diagnosis struck at the company's fundamental strength. Some industry experts contended that "age compression," the theory that youths of the late 1990s emulated teenage behavior at an earlier age than in decades past, was draining the strength of the Disney name. Rebellion against the wholesome Disney image was the result, reducing the size of Disney's target audience. "They've never gotten past the problem that their core audience is girls 2 to 8 and their moms," a former, unnamed, Disney executive explained in the September 6, 1999 issue of *Fortune* magazine. Sociological intricacies aside, the future financial health of Disney depended on the ability of the company to reap the rewards inherent in its operations, on its effectiveness in churning out profits from a powerful entertainment machine that looked good on the outside but internally was suffering. The continued attraction of the Disney name in the 21st century represented the foundation upon which the company's return to soaring profits would be built.

Disney's finances improved in 2000, with a 9 percent increase in total revenues and an impressive 39 percent jump in net income. The boost in growth was due particularly to the success of the ABC Network and ESPN. Parks and Resorts also had an impact on growth, achieving record results for the sixth consecutive year. Creatively, Disney had a positive year, with the premier of *The Emperor's New Groove*, as well as the Broadway premier of its musical *Aida*. But the success of 2000 would be short-lived.

The September 11, 2001 terrorist attacks in the U.S. immediately impacted Disney's financial situation. The hardest hit were Disney's Parks and Resorts, as vacation travel came to a halt. The recession that followed the attacks did not help matters. The suffering economy, coupled with a drop in ratings, led to a dramatic decrease in advertising rates for Disney's Media Networks, and in particular, the ABC Network. By 2001's end, Disney suffered a staggering $158 million loss in net income. Also contributing to a loss of income was a costly acquisition of Fox Family Worldwide, Inc. (FFW), for $5.3 billion.

In reaction to troubled times, Disney implemented a number of cost-cutting measures. Such measures included decreasing operations at Disney parks; cutting its annual investment in live-action films; and minimizing Internet operations. Additionally, Disney cut approximately 4,000 employees from its payroll. On a more positive note, Disney's *Monsters, Inc.* premiered at this time, quickly becoming a top 20 film for the studio.

Revenues for 2002 dropped slightly below those for 2001; yet, largely because of Disney's cost-cutting measures, the company's net income jumped to $1.2 billion. The year 2002 also witnessed creative successes for Disney, with the releases of *Peter Pan: Return to Neverland* and *Lilo & Stitch*. The latter, in particular, was hugely successful. The Walt Disney Studios reaped large rewards in 2003, becoming the first in history to exceed over $3 billion in worldwide box office sales. Contributing to this success were the premieres of *Pirates of the Caribbean: The Curse of the Black Pearl*, Bringing Down the House,; *Finding Nemo*, and *Brother Bear*.

But the mood was partly spoiled by turmoil within the company, between CEO Eisner and board members Roy E. Disney (son of Roy O. Disney) and Stanley Gold. Conflict came to the fore when Eisner pushed the board to deny the reelection of Disney to the board, claiming the latter, at age 72, was required to retire. In response, Gold resigned from the board, urging other board members to oust Eisner.

Eisner's difficulties did not lessen in 2004. For one, Pixar Animation Studios, creator of such hits as *Toy Story* and *Finding Nemo*, chose to look for another distributor. The end of the 12-year relationship between the two—spawned by Pixar's longstanding battles with Eisner over issues of control and money—was anticipated to further damage Disney's financial situation. Also in 2004, cable giant Comcast Corporation placed an unsolicited $54 billion bid to acquire the Walt Disney Company, which the latter refused, but which spread doubt concerning the company's future. Uncertainty seemed to surround Disney, even within its movie division. The 2004 movies *The Alamo* and *Home on the Range* yielded poor box office earnings, especially considering their high price tags (*The Alamo* alone cost $100 million). In the face of such difficulties and general dissatisfaction among certain board members, Eisner was forced to cede chairmanship, with some members desiring to see his resignation as CEO.

Principal Subsidiaries

ABC, Inc.; A&E Network (37.5%); Anaheim Sports; Buena Vista Home Video; Buena Vista International; Buena Vista Internet Group; Buena Vista Pictures Distribution, Inc.; Buena Vista Television; Childcraft Educational Corp.; The Disney Channel; The History Channel; Disney Consumer Products International, Inc.; Disney Development Co.; The Disney Store, Inc.; EDL Holding Co.; Euro Disney S.C.A. (49%); E! Entertainment Television (39.5%); ESPN (80%); Fairchild Publications; Hyperion; Infoseek Corporation; KHJ-TV, Inc.; Lake Buena Vista Communities; Lifetime Entertainment Services (50%); Miramax Films; Reedy Creek Energy Services, Inc.; Touchstone Films; Touchstone Television; Walt Disney Attractions; Walt Disney Imagineering; Walt Disney Pictures and Television; WCO Parent Corp.; WED Transportation Systems, Inc.

Principal Divisions

Broadcasting; Creative Content; Theme Parks; Resorts; Sports.

Principal Competitors

DreamWorks SKG; Fox Entertainment Group, Inc.; Liberty Media Corporation; Lucasfilm Ltd.; MGM; Microsoft Corporation; NBC Universal; Six Flags, Inc.; Sony Corporation; AOL Time Warner Inc.

Further Reading

Beard, Richard R., *Walt Disney's Epcot,* New York: Abrams, 1982.

Birnbaum, Steve, *The Best of Disneyland,* Boston: Houghton Mifflin, 1987.

"Disney Merges Television Production Arms," *MEDIAWEEK,* July 12, 1999, p. 3.

"Disney Profit Jumps 30%," *New York Times,* April 28, 1992.

"Disney Trimming Theme Park Staff As Par Gears Up," *Variety,* August 3, 1992.

"Eisner's Mousetrap," *Fortune,* September 6, 1999, p. 106.

Flower, Joe, *Prince of the Magic Kingdom: Michael Eisner and the Re-Making of Disney,* New York: John Wiley & Sons, 1991.

Gilpen, Kenneth N., "Comcast Withdraws Its Bid for The Walt Disney Company," *New York Times,* April 28, 2004.

Grover, Ron, *The Disney Touch: How a Daring Management Team Revived an Entertainment Empire,* Homewood, Ill.: Business One Irwin, 1991.

Holliss, Richard, *The Disney Studio Story,* New York: Crown, 1988.

Holstein, William J., "Mickey's Net Loss," *U.S. News & World Report,* June 21, 1999, p. 48.

La Franco, Robert, "Disney's Problems Go Well Beyond One Big Lawsuit," *Forbes,* July 5, 1999, p. 50.

Leebron, Elizabeth, *Walt Disney: A Guide to References and Resources,* Boston: G.K. Hall, 1979.

Maltin, Leonard, *The Disney Films,* New York: Crown, 1984.

Masters, Kim, *Keys to the Kingdom: The Rise of Michael Eisner and the Fall of Everybody Else,* HarperInformation, 2001.

Parkes, Christopher, "Inside the Magic Kingdom," *Financial Times,* June 4, 1999, p. 6.

Taylor, John, *Storming the Magic Kingdom: Wall Street, the Raiders, and the Battle for Disney,* New York: Knopf, 1987.

Thomas, Bob, *Walt Disney, an American Original,* New York: Simon & Schuster, 1976.

Toy, Stewart, Patrick Oster, and Ronald Grover, "The Mouse Isn't Roaring," *Business Week,* August 24, 1992.

"Walt Disney Co.," *Discount Store News,* June 21, 1999, p. 26.

Weinraub, Bernard, "2 Titans Clash and All of Filmdom Feels Shock Waves," *New York Times,* April 13, 1992.

—Cindy Pearlman
—updates: Jay P. Pederson, Jeffrey L. Covell,
Candice Mancini

Westport Resources Corporation

1670 Broadway, Suite 2800
Denver, Colorado 80202
U.S.A.
Telephone: (303) 573-5404
Fax: (303) 573-5609
Web site: http://www.westportresourcescorp.com

Public Company
Incorporated: 1991
Employees: 333
Sales: $813.88 million (2003)
Stock Exchanges: WRC
Ticker Symbol: New York
NAIC: 211111 Crude Petroleum and Natural Gas
    Extraction

Westport Resources Corporation is one of the 20 largest independent oil and gas exploration and production companies in the United States. Westport operates in North Dakota, Wyoming, Utah, Oklahoma, Texas, Louisiana, and the Gulf of Mexico, trying to strike a balance between lower-risk onshore properties and higher-risk offshore properties. The company's portfolio of assets is balanced between oil and gas.

Origins

Westport's definitive decade of development was a story of growth through acquisitions, a history punctuated by mergers that transformed a small, privately held company into one of the nation's largest independent oil and gas producers. The company was formed in 1991 as Westport Oil and Gas Company, Inc. During its inaugural decade, Westport completed a series of acquisitions that added to its reserve and production base. These acquisitions, which primarily consisted of oil- and gas-producing properties both onshore and offshore, served as a prelude to the mergers that later vaulted the company onto the national stage. From their base in Denver, Colorado, Westport executives built their company into a $35 million-in-sales concern by 1996, the year Westport's most influential leader arrived in Denver to lead it toward national prominence.

Donald D. Wolf joined Westport in June 1996, when he became the company's chairman and chief executive. A veteran of the oil and gas industry, Wolf previously had served in various capacities at a number of oil and gas companies, including Bow Valley Exploration, Tesoro Petroleum, Southland Royalty Co., and Sun Oil Co. In the years immediately preceding his arrival at Westport, Wolf served as president and chief operating officer at UMC Petroleum, a company that had acquired General Atlantic Resources Inc., which Wolf had founded in 1981. At Westport, Wolf presided over nearly all of the substantial transactions completed in the company's history, earning praise for his astute exploitation of the acquisitions he engineered. "Westport," the April 2001 issue of *Oil & Gas Investor* noted, "is a house built on acquisitions." Westport's success, the article explained, rested on the company's aggressive exploitation of its acquired assets, on what the company did with its acquired assets after they became part of the company's portfolio. Wolf, as the most influential individual at Westport, garnered much of the praise for the company's ability to add reserves at the same time it was increasing production from the acquired properties.

Westport's first growth surge actually began a year before Wolf's arrival. In 1995, the company completed its first sizable acquisition, purchasing properties in the Rocky Mountains owned by Conoco Inc. The assets acquired, which were located primarily in 76,000 acres spread across North Dakota and Wyoming, carried reserves of 55 billion cubic feet of gas equivalent (Bcfe). The acquisition of Conoco's Rocky Mountain assets touched off Westport's aggressive acquisition campaign, one that demanded roughly $250 million worth of investment during the ensuing four years. Nearly two years after the Conoco deal, Westport completed its next notable acquisition, purchasing the Axem companies in January 1997. The transaction added 82 Bcfe of reserves and 92,000 net acres in the Rocky Mountains, Texas, and the mid-continent region. By the end of the year, Westport's revenues reached nearly $64 million, far eclipsing the $35 million collected the previous year.

Mergers Fueling Rapid Growth: Late 1990s and Early 2000s

The addition of oil and gas properties steadily expanded Westport's foundation, helping the company build momentum

439

toward its evolution into a national contender. In October 1998, Westport joined forces with Energen Resources Corp. to jointly acquire Total Minatome Corporation, a deal that netted Westport 64 Bcfe of reserves in the Rocky Mountains, the Gulf Coast, and the Gulf of Mexico. Westport's next deal proved to be the linchpin of the company's maturation into a nationally recognized oil and gas company. In April 2000, a merger was completed between Westport Oil and Gas Co. and Equitable Production (Gulf) Company (EPGC). EPGC operated as an indirect, wholly owned subsidiary of Equitable Resources, Inc., representing Equitable Resources' Gulf of Mexico exploration and production business unit. The process of consummating the merger saw Westport Oil and Gas Co. become a wholly owned subsidiary of EPGC. EPGC, in turn, adopted a new name that reflected each of the merged companies, changing its corporate title to Westport Resources Corporation.

The "new" Westport embarked on a new era of existence, drawing the bulk of its senior executives from the "old" Westport. Wolf remained in charge of the newly combined company, retaining his titles of chairman and chief executive officer at a pivotal juncture in Westport's development. The merger added 134 Bcfe of gas reserves in the Gulf of Mexico, as well as 106 Bcfe of probable and possible reserves, doubling the company's exploitation inventory in the Gulf of Mexico. The merger also gave Westport a more balanced portfolio of assets, adding considerable gas reserves to a profile heavily slanted toward oil. In addition, the merger significantly bolstered Westport's involvement in offshore activities, giving it high-risk, high-yield properties in the Gulf of Mexico to complement its lower-risk, lower-output onshore properties.

The merger between EPGC and Westport convinced Wolf that he was ready to take his company into the public market. In October 2000, Westport completed its initial public offering (IPO) of stock, selling 10.2 million shares at $15 per share. The company collected net proceeds of $104 million from the IPO, giving it the resources to reduce its debt. Once the money from the IPO was used, Westport's debt was a paltry $162,000, leaving the company on a solid financial footing to pursue its expansion plans. By April 2001, a year after the EPGC merger, Westport's proved reserves were 454 Bcfe, a total that was balanced between oil and gas, with one-third of the reserves located offshore and the remainder found in onshore assets.

After a year's respite, Wolf was ready to pursue Westport's next large-scale transaction, a deal that promised to position the company as a national force. "This year should present us with excellent opportunities, and we will be an active consolidator," Wolf remarked in an April 2001 interview with *Oil & Gas Investor.* "I see an increased level of mergers and acquisitions between independents," he added, "because the public markets demand greater liquidity."

The pace of growth achieved during Wolf's first years of stewardship by far outstripped the financial increases recorded during Westport's first five years of existence. Sales, which totaled $35 million in 1996, leaped to $220 million in 2000 thanks in large part to the merger with EPGC. The first years of the 21st century witnessed equally robust growth, as Westport aggressively expanded its operations through mergers and acquisitions. By the summer of 2001, a new merger was being discussed, one Wolf referred to as a "watershed event" in a June 12, 2001 interview with the *Oil Daily.* The proposed merger involved wedding Westport with Belco Oil & Gas Corp., a $166.3 million-in-sales oil and gas company with its primary operating offices located in Dallas, Texas. Belco was formed in 1992 and, like Westport, developed its reserve base by following a program of acquisitions, exploration, exploitation, and development drilling. Belco also operated in many of the same regions as Westport, dividing its operations into four areas that included the Rocky Mountains, the Gulf Coast, the Permian Basin of west Texas, and the Midwest.

Merger discussions were held throughout the summer of 2001 and concluded in August 2001. The all-stock transaction, which was valued at $922 million, made Westport one of the 20 largest independent producers in the nation, increasing its estimated reserves by 726 Bcfe, or 193 percent. The merger, according to the July 2001 issue of *Oil & Gas Investor,* represented a "classic case of a financially strong, but opportunity strained producer [Westport] getting together with a competitor that has substantial exploration and development opportunities, but lacks the money to pursue them [Belco]." As part of the terms of the merger, Westport assumed responsibility for $588 million of Belco's debt.

Westport celebrated its 10th anniversary in 2001, collecting $428 million in revenues for the year, or more than 12 times the amount the company generated five years earlier. In the years immediately following the Belco merger, Westport concluded several small acquisitions and two major acquisitions. Briefly, it looked as if Westport might be acquired by another company, Australia's second largest oil company, Woodside Petroleum. In September 2002, Woodside confirmed that it was seriously considering several potential acquisitions, with Westport listed as one of two companies named in the business press. By the following month, however, Woodside announced that it was stopping its pursuit of Westport. Meanwhile, Westport executives were busy working out the details of a major acquisition.

Westport's financial strength during the early years of the decade was not a trait every energy company could claim to possess. El Paso Corporation, a more than $12 billion-in-sales energy company based in Houston, Texas, was experiencing severe financial difficulties during the early years of the decade.

In 2002, a year that would end with a nearly $1.5 billion loss for the company, El Paso was shedding assets to alleviate its financial problems. Westport benefited from the financial ailments of its much larger competitor, purchasing wells and pipelines and other natural gas assets located in Utah from El Paso. The acquisition, completed in December 2002, was valued at $507 million and gave Westport nearly all the assets that would form its Western division, one of four divisions comprising the company's operations. Westport's next major acquisition was completed a year after the El Paso purchase was completed. In December 2003, the company acquired oil and gas properties from United Resources, a privately held company. Westport paid $341 million to complete the deal, which increased its total proved reserves by 211 Bcfe.

Mergers and acquisitions described much of Westport's development, particularly during the late 1990s and the early years of the 21st century. The same corporate maneuvers that built the company also threatened to trigger its disappearance. In April 2004, Westport announced that it had agreed to a $3.4 billion merger with Oklahoma City, Oklahoma-based Kerr-McGee Corp., a more than $4 billion-in-sales oil and gas company with operations in the United States and abroad. The merger, if approved by shareholders, was expected to create the nation's fifth largest independent oil and gas producer, a company to be operated as Kerr-McGee Corp. The Westport name, after 13 years in existence, was expected to be dropped. In a Westport press release dated April 7, 2004, Wolf commented on the pending deal. "This transaction provides important benefits to our shareholders," he said. "It provides significant value while retaining the opportunity to participate in the exciting upside potential of Kerr-McGee. Our shareholders will benefit from becoming part of a larger, more diversified company with tremendous growth opportunities balanced with a substantial development portfolio and a strong balance sheet." Shareholders were expected to vote on the merger in late 2004.

Principal Subsidiaries

Westport Oil and Gas Co.; Westport Field Services, LLC.

Principal Divisions

Northern; Western; Southern; Gulf of Mexico.

Principal Competitors

Burlington Resources Inc.; Devon Energy Corporation; Pioneer Natural Resources Company.

Further Reading

"Australia's Woodside Petroleum Comes Up Empty Handed Again," *Oil Daily,* October 23, 2002.

Cleveland-Kappes, Crystal, "Westport Resources Corp.," *Oil & Gas Investor,* November 2001, p. 100.

Curry, Kerry, "Westport Buys Belco Oil & Gas," *Dallas Business Journal,* June 22, 2001, p. 25.

"Denver-Based Oil, Gas Firm to Merge with Oklahoma City-Based Company," *Knight Ridder/Tribune Business News,* April 8, 2004.

"Equitable Resources," *Petroleum Economist,* May 2000, p. 77.

"Equitable to Sell Gulf Assets," *Oil Daily,* March 13, 2000, p. 45.

"Equitable Wraps Up Westport Deal," *Oil Daily,* April 11, 2000, p. 32.

"Industry Restructuring—Australia's Woodside Confirmed Last Week That It Is Considering Several Potential Acquisitions," *Petroleum Intelligence Weekly,* September 30, 2002, p. 6.

Merolli, Paul, "Westport Buys Belco, Joins Top 20 Club for E&Ps," *Oil Daily,* June 12, 2001.

Snow, Nick, "Westport-Belco Combination Creates Top 200 Independent," *Oil & Gas Investor,* July 2001, p. 93.

"South Texas Reserves Fetching Strong Prices," *Oil & Gas Investor,* December 2003, p. 73.

Williams, Peggy, "A Sense of Balance," *Oil & Gas Investor,* April 2001, p. 70.

—Jeffrey L. Covell

The Ziegler Companies, Inc.

250 East Wisconsin Avenue, Suite 2000
Milwaukee, Wisconsin 53202-4298
U.S.A.
Telephone: (414) 978-6400
Toll Free: (800) 797-4272
Fax: (414) 978-6401
Web site: http://www.ziegler.com

Public Company
Incorporated: 1971 as The Ziegler Company, Inc.
Employees: 330
Total Assets: $121.1 million (2003)
Stock Exchanges: Pink Sheets
Ticker Symbol: ZCOI
NAIC: 523110 Investment Banking and Securities
    Dealing; 523120 Securities Brokerage; 523920
    Portfolio Management; 525910 Open-End Investment
    Funds; 551112 Offices of Other Holding Companies

The Ziegler Companies, Inc. provides a wide range of financial services, including investment banking, financial advisory, investment advisory, and asset management services. The firm caters particularly to several specific sectors of the nonprofit world: healthcare and senior living institutions, churches, and schools. Ziegler Capital Markets Group is one of the largest underwriters of church debt in the United States and, more generally, helps its institutional clients secure financing for building new facilities and expanding existing ones, refinancing debt, and purchasing land. This unit also advises hospitals on mergers and acquisitions. Ziegler Investment Services Group, serving both institutional and individual clients, offers investment planning, wealth accumulation, retirement planning, educational savings, and portfolio consulting services. This unit also manages North Track Funds, a mutual fund family that was among the first to introduce equity index funds, and offers 401(k) retirement plans for sole proprietors. At the end of 2003, total assets under management for Ziegler amounted to about $2.4 billion.

The Young Founder: "Ben" Ziegler

In 1902 West Bend, Wisconsin, was a small bustling mill town famous for the hotels it had built to put up travelers making the two-day trip between Milwaukee and Fond du Lac. The son of a hotelier and county treasurer, 18-year-old Bernhard C. "Ben" Ziegler had been selling fire insurance policies to area farmers and merchants to supplement his income as an assistant for the county's treasurer and register of deeds. In 1902 an insurance agency owned by a friend of Ziegler's father ran into financial trouble; as the agency's cosigner, Ziegler's father assumed its debt and the responsibility for finding a new agent for the business. Despite Ben's young age, Ziegler's father made Ben that new agent, and the young entrepreneur promptly began selling insurance policies to area businesses out of a room in his father's hotel. By 1905 Ben had saved $6,500, which he used to pay off his father's farm and saloon, and a home for him two years later. By 1906 Ziegler and his former employer in the insurance business, Henry Opgenorth, formed a new agency, Opgenorth and Ziegler, which fell apart only 18 months later after disagreements arose over the business. Opgenorth and Ziegler split the territories and went their separate ways.

"The Real Beginning": 1906–29

Still only 22, Ziegler had built a reputation as an enterprising, sharp-witted businessman, and in 1906 he was elected a director of the West Bend Mutual Fire Insurance Co. To drum up business, he began bicycling to the nearby Wisconsin communities of Grafton, Two Rivers, Manitowoc, and Sheboygan to sell fire insurance and farm mortgages to anyone who wanted them. In 1902 representatives of a land company convinced Ziegler to recruit West Bend home seekers to buy property in South Dakota. When Ziegler himself visited the South Dakota lands, however, he learned that the sellers were peddling $300 properties for a grossly inflated $1,600. Burned by the boondoggle, Ziegler vowed that any loan he made in the future would have to be secured by an owner who was "known to be responsible" in the West Bend area. Rather than offer the 6 or 7 percent return investors were promised in South Dakota, Ziegler's 4 to 4.5 percent return was smaller but far more secure. His reputation for conservatism was established.

Company Perspectives:

Our Mission: We advance health, wealth and well-being through tailored financial solutions.

This statement is the soul of our company; it tells why we are in business—to have a positive impact on the lives of the clients we serve. We improve health (physical, spiritual and mental) by creating funding to build churches, healthcare and senior living centers in communities throughout America. We help clients retire in prosperity and dignity. We help them generate and preserve wealth that they can use to improve their quality of life—by educating their children and grandchildren, giving to charities, realizing dreams of travel, recreation and financial freedom.

As the radius of his insurance territory grew in the early 1900s Ziegler traded in his bicycle for a horse and buggy so he could still make it back to West Bend every night to help his mother at the family's boarding house. By 1907, Ziegler's insurance business had grown to encompass virtually all of southeastern Wisconsin and its three largest cities, Milwaukee, Racine, and Kenosha. In the years that followed, Ziegler's business steadily expanded northward and westward. The so-called Roosevelt Panic of 1907 ironically turned out to be one of the biggest blessings of Ziegler's young career. The bank panic had caused depositors around the country to pull their savings from their neighborhood banks, and Ziegler was no exception. When the crisis passed and depositors began returning their savings to the nation's bank vaults, however, Ziegler decided to keep his, using the money instead to make loans to local farmers. "The net result," Ziegler later recalled, "was that I did more business in 60 days than I had done in the four years previous. This was the real beginning of the investment business for B.C. Ziegler and Co."

Ziegler also capitalized on his readiness to service his territory personally to learn more about the insurance needs of his far-flung customers. He soon counted among his customers such typical of the time Wisconsin businesses as elevator makers, gas engine plants, saloons, breweries, and malt houses. In 1911, two West Bend businessmen approached Ziegler for his advice on potentially profitable new businesses for the West Bend area. Having recently visited an aluminum manufacturing plant in Two Rivers, Ziegler recommended they start an aluminum plant, and in September 1911 Ziegler and his new associates formed the West Bend Aluminum Company, which was soon making pie plates, pudding pans, and dish pans. The company, with Ziegler at the helm, became the largest manufacturer of aluminum cooking utensils in the United States by the 1920s. Ziegler also helped establish the First National Bank of West Bend (later acquired by M&I Bank) and by 1917 had become its president as well.

But Ziegler's core business remained insurance and loans. By 1913 B.C. Ziegler and Co. was one of the largest insurance agencies and farm mortgage companies in eastern Wisconsin. The business that would eventually become Ziegler and Co.'s stock in trade—institutional lending—began modestly in 1913 when the pastor of West Bend's Church of the Holy Angels asked

Ziegler's father if his son would loan him the money to build a new church. Ziegler deemed the risk a reasonable one, and the pastor walked away with a $30,000 bond issue. Next, the pastor of Sacred Heart Church of Racine requested and received a $13,000 loan from Ziegler as well. Within a few years Ziegler was also doing business with the so-called building pastors of Milwaukee, and in 1922 Ziegler made his first major bond issue with a $100,000 offering for St. Sebastian's church. In 1928 Ziegler arranged its first institutional loan outside Wisconsin, extending a $485,000, 5 percent bond to the Missionary Sisters, Servants of the Holy Ghost, of Techny, Illinois, so they could erect a hospital in Waukegan. Without planning on it, Ziegler had initiated the business that would soon make his company the largest church bond issuer in the country's history.

While attending the Republican Party's national convention in Chicago in 1916 Ziegler ran into Delbert J. Kenny, the assistant principal back at West Bend High School. Ziegler and Kenny struck up a conversation and, impressed by Kenny's personality, Ziegler offered him a place with his firm on the spot. Kenny would eventually rise to become Ziegler and Co.'s third president. When the United States entered World War I in 1917 most of Ziegler's male employees left to join the fight in Europe. Business stagnated, but when Ziegler's men demobilized in 1919 Ziegler's firm began a renewed period of growth. In 1920 Ziegler incorporated B.C. Ziegler and Company and by the early 1920s the firm had become one of the state's leading farm financing companies, prudently extending loans only to the most stable dairy farmers of southern Wisconsin. As the U.S. economy boomed in the 1920s Ziegler expanded his company's bond business by charging a fair rate of interest on bonds, never offering "speculative" securities, paying investors their interest and principal on time, and willingly lending moneys to home and farm owners who could establish their "good reputations and good security." By the late 1920s Ziegler's customers numbered more than 5,000, and Ziegler was one of the 10 or 12 largest insurance agencies in Wisconsin, issuing primarily fire and tornado (though not life) insurance policies through the Mutual and Old Line insurance companies.

Growth Through Church Bonds: 1929–59

If Ziegler sought a new opportunity to demonstrate his business acumen, the great crash of 1929 gave it to him. While traveling in Kansas in early 1929, Ziegler saw firsthand the financial problems facing Kansas farmers. Figuring that if the country's farmers were facing difficulties, the national economy as a whole might not be as healthy as Wall Street wanted to believe, Ziegler concluded, he later recalled, "that business had just about reached its high point, and that we might be looking forward to a recession." He therefore sold all his stock and instructed his partner at West Bend Aluminum to commit to no new production and to cancel as many of his current commitments as he could. Moreover, he told his vice-president at Ziegler and Co. to pay off the company's $300,000 in debt within 60 days. By October 1929, when "the stock crash came," Ziegler recalled, "we had practically no commitments, no debts, and a nice cash position."

Ziegler also proved clairvoyant about the severity of the Great Depression. While attending a Rotary convention in Vienna, Austria, in mid-1931, Ziegler was struck by Europe's desperate economic conditions and on his return readied his company for the worst. By October 1931, when the post-crash downturn bottomed out into full-fledged depression Ziegler had liquidated $2.5 million in debts, and could confront the worst economic period in U.S. history with a war chest of cash. As the Depression staggered on, Ziegler managed to *increase* the size of its workforce, prevent its investors from losing money on their institutional bonds, and boast the best ratio of losses on farm loans of any lender in Wisconsin. In the last quarter of 1931, in fact, Ziegler issued more institutional bonds than in all of 1930. Ziegler's willingness to lend money to finance-strapped churches turned into a shrewdly conservative investment in the speculation-shy climate of the 1930s, for as one of Ziegler's lieutenants later recalled, "people were afraid of everything—except church bonds."

In 1936 Ziegler made the largest institutional bond issue in its history, a $3.1 million issue to St. Mary's College and

Academy and Marygrove College, both in Michigan. In the same decade, Ziegler established a subsidiary, Home Builders Inc., to build three to six homes a year in the West Bend area, and began acquiring farms that had gone bankrupt as the economy spoiled. Ziegler's Real Estate Department then began to sell the properties, adding another income stream to Ziegler's machine. Ziegler also established The Security Company, which in the 1940s and 1950s bought up land in the West Bend area and subdivided it into housing properties. In 1942, Ziegler's West Bend Aluminum Company was awarded Navy "E" for excellence awards for its munitions manufacturing achievements, and in 1944, with the war's end in sight, Ziegler and Co. made its first institutional underwriting on the West Coast—a $900,000 loan for the Lutheran Hospital Society of Southern California. By the time of founder Ben Ziegler's untimely death at age 62 in May 1946, his company's thriving institutional bond business was expanding nationwide through ongoing college and church loans (its two biggest categories) to communities in the Midwest and South. (Ziegler's partner, Delbert Kenny, who had assumed the firm's reins in 1942, continued on as president until 1965.)

As millions of U.S. servicemen began streaming home in 1945 and 1946, Ziegler and Co. had used its property purchases to create new parcels of home-sized lots ready for sale to them. In the postwar years, Ziegler's foray into the housing industry continued when the company became a distributor and builder for National Homes, a maker of $10,000-plus prefab homes for the booming residential housing market. With its bond and mortgage business expanding, Ziegler and Co. was forced to update its correspondence-based marketing network, and in 1949 opened its first sales office in Milwaukee, which was followed by offices in Fort Atkinson, Appleton, and Minneapolis by 1952. By the early 1960s, Ziegler's sales office network had grown to 12, extending from Toledo and St. Louis to as far west as San Francisco.

From Church to Hospital Bonds: 1961–77

Ziegler sold more church bonds between 1945 and 1965 than at any previous period in its history—most for the construction and modernization of church-owned schools and retirement homes. The early 1960s were a particularly active period for Ziegler's church bonds, and the period was quickly dubbed "the diocese financing." The diocese of Buffalo, New York, raised $16 million through Ziegler in 1960, for example, and between 1962 and 1964 the Archbishop of Boston raised $35 million with Ziegler bonds. In 1964 Ziegler was a pioneer of a new type of institutional financing instrument known as the collateral trust bond. Through its new subsidiary, First Church Financing Corporation of America (FCFCA), Ziegler acquired loans made to churches and other institutions that, because they were too small to justify issuing as individual bonds, were merged and marketed as collateral trust bonds. Between 1964 and 1967 alone, FCFCA issued and marketed $23.8 million of these bonds. Following founder Ben Ziegler's penchant for diversification, in the early 1960s Ziegler and Co. became the underwriter for the first institutional bond offering insured by the Federal Housing Authority, for a retirement home in Seattle.

By the time the son of Ben Ziegler's longtime partner Delbert Kenny assumed Ziegler's presidency in 1965 the construction boom in church and church-related educational facilities had topped out. Thomas Kenny thus began to focus the firm's energies on the still-growing niche of bond underwritings for the construction, enlargement, and modernization of hospitals. Despite the sophistication of the instruments Ziegler's sales force was selling, their methods were straightforward enough. A salesman would be assigned to a new hospital and set up camp in a hospital office for a few days, counting on the kind of local interest a large newly expanded facility attracts to bring customers to his door. As a Ziegler sales manager would later tell *Bond Buyer* magazine: "At that time [i.e., when a hospital has been enlarged or modernized] everybody had such a great feeling about their local hospital that we would get tons of people coming in. They wanted to buy it; they wanted to support it."

One instrument Ziegler used to finance its new hospital bond business was the short-term (three- to nine-month) construction note, which was sold to corporations across the country to fund the period early in a hospital's construction or modernization program before a bond sale or other form of "permanent" financing secured the project's capitalization. Stemming from this innovation, in 1969 Ziegler and Co. formed the Ziegler Financing Corporation (ZFC) as an operating company to provide similar short-term construction loans for commercial and industrial projects. In the years that followed, ZFC would underwrite short-term notes for the construction of nursing homes, condominiums, industrial buildings, retirement homes, mobile home parks, hotels, and housing projects authorized by the federal government's Housing and Urban Development (HUD) agency.

In 1971 another child of Ziegler's hospital underwriting business emerged, when the Ziegler Leasing Corporation (ZLC) was formed to design customized leases for hospitals seeking to lease medical equipment such as X-ray machines, intensive-care equipment, nuclear medicine devices, and other hospital technologies. This in turn led in 1972 to a new department within ZLC created specifically to handle leases for commercial and industrial equipment. With its stable of operating companies proliferating, Ziegler decided to create a new holding company structure to give its individual units free rein. The Ziegler Company, Inc. was thus formed in December 1971 and its stock issued to the over-the-counter market.

In June 1972 President Thomas J. Kenny, his wife, and four of his children were killed when their jetliner crashed in South Vietnam on a flight from Thailand to Hong Kong. The tragedy (which was apparently accidental and unconnected to the fighting on the ground) shocked the close-knit West Bend business community. Longtime Ziegler veteran Ken Marsden assumed the firm's presidency, and a year later founder Ben Ziegler's two sons, Bernard and R.D.—who had not planned to join their father's business—were named chairman of the board and president/CEO, respectively. The Ziegler Company's business was meanwhile showing no interruption. New branch sales offices had been opened in Kenosha and La Crosse, Wisconsin, and Springfield, Illinois, in 1967; Sheboygan, Wisconsin, in 1969; Green Bay, Wisconsin, and East Lansing, Michigan, in 1970; and Orlando, Florida, in 1971.

The firm also continued its historical penchant for scouting out new business opportunities by becoming the sole distributor of a mutual fund based in Milwaukee in 1967 and then three years later unveiling its own family of mutual funds. Taxable hospital bonds remained Ziegler's largest investment product in the late 1970s, but it also expanded into more conservative investment instruments during the period. In 1973, for example, it acquired a Chicago firm called Barcus, Kindred & Company, Inc. that specialized in originating and underwriting municipal and nonprofit revenue tax-exempt bonds. The addition, renamed Ziegler Securities in 1976, expanded still further Ziegler's portfolio in the management of tax-exempt financing in the healthcare industry. In 1974, Ziegler had also introduced its American Tax-Exempt Bond Trust and in the late 1970s unveiled the American Income Trust, a portfolio of corporate bonds designed to throw off high income while preserving the investor's principal.

Steady Growth: 1978–93

By the late 1970s, Ziegler remained the largest institutional bond underwriter in the United States (some 2,600 bond issues valued at almost $4 billion by 1977) and had solidified its claim to truly national status by opening branch sales offices in Denver and Portland in 1975 and Indianapolis and Grand Rapids in 1976. It had sold more hospital bonds than any other firm in U.S. history, and 625 of the nation's 3,364 private-sector, nonprofit general hospitals had used Ziegler as the underwriter of their bond issues by 1977. Ziegler continued to underwrite major bond issues for prominent U.S. institutions and corporations in the 1980s, including a $12 million mortgage bond issue for Associated Doctors Hospital and a $20 million notes issue for American Family Financial Services, both in 1980, and in 1982 a $10 million underwriting of senior notes for Northwestern Mutual Insurance. In the early 1980s, Ziegler Securities became a separately named division of the B.C. Ziegler and Company, and in 1984 the firm launched a "fully hedged" tax exempt bond fund to broaden its offerings of high-yield but capital-preserving investment vehicles. Similarly, in 1987 Ziegler and Co. teamed up with Wisconsin banking giant M&I Bank to serve as "co-advisers" of a new mutual fund. In April 1986, a third generation of Zieglers assumed command of the firm when Peter D. Ziegler (a first cousin of founder Ben Ziegler's grandson) was elected president of the holding company and all its subsidiaries, and in December 1989 Ben Ziegler's son R.D. finally stepped down as CEO after 16 years at the helm. Within a month Peter Ziegler was the new CEO.

In 1990 Ziegler's collateral trust bond subsidiary was newly incorporated as First Church Financing Corporation (FCFC) to issue, like its predecessor, mortgage-backed bonds collateralized by pools of notes secured by the first mortgages on church buildings and properties. That same year, Ziegler Securities marketed 47 healthcare financings—the most of any firm in the nation. In 1991 Ziegler's annual revenues, which had seesawed back and forth between $34 million and $40 million a year since 1986 finally reached the $40 million plateau for good and by 1993 were breaking the $50 million mark. In 1991 Ziegler began listing its stock on the American Stock Exchange and established two new subsidiaries: Ziegler Asset Management, Inc. (ZAM) and Ziegler Collateralized Securities, Inc. (ZCS). ZAM provided money management services (such as pension planning) in stocks and bonds to individual customers, institutions, and the parent firm's Principal Preservation Portfolio family of mutual funds. By late 1997 ZAM was managing some $1 billion in assets. ZCS was formed to issue bonds that were collateralized by pools or leases and other types of debt instruments packaged and sold to it by Ziegler Leasing Corporation, the firm's equipment leasing business. Meantime, in April 1993 the parent company was reincorporated in Wisconsin as The Ziegler Companies, Inc.

By 1993, two new subsidiaries had also joined the Ziegler stable. Ziegler Thrift Trading, Inc. (ZTT) was created to offer discount brokerage services to the booming stock, bond, mutual fund, and options market without the advice and research services that characterize full-service brokerage houses. Waste Research and Reclamation (WRR) reflected Ziegler's willingness—first reflected in Ben Ziegler's participation in the creation of West Bend Aluminum in 1911—to diversify into nontraditional areas of business. WRR (founded in 1970) operated hazardous waste treatment and waste solvent recycling facilities for industrial chemicals and solvents in Eau Claire, Wisconsin, and by 1995 was generating revenues of $3.8 million—or almost 9 percent of Ziegler's total 1995 revenues. Two of Ziegler's diversifying ventures were short-lived. Beginning in 1994, Ziegler held a one-third interest in Heartland Capital Company, a loan originator for the construction of affordable housing projects, and the same year it began purchasing automobile installment loans to be held until they could be pooled together and sold as securities. By 1997, however, Heartland had gone under and Ziegler had uncovered unpromising information about the quality of the auto loans it had purchased and began retreating from that line of business.

"Senior Living Debt," Stocks, and Restructuring: 1994–99

In 1993 Ziegler underwrote the largest church bond issue of its history, a $14 million issue for the Germantown Baptist Church of Memphis, Tennessee. By then the firm was also widely regarded as the largest investment banking firm for healthcare finance outside Wall Street. Just as Ziegler had seen the writing on the wall in the 1960s and switched its emphasis from church to hospital bonds, so too in the consolidating and chaotic healthcare climate of the early 1990s it looked for new, still growing bond markets. "Senior-living debt" was the answer. As the population aged, the demand for retirement facilities snowballed and Ziegler and its Senior Living Finance Group rushed in. As John Wagner, Ziegler's retail sales manager, told *Bond Buyer* in 1996, "maybe 10 years ago, we did very few issues in senior-care living, and the majority of our underwritings were in health care and hospitals. We've totally flip-flopped that now. . . . How many hospitals in your area do you see expanding anymore?" By the end of 1995, Ziegler's shift into senior living bonds was a fait accompli: it underwrote more than $450 million in retirement facility construction bonds versus only $220 million for its onetime meal ticket, healthcare. But its sales strategies remained the same: send a sales rep to the retirement center and attract the interest of local investors—including the often affluent residents of the retirement centers themselves. In 1997 Ziegler's Senior Living Finance Group completed 41 financings worth $175 million—making Ziegler the largest senior living facility bond underwriter in the United States. In the meantime, Ziegler disposed of its lease financing unit, Ziegler Leasing Corp., selling its assets to General Electric Capital Corporation for about $17 million.

Ziegler was also undertaking another even more fundamental shift in its business model—stepping gradually but firmly away from its historical image as a "bonds only" house. When some of its clients began to take their equity (or stock) investments elsewhere and the stock market boom of the 1990s began generating fortunes for equity brokerages, Ziegler decided to recast its image into a "full-service brokerage." As John Wagner told *Bond Buyer* magazine, "We also realized that to bring the younger client in, you've got to do more of the equity side of it and the mutual funds side. You still get their fixed-income business as they mature and age." In 1994 Ziegler began offering its customers stocks as well as bonds, and in 1997 Ziegler's Thrift Trading was set to launch the single feature perhaps most emblematic of the democratization of the U.S. stock market in the 1990s: low-commission online trading via the World Wide Web. Reflecting its decision to embrace the equity markets, in July 1997 Ziegler acquired Glaisner, Schiffarth, Grande & Schnoll, Ltd. and its GS^2 subsidiary, a Milwaukee-based institutional equity sales, trading, and research firm with more than $1 billion in managed assets. Dick Glaisner, the acquired firm's CEO, became the director of Ziegler's newly organized Ziegler Investment division with responsibility for its money management and equity sales operations. A newly reconstituted Ziegler Securities division would handle the firm's "capital formation, investment banking and institutional fixed-income [i.e., bond] sales and trading." In an indication of the early success of Ziegler's strategy to cover all the investment industry bases, sales of its mutual funds totaled $100 million in 1997. Also in 1997 R.D. Ziegler retired as chairman, a position that Peter Ziegler added to his existing responsibilities.

The Ziegler Companies continued restructuring in the late 1990s, and restructuring and other charges in 1998 resulted in a net loss of $2.8 million. The largest such charge totaled $1.6 million after tax and related to changes that were made in the firm's taxable fixed-income trading department. To bolster its money management capabilities Ziegler acquired investment advisory firm PMC International Inc. in a December 1998 deal valued at about $7.1 million. PMC, which was based in Denver and operated an office in Atlanta, added $2 billion in assets under management to Ziegler. In January 1999 the company aimed to unify more of its operations under its flagship name by changing the names of some of its operating divisions and units to B.C. Ziegler and Company. The most prominent name to be rebranded was that of GS^2. Two other subsidiaries were divested during the year as Ziegler pulled back somewhat from its diversification drive in order to concentrate on several core areas. In October 1999 discount brokerage service Ziegler Thrift Trading was sold to Strong Capital Management, Inc. for approximately $10 million. In December, WRR Environmental Services Co., Inc.—Ziegler's only nonfinancial business—was sold to a group of senior managers and private investors for about $6 million. Ziegler now had four main divisions: retail brokerage, mutual fund management, investment banking, and portfolio management for high net worth individuals.

Sharpening Focus Under New Management: Early 2000s

As Ziegler struggled to improve its earnings, which amounted to just $1.5 million in 1999 on record revenues of

$96.7 million, the company's management ranks were shaken up. In February 2000 John J. Mulherin was brought onboard as the new president and CEO, replacing Peter Ziegler. Mulherin had most recently served as chief administrative officer at Villanova Capital, the asset management group of Nationwide Insurance. The new leader's résumé also included earlier stints at Fidelity Investments Inc., First National Bank of Chicago, and the former Continental Bank, Chicago. Ziegler remained chairman but only until July 2000, when Peter R. Kellogg was elected to that position. Kellogg, who had been on the Ziegler board since 1995, was a senior partner of Spear, Leeds & Kellogg, a specialist firm on the New York Stock Exchange. He was the largest shareholder of the Ziegler Companies, owning a stake of more than 20 percent. Peter Ziegler remained involved in the company as a director and chairman of the firm's Principal Preservation family of mutual funds.

Soon after taking over, Mulherin cut two more small operations—both initiated in the 1990s—that were outside the company's core: an institutional research department and a preferred stock trading division. These cuts affected about 25 employees. He also continued an overhaul of the company's system of branches. Between 1999 and 2002, Wisconsin offices in Fond du Lac, Kenosha, La Crosse, and Port Washington were shut down, along with branches in Arlington Heights and Springfield, Illinois; Des Moines, Iowa; Indianapolis; and St. Louis. To better serve retirees relocating in the Sunbelt, Ziegler opened new offices in St. Petersburg, Florida, and Scottsdale, Arizona. Ziegler shifted its headquarters to Milwaukee in 2001 to be closer to the financial center of southeastern Wisconsin; its ties to West Bend were maintained through a branch office there. Also in 2001 Ziegler sold B.C. Ziegler and Company's insurance division and merged PMC into the Envestnet Group, Inc., a Chicago-based provider of individual managed accounts, mutual funds, and alternative investments to independent financial advisers. As part of the latter deal, Ziegler acquired a minority stake in the resulting EnvestnetPMC, Inc. Through the various divestments and closures, Ziegler between 2000 and 2002 reduced its workforce by nearly 40 percent, from 528 to 330. Such cost-cutting efforts helped turn around a company that had posted a net loss of $4.7 million in 2000. Ziegler returned to profitability in 2001, recording net income of $1.3 million, a figure that improved to $1.8 million in 2002.

Other initiatives launched by Mulherin during this period strengthened Ziegler's core operations and propelled the turnaround forward. The company upgraded its technology, introduced a new logo, instituted a new statement of values, and launched a new advertising and marketing campaign. During 2001 the Principal Preservation family of mutual funds was rebranded as North Track Funds, which emphasized the family's concentration on index funds, which track particular market indices or sectors, attempting to mimic their performance. Two new mutual funds were added to this family during 2001: the Dow Jones U.S. Healthcare 100 Plus Fund and the Dow Jones U.S. Financial 100 Plus Fund. Both funds were designed to track particular Dow Jones indexes. To support the new funds and the new family name, Ziegler more than doubled the number of sales representatives who marketed the funds to distributors nationwide. Also during 2002, the Ziegler Investment Services Group began offering a 401(k) retirement plan designed specifically for sole proprietors. In January 2002 Ziegler aimed

to leverage its strong base of experience in the healthcare field by launching a healthcare mergers and acquisitions practice through its Ziegler Capital Markets Group. The new practice would advise hospitals on mergers and acquisitions.

Results for 2003 provided further evidence for a sustained turnaround at Ziegler. Revenues increased 10 percent to $74.3 million, while net income jumped 19 percent to $2.2 million. Issuance of debt securities through Ziegler's investment banking division totaled $1.94 billion in 2003, compared to $1.81 billion the previous year. Assets under management through the North Track Funds family and other investment services increased from $1.8 billion to $2.4 billion. In December 2003 B.C. "Bernie" Ziegler III, grandson of the founder, was named chairman of the Ziegler Companies, replacing Kellogg, who nevertheless remained a director. That same month, Ziegler voluntarily delisted itself from the American Stock Exchange, and its shares began trading over the counter via the Pink Sheets electronic network. The company cited a number of reasons for taking this action: the small number of shareholders, the limited trading volume of the stock, the fact that no analysts were following the stock, and perhaps most importantly the increasing cost associated with meeting the reporting requirements, which grew more stringent under the Sarbanes-Oxley Act of 2002, a legislative response to the accounting scandals of the early 2000s. Among the company's initiatives going forward were to pursue strategic acquisitions, increase fee-based revenues, and further enhance its strong healthcare franchise within the Ziegler Capital Markets Group.

Principal Subsidiaries

B.C. Ziegler and Company; Ziegler Financing Corporation; Ziegler Healthcare Capital, LLC; First Church Financing Corporation; Ziegler Equity Funding I, LLC; ZHP I, LLC; Ziegler Healthcare Fund I, L.P.

Principal Operating Units

Ziegler Capital Markets Group; Ziegler Investment Services Group.

Principal Competitors

Piper Jaffray Companies; UBS Financial Services Inc.; RBC Dain Rauscher Corporation; Robert W. Baird & Co. Incorporated; Merrill Lynch & Co., Inc.; Raymond James Financial, Inc.

Further Reading

"B.C. Ziegler Co.: A 75-Year Niche in the World of Finance," *West Bend (Wis.) News,* October 15, 1977, p. 1.
"B.C. Ziegler Company Opens New Office," *West Bend (Wis.) News,* April 4, 1928, p. 1.
"B.C. Ziegler's Unfinished Autobiography Outlines Earliest Days," *West Bend (Wis.) News,* October 15, 1977, p. 6.
"Bernhard C. Ziegler, 1884–1946," West Bend, Wis.: B.C. Ziegler and Company, n.d.
Dymale, Nan, "Bernard C. Ziegler," West Bend, Wis.: B.C. Ziegler and Company, May 1988.
"Firm Expanding, Creating New Opportunities," *Main Street Journal,* West Bend, Wis.: B.C. Ziegler and Company, December 3–5, 1993.

Gallagher, Kathleen, ''B.C. Ziegler Expands Services to Add Advice on Stock Purchases,'' *Milwaukee Journal Sentinel,* September 13, 1995.

——, ''Changes in Compensation, Approach: B.C. Ziegler Expands Brokerage Services,'' *Milwaukee Journal Sentinel,* April 16, 1996.

——, ''Ziegler Companies Decides to Delist Itself,'' *Milwaukee Journal Sentinel,* October 29, 2003, p. 3D.

——, ''Ziegler Companies Shakes Up Its Management,'' *Milwaukee Journal Sentinel,* January 25, 2000, p. 1D.

Hoeschen, Brad, ''New Ziegler Executive Plans National Growth,'' *Business Journal of Milwaukee,* March 31, 2000.

——, ''Ziegler Cos. Restructures,'' *Business Journal of Milwaukee,* February 6, 1998, pp. 1+.

——, ''Ziegler's New CEO Serious About Changing Focus,'' *Business Journal of Milwaukee,* May 5, 2000.

Muckian, Michael, ''Mulherin Pilots Ziegler in Uncertain Times: Profits Improve As He Implements Turnaround Plan,'' *Business Journal of Milwaukee,* March 21, 2003.

Roberto, Sondra, ''Midwestern Firm Banks Its Future on Senior-Living Centers,'' *Bond Buyer,* July 2, 1996.

Schwab, Paul, ''Ziegler Revamps Mutual Funds,'' *Business Journal of Milwaukee,* March 16, 2001, p. 3.

''Two Ziegler Brothers Leave Dart to Join Father's Firm,'' *West Bend (Wis.) News,* October 2, 1972, p. 1.

''Ziegler Celebrates Centennial in 2002,'' special issue of *Investor's Edge,* Milwaukee, Wis.: B.C. Ziegler and Company, autumn 2002.

The Ziegler Story, 1902–1977, West Bend, Wis.: B.C. Ziegler and Company, 1977.

—Paul S. Bodine
—update: David E. Salamie

INDEX TO COMPANIES

Index to Companies

Listings in this index are arranged in alphabetical order under the company name. Company names beginning with a letter or proper name such as Eli Lilly & Co. will be found under the first letter of the company name. Definite articles (The, Le, La) are ignored for alphabetical purposes as are forms of incorporation that precede the company name (AB, NV). Company names printed in bold type have full, historical essays on the page numbers appearing in bold. Updates to entries that appeared in earlier volumes are signified by the notation **(upd.)**. Company names in light type are references within an essay to that company, not full historical essays. This index is cumulative with volume numbers printed in bold type.

Gerling-Konzern Versicherungs-
Beteiligungs-Aktiengesellschaft, **III**
695; **51** 139–43
Germaine Monteil Cosmetiques Corp., **I**
426; **III** 56
German American Bancorp, 41 178–80
German-American Car Company. *See*
GATX.
German-American Securities, **II** 283
The German Society. *See* The Legal Aid
Society.
Germania Refining Co., **IV** 488–89; **50**
351
Germplasm Resource Management, **III** 740
GERPI, **51** 16
Gerrard Group, **61** 270, 272
Gerresheimer Glas AG, II 386; **IV** 232;
43 186–89
Gerrity Oil & Gas Corporation, **11** 28; **24**
379–80
Gerry Weber International AG, 63
169–72
GESA. *See* General Europea S.A.
Gesbancaya, **II** 196
Geschmay Group, **51** 14
Gesparal, **III** 47; **8** 342
Gestettner, **II** 159
Gestione Pubblicitaria Editoriale, **IV** 586
GET Manufacturing Inc., **36** 300
Getchell Gold Corporation, **61** 292
Getronics NV, 39 176–78
Getty Images, Inc., 31 216–18
Getty Oil Co., **II** 448; **IV** 367, 423, 429,
461, 479, 488, 490, 551, 553; **6** 457; **8**
526; **11** 27; **13** 448; **17** 501; **18** 488; **27**
216; **41** 391, 394–95; **47** 436; **50** 353
Getz Corp., **IV** 137
Gevaert. *See* Agfa Gevaert Group N.V.
Gevity HR, Inc., 63 173–77
Geyser Peak Winery, **58** 196
Geysers Geothermal Co., **IV** 84, 523; **7**
188
GFI Informatique SA, 49 165–68
GfK Aktiengesellschaft, 49 169–72
GFL Mining Services Ltd., **62** 164
GFS. *See* Gordon Food Service Inc.
GFS Realty Inc., **II** 633
GGT Group, **44** 198
GHH, **II** 257
GHI, **28** 155, 157
Ghirardelli Chocolate Company, 24 480;
27 105; **30 218–20**
GI Communications, **10** 321
GI Export Corp. *See* Johnston Industries,
Inc.
GIAG, **16** 122
Gianni Versace SpA, 22 238–40
Giant Bicycle Inc., **19** 384
Giant Cement Holding, Inc., 23 224–26
Giant Eagle, Inc., **12** 390–91; **13** 237
Giant Food Inc., II 633–35, 656; **13** 282,
284; **15** 532; **16** 313; **22 241–44 (upd.)**;
24 462; **60** 307
Giant Industries, Inc., 19 175–77; 61
114–18 (upd.)
Giant Resources, **III** 729
Giant Stores, Inc., **7** 113; **25** 124
Giant TC, Inc. *See* Campo Electronics,
Appliances & Computers, Inc.
Giant Tire & Rubber Company, **8** 126
Giant Video Corporation, **29** 503
Giant Wholesale, **II** 625
GIB Group, V 63–66; **22** 478; **23** 231; **26**
158–62 (upd.)

Gibbons, Green, van Amerongen Ltd., **II**
605; **9** 94; **12** 28; **19** 360
Gibbs Construction, **25** 404
GIBCO Corp., **17** 287, 289
Gibraltar Casualty Co., **III** 340
Gibraltar Steel Corporation, 37 164–67
Gibson, Dunn & Crutcher LLP, 36
249–52; 37 292
Gibson Greetings, Inc., 7 24; **12 207–10**;
16 256; **21** 426–28; **22** 34–35; **59** 35,
37
Gibson Guitar Corp., 16 237–40
Gibson McDonald Furniture Co., **14** 236
GIC. *See* The Goodyear Tire & Rubber
Company.
Giddings & Lewis, Inc., 8 545–46; **10**
328–30; 23 299; **28** 455
Giftmaster Inc., **26** 439–40
Gil-Wel Manufacturing Company, **17** 440
Gilbane, Inc., 34 191–93
Gilbert & John Greenall Limited, **21** 246
Gilbert Lane Personnel, Inc., **9** 326
Gilde-Verlag, **IV** 590
Gildon Metal Enterprises, **7** 96
Gilead Sciences, Inc., 54 129–31
Gilkey Bros. *See* Puget Sound Tug and
Barge Company.
Gill and Duffus, **II** 500
Gill Industries, **II** 161
Gill Interprovincial Lines, **27** 473
Gillett Holdings, Inc., 7 199–201; **11** 543,
545; **43** 437–38
The Gillette Company, III 27–30, 114,
215; **IV** 722; **8** 59–60; **9** 381, 413; **17**
104–05; **18** 60, 62, 215, 228; **20 249–53**
(upd.); **23** 54–57; **26** 334; **28** 247; **39**
336; **51** 57; **52** 269
Gilliam Furniture Inc., **12** 475
Gilliam Manufacturing Co., **8** 530
Gilliam S.A., **61** 104
Gilman Fanfold Corp., Ltd., **IV** 644
Gilman Paper Co., **37** 178
Gilmore Steel Corporation. *See* Oregon
Steel Mills, Inc.
Gilroy Foods, **27** 299
Giltspur, **II** 587
Gimbel Brothers, Inc. *See* Saks Holdings,
Inc.
Gimbel's Department Store, **I** 426–27; **8**
59; **22** 72; **50** 117–18
Gindick Productions, **6** 28
Gingiss Group, **60** 5
Ginn & Co., **IV** 672; **19** 405
Ginnie Mae. *See* Government National
Mortgage Association.
Gino's East, **21** 362
Ginsber Beer Group, **15** 47; **38** 77
Giorgio Armani S.p.A., 45 180–83
Giorgio Beverly Hills, Inc., **26** 384
Giorgio, Inc., **III** 16; **19** 28
Girard Bank, **II** 315–16; **44** 280
Girbaud, **17** 513; **31** 261
Girl Scouts of the USA, 35 193–96
Girling, **III** 556
Giro Sport Designs International Inc., **16**
53; **44** 53–54
Girod, **19** 50
Girsa S.A., **23** 170
Girvin, Inc., **16** 297
Gist-Brocades Co., **III** 53; **26** 384
Git-n-Go Corporation, **60** 160
The Gitano Group, Inc., 8 219–21; **20**
136 **25** 167; **37** 81
Givaudan SA, 43 190–93

GIW Industries Inc., **62** 217
GJM International Ltd., **25** 121–22
GK Technologies Incorporated, **10** 547
GKH Partners, **29** 295
GKN plc, III 493–96; **38 208–13 (upd.)**;
42 47; **47** 7, 9, 279–80
Glacier Bancorp, Inc., 35 197–200
Glacier Park Co., **10** 191
Glacier Water Services, Inc., 47 155–58
Gladieux Corp., **III** 103
Glamar Group plc, **14** 224
Glamis Gold, Ltd., 54 132–35
Glamor Shops, Inc., **14** 93
Glanbia plc, 38 196, 198; **59 204–07**, 364
Glass Glover Plc, **52** 419
Glasstite, Inc., **33** 360–61
GlasTec, **II** 420
Glastron. *See* Genmar Holdings, Inc.
Glatfelter Wood Pulp Company, **8** 413
Glaxo Holdings plc, I 639–41, 643, 668,
675, 693; **6** 346; **9 263–65 (upd.)**; **10**
551; **11** 173; **20** 39; **26** 31; **34** 284; **38**
365; **50** 56; **54** 130
GlaxoSmithKline plc, 46 201–08 (upd.)
Gleason Corporation, 24 184–87
Glen & Co, **I** 453
Glen Alden Corp., **15** 247
Glen-Gery Corporation, **14** 249
Glen Line, **6** 416
Glencairn Ltd., **25** 418
Glencore International AG, **52** 71, 73
Glendale Federal Savings, **IV** 29
The Glenlyte Group, **29** 469
Glenlyte Thomas Group LLC, **29** 466
Glenn Advertising Agency, **25** 90
Glenn Pleass Holdings Pty. Ltd., **21** 339
GLF-Eastern States Association, **7** 17
The Glidden Company, I 353; **8 222–24**;
21 545
Glimcher Co., **26** 262
Glitsch International, Inc., **6** 146; **23** 206,
208
Global Access, **31** 469
Global Apparel Sourcing Ltd., **22** 223
Global Berry Farms LLC, 62 154–56
Global BMC (Mauritius) Holdings Ltd., **62**
55
Global Communications of New York,
Inc., **45** 261
Global Crossing Ltd., 32 216–19
Global Energy Group, **II** 345
Global Engineering Company, **9** 266
Global Health Care Partners, **42** 68
Global Industries, Ltd., 37 168–72
Global Information Solutions, **34** 257
Global Interactive Communications
Corporation, **28** 242
Global Marine Inc., 9 266–67; 11 87
Global Natural Resources, **II** 401; **10** 145
Global One, **52** 108
Global Outdoors, Inc., 49 173–76
Global Power Equipment Group Inc., 52
137–39
Global TeleSystems, Inc., **59** 208, 210. *See
also* Global Crossing Ltd.
Global Transport Organization, **6** 383
Global Vacations Group. *See* Classic
Vacation Group, Inc.
Global Van Lines. *See* Allied Worldwide,
Inc.
GlobalCom Telecommunications, Inc., **24**
122
GlobaLex, **28** 141
Globalia, **53** 301

Gulf Air Company, 6 63; **27** 25; **39** 137–38; **56 146–48**

Gulf Canada Ltd., **I** 262, 264; **IV** 495, 721; **6** 478; **9** 391; **13** 557–58

Gulf Canada Resources Ltd., **63** 110

Gulf Caribbean Marine Lines, **6** 383

Gulf Coast Sportswear Inc., **23** 65

Gulf Energy Development, **22** 107

Gulf Engineering Co. Ltd., **IV** 131

Gulf Exploration Co., **IV** 454

Gulf Island Fabrication, Inc., 44 201–03

Gulf Marine & Maintenance Offshore Service Company, **22** 276

Gulf of Suez Petroleum Co., **IV** 412–14

Gulf Oil Chemical Co., **13** 502

Gulf Oil Corp., **II** 315, 402, 408, 448; **IV** 198, 287, 385–87, 392, 421, 450–51, 466, 470, 472–73, 476, 484, 508, 510, 512, 531, 538, 565, 570, 576; **17** 121–22; **21** 494; **24** 521; **25** 444; **33** 253

Gulf Plains Corp., **III** 471

Gulf Power Company, **38** 446, 448

Gulf Public Service Company, Inc, **6** 580; **37** 89

Gulf Resources & Chemical Corp., **15** 464

Gulf States Paper, **IV** 345

Gulf States Steel, **I** 491

Gulf States Utilities Company, 6 495–97; 12 99

GulfMark Offshore, Inc., 49 180–82

Gulfstream Aerospace Corporation, 7 205–06; 13 358; **24** 465; **28 169–72 (upd.); 36** 190–91

Gulfstream Banks, **II** 336

Gulfwind Marine USA, **30** 303

Gulistan Holdings Inc., **28** 219

Gulton Industries Inc., **7** 297; **19** 31

Gump's, **7** 286

Gunder & Associates, **12** 553

Gunderson, Inc. *See* The Greenbrier Companies.

Gunfred Group, **I** 387

Gunite Corporation, 23 306; **51 152–55**

The Gunlocke Company, 12 299; **13** 269; **23 243–45**

Gunnebo AB, 53 156–58

Gunnite, **27** 203

Gunter Wulff Automaten, **III** 430

Gunther, S.A., **8** 477

Gupta, **15** 492

Gurneys, Birkbeck, Barclay & Buxton, **II** 235

Gurwitch Bristow Products, LLC, **49** 285

GUS plc, 47 165–70 (upd.); 54 38, 40

Gustav Schickendanz KG, **V** 165

Gustin-Bacon Group, **16** 8

Gutehoffnungshütte Aktienverein AG, **III** 563; **IV** 201

Guthrie Balfour, **II** 499–500

Guthy-Renker Corporation, 32 237–40

Gutteridge, Haskins & Davey, **22** 138

Gutzeit. *See* W. Gutzeit & Co.

Guy Degrenne SA, 44 204–07

Guy Motors, **13** 286

Guy Pease Associates, **34** 248

Guy Salmon Service, Ltd., **6** 349

Guyenne et Gascogne, 23 246–48

Guyomarc'h, **39** 356

GVN Technologies, **63** 5

GW Utilities Ltd., **I** 264; **6** 478

Gwathmey Siegel & Associates Architects LLC, II 424; **13** 340; **26 186–88**

GWC. *See* General Waterworks Corporation.

GWK GmbH, **45** 378

GWR Group plc, 39 198–200

Gymboree Corporation, 15 204–06

Gynecare Inc., **23** 190

Gynetics, Inc., **26** 31

Gypsum, Lime, & Alabastine Canada Ltd., **IV** 271

H&D. *See* Hinde & Dauch Paper Company.

H&H Craft & Floral, **17** 322

H & H Plastics Co., **25** 312

H & R Block, Incorporated, 9 268–70; 25 434; **27** 106, 307; **29 224–28 (upd.); 48** 234, 236; **52** 316

H.A. Job, **II** 587

H.B. Claflin Company, **V** 139

H.B. Fenn and Company Ltd., **25** 485

H.B. Fuller Company, 8 237–40; 32 254–58 (upd.)

H.B. Nickerson & Sons Ltd., **14** 339

H.B. Reese Candy Company, **II** 511; **51** 157

H.B. Tuttle and Company, **17** 355

H.B. Viney Company, Inc., **11** 211

H. Berlind Inc., **16** 388

H.C. Christians Co., **II** 536

H.C. Frick Coke Co., **IV** 573; **7** 550

H.C. Petersen & Co., **III** 417

H.C. Prange Co., **19** 511–12

H Curry & Sons. *See* Currys Group PLC.

H.D. Lee Company, Inc. *See* Lee Apparel Company, Inc.

H.D. Vest, Inc., 46 217–19

H. Douglas Barclay, **8** 296

H.E. Butt Grocery Company, 13 251–53; 32 259–62 (upd.); 33 307

H.E. Moss and Company Tankers Ltd., **23** 161

H.F. Ahmanson & Company, II 181–82; 10 342–44 (upd.); 28 167; **47** 160

H.F.T. Industrial Ltd., **62** 150

H.G. Anderson Equipment Corporation, **6** 441

H.H. Brown Shoe Company, **18** 60, **18** 62

H.H. Cutler Company, **17** 513

H.H. Robertson, Inc., **19** 366

H.H. West Co., **25** 501

H. Hamilton Pty, Ltd., **III** 420

H.I.G. Capital L.L.C., **30** 235

H.J. Heinz Company, II 414, 480, 450, 507–09, 547; **7** 382, 448, 576, 578; **8** 499; **10** 151; **11 171–73 (upd.); 12** 411, 529, 531–32; **13** 383; **21** 55, 500–01; **22** 147; **25** 517; **27** 197–98; **33** 446–49; **36 253–57 (upd.); 43** 217–18

H.J. Justin & Sons. *See* Justin Industries, Inc.

H.K. Ferguson Company, **7** 355

H.K. Porter Company, Inc., **19** 152

H.L. Green Company, Inc., **9** 448

H.L. Yoh Company. *See* Day & Zimmerman, Inc.

H. Lewis and Sons, **14** 294

H. Lundbeck A/S, 44 208–11

H.M. Byllesby & Company, Inc., **6** 539

H.M. Goush Co., **IV** 677–78

H.M. Spalding Electric Light Plant, **6** 592; **50** 37

H. Miller & Sons, Inc., **11** 258

H N Norton Co., **11** 208

H.O. Houghton & Company, **10** 355

H.O. Systems, Inc., **47** 430

H-P. *See* Hewlett-Packard Co.

H.P. Foods, **II** 475

H.P. Hood, **7** 17–18

H.P. Smith Paper Co., **IV** 290

H. Reeve Angel & Co., **IV** 300

H. Salt Fish and Chips, **13** 320

H. Samuel Plc, **61** 326

H.T. Cherry Company, **12** 376

H.W. Johns Manufacturing Co., **III** 663, 706–08; **7** 291

H.W. Madison Co., **11** 211

H.W.S. Solutions, **21** 37

H.W. Wilson Company, **17** 152; **23** 440

H. Williams and Co., Ltd., **II** 678

Ha-Lo Industries, Inc., 27 193–95

Häagen-Dazs, **II** 556–57, 631; **10** 147; **14** 212, 214; **19** 116; **24** 140, 141

Haake-Beck Brauerei AG, **9** 86

Haan Crafts Corporation, **62** 18

Haas, Baruch & Co. *See* Smart & Final, Inc.

Haas Publishing Companies, Inc., **22** 442

Haas Wheat & Partners, **15** 357

Habersham Bancorp, 25 185–87

Habitat for Humanity International, 36 258–61

Habitat/Mothercare PLC. *See* Storehouse PLC.

Hach Co., 14 309; **18 218–21**

Hachette Filipacchi Medias S.A., 21 265–67; 33 310

Hachette S.A., IV 614–15, **617–19**, 675; **10** 288; **11** 293; **12** 359; **16** 253–54; **17** 399; **21** 266; **22** 441–42; **23** 476; **43** 210. *See also* Matra-Hachette S.A.

Hachmeister, Inc., **II** 508; **11** 172

Haci Omer Sabanci Holdings A.S., 55 186–89

Hacker-Pschorr Brau, **II** 242; **35** 331

Hackman Oyj Adp, 44 204, **212–15**

Hadco Corporation, 24 201–03

Hadleigh-Crowther, **I** 715

Haemocell, **11** 476

Haemonetics Corporation, 20 277–79

Haftpflichtverband der Deutschen Industrie Versicherung auf Gegenseitigkeit V.a.G. *See* HDI (Haftpflichtverband der Deutschen Industrie Versicherung auf Gegenseitigkeit V.a.G.).

Hagemeyer N.V., 18 180–82; 39 201–04; 45 426; **54** 203

Hagemeyer North America, **63** 289

Haggar Corporation, 19 194–96; 24 158

Haggen Inc., 38 221–23

Haggie, **IV** 91

Hägglunds Vehicle AB, **47** 7, 9

Hahn Automotive Warehouse, Inc., 24 204–06

Hahn Department Stores. *See* Allied Stores Corp.

Hahn, Inc., **17** 9

Haile Mines, Inc., **12** 253

The Hain Celestial Group, Inc., 43 217–20 (upd.)

Hain Food Group, Inc., I 514; **27 196–98; 36** 256

Hainaut-Sambre, **IV** 52

Hakuhodo, Inc., 6 29–31, 48–49; **16** 167; **42 172–75 (upd.)**

Hakunetsusha & Company, **12** 483

HAL Inc., 6 104; **9 271–73**. *See also* Hawaiian Airlines, Inc.

Halcon International, **IV** 456

INDEX TO INDUSTRIES

Index to Industries

AUTOMOTIVE

ENGINEERING & MANAGEMENT SERVICES

FINANCIAL SERVICES: NON-BANKS

HEALTH & PERSONAL CARE PRODUCTS

INFORMATION TECHNOLOGY

PERSONAL SERVICES

PETROLEUM

PUBLISHING & PRINTING

REAL ESTATE

Telstra Corporation Limited, 50
Tiscali SpA, 48
The Titan Corporation, 36
Tollgrade Communications, Inc., 44
TV Azteca, S.A. de C.V., 39
U.S. Satellite Broadcasting Company, Inc., 20
U S West, Inc., V; 25 (upd.)
U.S. Cellular Corporation, 9; 31 (upd.)
United Pan-Europe Communications NV, 47
United Telecommunications, Inc., V
United Video Satellite Group, 18
USA Interactive, Inc., 47 (upd.)
Verizon Communications, 43 (upd.)
ViaSat, Inc., 54
Vivendi Universal S.A., 46 (upd.)
Vodafone Group PLC, 11; 36 (upd.)
The Walt Disney Company, 63 (upd.)
Watkins-Johnson Company, 15
The Weather Channel Companies, 52
West Corporation, 42
Western Union Financial Services, Inc., 54
Western Wireless Corporation, 36
Westwood One, Inc., 23
Williams Communications Group, Inc., 34
The Williams Companies, Inc., 31 (upd.)
Wipro Limited, 43
Wisconsin Bell, Inc., 14
Working Assets Funding Service, 43
Young Broadcasting Inc., 40
Zoom Technologies, Inc., 53 (upd.)

TEXTILES & APPAREL

Abercrombie & Fitch Co., 35 (upd.)
adidas-Salomon AG, 14; 33 (upd.)
Alba-Waldensian, Inc., 30
Albany International Corp., 8
Algo Group Inc., 24
American Safety Razor Company, 20
Amoskeag Company, 8
Angelica Corporation, 15; 43 (upd.)
AR Accessories Group, Inc., 23
Aris Industries, Inc., 16
ASICS Corporation, 57
Authentic Fitness Corporation, 20; 51 (upd.)
Banana Republic Inc., 25
Bata Ltd., 62
Benetton Group S.p.A., 10
Bill Blass Ltd., 32
Birkenstock Footprint Sandals, Inc., 12
Blair Corporation, 25
Brazos Sportswear, Inc., 23
Brooks Brothers Inc., 22
Brooks Sports Inc., 32
Brown Group, Inc., V; 20 (upd.)
Bugle Boy Industries, Inc., 18
Burberry Ltd., 17; 41 (upd.)
Burlington Industries, Inc., V; 17 (upd.)
Calcot Ltd., 33
Calvin Klein, Inc., 22; 55 (upd.)
Candie's, Inc., 31
Canstar Sports Inc., 16
Capel Incorporated, 45
Capezio/Ballet Makers Inc., 62
Carhartt, Inc., 30
Cato Corporation, 14
Chargeurs International, 21 (upd.)
Charming Shoppes, Inc., 8
Cherokee Inc., 18
Chic by H.I.S, Inc., 20
Chico's FAS, Inc., 45
Chorus Line Corporation, 30
Christian Dior S.A., 19; 49 (upd.)
Cintas Corporation, 51 (upd.)

Claire's Stores, Inc., 17
Coach Leatherware, 10
Coats plc, 44 (upd.)
Coats Viyella Plc, V
Collins & Aikman Corporation, 13
Columbia Sportswear Company, 19; 41 (upd.)
Concord Fabrics, Inc., 16
Cone Mills Corporation, 8
Converse Inc., 31 (upd.)
Cotton Incorporated, 46
Courtaulds plc, V; 17 (upd.)
Croscill, Inc., 42
Crown Crafts, Inc., 16
Crystal Brands, Inc., 9
Culp, Inc., 29
Cygne Designs, Inc., 25
Dan River Inc., 35
Danskin, Inc., 12; 62 (upd.)
Deckers Outdoor Corporation, 22
Delta and Pine Land Company, 59
Delta Woodside Industries, Inc., 8; 30 (upd.)
Designer Holdings Ltd., 20
The Dixie Group, Inc., 20
Dogi International Fabrics S.A., 52
Dolce & Gabbana SpA, 62
Dominion Textile Inc., 12
Donna Karan International Inc., 15; 56 (upd.)
Donnkenny, Inc., 17
Duck Head Apparel Company, Inc., 42
Dunavant Enterprises, Inc., 54
Dyersburg Corporation, 21
Ecco Sko A/S, 62
Edison Brothers Stores, Inc., 9
Eileen Fisher Inc., 61
Ellen Tracy, Inc., 55
Eram SA, 51
Ermenegildo Zegna SpA, 63
Esprit de Corp., 8; 29 (upd.)
Etam Developpement SA, 44
Etienne Aigner AG, 52
Evans, Inc., 30
Fab Industries, Inc., 27
Fabri-Centers of America Inc., 16
Fieldcrest Cannon, Inc., 9; 31 (upd.)
Fila Holding S.p.A., 20
Florsheim Shoe Group Inc., 31 (upd.)
Fossil, Inc., 17
Frederick's of Hollywood Inc., 16
French Connection Group plc, 41
Fruit of the Loom, Inc., 8; 25 (upd.)
Fubu, 29
G&K Services, Inc., 16
G-III Apparel Group, Ltd., 22
Galey & Lord, Inc., 20
Garan, Inc., 16
Gerry Weber International AG, 63
Gianni Versace SpA, 22
Giorgio Armani S.p.A., 45
The Gitano Group, Inc. 8
Greenwood Mills, Inc., 14
Groupe DMC (Dollfus Mieg & Cie), 27
Groupe Yves Saint Laurent, 23
Gucci Group N.V., 15; 50 (upd.)
Guess, Inc., 15
Guilford Mills Inc., 8; 40 (upd.)
Gymboree Corporation, 15
Haggar Corporation, 19
Hampton Industries, Inc., 20
Happy Kids Inc., 30
Hartmarx Corporation, 8
The Hartstone Group plc, 14
HCI Direct, Inc., 55
Healthtex, Inc., 17
Helly Hansen ASA, 25

Hermès S.A., 14
The Hockey Company, 34
Hugo Boss AG, 48
Hyde Athletic Industries, Inc., 17
I.C. Isaacs & Company, 31
Interface, Inc., 8; 29 (upd.)
Irwin Toy Limited, 14
Items International Airwalk Inc., 17
J. Crew Group, Inc., 12; 34 (upd.)
Jockey International, Inc., 12; 34 (upd.)
Johnston Industries, Inc., 15
Jones Apparel Group, Inc., 39 (upd.)
Jordache Enterprises, Inc., 23
Jos. A. Bank Clothiers, Inc., 31
JPS Textile Group, Inc., 28
K-Swiss, Inc., 33
Karl Kani Infinity, Inc., 49
Kellwood Company, 8
Kenneth Cole Productions, Inc., 25
Kinney Shoe Corp., 14
Klaus Steilmann GmbH & Co. KG, 53
Koret of California, Inc., 62
L.A. Gear, Inc., 8; 32 (upd.)
L.L. Bean, Inc., 10; 38 (upd.)
LaCrosse Footwear, Inc., 18; 61 (upd.)
Laura Ashley Holdings plc, 13
Lee Apparel Company, Inc., 8
The Leslie Fay Company, Inc., 8; 39 (upd.)
Levi Strauss & Co., V; 16 (upd.)
Liz Claiborne, Inc., 8
London Fog Industries, Inc., 29
Lost Arrow Inc., 22
Maidenform, Inc., 20; 59 (upd.)
Malden Mills Industries, Inc., 16
Marzotto S.p.A., 20
Milliken & Co., V; 17 (upd.)
Mitsubishi Rayon Co., Ltd., V
Mossimo, Inc., 27
Mothercare UK Ltd., 17
Movie Star Inc., 17
Naf Naf SA, 44
Nautica Enterprises, Inc., 18; 44 (upd.)
New Balance Athletic Shoe, Inc., 25
Nike, Inc., V; 8 (upd.)
Nine West Group, Inc., 39 (upd.)
Nitches, Inc., 53
The North Face, Inc., 18
Oakley, Inc., 18
OshKosh B'Gosh, Inc., 9; 42 (upd.)
Oxford Industries, Inc., 8
Pacific Sunwear of California, Inc., 28
Peek & Cloppenburg KG, 46
Pendleton Woolen Mills, Inc., 42
Pentland Group plc, 20
Perry Ellis International, Inc., 41
Phat Fashions LLC, 49
Pillowtex Corporation, 19; 41 (upd.)
Plains Cotton Cooperative Association, 57
Pluma, Inc., 27
Polo/Ralph Lauren Corporation, 12; 62 (upd.)
Prada Holding B.V., 45
PremiumWear, Inc., 30
Puma AG Rudolf Dassler Sport, 35
Quaker Fabric Corp., 19
Quiksilver, Inc., 18
R.G. Barry Corporation, 17; 44 (upd.)
Recreational Equipment, Inc., 18
Red Wing Shoe Company, Inc., 30 (upd.)
Reebok International Ltd., V; 9 (upd.); 26 (upd.)
Rieter Holding AG, 42
Rollerblade, Inc., 15
Russell Corporation, 8; 30 (upd.)
St. John Knits, Inc., 14
Salant Corporation, 51 (upd.)
Salvatore Ferragamo Italia S.p.A., 62

GEOGRAPHIC INDEX

Geographic Index

United States

NOTES ON CONTRIBUTORS

Notes on Contributors

COHEN, M. L. Novelist and researcher living in Paris.

COVELL, Jeffrey L. Seattle-based writer.

DINGER, Ed. Writer and editor based in Bronx, New York.

HALASZ, Robert. Former editor in chief of *World Progress* and *Funk & Wagnalls New Encyclopedia Yearbook*; author, *The U.S. Marines* (Millbrook Press, 1993).

INGRAM, Frederick C. Utah-based business writer who has contributed to *GSA Business, Appalachian Trailway News,* the *Encyclopedia of Business,* the *Encyclopedia of Global Industries,* the *Encyclopedia of Consumer Brands,* and other regional and trade publications.

LORENZ, Sarah Ruth. Minnesota-based writer.

MANCINI, Candice. Researcher and writer.

MEYER, Stephen. Writer living in Missoula, Montana.

MOZZONE, Terri L. Iowa-based writer.

PEIPPO, Kathleen. Minneapolis-based writer.

RHODES, Nelson. Editor, writer, and consultant in the Chicago area.

ROTHBURD, Carrie. Writer and editor specializing in corporate profiles, academic texts, and academic journal articles.

SALAMIE, David E. Part-owner of InfoWorks Development Group, a reference publication development and editorial services company.

TRADII, Mary. Writer based in Denver, Colorado.

WOODWARD, A. Wisconsin-based writer.